A HISTORY OF EUROPE
IN THE MODERN WORLD

TWELFTH EDITION

A HISTORY OF EUROPE IN THE MODERN WORLD

Lloyd Kramer   **R.R. Palmer**   **Joel Colton**

A HISTORY OF EUROPE IN THE MODERN WORLD, TWELFTH EDITION

Published by McGraw-Hill Education, 2 Penn Plaza, New York, NY 10121. Copyright © 2020 by McGraw-Hill Education. All rights reserved. Printed in the United States of America. Previous editions © 2014, 2007, and 2002. No part of this publication may be reproduced or distributed in any form or by any means, or stored in a database or retrieval system, without the prior written consent of McGraw-Hill Education, including, but not limited to, in any network or other electronic storage or transmission, or broadcast for distance learning.

Some ancillaries, including electronic and print components, may not be available to customers outside the United States.

This book is printed on acid-free paper.

2 3 4 5 6 7 8 9 LWI 21 20 19

ISBN 978-1-259-92249-7 (bound edition)
MHID 1-259-92249-9 (bound edition)

ISBN 978-1-260-68721-7 (loose-leaf edition)
MHID 1-260-68721-X (loose-leaf edition)

Product Developer: *Erika Lo*
Content Project Managers: *Lisa Bruflodt, Katie Reuter*
Buyer: *Susan K. Culbertson*
Designer: *Jessica Cuevas*
Content Licensing Specialist: *Brianna Kirschbaum*
Cover Image: *Library of Congress Prints and Photographs Division [LC-DIG-ppmsc-08576]*
Compositor: *Lumina Datamatics, Inc.*

All credits appearing on page or at the end of the book are considered to be an extension of the copyright page.

Library of Congress Cataloging-in-Publication Data

Names: Palmer, R. R. (Robert Roswell), 1909–2002, author. | Colton, Joel,
  1918–2011, author. | Kramer, Lloyd S., author.
Title: A history of Europe in the modern world / R. Palmer, Lloyd Kramer,
  Joel Colton.
Other titles: History of the modern world
Description: Twelfth edition. | Dubuque : McGraw Hill Education, 2019.
Identifiers: LCCN 2019021817 | ISBN 9781259922497 | ISBN 9781260687279 |
  ISBN 9781260687255
Subjects: LCSH: History, Modern–Textbooks. |
  Europe–History–1492–Textbooks.
Classification: LCC D209 .P26 2019 | DDC 909.08–dc23
LC record available at https://lccn.loc.gov/2019021817

The Internet addresses listed in the text were accurate at the time of publication. The inclusion of a website does not indicate an endorsement by the authors or McGraw-Hill Education, and McGraw-Hill Education does not guarantee the accuracy of the information presented at these sites.

mheducation.com/highered

About the Authors

LLOYD KRAMER was born in Maryville, Tennessee, and graduated from Maryville College. He received his PhD from Cornell University in 1983. Before entering Cornell, he was a teacher in Hong Kong and he traveled widely in Asia. After completing his graduate studies, he taught at Stanford University and Northwestern University. Since 1986 he has been a member of the faculty at the University of North Carolina at Chapel Hill, where he is currently a professor of history and the director of Carolina Public Humanities—a program that serves K–12 educators and other communities outside the university. He has served two terms as chair of his department and received two awards for distinguished undergraduate teaching. His writings include *Threshold of a New World: Intellectuals and the Exile Experience in Paris, 1830–1848* (1988); *Lafayette in Two Worlds: Public Cultures and Personal Identities in an Age of Revolutions* (1996), which won the Gilbert Chinard Prize from the Society for French Historical Studies and the Annibel Jenkins Biography Prize from the American Society for Eighteenth-Century Studies; and *Nationalism in Europe and America: Politics, Cultures, and Identities since 1775* (2011). He has also co-edited several books, including a collection of essays on historical education in America and *A Companion to Western Historical Thought* (2002). He has been a member of the School of Historical Studies at the Institute for Advanced Study and a Fellow at the National Humanities Center; and he served as president of the Society for French Historical Studies.

R. R. PALMER was born in Chicago. After graduating from the University of Chicago, he received his PhD from Cornell University in 1934. From 1936 to 1963 he taught at Princeton University, taking leave during World War II to work on historical projects in Washington, DC. In 1963 he moved to Washington University in St. Louis to serve as dean of arts and sciences but in 1969 resumed his career in teaching and research, this time at Yale. After his retirement he lived in Princeton, where he was affiliated with the Institute for Advanced Study, and then in a retirement community in Newtown, Pennsylvania. Of the numerous books he wrote, translated, and edited, three of the most important have been his *Catholics and Unbelievers in Eighteenth-Century France* (1939); *Twelve Who Ruled: The Year of the Terror in the French Revolution* (1941, 1989); and his two-volume *Age of the Democratic Revolution* (1959, 1964), the first volume of which won the Bancroft Prize. He served as president of the American Historical Association in 1970, received honorary degrees from universities in the United States and abroad, and was awarded the Antonio Feltrinelli International Prize for History in Rome in 1990. He was a long-time Fellow of the American Philosophical Society and of the American Academy of Arts and Sciences. He died in 2002, widely recognized as one of the preeminent historians of his generation.

JOEL COLTON was born in New York City. A graduate of the City College of New York, he served as a military intelligence officer in Europe in World War II, and received his PhD from Columbia University in 1950. He served on the faculty of Duke University for more than four decades, chairing the History Department from 1967 to 1974 and chairing the university's academic council from 1971 to 1973. On leave from Duke, he served from 1974 to 1981 with the Rockefeller Foundation in New York as director of its research and fellowship program in the humanities. In 1986 Duke voted him a distinguished teaching award. He received Guggenheim, Rockefeller Foundation, and National Endowment for the Humanities fellowships. He served on the editorial boards of the *Journal of Modern History, French Historical Studies*, and *Historical Abstracts,* and was co-president of the International Commission on the History of Social Movements and Social Structures. In 1979 he was elected a Fellow of the American Academy of Arts and Sciences. His writings include *Compulsory Labor Arbitration in France, 1936–1939* (1951); *Léon Blum: Humanist in Politics* (1966, 1987), for which he received a Mayflower Award; *Twentieth Century* (1968, 1980) in the *Time-Life Great Ages of Man* series; and numerous contributions to journals, encyclopedias, and collaborative volumes. He died in 2011, having served as the distinguished co-author of *A History of the Modern World* for every revision after the first edition.

Brief Contents

Contents

List of Chapter Illustrations

List of Chronologies, Historical Documents, Historical Interpretations and Debates, Maps, Charts, and Tables

Historical Interpretations and Debates

Maps, Charts, and Tables

Preface

Dramatic events in the contemporary world—wars, revolutions, political upheavals, terrorist attacks, catastrophic natural disasters, economic crises, and the endless stream of daily news—often obscure the long-developing historical processes that have created the societies in which we live and the current problems with which we have to cope. The mass media pay little attention to the broader historical patterns and contexts that shape the deeper meaning of swiftly moving public events and private lives. This new edition of *A History of Europe in the Modern World,* therefore, brings new information, documents, and interpretations to the ongoing search for historical perspectives on the complex, often bewildering, events of our own era. Although this book (as in past editions) focuses specifically on the history of Europe, it also emphasizes that modern European history has always evolved through interactions and exchanges with the wider world.

It is impossible to understand European history without placing it "in the modern *world,*" just as it is impossible to understand the modern world without knowing the history of Europe. This book thus carries the guiding assumption that events and ideas in modern European societies have often influenced people in every part of the world, but that Europeans have also been constantly influenced by their encounters with other peoples and cultures. The era of European colonial empires ended in the later twentieth century, but the economies, political cultures, and migrations of people within Europe have become ever more entangled with cultures, conflicts, and societies in other parts of the world. At the same time, however, Europe's endless exchange with "otherness" includes an endless dialogue with its own past; and this book also carries the presupposition that contemporary events and conflicts are deeply connected to the diverse cultures, institutions, social systems, economic exchanges, power struggles, empires, and ideas of earlier eras in human history. Nobody can truly understand present times, in short, without studying the past; and in modern times the history of Europe has often entered (for better or for worse) into the history of almost the whole world.

The multiple levels of human history and cross-cultural exchanges have created modern societies that both resemble and differ from the "modernity" that has evolved in Europe since about the fifteenth century. This book thus describes the main features of this dynamic modern history by examining specific nations and landmark events, such as great revolutions, economic transitions, and changing cultural beliefs; but it also emphasizes broad historical and social trends that have developed beneath the most prominent events, gradually creating what we now call "the modern world." Although the following narrative explores the rise of nation-states and the international conflicts that have reshaped modern societies over the last several centuries, it links such public events to the wider historical influence of the global economy, the development of science, technology, and new forms of knowledge, the rise of industry, the significance of religious and philosophical beliefs, the origin and diffusion of new political ideas, the changing mores of family and social life, the evolving views of human rights, and the complex relations between European cultures and other cultures around the world.

The term "modern," as it is used in this book, refers to a phase of human history that began about five or six centuries ago and steadily transformed both the material conditions of human societies and the meaning of individual identities or selfhood.

"Modern" ways of life have developed in diverse historical contexts, and they are now evolving more rapidly and in more places than ever before. This book affirms that every culture and historical era has made important contributions to the collective history of human beings, but it mostly discusses specific historical events and changes within Europe, even as it traces the growing European involvements with other peoples, economies, and political systems far beyond the relatively small continent of Europe itself. The narrative stresses the influence of European societies on the emergence of modern institutions and social practices, yet it also notes the worldwide exchanges that have contributed to the increasingly global culture of the contemporary era. Europeans were never the only influential actors in the global creation of modernity, but they were often present wherever the transitions to modernity were taking place. These historical transitions generated violence and oppression and political conflicts as well as social, cultural, and economic progress; and it is the combined effects of these modern developments on all human lives (and the natural environment) that provide the essential rationale for historical studies and for this new edition of *A History of Europe in the Modern World*.

ORGANIZATION OF THE BOOK: CHANGES AND CONTINUITIES

As in the past, the book is organized in chapters that describe events in specific chronological eras, moving steadily toward the present. Yet the clearly defined and numbered sections within each chapter often deal with themes, events, or issues that do not develop in simple chronological order. Each chapter focuses on a specific time frame but also on themes and problems of continuing historical importance. The chronological organization gives readers a broad historical framework and provides opportunities for further analysis and discussion of specific historical themes or problems—discussions that can draw, for example, on the Suggestions for Further Reading and other materials that can be found on Connect.

Although the history of political systems, state power, revolutions, and international conflicts remains important, *A History of Europe in the Modern World* goes beyond this kind of information by providing analytical overviews of cultural changes, social systems, and the ideas of influential European writers. This book seeks to engage both students and nonacademic readers who are looking for broad perspectives on more specific historical scholarship. The narrative therefore explains major events and also draws on the work of recent social, cultural, and intellectual historians who have contributed important new insights to modern historical studies. There are discussions of the evolving roles of women in various historical contexts; descriptions of cultural movements and intellectual debates from the early modern to the contemporary period; and analysis of the political, economic, and cultural interactions that took place in European empires and in the anticolonial movements that ultimately brought about the dissolution of imperial systems. Discussions of Europe's global empires thus emphasize the interactions between Europeans and other peoples as the opposition to European imperialism spread across the whole modern world.

An important new feature in this edition appears in a new selection of brief excerpts from historical documents, each of which expresses important cultural beliefs or political ideas that emerged in different historical contexts. Historical knowledge develops through detailed, analytical study of primary sources that describe the actions and worldviews of people who lived in past eras, so the historical documents in this new edition (scattered across numerous chapters and coming from different centuries) can be used as a "site" for critical-minded explorations of influential cultural or political movements, events, and conflicts.

These documents can also suggest how primary sources generate opposing historical interpretations, and this edition again provides examples of different explanations for important historical transitions. A series of exemplary "Historical Interpretations and Debates" shows how historians develop diverging analytical perspectives. These interpretations come from "classic" historical studies and from more recent revisions of past historical assumptions, but they all point to the diversity of historical analysis. Both the historical documents and the historical interpretations offer wide-ranging perspectives on the dynamic components of historical thinking and the constant evolution of historical viewpoints.

Well-informed historical thinking requires factual knowledge about past events, careful readings of historical documents, and critical evaluation of different historical interpretations. This book therefore provides materials for entry into all these levels of historical thought and into the constant expansion and revision of historical knowledge. Examining the specific history of Europe in the modern world, in other words, opens pathways toward the essential personal and public skills of all well-informed, analytical historical thinking.

This book describes major events such as the emergence of Renaissance humanism, the European expansion across the Atlantic world, the religious wars in early modern European societies, and the Scientific Revolution. Later chapters discuss the French and Russian Revolutions, the Industrial Revolution, the development of European nationalism and imperialism, the twentieth-century world wars and globalizing economy, the spread of democracy and the authoritarian challenges that democracies have faced, the collapse of European-dominated empires, the continuing search for international order, the emergence of the European Union, and the most recent nationalist challenges to Europe's transnational institutions. These broad thematic developments are always linked to particular places, people, or conflicts, and there are transnational comparisons in the discussions of every historical era.

The visual components of this new edition expand the historical narrative with new images and artwork. Like other kinds of primary sources, the images and creative arts from past cultures offer important, provocative historical information. Knowing how to "read" and critically evaluate the meanings of illustrations, paintings, and photographs is essential for analytical thought and for cross-cultural comparisons. The captions that accompany the illustrations thus connect the visual images and themes to the book's historical narrative and interpretations. There are also numerous maps and charts that show how the boundaries, populations, and economies of different regions or nations have changed across the centuries; and each chapter includes a chronological timeline that summarizes the most notable events.

The revised entries in the comprehensive Suggestions for Further Reading, a much-valued feature in each edition of this book, provide up-to-date listings of useful websites as well as the titles of significant new scholarly publications on specific national histories and on the themes of transnational historical research. For this new edition, the Suggestions for Further Reading can be found in the ebook, on Connect, or online at www.mhhe.com/kramer12e.

The changes in this edition of *A History of Europe in the Modern World* provide new historical documents, new thematic perspectives, and new information (especially on recent historical transitions), but this edition also continues to provide the prose style, factual content, and analytical qualities that have long appealed to both teachers and students of European history. Readers will find that the book strongly reaffirms the value of historical knowledge and perspectives for anyone who wants to live a well-informed and engaged life in the constantly changing modern world. This book achieves its overall purpose whenever it gives readers new insights into the meanings of European history or modern global history and whenever it helps readers gain new perspectives on their own lives, beliefs, cultures, and social experiences.

RESOURCES & SUPPLEMENTS

The twelfth edition of *A History of Europe in the Modern World* is now available online with Connect, McGraw-Hill Education's integrated assignment and assessment platform. Connect also offers SmartBook for the new edition, which is the first adaptive reading experience proven to improve grades and help students study more effectively.

FOR THE INSTRUCTOR

Instructor resources are available through Connect, including the following:

- **Test Bank**   The test bank is designed for use with Connect or EZ Test software and contains multiple-choice, essay, and identification question types. Instructors may also add their own questions in either system. Multiple versions of tests can be created, and tests can be exported for use with course management systems. Additional information is available at www.mheducation.com/connect.
- **Instructor's Manual**   This unique manual offers a chapter-by-chapter guide to some of the best documentaries, educational and feature films, videos, and audio recordings to enhance classroom discussion. Brief overviews help instructors select the films best suited to each course topic. The manual also provides instructors with chapter objectives, chapter overviews, and points for discussion for each chapter.
- **Maps**   An image bank offers instructors the opportunity to create custom-made, professional-looking presentations, handouts, and teaching tools by providing electronic versions of many maps from the text.

FOR THE STUDENT

Student resources are assignable through Connect, including the following:

- **Suggestions for Further Reading**   A bibliography provides up-to-date listings of useful websites, as well as the titles of significant new scholarly publications on specific national histories and on the themes of transnational historical research. (Suggestions for Further Reading is also available in the ebook or online at www.mhhe.com/kramer12e.)
- **Study Guide**   A chapter-by-chapter study guide provides students with study questions, discussion topics, and key terms.
- **SmartBook**   SmartBook is an adaptive reading experience proven to improve grades and help students study more effectively.

ACKNOWLEDGMENTS

It is a pleasure to acknowledge the assistance and valuable insights of the many people who have helped produce the new edition of this book. The editors and staff at McGraw-Hill, Inc., have provided much-appreciated assistance on every aspect of the production process. McGraw-Hill began publishing this book in its 7th edition, and its talented editors have offered their helpful expertise for each subsequent edition. The McGraw-Hill team for this edition included Erika Lo, Erica Longenbach, and Jasmine Staton, who helped to get the project launched. Brianna Kirschbaum, Traci Vaske, Jasmine Suarez, and Cathi Profitko later managed all of the complex editorial details with efficiency, insight, and diverse skills—for which I thank each of them. Jennifer Parker and Susan Landstrom provided valuable administrative support at UNC-Chapel Hill.

Catherine Conner, who received her PhD in the history department at the University of North Carolina-Chapel Hill and who is a talented teacher of modern history, contributed her careful research and bibliographical knowledge to the updated Suggestions for Further Reading. These suggestions include information on useful Web sites, and the whole bibliography can be found for this edition in the ebook, on Connect, or online at www.mhhe.com/kramer12e. I very much appreciate Dr. Conner's excellent work on this important, wide-ranging bibliographic project.

This new edition has also benefited from the advice of academic reviewers who offered ideas for revisions and clarifications that would improve the book. My deep appreciation to the reviewers of this edition:

David A. Meola, University of South Alabama
Julie Allen, South Carolina Governor's School for the Arts and Humanities
Ian W. Campbell, University of California, Davis

None of the people who assisted in preparing or evaluating the book's content are responsible for any of the book's shortcomings, but all have added to its strengths. Colleagues at UNC–Chapel Hill, teachers of advanced placement European history classes, and friends at other universities have all provided valuable assistance and advice during numerous conversations about this book. A special "thank-you" goes to Kyle Kramer for his helpful editorial suggestions and to Gwynne Pomeroy for her perspectives, advice, and encouragement during every phase of the work on this new edition (and also on many other shared projects and experiences).

The revisions for this book have been completed without the wise counsel of my two deceased co-authors and friends, R. R. Palmer and Joel Colton. The publication of this new edition, however, gives me another opportunity to acknowledge and thank Professors Palmer and Colton for their distinguished historical work and for our collaborations on earlier editions. Their remarkable knowledge of complex events and their exceptional ability to write clear, analytical prose remain a model for me and for many others who admired their historical scholarship. Their long collaboration on earlier versions of this narrative, which they always called *A History of the Modern World*, became an outstanding example of how intellectual partnerships can enhance historical knowledge and expand historical perspectives. They both knew how to connect the history of specific events to the broadest historical developments of modern times.

In revising another edition of a book that was often known in the past as simply Palmer-Colton, I have sought always to sustain the high quality of their previous work, even as I have changed the content or structure of various chapters and as I have added new sources, images, or interpretations. I learned from each of these historians about the rigorous standards of good intellectual work, the deep value of academic friendships, and the enduring importance of human knowledge. My many conversations with Joel Colton during his later years enriched my personal life as well as my understanding of the past. This book thus continues to convey the knowledge and insights of Professors Palmer and Colton in a revised narrative that must now also include the changing events in contemporary European societies, the changing perspectives on modern European history, and the changing themes of modern historical scholarship.

Lloyd Kramer

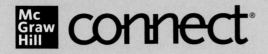

You're in the driver's seat.

Want to build your own course? No problem. Prefer to use our turnkey, prebuilt course? Easy. Want to make changes throughout the semester? Sure. And you'll save time with Connect's auto-grading too.

65%

Less Time Grading

Laptop: McGraw-Hill Education

They'll thank you for it.

Adaptive study resources like SmartBook® help your students be better prepared in less time. You can transform your class time from dull definitions to dynamic debates. Hear from your peers about the benefits of Connect at **www.mheducation.com/highered/connect**

Make it simple, make it affordable.

Connect makes it easy with seamless integration using any of the major Learning Management Systems— Blackboard®, Canvas, and D2L, among others—to let you organize your course in one convenient location. Give your students access to digital materials at a discount with our inclusive access program. Ask your McGraw-Hill representative for more information.

Padlock: Jobalou/Getty Images

Solutions for your challenges.

A product isn't a solution. Real solutions are affordable, reliable, and come with training and ongoing support when you need it and how you want it. Our Customer Experience Group can also help you troubleshoot tech problems— although Connect's 99% uptime means you might not need to call them. See for yourself at **status. mheducation.com**

Checkmark: Jobalou/Getty Images

SUPPORT AT
every step

FOR STUDENTS

Effective, efficient studying.

Connect helps you be more productive with your study time and get better grades using tools like SmartBook, which highlights key concepts and creates a personalized study plan. Connect sets you up for success, so you walk into class with confidence and walk out with better grades.

Study anytime, anywhere.

Download the free ReadAnywhere app and access your online eBook when it's convenient, even if you're offline. And since the app automatically syncs with your eBook in Connect, all of your notes are available every time you open it. Find out more at www.mheducation.com/readanywhere

> *"I really liked this app—it made it easy to study when you don't have your text-book in front of you."*
>
> - Jordan Cunningham, Eastern Washington University

No surprises.

The Connect Calendar and Reports tools keep you on track with the work you need to get done and your assignment scores. Life gets busy; Connect tools help you keep learning through it all.

Calendar: owattnphotos/Getty Images

Learning for everyone.

McGraw-Hill works directly with Accessibility Services Departments and faculty to meet the learning needs of all students. Please contact your Accessibility Services office and ask them to email accessibility@mheducation.com, or visit **www.mheducation.com/about/accessibility** for more information.

Top: Jenner Images/Getty Images, Left: Hero Images/Getty Images, Right: Hero Images/Getty Images

Geography, History, and the Modern World

History is the experience of human beings in time, but that experience takes place also in geographic space. Geography describes and maps the earth, but geographers also study the cultural practices that shape human interactions with the environments in which they live.

The universe, of which our planet earth and our solar system form but a small part, is now thought to be at least 12 billion years old. Most scientists believe the earth is over 4.5 billion years old. Yet the entire history (and prehistory) of humankind goes back only 3.5 to 5 million years, or perhaps only 2 million years, depending on how humans are defined. What we call history—the recorded cultures and actions of human beings—began with the invention of early forms of writing only about 5,500 years ago, though collective memories were shared through storytelling and artwork long before people could write.

Oceans and continents have moved about over time, changing in size, shape, and location. The continents as we know them took on their distinctive forms less than 100 million years ago. Dinosaurs, which became extinct some 60 million years before the first humans even emerged, could walk from North America to Europe (as we now call these continents) on solid land in a warm climate. It is only a few thousand years since the end of the most recent glacial age. That Ice Age, which began about 2 million years ago and reached its coldest point only 20,000 years ago, was caused by a slight shift in the earth's orbit around the sun.

Ice Age

Water froze into ice 1–2 inches thick and covered the northern parts of the planet (in North America as far south as present-day Chicago and in Europe across large parts of the British Isles and the nearby mainland). The melting of this ice produced the coastlines, offshore islands, inland seas, bays, and harbors that we know today, as well as some of the large river systems and lakes. The process of change in the earth's surface continues. Niagara Falls, on the border between the United States and Canada, has been receding because the ongoing cascade of water erodes the underlying rock. The ocean's tides and human construction are eroding our shorelines; and scientists have shown that human activity and climate change are gradually changing the oceans, altering coastal lands, and reducing biodiversity throughout the world.

Oceans presently cover more than two-thirds of the earth's surface, and many large land areas in the remaining third are poorly suited for habitation by human beings or most other animal and plant organisms. One-tenth of the land remains under ice, as in Antarctica and Greenland (but this ice is receding); much is tundra; much is desert, as in the Sahara; and much land lies along the windswept ridges of high mountains. Like the oceans, these regions have been important in human history, often acting as barriers to movement and settlement. Human history has therefore evolved in relatively small, scattered sections of the earth's total surface.

Researchers have found persuasive material evidence to show that human beings originated in Africa. Humans belonging to the species *Homo erectus,* the Latin term used by anthropologists and others to denote the upright, walking predecessors of modern humans, seem to

Origins of human beings

have migrated from Africa about 1.8 million years ago, perhaps because of environmental pressures or perhaps because of simple curiosity. Our own species *Homo sapiens,* the Latin term connoting increased cognitive and judgmental abilities, emerged about 200,000 years ago. When humans went beyond merely utilitarian accomplishments and demonstrated aesthetic and artistic interests as well as advanced toolmaking (about 35,000 years ago), we refer to them as the subspecies *Homo sapiens sapiens*. They were the remaining survivors of a very complex human family tree.

The great Ice Age lowered the seas by hundreds of feet and froze huge quantities of water. The English Channel became dry. Land bridges opened up between Siberia and North America over what we now call the Bering Strait. Hunters seeking game walked from one continent to the other. When the glaciers melted, forests sprang up, and many of the open areas in which humans had hunted disappeared, providing added motivation for movement.

Our human ancestors spread eventually to every continent except Antarctica. In doing so, human groups became isolated from each other for millennia, separated by oceans, deserts, or mountains. Wherever they wandered, they evolved slightly over time, developing superficial physical differences that modern cultures have defined as the characteris-

Race: a cultural concept

tics of various racial groups. But "race" is a cultural idea rather than a mark of biologically significant differences. All human beings belong to the *Homo sapiens* species, all derive from the same biological ancestry, and all are mutually fertile. Only a very few human genes are responsible for physical differences such as skin pigmentation, in comparison to the vast number of genes that are shared by all members of the human species.

Geography and culture

The basic anatomy and genetic makeup of modern humans has not changed over the last 100,000 years. Geographic separation accounts for the emergence over shorter time periods of distinctive cultures, which can be seen, for example, in the different historical and cultural development of the pre-Columbian Americas, Africa, China, India, the Middle East, and Europe. On a still smaller time scale, geographic separation also explains differences in languages and dialects.

Geographic distances and diversity of climate have also produced differences in flora and fauna, and hence in the plants and animals upon which humans depend. Wheat became the most common cereal in the Middle East and Europe, millet and rice in East Asia, sorghum in tropical Africa, maize in pre-Columbian America. The horse, first domesticated in north-central Asia about 4,500 years ago, was for centuries a mainstay of Europe and Asia for muscle power, transportation, and fighting. The somewhat less versatile camel was adopted later and more slowly in the Middle East, and the Americans long had only the llama as a load-carrying animal. Such differences did not begin to diminish until early modern travelers crossed the oceans, taking plants and animals with them and bringing others back to environments where they had never lived before.

Although much remains obscure about the origins of life, and new discoveries and chronologies are always displacing older hypotheses, paleontologists studying plant and animal fossils (including human ones) have used techniques such as radiocarbon dating to transform our knowledge of the earth and of the earliest human beings. In geography, aerial and satellite photography and computer technology have enabled us to refine older conceptions of continents and oceans. And astrophysicists are now studying vast amounts of new data about the universe, which have been sent to them from powerful telescopes mounted on unmanned spaceships.

Cartography, the art and science of mapmaking, has evolved rapidly, but we tend to forget how our maps often remain conventional and even parochial. Europeans and descendants of Europeans designed our most commonly used maps, which are oriented North-South and West-East from fixed points in their horizons, and which therefore reflect various European cultural assumptions. Similar biases can be found in the maps of other cultures too. The Chinese for centuries defined and visualized their country as the "Middle Kingdom." In the early modern centuries maps drawn in India typically represented South Asia as forming the major part of the world. One such map depicted the European continent as a few marginal areas labeled England, France, and "other hat-wearing islands."

Changing conceptualizations of the globe continue in our day. A map drawn and published in contemporary Australia, demonstrating the Australian perspective from "down under," shows South Africa at the top of the map and Capetown at the very tip, the large expanse of contemporary African nations in the middle, and the European countries crowded at the bottom, the latter appearing quite insignificant. The European-invented term "Middle East" has been called into question, and this region of the world is perhaps better designated as Western Asia. Even the traditional concept of Europe as one of the seven continents (Africa, Asia, Europe, North America, South America, Australia, and Antarctica) is now questioned. Why, for example, should the Indian peninsula be a "subcontinent" when it roughly matches the size and exceeds the population and diversity of the European "continent" (at least that part of the "continent" that lies west of the former Soviet Union)? Europe itself is, of course, actually a peninsula, in a way that the other continents are not. Some geographers ask us to consider it more properly as part of Asia, the western part of a great "Eurasian landmass." Defined in these terms, Europe becomes more of a cultural conception, arising out of perceived differences from Asia and Africa, than a continent in a strictly geographical sense.

Europe's Influence on Modern History

However we define its place on the globe, Europe has undoubtedly shaped much of modern world history—partly because of its overseas expansion, partly because of what it borrowed from other parts of the world, and partly because of its decisive economic and cultural influence on the emergence of an increasingly global civilization. Europe is of course only one of many important cultural spheres in human history. Its economy, political systems, religious traditions, and social institutions are not the sole historical path to modernity; indeed, people in other regions of the world have often challenged or rejected European forms of "modernization" as they have built their own modern societies. Yet even the critique or rejection of European institutions has usually required historical analysis of Europe's development and role in the world. Much of the modern global economy, for example, emerged in the international trade that Europe's imperial powers controlled and expanded after the sixteenth century. European political ideas, science, philosophy, cultural mores, and people also spread widely across the world, contributing to both the constructive and destructive patterns of modern political, social, and cultural life. Ideas and people have meanwhile flowed constantly into Europe from other parts of the world, so that European societies remain a vital center for cross-cultural exchanges and conflicts.

Europe and history

It is possible to narrate a "history of the modern world" from widely diverging perspectives and with an emphasis on quite different historical themes. This book, however, begins with the recognition that Europe developed and promoted many of the distinctive "modern" ideas and institutions that have now evolved in diverse forms throughout the contemporary world. Historical understanding of modernity must therefore include a comprehensive analysis of Europe—though an accurate history of the modern world must also

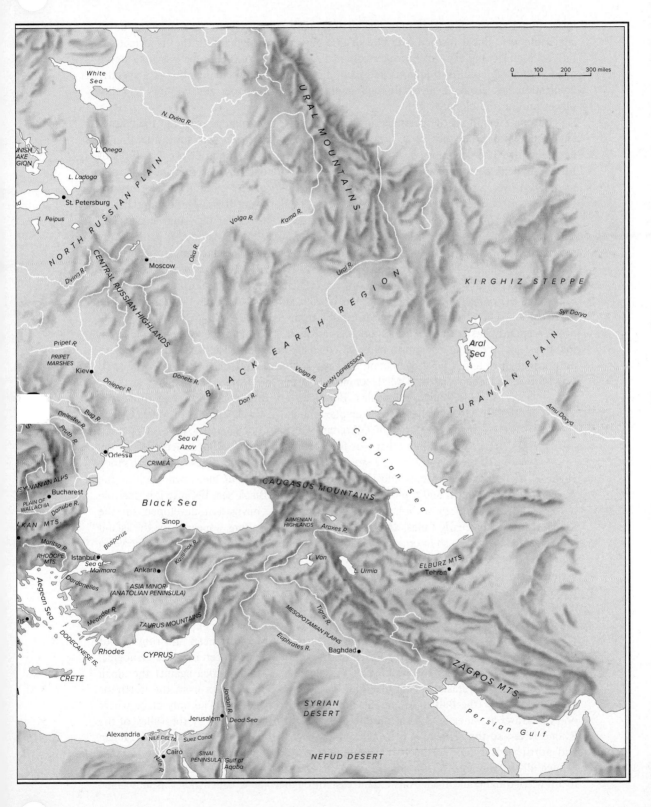

insist that Europe represents only one of the many complex cultures that continue to shape modern global history. The title of this book thus affirms both the historical significance and complexity of Europe's role in the modern world. Europe has long developed distinctive cultural traditions and institutions, but its modern identity as a specific civilization has always evolved through interactions with people and cultures in other places around the globe.

Europe exemplifies the perennial interactions between human activity and the natural environment, and the study of its historical evolution should begin with some attention to its geography. The accompanying topographical map shows the main physical features of Europe and its surrounding geographical space. This topography has remained virtually unchanged over historic time, despite the constant political and cultural transformations in European societies. Europe is not large. Even with European Russia, it contains hardly more than 6 percent of the earth's land surface, occupying about the same area as the United States mainland plus Alaska. It is only a little larger than Australia. It is physically separated from Africa by the Mediterranean Sea, although the Mediterranean historically has been as much a passageway as a barrier. A truer barrier emerged when the Sahara Desert dried up only a few thousand years ago, which suggests why northern Africa has often been as connected to southern Europe, or culturally to the Middle East, as to sub-Saharan Africa. The physical separation of Europe from Asia is even less clear. The conventional boundary has been the Ural Mountains in Russia, but they are a low and wide chain that does not stretch far enough to make an adequate boundary. The Russians themselves do not recognize any official distinction between European and Asian Russia.

Europe is indeed one of several peninsulas jutting off from Asia, like the Arabian and Indian peninsulas. But there are differences. For one thing, the Mediterranean Sea is unique among the world's bodies of water. Closed in by the Strait of Gibraltar, which is only 8 miles wide, it is more shielded than other seas from the open ocean and is protected from the most violent ocean storms. Though over 2,000 miles long, it is subdivided by islands and peninsulas into lesser seas with identities of their own, such as the Aegean and the Adriatic, and it provides access also to the Black Sea. Because it is possible to travel great distances without being far from land, navigation developed on the Mediterranean from early times, and one of the first civilizations appeared on the island of Crete. It is possible also to cross between Europe and Asia at the Bosporus and between Europe and Africa at Gibraltar. Populations and cultures became mixed by migration, and various historic empires—the Carthaginian, Roman, Byzantine, Arabic, Spanish, Venetian, and Ottoman—have effectively used the Mediterranean to govern their component parts. After the Suez Canal was built in the nineteenth century, the Mediterranean became an important segment in the "lifeline of empire" for the British Empire in its heyday.

The Mediterranean Sea

In southern Europe, north of the Mediterranean and running for its whole length, is a series of mountains, produced over the geological ages by the pushing of the gigantic mass of Africa against the small Eurasian peninsula. The Pyrenees close off Spain from the north, as the Alps do Italy; the Balkan Mountains are difficult to penetrate. The only place where one can travel at water level from the Mediterranean to the north is by the valley of the Rhone River, so that France is the only country that belongs both to the Mediterranean and northern Europe. North of the mountains is a great plain extending from western France all the way into Russia and on into Asia, passing south of the Urals. If one were to draw a straight line from Amsterdam east through what is called the Caspian Gate,

Mountains

north of the Caspian Sea, as far as western China, one would never in traveling these 3,500 miles be higher than 2,000 feet above sea level. This plain has at various times opened Europe to Mongol and other invasions, enabled the Russians to move east and create a huge empire, and made Poland a troubled battleground.

The European rivers are worth particular attention. Most are nav-   **Rivers** igable, and they also give access to the sea. With their valleys, they provided areas where intensive local development could take place. Thus the most important older cities of Europe developed on rivers—London on the Thames, Paris on the Seine, Vienna and Budapest on the Danube, Warsaw on the Vistula. In northern Europe it was often possible to move goods from one river to another, and then in the eighteenth century to connect them by canals. The importance of water is shown again by the location of Copenhagen, Stockholm, and St. Petersburg on the Baltic and of Amsterdam and Lisbon, which grew rapidly after Europeans began traversing the Atlantic Ocean.

There are important geographical conditions such as climate that a   **Climate** topographical map cannot show. Climate depends on latitude, ocean currents, and winds that bring or withhold rainfall. Europe lies as far north as the northern United States and southern Canada, but the parts of Europe near the sea have less extreme temperatures than the corresponding northerly regions of North America. The Mediterranean countries have more sunshine and less severe winters than either northern Europe or the northern United States. Like people on every continent, Europeans have struggled with weather conditions and diseases, but the winters in Europe are cold enough to suppress infectious pathogens and keep out certain diseases that may afflict people in warmer climates. The warm summers with their growing seasons have produced an annual cycle of agriculture, and rainfall has been adequate but not excessive. Europe is the only continent that has no actual desert. It is also for the most part a region of fertile soil. In short, since the end of the Ice Age, or since humans learned to survive winters, Europe has been one of the most favored places on the globe for human habitation.

If we say that climate and the environment not only set limits but also provide opportunities for what human beings can do, then there is no such thing as geographical determinism. Geography is not destiny. What happens   **Geographical** depends on the application of knowledge and abilities in any particular   **determinism** time and place and in any particular culture. What constitutes a natural resource varies with the state of technology and the possibilities of economic exchange. Even the disadvantages of distance can be overcome by developing new means of transportation. The oceans that long divided human beings became a highway for the Portuguese, Spanish, Dutch, French, and English, and later for others. Chinese and Arab sailors also used the oceans for trade across Asia and East Africa. For most of human history, however, neither persons, information, nor commands could travel much more than 30 miles a day. Localism prevailed, and large-scale commercial or governmental organizations were hard to create and maintain. Like most other regions of the world, therefore, Europe was long made up of small local units, pockets of territory each with its own customs, way of life, and manner of speech, largely unknown to or ignorant of others, and looking inward upon itself. A "foreigner" might come from a thousand miles away, or from only ten.

Agriculture, like commerce and industry, depends on human inven-   **Agriculture** tion and decision making. The state of agriculture obviously depends on natural conditions, but it has also depended historically on the invention of the plow, the planting of appropriate crops, the rotation of fields to prevent soil exhaustion, and the availability of livestock from which manure could be obtained as fertilizer. It benefits from stability and is affected by demographic changes. If population grows, new and less fertile or more distant areas must be brought under cultivation. Nor can agriculture be improved without the building of roads and a division of labor between town and country, in which agrarian workers produce surpluses for those not engaged in agriculture. And for agriculture, as for other productive enterprises, elementary security is essential. Farming cannot proceed, nor food be stored over the winter, unless the men and women who work the fields can be protected from attack.

The maps in the present volume cannot show in detail all of the waterways, mountains, and geographical barriers that have helped to shape the course of human history in Europe and the wider world, but they do point to the role of geography in the evolution of political and economic power, or what has become known as geopolitics. Human beings have always developed their institutions and cultures through a complex relation with the natural world, and maps remind us that all human activities take place in geographical space. Readers can also use their imaginations and the scale of maps to convert space into time, remembering that until the invention of the railroad both people and news traveled far more slowly than today. At a rate of 30 miles a day it would take three weeks to travel from London to Venice, and at least six weeks for an exchange of letters. Communication to places outside Europe took much longer. In our own day, when we travel at supersonic speeds and measure electronic communication in nanoseconds, or one-billionth of a second, the communication barriers of geographic space have virtually disappeared. Yet human beings remain profoundly dependent on their natural environments in even the most modern, technologically advanced societies, and human history remains firmly embedded in the geography of the planet earth.

The Transitions and Themes of "Modern" History

This book focuses on the history of Europe in the modern world, but it begins with a brief overview of ancient and medieval Europe because the meaning of "modern history" depends partly on its differences from previous historical eras. The distinctive aspects of modern Europe and its role in the modern world become more apparent when we note how historians have described modernity as a new phase of human history. Earlier institutions and beliefs often remained influential, but they were steadily transformed.

Over the centuries between roughly 1500 and 1900, Europe developed the most powerful combination of political, military, economic, technological, and scientific systems that the world had ever seen. In doing so, Europeans radically transformed their own societies. They also profoundly affected other societies and cultures in America, Africa, and Asia—sometimes destroying them, sometimes stimulating or enlivening them, and always presenting them with problems of resistance or adaptation. This European ascendancy gained global influence in the seventeenth and eighteenth centuries. It reached its zenith with the European colonial empires at the beginning of the twentieth century. Since then, the position of Europe has relatively declined, partly because of conflicts within Europe itself, but mainly because the transitions and structures that had made Europe so dominant can now be found in most other countries. Some, like the United States, first emerged as European colonies or as cultural and political offshoots of Europe. Others have very different and ancient backgrounds. But whatever their backgrounds and cultural differences, all peoples in the contemporary world have been caught up in processes of "modernization" or "development," which often means acquiring or adapting some of the technical skills, commercial systems, and state power first exhibited by Europeans.

Europe's early modern ascendancy

There is thus in our time a kind of global modern civilization that overlies or enters into the diverse, regional cultures of the world. This civilization is an interlocking global system, in that conditions and conflicts on one side of the globe have repercussions on the other. Communications are almost instantaneous, and news travels everywhere through new social media. If the air is polluted in one country, neighboring countries are affected; if oil ceases to flow from the Middle East or if oil prices suddenly change, the lives of people in distant societies may become very difficult. The modern world depends on elaborate, interlocking transportation systems; on science, industry, machines, and computers; on new sources of energy to meet insatiable demands; on scientific medicine, public hygiene, and efficient methods of raising food. Nations fight wars by advanced technological methods or maintain peace by global diplomacy. There is an earth-encompassing network of finance and trade, loans and debts, investments and bank accounts, with worldwide fluctuations in monetary exchanges and balances of payments. More than 190 very unequal and disunited members compose the United Nations and represent every region of the world, but the concept of modern sovereign nationhood, as represented in that body, is derived largely from Europe.

In most modern countries there have been social and political movements for more democratic political systems, and all modern governments, democratic or not, seek to mobilize the energies and support of their populations. In modern societies old customs loosen, and ancestral religions are often questioned or transformed. There are usually demands for individual liberation from various social traditions, and people expect a higher standard of living. Modern societies typically move toward more equality between sexes and races, between adherents of different religions, or between different regions within the same country; and most modern governments provide social and economic assistance for people with low incomes. Movements for social change may be slow and gradual, or revolutionary and catastrophic, but social change is constant and universal.

Modern social transitions

Such are a few of the historical trends of modernity. New "modernizing" forms of technology, culture, and economic organization now emerge in many different places around the world and affect people everywhere, but most of the early patterns of modernity appeared first in Europe or in the global expansion of European societies (including the United States). The present book thus deals mainly with the historical evolution of European societies and cultures, with increasing attention in later chapters to Europe's colonial systems and growing interactions with other cultures around the world. European encounters with diverse peoples and civilizations led to a wide range of cross-cultural exchanges and conflicts, including movements that criticized or rejected many aspects of "modernity" itself. Such anti-modern movements have often become influential in modern world history, and when they have occurred outside of Europe they have often been called anti-European or anti-Western, as if to show that Europe and the West embody most of the key problems or dangers of modern history. Even those movements that most vigorously challenge European social and cultural systems, however, must confront the institutions, ideas, and legacies of modern European history.

Cross-cultural exchanges

If "modern" refers especially to a global economic system or changing social values or more complicated, interconnected ways of living, it has also another sense—meaning merely what is recent or current. The word "modern" is used for very different time spans. A modern kitchen may be 5 years old, modern physics is more than 100 years old, modern science is almost 400 years old, and the modern European languages began to emerge about 1,000 years ago. Modern civilization, which is always changing and which continues to develop new social-cultural practices that are often called "postmodern," has evolved throughout the world over the last 250 years; but it still includes many ideas and social customs that are much older, sometimes dating back to antiquity.

Roughly speaking, it may be said that modern times began in Europe about 1500. Modern times were preceded by a period of 1,000 years called the Middle Ages, which set in about 500 C.E., and which were in turn preceded by about another 1,000 years of classical Greek and Roman civilization. The long histories of people in Egypt and Mesopotamia began much earlier, coinciding also with early civilizations (farther east) in the Indus Valley and China.

All times prior to the European Middle Ages are commonly called "ancient." But the whole framework—ancient, medieval, and modern—reflects historical conventions whose meanings developed mainly with reference to Europe before they became more common for categorizing historical eras throughout the world. We shall thus begin with a running start across the distant past, and then slow the pace as we more fully survey European history in modern times.

 Suggested Further Readings can be found in the ebook, on Connect, or online at www.mhhe .com/kramer12e.

Chapter 1

THE RISE OF EUROPE

Europeans were by no means the pioneers of human civilization. Half of recorded history had passed before anyone in Europe could read or write. The priests of Egypt began to keep written records between 4000 and 3000 B.C.E., but 2,000 years later the poems of Homer were still being circulated in the Greek city-states by word of mouth—a form of oral history that has sustained collective memories in many human cultures.

Shortly after 3000 B.C.E., while the pharaohs were building the pyramids, Europeans were laboriously setting up the huge, unwrought stones called megaliths, of which Stonehenge is the best-known example. In a word, until after 2000 B.C.E., Europe was in the Neolithic or New Stone Age. This was in truth a great age in human history, the age in which human beings learned to make and use sharp tools, weave cloth, build living quarters, domesticate animals, plant seeds, harvest crops, and sense the returning cycles of the months and years. But the Middle East—Egypt, the valley between the Euphrates and Tigris rivers, the island of Crete, and the shores of the Aegean Sea (which belonged more to Asia than to Europe)—had reached its Neolithic Age 2,000 years before Europe. By about 4000 B.C.E. the Middle East was already moving into the Bronze Age, and well-organized ancient societies began to evolve along the Nile, Tigris, and Euphrates rivers. The ancient history of Europe lagged behind, emerging long after other civilizations had developed complex social systems, enduring architectural monuments, government bureaucracies, religious priesthoods, and written texts.

1. ANCIENT TIMES: GREECE, ROME, AND CHRISTIANITY

After about 2000 B.C.E., in the dim, dark continent that Europe then was, great changes began that are now difficult to trace. Europeans, too, learned how to smelt and forge metals, with the Bronze Age setting in about 2000 B.C.E. and the Iron Age about 1000 B.C.E. There was also a steady infusion of new peoples into Europe. They spoke languages related to languages now spoken in India and Iran, to which similar peoples migrated at about

Chapter emblem: Portrait of St. Augustine by Lippo Memmi (c. 1291–1356). (©Photos.com/Getty Images)

the same time. All these languages (whose interconnection was not known until the nineteenth century) are now referred to as Indo-European, and the people who spoke them became the ancestors both of the classical Greeks and Romans and of the Europeans of modern times. All European languages today are Indo-European with the exceptions of Basque, which is thought to be a survival from before the Indo-European invasion, and of Finnish and Hungarian, which were brought into Europe from Asia some centuries later. It was these invading Indo-Europeans who diffused over Europe the kind of speech from which the Latin, Greek, Germanic, Slavic, Celtic, and Baltic languages were later derived.

The Greek World

The first Indo-Europeans to emerge into the clear light of history, in what is now Europe, were the Greeks. They filtered down through the Balkan peninsula to the shores of the Aegean Sea about 1900 B.C.E., undermining the older Cretan civilization and occupying most of what has since been called Greece by 1300 B.C.E. Beginning about 1150 B.C.E., other Greek-speaking tribes invaded from the north in successive waves. The newcomers included many restless and warlike tribes, and their coming ushered in several centuries of chaos and unrest before a gradual stabilization and revival began in the ninth century. The *Iliad* and the *Odyssey,* written down about 800 B.C.E., but composed and recited much earlier, probably refer to wars between the Greeks and other centers of civilization, of which one was at Troy in Asia Minor. The siege of Troy is thought to have occurred about 1200 B.C.E.

The ancient Greeks proved to be an exceptionally creative people, achieving new cultural heights in thought and letters. They absorbed the knowledge of earlier Eastern cultures, the mathematical lore of the ancient Chaldeans, and the arts and crafts that they found in Asia Minor and on voyages to Egypt. They added immediately to everything that they learned. It was the Greeks of the fifth and fourth centuries B.C.E. who formulated what later Europeans long meant by the beautiful, and who first speculated on political freedom.

Greek cultural accomplishments

As they settled down, the Greeks formed tiny city-states, all independent and often at war with one another, each only a few miles across, and typically including a coastal city and its adjoining farmlands. Athens, Corinth, and Sparta were such city-states. Many were democratic, which meant that all male citizens could congregate in the marketplace to elect officials and discuss their public business. They were not democratic in a modern sense because slaves, resident noncitizens (called "metics"), and women were excluded from political life, but male citizens participated in public debates and served in public institutions.

Politics was turbulent in the small Greek states. Democracy alternated with aristocracy, oligarchy, despotism, and tyranny. From this rich fund of experience was born systematic political science as set forth in the unwritten speculations of Socrates and in the *Republic* of Plato and the *Politics* of Aristotle in the fourth century B.C.E. The Greeks also were the first to write history as a subject distinct from myth and legend. Herodotus, "the Father of History," traveled throughout the Greek world and far beyond, ferreting out all he could learn of the past. Thucydides, in his account of the wars between Athens and Sparta, presented history as a guide to enlightened citizenship and constructive statecraft.

Classical Greek virtues

Perhaps because they were a restless and vehement people, the Greeks came to prize the "classical" virtues, which they were the first to define and which would have great influence in the subsequent history of European societies. For them, the ideal lay in moderation, or a golden mean. They valued order, balance, symmetry, clarity, and control. Their statues of idealized males revealed their conception of what humans ought to be—noble creatures,

The Parthenon, constructed in ancient Athens during the fifth century B.C.E. to honor the goddess Athena, gave architectural form to the Greek respect for balance, order, and symmetry.
(©Bruno Cossa/SOPA/Corbis)

dignified, poised, unterrified by life or death, masters of themselves and their feelings. Their architecture, as in the Parthenon, made use of exactly measured angles and rows of columns. The classical order, or set of carefully wrought pillars placed in a straight line at specified intervals, represented the firm impress of human reason on the brute materials of nature. The same sense of form and order was thrown over the torrent of human words. Written language became carefully planned and organized for effect. The epic poem, the lyric, the drama, the oration, along with history and the philosophical dialogue, each with its own rules and principles of composition, became the forms within which European writers long expressed their thoughts.

Reflecting on the world about them, Greek philosophers such as Plato concluded that something more enduring existed beyond the world of appearances, that true reality was not what met the eye in the material world. With other peoples, and with the Greeks themselves in earlier times, this same realization had led to the formation of myths, dealing with invisible but mighty beings known as gods and with faraway places on the tops of mountains, beneath the earth, or in a world that followed death. Greek thinkers set to criticizing the web of myth. They looked for rational or natural explanations behind the variety and confusion that they saw. Some, observing human sickness, said that disease was not a demonic possession, but a natural sequence of conditions in the body, which could be identified, understood, and even treated in a natural way. Others, turning to physical nature, said that all matter was in reality composed of a very few things—made up of atoms or elements—which they usually designated as fire, water, earth, and air. Some said that change was a kind of illusion, all basic reality being uniform; some, that only change was real, and that the world was in flux. Some, like Pythagoras, found the enduring reality in mathematics. The Greeks, in short, laid the foundations for scientific thinking. Studying also the way in which the rational mind worked, or ought to work, if it was to reach truthful conclusions, they developed the science of logic. The great codifier of Greek thought on almost all subjects in the classical period was Aristotle, who lived in Athens from 384 to 322 B.C.E.

Spread of Greek civilization

Greek influence spread widely and rapidly. Hardly were some of the city-states founded when their people, crowded within their narrow bounds, sent off some of their number with equipment and provisions to establish colonies. In this way Greek cities were very early established in south Italy, in Sicily, and even in the western Mediterranean, where Marseilles was founded about 600 B.C.E. Later the Greek city-states, unable to unite, succumbed to conquest by Philip of Macedon, who came from the relatively crude northern part of the Greek world, and whose son, Alexander the Great (356–323 B.C.E.), led a phenomenal, conquering march into Asia, across Persia, and on as far as India itself. Alexander's empire did not hold together, but Greek civilization, after having spread into the western Mediterranean, now began also to influence the ancient peoples of Egypt and the Middle East. Greek thought, Greek art, and the Greek language spread far and wide, drawing at the same time on the knowledge and creativity of other ancient cultures. The most famous "Greeks" after the fourth century B.C.E. and during the early centuries of the Christian era usually did not come from Greece but from the Hellenized Middle East, and especially from Alexandria in Egypt. Among these later Greeks were the great summarizers or writers of encyclopedias in which ancient science was passed on to later generations— Strabo in geography, Galen in medicine, Ptolemy in astronomy. All three lived in the first and second centuries C.E., and all would influence European views of knowledge during the cultural transitions of the early modern era.

The Forum was the vital center of Roman public life and a symbol of imperial power. Rome's sense of grandeur and social order can still be discerned in the Forum's ruins, which are pictured here with the famous coliseum in the background.

(©Jessica Byrne)

The Roman World

In 146 B.C.E. the Greeks who lived within Greece were conquered by the military forces of Rome, the expanding power that had already taken control of the western Mediterranean. The Romans kept their own Latin language but rapidly absorbed what they could of the intellectual and artistic culture of the Greeks. Over a period of two or three centuries they assembled an empire that included all of the ancient Mediterranean and Middle Eastern civilizations west of Persia. Egypt, Greece, Asia Minor, and Syria all became Roman provinces, but in them the Romans had hardly any deep influence except in a political sense. The Romans also used ruthless methods of conquest to build their empire in the western Mediterranean and far to the north—in what are now Tunisia, Algeria, Morocco, Spain, Portugal, France, Switzerland, Belgium, and England—where in the long run they acted as civilizing agents, transmitting to these hitherto isolated countries the age-old achievements of the East and the more recent culture of Greece and of Rome itself. So thorough was the Romanization that Latin became the commonly spoken language in most western Mediterranean cultures. It was later displaced by Arabic in Africa but survives to this day, transformed by time, in the Romance languages of France, Italy, Spain, Portugal, Romania, and Latin America.

In the Roman Empire, which lasted with many vicissitudes from about 31 B.C.E. to the latter part of the fifth century C.E., virtually the entire civilized world of the ancient West was politically united and

The Roman Empire

enjoyed generations of internal peace. Rome was the center, around which in all directions lay the "circle of lands," the *orbis terrarum,* the known world—that is, as known in the West, for the Han Empire at the same time in China (202 B.C.E. to 220 C.E.) was also a highly organized cultural and political entity. The Roman Empire consisted essentially of the coasts of the Mediterranean Sea, which provided the great artery of transport and communication, and from which no part of the empire, except northern Gaul (France),

Caesar Augustus became the first emperor of the Roman Empire after a protracted struggle for power in the first century B.C.E. He reorganized the earlier Roman republican government into a new imperial system during his long reign (31 B.C.E.-14 C.E.). As this statue suggests, Augustus was often portrayed as a powerful symbol of the pax Romana.

(©PaoloGaetano/Getty Images)

Britain, and the Rhineland, was more than a couple of hundred miles away. Civilization among the elites in this vast empire was remarkably uniform; there were no distinct nationalities, and the most significant cultural difference was linguistic. East of Italy the predominant language was Greek, whereas in Italy and to the west the predominant language was Latin. Cities grew up everywhere, engaged in a busy commercial life, exchanged ideas with one another, and, like the cities in other ancient cultures, relied on the labor of slaves. There were always more cities in the East, where most of the manufacturing crafts and the densest population were still concentrated, but they sprang up now in the West—indeed, most of the older cities of France, Spain, England, and western and southern Germany boast of origins under the Romans.

The distinctive aptitude and enduring influence of the Romans lay in organization, administration, government, and law. Never before had armies been so systematically formed, maintained over such long periods, dispatched at a word of command over such distances, or maneuvered so effectively on the field of battle. Never had so many peoples been governed from a single center. The Romans had at first possessed self-governing and republican institutions, but they lost them in the process of conquest, and the governing talents that they displayed in the days of the empire were of an authoritarian character—talents not for self-government but for managing, coordinating, and ruling the manifold and scattered parts of one enormous system. Locally, cities and city-states enjoyed a good deal of autonomy. But above them all rose a pyramid of imperial officials and provincial governors, culminating in the emperor at the top. The empire kept peace, the *pax Romana,* and even provided a certain justice for its many peoples. Lawyers worked on the body of principles known ever afterward as Roman law.

The pax Romana

Roman judges had somehow to settle disputes between persons of different regions, or between persons with conflicting local customs, for example, two merchants of Spain and Egypt. The Roman law came therefore to hold that no custom is necessarily right, that there is a higher or universal law by which fair decisions may be made, and that this higher, universal, or "natural" law, or "law of nature," will be understandable or acceptable to everyone, since it arises from human nature and reason. Here the lawyers drew on Greek philosophy for support. They held also that law derives its force from being enacted by a proper authority (not merely from custom, usage, or former legal cases); this authority to make law they called *majestas,* or sovereign power, and they attributed it to the emperor. Thus the Romans emancipated the idea of law from mere custom on the one hand and mere caprice on the other; they regarded it as something to be formed by enlightened intelligence, consistent with reason and the nature of things, and they associated it with the solemn action of official power. It must be added that Roman law favored the state, or the public interest as seen by the government, rather than the interests or liberties of individual persons, and it generally provided men with more legal privileges than women. These principles, together with more specific ideas on such matters as property, debt, marriage, and wills were in later centuries to have a great effect in Europe.

The Coming of Christianity

The thousand years during which Greco-Roman civilization arose and flourished were notable in another way even more momentous for all later human history. It was in this period that the great world religions came into being. Within the time bracket 800 B.C.E. to 700 C.E. the lives of Confucius and Buddha, of the major Jewish prophets, and of Muhammad are all included. At the very midpoint (probably about 4 B.C.E.), in Palestine in the Roman Empire, a man named Jesus was born, believed by his followers to be the Son of God. Jesus became a popular religious teacher who urged his disciples to assist the poor, alleviate suffering, and help all those in need, including strangers. A Roman governor, fearing social disruption, ordered Jesus's crucifixion, but his followers affirmed that Jesus arose from death and later appeared to some who had known him.

The new Christian religion thus began to develop in Palestine, and, like Jesus, the first Christians were Jews. But under the impulse of its own doctrine, which held that all people were alike in spirit, and under the strong early leadership of Paul, a man of Jewish birth, Roman citizenship, and Greek culture, Christianity began to make converts. The new religion, as described in the canonical gospel writings of the Christian Bible and the commentaries of early Christian thinkers, gradually fused the monotheism of Judaism and its ethical teachings with various themes in Greek philosophy, creating a new synthesis of Judeo-Greek thought that would shape much of the later history of ideas in Western cultures. Christianity gained adherents across most of the Roman Empire, and there were certainly a few Christians in Rome by the middle of the first century. Both Paul and the elder apostle, Peter, according to church tradition, died as martyrs at Rome in the time of Emperor Nero about 67 C.E.

The Christian teaching spread at first mainly among the poor, the people at the bottom of society, those whom Greek politics and Roman imperial powers had passed over or enslaved, and who had the least to delight in or to hope for in the existing world. Women were also drawn to the new religion, perhaps in part because early Christianity offered

Emergence and spread of Christianity

them more autonomy and more opportunities for leadership than they found in the traditional patriarchal order of Roman law and families. Gradually Christian ideas reached the upper classes; a few classically educated and well-to-do people became Christians; in the second century Christian bishops and writers were at work publicly in various parts of the empire.

In the late third century, with the empire in turmoil, the Roman Emperor Diocletian blamed the social troubles on the Christians and subjected them to wholesale persecution. This repression soon ended in the early fourth century, however, when the Emperor Constantine converted to Christianity and befriended Christian advisors. He also sought to create doctrinal unity by convening church leaders in a council at Nicaea (325 C.E.). The assembled clergy produced the Nicene Creed, affirming a trinitarian belief in the eternal existence of God the Father, God the Son, and the Holy Spirit. Later bishops and church councils gradually came to agree on 66 canonical books for the Old and New Testaments of the Christian Bible, which the late fourth-century scholar Jerome translated from Hebrew and Greek into Latin. By the fifth century the entire Roman world was formally Christian; no other religion was officially tolerated. The deepest thinkers were Christians who combined Christian beliefs with the now thousand-year-old tradition of Greco-Roman thought, philosophy, and social institutions.

It is impossible to exaggerate the importance of the coming of Christianity. It brought with it, for one thing, an altogether new sense of human life. Where the Greeks had demonstrated the powers of the

Christian beliefs

mind, the Christians explored the soul, and they taught that in the sight of God all souls were equal, that every human life was sacrosanct and inviolate, and that all worldly distinctions of greatness, beauty, and brilliancy were in the last analysis superficial. Where the Greeks had linked the beautiful with the good, thought ugliness to be bad, shrunk from disease as an imperfection, and viewed everything misshapen as horrible and repulsive, the Christians resolutely saw a spiritual beauty even in the plainest or most unpleasant exterior and sought out the diseased, the disabled, and the mutilated to give them help. Love, for the ancients, was never quite distinguished from Venus; for the Christians, who held that God was love, it took on deep overtones of sacrifice and compassion. Suffering itself was in a way divine, since God had also suffered on the Cross in human form. A new dignity was thus found for suffering that the world could not cure. Other ancient philosophies had offered ethical advice and guidance for living a "good life," but the Christians worked to relieve suffering as none had worked before. They protested against the massacre of prisoners of war, against the mistreatment and degradation of slaves, against the sending of gladiators to kill each other in the arena for another's pleasure. In place of the Greek and pagan self-satisfaction with human accomplishments they taught humility in the face of an almighty Providence, and in place of proud distinctions between high and low, slave and free, civilized and barbarian, they held that all men and women were spiritually alike because all were children of the same God.

On an intellectual level Christianity also marked a revolution. It was Christianity, not rational philosophy, that dispelled the ancient beliefs in greater and lesser gods and goddesses; the blood sacrifices and self-immolation; or the frantic resort to magic, fortune-telling, and divination. The Christians taught that there was only one God. The pagan conception of local, tribal, or national gods disappeared. For all the world there was only one plan of salvation and one Providence, and all human beings took their origin from one source. The idea of the world as one thing, a "universe," was thus affirmed with a new depth of meaning. The very intolerance of Christianity (which was new to the ancient world) came from this new sense of human unity, in which it was thought that all people should have, and deserved to have, the one true and saving religion.

The Christians were often denounced and sometimes persecuted for their political ideas. The Roman Empire was a world state, and the Romans accepted no rival to its power; no living human being except the emperor was sovereign; no one anywhere on earth was his equal. Between gods and human beings, in the pagan view, there was moreover no clear distinction. Some gods

Persecution of Christians

St. Augustine's influence on Christian theology was honored throughout the Middle Ages and early modern era. He appears here in an early fourteenth-century portrait by the Italian artist Lippo Memmi (c. 1291–1356).

(©Photos.com/Getty Images)

behaved very humanly, and some human creatures were more like gods than others. The emperor was held to be veritably a god. A cult of Caesar was established and regarded as necessary to maintain the state, which was the world itself. All this the Christians firmly refused to accept. It was because they would not worship Caesar that some Roman officials regarded them as mysterious social incendiaries who must be persecuted or even stamped out.

The Christian doctrine on this point went back to a saying from Jesus in the New Testament Gospel of Matthew, which advised that one should render to Caesar the things that were Caesar's, and to God those that were God's. The same dualism was presented more systematically by St. Augustine about 420 C.E. in his *City of God.* Few books were more influential in shaping the later development of European civilization.

The "world," the western Mediterranean world of Caesar, in the time of St. Augustine, was going to ruin. Rome itself was plundered in 410 C.E. by heathen barbarians. Augustine wrote the *City of God* with this event obsessing his imagination. He wrote to show that though the material world could perish there was yet another world that was more enduring and more important. | *St. Augustine*

There were, he said, really two "cities," the earthly and the heavenly, the temporal and the eternal, the city of man and the City of God. The earthly city was the domain of state and empire, of political authority and political obedience. It was a good thing, as part of God's providential scheme for human life, but it had no inherently divine character of its own. The emperor was human. The state was not absolute; it could be judged, criticized, or corrected from sources outside itself. It was, for all its majesty and splendor, really subordinate in some way to a higher and spiritual power. This power lay in the City of God. By the City of God Augustine meant many things, and readers found all sorts of meanings in later ages. The heavenly city might mean heaven itself, the abode of God and of blessed spirits enjoying life after death. It might mean certain elect spirits of this world, the good people as opposed to the bad. It might, more theoretically, be a system of ideal values or ideal justice, as opposed to the crude approximations of the actual world.

In any case, this Christian dualism gave the later European and Western world a theoretical escape from what is called Caesaropapism, a political system in which one person holds the powers of ruler and of pontiff. Instead, the spiritual power and the political power were held | *Rejection of Caesaropapism* | to be separate and independent. In later times popes and kings often quarreled with each other; the clergy often struggled for political power, and governments often attempted to dictate what people should believe, or love, or hope for. But speaking in general of European history, neither side has ever won out, and in the sharp distinction between the spiritual and the temporal has lain the germ of many liberties in later societies. At the same time, the idea that no ruler, no government, and no institution is too mighty to rise above moral criticism eventually opened the way to dynamic and progressive changes in European social and political systems.

2.   THE EARLY MIDDLE AGES: THE FORMATION OF EUROPE

There was really no Europe or "European civilization" in ancient times. In the Roman Empire we may see a Mediterranean world, or even a kind of early West and East in the Latin- and Greek-speaking portions. But the West included parts of Africa as well as of Europe, and Europe as we know it was divided by the Rhine-Danube frontier, south and west of which lay the civilized provinces of the empire, and north and east the "barbarians" of whom the Roman world knew almost nothing. To the Romans, "Africa" meant lands that are now called Tunisia and Algeria; "Asia" meant the Asia Minor peninsula; and the word "Europe," since it meant little, was scarcely used at all. It was in the half-millennium from the fifth to the tenth centuries that Europe as such for the first time emerged with its peoples brought together in a life of their own, clearly set off from Asia or Africa and beginning to create a culture that Europeans would later describe as "Western."

The Disintegration of the Roman Empire

The Roman Empire began to fall apart, especially in the West, and the Christianizing of the empire did nothing to impede its decline. The Emperor Constantine, who in embracing Christianity undoubtedly hoped to strengthen the imperial system, also took one other

Founding of Constantinople

significant step. In 330 C.E. he founded a new capital at the old Greek city of Byzantium, which he renamed Constantinople. (It is now Istanbul.) Thereafter the Roman Empire had two capitals, Rome and Constantinople, and was administered in two halves. Increasingly the center of gravity moved eastward, as if returning to the more ancient centers in the Middle East, as if the experiment of civilizing the West were to be given up as a failure.

Throughout its long life the empire had been surrounded on almost all sides by people whom the Romans called "barbarians"—wild Celts in Wales and Scotland, Germans in the heart of Europe, Persians or Parthians in the East (barbarian only in the ancient sense of speaking neither Greek nor Latin), and, in the southeast, the Arabs. These diverse peoples, with the exception of some Persians, had never been brought within the control of ancient Greek or Roman civilization. Somewhat like the Chinese, who about 200 B.C.E. built several walls to solve the same problem, the Romans simply drew a line beyond which they themselves rarely ventured and would not allow the barbarians to pass. Nevertheless outsiders filtered into the empire. As early as the third century C.E., emperors and generals recruited bands of them to serve in the Roman armies. Their service over, they would receive farmlands, settle down, marry, and mingle with the population. By the fourth and fifth centuries a good many such individuals were even reaching high positions of state.

At the same time, in the West, for reasons that are not fully understood, the activity of the Roman cities began to falter, commerce began to decay, local governments became

Decline in the West

paralyzed, taxes became more ruinous, and free farmers were bound to the soil. The army seated and unseated emperors. Rival generals fought with each other. Gradually the western Roman Empire fell into decrepitude, and the old line between the Roman provinces and the barbarian world made less and less difference.

After some centuries of relative stability, the barbarians themselves, pressed by more distant peoples from Asia, began to move. Sometimes they first sought peaceable access to the empire, attracted by the warmer Mediterranean climate, or desiring to share in the

Barbarian invasions

advantages of Roman civilization. More often, Germanic tribes moved swiftly and by force, plundering, fighting, and killing as they went. In 476, a barbarian chieftain deposed the last Roman emperor in the West. Sometimes in the general upheaval peoples from Asia rapidly intermixed with other populations in the old Roman Empire. The most famous of these invaders were the Huns, who cut through central Europe and France about 450 under their leader Attila, the "scourge of God"—and then disappeared. There were also other invasions. Two centuries

later new irruptions burst upon the Greco-Roman world from the southeast, where hitherto outlying peoples poured in from the Arabian deserts. The Arabs, mobilized by the
new faith of Islam (Muhammad died in 632), fell as conquerors upon Syria, Mesopotamia,
and Persia; occupied Egypt about 640 and the old Roman Africa about 700; and in 711
they reached Spain.

Beneath these blows the old unity of the Greco-Roman or Mediterranean world was
broken. The "circle of lands" divided into three segments. Three types of civilization now
confronted each other across the inland sea.

The Byzantine World, the Arabic World, and the West about 700

The Eastern Roman, Later Roman, Greek, or Byzantine Empire (all names for the same
empire) with its capital at Constantinople, and now including only the Asia Minor
peninsula, the Balkan peninsula, and parts of Italy, made up one segment of the circle of
lands. It represented the most direct continuation of the ancient civilizations of the Middle East. It was Christian in religion and Greek in   *Byzantine Empire*
culture and language. Its people viewed themselves as the truest heirs
both of early Christianity and of earlier cultures in Greece. Art and architecture, trades
and crafts, commerce and navigation, thought and writing, government and law, while not
so creative or flexible as in the classical age, were still carried on actively in the Eastern
empire, on much the same level as in the closing centuries of ancient times. For all
Christians, and for heathen barbarians in Europe, the emperor of the East stood out as
the world's supreme ruler, and Constantinople as the world's preeminent and most
fabulous city.

The second segment of the Mediterranean world was the Arabic
and Islamic. It became the most dynamic culture in the lands of the   *Arabic world*
old Roman Empire, reaching from the neighborhood of the Pyrenees
through Spain and all North Africa into Arabia, Syria, and the East. Arabic was its
language; it became, and still remains, the common speech from Morocco to the Persian
Gulf. Islam was its religion, and it looked to the prophet Muhammad (c. 570–632) and
the Qur'an (Koran) for its religious truths. Muhammad had spent his early adult years as
a merchant in Mecca on the Arabian peninsula, but he began to have a series of intense
religious revelations when he was about 40 years old. These revelations led Muhammad
to a devout and uncompromising monotheism, which stressed the great power of God—
Allah in Arabic—and the human duty to adhere to God's will. Muhammad saw himself
as a prophet in the Jewish and Christian tradition, but he soon came to define his
revelations and teachings as the beginning of a new religion. The messages that came to
Muhammad through revelation were written down in the sacred book of Islam, the Qur'an,
which was organized into 114 chapters (called *suras*). Emphasizing submission to God,
the importance of prayer, and an ethical obligation to help others, the Qur'an provided
directions for the affairs of daily life as well as a powerful, poetic vision of the grandeur
of God.

Muhammad's revelations attracted little early support in Mecca. Indeed, the hostility
there forced him to move north in 622 to the city of Medina. This famous flight (the
Hegira) brought him to a more receptive community, where his teachings quickly gained
numerous adherents and from where the first Muslims set out to spread the new faith
across all of Arabia, including Mecca. Muhammad died in 632, but the new religion
continued to expand rapidly in all directions. Leadership passed to a series of caliphs who
were initially relatives of Muhammad himself. As Muslims conquered new territories and

The sixth-century emperor Justinian built the great Hagia Sophia to display his commitment to the Christian religion and the power of his capital city, Constantinople. The church became a mosque after the Byzantine Empire fell to Muslim invaders in the fifteenth century, but it remains the most famous achievement of Byzantine architecture.

(©David Madison/Getty Images)

won new converts throughout the Middle East and North Africa, the lands of Islam came under the control of these caliphs. All Muslims were included in the caliphate. The ruling caliph exercised both spiritual and political authority, and he was regarded as the true religious and military successor of Muhammad himself.

Conflicts and lasting divisions nevertheless developed during the era of the third caliph, Uthman—one of the sons-in-law of Muhammad and a leader of the Umayyad family. Supporters of Ali, a rival leader and also a son-in-law of Muhammad, killed Uthman in 656, and Ali came to power as the fourth caliph. This violence did not resolve the conflict, however, and Ali himself was soon murdered. Ali's followers refused to accept the legitimacy of the Umayyad family, which now regained control of the caliphate. A minority faction, called Shiites, continued to honor Ali and to claim that all true leaders of Islam must descend from him. Although most Muslims supported the Umayyad caliphs, the Shiite minority remained a permanent presence within Islam, sustaining the memory of Ali and challenging the religious legitimacy of the dominant Sunnis (a term that emerged later). Meanwhile, the Umayyad dynasty set up its capital in Damascus, and some members of the family extended their power as far west as Spain. Meeting at such places on the European continent and in other Mediterranean lands, Muslims and Christians began a long-developing pattern of exchanges and conflicts that would help to shape both of these religious cultures through all later centuries.

The Arabic world, like the Byzantine, built upon the heritage of the Greco-Romans. In religion, the early Muslims regarded themselves as successors to the Jewish and Christian traditions. They considered the line of Jewish prophets since Abraham to be spokesmen of the true God, and they put Jesus in this line. But they added that Muhammad was the last and greatest of the prophets, that the Qur'an set forth a revelation replacing that of the Jewish Bible, that the Christian New Testament was mistaken because Christ was not divine, and that the Christian belief in a Trinity was erroneous because there was in the strictest sense only One True God. To the Muslim Arabs, therefore, all Christians were dangerous or misguided infidels.

In mundane matters, the Arabs speedily took over the civilization of the lands they conquered. In the caliphate, as in the Byzantine Empire, the civilization of the ancient world went its way without serious interruption. Huge buildings and magnificent palaces were constructed; ships plied the Mediterranean; Arab merchants ventured over the deserts and traversed the Indian Ocean; holy or learned men corresponded over thousands of miles. The government developed efficient systems to collect taxes, enforce the laws, and keep the provinces in order. In the sciences the Arabs not only learned from but also went beyond the Greeks. They | *Arab Muslim Culture* translated Greek scientific literature: we know some of it today only through these medieval Arabic versions. Arab geographers had a wider knowledge of the world than anyone had possessed up to their time. Arab mathematicians developed algebra so far beyond the Greeks as almost to be its creator (algebra is an Arabic word), and in introducing the "Arabic" numerals (through their contacts with India) they made arithmetic, which in Roman numerals had been formidably difficult, into something that every schoolchild could be taught.

The third segment of the ancient Greco-Roman world was Latin Christendom, which about 700 C.E. did not look very promising. It was what was left over from the other two segments—what the Byzantines were unable to hold and the Arabs were | *Latin Christendom* unable to conquer. It included only Italy (shared in part with the Byzantines), France, the Rhineland, Britain, and a few other territories in northwestern Europe. Barbarian kings were doing their best to rule small kingdoms, but in truth all government had fallen to pieces. Usually the invading barbarians remained a minority, eventually to be absorbed. Only in England, and in the region immediately west of the Rhine, did the Germanic element supersede the older Celtic and Latin. But the presence of violent invaders amid peasants and city dwellers reduced to passivity by Roman rule, together with the earlier disintegration of Roman institutions, left this region in chaos.

The Western barbarians, as noted, were Germanic-speaking peoples, and the Germanic cultural influence became another distinctive | *Germanic customs* contribution to the making of Europe. Some Germans were Christian by the fourth century, but most were still heathen when they burst into the Roman Empire. Their languages had not been written down, but they possessed an intricate folklore and religion in which fighting and heroic valor were much esteemed. Though now in a migratory phase, they were an agricultural people who knew how to work iron, and they had a rudimentary knowledge of the crafts of the Romans. They were organized in small tribes and had a strong sense of tribal kinship, which (as with many similar peoples) dominated their ideas of leadership and law. They enjoyed more freedom in their affairs than did the citizens of the Roman Empire. Many of the tribes were roughly self-governing in that all free men, those entitled to bear arms, met in open fields to hold council, and often the tribe itself elected its leader or king. They had a strong sense of loyalty to the acknowledged king or chief, but they had no sense of loyalty to large or general institutions. They had no sense of the state—of any distant, impersonal, and continuing source of law and rule. Law they regarded as the inflexible custom of each tribe. In the absence of abstract jurisprudence or trained judges, they settled disputes by rough and ready methods. In the ordeal, for example, a person who obstinately floated when thrown into water was adjudged guilty. In trial by battle, the winner of a kind of ritualistic duel was regarded as innocent. The gods, it was thought, would not allow wrong to prevail.

The Germans who overran the old Roman provinces found it difficult to maintain any political organization at more than a local level. Security and civil order all but disappeared. Peasant communities were at the mercy of wandering bands of habitual fighters. Fighters often captured peasant villages, took them under their protection, guarded them from further marauders, and lived off their produce. Sometimes the same great fighting man came to possess many such villages, moving with his retinue of horsemen from one village to another to support himself throughout the year. Thus originated a new distinction between lord and servant, noble and commoner, martial and menial class. Life became local and self-sufficient. People ate, wore, used, and dwelled in only what they themselves and their neighbors could produce. In contrast to the economies of the Byzantine and Islamic worlds, western European trade died down, the cities became depopulated, money went out of circulation, and almost nothing was bought or sold. The Roman roads fell into neglect; people often used them as quarries for ready-cut building blocks for their own crude purposes. Western Europe not only broke up into localized villages but also ceased to have habitual exchanges across the Mediterranean. It lost contact with the eastern centers from which its former civilization had always been drawn. From roughly 500 C.E. on, most of Europe fell into what some later historians would call the "Dark Ages."

The Church and the Rise of the Papacy

Only one organized institution maintained a tie with ancient civilization. Only one institution, reaching over the whole West, could receive news or dispatch its agents over the whole area. This institution was the Christian Church. Its framework still stood; its network of bishoprics, as built up in late Roman times, remained intact except in places such as England, where the barbarian conquest was complete.

Growth of monasteries	In addition, a new type of religious institution spread rapidly with the growth of monasteries. The serious and the sensitive rejected the savagery about them, and both men and women retired into communities of their own (though not together, to be sure). Usually they

were left unmolested by rough neighbors who held them in religious awe. In a world of violence they formed islands of quiet, peace, and contemplation. Their prayers, it was believed, were of use to all the world, and their example might at the least arouse pangs of shame in more worldly people. The male religious houses, which came to be called monasteries or abbeys, generally adopted the rule of St. Benedict (c. 480–543), and the monks who lived there were governed by an abbot. Dedicated to the same ideals, they formed unifying filaments throughout the chaos of the Latin West. Female religious houses came to be called convents or abbeys, and the nuns in these communities were governed by an abbess.

Bishops, abbots, monks, nuns, and abbesses looked with veneration to Rome as the spot where St. Peter, the first apostle, had been martyred. The bishop of Rome corresponded with other bishops, sent out missionaries, gave advice on doctrine when he could, and attempted to oversee the situation throughout the Latin world as a whole. Moreover, with no emperor in Rome, the bishop took over the government and public affairs of the city. Thus the bishop of Rome, while claiming a primacy over all Christians, was not dominated by any secular power. In the East, the great church functionaries, the patriarchs, fell under the influence of the emperor who continued to rule at Constantinople. A tradition of Caesaropapism grew up in the East, but in the West the independence of the bishop of Rome now confirmed in practice a principle always maintained by the great churchmen of the West—the independence of the spiritual power from the political or temporal.

The growing authority of the popes was fortified by various arguments. St. Peter, it was held, had imparted the spiritual authority given to him by Christ himself to the Roman bishops who were his successors. This doctrine of the "Petrine supremacy" was based on two verses in the Bible (Matthew 16: 18–19), according to which Christ designated Peter as the head of the church, giving him the "power of the keys" to open and close the doors of eternal salvation. As for the pope's temporal rule in Rome, it was affirmed that the Emperor Constantine had given the bishop of Rome an enduring authority to govern the city. This "Donation of Constantine" was accepted as historical fact from the eighth century to the fifteenth, when it was proved to be a forgery.

Papal authority

It was the church that incorporated Germanic tribal groups such as the Goths, Franks, and Anglo-Saxons into new forms of social life; and when such groups embraced a more settled, civilized way of living, it was the church that they entered. As early as about 340 C.E., the church sent a missionary named Ulfilas to convert the Goths; his translation of the Bible represents the first writing down of any Germanic language. About 496, the king of the Franks, Clovis, was converted to Christianity. A hundred years later, in 597, the king of Kent in southeast England yielded to the persuasions of Augustine of Canterbury, another missionary dispatched from Rome, and the Christianization of the Anglo-Saxons gradually followed. Missionaries from Ireland, to which Christians of the Roman Empire had fled to escape the heathen barbarians, now returned to both Britain and the Continent to spread the gospel. By 700, after three centuries of turmoil, the borders of Christianity in the West were again roughly what they had been in late Roman times. Then in 711, as we have seen, Arab Muslims entered Spain. They crossed the Pyrenees and moved on toward central Europe, but were stopped by a Christian and Frankish army in 732 near Tours on the river Loire. Islam was turned back into Spain, thereby allowing the people of western Europe to expand their emerging Latin Christian culture.

Conversion of the Germanic tribes

The Empire of Charlemagne, 800–814

Among the Franks, in what is now northern France and the German Rhineland, there had arisen a line of capable rulers of whom the greatest was Charlemagne. The Frankish kings made it their policy to cooperate with the pope. The pope needed a protector against the military threats of his plundering neighbors and against the political claims of the Byzantine Empire upon the city of Rome. The Frankish kings, in return for protection thus offered, won papal support to their side. This made it easier for them to control their own bishops, who were more often seen on horseback than in the episcopal chair, and the papal alliance helped the kings pacify their own domains and wage wars of conquest against the heathen. In the year 800, in Rome, the pope crowned Charlemagne as emperor

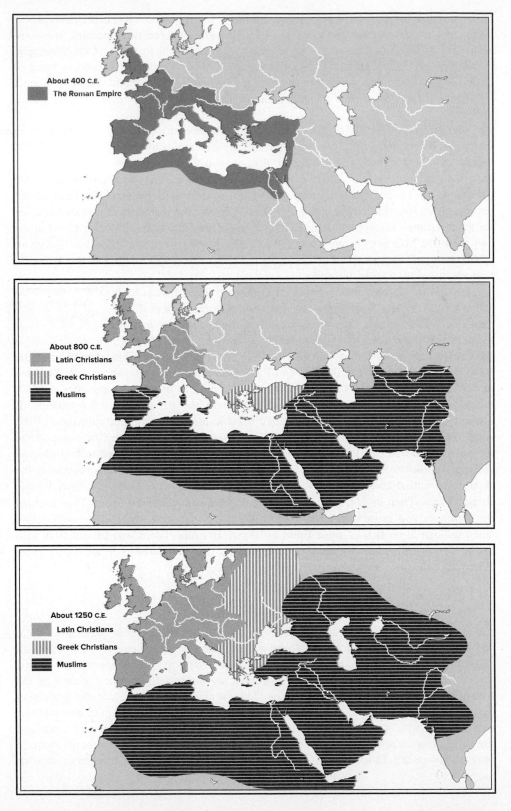

About 400 C.E.
The Roman Empire

About 800 C.E.
Latin Christians
Greek Christians
Muslims

About 1250 C.E.
Latin Christians
Greek Christians
Muslims

of the West. Frankish king and Roman bishop both believed that if only the Roman Empire could be restored peace and order might once more reign. Church and empire, religion and the state, were to be as two mighty swords employed in the same holy cause.

Charlemagne crossed the Pyrenees with an army that regained Christian control of northeastern Spain. He overthrew and subordinated the barbarian kings who had set themselves up in northern Italy. *Charlemagne*
He sent forces down the Danube, penetrated into Bohemia, and proceeded against some of the still heathen Germans (the Saxons) who lived along the river Elbe, and whom he either massacred or converted to Christianity. All these regions he brought within his new empire. Except for England and Ireland, which remained outside, the borders of his empire were coextensive with those of the Latin Christian world.

Once more, the diverse peoples of western Europe were loosely united under an empire. But a momentous change had occurred. Its *Revival of learning* capital did not lie in the ancient world of the Mediterranean. Its capital was now in northern Europe at Aix-la-Chapelle, or Aachen, near the mouth of the Rhine. Its ruler, Charlemagne, was a German of an ethnic group that had remained outside ancient civilization. Its people were Germans, French, and Italians, or, more precisely, the ancestors from whom these nationalities would later emerge. In the Greco-Roman world the north had always been at best provincial. Now the north became a center in its own right. Charlemagne dispatched embassies to the Byzantine emperor at Constantinople and to Harun al-Rashid, the great Muslim caliph at Baghdad. In intellectual matters, too, the north now became a capital. Centuries of violence and confusion had virtually destroyed education and systematic learning, even for the most powerful families in Europe. Charlemagne himself, though he understood Latin, could barely read and never learned to write. He used his authority, however, to revive the all but forgotten ancient learning and to spread education at least among the clergy. To his palace school came scholars from England, Germany, France, Italy, and Spain. They wrote and spoke in Latin, the only Western language in which complicated ideas could at the time be expressed. Disintegrating ancient manuscripts were copied and recopied to assure a more abundant supply for study—always by hand, but in a more rapid script than had been used before. This so-called Carolingian minuscule evolved into the small letters of the modern Western alphabet, only the capital letters being Roman. Meanwhile, Charlemagne sought to foster commerce by creating a new and more reliable coinage, which was based on silver, the gold coins of the Roman Empire having long since vanished.

THE MEDITERRANEAN WORLD about 400, 800, and 1250 C.E.
Greco-Roman civilization, centered about the Mediterranean, was officially Christian and politically unified under the Roman Empire in 400 C.E., but it broke apart into three segments in the early Middle Ages. Each segment developed its own type of life. Each segment also expanded beyond the limits of the ancient Mediterranean culture. By 1250, Latin Christendom reached to the Baltic and beyond. Greek Christendom expanded north of the Black Sea to include the Russians. The Muslim world spread into inner Asia and Africa. In 1250, and until 1492, the Muslims, or Moors, still held the southern tip of Spain. Jews lived in varying numbers throughout the Mediterranean world, and Jewish communities were important within each of the religious spheres on these maps.

This image of a monastery in a medieval Spanish manuscript shows how early Christian monks became known for their learning as well as their religious contemplation and disciplined labor.

(©The Pierpont Morgan Library/Art Resource, NY)

Ninth-Century Invasions; Europe by 1000

Second wave of invaders

In Charlemagne's empire we first see the emerging historical shape of Europe as a society and culture distinct from the Mediterranean world of antiquity, but the empire soon fell apart. New waves of invaders assailed Western Christendom in the ninth century. The Magyars (called in Latin "Hungarians") terrified various parts of Europe until they settled down on the middle Danube about the year 900. New Germanic tribes uprooted themselves, coming this time from Scandinavia, and variously known as Norse, Vikings, or Danes. Bursting out in all directions, they reached Kiev in Russia in 864, discovered Iceland in 874, and even touched America in 1000. In the Christian world they assaulted the coasts and pushed up the rivers but settled in considerable numbers only in the Danelaw in England and in Normandy in France. Meanwhile the Arabs raided the shores of France and Italy and occupied Sicily. Nowhere was the power of government strong enough to ward off such attacks. Everywhere the harassed local population found its own means of defense or, that failing, was slaughtered, robbed, or carried off into slavery.

Gradually the second wave of invaders was incorporated as the first had been, by the same process of conversion to Christianity. By the year 1000, this process was nearly complete. In 1001, the pope sent a golden crown to the Magyars to crown St. Stephen as their first king, thus bringing Hungary within the orbit of the Latin West. Poland, Bohemia, and the Scandinavian homelands of the Norse were Christianized during the same era. In older Christian countries, such as France, the last remote and isolated rustics—the "heathen" who lived in the "heath"—were finally ferreted out by missionaries and brought within the Christian fold. In Christian countries, Christianity now permeated every corner, and (despite the local differences that existed everywhere) the historic peoples of western Europe had come together within the spreading religious and cultural system of the Latin church.

Meanwhile the cultures of eastern and western Europe continued to drift apart. The refusal of Greek patriarchs at Constantinople to recognize the claims to primacy of the bishop of Rome, whom they regarded as a kind of Western barbarian, and the refusal of the Roman *"Great Schism of East and West"* pontiff to acknowledge the political pretensions of the Byzantine Empire, led to the Great Schism of East and West. This schism, after developing for three centuries, became definite in 1054. It divided the Christian world into the Latin or Roman Catholic and the Greek Orthodox churches. It was from Constantinople that Christianity reached the peoples of Russia. The Russians, like the Balkan peoples, remained out of contact with most of Europe during the centuries when spiritual and intellectual contacts were carried through the clergy. They believed, indeed, that the Latin West was evil, heretical, and unholy. The Latin West, at the same time, by the schism, cut one more of its ties with antiquity and emerged more clearly as an independent center of its own civilization.

By the year 1000 or soon thereafter, the entity that we now call Europe had come into existence. From the turbulence that followed the collapse of the Greco-Roman civilization had issued the peoples and the countries that would evolve into the cultures and societies of modern Europe. A kingdom of France had emerged, adjoining the great ill-defined bulk of Germany to the east. *Emerging European identities* There were small Christian kingdoms in northern Spain and a number of city-states in the Italian peninsula. In the north there were now a kingdom of England and a kingdom of Scotland; Denmark, Norway, and Sweden had also taken form. In the east rose the three great kingdoms of Poland, Bohemia, and Hungary, the first two predominantly Slavic, Hungary predominantly Magyar, but all were Latin and Catholic in culture and religion. The east Slavs, or Russians, and the Slavs and other peoples of the Balkan peninsula also formed kingdoms of their own. Their languages and religion were diverging from the cultures of western Europe. Christianized by Byzantine missionaries, they were Greek and Orthodox in culture and religion, and oriented toward Constantinople.

The civilization of western Europeans in the year 1000 was still unimpressive in comparison to the more polished circles of Byzantium or Baghdad. It might still seem that the West would suffer more than the East from their separation. But western Europeans began at this time to develop new social and economic activity, ushering in the European civilization of the High Middle Ages.

3.   THE HIGH MIDDLE AGES: SECULAR CIVILIZATION

Agriculture and the Feudal System after 1000

Some historical periods are so dynamic that a person who lives to a mature age can remember sweeping changes that have come in one's own lifetime. Such a time began in Europe in the eleventh century. People could see new towns rise and grow before their eyes. They could observe new undertakings in commerce or government. Most of the cities that became influential in Europe before the modern industrial era sprang up between about 1050 and 1200. The population of western Europe, which had been sparse even in Roman days, and which was even sparser after 500, suddenly began to grow denser about the year 1000, and it expanded steadily for two or three hundred years. The people of the High Middle Ages did not develop a new conception of progress because their minds were set upon timeless values and personal salvation in another world, but the period was nevertheless one of rapid progress in nonreligious or "secular" matters. Much was created that remained fundamental for European cultures far into modern times.

Agriculture and
population growth

The new era was made possible by a growth in population that went along with agricultural changes. After the Norse and Magyar attacks had stopped, Europe was spared the assaults of other outside invaders. There came to be more security of life and limb. Farmers could plant with more confidence that they would reap, and people could build houses with the expectation of passing them on to their children. Hence there was more planting and building. Sometime before the year 1000 a heavier plow was invented, which cut a deeper furrow. Better methods of harnessing horses made agriculture and transportation more efficient. The ancient Romans had continued simply to throw a yoke over a horse's neck, so that the animal in pulling a weight easily choked. Europeans, before the year 1000, began to use a horse collar that rested on the animal's shoulders. The single horse could pull a greater load, or several horses could now for the first time be hitched in tandem. The amount of available animal power was thus multiplied, at a time when animals were the main source of power other than human muscle. Windmills, unknown to the ancients, were developed in the Low Countries about this time. They too offered a new source of power. Thus at the very beginning of a specifically "European" history, one may detect characteristics that would also shape subsequent European civilization—a search for technological invention, a quest for new sources of energy.

With such labor-saving devices people continued to work very hard, but they obtained more results by their efforts. Probably the use of such inventions, together with the influence of the Christian clergy, accounts for the gradual disappearance of slavery from Europe and its replacement by the less-abject and less-degrading status of serfdom. It is true that medieval Christians, when they could, continued to enslave whites as they were later to do with blacks. Usually such slaves were captured in wars with tribes not yet converted to Christianity, and sometimes they were exported as a form of merchandise to the Byzantine and Muslim worlds. As the successive European peoples became Christianized, the supply of non-Christian slaves dried up within Europe. Medieval Christians did not enslave each other, nor was slavery essential to any important form of production.

Not only did population increase, and work become more productive, but also groups of people became less isolated from one another. Communications improved. The roads remained poor or nonexistent, but bridges were built across European rivers, and settlers filled in the wildernesses that had formerly separated the inhabited areas. Trees were felled, land was cleared, and the rural population clustered in village communities. The "nucleated" village gave more security, more contact between families, and readier access to the blacksmith or the priest. It also made possible a communally organized agriculture.

Better ways of using land were introduced in the "three-field" system, which spread to almost every region where cereal crops were the staple. In this system the peasant

Three-field system

village divided its arable fields into three parts. The first part was then sown with one crop, such as wheat; a second part with another, such as barley; and the third was left to lie fallow. The three parts were rotated from year to year. Thus soil exhaustion was avoided at a time when fertilizers were unknown. Formerly, half or less of the available fields had been cultivated at any one time. With the three-field system two-thirds of the land came into annual use. This change, reinforced by better plowing and more effective employment of animals, led to a huge increase in the supply of food.

The peace and personal security necessary to agriculture also advanced, in the absence of effective public authority, through the growth of institutions that we know as "feudalism." Feudalism was

Feudalism

intricate and diverse, but in essence it was a means of carrying on some kind of government on a local basis where no organized state existed. After Charlemagne's empire collapsed in the ninth century the real authority fell into the hands of persons who were most often called "counts." The count was the most important man of a region covering a few hundred square miles. To build up his own position, and strengthen himself for war against other counts, he tried to keep the peace and maintain control over the lesser lords in his county, those whose possessions extended over a few hundred or a few thousand acres. These lesser lords accepted or were forced to accept his protection. They became his vassals, and he became their lord. The lord and vassal relation was one of reciprocal duties. The lord protected the vassal and assured him justice and firm tenure of his land. If two vassals of the same lord disputed the possession of the same village, the lord decided the case, sitting in council (or "court") with all his vassals assembled and judging according to the common memory or customary law of the district. If a vassal died young, leaving only small children, the lord took the family under his "wardship" or guardianship, guaranteeing that the rightful heirs would inherit in due time. Correspondingly the vassal agreed to serve the lord as a fighting man for a certain number of days in the year. The vassal also had to advise and serve the lord in other ways, including service in his court for the judging of disputes. Usually he owed the lord no money or material payment, but if the lord had to be ransomed from captivity, or when the lord's children married, the vassal paid a fee. The vassal also paid a fee on inheriting an estate, and the income of estates under wardship went to the lord. Thus the lord collected sporadic revenues with which to finance his somewhat primitive government.

This feudal scheme gradually spread across northern Europe. Lords at the level of counts became in turn the vassals of dukes. In the year 987, the great lords of France chose Hugh Capet as their king and became his vassals. The kings of France enjoyed little real power for another 200 years, but the descen-

Capetian kings

dants of Hugh occupied their throne for eight centuries, until the French Revolution. Similarly the magnates of Germany elected a king in 911. In 962, the German King Otto I was crowned emperor by the pope, as Charlemagne had been before him. Otto's Roman coronation launched a new "Holy Roman Empire" in central Europe, of which much will be heard in the following chapters.

England in these formative centuries did not choose a king by election. England was conquered in 1066 by the Duke of Normandy, William. The Normans (the Norse reshaped by a century of Christian and French influences) imposed upon England a centralized and efficient type of feudalism that they had developed in Normandy. In England, from an early date, the king and his officials therefore had considerable power, which led to more civil

The Normans in England

peace and personal security than on the Continent. Within the framework of a strong monarchy self-governing institutions could eventually develop with a minimum of disorder.

The notable feature of feudalism was its mutual or reciprocal character. In this it differed from the old Roman imperial principle, by which the emperor had been a majestic and all-powerful sovereign. Under feudalism no one was sovereign. King and people, lord and vassal, were joined in a kind of contract. Each owed something to the other. If one defaulted, the obligation ceased. If a vassal refused his due services, the king had the right to enforce compliance. If the king violated the rights of the vassal, the vassals could join

Most people in the Middle Ages worked in the fields, coping like the peasants in these late medieval illustrations with the seasons, soil, seeds, and animals that shaped agricultural life.
(©Print Collector/Hulton Archive/Getty Images)

together against him. The king was supposed to act with the advice of the vassals, who formed his council or court. If the vassals believed the king to be exceeding his lawful powers, they could impose terms upon him. Although feudalism was always a hierarchical system of lords and vassals, its mutual or contractual character contributed to later European ideas of constitutional government.

Feudalism applied in the strict sense only to the military or noble class. Below the feudal world lay the vast mass of the peasantry. In the village, the lowliest vassal of a higher noble was lord over his own subjects. The village, with its people and surrounding farmlands, constituted a "manor," the estate of a lord. In the eleventh century most people of the manor were serfs. They were "bound to the soil" in that they could not leave the manor without the lord's permission. Few wanted to leave anyway, at a time when the world beyond the village was unknown

The manor and serfs

and dangerous, when food supplies were precarious, and when other lands were filled at best only with other similar manors. The lord, for his part, could not expropriate the villagers or drive them away. He owed them protection and the administration of justice. They in turn worked his fields and gave him part of the produce of their own. No money changed hands, because there was virtually no money in circulation. The manorial system was the agricultural base on which a ruling class was supported. It supported also the clergy, for the church held much land in the form of manors. It gave the protection from physical violence and the framework of communal living without which the peasants could not grow crops or tend livestock.

With the rise of agricultural productivity, lords and even a few peasants began to produce a surplus, which they might sell if they could find a market. The country was thus able to produce enough food to support a town population. And since population grew with the increase of the food supply, a surplus rural population also began to exist. Restless spirits among the peasants now wanted to get away from the manor. And many went off to the new towns.

The Rise of Towns and Commerce

We have seen how the ancient cities had decayed. In the ninth and tenth centuries, with few exceptions, there were none left in western Europe. Here and there one would find a cluster of population around the headquarters of a bishop, a great count, or a king. But there were no commercial centers. There was no merchant class. The simple crafts—weaving, metalworking, harness making—were carried on locally on the manors. Rarely, an itinerant trader might appear with such semiprecious goods as he could carry for long distances on donkeys—Eastern silks or a few spices for the wealthy. Among these early traders Jews were often important, because Judaism, part of the Byzantine and Arabic worlds as well as the Western, offered one of the few channels of communication among the different Mediterranean cultures, and many Jewish traders were connected through long-distance commercial networks.

Long-distance trading was in fact the first economic activity to revive and develop. The city of Venice was founded about 570 when refugees fled from invaders and settled in its islands. The Venetians, as time went

Long-distance trade

on, brought Eastern goods up the Adriatic and sold them to traders coming down from central Europe. In Flanders in the north, in what is now Belgium, manufacturers of woolen cloth emerged. Flemish woolens were of a unique quality, owing to peculiarities of the atmosphere and the skill of the weavers. They could not be duplicated elsewhere. Nor could Eastern goods be procured except through the Venetians—or through the merchants of Genoa or Pisa. Such goods could not possibly be produced locally, yet they were in demand wherever they became known. Merchants traveled in increasing numbers to sell them. Money came back into more general circulation; where it came from is not quite clear, since there was little mining of gold or silver until the end of the Middle Ages. Merchants began to establish permanent headquarters, settling within the deserted walls of ghostly Roman towns or near the seat of a lord or ecclesiastic, whose numerous retainers might become customers. Craftsmen moved from the overpopulated manors to these same growing centers, where they might produce wares that the lords or merchants would wish to buy. The process, once started, tended to snowball: the more people settled in such an agglomeration, the more they needed food brought to them from the country. The more craftsmen left the villages, the more the country people, lords, and serfs had to obtain clothing and simple tools and utensils from the towns. Hence a busy local trade developed also.

Growth of towns
By 1100, or not long thereafter, such centers existed all over Europe, from the Baltic to Italy, from England as far east as Bohemia. Usually there was one about every 20 or 30 miles. The smallest towns had only a few hundred inhabitants; the larger ones had two or three thousand, or sometimes more. Each carried on a local exchange with its immediate countryside, provided markets for local artisans, and purveyed goods of more distant origin to local consumers. But their

A GOLDSMITH IN HIS SHOP
by Petrus Christus (Netherlandish, c. 1410–1476)

Merchants and artisans held influential social positions in medieval European towns. The goldsmith in this painting may have worked in Bruges, the prosperous Flemish city where Petrus Christus painted during the 1400s and where craftsmen made a good living throughout the medieval era. The goldsmith's wealthy clients were likely purchasing a ring for their wedding.

(©Metropolitan Museum of Art, New York, Robert Lehman Collection, 1975) importance was by no means merely economic. What made them "towns" in the full sense of the word was their acquisition of political rights.

The merchants and craftsmen who lived in the towns did not wish to remain, like the country people, subject to neighboring feudal lords. At worst, the feudal lords regarded merchants as a convenient source of ready money; they might hold them up on the road, plunder their mule trains, collect tolls at river crossings, or extort cash by offering "protection." At best, the most well-meaning feudal lord could not supervise the affairs of merchants, for the feudal and customary law knew nothing of commercial problems. The traders in the course of their business developed their own commercial law, having to do with money and moneychanging, debt and bankruptcy, contracts, invoices, fraudulent goods, and bills of lading. They strove, therefore, to get recognition for their own law, their own courts, their own judges and magistrates. They wished, too, to govern their towns themselves and to avoid payment of fees or taxes to nearby nobles.

Everywhere in Latin Christendom, after about 1100, the new towns struggled to free themselves from the encircling feudalism and to set themselves up as self-governing little republics. Where the towns were largest and closest together—along the highly urbanized arteries of the trade routes, in north Italy, on the upper Danube and Rhine rivers, in Flanders, or on the Baltic coast—they emancipated themselves the most fully. Venice, Genoa, Pisa, Florence, and Milan became virtually independent city-states, each governing a substantial tract of its surrounding country. In Flanders also, towns like Bruges and Ghent dominated their localities. Along the upper Danube, the Rhine, the North Sea, the Baltic, many towns became imperial free cities within the Holy Roman Empire, each a kind of small republic owing allegiance to *Town charters* no one except the distant and usually ineffectual emperor. Nuremberg, Frankfurt, Augsburg, Strasbourg, Hamburg, and Lübeck were free cities of this kind. In France and England, where the towns in the twelfth century were somewhat less powerful, they obtained less independence but received charters of liberties from the king. By these charters they were assured the right to have their own town governments and officials, their own courts and law, and to pay their own kind of taxes to the king in lieu of ordinary feudal obligations.

Often towns formed leagues or urban federations, joining forces to repress banditry or piracy or to deal with ambitious monarchs or predatory nobles. The most famous such league was the Hanse; it was formed mainly of German towns, fought wars under its own banner, and dominated the commerce of the North Sea and the Baltic until after 1300. Similar tendencies of the towns to form political leagues, or to act independently in war and diplomacy, were suppressed by the kings in England, France, and Spain.

The fact that Italy, Germany, and the Netherlands were commercially more advanced than the Atlantic countries in the Middle Ages, and so had a more intensive town life, was to be one cause (out of many) impeding political unification in the early modern era. In other areas of western Europe, where more of a balance was kept between town and country, the towns were absorbed into larger territorial governments that were arising under the kings. This early difference between central and western Europe would later shape much of Europe's history in modern times.

The liberties won by the towns were corporate liberties. Each town was a collective entity. The people in towns did not possess individual *Corporate liberties* rights, but only the rights that followed from being a resident of a particular town. Among these were personal liberty; no townsman could be a serf, and fugitive serfs who lived over a year in a town were generally deemed to be free. But townspeople did not seek individual liberty in the modern sense. The social world was still too unsettled for the individual to act alone. Townspeople wanted to join together in a compact body and to protect themselves by all sorts of regulations and controls.

The most obvious evidence of this communal solidarity was the wall within which most towns were enclosed. The citizens in time of trouble looked to their own defense. As the towns grew, they built new walls farther out. In many European cities today one may still see remains of walls that were in use from the tenth to the thirteenth centuries.

Economic solidarity was of more day-to-day importance. The towns required neighboring peasants to sell foodstuffs only in the town marketplace. They thus protected their food supply against competition from other towns. Or they forbade the practice of certain trades in the country; this was to oblige peasants to make purchases in town and to protect the jobs and livelihood of the town craftsmen. They put up tariffs and tolls on the goods of other towns brought within their own walls. Or they levied special fees on merchants from outside who did business in the town. In Italy and Germany they often coined their own money, and the typical town fixed the rates at which various moneys should be exchanged. The medieval towns, in short, at the time of their greatest liberty, followed in a local way the same policies of protectionism and exclusiveness that later national governments would often follow in modern times.

Guilds

Within each town merchants and craftsmen formed associations called "guilds," whose "masters" supervised the affairs of a specific trade or craft. Merchants formed a merchant guild. Stonemasons, carpenters, barbers, dyers, goldsmiths, coppersmiths, weavers, hatters, tailors, shoemakers, grocers, and apothecaries formed craft guilds of their own. The guilds served a public purpose. They provided that work should be done by reliable and experienced persons, thereby protecting people from the pitfalls of shoddy garments, clumsy barbers, poisonous drugs, or defective and poorly built houses. They also provided a means of vocational education and marked out a career for young men. Women also worked in many trades and could belong to guilds; they were particularly numerous in certain guilds of the

Stonemasons and other craftsmen built the protective walls that surrounded many medieval cities, as in the sturdy towers and walls at Avila, Spain, which appear in this modern picture of the old city.
(©Pixtal/AGE Fotostock)

The crafts and trade in medieval towns were dominated by the guilds, whose symbols conveyed the nature of their work. The sheep on this emblem represents the wool guild in Florence.
(©Alinari/Art Resource, NY)

clothing trades. Women were nevertheless excluded from some of the guilds' social activities, and they were not granted the political privileges that men received as they moved up through the ranks of the guild hierarchy. Typically a boy became an apprentice to some master, learned the trade, and lived with and was supported by the master's family for a term of years, such as seven. Then he became a journeyman, a qualified and recognized worker, who might work for any master at a stated wage. Most workers remained journeymen throughout their lives, especially in the later Middle Ages. The guild system enabled some workers to improve their social position, however, and a lucky young man might eventually become a master, open his own shop, hire journeymen, and take apprentices. So long as the towns were growing, a boy had some chance to become a master, but as early as 1300 many guilds were becoming frozen, and the masters were increasingly chary of admitting new persons to their own status. Although widows often continued to work in the trades or artisanal crafts of their husbands, women almost never became masters. From the beginning, in any case, it was an important function of the guilds to protect their own members. The masters, assembled together, preserved their reputation by regulating the quality of their product. They divided work among themselves and fixed the terms of apprenticeship, the wages to be paid to journeymen, and the prices at which their goods must be sold. Or they took collective steps to meet or keep out the competition of the same trade in nearby towns.

Whether among individuals within the town itself, or between town and country, or between town and town, the spirit of the medieval economy was to prevent competition. Risk, adventure, and speculation were not wanted. Almost no one thought it proper to work for monetary profit. The few who did, big merchants trading over large areas, met with suspicion and disapproval wherever they went.

The towns tried in many ways to subject the peasants' interests to their own but nevertheless had an emancipating influence on the country. Some peasants were able to escape from serfdom by settling for more than a year in a town. But the town influence was more widespread and far out of proportion to the relatively small number of people who could become town dwellers. The growth of towns increased the demand for food. Lords began to clear new lands, and western Europeans set about developing a kind of internal frontier.

Towns and the decline of serfdom

Formerly villages had been separated by dark tracts of roadless woods, in which wolves roamed freely, shadowed by the gnomes, elves, and fairies of popular folklore. Now pioneers with axes cleared farmlands and built villages. The lords who usually supervised such operations (since their serfs were not slaves and could not be moved at will) offered freer terms to entice peasants to settle on the new lands. It was less easy for the lord of an old village to hold his people in serfdom when people in an adjacent village, within a few hours' walk, were legally free.

The peasants, moreover, were now able to obtain a little money for themselves by selling produce in town. The lords wanted money because the towns were producing more articles that money could buy. It became common for peasants to obtain personal freedom, holding their own lands, in return for an annual money payment to the lord for an indefinite period into the future. As early as the twelfth century, serfdom began to disappear in northern France and southern England, and by the fifteenth century it had disappeared from most of western Europe. Peasants could now, in law, move freely about. But the manorial organization remained; the peasants owed dues and fees rather than older forms of direct labor, but they were still under the lord's legal jurisdiction.

The Growth of Monarchies and Government Institutions

Changes in monarchical rule

Meanwhile the kings were busy, each trying to build his kingdom into an organized monarchy that would outlast his life. Monarchy became hereditary; the king inherited his position like any other feudal lord or possessor of an estate. Inheritance of the crown made for peace and order, for elections under conditions of the time were usually turbulent and disputed, and where the older Germanic principle of elective monarchy remained alive, as in the Holy Roman Empire, there was periodic commotion. The kings sent out executive officers to supervise their interests throughout their kingdoms. The kings of England, adopting an old Anglo-Saxon practice, had a sheriff in each of the 40 shires; the kings of France created similar officers who were called bailiffs. The kings likewise instituted royal courts, under royal justices, to decide property disputes and repress crime. This assertion of legal jurisdiction, together with the military might necessary to enforce judgments upon obstinate nobles, became a main pillar of the royal power. In England especially, and in lesser degree elsewhere, the kings required local inhabitants to assist royal judges in the discovery of relevant facts in particular cases. It is from this enforced association of private persons with royal officers that the court jury developed.

The kings needed money to pay for their governmental machinery or to carry on war with other kings. Taxation, as known in the Roman Empire, was quite unknown to the Germanic and feudal tradition. In the feudal scheme each person was responsible only for the customary fees that arose on stated occasions. The king, like other lords, was supposed to live on his own income—on the revenue of manors that he owned himself, the proceeds of estates temporarily under his wardship, or the occasional fees paid to him by his vassals. No king, even for the best of reasons, could simply decree a new tax and collect it. At the same time, as the use of money became more common, the kings had to assure themselves of a money income. As the towns grew up, with a new kind of wealth and a new source of money income, they agreed to make stipulated payments in return for their royal charters.

Taxation

Historical Documents
The *Magna Carta* (1215)

Medieval kings often provoked resistance from church officials and noble lords when they tried to restrict the autonomy of church institutions, demanded more money, or altered customary legal practices. The English King John faced such opposition among the high churchmen and barons who viewed his policies as violations of historic religious and legal liberties, and the king responded to their complaints by reluctantly signing the famous Magna Carta in 1215. Note how the following excerpts confirm the king's recognition of church rights, regular legal procedures for all English free men, and the importance of well-qualified government officials.

JOHN, by the grace of God King of England . . . to his archbishops, bishops, abbots, earls, barons, justices, foresters, sheriffs, stewards, servants, and to all his officials and loyal subjects, greeting. . . .

WE HAVE GRANTED TO GOD, and by this present charter have confirmed for us and our heirs in perpetuity, that the English Church shall be free, and shall have its rights undiminished, and its liberties unimpaired. . . .

TO ALL FREE MEN OF OUR KINGDOM we have also granted, for us and our heirs for ever, all the liberties written out below, to have and to keep for them and their heirs, of us and our heirs. . . .

For a trivial offence, a free man shall be fined only in proportion to the degree of his offence, and for a serious offence correspondingly, but not so heavily as to deprive him of his livelihood. . . .

No free man shall be seized or imprisoned, or stripped of his rights or possessions, or outlawed or exiled, or deprived of his standing in any way, nor will we proceed with force against him, or send others to do so, except by the lawful judgment of his equals or by the law of the land. . . .

We will appoint as justices, constables, sheriffs, or other officials, only men that know the law of the realm and are minded to keep it well. . . .

To any man whom we have deprived or dispossessed of lands, castles, liberties, or rights, without the lawful judgment of his equals, we will at once restore these. . . .

All these customs and liberties that we have granted shall be observed in our kingdom in so far as concerns our own relations with our subjects. Let all men of our kingdom, whether clergy or laymen, observe them similarly in their relations with their own men. . . .

Both we and the barons have sworn that all this shall be observed in good faith and without deceit. Witness the abovementioned people and many others.

Given by our hand in the meadow that is called Runnymede.

G.R.C. Davis, *Magna Carta* (London, British Museum, 1963), pp. 23–33.

The royal demands for money and the claims to exercise legal jurisdiction were regarded as innovations. They were constantly growing and sometimes were a source of abuse. They met with frequent resistance in all countries. A famous case historically (though somewhat commonplace in its own day) was that of Magna Carta in England in 1215, when a group of English lords and high churchmen, joined by representatives of the city of London, required King John to confirm and guarantee their historic liberties.

The king, as has been said, like any lord, was supposed to act in council or court with his vassals. The royal council became the egg out of which departments of government were hatched—such as the royal judiciary, exchequer, and military command. From it also was hatched the institution of parliaments. The kings had always, in a way, held great parleys or "talks" (the Latin *parliamentum* meant simply a "talking") with their chief retainers. In the twelfth and thirteenth centuries the growth of towns added a new element to European life. To the lords and bishops was now added a burgher class, which, if of far inferior dignity, was too stubborn, free-spirited, and well furnished with money to be overlooked. When representatives of the towns began to be summoned to the king's great talks, along with lords and clergy, parliaments may be said to have come into being.

Parliaments, in this sense, sprouted all over Europe in the thirteenth century. The new assemblies were called *cortes* in Spain, diets in Germany, Estates General or provincial estates in France, parliaments in the British Isles. Usually they are referred to generically as "estates," the word "parliament" being reserved for Britain, but in origin they were all essentially the same.

The kings called these assemblies as a means of publicizing and strengthening the royal rule. They found it more convenient to explain their policies, or to ask for money, to a large gathering brought together for that purpose than to have a hundred officials make local explanations and strike local bargains in a hundred different places. The kings did not recognize, nor did the assemblies claim, any right of the parliament to dictate to the king and his government. But usually the king invited the parliament to state grievances; his action upon them was the beginning of parliamentary legislation.

The parliaments represented neither the "nation" nor the "people" nor yet the individual citizen, but they embodied the "estates of the realm," the great collective interests of the country. The first and highest estate was the clergy; the second was the landed or noble class; to these older ruling groups were added, as a "third estate,"

the burghers of the chartered towns. Quite commonly these three types of people sat separately as three distinct chambers. But the pattern varied from country to country. In England, Poland, and Hungary the clergy as a whole ceased to be represented; only the bishops came, sitting with lay magnates in an upper house. Eventually the burghers dropped out in Poland, Bohemia, and Hungary, leaving the landed aristocracy in triumph in eastern Europe. In Castile and Württemberg, on the other hand, the noble estate eventually refused to attend parliament, leaving the townspeople and clergy in the assemblies. In some countries—in Scandinavia, Switzerland, and in the French Estates General—even peasants were allowed to have delegates.

In England, the Parliament developed eventually in a distinctive way. After a long period of uncertainty there came to be two houses, known as the Lords and the Commons.

The Lords, as in Hungary or Poland, included both great prelates and lay magnates. The House of Commons developed features not found on the Continent. Lesser landholders, the people who elsewhere counted as small nobles, sat in the same House of Commons with representatives of the towns. This mingling of classes in England, the willingness of townsmen to follow the leadership of the gentry, and of the gentry to respect the interests of townsmen, helped to root representative institutions in England more deeply than in other countries during the medieval era. Moreover, England was a small country in the Middle Ages. There were no provincial or local parliamentary bodies (as in France, the Holy Roman Empire, or Poland) which might jealously cut into the powers of the central body or with which the king could make local arrangements. And finally, as another explanation for the growing strength of Parliament in England, the elected members of the House of Commons very early obtained the power to *commit* their constituents. If they voted a tax, those who elected them had to pay it. The king, in order to get matters decided, insisted that the votes be binding. Constituents were not allowed to repudiate the vote of their deputies, nor to punish or harass them when they came home, as often happened in other countries. Parliament thus exercised power as well as rights.

In summary, the three centuries of the High Middle Ages laid foundations both for order and for freedom. Slavery was defunct and serfdom was expiring. Politically, the multitude of free chartered towns, the growth of juries in some places, and the rise of parliaments everywhere provided means by which peoples could take some part in their governments. The ancient civilizations had never created a free political unit larger than the city-state. The Greeks had never carried democracy beyond the confines within which people could meet in person, nor had the Romans devised means by which, in a large state, the governed could share any responsibilities with an official bureaucracy. The ancients had never developed the idea of representative government, or of government by duly elected and authorized representatives acting at a distance from home. The idea is by no means as obvious or simple as it looks. It first appeared in the realms of medieval European monarchies, and, after much subsequent development, it would become a fundamental principle for political systems in most of the modern world.

4. THE HIGH MIDDLE AGES: THE CHURCH

So far in our account of the High Middle Ages we have left aside the church, except, indeed, when some mention of it could not be avoided. In the real life of the time, the church was omnipresent. Religion permeated every sphere of political, social, and cultural life. In feudalism the mutual duties of lord and vassal were confirmed by religious oaths, and bishops and abbots, as holders of lands, became feudal personages themselves. In the monarchies, the king was crowned by the chief churchman of his kingdom, adjured to rule with justice and piety, and anointed with holy oils. In the towns, guilds served as lay religious brotherhoods; each guild chose a patron saint and marched in the streets on holy days. For amusement the townspeople watched religious dramas, the morality and miracle plays in which religious themes were enacted. The rising town, if it harbored a bishop, took special care to erect a new cathedral. Years of effort and of religious fervor produced the Gothic cathedrals that still stand as the best-known memorials of medieval civilization. Intellectual life was also closely tied to the church, so that religious thinkers shaped the main philosophical debates of the era, and the most influential writers were clergymen.

The Development of the Medieval Church and Papacy

If, however, we turn back to the tenth century, the troubled years before 1000, we find the church in as dubious a condition as other institutions. It was fragmented and localized. Every bishop went his own way.

The church in crisis

Though the clergy was the only literate class, many of the clergy themselves could not read and write. Christian belief was mixed with the old pagan magic and superstition, and most Christians knew nothing about the theology that had shaped the traditions of the Catholic Church. The monasteries were in decay. Priests often lived in a concubinage that was generally condoned. It was customary for them to marry, so that they had recognized children, to whom they intrigued to pass on their churchly position. Powerful laymen

CHRONOLOGY OF NOTABLE EVENTS, 500 B.C.E.–1300 C.E.

500–300 B.C.E.	Creative era of Classical Greek Civilization: Plato, Aristotle
46 B.C.E.	Roman Republic conquers Greece
45–31 B.C.E.	Roman Republic evolves into the Roman Empire
c. 26–29 C.E.	Jesus is active in Palestine; beginnings of Christianity
306–337	Roman Emperor Constantine: toleration of Christianity
c. 420	St. Augustine writes *City of God*
476	End of Roman Empire in the West
450–750	Roman Catholic Church gains converts and influence in western Europe
610–632	Prophet Muhammad teaches the new religion of Islam
635–750	Islam spreads across Middle East, North Africa, and Spain
800	Coronation of Emperor Charlemagne; the Carolingian Empire
1000–1200	Improvements in European agriculture and rise of towns
1054	Schism of Roman Catholic Church and Orthodox Eastern Church
1095–1099	First Christian Crusade in Palestine
1100–1200	Arabic and Greek science enters European Culture
1147–1272	Second-Ninth Christian Crusades
1198–1216	Pope Innocent III: height of medieval papacy
1215	Magna Carta defines limits of royal power in England
1100–1300	Development of universities and scholasticism
1267–1273	Thomas Aquinas writes the *Summa Theologica*

often dominated their ecclesiastical neighbors, with the big lords appointing the bishops and the lesser ones appointing the parish priests. When people thought about Rome at all, they could barely imagine a place that was legendary and far away, but the bishop of Rome, or pope, had no influence in local villages and was treated in unseemly fashion by nobles in his own city.

The Roman Catholic Church is in fact unrecognizable in the jumble of the tenth century. So far at least as human effort was concerned, it was virtually recreated in the eleventh century along with the other institutions of the High Middle Ages.

The impulse to reform came from many quarters. Sometimes a secular ruler undertook to correct conditions in his own domains. For this purpose he asserted a strict

Reform efforts

control over his clergy. In 962, as noted earlier, King Otto I was crowned as a new emperor in Rome, though the empire he established was not commonly called the "Holy Roman Empire" until the twelfth century. This empire, like the Carolingian and Roman empires that it was supposed to continue, was in theory coterminous with Latin Christendom itself and endowed with a special mission to preserve and extend the Christian faith. Neither in France nor in England (nor in Spain, Hungary, Poland, or Scandinavia) was this claim of the Holy

Roman Empire ever acknowledged. But the empire did for a time embrace Italy as well as Germany. The first emperors, in the tenth and eleventh centuries, denouncing the conditions of the church in Rome, strove to make the pope their appointee.

At the same time a reform movement arose from spiritual sources. Serious Christians took matters into their own hands. They founded a new monastery at Cluny in France, which soon had many affiliated houses. It was their purpose to purify monastic life and to set a higher Christian ideal to which all clergy and laity might aspire. To rid themselves of immediate local pressures, the greed, narrowness, ignorance, family ambition, and self-satisfied inertia that were the main causes of corruption, the Cluniacs refused to recognize any authority except that of Rome itself. Thus, at the very time when conditions in Rome were at their worst, Christians throughout Europe built up the prestige of Rome, of the idea of Rome, as a means to raise all Latin Christendom from its depths.

As for the popes in Rome, those who preserved any independence of judgment or respect for their own office, it was their general plan to free themselves from the Roman mobs and aristocrats without falling into dependence upon the Holy Roman Emperor. In 1059, Pope Nicholas II issued a decree providing that future popes should be elected by the cardinals, who at that time were the priests of churches in the city of Rome or bishops of neighboring dioceses. By entrusting the choice of future popes to them, Pope Nicholas hoped to exclude all influence from outside the clergy itself. Popes have been elected by cardinals ever since, though not always without influence from outside.

One of the first popes so elected was Gregory VII, known also as Hildebrand, a dynamic and strong-willed man who was pope from 1073 to 1085. He had been in contact with the Cluniac reformers, and he _Gregory VII_ dreamed of a reformed and reinvigorated Europe under the universal guidance of the Roman pontiff. Gregory believed that the church should stand apart from worldly society, that it should judge and guide all human actions, and that a pope had the supreme power to judge and punish kings and emperors if he deemed them sinful. His ideal was a world church with a disciplined clergy, centralized under a single authority. He began by insisting that the clergy free itself of worldly involvements. He required married priests to put aside their wives and families. Celibacy of the clergy, never generally established in the Greek Orthodox Church, and later rejected by Protestant churches, became the rule for the Roman Catholic priesthood. Gregory insisted also that no ecclesiastic might receive office through appointment by a layman. In his view only clergy might institute or influence clergy, for the clergy must be independent and self-contained.

Gregory soon faced a battle with that other aspirant to universal supremacy and a sacred mission, the Holy Roman Emperor, who at _Lay investiture_ this time was Henry IV. In Germany the bishops and abbots possessed a great deal of the land, which they held and governed under the emperor as feudal magnates in their own right. To the emperor it was vitally important to have his own men, as reliable vassals, in these great positions. Hence in Germany "lay investiture" had become very common. Lay investiture meant the practice by which a layman, the emperor, conferred upon the new bishop the signs of his spiritual authority, the ring and the staff. Gregory prohibited lay investiture. He supported the German bishops and nobles when they rebelled against Henry, but the emperor remained obstinate. Gregory then excommunicated him—that is, outlawed him from Christian society by forbidding any priest to give him the sacraments. Henry, baffled, sought out the pope at Canossa in Italy to do penance. "To go to Canossa" in later times became a byword for submission to the will of Rome.

In 1122, after both original contenders had died, a compromise on the matter of lay investiture was effected by which bishops recognized the emperor as their feudal head but looked to Rome for spiritual authority. But the struggle between popes and emperors went on unabated. The magnates of Germany, lay lords as well as bishops, often allied with the pope to preserve their own feudal liberties from the emperor. The emperor in Germany was never able to consolidate his domains as did the kings in England and France. The unwillingness of lords and churchmen (and of towns also, as we have seen) to let the emperors build up an effective government left its mark permanently upon Europe in two ways. It contributed to the centralization of Latin Christendom under Rome, while it blocked the development of a more unified monarchical state in central Europe.

The height of the medieval papacy came with Innocent III, whose

| Innocent III |

pontificate lasted from 1198 to 1216. Innocent virtually realized Gregory's dream of a unified Christian world. He intervened in politics everywhere. He was recognized as a supreme arbiter. Responding to his demands, a king of France took a wife, a king of England accepted an unwanted archbishop, a king of León put aside the cousin whom he had married, and a claimant to the crown of Hungary deferred to his rival. The kings of England, Aragon, and Portugal acknowledged him as feudal overlord within their realms. Huge revenues now flowed to Rome from all over Latin Christendom, and an enormous bureaucracy worked there to dispatch the voluminous business of the papal court. As kings struggled to repress civil rebellion, so Innocent and his successors struggled to repress heresy, which, defined as doctrine at variance with that of the church at large, was becoming alarmingly common among the Albigensians who vehemently condemned impious priests in southern France.

In 1215, Innocent called a great church council, the greatest since antiquity, attended by 500 bishops and even by the patriarchs of Constantinople and Jerusalem. The council convened in Rome and labored at the perplexing task of keeping the clergy from worldly temptations. By forbidding priests to officiate at ordeals or trials by battle, it virtually ended these survivals of pre-Christian judgments and punishments. It attempted to regularize belief in the supernatural by controlling the traffic in holy relics. It declared the sacraments to be the channel of God's saving grace and defined them authoritatively.[1] In the chief sacrament, the Eucharist or Mass, it promulgated the dogma of transubstantiation, which held that, in the Mass, the priest converts the substance of bread and wine into the substance of Christ's body and blood. Except for heretics, who were suppressed, the reforms and doctrines of Innocent's council were accepted by Christians throughout Latin Europe.

Intellectual Life: The Universities, Scholasticism

Under the auspices of the church, as rising governments gave more civil security, and as the economy of town and country became more able to support people devoted to a life of thought, European intellectual horizons began to widen. The twelfth and thirteenth centuries saw the founding of the first universities. These originated in the

---

[1] A sacrament is understood to be the outward sign of an inward grace. In Catholic doctrine the sacraments were and are seven in number: baptism, confirmation, penance, the Eucharist, extreme unction, marriage, and holy orders. Except for baptism, a sacrament may be administered only by a priest. A dogma is the common belief of the church, in which all the faithful share and must share so long as they are members of the church. Dogmas are regarded as implicitly the same in all ages; they cannot be invented or developed, but may from time to time be clarified, defined, promulgated, or proclaimed.

natural and spontaneous coming together of teachers and students that had never wholly disappeared even in the most chaotic era of the early Middle Ages. By 1200, there was a center of medical studies at Salerno in south Italy, of legal studies at Bologna in north Italy, of theological studies at Paris. Oxford was founded about 1200 by a secession of disgruntled students and professors from Paris; Cambridge, shortly thereafter. By 1300, there were a dozen such universities in Latin Europe; by 1500, there were almost a hundred.

The founding of universities

As the early agglomerations of traders developed into organized towns and guilds, so the informal concourses of students and teachers developed into organized institutions of learning, receiving the sharp corporate stamp that was characteristic of the High Middle Ages. It was in having this corporate identity that medieval universities resembled our own and differed from the schools of Athens or Alexandria in ancient times. A university, the University of Paris, for example, was a body of individuals, young and old, interested in learning and endowed by law with a communal name and existence. It possessed definite liberties under some kind of charter, regulated its own affairs through its own officials, and kept its own order among its often boisterous population. It gave, and even advertised, courses and lectures, and it decided collectively which professors were the best qualified to teach. It might consist of distinct schools or "faculties"—the combination of theology, law, and medicine, as at Paris, was the most usual. It held examinations and awarded degrees, whose meaning and value were recognized throughout the Latin West. The degree, which originated as a license to teach, admitted its holder to certain honors or privileges in the same way that members of other guilds were authorized to practice a specific craft. With such degrees, professors might readily move from one university to another. Students moved easily also because all universities used the Latin language and offered a similar curriculum. The university, moreover, though typically beginning in poverty, was a corporate body capable of holding property, and the benefactions of pious donors often built up substantial endowments in lands and manors. So organized, free from outside control, and enjoying an income from property, the university lived on as a permanent institution, through good times and bad.

The queen of the sciences was theology, the intellectual study of religion. By the eleventh century, many people in Europe were beginning to reflect upon their beliefs with new intellectual methods. They continued to believe in God, but they sought to base their beliefs on more systematic analytical foundations. It was accepted as a fact, for example, that the Son of God had been incarnated as a man in Jesus Christ. But in the eleventh century an Italian named Anselm, who became archbishop of Canterbury, wrote a treatise called *Cur Deus Homo?—Why Did God Become Man?*—giving reasoned explanations to show why God had taken human form to save sinful human beings. Anselm argued that reason strongly supported the Christian faith in God. Soon afterward Abelard, who taught at Paris, wrote his *Sic et Non—Yes and No* or *Pro and Con*—a collection of inconsistent statements made by St. Augustine and other fathers of the church. Abelard's purpose was to apply logic to the inherited mass of patristic writings, show wherein the truth of Christian doctrine really lay, and so make the faith consistent with reason and reflection.

Theology

Meanwhile, in the twelfth century a great stream of new knowledge poured into Europe, bringing about a veritable intellectual revolution. It was derived from the Arabs, with whom Christians exchanged ideas and texts in Sicily and Spain. The Arabs, as has been seen, had taken over the ancient Greek science, translated Greek writings into Arabic, and in many ways added further

Arabic and Greek learning

THE MEETING OF ST. ANTHONY AND ST. PAUL
by Sassetta (Italian, 1392–1450)

This picture conveys the abstractness of medieval thought in which "realism" meant a belief in the reality of permanent ideas (a belief that might now be called "idealism"). There is no attempt to portray the figures as unique individuals; they are typical saints with the halos designating sacred persons. St. Anthony appears in three places—walking alone, converting a centaur, and embracing St. Paul. The forest and hills represent the general idea of trees or mounds of earth, but there is no physical specificity in these representations of nature.

(*Source:* National Gallery of Art)

THOMAS AQUINAS
by Fra Bartelemo (Italian, 1472–1517)

Thomas Aquinas combined Aristotelian knowledge with Christian faith in his scholastic theology, thus gaining permanent respect (and sainthood) from the Catholic Church and artistic recognition from painters such as Fra Bartelemo.

(©Nicolo Orsi Battaglini/Art Resource, NY)

refinements of their own. Bilingual Christians (assisted by numerous learned Jews who traveled readily between the Christian and Muslim worlds) translated these works into Latin. Above all, they translated Aristotle, the great codifier of Greek knowledge who had lived and written in the fourth century B.C.E. The Europeans, drawing on the commentaries of Muslim scholars such as Averroës (1126–1198), were overwhelmed by this sudden disclosure of an undreamed universe of knowledge. Aristotle became The Philosopher, the unparalleled authority on all branches of knowledge other than religious.

The great problem for Europeans was how to digest Aristotle's vast writings, or, in more general terms, how to assimilate or reconcile the body of Greek and Arabic learning to the Christian faith. The universities, with their "scholastic" philosophers or "schoolmen," performed this function. Most eminent of scholastics was Thomas Aquinas (1225–1274), the Angelic Doctor, known also to his own contemporaries as the Dumb Ox from the slow deliberation of his speech. His chief work, appropriately called the *Summa Theologica,* was a survey of all knowledge.

The chief accomplishment of Thomas Aquinas was his demonstration that faith and reason could not be in conflict. By reason he meant a severely logical method, with exact definition of words and concepts,

Thomas Aquinas

deducing step by step what must follow if certain premises are accepted. His philosophy is classified as a form of moderate "realism," a term whose medieval meaning differed from its common usage today. For medieval philosophers realism meant that the general idea or abstraction is more "real" than the particular—that "man" or "woman" is more real than this or that man or woman, that "law" as such is more real and binding than this or that particular law. He derived his philosophy from what he took to be the

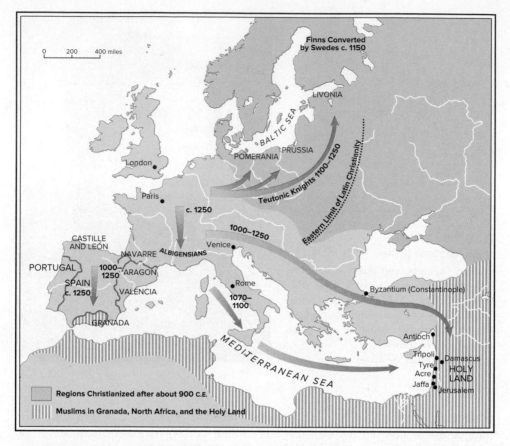

CRUSADING ACTIVITY, 1100–1250
Medieval Christendom expanded geographically until about 1250. Darker regions are those christianized shortly before and after 1000. Arrows indicate organized military-religious expeditions, which by
1250 had ended the Muslim control in most of Spain but had failed to do so in the Holy Land. Dates
are rounded and very rough.

enduring, transcendent nature of God, of law, of reason, of human life, and of beings in
general. Thomas taught a hierarchic view of the universe and of society, of which God
was the apex. All things and all people were subordinated to God in a descending order,
each bound to fulfill the role set by its own place and nature. It was the emphasis on the
superior reality of abstractions that enabled people in the Middle Ages to believe steadfastly in the church while freely attacking individual churchmen, to have faith in the
papacy while denouncing the popes as scoundrels—or to accept without difficulty the
mystery of transubstantiation, which declared that what admittedly looked and tasted like
bread and wine was, in real inner substance, the body of Christ.

Scholasticism
                    The scholastic philosophy, as perfected by Thomas Aquinas, was
                    not very favorable to the growth of natural science, because its empha-
                    sis on an inner reality drew attention away from the actual details and
behavior of concrete things. On the other hand, the scholastic philosophy described nature
as material evidence of God's power, which could be analyzed like other evidence of divine
influence. More generally, as a method of making systematic arguments, scholasticism

laid foundations on which later European thought was to be reared. It habituated Europeans to great exactness, to careful distinctions, even to the splitting of hairs. It called for disciplined thinking. And it made the world safe for reason. If any historical generalization may be made safely, it may be said that any society that believes reason to threaten its foundations will suppress reason. In Thomas's time, there were some who said that Aristotle and the Arabs were infidels, dangerous influences that must be silenced. Any reasoning about the faith, they warned, was a form of weakness. Thomas's doctrine that faith could not be endangered by reason gave a freedom to thinkers to go on thinking.

The Crusades; New Invasions; Europe by 1300

Meanwhile, Europeans were beginning to expand beyond Europe. In the late eleventh century, they launched a military offensive against Islam, and most of Latin Christendom's military forces went on the Crusades. War itself was subordinated to the purposes of religion.

The most ambitious, best remembered, and least successful of such expeditions were the nine Crusades to win back the Holy Land to Christian control (1095–1272). The First Crusade was proclaimed as a holy religious mission in 1095 by Pope Urban II, who hoped thereby to advance the peace of God by draining off bellicose nobles to fight the infidels and to build up the pope's leadership in Europe. Crusades to the Holy Land, with varying success, and sometimes departing woefully from their religious aims, went on intermittently for 200 years. The growth of Italian shipping in the Mediterranean, the rise of more orderly feudal monarchies, and the increasing sense of a Europe-wide common purpose made possible the assembly and transport of considerable forces over a great distance. But the motivation for such Crusades, especially in the beginning, came mostly from a wave of religious fervor that brought nobles and commoners alike into the Crusader armies. This fervor contributed to brutal, deadly attacks on Jewish communities within Europe as well as to the extraordinary violence against entire Muslim populations in cities such as Antioch and Jerusalem. At the same time, however, the Crusades gave Europeans a new awareness of the world beyond their own local realms of religion and small-town economies. Historians have argued that the Crusaders' contacts with Arab societies in the Middle East stimulated subsequent European economic development and a new cultural identity among "Western" peoples. Although this argument points to important consequences of the Crusades, it is also true that the campaigns against Islam grew out of Europe's own growing political and military strength. For a century the Latin Christians occupied parts of Palestine and Syria. But military defeats forced them to withdraw in the thirteenth century, and the Muslims remained in possession.

Crusades to the Holy Land

Other crusades (for such they were) had more lasting results. A party of Normans won Sicily from the Arabs about 1100. Iberian Christians, descending from the mountains of northern Spain, carried on a *reconquista* of two centuries against the Moors. By 1250, they had staked out the Christian kingdoms of Portugal, León, Castile, Aragon, and Valencia, leaving the Muslims only Granada in the extreme south, which was conquered much later, in 1492. In southern France, a thirteenth-century crusade against the Albigensians put down the heretics, those born in the Christian faith but erring from the church's reigning interpretations of it. The Albigensians, for example, believed that the moral corruption of the clergy betrayed the spiritual essence of Christianity—a claim that church officials could never accept. Crusading expeditions were also launched against a few remaining "heathen" populations in

Other crusades

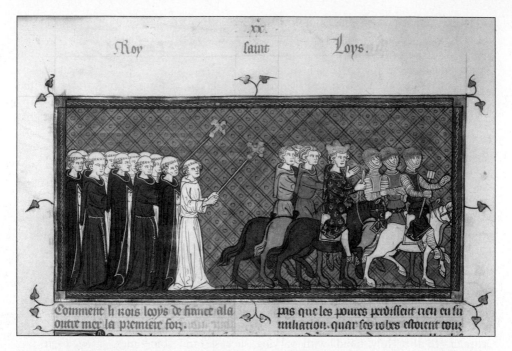

Roman Catholic popes preached in the Middle Ages that Europeans should expel the Muslims from Christian holy sites in the Middle East, thereby launching numerous military crusades that ultimately failed to achieve a lasting Christian conquest. The clergy portrayed in this medieval manuscript are blessing Christian soldiers as they set off on a crusading religious expedition.

(©Europeana Collections/The British Library)

northeastern Europe. The Teutonic Order, a military-religious society of knights founded originally to fight in the Holy Land, transferred its operations to the north. Christianity was thus brought by the sword to eastern Prussia and the east Baltic regions.

About the year 1250, there developed a new threat of invasion from Asia. As the Huns had burst out of Asia in the fifth century, and the Magyars in the ninth, so now the Tartars appeared in the thirteenth century, to be followed in the fourteenth by the Ottoman Turks. We shall see how the Turks long continued to press upon central Europe. But, on the whole, by the thirteenth century, Europe was capable of resistance. Always until then it had been vulnerable as an outlying, backward, thinly populated protuberance from the Eurasian land mass. It had lain open in the remote past to wandering Indo-Europeans, then to Roman imperial conquerors, to Germanic barbarians, to Huns, Magyars, and, in part, the Arabs. All these were gradually assimilated by the Roman Catholic Church, the Latin language, the common institutions of feudalism, monarchy, a free town life, parliamentary assemblies, and scholastic learning. An increasingly connected and coherent culture ran from England to Sicily and from Portugal to Poland.

By 1300, the "rise of Europe" was an accomplished fact. The third of the three segments into which the ancient Greco-Roman world had divided, the one that in 700 C.E.

The "rise of Europe"

had been the most isolated and fragmented, now some 600 years later had a civilization of its own. It was still only one among the several great cultures of the world, such as the Islamic, Byzantine, Indian, and Chinese. It enjoyed no preeminence. The Chinese Empire, for example, in the thirteenth century, had cities whose population reached into millions. It had an affluent merchant class, great textile manufacturers, and an iron industry that produced over 100,000 tons a year. The arts and sciences were assiduously pursued. Government was centralized and complex; it issued paper money and employed a civil service recruited by competitive examinations. Books on religious, technical, and agricultural subjects, including whole multivolume encyclopedias, were printed in enormous numbers. The Venetian Marco Polo was dazzled by the China that he lived in from 1275 to 1292.

Many have asked why China did not generate, as Europe did in these centuries, the main forces that ultimately led to the modern scientific and industrial world. One answer is suggested by the fact that it was Europeans such as Marco Polo who went to China, not Chinese who went to Europe. In the fifteenth century, over the years 1405 to 1433, a Ming emperor launched a large-scale series of long-range naval expeditions, seven in all, headed by his admiral Zheng He (also known in English as Cheng Ho). The expeditions sailed to ports in Southeast Asia, India, the Persian Gulf, and East Africa, exchanging gifts in transactions that recognized the emperor's power and prestige. But the emperor and his advisers ultimately terminated the entire venture. China turned away from distant overseas commercial opportunities in this period, and the Chinese government turned inward to the protection and expansion of its vast land frontiers. It was the Europeans who later pursued the development of trade in India and also crossed the Atlantic to colonize the Americas. Europeans gradually became more interested in exploring other lands and developing new kinds of trade, perhaps because in Europe there was no all-embracing empire as in China, but kings, lords, bishops, and towns that competed with each other for political power. With religion and the church kept distinct from the state, the search for what one should do with one's life became less dependent on the power of a unifying imperial or religious system. Europe was disorderly and full of conflict—rivalries and wars between kings, quarrels between kings and their barons, disputes between church and state, clashes between lords and their peasant workers. Much of this conflict was destructive, yet there was also a kind of opportunity or freedom in such disorder and a dynamism that promoted change.

European civilization in 1300 was by no means a modern society, yet the ancient and medieval cultures on European lands had created institutions and traditions that have remained influential even in the most recent eras of modern world history. By 1300, people in Europe *European civilization in 1300* had developed separate (at times contending) institutions of church and state to control a growing population, economic institutions to promote urban commerce and long-distance trade, judicial and parliamentary councils to codify or revise the law, and universities to teach or redefine their intellectual traditions. These traditions included a pervasive faith in Christianity, but the ancient Christian beliefs were challenged, revised, and extended by other ancient traditions of rhetoric, philosophy, and rational inquiry—all of which contributed to the emergence of what is now called "early modern" European history.

 Suggested Further Readings can be found in the ebook, on Connect, or online at www.mhhe .com/kramer12e.

THE UPHEAVAL IN WESTERN CHRISTENDOM, 1300–1560

In the transition from traditional to more modern forms of society, people in all the older civilizations have reexamined their religious base. People in modern societies do not necessarily reject their ancestral religions. In fact, they may strongly reaffirm their religious beliefs, but they usually try also to adapt their religions to modern economic and political conditions and to make room for new and nonreligious interests. The process of developing various activities outside the sphere of religion is called "secularization."

Latin Christendom was the first of the world's major religious cultures to become increasingly secularized. In the very long run it was those aspects of European civilization that were least associated with Christianity, such as natural science and industrial technology, or military and economic power, that the non-European world proved to be most willing to adopt. This secularization of human cultures, although often challenged by popular religious movements in the contemporary world, remains one of the decisive trends in modern world history, and it is a trend that began to appear in Europe at the end of the Middle Ages.

The Europe that had become both expansive and more prosperous by the thirteenth century entered upon a series of new disasters over the following two centuries. The Mongols after about 1240 held Russia in subjugation for 200 years. The Ottoman Turks, who had originated in central Asia, penetrated the Byzantine Empire, crushed the medieval Serbian kingdom at the battle of Kosovo in 1389, and spread over the Balkans. They took Constantinople itself in 1453. Eastern Christianity continued to exist, but under alien political domination. Latin Christianity, reaching from Poland and Hungary to the Atlantic, remained independent but was beset with troubles. The authority of the papacy and of the Roman Catholic Church was called into question. Eventually new Protestant churches emerged, and the religious unity of medieval Christian civilization disappeared.

Chapter emblem: Detail from *A Portrait of a Family* by Lavinia Fontana (1552-1614). (©Scala/Art Resource, NY)

Yet new forces also asserted themselves alongside or outside the religious tradition. Government, law, philosophy, science, the arts, material interests and economic activities were pursued with less regard for older Christian values. Power, order, beauty, wealth, knowledge, and control of nature were regarded as desirable in themselves.

In this mixture of decline and revival, of religious revolution and secularization, medieval Christendom evolved into the social, political, and cultural world of early modern Europe.

5.   DISASTERS OF THE FOURTEENTH CENTURY

The Black Death and Its Consequences

During the fourteenth century, and quite abruptly, about a third of the population of Europe was wiped out. Although it is impossible to know exactly how many people lived in medieval Europe, modern demographic historians have estimated that the total population fell from more than 80 million in the early 1300s to roughly 60 million in 1400, and Europe's population did not return to pre-plague levels until the sixteenth century (see the graph on p. 55). Some died in sporadic local famines that began to appear after 1300. The great killer, however, was the plague, or Black Death, which first struck Europe in 1348. The precise medical cause of the plague is still debated. Most modern historians believe that the disease was carried by rats and transmitted by fleas, but this theory may not explain how the contagion moved so quickly across Europe or why so many humans became vulnerable to a bacillus that normally lives in rodents. A pneumonic form of the plague, which caused severe lung infections, also spread quickly through coughs or other human contacts. Despite the uncertainty about its physiological origins, historians agree that the plague caused painful lymphatic swelling, intense fevers, and other lethal effects in almost everyone who fell ill. It also had decisive effects on European social life. Since the plague returned at irregular and unpredictable intervals, and killed off the young as well as the old, it disrupted marriage and family life and made it impossible for many years for Europe to regain the former level of population. In some places whole villages disappeared. Cultivated fields were abandoned for want of able-bodied men and women to work them. The towns were especially vulnerable, because the contagion spread quickly through populations crowded within town walls. Trade and exchange were obstructed; prices, wages, and incomes moved erratically; famine made its victims more susceptible to disease; and deaths from the plague contributed to famine. The living were preoccupied with the burial of the dead and with fears for their own future.

There were immediate social and political repercussions. In some cases, survivors benefited because the scarcity of labor led to higher wages. On the other hand, in the general disorganization, and with landowners and urban employers decimated also, many of the poor could find no work or took to vagabondage and begging. The upper classes, acting through governments, attempted to control wages and prices. Rebellions of workers broke out in various towns, especially in Flanders, and there were massive insurrections of peasants in many parts of Europe. In France these were called "jacqueries" (from Jacques, a nickname for a peasant), of which the first was in 1358. In England a similar large-scale uprising in 1381 came to be known as Wat Tyler's rebellion. Sometimes the spokesmen for these movements went beyond their immediate grievances to raise broader social

The Black Death

Revolts and repression

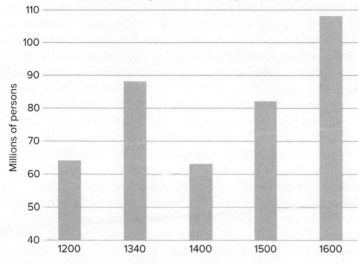

Estimated Population of Europe, 1200–1600

This graph shows the growth of Europe's population after 1200, the far-reaching demographic impact of the Black Death in the fourteenth century, and the gradual revival of the European population during the fifteenth century.

Source: Massimo Livi-Bacci, *A Concise History of World Population,* 5th ed. (Oxford: Wiley Blackwell, 2012).

questions about why some should be rich and others poor. Governments and the upper classes replied to this menace with ferocious repression. The peasants generally returned to their usual labors. Yet something was gained for the rural workers, at least in the long run, as underlying economic and demographic forces continued to assert themselves. The landowners, or feudal class, in order to get the work done on their manors and assure their own incomes, had to offer more favorable terms. These included, for example, the giving of lifetime tenures to peasant families, in return for fixed payment of sums of money. Over the years many of these peasant holdings became hereditary and the value of money decreased, so that payment of a shilling, for example, which in 1400 represented a significant amount, became much less burdensome for the rural worker by 1600. In effect, a class of small peasant property owners began to emerge in much of Europe.

The kings, who had been building up their position against the church and the feudal lords since the eleventh century, also found their problems complicated by the disasters of the fourteenth. They still had their governments to maintain, and their ambitions to satisfy, even if death removed large fractions of their subjects. They even had to increase their incomes, as it became usual for kings to employ royal armies of foot soldiers against the recurring possibility of feudal resistance. Various means of increasing the royal spending power were devised. Currency was debased; that is, the king ordered a given weight of gold or silver to represent a larger number of monetary units. Thus he temporarily had more money, but the result was inflation and higher prices, which led to further declines in the value of money. New taxes were introduced. About 1300 the kings of both England and France undertook to tax the landowning clergy of their respective kingdoms. The kings made increasing demands as well on great noble landholders and urban merchants. These demands were resisted, or made subject to bargains by the representative bodies whose origin was described in the last chapter, so that the fourteenth century, and still more the fifteenth, has been called the "golden age" of the medieval parliaments.

In 1337 the Hundred Years' War began between England and France. The war grew out of a dynastic struggle between English and French rulers who both claimed the right to be king of France, but the war between their royal families continued long after the first claimants had died. The battles all took place in France, which was internally divided, some parts, like Aquitaine, having long belonged to the English crown. France was ravaged by marauding bands of English soldiers and their French adherents.

The Hundred Years' War

Eventually, however, French forces began to achieve military victories under the inspired leadership of Joan of Arc, the young woman whom the English burned at the stake in Rouen in 1431 after she was convicted by the church of heresy and witchcraft. The war finally ended in 1453, when the English lost a final, decisive battle and gave up their long campaign to control territories on the continent, but the French suffered the greatest human and material losses during the many decades of fighting and social disruption. The costly century of warfare also had important consequences in England, where a kind of early patriotism arose among the English as their soldiers used longbows to defeat the mounted French knights at places such as Agincourt. Parliament widened its powers because the kings needed money for their campaigns. But the great English barons also became more unruly, and internal disorders fractured England throughout the fifteenth century. Dukes and earls and their followers formed private armies and fought with each other; they defied the royal law courts and intimidated juries, used Parliament and government for their own purposes, and exploited their peasants. From about 1450 until 1485 England was beset by upper-class turmoil that came to be called the Wars of the Roses, because the opposing noble factions adopted red and white roses as their symbols.

Troubles of the Medieval Church

Meanwhile similar calamities afflicted the church. In 1300, the church of the High Middle Ages, centralized in the papacy, stood at its zenith. But the church was weakened by its very successes. It faced the danger that besets every successful institution—a form of government or a university, to choose modern examples—the danger of believing that the institution exists for the benefit of those who conduct its affairs. The papacy, being at the top, was the most liable to this danger. It became "corrupt," set in its ways, out of touch with public opinion, and controlled by a self-perpetuating bureaucracy. It was unable to reform itself, and unwilling to let anyone else reform it.

Both Edward I of England and Philip the Fair of France, in the 1290s, assessed taxes on the landed estates belonging to the great abbeys, bishoprics, and other components of the church. The pope, Boniface VIII, prohibited the taxation of clergy by the civil ruler.

The "Babylonian Captivity"

In the ensuing altercation, in 1302, he issued the famous bull *Unam Sanctam,* the most extreme of all assertions of papal supremacy, which declared that outside the Roman church there was no salvation, and that "every human creature" was "subject to the Roman pontiff."[1] The French king sent soldiers to arrest Boniface, who soon died. French influence in the College of Cardinals brought about the election of a pope who was expected to be subservient to King Philip, and who took up his residence, with his court and officials, at Avignon on the lower Rhone River, on what were then the borders of France. Thus began

---

[1]Bulls, so-called from the Latin word for their seal, are known by their first one or two Latin words, which in this case mean "one holy (Church)." A "bull," while the most solemn form of papal edict, does not as such embody a dogma, and it is not Catholic practice today to affirm this policy of Boniface VIII.

the "Babylonian Captivity" of the church. The rest of Europe regarded the popes at Avignon throughout the century as tools of the French monarchy, and the papacy lost much of its prestige as a universal institution.

Attempts to correct the situation made matters worse. In 1378 the College of Cardinals, torn by French and anti-French factions within it, elected two popes. Both were equally legitimate, being chosen by cardinals, but one lived at Rome, one at Avignon, and neither would resign. The French and their supporters recognized the Avignon pope; England and most of Germany, the Roman. For forty years both lines were perpetuated. There were now two papacies, estranged by the Great Schism of the West.

Never had the papacy been so externally magnificent as in the days of the Captivity and the Schism. The papal court at Avignon surpassed the courts of kings in splendor. The papal officialdom grew in numbers, *The Great Schism* ignoring the deeper problems while busily transacting each day's business. Papal revenues mounted, and new papal taxes were devised. In the continuing movement of funds from all over Europe to the papal court, from the thirteenth century on, a new class of international bankers rose and prospered.

But the papacy, never so sumptuous, had never since the tenth century rested on such shaky foundations. People pay willingly for institutions in which they believe, and admire magnificence in leaders whom they respect. But before 1378, with the pope submissive to France, and after 1378, with two popes and two papacies to support, there was growing complaint at the extravagance and worldliness of papal rule. It must be remembered that all this happened in a Europe traumatized by the plague, and with a declining number of people expected to bear increasing financial burdens. The most pious Christians were the most shocked. They recognized the vital necessity of obtaining God's grace, but with two churches under two popes, each claiming to hold the keys to heaven from Peter, how could they be certain that their church gave true salvation? In a society that was still primarily a religious community, this sense of religious insecurity was a source of uneasiness and dread.

The old moorings were weakened, the wrath of God seemed to be raining upon the earth, and no one knew how to escape from the crisis. Symptoms of mass neurosis appeared. Some people sought refuge in a hectic merriment or luxury and self-indulgence. Others became preoccupied with grisly subjects. *Responses to crisis* Some frantically performed the Dance of Death in the cemeteries, while others furtively celebrated the Black Mass, parodying religion in a mad desire to appease the devil. The Order of Flagellants grew up; its members went through the streets, two by two, beating each other with chains and whips. Religious anxieties and fearful religious rumors contributed also to waves of anti-Jewish violence, murder, and expulsion that spread across parts of France and Germany in the fourteenth century. And it was at this time that people first became obsessed with the fear of witches, a delusion that would ultimately cause thousands of persons (often older women) to be tortured and executed over the following three centuries.

Disaffection with the church, or the thought that it might not be the true or the only way to salvation, spread in all ranks of society. It was not only kings who disputed the claims of the clergy but also obscure parish priests, close to the distress of ordinary people, who began to doubt the powers of their ecclesiastical superiors. One of these humble clerics was William Langland, who in his *Piers Plowman,* in the 1360s, contrasted the sufferings of the honest poor with the hypocrisy and *Lollards and Hussites* corruption in high places. Such unsettling ideas spread very widely; in England those who held them were known as Lollards. Since the actual poor left no records, it is hard to say exactly what they thought, but some of their ideas were probably

Extreme expressions of religious anxiety appeared in the later Middle Ages among the flagellants who wandered through towns beating themselves to appease the wrath of God. They are portrayed here in a later sixteenth-century engraving of their processions.

(©Bridgeman-Giraudon/Art Resource, NY)

expressed by John Wyclif, who taught at Oxford. About 1380, Wyclif was saying that the true church could do without elaborate possessions, and even that an organized church might not be necessary for salvation, since ordinary, devout persons could do without priests and obtain salvation by reading the Bible, which he translated into English. Similar ideas appeared in Bohemia in central Europe, with Jan Hus as their spokesman. Here they became a national movement, for the Hussites were both a religious party and at the same time a Slavic or Czech party protesting against the supremacy of the Germans who lived in Bohemia. The Hussite wars ravaged central Europe for decades in the fifteenth century. The ideas of the Lollards and of Hus and Wyclif were branded as heresy, or unacceptable deviations from the true doctrine of the church.

Influential and established persons did not yet turn to heresy, and still less to witchcraft or flagellation. Their answer to the needs of the day was to assemble a great Europe-wide or general council of the church, in which reforms could be pressed by the whole body of Christians upon the reluctant and rival popes.

The Conciliar Movement

In 1409 such a church council met at Pisa. All parts of the divided Roman Catholic Church were represented. The council declared both reigning popes deposed and obtained the due election of another, but since the first two refused to resign there were now three. In 1414 an even greater and more fully attended council met at Constance. Its aims were three: to end the now threefold schism, to extirpate heresy, and to reform the church "in head and members," or from top to bottom. Not much was accomplished in reform. To discourage heresy, Jan Hus was interrogated, condemned, and burned at the stake. The schism was ended. All three popes were at last persuaded or compelled to withdraw, and another, Martin V, was elected. The unity of the church, under the papacy, was at last restored.

The majority of the Council of Constance wished to make general councils part of the permanent apparatus of the church. Martin V, however, soon reaffirmed the prerogatives of the papal office, dissolved the Council of Constance, repudiated its decrees, and reestablished papal authority in Rome. The next 30 years saw a continuing contest of wills between successive popes and successive councils.

General councils

In this battle for jurisdiction few reforms could be adopted, and fewer still could be enforced. Increasingly the life of the church was corrupted by money. No one believed in bribery, but everyone knew that many high churchmen (like many high civil officials of the day) could be bribed. To buy or sell a church office was a crime in the canon law known as "simony," but it was a crime that in the fifteenth century could not be suppressed. For churchmen to live with mistresses was considered understandable, if unseemly; the standards

Church corruption and indulgences

of laymen in such matters were not high. But for a bishop or other ecclesiastic to give lucrative church positions to his own children (or other relatives) was the abuse known as nepotism, and it, too, could not be eradicated. To sell divine grace for money, all agreed, was not only wrong but also impossible. But in 1300 Boniface VIII had given encouragement to the practice of "indulgences." A person, if properly confessed, absolved, and truly repentant, might, by obtaining an indulgence, be spared certain of the temporal punishments of purgatory. One usually obtained such an indulgence in return for a donation of money. The practice proved to be a fatally easy method of fundraising, despite complaints against the sale of indulgences simply for money.

Gradually the popes prevailed over the councils. The conciliar movement was greatly weakened for Christendom as a whole when the powerful French element secured its own independence after 1438 by a special arrangement in which the Gallican (or French) church declared its administrative independence from the Holy See, suppressed the payment of some church taxes to Rome, and forbade papal intervention in the appointment of French prelates. The papacy thus lost influence in France, but the popes remained preeminent in Europe as a whole. In 1449, with the dissolution of the Council of Basel, the conciliar movement came to an end. In 1450 a great Jubilee was held in Rome to celebrate the papal triumph.

The papacy, its prestige and freedom of action thus secured, now passed into the hands of a series of cultivated gentlemen, men of the world and men in tune with the evolving cultural values of their times—the famous popes of the Renaissance. Some, like Nicholas V (1447–1455) or Pius II (1458–1464), were accomplished scholars and connoisseurs of books. Some were like Innocent VIII (1484–1492), a pleasant man who was the first pope to dine in public with ladies. Alexander VI (1492–1503), of the Spanish Borgia

The Renaissance popes

family, exploited his office for the benefit of his relatives, trying to make his son Cesare Borgia the ruler of all Italy, while his daughter, Lucretia Borgia, became duchess of Ferrara and gathered literary men and artists at her famous Renaissance court. Alexander VI's successor, Julius II (1503–1513), was a capable general, and Leo X (1513–1521) was a superb patron of architects and painters. But we must now describe the Italian Renaissance, in which worthies of this kind were elevated to the Holy See.

6.   THE RENAISSANCE IN ITALY

In Italy in the fifteenth century, and especially at Florence, we observe not merely a decay of medieval certainties but the appearance of a new and invigorating attitude toward the world. The Renaissance, a French word meaning "rebirth," received its historical name in the nineteenth century from those who thought of the Middle Ages as a dark time from which the human spirit had to be awakened. It was called a *re*birth because of the belief that people in Italy, after a long interruption, had taken up and resumed a civilization like that of the Greco-Romans. Medieval people had thought of the times of Aristotle or Cicero as not sharply distinct from their own. In the Renaissance, with a new historical sense, arose the conception of "modern" and "ancient" times, separated by a long period with a different lifestyle and appropriately called the Middle Ages.

The basic institutions of Europe, the distinctive languages and national cultures, the great frameworks of collective action in law, government, and economic production—all originated in the Middle Ages. But the Renaissance marked a new era in thought and feeling, by which Europe and its institutions were in the long run to be transformed. The origins of modern natural science can be traced more to the medieval universities than to the Renaissance thinkers. But it was in the Italy of the Quattrocento (as Italians call the fifteenth century) that other fields of thought and cultural expression were first cultivated. The Italian cultural influence in other countries remained very strong for at least

The Italian influence

200 years. It pertained to high culture, and hence to a limited number of persons, but extended over the whole area represented by literature and the arts—literature meaning all kinds of writing and the arts including all products of human skill. The effects of the Italian Renaissance, though much modified with the passage of time, were evident in the books and later art galleries of Europe and America, and in the architecture of their cities, even after the revolution of modern art in the early twentieth century. They involved the whole area of culture that was neither theological nor scientific but concerned with moral and civic questions about what human beings ought to be or ought to do, with the answers reflected in matters of taste, style, propriety, decorum, personal character, and education. In particular, it was in Renaissance Italy that an almost purely secular attitude first appeared, in which leading thinkers no longer viewed life as a brief preparation for the hereafter.

The Italian Cities and the New Conception of Life

The towns of Italy, so long as long-distance trade converged in the Mediterranean, were the biggest and most bustling of all the towns that rose in Europe during the Middle Ages. The crafts of Italy included many refined trades such as those of the goldsmith or stonecarver, which were so zealously pursued that artisanship turned into art, and a delight in the beautiful became common among all classes. Merchants made fortunes in commerce: they lent their money to popes or princes and so made further fortunes as bankers. They bought the wares of the craftsmen-artists. They rejoiced not so much in money or the making of money, as in the beautiful things and psychological satisfactions that money could buy. And if they forgot the things that money could not buy, this is only to say again that their outlook was becoming more secular.

The Italian city-states

The Italian towns were independent city-states. There was no king to build up a government for Italy as a whole, and for several generations the popes were either absent at Avignon or engaged in disputes arising from the Great Schism, so that the influence of Rome was unimportant.

The wealthiest persons in Italian towns were often bankers who made money from the kind of financial exchange that is portrayed in this fifteenth-century illustration.

(©Scala/Art Resource, NY)

The merchant oligarchies, each in its own city, enjoyed an unhampered stage on which they could use their money to pursue interests other than those of business. In some, as at Milan, they succumbed to or worked with a local prince or despot. In others, as at Florence, Venice, and Genoa, they continued to govern themselves as republics. They had the experience of contending for public office, of suppressing popular revolt or winning popular favor, of producing works of public munificence, of making alliances, hiring armies, outwitting rivals, and conducting affairs of state. In short, Italy offered a social environment in which human personalities could develop in many secular directions.

All this was especially true in Florence, the chief city of Tuscany, which had grown wealthy in the later Middle Ages from the production of woolens. In the fifteenth century it had a population of about 60,000, which made it only moderately large as Italian cities went. Yet, like ancient Athens, Florence produced an extraordinary sequence of gifted individuals. From the years of Dante, Petrarch, and   *The Medici family* Boccaccio, who all died before 1375, to those of Machiavelli, who lived until 1527, an amazing number of the leading figures of the Italian Renaissance were Florentines. Like Athens also, Florence lost its republican liberty as well as its creative powers. Its history can be summarized in that of the Medici family. The founder of the family fortunes was Giovanni (1360-1429), a merchant and banker of Florence. His son, Cosimo de' Medici (1389-1464), allying himself with the popular element against some of the leading families of the republic, soon became unofficial ruler himself. Cosimo's

Two wool merchants display their goods and bags of wool. This illustration, which is from a 1492 book on arithmetic, shows the use of both Arabic and Roman numerals.

(©Biblioteca Riccardiana, Florence/Art Resource, NY)

grandson, Lorenzo the Magnificent (1449–1492), also used his great wealth to govern but is chiefly remembered as a poet, connoisseur, and lavish benefactor of art and learning. In the next century Tuscany became a grand duchy, of which the Medici were hereditary grand dukes until the family died out in 1737. Thus established, they furnished numerous cardinals and two popes to the church, and two Medici women became queens of France.

What arose in Italy, in these surroundings, was a new, more secular conception of life. It seemed very doubtful to many Italians that a quiet, cloistered, or celibate life was

A secular conception of life

on a higher plane than an active gregarious life, or family life, or even a life of promiscuity and adventure. It was hard to believe that clergy were any better than laity or that life led to a stern divine judgment in the end. That human will and intelligence might prove misleading seemed a gloomy doctrine. The belief that human beings were frail creatures, in need of God's grace and salvation, though perhaps said aloud and in public places, seemed to evoke less feeling in the heart. Instead, what captivated the Italians of the Renaissance was a sense of the vast range of human powers.

Formerly, the ideal behavior had been seen in renunciation, in a certain disdain for the concerns of this world. Now a life of public involvement was also prized. Formerly, poverty had been greatly respected, at least in Christian doctrine. Now there was more praise for a proper enjoyment of wealth. Medieval Europeans had admired a life of contemplation, or meditative withdrawal. Now the humanist Leonardo Bruni could write, in 1433, "The whole glory of man lies in activity." Often, to be sure, the two attitudes existed in the same person. Sometimes they divided different groups within the same city. As always, the old persisted along with the new. The result might be psychological stress and civil conflict.

Individualism

The new esteem for human activity took both a social and an individualistic turn. In cities maintaining their republican forms, as at Florence in the early fifteenth century, a new civic consciousness or sense of public duty was expressed. For this purpose the writings of Cicero and other

This procession is part of a fresco that Benozzo Gozzoli painted in 1469 for a Medici chapel. Although its title refers to the three kings on their way to Bethlehem, it actually represents important personages in fifteenth-century Florence. Cosimo de' Medici is on a white horse, followed by a throng of supporters.
(©Alinari/Art Resource, NY)

ancients were found to be highly relevant, since they provided an ethics independent of the Christian and medieval tradition. There was also a kind of cult of the great individual, hardly known to the ancients, which gave little attention to collective responsibility. Renaissance individualism emphasized the outstanding attainments of extraordinary men (women, by contrast, were usually expected to pursue the ordinary tasks of domestic life). The great man shaped his own destiny in a world governed by fortune. He had *virtù,* the quality of being a man (*vir,* "man"), and although a few women might also exhibit *virtù,* it was a quality that in the society of the day was more to be expected in the most aggressive adult males. It meant the successful demonstration of human powers. A man of *virtù,* in the arts, in war, or in statecraft, was a man who knew what he was doing, who, from resources within himself, made the best use of his opportunities, hewing his way through the world and excelling in all that he did. For the arts, such a spirit is preserved in the autobiography of Benvenuto Cellini.

The growing preoccupation with human actions can be traced in new forms of painting, sculpture, and architecture that arose in Italy at this time. These arts likewise

Lorenzo de Medici, known as the Magnificent, was a Florentine political leader whose famous patronage of the arts helped to give Florence its prominence in Renaissance painting, architecture, and sculpture. This bust of Lorenzo, likely based on a model by the late fifteenth-century artists Andrea del Verrocchio and Orsino Benintendi, exemplifies the era's interest in portraying worldly power and human achievements.
(Source: National Gallery of Art)

reflected an increasing this-worldliness—a new sense of reality and a new sense of space—that was different from that of the Middle Ages and would underlie much European thought until the early twentieth century. Space was no longer indeterminate, unknowable, or divine; it was a zone occupied by physical human beings. Reality meant visible and tangible persons or objects in this physical space, "objective" in the sense that they looked or felt the same to all normal persons who perceived them. It was a function of the arts to convey this reality, however idealized or suffused by the artist's individual feeling, in such a way that observers could recognize in the image the identity of the subject portrayed. Despite the growing emphasis on individual achievements, knowledge itself was understood to be more than a subjective perception or the unique vision of a creative genius.

Architecture reflected the new tendencies. Although the Gothic cathedral at Milan was built as late as 1386, at Florence and elsewhere architects preferred to adapt Greco-Roman principles of design, such as the classical column, the arch, and the dome. More public buildings of a nonreligious character were built, and more substantial town houses were put up by wealthy merchants, in styles meant to represent grandeur, or civic importance, or availability and convenience for human use. Gardens and terraces were added to many such buildings.

Realism in sculpture and painting

Sculpture, confined in the Middle Ages to the niches and portals of cathedrals, now emerged as an independent and freestanding art. Its favored subjects were human beings, now presented so that the viewer could walk around the object and see it from all directions. The difference from the religious figures carved on medieval churches was very great. Like the architects, Renaissance sculptors found much in the Greek and Roman tradition that was modern and useful to their purpose. They produced portrait busts of eminent contemporaries, or figures of great leaders, sometimes on horseback, or statues depicting characters from Greco-Roman history and mythology. The use of the nude, in mythological or allegorical subjects, likewise showed a conception of humanity that was more in keeping with the Greek than with the Christian tradition.

Painting was less influenced by the ancients, since the little of ancient painting that had survived was unknown during the Renaissance. The invention of painting in oils opened new pathways for the art. Merchants, ecclesiastics, and princes provided a mounting demand for portraits and new interpretations of biblical or ancient events. In subject matter painting remained conservative, dealing most often with religious themes. It was the conception and presentation that were new. The new feeling for space became evident.

LA PIETA

by Michelangelo Buonarroti (Italian, 1475–1564)

Michelangelo's marble representation of Mary with the body of Jesus shows the carefully crafted details of Renaissance Italian sculpture and fuses religious themes with the material depiction of human beauty and suffering.

(©pandapaw/Shutterstock)

With the discovery of the mathematics of perspective, space was presented in exact relation to the beholder's eye. The viewer, in a sense, entered into the world of the painting. A three-dimensional effect was achieved, with careful representation of distance through variation of size, and techniques of shading or chiaroscuro added to the illusion of physical volume. Human figures were often placed in a setting of painted architecture, or against a background of landscape or scenery, showing castles or hills, which though supposedly far away yet framed the composition with a knowable boundary. In such a painting everything was localized in place and time; a part of the real world was caught and put in the picture. The artistic aspiration was not to suggest eternity or transcendent ideas, as in earlier religious painting, nor yet to express private fantasy or the workings of the unconscious, as in much modern art, but to present a familiar theme in an understandable setting, often with a narrative content, that is, by the telling of a story.

Like the sculptors, painters studied human anatomy and also portrayed people in distinctive and living attitudes. Faces took on more expression as artists sought to depict individual personalities. Painting became less symbolic, less an intimation of general or abstract truths, more a portrayal of concrete realities as they met the eye. In Giovanni Bellini's portrait of a *condottiere* (p. 67), for example, the reader can see how a strong, real, and vivid personality looks out from the canvas. Similarly, the great religious paintings were peopled with human beings. In Leonardo da Vinci's *The Last Supper,* Christ and his disciples are seen as a group of men, each with his own characteristics. Raphael's Madonnas seem to be young Italian women, and in the mighty figures of Michelangelo the attributes of humanity invade heaven itself.

Humanism: The Birth of "Literature"

The literary movement in Renaissance Italy is called humanism because of the rising interest in humane letters, *litterae humaniores.* There had indeed been much writing in the later Middle Ages. Much of it had been of a technical character, as in theology, philosophy, or law; some of it had been meant to convey information, as in chronicles, histories, and descriptions of the physical world. Great hymns had been composed, lively student songs had been sung at the universities, plays had been performed in cathedrals, and the old English and French legends of King Arthur and Roland had been written down. Troubadours had praised the wonders of true love. Yet a new kind of literature and literary culture began to appear in the fourteenth and fifteenth centuries in Italy. A new class of writers looked upon literature as their main life's work, wrote for each other and for a somewhat larger public, and used writing to deal with general questions, to examine their own states of mind, or to resolve their own difficulties. They used words to achieve artistic effects or simply to please and amuse their readers. Almost all of the writers were men, but a few women also entered the new literary culture and contributed to the era's expanding literary themes. The writings of Christine de Pisan, for example, helped to spread humanist ideas in France during the early fifteenth century (her family had moved to France from Italy) and also demonstrated to skeptical male critics that women could participate in the debates of European intellectual life.

The Italian humanists, like their medieval predecessors, often wrote in Latin. They differed from earlier literate persons, however, in that they were usually not members of the clergy. They complained that Latin had become monkish, barbaric, and "scholastic," a jargon of the schools and universities, and they greatly preferred the classic style of Cicero or Livy. Medieval Latin was a vigorous living language that used words in new senses, many of which have passed

Humanists and Latin

**PORTRAIT
OF A CONDOTTIERE
by Giovanni Bellini (Italian,
1430–1516)**

**This portrait provides an emphatic
statement of Renaissance individualism. The artist represents here a
concrete, strong-willed human
being rather than an abstract
type, stressing his subject's
independence and self-sufficiency
by placing him against a dark and
entirely vacant background.**

(Source: National Gallery of Art)

into English and the Romance languages as perfectly normal expressions. Yet in the ancient writers the humanists found qualities that medieval writing did not have. They discovered a new range of interests, a new sensibility, a complex discussion of political and civic questions, a world presented without the overarching framework of religious belief. In addition, the Greeks and Romans unquestionably had style—a sense of form, a taste for the elegant and the epigrammatic. They had also written many of their works for practical ends, in dialogues, orations, or treatises that were designed for purposes of persuasion.

If the humanists therefore made a cult of antiquity, it was because they saw kindred spirits in ancient cultures. They sensed a thematic relevance for their own time. The classical influence, never wholly absent in the Middle Ages, now reentered as a main force in the higher culture of European writers. The humanists polished their Latin, and increasingly they learned Greek. They searched assiduously for classical texts hitherto unknown. Many were found; they had of course been copied and preserved by the monks of an earlier era.

But while a special dignity attached to writing in Latin, known throughout Europe, most of the humanists wrote in Italian also. Or rather, they used the mode of speech current in Florence. This had also been the language of Dante's early fourteenth-century epic poem, the *Divine Comedy*. To this vast poem the humanists now added many writings in Florentine or Tuscan prose. The result was that Florentine became the standard form of modern Italian. It was the first

Vernacular languages

time that a European vernacular—that is, the common spoken tongue as opposed to Latin—became thus standardized amid the variety of its dialects and adapted in structure and vocabulary to the more formal requirements of a written language. French and English soon followed, and most of the other European languages somewhat later.

Petrarch

The Florentine exile Francesco Petrarca, or Petrarch, has been called the first man of letters. The son of a merchant who had moved to the papal city of Avignon, Petrarch spent his life in travel throughout France and Italy. Although he trained for the law and was ordained as a clergyman, he became a somewhat rootless critic of these two esteemed professions, which he denounced for their scholasticism. He lived in the generation after Dante, dying in 1374, and he anticipated the more fully developed humanism that was to come. His voluminous writings show the complex, contradictory attitudes of early Renaissance thought. Attracted by life, love, beauty, travel, and connections with people of importance in church and state, he could also spurn all these things as ephemeral and deceptive. He loved Cicero for his common sense and his commitment to political liberty; indeed, he discovered a manuscript of Cicero's letters in 1345. He loved St. Augustine for his otherworldly vision of the City of God. But in Cicero's writings he also found a deep religious concern, and in St. Augustine he esteemed the active man who had been a bishop and writer heavily engaged in the controversies of his time.

Petrarch wrote sonnets in Italian, an epic in Latin, an introspective study of himself, and a great many letters that he clearly meant to be literary productions. He aspired to literary fame. In all this we see a new kind of writer, who uses language not merely as a practical tool but as a medium of more subtle expression, to commune with himself, to convey moods of discouragement or satisfaction, to clarify doubts, to improve his own understanding of the choices and options that life affords. With Petrarch, in short, literature became a kind of calling, and also a consideration of moral philosophy, still related but no longer subordinate to religion. It was moral philosophy in the widest sense, raising questions of how human beings should adjust to the world, what a good life ought to be, and where the ultimate rewards of living were to be found.

Petrarch was an indication of things to come. Boccaccio, his contemporary and also a Florentine, wrote *The Decameron* in Italian, a series of tales designed both to entertain and to impart a certain wisdom about human character and behavior. They were followed by the main group of humanists, far more numerous but less well remembered. Men of letters began to take part in public life, to gather students and found schools, to serve as secretaries to governing bodies or princes, and even to occupy office

The humanists

themselves. Thus the humanist Coluccio Salutati became chancellor of Florence in 1375. During the following decades Florence was threatened by the expansive ambitions of Milan, where the princely despotism of the Visconti family controlled the city-state. Against such dangers a new and intense Florentine civic consciousness asserted itself. Salutati, in addition to the usual duties of chancellor, served the state with his pen, glorifying Florentine liberty and identifying it with the liberties of ancient republican Rome before they were undermined by the Caesars. Another humanist, Leonardo Bruni, later succeeded him as chancellor. Bruni wrote a history of Florence that marked a new achievement in historical writing, when compared with the annals and chronicles of the Middle Ages. He saw the past as clearly different from but relevant to the present, and he introduced a new division of historical periods. On the model of such ancient writers as Livy, he adopted a flowing narrative form. And he used history for a practical political purpose, to show that Florence had a long tradition of liberty and possessed values and

The three men in this painting were Florentine humanists around 1490. They appear in a larger work that the artist Domenico Ghirlandaio painted for a chapel. Ghirlandaio followed the typical Renaissance practice of using religious stories or events to convey secular subjects and ideas.
(©Alinari/Art Resource, NY)

attainments worth fighting for against menacing neighbors. History became a new kind of useful knowledge. It took on a public value that it had once had for the Greeks and Romans and that it would retain in the future in Europe and eventually in other parts of the world: the function of heightening a sentiment, not yet of nationalism, but of collective civic consciousness or group identity. It was meant to arouse its readers to a life of commitment and public participation.

All this literary activity was of a scholarly type, in which authors broadened their understanding as much by reading as by personal experience of the world. And scholarly activity, the habit of attending closely to what a page really said, had consequences that went beyond either pure literature or local patriotism. A new critical attitude developed. Bruni, in his history, showed a new analytical sense of the need for authentic sources. Lorenzo *Modern critical methods* Valla became one of the founders of textual criticism. Studying the Latin language historically, he observed that its characteristic words and expressions varied from one time to another. He put this knowledge to the service of the king of Naples in a dispute with the pope. Valla showed, by analysis of the language used in the document, that the Donation of Constantine, on which the papacy then based its temporal claims, could not have been written in Constantine's time in the fourth century, and so was a forgery. Such scholarship helped establish modern methods for assessing the truth of written texts, and it contributed also to humanist optimism about the range and utility of human knowledge. Pico della Mirandola and others looked for aspects of truth not revealed in the Christian scriptures. In 1486, the enthusiastic and very learned Pico, for example, claimed at the age of 23 that he could summarize all human knowledge in 900 theses, which he had drawn from "the Chaldaic, Arabic, Hebrew, Grecian, Egyptian, and Latin sages."

Schooling, Manners, and Family Life

While Italian humanism thus contributed new themes, vernacular texts, and analytical methods to literature and scholarship, to classical learning, and to the formation of modern national languages, it also had tangible and lasting effects in education. Here its impact persisted in all European cultures down to the present. The medieval universities were essentially places for professional training in theology, medicine, and law. Except in England this continued to be their primary function. What came to be known as second-ary education, the preparation of young men either for the universities or for life, owes more to the Renaissance. The organized education of women came much later; some girls learned to read at home or in one of the few female primary schools, but young women were excluded from humanist academies and Renaissance universities.

Medieval schooling had been chaotic and repetitious. Young male students of all ages sat together with a teacher, each absorbing from the confusion whatever could be under-stood of Latin rules and vocabulary. The Renaissance launched the idea of putting different age groups or levels of accomplishment into sepa-rate classes, in separate rooms, each with its own teacher, with periodic promotion of the pupil from one level to the next. Latin remained the principal subject, with Greek now added. But many new purposes were seen in the study of Latin. It was intended to give skill in the use of language, including the pupil's native tongue. Rhetoric was the art of using language to influence others. It heightened commu-nication. Knowledge alone was not enough, said the historian and chancellor Bruni, who also wrote a short work on education—"to make effectual use of what we know we must add the power of expression." Nor was Latin merely the necessary professional tool for the priest, the physician, the lawyer, or the government servant. The student learned Latin (and Greek) in order to read the ancient writings—epics, lyrics, orations, letters, histories, dialogues, and philosophical treatises—and it was assumed that such writings offered practical lessons for the educated elites of every generation. Readers therefore learned how to find relevant historical models or failures in the rise and decline of the Roman republic and the troubles of the Greek city-states. The classics were meant also to have a moral impact, to produce a balanced personality, and to form character. Not everyone could be important or gifted, said the humanist Vittorino, but we all face a life of "social duty" and are responsible for our "personal influence" on others. This emphasis on character formation became a permanent theme in the educational systems that trained the young men of early modern Europe.

Young people were trained also for a more civilized deportment in everyday social living. Personal style in the upper classes became somewhat more studied. Hitherto Europeans had generally acted like big children; they spat, belched, and blew their noses without inhibition, snatched at food with their fingers, bawled at each other when they were unhappy, or sulked when their feelings were offended. It was Italians of the Renaissance who first taught more polite habits. Books of etiquette began to appear, of which the most successful was Baldassare Castiglione's *Book of the Courtier* (1528). The "courtier" was ancestor to the "gentleman"; "courtesy" was originally the kind of behavior suited to princely courts.

The "courtier," according to Castiglione, should be a man of good birth but is chiefly the product of training. His education in youth, and his efforts in mature years, should be directed toward mixing agreeably in the company of his equals. His clothes should be neat, his movements graceful, his approach to other people perfectly poised. He must converse with facility, be proficient in sports and arms,

Renaissance education

The "courtier"

This painting by the Italian artist Lavinia Fontana (1552–1614) portrays an appreciation for the generations and social roles that constituted late Renaissance family life. Entitled simply *Portrait of a Family,* it arranges people by age and gender, thus suggesting a different identity and destiny for each person and each group. Fontana was one of the most prolific and successful women artists of the early modern era, and she conveyed her own knowledge of family life (having 11 children of her own) through her detailed artistic representations of specific individuals and their social relationships.

and know how to dance and appreciate music. He should know Latin and Greek. With literary and other subjects he should show a certain familiarity but never become too engrossed. Pedantry and heaviness must yield to an air of effortless superiority, so that even when the courtier knows or does something seriously, he must treat it lightly as one of many accomplishments. At its best, the code taught a consideration for the feelings of others and incorporated some of the moral ideas of the humanists, aiming at a good and successful life in active society. Castiglione's book was translated into numerous languages, and a hundred editions were printed before 1600.

Castiglione's ideal court also included women, whose civilizing influence was supposed to encourage the good manners, polite conversation, and cultural graces that rough-edged men might otherwise ignore. Expressing common views of men and women that shaped much of Renaissance culture, Castiglione expected men to cultivate a "robust and sturdy manliness," which would be balanced in court society by the "soft and delicate tenderness" of women. Such distinctions suggested also the gender divisions in Renaissance families and households, including those that were far removed from the courts of princes.

Historical Documents
Baldesar Castiglione, *The Book of the Courtier* (1528)

Renaissance humanists developed new descriptions of good behavior and successful human lives. The following excerpts from Baldesar Castiglione's influential book about how to succeed at a princely court suggest in typical humanist fashion that individuals can shape their own reputations and create plans for achieving their goals. To be sure, these goals were more available to men than to women, but could these ideas also be useful for ambitious women? Note how Castiglione advises the would-be courtier to appear "nonchalant" as he seeks to impress others and gain recognition within a status-conscious social community.

I have discovered a universal rule which seems to apply more than any other in all human actions or words: namely, to steer away from affectation at all costs, as if it were a rough and dangerous reef, and . . . to practice in all things a certain nonchalance which conceals all artistry and makes whatever one says or does seem uncontrived and effortless. I am sure that grace springs especially from this. . . . So we can truthfully say that true art is what does not seem to be art; and the most important thing is to conceal it, because if it is revealed this discredits a man completely and ruins his reputation. . . .

So this quality which is the opposite of affectation, and which we are now calling nonchalance, . . . brings with it another advantage: for whatever action it accompanies . . . not only reveals the skill of the person doing it but also very often causes it to be considered far greater than it really is. . . . Our courtier, therefore, will be judged to be perfect and will show grace in everything, and especially in his speech, if he shuns affectation.

Baldesar Castiglione, *The Book of the Courtier*, translated by George Bull (London: Penguin Books Ltd, 1967), pp. 67, 69–70.

The marriages that created Renaissance households grew out of careful negotiations in which the families of prospective brides and grooms sought to enhance their respective social positions. In Florence, for example, parents typically arranged for their daughters to be married by age 18 to older men whose economic or political connections would be advantageous to the young woman's own family. Florentine husbands, who had usually reached age 30 before their first marriage, were well advanced in trades or professions before they established their new households, which depended also on the dowries that they received through their marriage contracts. The different ages of husbands and wives reinforced the gender divisions in Renaissance families; men pursued their public careers with their professional peers while their much younger wives raised children in the home. The high mortality rates in Renaissance cities, however, meant that women often outlived their older husbands, and, as young widows, they were forced to raise the children and manage the household. The young men who attended the new Renaissance schools therefore came from families in which mothers usually provided the most important training during their early years. Renaissance education and manners, as taught in the new schools and academies, thus developed within the distinctive patterns of Italian family life and extended the other "lessons" that women were also teaching at home.

Renaissance marriages

Politics and the Italian Renaissance

The Italian Renaissance, for all its cultural accomplishments, produced no institution or great idea by which masses of people living in society could be held together. Indeed, the greatest of Europe's institutions, the Roman Catholic Church, in which Europeans had lived for centuries, and without which they did not see how they could live at all, fell into neglect under the Renaissance popes. Nor did Italy as a whole develop any effective political institutions. Florence during the fifteenth century passed from a high-spirited republicanism to acceptance of one-man rule. Throughout the peninsula the merchants, bankers, connoisseurs, and courtly classes who controlled the city-states could not fight for themselves, nor arouse their citizens to fight for them. They therefore hired professional fighting men, *condottieri,* private leaders of armed bands, who contracted with the various city-states to carry on warfare and often raised their price or changed sides during hostilities. Italian politics became a tangled web, a labyrinth of subterfuge and conspiracy, a platform on which powerful individuals might exhibit their *virtù.* Dictators rose and fell. The Medici became dukes in Florence, the Sforza in Milan, while in Venice and Genoa, where the republics survived, narrow oligarchies held tight control. These states, along with the states of the church, jockeyed for influence within an intricate, shifting, and purely local balance of power.

Italy was the despair of its patriots, or of such few as remained. One of these was Niccolò Machiavelli, who, in *The Prince* (1513), wrote the most lasting work of the Italian Renaissance. He dreamed of the day when the citizens of his native Florence, or indeed of all Italy, should behave like early Romans—show virility in their politics, fight in citizen armies for patriotic causes, and uphold their dignity before Europe. It was outside Italy, in kings Ferdinand of Aragon, Louis XI of France, and Henry VII of England, that Machiavelli was obliged to find

NICCOLÒ MACHIAVELLI
by Cristofano dell'Altissimo
(Italian, c. 1525–1605)

Niccolò Machiavelli's famous book, *The Prince,* developed a new, secular account of how political rulers gained and consolidated their control of state power. Although his writings were criticized for ignoring Christian ethical values, Machiavelli's ideas marked a key starting point for modern European political thought.

(©Fine Art/Getty Images)

Machiavelli

his modern monarchical heroes. He admired them because they knew how to exercise power and how to build strong states. In *The Prince* he produced a handbook of statecraft that he hoped Italy might find useful. He produced also the first purely secular treatise on politics.

Medieval writings on politics, those of Thomas Aquinas or Marsiglio of Padua, for example, had always talked of God's will for the government of people, with such accompanying matters as justice and right, or divine and natural law. All this Machiavelli put

Uses of political power

aside. He emancipated politics from theology and moral philosophy. He undertook to describe simply what rulers actually did. What really happens, said Machiavelli, is that effective rulers and governments use their power to act only in their own political interest. They keep faith or break it, observe treaties or repudiate them, are merciful or ruthless, forthright or sly, peaceable or aggressive, according to their estimates of their political needs. Machiavelli was prepared to admit that such behavior was bad; he only insisted that it was in this way, however regrettably, that successful rulers behaved. He was thought unduly cynical even in an age that lacked political delicacy. He had nevertheless diagnosed the new era with considerable insight. It was an age when politics and political theory were in fact breaking off from religion, with the building up of state power and authority emerging as goals that required no other justification.

But the most successful states of the time, as Machiavelli saw, were not in Italy. They were what history knows as the New Monarchies, and they owed their strength to something more than princely craft, for they enjoyed a measure of loyalty from the people they governed. The city-states in Renaissance Italy failed to sustain even this limited sense of loyalty between governments and their people. Italian politics became an affair of individual or elite *virtù;* and, as outsiders began to realize, the people of Italy lost interest in both the politics and the wars of their own city-states.

So Italy, the sunny land of balmy Mediterranean skies, rich in the busy life of its cities, its moneyed wealth, its gorgeous works of art, became vulnerable to the depredations of other more unified peoples, from Spain and the north, who possessed political

Italian vulnerability

and military institutions in which men could act together in large numbers. In a new age of rising national monarchies the city-states of Italy were too small to compete. In 1494 a French army crossed the Alps. Italy became a bone of contention between France and Spain. In 1527, during a later phase of this long conflict, an army of undisciplined Spanish and German mercenaries, joined by footloose Italians, fell upon Rome itself. Never, not even from the barbarian Goths of the fifth century, had Rome experienced anything so horrible and degrading. The city was sacked, thousands were killed, soldiers milled about in an orgy of rape and loot, the pope was imprisoned, and cardinals were mockingly paraded through the streets facing backward on the backs of mules.

After the sack of Rome the Italian Renaissance faded away. Politically, for over three hundred years, Italy remained divided, the passive object of the ambitions of outside powers. Meanwhile its culture permeated the rest of Europe.

7.   THE RENAISSANCE OUTSIDE ITALY

Outside Italy people were much less conscious of any sudden break with the Middle Ages. Developments north of the Alps, and in Spain, were more an outgrowth of what had gone before. There was indeed a cultural Renaissance in the Italian sense, and some Flemish masters introduced artistic innovations even before the new techniques were used by painters in Italy. In the north also, as in Italy, writers favored a revival of classical Latin, but the modern written languages also began to develop.

The northern Renaissance resembled the earlier southern Renaissance in blending the old and the new, but the religious element was much stronger than in Italy. The most important northern humanists were writers such as Thomas More in England and Erasmus in Holland. The French humanism that produced the earthy François Rabelais also produced the austere John Calvin.

Religious Scholarship and Science

Historians like to distinguish between the "pagan" humanism of Italy and the Christian humanism of the north. In the north, Christian humanists studied the Hebrew and Greek texts of the Bible and read the

Christian humanists

Church Fathers, both Latin and Greek, in order to deepen their understanding of Christianity and to restore its moral vitality. Among people without pretense to humanistic learning, religion also remained a force. Medieval intellectual interests persisted. This is apparent from the continuing foundation of universities. The humanists generally regarded universities as centers of a pedantic, monkish, and scholastic learning. Concentrating upon theology, or upon medicine and law, the universities gave little encouragement to experimental science and still less to purely literary studies. In Italy in the fifteenth century no new universities were established. But in Spain, in France, in Scotland, in Scandinavia, and above all in Germany, new universities continued to develop. Between 1386 and 1506 no less than 14 universities were established in Germany. At one of the newest, Wittenberg, founded in 1502, Martin Luther was to launch the Protestant Reformation.

Germany at this time, on the eve of the great religious upheaval, and before the shift of the principal commercial arteries from central Europe to the Atlantic seaboard, was a main center of European life. Politically, the German-speaking world was an ill-defined and ill-organized region, composed of many diverse parts, from which the Netherlands and Switzerland were not yet differentiated. Economically, nevertheless, western and southern Germany enjoyed a lead over most of Western Europe; the towns traded busily, and German banking families, like the famous Fugger, controlled more capital than any others in Europe. Technical inventiveness was alive; mining was developing; and it was in the Rhineland, at Mainz, that Gutenberg, about 1450, produced the first European books printed with movable type. In painting, the western fringe of the Germanic world produced the Flemish masters, and south Germany gave birth to imaginative artists such as Albrecht Dürer and the Holbeins.

Intellectually, Germany shared in the Latin culture of Europe, a fact often obscured by the Latin names that German authors used in the early modern era. Regiomontanus (the Latin name of Johann Müller) laid the foundations during his short lifetime (1436–1476) for a mathematical conception of the universe. He was probably the most influential scientific worker of the fifteenth century, especially since Leonardo da Vinci's scientific labors remained unknown. Nicholas of Cusa (1401?–1464), a Rhinelander, was a

German contributions to early modern science

churchman whose mystical philosophy entered into the later development of mathematics and science. From such a background of mathematical interests came Copernicus (Niklas Koppernigk, 1473–1543), who believed that the earth moved about the sun; he was indeed a Pole, but he came from the mixed German-Polish region of East Prussia. Fortified by the same mathematical interests, Europe's best-known cartographers were also Germans, such as Behaim and Schöner, whose world maps represented the most advanced geographical knowledge of the time. Paracelsus (Latin for

Hohenheim) undertook to revolutionize medicine at the University of Basel. His wild prophecies made him a mixture of scientist and charlatan; but, in truth, science was not yet clearly distinguished from the occult, with which it shared the idea of control over natural forces. A similar figure, remembered in literature and the arts, was the celebrated Dr. Faustus. In real life, Faust, or Faustus, was perhaps a learned German of the first part of the sixteenth century. He was rumored to have sold his soul to the devil in return for knowledge and power. The Faust story was dramatized in England as early as 1593 by Christopher Marlowe, and, much later, by Goethe in German poetry. In the legend of Faust later generations were to see a symbol of the inordinate ambitions of modern people.

The idea that human powers could understand and control physical nature developed especially north of the Alps, but this idea also corresponded in many ways to the more purely Italian and humanistic emphasis on the infinite richness of human personalities. Together, these ideas constituted the new Renaissance spirit, for both stressed the emancipation of humanity's limitless potentialities. The two ideas constantly interacted; in fact, most of the scientific workers just mentioned—Regiomontanus, Nicholas of Cusa, Copernicus—spent many years in Italy, receiving the stimulus of Italian thought.

Mysticism and Lay Religion

In the north a genuine religious impulse went beyond the religious humanistic scholarship and sustained a stronger interest in Christian mysticism. Where in Italy the religious sense, if not extinct, seemed to pass into a joyous and public cult in which God was glorified by works of art, in the north it took on a more spiritual and moral tone. Germany in the fourteenth century produced a series of mystics. The mystic tendencies of Nicholas of Cusa have been mentioned. More typical mystics were Meister Eckhart (d. 1327) and Thomas à Kempis (d. 1471), author of the *Imitation of Christ*. The essence of mysticism lay in the belief, or experience, that the individual soul could in perfect solitude commune directly with God. The mystic had no need of reason, nor of words, nor of joining with other people in open worship, nor of the sacraments administered by the priests—nor even of the church. The mystics did not rebel against the church; they accepted its pattern of salvation; but they also offered, to those who could follow, a deeper religious experience in which the church as a social institution had no place. All social institutions, in fact, were transcended in mysticism by the individual soul; and on this doctrine, both profound and socially disruptive, Martin Luther was later to draw.

Mysticism and the individual soul

For the church, it was significant also that religion was felt deeply outside the clergy. Persons stirred by religion, who in the Middle Ages would have taken holy orders, now frequently remained laymen. In the past the church had often needed reform. But in the past, the clergy had found influential reformers within their own ranks. The church had thus been repeatedly reformed and renewed without revolution. Now, in the fifteenth and early sixteenth centuries an ominous line seemed to be increasingly drawn: between the clergy as an established interest, inert and set in its ways, merely living, and living well, off the church; and groups of people outside the clergy—religious laypersons, religiously inclined humanists and writers, impatient and headstrong rulers—who were more influential than ever before and more critical of ecclesiastical abuses.

Lay religion was especially active in the Netherlands. A lay preacher, Gerard Groote, attracted followers there by calling for spiritual regeneration. In 1374 he founded a religious sisterhood, which was followed by establishments for religiously minded men. They called themselves, respectively, the Sisters and the Brothers of the Common Life, and they eventually received papal approval. They lived communally, but not as monks and nuns, for they took no vows, wore ordinary clothing, and were free to leave at will. They worked at relieving the poor and in teaching. The schools of the Brothers, since some of them came to have as many as a thousand boys, were the first to be organized in separate classes, each with its own room and its own teacher, according to the pupil's age or

The Sisters and Brothers of the Common Life

level of advancement. The Sisters maintained similar though less elaborate schools for girls. Students learned to read and write, but the emphasis was on a Christian ideal of character and conduct, and the goal was to instill such qualities as humility, tolerance, reverence, love of one's neighbor, and the conscientious performance of duty. This Modern Devotion, as it was called, spread widely in the Netherlands and adjoining parts of Germany.

Erasmus of Rotterdam

In this atmosphere grew up the greatest of all the northern humanists, and indeed the most notable figure of the entire humanist movement, Erasmus of Rotterdam (1466–1536). Like all the humanists, Erasmus

Erasmus of Rotterdam

chose to write in a "purified" and usually intricate Latin style. He regarded the Middle Ages as benighted, ridiculed the scholastic philosophers, and studied deeply the classical writers of antiquity. He had the strength and the limitations of the pure man of letters. To the hard questions of serious philosophy he was largely indifferent; he feared the unenlightened excitability of the common people, and he was almost wholly unpolitical in his outlook. He rarely thought in terms of worldly power or advantage and made too little allowance for those who did. An exact contemporary to the most worldly Renaissance popes, Erasmus was keenly aware of the need for reform of the clergy. He put his faith in education, enlightened discussion, and gradual moral improvement; and he counseled against all violence or fanaticism. He prepared new Greek and Latin editions of the New Testament. Urging people to read the New Testament in the vernacular languages, he

ERASMUS OF ROTTERDAM
by Hans Holbein the Younger
(German, 1497–1543)

This portrait from 1532 portrays the famous humanist toward the end of his lifelong campaigns to promote tolerance and careful scholarship, suggesting perhaps his dismay as Christians divided into bitterly warring factions in the early sixteenth century.

(©The Metropolitan Museum of Art, New York, Robert Lehman Collection, 1975)

hoped that a better understanding of Christ's teaching might turn them from their evil ways. In his *Praise of Folly* he satirized all worldly pretensions and ambitions, those of the clergy most emphatically. In his *Handbook of a Christian Knight* he showed how a man might take part in the affairs of the world while remaining a devout Christian. Tolerance, restraint, good manners, scholarly understanding, a love of peace, a critical and reforming zeal, and a reasonable tone from which shouting and bad temper were always excluded—such were the Erasmian virtues.

Erasmus achieved an international eminence such as no one of purely intellectual attainments had ever enjoyed. He corresponded with the most powerful kings and church officials in Europe. Theologians found fault with Erasmus's ideas (in which, indeed, the supernatural had little importance), but among the leaders of the church, the popes and prelates, he had many admirers. Erasmus, it must be noted, attacked only the abuses in the church, the ignorance or sloth of the clergy, and the moral or financial corruption of their lives. The essence and principle of the Roman Catholic Church he never called into question. The Erasmian spirit, so widely diffused about 1520, might have helped to reform the church without far-reaching social or spiritual upheaval, but the revolutionary impact of Protestantism soon drove Erasmian tolerance and restraint out of Europe's intensely divisive religious debates.

8.   THE NEW MONARCHIES

Meanwhile, in Europe outside Italy, kings were actively building the institutions of the modern state. It was these states, more than any other single factor, that were to determine the course of the sixteenth-century religious revolution. Whether a country turned Protestant, remained Catholic, or divided into separate religious communities would depend very largely upon political considerations.

War, civil war, class war, feudal rebellion, and plain banditry afflicted a good deal of Europe in the middle of the fifteenth century. In this formless violence central governments had become very weak. Various rulers now tried to impose a more orderly civil peace. They have been conveniently called the New Monarchs, but they were not really very new because they resumed the interrupted labors of kings in the High Middle Ages. They thus laid foundations for later national, or at least territorial, states.

The New Monarchs offered the institution of monarchy as a guarantee of law and order. Arousing latent sentiments of loyalty to the reigning dynasty, they proclaimed that hereditary monarchy was the only legitimate form of public power. They especially enlisted the support of middle-class people in the towns, who were tired of the private wars and marauding habits of the feudal nobles. Townspeople were willing to let parliaments be dominated or even ignored by the king, for parliaments had proved too often to be strongholds of unruly barons, or had merely accentuated class conflict. The king, receiving money in taxes, was able to organize armies with which to control the nobles. The use of the pike and the longbow, which enabled the foot soldier to stand against the horseman, was here of great potential value. The king, if only he could get his monarchy sufficiently organized and his finances into reliable order, could hire large numbers of foot soldiers, who generally came from the growing population of commoners, unlike the knightly horsemen. But to organize his monarchy, the king had to break down the mass of feudal, inherited, customary, or "common" law in which the rights of the feudal classes were entrenched. For this purpose, at least on the Continent, the New Monarch made use of Roman law, which was now actively studied in the universities. He called himself a "sovereign"—it was at this time that kings began to be addressed as "majesty." The king, said the experts in Roman law, incorporated the will and welfare of the people in his own person. He could therefore *make* law by his own authority, regardless of previous custom or even of historic liberties—and they quoted Latin phrases to argue that "what pleases the prince has the force of law."

The New Monarchy in England, France, and Spain

The New Monarchy came to England with the dynasty of the Tudors (1485–1603), whose first king, Henry VII (1485–1509), after gaining the throne by force, put an end to the civil turbulence of the Wars of

The Tudors

the Roses. In these wars the great English baronial families had seriously weakened each other, to the great convenience of the king and most of the common people. Henry VII passed laws against "livery and maintenance," the practice by which great lords maintained private armies wearing their own livery or insignia, and he used his royal council as a new court to deal with property disputes and infractions of the public peace. It met in a room decorated with stars, whence its name, the Star Chamber. It represented the authority of the king and his council, and it operated without a jury. Later denounced as an instrument of despotism, it was popular enough at first, because it preserved order and rendered substantial justice. Henry VII, though miserly and unpleasant in person, was accepted as a good ruler. National feeling in England consolidated around the house of Tudor.

In France the New Monarchy was represented by Louis XI (1461–1483), of the Valois line, and his successors. In the five centuries after the first French king was crowned, the royal domain had steadily expanded from its original small nucleus around Paris through a combination of inheritance, marriage, war,

The Valois

intrigue, and conquest. Louis XI continued to round out the French borders. Internally, he built up a royal army, suppressed brigands, and subdued rebellious nobles. He acquired far greater powers than the English Tudors to raise taxation without parliamentary consent. The French monarchy also enlarged its already exceptional powers over the clergy. In 1516 King Francis I reached an agreement with Pope Leo X in the Concordat of Bologna, which gave the pope financial income from the French church but allowed the French king to appoint the church bishops and abbots within France. The fact that, after 1516, the kings of France already controlled their own national clergy was one reason why, in later years, they were never tempted to turn Protestant.

Strictly speaking, there was no kingdom of Spain. Various Spanish kingdoms had combined into two, Aragon and Castile. To Aragon, which lay along the Mediterranean side of the peninsula, belonged the

Aragon and Castile

Balearic Islands, Sardinia, Sicily, and the south Italian kingdom of Naples. To Castile, after 1492, belonged the newly discovered Americas. The two were joined in a personal union by the marriage of Ferdinand of Aragon and Isabella of Castile in 1469. The union was personal only; that is, both kingdoms recognized the two monarchs, but they had no common political, judicial, or administrative institutions. There was little or no Spanish national feeling; indeed, the Catalans in northern Aragon spoke a language quite different from Castilian Spanish. The most significant common feeling throughout Spain came from the sense of belonging to the Spanish Catholic Church. The common memory was that of the Christian crusade against the Muslims (Moors) who had long lived on the southern Iberian peninsula. The one common institution, whose officials had equal authority and equal access to all the kingdoms, was a church court, the Inquisition. Meanwhile, the *reconquista* was at last completed when the southern tip of Spain, Granada, was conquered from the Moors in 1492. Its annexation added to the heterogeneous character of the Spanish dominions.

In these circumstances the New Monarchy in Spain followed a religious bent. Unification took place around the church. The rulers, though they made efforts at political centralization, worked largely through facilities offered by the church, and the early sense of "Spanishness" was linked to a sense of Catholicity. Formerly the Spanish had been among the most tolerant of Europeans; Christians, Muslims, and Jews had managed to live together. But in the wave of religious excitement that accompanied the conquest of Granada both the Jews and the Moors were expelled. The expulsion of the Jews by a decree of 1492 was actually a sign of former toleration in Spain, for the Jews had been earlier expelled from England in 1290 and from France in 1306. They were not again legally allowed in England until the mid-seventeenth century, nor in France (with some exceptions) until the French Revolution. In Spain, as in the history of many European peoples, the emergence of an early "national" consciousness seemed to express or produce an anti-Semitism that defined Jews as "outsiders."[2]

All persons in Spain were now supposed to be Christians. In fact, however, Spain was one of the places in Europe where a person's Christianity could not be taken for granted, because many Spanish families had been Jewish or Muslim for centuries and had only accepted Christianity to avoid expulsion. Hence arose a fear of false Christians, of an unassimilated element secretly hostile to the foundations of Spanish life. It was feared that Moriscos (Christians of Moorish background) and Marranos (Christians of Jewish background) retained a clandestine sympathy for the religion of their forebears. Thousands of such persons were brought before the Inquisition, where, as in the civil courts under Roman procedure, torture could be employed to extort confessions. It was thus safest to be profuse in one's external religious devotions because adherence to the Catholic Church became the way of proving oneself to be a good Spaniard.

Fusing the national and the Catholic

The life of Spain carried forward some of the long-existing commitment to a crusade—which had now evolved into a campaign within Spain against Moriscos and Marranos, and a new campaign against the Moors in northern Africa itself, which the Spanish invaded immediately after the conquest of Granada. The Spanish also extended their religious energies into the Americas, where the Spanish church set about gathering the Indians into the Christian fold. And Spain's strong religious identity would soon contribute to its growing role in the wider political and religious conflicts of sixteenth-century Europe. The Spanish history of crusades against Muslims had prepared the country (before Protestantism ever appeared) to become a leading defender of Roman Catholic traditions as well as an advocate for Catholic renewal and internal reforms.

The Holy Roman Empire and the Habsburg Supremacy

Ideas of the New Monarchy were at work even in Germany, which is to say, in the Holy Roman Empire. There were three kinds of states in the empire. There were the princely states such as Saxony, Brandenburg, or Bavaria, each of which was a small hereditary dynastic monarchy in itself. There were also ecclesiastical states—bishoprics, abbacies, etc.—in which the bishop or abbot, whose rule was of course not hereditary, conducted

---

[2]The Jews who left Spain (the Sephardic Jews) went to North Africa and the Middle East, and in smaller numbers to the Dutch Netherlands and even to southwestern France (one of the exceptions noted above). Those who left England two centuries earlier generally went to Germany, the great center of Ashkenazic Jewry in the Middle Ages. Driven from Germany in the fourteenth century they concentrated in Poland, which remained a great center of European Jews until the Nazi massacres of the 1940s.

the government. A large portion of the area of the empire consisted of these church-states. Third, there were the imperial free cities, some 50 in number; their collective area was not large, but they dominated the commercial and financial life of the country.

The German states, over the centuries, had prevented the emperor from infringing upon their local liberties. They had taken care to keep the emperorship an elective office, so that with each election local liberties could be reaffirmed. After 1356 the right of electing an emperor was vested in seven electors: four of the princely lords—the Count Palatine, Duke of Saxony, Margrave of Brandenburg, and King of Bohemia—and three of the ecclesiastical lords—the arch-bishops of Mainz, Trier, and Cologne. In 1452 the electors chose the Archduke of Austria to be emperor. His family name was Habsburg. The Habsburgs, by using the resources of their hereditary possessions in Austria (and later elsewhere) and by delicately balancing and bribing the numerous political forces within Germany, managed to get themselves consistently reelected to the Holy Roman emperorship in every generation, with one exception, from 1452 until 1806. The Habsburg emperors also tried to introduce the centralizing principles of the New Monarchy into an empire that lacked institutions for the exercise of centralized power.

The Habsburgs

Under Maximilian I (1493–1519) there seemed to be progress in that direction: the empire was divided into administrative "circles," and an Imperial Chamber and Council were created, but they were all doomed to failure before the immovable obstacle of regional states' rights. Maximilian was also the author of the Habsburg family fortunes through his strategic use of royal marriages, which brought the Habsburgs into control of a vast empire. Maximilian's grandson, Charles, thus inherited from his four grandparents the lands of Austria, the Netherlands, and part of Burgundy; Castile and Aragon in Spain; the whole of Spanish America; and scattered possessions in Italy and the Mediterranean. In addition, in 1519, Charles was elected Holy Roman Emperor and so became the symbolic head of all Germany.

Charles V of the empire (he was known as Charles I in Spain) was thus beyond all comparison the most powerful ruler of his day. But still other fortunes awaited the house of Habsburg. The Turks, who had occupied Constantinople in 1453, were at this time pushing through Hungary and menacing central Europe. In 1526 they defeated the Hungarians at the battle of Mohacs. The parliaments of Hungary, and of the adjoining kingdom of Bohemia, hoping to gain allies in the face of the Turkish threat, thereupon elected Charles V's brother Ferdinand as their king. Ferdinand soon lost much of Hungary to the Turkish Sultan, Suleiman I, but he retained his royal crown and gradually expanded Habsburg influence in central Europe. No royal family since Charlemagne had stood so far above all rivals. Contemporaries cried that Europe was threatened with "universal monarchy," with a kind of imperial system in which no people could preserve its independence from the Habsburgs.

Charles V

The reader who wishes to understand the early modern European religious revolution and the spreading support for Protestantism must bear in mind the intricate interplay of the factors that have now been outlined: the declining respect for the Roman church; the growth of secular and humanistic feeling; the spread of lay religion outside the official clergy; the rise of monarchs who wished to control everything in their kingdoms, including the church; the resistance of feudal elements to these same monarchs; the lassitude of the popes and their fear of church councils; the division of Germany; the Turkish entry into central Europe; the crusading traditions in Spain; the preeminence of Charles V; and the fears felt in other countries, especially in France, of absorption by the amazing empire of the Habsburgs.

9.   THE PROTESTANT REFORMATION

Three streams contributed to the religious upheaval in sixteenth-century Europe. First, among common people, or the laboring poor, who might find their spokesmen among local priests, there was an endemic dissatisfaction with all the grand apparatus of the church, or a belief that its bishops and abbots were part of a wealthy and oppressive ruling class. For such people, religious ideas became mixed with a protest against the whole social order. They found expression in the great peasant rebellion in Germany in the 1520s. The sects that emerged from these social groups are known historically as Anabaptists, and the modern Baptists, Mennonites, and Moravian Brothers are among their descendants. Second, and forming a group generally more educated and with broader views of the world, were the middle classes of various European cities, especially of cities that were almost autonomous little republics, as in Germany, Switzerland, and the Netherlands. They might wish to manage their own religious affairs as they did their other business, believing that the church hierarchy was too much embedded in a feudal, baronial, and monarchical system with which they had little in common. The modern churches of Calvinist origin came in large part from this stream. Third, there were the ruling sovereigns and princes, who had long disputed with the church on matters of property, taxes, legal jurisdiction, and political influence. All such rulers wanted to be masters in their own territory. In the end it was the power of such

Political and social discontents

This painting entitled *Confession of Jewish Judas*, **by the Spanish artists Martin Bernat and Miguel Ximenez (c. 1480s), suggests the dangers that non-Christian people faced in late fifteenth-century Spain. Influential, wealthy interrogators questioned the beliefs or behavior of persons whose religion made them "suspicious" and vulnerable to the powerful people who distrusted them.**

(©PHAS/Getty Images)

EUROPE, 1526
The main feature of the political map of Europe about 1526 is the predominance of the house of Habsburg. Much of Europe was ruled by the Habsburg Emperor Charles V, who was at the same time King Charles I of Spain. Charles left his possessions in Austria, Hungary, and Bohemia to his brother and those in Spain, the Netherlands, Italy, and America to his son, thereby establishing the Austrian and Spanish branches of the Habsburg dynasty. France was nearly encircled by Habsburg dominions and habitually formed alliances to oppose the Habsburg kings.

rulers that determined which form of religion should officially prevail. The Lutheran and Anglican churches were in this tradition, and to some extent the Gallican church, as the French branch of the Roman Catholic Church was called. As it turned out, by 1600, the second and third streams had won many successes, but the first was suppressed. Socio-religious radicalism was reduced to an undercurrent in countries where Anglican, Lutheran, Calvinist, or Roman Catholic churches were established during the sixteenth century.

Strands of Protestantism

Since northern Europe became Protestant while the south remained Catholic, it may look as if the north had broken off in a body from a once solid Roman church. The reality was not so simple. Let us for a moment put aside the term "Protestant," and think of the adherents of the new religion as religious revolutionaries.[3] Their ideas were revolutionary because they held, not merely that abuses in the church must be corrected, but also that the Roman church itself was wrong in principle. Even so, there were many who hoped, for years, that old and new ideas of the church might be combined. Many deplored the extremes but gradually in the heat of struggle had to choose one side or the other. The issues became drawn, and each side aspired to destroy its adversary. For over a century the revolutionaries maintained the hope that "popery" would everywhere fall. For over a century the upholders of the old order worked to annihilate or reconvert "heretics." Only slowly did Catholics and Protestants come to accept each other's existence as an established fact of European society. Though the religious frontier that was to prove permanent appeared as early as 1560, it was not generally accepted until after the Thirty Years' War, which ended in 1648.

Luther and Lutheranism

The first who successfully defied the older church authorities was Martin Luther (1483–1546). He was a monk, and an earnest one, until he was almost 40 years old. A vehement and spiritually uneasy man, with many dark and introspective recesses in his person-

Luther's "justification by faith"

ality, Luther was terrified by the thought of the omnipotence of God, distressed by his own sense of inadequacy, apprehensive of the devil, and suffering from the chronic conviction that he was damned. The means offered by the church to allay such spiritual anguish—the sacraments, prayer, attendance at Mass—gave him no satisfaction. From a reading and pondering of St. Paul (Romans 1: 17)—"the just shall live by faith"—there dawned upon him a new realization and sense of peace. He developed the doctrine of justification by faith alone. This held that what "justifies" a person is not what the church knew as "works" (prayer, alms, the sacraments, holy living) but "faith alone," an inward bent of spirit given to each soul directly by God. Good works, Luther thought, were the consequence and external evidence of this inner grace, but in no way its cause. People did not "earn" grace by doing good; they did the good because they possessed the grace of God. With this idea Luther for some years lived content. Even years later some high-placed churchmen believed that in Luther's doctrine of justification by faith there was nothing contrary to the teachings of the Catholic Church.

Luther, now a professor at Wittenberg, was brought out of seclusion by an incident of 1517. A friar named Tetzel was traveling through Germany distributing indulgences, authorized by the pope to finance the building of St. Peter's in Rome. Tetzel claimed that

Indulgences

purchasing indulgences would free people from some of the punishments of purgatory, so the faithful were paying stipulated sums of money to buy them. Luther thought that people were being deluded, that no one could obtain grace in this way, or ease the pains of relatives in purgatory, as was officially claimed. In the usual academic manner of the day, he posted 95 theses on the door of the castle church at Wittenberg. Reviewing the Catholic sacrament of penance, Luther held in these theses that, after confession, the sinner is freed of sinful burdens not by the priest's absolution but by inner grace and faith alone. Increasingly, as Luther described his view of Christian faith, it seemed that the priesthood performed no necessary function in the spiritual relation between human beings and God.

---

[3]The word "Protestant" arose as an incident in the struggle, at first denoting certain Lutherans who drew up a formal protest against an action of the diet of the empire in 1529. Only very gradually did the various groups of anti-Roman reformers think of themselves as collectively Protestant.

Martin Luther and his wife Catherine von Bora, portrayed here by the artist Lucas Cranach, the Elder, represent the acceptance of marriage among the clergy and religious leaders of the new Protestant churches. Catherine had lived in a convent before she married Luther and took on the new tasks of a religious wife in a Protestant minister's household.
(Source: Statens Museum for Kunst/National Gallery of Denmark; © ullstein bild/Getty Images)

Luther at first appealed to the pope, Leo X, to correct the abuse of indulgences in Germany. When the pope refused action Luther (like many before him) urged the assembly of a general church council as a religious authority above the pope. He was obliged, however, to admit in public debate that even the decision of a general council might be mistaken. The Council of Constance, he said, had in fact erred in its condemnation of Jan Hus. But if neither the pope, nor yet a council, had authority to define true Christian belief, where was such authority to be found? Luther's answer was, in effect: there is no such authority. He held that individuals might read the Bible and freely make their own interpretations according to their own conscience. This idea was as revolutionary for the church as would be the assertion today that neither the Supreme Court nor any other body may authoritatively interpret or enforce the Constitution of the United States, since each citizen may interpret the Constitution in his or her own way.

From his first public appearance Luther's critique of the Roman church won ardent supporters, for there was a good deal of resentment in Germany against Rome. In 1519 and 1520 he rallied public opinion in a series of tracts that profoundly challenged key tenets of the Roman Catholic Church. He especially urged people to find Christian truth in the Bible for themselves, and in the Bible only. He denounced the reliance on fasts, pilgrimages, saints, and Masses. He rejected the belief in purgatory. He reduced the seven sacraments *Luther's criticisms of the church* to two—baptism and the communion, as he called the Mass. In the latter he repudiated the doctrine of transubstantiation, which held that the priest's consecration of bread and wine during the Mass transformed these substances into the actual body and blood of Christ. At the same time, however, he affirmed that God was still somehow mysteriously present in the bread and wine. He declared that the clergy should marry, upbraided the prelates for their luxury, and demanded that monasticism be eliminated. To drive through such reforms he called upon the temporal power, the princes of Germany. He thus issued an invitation to the state to assume control over religion, an invitation which, in the days of the New Monarchy, a good many rulers were enthusiastically willing to accept.

Threatened by a papal bull with excommunication unless he recanted, Luther solemnly and publicly burned the bull. Excommunication followed. To the emperor, Charles V, now fell the duty of apprehending the heretic and repressing the heresy. Luther was summoned to appear before an assembly of the governing officials of the Holy Roman Empire (called a Diet), which met at Worms, an imperial city in the Rhineland. He declared that he could be convinced only by Scripture or right reason; otherwise "I neither can nor will recant anything, since it is neither right nor safe to act against conscience. God help me! Amen." He was placed under the ban of the empire. But the Elector of Saxony and other north German princes took Luther under their protection after he left Worms. In safe seclusion, he began to translate the Bible into German.

Social revolution

Lutheranism quickly swept over Germany, assuming the proportions of a national upheaval. It became mixed with all kinds of political and social revolution. A league of imperial knights, adopting Lutheranism, attacked their neighbors, the church-states of the Rhineland, hoping by annexations to enlarge their own meager territories. In 1524 the peasants of a large part of Germany revolted. They were stirred by new religious ideas, worked upon by preachers who went beyond Luther in asserting that each individual could readily understand what was right or wrong. Their aims, however, were social and economic; they demanded a regulation of rents and security of common village rights and complained of oppressive rule by their manorial overlords. Luther repudiated all connection with the peasants, called them filthy swine, and urged the princes to suppress them by the sword. The peasants were unmercifully put down, but popular unrest continued to stir the country, expressing itself, in a religious age, in various forms of extreme religious frenzy.

Various religious leaders attracted devout followers, who came to be known collectively as Anabaptists. Some said that all the world needed was love, some that Christ would soon come again, some that they were saints and could do no wrong, and some that infant baptism was useless, immersion of full-grown adults being required, as described in the Bible. The roads of Germany were alive with religious radicals, of whom some tens of thousands converged in 1534 on the city of Münster. There they proclaimed the reign of the saints, abolished property, and introduced polygamy as sanctioned in the Old Testament. A Dutch tailor, John of Leyden, claimed that authority came to him directly from God. Hemmed in by besieging armies, he ruled Münster by a revolutionary terror. Luther advised his followers to join even with Catholics to repress such a dangerous religious and social menace. After a full year Münster fell to the forces of its former rulers. The "saints" were pitilessly rooted out; John of Leyden died in torture.

Luther, horrified at the way in which religious revolution became confused with social revolution, defined his own position more conservatively. He restricted, while never denying, the right of private judgment in matters of conscience, and he made a larger place for

Luther's reaction

an established Lutheran clergy who served as teachers and religious leaders over the laity. Always well disposed to temporal rulers, having called upon the princes to act as religious reformers, he was thrown by the peasant and Anabaptist uprisings into an even closer alliance with the state. Christian liberty, Luther insisted, was an internal freedom, purely spiritual, known only to God. In worldly matters, he said, the good Christian owed obedience to established authority. Lutheranism thus came to view the state with more deference and respect than governments usually received from either Roman Catholicism or the Calvinism that soon arose.

The radical Anabaptist movement in Münster was severely repressed after the city's former rulers regained control in early 1536. This illustration depicts the public torture and death of John of Leyden, whose punishment served as a vivid warning to other revolutionary Protestants throughout Germany.
(©FALKENSTEINFOTO/Alamy Stock Photo)

In the revolution that was rocking Germany it was not the uprising of imperial knights, nor that of peasants or tailors and journeymen, that was successful, but the rebellion of the higher orders of the Empire against the emperor. Charles V, as Holy Roman Emperor, was bound to uphold Catholicism because only in a Catholic world did the Holy Empire have any meaning. The states of the empire, always fearing the loss of local liberty, saw in Charles's efforts to repress Luther a threat to their own freedom. Many imperial free cities, and

Political rebellion

most of the dynastic states of north Germany, now insisted on adding to their other rights and liberties the right, or liberty, to determine their own religion. The right or power to reform, they said, belonged to member states, not to the empire itself. They became Lutheran, locally, introducing Lutheran bishops, doctrines, and forms of worship. Where a state turned Lutheran it usually confiscated the church properties within its borders, a process that considerably enriched some of the Lutheran princes and gave them a strong material interest in the success of the Lutheran movement. In most of the church-states, since the Catholic archbishop or bishop was himself the government, Catholicism prevailed. But a few church-states turned Lutheran. A good example of the secularization of a church-state was afforded in East Prussia, just outside the empire. This territory belonged to the Teutonic Order, a Catholic organization of which the grand commander, an elective official, was at this time Albert of Brandenburg. In 1525 Albert declared for Luther and converted East Prussia into a secular duchy, of which he and his descendants became hereditary dukes.

CHRONOLOGY OF NOTABLE EVENTS, 1309–1555

1309–1378	"Babylonian Captivity": Papacy in Avignon
1337–1453	Hundred Years' War between England and France
1348–1350	Black Death decimates European population
c. 1350–1500	Renaissance Humanism and Art
1378–1417	Schism of Roman Catholic Church: Popes in Avignon and Rome
1454	Johann Gutenberg begins printing books with movable type
1494	French invasion of Italy destroys independence of city-states
1513	Niccolò Machiavelli writes *The Prince*
1517	Martin Luther posts his "95 theses"; beginning of Protestant Reformation
1545–1563	Roman Catholic Council meets at Trent; promotes Catholic reforms
1555	Peace of Augsburg recognizes Protestant and Catholic states in Germany

Against the emperor, a group of Lutheran princes and free cities formed the League of Schmalkald. The king of France, Francis I, though a Catholic in good standing, allied with and supported the League. Political interests overrode religious ones. Against the "universal monarchy" of the swollen Habsburgs the French found alliances where they could, allying with the Turks as with the Lutherans, building up a balance of power against their mighty foe. It became the studied policy of Catholic France to maintain the religious division of Germany.

Threatened by French and Turkish armies and challenged by the resistance of German princes within his own empire, Charles appealed to the pope, urging him to assemble a Europe-wide council in which all disputed matters could be considered, the Protestants could be heard, compromises could be effected, and church unity and German unity (such as it was) could be restored. The king of France schemed at Rome to prevent the pope from calling any such council.

Charles's appeals to the papacy

The kings of both France and England urged national councils instead, in which religious questions could be settled on a national basis. Pope after pope delayed. The papacy feared that a council of all Latin Christendom might get out of control, since Catholics as much as Protestants demanded reform. To the papacy, remembering the Council of Constance, nothing was more upsetting than the thought of a council, not even the Protestants, not even the Turks. So the popes procrastinated, no council met, years passed, and a new generation grew up in Lutheranism. Meanwhile the Schmalkaldic League, allied with France, actually went to war with the emperor in 1546. Germany fell into an anarchy of civil struggle between Catholic and Protestant states, the latter aided by Catholic France. The war was ended by the Peace of Augsburg of 1555.

The terms set at Augsburg signified a complete victory for the cause of Lutheranism and states' rights. Each state of the empire received the liberty to be either Lutheran or Catholic as it chose. No individual freedom of religion was permitted; if a ruler or a free city decided for Lutheranism, then all persons had to be Lutheran. Similarly in Catholic states all had to be Catholic. The Peace of Augsburg provided also, by the so-called Ecclesiastical Reservation, that any Catholic bishop or other churchman who turned Lutheran in the future should not carry his territory with him, but should turn Lutheran as an individual and

The Peace of Augsburg

move away, leaving his land and its inhabitants Catholic. Since the issues in Germany were still far from stabilized, this proviso was often disregarded in later years.

The Peace of Augsburg was thus, in religion, a great victory for Protestantism, and at the same time, in German politics and constitutional matters, a step in the disintegration of Germany into a mosaic of increasingly separate states. Lutheranism prevailed in the north and in the south in the duchy of Württemberg and various detached islands formed by Lutheranized free cities. Catholicism mostly prevailed in the south, in the Rhine valley, and in the direct possessions of the house of Habsburg, which in 1555 reached as far north as the Netherlands. The Germans, because of conditions in the Holy Roman Empire, were the one large European people to emerge from the religious conflict almost evenly divided between Catholic and Protestant.

Lutheranism was also adopted by the kings of Denmark and Sweden as early as the 1520s. Since Denmark controlled Norway, and Sweden ruled Finland and the eastern Baltic, all Scandinavia and the Baltic regions became, like north Germany, Lutheran. Beyond this area Lutheranism failed to take root. Like Anglicanism in England (to be described shortly), Lutheranism was too closely associated with established states to spread easily as an international movement. Another group of religious revolutionaries, the followers of John Calvin, thus became the most successful international form of the Protestant movement. Within German territories, however, neither Lutherans nor Catholics were willing to tolerate the Calvinists; and the Peace of Augsburg granted no political or religious rights to Calvinism.

Calvin and Calvinism

John Calvin (1509-1564) was a full generation younger than Luther. Born in northern France and educated in French Catholic schools, Calvin gained a humanist knowledge of Latin, Greek, and Hebrew. He was trained both as a priest and as a lawyer, but at the age of 24, experiencing a sudden conversion, he joined with religious revolutionaries who were beginning to emerge in France. Moving to Switzerland for safety, Calvin published in 1536 his *Institutes of the Christian Religion*. This book, published first in the international language of Latin and later in French, launched a new kind of Protestant theology. Where Luther had aimed much of his writing either at the existing rulers of Germany, or at the German *Calvin's life and ideas* national feeling against Rome, Calvin addressed his *Institutes* to all the world. He seemed to appeal to human reason itself; he wrote in the severe, logical style of the trained lawyer; he dealt firmly, lucidly, and convincingly with the most basic theological issues. In the *Institutes* people in all countries, if dissatisfied with the existing Roman church, could find cogent expression of universal propositions, which they could apply to their own local circumstances as they required.

With Luther's criticisms of the Roman church, and with most of Luther's fundamental religious ideas, such as justification by faith and not by works, Calvin agreed. In what they retained of the Catholic Mass, the communion or Lord's Supper as they called it, Luther and Calvin developed certain doctrinal differences. Both rejected transubstantiation, but where Luther insisted that God was somehow actually present in the bread and wine used in the service ("consubstantiation"), Calvin and his followers tended more to regard it as a pious act of symbolic or commemorative character.

There were two chief differences between Calvin and Luther. Calvin made far more of the idea of predestination. Both, drawing heavily on St. Augustine, held that human beings could never earn salvation by their own actions, that any grace that anyone

Predestination

possessed came from the free action of God alone. God, being Almighty, knew and willed in advance all things that happened, including the way in which every life would turn out. God thus knew and willed that some were saved and some were damned. Calvin, a severe critic of human nature, felt that those who had grace were relatively few. They were the "elect," the "godly," the small group chosen without merit of their own for salvation. People could feel in their own minds that they were among the saved, God's chosen few, if throughout all trials and temptations they persisted in pursuing a saintly life. Thus the idea of predestination, of God's omnipotence, instead of turning to fatalism and resignation, became a challenge to unrelenting effort, a sense of burning conviction, a conviction of being on the side of that Almighty Power which must in the end be everlastingly triumphant. Calvinists, in all countries, were militant, uncompromising, perfectionist—or Puritan, as they were called first in England and later in America.

The second way in which Calvinism differed from Lutheranism was in its attitude to society and to the state. Calvinists refused to recognize the subordination of church to state, or the right of any government to lay down laws for religion. On the contrary, they insisted that true Christians, the elect or godly, should Christianize the state. They wished to remake society itself into the image of a religious community. They rejected the institution of bishops (which both the Lutheran and Anglican churches retained) and provided instead that the church should be governed by presbyteries, elected bodies made up of ministers and devout laymen. By thus bringing an element of lay or secular control into church affairs, they broke the monopoly of priestly power. On the other hand, they were the reverse of secular, for they wished to Christianize all society.

Calvin, called in by earlier reformers who had driven out their bishop, was able to set up his model Christian community at Geneva in Switzerland. A body of ministers ruled the church; a consistory of ministers and elders ruled the town. The rule was strict;

Calvin's Geneva

all loose, light, or frivolous living was suppressed; disaffected persons were driven into exile. The form of worship was severe and favored the intellectual rather than the emotional or the aesthetic. The service was devoted largely to long sermons elucidating Christian doctrine, and all appeals to the senses—color, music, incense—were rigidly subdued. The black gown of Geneva replaced brighter clerical vestments. Images, representing the saints, Mary, or Christ, were taken down and destroyed. Chanting was replaced by the singing of hymns. Instrumental music was frowned upon, and many Calvinists thought even bells to be a survival of popery. In all things Calvin undertook to regulate his church by the Bible. Nor was he more willing than Luther to countenance any doctrine more radical than his own. When a Spanish refugee, Michael Servetus, who rejected the doctrine of the Trinity and thus denied the coeval divinity of Christ, sought asylum at Geneva, Calvin pronounced him a heretic and had him burned at the stake.

Reformers of all nationalities flocked to Geneva to see and study a true scriptural community so that they might reproduce it in their own countries. Geneva became the Protestant Rome, the one great international center of Reformed doctrine. Everywhere

The spread of Calvinism

Calvinists made their teachings heard (even in Spain and Italy in isolated cases), and everywhere, or almost everywhere, little groups that had locally and spontaneously broken with the old church found in Calvin's *Institutes* a reasoned statement of doctrine and a suggested method of organization. Thus Calvinism spread very widely. In Hungary and Bohemia large elements turned Protestant, and usually Calvinist, partly as a way of opposing the Habsburg rule. In Poland there were many Calvinists, along with less-organized

This portrait of John Calvin conveys the determination and serious religious vision that characterized his leadership of Protestants in Geneva. Based on a painting by Hans Holbein the Younger (1497–1543), this engraving by the nineteenth-century American artist John Sartain also exemplifies Calvin's later international and transatlantic influence.

(Source: Library of Congress Prints & Photographs Division [LC-USZ62-72002])

Anabaptists and Unitarians, or Socinians, as those who denied the Trinity were then called. Calvinists spread in Germany, where, opposing both Lutheran and Catholic churches as ungodly impositions of worldly power, they were disliked equally by both. In France the Huguenots were Calvinist, as were the Protestants of the Netherlands. John Knox in the 1550s brought Calvinism to Scotland, where Presbyterianism became and remained the established religion. At the same time Calvinism began to penetrate England, from which it was later to reach British America, giving birth to the Presbyterian and Congregationalist churches of the United States.

Calvinism was far from democratic in any modern sense. It carried an almost aristocratic outlook, in that those who sensed themselves to be God's chosen few felt free to dictate to the wider population of lost souls. Yet in many ways Calvinism entered into the development of later democratic ideas. For one thing, Calvinists never venerated the state; they always held that the sphere of the state and of public life was subject to moral judgment. For another, the Calvinist doctrine of the "calling" taught that a person's labor had a

Calvinism and democracy

religious dignity and that any form of honest work was pleasing in the sight of God. In the conduct of their own affairs Calvinists developed a type of self-government. They formed "covenants" with one another and devised machinery for the election of presbyteries. They refused to believe that authority was transmitted downward through bishops or through kings. They were inclined also to a more democratic or antimonarchical outlook, because in most countries they remained an unofficial minority. Only at Geneva, in the Dutch Netherlands, in Scotland, and in New England (and for a few years in England in the seventeenth century) were Calvinists ever able to prescribe the mode of life and religion of a whole country. In England, France, and Germany, Calvinists remained in opposition to the established authorities of church and state and hence were disposed to favor limitations upon established power. In Poland and Hungary many Calvinists were nobles who disliked royal authority.

The Reformation in England

England was peculiar in that its government broke with the Roman church before adopting any Protestant principles. Henry VIII (1509–1547) in fact prided himself on his ortho-doxy. When a few obscure persons, about 1520, began to whisper Luther's ideas in

Henry VIII

England, Henry himself wrote a *Defense of the Seven Sacraments* in refutation, for which a grateful pope conferred upon him the title "Defender of the Faith." But the king had no male heir. Recalling the violent anarchy from which the Tudor dynasty had extricated England, and determined as a New Monarch to build up a durable monarchy, he decided that he must remarry in order to have a son. He therefore requested the pope, Clement VII, to annul his existing marriage to Catherine of Aragon. Popes in the past had obliged monarchs in similar situations. The pope now, however, was embarrassed by the fact that Catherine, who objected, was the aunt of the Habsburg emperor, Charles V, whom the pope needed for support in his conflict with German Lutheranism. Henry, not a patient man, pushed matters forward. He appointed a new archbishop of Canterbury, repudiated the Roman connection, secured the annulment of his earlier marriage, and married the youthful Anne Boleyn. The fact that only three years later he put to death the unfortunate Anne, and thereafter in quick succession married four more wives, threw considerable doubt on the original character of his motives.

Henry acted through Parliament, believing, as he said, that a king was never stronger than when united with representatives of his kingdom. In 1534 Parliament passed the Act of Supremacy, which declared the English king to be the "Protector and Only Supreme

The Act of Supremacy

Head of the Church and Clergy of England." All subjects were required, if asked, to take the oath of supremacy acknowledging the religious headship of Henry and rejecting that of the pope. For refusing this oath Sir Thomas More, a statesman and humanist best known as the author of *Utopia,* was executed for treason. The Roman Catholic Church, in the twentieth century, would pronounce More to be a saint, but Henry won English support for most of his policies. He closed all the monasteries in England, seized the extensive monastic lands, and passed them out to numerous followers. He thus strengthened and reconstituted a landed aris-tocracy that had been seriously weakened in the Wars of the Roses. This new landed gentry remained firm supporters of the house of Tudor and the English national church, whatever its doctrines.

It was Henry's intent not to change the doctrines at all. He simply wished to be the supreme head of an English Catholic church. On the one hand, in 1536, he forcibly suppressed a predominantly Catholic rebellion, and, on the other, in 1539, through the Six Articles, required everybody to believe in transubstantiation, the celibacy of the clergy, the need of confession, and a few other aspects of Catholic faith and practice. But it proved impossible to maintain this position, for a great many people in England began to favor various ideas of Continental Reformers, and a small minority were willing to accept the entire Protestant position.

For three decades after 1530 the government's religious policies veered about. Henry died in 1547 and was succeeded by his 10-year-old son, Edward VI, the child of his third wife, Jane Seymour. The Protestant party now came to the fore. But Edward died in 1553 and was succeeded by his much older half-sister, Mary, the daughter of Catherine of

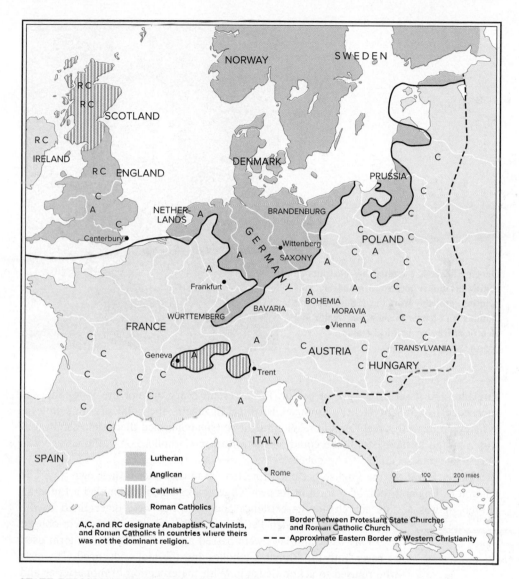

STATE RELIGIONS IN EUROPE ABOUT 1560

This map shows the legally authorized, established churches about 1560, but it does not show the precise distributions of religious communities. Many Catholics lived north of the heavy line, and many Protestants south of it. Most widely dispersed were the Calvinists and the more radical Protestants or Anabaptists. In Germany, under the Holy Roman Empire, each principality and free city chose its own religion; hence, the Germans were the only large European population to emerge from the Reformation almost evenly divided between Catholics and Protestants.

Aragon and a devout Roman Catholic whose whole life had been embittered by the English break with Rome. Mary tried to re-Catholicize England, but she actually made Catholicism more unpopular among the English people. In 1554 she married Philip of Spain, who became king of England, though only in name. The English did not like Philip, nor the Spanish, nor the intense Spanish Catholicism that Philip represented. Under Mary, moreover, some 300 persons were burned at the stake, as heretics, in public mass executions. It was the first (and last) time that such religious executions had happened in

Queen Elizabeth I wanted her portraits to convey her power and royal grandeur. This painting, probably from the 1580s, uses her clothing and jewels to show her wealth and also to affirm her political stature.
(©Print Collector/Getty Images)

England, and it set up a wave of horror. In any event, Mary did not live long. She was succeeded in 1558 by Henry's younger daughter, Elizabeth, the child of Anne Boleyn. Whatever Elizabeth's real views in religion might be (she concealed them successfully and was rumored to have none), she could not be a Roman Catholic. For Catholics she was illegitimate and so unable to be queen.

Under Elizabeth the English became Protestant, gradually and in their own way. The Church of England took on a form of its own. Organizationally, it resembled a Lutheran church. It was a state church, for its existence and doctrines were determined by the monarch acting through Parliament. All English subjects were obliged to belong to it, and laws were passed against "recusants," a term used to cover both the Roman Catholics and the more advanced Calvinists who refused to acknowledge it. With the exception of monasteries and certain other church foundations, the Church of England retained the physical possessions, buildings, and internal organization of the medieval church—the bishops and the archbishops, who continued to sit in the House of Lords, the episcopal courts with their jurisdiction over marriage and wills, the tithes or church taxes paid by all landowners, the parish structure, the universities of Oxford and Cambridge.

The Church of England

In religious practice, the Church of England was definitely Protestant: English replaced Latin as the language of the liturgy, there was no cult of the saints, and the clergy married, though Elizabeth confessed to some embarrassment at the thought of an archbishop having a wife. In doctrine, it was Elizabeth's policy to make the dogmas broad and ambiguous, so that persons of all shades of belief could be more readily accommodated. The Thirty-nine Articles (1563), composed by a committee of bishops, defined the Protestant creed of the Anglican Church. All but one of the Anglican bishops had been newly appointed by Elizabeth at her accession; many had lived in exile among Continental Protestants in the reign of Mary Tudor; and except on the matter of church government through bishops (known as episcopacy) a strong Calvinist influence entered Anglican belief in the time of Elizabeth.

The same ecclesiastical settlement was prescribed for Ireland, where English or rather Anglo-Norman conquerors had settled since the twelfth century, shortly after the Norman conquest of England. A replica of the Church of England was now established, called the Church of Ireland, which took over the properties and position of the Roman church. The native Irish, however, remained almost solidly Roman Catholic. As in Hungary or Bohemia people who resented the Habsburgs were likely to turn Protestant rather than share in the ruler's religion, so in Ireland the fact that the ruling English were Protestant only confirmed the Irish in their attachment to the Roman church. The Catholic priests, deprived of status, income, and church buildings, and often in hiding, became national leaders of a discontented people.

The Consolidation of Protestantism by 1560

Neither in England, nor in Germany, nor in international Calvinism were the religious issues regarded as settled in 1560. Nor had the Roman Catholic Church accepted the new situation. But by 1560 the chief Protestant doctrines had been affirmed, and geographically Protestantism had made many conquests. The institutional unity of Latin Christendom had been broken. A world of separate churches, states, and nations was taking its place.

Protestants differed in many of their religious ideas, yet certain core beliefs shaped the theology and social practices in almost every Protestant church. There was no single international Protestant organization, and even the ascendancy of Calvinist Geneva proved to be only temporary. Shared beliefs and national churches rather than a transnational institution sustained Protestant communities. All Protestants believed that the clergy were much like other people, which meant that the priests (whom they generally called ministers) had no special or supernatural character. Indeed, the Protestant movement was perhaps most fundamentally a revolt against the separate, elevated position of the medieval clergy. There were no Protestant monks, nuns, or friars, and all Protestant clergy could marry. Protestant churches all replaced Latin with local vernacular languages—English, French, German, Czech, as the case might be.

What Protestants held in common

All Protestants reduced their holy liturgies from seven sacraments to two or three, stressing that the retained sacraments of baptism and communion (or the Eucharist) were to be regarded more as symbols than as actual carriers of divine grace. All declared that the one true source of Christian belief was the Holy Scripture, and all believed, in one way or another, in justification by faith and in some kind of private religious conscience—while usually insisting that the members of their own churches conform to specified doctrines. These widely affirmed ideas created a shared Protestant religious identity.

At the same time, Protestants created new identities by clearly stating what they rejected. All rejected the papal authority. All denied transubstantiation or the miracle of the Mass, by which Catholics claimed that bread and wine actually became the body and blood of Christ. All Protestants gave up the obligatory confessional and the priestly absolution that accompanied it. They rejected the belief in purgatory as a kind of temporary zone between heaven and hell, which meant that they also gave up special prayers and services that were to help deceased persons move on to heaven. Nothing like indulgences remained, and all Protestants gave up the cult of the saints and of the Virgin Mary, whose intercession in Heaven was no longer expected.

What Protestants rejected

Some English Protestants wanted to move toward a more Calvinist-style or "purified" Protestant church. This portrayal of a sixteenth-century English family may represent this kind of emerging Puritanism because the father is teaching his children to memorize the psalms and the family's appearance and home suggest a firm rejection of frivolity and trifling entertainments.

(©Print Collector/Getty Images)

It has sometimes been maintained that one of the motivations for the spread of Protestantism was economic—that a new acquisitive, dynamic, capitalistic impulse shook off the restrictions imposed by medieval religion. The fact that Protestant England and Holland soon underwent a rapid capitalistic development gives added credibility to this idea. The alacrity with which Protestant governments confiscated church lands shows a keen material interest; but in truth, both before and after the Reformation, governments confiscated church properties without breaking with the Roman church. Other economic changes, ranging far beyond land confiscations, also disrupted European societies throughout this era. Yet it seems that economic conditions were far less decisive than religious convictions and political circumstances. Calvinism won followers not only in cities but also in agrarian countries such as Scotland, Poland, and Hungary. Lutheranism spread more successfully in the less economically active regions of north Germany than in the busy south. The English were for years no more inclined to Protestantism than the French, and in France, while many lords and peasants turned Protestant, Paris and many other towns remained as steadfastly Catholic. It is possible that Protestantism, by casting a moral glow of religious righteousness over a person's daily business and material prosperity, later contributed to the cultural meaning of economic success among Protestant peoples and to new cultural assumptions about the moral failings of poor people. It does not seem, however, that a Protestant work ethic or other economic factors were of distinctive importance in shaping the first stages of Protestantism.

The new religious movements had a more immediate influence on attitudes about marriage and the family. In contrast to medieval Catholicism, which had praised sexual abstinence and celibacy as key traits of the most exalted religious persons, Protestantism strongly promoted marriage as the ideal social institution for clergy and lay people alike. Parenthood became honorable for even the most pious Protestant leaders. Although women sometimes wrote hymns or preached in the more radical Protestant churches, the model Protestant woman was the conscientious mother in a devout, religious household. The opportunities for institutional leadership, even if limited, that some women had found in medieval convents and religious communities disappeared in Protestant societies, which may explain why nuns in Protestant territories were often among the last persons to accept the new religious ideas.

Protestants and family life

Apart from the new emphasis on marriage, however, Protestants did little to change the role of women in Christian churches or in the wider social order. The pastors in Protestant communities were all men, and though more women may have become literate in order to read the Bible, they became less visible in Protestant rituals as the long venerated female saints vanished from prayers, religious writings, and charitable institutions. Meanwhile, women in the convents of Catholic countries were more strictly cloistered and controlled as Catholicism developed its own powerful movements for reform and reorganization.

10. CATHOLICISM REFORMED AND REORGANIZED

The Catholic movement corresponding to the rise of Protestantism is known as the Catholic Reformation or the Counter Reformation. Catholics have usually preferred the former term and Protestants have usually preferred the latter, but both are applicable. On the one hand the Catholic Church underwent a genuine reform, which might have worked itself out in one way or another even if the stimulus of revolutionary Protestantism had been absent. On the other hand the character of the reform, the measures adopted, and the new sense of urgency became an explicit response to the Protestant challenge; and certainly, also, there was a good deal of purely "counter" activity aimed at the elimination of Protestantism as such.

The demand for reform was as old as the abuses against which it was directed. Characteristically, it had expressed itself in the demand for a general or ecumenical church council. The conciliar movement, defeated by the popes about 1450, showed signs of revival after 1500. The Lutheran upheaval thus provoked new calls for a general council of the church, and we have seen how Charles V, in the interests of German unity, sought to persuade the pope to assemble an adequately empowered council, which might remove some of the abuses in the church and take away the grounds upon which many Germans were turning to Lutheranism. But meanwhile the king of France found reason to favor the pope and to oppose the emperor. The French king, Francis I (1515–1547), could support the pope because he had obtained from the papacy what he wanted, namely, control over the Gallican church, as acquired in the Concordat of Bologna of 1516. And he had reason to oppose Charles V, because the Habsburgs ruled not only in Germany but also in the Netherlands, Spain, and much of Italy, thus encircling France and threatening Europe with what contemporaries called "universal monarchy." Francis I therefore actively encouraged the Protestants of Germany, as a means of maintaining dissension there, and used his influence at Rome against the calling of a council by which the troubles of the Catholic world might be relieved.

The call for reform

Gradually there arose a party of reforming cardinals who concluded that the need for reform was so urgent that all dangers of a council must be risked. Pope Paul III thus summoned a council to meet in 1537, but the wars between France and the empire forced its abandonment. Finally, in 1545, a council assembled and began deliberations at Trent, on the Alpine borders of Germany and Italy. The Council of Trent, which shaped the destiny of modern Catholicism, sat at irregular intervals for almost 20 years. It was not until the Second Vatican Council in the 1960s that some of the main decisions made at Trent were substantially modified.

The Council of Trent

The council was beset by pressing political difficulties, which seemed to show that under troubled conditions an international council was no longer a suitable means of regulating Catholic affairs. Significantly, it was not well attended. Whereas earlier councils of the church had assembled as many as 500 prelates, the attendance at Trent was never nearly so great; it sometimes fell as low as 20 or 30, and the important decree on "justification," the prime issue raised by Luther, and one on which some good Catholics had until then believed a compromise to be possible, was passed at a session where only 60 prelates were present. Even with the small attendance, the old conciliar issue was raised. A party of bishops believed that the bishops of the Catholic Church, when assembled in council from all parts of the Catholic world, collectively constituted an authority superior to that of the pope. To stave off this "episcopal" movement was one of the chief duties of the cardinal legates deputed by the pope to preside over the sessions.

The popes managed successfully to resist the idea of limiting the papal power. In the end they triumphed, through a final ruling voted by the council, that no act of the council should be valid unless accepted by the Holy See. It is possible that had the conciliar theory won out, the Catholic Church might have become as disunited in modern times as the Protestant. It was clear, at Trent, that the various bishops tended to see matters in a national way, in the light of their own problems at home, and to be frequently under strong influence from their respective secular monarchs. In any case, the papal party prevailed, which is to say that the centralizing element, not the national, triumphed. The Council of Trent thus preserved the papacy as a unifying center for the Catholic Church and helped prevent the very real threat of its dissolution into state churches.

Preserving papal authority

Questions of national politics and of church politics apart, the Council of Trent addressed itself to two kinds of labors—to a statement of Catholic doctrine and to a reform of abuses in the church. When the council began to meet in 1545, the Protestant movement had already gone so far that any reconciliation was probably impossible: Protestants, especially Calvinists, simply did not wish to belong to the church of Rome under any conditions. In any case, the Council of Trent made no concessions.

The Council of Trent: defining Catholic doctrine

It declared that justification or salvation by God's grace came to humans through their works and faith combined. It enumerated and defined the seven sacraments, which were held to be vehicles of grace independent of the spiritual state of those who received them. The priesthood was declared to be a special estate set apart from the laity by the sacrament of holy orders. The procedures of the confessional and of absolution were clarified. Transubstantiation was reaffirmed. As sources of Catholic faith, the council put Scripture and tradition on an equal footing. It thus rejected the Protestant claim to find true faith in the Bible alone and reasserted the validity of church development since New Testament times. The Vulgate, a translation of the Bible into Latin by St. Jerome in the fourth century, was declared to be the only version on which authoritative teaching could be based. The right of individuals to believe that their own interpretation of Scripture was more true than that of church authorities (private judgment) was denied. Latin, as against the national languages, was prescribed as the language of religious worship—a requirement that would continue to shape Catholic liturgy until the Second Vatican Council in the 1960s. Celibacy of the clergy was maintained, and monasticism was upheld. The existence of purgatory was reaffirmed. The theory and correct practice of indulgences were restated. The veneration of saints, the cult of the Virgin, and the use of images, relics, and pilgrimages were approved as spiritually useful and pious actions.

It was easier for a council to define doctrines than to reform abuses, since the latter consisted in the rooted habits of people's lives. The Council of Trent decreed, however, a drastic reform of the monastic orders. It acted against the abuse of indulgences while upholding the principle. It ruled that bishops should reside habitually in their dioceses, attend more carefully to their proper duties, and exercise more administrative control over clergy in their own dioceses. The abuse by which one man had held numerous church offices at the same time (pluralism) was checked, and steps were taken to assure that church officials should be competent. To provide an educated clergy, the council ordered that a seminary should be set up in each diocese for the training of priests.

The New Catholicism

As laws in general have little force unless sustained by shared opinions, so the reform decrees of the Council of Trent would have remained ineffectual had not a renewed sense of religious seriousness been growing at the same time. Herein lay the inner force of the Catholic Reform. In Italy, as the Renaissance became more undeniably pagan, and as the sack of Rome in 1527 showed that even many Catholics had lost respect for the Roman clergy, the voices of moralists began to be heeded. The line of Renaissance popes was succeeded by a line of reforming popes, of whom the first was Paul III (1534–1549). The reforming popes insisted on the primacy of the papal office, but they regarded this office, unlike their predecessors, as a moral and religious force. In many dioceses the bishops began on their own initiative to be stricter. The new Catholic religious sense, more than the Protestant, centered in a reverence for the sacraments and a mystical awe for the church itself as a divine institution. Both men and women founded many new religious orders, of which the Jesuits became the most famous. Others were the Oratorians for men and the Ursulines for women. The new orders dedicated themselves to a variety of educational and philanthropic activities. Missionary fervor for a long time was more characteristic of Catholics than of Protestants. It reached into Asia and the Americas, and in Europe expressed itself as an intense desire for the reconversion of Protestants. It showed itself, too, in missions among the poor, as in the work of St. Vincent de Paul among the human wreckage of Paris, for which the established Protestant churches failed to produce anything comparable. In America, as colonies developed in the sixteenth and seventeenth centuries, the Protestant clergy tended to take the European settlers' hostile view of the Indians, while the Catholic clergy labored to convert and protect them; and the Catholic Church generally worked to mitigate the brutal treatment of enslaved Africans, to which the pastors in English and Dutch colonies, perhaps because they were more dependent upon the laity, remained largely indifferent.

Catholic religious renewal

St. Ignatius Loyola's religious inspiration is portrayed in this painting by Peter Paul Rubens, whose work often represented the religious and political leaders of Catholic countries.
(©Print Collector/Getty Images)

We have seen how in Spain, where the Renaissance had never taken much hold, the very life of the country was connected to a kind of ongoing Christian crusade. It was in Spain that much of the new Catholic feeling first developed; and it was Spain that now generated a new surge of Catholic missionary activity. Spanish writers provided the most influential sixteenth-century accounts of Catholic mysticism, including Teresa of Avila's famous descriptions of her encounters with Christ. Spain was also the home country of St. Ignatius Loyola (1491–1556). A soldier in youth, he too, like Luther and Calvin, had a religious experience or conversion, which occurred in 1521, before he had heard of Luther and while Calvin was still a boy. Loyola resolved to become a soldier of the church, a militant crusader for the pope and the Holy See. On this principle he established the Society of Jesus, commonly known as the Jesuits. Authorized by Pope Paul III in 1540, the Jesuits constituted a monastic order of a new type, less attached to the cloister, more directed toward active participation in the affairs of the world. Only men of proven strength of character and intellectual force were admitted. Each Jesuit had to undergo an arduous mystical training, set forth by Loyola in his *Spiritual Exercises*. The order was ruled by an iron discipline, which required each member to see in his immediate superior the infallibility of the Holy

The Jesuits

Church. As Loyola explained in his *Spiritual Exercises,* if the church teaches to see something as black even when the eye sees it as white the mind must believe it to be black.

For 200 years the Jesuits were the most famous schoolmasters of Catholic Europe, eventually conducting some 500 schools for boys of the upper and middle classes. These schools taught the Catholic faith, but they also taught the principles of gentlemanly deportment (their teaching of dancing and dramatics became a scandal to more puritanical Catholics), and they carried over the Renaissance and humanist idea of the Latin classics as the main substance of adolescent education. The Jesuits made a specialty of work among the ruling classes. They became confessors to kings and hence involved in political intrigue. In an age when Protestants subordinated an organized church either to the state or to an individual conscience, and when even Catholics frequently thought of the church within a national framework, the Jesuits seemed almost to worship the church itself as a divine institution that must remain internationally organized and governed by the Roman pontiff. All full-fledged Jesuits took a special vow of obedience to the pope. Jesuits in the later sessions of the Council of Trent fought obstinately, and successfully, to uphold the position of Rome against that of the national bishops.

By 1560 the Catholic Church, renewed by a deepening of its religious life and by an uncompromising restatement of its dogmas and discipline, had devised also the practical machinery for a counteroffensive against Protestantism. The Jesuits acted as an international missionary force. They recruited members from all countries, including those in which the governments had turned Protestant. English Catholics, for example, trained as Jesuits on the Continent, returned to England to attempt to overthrow the heretic usurper, Elizabeth, seeing in the universal church a higher cause than national independence in religion. Jesuits poured also into the most hotly disputed regions where the religious issue still swayed in the balance—France, Germany, Bohemia, Poland, Hungary. As after every great revolution, many people moved from an initial burst of Protestantism toward a revived interest in the old religious order, especially as the more crying evils within the Catholic church were corrected. The Jesuits reconverted many who thus hesitated.

The more recalcitrant religious dissidents were repressed everywhere by new kinds of social control. All countries censored books; Protestant authorities labored to keep "papist" works from the eyes of the faithful, and Catholic authorities took the same pains to suppress all knowledge of "heretical" authors and texts. All bishops, Anglican, Lutheran, and Catholic, regulated reading matter within their dioceses. In the Catholic world, with the trend toward centralization under the pope, a special importance attached to the list published by the bishop of Rome, the papal Index of Prohibited Books. Only with special permission, granted to reliable persons for special study, could Catholics read books listed on the Index, which was not abandoned until the 1960s.

All countries, Protestant and Catholic, also set up judicial and police machinery to enforce conformity to the accepted church. In England, for example, Elizabeth established the High Commission to bring "recusants" into the Church of England. All bishops, Protestant and Catholic, likewise possessed machinery of enforcement in their episcopal courts. But no court made itself so dreaded as the *Enforcing religious* Inquisition. In reality two distinct organizations went under this name, *conformity* the word itself being simply an old term of the Roman law, signifying a court of inquest or inquiry. One was the Spanish Inquisition, established originally, about 1480, to ferret out Jewish and Muslim survivals in Spain. It was then introduced into all countries ruled by the Spanish crown and employed against Protestantism, particularly in the Spanish Netherlands, which was an important center of Calvinism. The other was the

Roman or papal Inquisition, established at Rome in 1542 under a permanent committee of cardinals called the Holy Office. Both the Spanish and the Roman Inquisitions employed torture, for heresy was regarded as the supreme crime, and all persons charged with crime could be tortured, in civil as well as ecclesiastical courts, under the existing laws. In the use of torture, as in the imposition of the harshest sentence, burning alive, the Roman Inquisition was less severe than the Spanish. The Roman Inquisition in principle offered a court to protect purity of faith in all parts of the Catholic world. But the national resistance of Catholic countries proved too strong; few Catholics wished the agents of Rome inquiring locally into their opinions; and the Roman Inquisition never functioned for any length of time outside of Italy.

In the "machinery" of enforcing religious belief, however, no engine was to be so powerful as the apparatus of state. Where Protestants won control of government, people became Protestant. Where Catholics retained control of governments, Protestants became in time small minorities. And it was in the clash of governments, which is to say in war, for about a century after 1560, that the fate of European religion was worked out. In 1560 the strongest powers of Europe—Spain, France, Austria—were all officially Catholic. The Protestant states were all small or at most middle-sized. The Lutheran states of Germany, like all German states, were individually of little weight. The Scandinavian monarchies were far away. England, the most considerable of Protestant kingdoms, was a country of only 4 million people, with an independent and hostile Scotland to the north, and with no sign of colonial empire yet in existence. In the precedence of monarchs, as arranged in the earlier part of the century, the king of England ranked just below the king of Portugal, and next above the king of Sicily. Clearly, had a great combined Catholic crusade ever developed, Protestantism could have been wiped out. Yet such a crusade, partially launched on various fronts by the king of Spain, never succeeded. Religious divisions became a permanent reality in European culture, contributing eventually, like Renaissance humanism and the new European monarchies, to a gradual secularization of modern societies. And in later, more secular times, the idea and practice of religious tolerance would develop as a stabilizing solution for the intractable conflicts that long threatened the lives of individual believers as well as the survival of entire religious communities.

Suggested Further Readings can be found in the ebook, on Connect, or online at www.mhhe .com/kramer12e.

Chapter 3

THE ATLANTIC WORLD, COMMERCE, AND WARS OF RELIGION, 1560–1648

European history in the period following 1560 is often described as the age of the Wars of Religion, which may be said to have ended with the Peace of Westphalia in 1648. France, England, the Netherlands, and the Holy Roman Empire fell into internal and international struggles in which religion was often the most burning issue, but in which political, constitutional, economic, and social questions were also involved. This time of long, drawn-out conflicts between Catholics and Protestants, however, was also a time of important economic transitions. From the beginning of the sixteenth century European society was transformed by contacts with diverse peoples whom Europeans had never before encountered. These new cross-cultural contacts on previously unknown continents contributed decisively to the expansion of global trade routes, the emergence of a new commercial capitalism, and the formation of new social classes in most European societies.

This was the era in which the modern global economic system began to develop and in which new exchanges with people in Asia, Africa, and the Americas began to reshape social, economic, and political power within Europe itself. The effects of these profound global changes, however, were obscured and delayed by Europe's internal politico-religious struggles. In the present chapter we first examine the most important European geographical discoveries, then survey the broad new economic and social developments under way, and finally trace the impact of the religious wars on various parts of Europe. The wars, as we shall see, left Spain and Germany very much weakened, and opened the way for the English, Dutch, and French to profit from the global economic changes and to play leading roles in the transnational conflicts of early modern times.

Chapter emblem: Detail from Jean Bourdichon (1457–1521), *The Four Estates of Society: Work*, which shows a carpenter working with the tools of his craft. (Bridgeman-Giraudon/Art Resource, NY)

11.   THE OPENING OF THE ATLANTIC

In all the centuries before 1500, the Atlantic Ocean had been an impassable barrier that blocked the western movement of European peoples and commerce. During the centuries after 1500, however, the Atlantic became a great bridge that connected Europe with Africa and the Americas, thus opening a vast geographical space for new cross-cultural communications, conflicts, and colonization. This was the era in which European history began to intersect with and influence the wider history of the whole world. The consequences were enormous for all concerned. In general, they were favorable for Europeans but devastating for peoples elsewhere—in America through massive depopulation by diseases such as smallpox brought from Europe, in Africa through the transatlantic slave trade, and ultimately in places as far away as Australia through the destruction of long-existing cultures or languages. Older, celebratory accounts of Europe's "overseas discoveries" have therefore been widely challenged in recent decades as historians have revised the story of European expansion from the perspective of Native Americans or African Americans. Viewed from these perspectives, Columbus's first voyage to America in 1492 launched a history of terrible losses rather than an era of heroic European explorations and conquests.

But few would deny that the new, complex association of the Old and New Worlds, as Europeans called them, became a momentous event in human history. The endless migration of people, the worldwide movement of trade, and the disorienting

Cultural transformation and destruction

experiences of cross-cultural encounters marked the true beginning of modern global history. Europeans transformed or even destroyed numerous other cultures, but their own culture was also transformed through steadily expanding contacts with other peoples, social traditions, and religions in every part of the world. A new wealthy commercial class grew up in cities along Europe's Atlantic coast. Naval power became decisive. European populations grew with the adoption of the American potato, and people in Europe became dependent on imported commodities such as sugar and tobacco. European writers took increasing pride in their understanding of the world and in what they regarded as the superiority of their own cultural or religious traditions. There was also much speculation on the diversity of the human races and cultures, which sometimes led to a new kind of race consciousness on the part of Europeans and sometimes to a cultural relativism in which European customs were seen as only one variant of human behavior as a whole. Meanwhile, people in the Americas and Africa struggled to defend their own evolving cultures and institutions as European soldiers, traders, and missionaries entered the various civilizations of an increasingly interconnected transatlantic economic system.

The Portuguese in the East

Europeans had skirted their Atlantic coast since prehistoric times. Vikings had settled in Iceland in the ninth century and had even reached North America soon thereafter. In 1317 Venetians had established the Flanders galleys, commercial flotillas that regularly made the passage between the Adriatic and North seas. In the fifteenth century, improvements in shipbuilding, the rigging of sails, and the adoption of the mariner's compass made it feasible to sail on the open ocean out of sight of land. When the Portuguese about 1450 settled in the Azores Islands, in the mid-Atlantic, they found steady westerly winds to assure a safe return to Europe. It seemed that the ocean might even lead to Asia.

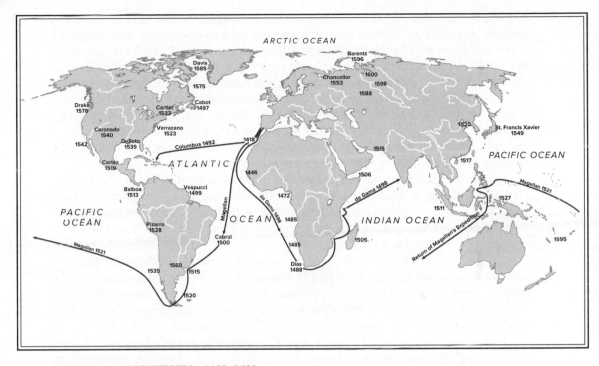

EUROPEAN DISCOVERIES, 1450–1600

Discovery means the bringing of newly encountered countries within the habitual knowledge or permanent commercial activity of the society from which the discoverer comes. Although sailors and travelers from Asia had long made voyages to distant places and engaged in trade across the Indian Ocean or South Pacific, it was the Europeans who discovered much of the Atlantic world in the sense indicated here. They did so in the period between 1450 and 1600, using maritime skills and geographical knowledge developed in the Mediterranean and off the Atlantic coast. Dates on the map show the years of first significant European arrival at the points indicated.

For centuries Asia had been a source for European imports of highly valued commodities, partly manufactured materials in which Europe could not compete, such as silk and cotton fabrics, rugs, jewelry, porcelains, and fine steel, and partly raw or semimanufactured drugs and foodstuffs, such as sugar and, above all, spices. Europeans had never themselves gone to the sources of supply of Eastern goods. Somewhere, east of Suez, barely known to Europeans, was another world of other merchants who moved the wares of China, India, and the East Indies Spice Islands by caravan over land and by boat through the Red Sea or Persian Gulf to the markets of the eastern Mediterranean. Traders of the two worlds met and did business at such thriving centers as Alexandria, Beirut, and Constantinople.

In 1498 the Portuguese navigator Vasco da Gama, having rounded Africa in the wake of other intrepid explorers, found himself in the midst of the unknown world of Arab commerce. He landed on the Malabar Coast (the southwest coast of India), where he found a busy commercial population of heterogeneous religious background. These people knew at least as much about Europe as Europeans knew about India (a Jewish translator was able to act as da Gama's interpreter), and they realized that the coming of the Portuguese would disturb their established channels of commerce. Da Gama, playing upon local rivalries, managed to load his ships with the coveted wares, but on his second voyage, in 1502, he came better prepared, bringing a fighting fleet of no less than 21 vessels. A ferocious war broke out between the Portuguese and Arab merchants, the latter supported in one way or another by the Egyptians, the Turks, and even the distant Venetians, all of whom had an interest in maintaining the old routes of trade. For the Portuguese, trained like the Spaniards in long wars against the Moors at home, no atrocities were too horrible to commit against the "infidels" whom they found as competitors at the end of their long commercial quest. Cities were devastated along the Malabar Coast, ships were burned at their docks, prisoners were butchered, and their dismembered hands, noses, and ears were sent back as derisive trophies. Such, unfortunately, was India's introduction to the highly assertive, brutal methods of early modern Europe's transoceanic trade.

In the following years the Portuguese built permanent fortified stations at Goa on the Malabar Coast, at Aden near the mouth of the Red Sea, at Hormuz near the mouth

Portuguese trading empire

of the Persian Gulf, and in East Africa. In 1509 they reached Malacca, near modern Singapore, from which they passed northward into China itself and eastward to Amboina, the heart of the Spice Islands, just west of New Guinea. Thus an empire was created, the first of Europe's commercial-colonial empires, maintained by superiority of firearms and sea power and by forceful economic interventions that combined trade with war and plunder. The early European traders were soon followed by bold Jesuits, including St. Francis Xavier, who, by 1550, had baptized thousands of souls in India, Indonesia, and even Japan.

By the new sea route the European cost of Asian goods was much reduced, for the old route had involved many transshipments, unloadings, and reloadings, movements by sea and by land, through the hands of many merchants. In 1504 spices could be bought in Lisbon for only a fifth of the price demanded in Venice. The Venetians (who in their desperation even talked of digging a Suez canal) were hopelessly undersold in western European markets: their trade thereafter was confined to products of the Middle East. As for the Portuguese, never was a commercial monopoly built so fast. The lower prices added enormously to European demand and consumption. Beginning in 1504, only five years after da Gama's first return, an average of 12 ships a year left Lisbon for the expanding Asian trade.

The European Discovery of America

Meanwhile, the same quest for a route to the East had led to the somewhat disappointing discovery of America. Like most such discoveries, this was no chance hit of an isolated genius. Behaim's globe, constructed in 1492, the very year of Columbus's first voyage, suggested that China could be reached by crossing the Atlantic and thus supported the idea of sailing westward to arrive in the East. Nevertheless, it was Christopher Columbus who had the persistence and daring to undertake the unprecedented westward voyage. Before the invention of sufficiently accurate clocks (in the eighteenth century) mariners had no way of determining longitude, that is, their east-west position, and learned geographers greatly underestimated the probable distance from Europe westward to Asia. When Columbus struck land, he naturally supposed it to be an outlying part of the Indies. The people were soon called Indians, and the islands where Columbus landed became known in Europe as the West Indies.

Columbus had sailed with the backing of Queen Isabella of Castile, and the new lands were brought into the composite dominions of the crown of Spain. The Spaniards, hoping to find a sea route that would enable them to beat the Portuguese to the East (which da Gama had not yet reached), received Columbus's first reports with enthusiasm.

Landscape of the West Indies **was painted by the Dutch artist Jan Mostaert about 1540. In this detail from an early European visualization of the New World, the American Indians are seen as naked, helpless, confused, and very different from Europeans.**
(©DEA PICTURE LIBRARY/Getty Images)

For his second voyage they gave him 17 ships, filled with 1,500 workmen and artisans. Columbus himself, until his death in 1506, kept probing about in the Caribbean, baffled and frustrated, still believing he had discovered a route to Asia and hoping to find something that looked like the fabulous East. Other Europeans were more willing to see the new lands as a previously unknown place in which they could pursue new wealth and power. Indeed, the lands were soon given a new European name—America—after the Italian explorer Amerigo Vespucci reported that neither the islands nor the mainland seemed to be connected with Asia. Spanish churchmen began to view America as a new field for crusading and conversion. The Spanish government saw it as a source of gold and silver for the royal exchequer. Footloose gentry with military ambitions, left idle by the end of war with the Moors in Iberia, turned to America to make their fortunes. The *conquistadores* fell upon the new lands. Hernando Cortés led a small Spanish army that conquered the Aztecs in Mexico between 1519 and 1521. Taking advantage of divisions among peoples within Aztec territories, the *conquistadores* used massacres and sieges to complete a conquest that brought "New Spain" into a growing Spanish Empire. Francisco Pizarro's later expedition into the Inca Empire in Peru also resorted to brutal tactics of deception and murder to remove the Inca emperor, Atahualpa, and thereby expand Spain's imperial control across the Andes during the 1530s. The colonizing Spanish forces quickly despoiled the native empires in both Mexico and Peru. Mines for precious metals were opened almost immediately. The Indians were put to forced labor, in which many died. The rapid decline in the Indian population, the attempts of the church to protect its Indian converts, and the restrictions set by royal authorities on their exploitation soon led to the importation of African slaves. Europeans thus turned to the forced labor of enslaved

Conquest begins in the Americas

Africans to replace and expand the forced labor of Indians. More than 120,000 enslaved Africans were brought to America by 1575, and another 500,000 arrived over the next 50 years. This massive, forced migration of Africans continued for more than two centuries via a far-reaching European-managed slave trade that would carry 12.5 million enslaved Africans to the Americas by the middle of the nineteenth century. The great majority would be transported to Portuguese-controlled Brazil and to the various West Indian sugar islands, but many also went to the Spanish Empire and to the later British Empire in North America. Indeed, the number of enslaved Africans reaching America, including the two continents and the West Indies, was far greater than the number of Europeans who settled there before 1800; and some enslaved persons were also taken from Africa into Portugal, Spain, England, and other parts of Europe.

Further explorations

Meanwhile, explorers began to make their way along the vast American continent that barred them from Asia. A Spanish expedition, led by Ferdinand Magellan, found a southwestern passage in 1520, sailed from the Atlantic into the Pacific, crossed the Pacific, reached the Philippine Islands (where Magellan died in battle), and finally made its way across the Indian Ocean back to Spain. The globe was thus circumnavigated for the first time, and new ideas about the true size and interconnection of the oceans were brought back to Europe. Geographical experts immediately incorporated the new knowledge. Europeans still knew little about the vast, newly discovered continents, however, and other explorers sailing for Spain, for England, and for France, began the long and fruitless search for northwest passage to the Pacific. An English expedition, looking for an alternative northeast passage, discovered the White Sea in 1553. English merchants immediately began to take the ocean route to Russia, and Archangel became a Russian port for international trade.

For a century it was only the Spanish and Portuguese who developed the new ocean trading routes to America and the East. The monarchs of these two peoples, in a treaty of 1494, asserted that the globe should be divided between them by an imaginary north-and-south line that ran from a point in the middle of the North Atlantic Ocean through the North Pole and across eastern Asia. Spain claimed all the Americas by this treaty, and Portugal, all rights of trade in Africa, Asia, and the East Indies. But when the Portuguese explorer Pedro Cabral discovered Brazil in 1500, it was found to be far enough east to lie within the Portuguese area, and after Magellan landed on the Philippine Islands in 1521, they were claimed to be in the Spanish zone.

In the populous, long-established civilizations of the East the Portuguese were never more than a handful of outsiders who could not impose their language, their religion, or their way of life. It was otherwise in the Americas, where previously unknown diseases such as smallpox decimated the native populations, and where Spanish invaders set about imposing European culture on the weakened and demoralized survivors.

The Spanish Empire in America

In South America, Mexico, and the Caribbean, after the first ferocity of the *conquista,* the Spanish established their own civilization. In Protestant countries, and also in France, as the years went on there arose an extremely unfavorable idea of the Spanish regime in America, where, it was noted, the Inquisition was soon established and the native peoples were reduced to servitude by the conquerors. The Spanish themselves came to dismiss this grim picture as a false legend concocted by their rivals. The true character of the Spanish Empire in America is not easy

Spanish colonial rule

to portray. The Spanish government (like the home governments of all colonial empires) regarded its empire as existing primarily for the benefit of the mother country. The Indians were put into servitude, to work in mines or in agriculture. They also died in large numbers from infections brought by Europeans to which Europeans over past centuries had developed immunities but against which the native American peoples had no such protection. The same was true farther north in what later became the United States. Religious critics of Spanish brutality, including, most notably, Bartolomé de las Casas, condemned the pervasive abuse of the native populations, and the Spanish government made efforts to moderate the exploitation of Indian labor. It attempted to regulate the encomienda, a labor and land system in which Indians were required to work for an owner a certain number of days in the week, while retaining parcels of land on which to work for themselves. How much the royal regulations were enforced on remote encomiendas is another question, to which answers vary. Black African slavery became somewhat less important in most of the Spanish American economy than it later became in the Dutch, French, and English colonies or in Portuguese Brazil. But the European and American-born white population remained relatively small. Castilian Spaniards looked down on American-born whites, called Creoles. Since fewer women than men emigrated from Spain, there arose a large class of mestizos, of mixed white and Indian descent.

The mestizos, along with many Indians, adopted to a considerable degree the Spanish language and the faith of the Spanish church. The Indians, while unfree, had also usually lacked individual freedoms under their own tribal chiefs. The sufferings of Indians, however, took new forms under the Spanish colonial system. They faced the harsh conditions of the Spanish labor system, but they were now spared from the violence of recurring tribal wars; they also fell under the strict religious controls of the Spanish Inquisition, but they were no longer threatened by traditional Aztec or Inca rituals of human sacrifice. Meanwhile, new forms of education began to develop within the Spanish Empire. The printing press was brought to Mexico in 1544. By the middle of the sixteenth century Spanish America consisted of two great viceroyal ties, those of Mexico and Peru, with 22 bishoprics, and with a university in each viceroyalty; the University of Lima was established in 1551, that of Mexico in 1553. When Harvard College was founded in New England (in 1636), there were five universities on the European model in Spanish America.

In 1545 a great discovery was made, the prodigiously rich silver deposits at Potosí in Peru. (It is now in Bolivia.) Almost simultaneously, better methods of extracting silver from the ore by the use of mercury were developed. American production of precious metals shot up suddenly and portentously. For years, after the midcentury, 500,000 pounds of silver and 10,000 pounds of gold flowed annually from America to Spain. The riches of Potosí financed the European projects of the king of Spain. Peruvian ores, Indian labor, and Spanish management combined to make possible the militant, anti-Protestant phase of the Counter Reformation within Europe.

The Potosí silver mines

But the Spanish also found American natural resources that would become more valuable in Europe than all of the gold and silver in colonial mines, because the Indians introduced Europeans to new plants such as beans, potatoes, maize, tomatoes, and squash. These nutritious foods were taken back to Europe, where, in the long run, they became much more useful than any precious metal in the daily lives and meals of everyone in Europe. American food plants eventually transformed European agriculture, changed the cuisine in every European country, and improved the diets of people in even the poorest social classes.

Europeans negotiate with an African chief and his council on the Guinea coast, perhaps for the purchase of enslaved people who will be transported to America. The Europeans have guns while the Africans have only spears, but in contrast to early European images of American Indians the Africans are fully clothed and seated in a dignified manner.

(©The New York Public Library/ Art Resource, NY)

Enslaved black workers are stooped over in a diamond-processing operation in Brazil, while white overseers watch with whips.

(©The New York Public Library/ Art Resource, NY)

Historical Interpretations and Debates
Europe and the Americas

Historians have long argued that the European encounter with the New World transformed Old World societies as well as cultures in the Americas. As these two influential historians explain in their accounts of cross-cultural exchanges and perceptions, the discovery of previously unknown lands and peoples profoundly altered both the material lives and the intellectual perspectives of early modern Europeans. Note the contrasting themes of social and cultural history that Alfred Crosby Jr. and J. H. Elliott develop in their interpretations of how European contacts with American Indians changed the history of Europe.

Alfred W. Crosby Jr., *The Columbian Exchange: Biological and Cultural Consequences of 1492* (1972, 2003)

The [American] Indian produced some of the most important of all food plants. He also gave humanity such nonfoods as tobacco, rubber, and certain cottons, but let us restrict ourselves to . . . his most valuable food crops. . . .

American plants [enabled the European] farmer to produce food from soils that, prior to 1492, were rated as useless because of their sandiness, altitude, aridity, and other factors. . . .

The American crops of primary importance in Europe have been beans, maize, and, above all, potatoes. . . . String beans and lima beans were among the chief products of seventeenth-century Spain. . . . The bean spread to almost all the latitudes of Europe, but the impact of maize was . . . restricted almost entirely to the southern half of that continent. . . .

Maize has had an important influence on population growth in southern Europe. . . . [But] another factor . . . has been Europe's love affair with the common American potato. . . . It was the Irish, of course, who first wholeheartedly adopted the potato. . . . As the crop spread in Ireland, the population grew, which made further spread of the tuber almost compulsory, for no other plant could feed so many Irishmen on such small plots of land. One-and-a-half acres, planted with potatoes, would provide enough food, with the addition of a bit of milk, to keep a family hearty for a year.

J. H. Elliott, *The Old World and the New 1492-1650* (1970)

The temptation was almost overpoweringly strong [for Europeans] to see the newly-discovered lands in terms of the enchanted isles of medieval fantasy. . . . [And] the Christian and the classical tradition were likely to prove the obvious points of departure for any evaluation of the New World and its inhabitants. . . .

The reverence . . . for their Christian and classical traditions had salutary consequences for their approach to the New World, in that it enabled them to set it into some kind of perspective in relation to themselves. . . . Christendom's own sense of self-dissatisfaction found expression in the longing for a return to a better state of things. The return might be to the lost Christian paradise, or to the Golden Age of the ancients, or to some elusive combination of both these imagined worlds. With the discovery of the Indies . . . it was all too easy to transpose the ideal world from a world remote in time to a world remote in space. . . .

It was an idyllic picture, and the humanists made the most of it, for it enabled them to express their dissatisfaction with European society, and to criticize it by implication. America and Europe became antitheses—the antitheses of innocence and corruption. . . .

But by treating the New World in this way, the humanists were closing the door to understanding an alien civilization. America was not as they imagined it. . . . But the dream was a European dream, which had little to do with the American reality.

Sources: Alfred W. Crosby Jr., *The Columbian Exchange: Biological and Cultural Consequences of 1492* (Westport, CT: Praeger, 2003), pp. 170, 176-78, 181-83; J. H. Elliott, *The Old World and the New 1492-1650* (Cambridge and New York: Cambridge University Press, 1970, 1992), pp. 24-27.

Meanwhile, beginning in 1565, the Spanish also established a lucrative trade route between their colonies in Mexico and the Philippines. Large ships called the "Manila Galleons" carried vast cargoes of silver from Acapulco to Manila, where the silver was traded for Chinese luxury goods—spices, porcelain, silks, and ivory—all of which were transported back to Mexico and on to Europe. This valuable trade continued until the early nineteenth century. It carried perhaps a third of all the silver extracted from Spain's American colonies off to Asia; and it helped to create the first modern global network for commercial exchange, in part because it brought Chinese consumers the only commodity that they wanted to buy from Europeans during this era. Silver from New World mines therefore sustained the whole Asian-American-European trading system and enabled Spain to control much of the burgeoning global market for Chinese products.

The opening of the Atlantic thus reoriented Europe. In an age of oceanic communications Europe became a center from which America, Africa, and Asia could all be reached. In Europe itself, the Atlantic coast now enjoyed great advantages over the older Mediterranean ports and the towns in central Europe. As the Portuguese began to bring spices from the East Indies into Western Europe, Antwerp began to flourish in Flanders as the point of redistribution for northern Europe. But for a century after the Spanish and Portuguese began to build their empires, the northern peoples did not take to the oceans. French corsairs did indeed put out from Bayonne or Saint-Malo, and Dutch prowlers and English "sea dogs" followed at the close of the century, all bent upon plundering the Iberian treasure ships. Still the Spanish and Portuguese kept their monopoly. No organized effort, backed by governments, came from the north until about 1600. For it is by no means geography alone that determines economic development; the English, Dutch, and French could not make use of the new Atlantic opportunities until they had cleared up their domestic troubles and survived the perils and hazards of the Wars of Religion.

12.   THE COMMERCIAL REVOLUTION

Population growth

In the great economic readjustment that was taking place in Europe, the opening of ocean trade routes was important, but it was by no means the only factor in shaping what historians call the early modern "Commercial Revolution." Two other key factors were the growth of population and a long, gradual rise in prices, or a slow inflation.

European population again grew rapidly, as in the High Middle Ages, reaching about 108 million in 1600, of which more than 20 million represented the growth during the sixteenth century. The increase took place in all countries, though the distribution was quite different from the population increases in more recent times. England in 1600 had less than 5 million inhabitants. France had four times as many, and the German states altogether almost as many as France. Italy and Spain had fewer than France, and distant Russia, within its sixteenth-century boundaries, may have had no more than 10 million people. Some cities grew substantially, with London and Paris approaching 200,000; Antwerp, Lisbon, and Seville, thanks to the ocean trade, jumped to 100,000 by 1600. But smaller towns remained much the same; Europe as a whole was probably no more urbanized than in the later Middle Ages. Most of the population growth represented an increasing density in the rural regions.

The price revolution

The steady rise in prices, which is to say the steady decline in value of a given unit of money (such as an English shilling), constituted a

The Spaniards stamped out many Indian religious practices, which they viewed as idolatrous. Yet it is to Spanish priests that we owe the preservation of much of our knowledge of the pre-conquest culture. This page is from a book in which a Spanish missionary wrote down the Aztec language in the Latin alphabet. A human sacrifice is also depicted.

(©De Agostini Picture Library/Getty Images)

gradual inflation. It has been called a "price revolution," but it was so slow as to be hardly comparable to the kinds of inflation known in some modern societies. One cause seems to have emerged from the growth of population itself, which set up an increasing demand for food. This meant that new land was brought under cultivation, including land that was less fertile, more inaccessible, or more difficult to work than the fields that had been cultivated previously. With increasing costs of production, agricultural prices rose; in England, for example, they about quadrupled during the sixteenth century. Prices were also pushed upward by the increase in the volume of money. The royal habit of debasing the currency brought a larger amount of money into circulation, since larger numbers of florins, *reals,* or *livres* were obtained from the same amount of bullion. The flow of gold and silver from America also made money more plentiful, but the impact of Peruvian and Mexican mines can easily be exaggerated. Even before the discovery of America, the development of gold and silver mines had augmented the European money supply. Although the expansion of both population and commerce checked the inflationary forces, the long trend of prices was upward. It affected all prices, including rents and other payments that were set in money values, but the price of hired labor, that is, wages, rose the least. The price changes thus had different effects on the well-being of different social classes.

The rising prices and growing population enhanced the economic opportunities for commercial enterprises. Merchants could count on increasing numbers of customers, new people could enter trade with hope of success, stocks of goods could rise in value with the passage of time, and borrowed money could more easily be repaid. Governments benefited also, insofar as kings could count on having more taxpayers and more soldiers.

The economic changes in Europe in the early modern period thus led to the Commercial Revolution, a broad term signifying the rise of a capitalistic economy and

The silver mines at Potosí, portrayed here in an eighteenth-century illustration, sent over 500,000 pounds of silver to Spain every year during most of the colonial era. American precious metals and the labor of American Indians enabled the Spanish government to wage its costly European wars and to maintain a lucrative trade with Chinese merchants in Asia.

(©Photo 12/Getty Images)

the transition from a town-centered to a nation-centered economic system. This "revolution" was an exceptionally slow and protracted one; it began at least as early as the fourteenth century and lasted until machine industry began to overshadow commerce in the early nineteenth century.

Changes in Commerce and Production

The early modern transformation of the European economy gradually changed the balance of commercial power from a local, medieval trading system to a more global, long-distance trading system. In the Middle Ages the town and its adjoining country had formed a closely connected economic unit. Craftsmen, organized in guilds, produced common articles for local use. Peasants and lords sold their agricultural products to the local town, from which they bought what the craftsmen produced. The town protected itself by its own tariffs and regulations. In the workshop the master both owned his "capital"—his house, workbench, tools, and materials—and acted as a workman himself along with half a dozen journeymen and apprentices. The masters owned a modest capital, but they were hardly capitalists. They produced only upon order, or at least for customers whose tastes and number were known in advance. There was little profit, little risk of loss, and not much innovation.

All this changed with the widening of the early modern trading area, or commercial market. Even in the Middle Ages, as we have seen, there was a certain amount of long-distance trading in articles that could not be produced as well in one place as in another. Gradually more articles came within this category. Where goods were produced to be sold at some time in the future, in faraway places, to persons unknown, the local guildmaster could not manage the operation. He lacked the money to tie up capital in stocks of unsold wares; he lacked the knowledge of what distant customers wanted, or where, in what quantities, and at what price people would buy. In this new type of long-distance business, new kinds of entrepreneurs became prominent in European commercial life. They usually started out as merchants working in an extensive market and ended up as bankers, like the Medici family in Renaissance Florence. Equally typical were the German Fuggers.

New entrepreneurs

JAKOB FUGGER, "THE RICH"
by Albrecht Dürer (German, 1471–1528)
This portrait of the German merchant and banker Jakob Fugger (1459–1525) suggests that the wealth of early modern commercial families attracted the interest of prominent artists as well as the attention of powerful monarchs. Dürer's painting conveys both the status and sense of purpose that characterized Fugger's wide-ranging economic career.
(©DEA PICTURE LIBRARY/Getty Images)

The first of this family, Johann Fugger, a small-town weaver, came to Augsburg in 1368. He established a business in a new kind of cloth, called fustian, in which cotton was mixed with other fabrics to produce clothing that was thicker or heavier than the woolens and linens in which people then clothed themselves. Fugger thus enjoyed a more than local market. Gradually the family began to deal also in spices, silks, and other Eastern goods obtained at Venice. Later generations invested their large profits in other enterprises, notably mining. They lent money to the Renaissance popes. They lent Charles V the money he needed to obtain election as Holy Roman Emperor in 1519. They became bankers to the Habsburgs in both Germany and Spain. Together with other German and Flemish bankers, the Fuggers financed the Portuguese trade with Asia, either by outright loans or by providing in advance, on credit, the cargoes that the Portuguese traded for spices. The wealth of the Fuggers became proverbial and declined only through repeated Habsburg bankruptcies and with the general economic decline that beset Germany in the sixteenth century. By that time, however, the family had become a kind of model for the transnational, commercial practices that were reshaping the sixteenth-century European economy.

Other dealers in cloth, less spectacular than the first Fugger, broke away from the town-and-guild framework in other ways. England until the fifteenth century was an exporter of raw wool and an importer of finished woolens from Flanders. In the fifteenth century certain English entrepreneurs began to develop the spinning, weaving, and dyeing of wool in England. To avoid the restrictive practices of the towns and guilds they "put out" the work to people in the country, providing them with looms and other equipment for the purpose, of which they generally retained the ownership themselves. This "putting out" or domestic system spread very widely outside the guild system, and, by the early modern

The "putting out" system

PORTRAIT OF AN AFRICAN MAN
by Jan Mostaert, (Dutch, c. 1473–c. 1556)
Europe's new international commerce included
an expanding slave trade that transported
enslaved Africans to the Americas. Both enslaved
and free Africans also arrived in Europe, however, and Mostaert met this unidentified African
man either in the Netherlands or in his European
travels. Although his clothing and sword convey
a status that differed from the position of
enslaved workers in the Americas, he surely had
to cope with the social and racial hierarchies
that all Africans encountered in early modern
Europe.

(©Heritage Images/Getty Images)

period, typically depended on a gendered division of labor. Women usually did the work
of spinning wool into thread (hence the later English term for an unmarried woman,
"spinster"); men usually wove the thread into cloth. In France the cloth dealers of Rouen,
feeling the competition of the new silk trade, developed a lighter, cheaper, and more simply
made type of woolen cloth. Various guild regulations in Rouen, to protect the workers
there, prohibited the manufacture of this cheaper cloth. The Rouen dealers, in 1496, took
the industry into the country, installed looms in peasant cottages, and farmed out the
work to the peasants. The new commercial enterprises therefore weakened the guilds'
economic influence and created new processes for both the production of goods and the
accumulation of capital.

Capital and Labor

The system of rural household industry remained typical of production in cloth, hardware,
and other western European goods until the introduction of factories in the late eighteenth
century. It signified a new divergence between capital and labor. On
the one hand were the workers, men and women who worked as the
employer needed them, received wages for what they did, and had little
interest in or knowledge of more than their own task. Living both by
agriculture and by cottage industry, they formed an expansible labor force, available when
labor was needed, left to live by farming or local charity when times were bad. On the
other hand was the manager or entrepreneur (almost always a man) who directed the
whole affair. He had little or no personal acquaintance with the workers. Estimating how

*Divergence between
capital and labor*

much of a product such as woolens he could sell in a national or even international market, he purchased the needed raw materials, passed out wool to be spun by one group of peasants, took the yarn to another group for weaving, collected the cloth and took it still elsewhere to be dyed. Paying wages on all sides for services rendered, he retained ownership of the materials and the equipment and kept the coordination and management of the whole enterprise in his own head. Much larger business enterprises could be established in this way than within the municipal framework of guild and town. Indeed, the very master weavers of the guilds often sank to the status of subcontractors, hardly different from wage employees, of the great clothiers and drapers by whom the business was dominated. The latter, with the widening market, became personages of national or even international repute. And, of course, the bigger the business the more of a capital investment it represented.

Certain other industries, new or virtually new in the fifteenth and sixteenth centuries, could by their nature never fit into a town-centered system and were capitalistic from the start, in that they required a large initial outlay before any income could be received. Mining was one such industry, and another was printing and the book trade. Books had a national and even international market, being mainly in Latin; and no ordinary craftsman could afford the outlay required for a printing press, for fonts of type, supplies of paper, and stocks of books on hand. Printers therefore borrowed from capitalists or shared with them an interest in business. Shipbuilding was so stimulated by the shift to transoceanic trade as almost to become a new industry, and still another was the manufacture of cannons and muskets. For the latter the chief demand came from the state, from the New Monarchies that were organizing national armies. In the rise of capitalism the needs of the military were in fact fundamentally important. Armies, which started out by requiring thousands of weapons, required thousands of new uniforms as well as many new barracks and fortifications throughout the seventeenth and eighteenth centuries. These heavy demands were the first to require mass production. Where governments themselves did not take the initiative, private middlemen stepped in as links to the many small handicraft workers and families who before the industrial age still manufactured the actual product.

New industries

The new sea route to the East and the discovery of America brought a vast increase in trade not only of luxury items but of imported commodities like rice, sugar, tea, and other consumer goods. Older commercial activities within Europe were also transformed by the widening of markets. Spain increasingly drew cereals from Sicily. The Netherlands were fed from Poland; the French wine districts lived on food brought from northern France. With the growth of shipping, the timber, tar, pitch, and other naval stores of Russia and the Baltic entered the commercial scene. There was thus an ever-growing movement of heavy staple commodities, in which again only persons controlling large funds of capital could normally take part.

Not all capital was invested; some was simply lent to the church, to governments, to impecunious nobles, or to persons engaged in trade and commerce—though commercial loans were still the least common type of lending in the sixteenth century. Bankers and others who lent money expected to receive back, after a time, a larger sum than that of the loan. They expected "interest"; and they sometimes received as much as 30 percent a year. In the Middle Ages the taking of interest had been frowned upon as usury, denounced as avarice, and forbidden in the canon law. It was still frowned upon in the sixteenth century by almost all but the lenders themselves. The Catholic Church maintained its prohibitions.

New banking practices

The growing production of cloth in early modern Europe depended on the labor of families in rural cottage industries. Spinning thread became an important economic activity for many women, as Jean Bourdichon (1457–1521) demonstrates in this illustration of a family at work. The man is apparently a skilled woodworker, and the child is gathering wood chips that can be used for cooking food or heating the house. The solid walls and ceiling show that this is a prosperous, hard-working family.
(©Bridgeman-Giraudon/Art Resource, NY)

The theologians of the University of Paris also ruled against it in 1530. Luther, who hated bankers like the Fuggers, continued to preach against usury. Calvin made allowances, but as late as 1640, in capitalist Holland itself, the stricter Calvinist ministers still denounced lending at interest.

Religious interventions, however, could never stop the practice. Borrowers compounded with lenders to evade prohibitions, and theologians of all churches began to distinguish between "usury" and a "legitimate return." Gradually, as interest rates fell, as banking became more established, and as loans were made for economically productive uses rather than to sustain ecclesiastics, princes, and nobles in their personal habits, the feeling against a "reasonable" interest died down and interest became an accepted feature of capitalism. The Bank of Amsterdam, for example, attracted depositors because they knew their money was safe, would earn interest, and could be withdrawn at will. Deposits thus flowed into the bank from all countries and enabled it to make low-interest loans that financed new commercial activities.

The net effect of all these developments was a commercialization of industry. The dynamic, entrepreneurial persons in commercial life were the merchants. Industry, the actual processes of production, still in an essentially handicraft stage, was subordinate to the buyers and sellers. Producers—spinners, weavers, hatters, metalworkers, gunsmiths, glassworkers—worked to fill the orders of the merchants, and often with capital that the merchants supplied and owned. The entrepreneur who knew where the article could be sold prevailed over the person who simply knew how to produce it. This commercial capitalism remained the typical form of capitalism until after 1800, when, with the introduction of power machinery, it yielded to industrial capitalism, and merchants became dependent on industrialists who owned, understood, and organized the machines.

Mercantilism

There was still another aspect of the Commercial Revolution, which is described historically under the name of "mercantilism." Mercantilist economic theories of the sixteenth and seventeenth centuries assumed that capital accumulation in one country would reduce the available capital in others. Drawing on such theories, mercantilism was a government economic policy that used high tariffs to reduce imports, protect key industries, and create a favorable balance of trade. The goal was always to promote the internal growth of national wealth. Rulers were hard pressed for money, and they needed more of it as their coins fell in value. The desire of kings and their advisers to force gold and silver to flow into their own kingdoms was thus one of the first impulses leading to mercantilist regulation. Gradually this desire for more gold and silver was expanded or replaced by the more general idea of building up a strong and self-sufficient economy. Mercantilist policies were supposed to turn the country into a hive of industry and to discourage idleness, begging, vagabondage, and unemployment. New crafts and manufactures were introduced, and government favors were given to merchants who provided work for the poor or who sold the country's products abroad. It was thought desirable to raise the export of finished goods and reduce the export of unprocessed raw materials, to curtail all imports except of needed raw materials, and thus to obtain the favorable balance of trade that would follow when other countries had to pay their debts in bullion. Since all this was done by a royal or nationwide system of government regulations, mercantilism became in the economic sphere what the state building of the New Monarchies was in the political, signifying the transition from town to national units of social living.

Mercantilists frowned upon the localistic and conservative outlook of the guilds. In England, where mercantilist policies first advanced most rapidly, the guilds ceased to have importance. Parliament, in the

Opposition to guilds

time of Elizabeth, did on a national scale what guilds had once done locally when it enacted the Statute of Artificers of 1563, regulating the admission to apprenticeship and the level of wages in various trades. In France the royal government maintained the legal existence of the guilds, because they were convenient bodies to tax, but it deprived them of most of their old independence and used them as organizations through which royal control of industry could be enforced. In both countries the government assisted merchants who wished to set up domestic or cottage industry in the country, against the protests of the town guilds, which in their heyday had forbidden rural people to engage in crafts. Governments generally tried to suppress idleness. The famous English Poor Law of 1601 (which remained in effect, with amendments, until 1834) was designed to force able-bodied people to work and to relieve the absolute destitution of those who could not.

Governments likewise took steps to introduce new industries. The silk industry was brought from Italy to France under royal protection, to the dismay of French woolen and linen interests. The English government assisted in turning England from a producer of raw wool into a producer of finished woolens, supervising the immigration of skilled Flemish weavers and even fetching from faraway Turkey, about 1582, two youths who understood the more advanced dyeing arts of the Middle East. Generally, under mercantilism, governments fought to steal skilled workers from each other while prohibiting or discouraging the emigration of their own skilled workers, who might take their trade secrets to foreign places.

National markets

By such means governments helped to create a national market and an industrious nationwide labor supply for their great merchants.

Without such government support and government-imposed tariffs the great merchants, such as the drapers or clothiers, could never have risen and prospered. The same help was given to merchants operating in foreign markets. Henry VII of England, for example, negotiated a commercial treaty with Flanders in 1496; and in the next century the kings of France signed treaties with the Ottoman Empire by which French merchants obtained privileges in the Middle East. A merchant backed by a national monarchy was in a much stronger position than one backed merely by a city, such as Augsburg or Venice. This backing on a national scale was also provided when national governments subsidized exports, paying bounties for goods whose production they wished to encourage, or when they erected tariff barriers against imports to protect their own producers from competition.

A national tariff system was thus superimposed on the old network of provincial and municipal tariffs. These latter were now thought of as "internal tariffs," which mercantilists usually wished to abolish by creating an area of free trade within the state as a whole. But local interests were so strong that for centuries the European monarchies were unable to get rid of local tariffs except in England. Meanwhile, however, the new commercial capitalism developed everywhere with the support of government protections, subsidies, and economic interventions.

In distant parts of the world, or in less accessible regions nearer home, such as the Middle Eastern Muslim lands or Russia, it was not possible for individual European merchants to act by merely private initiative. Merchants trading with such countries needed a good deal of capital, they often had to obtain special privileges and protection

Chartered trading companies

from native rulers, and they had to arm their ships against Barbary or Malay pirates or against hostile Europeans. Merchants and their respective governments came together to found official companies for the transocean trade. In England, soon after the English discovery of the White Sea in 1553, a Russia Company was established. A Turkey Company soon followed. Shortly after 1600 a great many such companies were operating out of England, Holland, and France. The most famous of all were the East India Companies, which the English founded in 1600, the Dutch in 1602, the French not until 1664. In 1672 the English also chartered the Royal African Company, which for a time controlled the English slave trade and the gold imports from west Africa. Each of these companies was a state-supported organization with special rights. Each was a monopoly in that only merchants who belonged to the company could legally engage in trade in the region for which the company had a charter. Each was expected to find markets for the national products, and most of them were expected to bring home gold or silver. With these companies the northern European peoples began to encroach on the Spanish and Portuguese monopoly in America, Africa, and the East. With them new commercial-colonial empires would be launched and expanded after various domestic and transnational European conflicts were settled in outcomes that strengthened the northwestern European states.

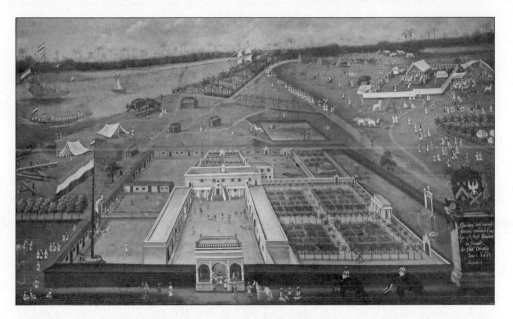

The headquarters of the Dutch East India Company in Bengal in 1665, long before the British gained predominance there. It is wholly walled off from the Indian life around it, with offices, living quarters, and spacious gardens for employees of the company.
(©Universal History Archive/Getty Images)

13.   CHANGING SOCIAL STRUCTURES

Social structure, for present purposes, refers to the composition, functions, and interrelationships of social classes. Because changes in social structure are slow, they are hard to identify in specific decades or particular periods of time. In general, however, with the effects of the Commercial Revolution, population growth, and the falling value of money, the classes of Europe, broadly defined, took on forms that were to last until the industrializing era of the nineteenth and twentieth centuries. These classes were the landed aristocracy, the peasantry or mass of agricultural workers, the miscellaneous middle classes, and the urban poor.

While all prices rose in the sixteenth century, it was agricultural prices that rose the most. Anyone who had agricultural products to sell was likely to benefit. Among such beneficiaries were peasants who held small plots of land in return for fixed payments to a manorial lord. Many such payments were set in unchangeable sums of money, in the old values of the fourteenth or even thirteenth century, so the price inflation of the sixteenth century enabled some peasants in effect to pay much less to the lord than in the past. Other rural workers, however, either held no land of their own or produced only at a subsistence level with nothing to sell in the market. Such peasants, and hired hands dependent on wages, found their situation worsened. Village life became less egalitarian than it had been in the Middle Ages. In England a class of small freeholders (the "yeomanry") developed between the landed gentry and the rural poor. On the Continent, at least in France, western Germany, and the Netherlands, an increasingly prosperous class of peasants acquired more secure property rights, resembling those of small freeholders in England. But both in England

Small freeholders

and on the Continent a large class of unpropertied rural workers remained in poverty and excluded from the emerging international markets for agricultural products.

Land rents in the countryside went up as rising agricultural prices increased the value of arable soil. Inflation and population growth also drove up rentals for housing in the more crowded towns. Owners of real property (that is, land and buildings) were favored by such changes, but within the former class of feudal lords the effects were mixed. If one's great-grandfather had let out land in earlier times in exchange for fixed sums of money, the value of the income received from that land had actually declined. But those landowners who received payments in kind from their tenants, for example, in bushels of wheat or barley, or who managed their large estates themselves, could sell their actual agricultural products at current prices and so increase their money income.

Social Classes

The former feudal class, or land-based nobility, thus gradually turned into a new kind of service-based or commercial aristocracy. If income from their estates declined, they sought paid service in the king's army or government or appointment to the more prestigious offices in the church. If landed income increased, they used the new trading systems to become more wealthy. In either case, and even if they served as military commanders, they became more concerned with civilian pursuits; and they were likely to develop more refined tastes and pay more attention to the education of their children.

The nobility

Like the peasants, the landowning class became more heterogeneous, ranging from the small gentry to the great peers of England and from small or impoverished nobles to the *grands seigneurs* of France. Some led a life of leisure; others were eager to work in the higher reaches of organized government. The most impoverished nobles sometimes had the longest pedigrees. As their social functions changed, and as persons of more recent family background competed for education, government employment, and even military service, there came to be an increasing importance set upon ancestry as a badge of status. Among the upper class, there was more insistence on high birth and distinguished forebears in the seventeenth and eighteenth centuries than there had been before. But many nobles also claimed that they deserved special privileges because they contributed meritorious service to kings or the expanding national governments.

The bourgeoisie

Below the aristocracy were the middle classes, or "bourgeoisie." *Bourgeois* was a French word, which, like the English "burgher," originally meant a person living in a chartered town or borough and enjoying its liberties. The bourgeoisie was the whole social class made up of individual bourgeois. In a much later sense of the word, derived from Karl Marx in the nineteenth century, the term "bourgeoisie" was applied to the class of owners of capital. This Marxist concept of the bourgeoisie must be kept distinct from the meaning of the word in an earlier era. "Bourgeoisie" referred in preindustrial times to the middle levels of society between the aristocracy, which mostly drew its income from land, and the laboring poor, who depended on wages or charity, or who often went hungry. Class lines tended to blur as aristocratic families formed the habit of living in towns and middle-class burghers began to buy land in the country. Some bourgeois thus came to live on landed rents, while some of the gentry and aristocracy, most notably in England, bought shares in the great overseas trading companies or engaged in other forms of business enterprise. Aristocrats possessing large agricultural estates, timberlands, or mines increasingly brought their products to market to be sold at a profit. But even when aristocrat and bourgeois became economically more alike, a consciousness of social difference between them remained.

The middle class became more numerous in the sixteenth century, and increasingly so thereafter. It was an indefinite category, because the countries of Europe differed in the size and importance of their middle classes, in the kinds of persons who belonged to them, and in the types

of occupations that bourgeois people pursued. Near the top were the urban elites who governed the towns; they might draw their incomes from rural property, from commerce, or from the emoluments of government itself, and they sometimes intermarried with persons of noble status. Especially where the towns were strong or royal government was weak, as in the Netherlands, the German free cities, or north Italy, such urban patriciates formed virtual aristocracies in themselves. But in a larger social perspective, or in the context of the more powerful monarchical states, the families of merchants, bankers, and shipowners were middle class, as were those of the traditional learned professions, law and medicine. So, in general, were judges, tax officials, and other employees of governments, except in the highest ranks. In the professions and in government service the younger sons of the aristocracy might be found alongside the offspring of the middle classes, most commonly in England, less so in France, and even less as one moved into Germany or Spain.

The clergy was drawn from all classes. There were poor parish priests, who might be the sons of peasants, and there were bishops and abbots from the most prominent noble families; but the bulk of the clergy was recruited from middle-class families. In Protestant countries, where the clergy married, their sons and daughters became an important element in the middle class. Members of trade guilds were middle class, though the guilds differed widely in social status, from those of the great wholesale merchants or the goldsmiths, down through the guilds of such humble occupations as the tanners and barrel makers. At the bottom of bourgeois social life, the middle class faded into the socioeconomic world of small retail shopkeepers, innkeepers, owners of workshops in which ordinary articles were manufactured by hand, the lesser skilled tradespeople, and their employees, journeymen, and apprentices.

The mass of the population in all countries was composed of the working poor. These included not only the unskilled wage laborers but the unemployed, unemployable, and paupers, with a large fringe that turned to vagabondage and begging. They were unable to read or write

and were often given to irregular habits that distressed both middle-class persons and government officials. Poverty was increasingly viewed as an example or outcome of immorality. Mercantilist governments tried to make poor people work, but charitable relief also developed toward the end of the sixteenth century, as shown in the English Poor Law of 1601 and in similar efforts on the Continent. The idea gained ground that begging was a public nuisance and that the poor should thus be segregated in workhouses or hospices from the rest of society. Most of the poor were of course not recipients of such relief, and most did hard work. They were the working men and women who tilled the fields, wove the cloth, tended the livestock, dug in the mines, or went to sea as fishermen and common sailors. They also found work in the towns as casual laborers, porters, water carriers, or removers of excrement; or they entered the domestic service of noble and upper-middleclass families, whose rising standard of living required a growing number of chambermaids, cooks, washerwomen, footmen, lackeys, coachmen, and stable boys. Domestic service was in fact the most common job for women during the entire period of early modern history, and the pay for such work remained extremely low. Wages rose less than

PEASANTS AT LUNCH
by Diego Velázquez (Spanish, 1599–1660)

Velázquez was best known for his portraits of people at the Spanish royal court, but he also portrayed
the lives and character of the lower classes—as in this detail from a seventeenth-century painting of
peasants sharing food at a table.

(©Imagno/Getty Images)

prices in the sixteenth century. The poor, if not positively worse off than in former times, gained the least from the great commercial developments with which economic history is usually concerned. The very growth of social differentiation, the fact that the middle and upper classes made such advances, left the condition of the poor correspondingly worse.

Social Roles of Education and Government

Education in the latter part of the sixteenth century took on an altogether new importance for the social system. One consequence of the Reformation, in both Protestant and Catholic countries, was the attempt to put a serious and effective pastor in each parish. This set up a demand for a more educated clergy. The growth of commerce made it necessary to have literate clerks and agents. Governments wanted men from both the noble and middle classes who could cooperate in large organizations, be reliable, understand finance, keep records, and draft proposals. There was also a widespread need for lawyers. Every profession, commercial enterprise, and government institution, in short, was seeking better-educated persons to manage and advance their interests.

The new demand for education was met by an outburst of philanthropy, which reached a high point in both England and France between about 1580 and 1640. Many endowed scholarships were established. At what would now be called a secondary level, hundreds of "grammar schools" were founded at this time in England. In France the *collèges* combined the work of the English grammar school with what corresponded to the first year or two of university work at Oxford or Cambridge. Of the 167 most important French colleges still existing at the time of the Revolution in 1789, only 36 had been founded in the centuries before 1560, and 92 were established in the years between 1560 and 1650. Provision for girls' schools was more sporadic, but the Ursuline sisters, for example, founded in Italy in 1535, had established about 350 convents by the year 1700 in Catholic Europe and even in Canada, in most of which the education of girls was a principal purpose and occupation of the sisters.

New schools and universities

Dutch and Swiss Protestants founded the universities of Leyden and Geneva. New universities, both Protestant and Catholic, appeared in Germany. In Spain the multiplication of universities was phenomenal. Castile, with only 2 universities dating from the Middle Ages, had 20 by the early seventeenth century; Salamanca was enrolling over 5,000 students a year. Five universities also existed in Spanish America by 1600. In England, new colleges were founded at Oxford and Cambridge, and it was especially in these years that some of the Oxford and Cambridge colleges became very wealthy. Annual admissions of new students at Oxford, barely 100 in 1550, rose to over 500 in the 1630s, a figure not exceeded, or even equaled, during the following 200 years.

The schools, colleges, and universities drew their students from a wide range of social classes. There was less organized schooling for girls than for boys, but an intelligent and lucky boy of poor family had perhaps a better chance for education than at any time in Europe until the later twentieth century. In Spain most of the students seem to have been lesser nobles, or "hidalgos," aspiring to positions in the church or government; but hidalgos were very numerous in Spain, overlapping with what might be called the middle class in other countries. The French colleges, including those operated by the Jesuits, recruited their students very widely, taking in the sons of nobles, merchants, shopkeepers, artisans, and even, more rarely, of peasants. English grammar schools did likewise; it was in later times that a few of them, like Eton and Harrow, became more exclusive public schools. As for universities, we have detailed knowledge for Oxford, which recorded the status of its

Wider access to education

A seventeenth-century monk is teaching in Spain at the University of Salamanca, one of the largest European universities of the time and an example of how such institutions expanded in both Catholic and Protestant countries during the century after the Protestant Reformation. Many students are more interested in their friends or other distractions than in the instructor's lecture–which suggests the continuities of classroom experiences across the centuries.
(©DEA/G. DAGLI ORTI/Getty Images)

students at matriculation, classifying them as "esquires," "gentlemen," "clergy," and "plebeians." From 1560 to 1660 about half of the Oxford students were plebeians, which in the language of that time could embrace the whole middle class from big merchants down to quite modest social levels. It seems certain that Oxford and Cambridge were more widely representative of the English people in 1660 than in 1900.

Social classes were formed not only by economic forces, and not only by education, but also by the actions of governments. We have noted how kings contributed to the rise

Government and social classes

of commercial capitalism and a new business class by granting monopolies, borrowing from bankers, and issuing charters to trading companies. In many countries, and notably in France, many families owed their middle-class position to the holding of government offices, some of which might become a form of inheritable property. It might also be the action of governments, as much as economic conditions, that defined or promoted distinctions between nobles and commoners, or privileged and unprivileged social classes. Where peasants suffered heavily from royal taxes, it was more from political than from economic causes. The king, by "making" nobles—that is, by conferring titles of nobility on persons who did not inherit them—could raise a few in the middle class to higher status. Tax exemption could also be a sign of high social standing. The king exercised political power, but he was simultaneously the fountain of social honor at the top of society. The royal court formed the apex of a pyramid of social rank, in which each class looked up to or down upon the others. Those favored with the royal presence disdained the plain country nobility, who sniffed at the middle classes, who patronized or disparaged the hired servants, day laborers, and the poor. Looking upward in the social hierarchy, people were expected to show deference toward those with higher social status.

Eastern and Western Europe

One other remark may be made on social structure. It was in the sixteenth century that important social differences developed between eastern and western Europe. In the west, the Commercial Revolution and the gradual emergence of global trading systems brought advantageous changes to the middle class and even to many of the peasants for whom the old burdens of the manorial system were lightened. In eastern Europe, it was the lords who benefited from rising prices and the growing market for grain and forest products. Here too the institution of the manor existed; but the peasants' land tenures were more precarious than in the west and more dependent on accidents of death or on the wishes of the lord. The lords in eastern Europe also tended to work a larger part of their manors with their own workforces for their own use or profit.

The rise of prices and expansion of Baltic shipping gave the lords a strong incentive to increase their output. In northeast Germany (where such lords were called Junkers), in Poland, and later in Russia, Bohemia, and Hungary, beginning in the sixteenth century and continuing into the eighteenth, a vast process set in by which most of the peasantry sank into more restrictive forms of serfdom. This process was hastened in many regions by the violence and insecurity engendered by the religious wars. Typically, peasants lost their individual parcels of land or received them back on the condition that they render unpaid labor services to the lord. Usually peasants owed three or four days a week of such forced labor (called *robot* in Bohemia and adjoining territories), remaining free to work during the remainder of the week on their own parcels. Often the number of days of *robot* exacted by the lord was greater, since in eastern Europe, where centralized legal systems were almost unknown, the lord himself was the final court of appeal for his people. His people were in fact his "subjects."

Serfdom in eastern Europe

Serfdom in Germany was not called serfdom, but "hereditary subjection." By whatever name they were known throughout eastern Europe, serfs, or hereditary subjects of the manorial lord, could not leave the manor, marry, or learn a trade without the lord's express permission. Lords used this compulsory labor mainly for agriculture, though some serfs learned handicrafts that were needed on the estate. The large property owners sold the estate's produce, however, and retained the profits for themselves.

Thus, in eastern Europe at the beginning of modern times, the rural masses lost personal freedoms and lived in a poverty that was mostly unknown among the peasants to the west, poor as the latter were. In western Europe there were peasants who were already on the way to becoming small proprietors. They were free people under the law. They could migrate, marry, and learn trades as opportunity offered. Those who held land could defend it in the royal courts and raise crops and take part in the market economy on their own account. They owed the lord no forced labor—or virtually none, for the 10 days a year of forced labor (called the *corvée*) still found in parts of France hardly compared with the almost full-time *robot* of the peasant in eastern Europe.

The landlord in the east, from the sixteenth century onward, was solidly entrenched in his own domain, monarch of all he surveyed, with no troublesome urban bourgeoisie to annoy him, and with kings and territorial rulers solicitous of his wishes. Travelers from the west were impressed with the wealth of great Polish and Lithuanian magnates, with their palatial homes, private art galleries, well-stocked libraries, collections of jewels, gargantuan dinners, and lavish hospitality. The Junkers of northeast Germany lived more modestly, but enjoyed the same kind of independence and social superiority.

The growing power of wealthy landlords and the weakening position of impoverished peasants would have decisive social and political consequences for the later history of Prussia, Poland, Russia, and the Austrian world. But meanwhile, amidst all the economic growth, social development, and overseas conquests that have been described in the preceding pages, Europe was torn by the destructive ferocity of the Wars of Religion.

14. THE WARS OF CATHOLIC SPAIN: THE NETHERLANDS AND ENGLAND

The Ambitions of Philip II

Charles V, having tried in vain for 35 years to preserve religious unity in Germany, abdicated his many crowns and retired to a monastery in 1556, the year after the Peace of Augsburg had given the ruler of each German state the right to choose its own religion. He left Austria, Bohemia, and Hungary (or the small part of it not occupied by the Turks) to his brother Ferdinand, who was soon elected Holy Roman Emperor (see map, p. 83). All his other possessions Charles left to his son Philip, who became Philip II of Spain. The Habsburg dynasty remained thereafter divided into two branches, the Austrian and the Spanish. The two cooperated in European affairs. The Spanish branch for a century was the more important. Philip II (1556–1598) not only possessed the Spanish kingdoms but in 1580 inherited Portugal, so that the whole Iberian peninsula was brought under his rule. He possessed the 17 provinces of the Netherlands and the Free County of Burgundy, which were member states of the Holy Roman Empire, lying on its western border, adjacent to France. Milan in north Italy and Naples in the south belonged to Philip, and since he also held the chief islands, as well as Tunis, he enjoyed a naval ascendancy in the western Mediterranean that was threatened only by the Turks. For five years, until the death of Queen Mary in 1558, he was titular king of England, and in 1589, in the name of his daughter, he laid claim to the throne of France. Almost all of Central and South America belonged to Philip II, and after 1580 all the Portuguese Empire as well, so that except for a few nautical daredevils all ships plying the open ocean were the Spanish king's.

Philip II therefore naturally regarded himself as an international figure, and even more so because he combined the organizing methods of a new monarchy with a profound interest in the political and religious issues that were dividing post-Reformation Europe. He saw Spain as a leader of European Catholicism, and he believed that the advance of Spanish power in Europe served the cause of the universal church as well as the interests of his own monarchy and the people of Spain. Yet his attempts to protect and enhance Spanish power in Italy sometimes led to conflicts with the popes, and much of his foreign

Philip's goals

policy was directed against the Ottoman Empire in a continuing struggle for control of the Mediterranean Sea. European Protestantism was thus only one of Philip's many international concerns.

Philip's active participation in Europe's religious wars should therefore be seen as part of his wider military and political campaigns to protect Spanish and Habsburg interests rather than a single-minded crusade for Catholicism. In his personal life, he was serious, devout, and hardworking. He gave the most detailed attention to the management of his far-flung territories. The wealth that flowed to his country from Potosí and other mines in South America enabled Philip to pursue his goals throughout Europe and the Mediterranean. Meanwhile, Spain also entered upon the Golden Age of its early modern culture.

In this period, the *siglo de oro,* running in round dates from 1550 to 1650, Cervantes wrote his *Don Quixote* (in two parts, 1605, 1615) and Lope de Vega wrote his 200 dramas, while El Greco, Murillo, and Velázquez painted their renowned pictures, and the Jesuit Francisco Suarez composed works on philosophy and law that were read even in Protestant countries. As Cervantes showed in *Don Quixote,* many Spaniards were highly aware of the enduring tensions between high ideals and the difficult realities of social, political, and religious life. But Catholic traditions and the Catholic Church remained a powerful force in Spanish culture. The church was vitally present at every social level, from the archbishop of Toledo, who ranked above grandees and could address the king as an equal, down to a host of penniless and mendicant friars, who mixed with the poorest people in Spain.

Philip II built himself a new royal residence, the Escorial, which well expressed in solid stone its creator's political and religious determination. Madrid itself was a new town, merely a government center, far from the worldly distractions of Toledo or Valladolid. But it was 30 miles from Madrid, on the bleak arid plateau of central Castile, overlooked by the jagged Sierra, that Philip

The Escorial

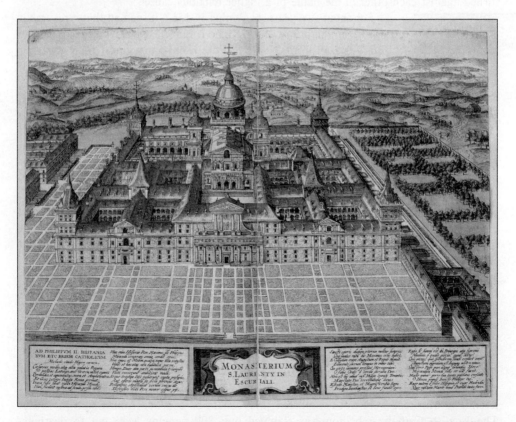

Philip II's Spanish palace, the Escorial, was a monastery as well as a royal residence. The buildings, which honored St. Lawrence, were laid out in the shape of a grill, since Catholic martyrologists reported that this saint had been burned alive on a grill over burning coals in the third century.
(©DEA/G. DAGLI ORTI/Getty Images)

chose to erect the Escorial. Somber and vast, made of blocks of granite meant to last forever, and with its highest spire rising 300 feet from the ground, the Escorial was designed not only as a palace but as a center for religious life and the efficient management of a vast empire. Working constantly in this somber setting, Philip II dispatched his couriers to Mexico, to Manila, to Vienna, and to Milan. He sent his troops off to Italy and the Netherlands, his diplomats to all the royal courts of Europe, and his spies wherever they were needed—seeking to extend the influence of his powerful state and (when possible) to promote the Catholicism in which he devoutly believed.

The first years of Philip's reign were also the first years of Elizabeth's reign in England, where the religious issue was still in flux; they were years in which Calvinism agitated the Netherlands, and when France, ruled by teenaged boys, fell into implacable civil war. Religious loyalties that knew no frontiers overlapped all political boundaries. Everywhere there were people who looked for guidance outside their own countries. Fervent Calvinists in England, France, and the Netherlands felt more connected to one another than to their own monarchs or their own neighbors. Fervent Catholics, in all three countries, welcomed the support of international Catholic forces—the Jesuits, the king of Spain, the pope. National unity threatened to dissolve or was not yet formed. The sense of mutual trust between people who lived side by side was eaten away; and people who lived not only in the same country, but in the same town, on the same street, or even in the same house, turned against each other in the name of a higher religious cause.

The Catholic offensive

For about five years, beginning in 1567, it seemed that a resurgent Catholicism might prevail throughout Europe. Catholic forces took the offensive on all fronts. In 1567 Philip sent a new and firmer governor general to the Netherlands, the Duke of Alva, with 20,000 Spanish soldiers; the duke proceeded to suppress religious and political dissidents by establishing a Council of Troubles. In 1569 Philip, who was preparing for a new war with the Ottoman Turks, put down a revolt of the Moriscos (converted Muslims) in Spain. In the same year the Catholics of northern England, led by the Duke of Norfolk and sewing the cross of crusaders on their garments, rose in an unsuccessful armed rebellion against Queen Elizabeth, but English Catholics continued to plot against their heretic queen. In the next year, 1570, the pope excommunicated Elizabeth and absolved her subjects from allegiance to her, so that English Catholics, if they wished, could henceforth in good religious conscience conspire to overthrow her. In 1571 the Spanish joined with the Venetians and others to win a great naval battle against the Turks, at Lepanto off the coast of Greece. Although this battle was part of the ongoing military struggle for political and economic control of the Mediterranean, some Spanish sailors wove a cross on their sails and portrayed their war with the Ottomans as a new Christian resistance to Islam. In the next year, 1572, the Catholic leaders of France, with the advice of the pope and of Philip II, decided to make an end of the Huguenots, or French Protestants. Over 3,000 were seized and put to death on the eve of St. Bartholomew's Day in Paris alone; and this massacre was followed by other violence and lesser liquidations throughout the provinces.

But none of these victories proved enduring. The Turks soon recovered from their defeat at Lepanto and built a new fleet. In fact, they took Tunis from Philip two years later. The Moriscos were not assimilated (they would be expelled from Spain in 1609). The English Catholic rebellion was stamped out; 800 persons were put to death by Elizabeth's government. The revolt in the Netherlands remained very much alive, as did the French Huguenots. Twenty years later England was Protestant, the Dutch were winning independence, a Huguenot had become king of France, and the Spanish fleet had

KING PHILIP II OF SPAIN
by Titian (Italian, 1488–1576)
**This portrait of the Spanish king conveys the
highly focused political, religious, and military
commitments of this devout Catholic monarch.**
(©Universal History Archive/Getty Images)

gone to ruin in northern waters. Despite the global power and wealth of the vast Spanish Empire, Spain's armies and naval forces would finally abandon their long campaign to drive the Muslims from the Mediterranean and the Protestants from northern Europe.

The Revolt of the Netherlands

The Netherlands, or Low Countries, roughly comprised the area of the modern kingdoms of the Netherlands and Belgium and the grand duchy of Luxembourg. They consisted of 17 provinces, which in the fifteenth century, one by one, had been inherited, purchased, or conquered by the dukes of Burgundy, from whom they were inherited by Charles V and his son, Philip II. In the mid-sixteenth century neither a Dutch nor a Belgian nationality yet existed. In the northern provinces the people spoke German dialects; in the southern provinces they spoke dialects of French; but neither here, nor elsewhere in sixteenth-century Europe, was it felt that language boundaries had anything to do with political borders. The southern provinces had for centuries been busy commercial centers, and we have seen how Antwerp, having once flourished in trade with Venice, now flourished in trade with Lisbon. The northern provinces that were most open to the sea, the counties of Holland and Zeeland, had developed rapidly in the fifteenth century. They had a

The Netherlands provinces

popular literature of their own, written in their own kind of German, which came to be called Dutch. The wealth of the northern provinces was drawn from deep-sea fishing. Amsterdam was said to be built on herring bones, and the Dutch, when they added trading to fishing, still lived by the sea.

The northern provinces felt no tie with each other and no sense of difference from the southern provinces. Each of the 17 provinces was a small state or country in itself, and each enjoyed typical medieval liberties and privileges. The only common bond of all 17 provinces was simply that beginning with the acquisitive dukes of Burgundy they had the same ruler. Their adherence to this ruler meant that each province was called upon from time to time to send delegates to the same estates general, and so they developed an embryonic sense of federal collaboration. The feeling of Netherlandish identity was heightened with the accession of Philip II, for Philip, unlike his father, was thought of as foreign, a Spaniard who lived in Spain; and after 1560 Spanish governors general, Spanish officials, and Spanish troops were seen more frequently in the Netherlands. Moreover, since the Netherlands was the crossroads of Europe, with a tradition of earnestness in religion, Protestant ideas took root very early, and after 1560, when religious wars began in France, a great many French Calvinists fled across the borders. At first, there were probably more Calvinists in the southern provinces than in the northern, more among the people whom we now call Belgians than among those whom we now call Dutch.

| *Revolt of the Netherlands* | The Dutch revolt against Philip II was inextricably political and religious at the same time, and it became increasingly an economic struggle as the years went by. It began in 1566, when some 200 nobles |

of the various provinces founded a league to check the "foreign" or Spanish influence in the Netherlands. The league, to which both Catholic and Protestant nobles belonged, petitioned Philip II not to employ the Spanish Inquisition in the Netherlands. They feared the trouble it would stir up; they feared it as a foreign court; they feared that in the enforcement of its rulings the liberties of their provinces would be crushed. Philip's agents in the Netherlands refused the petition. A mass revolt now broke out. Within a week fanatical Calvinists pillaged 400 churches, pulling down images, breaking stained-glass windows, defacing paintings and tapestries, making off with gold chalices, destroying with a fierce contempt the symbols of "popery" and "idolatry." The rank and file for these anti-Catholic and anti-Spanish demonstrations consisted chiefly of journeymen wage earners, whose fury was driven by social and economic grievances as well as religious belief. Before such vandalism the more moderate petitioning nobles recoiled; the Catholics among them, as well as less militant Protestants, unable to control their revolutionary followers, began to look upon the Spanish authorities with less disfavor.

Philip II, appalled at the sacrilege, forthwith sent in the Inquisition, the Duke of Alva, and reinforcements of Spanish troops. Alva's Council of Troubles, nicknamed the Council of Blood, sentenced some thousands to death, levied new taxes, and confiscated the estates of a number of important nobles. These measures united people of all classes in opposition. What might otherwise have been primarily a conflict between social classes now took on the character of a national opposition. At its head emerged one of the noblemen whose estates had been confiscated by Spanish forces, William of Orange (called William the Silent), Philip II's stadholder or lieutenant in the County of Holland. Beginning to claim the authority of a sovereign, William authorized ship captains to make war at sea. Fishing crews, "sea dogs," and downright pirates began to raid the small port towns of the Netherlands and France, descending upon them without warning, desecrating the churches, looting, torturing, and killing, in a wild combination of religious rage, political hatred, and lust for booty. The Spanish reciprocated by renewing their land confiscations, their inquisitorial tortures, and their burnings and hangings. The Netherlands was torn by anarchy, revolution, and civil war. No lines were clear, either political or religious. But in 1576 the anti-Spanish feeling prevailed over religious difference. Representatives of all 17 provinces, putting aside the religious question, formed a union to drive out the Spanish at any cost.

The Involvement of England

But the Netherlands revolution, though it was becoming a national revolution with political independence as its first aim, was only part of the international politico-religious struggle. All sorts of other interests became involved in it. Queen Elizabeth of England lent aid to the Netherlands, though for many years surreptitiously, not wishing to provoke a war with Spain, in which it was feared that English Catholics might side with the Spaniards. *England lends support to the Dutch* Elizabeth was troubled by having on her hands an unwanted guest, Mary Stuart, Queen of Scots. Mary had remained a Catholic and had been queen of France until her husband's premature death, and queen of Scotland until driven out by irate Calvinist lords, and who—if the pope, the king of Spain, the Jesuits, and many English Catholics were to have their way—would also be queen of England instead of the Protestant usurper Elizabeth.[1] Elizabeth under these circumstances kept Mary Stuart imprisoned. Many intrigues were afoot to put Mary on the English throne, some with and some without Mary's knowledge.

In 1576 Don Juan, hero of the Spanish naval victory at Lepanto and half-brother of Philip II, became governor general of the embattled Netherlands. He developed a grandiose plan to subdue the Netherlands and then to use that country as a base for an invasion of England. After overthrowing Elizabeth with Spanish troops, he would put Mary Stuart on the throne, marry her himself, and so become king of a re-Catholicized England. Thus the security of Elizabethan and Protestant England was coming to depend on the outcome of fighting in the Netherlands. Elizabeth signed an alliance with the Netherlands patriots.

Don Juan died in 1578 and was succeeded as governor general of the Netherlands by the prince of Parma. A diplomat as well as a soldier, Parma broke the solid front of the 17 provinces by a mixture of force and persuasion. He promised that the historic liberties of the provinces would be respected, and he appealed not only to the more zealous Catholics but also to moderates who were wearying of the struggle and repelled by mob violence and religious vandalism. On this basis he rallied the southernmost provinces to his side. The seven northern provinces, led by Holland and Zeeland, responded by forming the Union of Utrecht in 1579. In 1581 they formally declared their independence from the king of Spain, calling themselves *The Union of Utrecht* the United Provinces of the Netherlands. Thus originated what was more commonly called the Dutch Republic, or simply "Holland" in view of the predominance of that county among the seven. The great Flemish towns—Antwerp, Ghent, and Bruges—at first sided with the "Dutch" Union.

Where formerly all had been turmoil, a geographical line was now drawn. The south rallying to Philip II now faced a still rebellious north. But neither side accepted any such partition. Parma still fought to reconquer the north, and the Dutch, led by William the

---

[1]Mary Stuart, a great-granddaughter of Henry VII, was the next lawful heir to the English throne after Elizabeth, since Elizabeth had no children.

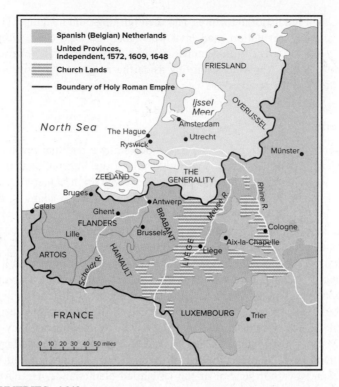

THE LOW COUNTRIES, 1648

This group of towns and provinces, along the lower reaches of the Rhine, Meuse, and Scheldt rivers, originated in the Middle Ages as part of the Holy Roman Empire. The northern or Dutch provinces were recognized as independent of the empire in 1648. Early in the seventeenth century a political frontier emerged between the "Dutch" and "Belgian" parts, but the word "Belgium" was not used until much later, the southern or Habsburg provinces being called the Spanish Netherlands in the seventeenth century and the Austrian Netherlands in the eighteenth. The large bishopric of Liège remained a separate church-state until the French Revolution. The language frontier, then as now, ran roughly east and west somewhat south of Brussels, with French to the south and Flemish (a form of Dutch, and hence Germanic) to the north of the line.

Silent, still struggled to clear the Spanish out of all 17 provinces. Meanwhile the two sides fought to capture the intermediate Flemish cities. When Parma moved upon Antwerp, still the leading port of the North Sea, and one from which an invasion of England could best be mounted, Elizabeth at last openly entered the war on the side of the rebels, sending 6,000 English troops to the Netherlands in 1585.

England was now clearly emerging as the chief bulwark of Protestantism and of anti-Spanish feeling in northwestern Europe. In England itself, the popular fears of Spain, the popular resentment against Catholic plots revolving about Mary Stuart, and the popular indignation at foreign and outside meddling in English matters produced an unprecedented sense of national solidarity. The country rallied to Protestantism and to Elizabeth, and even the Catholic minority for the most part disowned the conspiracies against her. The English were now openly and defiantly allied with the Protestant Dutch. Not only were they

England as bulwark of Protestantism

The vast size of the Spanish naval armada and the English opposition to it are portrayed in this illustration by an unknown artist. Both navies had crosses on the flags of their ships, thereby claiming divine support for their cause and indicating the religious and national stakes in this epic conflict.
(©Universal History Archive/ Getty Images)

fighting together in the Netherlands, but both English and Dutch sea raiders also fell upon Spanish shipping, captured the treasure ships, and even pillaged the mainland coast of northern South America. Elizabeth was negotiating with Scotland, with German Calvinists, and with French Huguenots. At the Escorial it was said that the Netherlands could only be rewon by an invasion of England, that the queen of the heretics must be dethroned, that it was cheaper to launch a gigantic attack upon England than to pay the cost of protecting Spanish galleons year after year against the depredations of piratical sea dogs.

Philip II therefore prepared to invade England. The English retorted with vigor. Mary Stuart, after almost 20 years of imprisonment, was executed in 1587; an aroused Parliament, more than Elizabeth herself, demanded her life on the eve of foreign attack. Sir Francis Drake, most spectacular of the sea dogs, sailed into the port of Cádiz and burned the very ships assembling there to join the Armada. This was jocosely described as singeing the beard of the king of Spain.

The great Armada, the *armada católica,* was ready early in 1588, with crosses on the sails and banners bearing the image of the Holy Virgin. It consisted of 130 ships, weighing 58,000 tons, carrying 30,000 men and 2,400 pieces of artillery—the most prodigious assemblage of naval power that the world had ever seen. The plan was for the fleet to sail to the Netherlands, from which it was to escort the prince of Parma's army across the straits to the English coast.

The Spanish Armada

But the Armada never reached the Spanish army. It was met in the English Channel by some 200 English vessels, which encircled the Spanish fleet near Calais. The English craft—lighter, smaller, and faster, though well furnished with guns—harried the lumbering mass of the Armada, broke up its formations, and attacked its great vessels one by one. It found no refuge at Calais, and English fireships drove it out again to sea. Then arose a great storm, which the English would later call the "Protestant wind." The storm blew the broken Armada northward around the tip of Scotland, the Orkneys, the Hebrides, and northern Ireland—forbidding coasts that the Spaniards had to skirt without charts or pilots or adequate provisions, and which they strewed with their wreckage and their bones.

CHRONOLOGY OF NOTABLE EVENTS, 1492–1648

1492	Christopher Columbus reaches America
1519–1522	Ferdinand Magellan circumnavigates the globe
1519–1533	Spanish conquests of Native American empires in the Americas
1556–1598	Reign of King Philip II in Spain
1562–1598	Religious and civil wars in France
1565	"Manila Galleons" open Spanish trade route between Asia and America
1566	Revolt against Spanish control begins in the Netherlands
1588	Spanish Armada is destroyed off the coast of England and Scotland
1598	King Henry IV issues Edict of Nantes; grants religious rights to French Protestants
1618–1648	The Thirty Years' War in Germany
1648	Peace of Westphalia recognizes system of sovereign European states

The Results of the Struggle

The war for control of the Netherlands went on for several years, even after Philip died in 1598. In the wars with Spain the English had, above all else, assured their national independence. They had acquired an intense national spirit, a love of "this other Eden, demi-paradise," "this precious stone set in the silver sea," as Shakespeare wrote; and they had become more solidly Protestant, almost unanimously set against "popery." With the ruin of the Armada, they were more free to take to the sea; we have seen how the English East India Company was founded in 1600.

Partition of the Netherlands

In the Netherlands, the battle lines swayed back and forth until 1609, when the two sides agreed to a Twelve Years' Truce. By this truce the Netherlands were partitioned. The line of partition ran somewhat farther north than it had in Parma's time, for the Spaniards had retaken Antwerp and other cities in the middle zone. The 7 provinces north of the line, those that had formed the Union of Utrecht in 1579, were henceforth known as Dutch. The 10 provinces south of the line were known as the Spanish Netherlands. Protestants in the south either became Catholics or fled to the north, so that the south (the modern Belgium) became solidly Catholic, while the number of Protestants in the north was increased. Even so, the Dutch were not a completely Protestant people, for probably as many as a third of them remained Catholic. Calvinism was the religion of most Dutch burghers and the religion favored by the state; but in response to an exceptionally large religious minority the Dutch Netherlands adopted a policy of toleration.

The southern Netherlands were ruined by almost 40 years of war. The Dutch, moreover, occupied the mouth of the Scheldt River and refused to allow oceangoing vessels to proceed upstream to Antwerp or to Ghent. The Scheldt remained closed for two centuries, and the Flemish cities never recovered their old position. Amsterdam became the commercial and financial center of northern Europe; it retained its commercial supremacy for a century and its financial supremacy for two centuries. For the Dutch, as for the

English, the weakening of Spanish naval power opened the way to the sea. The Dutch East India Company was organized in 1602. Both the Dutch and the English began to found overseas colonies. The English established a colony in Virginia in 1607, the Dutch launched the colonization of New York in 1612.

As for Spain, while it remained the most formidable military power of Europe for another half-century, its political and economic decline had already begun. At the death of Philip II the monarchy was living from hand to mouth, habitually depending on the next arrival of trea-

The beginnings of Spanish decline

sure from America or the Indies. The productive forces of the country were weakened by inflation, taxation, emigration, and depopulation. At Seville, for example, only 400 looms were in operation in 1621, where there had been 16,000 a century earlier. Spain suffered from the very circumstances that made it great. Qualities that developed in the centuries of religious war and in the reliance upon imported gold or silver from America were not those on which a more modern economy and society could easily be built. Spanish aristocrats were often relatively indifferent to the newer, expanding institutions of European commercial activity, and their attitudes may have influenced the country as a whole. In any case, many of the ablest Spaniards continued to enter the church, and there were few innovations in Spain's political and economic life.

The very unity accomplished under Ferdinand and Isabella threatened to dissolve. After more than a century of the Inquisition people were still afraid of false Christians and crypto-Muslims. The lingering hostility for the Moriscos thus rose again after 1600. The Moriscos included some of the best farmers and most skilled artisans in the country. They lived in almost all parts of

The Moriscos

Spain and were in no sense a "foreign" element, since they were simply the descendants of those Spaniards who, in the Muslim period, which had begun 900 years before, had adopted the Muslim religion and Arabic language and culture. They had later converted to Christianity, but many other Spanish Christians accused them of hiding their anti-Christian beliefs, of preserving in secret the rites of Islam, and of sympathizing with the North African Barbary pirates. They were thought to be clannish, marrying among themselves; and they were so efficient, sober, and hardworking that they outdistanced other Spaniards in competition. In 1609 some 150,000 Moriscos were driven out of Valencia; in 1610 some 64,000 were driven from Aragon; and in 1611 there were also mass expulsions from Castile. About 300,000 people were expelled from the whole of Spain. They were men, women, and children of every age and social level, but all were simply put on boats and sent off with what they could carry. A few Moriscos went to other parts of southern Europe, but most settled in North Africa. Spain, whose total population was rapidly falling in any case, thus passed through another phase of abrupt religious expulsions in which the country lost one of its most productive and socially valuable minorities.

Nor could the diverse territories under Spanish control be held together in peaceable alliance, despite the centralizing projects of the main government minister, the Count of Olivares. Coming to power under King Philip IV in 1621, Olivares sought to curb the independence of the church, increase the king's revenues, control the aristocracy, and send the Spanish army into both the Netherlands and the religious wars in Germany. His policies provoked strong opposition throughout Spain. In 1640 Portugal, which had been joined to the Spanish crown since 1580 when its own ruling line had run out, reestablished its independence. That same year Catalonia rose in an armed rebellion that would continue (with French support) for almost 20 years. Catalonia was at last reconquered, but it managed to preserve its old privileges and separate identity. Castile and Catalonia were now almost as disunited, in spirit and in institutions, as in the days of Isabella and

Ferdinand. They suffered, too, during the seventeenth century from a line of kings whose mental weaknesses reached a stage of extreme incompetence. Meanwhile, however, the might of Spain could still be felt in both Germany and France.

15. THE DISINTEGRATION AND RECONSTRUCTION OF FRANCE

Both France and Germany, in the so-called Wars of Religion, fell into an advanced state of decomposition. France was torn apart by almost 40 years of civil war between 1562 and 1598, while Germany entered a long period of civil troubles that culminated in the Thirty Years' War between 1618 and 1648. From this decomposition France recovered in the seventeenth century, but Germany did not.

Political and Religious Disunity

The Wars of Religion in France, despite the religious savagery shown by partisans of both sides, were also the sixteenth-century recurrence of a long French political struggle. They were essentially a new form of the old phenomenon of feudal rebellion against a higher central authority. "Feudal," in this postmedieval sense, generally refers not to nobles only, but to all sorts of groups having rights within the state, and so includes towns and provinces, and even craft guilds and courts of law, in addition to the church and the noble class. It remained to be seen whether all these elements could be welded into one body politic.

In France the early modern New Monarchy, building on the work of medieval kings, had imposed a certain unity on the country. Normally the country acted as a unit in foreign affairs. The king alone made treaties, and in war his subjects all fought on his side, if they fought at all. Internally, the royal centralization was largely administrative; that is, the king and those who worked for him dealt with subordinate bodies of all kinds, while these subordinate bodies remained in existence with their own functions and personnel. France by the ideas of the time was a very large country. It was three times as large as England and more than four times as populous—roughly 18 million in the sixteenth century. At a time when travelers could move hardly 30 miles a day, it took three weeks of steady plodding to cross the kingdom. Local influence was therefore very strong. Beneath the platform of royalty there was almost as little substantial unity in France as in the Holy Roman Empire. When the empire had 300 states, France had some 300 areas with their own legal systems. Where the empire had free cities, France had *bonnes villes,* the king's "good towns," each with its stubbornly defended corporate rights. Where the empire had middle-sized states like Bavaria, France had provinces as great as some European kingdoms—Brittany, Burgundy, Provence, Languedoc—each ruled by the French king, to be sure, but each with its own identity, autonomy, laws, courts, tariffs, taxes, and parliament or provincial estates. To all this diversity, in France as in Germany, was now added diversity of religion. Calvin himself was by birth and upbringing a Frenchman; and Calvinism spread very rapidly in France during the 1550s.

Nor was France much attached to a papal or international Catholicism. The French clergy had long struggled for its national or Gallican liberties; the French kings had dealt rudely with popes, ignored the Council of Trent, and allied for political reasons with both the Lutherans and the Turks. Since 1516 the king of France had the right to nominate

Centralization vs. localism

the French bishops. The fact that both the French monarchy and clergy already felt independent of Rome held them back from the revolutionary solutions of Protestantism. The Protestantism that eventually spread in France therefore developed without government support and embraced the most radical theological wing of the Reformation, namely Calvinism, which preached at kings, attacked bishops, smashed religious images, and desecrated Catholic churches. Within the main countries that became Protestant—England, north Germany, even the Netherlands—this kind of Protestantism was the doctrine of an extremist minority. In France there was no middle-of-the-road Protestantism, no broad and comfortable Anglicanism, no halfway Lutheranism inspired by governments; and in the long run, as will be seen, the middle of the road was occupied by Catholics.

At first, however, the Huguenots, as the French Calvinists were called, though always a minority, were neither a small group nor modest in their demands. In a class analysis, it is clear that it was chiefly the

The Huguenots

nobility that was attracted to Protestantism, though of course it does not follow that most French Protestants were nobles, since the nobility was a small class. More than a third, and possibly almost a half, of the French nobility was Protestant by the 1560s or 1570s. Frequently the seigneur, or lord of one or more manors, believed that he should have the right to regulate religion on his own estates, as the princes of Germany decided the religion of their own territories. It thus happened that a lord might defy the local bishop, put a Calvinist minister in his village church, throw out the images, simplify the sacraments, and have the service conducted in French. In this way peasants also became Huguenots. Occasionally peasants turned Huguenot without encouragement by the lord. It was chiefly in southwestern France that Protestantism spread as a general movement affecting whole areas. But in all parts of the country, north as well as south, many towns converted to Protestantism. Usually this meant that the bourgeois oligarchy, into whose hands town government had generally fallen, went over to Calvinism and thereupon banned Catholic services. The journeymen wage earners might follow along; or estranged by class differences arising from within the local economy, they might remain attached to their old priests. In general, the unskilled laboring population probably remained the least touched of all classes by Calvinist doctrine.

Both Francis I and Henry II opposed the spread of Calvinism—as did Lutheran and Anglican rulers—for Calvinism, rising spontaneously among laity and reforming ministers, seemed to threaten not only the powers of monarchy but also the very idea of a nationally established

Opposition to Calvinism

church. The fact that in France the nobility, a traditionally ungovernable class, figured prominently in the movement only made it look more like political or feudal rebellion. Persecution of Huguenots, with burnings at the stake, began in the 1550s.

Then in 1559 King Henry II was accidentally killed in a tournament. He left three sons, of whom the eldest in 1559 was only 15. Their mother, Henry's widow, was Catherine de' Medici, an Italian woman who brought to France some of the polish of Renaissance Italy, along with some of its taste for political intrigue, with which she attempted to govern the country for her royal sons. (Their names were Francis II, who died in 1560, Charles IX, who died in 1574, and Henry III, who lasted until 1589.) With no firm hand in control of the monarchy, the country fell apart; and in the ensuing chaos both Catholic and Huguenot factions tried to get control of the youthful monarchs for their own purposes. The Huguenots, under persecution, were too strong a minority to go into hiding. Counting among their number a third or more of the professional warrior class, the nobles, they took naturally and aggressively to arms.

The Civil and Religious Wars

The civil wars in sixteenth-century France were not wars in which one region of a country takes up arms against another, each retaining some apparatus of government, as in the American Civil War or the civil wars of the seventeenth century in England. They were civil wars of the kind fought in the absence of government. Roving bands of armed men, without territorial base or regular means of subsistence, wandered about the country, fighting and plundering, and joining or separating from other similar bands that were quickly formed or quickly dissolved. The changing economic and social conditions of the era detached many people from their old routines and threw them into a life of adventure. The more prominent leaders could thus easily obtain followers, and at the coming of such cohorts the peasants usually took to the woods, while bourgeois townspeople would lock the gates of their cities. Peasants would form protective leagues, like vigilantes; and even small towns maintained diminutive armies.

The Huguenots were led by various personages of rank, such as Admiral de Coligny and Henry of Bourbon, king of Navarre, a small independent kingdom at the foot of the Pyrenees between Spain and France. A pronounced Catholic party arose under the Guise family, headed by the Duke of Guise and the Cardinal of Lorraine. Catherine de' Medici was left in the middle, opposed like all monarchs to Calvinism but unwilling to fall under the domination of the Guises. While the Guises wished to extirpate heresy, they wished even more to govern France. Among the Huguenots some fought for local liberties in religion, while the more ardent spirits hoped to drive "idolatry" and "popery" out of all France, and indeed out of the world itself. Catherine de' Medici for a time tried to play the two parties against each other. But in 1572, fearing the growing influence of Coligny over the king, and taking advantage of a great gathering of influential Huguenots in Paris to celebrate the marriage of Henry of Navarre, she decided to rid herself of the Huguenot

St. Bartholomew's Day massacre

leaders at a single blow. In the resulting massacre of St. Bartholomew's Day some thousands of Huguenots were dragged from their beds after midnight and unceremoniously murdered. Coligny was killed; Henry of Navarre escaped by temporarily changing his religion.

This outrage only aroused Huguenot fury and led to a renewal of civil war throughout the country, with mounting atrocities committed by both sides. The armed bands slaughtered each other and terrorized noncombatants. Both parties hired companies of mercenary soldiers, mainly from Germany. Spanish troops invaded France at the invitation of the Guises. Protestant towns, such as Rouen and La Rochelle, appealed for armed support from Elizabeth of England, but Elizabeth was too preoccupied with her own problems to give more than very sporadic and insignificant assistance. Neither side could subdue the other, and hence there were numerous truces, during which fighting still flared up, since no one had the power to impose peace.

The Politiques

Gradually, mainly among the more perfunctory Catholics, but also among moderate Protestants, there developed still another group who thought of themselves as the "politicals" or *politiques*. The *politiques* concluded that too much was being made of religion, that no doctrine was important enough to justify everlasting war, that perhaps after all there might be room for two churches, and that what the country needed above all else was civil order. Theirs was a secular rather than a religious view. They believed that people lived primarily in the state, not in the church. They were willing to overlook the religious ideas of people in different churches if such persons would simply obey the king and go peaceably about their business. To escape anarchy they put their hopes in the institution of monarchy. Henry of Navarre,

THE ST. BARTHOLOMEW'S DAY MASSACRE

by François Dubois (French, 1529-1584)

This massacre of Protestants in Paris in 1572 sparked further atrocities and massacres by both sides in France's religious wars. As the Huguenot painter François Dubois showed in this portrayal of the killings, the St. Bartholomew's Day Massacre also became an enduring symbol of the brutal conflicts that divided the nation throughout the late sixteenth century.

(©DEA/G. DAGLI ORTI/Getty Images)

now again a Protestant, was at heart a *politique.* Another was the political philosopher Jean Bodin (1530-1596), the first thinker to develop the modern theory of sovereignty. He held that in every society there must be one power strong enough to give law to all others, with their consent if possible, without their consent if necessary. Thus from the disorders of the religious wars in France was germinated the idea of royal absolutism and of the sovereign state.

The End of the Wars: Reconstruction under Henry IV

In 1589 both Henry III, the reigning king, and Henry of Guise, the Catholic party chief who was trying to depose him, were assassinated by a partisan of the other. The throne now came by legal inheritance to the third of the three Henrys, Henry of Navarre, the Huguenot leader who was quite willing to work with Catholics and even to change his religious affiliations. He reigned as Henry IV. Most popular and most amiably remembered of all French kings, except for medieval St. Louis, he was the first of the Bourbon dynasty, which was to last until the French Revolution.

The civil wars did not end with the accession of Henry IV. The Catholic party refused to recognize him, set up a pretender against him, and called in the Spaniards. Henry, the *politique,* sensed that the majority of the French people were still Catholic and that the Huguenots were not only a minority but, after 30 years of civil strife, an increasingly unpopular minority. Paris especially, Catholic throughout the wars, refused to admit the

Henry IV accepts Catholicism

heretic king within its gates. Supposedly remarking that "Paris is well worth a Mass," Henry IV in 1593 publicly abjured the Calvinist faith, and subjected himself to the elaborate processes of papal absolution. Thereupon the *politiques* and less excitable Catholics consented to work with him. The Huguenots, at first elated that their leader should become king, were now not only outraged by Henry's abjuration but also alarmed for their own safety. They demanded positive guarantees for their personal security as well as protection of their religious liberty.

The Edict of Nantes

Henry IV in 1598 responded by issuing the Edict of Nantes. The Edict granted to every seigneur, or noble who was also a manorial lord, the right to hold Protestant services in his own household. It allowed Protestantism in towns where it was in fact the prevailing form of worship, and in any case in one town of each *bailliage* (a unit corresponding somewhat to the English shire) throughout the country; but it barred Protestant churches from Catholic episcopal towns and from a zone surrounding and including the city of Paris. It promised that Protestants should enjoy the same civil rights as Catholics, the same chance for public office, and access to the Catholic universities. In certain of the superior law courts it created mixed chambers of both Protestants and Catholics—somewhat as if a stated minority representation were to be legally required in United States federal courts today. The Edict also gave Protestants their own means of defense, granting them about 100 fortified towns to be held by Protestant garrisons under Protestant command.

The Huguenot minority, reassured by the Edict of Nantes, became less of a rebellious element within the state. The majority of the French people, however, viewed the Edict with suspicion. The parlements, or supreme law courts, of Paris, Bordeaux, Toulouse, Aix, and Rennes all refused to recognize it as the law of the land. It was the king who forced toleration upon the country. He silenced the parlements and subdued Catholic opposition by doing favors for the Jesuits. France's chief religious minority was thus protected by the central government, not by popular wishes. Where in England the Catholic minority had no rights at all, and in Germany the religious question was settled only by cutting the country into small and hostile fragments, in France a compromise was effected, by which the Protestant minority had both individual and territorial rights. A considerable number of French statesmen, generals, and other important persons in the seventeenth century were Protestants.

Henry IV, having appeased the religious controversy, did everything that he could to let the country gradually recover from its decades of civil war. His ideal, as he breezily put it, was a "chicken in the pot" for every Frenchman. He worked also to restore the ruined government, to collect taxes, pay officials, discipline the army, and supervise the administration of justice. Roads and bridges were repaired and new manufactures were introduced under mercantilist principles. Never throughout his reign of 21 years did he summon the Estates General. A country that had just hacked itself to pieces in civil war was scarcely able to govern itself, and so, under Henry IV, the foundations of the later royal absolutism of the Bourbons were laid down.

The foundations of absolutism

Henry IV was assassinated in 1610 by a crazed fanatic who believed him a menace to the Catholic Church. Under his widow, Marie de' Medici, the nobility and upper Catholic clergy again grew restless and forced the summoning of the Estates General, in which so many conflicting and mutually distrustful interests were represented that no program could be adopted. Marie dismissed them in 1615 to the general relief of all concerned. No Estates General of the kingdom as a whole thereafter met until 1789. Remembering the violent chaos of the previous century, most people in France, even many nobles, became more willing to accept a national government that would be conducted by and through the king.

Cardinal Richelieu

In the name of Marie de' Medici and her young son, Louis XIII, the control of affairs gradually came into the hands of an ecclesiastic, Cardinal Richelieu. In the preceding generation Richelieu might have been called a *politique*. It was the state, not the church, whose interests he worked to further. He tried to strengthen the state economically by issuing mercantilist edicts and by allowing nobles to engage in maritime commerce without loss of noble status. He also made it possible for wholesale merchants to become nobles in return for payments into the royal exchequer. Seeking to expand France's international trade, he founded and supported many commercial companies on the Anglo-Dutch model.

For a time, however, it seemed that feuding nobles might cause civil war to break out again. Richelieu therefore prohibited private warfare and ordered the destruction of all fortified castles not manned and needed by the king himself. He even prohibited dueling, a custom

Renewed threat of civil war

much favored by the nobles of the day, but regarded by Richelieu as a mere remnant of private war. The Huguenots, too, with their own towns and their own armed forces under the Edict of Nantes, had become something of a state within the state. In 1627 the Duke of Rohan led a Huguenot rebellion, based in the city of La Rochelle, which received military support from the English. Richelieu after a year suppressed the rebellion and in 1629, by the Peace of Alais, amended the Edict of Nantes. For this highly secularized cardinal of the Catholic Church it was agreeable for the Protestants to keep their religion but not for them to share in the instruments of political power. The Huguenots lost, in 1629, their fortified cities, their Protestant armies, and all their military and territorial rights, but in their religious and civil rights they were not officially disturbed for another 50 years.

The French monarchy, having reestablished its centralizing powers and aspirations after the civil wars, now began to revive the old foreign policy of Francis I, who had opposed on every front the European supremacy of the house of Habsburg. The Spanish power still encircled France at the Pyrenees, in the Mediterranean, in the Free County of Burgundy (the Franche-Comté), and in Belgium. The Austrian branch had pretensions to supremacy in Germany and all central Europe. Richelieu found his opportunity to assail the Habsburgs in the civil and religious struggles that now began to afflict Germany.

16.   THE THIRTY YEARS' WAR, 1618–1648: THE DISINTEGRATION OF GERMANY

The Holy Roman Empire extended from France on the west to Poland and Hungary on the east. It included the Czechs of Bohemia and sizable French-speaking populations in what are now Belgium, Lorraine, eastern Burgundy, and western Switzerland; but with these exceptions the empire consisted of people who spoke various dialects of the German language (see maps, pp. 83, 148–149). For most people at this time, however, language was far less important than religion as the uniting or shared identity of a community; and in religion the empire was almost evenly divided. Where in England, after stabilization set in, Roman Catholics sank to a minority of some 3 percent, and in France the

Huguenots fell in the seventeenth century to not much over 5 percent, in Germany there was no true minority, and hence no majority, and religion gave no foundation for German or imperial unity. Possibly there were more Protestants than Catholics in the empire in 1600, for not only was Protestantism the state religion in many of the 300 states, but individual Protestants were also numerous in the legally Catholic states of the Austrian Habsburgs. Bohemia had a Protestant majority, rooted in the Czech people. Farther east, outside the Holy Roman Empire, the Hungarian nobles were mainly Protestant, and Transylvania, in the elbow of the Carpathian Mountains, was an active center of Calvinism.

German decline

In 1500 Germany had led in many aspects of European life, but by 1600 it had lost much of its former cultural creativity and leadership.

Where both Catholics and Calvinists recognized international affiliations, Lutherans were suspicious of the world outside the Lutheran states of Germany and Scandinavia, and hence suffered from a cultural isolation. The German universities, both Lutheran and Catholic, attracted fewer students than formerly, and their intellectual effort was consumed in combative dogmatics, each side demonstrating the truth of its own ideas. Many of the most deadly, large-scale campaigns against witchcraft took place in the small German states, and more women were burned as witches in Germany than in other countries in western Europe. The commerce of south Germany and the Rhineland was in decay, both because of the shift of trade to the Atlantic and because the Dutch controlled the mouth of the Rhine in their own interests. German bankers, such as the Fuggers, were of slight importance after 1600. Capital was now being formed in the centers of maritime trade.

Background of the Thirty Years' War

The Peace of Augsburg in 1555 had provided that in each state the government could prescribe the religion of its subjects. In general, over the following decades, the Lutherans made considerable gains, putting Lutheran administrators into the church states, or "secularizing" them and converting them into lay principalities. In addition, Calvinism spread into Germany. Though Calvinists had no rights under the Peace of Augsburg, a number of states became Calvinist. One of these was the Palatinate, important because it was strategically placed across the middle Rhine in southwestern Germany, and because its ruler, the Elector Palatine, was one of the seven persons who elected the Holy Roman Emperor. In 1608 the Protestant states, urged on by the Elector Palatine, formed a Protestant union to defend their gains. To obtain support, they negotiated with the Dutch, with the English, and with Henry IV of France. In 1609 a league of Catholic German states was organized by Bavaria. It looked for help from Spain.

Lutheran gains

The Germans were thus falling apart, or rather coming together, into two parties in anticipation of religious conflicts, and each party solicited foreign assistance against the other. Other issues were also maturing. The Twelve Years' Truce between Spain and the Dutch, signed in 1609, was due to expire in 1621. The Spanish (whose international military power was still unaffected by internal decline) were again preparing to crush the Dutch Republic. Since the Dutch insisted on independence, a renewal of the Dutch-Spanish war appeared to be inevitable. The Spanish also wished to consolidate the Habsburg position in central Europe and enhance their access to the Netherlands by gaining control of new territories along the Rhine River and in various Swiss cantons (see map, pp. 148–149).

These Spanish designs in the Rhineland and Switzerland aroused the usual opposition of France. Moreover, the Austrian branch of the Habsburg family was slowly bestirring itself to eradicate Protestantism in its own domains and to turn the Holy Roman Empire into a more modern type of state. The idea of a strong power in Germany was abhorrent to the French. Through its opposition to the Habsburgs, Catholic France was again put in the position of chief protector of Protestantism. France was a giant of Europe, over four times as populous as England, over 10 times as populous as Sweden or the Dutch Republic, incomparably more populous than any single German state. And France after 1600 was at last relatively unified within.

The Thirty Years' War, resulting from all these pressures, was therefore exceedingly complex. It was a German civil war fought over the Catholic-Protestant issue. It was also a German civil war fought over constitutional issues, between the emperor striving to build up the *The complexity of the Thirty Years' War* central power of the empire and the member states struggling to maintain independence. These two civil wars by no means coincided, for Catholic and Protestant states were alike in objecting to imperial control. It was also an international war, between France and the Habsburgs, between Spain and the Dutch, with the kings of Denmark and Sweden and the prince of Transylvania becoming involved, and with all these outsiders finding allies within Germany, on whose soil most of the battles were fought. The wars were further complicated by the fact that many of the generals were soldiers of fortune who aspired to create principalities of their own and who fought or refused to fight whenever it suited their own convenience.

The Four Phases of the War

The fighting began in Bohemia. It is in fact customary to divide the war into four phases, the Bohemian (1618–1625), the Danish (1625–1629), *The Bohemian war* the Swedish (1630–1635), and the Swedish-French (1635–1648).

In 1618 the Bohemians, or Czechs, fearing the loss of their Protestant liberties, dealt with two emissaries from the Habsburg Holy Roman Emperor, Matthias (who was also their king), by a method occasionally used in that country—throwing them out of the window. After this "defenestration of Prague" the king-emperor sent troops to restore his authority, whereupon the Bohemians deposed him and elected a new king. In order to obtain Protestant assistance, they chose the Calvinist Elector Palatine, the head of the Protestant Union, who assumed the title of Frederick V. He brought aid to the Bohemians from the Protestant Union, the Dutch, and the Protestant prince of Transylvania (who was at this time supported by the Ottoman Empire). The Emperor Ferdinand, Matthias's successor, assisted by money from the pope, by Spanish troops sent from Milan, and by the forces of Catholic Bavaria, managed to overwhelm the Bohemians at the battle of the White Mountain in 1620. Frederick fled, jeered or pitied as the "winter king." His ancestral domains in the Palatinate were overrun by the Spaniards who soon moved into southwestern Germany.

The Habsburgs now set out to reconquer and revolutionize Bohemia. The Emperor Ferdinand got himself elected as king of Bohemia and soon confiscated the estates of almost half the Bohemian nobles. He granted these lands as endowments for Catholic churches and monasteries or as gifts to adventurers of all nationalities who had entered his service and who became the new landed aristocracy of Bohemia.

With Protestant fortunes at a low ebb, the Bohemian lands around Prague under Habsburg-Catholic control, and the Protestant Union itself dissolved in 1621, the lead in

A la fin ces Voleurs infames et perdus,   Monstrent bien que le crime (horrible et noirs engeance)   Et que cest le Destin des hommes vicieux
Comme fruits malheureux a cet arbre pendus   Est luy mesme instrument de honte et de vengeance,   Desprouuer tost ou tard la iustice des Cieux.

The violence of the Thirty Years' War in Germany, depicted here in a vivid illustration by Jacques Callot entitled simply *The Hanging Tree* (1633), produced terror, bitter memories, and political divisions in central Europe that lasted long after the fighting finally ended in 1648.
(©Photo 12/Getty Images)

Protestant affairs was now taken by the king of Denmark, who was also Duke of Holstein, a state of the Holy Roman Empire. With a little aid from the Dutch and English, and with promises from Richelieu, he entered the fray. Against him the Emperor Ferdinand raised another army, or, rather, commissioned Albert of Wallenstein to raise one on his own private initiative. Wallenstein assembled a force of professional fighters, of all nationalities, who lived by pillage rather than by pay. His army was his personal instrument, not the emperor's, and he therefore followed a policy of his own, which was so tortuous and well concealed that the name of Wallenstein has always remained an enigma. Wallenstein and other imperial generals soon defeated the king of Denmark, reached the Baltic coast, and even invaded the Danish peninsula.

The full tide of the Counter Reformation now flowed over Germany. Not only was Catholicism again seeping into the Palatinate, and again flooding Bohemia, but it also rolled northward into the inner recesses of the Lutheran states. By the Edict of Restitution, in 1629, the emperor declared all church territories secularized since 1552 automatically restored to the Catholic Church. Some of these territories had been Protestant since the oldest person could remember. Terror swept over Protestant Germany. It seemed that the whole Protestant Reformation, now a century old, might be undone.

French and Swedish alarm

The Habsburg-Catholic advance raised alarms across northern Europe, especially in France and Sweden. Richelieu, however, was still putting down fractious nobles and Huguenots. He had not yet consolidated France to his satisfaction and believed that France, without sending its own armies into military campaigns, could counter the Habsburg ambitions through the use of allies. He sent diplomats to help extricate the king of Sweden from a war with Poland, and he promised him financial assistance, which soon rose to a million livres a year in return for the maintenance in Germany of 40,000 Swedish troops. The Dutch subsidized the Swedes with some 50,000 florins a month.

Gustavus Adolphus

The king of Sweden was Gustavus Adolphus, a ruler of superlative ability, who had extended Swedish holdings on the east shore of the Baltic. Using Dutch and other military experts, he had created the most modern army of the time, noted for its firm discipline, high courage, and mobile cannon. Himself a religious man, he had his troops march to battle singing Lutheran hymns. He was ideally suited to be the Protestant champion, a role he now willingly took up, landing in Germany in 1630. Richelieu, besides giving financial help, negotiated with the Catholic states of Germany, playing on their fears of imperial centralization and seeking to isolate the emperor, against whom the well-disciplined Swedish army was now hurled.

The Swedes, with military aid from Saxony, won a number of spectacular victories, at Breitenfeld in 1631 and Lützen in 1632, where, however, Gustavus Adolphus was killed. His chancellor, Oxenstierna, carried on. The Swedish army penetrated into Bohemia and as far south as the Danube. But the brilliant Swedish victories came to little. Both sides were weakened by disagreement. Wallenstein, who disliked the Spanish influence in Germany, virtually ceased to fight the Swedes and Saxons, with whom he even entered into private talks hoping to create an independent position for himself. He was finally disgraced by the emperor and assassinated by one of his own staff. On the Swedish-Saxon side, the Saxons decided to make a separate peace. Saxony therefore signed with the emperor the Peace of Prague of 1635. The other German Protestant states concurred in it and withdrew their support from the Swedes. The emperor, by largely annulling the Edict of Restitution, allayed Protestant apprehensions. The Swedes were left isolated in Germany. It seemed that the German states were coming together, that the religious wars might be nearing an end. But, in fact, in 1635, the Thirty Years' War was still evolving into a protracted final phase. Neither France nor Spain wished peace or reconciliation in Germany.

Richelieu renewed his assurances of support to the Swedes, hired a German prince-ling, Bernard of Saxe-Weimar, to maintain an army of Germans in the French service, and at last brought Catholic France into open support of the German Protestants.

So the French finally moved toward the Rhine, though not at first with the success for which the French or Protestants had hoped. The Spanish, from their bases in Belgium and Franche-Comté, drove instead *European involvement* deep into France. Champagne and Burgundy were ravaged, and Paris itself was seized with panic. The Spanish also raided the south. The French had a taste of the plunder, murder, burnings, and stealing of cattle by which Germany had been afflicted. But the French soon turned the tables. When Portugal and Catalonia rebelled against Philip IV in 1640, France immediately recognized the independence of Portugal under the new royal house of Braganza—as did England, Holland, and Sweden with equal alacrity. French troops streamed over the Pyrenees into Catalonia, spreading the usual devastation. Richelieu even recognized a Catalan republic.

In Germany this last Swedish-French phase of the war was not so much a civil war among Germans as an international struggle on German soil. Few German states now sided with the French and Swedes. A feeling of national resentment against foreign invasion even seemed to develop.

The Peace of Westphalia, 1648

Peace talks began in 1644 in Westphalia, at the two towns of Münster and Osnabrück. The German states were crying for peace, for a final religious settlement, and for reform of the Holy Roman Empire. France and Sweden insisted that the German states should individually take part in the negotiations, a disintegrating principle that the German princes eagerly welcomed and which the emperor vainly resisted. Hundreds of diplomats joined the protracted negotiations in Westphalia, representing the empire, its member states,

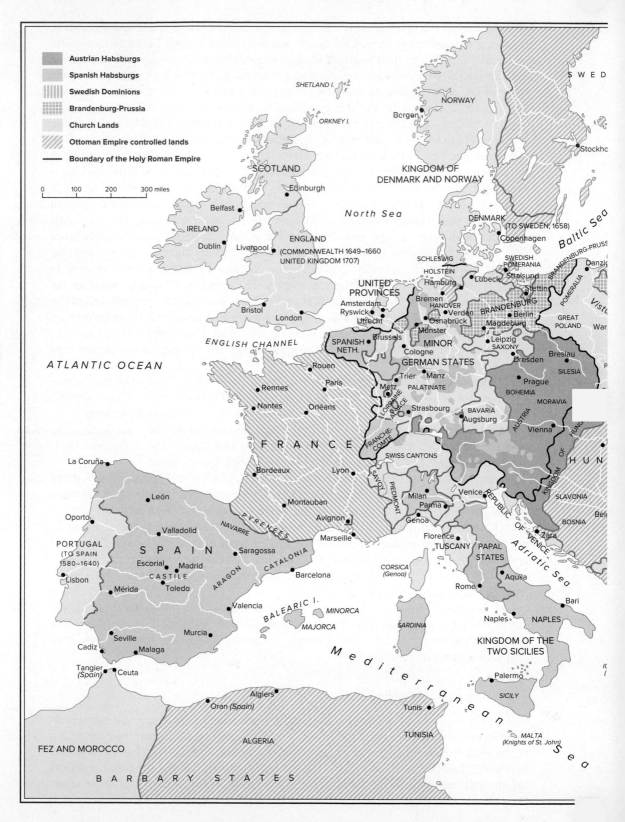

Austrian Habsburgs

Spanish Habsburgs

Swedish Dominions

Brandenburg-Prussia

Church Lands

Ottoman Empire controlled lands

Boundary of the Holy Roman Empire

0   100   200   300 miles

SHETLAND I.

ORKNEY I.

NORWAY

Bergen

KINGDOM OF
DENMARK AND NORWAY

SWED

Stockho

SCOTLAND

Edinburgh

North Sea

DENMARK

(TO SWEDEN, 1658)

Copenhagen

Baltic Sea

Belfast

IRELAND

Dublin   Liverpool

Bristol

ENGLAND
(COMMONWEALTH 1649–1660
UNITED KINGDOM 1707)

London

SCHLESWIG

HOLSTEIN

Hamburg   Lübeck

SWEDISH
POMERANIA

Stralsund

Stettin

BRANDENBURG-PRUSS

Danzig

Vistu

UNITED
PROVINCES

Amsterdam
Ryswick
Utrecht

Bremen
HANOVER
Verden
Osnabrück
Münster

POMERANIA

BRANDENBURG

Berlin

GREAT
POLAND

War

Magdeburg

ENGLISH CHANNEL

SPANISH
NETH.

Brussels

Cologne

MINOR
GERMAN STATES

Leipzig
SAXONY

Dresden

Breslau

SILESIA

ATLANTIC OCEAN

Rouen

Paris

Metz

Trier   Manz

PALATINATE

Prague

BOHEMIA

MORAVIA

Rennes

Nantes

Orléans

LORRAINE
ALSACE

Strasbourg

BAVARIA
Augsburg

AUSTRIA

Vienna

KINGDOM OF HUN

H U N

F R A N C E

FRANCHE-
COMTÉ

SWISS CANTONS

SAVOY

PIEDMONT

SLAVONIA

La Coruña

León

Bordeaux

Lyon

Milan

Parma

Venice

REPUBLIC OF VENICE

BOSNIA

Bel

Oporto

Valladolid

Montauban

Avignon

Genoa

Adriatic Sea

Zara

NAVARRE

PYRENEES

Marseille

Florence

TUSCANY

PAPAL
STATES

PORTUGAL
(TO SPAIN
1580–1640)

Lisbon

S P A I N

Escorial   Madrid

CASTILE

Mérida   Toledo

Saragossa

ARAGON

CATALONIA

Barcelona

*CORSICA
(Genoa)*

Rome

Aquila

Bari

Valencia

BALEARIC I.   *MINORCA*

MAJORCA

SARDINIA

Naples   NAPLES

Seville   Murcia

Cadiz   Malaga

Tangier
(Spain)   Ceuta

KINGDOM OF THE
TWO SICILIES

Palermo

SICILY

M e d i t e r r a n e a n

Algiers

Oran *(Spain)*

FEZ AND MOROCCO

ALGERIA

Tunis

TUNISIA

MALTA
(Knights of St. John)

Sea

B A R B A R Y   S T A T E S

EUROPE, 1648

This map shows the European states at the time of the Peace of Westphalia. A plurality of independent sovereign states was henceforth considered normal. The plurality of religions was also henceforth taken for granted within Europe as a whole, though each state continued to require or favor religious uniformity within its borders. By weakening the Habsburgs and furthering the disintegration of Germany, the Peace of Westphalia opened the way for a (short-term) seventeenth-century expansion of the Ottoman Empire in southeastern Europe and the later political ascendancy of France.

Spain, France, Sweden, the Dutch, the Swiss, the Portuguese, the Venetians, numerous other Italians, and the pope. There had been no such European congress since the Council of Constance, and the fact that a European assemblage had in 1415 dealt with affairs of the church, and now in the 1640s dealt with affairs of the state, war, and power, was a measure of the secularization that had come over Europe.

Lengthy peace negotiations

The negotiations dragged on, because the armies were still fighting, and after each battle one side or the other raised its terms. France and Spain refused to make peace with each other at all and in fact remained at war until 1659. But for the Holy Roman Empire a settlement was reached in 1648 in the two treaties of Münster and Osnabrück, which became commonly known as the Peace of Westphalia.

The Peace of Westphalia represented a general checkmate to the Catholic Counter Reformation in Germany. It not only renewed the terms of the Peace of Augsburg, granting each German state the right to determine its own religion, but it also added Calvinism to Lutheranism and Catholicism as an acceptable faith. On the controversial issue of church territories secularized after 1552 the Protestants won a complete victory; Catholic claims to the territories were abandoned.

Dissolution of the Holy Roman Empire

The dissolution of the Holy Roman Empire, which had been advanced by the drawing of internal religious frontiers in the days of Luther, was now confirmed in politics and international law. Borderlands of the empire fell away. The Dutch and Swiss ceased to belong to it, and both the United Provinces and Swiss cantons (or Helvetic Body) were recognized as sovereign and independent. From the disintegrating western frontier of the Holy Roman Empire the French cut off small pieces, receiving permanent sovereignty over three Lorraine bishoprics and certain rights in Alsace. The king of Sweden received new territories in northern Germany, thus adding to Sweden's trans-Baltic possessions; and Spain finally recognized the independence of the Dutch Republic.

Germany fragmented

It was in the new constitution of the empire itself, not in territorial changes, that the greatest victory of the French and their Swedish and Dutch allies was to be found. The German states, over 300 in number, became virtually sovereign. Each received the right to conduct diplomacy and make treaties with foreign powers. The Peace of Westphalia further stipulated that no laws could be made by the empire, no taxes could be raised, no soldiers could be recruited, no war could be declared or peace terms ratified except with the consent of the imperial estates—the 300-odd princes, ecclesiastics, and free cities in the Reichstag assembled. Since it was well known that agreement on any such matters was impossible, the principle of self-government, or of medieval constitutional liberties, was used to destroy the empire itself as an effective political entity. While most other European countries were consolidating under royal absolutism, Germany sank back toward fragmentation and localism.

The Peace of Westphalia blocked the Counter Reformation, frustrated the Austrian Habsburgs, and forestalled for almost two centuries any movement toward German national unification. Within Europe as a whole, however, it marked the advent in interna-

System of sovereign states

tional law of the modern system of sovereign states. The diplomats who assembled at Westphalia represented independent powers that recognized no superior or common tie. No one any longer pretended that Europe had any significant religious or political unity. Statesmen delighted in the absence of any such unity, in which they sensed the menace of "universal monarchy." Europe was understood to consist of a large number of unconnected sovereignties, free and detached states, which acted according to their own laws, following their own political interests, forming and dissolving alliances, exchanging embassies and legations, alternating between war and peace, and shifting positions within a shifting balance of power.

Physically Germany was wrecked by the Thirty Years' War. Cities were sacked by mercenary soldiers with a rapacity that their commanders could not control; or the commanders themselves, drawing no supplies from their home governments, systematically looted whole areas to maintain their armies. Magdeburg was besieged ten times; Leipzig, five. In one woolen town of Bohemia, with a population of 6,000 before the wars, the citizens fled and disappeared, the houses collapsed, and eight years after the peace only 850 persons were found there. The peasants, murdered, put to flight, or tortured by soldiers to reveal their few valuables, ceased to farm; agriculture was ruined; starvation followed, and with it came pestilence. Even revised modern estimates allow that in many extensive parts of Germany as much as a third of the population may have perished. The effects of fire, disease, undernourishment, homelessness, and exposure in the seventeenth century were terrible because of the lack of means to combat them. The horrors that civilians have suffered in modern wars are thus not wholly different from horrors that men and women experienced in the past.

Germany as such, physically wrecked and politically cut into small pieces, ceased for a long time to play any significant part in European affairs. A kind of political and cultural vacuum existed in central Europe. On the one hand, the western or Atlantic peoples—French, English, Dutch—began in the seventeenth century to take the lead in European politics, trade, and culture. On the other hand, in eastern Germany, around Berlin and Vienna, new and only half-German centers of power began to form. These themes will be traced in the two following chapters.

With the close of the Thirty Years' War the Wars of Religion came to an end. While religion remained an issue in some later conflicts and within some countries, it was never again an important cause of conflicts in the transnational political affairs of Europe as a whole. In general, by the close of the seventeenth century, the division between Protestant and Catholic had become stabilized. Neither side any longer expected to make territorial gains at the expense of the other. Both the Protestant and the Catholic reformations were accomplished facts. The political struggle for territory, wealth, and strategic alliances had become secularized in that "reasons of state" now prevailed over religious allegiances in shaping both the foreign policies of governments and the military conflicts of sovereign powers.

 Suggested Further Readings can be found in the ebook, on Connect, or online at www.mhhe .com/kramer12e.

Chapter 4

THE GROWING POWER OF WESTERN EUROPE, 1640–1715

If the reader were to take a map of Europe, set a compass on the city of Paris, and draw a circle with a radius of 500 miles, a zone would be marked out from which much of modern European and "Western" civilization radiated after about 1640. It was within this zone that a secular society, modern natural science, global capitalism, the modern state, parliamentary government, democratic ideas, machine industry, and much else either originated or received their first full expression over the following 250 years. The extreme western parts of Europe—Ireland, Portugal, and Spain—were somewhat outside the zone in which the most rapid changes occurred. But within it were England, southern Scotland, France, the Low Countries, Switzerland, western and central Germany, and northern Italy. This area, beginning in the seventeenth century, was for more than two centuries the earth's principal center of what anthropologists might call cultural diffusion. Although the economy and culture of western Europe were deeply influenced by the expanding trade and contacts with people outside Europe, the growing power of western European states, trading companies, science, and cultural institutions had a profound and spreading impact on the rest of Europe, the Americas, and ultimately the whole world.

This western European influence grew steadily in the half-century following the Peace of Westphalia. The fading out of the Italian Renaissance, the subsiding of religious wars, the ruin of the Holy Roman Empire, and the decline of Spain all cleared the stage on which the Dutch, English, and French were to become the principal political, economic, and cultural actors. But the Dutch were few in number, and the English during most of the seventeenth century were weakened by domestic discord. It was France that for a time played the most imposing role. The whole half-century of European history following the Peace of Westphalia is in fact often called the Age of Louis XIV.

Chapter emblem: Detail from a portrait of King Louis XIV by Hyacinthe Rigaud (1659–1743). (Universal History Archive/Getty Images)

17.   THE *GRAND MONARQUE*
AND THE BALANCE OF POWER

This king of France inherited his throne in 1643 at the age of 5, assumed the personal direction of affairs in 1661 at the age of 23, and reigned for 72 years until his death in 1715. No one else in modern history has held so powerful a position for so long a time. Louis XIV was more than a figurehead. For over half a century, during his whole adult life, he was the actual and working head of the French government. Inheriting the state institutions that Richelieu had developed earlier in the seventeenth century, he made France the strongest country in Europe. Using French money, by bribes or other induce-ments, he built up pro-French groups in virtually every country from England to Turkey. His policies and the counterpolicies that others adopted against him (for he also provoked opposition throughout Europe) set the pace of public events, and his methods of govern-ment and administration, war and diplomacy, became a model for other rulers to copy. During this time the French language, French thought and literature, French architecture and landscape gardens, and French styles in clothes, cooking, and etiquette became the accepted standard for Europe. Louis XIV was called by his fascinated admirers Louis the Great, the *Grand Monarque,* and the Sun King.

Internationally, the consuming political question of the last decades of the seventeenth century (at least in western Europe—eastern Europe we reserve for the next chapter) was

The weakness of Spain

the fate of the still vast possessions of the Spanish crown. Spain was drifting into a condition that nineteenth-century western Europeans would later ascribe to Turkey, "the sick man of Europe." To its social and economic decline was added the hereditary physical deterioration of its rulers. In 1665 the Spanish throne was inherited by Charles II, an incompetent ruler afflicted by many ills of mind and body, impotent, mentally deficient, the pitiable product of generations of intermarriage among various branches of the extended Habsburg family. His rule was irresolute and feeble. It was known from the moment of his accession that he could have no children and that the Spanish branch of the Habsburg family would die out with his death. The whole future not only of Spain but also of the Spanish Nether-lands, the Spanish holdings in Italy, and all Spanish America was therefore in question. Charles II dragged out his miserable days until 1700, the object of jealousy and outright assault during his lifetime, and precipitating a new European war by his death.

The ambitions of Louis XIV

Louis XIV, who in his youth married a sister of Charles II, intended to benefit from the debility of his royal brother-in-law. His expansionist policies followed two main lines. One was to push the French borders eastward to the Rhine, annexing the Spanish Netherlands (which later became Belgium) and the Franche-Comté or Free County of Burgundy, a French-speaking region lying between ducal Burgundy and Switzerland (see maps, pp. 148–149, 155). Such policies along France's eastern frontier involved the further dismemberment of the Holy Roman Empire. The other line of Louis XIV's ambitions, increasingly clear as time went on, was his hope of obtaining the entire Spanish inheritance for himself. By combining the resources of France and Spain he would make France supreme in Europe, in America, and on the sea. To promote these ends Louis XIV intrigued with the smaller and middle-sized powers of Europe and also contacted dissidents (i.e., potential allies) in all the coun-tries whose governments opposed him.

If Louis XIV had achieved his aims, he would have created the "universal monarchy" dreaded by diplomats, that is to say, a political situation in which one state might

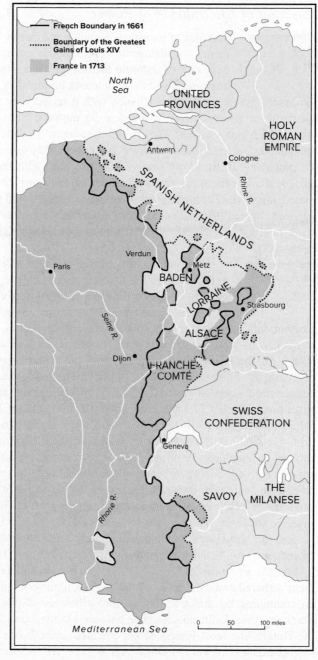

THE EXPANSION OF FRANCE, 1661–1713

The map shows how the foreign policy and wars of King Louis XIV gradually extended France's borders toward the east and north-east, bringing the Franche-Comté and new lands in both Alsace and Lorraine under French control. Louis also gained other territories in the Spanish Netherlands and expanded French holdings in the south along the frontier with Savoy. In addition to the expansion shown here, Louis XIV's other great ambition was to obtain control of Spain and the Spanish Empire in the Americas.

subordinate all others to its will. The technique used against universal monarchy was the balance of power. Universal monarchy had formerly been almost achieved in Europe by the Austro-Spanish Habsburgs. The Habsburg supremacy had been blocked mainly by a balance of power headed by France, for which the Thirty Years' War and the Peace of Westphalia were the outstanding triumphs. Now, in the later seventeenth century, the danger of universal monarchy came from France, and it was against France that the balance of power was directed.

The Idea of the Balance of Power

The aim of statesmen pursuing policies of balance of power in the seventeenth and eighteenth centuries was generally to preserve their own independence of action to the utmost. Hence the basic rule was to ally against any powerful state threatening domination. If one state seemed to dictate too much, others would shun alliance with it unless they were willing (from ideological sympathy or other reasons) to become its puppets. They would seek alliance with the other weaker states instead. They would thus create a balance or counterweight, or "restore the balance," against the state whose ascendancy they feared. Another more subtle reason for preferring alliance with the weak rather than with the strong was that in such an alliance the leaders of each state could believe their own contribution to be necessary and valued, and by threatening to withdraw their support could win consideration of their own interests. Indeed, the balance of power may be defined as a system in which each state tends to throw its weight where it is most needed, so that its own importance may be enhanced.

The purpose of balance-of-power politics was not to preserve peace but to preserve the sovereignty and independence of the states of Europe, or the "liberties of Europe," as they were called, against potential aggressors. The system was effective as a means to protect most sovereign governments in the seventeenth and eighteenth centuries. Combinations were intricate, and alliances were readily made and unmade to deal with emerging situations. One reason for the effectiveness of the system lay in the great number of states capable of pursuing an independent foreign policy. These included not only the greater and middle-sized states of Austria, Spain, France, England, Holland, Sweden, and Bavaria, but a great number of small independent states, such as Denmark, the German principalities, Portugal after 1640, and Savoy, Venice, Genoa, and Tuscany. States moved easily from one alliance to another or from one side of the balance to another. They were held back by no ideologies or historic sympathies, especially after the religious wars subsided, but could freely choose or reject allies, aiming only to protect their own independence or enlarge their own interests. Moreover, owing to the military technology of the day, small states might count as important military partners in an alliance. By controlling a strategic location, like the king of Denmark, or by making a contribution of ships or money, like the Dutch Republic, they might add just enough strength to an alliance to balance and overbalance the opposing great power and its allies.

As the ambitions of Louis XIV became bolder, and as the capacity of Spain to resist them withered away, the prevention of a French universal monarchy depended increasingly on combining the states of Europe into a balance of power that could effectively block France's expansionist policies. The balance against Louis XIV was engineered mainly by the Dutch. The most tireless of his enemies, and the one who did more than any other to checkmate him, was the Dutchman William III, the prince of Orange, who in his later years was king of England and Scotland as well.

Beginning with a survey of the influential Dutch role in seventeenth-century global affairs, we shall examine the leading western European powers of the era. Each power went through long, disruptive conflicts, which included a momentous struggle between Parliament and king in the British Isles and the protracted wars of Louis XIV. These wars, culminating in the War of the Spanish Succession, mobilized a collective resistance to French ambitions that ultimately restored the European balance of power.

18.   THE DUTCH REPUBLIC

Dutch Culture and Government

The ambassadors of kings, strolling beside a canal at The Hague, might on occasion observe a number of burghers in plain black garments step out of a boat on to a well-maintained Dutch lawn, and they would recognize in these serious, black-clad figures the provincial delegates of the Estates General of the United Provinces, as the Dutch government was known in the diplomatic language of the day. Though noblemen lived in the country, the Dutch were the most bourgeois of all peoples. They were not the only republicans in Europe, because the Swiss cantons, Venice, Genoa, and even England for a few years were republics, but of all republics the United Provinces was by far the most wealthy, the most flourishing, and the most important in international diplomacy and culture.

The Dutch acquired a nationality of their own in the long struggle against Spain, and the memories of that war contributed to a pride in their own freedom and independence. In the later phases of the war with Spain, notably during the Thirty Years' War, they were able to rely more on their wealth and diplomacy than on actual fighting, so that during the whole seventeenth century they enjoyed a degree of comfort, and of intellectual, artistic, and commercial achievement unexcelled in Europe. The classic Dutch poets and dramatists wrote at this time, making a literary language of what had formerly been a dialect of Low German. Hugo Grotius produced, in his *Law of War and Peace* (1625), a pioneering treatise on international law. Baruch Spinoza (1632–1677) who grew up in family of refugee Portuguese Jews in Amsterdam, quietly turned out works of philosophy, examining the nature of material reality, of God, of human ethics, and religious institutions. Spinoza questioned inherited religious beliefs, but he made his living by grinding lenses; there were many other lens grinders in Holland; some of them developed the microscope, and some of these, in turn—Leeuwenhoek, Swammerdam, and others—peering through their microscopes and beholding for the first time the world of microscopic life, became founders of modern biological science. The greatest Dutch scientist was Christian Huyghens (1629–1695), who worked mainly in physics and mathematics; he improved the telescope (a Dutch invention), made clocks move with pendulums, discovered the rings of Saturn, and launched the wave theory of light. A less famous writer, Balthasar Bekker, in his *World Bewitched* (1691) delivered a decisive blow against the expiring superstition of witchcraft. Meanwhile, the extraordinarily learned scholar and artist Anna Maria van Schurman (1607–1678) developed an important seventeenth-century argument for the education of women in her influential treatise *The Learned Maid or Whether a Maid May Be Called a Scholar* (1638).

Dutch achievements

But the most eternally fresh of the Dutch creations, suffering from no barrier of time or language, were the superb canvases of the painters. Frans Hals produced bluff portraits of the common people. Jan Vermeer threw a spell of magic and quiet dignity over men, and especially women, of the burgher class, many of whom he portrayed in typical domestic scenes. Rembrandt conveyed the mystery of human consciousness itself. In Rembrandt's *Masters of the Amsterdam Drapers' Guild* (see p. 158) we face a group of six men who seem about to speak from the canvas, inclined slightly forward, as intent on their business as judges on the proceedings in a courtroom. Such men conducted the affairs of Holland, in both commerce and government; intelligent, calculating, and honest but determined to drive a hard bargain; the sober black cloaks, with the clean white collars,

THE MASTERS OF THE AMSTERDAM DRAPERS' GUILD
by Rembrandt van Rijn (Dutch, 1606–1669)
This painting was done on commission for the guild of drapers or "clothiers" in Amsterdam. These men were the prosperous leaders of the guild; and they were members of a dynamic merchant class that supported both a flourishing community of creative artists and the expanding Dutch role in global commercial systems.
(Source: Rijksmuseum, Amsterdam)

set against the carved woodwork and rich table covering of the Cloth Hall, seem to suggest that personal vanity must yield to collective undertakings and that personal simplicity must be maintained in the midst of material opulence. And in Vermeer's *Geographer* (see p. 163), painted in 1669, there appears not only an immaculately scrubbed Dutch interior, but something of a symbol of the early modern world—the pale northern sunlight streaming through the window, the globe and the map, the dividers in the scholar's right hand, instrument of science and mathematics, the tapestry flung over the table (or is it a new rug brought from Asia?), the head lifted in thought, and eyes resting on an invisible world of fresh discoveries and opening horizons. The same interest in the complexities of human character and the details of household objects appears in many of Vermeer's paintings, including *Girl Reading a Letter at an Open Window* (see p. 160), which he painted in the late 1650s, and *The Milkmaid* (c. 1660, see p. 161). Like other Dutch artists in this era, Vermeer discovered and portrayed the aesthetic pleasures in the common experiences of daily life.

Dutch paintings also showed certain characteristics of the wider seventeenth-century artistic style that came to be known as Baroque. The fascination with lighting, the representation of interior spaces, the use of distinctive colors or subtle hues, and a more naturalistic image of human beings often shaped the distinctive appearance of Baroque paintings. In contrast to most Dutch artists, however, many of the best-known Baroque painters identified with the Catholic Church or the Counter Reformation. The Flemish painter

PORTRAIT OF THE ARTIST WITH ISABELLE BRANT
by Peter Paul Rubens (Flemish, 1577–1640)

Isabelle Brant married Rubens about the time he painted this dual portrait (c. 1610), which conveys the affection in an early seventeenth-century marriage. This painting suggests the importance of family relationships for an artist whose best-known works often portrayed famous public figures or Catholic religious themes.

(©Print Collector/Getty Images)

Peter Paul Rubens was one prominent example of this identification with Catholicism in the Low Countries (though the portrait on this page depicts his personal life). Rubens often painted influential Catholic political figures as well as dramatic biblical scenes, but art in the Netherlands tended to emphasize the quotidian scenes of urban life rather than the passions of religious ecstasy or the grandeur of royal families.

In religion, after initial disputes, the Dutch Republic adopted toleration. Early in the seventeenth century the Dutch Calvinists divided. One group favored a modification of Calvinism, with a toning down of the doctrine of absolute predestination. This more moderate Calvinism drew its main support from the comfortable burghers and its doctrines from a theologian of Leyden

Religious toleration

WOMAN READING A LETTER AT AN OPEN WINDOW
by Jan Vermeer (Dutch, 1632–1675)
Vermeer's characteristic interest in the mysteries of human character, the subtle shades of light, and the complex folds of a curtain appear in this painting of a young woman who seems to have received a disconcerting message or perhaps long anticipated news from afar.
(©Heritage Images/Getty Images)

named Arminius, whose ideas were condemned at an international Calvinist synod in 1618. But beginning in 1632 the Arminians were tolerated. Rights were granted to the large Catholic minority. Jews had long been welcomed in the republic; and Christian sects despised everywhere else, such as the Mennonites, found a refuge in Dutch towns. Although none of these people had as many political or economic rights as the Calvinists, the resulting mixture stimulated both the intellectual life and the commercial enterprise of the country.

THE MILKMAID
by Jan Vermeer (Dutch, 1632–1675)
This portrayal of a woman pouring milk and preparing food at a table shows Vermeer's fascination with the activities of daily life, which he represented with remarkable attention to details, respect for the humanity of the working woman, and the simplicity of a well-lighted Dutch room.
(Source: Johannes Vermeer/Rijksmuseum Amsterdam)

The Dutch as early as 1600 had 10,000 ships, and throughout the seventeenth century they owned most of the shipping of northern Europe. They were the carriers between Spain, France, England, and the Baltic. They also settled in Bordeaux to buy wines, lent money to vintners, and soon owned many vineyards in France itself. They sailed on every sea. They entered the Pacific by way of South America, where they rounded Cape Horn and named it after Hoorn in Holland. Organized in the East India Company of

Dutch explorations and settlements

1602, their merchants increasingly replaced the Portuguese in India and the Far East. In Java, in 1619, they founded the city of Batavia—the Latin name for Holland. (The city is now called Jakarta.)

Not long after 1600 the Dutch reached Japan. But the Japanese, fearing the political consequences of Christian traders, in 1641 expelled all other Europeans and confined the Dutch to limited operations on an island near Nagasaki. The Dutch remained for over two centuries the sole link of the West with Japan. In 1612 the Dutch founded their first settlement on Manhattan Island, and in 1621 they established a Dutch West India Company to exploit the loosely held riches of Spanish and Portuguese America. The new West India company also entered the expanding Atlantic slave trade and transported enslaved Africans to recently founded Dutch colonies at Pernambuco and Bahia in Brazil (lost soon thereafter) and at Curaçao and Guiana in the Caribbean. In 1652 the Dutch captured the Cape of Good Hope in South Africa from the Portuguese. Dutch settlers soon appeared. Moving inland, they occupied the territory of the Khoikhoi and displaced or enslaved the people whose ancestors had lived there for centuries. These Dutch settlers mixed with French Huguenots and others in southern Africa and gradually became the Afrikaner people, whose modern language and religion still reflect their mainly Dutch origins.

The Bank of Amsterdam

In 1609 the Dutch founded the Bank of Amsterdam. European money was in chaos; coins were minted not only by great monarchs but also by small states and cities in Germany and Italy, and even by private persons. In addition, under inflationary pressures, kings and others habitually debased their coins by adding more alloy, while leaving the old coins in circulation along with the new. Anyone handling money thus accumulated a miscellany of uncertain value. The Bank of Amsterdam accepted deposits of such mixed money from all persons and from all countries, assessed the gold and silver content, and, at rates of exchange fixed by itself, allowed depositors to withdraw equivalent values in gold florins minted by the Bank of Amsterdam. These were of known and unchanging weight and purity. They thus became an internationally sought money, an international measure of value, acceptable everywhere. Depositors were also allowed to draw checks against their accounts. These conveniences, plus a safety of deposits guaranteed by the Dutch government, attracted capital from all quarters and made possible loans for a wide range of purposes. Amsterdam remained the financial center of Europe until the French Revolution.

Under their republican government the Dutch enjoyed great freedom, but it can hardly be said that their government met all the requirements of a modern democratic state. The seven provinces that sent representatives to the Estates General of the United Provinces were all jealous of their own independence. Each province had, as its executive, an elected stadholder, but there was no stadholder for the United Provinces as a whole. This difficulty was overcome by the fact that most of the various provinces usually elected the head of the house of Orange as their own stadholder. This family had enjoyed exceptional prestige in the republic since the days of William the Silent and the wars for independence, but the prince of Orange, apart from being stadholder, was simply one of the traditional noblemen of the country. In general, however, the commercial class had more wealth than the older noble families, and affairs were usually managed by the burghers.

Politics in the Dutch Republic was a seesaw between the burghers, pacifistic and absorbed with business, and the princes of Orange, to whom the country owed most of

THE GEOGRAPHER

by Jan Vermeer (Dutch, 1632–1675)

The impact on Europe of the opening of the Atlantic may be seen in this painting. For the first time in human history it had become possible to understand with some accuracy the relationships of the oceans and continents around the globe. The Dutch built up a large ocean-going trade, and many of the leading cartographers lived in the Netherlands.

(©DEA PICTURE LIBRARY/Getty Images)

its military security. When foreigners threatened invasion, the power of the stadholder increased. When all was calm, the stadholder could do little. The Peace of Westphalia produced a mood of confidence in the burghers, followed by a constitutional crisis, in the course of which the stadholder William II died, in 1650. No new stadholder was elected for 22 years. The burgher, civilian, and decentralizing tendencies prevailed.

In 1650, eight days after his father's death, the third William was born in the house of Orange, seemingly fated never to be stadholder and to pass his life as a private noble-man on his own estates. William III grew up to be a grave and reserved young man, small and rather stocky, with a determined spirit. He learned to speak Dutch, German, English,

William of Orange

and French with equal facility and to understand Italian, Spanish, and Latin. He observed the requirements of his religion, which was Dutch Calvinism, with sober regularity. He had a strong dislike for everything magnificent or pompous; he lived plainly, hated flattery, and took no pleasure in social conversation. In these respects he was the opposite of his lifelong enemy the Sun King, whom he resembled only in his diligent preoccupation with affairs. In 1677 William married the king of England's niece, Mary Stuart.

Foreign Affairs: Conflict with the English and French

Meanwhile matters were not going favorably for the Dutch Republic. In 1651 the revolutionary government then ruling England passed a Navigation Act. This act may be considered the first of a long series of political measures by which the British began to build their colonial empire. It was aimed against the Dutch carrying trade. It provided that goods imported into England and its dependencies must be transported on English ships or on ships belonging to the country exporting the goods. Because the Dutch were too small a

Threats by sea and land

people to be great producers and exporters themselves, and lived largely by carrying the goods of others, they saw in the new English policy a threat to their economic existence. The Dutch and English soon entered into a series of three wars, running with interruptions from 1652 to 1674 and generally indecisive, though in 1664 the English annexed New Amsterdam and renamed it New York.

While thus assaulted at sea by the English, the Dutch were menaced on land by the French. Louis XIV made his first aggressive move in 1667, claiming the Spanish Netherlands and Franche-Comté by alleging certain rights of his Spanish wife, and overrunning the Spanish Netherlands with his army. The Dutch, to whom the Spanish Netherlands were a buffer against France, set into motion the mechanism of the balance of power. Dropping temporarily their disputes with the English, they allied with them instead; and because they were able also to secure the adherence of Sweden, the resulting Triple Alliance was sufficient to give pause to Louis XIV, who withdrew from the Spanish Netherlands. But in 1672 Louis XIV again rapidly crossed the Spanish Netherlands, attacked with forces five times as large as the Dutch, and occupied three of the seven Dutch provinces.

The election of William as stadholder

A popular clamor now arose among the Dutch for William of Orange, demanding that the young prince, who was 22 years of age, be installed in the old office of stadholder, in which his ancestors had defended them against Spain. He was duly elected stadholder in six provinces. In 1673 these six provinces voted to make the stadholderate hereditary in the house of Orange. William, during his whole "reign" in the Netherlands, attempted to centralize and consolidate his government, put down the traditional liberties of the provinces, and move generally in the direction of absolute monarchy. He was unable, however, to go far in this course, and the United Provinces remained a decentralized patrician republic until 1795.

Meanwhile, to stave off the immediate menace of Louis XIV, William resorted to a new manipulation of the balance of power. He formed an alliance this time with the minor powers of Denmark and Brandenburg (the small German state around Berlin) and with the Austrian and Spanish Habsburgs. Nothing could indicate more clearly the new European concern about the balance of power than this coming over of the Dutch to the Habsburg side. This alliance presented a forceful new challenge to Louis XIV and pushed him into negotiations that ended this phase of his expansionist wars. Peace was signed in 1678 (by the treaty of Nimwegen), but only at the expense of Spain and the Holy Roman Empire, from which Louis XIV took the long coveted Franche-Comté, together with another batch of towns in Flanders (see map, p. 155). The Dutch preserved their territory intact.

In the next ten years came the great windfall of William's life. In 1689 he became king of England. He was now able to bring the British Isles into his perpetual combinations against France. Because the real impact of France was yet to be felt, and the real bid of Louis XIV for *William comes to the English throne* universal monarchy was yet to be made, and because the English at this time were rapidly gaining in strength, the entrance of England was a decisive addition to the balance formed against French expansion. In this way the political upheavals in seventeenth-century England, by bringing a determined Dutchman to the English throne, entered into the general stream of European affairs and helped to assure that western Europe and its overseas offshoots should not be dominated totally by France.

19.   BRITAIN: THE CIVIL WAR

After the defeat of the Spanish Armada and recession of the Spanish threat the English were for a time less closely involved with the affairs of the Continent. They played no significant part in the Thirty Years' War and were almost the only European people west of Poland who were not represented at the Congress of Westphalia. At the time of the Westphalia negotiations in the 1640s they were in fact engaged in a civil war of their own. This English civil war was a milder variant of the Wars of Religion that desolated France, Germany, and the Netherlands. It was fought not between Protestants and Catholics as on the Continent, but between the more extreme or Calvinistic Protestants called Puritans and the more moderate Protestants, who adhered to the established Church of England. As in the wars on the Continent, religious differences were mixed indistinguishably with political and constitutional issues. As the Huguenots represented to some extent feudal rebelliousness against the French monarchy, as German Protestants fought for states' rights against imperial centralization, and the Calvinists of the Netherlands for provincial liberties against the king of Spain, so the Puritans asserted the rights of Parliament against the mounting claims of royalty in England.

The civil war in England took many lives, but was less destructive than most such wars on the Continent; and England escaped the worst horrors of the Wars of Religion. The same was not true of the British Isles as a whole. After 1603 the kingdoms of England and Scotland, while otherwise separate, were ruled by the same king; the kingdom of Ireland remained, as before, a dependency of the English crown. Between England and Presbyterian Scotland there was constant friction, but the worst trouble was between England and Catholic Ireland, which was the scene of religious warfare as savage as that on the Continent.

England in the Seventeenth Century

For the English the seventeenth century was an age of great achievement, during which they made their debut as one of the chief peoples of modern Europe. In 1600 only 4 or 5 million persons, in England and Lowland Scotland, spoke the English language. The number did not rise rapidly for another century and a half. But the population began to spread. Religious discontents, reinforced by economic pressures, led to considerable emigration. Twenty thousand Puritans settled in New England between 1630 and 1640, and a similar number went to Barbados and other West India islands during these same years.

English emigration to North America

A third stream, again roughly of the same size, but made up mainly of Scottish Presbyterians, settled in northern Ireland under government auspices, driving away or expropriating the native Celts. English Catholics were allowed by the home government to settle in Maryland. A great many members of the Church of England went to Virginia during and after the midcentury civil war, adding to the small settlement made at Jamestown in 1607. Except for the movement to northern Ireland, called the "plantation of Ulster," these migrations took place without much attention on the part of the government, through private initiative organized in commercial companies. After the middle of the century the government began deliberately to build an empire. New York was conquered from the Dutch, Jamaica from the Spanish, and Pennsylvania and the Carolinas were established as new colonies. All of Britain's thirteen North American colonies except Georgia were founded before 1700, but there were at that time still fewer than half a million Europeans and Africans living in these colonial settlements.

The English also, like the Dutch, French, and Spanish at the time, were creating a new national culture. Throughout western Europe the national languages, encroaching upon international Latin on the one hand and local dialects on the other, were becoming new linguistic vehicles for the expression of thought and feeling. William Shakespeare helped to shape the evolving English language through the enduring influence of his great plays, including the famous tragedies *Hamlet, Macbeth,* and *King Lear*—all of which were

The English playwright William Shakespeare helped to shape the modern English language as well as much of the later history of English theater and literature. This image of the famous author appeared on an early seventeenth-century edition of his collected works.

(©Hulton Archive/Getty Images)

first performed and published in the early years of the seventeenth century. John Milton published his influential epic poems *Paradise Lost* and *Paradise Regained* later in this same century, after the bitter conflicts of the English Civil War. Shakespeare and Milton projected their complex conceptions of human experience, aspirations, and tragedy with the imaginative power of both new and old words. The English classical literature, rugged in form but deep in content, vigorous yet subtle in insight, majestic, abundant, and sonorous in expression, was almost the reverse of French classical writing, with its virtues of order, economy, propriety, and graceful precision. Proud of their literary culture and their own great writers, the English could never thereafter quite yield to French standards, nor be dazzled or dumbfounded, as some peoples were, by the cultural glories of the Age of Louis XIV. There were no seventeenth-century painters comparable to those on the Continent, but in music it was the age of Thomas Campion and Henry Purcell, and in architecture the century closed with the great London buildings of Christopher Wren.

Economically the English were enterprising and affluent, though in 1600 far outdistanced by the Dutch. They had a larger and more productive country than the Dutch, and were therefore not as limited to purely mercantile and seafaring occupations. Coal was mined around Newcastle, but it was not yet a leading source of English wealth. The great industry was the growing of sheep and manufacture of woolens, which were the main export. Spinning and weaving were done mostly by workers in the country, under the putting-out system, and organized by merchants according to the methods of commercial capitalism. Since 1553 the English had traded with Russia by way of the White Sea; they were increasingly active in the Baltic and eastern Mediterranean; and with the founding of the East India Company, in 1600, they competed with the Dutch in assaulting the old Portuguese monopoly in India and East Asia. But profitable as such overseas operations were becoming, the main wealth of England was still in the land. The richest men were not merchants but landlords, and the landed aristocracy formed the richest class.

Economic activity

Background to the Civil War. Parliament and the Stuart Kings

In England, as elsewhere in the seventeenth century, the kings clashed with their old medieval representative institutions. In England the old institution, Parliament, won out against the king. But this was not the unique feature in the English development. In Germany the estates of the Holy Roman Empire triumphed against the emperor, and much the same thing, as will be seen, occurred in Poland. But on the Continent the triumph of the old representative institutions generally meant political dissolution or even anarchy. Successful governments were generally those in which kingly powers increased; this was the strong tendency of the time, evident even in the Dutch Republic after 1672 under William of Orange. The unique thing about England was that Parliament, in defeating the king, arrived at a workable form of strong government under parliamentary control. This determined the character of modern England and launched into the history of Europe and of the world the great movement of liberalism and representative institutions.

The violent struggles that ultimately produced England's new political order emerged from the conflicting ambitions of the Stuart kings and the most powerful social groups in the English Parliament. In 1603, on the death of Queen Elizabeth, the English crown was inherited by the son of Mary Stuart, James VI of Scotland. As a descendant of Henry VII he became king of England also, taking there the title of James I. James was a philosopher of royal absolutism. He had even written a book on the subject, *The True Law*

The Stuarts and Parliament

of Free Monarchy. By a "free" monarchy James meant a monarchy free from control by Parliament, churchmen, or laws and customs of the past. It was a monarchy in which the king, as father to his people, looked after their welfare as he saw fit, standing above all parties, private interests, and pressure groups. He even declared that kings drew their authority from God and were responsible to God alone, a doctrine known as the divine right of kings.

Any ruler succeeding Elizabeth would probably have had trouble with Parliament, which had shown signs of restlessness in the last years of her reign but had deferred to her as an aging queen and a national symbol. She had maintained peace within the country and fought off the Spaniards, but these very accomplishments persuaded many people that they could now bring their grievances into the open. James I was a foreigner, a Scot, who lacked the touch for dealing with the English and who was moreover a royal pedant, the "wisest fool in Christendom," as he was uncharitably called. Not content with the actual or implicit methods of political control, as Elizabeth had been, he read the Parliament tiresome lectures on the royal rights. He also was in constant need of money because the wars against Spain had left a considerable debt. James was far from economical, and, in any case, in an age of rising prices, he could not live within the fixed and customary revenues of the English crown. These revenues were still set by medieval traditions that were increasingly quaint under the new national and international conditions.

Neither to James I nor to his son Charles I, who succeeded him in 1625, would Parliament grant adequate revenue. It distrusted them both, partly for legal and financial reasons and partly on religious grounds. Many members of Parliament were lawyers. They feared that the centralizing power of the kings was threatening the historic common law of England. They disliked the "prerogative" courts that had expanded royal authority—the Star Chamber set up by Henry VII to settle disputes without the deliberations of a jury and the High Commission set up by Elizabeth to ensure conformity to the theology of the Church of England. They thus opposed the new doctrine of divine right, which claimed that a sovereign king could make laws and decide cases at his own discretion. Practically all members of Parliament were also property owners. Landowners, supported by the merchants, feared that if the king could raise taxes on his own authority, their wealth would be insecure. Finally, many Parliament members were staunch Puritans, whose Calvinist beliefs made them dissatisfied with the organization and doctrine of the Church of England. King James threatened to "harry the Puritans out of the land," and Charles supported the Church hierarchy's desire to enforce religious conformity. Hence there were multiple causes for a growing parliamentary resistance.

Parliamentary resistance

In England the Parliament was so organized as to make resistance effective. There was only one Parliament for the whole country. There were no provincial or local estates, as in the Dutch Republic, Spain, France, Germany, and Poland. All parliamentary opposition was therefore concentrated in one place. In this one Parliament, there were only two houses, the House of Lords and the House of Commons. The landed interest dominated in both houses, the noblemen in the Lords and the gentry in the Commons. In the Commons the gentry, who formed the bulk of the aristocracy, mixed with representatives of the merchants and the towns. Indeed the towns frequently chose country gentlemen to represent them. These connections suggest why the houses of Parliament (especially the Commons) did not accentuate, as did the estates on the Continent, the class division within the country.

Nor was the church present in Parliament as a separate force. Before Henry VIII's break with Rome the bishops and abbots together had formed a large majority in the

House of Lords. Now there were no abbots left, for there were no monasteries. The House of Lords was now predominantly secular; in the first Parliament of James I there were 82 lay peers and 26 bishops. The great landowners had captured the House of Lords. The smaller landowners of the Commons had been enriched by receiving former monastic lands and had prospered by raising wool. The merchants had likewise grown up under mercantilistic protection. Parliament was strong not only in organization but also in the social interests and wealth that it represented. No king could long govern against its will. Parliament affirmed its expectations in a "Petition of Right" (1628), which asserted that taxes could only be raised through Parliamentary consent. Charles at first accepted the petition as a necessary compromise for receiving much-needed revenues.

In 1629, however, king and Parliament came to a deadlock. Charles I, soon ignoring the Petition of Right, attempted to rule without Parliament, which could legally meet only at the royal summons. He intended to give England a good and efficient government. Had he succeeded, the course of English constitutional development would have paralleled that of France. But by certain reforms in Ireland he antagonized the English landlords who had interests in that country. By supporting the leadership and theology of the Church of England he made enemies of the Puritans. And by attempting to modernize the navy with funds raised without parliamentary consent (called "ship money") he alarmed all property owners, who feared that they would be forced to pay for policies they opposed.

The ship-money dispute illustrates the best arguments of both sides. It was the old custom in England for coastal towns to provide ships for the king's service in time of war. More recently, these coastal towns had provided money instead. Charles I wished to maintain a navy in time of peace and to have ship money paid by the country as a whole, including the inland counties. In the old or medieval view it was the function of the towns that were directly affected to maintain a fleet. In the new view, sponsored by the king, the whole nation was the unit on which a navy should be based. The country gentlemen whom Parliament mainly represented, and most of whom lived in inland counties, had less interest in the navy, and in any case were unwilling to pay for it unless they could control the foreign policies for which a navy might be used. The parliamentary class represented the idea, derived from the Middle Ages, that taxes should be authorized by Parliament. The king represented the newer ideas of monarchy that were developing on the Continent, which included a belief in the king's right to collect revenues that were needed by the state. The politically significant classes in England would not accept such ideas. Until the king could govern with the confidence of Parliament, or until Parliament itself was willing to assume the financial responsibilities of government under modern conditions, neither a navy nor any effectual government could be maintained.

The ship-money dispute

The Scots were the first to rebel. In 1637 they rioted in Edinburgh against attempts to impose the Church of England's prayer book and episcopal organization in Scotland. Charles, to raise funds to put down the Scottish rebellion, finally convoked the English Parliament in 1640, for the first time in 11 years. When it proved hostile to him, he dissolved it and called for new elections. The same men were returned. The resulting body, because it sat theoretically for 20 years without new elections, from 1640 to 1660, is known historically as the Long Parliament. Its principal leaders were small or moderately well-to-do landowning gentry. The merchant class, while furnishing no leaders, lent its support.

The Long Parliament

The Long Parliament, far from assisting the king against the Scots, used the Scottish rebellion as a means of pressing its own demands. These were revolutionary from the outset. Parliament insisted that the chief royal advisers be not merely removed but impeached and put to death. It abolished the Star Chamber and the High Commission. The most extreme Calvinist element, the "root and branch" men or "radicals," drove through a bill for the abolition of bishops, revolutionizing the Church of England. In 1642 Parliament and king came to open war: the king drawing followers mainly from the north and west; the Parliament, from the commercially and agriculturally more advanced counties of the south and east (see map, p. 178). A series of bloody battles steadily weakened the king's position, and his army dissolved in 1646. During the war, as the price of support from the Scottish army, Parliament also transformed the government's official Protestantism by adopting the Solemn League and Covenant, which made Presbyterianism the established legal religion of England, Scotland, and Ireland.

The Emergence of Cromwell

The parliamentary forces, called Roundheads from the close haircuts favored by Puritans, gained their major military victories with an efficient new army, the New Model Army, and a highly competent commander, Thomas Fairfax. The wars also brought a hitherto unknown gentleman named Oliver Cromwell to the foreground. A devout Protestant, he organized an especially effective regiment in the New Model Army, the Ironsides, in which extreme Protestant exaltation provided the basis for morale, discipline, and the will to fight. By the late 1640s Cromwell had become the most powerful political and military leader of the parliamentary forces. The army, in which a more popular class was represented than in the Parliament, became the center of advanced democratic ideas. Many of the soldiers objected to Presbyterianism as much as to the Church of England. They favored a free toleration for all "godly" forms of religion, with no superior church organization above local groups of like-minded spirits.

Cromwell concluded that the defeated king, Charles I, could not be trusted, that "ungodly" persons of all kinds put their hopes in him (what later ages would call counter-revolution), and that he must be put to death. Because Parliament hesitated, Cromwell with the support of the army moved against Parliament. The Long Parliament, having started in 1640 with some 500 members, had sunk by 1649 to about 150 (for this revolution, like others, was pushed through by a minority); of these Cromwell now drove out almost 100, leaving a Rump of 50 or 60. This operation was called Pride's Purge,

Pride's Purge

after Colonel Thomas Pride, who commanded the armed force that intimidated Parliament; and in subsequent revolutions such forced removals have been commonly known as purges, and the residues, sometimes, as rumps. The Rump condemned King Charles for treason and sent him to death on the scaffold in 1649.

England, or rather the whole British Isles, was now declared a republic. It was named the Commonwealth. Cromwell tried to govern as best he could. Religious toleration was decreed except for Unitarians and atheists on the one hand, and except for Roman Catholics and the most obstinate supporters of the Church of England on the other. Cromwell had to subdue both Scotland and Ireland by force. In Scotland the execution of the king, violating the ancient national Scottish monarchy of the Stuarts, had swung the country back into the royalist camp. Cromwell crushed the Scots in 1650.

Religious violence in the Commonwealth

Meanwhile the Protestant and Calvinist fury swept over Ireland. A massacre of newly settled Protestants in Ulster in 1641 had left bitter memories that were now avenged. The Irish garrisons of Drogheda and Wexford were defeated and massacred. Thousands of Catholics were killed; priests were put to the sword, and women and small children were dispatched in cold blood. Where formerly, in the "plantation" of Ulster, a whole Protestant population

The execution of King Charles I marked the dramatic triumph of the radical, parliamentary forces in 1649, but the king's death—portrayed here in a seventeenth-century engraving—raised unprecedented questions about the proper limits for political authority and religious radicalism in English society.
(©De Agostini Picture Library/Getty Images)

had been settled in northern Ireland, bodily replacing the native Irish, now Protestant landlords were scattered over the country as a whole, replacing the Catholic landlords and retaining the Catholic peasantry as their tenants. Ireland's native religion and clergy were driven underground, a foreign and detested church was established, and a new and foreign landed aristocracy, originally recruited in large measure from military adventurers, was settled upon the country, in which it ceased to reside as soon as it assured the payment of its rents.

In England itself Cromwell ruled with great difficulty. His regime was more successful in pursuing English commercial and colonial interests abroad, for he not only completed the violent subjugation of Ireland, but in the Navigation Act of 1651, which barred Dutch ships from carrying goods between other countries and England or its colonies, he also opened the previously noted English attack on the Dutch maritime supremacy. He further waged a war with Spain in which England acquired Jamaica, thereby expanding England's involvement in the new slave-based sugar production system in the Caribbean and launching an English campaign for some of the vast inheritance of the Spanish Habsburgs. But he failed to gain the support of a majority of the English. The Puritan Revolution, like others, produced its extremists. It failed to satisfy the most ardent and could not win over the truly conservative, so that Cromwell found himself reluctantly more autocratic, and more alone.

A party arose called the Levellers, who were in fact what later times would call radical political democrats. They were numerous in the Puritan army, though their chief spokesman, John Lilburne, was a civilian. Appealing to natural rights and to the rights of Englishmen,

Religious and social radicalism

Among the many religious groups that emerged during the era of the English Revolution, the Quakers became especially notorious for their critique of religious hierarchies and their willingness to let women speak at their meetings. The novelty of the group is suggested in this seventeenth-century illustration of a woman addressing a Quaker meeting.

(©Universal History Archive/Getty Images)

they asked for a nearly universal manhood suffrage, equality of representation, a written constitution, and subordination of Parliament to a reformed body of voters. The Levellers thus anticipated many ideas of the American and French revolutions over a century later, but they were at this time repressed and expelled from the army. There were others in whom religious and social radicalism were indistinguishably mixed. George Fox, going beyond Calvinism or Presbyterianism, led a new movement of radical religious dissenters who became known as the Society of Friends, or "Quakers." The Quakers were condemned by the established Protestant clergy and many were imprisoned, but the movement continued to attract inspired adherents by insisting that all believers could have new revelations of spiritual truth, by rejecting various social and religious hierarchies, and by allowing or even encouraging women to preach at their meetings. A more ephemeral group, the "Diggers," proceeded to occupy and cultivate common lands, or lands privately owned, in a general repudiation of property. The Fifth Monarchy Men were a millennial group who felt that the end of the world was at hand. They were so called from their belief, as they read the Bible, that history has seen four empires, those of Assyria, Persia, Alexander, and Caesar; and that the existing world was still "Caesar's" but would soon give way to the fifth monarchy, of Christ, in which justice would finally prevail.

Cromwell opposed all such radical movements, which threatened both well-established persons and long-established social and religious hierarchies. As a regicide and a Puritan, however, he could not seek support from the royalists or the former leaders of the Church of England. Unable to agree even with the Rump, he abolished it also in 1653, and thereafter vainly attempted to govern, as Lord Protector, through representative bodies devised by himself and his followers, under a written constitution, the Instrument of Government. Actually, he was driven to place England under military rule, the regime of the "major generals." These officials, each in his district, repressed malcontents, vagabonds, and bandits, closed ale houses, and prohibited cockfighting, in a mixture of moral puritanism and political dictatorship. Cromwell died in 1658; and his son was unable to maintain the Protectorate. Two years later, with all but universal assent, monarchy was restored. Charles II, son of the recently executed Charles I, became king of England and of Scotland.

Cromwell, by beheading a king and keeping his successor off the throne for 11 years, left a lesson that was not forgotten. Though he favored constitutional and parliamentary government and had granted a measure of religious toleration, he had in fact ruled as a dictator in behalf of a stern Puritan minority. The English people now began to blot from their memories the fact that they had ever had a real revolution. The fervid dream of a "godly" England was dissipated forever. What was remembered was a nightmare of standing armies and major generals, of grim Puritans and overwrought religious enthusiasts. The English lower classes ceased to have any political role or consciousness for over a century, except in sporadic rioting over food shortages or outbursts against the dangers of "popery." Democratic ideas were rejected as "levelling." They were generally abandoned in England after 1660 or were cherished by obscure radicals who could not make themselves heard. Such ideas, indeed, had a more continuous history in the English colonies in America, where some leaders of the discredited revolution took refuge.

Legacy of the revolution

20.   BRITAIN: THE TRIUMPH OF PARLIAMENT

The Restoration, 1660–1688: The Later Stuarts

What was restored in 1660 was not only the monarchy, in the person of Charles II, but also the Church of England and the Parliament. Everything, legally, was supposed to be as it had been in 1640. The difference was that Charles II, knowing the fate of his father, was careful not to provoke Parliament to extremes and that the classes represented in Parliament, frightened by the disturbances of the past 20 years, were now more warmly loyal to the king and more willing to uphold the established Church of England.

New legislation

Parliament during the Restoration enacted some far-reaching legislation. It changed the legal basis of land tenure, abolishing certain old feudal payments owed by landholders to the king. The possession of land thus came to resemble modern private property, and the landowning class became more definitely a propertied aristocracy. In place of the feudal dues to the king, which had been automatically payable, Parliament arranged for the king to receive income in the form of taxation, which Parliament could raise or reduce in amount. This gave a new power to Parliament and a new flexibility to government. The aristocracy thus cleared their property of customary restrictions and obligations, and at the same time undertook to support the state by imposing taxes on themselves. The English aristocracy proved more willing than the corresponding classes on the Continent to pay a large share of the expenses of government. Its reward for this taxation was that, for a century and a half, it virtually ran the government to the exclusion of everyone else. Landowners in this period directed not only national affairs through Parliament but also local affairs as justices of the peace. The justices, drawn from the gentry of each county, decided small lawsuits, punished misdemeanors, and supervised the parish officials charged with poor relief and care of the roads. The regime of the landlord-justices came to be called the "squirearchy."

Other classes drew less immediate advantage from the Restoration. The Navigation Act of 1651 was extended, so that commercial, shipping, and manufacturing interests were well protected. But in other ways the landed classes now in power showed themselves unsympathetic to the business classes of the towns. Many people in the towns were Dissenters, including the Puritans who refused to accept the restored Church of England.

Exclusion of Dissenters

Parliament excluded Dissenters from the town "corporations," or governing bodies and forbade any dissenting clergymen to teach school or come within five miles of an incorporated town. New laws prohibited all kinds of religious meetings, which were called "conventicles," not held according to the forms and by the authority of the Church of England. The effect was that many middle-class townspeople found it difficult or impossible to follow their preferred religion, to obtain an education for their children, either elementary or advanced (for Oxford and Cambridge were a part of the established church), to take part in local affairs through the town corporations, or to sit in the House of Commons. The lowest classes, the very poor, were discouraged by the same laws from following sectarian and visionary preachers.

Another enactment fell upon poor people alone and reduced their economic opportunities by impeding their movement around the country. The Act of Settlement of 1662, which decentralized the administration of the Poor Law, made each parish responsible only for its own paupers. Poor people, who were very numerous, were condemned to remain in the parishes where they lived. A large group of English people was thus immobilized within their home towns.

But it was not long after the Restoration that Parliament and king were again at odds. The main issue was again religion. Many Protestants throughout Europe at this time were returning voluntarily to Roman Catholicism, a tendency naturally dreaded by the Protestant churches. This kind of conversion was most conspicuously illustrated when the daughter of Gustavus Adolphus himself, Queen Christina of Sweden, abdicated her throne and was received into the Roman church. In England the national feeling was excitedly anti-Catholic. No measures were more popular than those against "popery"; and the squires in Parliament, stiffly loyal to the Church of England, dreaded papists even more than Dissenters. The king,

Catholic Conversions

Charles II, was personally inclined to Catholicism. He admired the magnificent monarchy of Louis XIV, which he would have liked to duplicate, insofar as possible, in England. At odds with his Parliament, Charles II made overtures to Louis XIV. The secret treaty of Dover of 1670 was the outcome. Charles thereby agreed to join Louis XIV in his expected war against the Dutch; and Louis agreed to pay the king of England 3 million livres a year during the war. He hoped also that Charles II would soon find it opportune to rejoin the Roman church.

While these arrangements were unknown in detail in England, it was known that Charles II was well disposed to the French and to Roman Catholicism. England went to war again with the Dutch. The king's brother and heir, James, Duke of York, publicly announced his conversion to Rome. Charles II, in a "declaration of indulgence," announced the nonenforcement of laws against Dissenters. The king declared that he favored general toleration, but it was rightly feared that his real aim was to promote Roman Catholicism in

Charles II and the Test Act

England. Parliament retorted in 1673 by passing the Test Act, which required all office-holders to take communion in the Church of England. The Test Act renewed the legislation against Dissenters and also made it impossible for Catholics to serve in the government or in the army and navy. The Test Act remained on the English statute books until 1828.

Although Charles's pro-French and pro-Catholic policies were extremely unpopular, the situation might not have come to a head except for the avowed Catholicism and French orientation of Charles's brother James, due to be the next king because Charles had no legitimate children. This impending transition shaped the emergence of opposing political factions who came to be known as "Whigs" and "Tories." A strong movement developed in Parliament to exclude James by law from the throne. The exclusionists—and those generally who were most suspicious of the king, Catholics, and the French—received the nickname of Whigs. The king's supporters were popularly called Tories. The Whigs, while backed by the middle class and merchants of London, drew their main strength from the upper aristocracy, especially certain great noblemen who might expect, if the king's power were weakened, to play a prominent part in ruling the country themselves. The Tories were the party of the lesser aristocracy and gentry who were suspicious of the "moneyed interest" of London and who felt a strong loyalty to church and king. These two parties, or at least their names, became permanently established in English public life. But all the Whigs and Tories together, at this time, did not number more than a few thousand persons.

The Revolution of 1688

James II, despite Whig vexation, became king in 1685. He soon antagonized even the Tories, who strongly supported the Church of England. As landowners they appointed most of the parish clergy, who imparted Tory sentiments to the rural population; and members of landowning Tory families frequently became bishops, archdeacons, university functionaries, and other high personnel of the church. The laws keeping Dissenters and Catholics from office had given Anglicans (i.e., members of the Church of England) a monopoly in local and national government and in the army and navy. James II acted as if there were no Test Act, claiming the right to suspend its operation in individual cases, and appointed a good many Catholics to influential and lucrative positions. He offered a program, as his brother had done, of general religious toleration, to allow Protestant Dissenters as well as Roman Catholics to participate in public life.

Such a program was repugnant to the Church of England. Seven bishops refused to endorse it. They were prosecuted for disobedience to the king but were acquitted by the jury. James, by these actions, violated the liberties of the established church, threatened the Anglican monopoly of church and state, and aroused the popular terrors of "popery."

Whigs and Tories in opposition to the crown

He was also forced to take the position philosophically set forth by his grandfather James I, that a king of England could make and unmake the law by his own will. The Tories joined the Whigs in opposition. In 1688, a son was born to James II and baptized into the Catholic faith.

The prospect now opened up of an indefinite line of Catholic rulers in England. The leaders of both parties thereupon abandoned James II and offered the throne to his grown daughter Mary, who was brought up a Protestant before her father's conversion to Rome.

Mary was the wife of William of Orange. William, it will be recalled, had spent his adult life blocking the ambitions of the king of France, who had threatened Europe with a "universal monarchy" by absorbing or inheriting the global territories of Spain. To William III it would be a mere distraction to be husband to a queen of England, or even to be king in his own name, unless England could be brought to serve his own purposes.

William invades England

He was immutably Dutch; his purpose was to save Holland and hence to ruin Louis XIV. His chief interest in England was to bring the English into his balance of power against France. Because the English were generally anti-French, and had chafed under the pro-French tendencies of their kings, William quickly reached an understanding with the discontented Whigs and Tories. Protected by a written invitation from prominent Englishmen, he invaded England with a considerable army. James II fled, and William was proclaimed co-ruler with Mary over England and Scotland. In the next year, 1690, at the Boyne River in Ireland, a motley army of Dutchmen, Germans, Scots, and French Huguenots under William III defeated a French and Irish force led by James II. Thus the constitutional power of the English Parliament was reaffirmed, and Anglican Protestantism remained the official religion of the English nation. James II fled to France.

Louis XIV of course refused to recognize his inveterate enemy as ruler of England. He maintained James at the French court with all the honors due the English king. It was thereafter one of his principal war aims to restore the Catholic and Stuart dynasty across the Channel. The English now had new reasons to fight the French. A French victory would mean counterrevolution and royal absolutism in England. The whole Revolution of 1688 was at stake in the French wars.

Bill of Rights and the Toleration Act

In 1689, Parliament enacted a Bill of Rights, stipulating that no law could be suspended by the king (as the Test Act had been), no taxes could be raised or army maintained except by parliamentary consent, and no subject (however poor) could be arrested and detained without legal process. William III accepted these articles as conditions to receiving the crown. Thereafter the relation between king and people was a kind of contract. It was further provided, by the Act of Settlement of 1701, that no Catholic could be king of England; this excluded the descendants of James II, known in the following century as the Pretenders. Parliament also passed the Toleration Act of 1689, which allowed Protestant Dissenters to practice their religion but still excluded them from political life and public service. Because ways of evading these restrictions were soon found, and because even Catholics were not molested unless they supported the Pretenders, there was thereafter no serious trouble over religion in England and Lowland Scotland.

Historical Interpretations and Debates
The Meaning of the English Revolution

Debates about the significance of the mid-seventeenth-century English Revolution often focus on how the Revolution transformed the political or economic influence of various social groups. Although many historians have argued that landed, aristocratic elites emerged from the seventeenth-century upheavals as the dominant power in English society, there is much disagreement about whether the revolutionary events also enhanced or weakened the political position of other people in the multiple layers of English social life. Such differences appear in the writings of Hugh R. Trevor-Roper and Phyllis Mack, who seek to explain the Revolution's historical meaning for some of its diverse social groups and participants.

Hugh R. Trevor-Roper, "The Social Causes of the Great Rebellion" (1957)

The Great Rebellion . . . [was] not the clear-headed self-assertion of the rising bourgeoisie and gentry, but rather the blind protest of the depressed gentry. . . .

It was the blind revolt of the gentry against the Court, of the provinces against the capital; the backwash against a century of administrative and economic centralization. Since they were animated by passion, not by positive political ideas, . . . the radical gentry, when they were in power, found themselves without a policy. Ultimately, after a period of fumbling experiments, they gave up the effort, accepted back the old political system, and sank into political quietism. . . .

The rebellion itself . . . took place because a failure of political ability coincided with a general economic crisis. . . . Perhaps *indirectly* the rebellion may have forwarded the undoubted change of mentality between the early and the late seventeenth century in England. . . . But, equally, it may have impeded that progress for a generation. . . . What we can say . . . is that it was not, in itself, a successful stage in the rise of the bourgeoisie.

Phyllis Mack, *Visionary Women: Ecstatic Prophecy in Seventeenth-Century England* (1992)

The [religious] prophets of the Civil War period, many of them laborers, farmers, or artisans, understood their condemnation of an engorged clergy and aristocracy as both a spiritual and social protest. And since women were commonly identified with the poor and deprived, . . . one would expect that those radical movements that championed the poor and deprived would also champion the increased authority of women. Yet . . . those sects that were most radical in challenging traditional social and economic relationships were least likely to be attentive to the needs and rights of oppressed people who were female. Conversely, those women who were most conscious of their authority as females, Quaker and non-Quaker, were also those middle and upper class women who had the least affinity with the plight of the laboring classes. . . .

Women as [religious] prophets enjoyed virtually the only taste of public authority they would ever know. Some of them used that authority to write and publish their own works, to organize separate women's meetings, or to challenge the greater authority of the male leaders. . . .

The historian's attentiveness to the issue of gender is likely to raise more questions than it answers. . . . [But] it suggests . . . that the private actions of ordinary individuals have affected larger social and political movements as profoundly as the deeds of great and famous men, forcing us to broaden our definition of the term "politics."

Sources: H. R. Trevor-Roper, "The Social Causes of the Great Rebellion," in *Men and Events: Historical Essays* (New York: Harper and Brothers, 1957), pp. 200, 204–205; Phyllis Mack, *Visionary Women: Ecstatic Prophecy in Seventeenth-Century England* (Berkeley, CA: University of California Press, 1992), pp. 4–5.

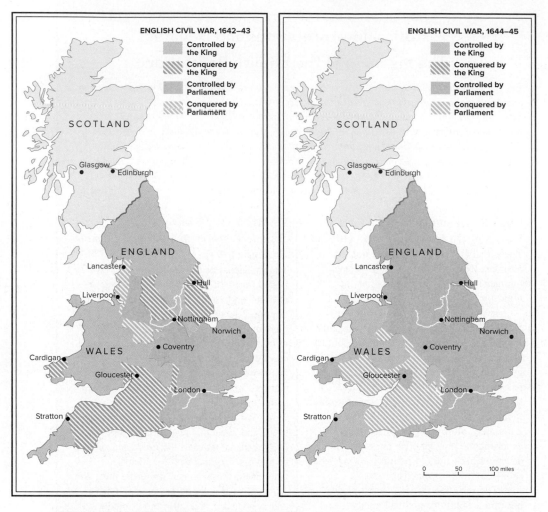

ENGLAND IN THE SEVENTEENTH CENTURY

The maps show the principal seventeenth-century English towns and the rough division of the country into royalist and parliamentary regions during the English Civil War. King Charles I drew his strongest support from the north and west; Parliament drew its strongest support from the southeast and from London. Similar regional political patterns emerged in later conflicts between the Royalist "Tories" and the Parliamentary "Whigs." The Whigs were generally supported by the upper aristocracy and the commercial classes of London, who opposed the pro-French, pro-Catholic policies of the Stuart kings Charles II and James II.

The English Parliament could make no laws for Scotland, however, and it was feared that James II might someday be restored in his northern kingdom. The securing of the parliamentary revolution in England, and of the island's defenses against France, required that the two kingdoms be organically joined; but there was little sentiment in Scotland for a merger with the English. The English tempted Scottish political leaders with economic advantages. The Scots still had no rights in the English East India Company, nor in the English colonies, nor within the English system of mercantilism and Navigation Acts. They obtained such rights by consenting to a union. Although anti-merger sentiment remained strong in much of Scotland, the United Kingdom of Great Britain was created

CHRONOLOGY OF NOTABLE EVENTS, 1642–1713

1642–1648	Civil War in England
1649	Execution of King Charles I in London
1649–1658	Oliver Cromwell leads the English "Commonwealth" and "Protectorate"
1660	Restoration of English monarchy, King Charles II
1661	King Louis XIV takes personal control of French government; reign continues to 1715
1685	Revocation of Edict of Nantes; persecution of French Protestants
1688	"Glorious Revolution" brings William and Mary to English throne and strengthens power of Parliament
1702–1713	War of Spanish Succession; "balance of power" limits French expansion
1713	Peace of Utrecht

in 1707. The Scots retained their own legal system and established Presbyterian church, but their government and parliament were merged with those of England. The term "British" came into use to refer to both English and Scots.

As for Ireland, it was now feared as a center of Stuart and French intrigue. The Revolution of 1688 marked the climax of a long record of trouble. Ireland had never been simply conquered by England, though certain English or rather Anglo-Norman families had carved out estates there since the twelfth century. By the end of the Middle Ages Ireland was organized as a separate kingdom with its own parliament, subordinate to the English crown. During the Reformation the Irish remained Catholic while England turned Protestant, but the monasteries were dissolved in Ireland as in England; and the organized church as such, the established Church of Ireland, with its apparatus of bishoprics, parishes, and tithes, became an Anglican communion in which the mass of native Irish had no interest. Next came the plantation of Ulster, already mentioned, in which a mass of newcomers, mainly

The Irish threat to the Revolution of 1688

Scottish and Presbyterian, settled in the northern part of the island. Then, in Cromwell's time, English landlords spread through the rest of the country; or rather, a new Anglo-Irish upper class developed, in which English landowning families, residing most often in England, added the income from Irish estates to their miscellaneous revenues.

Ireland therefore by the close of the seventeenth century was a very mixed country. Probably two-thirds of its population was Catholic, of generally Celtic ethnic background; perhaps a fifth was Presbyterian, with recent Scottish connections; the small remainder was made up of Anglicans, largely Anglo-Irish of recent or distant origin in England, who controlled most of the land, manned the official church, and were influential in the Irish parliament. It was essentially a landlord and peasant society, in which the Presbyterian and Catholic populations were overwhelmingly agricultural and poor, towns were small, and the middle class scarcely developed.

After the Revolution of 1688, in which the final overthrow of James II took place in Ireland at the Boyne River, the English feared Ireland as a source of danger to the post-revolutionary arrangements in England and as a likely site for anti-English resistance to develop among subjugated Catholics. English elites who were defending their own liberties

*Restrictions for
Irish Catholics*

at home thus set about destroying the religious, political, and social liberties of Irish Catholics. In addition to the burden of an alien church and absentee landlordism, the Irish were now subjected to a new "penal code." Catholic clergy were banished, and Catholics were forbidden to vote or to sit in the Irish parliament. Catholic teachers were forbidden to teach, and Catholic parents were forbidden to send children overseas to be educated in Catholic schools. No Catholic could take a degree at Trinity College (Dublin University), an Anglican institution. Catholics in Ireland were forbidden to purchase land, to lease it for more than 31 years, to inherit it from a Protestant, or even to own a horse worth more than £5. Catholics were forbidden to be attorneys, to serve as constables, or, in most trades, to have more than two apprentices. Some disabilities fell on the Protestant Irish also. Thus Irish shipping was excluded from the British colonies, nor could the Irish import colonial goods except through England. Export of Irish woolens and glass manufactures was prohibited. No import tariff on English manufactures could be levied by the Irish parliament. About all that was left to the Irish, in international trade, was the export of agricultural produce; and the foreign exchange acquired in this way went very largely to pay the rents to absentee landlords.

The purpose of the penal code was in part strategic, to weaken Ireland as a potentially hostile country during a long period of English wars with France. In part it was commercial, to favor English manufactures by removing Irish competition. And in part it was social, to confirm the position of the Anglican interest, or "ascendancy" as it came to be called. Parts of the code were removed piecemeal in the following decades, and a Catholic merchant class grew up in the eighteenth century; but much remained in effect for a long time, so that, for example, a Catholic could not vote for members of the Irish parliament until 1793, and even then could not be elected to it. In general, the Irish emerged from the seventeenth century as the most repressed people of western Europe.

*Coalition against
France*

England, immediately after the expulsion of James II, joined William III's coalition against France. To the alliance England brought a highly competent naval force, together with very considerable wealth. William's government, to finance the war, borrowed £1,200,000 from a syndicate of private lenders, who in return for holding government bonds were given the privilege of operating a bank. Thus originated, in 1694, both the Bank of England and the British national debt. Owners of liquid assets, merchants of London and Whig aristocrats, having lent their money to the new regime, had a compelling reason to defend it against the French and James II. And having at last a government whose policies they could control, they were willing to entrust it with money in large amounts. The national debt rapidly rose, while the credit of the government held consistently good; and for many years people on the Continent were astonished at the wealth that the British government could tap at will and the quantities of money that it could pour into the wars of Europe.

*The Glorious
Revolution*

The events of 1688 came to be known to the English as the Glorious Revolution. The Revolution was portrayed as vindicating the principles of parliamentary government, the rule of law, and even the right of rebellion against tyranny (though, as noted above, England's governing classes denied all such rights in Ireland and in their overseas colonies). The overthrow of James II and the enactment of new parliamentary restrictions on the power of English kings have often been depicted as key moments in the growth of English constitutional self-government. Political writers like John Locke, shortly after the events, helped to give wide currency to these ideas. There was some justification for these views even though in more recent times some writers have "deglorified" the Revolution of 1688. They point out that it was an upper-class movement, promoted and maintained by an exclusionary landed aristocracy. The Parliament that boldly asserted itself against the king was at the same time closing itself to large segments of the English people. Where in the Middle Ages members of the House of Commons had usually received pay for their services, this custom disappeared in the seventeenth century, so that thereafter only men with independent incomes could sit. After the parliamentary triumph of 1688 this tendency became a matter of law. An act of 1710 required members of the House of Commons to possess private incomes at such a level that only a few thousand persons could legally qualify. This income had to come from the ownership of land. England from 1688 to 1832 was the best example in modern times of a true aristocracy, that is, of a country in which the men of an aristocratic landowning class not only enjoyed privileges but also conducted the government. But the landowning interest was then the only social group that was sufficiently wealthy, numerous, educated, and self-conscious to stand politically on its own feet. Although it depended on the labor and trade of men and women who could never vote or hold office, the rule of the "gentlemen of England" was, within its strict social limits, an evolving, early regime of political liberty.

21. THE FRANCE OF LOUIS XIV, 1643–1715: THE TRIUMPH OF ABSOLUTISM

French Culture in the Seventeenth Century

Having traveled in the outer orbits of the seventeenth-century European political system, we come now to its radiant and mighty center, the domain of the Sun King himself, the France against which the rest of Europe felt obliged to combine because its power threatened the interests of so many other countries—the future of the Spanish possessions, the independence of Holland, the maintenance in England of the parliamentary revolution. The France of Louis XIV owed much of its ascendancy to the quantity and quality of its people. Population was stabilized or possibly even falling in the seventeenth century, the last century in which France was seriously disturbed by famines and peasant rebellions. With 19 million inhabitants in 1700 France was still over three times as populous as England and twice as populous as Spain. Its fertile soil, in an agricultural age, made it a wealthy country, though the wealth was very unevenly distributed.

France was big enough to harbor many contradictions. Millions of its people lived in poverty, yet the number in comfortable or even luxurious circumstances was very large. There were both modest country nobles and cosmopolitan *grands seigneurs*. The middle class included *The contradictions of French society* an inordinate number of lawyers, officeholders, and bureaucrats. The country was less commercial than Holland or England, yet in sheer numbers there may have been more merchants in France than in either of the other two countries. Protestants were a declining minority, yet in the mid-seventeenth century there were still more French Huguenots than Dutch Calvinists. It was a self-sufficient country, yet the French in this century began trading in India and Madagascar, founded colonial settlements in Canada, explored the Great Lakes and the Mississippi Valley, set up sugar plantations in the West Indies, expanded their ancient commerce with the Levant, enlarged their mercantile marine, and for a time had the leading navy of Europe. France, in short, became a highly active participant in the widening networks of global trade and European colonization.

The dominance of France meant the dominance not merely of political or military power but of a people whom most Europeans viewed as the forefront of seventeenth-century art, literature, and social etiquette. They carried over the earlier versatility of the Italian Renaissance. In Nicholas Poussin and Claude Lorrain they produced a notable school of painters, their architecture was emulated throughout Europe, and they excelled in military fortification and engineering. Much of their literature, though often written by bourgeois writers, was designed for an aristocratic and courtly audience, which had put aside the uncouth manners of an earlier day and prided itself on the refinement of its tastes and perceptions. Corneille and Racine wrote austere tragedies on the personal conflicts and social relations of human life. Molière, in his comedies, ridiculed bumbling doctors, religious hypocrites, new-rich bourgeois, and foppish aristocrats. La Fontaine gave the world his animal fables, and La Rochefoucauld, in his witty and sardonic maxims, offered a nobleman's candid judgment on human nature. In Descartes the French produced a great mathematician and scientific thinker; in Pascal they found a scientist who was also a profound spokesman for Christianity; and in Bayle they brought forward an intellectual advocate of early modern skepticism. It was French thought and the French language, not merely the armies of Louis XIV, which in the seventeenth century were sweeping the European world.

Patronage of the arts by Louis XIV

Louis XIV understood that France's dominant position in Europe required more than large armies and that a flourishing cultural life greatly enhanced the international prestige of even the wealthiest or most powerful sovereign state. He therefore gave generous financial

The French playwright Molière often performed in his own plays, including some that were staged at the court of Louis XIV. He is portrayed here as a character in *The School for Wives,* **a popular comedy about conflicts and deceptions in the relations between women and men.**

(©Bridgeman-Giraudon/Art Resource, NY)

MOLIERE.

dans le rôle d'Arnolphe, de l'École des femmes

(Coméd.ᵉ Française.)   (Année 1670.)

support to his favorite writers and artists, especially those who produced works for his new palace at Versailles. He also brought the arts and sciences into the state's administrative system by establishing royal academies in which various theorists taught the correct principles for art, literature, music, dance, and scientific knowledge. The favored or official aesthetic theory in these academies was called classicism, a theory that emphasized order, harmony, and the artistic achievements of antiquity. Following the example of painters such as Poussin, young artists learned to portray scenes from classical Roman history or mythology with harmonious and almost geometric precision. The great literary theorist of the day, Nicolas Boileau, urged writers to emulate the poetic works of ancient writers who had shown how literature addresses the timeless themes of human knowledge and transcendent truths rather than the frivolities of daily life. The classicism of French artists and writers thus fit comfortably with the Sun King's appreciation for order and hierarchy in every sphere of social, political, and cultural life.

Yet neither the king nor his official academies could control all of France's artistic and intellectual activity. Some literary critics, soon known as the "Moderns," began to argue that modern literature and knowledge had in fact surpassed the achievements of ancient cultures and that Boileau's academic writers, soon called the "Ancients," deferred much too rigidly to ancient authorities. Meanwhile, other centers of intellectual life emerged outside the royal academies in the new salons of Paris. Developing rapidly in the second half of the seventeenth century, the salons became the unofficial gathering places for Parisian nobles, wealthy professional persons, and creative writers or artists. They were organized by upper-class women who invited people into their homes to discuss philosophy, literature, and art—all of which could be debated without the formal constraints and solemnity of the academies. The salons attracted criticism and even ridicule from some people in the government and academies, partly because they were created by energetic women and partly because they flourished outside the official cultural institutions of the state. But the Parisian salons, like the royal academies, became an enduring, distinctive institution in French cultural life. They also welcomed distinguished foreign visitors, thus contributing to the spread of French ideas and social mores throughout Europe. Parisian-style salons eventually appeared in other European cities, along with French fashion, French manners, and the French language.

Salons

The Development of Absolutism in France

This ascendancy of French culture went along with a regime in which political liberties were at a discount. The culture embellished what historians have often called the "absolute monarchy" of Louis XIV, though the king's power was never as far-reaching as the term "absolutism" suggests. The Sun King had to secure the cooperation of the nobility and other social classes; and his power was constrained in various ways by regional institutions, French legal traditions, and a fragmented system of local economies. Like other European countries, France had a tradition of political rights and liberties that were associated with older, even feudal, political and legal institutions. It had an Estates General, which had not met since 1615 but was not legally abolished. In some regions Provincial Estates, still meeting frequently, retained a measure of self-government and of power over taxation. There were about a dozen bodies known as parlements,[1] which, unlike the English Parliament,

The "parlements"

---

[1] Spelled *parlements* in French, to distinguish from the English Parliament.

had developed as courts of law, each being the supreme court for a certain area of the country. The parlements upheld certain "fundamental laws" that they said the king could not overstep, and they often refused to enforce royal edicts that they declared to be unconstitutional. France, beneath the surface, was almost as diverse as Germany (see map, p. 191). French towns had won charters of acknowledged rights, and many of the great provinces enjoyed liberties written into old agreements with the crown. These local liberties created institutional complications for a would-be "absolute" monarch. There were some 300 "customs" or regional systems of law; it was observed that travelers sometimes changed laws more often than they changed horses. Internal tariffs ran along the old provincial borders. Tolls were levied by manorial lords. The king's taxes fell less heavily on some regions than on others. Neither coinage nor weights and measures were uniform throughout the country. France was a bundle of territories held together by allegiance to the same king.

This older kind of feudal freedom discredited itself in France at the very time when in Germany a neo-feudal localism was pulling the Holy Roman Empire to pieces, and when in England the older feudal liberties were making a transition to a more modern form of political liberty, embodied in the parliamentary system of an aristocratic state. In France the old medieval or local type of liberty became associated with disorder. It has already been related how after the disorders of the sixteenth-century religious wars people had turned with relief to the monarchy and how Henry IV and then Richelieu had begun to make the monarchy strong. The troubles of the Fronde, beginning in 1648, provided additional incentive for the centralization of political power in France.

| The Fronde | The Fronde broke out immediately after the Peace of Westphalia, while Louis XIV was still a child, and was directed against Cardinal Mazarin, who was governing in his name. It was an abortive revolution, |

led by the same elements, the parlements and the nobility, which were to initiate the great French Revolution in 1789. The parlements, especially the Parlement of Paris, insisted in 1648 on their right to pronounce certain royal edicts unconstitutional. Barricades were thrown up and street fighting broke out in Paris. The nobility rebelled, as it had often in the past. Leadership was assumed by some prominent noblemen who had enough wealth and influence to believe that, if the king's power were contained, they might govern the country themselves. The rebelling nobles demanded a calling of the Estates General, expecting to dominate over the bourgeoisie and the clergy in that body. Armed bands of soldiers, unemployed since the Peace of Westphalia and led by nobles, roamed about the country terrorizing the peasants. If these nobles had expanded their power, the manorial system would likely have fallen on the peasants more heavily, as in eastern Europe, where triumphant lords were at this very time exacting increased labor services from the peasants. Finally the rebellious nobles called in Spanish troops to bolster their uprising, though France was still at war with Spain. By this time the bourgeoisie, together with the parlements, had withdrawn support from the rebellious nobles. The agitation subsided in total failure. Urban commercial groups could not work together with an assertive nobility; the nobles outraged people throughout France by bringing Spanish soldiers into their rebellion; and the *frondeurs,* especially after the parlements deserted them, had no base of popular support and no systematic or constructive program, aiming only at the overthrow of the unpopular Cardinal Mazarin and at obtaining offices and favors for themselves.

After the Fronde, as after the religious wars, the townspeople and peasantry of France, to protect themselves against the claims of the aristocracy, were in a mood to

INSPIRATION OF THE EPIC POET
by Nicolas Poussin (French, 1594–1665)

Poussin's interest in both the themes and forms of classicism appear in this image of a poet who yearns for the honor of a laurel crown as he meditates on the Greek god Apollo (with his lyre) and Calliope, the muse of epic poetry. The painting shows the careful symmetry and balance of much seventeenth-century French art.

(©Print Collector/Getty Images)

welcome the exercise of strong power by the kings. And in the young Louis XIV they had a man more than willing to grasp all the power he could get. Louis, at age 23, on Mazarin's death in 1661, announced that he would govern the country himself. He was the third king of the Bourbon line. It was the Bourbon tradition, established by Henry IV and by Richelieu, to draw the teeth from independent aristocrats, and this was a tradition that Louis XIV now followed. He was not a man of any transcendent abilities, though he had the capacity, often found among successful executives, of learning a good deal from conversation with experts. His education was somewhat limited, having been made purposely easy; but he had the ability to see and stick to definite lines of policy, and he was extremely methodical and industrious in his daily habits, scrupulously loading himself with administrative business throughout his reign. He was extremely fond of himself and his position of kingship, with an insatiable appetite for admiration and flattery; he loved magnificent display and elaborate etiquette, though to some extent he simply adopted them as instruments of policy rather than as a personal whim.

With the reign of Louis XIV the state in its modern administrative form took a long step forward. The state in the abstract has always seemed somewhat theoretical to the English-speaking world. Let us say, for simplicity, that the state represents a fusion of justice and power. A sovereign state possesses, within its territory, a monopoly over the administration of justice and the use of force. Private persons neither pass legal judgments on others nor control private armies of their own. For private and unauthorized persons to do so, in an orderly state, constitutes rebellion. This was in contrast to the older feudal practice, by which feudal lords maintained manorial courts and led their own followers into battle. Against these feudal practices Louis XIV energetically worked, though not with complete success, claiming to possess in his own person, the sovereign ruler, a monopoly over the lawmaking processes and the armed forces of the kingdom. This is

"L'etat, c'est moi"

the deeper meaning of his reputed boast, *L'état, c'est moi*—"the state is myself." In the France of the seventeenth century, divided by classes and by regions, there was in fact no practical means of consolidating the powers of state except in a shared deference to one individual.

The state, however, while representing law and order within its borders, has generally stood in a lawless and disorderly relation to other states, because no higher monopoly of law and force has existed. Louis XIV, personifying the French state, had no particular regard for the claims of other states or rulers. He was constantly either at war or preparing for war with his neighbors. The modern state, indeed, was created by the needs of peace at home and war abroad. Machinery of government, as devised by Louis XIV and others, was a means of giving order and security within the territory of the state, and of raising, supporting, and controlling armies for use against other states.

The idea that law and force within a country should be monopolized by the lawful king was the essence of the seventeenth-century doctrine of absolutism. Its principal theorist in the time of Louis XIV was the French bishop Jacques-Bénigne Bossuet, who advanced the old Christian teaching that all power comes from God and that all who hold power are responsible to God for the way they use it. He held that kings were God's representatives in the political affairs of earth. Royal power, according to Bossuet, was absolute but not arbitrary. The use of power could not be arbitrary because it must be reasonable and just, like the will of God that it reflected; but it was absolute in that it was free from dictation by parlements, estates, or other subordinate elements within the country. Law, therefore, was the will of the sovereign king, so long as it conformed to the higher law that was the will of God.

Absolutism

This doctrine, affirming the divine right of kings, was popularly held in France at the time and was taught in the churches. Absolutism and absolute monarchy became the prevailing concepts of government on much of the European continent in the seventeenth and eighteenth centuries. It must be remembered, however, that these terms referred more to legal theories than to facts. A ruler, in theory, could be absolute because he was not legally bound by any other persons or institutions in the country. In reality he became dependent upon a host of advisers and bureaucrats; he often had to compromise with vested interests; and he could be thwarted by the sheer weight of local custom or meet resistance from lawyers, ecclesiastics, nobles, grandees, hereditary officeholders, and miscellaneous dignitaries. And the slow pace of both transportation and communication prevented early modern "absolutist" rulers from controlling their subjects as quickly or as efficiently as governments have controlled their people in modern nation-states.

Government and Administration

Louis XIV's early and perhaps most important administrative steps assured his tight control of the army. Armed forces in Europe had long been almost a private enterprise. Specialists in fighting, leading their own troops, worked for governments more or less as they chose, either in return for money or to pursue political aims of their own. This was especially common in central Europe, but even in France great noblemen had strong private influence over the troops, and in times of disorder nobles led armed retainers about the country. Colonels were virtually on their own. Provided with a general commission and with funds by some government, they recruited, trained, and equipped their own regiments, and likewise fed and supplied them, often by preying upon civilian populations in the vicinity. In these circum- *War: a state activity* stances it was often difficult to say on whose side soldiers were fighting. It was hard for governments to set armies into motion and equally hard to make them stop fighting, for commanders fought for their own interests and on their own momentum. War was not a "continuation of policy"; it was not an act of the state; it easily degenerated, as in the Thirty Years' War, into a kind of aimless and perpetual violence.

Louis XIV made war an activity of state. He compelled all armed persons in France to fight only for him. This produced peace and order within France, while strengthening the fighting power of France against other states. Under the older conditions there was also little integration among different units and branches of the army. Infantry regiments and cavalry went largely their own way, and the artillery was supplied by civilian technicians under contract. Louis XIV created a stronger unity of control, put the artillery

LOUIS XIV

by Hyacinthe Rigaud (French, 1659–1743)

The grandeur of the Sun King is conveyed in this portrait by Rigaud. He uses the king's clothing, stance, and royal emblems to express the power of the French monarchy.

(©UniversalImagesGroup/Getty Images)

organically into the army, systematized the military ranks and grades, and clarified the chain of command, placing himself at the top. The government supervised recruiting, required colonels to prove that they were maintaining the proper number of soldiers, and assumed most of the responsibility for equipping, provisioning, clothing, and housing the troops. Higher officers, thus becoming dependent on the government, could be subjected to discipline. The soldiers were put into uniforms, taught to march in step, and housed in barracks; thus they too became more susceptible to discipline and control.

Armed forces became less of a terror to their own people and a more effective weapon in the hands of the centralizing government. They were employed usually against other governments but sometimes to suppress rebellion at home. Louis XIV also increased the French army in size, raising it from about 100,000 to about 400,000. These changes, both in size and in degree of government control, were made possible by the growth of a large civilian administration, the heads of which were also civilians under the control of Louis XIV. They were in effect the first ministers of war, and their assistants, officials, inspectors, and clerks constituted the first organized war ministry.

Louis XIV was a vain man, but he connected his vanity to a broader political strategy to overawe the country with his own grandeur. He built himself a whole new city at the old village of Versailles about 10 miles southwest of Paris. Where the Escorial in Spain had the atmosphere of a monastery, Versailles was a monument to worldly splendor. Tremendous in size, fitted out with polished mirrors, gleaming chandeliers, and magnificent tapestries, opening on to a formal park with fountains and shaded walks, the palace of Versailles became the marvel of Europe and the envy of lesser kings. It was virtually a public building, much of it used for government offices, with nobles, churchmen, notable bourgeois, and servants milling about on the king's affairs. The more exclusive honors of the château were reserved for the higher nobles. The king surrounded his daily routine of rising, eating, and going to bed (known as the *lever, dîner,* and *coucher*) with an infinite series of ceremonial acts, so minute and so formalized that there were, for example, six different entries of persons at the *lever,* and a certain gentleman at a specified moment held the right sleeve of the king's nightshirt as he took it off. The most exalted persons thought themselves the greater for thus waiting on so august a being. With such honors, and by more material favors, many great nobles were induced to live habitually at court. Here, under the royal eye, they might engage in palace intrigue but were kept away from real political agitation in the provinces. Versailles had a debilitating effect on the French aristocracy.

The splendor of Versailles

For most positions in the government, as distinguished from his personal entourage, Louis XIV preferred to use men whose upper-class status was recent. Such men, unlike hereditary nobles, could aspire to no independent political influence of their own. He never called the Estates General, which in any case no one except some of the nobility wanted. Some of the Provincial Estates, because of local and aristocratic pressures, were allowed to remain functioning. He temporarily destroyed the independence of the parlements, commanding them to accept his orders, as Henry IV had commanded them to accept the Edict of Nantes. He developed a strong system of administrative coordination, centering in a number of councils of state, which he attended in person, and in "intendants" who represented these councils throughout the country. Councilors of state and the intendants in provincial districts were generally of bourgeois origin or newly ennobled. Each intendant, within his district, embodied all aspects of the royal government—supervising the flow of taxes and recruiting of soldiers, keeping an eye on the local nobility, dealing with towns and guilds, controlling the more or less hereditary officeholders, policing the

Administrative tactics of Louis XIV

marketplaces, relieving famine, watching and often participating in the local law courts. A firm and uniform administration was superimposed upon the heterogeneous mass of the old France. In contrast to England, many local questions were handled by agents of the central government, usually honest and often efficient, but essentially bureaucrats constantly instructed by, and reporting back to, their superiors at Versailles.

Economic and Financial Policies: Colbert

To support the reorganized and enlarged army, the panoply of Versailles, and the growing civil administration, the king needed a good deal of money. Finance was always the weak spot in the French monarchy. Methods of collecting taxes were costly and inefficient. Direct taxes passed through the hands of many intermediate officials; indirect taxes were collected by private concessionaries called tax farm-

Taxation

ers, who made a substantial profit. The state always received far less than what French taxpayers actually paid. But the main weakness arose from an old bargain between the French crown and nobility; the king might raise taxes without consent only if he refrained from taxing the nobles. Only the "unprivileged" classes paid direct taxes, and these came almost to mean the peasants only, because many merchants and urban professions in one way or another also obtained exemptions. The system was outrageously unjust in throwing a heavy tax burden on the poor and helpless. Louis XIV was

Thirty thousand workers were employed at one time in the building of the great royal château at Versailles. This seventeenth-century image by an unknown artist shows the activity at Versailles when the king, government ministers, and nobles were assembled in the vast buildings and gardens. The grandeur and scale of these buildings were designed to symbolize the king's power and to create a sense of awe in the foreign visitors who came to meet Louis XIV or his advisors.

(©Digital image courtesy of the Getty's Open Content Program)

willing enough to tax the nobles but was unwilling to fall under their control, and only toward the close of his reign, under extreme stress of war, was he able, for the first time in French history, to impose direct taxes on the aristocratic elements of the population. This was a step toward equality before the law and toward sound public finance, but the nobles and wealthiest bourgeois taxpayers received numerous concessions and exemptions that greatly reduced the financial value of the reforms.

Like his predecessors, Louis resorted to all manner of expedients to increase his revenues. He raised the tax rates, always with disappointing results. He devalued the currency. He sold patents of nobility to ambitious bourgeois. He sold government offices, judgeships, and commissions in the army and navy. For both financial and political reasons the king used his sovereign authority to annul the town charters, then sold back reduced rights at a price; this produced a little income but demoralized local government and civic spirit. The need for money arose from the fundamental inability to tax the wealthy. This problem reflected the weakness and limitations of absolutism because the government's refusal to share its rule with the propertied classes corrupted much of French public life and undermined the political aptitude of the French people.

Louis XIV wished, if only for his own purposes, to make France economically powerful. His great finance minister Jean-Baptiste Colbert worked for 20 years to do so. Colbert went beyond Richelieu in the application of mercantilism, aiming to make France a self-sufficing economic unit, to expand the export of French goods, and to increase the wealth from which government income was drawn. There was not much that he could do for agriculture, the principal industry of the kingdom, which remained less developed than in England and the Netherlands.

The Five Great Farms

But he managed to reduce internal tariffs in a large part of central France, where he set up a tariff union oddly entitled the Five Great Farms (because the remaining tolls were collected by tax farmers); and although vested interests and provincial liberties remained too strong for him to do away with all internal tariffs, the area of the Five Great Farms was in itself one of the largest free-trade areas in Europe, being about the size of England.

Colbert's Commercial Code

For the convenience of business Colbert promulgated a Commercial Code, replacing much of the local customary law with a new model of business practice and regulation. He improved communications by building roads and canals. Working through the guilds, he required the handicraft manufacturers to produce goods of specified kind and quality, believing that foreigners, if assured of quality by the government, would purchase French products. He gave subsidies, tax exemptions, and monopolies to expand the manufacture of silks, tapestries, glassware, and woolens.

Colbert also helped to found colonies, built up the navy, and established the French East India Company, which soon expanded the French presence in India. During this same era, the East India Company occupied and began to develop a new Caribbean colony in Saint-Domingue, a territory on the western side of the island of Hispaniola that Spain would officially cede to France in 1697. Enslaved Africans were taken to Saint-Domingue, where they became the labor force in a colonial plantation economy that would later produce very large and profitable shipments of sugar, coffee, and indigo for European markets. Within France itself, export of some goods, notably foodstuffs, was forbidden, for the government wished to keep the populace quiet by holding down the price of bread. Export of other goods, mainly manufactures, was encouraged, partly as a means of bringing money into the country, where it could be funneled into the royal treasury. The growth of the army, and the fact that under Louis XIV the government placed unprecedentedly

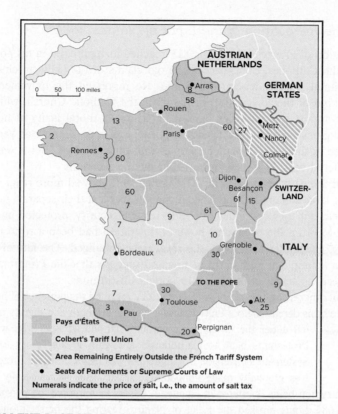

FRANCE FROM THE LAST YEARS OF LOUIS XIV TO THE REVOLUTION OF 1789
The map gives an idea of the diversity of law and administration before the Revolution. Dark areas are "pays d'etats," provinces in which representative bodies ("estates") continued to meet. Cities named are the seats of what the French called parlements (see pp. 181–182). The key indicates Colbert's tariff union, the Five Great Farms. The area marked with hatching remained outside the French tariff system entirely; it continued to trade with the states of the Holy Roman Empire (from which it had been annexed) without interference by the French government. Numerals indicate the price of salt, i.e., the varying burden of the salt tax, in various regions. In general, regions farthest from Paris enjoyed the most "privileges" or "liberties," preserving their legal and judicial identity, Provincial Estates, local tariffs, and a favored position in national taxation.

large orders for military uniforms, overcoats, weapons, and ammunition, greatly stimulated the employment of weavers, tailors, and gunsmiths and advanced the commercial capitalism by which such labors were organized. Trade and manufacture thus developed in France under more direct government guidance than in England; and the French gave the English an extremely brisk competition throughout the early modern era. Not until the age of iron and coal did France begin economically to lag.

In general, the system elaborated in the two centuries of Bourbon rule, known in retrospect as the Old Regime, was a society in which groups of many kinds could connect their own special interests with those of the absolute monarchy. But it rested on a precarious inconsistency. On the one hand, the royal government, through its intendants and bureaucracy, worked to restrict the privileges of provinces, nobles, and others. On the other hand, it multiplied and protected these and other privileges in its perpetual need for money. The inconsistency was not resolved until the Revolution of 1789, when the principle of equality of rights would replace the regime of privilege.

Religion: The Revocation of the Edict of Nantes, 1685

The consolidation of France under Louis XIV reached its high point in his policies toward religion. For the Catholics, Louis backed the old claims of the Gallican church to enjoy a certain national independence from Rome. He repressed the movement known as Jansenism, a kind of theological Calvinism within the Catholic Church, which remained influential for almost two centuries. Jansenists criticized moral laxity in high places as well as the religious power of the Jesuits, so there was wide support at Versailles when the king moved against all the main centers of Jansenist theology. But it was the Protestants who suffered most in a new wave of religious persecutions.

France, in the early years of Louis XIV's reign, still allowed more religious toleration than any other large state in Europe. The Huguenots had lost their separate political status under Richelieu, but they continued to live in relative security, protected by the Edict of Nantes of 1598. From the beginning, however, toleration had been a royal rather than a popular policy, and under Louis XIV the royal policy changed. The fate of Catholics at the hands of a triumphant Parliament in England suggests that the Protestants in France would have been no better off under more popular institutions.

Bending all other institutions to his will, Louis XIV resented the presence of heretics among his subjects. He considered religious unity necessary to the strength and dignity of his rule. He

Louis XIV seeks religious unity

fell under the influence of certain Catholic advisers who wished to turn Protestants back to Catholicism and gain greater glory for themselves. Systematic conversion of Huguenots was begun. Life for Protestant families was gradually made unbearable. Finally they were literally "dragooned," mounted infantrymen being quartered in Huguenot homes to reinforce the persuasions of missionaries. In 1685 Louis revoked the Edict of Nantes. During the persecutions hundreds of thousands of Protestants left France, migrating to Holland, Germany, and America. Their loss was a severe blow to French economic life, for although Protestants were found in all levels of French society, those of the commercial and industrial classes were the most mobile. With the revocation of the Edict of Nantes France embarked on a century of official intolerance (slowly mitigated in practice), under which Protestants in France were in much the same position as Catholics in the British Isles. The fact that 100 years later, when Protestants were again tolerated, many of them were found to be both commercially prosperous and politically loyal suggests that they actually fared far better than the Catholic Irish.

Accomplishments of Louis XIV

All things considered, the reign of Louis XIV brought considerable advantages to the French middle and lower classes. His most bitter critics, with the natural exception of Protestants, were disgruntled nobles such as the duke of Saint-Simon, who thought that he showed too many favors to persons of inferior social rank. Because Protestants were an unpopular minority, his repression of them won much approval. Colbert's system of economic regulation, and perpetuation of the guilds, meant that innovation and private enterprise developed less fully than in England, but France was economically stronger in 1700 than in 1650. Peasants were heavily taxed to pay for Louis XIV's wars, and they suffered through devastating famines after 1690 (also caused partly by the wars). But they did not sink into the serfdom that was rising in eastern Europe. Compared to later times, France was still a hodgepodge of competing jurisdictions, special privilege, and bureaucratic ineptitude. The king was in truth far from absolute but France was nevertheless the best organized of the large monarchies on the Continent. Louis XIV, in turning both high and low into dutiful subjects, may even have advanced the cause of abstract civil equality. For a long time he was generally popular. What finally turned his people against him in his last years was the strain of his incessant wars.

The systematic repression of French Huguenots after 1685 was widely condemned in Protestant countries. Images such as this gruesome depiction of torture contributed to the international hostility for Louis XIV and to the foreign acceptance of French refugees who scattered into Protestant states throughout Europe and North America.
(©DEA PICTURE LIBRARY/Getty Images)

22.   THE WARS OF LOUIS XIV: THE PEACE OF UTRECHT, 1713

Before 1700

From the outset of his reign Louis pursued a vigorous foreign policy. The quarrel between the house of France and the house of Habsburg had gone on for more than a century. When Louis XIV assumed his personal rule in 1661, Spanish territories still faced France on three sides (northeast, east, and south), but Spain was so weakened that this fact was no longer a menace to France; indeed, the surrounding Spanish territories were now a temptation to French expansion. Louis XIV could count on popular support in France, for the dream of a frontier on the Rhine and the Alps was captivating to Frenchmen. He struck first in 1667 by sending a large army into the Spanish Netherlands. He was blocked, as noted earlier, by the Triple Alliance of the Dutch, the English, and the Swedes. With strength renewed by reforms at home, and in alliance now with Charles II of England, Louis struck again in 1672 (the "Dutch War"), invading the Dutch provinces on the lower Rhine, and this time raising up against him his great adversary, the prince of Orange. William III, bringing the Austrian and Spanish Habsburgs, Brandenburg, and Denmark into alliance with the Dutch Republic, forced Louis to sign the treaty of Nimwegen in 1678. The French gave up their ambitions against Holland but took from Spain the rich province of Franche-Comté, which outflanked Alsace on the south and brought French power to the borders of Switzerland (see map, p. 155).

French incursions into the Holy Roman Empire

In the very next year, Louis further infiltrated the dissolving frontier of the Holy Roman Empire, this time in Lorraine and Alsace. By the Peace of Westphalia the French king had rights in this region, but the terms of that treaty were so ambiguous that claims could be made in contrary directions. In 1681 French troops occupied the city of Strasbourg, which, as a free city of the Holy Roman Empire, regarded itself as an independent little republic. A protest went up throughout Germany against this unprovoked invasion. But Germany was not a political unity. Since 1648 each German state conducted its own foreign policy, and at this very moment, in 1681, Louis XIV had an ally in the Elector of Brandenburg (forerunner of the kings of Prussia). The diet of the Holy Roman Empire was divided between an anti-French and a pro-French party. The emperor, Leopold I, was distracted by developments in the East. The Hungarians, incited and financed by Louis XIV, were again rebelling against the Habsburgs. They appealed to the Ottoman Turks, and Ottoman forces in 1683 moved up the Danube and besieged Vienna. Louis XIV, if he did not on this occasion positively assist the Turks, ostentatiously declined to join the proposed crusade against them.

The Habsburg emperor, with Polish assistance, was able to push the Ottoman army out of Austria. Returning to his western problems and observing the western border of the empire crumbling, Franche-Comté already lost, the Spanish Netherlands threatened, and Lorraine and Alsace absorbed bit by bit, the Emperor Leopold gathered the Catholic powers into a combination against the French. The Protestant states at the same time, aroused by the French revocation of the Edict of Nantes in 1685 and by Huguenot émigrés who called down the wrath of God on the perfidious Sun King, began to ally the more readily with William of Orange. Catholic and Protestant enemies of Louis XIV thus came together in 1686 in the League of Augsburg, which comprised the Holy Roman Emperor, the kings of Spain and of Sweden, the electors of Bavaria, Saxony, and the Palatinate, and the Dutch Republic. In 1686 the king of England was still a protégé of France, but three years later, when William became king in England, that country too joined the League.

The War of the League of Augsburg

The War of the League of Augsburg began in 1688. The French armies won battles but could not drive so many enemies from the field. The French navy could not overpower the combined fleets of the Dutch and English. Louis XIV found himself badly strained (it was at this time that he first imposed direct taxes on the French nobles) and finally made peace at Ryswick in the Netherlands in 1697, leaving matters about where they had been when the war began.

In all the warring and negotiating the question had not been merely the fate of this or that piece of territory, nor even the French thrust to the east, but the eventual disposition of the whole empire of Spain. The Spanish king, Charles II, prematurely senile, defied all expectations by living on year after year. The greatest diplomatic issue of the day was thus still unsettled, and his long-awaited death, in 1700, soon led to a long war for control of the Spanish throne and Spain's vast colonial empire.

The War of the Spanish Succession

The War of the Spanish Succession lasted 11 years, from 1702 to 1713. It was less destructive than the Thirty Years' War, for armies were now supplied in more orderly fashion, subject to more orderly discipline and command, and could be stopped from fighting at the will of their governments. Except for the effects of civil war in Spain and of deadly famines in France, the civilian populations were generally spared from violence and destruction. In this respect the war foreshadowed the typical warfare of the eighteenth century, fought by professional armies rather than by whole peoples. Among wars of the largest scale, the War of the Spanish Succession was the first in which religion counted for little, the first in which commerce and sea power were the principal stakes, and the first in which English money was liberally used in Continental politics. It was also the first that can be called a "world war," because it involved the overseas world together with the leading powers of Europe. Wars within Europe were becoming linked to the global competition for colonies and trade.

The struggle had long been foreseen. The two main aspirants to the Spanish inheritance were the king of France and the Holy Roman Emperor. Each had married a sister of the perpetually moribund Charles II, and each could hope to place a younger member of his family on the throne of Spain. During the last decades of the seventeenth century the powers had made various treaties agreeing to partition the Spanish possessions. The idea was, by dividing the Spanish heritage between the two claimants, to preserve the balance of power in Europe. But when Charles II finally died, it was found that he had made a will, which stipulated that the empire of Spain should be kept intact, that all Spanish territories throughout the world should go to the grandson of Louis XIV, and that if Louis XIV refused to accept in the name of his 17-year-old grandson, the entire inheritance should pass to the son of the Habsburg emperor in Vienna. Louis XIV decided to accept. With Bourbons reigning in Versailles and Madrid, even if the two thrones were never united, French influence would now run from Belgium to the Straits of Gibraltar, and from Milan to Mexico and Manila. At Versailles the word went out: "The Pyrenees exist no longer."

"The Pyrenees exist no longer"

Never, at least in almost two centuries, had the political balance within Europe been so threatened. Never had the other states faced such a prospect of relegation to the sidelines. William III acted at once; he gathered the stunned or hesitant diplomats into the last of his coalitions, the Grand Alliance of 1701. Although he died the next year, before hostilities began, and with Louis XIV at the seeming apex of his grandeur, William had in fact launched the engine that was to crush the Sun King. The Grand Alliance included England, Holland, and the Austrian emperor, supported by Brandenburg and eventually by Portugal and the Italian duchy of Savoy. Louis XIV could count on Spain, which was generally loyal to the late king's will. Otherwise his only ally was Bavaria, whose rivalry with Austria made it a habitual satellite of France. The Bavarian alliance gave the French armies an advanced position toward Vienna and maintained that internal division within Germany that was fundamental to both the French ascendancy and the ongoing struggle to maintain an international balance of power.

Threats to political balance

The war was long, mainly because each side no sooner gained a temporary advantage than it raised its demands on the other. The English, though they sent relatively few troops to the Continent, produced in John Churchill, Duke of Marlborough, a preeminent military commander for the Allied forces. The Austrians were led by Prince Eugene of Savoy. The Allies won notable battles at Blenheim in Bavaria (1704), and at Ramillies (1706), Oudenarde (1708), and Malplaquet (1709) in the Spanish Netherlands. The French were routed; Louis XIV asked for peace but then would not agree to a treaty because the Allied terms were so enormous. Louis fought to hold the two crowns, to conquer the Spanish Netherlands, to get French merchants into Spanish America, and at the worst in self-defense. After minor successes in 1710 he again insisted on controlling the crown of Spain. The Spanish fought to uphold the will of the deceased king, the unity of the Spanish possessions, and even the integrity of Spain itself—for the English moved in at Gibraltar and made a menacing treaty with Portugal. Meanwhile, the Austrians landed at Barcelona and invaded Catalonia, which (as in 1640) again rose in rebellion, recognizing the Austrian claimant to the Spanish throne, so that all Spain fell into civil war.

Motives of the warring states

The Austrians fought to keep Spain under the control the Habsburg family, to crush Bavaria, and to carry Austrian influence across the Alps into Italy. The Dutch fought as always for their security, to keep the French out of Belgium, and to control access to the river Scheldt. The English fought for these same reasons and also to keep the French-supported Catholic Stuarts out of England and preserve the Revolution of 1688. It was to be expected that the Stuarts, if they returned, would ruin the Bank of England and repudiate the national debt. Both maritime powers, England and Holland, fought to keep French merchants out of Spanish America and to advance their own commercial position in America and the Mediterranean. These war aims made the Whigs the implacable war party in England, whereas the vaguely pro-Stuart and anticommercial Tories were quite willing to make peace at an early date. As for the minor allies, Brandenburg and Savoy, their rulers had simply entered the alliance to gain such advantages as might turn up.

The Peace of Utrecht

The partition of Spain's holdings

Peace was finally made at the treaties of Utrecht and Rastatt of 1713 and 1714. The treaty of Utrecht, with its allied instruments, in fact partitioned the world of Spain. But it did not divide it between the two legal claimants only. The British remained at Gibraltar, to the great irritation of the Spaniards, and likewise annexed the island of Minorca. The Duke of Savoy eventually gained the former Spanish island of Sardinia in return for his contribution to the Allied cause. The rest of the Spanish Mediterranean holdings—Milan, Naples, and Sicily—passed to the Austrian Habsburgs, as did the Spanish Netherlands (or Belgium), subsequently referred to as the Austrian Netherlands. In Spain itself, shorn of its European possessions but retaining America, the grandson of Louis XIV was confirmed as king (Philip V of Spain), on the understanding that the French and Spanish thrones should never be inherited by the same person. The Bourbons reigned in Spain, with interruptions, from Philip V to the republican revolution of 1931. French influence was strong in the eighteenth century, for a good many French courtiers, advisers, administrators, and merchants crossed the Pyrenees with Philip V. They helped somewhat to revive the Spanish monarchy by applying the methods of Louis XIV, and they passed a swelling volume of French manufactures through Seville into Spanish America.

Consequences of the war for France

The old objective of William III, to prevent French domination of the Netherlands and of Europe, was realized at last. The war itself was the main cause of French loss of strength. It produced poverty, misery, and depopulation, and it exposed Louis XIV to severe criticism at home. Recurring famines and tax increases provoked peasant uprisings, which were brutally repressed. Dissatisfaction with the war led also to a revival of aristocratic and parliamentary opposition. By the peace treaties the French abandoned, for the time being, their efforts to conquer what now became the Austrian Netherlands. They ceased to recognize the Stuart pretender as king of Great Britain. They surrendered to the British two of their colonies, Newfoundland and Nova Scotia (called Acadia), and recognized British sovereignty in the disputed American northwest, known as the Hudson Bay

The battle of Blenheim, portrayed here by the French émigré artist Louis Laguerre (1663–1721), was fought in Bavaria in 1704. It was a great victory for the English and the Allied forces that had joined to oppose the French in the War of Spanish Succession. The English commander, John Churchill, Duke of Marlborough, is the central figure in Laguerre's painting. Blenheim brought fame and rewards to Marlborough, but for the French it was the first in a series of military defeats that steadily weakened the power of Louis XIV.

(©Print Collector/Getty Images)

territory. But the French were only checked, not downed. They retained the conquests of Louis XIV in Alsace and the Franche-Comté. Their influence was strong in Spain. Their deeper strength and capacity for recovery were soon evident in renewed economic expansion. Their language and civilization continued to spread throughout Europe.

The Dutch received guarantees of their security. They were granted the right to garrison the "Dutch Barrier," a string of forts in the Austrian Netherlands on the side toward France. But the Dutch, strained by the war and outdistanced by England, never again played a primary role in European political affairs. Two other small states ascended over the diplomatic horizon, Savoy (or Piedmont) and Brandenburg. The rulers of both, for having sided with the victors, were recognized as "kings" by the treaty of Utrecht. Savoy came to be known as "Sardinia," and Brandenburg as "Prussia."

The greatest winners were the British. Great Britain made its appearance as a great power. The union of England and Scotland had taken place during the war. Based at Gibraltar and Minorca, Britain was now a power in the Mediterranean. The Southern Netherlands, the "pistol *Britain becomes a great power* pointed at the heart of England," was in the innocuous hands of the Austrians. The British added to their American holdings, but far more valuable than Newfoundland and Nova Scotia was the *asiento* extorted from Spain. The *asiento* granted the lucrative privilege (which the French had sought) of providing Spanish America with African slaves. Much of the wealth of Bristol and Liverpool in the following decades was to be built upon the slave trade. The *asiento,* by permitting one shipload of British goods to be brought each year to Porto Bello in Panama, also provided opportunities for illicit trade in nonhuman cargoes.

A PEASANT INTERIOR
by Louis Le Nain (French, c. 1600–1648)
Although Le Nain portrayed this peasant family in the 1640s, the people in this painting resemble the peasants who later suffered through wars, famines, and tax increases in the last decades of the long reign of Louis XIV.
(Source: National Gallery of Art)

The Spanish Empire was pried open, and British merchants entered on an era of wholesale smuggling into Spanish America, competing strenuously with the French, who because of their favored position in Spain were usually able to go through more legal channels. Moreover, the British, by defeating France, assured themselves of a line of Protestant kings and of the maintenance of constitutional and parliamentary government. The ratification of the Peace of Utrecht actually marked a further step in the evolution of English constitutional history. The Whigs, who were the main supporters of the war with France, thought the treaty insufficiently favorable to England. The Tories, pledged to peace, had won the House of Commons in 1710, but the Whigs continued to control the House of Lords. Queen Anne, at the request of Tory leaders and in the interests of peace, raised 12 Tory commoners to the peerage in order to create a Tory majority in the Lords and hence to obtain ratification of the treaty. This established itself as a precedent; it became an unwritten article of the British constitution that when the Lords blocked the Commons on an important issue, the monarch could create enough new lords to make a new majority in that House. After 1713, the Lords never again allowed themselves to

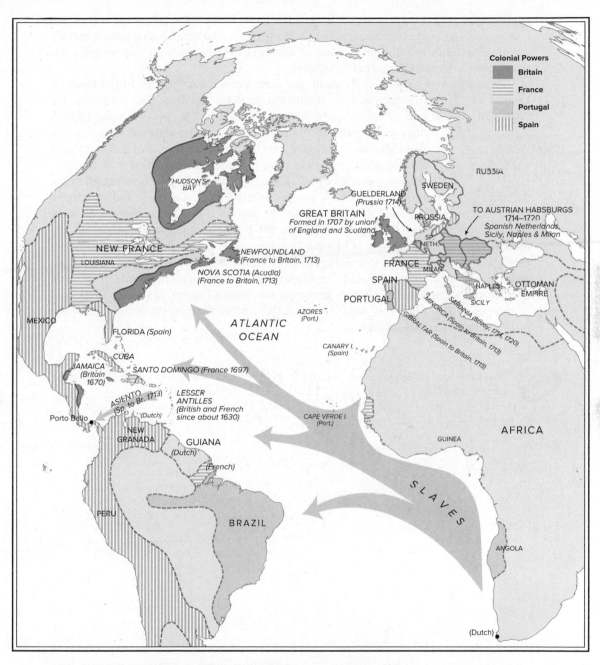

Colonial Powers

- Britain
- France
- Portugal
- Spain

HUDSON'S BAY

GUELDERLAND *(Prussia 1714)*

SWEDEN

RUSSIA

GREAT BRITAIN
Formed in 1707 by union of England and Scotland

PRUSSIA

TO AUSTRIAN HABSBURGS 1714–1720
Spanish Netherlands, Sicily, Naples & Milan

NEW FRANCE

LOUISIANA

NEWFOUNDLAND (France to Britain, 1713)

NOVA SCOTIA (Acadia) (France to Britain, 1713)

SP. NETH.

FRANCE

MILAN

SPAIN

PORTUGAL

NAPLES

OTTOMAN EMPIRE

SICILY

SARDINIA *(Savoy, 1714, 1720)*

MINORCA *(Spain to Britain, 1714, 1720)*

GIBRALTAR *(Spain to Britain, 1713)*

ATLANTIC OCEAN

AZORES (Port.)

MEXICO

FLORIDA *(Spain)*

CUBA

JAMAICA *(Britain 1670)*

SANTO DOMINGO (France 1697)

CANARY I. *(Spain)*

ASIENTO (Sp. to Br. 1713)

LESSER ANTILLES (British and French since about 1630)

(Dutch)

CAPE VERDE I. *(Port.)*

AFRICA

GUINEA

Porto Bello

NEW GRANADA

GUIANA *(Dutch)* *(French)*

PERU

BRAZIL

SLAVES

ANGOLA

(Dutch)

THE ATLANTIC WORLD AFTER THE PEACE OF UTRECHT, 1713

The map shows the partitioning of the Spanish Empire and the rise of the British. Spain and its American possessions went to the Bourbon Philip V; the European possessions of Spain—the Netherlands, Milan, Naples, and Sicily—went to the Austrian Habsburgs. Britain meanwhile was strengthened by the union of England and Scotland, the acquisition of Minorca, Gibraltar, and the commercial privilege of the *asiento* from Spain, and of Newfoundland and Nova Scotia from France. The French, for their part, had taken control of rich, Caribbean lands in Saint-Domingue (Santo Domingo) through an earlier treaty with Spain.

be swamped by newcomers and thus acceded in all future disputes to the will of the Commons. The landed aristocracy and their merchant allies could now govern as they saw fit. The result was a rapid increase of wealth in England, precipitating within a few generations a veritable Industrial Revolution.

Except for the addition of England, the same powers were parties to the treaty of Utrecht in 1713 as to the Peace of Westphalia in 1648, and they now confirmed the system of international relations established by Westphalia. The powers accepted each

Confirmation of the European system

other as members of the European system; recognized each other as sovereign states connected only by free negotiation, war, and treaty; and adjusted their differences through rather facile exchanges of territory, made in the interests of a balance of power, and without regard to the nationality or presumed wishes of the peoples affected. With Germany still in extreme fragmentation, Italy divided into minor states or controlled by foreign kings, and Spain subordinated to France, the treaty of Utrecht left France and Great Britain as the two most vigorous imperial powers of Europe. These countries soon became the two principal carriers and exporters of the European civilization that would spread its empires, commerce, institutions, and ideas throughout much of the modern world. In the next chapter we look at how the societies of central and eastern Europe, developed along lines of their own, even when they were strongly influenced by the growing power and wealth of the western European states.

 Suggested Further Readings can be found in the ebook, on Connect, or online at www.mhhe .com/kramer12e.

Chapter 5

THE TRANSFORMATION OF EASTERN EUROPE, 1648–1740

In eastern Europe, in the century after the Peace of Westphalia of 1648, it became apparent that political systems that failed to become more "modern" might be in danger of going out of existence. In the mid-seventeenth century most parts of eastern Europe belonged to one or another of three older, decentralized political organizations—the Holy Roman Empire, the Republic of Poland, and the empire of the Ottoman Turks (see maps, pp. 205, 206). All three were loosely organized and increasingly ineffective. They were challenged and gradually superseded by three new and stronger powers—Prussia, Austria, and Russia. These three, by overrunning the intermediate ground of Poland, came to adjoin one another and cover all eastern Europe except the Balkans, which remained within the Ottoman Empire. It was in this same period that Russia expanded territorially, adopted some of the technical and administrative apparatus of western Europe, and became an active participant in European affairs.

East and west are of course relative terms. For the Russians Germany and even Poland were "western." But for Europe as a whole a significant though indefinite social and economic line ran roughly along the Elbe River and the Bohemian Mountains to the head of the Adriatic Sea. East of this line towns were fewer than in the west, human labor was less productive, and the middle classes were less strong. Above all, the peasants were governed by their landlords. From the sixteenth to the eighteenth century, in eastern Europe in contrast to what happened in the west, the peasants increasingly lost many of their older, feudal-type rights and freedoms. The commercial revolution and widening of the market created a strong merchant class in western Europe and tended to turn working people into a legally free and mobile labor force. In eastern Europe these changes strengthened the great landlords who produced for export and who secured their labor force by the institutions of serfdom and "hereditary subjection." The main social unit was the agricultural estate. The lord exploited his estate with uncompensated compulsory labor (or *robot*) furnished by his people, who could not migrate, marry, or learn a trade except

Chapter emblem: Russian workers building the new city of St. Petersburg during the reign of Tsar Peter I (1689–1725). (©Bettman/Getty Images)

as he permitted, and who, until the eighteenth century, had no legal protector or court of appeal other than himself. In the east, therefore, the landlords were exceedingly powerful. They were the only significant political class. And the three new states that grew up during this era—Prussia, Austria, Russia—were alike in being landlord states.

23. THREE AGING EMPIRES

In 1648 the whole mainland of Europe from the French border almost to Moscow was occupied by the three large and loosely built structures that have been mentioned—the Holy Roman Empire, the Republic of Poland, and the empire of the Ottoman Turks. The Ottoman power reached deeply into Europe, to about 50 miles from Vienna, and it extended over what is now Romania and over the Tartars on the north shore of the Black Sea. Even so, its European holdings were but a projection from the main mass of the Ottoman Empire in the Middle East and North Africa. Poland extended from roughly 100 miles east of Berlin to a hundred miles west of Moscow and virtually from "sea to sea" in the old phrase of its patriots, from the Baltic around Riga almost to the Black Sea coast. The Holy Roman Empire extended from Poland and Hungary to the North Sea.

These three empires were by no means alike. The Holy Roman Empire bore some of the oldest traditions of Christendom. Poland too had old connections with western Europe and Christian religious institutions. Ottoman Turkey was a Muslim power, closely connected

Weaknesses of the empires

to the Islamic civilization of the Middle East and filled with peoples who generally lived outside European cultural or religious traditions (despite a long history of Mediterranean trade and commerce). Yet in some ways the three resembled each other. In all of them central authority had become weak, consisting largely of collaborations between a nominal head and outlying dignitaries or potentates. All lacked efficient systems of administration and government. All faced challenges from the newer, centralizing states that were now developing in countries such as France. All, but especially Poland and the Ottoman Empire, were made up of diverse ethnic or language groups. The whole immense area was therefore politically fragmented and weak. It was malleable in the hands of kings or ruling elites who might become a little stronger than their neighbors. We must try to see in what this weakness consisted, and how newer, stronger state forms were created.

The Holy Roman Empire after 1648

The Holy Roman Empire, especially after the Peace of Westphalia, was little more than an impressive name. It had no real power because it lacked almost all the resources of a functioning imperial system. It possessed no real army, revenues, or working organs of a central government; and as Voltaire later observed, it was neither holy nor Roman nor an empire. Created in the Middle Ages, it had been ruined by the Reformation, which left the Germans divided almost evenly between Protestant and Catholic, with each side thereafter demanding special safeguards against the other. The empire still claimed to be universal, however, in that it had no relation to a specific nationality. In theory, the Holy Roman Empire was a form of government suitable to all peoples, although it had never lived up to this theoretical claim and had not expanded since the Middle Ages. In actuality, the empire was roughly coterminous with the German states and the region of the German language, except that it excluded after 1648 the

Dutch and Swiss, who no longer considered themselves German; and it likewise excluded those Germans who since the fourteenth century had settled along the eastern shores of the Baltic.

Large parts of the empire had suffered repeatedly from the Thirty Years' War. Yet the war, and the peace terms that followed it, only accentuated an economic situation that had already become unfavorable. Postwar revival was difficult; the breakup of commercial

Effects of the Thirty Years' War

connections and the wartime losses of savings and capital were hard to overcome. Germany fell increasingly out of step with the economic expansion and cultural changes in western Europe. The burgher class, its ambitions blocked, lost much of its old vitality while western European traders were expanding their commerce across the Atlantic world. No overseas colonies could be founded, for want of strong enough government backing, as was shown when a colonial venture of Brandenburg came to nothing. There were no stock exchanges in German cities until one was established at Vienna in 1771, half a century after those of London, Paris, and Amsterdam. Laws, tariffs, tolls, and coinage were more diverse than in France. Even the calendar varied. It varied, indeed, throughout Europe as a whole, because Protestant states long declined to accept the corrected calendar issued by Pope Gregory XIII in 1582; in parts of divided Germany the holidays, the date of the month, and the day of the week changed every few miles. The arts and letters, flourishing in western Europe as never before, were at a low ebb in Germany during the seventeenth century. In science the Germans during and after the Thirty Years' War accomplished less than the English, Dutch, French, or Italians, despite the great mathematician and philosopher Gottfried Wilhelm Leibniz, one of the influential intellectual leaders of the age. Only in music, in the work of performers and composers such as the Bach family, did the Germans at this time excel. But music was not then much heard beyond the place of its origin. Germany was thus mostly a byway in the new creative arts and culture of seventeenth-century Europe.

After the Thirty Years' War each German state had sovereign rights. These states numbered some 300 or 2,000, depending on how they were counted. The higher figure included the "knights of the empire," found in south Germany and the Rhineland. They were persons who acknowledged no overlordship except that of the emperor himself. The knights held tiny estates, averaging not over 100 acres apiece, consisting of an "independent" castle and a manor or two, completely enclosed by the territory of a larger surrounding state. But even without the knights there were about 300 states capable of some independence of action—free cities, abbots without subjects, archbishops and bishops ruling with temporal power, landgraves, margraves and dukes, and one king, the king of Bohemia.

All these states were intent on preserving what were called the "Germanic liberties." They were gladly assisted by outside powers, notably but not exclusively France. The Germanic liberties meant freedom of the member states from control by emperor or empire. The

The "Germanic liberties"

rulers of the most important states within the empire elected the emperor (there were nine electors by the end of the seventeenth century), and they always required the successful candidate to accept certain "capitulations," in which he promised to safeguard all the privileges and immunities of the states. The Habsburgs, though consistently elected after 1438, had none of the advantages of hereditary rulers who passed increasing governmental powers to their heirs. The elective principle meant that imperial power could not be accumulated and transmitted from one generation to the next. It opened the doors to foreign intrigue, because the electors were willing to consider whichever candidate would promise them most. The French repeatedly supported a rival candidate to the Habsburgs. After 1648 they had supporters in the electoral college, Bavaria and Cologne being the most consistently pro-French. In 1742 the French obtained the elevation of their Bavarian ally to the imperial throne. The office of emperor became a political football for Germans and non-Germans alike.

Nor would the German states, after the Thirty Years' War, allow any authority to the imperial diet. The diet possessed the power to raise troops and taxes for the whole empire, but this power remained unused because the various states feared that any such action would diminish their own authority and independence. Meanwhile, the states that insisted with such obstinacy on their liberties from the empire gave few liberties to their own subjects. The free cities were closed urban oligarchies, as indeed were most cities in other countries, but in Germany the burgher oligarchs controlled free cities that were almost like sovereign states. Most of the other European countries, large or small, developed in the direction of a centralizing absolutism. Such absolutism was checked for Germany as a whole, only to reappear in miniature in hundreds of different places. Each ruler thought himself a little Louis XIV, each court a small Versailles. Subjects became attached by ties of sentiment to their rulers, who almost always lived in the neighborhood and could be readily seen by passersby. People liked the small courts, the small armies, the gossipy politics, and the familiar officials of their tiny states; and despite all its flaws, the empire had the merit of holding this conglomeration of states in a lawful relation to one another. For a century and a half after 1648 small states existed alongside larger ones, or often totally enclosed within them, without serious fear for their security and without losing their independence.

Yet there were many ambitious rulers in Germany after the Peace of Westphalia. They had won recognition of their sovereignty in 1648. They were busily building absolutist monarchies, and they aspired also to expand their dominions. There were other ways of doing this than by devouring their smaller neighbors outright. One was by marriage and inheritance. The empire in this respect was a paradise for fortune hunters; the variety of possible marriages was enormous because of the great number of ruling families. Another outlet for ambition lay in the high politics of the empire. The Wittelsbach family, which ruled in Bavaria, managed to win an electorate in the Thirty Years' War. Using this political influence, they consistently placed family members in prominent ecclesiastical posts throughout the Rhineland and attracted support from France, which in turn backed them against the Habsburgs. The Guelph family, ruling in Hanover, schemed for years to obtain an electorate, which they finally extorted from the emperor in 1692; in 1714 they inherited the throne of Great Britain with King George I, preferred by the British as Protestants to their Catholic Stuart cousins. The Hohenzollerns, electors of Brandenburg, inherited territories as far apart as the Rhine and Vistula rivers.

CENTRAL AND EASTERN EUROPE, 1660–1795
The upper panel of this map indicates boundaries as of 1660; the lower panel those of 1795, by which time the Ottoman Empire had been pushed back toward the Balkans and the Republic of Poland had been destroyed by Prussia, Austria, and Russia. Both panels show the evolving social border between the eastern and western agrarian zones, running from the mouth of the Elbe River into central Germany and down to Trieste. East of this line, from the sixteenth to the eighteenth centuries, the peasants sank toward a new kind of serfdom in which they rendered forced labor to their lords on large farms. West of the line the peasants owed little or no forced labor and tilled small farms that they owned or rented. This line marks a somewhat imprecise but significant social boundary that would also have an important influence on the political and economic history of modern Europe. This complex area is also shown in simplified form on p. 206.

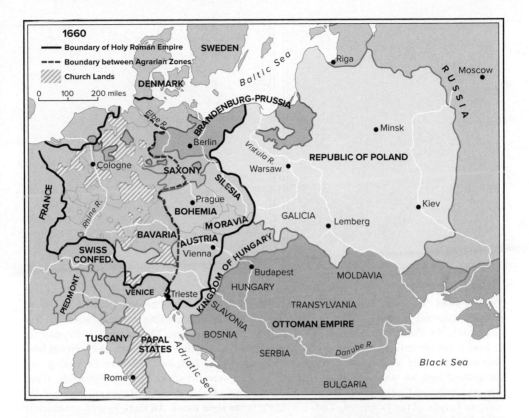

1660

— Boundary of Holy Roman Empire
- - - Boundary between Agrarian Zones
▨ Church Lands

0   100   200 miles

SWEDEN
Baltic Sea
• Riga
RUSSIA
• Moscow
DENMARK
BRANDENBURG-PRUSSIA
Elbe R.
• Berlin
• Minsk
Vistula R.
REPUBLIC OF POLAND
• Cologne
SAXONY
• Warsaw
SILESIA
FRANCE
Rhine R.
• Prague
BOHEMIA
GALICIA
• Lemberg
MORAVIA
• Kiev
BAVARIA   AUSTRIA
SWISS
CONFED.
• Vienna
KINGDOM OF HUNGARY
• Budapest
MOLDAVIA
VENICE
PIEDMONT
Trieste
HUNGARY
TRANSYLVANIA
SLAVONIA
OTTOMAN EMPIRE
BOSNIA
TUSCANY   PAPAL
STATES
SERBIA
Danube R.
Black Sea
Adriatic Sea
• Rome
BULGARIA

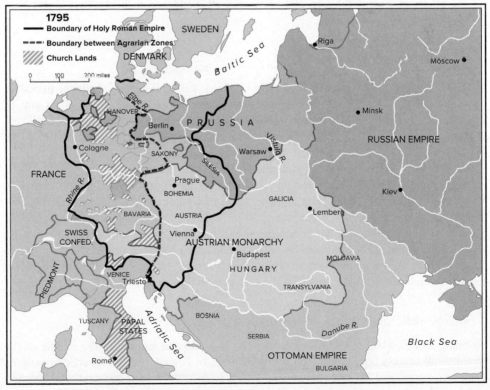

1795

— Boundary of Holy Roman Empire
- - - Boundary between Agrarian Zones
▨ Church Lands

0   100   200 miles

SWEDEN
Baltic Sea
• Riga
DENMARK
• Moscow
HANOVER
Elbe R.
• Berlin
P R U S S I A
• Minsk
RUSSIAN EMPIRE
• Cologne
SAXONY
Vistula R.
FRANCE
SILESIA
• Warsaw
Rhine R.
• Prague
BOHEMIA
GALICIA
• Kiev
BAVARIA
AUSTRIA
• Lemberg
SWISS
CONFED.
• Vienna
AUSTRIAN MONARCHY
MOLDAVIA
VENICE
PIEDMONT
Trieste
• Budapest
H U N G A R Y
TRANSYLVANIA
TUSCANY   PAPAL
STATES
BOSNIA
SERBIA
Danube R.
Black Sea
Adriatic Sea
• Rome
OTTOMAN EMPIRE
BULGARIA

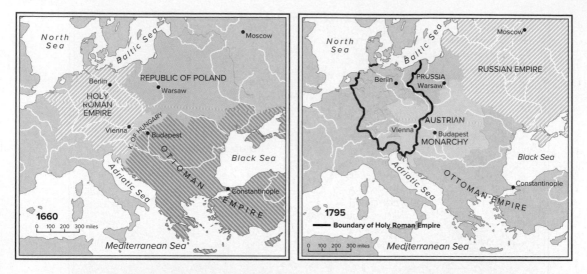

AGING EMPIRES AND NEW POWERS

The left panel shows the "three aging empires" that occupied much of central and eastern Europe in the seventeenth century. Though maintaining themselves with growing difficulty under modern conditions, the Polish Republic lasted until 1795, the Holy Roman Empire until 1806, and the Ottoman Empire until 1923. Meanwhile, beginning in the seventeenth century, the political leadership in this area was assumed by three rising monarchical states that were developing new institutions such as standing armies and professional bureaucracies. These reorganizing states were the Austrian Empire of the Habsburgs, the Prussian kingdom of the Hohenzollerns, and the Russian Empire of the Romanovs. They are shown in the right panel. All three figured prominently in the affairs of Europe for over 200 years; and all would perish in the First World War, 1914–1918.

The half-century after the Peace of Westphalia was thus a highly critical period in central Europe. The situation in Germany was fluid. No one could tell which, if any, of the half-dozen chief German states would emerge in the lead. Nothing was crystallized;

Austria and Prussia

anything might happen. Two states definitely came forward after 1700, built by the skill and persistence of their rulers—Austria and Prussia. It is a curious and revealing fact that neither really had a political or cultural name of its own. They were for a long time known most commonly as "houses"— the house of Austria or Habsburg and the house of Brandenburg or Hohenzollern. Each house put together a certain combination of territories. Each would have been as willing to possess any other territorial combination had the course of events been different. By extension of meaning, one came to be called "Austria," which for centuries had been simply an archduchy on the upper Danube. The other, "Prussia," for centuries had meant only a certain stretch of the Baltic coast. To these two expanding states we shall shortly turn.

The Republic of Poland about 1650

Running almost 1,000 miles eastward from the Holy Roman Empire in the middle of the seventeenth century lay the vast tract of the Republic of Poland, called a republic because its king was elected and because the political classes took pride in their constitutional liberties.

COUNT STANISLAS POTOCKI
by Jacques-Louis David (French, 1748–1825)
This portrait of a well-known eighteenth-century Polish nobleman—painted by David in 1781—expresses the sense of independent grandeur that characterized the Polish aristocracy for several centuries in the early modern era.
(©Erich Lessing/Art Resource, NY)

Its vast size was one cause of its internal peculiarities. No administrative system could have kept up with the expansion of its frontiers, so that a large degree of freedom had always been left to outlying lords. In addition, this geographical expansion had given the Republic of Poland a heterogeneous population with diverse cultures, languages, and religions.

The Polish state was a far more recent and less substantial creation than the Holy Roman Empire. It was made up of two main parts, Poland proper (the Kingdom of Poland) in the west and the Grand Duchy of Lithuania in the east. They had been joined by a union of their crowns (see maps, pp. 205, 206). Only in the west was there a large Polish population. The Duchy of Prussia, a fief of the Polish crown, was peopled mainly by Germans. Further east a Byelorussian and Ukrainian peasantry was subject to a scattering of Polish and Lithuanian landlords.

Poland and Lithuania

Even in Poland itself the town population was not generally "Polish" in its language or culture. Most townspeople were Germans and Jews. The Jews spoke Yiddish, derived from German, and were very numerous because a king of Poland in the later Middle Ages had welcomed Jewish refugees fleeing from anti-Jewish violence in Germany. They lived in separate communities with their own law, language, and religion, forming large vibrant islands of Orthodox Jewish life in the Gentile ocean. The Germans too held to their own linguistic and cultural traditions, resisting assimilation to the communities that surrounded them. An unsurpassable barrier thus existed between town and country. There was no national middle class. The official and political language was Latin. Roman Catholicism was the leading religion.

Poland was the region in which the landed aristocracy prevailed most successfully over all other groups in the country, neither allowing the consolidation of the state on absolutist lines nor yet creating an effective constitutional or parliamentary government. The Polish aristocracy, or *szlachta,* made up some 8 percent of the population, a far higher proportion than the aristocracy of any country in western Europe. On this ground the old Polish kingdom has sometimes been considered, especially by later Polish nationalists, as the possessor of an early form of democracy. The aristocracy were sticklers for their liberties, which resembled the German liberties in that they consisted largely of a fierce suspicion of central authority and were a perpetual invitation to foreign interference. As in the Holy Roman Empire, the monarchy was elective, and the king upon election had to accept certain contractual agreements, which, like the German "capitulations," prevented the accumulation of monarchical authority. The Poles were too politically divided to accept one of their own number as king, so from 1572 to the extinction of Poland over two centuries later there were only two native Polish kings who reigned for any length of time. One of these kings was the national hero John Sobieski, who led a decisive campaign against the army of the Ottoman Empire during the 1680s.

Weakness of central government

As in Germany, the central diet was ineffective, so the centers of political action were local. The aristocracy met in 50 or 60 regional diets, turbulent assemblages of warlike gentry, in which the great lords used the lesser lords for their own purposes. The central diet, from which the towns were excluded, was a periodic meeting of emissaries, under binding instructions from the regional diets. It came to be recognized, as one of the liberties of Poland, that the central diet could take no action to which any member objected. Any member, by stating his unalterable opposition, could oblige a diet to disband. This was the famous *liberum veto,* the free veto, and to use it to break up a diet was called "exploding" the diet. The first diet was exploded in 1652. Of 55 diets held from that year to 1764, 48 were exploded.

Government under these conditions became a paralyzing stalemate. The monopoly of law and force, characteristic of the modern state, failed to develop in Poland. The king of Poland had practically no army, no law courts, no officials, and no income. The nobility paid no taxes, and no institution had the authority or power to make reforms. By 1750 the revenues of the king of Poland were about one-thirteenth those of the tsar of Russia and one seventy-fifth those of the king of France. Armed force was in the hands of a dozen or so aristocratic leaders, who also conducted their individual foreign policies, pursuing their own adventures against the Turks, or bringing in Russians, French, or Swedes to help them against other Poles. The landlords became local monarchs on their manorial estates. The mass of the rural population fell deeper into a serfdom scarcely different from slavery, bound to compulsory labor on estates resembling plantations, with police and disciplinary powers in the hands of the lords and with no outside legal or administrative system to set the limits of exploitation.

The huge expanse comprised under the name of Poland was, in short, a political vacuum; and as more powerful centers developed, notably around Berlin and Moscow, the push against the Polish frontiers became steadily stronger. It was facilitated by the Poles themselves. As early as 1660 the East Prussian fief became independent of the Polish crown. As early as 1667 the Muscovites reconquered Smolensk and Kiev. Already there was confidential talk of partitioning Poland, which, however, was deferred for a century. Much of the history of modern Europe would have been different had the seventeenth-century Republic of Poland held together or built a more powerful, centralized state. There may have been no kingdom of Prussia and no Prussian influence in Germany; nor would Russia have become the chief Slavic power or reached so far into central Europe.

Pressures on Poland

The Ottoman Empire about 1650

The Ottoman state, the third of the three multicultural empires that together spread over so much of central and eastern Europe, was larger than either of the others, and in the seventeenth century it was much more solidly organized and powerful. In 1529 the Ottoman Turks had attacked Vienna and seemed about to move into Germany, where the bitter conflicts of the Lutheran Reformation were then dividing and distracting the German princes. To most people in Europe the Turks were a mystery as well as a commercial rival or a looming military threat. We have seen, for example, how Philip II of Spain sent his navy to wage war against Ottoman forces in the Mediterranean during the sixteenth century. But Turkish culture and institutions were still not well known in Europe. The Turks had lived originally in central Asia, from where they migrated into Anatolia during the Middle Ages and eventually conquered Constantinople in 1453. They were Muslims who drew much of their Islamic civilization from the Arabs and Persians, whom they had also conquered and with whom they had developed extensive cultural and economic exchanges over several centuries. Turkish armies had entered the Balkans even before their conquest of Constantinople, and they steadily gained control of new Balkan territories after military victories, such as the Battle of Kosovo (1389). The Ottoman Empire later expanded deeper into Europe under the skillful leadership of Suleiman the Magnificent, who introduced important legal reforms and also led the army that was turned back from Vienna in 1529.

The Ottoman Empire remained the dominant power in the eastern Mediterranean and southeastern Europe throughout the seventeenth century, and their dominions extended, about 1650, from the Hungarian plain and the south Russian steppes as far as Algeria, the upper Nile, and the Persian Gulf. The empire was based to a large degree on military proficiency.

Long before the European states had established permanent military forces, the Turks already had a standing army, of which the well-disciplined janissaries were the main striking force. The janissaries were originally recruited from Christian children taken from their families in early childhood, brought up as Muslims, reared in military surroundings, and forbidden to marry (this restriction was gradually dropped in the late sixteenth century). Without social ties, interests, or ambitions outside the military organization to which they belonged, the janissaries were an ideal professional fighting force under the control of political leaders. The Turkish forces were long as well equipped as the Christian armies, being especially strong in heavy artillery. But by the mid-seventeenth century they were beginning to fall behind. Their armies had changed little, or for the worse, since the

Suleiman the Magnificent was the most important sultan in the sixteenth-century Ottoman Empire. During his long reign (1520–1566) Suleiman introduced numerous imperial reforms and expanded Ottoman power deep into the Balkans and central Europe, where his forces came into repeated conflict with the Austrian Habsburgs. This Turkish miniature shows Suleiman in his exalted position as he receives a visiting emissary.

(©DEA/G. DAGLI ORTI/Getty Images)

days of Suleiman the Magnificent a century before, whereas in the better-organized Christian states discipline and military administration had been improved, and firearms, land mines, and siegecraft had become more effective.

The Turks cared little about assimilating subject peoples to their language or institutions. Local populations within the empire thus retained most of their cultural traditions and autonomy. Law was based on religious law derived from the Qur'an. Law courts and judges were hard to distinguish from religious authorities, for there was no separation between religious and secular spheres. The sultan was also the caliph, the commander of the faithful; while on the one hand there was no clergy in the European sense, on the other hand religious influences affected all aspects of life. The Turks, for the most part, applied the Muslim law only to Muslims; and the overall administration of imperial policies was controlled by a powerful government official called the grand vizier.

Tolerance of non-Muslim subjects

The Ottoman government left its non-Muslim subjects to settle their own affairs in their own way, not according to nationality, which was generally indistinguishable, but according to religious groupings. The Greek Orthodox Church, to which most Christians in the empire belonged, thus became an almost autonomous intermediary between the sultan and a large fraction of its subjects. Armenian Christians and Jews formed other separate bodies. Except in the western Balkans (Albania and Bosnia) there was no general conversion of Christians to Islam during the Turkish rule, although there were many individual cases of Christians turning Muslim to obtain the privileges of the ruling faith. North of the Danube the

Christian princes of Transylvania, Wallachia, and Moldavia (later combined into modern Romania) continued to rule over Christian subjects. They were kept in office for that purpose by the sultan, to whom they paid tribute. In general, because their subjects were more profitable to them as Christians, the Turks were not eager to proselytize for Islam.

The Ottoman Empire was therefore a relatively tolerant empire, far more so than the states of Europe. Christians in the Ottoman Empire fared better than Muslims would have fared in Christendom or than the Moors and Jews had in fact fared in Spain. Christians were less disturbed in Turkey than were Protestants in France, after 1685, or Catholics in Ireland. The empire was tolerant because it was composite, an aggregation of peoples, religions, and laws, having no drive, as did the Western states, toward internal unity and complete legal sovereignty. The same tolerance was evident in the attitude toward foreign merchants, who were active throughout most of the empire.

The kings of France had maintained treaty arrangements with Turkey since 1535, partly because the Ottoman Empire challenged the expanding power of the Austrian Habsburgs and partly because the Ottoman government granted French traders special privileges (called "capitulations") in the Empire's ports and commercial exchanges. Many traders from Marseilles had thus spread over the port towns of the Middle East. They were exempted by treaty from the laws of the Ottoman Empire and were liable to trial only by their own judges, who though residing in Turkey were appointed by the king of France. They were free to exercise their Roman Catholic religion, and if disputes with Muslims arose, they appeared in special courts where the word of an infidel received equal weight with that of a follower of the prophet. Similar rights in Turkey were obtained by other European states. Thus began "extraterritorial" privileges of the kind that Europeans obtained in later centuries in China and elsewhere, wherever the local laws were regarded as "backward," or hostile to Europeans. To the Turks of the seventeenth century there was nothing exceptional about such arrangements. Only much later, under the influence of the rise of modern nationalism, did the Turks come to resent these capitulations as impairments of their own sovereignty.

"Extraterritorial" privileges

Yet the Turkish rule was often oppressive to specific groups within the Empire, and the "terrible Turk" was the recurring religious and military nightmare of eastern Europe. Ottoman rule was oppressive to Christians if only because it relegated them to a secondary position and because Christian beliefs or holy sites were viewed by the Turks with little respect and even (at times) with contempt. But Ottoman rule could become oppressive also in that it veered at times toward policies that were arbitrary and brutal, even by the none too sensitive standards of Europeans. It was worse in these respects in the seventeenth century than formerly, for the central authority of the sultans gradually declined, and the outlying governors, or pashas, had a virtual free hand with their subjects.

Those parts of the Ottoman Empire that adjoined the Christian states were among the least firmly attached to Constantinople. The Tartar Khans of south Russia, like the Christian princes of the Danubian principalities, were simply protégés who paid tribute. Hungary was occupied by the Ottomans, but it was more a battlefield than a province. These regions were disputed by Germans, Poles, and Russians. It seemed in the middle of the seventeenth century as if the grip of the Turks might be relaxing. But a series of capable grand viziers, of the Köprülü family, came to power and retained it contrary to Turkish customs for 50 years. Under them the empire again launched a military campaign to expand into the Habsburg lands in central Europe. By 1663 the janissaries were again mobilizing in Hungary. Tartar horsemen were on the move. The people of central Europe again felt the old fears. The pope also feared that the dreaded Ottoman enemy might break into Italy. Throughout Germany by the

Disputed regions

emperor's order special "Turk bells" sounded the alarm. The states of the empire voted to raise a small imperial army. The Holy Roman Empire thus bestirred itself temporarily against the historic enemy of European Christians. However, it was not under the auspices of the Holy Roman Empire, but by the house of Austria that the Turks were repelled.

24.   THE FORMATION OF AN AUSTRIAN MONARCHY

The Recovery and Growth of Habsburg Power, 1648–1740

The Austria that was gaining international influence by 1700 was actually a new creation, though not as obviously so as the two other rising states in Prussia and Russia. The Austrian Habsburgs had long enjoyed an eminent role. Formerly their position had rested on their headship of the Holy Roman Empire and on their family connection with the wealthy Habsburgs of Spain. In the seventeenth century these two supports collapsed. The hope for an effective Habsburg Empire in Germany disappeared in the Thirty Years' War. The connection with Spain lost its value as Spain declined, and it vanished when in 1700 Spain passed to the Bourbon family of France. The Austrian royal family in the latter half of the seventeenth century stood at the great turning point of its fortunes. It successfully made a difficult transition, emerging from the husk of the Holy Roman Empire and building an empire of its own. At the same time the Habsburgs continued to be Holy Roman Emperors and remained active in German affairs, using resources drawn from outside Germany to maintain their influence over the German princes. The relation of Austria to the rest of Germany remained a political conundrum down to the twentieth century.

Dominions of Austria

The Austrian Habsburgs held direct control over three main geographical regions of Europe. Their oldest territories were the "hereditary provinces"—Upper and Lower Austria, with the adjoining Tyrol, Styria, Carinthia, and Carniola. Second, they controlled the kingdom of Bohemia—Bohemia, Moravia, and Silesia joined under the crown of St. Wenceslas. Third, there was the kingdom of Hungary—Hungary, Transylvania, and Croatia joined under the crown of St. Stephen. Nothing held all these regions together except the fact that the Austrian Habsburg dynasty, in the seventeenth century, reaffirmed its political grip upon them all. During the Thirty Years' War the dynasty rooted Protestantism and feudal rebelliousness out of Austria and the hereditary provinces. It also reconquered and re-Catholicized Bohemia, and in the following decades it was able to conquer Hungary.

Since 1526 most of Hungary had been occupied by the Turks. For generations the Hungarian plain was a theater of intermittent warfare between the armies of Vienna and Constantinople. The struggle had flared up again in 1663, when, as noted earlier, the armies of the Ottoman Empire began to move up the Danube. A mixed force, assembled from the empire and its various European allies, stopped this advance and obliged the Turks in 1664 to accept a 20-year truce. But Louis XIV, who in these years was busily dismembering the western frontier of the Holy Roman Empire, stood to profit greatly from an Ottoman diversion on the Danube. He incited the Turks (old allies of France through common hostility to the Habsburgs) to resume their assaults, which they did as the 20-year truce came to a close.

Vienna besieged by the Turks

In 1683 a large Turkish army reached Vienna and set up an extended siege of the city. The Turks again, as in 1529, threatened to break through to the main centers of German culture and political power. The garrison and people of Vienna, greatly outnumbered, held off the besiegers for two months, enough time for a defending force to arrive from other parts of eastern Europe. Both sides showed the "international" character of the conflict. The Turkish army included Christians—Romanian and Hungarian—the latter in rebellion against Habsburg rule in Hungary. The anti-Turkish force was composed mainly of Poles, Austrian dynastic troops, and Germans from various states of the Holy Roman Empire. It was financed largely by Pope Innocent XI; it was commanded in the field by the Habsburg general, Duke Charles of Lorraine, who hoped to protect his inheritance on the eastern borders of France from annexation by Louis XIV, and its higher command was entrusted to John Sobieski, king of Poland. Sobieski contributed greatly to the victory of the Habsburg allies at the battle of Vienna, which broke the Ottoman siege and also was the last great military effort of the moribund Republic of Poland. After the Turks abandoned their siege, a general anti-Turkish counteroffensive developed across southeastern Europe. Armed forces of the pope, Poland, Russia, and the republic of Venice joined with the Habsburgs in new campaigns. It was in this war, in fighting between Turks and Venetians, that the Parthenon at Athens, which had survived for 2,000 years but which the Turks now used as a citadel for storing ammunition, was severely damaged when a Venetian bombardment set off an explosion of the Turkish munitions.

The Habsburgs had the good fortune to obtain the services of a man of remarkable talent, Prince Eugene of Savoy. Eugene, like many other servants of the Austrian house, was not Austrian at all; he was in fact French by origin and education but like many aristocrats of the time he was an international personage. More than anyone else he was the founder of the modern Austrian state. Distinguished both as a military administrator and as a commander in the field, he led the Habsburg forces to a decisive victory in 1697 at the battle of Zenta, driving the Ottoman forces out of Hungary. At the Peace of Karlowitz (1699) the Turks yielded most of Hungary, together with Transylvania and Croatia, to the Habsburg house; and the Ottoman Empire was pushed back permanently into Romania and the Balkans.

Prince Eugene of Savoy

The Habsburgs were now free to pursue their ambitions in the west. They entered the War of the Spanish Succession to win the Spanish crown, but they had to content themselves by the treaty of Rastatt in 1714 with the annexation of the old Spanish Netherlands and with Milan and Naples. Prince Eugene, freed now in the west, again turned eastward. Never before or afterward were the Austrians so brilliantly successful. Eugene captured Belgrade and pushed through the Iron Gate into Wallachia. But the Ottoman Empire was by no means helpless, and Turkish armies later drove the Austrians from much of the Balkan territory they had recently occupied. The Peace of Belgrade (1739) drew a new frontier that on the Austrian side remained unchanged until the twentieth century. The Turks continued to hold Romania and the whole Balkan peninsula except Catholic Croatia, which was incorporated into the Habsburg Empire. The Habsburg government, to open a window on the Mediterranean, developed a seaport at Trieste. Meanwhile the Ottoman Empire remained an important contributor to the cross-cultural exchanges, contacts, and conflicts that constantly influenced the political and economic life of every European country in the Mediterranean world.

The Austrian Monarchy by 1740

Thus the royal house of Austria, in two or three generations after its humiliation at the Peace of Westphalia, acquired a new empire of considerable proportions. Though installed in the southern Netherlands and Italy, it was essentially an empire of the middle

The Austrian Habsburgs mobilized a large force of military alllies, including Polish troops under King John Sobieski, to repel the Turkish army that besieged Vienna in 1683. This painting by Franz Geffels (1635–c. 1699) portrays the final, decisive clash that forced the Turks to abandon their siege of the city.
(©DEA/G. DAGLI ORTI/Getty Images)

Danube, with its headquarters at Vienna in Austria proper, but possessing also the sizable kingdoms of Hungary and Bohemia. Though German influence was strong, the empire was impressively international. At the Habsburg court, and in the Habsburg government and army, the names of Czech, Hungarian, Croatian, and Italian noblemen were common. When nationalist movements later swept over Europe in the nineteenth century, the empire was denounced as tyrannical by Hungarians, Croats, Serbs, Romanians, Czechs, Poles, Italians, and even by some Germans, whose national ambitions were blocked by its existence. In more recent times, disillusioned by nationalism in central and eastern Europe, some historians tended to romanticize unduly the old Habsburg monarchy, noting that it had at least the merit of holding many discordant peoples together.

The international Habsburg empire

The empire was based on a cosmopolitan aristocracy of landowners who felt closer to each other, despite differences of language, than to the laboring masses who worked on their estates. Not for many years, until after 1848, did the Habsburg government really touch these rural masses; it dealt with the landed class and with the relatively few cities, but it left the landlords to control the peasants. The old diets, or assemblies, survived in Bohemia, Hungary, and the Austrian provinces. No diet was created for the empire as a whole. The regional diets were essentially assemblages of landlords; and though they no longer enjoyed their medieval freedoms, they retained powers over taxation and administration and a sense of constitutional liberty against the crown. So long as they produced taxes and soldiers as needed, and accepted the wars and foreign policy of the ruling house, no

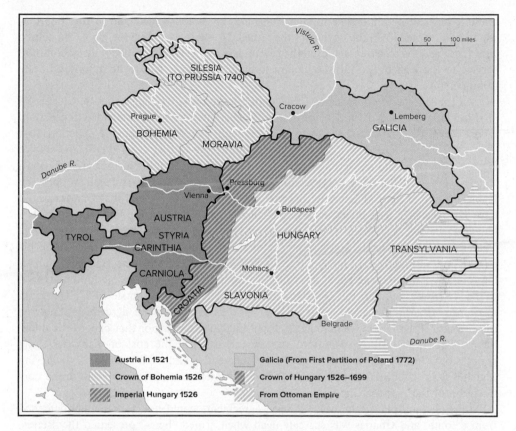

THE GROWTH OF THE AUSTRIAN MONARCHY, 1521–1772

The map shows the main body of the Austrian monarchy as it evolved in the eighteenth century and endured until the collapse of the empire in 1918. There were three main parts: (1) a nucleus, composed of Austria and adjoining duchies, often called the "hereditary provinces"; (2) the lands of the Bohemian crown, which became Habsburg in 1526 and where the Habsburgs reasserted their power during the Thirty Years' War; and (3) the lands of the Hungarian crown, where at first the Habsburgs held only the segment called Imperial Hungary, the rest remaining within the Ottoman Empire until the Habsburgs gained almost full control in 1699. In the first partition of Poland (1772) the Habsburgs annexed Galicia. Silesia was lost to Prussia in 1740.

questions were asked at Vienna. Religion was a different matter, however, for the Habsburgs forcefully repressed the Protestantism that had spread widely across both Bohemia and Hungary. Many of the estates of Protestant nobles and rebels were confiscated, giving the Habsburgs valuable lands with which to reward soldiers and supporters from all parts of Europe. An increasingly heterogeneous population of Germans, Croats, and Serbs settled in Habsburg territories, especially in Hungary. Meanwhile, the peasants remained in, or reverted to, serfdom.

Despite the concerted political, religious, and military policies of the Habsburg rulers, the Austrian Empire was still a collection of territories held together by a political allegiance to the same Habsburg monarch. Inhabitants of Austria proper considered their ruler as archduke, Bohemians saw in him the king of Bohemia; Magyars, the apostolic king of Hungary. Each country retained its own law, diet, and political life, all of which made it difficult or impossible for the Habsburgs to establish laws and institutions that would be accepted in all the territories they ruled. No shared national feeling in the people held these regions together, and even the several aristocracies were joined only by common service to the Habsburgs. For the empire to exist, all crowns had to be inherited by the same person.

As the Habsburgs consolidated their control of Hungary, the king-archduke, Charles VI (1711–1740), devised a form of insurance to guarantee such an undivided succession.

Charles VI and the Pragmatic Sanction

This took the form of a document called the Pragmatic Sanction, first issued in 1713. This document proposed that every diet in the empire and the various archdukes of the Habsburg family would agree to regard the Habsburg territories as indivisible and to recognize only the Habsburg line of heirs. The matter became urgent when it developed that Charles would have no male heir. The direct male line of the Austrian Habsburgs, as of the Spanish a few years before, was about to become extinct. But Charles did have a daughter, Maria Theresa, and he gradually won acceptance of the Pragmatic Sanction by all parts of his empire and all members of his family. Women had never inherited the Habsburg monarchy, and, by law, a woman could not rule Austria; but the Pragmatic Sanction recognized Maria Theresa's right to the Habsburg throne and to the inheritance of all Habsburg territories. Charles set about having foreign powers guarantee the agreement, knowing that Bavaria, Prussia, or others might well put in claims for this or that part of the inheritance. This process took years, and was accomplished at the cost of many damaging concessions. Finally all powers signed the agreement. Charles VI died in 1740, having done all that could be done, by domestic law and international treaty, to assure the continuation of the Austrian Empire.

Like all such plans, however, the legal agreements could not be forcefully defended from a tomb, and Charles was scarcely dead when armed "heirs" presented themselves. A great war broke out to partition the Austrian Empire, as the Spanish Empire had been partitioned shortly before. Bohemia threw off its allegiance. Hungary almost did the same. But these events became connected to wider European conflicts during "The War of the Austrian Succession," which will be discussed in a later chapter. At the moment it is enough to know that by 1740 a populous empire of great military strength existed on the Danube.

25.   THE FORMATION OF PRUSSIA

It was characteristic of the seventeenth century that very small states were able to play an influential part in European affairs, seemingly out of all proportion to their size. The main reason why small states could act as great powers was that armies were small and weapons were simple. Difficulties of supply and communications, the poor condition of the roads, the lack of maps, the absence of general staffs, together with many other administrative and technical difficulties, reduced the number of soldiers who could be successfully managed in a campaign. The battles of the Thirty Years' War, on the average, were fought by armies of less than 20,000 men. And while Louis XIV, by the last years of his reign, built up a military establishment aggregating some 400,000, the actual field armies in the wars of Louis XIV did not exceed, on the average, 40,000. Armies of this size were well within the reach of smaller powers. If especially well trained, disciplined, and equipped, and if ably commanded, the armies of smaller states could defeat those of much larger neighbors. On this fact, fundamentally, the German state of Prussia would be built. But Sweden was actually the first such smaller power to exploit this kind of military opportunity with spectacular consequences.

Sweden's Short-Lived Empire

Sweden almost, but not quite, formed an empire in central and eastern Europe in the seventeenth century. The population of Sweden at the time was not over a million; it was smaller than that of the Dutch Republic. But the Swedes produced a line of extraordinary rulers, ranging from genius in Gustavus Adolphus (1611-1632) through the brilliantly unconventional Queen Christina (1632-1654) to the amazing military exploits of Charles XII (1697-1718). The elective Swedish kingship was made hereditary, so that the royal power was freed from control by the estates. Craftsmen and experts were brought from western countries notably Holland; war industries were subsidized by the government; and an army was created with many novel features in weapons, organization, and tactics.

With this army Gustavus Adolphus crossed the Baltic in the Thirty Years' War, made alliances with Protestant German princes, cut through the Holy Roman Empire, and helped to ward off the Habsburg unification of Germany. The Swedish crown, by the Peace *Swedish territorial victories* of Westphalia, received certain coastal regions of Germany. Subsequently, in a complex series of wars, the Swedes won control of virtually all the shores and cities of the Baltic. Only Denmark at the mouth of that sea and the territories of the house of Brandenburg, which had almost no ports, remained independent. For a time the Baltic was a Swedish lake. The Russians were shut off from it, and the Poles and even the Germans, who lived on its shores, could use the Baltic only on Swedish terms.

The final Swedish campaign for imperial expansion took place during the meteoric reign of Charles XII. As a young man he found his dominions attacked by Denmark, Poland, and Russia; he won *Charles XII* remarkable victories over them but would not make peace; he then led an army back and forth across the eastern European plain, only to be crushed by the Russians. He fled to the Ottoman Empire and spent several years as a guest and protégé of the Turks before he eventually returned to Sweden. By the time Charles died in 1718 the Swedish sphere had contracted to Sweden itself, except that Finland and reduced holdings in northern Germany remained Swedish for a century more. The Swedes in time proved themselves exceptional among European peoples in not harping on their former greatness. They successfully and peaceably made the transition from the role of an important military state to that of a small power.

The Territorial Growth of Brandenburg-Prussia

In the long run it was to be Prussia that dominated the northern part of central Europe. Prussia became famous for its "militarism," which may be said to exist when military needs and military values permeate all other spheres of life. Through its influence on Germany over a period of two centuries Prussia played a momentous part in modern European and world history. The south coast of the Baltic, where Prussia was to arise, was an unpromising site for the creation of a strong political power. It was an uninviting country, thinly populated, with poor soil and without mineral resources, more backward than Saxony or Bohemia, not to mention the busy centers of south Germany and western

Europe. It was a flat open plain, merging imperceptibly into Poland, without prominent physical features or natural frontiers (see maps, pp. 4–5, 206, 220–221). The coastal region directly south from Sweden was known as Pomerania. Inland from it, shut off from the sea, was Brandenburg, centering about Berlin. Brandenburg had been founded in the Middle Ages as a border state, a "mark" or "march" of the Holy Roman Empire, to fight the battles of the empire against the then heathen Slavs. Its ruler, the margrave, was one of the seven princes who, after 1356, elected the Holy Roman Emperor. Hence he was commonly called the Elector of Brandenburg. After 1415 the electors were always of the Hohenzollern family.

Germans expand eastward

All Germany east of the Elbe, including Brandenburg, represented a medieval conquest by German-speaking peoples—the German *Drang nach Osten,* or drive to the east. From the Elbe to Poland, German conquerors and settlers had replaced the Slavs, eliminating them or absorbing them by intermarriage. Eastward from Brandenburg, and outside the Holy Roman Empire, stretched a region inhabited by Slavic peoples. Next to the east came "Prussia," which eventually was to give its name to all territories of the Hohenzollern monarchy. This original Prussia formed part of the lands of the Teutonic Knights, a military crusading order that had conquered and Christianized the native peoples in the thirteenth century. Except for its seacoast along the Baltic, the duchy of Prussia was totally enclosed by the Polish kingdom. To the north, along the Baltic, as far as the Gulf of Finland, German minorities lived among Lithuanians, Latvians (or Letts), and Estonians. The towns were German, founded as German commercial colonies in the Middle Ages, and many of the landlords were German also, descendants of the Teutonic Knights, and later known as the "Baltic barons."

Territorial acquisitions of the Hohenzollerns

Modern Prussia began to emerge in the seventeenth century when a number of territories came into the hands of the Hohenzollerns of Brandenburg. In 1618 the Elector of Brandenburg inherited the duchy of Prussia. Another important development occurred when the old ruling line in Pomerania expired during the Thirty Years' War. Although the Swedes succeeded in taking the better part of Pomerania, the Elector of Brandenburg received at the Peace of Westphalia eastern Pomerania. Barren, rural, and harborless though it was, it at least had the advantage of connecting Brandenburg with the Baltic. The Hohenzollerns no sooner obtained it than they began to dream of joining it with their duchy of Prussia to the east, a task that required the absorption of an intermediate and predominantly Slavic area, which was part of Poland, a task not accomplished until 1772.

Had the duchy of Prussia and eastern Pomerania been the only acquisitions of the Hohenzollerns, their state would have been oriented almost exclusively toward eastern Europe. But at the Peace of Westphalia they received, in addition to eastern Pomerania, new territories on the west bank of the Elbe. Moreover, through the play of family inheritances common in the Holy Roman Empire, the Hohenzollerns had earlier, in 1614, come to control the small state of Cleves on the Rhine at the Dutch border and a few other small territories also in western Germany. These were separated from the main Hohenzollern lands around Brandenburg by many intermediate German principalities, but the western territories provided direct contact with the more advanced regions of western Europe and a base from which larger holdings in the Rhineland were eventually to be built up.

In the seventeenth century the dominions of the house of Brandenburg were therefore developing in three disconnected territories. The main one was Brandenburg, with

Frederick William, who became known as the Great Elector, governed Prussia for almost 50 years (1640–1688) and set his country on a course toward new power and military influence in central Europe.
(©Foto Marburg/Art Resource, NY)

adjoining Pomerania and territories along the Elbe. There was also a detached eastern territory in the duchy of Prussia and another small detached western territory on and near the Rhine. To connect and unify these three territorial possessions became the long-range policy of the Brandenburg house.

In the midst of the Thirty Years' War, in 1640, a young man of 20, named Frederick William, succeeded to these diverse possessions. Known later as the Great Elector, he was the first of the several influential leaders who shaped modern Prussia. He had grown up under trying conditions. Brandenburg was one of the parts of Germany to suffer most heavily from the war. Its location made it the stamping ground of Swedish and Habsburg armies. In 1640, in the 22 years since the beginning of the war, the population of Berlin had fallen from about 14,000 to about 6,000. Hundreds of villages had been completely wiped out.

The Great Elector

Frederick William concluded that in his position, ruling a small and open territory, without natural frontiers or the strategic possibility of defense in depth, he must put his main reliance on a competent army. With an effective army, even if small, he could force the stronger states to take him into their calculations and thereby enter with some hope of advantage into the politics of the balance of power. This long remained the program of the Brandenburgers—to have an army but not to use it, to conserve it with loving and even miserly care, to keep an "army in being," and to gain their ends by diplomatic maneuver. They did so by siding with France against the Habsburgs, or with Sweden against Poland. They aspired also to the title not merely of margrave or elector, but to the rank of king. The opportunity came in 1701, when the Habsburg emperor was preparing to enter the War of the Spanish Succession. The emperor requested the elector of Brandenburg, who was then Frederick III, to support him with 8,000 troops. The elector named his price: recognition of himself, by the emperor, as king "in Prussia." The emperor yielded; the title, at first explicitly limited to the less honorable king *in* Prussia, soon became king *of* Prussia. The elector Frederick III of Brandenburg became King Frederick I of Prussia. Another thread was torn from the fraying fabric of the Holy Roman Empire; and there was now a German king above all the other German princes.

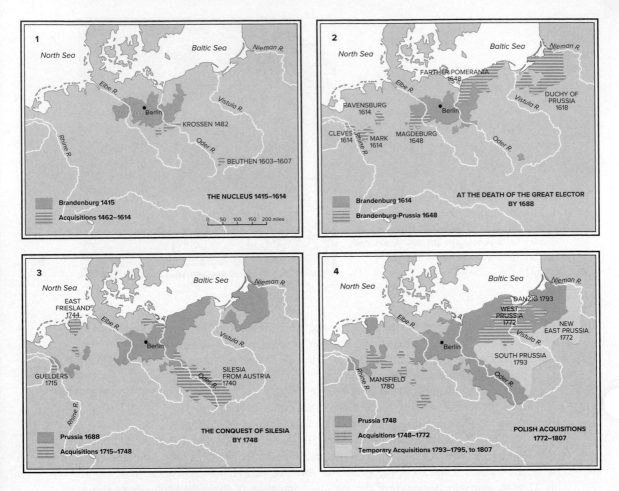

THE GROWTH OF PRUSSIA, 1415–1918

The maps shown here, going well beyond the scope of this chapter, give an overview of Prussian history from the time when Brandenburg began to expand in the seventeenth century. One may see, by looking at all the panels together, how Prussia was really an east-European state until 1815; its center of gravity shifted westward, in significant degree, only in the nineteenth century. Panel 2 shows the early formation of three unconnected territories; Panel 3, the huge bulk of Silesia relative to the small kingdom that annexed it; Panel 4, the fruits of the partitions of Poland; Panel 5, Napoleon pared Prussia down. The main crisis at the Congress of Vienna, and its resolution, are shown in Panels 6 and 7. Bismarck's enlargement of Prussia appears in Panel 8. The boundaries established by Bismarck remained unchanged until the fall of the monarchy in 1918.

The Prussian Military State

The preoccupation of Prussia with its army was unquestionably defensive in origin, arising from the horrors of the Thirty Years' War. But the military emphasis outlasted its cause and shaped the evolving character of the country. Prussia was not unique in the attention it paid to its armed forces. The unique thing about Prussia was the disproportion between the size of the army and the size of the resources on which the army was based. The government, to maintain the army, had to direct and plan the life of the country for this purpose. Nor was Prussia the originator of the "standing" army, kept

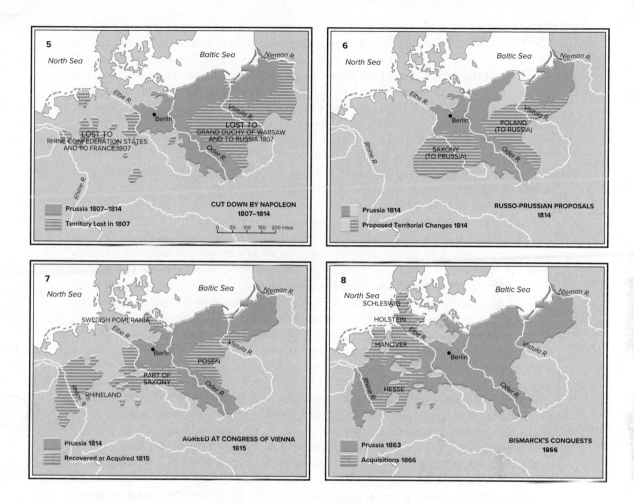

active in time of peace and always preparing for war. Most governments adopted the methods of Louis XIV in establishing standing armies, not merely to promote foreign ambitions but to keep armed forces out of the hands of nobles or military adventurers and under control by the state.

But Prussia was unique in that, more than in any other country, the army developed a life of its own, almost independent of the life of the state. It was older than the Prussian state itself. In 1657 the Great

The Prussian army

Elector fought a great battle at Warsaw with soldiers from all parts of his dominions. It was the first time that people from Cleves, Brandenburg, and ducal Prussia had ever done anything together. The army was the first "all Prussian" institution. Institutions of civilian government developed later and largely to meet the needs of the army. And in later generations the army proved more durable than the state. When Prussia collapsed during the Napoleonic wars in 1806, the spirit and morale of the Prussian army carried on; and when the Hohenzollern Empire finally crashed in 1918, the Prussian-shaped army still maintained its life and traditions within the Weimar Republic, which again it survived. Not until the defeat of Adolf Hitler in the Second World War and the establishment of a new republican regime was the army and its military traditions totally subordinated to civilian authority.

Financing the army

In all countries, to some extent, the machinery of the modern state developed as a means of supporting armed forces, but in Prussia the process was exceptionally clear and simple. In Prussia the rulers drew roughly half their income from the crown domain and only about half from taxes. The crown domain, consisting of manors and other productive enterprises owned directly by the ruler as a traditional lord, was in effect a kind of government property, for the Prussian rulers used their income almost entirely for state purposes, being personally simple and even Spartan in their habits. The rulers of Prussia, until a century after the accession of the Great Elector, were able to pay the whole cost of their civil government from their own income, the proceeds of the crown domain. To develop the domain and transfer the funds into government expenditures, they created a large body of civilian officials. The domain bulked so large that much of the economy of the country was not in private hands but consisted of enterprises owned and administered by the state. For additional income the Great Elector introduced taxes of the kind used in France, such as excise taxes on consumers' goods and a government monopoly on the sale of salt. All taxes, for a century after the accession of the Great Elector, were levied specifically for the use of the army.

Economic life grew up under government sponsorship, rather than through the enterprise of a venturesome business class. This was because, for a rural country to maintain an organized army, productive and technical skills had to be imported, mainly from the West. The Great Elector in his youth spent a number of years in Holland, where he was impressed by the wealth and prosperity that he saw. After becoming elector he settled Swiss and Frisians in Brandenburg (the Frisians were akin to the Dutch); he welcomed Jews from Poland; and when Louis XIV began to persecute the French Protestants, he provided funds and special officials to assist the immigration of 20,000 Huguenots to Brandenburg. French immigrants for a time formed a sixth of the population of Berlin and were the most advanced commercial element of that comparatively undeveloped city. The government, as in France under Colbert, initiated and helped to finance various industries; but the importance of such government participation was greater than in France, because the amount of privately owned capital available for investment was incomparably less. Military needs, more than elsewhere, dominated the market for goods, because civilian demand in so poor a country was relatively low; the army, in its requirements for food, uniforms, and weapons became a strong force in shaping the early modern economic growth of the country.

*The army and
Prussian society*

The army had a profound effect also on the social development and class structure of Prussia. The civilian middle class was generally willing to accept the military priorities, and it became the policy of the rulers to absorb practically the whole landed aristocracy, the Junkers, into military service. They used the army, with conscious purpose, as a means of implementing an "all Prussian" psychology in the landed families of Cleves, Brandenburg, Pomerania, and the former dominions of the Teutonic Knights. The fact that Prussia was a very recent and artificial combination of territories, so that identification with it was not a traditional sentiment, made it all the more necessary to instill loyalty by martial means. Emphasis fell on duty, obedience, service, and sacrifice. That military virtues became characteristic of the whole male Prussian aristocracy was also due, like so much else, to the small size of the population. In France, for example, with perhaps 50,000 male adult nobles, only a small minority served as army officers. In Prussia there were few Junker families that did not have some of their members in uniform.

The Great Elector and his successors, like all absolutist rulers of the era, repressed the estates or parliamentary assemblages in which the landed aristocracy was the main element. To mollify the squires, the rulers promised commissions in the army to men of their class. They promised them also a free hand over their peasants. The Prussian monarchy was largely based on an understanding between the ruler and the landlord gentry—the latter agreed to accept the ruler's government and to serve in his army, in return for holding their own peasants in hereditary subjection. Serfdom spread in Prussia as elsewhere in eastern Europe. In East Prussia the peasants fell into conditions that were as deplorable as the agricultural conditions in Poland.

The Prussian rulers believed that the Junkers made better army officers because they were accustomed to the habit of commanding their own peasants. To preserve the officer class, legislation forbade the sale of "noble" lands, that is, manors, to persons not noble. In France, again by way of contrast, where manorial rights had become simply a form of property, bourgeois persons and even peasants could legally acquire manors and enjoy a lordly or seigneurial income. In Prussia this was *Limited social mobility* not possible; classes were frozen by owning nonexchangeable forms of property. It was thus harder for middle-class people to enter the aristocracy by setting up as landed gentry. The bourgeois class in any case had little spirit of independence. Few of the old towns of Germany were in Prussia. The Prussian middle class was not wealthy, and it had not gained much influence through the possession of private property. The typical middle-class man was an official who worked for the government as an employee of the large crown domain or in an enterprise subsidized by the state. The civil service in Prussia, from the days of the Great Elector, became notable for its honesty and efficiency. But the middle class, more than elsewhere, deferred to the nobles, served the state, and accepted the pervasive public role of the army.

These distinctive features of Prussian social life and military service developed especially under Frederick William I, who was king from *Frederick William I* 1713 to 1740. He was an earthy, uncouth man, who disdained whatever savored of "culture," to which his father, his grandfather (the Great Elector), and also his son (Frederick the Great) were all strongly attracted. He begrudged every penny not spent on the army. He cut the expense of the royal household by three-fourths. On his coronation journey to Königsberg he spent 2,547 thalers, where his father had spent 5 million. He ruled the country in a fatherly hierarchical style, supervising it like a private estate, prowling the streets of Berlin in an old seedy uniform, and disciplining negligent citizens with blows of his walking stick. He worked all the time and expected everyone else to do likewise.

He loved the army, which all his policies were designed to serve. He was the first Prussian king to appear always in uniform. He rearranged the order of courtly precedence, moving army officers up and civilians down. His love of tall soldiers is famous; he collected a special unit, men between 6 and 7 feet tall, from all over Europe, and indeed the Russian Tsar Peter the Great sent him some from Asia. He devised new forms of discipline and maneuver, founded a cadet corps to train the sons of the Junkers, and invented a new system of recruiting (the canton system, long the most effective in Europe), by which each regiment had a particular district or canton assigned to it as a source of soldiers. He raised the size of the army from 40,000 at his accession to 83,000 at his death. During his reign Berlin grew to be a city of 100,000, of whom 20,000 were soldiers, a proportion probably unmatched in any other city of Europe. He likewise left to his successor (for he fought practically no wars himself) a war chest of 7,000,000 thalers.

With this army and war chest Frederick II, later called the Great, who became king in 1740, startled Europe. Charles VI of Austria had just died. His daughter Maria Theresa entered upon her manifold inheritance, which depended on the long-negotiated guarantees of the Pragmatic Sanction. While others waited, Frederick struck. Serving no notice, he quickly moved his military forces into Silesia, which was a part of the kingdom of Bohemia on the side toward Poland, lying in the upper valley of the Oder River and adjoining Brandenburg on the north. The addition of Silesia to the kingdom of Prussia almost doubled the population and added valuable industries, so that Prussia now, with 6 million people and an army that Frederick raised to 200,000, at last established itself as a great power. It must be added that, judged simply as a human accomplishment, Prussia was a remarkable political and military creation, a state made on a shoestring, a triumph of work and duty.

The advances of Frederick the Great

26.   THE TRANSFORMATION OF RUSSIA

The affairs of central and eastern Europe, from Sweden to Turkey and from Germany to the Caspian Sea, were profoundly interconnected. The underlying theme of the present chapter, it may be recalled, is that this whole great area was fluid, occupied by the weakening political bodies of the Holy Roman Empire, Poland, and the Ottoman Empire and that in this fluid area three new powers gradually developed—the modern Austrian monarchy, the kingdom of Prussia, and the Russian Empire. All, too, in varying degree, became modern eighteenth-century states by borrowing various ideas and administrative systems from western Europe, though each of these new eastern states also retained its own distinctive political, social, and cultural characteristics.

In the century after 1650 the old tsardom of Muscovy evolved into modern Russia. Moving out from the region around Moscow, the Russians not only established themselves across northern Asia, reaching the Bering Sea about 1700, but also entered into closer relations with Europe, undergoing especially in the time of Tsar Peter the Great (1682–1725) a rapid process of European-style state-building. To what extent Russia became truly European has always been an open question, disputed both by western Europeans and by Russians themselves. In some ways the Russians had been European from as far back as Europe itself can be said to have existed, that is, from the early Middle Ages. Ancient Russia had been colonized by Vikings, and the Russians had become Christian long before the Swedes, the Lithuanians, or the Finns.

Europeanization

Yet Russia had not been part of the general development of medieval and early modern Europe for a number of reasons. Russia had been converted to the Greek Orthodox branch of Christianity; therefore, the religious and cultural influence of Constantinople, not of Rome, had predominated. Second, the Mongol invasions and conquest about 1240 had kept Russia under Asian domination for about 250 years, until 1480 when a grand duke of Muscovy, Ivan III (1462–1505), was able to throw off the Mongol overlordship and cease payment of tribute. Last, Russian geography, especially the lack of warm-water or ice-free seaports, had made commerce and communication with western Europe difficult. Russia had therefore not shared in the general European economic development after about 1100, and the changes that took place in the seventeenth and eighteenth centuries may accurately be called a kind of "Europeanization." There was in this era a wholesale Russian borrowing of the new knowledge and institutions that had developed in the early modern European states; and this Europeanizing of many Russian institutions was by no means a unique thing. It was a step in the expansion of modern European forms of social organization and hence in the formation of the modern

The rising power of Prussia was closely linked to the influence of its military culture. King Frederick II (1740–1786), who is shown here at a parade of his soldiers, sent his army into Bohemia in 1740 to seize Silesia from the Austrian Habsburgs. Defending this conquest during the later Seven Years War, Frederick used his well-disciplined army to symbolize the stature of Prussia's military class as well as the kingdom's expanding role in European affairs.

(©UniversalImagesGroup/Getty Images)

world as we have known it in recent centuries. Developing strategies for reform that other societies would also follow in later historical eras, the Russians began to introduce western European methods of state and economic organization while also seeking to protect their own interests and distinctive cultural traditions.

In some ways the new Russian Empire resembled the new kingdom of Prussia. Both took form in the great plain that runs uninterruptedly from the North Sea into inner Asia. Both lacked natural frontiers and grew by addition of territories to an original nucleus. In both countries the state arose primarily as a means of supporting a modern army. In both the government developed autocratically, in conjunction with a landlord class that was brought into state service and which in turn held the peasantry in serfdom. Neither Russia nor Prussia had a strong commercial class or an urban banking system that could exert political influence. In neither country could the modern state and army have been created in this era without the importation of new skills from western Europe. Yet Prussia, with its German connections, its Protestant religion, its universities, and its proximity to the busy commercial artery of the Baltic, was far more European than Russia, and the Europeanization of Russia may perhaps better be compared with the later "westernization" of Japan. In the Russia of 1700, as in the Japan of 1870, the main purpose of the administrative and

Parallels with Prussia

social reformers was to obtain scientific, technical, and military knowledge from the West, in part with a view to strengthening their own countries against penetration or conquest by Europeans. Yet here too the parallel must not be pushed too far. In time, the Russian upper classes intermarried with Europeans and entered more widely than the later Japanese elites into European cultural life. Russian music and literature eventually became well known and influential among modern European intellectuals, and Russia itself developed a unique blend of European and central Asian cultural traits.

Russia before Peter the Great

The Russians in the seventeenth century, as today, were a medley of peoples distinguished by their language, which was of the Slavic family, of the great Indo-European language group. The Great Russians or Muscovites lived around Moscow. Moving out from that area, they had penetrated the northern forests and had also settled in the southern steppes and along the Volga, where they had assimilated various Asian peoples known as Tartars. After two centuries of expansion, from roughly 1450 to 1650, the Russians had almost but not quite reached the Baltic and the Black seas. The Baltic shore was held by Sweden. The Black Sea coast was still held by Tartar Khans under the protection of Ottoman Turkey. In the rough borderlands between Tartar and Russia lived the semi-independent cowboy-like Cossacks, largely recruited from migratory Russians. West of Muscovy were the White Russians (or Byelorussians) and southwest of Muscovy the Little Russians (Ruthenians or Ukrainians), both in the seventeenth century under the rule of Poland, which was then the leading Slavic power.

Russian expansion to the east

The energies of the Great Russians were directed principally eastward. They conquered the Volga Tartars in the sixteenth century and reached the Ural Mountains, which they immediately crossed. Muscovite pioneers, settlers, and townbuilders streamed along the river systems of Siberia, felling timber and trading in furs as they went. In the 1630s, while the English were building Boston and the Dutch New York, the Russians were establishing towns in the vast Asian stretches of Siberia, reaching to the Pacific itself. A whole string of settlements, remote, small, and isolated—Tomsk and Tobolsk, Irkutsk and Yakutsk—extended for 5,000 miles across northern Asia.

It was toward the vast heartland of central Asia that Muscovy really faced, looking out upon Persia and China across the deserts. The bazaars of Moscow and Astrakhan were frequented by Persians, Afghans, Indians, and Chinese. The Caspian Sea, into which flowed the Volga, the greatest of Russian rivers, was better known than was the Baltic. Europe as viewed from Moscow was more distant and less accessible than other busy trading centers to the south and east. During most of the seventeenth century even Smolensk and Kiev belonged to Poland. Yet the Russians were not totally shut off from Europe. In 1552, when Ivan the Terrible conquered Kazan from the Tartars, he had a German engineer in his army. In the next year, 1553, Richard Chancellor arrived in Moscow from England by the roundabout way of Archangel on the White Sea. Thereafter trade between England and Muscovy was continuous. The tsars valued Archangel as their only inlet from the West through which military materials could be imported. The English valued it as a means of reaching the wares of Persia.

Russian separation from Europe

Russia in the seventeenth century reflected its long separation from the culture and social mores that had been developing in Europe. Women of the upper classes were secluded and often wore veils. Men wore beards and skirted garments that seemed exotic to Europeans.

CHRONOLOGY OF NOTABLE EVENTS, 1640–1740

1640–1688	Frederick William, the Great Elector, develops state and military power in Prussia
1663	Ottoman Empire begins new phase of expansion in Central Europe
1667–1671	Stephen Razin leads rebellion of rural population in Russia
1683	Ottoman imperial army is forced to abandon siege of Vienna
1698–1725	Tsar Peter the Great introduces European reforms in Russia
1711–1740	Habsburg King-Archduke Charles VI builds the Austrian Empire
1713–1740	King Frederick William I expands the army and wealth of the Prussian state

Customs also seemed crude to European visitors; wild drunkenness and revelry alternated with mysterious rituals of repentance and religious prostration. Traditional superstitions remained influential among many people in the highest classes of church and state; and murder, kidnapping, torture, and elaborate physical cruelty were common forms of social control. The Russian church did not support the kinds of educational or charitable institutions that the Catholic and Protestant churches had established in western Europe. Churchmen feared the incipient European influences. "Abhorred of God," declared a Russian bishop, "is any who loves geometry; it is a spiritual sin." Even arithmetic was hardly understood in Russia. Arabic numerals were not used, and merchants computed with the abacus. The calendar was dated from the creation of the world. Ability to predict an eclipse seemed a form of magic. Clocks, brought in by Europeans, seemed as extraordinary in Russia as they did in China, where they were brought in by Jesuits at about the same time.

Yet this great, non-European Russia, which fronted on inner Asia, was European in some of its fundamental social institutions. It possessed a variant of the manorial and feudal systems. It experienced the same wave of constitutional crises that was sweeping over Europe at the same time. Russia had a duma or council of retainers and advisers to the tsar, and the rudiments of a national assembly corresponding to meetings of the estates in western Europe. In Russia as in Europe the question was whether power should remain in the hands of these bodies or become concentrated in the hands of the ruler. Ivan the Terrible, who ruled from 1533 to 1584 and was the first grand duke of Muscovy to assume the title of tsar,[1] was a shrewd observer of contemporary events in Poland. He saw the dissolution that was overtaking the Polish state and was determined to avoid it in Muscovy. His ferocity toward those who opposed him made him literally terrible, but though his methods differed from the methods commonly used in Europe, his aims were the aims of his European contemporaries. Not long after his death Russia passed into a period known as the Time of Troubles (1604–1613), during which the Russian nobles elected a series of tsars and demanded certain assurances of their own liberties. But the country

---

[1]The Slavic word *tsar*, like the German *Kaiser*, derives from *Caesar*, a title used as a synonym for *emperor* in the Roman, the Holy Roman, and the Byzantine (or eastern Roman) Empires. The spelling *czar*, also common in English, reveals the etymology and the current English-language pronunciation, *zar*. Some recent translators have used terms such as "Ivan the Fearsome" for the most famous sixteenth-century tsar, but we have retained "Ivan the Terrible" because this is the name by which he is traditionally known in English.

was racked by contending factions and a civil war in which the violence resembled the religious wars in France or the Thirty Years' War in central Europe.

The Romanovs

In 1613 a national assembly, hoping to settle the troubles, elected a 17-year-old boy as tsar, or emperor, believing him young enough to have no connection with any of the warring factions. The new boy tsar was Michael Romanov, of a gentry family, related by marriage to the old line of Ivan the Terrible. Thus was established, by vote of the political classes of the day, the Romanov dynasty that ruled in Russia until 1917. The early Romanovs, aware of the fate of elective monarchy in Poland and elsewhere, soon began to repress the representative institutions of Russia and set up as absolute monarchs. Here again, though they were often more lawless or violent than most European kings, the Russian monarchs followed the general pattern of contemporary rulers who were also suppressing older political institutions throughout much of Europe.

Serfdom in Russia

Nor can it be said that the main social development of the seventeenth century in Russia, the sinking of the peasantry into an abyss of helpless serfdom, was exclusively a Russian phenomenon. The same process generally took place in eastern Europe. Serfdom had long been overtaking the older free peasantry of Russia. In Russia, as in the American colonies, land was abundant and labor was scarce. Labor therefore tended to migrate over the great Russian plain. In the Time of Troubles, especially, there was a good deal of movement. The landlords, wishing to assure themselves of their labor force, obtained the support of the Romanov tsars.

The manor, or what corresponded to it in Russia, came to resemble the slave plantations in the New World. Laws against fugitive serfs were strengthened; lords won the right to recover fugitives up to 15 years after their flight, and finally the time limit was abolished altogether. Peasants came to be so little regarded that a law of 1625 authorized anyone killing another man's peasant simply to give him another peasant in return. Lords exercised police and judicial powers. By a law of 1646 landowners were required to enter the names of all their peasants in government registers; peasants once so entered, together with their descendants, were regarded as attached to the estate on which they were registered. Thus the peasants lost the freedom to move at their own will. For a time they were supposed to have secure tenure of their land; but a law of 1675 allowed the lords to sell peasants without the land, and thus to move peasants like chattels at the will of the owner. This sale of serfs without land, which made their condition more like slavery as then practiced in America, became indeed a distinctive feature of serfdom in Russia, because in Poland, Prussia, Bohemia, and other regions of serfdom, the serf was generally regarded as "bound to the soil," inseparable from the land.

Against the loss of their freedom the rural population of Russia protested as best it could, murdering landlords, fleeing to the Cossacks, taking refuge in a vagrant existence, countered by wholesale government-organized manhunts and by renewed and more stringent legislation. A tremendous uprising was led in 1667 by Stephen Razin, who gathered a host of fugitive serfs, Cossacks, and adventurers, outfitted a fleet on the Caspian Sea, plundered Russian vessels, defeated a Persian squadron, and invaded Persia itself. He then turned back, ascended the Volga, killing and burning as he went and proclaiming a war against landlords, nobles, and priests. Cities opened their gates to him; an army sent against him went over to his side. He was finally captured and put to death in 1671. The consequence of the rebellion, for over a century, was that serfdom was clamped on the Russian peasants more firmly than ever.

Stephen Razin became an almost mythic figure in Russian popular memory after leading a vast peasant rebellion in the late 1660s. This painting by Vasily Ivanovich Surikov (1848–1916) suggests Razin's later prominence in Russian culture and his symbolic status in modern social and political movements.

(©Sovfoto/Getty Images)

Even from the church the increasingly wretched rural people drew little comfort. The Russian Orthodox Church at this time went through a great internal crisis, and ended up as hardly more than a department of the tsardom, useful to the government in instilling a pervasive, unquestioning reverence for Holy Russia. The Russian church had historically looked to the Patriarch of Constantinople as its head. But the conquest of Constantinople by the Turks made the head of the Greek Orthodox Church a merely tolerated inferior to the Muslim sultan-caliph, so that the Russians in 1589 set up an independent Russian patriarch of their own. In the following generations the Russian patriarchate first became dependent on, then was abolished by, the tsarist government.

The Russian Orthodox Church

In the 1650s the Russian patriarch undertook certain church reforms, mainly to correct mistranslations in Russian versions of the Bible and other sacred writings. The changes aroused the horror and indignation of the general body of believers. Deeply attached to the mere form of the written word and believing the faith itself to depend on the customary spelling of the name of Jesus, the malcontents saw in the reformers a band of cunning Greek scholars perpetrating the work of Antichrist and the devil. The patriarch and higher church officials forced through the reforms but only with the help of the government and the army. Those who rejected the reforms came to be called Old Believers, and they vehemently denounced every change in the texts and rituals of the established church. More fanatical than the reform-minded clergy, agitated by visionary preachers and dividing into innumerable sects, the Old Believers became very numerous, especially among the peasants. Old Believers were active in Stephen Razin's rebellion and in all the sporadic peasant uprisings that followed. The peasants, already placed by serfdom outside the protection of law, were now also estranged from the established religion. A distrust of all organized authority settled over the Russian masses, to whom both church and government seemed to serve as mere engines of repression.

Old Believers

But while willing enough to modernize sacred texts by correcting mistranslations from the Greek, the Russian church officials resisted other kinds of modernization that were coming in from western Europe. They therefore opposed Peter the Great at the end of the century. After 1700 no new patriarch was appointed. Peter put the church under a committee of bishops called the Holy Synod, and to the Synod he attached a civil official called the Procurator of the Holy Synod. The Procurator was not a churchman but head of a government bureau whose task was to see that the church did nothing displeasing to the tsar. Peter thus secularized the church, making himself in effect its head. But while the consequences of state control were more extreme in Russia than elsewhere, it must again be noted that Peter's control of the church followed the general pattern of early modern Europe. Secular supervision of religion had become the rule almost everywhere, especially in Protestant countries. Indeed an Englishman of the time thought that Peter the Great, in doing away with the patriarchate and putting the church under his own control, was wisely imitating England, which he had visited in his youth.

Peter the Great: Foreign Affairs and Territorial Expansion

The Russia in which Peter the Great became tsar in 1682 was thus already European in some ways and had in any case been in contact with western Europeans for over a century. Without Peter, Russia would have developed its European connections more gradually. Peter, by his tempo and methods, made the process a social revolution.

Exposure to the West

Peter obtained his first knowledge of western Europe in Moscow itself, where a part of the city known as the German quarter was inhabited by Europeans of various nationalities, whom Peter often visited as a boy. Peter also in his early years mixed with Western travelers at Archangel, still Russia's only port, for he was fascinated by the sea and took lessons in navigation on the White Sea from Dutch and English ship captains. Like the Great Elector of Brandenburg, Peter as a young man spent over a year in western Europe, especially Holland and England, where he became profoundly aware of how his own country lagged far behind the commercial and technical advances in other societies. He had considerable talents as a mechanic and organizer. He labored with his own hands as a ship's carpenter in Amsterdam and talked with political and business leaders about the means for introducing the newer European organization and technology into Russia. He visited workshops, mines, commercial offices, art galleries, hospitals, and forts. Europeans saw him as a kind of alien genius, a giant of a man standing a head above most others, bursting with physical vitality and plying all he met with interminable questions on their manner of working and living. He had neither the refinement nor the pretension of Western monarchs; he mixed easily with workmen and technical people, dressed cheaply and carelessly, loved horseplay and crude practical jokes, and dismayed his hosts by the squalid disorder in which he and his companions left the rooms put at their disposal. A man of acute practical mind, he was as little troubled by appearances as by moral scruples.

Peter on his visit to Europe in 1697–1698 recruited almost 1,000 experts for service in Russia, and many more followed later. He cared nothing for the civilization of Europe except as a means to an end, and this end was to create an army and a state that could stand against the most powerful European states. His aim from the beginning was in part defensive, to ward off the Poles, Swedes, and Turks who had long pushed against Russia; and in part expansionist, to obtain warm-water seaports on the Baltic and Black seas, which would offer year-round access to trade with Europe. For all but two years of his four-decade reign Peter was at war.

The aspirations of Peter the Great are represented in this formal portrait of a monarch whose clothing and appearance resemble the style of western European elites in the early eighteenth century.

(©Hulton Archive/Getty Images)

The Poles were a receding threat to Peter's ambitions. A Polish prince had indeed been elected tsar of Muscovy during the Time of Troubles, and for a while the Poles aspired to conquer and Catholicize the Great Russians. But in 1667 the Russians had regained Smolensk and Kiev, and the growing anarchy in Poland made that country no longer a menace, except as the Swedes or others might install themselves in Polish territories. The Ottoman Turks and their Tartar dependencies, though no longer expanding, were still obstinate foes. Peter before going to Europe managed in 1696 to capture Azov at the mouth of the Don, but he was unable to hold any of the Black Sea coast; and he came to recognize the inferiority of the Russian army during these campaigns. The Swedes were at this time the main enemy of Russia. Their army, for its size, was still probably the best in Europe. They controlled the whole eastern shore of the Baltic including the Gulf of Finland. In 1697, the Swedish king having died, Peter entered into an alliance with Poland and Denmark to partition the overseas possessions of the Swedish house.

Polish threat recedes

The new king of Sweden, the youthful Charles XII, was in some ways as crude as Peter (as an adolescent he had sheep driven into his rooms in the palace in order to enjoy the warlike pleasure of killing them), but he proved also to have remarkable aptitude as a general. In 1700, at the battle of Narva, with an army of 8,000 men, he routed Peter's 40,000 Russians. The tsar thus learned another lesson on the need to reform and westernize his state and army. Fortunately for the Russians Charles XII, instead of immediately pressing his advantage in Russia, spent the following years promoting Swedish interests in Poland, where he forced the Poles to elect his preferred Polish ally as their king.

The Swedes

Peter meanwhile, with his imported officers and technicians, reformed the training, discipline, and weapons of the Russian army.

Eventually, Charles XII invaded Russia with a large and well-prepared force. Peter used against him the strategy later used by the Russians against Napoleon and Adolf Hitler; he drew the Swedes into the endless plains, exposing them to the Russian winter, which happened to be an exceptionally severe one, and in 1709, at Poltava in south Russia, he met and overwhelmed the demoralized remainder. The entire Swedish army was destroyed at Poltava, only the king and a few hundred fugitives managing to escape across the Turkish frontier. Peter in the next years was thus able to conquer Livonia and part of eastern Finland. He landed troops near Stockholm itself. He campaigned in Pomerania almost as far west as the Elbe. Never before had Russian influence reached so deeply into Europe. The imperial day of Sweden was now over, terminated by Russia. Peter had won for Russia a piece of the Baltic shore and with it warm-water outlets. These significant developments were confirmed in the treaty of Nystadt, which ended the Great Northern War (1700–1721) and opened the eastern Baltic to the ascending power of Russia.

War and imperial Russia

War is surely not the father of all things, as has been sometimes claimed, but these wars did a good deal to shape imperial Russia. The undisciplined, poorly organized Russian army was transformed into a professional force of the kind maintained by Sweden, France, or Prussia. The elite of the old army had been the *streltsi,* a kind of Moscow guard, composed of nobles and constantly active in politics. A rebellion of the *streltsi* in 1698 had cut short Peter's tour of Europe; he had returned and quelled the mutiny by ferocious use of torture and execution, killing five of the rebels with his own hands. The *streltsi* were liquidated only two years before the great Russian defeat at Narva. Peter then rebuilt the army from the ground up. He employed European officers of many nationalities, paying them half again as much as native Russians of the same grades. He filled his ranks with soldiers supplied by districts on a territorial basis, somewhat as in Prussia. He put the troops into uniforms resembling those of the western European armies, and he organized them in standardized regiments. He armed them with muskets and artillery of the kind used in Europe and tried to develop a new service of supply.

With this army he not only drove the Swedes back into Sweden but also dominated Russia itself. At the very time of the Swedish invasion large parts of the country were in rebellion, as in the days of Stephen Razin, for the whole middle and lower Volga, together with the Cossacks of the Don and Dnieper, rose against the tsar and rallied behind slogans of class resentment and hatred of the tsar's foreign experts. Peter crushed these disturbances with the usual ruthlessness. The Russian Empire, loose and heterogeneous, was held together by military might.

While the Swedish war was still in progress, even before the decisive battle of Poltava, Peter laid the foundations of a wholly new city in territory conquered from the

The founding of St. Petersburg

Swedes and inhabited not by Russians but by various Baltic peoples. Peter named it St. Petersburg after himself and his patron saint. From the beginning it was more truly a city than Louis's spectacular creation at Versailles established at almost the same time. Standing at the head of the Gulf of Finland, it was Peter's chief window on the West. Here he established the offices of government, required noblemen to build town houses, and gave favorable terms to foreign merchants and craftsmen to settle. Peter meant to make St. Petersburg a symbol of the new Russia. It was a new city facing toward Europe and drawing the minds of the Russians westward, replacing the old capital, Moscow, which faced toward Asia and was the stronghold of opposition to his westernizing program. St. Petersburg soon became one of the leading cities of northern Europe. It remained the capital of Russia (renamed Petrograd in 1914) until the Revolution of 1917, when Moscow resumed its old role. After the Revolution Petrograd became Leningrad. Its name reverted to St. Petersburg on the eve of the dissolution of the Soviet Union in 1991.

Internal Changes under Peter the Great

The new army, the new city, the new and expanding government offices all required money, which in Russia was very scarce. Taxes were imposed on an inconceivable variety of objects—on heads, as poll taxes; on land; on inns, mills, hats, leather, cellars, and coffins; on the right to marry, sell meat, wear a beard, or be an Old Believer. The tax burden fell mainly on the peasants; and to assure the payment of taxes the mobility of peasants was further restricted. Borderline individuals were classified as peasants in the government records, so that serfdom became both more onerous and more nearly universal.

To raise government revenues and to stimulate production, Peter adopted the mercantilist policies that Colbert had promoted in France. He encouraged exports, built a fleet on the Baltic, and developed mining, metallurgy, and textiles, which were indispensable to the army.

Mercantilism encouraged

He organized mixed groups of Russians and foreigners into commercial companies, provided them with capital from government funds (little private capital being available), and gave them a labor supply by assigning them the use of serfs in a given locality.

Serfdom, in origin mainly an agricultural institution, began to spread in Russia as an industrial institution also. Serf owners obtained the right to sell serfs without land, or to move them from landed estates

Serfs in industry

into mines or towns, which made it easier for industry in Russia to develop on the basis of unfree labor. Nor were the employers of serfs, in these government enterprises, free to modify or abandon their projects at will. They too were simply in the tsar's service. The economic system rested largely on impressment of both management and labor, not on private profit and wages as in the increasingly capitalistic economies of western Europe. In this way Peter's efforts to force Russia to a European level of material productivity widened the social differences between Russia and western Europe.

To oversee and operate this system of tax collecting, recruiting, economic controls, serf impressment, and repression of internal rebellion Peter created a new administrative system. The old organs of local self-government wasted away. The duma and the national assem-

New administrative system

bly, ineffective in that they could not function without disorder, now disappeared. In their place Peter put a "senate" dependent on himself, and 10 territorial areas called "governments," or *gubernii*. The church he ruled through his Procurator of the Holy Synod. At the top of the whole structure was the tsar himself, an absolute ruler and autocrat of "All the Russias." Dissatisfied with his son, he asserted the right for each tsar to name his own successor. Transmission of supreme power was thus put outside the domain of law, and in the following century the accession of tsars and tsarinas was marked by strife, conspiracy, and assassination. The whole system of centralized absolutism, while in form resembling that of the absolutist European monarchies, notably France, was in fact significantly different, for it lacked legal regularity, was handicapped by the poor education of many officials, and was imposed on a turbulent and largely unwilling population. The empire of the Romanovs has been called a state without a people.

The construction of the city of St. Petersburg became the most important architectural project in Peter the Great's long-term campaign to westernize Russian society. This new city was designed to be a western-looking capital and a new center for commercial contacts with western Europe; like the construction of the French palace at Versailles, the Russian tsar's architectural goals required the labor of thousands of poor workers and peasants.

(©Bettmann/Getty Images)

Peter sought to assure the success of his reforms by developing what was called "state service," which his predecessors had already begun. Virtually all landowning and serf-owning aristocrats were required to serve in the army or civil administration. Offices were multiplied to provide places for all. In the state service birth counted for nothing. Peter used men of all classes; Prince Dolgoruky was of the most ancient nobility, Prince Menshikov had been a cook, the tax administrator Kurbatov was an ex-serf, and many others were foreigners of unknown background. Status in Peter's Russia depended not on inherited rank, which Peter could not control, but on rank in his state service. "History," wrote a Scot serving in Peter's army, "scarcely affords an example where so many people of low birth have been raised to such dignities as in tsar Peter's reign, or where so many of the highest birth and fortune have been leveled to the lowest ranks of life."

Peter's social revolution

In this respect especially, Peter's program resembled a true social revolution. It created a new governing element in place of the old, almost what in modern terms would be called a party, a body of radical reformers working zealously for the new system with a personal interest in its preservation. These men, during Peter's lifetime and after his death, were the bulwarks against an anti-reform reaction; and they became the main agents in making Peter's revolution endure after he died. In time the new families evolved into hereditary positions themselves. The priority of state service over personal position was abandoned a generation after Peter's death. Offices in the army and government were filled by men of property and birth. After Peter's revolution, as after some others, the new upper class became merged with the old.

Revolutionary also, suggesting the great French Revolution or the Russian Revolution of 1917, were Peter's unconcealed contempt for everything reminiscent of the old Russia and his zeal to reeducate his people in the new ways. He required all gentry to put their sons in school. He sent many abroad to study. He simplified the Russian alphabet. He edited the first newspaper to appear in Russia. He ordered the preparation of the first Russian book of etiquette, teaching his subjects not to spit on the floor, scratch themselves, or gnaw bones at dinner, to mix men and women in social events, to converse pleasantly, and to look at people while talking. The beard he took as a symbol of Muscovite backwardness; he forbade it in Russia, and himself shaved a number of men at his court. He forced people to attend evening parties to teach them manners. He had no respect for hereditary aristocracy, torturing or executing the highborn as readily as the peasants. As for religion, Peter was described as a pious man who enjoyed singing in church, but he was contemptuous of ecclesiastical dignity. Like many revolutionists since his time, he was aggressively secular.

The Results of Peter's Revolution

Peter's tactics provoked a strong reaction. Some adhered strictly to the old ways; others simply thought that Peter was moving too fast and too indiscriminately toward new and alien social behaviors. Many Russians resented the inescapable presence of foreigners, who often looked down on Russians and who enjoyed special privileges such as the right of free exit from Russia and higher pay for similar employment. One center around which malcontents rallied was the church. Another was Peter's son Alexis, who declared that when he became tsar he would put a stop to the innovations and restore respect for the customs of old Russia. Peter, fearing his own son's collaboration with anti-reform conspirators, had Alexis tortured to death. This was the violent familial context in which Peter abolished the rule of hereditary succession to the tsardom. He would stop at nothing to remake Russia in his own fashion.

Resistance to reforms

Peter died in 1725, proclaimed "the Great" in his own lifetime by his admiring Senate. Few persons in all history have exerted so strong an individual influence, which indirectly became more far-reaching as the stature of Russia itself grew in later centuries. Though the years after Peter's death were years of turmoil and vacillation, his revolutionary changes held firm against those who would undo them. It was not simply that he imposed European reforms on Russia and conquered a place on the Baltic; these developments might have come about in any case. It was his autocratic methods, his impatient forcing of a new culture on Russia, that decisively influenced the future autocratic character of his empire. His harsh methods fastened autocracy, serfdom, and bureaucracy more firmly upon the country. Yet he was able to reach only the upper classes. Many of these became more Europeanized than he could dream, habitually speaking French and living spiritually in France or in Italy. But as time went on many upper-class Russians, because of their very knowledge of Europe, became impatient of the stolid immovability of the peasants around them, felt estranged from their own country, or were troubled that their position rested on the degradation and enslavement of other human beings. Russian psychology, often mysterious to later generations in western Europe, could perhaps be explained in part by the violent paradoxes set up by rapid Europeanization. As for the peasant masses,

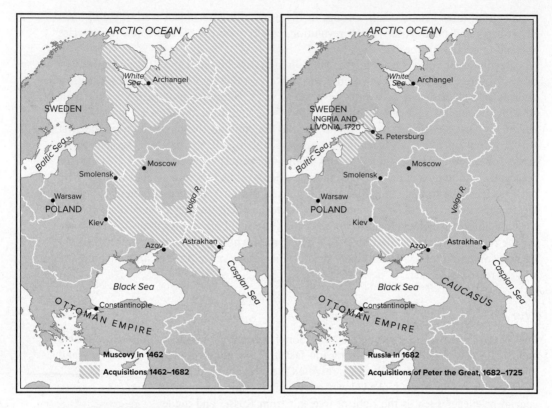

THE GROWTH OF RUSSIA IN THE WEST

At the accession of Peter the Great in 1682 the Russian Empire, expanding from the old grand duchy of Muscovy, had almost reached the Black and Baltic seas. Most of Peter's conquests were in the Baltic region where he pushed back the Swedes and built St. Petersburg. Under Catherine the Great (1762–1796) Russia took part in the three partitions of Poland and also reached the Black Sea. Tsar Alexander I (1801–1825), thanks largely to the Napoleonic wars, was able to acquire still more of Poland and annex Finland and Bessarabia; he also made conquests in the Caucasus. In the nineteenth century the western boundary of Russia remained stabilized, but additional gains were made in the Caucasus. Russia also spread over northern Asia in the seventeenth century, first reaching the Pacific as early as 1630.

Exclusion of peasants

they remained outside the new system, egregiously exploited, separated from their rulers and their social superiors, regarded by them as brutes or children, never sharing in any comparable way in their increasingly Europeanized civilization. Much of this worked itself out in the social conflicts of later times. As for Peter's own time, Russia by his efforts came clearly out of its isolation, its social elites and government reorganized to play a part in international affairs; and its history thenceforward was a part of the history of Europe and increasingly of the world. Russia, like Prussia and the Austrian monarchy, was to be counted among the powers of Europe.

The rising influence of these three monarchies depended in part on their ability to acquire modern weaponry, organize more efficient bureaucracies, and bring new forms of European knowledge into their government institutions. By the beginning of the eighteenth century, European science and technologies often gave European states a

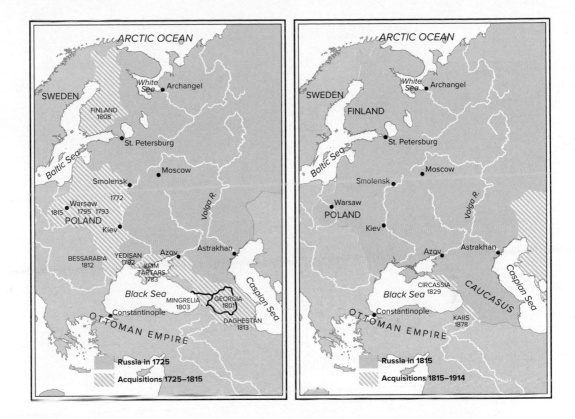

comparative advantage in their economic, political, and military encounters with other peoples or governments—as the ruling elites in Austria, Prussia, and Russia had learned from their own struggles for power in central Europe. Indeed, the new science would ultimately become one of the most distinctive, transformative forces in modern world history. Science helped to reshape economic production, military strategies, and traditional cultures as well as imperial conflicts in Europe and around the world. We must therefore look more closely at the ways in which the development of modern scientific thought increasingly influenced the knowledge and control of both nature and human beings.

Suggested Further Readings can be found in the ebook, on Connect, or online at www.mhhe .com/kramer12e.

CALILEO.

Chapter 6

THE SCIENTIFIC VIEW OF THE WORLD

The seventeenth century has been called the century of genius, in part because it was the age when science became "modern." It was the great age of Galileo and Sir Isaac Newton, whose combined lifetimes spanned the century, with Galileo dying and Newton being born in the same year, 1642. When Galileo was young, those who studied the natural world still labored largely in isolation from one another and from the general public, working oftentimes by methods of trial and error, not altogether clear on what they were trying to do, with their thinking still complicated by ideas not nowadays considered scientific. They had nevertheless accomplished a good deal, without which the intellectual revolution of the seventeenth century would not have occurred.

But in a way all scientific investigators before Galileo seem to be precursors, patient workers destined never to enter into the world toward which they labored. By 1727, when Newton died, a new international scientific community had emerged. Scientists, or "natural philosophers" as they were then called, communicated regularly with one another, and science was recognized as one of the principal enterprises of European society. Although the word "scientist" was not used until the early nineteenth century, scientific methods of inquiry had been defined. The store of factual knowledge had become very large. The first modern scientific synthesis, or coherent theory of the physical universe, had been presented by Newton. Scientific knowledge was applied increasingly to navigation, mining, agriculture, and many branches of manufacture. Science and invention were joining hands. Science was accepted as the main force in the advancement of civilization and progress. And science was becoming popularized; many people who were not themselves scientists believed in science and attempted to apply scientific habits of thought to diverse problems of social and political life.

The history of science is too complex a story to be told in this book, but there are a few ideas about it that even a book of this kind must attempt to make clear. First, science, purely as a form of thought, is one of the supreme achievements of the human mind, and to have a historical

Science

Chapter emblem: Galileo with his telescope. (©Popperfoto/Getty Images)

understanding of human intellectual powers one must sense the importance of science, as of philosophy, literature, or the arts. Second, science has increasingly affected practical affairs, entering into the health, wealth, and happiness of humankind. It has changed the size of populations and the use of raw materials, revolutionized methods of production, transport, business, and war, and so helped to relieve some human problems while aggravating others. Third, in the modern world ideas have had a way of passing over from science into other domains of thought. Many people today, for example, in their notions of themselves, their neighbors, or the meaning of life, are influenced by ideas that they believe to be those of Freud or Einstein—they talk of repressions or relativity without necessarily knowing much about them. Ideas derived from biology and from Darwin—such as evolution and the struggle for existence—have likewise spread far and wide. Similarly the scientific revolution of the seventeenth century had repercussions far beyond the realm of pure science. It changed many European ideas about religion, God, nature, and human beings. It helped to shape and spread influential new beliefs, such as that the physical universe is essentially orderly and harmonious, that human reason is capable of understanding and using it for social purposes, and that human affairs can be conducted by methods of peaceable exchange of ideas and rational discussion. Thus was laid a foundation for belief in free and democratic institutions.

The historical influence of modern science therefore extended far beyond the specific knowledge that transformed the human understanding and use of nature. Scientific methods for establishing truth or defining progress shaped a wide range of modern social institutions, including armies, hospitals, universities, trading companies, government bureaucracies, law courts, and even literary journals. The meaning of the word "modern" became linked to the intellectual prestige of science, and scientific knowledge became the most distinctive and important new intellectual force in modern Europe and the wider modern world. The purpose of this chapter is to sketch the rise of modern science in the seventeenth century and the emergence of the scientific view of the world and of human affairs. The chapters that follow will describe the increasing application of this new knowledge in the expanding global economy and the influence of scientific thought in eighteenth-century European culture, which is generally known as the Age of Enlightenment.

27.   THE EMERGENCE OF A SCIENTIFIC CULTURE: BACON AND DESCARTES

Science before the Seventeenth Century

The scientific view became characteristic of elite European society about the middle of the seventeenth century. There had, indeed, been a few in earlier times who caught glimpses of a whole civilization reared upon science. To us today the most famous of these earlier scientific thinkers is Leonardo da Vinci (1452-1519), the universal genius of the Italian Renaissance, who had been artist, engineer, and scientific theorist all in one. Leonardo, by actual dissection of dead bodies, had obtained an accurate knowledge of human anatomy; he had conceived of the circulation of the blood and the movement of the earth about the sun; and he had drawn designs for submarines and airplanes and speculated on the use of parachutes and poison gases. But Leonardo had not published his scientific ideas. He was known almost exclusively as an artist. His work in science remained outside the stream of scientific thought, without influence on its course. It was not even known until

Leonardo da Vinci

the discovery of his private notebooks in the twentieth century. Leonardo thus figures in the history of science as an isolated genius, a man of brilliant insights and audacious theories, which died with their author's death, whereas science depends on a transmission of ideas in which investigators build upon one another's discoveries, test one another's experiments, and fill in the gaps in one another's knowledge. Modern science evolved as a kind of new cultural system, more dependent on communications and widely shared cultural beliefs than on the brilliance of isolated thinkers. Leonardo's scientific work, remaining unpublished, never entered the cultural institutions in which new scientific knowledge would be produced, challenged, and revised.

A century after the death of Leonardo da Vinci educated Europeans were by no means scientifically minded. Among thoughtful persons many currents were stirring. On the one hand there was a great deal of skepticism, a constantly doubting frame of mind, which held that no certain knowledge is possible for human beings at all, that all beliefs are essentially only customs, that some people believe one thing and some another, and that there is no sound way of choosing between them. This attitude was best expressed by the French essayist Michel de Montaigne (1533-1592), whose thought distilled itself into an eternal question, *Que sais-je?* "What do I know?" with the always implied answer, "Nothing or very little." Montaigne's philosophy led to a new interest in self-analysis and

---

Historical Documents
Michel de Montaigne, *The Essays* (1580)

A new generation of skeptical thinkers arose after the Wars of Religion in the sixteenth century. The French writer Michel de Montaigne became one of the most important advocates for a new kind of self-conscious, analytical approach to all human experiences, stressing the discovery of selfhood as essential for a meaningful life. This skeptical self-fashioning helped to encourage a new tolerance as well as a new search for knowledge that would later shape the ideas of scientists such as René Descartes. In these excerpts from two of his famous essays, Montaigne emphasizes that a good life requires quiet reflection and times of withdrawal from the busy activities of daily life.

Choose treasures which no harm can corrupt and . . . hide them in a place which no one can enter, no one betray, save we ourselves. We should have . . . children, property, and, above all, good health . . . if we can: but we should not become so attached to them that our happiness depends on them. We should set aside a room, just for ourselves, . . . keeping it entirely free and establishing there our true liberty, our principal solitude and asylum. Within it our normal conversation should be of ourselves, with ourselves, so privy that no commerce with or communication with the outside world should find a place there . . . . We have a soul able to turn in on herself; she can keep herself company . . . .

Let us bring our thoughts and reflections back to our ourselves and to our own well-being.

I was born for company and loving relationships. The solitude which I advocate is, above all, . . . the bringing of my emotions and thoughts back to myself, restricting and restraining not my wandering footsteps but my anxiety and my desires, abandoning disquiet about external things and . . . running away not so much from the throng of people as from the throng of affairs.

Michel de Montaigne, "On Solitude" and "On Three Kinds of Social Intercourse," *The Essays: A Selection,* translated and edited by M. A. Screech (London: Penguin Books Ltd., 1987), pp. 100-101, 253.

to a tolerant, humane, and broad-minded outlook, but as a system of thought it was not very constructive in shaping new scientific knowledge or new institutions for scientific research. On the other hand, there was also a tendency to overbelieve in mysterious, supernatural powers, arising from the same inability to distinguish between true and false. There was no accepted line between chemistry and alchemy or between astronomy and astrology; all alike were regarded as ways of penetrating the "secrets" of nature. The sixteenth century had been a great age of charlatans, such as Nostradamus and Paracelsus, some of whom, notably Paracelsus, mixed magic and valid science in a way hardly understandable to modern scientists. As late as the seventeenth century, especially in central Europe where the Thirty Years' War produced chaos and terror, kings and generals kept private astrologers to divine the future.

Witchcraft panic

The two centuries from about 1450 to about 1650 were also the period when fear of witches was at its height. The great campaign against witches thus coincided with Europe's brutal religious wars and also with the early development of the new scientific culture among members of Europe's educated elite, but even highly educated persons often believed that witches actually existed. Witches were blamed for all kinds of natural disasters and personal tragedies—bad harvests, epidemics, the mysterious deaths of children. Although most of the persons prosecuted for witchcraft were women, men were also imprisoned or executed for various crimes of "sorcery." The witchcraft panic lasted longest in Germany and central Europe, probably kept alive by the insecurities engendered by the Thirty Years' War. But about 20

Women were executed on charges of witchcraft from the later Middle Ages down through the seventeenth century, when a new fear of witches happened to coincide with the early modern scientific revolution. This mid-seventeenth-century English illustration shows a typical pattern of persecution in which several women were put to death at the same time for the alleged crime of "sorcery" or conspiring with "witches."

(©Topham/The Image Works)

persons were hanged as witches in Massachusetts as late as 1692, for the English colonies, as a remote and outlying part of the European world, were among the last to feel the newer intellectual currents that were spreading across Europe. The last known execution for witchcraft took place in 1722 in Scotland.

It was by no means clear, in the early part of the seventeenth century, how European societies were going to develop. Europe might conceivably have fallen into a kind of pervasive political chaos. We have seen how much of Europe was racked by chronic and marauding violence, which was gradually ended by the consolidation of the modern state and the conversion of armed bands into organized and disciplined armies; but this more orderly political outcome was not yet apparent during the decades of the Thirty Years' War and the revolutionary upheavals in England. Similarly, in matters of the mind, there was no settled order. Doubt went with superstition, indifference with persecution. Science in time provided Europe with a new faith in its cultural achievements. The rise of science in the seventeenth century possibly saved Europeans from drifting into a long postmedieval afterglow or from wandering off into the diverse, dead-end paths of endless skepticism, ineffectual philosophizing, desultory magic, or mad fear of the unknown.

Bacon and Descartes

Two men stand out as prophets of an intellectual world reconstructed by science. One was the Englishman Francis Bacon (1561–1626); the other was the Frenchman René Descartes (1596–1650). Both published their most influential books between 1620 and 1640. Both addressed themselves to the problem of knowledge. Both asked themselves how it is possible for human beings to know anything with certainty or to have a reliable, truthful, and usable knowledge of the world of nature. Both shared in the doubts of their day. They branded virtually all beliefs of preceding generations (outside religion) as worthless. Both ridiculed the tendency to put faith in ancient books, to cite the writings of Aristotle or others, on questions having to do with the workings of nature. Both attacked earlier methods of seeking knowledge; they rejected the methods of the "schoolmen" or "scholastics," the thinkers in the academic tradition of the universities founded in the Middle Ages. On the whole, medieval philosophy had been deductive. That is, its characteristic procedure was to start with definitions and general propositions and then discover what further knowledge could be logically deduced from the broad definitions thus accepted. Or it proceeded by affirming the inherent nature of an object (e.g., "man is a political animal") and then describing how objects of such a nature do or should behave. These methods, which owed much to Aristotle and other ancient codifiers of human thought, had generally ceased to be fruitful in producing new knowledge of nature. Bacon and Descartes held that the medieval (or Aristotelian) methods approached truth from the wrong direction. They held that truth is not something that we postulate at the beginning and then explore in all its ramifications, but that it is something that we find at the end, after a long process of specific investigation, experiment, and intermediate thought.

Bacon and Descartes therefore went beyond mere doubt and proposed a new analytical method to challenge the cultural drift toward skepticism. They offered a constructive program, and though their programs were different, they both became advocates for a scientific conception of objective truth. They maintained that there was a true and reliable method of knowledge. And they maintained in addition that once this true method was known and practiced, once the real workings of nature were understood, people would be able to use this knowledge for their own purposes, control nature in their own interests, make useful inventions, improve their mechanical arts, and add generally to human wealth and comfort. Bacon and Descartes thus argued that science provided a new foundation for human progress as well as objective knowledge about the natural world.

Francis Bacon and empiricism

Francis Bacon planned a great work in many volumes, to be known as the *Instauratio Magna* or "Great Renewal," calling for a complete new start in science and civilization. He completed only two parts. One, published in 1620, was the *Novum Organum* or new method of acquiring knowledge. Here he insisted on the *inductive* method. In the inductive method we proceed from the particular to the general, from the concrete to the abstract. For example, in the study of leaves, if we examine millions of actual leaves of all sizes and shapes and if we assemble, observe, and compare them with minute scrutiny, we are using an *inductive* method in the sense meant by Bacon; if successful, we may arrive at a knowledge, based on observed facts, of the general nature of a leaf as such. If, on the other hand, we begin with a general idea of what we think all leaves are like, that is, all leaves have stems, and then proceed to describe an individual leaf on that basis, we are following the *deductive* method; we draw logical implications from what we already know, but we learn no more of the nature of a leaf than what we knew or thought we knew at the beginning.

Bacon advised his readers to put aside all traditional ideas, to rid themselves of prejudices and preconceptions, to look at the world with fresh eyes, to observe and study the innumerable things that are actually perceived by the senses. Thinkers before Bacon used the inductive method, but he formalized it as a method and became a leading philosopher of empiricism, which asserted that reliable knowledge must be based on observation and experience. This philosophy has always proved a useful safeguard against fitting facts into preconceived or purely abstract patterns. It demands that we let our ideas and actions be shaped by actual facts as we observe them. The new scientific knowledge thus linked particular facts to general principles and typically combined inductive method with the broader claims of deductive thought. The knowledge that developed from such empirical and analytical methods came to be viewed as stable truths that did not simply express the subjective beliefs of a particular person or cultural tradition; indeed, such knowledge seemed to offer truths that all people could accept, no matter how they might otherwise differ in their religious beliefs, cultural traditions, or social ranks.

The other completed part of Bacon's great work, published in 1623, was called in its English translation *The Advancement of Learning*. Here Bacon developed the same ideas and insisted also that true knowledge was useful knowledge. In *The New Atlantis* (1627), he portrayed a scientific utopia whose inhabitants enjoyed a perfect society through their knowledge and command of nature. This emphasis on the usefulness of knowledge became the other main element in the Baconian tradition. In this view there was no sharp difference between pure science and applied science or between the work of the purely scientific investigators and that of the inventors who in their own way probed into nature and devised instruments or machines for putting natural forces to work. The fact that knowledge could be used for practical purposes became a sign or proof that it was true knowledge. For example, the fact that soldiers could aim their cannon and hit their targets more accurately in the seventeenth century became a proof of the theory of ballistics that scientists had worked out in research that was far removed from a battlefield. Enthusiastic Baconians believed that knowledge was power. True knowledge could be put to work, if not immediately at least in the long run, after more knowledge was discovered. It was useful to mankind, unlike the "delicate learning" of the misguided scholastics. In this coming together of knowledge and power arose the far-reaching modern idea of progress. And in it arose many modern problems, because scientific knowledge and power can be used for either good or evil.

But Bacon, though a force in redirecting the European mind, never had much influence on the development of actual science. Kept busy as Lord Chancellor of England and in other government duties, he was not even fully abreast of the most advanced scientific thought of his day. Bacon's greatest intellectual weakness was his failure to understand the role of mathematics. Mathematics, dealing with pure abstractions and proceeding deductively from axioms to theorems, was not an empirical or inductive method of thought such as Bacon demanded. Yet science in the seventeenth century went forward most successfully in subjects where mathematics could be applied. Even today the degree to which a subject is truly scientific depends on the degree to which it can be made mathematical. We have pure science where we have formulas and equations, and the scientific method itself is both inductive and deductive.

Descartes was a great mathematician in his own right. He is considered the inventor of coordinate geometry. He showed that by use of coordinates (or graph paper, in simple language) any algebraic formula

René Descartes

could be plotted as a curve in space, and contrariwise that any curve in space, however complex, could be converted into algebraic terms and thus dealt with by methods of calculation. His general philosophy therefore contributed to the growing scientific belief that the vast world of nature could be reduced to mathematical form.

Descartes set forth his ideas in his *Discourse on Method* in 1637 and in other more technical writings. He advanced the principle of systematic doubt. He began by trying to doubt everything that could reasonably be doubted, thus sweeping away past ideas and clearing the ground for his own "great renewal," to use Bacon's phrase. Despite this far-reaching skepticism, however, he held that he could not doubt his own existence as a

RENÉ DESCARTES
After a portrait by Frans
Hals (1584–1666)

Descartes worked for many
years in Amsterdam, where
he developed his work in
mathematics, described his
philosophical methods of
systematic doubt, and sat
for a portrait by Frans Hals—
which was lost sometime
after another (unknown)
artist replicated the portrait
with the version shown here.
(©Everett - Art/Shutterstock)

thinking and doubting being (*cogito ergo sum,* "I think, therefore I exist"). He then deduced, by systematic reasoning, the existence of God and much else. He arrived at a philosophy of dualism, the famous "Cartesian dualism," which held that God has created two kinds of fundamental reality in the universe. One was "thinking substance"—mind, spirit, consciousness, subjective experience. The other was "extended substance"—everything outside the mind and hence a material reality that could be understood through objective knowledge. Of everything except the mind itself the most fundamental and universal quality was that it occupied a portion of space, minute or vast. Space itself was conceived as infinite and everywhere geometric.

This philosophy had profound and long-lasting effects. For one thing, the seemingly most real elements in human experience, color and sound, joy and grief, seemed somehow to be shadowy and unreal, or perhaps illusory, with no objective existence outside the mind itself. But all else was quantitative, measurable, reducible to formulas or equations. Over all else, over the whole universe or half-universe of extended substance, the most powerful instrument available to the human understanding, namely, mathematics, reigned supreme. "Give me motion and extension," said Descartes, "and I will build you the world."

Descartes also shared Bacon's belief in empirical research, useful knowledge, and human progress. Instead of the "speculative philosophy of the schools," he wrote in the *Discourse on Method,* one might discover a "practical philosophy by which, understanding the forces and action of fire, water, air, the stars and heavens and all other bodies that surround us, . . . we can use these forces . . . and so make ourselves the masters and possessors of nature. And this is desirable not only for the invention of innumerable devices . . . , but mainly also for the preservation of health, which is undoubtedly the principal good and foundation of all other good things in this life." Science, in short, opened the way to a better life than philosophy alone could ever produce.

28.   THE ROAD TO NEWTON: THE LAW OF UNIVERSAL GRAVITATION

Scientific Advances

Botany, anatomy, and physiology

Meanwhile actual scientific discovery was advancing on many fronts as new "natural philosophers" shared information in the emerging networks of scientific communication. The new knowledge did not advance on all fronts with equal speed. Some of the sciences were, and long remained, dependent mainly on the collection of specimens. Botany was one of these; Europe's knowledge of plants expanded enormously with the explorations overseas. New edible plants were brought from the Americas, and the botanical gardens and herb collections in Europe also became far more extensive than ever before, bringing important enlargements in the stock of medicinal drugs as well as new foods. Other sciences drew their impetus from intensive and open-minded observation. In 1543 the Flemish physician Andreas Vesalius published *The Structure of the Human Body,* an influential book that renewed and modernized the study of anatomy. Formerly anatomists had generally held that the writings of Galen, dating from the second century C.E., contained an authoritative description of all human muscles and tissues. They had indeed dissected cadavers but had dismissed those not conforming to Galen's description as somehow abnormal or not typical. Vesalius, by contrast, decided on the basis of his own careful dissections that

Galen's descriptions of the human body were often wrong. Developing comprehensive accounts of the human skeleton, organs, and circulatory system with detailed references to the actual bodies he examined, Vesalius constructed what historians of science would describe as a new "paradigm" for the later study of human anatomy.

In physiology also, dealing with the functioning rather than the structure of living bodies, there was considerable progress. William Harvey, after years of laboratory work in England (which included the vivisection of animals), published in 1628 a book *On the Movement of the Heart and Blood,* which set forth the doctrine of the continual circulation of the blood through arteries and veins. The Italian Marcello Malpighi, using the newly invented microscope, confirmed Harvey's findings by the discovery of capillaries in 1661. The Dutch scientist Antoine van Leeuwenhoek, also by use of the microscope, provided new information about blood corpuscles, spermatozoa, and bacteria, of which he left published drawings. Another seventeenth-century Dutch scientist, Régnier de Graaf, published the first description of the female ovaries, thus challenging Galen's ancient theories of human sexuality and the long-accepted idea that women contributed less than men to the biological processes of reproduction.

These sciences, and also chemistry, although work in them went forward continually, did not come fully into their own until after 1800. They were long overshadowed by astronomy and physics. Here mathematics could be most fully applied, and mathematics underwent a rapid *Astronomy and physics* development in the seventeenth century. Decimals came into use to express fractions, the symbols used in algebra were improved and standardized, and in 1614 logarithms were invented by the Scot John Napier. Coordinate geometry was mapped out by Descartes, the theory of probabilities was developed by Blaise Pascal, and calculus was invented simultaneously in England by Newton and in Germany by Leibniz. These advances made it more generally possible to think about nature in purely quantitative terms, to measure with greater precision, and to perform complex and laborious computations. Physics and astronomy were remarkably stimulated, and it was in this field that the most influential scientific revolution of the seventeenth century took place.

The Scientific Revolution: Copernicus to Galileo

Ever since Ptolemy had codified ancient astronomy in the second century C.E., educated Europeans had held a conception of the cosmos that we call Ptolemaic. The earth, as described in the Ptolemaic conception, was at the center of the universe. The cosmos in this ancient Greek view was a group of concentric spheres, a series of *The Ptolemaic system* balls within balls each having the same center. The innermost ball was the earth, made up of hard, solid, earthy substance such as people were familiar with underfoot. The other spheres, encompassing the earth in series of closer or more distant geometric circles, were all transparent. They were the "crystalline spheres," all of which revolved about the earth. Each sphere contained within it a luminous heavenly body or orb that also moved about the earth with the movement of its transparent sphere. Nearest to the earth was the sphere of the moon; then, in turn, the spheres of Mercury and Venus, then the sphere of the sun, then those of the outer planets. Last came the outermost sphere containing all the fixed stars studded in it, all moving majestically about the earth in daily motion, but motionless with respect to each other because they were held firmly in the same sphere. Beyond the sphere of the fixed stars, in general belief, lay the "empyrean," the home of angels and immortal spirits; but this was not a matter of natural science.

An earth-centered
cosmos

Persons standing on the earth and looking up into the sky thus felt themselves to be enclosed by a dome in which their own position was the center. In the blue sky of day they could literally see the crystalline spheres; in the stars at night they could behold the orbs that these spheres carried with them. All revolved about the observer, presumably at no very alarming distance. The celestial bodies were commonly supposed to be of different material and quality from the earth. The earth was of heavy dross; the stars and planets and the sun and moon seemed made of pure and gleaming light, or at least of a bright ethereal substance almost as tenuous as the crystal spheres in which they moved. The cosmos was a hierarchy of ascending perfection. The heavens were purer than the earth.

This Ptolemaic or geocentric system corresponded to actual appearances, and except for scientific knowledge would be highly believable today. It was formulated also in rigorous mathematical terms. Ever since the Greeks, and becoming increasingly intricate in the Middle Ages, a complex geometry had grown up to explain the observed motion of the heavenly bodies. The Ptolemaic system was a mathematical system. And it was for purely mathematical reasons rather than from empirical observations that it first came to be reconsidered. There was a marked revival of mathematical interest at the close of the Middle Ages, in the fourteenth and fifteenth centuries, a renewed concentration on the philosophical traditions of Pythagoras and Plato. These philosophies proposed the doctrine that numbers might be the final key to the mysteries of nature. With them went a metaphysical belief that simplicity was more likely to be a sign of truth than complexity and that a simpler mathematical formulation was better than a more complicated one.

Nicholas Copernicus

These ideas motivated Nicholas Copernicus (1473–1543), born in Poland of German and Polish background, who, after study in Italy, wrote his epochal work *On the Revolutions of the Heavenly Orbs*. In this book, published in 1543 after his death, he held the sun to be the center of the solar system and of the whole universe; the earth, he argued, was one of the planets revolving in space around it. This view had been entertained by a few isolated thinkers before. Copernicus gave a mathematical demonstration. To him it was a purely mathematical problem. With increasingly detailed knowledge of the actual movement of the heavenly bodies it had become necessary, as the years passed, to make the Ptolemaic system more intricate by the addition of new "cycles" and "epicycles," until, as John Milton expressed it later, the cosmos was

> With Centric and Concentric scribbled o'er,
> Cycle and Epicycle, Orb in Orb.

Copernicus needed fewer such hypothetical constructions to explain the known movements of the heavenly bodies. The heliocentric or sun-centered theory was mathematically simpler than the geocentric or earth-centered theory that it would gradually displace.

The Copernican doctrine long remained a hypothesis known only to experts. Most astronomers for a time hesitated to accept it, seeing no need, from the evidence yet produced, to make such a radical readjustment of the older Ptolemaic paradigm. Tycho Brahe (1546–1601), the greatest authority on the actual positions and movements of the heavenly bodies in the generations immediately after Copernicus, never accepted the Copernican system in full. But his assistant and follower, Johannes Kepler (1571–1630), building on Tycho's exact observations, not only accepted the Copernican theory but carried it further.

Johannes Kepler

Kepler, a German, was a kind of mathematical mystic, part-time astrologer, and scientific genius. Copernicus had believed the orbits of the planets about the sun to be

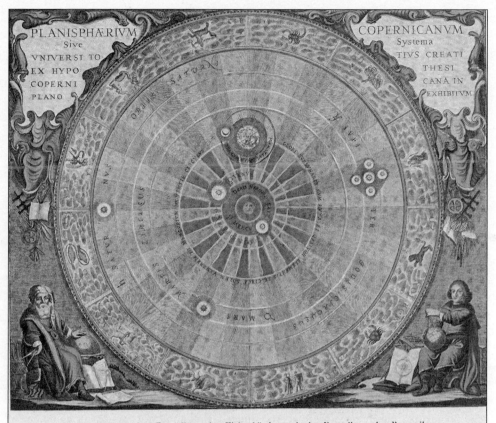

Faksimile einer alten Darstellung des Weltgebäudes nach der Vorstellung des Kopernikus
Nach Andreae Cellarii „Harmonia Macrocosmica" vom Jahre 1660

The Copernican conception of a solar system revolving around the sun was long unknown outside a small circle of experts, and few persons understood the mathematics upon which it was based. But the meaning of the Copernican theories later spread in visual images that depicted the new astronomical view of the sun, earth, and other planets.

(©Time Life Pictures/Getty Images)

perfect circles. Tycho showed that this belief did not fit the observable facts. It was Kepler who discovered that the orbits of the planets were ellipses. The ellipse, like the circle, is an abstract mathematical figure with knowable properties. Kepler demonstrated that the closer a planet is to the sun in its elliptical orbit, the faster it moves; and he showed that the length of time in which the several planets revolve about the sun varies proportionately with their distance from the sun.

Most people could not understand the mathematics involved, but it was possible to realize the astounding implications of Kepler's laws of planetary motion. Kepler showed that the actual world of stubborn facts, as observed by Tycho, and the purely rational world of mathematical harmony, as surmised by Copernicus, were not really in any contradiction to each other—that they really corresponded exactly. He digested an overwhelming amount of hitherto unexplained information into a few brief statements. He showed a cosmic mathematical relationship between space and time. And he described the movement of the planets in explicit formulas, which any competent person or scientific community could verify at will.

Galileo's scientific research, which included the use of a telescope and led to a clash with church authorities, gave him an enduring stature in European intellectual history. This later image of Galileo portrays him as the idealized early modern "man of science," working alone to discover and describe new knowledge.
(©Popperfoto/Getty Images)

Galileo

The international character of early modern scientific culture can be seen in the next important contributions of the Italian Galileo Galilei (1564–1642). So far the question of the substance of the heavenly bodies had hardly been reconsidered. Indeed, they were not thought of as bodies at all, but rather as luminous orbs. Only the sun and moon had any dimension; stars and planets were only points of light; and the theories of Copernicus and Kepler, like those of Ptolemy, might apply to insubstantial luminous objects in motion.

Telescopes and new knowledge

In 1609 Galileo built a telescope. Turning it to the sky, he perceived that the moon had a rough and apparently mountainous surface, as if made of the same kind of material as the earth. Seeing clearly the dark part of the moon in its various phases, and noting that in every position it only reflected the light of the sun, he concluded that the moon was not itself a luminous object, another indication that it might be made of earthlike substance. He saw spots on the sun, as if the sun were not pure and perfect. He found that the planets had visible breadth when seen in the telescope but that the fixed stars remained only points of light, as if incalculably further away. He discovered also that Jupiter had satellites, moons moving around it like the moon around the earth. These discoveries reassured him of the validity of the Copernican theory, which he had in any case already accepted. They suggested also that the heavenly bodies might be of the same substance as the earth, masses of matter moving in space; and if the heavenly bodies consisted of matter, it became easier to think of the earth itself as simply another heavenly body revolving about the sun. The difference between the earth and the heavens was disappearing. This struck a terrifying blow at all earlier philosophy and theology. Some professors were afraid to look through the telescope, and Galileo was condemned for heresy and forced by his church to renounce his description of the solar system; but he never really changed his scientific views.

Moreover, where Kepler had found mathematical laws describing the movement of planets, Galileo now found mathematical laws describing the movement of bodies on the earth. Formerly it had been thought that some bodies were by nature heavier than others and that heavier bodies fell to the ground faster than light ones. Galileo in 1591, according to the traditional story, dropped a 10-pound and a 1-pound weight simultaneously from the top of the Leaning Tower of Pisa. The truth of this story has been questioned, but in any case Galileo showed that two bodies of different weights, when allowance was made for the different air resistance of differently shaped objects, struck the ground at the same time. His further work in dynamics, or the science of motion of bodies, took many years to accomplish. He had to devise more refined means for measuring small intervals of time, find means of estimating the air resistance and friction that always occur in nature, and conceive of absolute motion, and of force and velocity, in abstract mathematical terms. Yet Galileo could still not answer certain questions about the motion of objects—questions that would soon be examined again by Isaac Newton.

The Achievement of Newton: The Promise of Science

Historians of science now tend to stress the collective and cultural components of scientific advances rather than "Great Man" accounts of the lone scientific genius, but it was the supreme creative achievement of Isaac Newton (1642–1727) that brought Kepler and Galileo together in a new explanation of universal motion. Connecting the breakthroughs of his influential predecessors, Newton was able to show that Kepler's laws of planetary motion and Galileo's laws of terrestrial motion were two aspects of the same laws. Galileo's discovery that moving bodies move uniformly in a straight line unless deflected by a definite force made it necessary to explain why the planets, instead of flying off in straight lines, tend to

Universal gravitation

fall toward the sun, the result being their elliptical orbits—and why the moon, similarly, tends to fall toward the earth. Newton seems early to have suspected that the explanation would be related to Galileo's laws of falling bodies and that the pull of the earth upon objects on earth might resemble a pull characterizing all bodies in the solar system. Great technical difficulties stood in the way, but finally, after inventing calculus, and using a new measurement of the size of the earth made by a Frenchman and experiments with circular motion made by the Dutch Huyghens on the pendulum, Newton was able to bring his calculations to fruition. He soon published, in Latin, his *Mathematical Principles of Natural Philosophy* (1687), a book that would bring the "law of universal gravitation" into both the science and the wider intellectual debates of early modern Europe.

This stupendous book showed that all motion that could be timed and measured, whether on the earth or in the solar system, could be described by the same mathematical formulas. All matter moved as if every particle attracted every other particle with a force proportionate to the product of the two masses and inversely proportionate to the square of the distance between them. This force was universal gravitation. What it was Newton did not pretend to explain. For 200 years the law stood unshaken, always verified by every new relevant discovery. Only in the last century were its limitations found; it does not hold good in the infinitesimal world of subatomic structure or in the macrocosm of the whole physical universe as now conceived.

It was in Newton's time that the pursuit of natural knowledge became institutionalized, and Newton himself first presented his theories at London's Royal Society for Improving Natural Knowledge. Such institutions, possessing equipment and funds, were engaged in scientific study, most notably at the Royal Society of London, founded in 1662, and the Royal Academy of Sciences in France, founded in 1666. Both originated when earlier and informal groups, usually gentlemen of the landed class, received official charters from their governments to pursue scientific interests. Scientific periodicals began to be published. Scientific societies provided the medium for prompt interchange of ideas

Historical Interpretations and Debates
Continuity and Discontinuity in the Scientific Revolution

Historians have waged spirited debates about the ways in which early modern scientists both reaffirmed traditional religious beliefs and launched a modern method for understanding the natural world. Such discussions therefore focus on broad questions about the nature of historical continuity and change and about the relation between deep structures of belief and revolutions in thought. A contrasting emphasis on continuity and change thus becomes one of the themes in the interpretations of B. J. T. Dobbs and Richard Westfall as they analyze the significance of Isaac Newton and the Scientific Revolution.

Betty Jo Teeter Dobbs, "Newton as Final Cause and First Mover" (2000)

I intend to undermine one of our most hallowed explanatory frameworks, that of the Scientific Revolution. . . .

No matter what one chooses to emphasize from the sixteenth and seventeenth centuries, . . . one must, it seems, bring the action to a dramatic climax in the work of Isaac Newton. The narrative has assumed all the characteristics of an inevitable progression. . . .

We choose for praise the thinkers that seem to us to have contributed to modernity, but we unconsciously assume that their thought patterns are fundamentally just like ours. Then we look at them . . . and discover . . . that our intellectual ancestors are not like us at all. . . .

[So] how could Newton . . . have pursued alchemy as he did . . .? What Newton hoped to gain from alchemy was a precise knowledge of the Deity. . . . If he, Newton, could but demonstrate the laws of divine activity in nature . . . then he could demonstrate in an irrefutable fashion the existence and providential care of the Deity—a grand goal, though hardly a modern one. . . .

I would like to suggest that [we evaluate] . . . Newton . . . not as the Final Cause of *the* Scientific Revolution, but as . . . a loser in a titanic battle between the forces of religion and the forces of irreligion.

Richard S. Westfall, "The Scientific Revolution Reasserted" (2000)

Dobbs announces her intention to undermine the concept of the Scientific Revolution. In contrast, I intend to defend it. . . .

Before the Scientific Revolution, theology was queen of all the sciences. As a result of the Scientific Revolution, we have redefined the word "science," and today other disciplines . . . strive to expand their self-esteem by appropriating the word . . . to themselves. . . . The focus of the change . . . was the Scientific Revolution of the sixteenth and seventeenth centuries. . . . I am convinced that there has been no more fundamental change in the history of European civilization . . . .

For those who accepted the new astronomy and the new mechanics, Aristotelian natural philosophy had become untenable. If the transformation of scientific thought were to proceed, a new natural philosophy had become a necessity. . . .

[W]ith Newton the new science and the new philosophy of nature found their definitive form in which they shaped the scientific tradition in the West for the coming two centuries. The very nature of the new enterprise . . . insured that the Newtonian system would be modified. . . . As long as we remember those modifications, it does appear to me that the system . . . continues to reign, and I see no prospect whatever that the reign will terminate.

Sources: Teeter Dobbs, Betty Jo, "Newton as Final Cause and First Mover," in *Rethinking the Scientific Revolution,* edited by Margaret J. Osler (Cambridge: Cambridge University Press, 2000), pp. 25, 29, 34, 36, 38–39; Westfall, Richard S. "The Scientific Revolution Reasserted," in *Rethinking the Scientific Revolution,* edited by Margaret J. Osler (Cambridge: Cambridge University Press, 2000), pp. 41, 43, 47–48.

indispensable to the growth of scientific knowledge. They held meetings, proposed projects for research, and published articles on the natural sciences and mathematics, but they also studied and wrote about paleography, numismatics, chronology, legal history, and natural law. The work of the learned had not yet evolved into modern academic specializations.

In all these activities the promise of science seemed fulfilled. Even in practical affairs conveniences followed, as anticipated by the Baconians. The tides could now be understood and predicted by the gravitational interplay of earth, moon, and sun. Exact mathematical knowledge of the celestial bodies, together with the invention of more accurate timepieces, was of great help to navigation and mapmaking. Measures of latitude, or of north-south distances on the spherical earth, had been known to the ancient Greeks. But longitude, or east-west distances, could not be measured until the eighteenth century, when it became possible to determine it by use of a chronometer and observation of heavenly bodies at a known time. Merchant ships and naval squadrons could thus operate with more assurance about where they were sailing. Places on land could be located and mapped more exactly. Eighteenth-century Europeans were the first human beings to have a fairly accurate idea of the shapes and sizes of all the continents and oceans. Better local and regional maps of places in Europe also became available.

Uses of scientific knowledge

Mathematical advance, including the development of calculus, which allowed an exact treatment of curves and trajectories, reinforced by technical discoveries in the working of metals, led to an increased use of artillery. Armies in 1750 used twice as many cannons per soldier as in 1650. Naval ordnance also improved. These items made armed forces more expensive to maintain, requiring governments to increase their taxes, and hence contributing to constitutional crises. Improved firearms heightened the advantage of armies over insurrectionists or private fighting bands, thus strengthening the sovereignty of the state. They also gave Europeans the military advantage over other peoples, in America, India, or elsewhere, on which the world ascendancy of Europe was built in the eighteenth century. The new scientific knowledge thus contributed to the expansion of Europe's colonial empires as well as the growing internal power of European governments.

Improved military weaponry

The significance of the steam engine may also be cited. In 1700 steam power was only in its earliest stages, but it would eventually almost literally move the world. A Frenchman, Denis Papin, in 1681 invented a device in which steam moved a piston, but with so little power that it could be used only in cooking. British scientists also turned their minds to the possible uses of steam. Robert Boyle, discoverer of "Boyle's Law" on the pressure of gases, studied the problem; scientists, mechanics, and instrument makers collaborated. In 1702 Thomas Newcomen, a man without scientific training who associated with scientists, produced the steam engine known thereafter as Newcomen's engine, from which James Watt later developed the steam engine as we know it. Newcomen's engine was primitive according to later ideas. It burned so much fuel that it could be used only in coal mines. But it began to be used, and not long after 1700 it was widely employed to pump water from the coal pits. It saved labor, cheapened production, and opened hitherto unusable deposits to exploitation. It was the first application of steam to an economic purpose.

No distinction was yet felt between pure and applied science. The modern sense of the word hardly existed, even in the early eighteenth century; what we call "science" was still called natural philosophy or "useful knowledge." Traveling public lecturers, in explaining the laws of force and motion, showed their application in devices such as pulleys, scales, levers, cogwheels, waterwheels, and pumps. Such lectures were attended, especially in England, by a mixed audience of philosophers, experimenters, inventors, artisans, landed gentlemen who wished to develop their estates, and small businessmen wishing to enlarge their markets. The scientific movement thus opened the way to agricultural and industrial improvements in Great Britain and other places where the new knowledge was brought into economic activities.

The Scientific Revolution and the World of Thought

The influence of the Scientific Revolution extended far beyond the era's new technologies, and the changing scientific knowledge soon began to challenge or revise some of the oldest religious and intellectual traditions of European culture. The new astronomy and physics led to what has been called the greatest spiritual readjustment that human beings have been required to make. The old heavens were exploded. Humans were no longer the center of creation. The luminaries of the sky no longer shone to light their way or to give them beauty. The sky itself was an illusion, its color a thing in the mind only, for anyone looking upward was really looking only into the darkness of endless space. The old cosmos, comfortably enclosed and ranked in an ascending order of purity, gave way to a new cosmos that seemed to consist of an infinite emptiness through which particles of matter were distributed. Humans were the puny denizens of a material object moving through space along with other very distant material objects of the same kind. About the physical universe there was nothing especially Christian, nothing that could clearly prove the shaping presence of the God portrayed in the Hebrew or the Christian Bible. The gap between religious and scientific explanations for the natural world, always present yet always bridged in the Middle Ages, now began to produce new public conflicts and new personal struggles to reconcile faith and reason. Such tensions were felt with growing anguish by some seventeenth-century writers. The Frenchman Blaise Pascal (1623–1662), for example, was an accomplished scientist, a preeminent mathematician, and a deep but often troubled Christian believer. He left a record of his religious beliefs, anxieties, and fears in his *Pensées,* or *Thoughts,* jottings and personal reflections from which he hoped some day to write a great book on the Christian faith. "I am terrified," he said in one of these jottings, "by the eternal silence of these infinite spaces."

But on the whole the cultural reaction was more optimistic. Man might be merely a tiny reed, as Pascal said, but Pascal added, he had the mental powers of "a thinking reed." Human beings might be no longer the physical center of the universe. But it was the human mind that had penetrated the universal laws by which the planets and the earth itself were put in motion. The Newtonian system, as it became popularized, a process that took about 50 years, led to a great intellectual confidence. Never had there been so much optimism about the intellectual abilities of human beings. As the English poet Alexander Pope put it,

The Newtonian system

> Nature and nature's laws lay hid in night;
> God said, "Let Newton be," and all was light.

Or, according to another epigram on the subject, there was only one universe to discover, and this universe had been discovered by Newton. Everything seemed possible to human reason. Although Newton and most other scientists continued to believe in the existence of God, the old feeling of dependency on divine powers and judgments lost much of its force or became something to be discussed by clergymen in church on Sunday. Most

COLBERT PRESENTING THE MEMBERS OF THE ROYAL ACADEMY OF SCIENCES TO LOUIS XIV
by Henri Testelin (1616–1695)

Testelin was an instructor at the Royal Academy of Painting and a strong defender of the academic traditions in French art. He portrayed King Louis XIV meeting members of the new Royal Academy of Sciences in 1667. This painting expresses his respect for both the king and the new scientific knowledge, but Testelin's life also exemplified another side of late seventeenth-century French culture. He was a Protestant who eventually had to give up his academic position and move to the Netherlands to practice his religion.

(©Photo Josse/Leemage/Corbis Historical/Getty Images)

advocates of the new scientific knowledge could no longer view human beings as little creatures, spiritual wayfarers in an alien natural world, yearning for a reunion with God that would bring peace. They were creatures of great capacity in their own right, living in a natural world that was understandable and manageable. These ideas contributed greatly to the secularizing of European society, gradually pushing religion and churches to the sidelines of European political power and many of the era's new intellectual debates.

The scientific discoveries also reinforced the old philosophy of natural law. This philosophy, developed by the Greeks and renewed in the Middle Ages, held that the universe is fundamentally orderly and that there is a natural rightness or justice, universally the same for all people and knowable by reason. It was very important in

ISAAC NEWTON
by Godfrey Kneller (English, 1648-1723)

Isaac Newton became the famous public symbol of the new scientific knowledge and the new scientific researcher. This portrait by Godfrey Kneller emphasizes the focused brilliance that made Newton an icon in the expanding institutions of scientific culture and in the wider development of eighteenth-century intellectual life.

(©Bettmann/Getty Images)

political theory, where it stood out against arbitrariness and the merely random claims of self-interested power. The laws of nature as discovered by science were somewhat different, but they taught the same lesson, namely, the orderliness and minute regularity of the world. It was reassuring to feel that everywhere throughout an infinite space every particle of matter was quietly attracting every other particle by a force proportionate to the product of the masses and inversely proportionate to the square of the distance. The physical universe laid bare by science—orderly, rational, balanced, smoothly running, without strife or rivalry or contention—became a model on which many later thinkers hoped to refashion human society. They hoped to make society also fulfill the rational rule of law, much like scientists had shown how material objects adhere to the laws of nature.

In some ways it would be possible to exaggerate the impact of pure science. Scientists themselves did not usually apply their scientific ideas to religion and society. Few suffered the spiritual torment of Pascal. Both Descartes and Newton wrote carefully argued tracts that asserted the truth of certain religious doctrines. Bacon and Harvey were conservative politically, upholders of king against Parliament. The Englishman Joseph Glanvill, in the 1660s, used Cartesian dualism to demonstrate the probable existence of witches. Descartes, despite his systematic doubt, held that the customs of one's country should usually be accepted without question. Natural science, in the pure sense, was not inherently revolutionary or even upsetting. If Europeans in the seventeenth century began to waver in many old beliefs, it was not only because of the stimulus of pure science but also because of an increasing study and knowledge of humanity itself.

29. NEW KNOWLEDGE OF HUMAN BEINGS AND SOCIETY

The discovery and exploration of the world overseas became a decisive new influence on European views of human cultures and the nature of human beings. Europe was already becoming part of the world as a whole, and Europeans could henceforth understand themselves only by comparisons with non-European regions. Great reciprocal influences were at work, and the cultural exchanges flowed in both directions. The influences of European expansion on other parts of the world are easily seen: the Indian societies of America were modified or sometimes almost extinguished; the indigenous societies of Africa were dislocated and many of their members were enslaved and transported; in the long run the ancient societies of Asia were also to be disrupted or undermined. European ideas and institutions altered the ways in which other peoples described their own cultures, and the exchanges or conflicts with Europe reshaped identities wherever such

Cross-cultural encounters

interactions occurred. From the beginning, however, the counterinfluence of the rest of the world upon Europe was equally great. It took the form of new medicines, new diseases, new foods, new and exotic manufactures brought to Europe, and the growth of material wealth in western European countries, but it also affected European thinking. New questions were raised about the diversity of religious traditions, the history of languages, and the origins of human civilizations. The growing involvement with other cultures undermined the old Europe and its ideas, just as Europe was undermining the old cultures beyond the oceans. Vast new horizons opened before Europeans in the sixteenth and seventeenth centuries. Europeans of this period were the first people to know the whole globe, to establish colonial outposts around most of the world, or to realize the variety of the human race and its multifarious manners and customs.

The Current of Skepticism

This encounter with the diversity of human cultures was very unsettling. The realization of human differences had the effect, in Europe, of breaking what has been called the "cake of custom." A new sense of the relative nature of social institutions developed. It became harder to believe in any absolute rightness of one's own ways. Montaigne, already mentioned, expressed the relativist outlook clearly, and nowhere more clearly than in his famous essay on cannibals. The cannibals, he said humorously, did in fact eat human flesh; that was their custom, and they have their customs as Europeans also have theirs; they would think some European ways odd or inhuman; peoples differ, and who are we to judge? The cannibals cooked human bodies after the people were dead, but Europeans burned human beings when they were still alive. Travelers' books spread the same message increasingly through the seventeenth century. As one of them observed (whether or not rightly), in Turkey it was the custom to shave the hair and wear the beard, in Europe to shave the beard and wear the hair; what difference does it really make?

Travelers' tales and cultural relativism

That the ways of non-Europeans might be good ways was emphasized by Jesuit missionaries. Writing from the depths of the Mississippi Valley or from China, the Jesuit fathers often dwelt on the natural goodness and mental alertness of native peoples they encountered, perhaps hoping in this way to gain support in Europe for their missionary labors. Meanwhile, people coming from the American wilderness or from Asia sometimes appeared in Europe itself. In 1684 a delegation of aristocratic Siamese arrived in Paris, followed by another in 1686. The Parisians went through a fad for Siam (now Thailand); they recounted how the king of Siam, when asked by a missionary to turn Christian, replied that divine Providence, had it wished a single religion to prevail in the world, could easily have so arranged it. The philosophical Siamese seemed civilized and wise; they allowed Christians to preach in their own country, whereas it was well known what would happen to a Siamese missionary who undertook to preach in Paris. China also was seen at this time as a civilized center of learning, tolerance, and wise ethical traditions. By 1700 there were even professors of Arabic, at Paris, Oxford, and Utrecht, who said that Islam was a religion to be respected, as good for Muslims as Christianity was for Christians.

Skepticism

Thus was created a strong current of skepticism, holding that all beliefs are relative, varying with the time, place, and culture in which they develop. The greatest spokesman for this kind of relativism or skepticism at the end of the century was Pierre Bayle (1647–1706). Bayle was also influenced by the scientific discoveries; not exactly that he understood them, for he was an almost purely literary scholar, but he realized that many popular beliefs were without scientific foundation. Between 1680 and 1682 a number of comets were seen. The one of 1682 was studied by a friend of Newton's, Edmond Halley, the first man to predict the return of a comet. He identified the comet of 1682 with the one observed in 1302, 1456, 1531, and 1607, and predicted its reappearance in 1757 (it appeared in 1759); it was seen again in 1910 and 1986 and is still called Halley's Comet. In the 1680s people were talking excitedly about the significance of comets. Some said that comets emitted poisonous exhalations; others, that they were supernatural omens of future events.

Bayle, in his *Thoughts on the Comet,* argued that there was no basis for any such beliefs except human credulity. In 1697 he published his *Historical and Critical Dictionary,* a tremendous repository of miscellaneous lore, conveying the message that what is called truth is often mere opinion, that most people are amazingly gullible, that many things firmly believed are really ridiculous, and that it is very foolish to hold too strongly to

Bayle's Critical Dictionary

one's own views. Bayle's *Dictionary* remained a reservoir on which skeptical writers continued to draw for generations. Bayle himself, having no firm basis in his own mind for settled judgment, mixed skepticism with an impulse to faith. Born a Protestant, he was converted to Roman Catholicism, then returned to his Calvinist background. In any case his views made for toleration in religion. For Bayle, as for Montaigne, no opinion could justify burning your neighbor at the stake.

The New Sense of Evidence

But in the study of humankind, as in the study of physical nature, Europeans of the seventeenth century were not generally content with skepticism. They usually sought to go beyond a doubting mood, important and salutary as such an attitude was. In the subjects collectively called the humanities, as in pure science, they were looking for a more advanced understanding of human behavior. They wanted new means of telling the true from the false, a new method for arriving at some degree of certainty of conviction. And here, too, a kind of scientific view of the world arose, if that term is understood in a general sense. The new human sciences took the form of a new interest in observable evidence. Evidence is that which gives one good reasons to believe that a statement is true, or at least truer than something else for which the evidence is weaker. And if to

The arrival of a second delegation of ambassadors from Siam at Versailles in 1686 made a vivid impression on a French generation that often read about distant lands and peoples. Although this portrayal of the visit by the French artist Charles le Brun confirmed that the bowing ambassadors showed the requisite respect for the Sun King, their presence in France contributed to a growing speculation on cultural differences and the relativism of cultural customs.
(©Print Collector/Getty Images)

believe without evidence is the sign of nonscientific or irrational thinking, to require observable evidence before believing is in a way to be scientific, or at least to trust and use the power of human intelligence.

The new belief in the need for evidence revealed itself in many ways. One of the clearest was in the law. The English law of evidence, for example, began to take on its modern form at the close of the seventeenth century. It was long believed that less evidence should be necessary in arriving at

English law of evidence

a verdict of guilty in trials for the most atrocious crimes; this was thought necessary to protect society from the more hideous offenses. From the end of the seventeenth century, in English law, the judge lost his power of discretion in deciding what should constitute evidence, and the same rules of evidence were applied in all forms of accusation, the essential legal question becoming always the same—did such-and-such a fact (however outrageous) occur or did it not? After 1650 mere hearsay evidence, long vaguely distrusted, was ruled definitely out of court. After 1696 even persons charged with felony were allowed legal counsel.

The new emphasis on empirical evidence was probably the main force in putting an end to the delusionary charges of witchcraft. What made witchcraft so credible and so fearsome was that many persons confessed themselves to be witches, admitting to supernatural powers

Evidence and witchcraft

and to evil designs upon their neighbors. Many or most such confessions were extracted under torture. Reformers urged that confessions obtained under torture were not evidence, that people would say anything to escape unbearable pain, so that no such confessions offered the slightest ground for believing in witches. As for the voluntary confessions, and even the boastings of some people of their diabolical powers, it was noted that such statements often came from persons who would today be called psychotic. Witches came to be regarded as self-deluded. Their ideas of themselves were no longer accepted as reliable or objective evidence. But it must be added that, except in England, the use of legal torture lasted through most of the eighteenth century in criminal cases in which the judge believed the accused to be guilty.

History and Historical Scholarship

The systematic study of past human societies, which would come to be called the historical sciences, also developed rapidly at this time. History, like the law, depends on the discovery and use of factual evidence. The historian and the judge must answer the same kind of question—did such-and-such a fact really occur? All knowledge of history, insofar as it disengages itself from legend, propaganda, or wishful thinking, rests ultimately on pieces of evidence, written records, and other material objects created in the past and surviving in some form or other down to the present. On this mass of material the vast picture of the past is built, and without it people would be ignorant of their own antecedents or would have only folktales and unconfirmed oral traditions. Oral history often shapes personal and collective memories, and it provides important information; but judges and historians know that people remember the same events with very different facts and perspectives.

There was thus much skepticism about history in the seventeenth century. Some said that history was not a form of true knowledge because it was not mathematical. Others said that it was useless because Adam, the perfect man, neither had nor needed any history. Many felt that what passed for history was only a mass of fables. History was distrusted also because historians were often pretentious, claiming to be high-flying men of letters, writing for rhetorical or inspirational appeal or for argumentative reasons, disdaining the hard labor of empirical study. History was losing the confidence of thinking people who came to view science as the model for reliable knowledge. How was it possible, they asked, to feel even a modicum of certainty about alleged events that had happened long before any living person had been born?

This doubting attitude itself arose from a stricter sense of evidence, or from a realization that there was really no proof for much of what was said about the past. But scholars set to work to assemble what evidence they could find. They hoped to create a new history, one that should contain only reliable statements. Europe was littered with old papers and parchments. Abbeys, manor houses, and royal archives were full of written documents, many of them of unknown age or unknown origin, often written in a handwriting that people could no longer read. Learned and laborious enthusiasts set to work

New historical scholarship

to explore this accumulation. They added so much to the efforts of their predecessors as virtually to create modern critical scholarship and erudition. The French Benedictine monk Jean Mabillon, in 1681, in his book *On Diplomatics* (referring to ancient charters and "diplomas") established the science of paleography, which deals with the deciphering, reading, dating, and authentication of manuscripts. The Frenchman DuCange in 1678 published a dictionary of medieval Latin that is still used. Other historians spent whole lifetimes exploring archives, collecting, editing, or publishing masses of documents, comparing manuscript copies of the same text and trying to discover what the author had

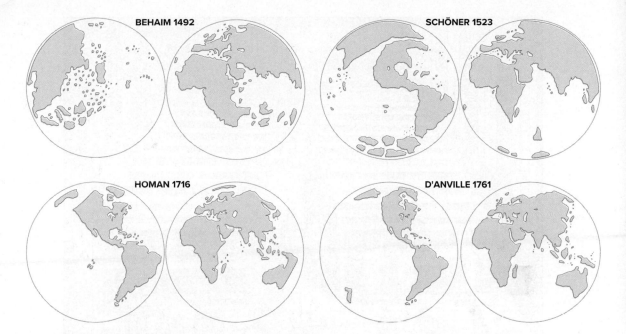

THE GROWTH OF GEOGRAPHICAL KNOWLEDGE

The four maps show the best scientific knowledge at their respective dates. Behaim has no inkling of the existence of America and has filled in the hemisphere opposite to Europe with a mass of islands, representing what he has heard of the East Indies and Japan. He knows pretty well the limits of Africa. Schöner in 1523 fills in America and even distinguishes two American continents. He knows of the Gulf of Mexico but fails to realize the narrowness of the Isthmus of Panama. He knows of the Straits of Magellan (but not Cape Horn) and hopefully fills in a corresponding Northwest Passage in the north. His conception of the Indian Ocean is quite accurate. To Homan, two centuries later, the size and shapes of oceans and continents are well known, but he believes New Guinea is joined to Australia and is frankly ignorant of the northwest coast of North America, representing it by a straight line. The Great Lakes and the interior of North America have become known to people in Europe. D'Anville in 1761 has no island of Tasmania, does not understand that Alaska is a peninsula, and believes the American polar regions to be impassable by sea. Otherwise his map is indistinguishable from one on the same scale today—though the cultural interpretations or meanings of geographical spaces have continued to evolve.

really written, rejecting some texts as fabrications or forgeries, pronouncing others to be genuine pieces of historical evidence. Others made themselves experts in ancient coins, many of which were far more ancient than the oldest manuscripts; they founded the science of numismatics. Still others, or indeed the same persons, turned to a critical examination of the inscriptions on old buildings and ruins, looking for the earliest possible information about specific people or events.

Another important but little-known historical "science," namely, chronology, was also pursued with new attention to precise evidence and dates. Chronology deals with the age of the world and with finding a common denominator between the dating systems of various peoples. Probably it is not natural for the human mind to think in terms of dates at all. For nonhistorically minded people, or for people who are little concerned with verifiable evidence, it is enough to know that some things happened "long ago." In the seventeenth century the new interest in numbers, evident in physical science, turned also

The early modern interest in the preservation and study of historical materials led to a systematic organization of the libraries and sources that careful scholarship would require. This Dutch engraving of a library in Leiden, based on a seventeenth-century painting by Jan Cornelius Woudanis, shows the subjects that scholars studied and the tables at which they stood to read the books. Although women were not present in this scholarly meeting place, the engraving shows that dogs apparently had free access to the library's main reading room.

(©Culture Club/Getty Images)

to the human past. Archbishop James Ussher, an Anglican prelate of Ireland, after much study of the Bible, announced the date of 4004 B.C.E. as the year in which the world was created. His chronological system was later printed in the margins of the authorized version of the English Bible and some fundamentalist Christians still adhere to it as if it were part of the Bible itself. But Ussher's system was not accepted by scholars even in his own time. New geographical knowledge was revealing China and its dynasties to Europe; historical knowledge was beginning to discover ancient Egypt. The Chinese and Egyptian records claimed a greater antiquity for their countries than the Old Testament seemed to allow for the human race. There was much erudite conjecture; one scholar about 1700 counted 70 estimates of the age of the world, ranging as high as 170,000 years, a figure that then seemed fantastic and appalling.

The difficulty was not only in the language of the Old Testament. It was in finding the correspondence between the chronological systems of different peoples. A Chinese system of dating by dynasties might be coherent within itself, but how could it be equated with the European system of dating from the birth of Christ, a date as little known to the Chinese as the date of Wu Wang was to Europeans? Even European records presented the same difficulty; the Romans counted by consulships, or from the supposed year of the founding of Rome; many medieval documents told only the year of an obscure ruler's reign. Only infinite patience, interminable research, and endless calculation could reduce such a jumble to the simple system of modern textbooks. This is of more importance than may be at first recognized. A common system of dating is a great aid to thinking of human history as an interconnected whole. An overall conception of the human race is made easier by the dating of all events according to what Europeans called the Christian era. This itself, it may be pointed out, is an arbitrary and conventional scale, because Christ is now thought to have been born not in 1 C.E., but in 4 B.C.E.

Common dating was increasingly important for practical affairs as well as for historical knowledge. Europe was disunited even on the Christian calendar. Protestant and some Orthodox countries followed the old or Julian calendar; Catholic countries, the corrected or Gregorian calendar issued in the sixteenth century under authority of Pope Gregory XIII. The two calendars varied in the seventeenth century by 10 days. Only gradually was the Gregorian calendar accepted, by England in 1752, by Russia in 1918. Most other peoples today, in China, India, the Arabic world, and elsewhere, use or recognize the Gregorian calendar as a shared calendar for modern global life. Without a uniform way of specifying days and years it would be difficult to transact international affairs, hold international conferences, make plans, or pay and receive money; a global system for defining time and dates thus became essential for global economic exchanges and communications. This common dating, easily taken for granted, was a consequence of the expanding global influence of Europe in modern times; and it became both a symbolic and a practical expression of the exchanges between different cultures in the modern world.

A common system of dating

The Questioning of Traditional Beliefs

The historical sciences provided a foundation on which a knowledge of human activities in the past could be built, and the growing geographical knowledge provided a panorama of human diversity in the present. This new knowledge shared with natural science the view that many traditional ideas were erroneous but that much could now be known by a more disciplined use of the human mind. The humanities and the sciences were alike in demanding evidence for belief and in trusting the power of reason. In their impact on the traditional certainties of European life, the studies of human cultures exerted possibly a greater direct force than those of nature. Pascal, in his defense of the Christian faith, feared the spirit of Montaigne, the mood of skepticism and the denial of universal certainties, which he himself feared more than he feared the findings of mathematical and physical science. And the movement of historical thought, with its insistence on textual criticism and verifiable evidence, threw doubt on much of the Christian religion, or at least on the sacred history and miracles related in the Bible, which was considered to be part and parcel of religion itself.

In 1678 a French priest, Richard Simon, published a pioneering work in Biblical criticism, his *Critical History of the Old Testament.* Although his book was condemned both by the church and by the government of Louis XIV, Simon always felt himself to be an orthodox Christian; Catholic faith, he insisted, depended more on church tradition than on the literal statements of the Bible. He simply applied to the Old Testament the methods of textual criticism that others were applying to secular documents. He concluded that the Old Testament, as known, rested on medieval manuscripts, many of which were of

Biblical scholarship and criticism

CHRONOLOGY OF NOTABLE EVENTS, 1543-1697

1543	Publication of Copernicus's *On the Revolution of the Heavenly Orbs* and Vesalius's *The Structure of the Human Body*
1609	Galileo builds a telescope
1620-1627	Francis Bacon argues for empirical method to advance knowledge
1637	René Descartes publishes *Discourse on Method*
1651	Thomas Hobbes publishes *Leviathan*
1662	Royal Society for Improving Natural Knowledge is chartered in London
1666	Royal Academy of Sciences is founded in Paris
1687	Isaac Newton publishes *Mathematical Principles of Natural Philosophy*
1690	John Locke publishes *Essay Concerning Human Understanding* and *Two Treatises of Government*
1697	Pierre Bayle publishes *Historical and Critical Dictionary*

unknown or doubtful origin, that monkish copyists had introduced errors and corruptions, and that the books thought to have been written by Moses could not have been written by him, because they contained obvious contradictions and matter clearly inserted after his death. Others went further, questioning not merely the evidence of the Biblical text, but the very possibility of some events that it related. From the scientific idea of the absolute regularity of nature on the one hand, and from a strong sense of human credulity on the other, they denied that miracles could have ever occurred; and they looked upon oracles and prophecies among either the Greeks or the Hebrews with a dubious eye.

Baruch Spinoza

The most profoundly disturbing of all thinkers of the time was Baruch Spinoza (1632-1677), the lens grinder of Amsterdam, a Jew whose ancestral family had emigrated from Portugal to escape the repression of Jewish communities in Iberia. Spinoza became an independent-minded, skeptical philosopher who was excommunicated by his own synagogue and who refused a professorship at the University of Heidelberg, craving only the quiet to think in peace. He drew on both the scientific and humanistic thought of his day to develop a philosophy holding that God had no existence apart from the world, that everything was itself an aspect of God—a philosophy technically called pantheism but considered by many to be really atheistic. Spinoza therefore rejected Cartesian dualism, but he also denied the inspiration of the Bible, disbelieved in miracles and the supernatural, rejected all revelation and revealed religion, Jewish or Christian, and held that few if any governments of the day were really just. He taught a pure, stern, and intellectual ethical code, and one that had few consolations for the average person. His name became a byword for impiety and horrendous unbelief. People were literally afraid to read his works, even when they could find them, which was not often because of the censorship. His influence spread slowly, through the mediation of other writers, contributing to the development of eighteenth-century rationalist philosophy.

More widely read, less abstruse, were the writings of the Englishman John Locke (1632-1704), who summarized many of the intellectual trends of his lifetime and exerted a strong influence for the following hundred years. He combined practical experience and theorctical interests in a philosophy that dwelled on the merits of common sense. Educated in medicine, he kept in touch with the sciences and was acquainted with Newton. He was associated with the great Whig noblemen who were the main authors of the English revolution in 1688. For political reasons he spent several years in the 1680s in the Netherlands, where he became familiar with new philosophical work on the Continent. He wrote on many subjects—finance, economics, education, religious policy, political theory, general philosophy—always with an engaging directness and the sober air of a sensible man of the world. In his *Letter on Toleration* (1689) he advocated an established church but with toleration of all except Roman Catholics and atheists; these he held to be dangerous to society: the former because of a foreign allegiance; the latter because they lacked a basis of moral responsibility. In his *Reasonableness of Christianity* he argued that Christianity, rightly considered, is after all a reasonable form of religion; this softened the friction between religion and natural knowledge but tended to shut out the supernatural and merge religious feeling into an unruffled common sense.

Locke's deepest book was his *Essay Concerning Human Understanding* (1690). Here he faced the great philosophical problem of the day, the problem of knowledge and skepticism; he asked if it was possible to know anything with certainty, and how certain knowledge was arrived at. His answer was that true or certain knowledge is derived from experience—from perceptions by the sense organs and reflection of the mind on these perceptions. Locke at the end of the century thus echoes Bacon at the beginning; they became the two great pillars of empirical philosophy, insisting on experience and observation as the source of truth. Locke denied Descartes's doctrine of innate ideas, or inevitable disposition of the human mind to think in certain ways. He held that the mind at birth is a blank tablet or *tabula rasa* and that the social environment shapes what people think or believe. Locke's environmentalist philosophy became fundamental to liberal and reforming thought in later years. It seemed that false ideas or superstitions were the result of bad

Locke's view of knowledge

The Dutch, Jewish philosopher Baruch Spinoza (1632–1677), portrayed here in a painting by Samuel Van Hoogstraten, developed a materialist or pantheistic philosophy that provoked strong opposition from many of his contemporaries; but Spinoza became an influential thinker for later writers who expressed skepticism about traditional religious beliefs.
(©Bettmann/Getty Images)

environment and bad education. It seemed that the evil in human actions was due to bad social institutions and that an improvement in human society would improve human behavior. This philosophy, whether or not wholly true in the final analysis, was largely true with respect to many practical conditions. A better education, for example, seemed to offer better opportunities for personal advancement and social well-being. Locke's philosophy thus gave confidence in the possibility of social progress and turned attention to a sphere in which planned and constructive action was possible, namely, the sphere of government, public policy, and legislation. Here we touch on political theory, to which Locke contributed *Two Treatises of Government* (these works are discussed later in this chapter).

30.   POLITICAL THEORY: THE SCHOOL OF NATURAL LAW

Political theory can never be strictly scientific. Science deals with what currently exists or has existed. It does not tell what ought to exist. To describe what society and government ought to be like, in view of human nature and the capacity to be miserable or contented, is a main purpose of political theory. Political theory is in a sense more practical than science. It is the scientists and scholars who are most content to observe facts as they are; and even when they seek to improve material conditions, they do not seek (or expect) to change the basic structures of the natural world. Practical people, however, and those scientists and scholars who have practical interests, must always ask themselves what ought to be done, what institutional structures ought to be changed, what policies ought to be adopted, what measures ought to be taken, what state of affairs ought to be maintained or brought about. Conservatives and radicals, traditionalists and innovators, are alike in this respect. It is impossible in human affairs to escape the ethical and political implications of "ought," or to stop thinking about possible changes in social and political systems.

But political theory was also affected by the scientific view. The Renaissance Italian, Niccolò Machiavelli (1469–1527), whom we have discussed earlier, had opened new critical thinking in this direction.

Niccolò Machiavelli

Machiavelli too had his "ought"; he preferred a republican form of government in which citizens felt a patriotic attachment to their state. But in his book *The Prince* he focused on the best strategies for exercising political power rather than on more abstract questions about the best form of government, a favorite question of Christian and scholastic philosophers in the Middle Ages. He separated the study of politics from theology and moral philosophy. He undertook to describe how governments and rulers actually behaved. He observed that successful rulers behaved as if holding or increasing power were their only object, that they regarded all else as means to this end. Princes, said Machiavelli, kept their promises or broke them, told the truth or distorted it, sought popularity or ignored it, advanced public welfare or disrupted it, conciliated their neighbors or destroyed them—depending merely on which course of action seemed the best means of advancing their political interests. All this was bad, said Machiavelli; but that was not the question, for the question was to find out what rulers really did to gain and hold power. Drawing his conclusions from the observable evidence of history, Machiavelli chose to be nonmoral in order to produce what might be called a "scientific" account of political power. To most readers he seemed to be simply immoral. Nor was it possible to draw the line between *The Prince* as a scientific description of fact and *The Prince* as a book of maxims of conduct. In telling how successful rulers obtained their successes, Machiavelli also suggested how rulers *ought* to proceed. And though governments did in fact continue to behave for the most part as Machiavelli said, most people refused to admit that they ought to.

Natural Right and Natural Law

Political theory in the seventeenth century did not generally embrace the cynicism attributed to Machiavelli. Nor did it fall into the skepticism of those who said that the customs of one's country should be passively accepted or that one form of government was about as good as another. It directly faced the question, What is right? The seventeenth century was the classic age of the philosophy of natural right or of natural law.

The early modern idea of natural law underlies a good deal of modern democratic development, and the decline of this idea became a philosophical aspect of most antidemocratic movements in more recent times. It is not easy to say in what the philosophy of natural law essentially consisted. It held that there is, somehow, in the structure of the world, a law that distinguishes right from wrong. It held that right is "natural," not a mere human invention or cultural construction. This right is not determined, for any country, by its heritage, tradition, or customs, nor yet by its actual laws (called "positive" laws) of the kind that are enforced in the law courts. All these may be unfair or unjust. We detect unfairness or injustice in them by comparing them with natural law as we understand it; thus we have a basis for saying that cannibalism is bad or that a law requiring forced labor from orphan children is unjust. Nor is natural law, or the enduring rightness of something, determined by the authority of any person or people. No king can make right that which is wrong. No people, by its will as a people, can make just that which is unjust. Right and law, in the ultimate sense, exist outside and above all peoples. They are universal, the same for all. No one can make them up to suit themselves. A good king or a just people is a king or people whose actions correspond to the objective standard. But how, if we cannot trust our own positive laws or customs, or our leaders, or even our collective selves, can we know what is naturally right? How do we discover natural law?

Natural law and natural right

The answer, in the natural law philosophy, is that we discover it by reason. Philosophers of natural law said that human beings are rational animals. And they assumed that all human beings have, at least potentially and when better enlightened, the same powers of reason and understanding—Germans or English, Asians, Africans or Europeans. This view favored a cosmopolitan outlook and made international agreement and general world progress seem realizable goals. As time went on, the premises of this philosophy came to be questioned. By the twentieth century it was widely thought that the human mind was not especially rational but was motivated by unconscious drives or urges or instincts and that human cultural differences were so fundamental that people of different nationalities or classes could never expect to see things in the same way. Challenged by such theories of human irrationality and cultural difference (which could be promoted with much ancient and modern evidence), the older philosophy of a universal natural law lost its hold on many minds.

Critiques of natural law

In the seventeenth and eighteenth centuries, however, it was generally accepted. Some, carrying over the philosophy of the Middle Ages, thought of natural law as an aspect of the law of God. Others, more secular in spirit, held that the natural law stood of itself. These included even some churchmen; a group of theologians, mainly Jesuits, were condemned by the pope in 1690 for holding that universal right and wrong might exist by reason only, whether God existed or not. The idea of natural law and the faith in human reason went side by side, and both were fundamental in the thought of the time. They were to be found everywhere in Europe, in their religious or their secular form.

On the basis of natural law some thinkers tried to create a new international law or "law of nations," to bring order into the maze of sovereign territorial states, great and small, that was developing in Europe. Hugo Grotius, in 1625, published the first great book devoted exclusively to this subject, his *Law of War and Peace.*

"Law of nations"

Samuel Pufendorf followed with his *Law of Nature and of Nations* in 1672. Both held that sovereign states, though bound by no positive law or authority, should work together for the common good, that there was a community of nations as of individuals, and that in the absence of a higher international sovereignty they were all still subordinate to natural reason and justice. Certain concrete doctrines, such as the freedom of the seas or the immunity of ambassadors, were put forward. The principles of international law were seen as an extension of natural law. The content came to include specific agreements between governments, certain kinds of admiralty and maritime law, and the terms of treaties such as the treaties of Westphalia, Utrecht, and others. Such laws and treaties expressed transnational principles or agreements, even though the means for enforcing such principles remained weak or nonexistent in the era's endless political conflicts and wars. They could nevertheless be viewed historically as the first halting steps toward a more legally coherent, international, and secular management of political affairs among the emerging, modern European states.

Hobbes and Locke

No philosopher at the time thought the state could have an absolute value in itself. Natural right and natural law were held to be in the nature of things, beyond human power to change. Forms of government were thus viewed as the means to an end—the institutional adherence to natural law. The state had to be "justified" by making it acceptable to moral consciousness or to reason. In domestic affairs the philosophy of natural law, though it rather favored constitutionalism, was used to justify both absolutist and constitutional governments. On the side of absolutism was the doctrine of the divine right of kings. On the side of constitutionalism were arguments based on heritage or custom, emphasizing the charters or compacts of former times and the historic powers of towns, parliaments, and estates. But neither the supernatural argument of the divine right of kings nor the

Competing views of natural law

historical argument pointing back to liberties of the Middle Ages was entirely satisfactory in the scientific atmosphere of the seventeenth century. Neither argument could be completely justified within the frameworks of reason or morality that now shaped the ideas of the most acute European thinkers. Both the absolutist and the constitutional

views of government were therefore reinforced in the seventeenth century by the concept of natural law; and two English political theorists showed most clearly how both sides in this debate built their opposing arguments on similar foundations of natural law. Absolutism was philosophically justified by Thomas Hobbes; constitutionalism, by John Locke.

Absolutism and Thomas Hobbes

Hobbes (1588–1679) followed the scientific and mathematical discoveries of his time with more than an amateur interest. In philosophy he held to a materialistic and even atheistic system. In English politics he sided with the king against Parliament; he disliked the disorder and

violence of the civil war of the 1640s and the unstable conditions of the English republic of the 1650s. He concluded that humans have no capacity for self-government. His opinion of human nature was low; he held that people in the state of nature, or as they could be imagined to exist without government, were quarrelsome and turbulent, forever locked in a war of all against all. In his famous phrase, life in the state of nature was "solitary, poor, nasty, brutish and short." Acting on their fear of each other and seeking to obtain order or enjoy the advantages of law and right, people came to a kind of agreement or "contract" by which they surrendered their freedom of action into the hands of a ruler. It was necessary for this ruler to have unrestricted authority, because order could be maintained only by the exercise of absolute government powers. It was intolerably dangerous, according to Hobbes, for anyone to question the actions of government, for such questioning might reopen the way to chaos. Government must therefore be a kind of Leviathan (the monster mentioned in the Bible, Job 41); and Hobbes in fact used the word *Leviathan* for the title of his principal book, published in 1651, two years after the execution of King Charles I.

By this book Hobbes became the leading secular exponent of absolutism and one of the principal theorists of the unlimited sovereignty of the state. His influence on later thinkers was very great. He accustomed political theorists to the use of purely natural arguments. He quoted freely from the Bible, but the Bible had no influence on his thought. After Hobbes, all advanced political theorists regarded government as a device created by human purpose rather than as part of God's divine dispensation to human history. Hobbes also affected later theorists by his arguments for a sovereign authority, which obliged them to refute his idea of an unlimited personal sovereign. But he was never a popular writer. In England the cause that he favored lost influence in the course of the seventeenth-century revolutions. In those continental countries where royal absolutism prevailed his arguments were received with secret gratification, but his irreligion was too dangerous to make public, and the absolutist argument, on the popular level, remained that of the divine right of kings. In any case Hobbes's arguments were in some ways insufficient for real monarchs. Hobbes abhorred struggle and violence. He believed that absolutism would produce civil peace, individual security, and a rule of law. He also held that absolute power depended on, or had at least originated in, a free and rational agreement by which people accepted it. An absolute monarchy that flagrantly violated these conditions could with difficulty be justified even by the doctrines of Hobbes. It is in these respects that Hobbes differs from totalitarian theorists of more recent times. For Hobbes, in the final analysis, absolute power was an expedient to promote individual welfare. It was a means to advance or protect the realization of natural law.

John Locke (1632–1704), as has been seen, also stood in the main current of scientific thought and discovery. But in his political philosophy he carried over many ideas of the Middle Ages, as formulated in the thirteenth century by St. Thomas Aquinas and kept alive in England by successive thinkers of the Anglican church. Medieval philosophy had never favored an absolute power. With Hobbes, Locke shared the idea that good government is an expedient of human purpose, neither provided by divine Providence nor inherited by a national tradition. He held, too, like Hobbes and the whole school of natural law, that government was based on a kind of contract, or rational and conscious agreement upon which authority was based. In contrast to Hobbes, he sided with Parliament against the king in the practical struggles of politics. About 1680, in the course of these disputes, he wrote *Two Treatises of Government,* which, however, were not published until shortly after the parliamentary revolution of 1688–1689.

Constitutionalism and John Locke

Locke took a more genial view of human nature than Hobbes. As he showed in his other books, he believed that a moderate religion was a good thing and above all that people could learn from experience and hence could be educated to an enlightened way of life. These ideas favored a belief in self-government and a more constitutional conception of state power. Locke declared (in contradiction to Hobbes) that people in the "state of nature" were reasonable and well disposed, willing to get along with one another though handicapped by the absence of public authority. They likewise had a moral sense, quite independently of government; and they also possessed by nature certain individual rights, quite apart from the state. These rights were the rights to life, liberty, and property.

Locke placed heavy emphasis on the right of property, by which he usually meant the possession of land. His philosophy can in fact be regarded as an expression of the landed classes of England, who challenged the power of kings by defending the political and social rights of private property. Individuals in the state of nature are not altogether able, according to Locke, to win general respect for their individual natural rights. They cannot by their own efforts protect what is "proper" to them, that is, their property. They agree to set up government to enforce observance of the rights of all. Government is thus created by a contract, but the contract is not unconditional, as claimed by Hobbes. It imposes mutual obligations. The people must be reasonable; only rational beings can be politically free. Liberty is not an anarchy of undisciplined will; it is the freedom to act without compulsion by another. Only rational and responsible creatures can exercise true freedom; but adult human beings, according to Locke, are or can be educated to be rational and responsible. They therefore can and should be free. Locke never really explained how these political rights, obligations, and freedoms might apply to women as well as to men, so there has been much modern debate about Locke's theoretical contributions to later campaigns for women's rights. In his own early modern context, however, Locke's writings explicitly supported the political rights and obligations of men who were claiming an active role in government affairs.

On government, also, as Locke described it, certain conditions and obligations are imposed. If a government breaks the contract, if it threatens the natural rights that it is the sole purpose of government to protect, if, for example, it takes away a man's property without his consent, then the governed have a right to reconsider what they have done in creating the government and may even in the last extremity rebel against it. The right to resist government, Locke admits, is very dangerous, but it is less dangerous than its opposite, which would lead to the loss of all liberty; and in any case Locke assumes that those who might resist the government in such situations would still be reasonable and responsible people.

If Locke's ideas seem familiar, especially to Americans, it is because of the wide popularizing of his philosophy in the century after his death. Nowhere was his influence

Locke's influence

greater than in the British colonies. The authors of the American Declaration of Independence and of the Constitution of the United States knew the writings of Locke very thoroughly. Some phrases of the Declaration of Independence echo his very language. In Great Britain also, and in France and elsewhere, in the course of time, Locke's influence was immense. But it should be noted that his ideas did not always mean the same thing for all people or in all places. Locke did not extend his ideas of human liberty to enslaved Africans, apparently because he viewed slavery as a legitimate form of private property. Locke himself invested in the slave-trading Royal African Company and endorsed the development of slavery in the American colonies. The growing influence of Locke's political theories may also have contributed indirectly to the emergence of new racist ideas in the eighteenth century. New justifications for slavery became necessary when the political classes of England and America began to believe that human beings possessed natural rights to life, liberty,

JOHN LOCKE
by Godfrey Kneller (English,
1646–1723)
Locke's writings on government
and natural rights summarized the
arguments against royal power in
England and also won adherents
wherever political theorists challenged monarchical absolutism.
(©Heritage Images/Getty Images)

and property. How could slavery be reconciled with such beliefs? The answer appeared in new forms of racism, which justified the enslavement of Africans by arguing that the African "race" lacked certain rational human traits of the European "race" and that black people could be denied fundamental human rights because they differed from other human beings.

In general, however, Locke's ideas of natural rights and human liberty were later used to challenge absolutist or repressive institutions, including also the slave trade and the legal systems that supported slavery. The right to human liberty, including the liberty of enslaved persons, would eventually be viewed as more universal, or more natural, than certain "property rights" of slaveholders—though slavery would not be abolished in most European colonies or postcolonial nations until the nineteenth century. Meanwhile, Locke's theories of contractual government gained international influence in the evolving debates about monarchical power. What Locke did was to convert an episode in English history into an event of universal political meaning. In England, in 1688, certain great lords, winning the support of the established church, gentry, and merchants, deposed one king and brought in another. On the new king they imposed certain obligations—specified in the Bill of Rights of 1689 and all dealing with legal or technical interpretations of the English constitution. The Revolution of 1688 was a very English affair. England in 1688 was still little known to the rest of Europe. The proceedings in England, insofar as they were known to most Europeans, might seem no different from a rebellion of the magnates of Hungary. Locke, in arguing that Parliament had been right to eject James II, put the whole affair on a level of reason, natural right, and human nature. It thus came to have meaning for people who had no connection with the specific problems of English political history.

Locke on the English revolution

Locke made the English revolution of 1688 a sign of progress rather than reaction. The new and modern form of government in 1690 was royal absolutism, with its professional bureaucracy and corps of paid officials. Almost everywhere there was resistance to the kings, led by landed interests and harking back to earlier freedoms. Such resistance seemed to many Europeans to be feudal and medieval. Locke checked the prestige of absolutism by showing how the resistance to an English king was a forward-looking movement. He gave new prestige to constitutional principles. He carried over, in modified form, many ideas from the scholastic philosophers of the Middle Ages, who had generally maintained that kings had only a relative and restricted power and were responsible to their peoples. To these ideas he added the force of the newer scientific view of the world. He did not rest his case on supernatural or providential arguments. He did not say that constitutional government was the will of God. He said that it rested on experience and observation of human nature, on recognition of certain individual rights and especially the right of property, and on the existence of a purely natural law of reason and justice. He was an almost entirely secular thinker, and, as such, he developed ideas that could be drawn into the political and social conflicts of most modern nations.

One must not claim too much for Locke, or for any writer. England was in fact, in 1688, already more inclined toward constitutional government than other countries in Europe. The Glorious Revolution was in fact not exactly like uprisings of the landed and propertied classes elsewhere. England in the following century did in fact develop a form of parliamentary government that was unique. But facts go together with the theories that give them an understandable meaning. Events in England, as explained by Locke, and as seen in other countries and even in England and its colonies through Locke's eyes, launched into the mainstream of modern history the superb tradition of constitutional government, which has been one of the principal themes in the history of the modern world ever since.

By 1700, at the close of the "century of genius," some beliefs that would become widely characteristic of modern times had clearly taken form, notably a faith in science, in human reason, in natural human rights, and in progress. The new scientific knowledge was beginning to transform the global economy, the culture of European elites, and the conflicts within or among European empires. Meanwhile, the cultural institutions of modern science were spreading across Europe, and new scientific theories in physics, astronomy, and physiology were challenging both the theology and thought systems of earlier generations. The following period, generally known as the Age of Enlightenment, was to be a time of clarifying and popularizing ideas that the more creative seventeenth century had produced. These ideas were eventually to revolutionize Europe, America, and the world. They were also in subsequent years to be modified, amended, challenged, or denied. Indeed, modern critics and governments have often ignored or rejected early modern ideas about reason, rights, and science. But these ideas are still very much alive today.

Suggested Further Readings can be found in the ebook, on Connect, or online at www.mhhe .com/kramer12e.

Chapter 7

THE GLOBAL STRUGGLE FOR WEALTH AND EMPIRE

In earlier chapters we have seen how western Europe, and especially England and France, by about 1700 came to occupy a position of power and influence in Europe as a whole. We have traced the political history of western Europe through the War of the Spanish Succession, terminated in 1713–1714 by the treaties of Utrecht and Rastatt. Affairs of central Europe and Germany have been described for the period up to 1740. In that year a new kingdom of Prussia and a new or renovated Austrian monarchy, each passing into the hands of a new ruler, stood on the eve of a struggle for ascendancy in central Europe. As for eastern Europe, we have observed the growing western European influence on the government and commerce of an expanding Russian Empire.

More important in the long run than these political events, and continuing throughout the seventeenth and eighteenth centuries, was the cumulative expansion of all forms of knowledge, which we saw in the rapid development of seventeenth-century science and new social theories. Equally important was the growing wealth of Europe, or at least of the Atlantic region north of Spain. The new wealth, in the widest sense, meaning conveniences of every kind, resulted partly from the new technical and scientific knowledge, which in turn it helped to produce; and the two together, more wealth and more knowledge, helped to form one of the most far-reaching ideas of modern times, the idea of progress. This idea challenged the traditional deference to ancient authorities and fostered critical inquiry, creative innovations, and remarkable optimism in most spheres of social and intellectual life. "Progress" could include changes in the economy, in science and intellectual life, in education, in political institutions, and in most other forms of human activity, but in every context a belief in the progressive direction of human history encouraged Europeans to assume that the future would be better than the past. Although the world wars and environmental problems of more recent times would eventually

Chapter emblem: Detail from an Indian miniature (c. 1785), showing an Englishwoman and one of her servants in India. (©Werner Forman/Getty Images)

provoke widespread anxieties about the historical consequences of new technologies, a belief in progress, even if somewhat chastened, remains a powerful cultural force in all modern societies.

The new wealth of Europe was not like the age-old wealth of the great empires in the East, said by Milton to "shower on her kings barbaric pearl and gold." It consisted of gold, to be sure, but even more of bank deposits and facilities for credit, of more and better devices for mining coal, casting iron, and spinning thread, more productive agriculture, better and more comfortable houses, a wider variety of foods on the table, more and improved sailing ships, warehouses, and docks; more books, more newspapers, more medical instruments, more scientific equipment; greater government revenues, larger armies, and more numerous government employees. The new wealth also flowed from the labor of enslaved workers and the commodities they produced in the Americas, but in the wealthier European countries, and because of the growing accumulation of capital, more people were freed from the necessity of toiling for food, clothing, and shelter. Drawing on the profits of an increasingly global economy, more Europeans were able to devote themselves to all sorts of specialized callings in government, management, finance, war, teaching, writing, inventing, exploring, and researching, and in producing the amenities rather than the barest necessities of life. These new forms of mechanical production, social organization, and specialized knowledge also began to spread to European colonies around the world, thus contributing to the expanding systems of transoceanic trade and to the growing belief in human progress.

31. ELITE AND POPULAR CULTURES

The accumulation of wealth and knowledge was not evenly distributed among the various social classes. There had always been differences between rich and poor, with many gradations between the extremes, but at the time we are now considering, as the seventeenth century turned into the eighteenth, there came to be a more obvious distinction between elite and popular cultures. The terms are hard to define. The elite culture was not exactly the culture of the rich and well-to-do, nor was the popular culture limited to the poor and lower economic classes. The word "elite" suggests a minority within a given range of interests; thus there were elites not only of wealth, but of social position and of power; elites of fashion, of patronage and connoisseurship in the arts, and of artists themselves; elites of education, of special training as in medicine and law, and of discovery and accomplishment in technology and the sciences. In general, persons taking part in an elite culture could share in the popular culture by attending public amusements or simply by talking with their servants and other less-educated persons who lived around them. But the relation was asymmetric. Those born into and living within popular culture could not easily share in the intellectual or social culture of the elites, at least not without transforming themselves, through education or marriage, which could occur only in exceptional cases.

A main difference was simply one of language. At the popular level people generally used a local form of speech, varying from one place to another, with a distinctive accent, and with words that had become obsolete elsewhere or that might not be understood even a few miles away. In the Middle Ages the use of Latin helped to overcome this linguistic diversity among educated elites, but Latin was becoming less common in even the most elite cultural groups by the late seventeenth century. After the invention of printing, the rise of national literatures, and the establishment of new schools (many of which were founded between 1550 and 1650), there came to be standard forms of English, French,

Italian, and other languages that all educated persons could speak and read. Grammar and spelling became regularized. Virtually all printing was in a national language when it was not in Latin. Because only a minority were able to get the necessary education, however, the mass of the people continued to speak as they did before. Their way of talking was now considered a dialect, a peasant language, or what was called *patois* in French or *Volkssprache* in German. And while it may be true, as some scientific philologists have long argued, that no form of speech is inherently "better" than another, it is also true that facility in the national language was a sign and privilege of elite culture until the spread of universal elementary schooling in the nineteenth century. It gave access to at least certain segments of the elite culture, as it continues to do today, and it enabled educated persons to participate in the elite institutions of government, commerce, and the professions.

National languages

The elite culture was transmitted largely by way of books, but it could also be acquired by word of mouth within favored families and social circles. The popular culture, by contrast, was predominantly oral, although it was also expressed in cheaply printed almanacs, chapbooks, woodcuts, and broadsides. Because it was so largely oral, and left so few written records, popular culture is often difficult for historians to reconstruct, but it made up the daily lives, interests, and activities of the great majority in all countries. It must always be remembered that what we read as history, in this as in most other books, is mostly an account of the actions of small minorities, either of power-wielders, decision-makers, and innovators whose public actions affected whole peoples, or of writers and thinkers whose ideas appealed to a limited audience. Persons who were illiterate or barely literate changed their ideas more slowly than the more mobile and more informed members of the elite. Cultural changes initiated by such elites spread slowly, generation after generation, to wider social classes, so that what was characteristic of popular culture at a given moment, such as a belief in magic, had often been common to all classes a century or two before. All people and social classes make history and actively participate in the processes of historical change, but the new knowledge and wealth in early modern societies created new social distinctions, new hierarchies of cultural power, and new opportunities for educated persons.

Oral vs. print culture

The humanism of the Renaissance, being transmitted so largely through books and the study of Greek and Latin, remained limited to persons who were educated in the elite culture. The strength of the Protestant Reformation lay in combining the efforts of highly educated leaders, such as Luther and Calvin, with the anger, distress, disillusionment, and hopes of many very ordinary people. The new science and the ensuing eighteenth-century Enlightenment emerged in the work of small numbers of researchers and writers, but their ideas slowly reshaped the thinking of others. The process of diffusion might be slow and uncertain. Astrology, for example, was in the Middle Ages a branch of scientific inquiry; in the seventeenth century astrologers were still consulted by emperors and kings; then both the clergy and secular thinkers denounced divination by the stars as a superstition, and astrology was expelled from astronomy, but horoscopes still appear today in American and European newspapers.

The differences of wealth, if not wholly decisive, were of great importance. Culture in the broader or anthropological sense of the word includes material circumstances of food, drink, and shelter. In some respects the lot of the poor in the seventeenth century was worse than in the Middle Ages. Less meat was eaten in Europe, because as population grew there was less land available for the raising of livestock. With the growth of a market economy many peasants raised wheat, but ate bread made of rye, barley, or oats, or even looked for acorns and

Living standards

THE SCHOOL TEACHER PUNISHES THE STUDENT
by Jan Miense Molenaer (Dutch, 1610–1668)
New schools were founded throughout Europe during the seventeenth century. Segregated by gender
and mainly educating boys from the upper classes, these schools created a new cultural foundation for
social status and political influence. As this painting by the Dutch artist Molenaer clearly shows, the
schools of this era also taught proper social behaviors and punished students harshly whenever they
acted in the wrong way.
(©Mondadori Portfolio/Getty Images)

roots in times of famine. The consumption of bread by working people in France in the
eighteenth century was about a pound per day per person, because little else except cab-
bages and beans was eaten on ordinary days; after 1750 the use of white bread became
more usual. Meanwhile the rich, or the merely affluent, developed more delicate menus
prepared by well-trained professional cooks, one of whom is said to have committed
suicide when his soufflé fell before it was served.

In the towns the poor lived in crowded, unsanitary buildings, and in the country they
lived in dark and shabby cabins where stoves only gradually replaced holes in the roof

Housing conditions

for the escape of smoke. The poor had no glass in their windows, the
middle classes usually had a few glass windows, and the rich displayed
their wealth, in part, by installing glass windows and mirrors throughout both their urban apartments and their country estates. In humble homes the dishes
were wooden bowls, slowly replaced by pewter, while china plates began to appear on the
tables of the more well-to-do. Table forks, with one for each diner, originating in Italy,
were brought to France in the sixteenth century by Catherine de Medici along with other
items of Italian culture, and soon spread among those able to afford them, though
Louis XIV still preferred to use his fingers. Silver bowls and pitchers were ancient but

became more elaborate and more often seen in upper-class circles. The poor had no furniture, or only a few benches and a mat to sleep on; the middle classes had chairs and beds; the rich not only had substantial furniture but were becoming more conscious of style. Among higher-income families it became usual to have houses with specialized rooms, such as separate bedrooms, and a dining room. New ideas about privacy, the meaning or autonomy of childhood, and the health of the human body began to influence eighteenth-century architecture, so that well-to-do people wanted more private spaces for themselves and their children. The prominent and the fashionable also fitted out larger rooms for social receptions and public entertainments, called salons in France, with walls of wood paneling, lighted by chandeliers reflected in mirrors, and provided with sofas and armchairs, which the invention of upholstery made more comfortable. The poor, after dark, huddled on chests or still sat together on the floor by a single candle.

In the use of beverages the seventeenth century saw a different kind of progress, if that is the right word. Coffee and tea, along with sugar and tobacco, all imported to Europe from overseas, were exotic rarities in 1600, more widely enjoyed in 1700, and available to all but the very destitute by the late eighteenth century. Coffee shops developed and taverns multiplied. Cheap wines became more plentiful in southern Europe, as did beer in the north. The distillation of alcohol had been developed in the Middle Ages, when brandy, a distilled wine, was used *Coffee and alcohol* as a medicine; by the seventeenth century it was a familiar drink. Whisky and gin also came into use at about this time. The taverns and coffee shops offered a place for neighborly gatherings for the middling and lower social classes; and writers began meeting in coffeehouses to discuss their work, share gossip, or argue about public events. During this same era, drunkenness became a more visible problem in European cities, especially among workers who could buy cheap gin or whisky but could not drink in domestic

GIN LANE
by William Hogarth
(English, 1697–1764)

Hogarth showed both the popularity and dangers of alcohol in the lives of Britain's working classes, as in this illustration of drunkenness in the streets of London.

(©UniversalImagesGroup/Getty Images)

The increasing import of coffee and tea made the eighteenth-century coffeehouse a popular meeting place in large cities such as London and Paris. The London establishment portrayed here attracted an upper-class clientele, but coffee was becoming less expensive and many coffeehouses also catered to the lower classes.
(©Culture Club/Getty Images)

privacy. Drunken people were therefore often seen in the streets, as shown by Hogarth's pictures of "Gin Lane" in London about 1750. The migrations of displaced rural workers and the poverty in large cities also contributed to an increase in out-of-wedlock births and the abandonment of children. It was calculated that in Paris in 1780 there were 7,000 abandoned children for 30,000 births, but many of these infants were brought from the country to be deposited in the foundling hospitals of the city, which were overwhelmed.

Despite the growing differences in wealth, housing, and education, there was much that persons of all classes and cultures still shared. Most important, in principle, was religion. The refined and the rude, the learned and the untutored, heard the same sermons in church, were baptized, married, and buried by the same sacraments, often by the same priest, and were subject to religious and moral obligations that transcended the boundaries of social class. Such was most likely to be the case in small communities of unmixed religion or where the lord and lady of the manor attended the same church as the villagers. Where different churches existed in fact, whether or not officially tolerated, religion played less of a role in social cohesion. In England, for example, the Nonconformists, who succeeded the old Puritans after the Stuart Restoration, developed a kind of middle-class culture that was noticeably different from the culture of the Anglican gentry. Rich people in both Protestant and Catholic countries sometimes had their own private chaplains or built their own family chapels. In towns that were big enough for socially diverse neighborhoods some churches became fashionable and others merely popular. In any case some people in the seventeenth century were not very religious at all; these less religious persons included those in inaccessible rural areas as well as some of the poorest in the larger towns, who were often homeless migrants from an overcrowded countryside. Reforming bishops, especially in France, undertook to ameliorate the situation, so that the seventeenth century was a great age of internal missionary work, and it may be that in the following century, as skepticism began to pervade the elite culture, the popular culture became more Christianized than it had been in the past.

Religion

Rich and poor were subject to the same diseases, the same dangers of tainted food and polluted water, and the same smells and filth in noisy streets littered with horse droppings, puddles, and garbage. But here too, of course, there were many social differences. In the elite culture people depended on the daily assistance of servants and called on the medical advice of doctors, who had

Health

been trained in the universities, while ordinary sufferers sought out popular healers, who were often women and whose remedies consisted of strange herbs or mysterious potions (women did not become doctors because they could not attend universities). It also made a difference whether one rode through the streets in a coach, as the affluent did, or picked one's way on foot with the common people. Congestion was worst in rapidly growing cities, such as London, Paris, Amsterdam, and Naples, where the differences between wealth and poverty were both more extreme and more shockingly visible. There were recurrent fears of food shortages, as crop failure and local famine struck this or that region, in which case some starved and some ate less, while those able to do so simply paid higher prices. In some towns charitable organizations developed, often on the initiative of upper-class women, to finance and assist religious sisters in relief of the poor. Hunger and the fear of hunger sometimes produced riots, which however had little political significance except insofar as upper-class people tried to make use of them for their own purposes.

It was also in less material aspects that the elite and popular cultures increasingly diverged. The upper strata set a new importance on polite manners, in which the French now set the tone, with much bowing, doffing of hats, and exchange of compliments, beside which the manners of ordinary people now seemed *Politeness, etiquette,* uncouth. The etiquette of princely courts became more formal, the *entertainment* court fools and jesters disappeared, and royalty surrounded itself not with rough retainers but with ladies and gentlemen. About 1600 the plays of Shakespeare were staged in public theaters where all classes mixed and enjoyed the same performance, but in the following century it became usual for the upper classes to have private theaters. People of higher social position took to stylish dancing, which their children had to learn from dancing teachers, while plain people continued to cavort more spontaneously in country dances and jigs. For evening parties, the polite world met in salons to engage in the art of cultured conversation, while working people, especially in the country, met in a neighbor's house after the day's labors were over. Conversation was as important for the rural poor as for the educated elites; and while some of the men and women repaired their tools or mended their clothes, the gathered families engaged in local gossip, listened to storytellers, or learned something about the wider world when a literate person read aloud from one of the cheaply printed books that were now circulating in even the smallest villages. The traveling peddlers who sold such books became a kind of early precursor to modern Internet communications as they carried new information and practical advice to widely scattered communities across the European countryside.

Enough of these books have survived, along with popular almanacs, to make it possible to form some ideas of the mental horizons of the nonliterate and inarticulate classes. They were often written by printers or their employees or by others who were in effect intermediaries between the elite and popular cultures and who purposely addressed themselves to what they knew of popular interests. The almanacs purveyed astrological observations, advice on the weather, proverbs, and scraps of what had once been science but was now offered as occult wisdom. Other little books *Popular books* undertook to teach the ABCs or told how to behave in church; how to approach persons of the other sex; how to show respect for superiors; or how to compose a proper letter of love, thanks, or condolence, or have such a letter written by the professional letter writers to whose services illiterate persons resorted. Still others put into print the stories that had long circulated in the oral tradition, fairy tales, saints' lives, or accounts of outlaws such as Robin Hood. Miracles, prodigies, witches, ogres, angels, and the devil figured prominently in such narratives.

It is a curious fact that where educated persons were now schooled in Greek mythology and admired the heroes of ancient Rome, the plain people were still engrossed by tales of medieval chivalry, knights errant, and holy hermits that had once been told in baronial halls. Memories of the times of King Arthur and Charlemagne lingered in the popular consciousness. There were long and complex European tales of the exploits of Roland and other paladins who had fought for Christianity against the infidels, all set in a world of faraway adventure without definite location in time or place. Saracens, Moors, Turks, and Muslims, and at times Jews, were generally portrayed in such stories as menacing figures.

Witchcraft and magic

Belief in witchcraft and magic was to be found in 1600 in all social classes. The witches in *Macbeth* were perfectly believable to Shakespeare's audience. Learned books were still written on these subjects, and indeed the learned writers and the judges in law courts may have stirred up more anxiety about witches and magicians than ordinary people would otherwise have felt. By 1700, however, a great change was evident: witches, magicians, and miscellaneous enchantments were disappearing from the elite culture, but they still figured in the popular mind. Unaffected as yet by either science or doubt, most ordinary people inclined to think that there was something true about magic, which they distinguished as good and bad. Good magic unlocked the "secrets" of nature; popular writings on alchemy told of famous sages of the past who knew how to turn base metals into gold; there were special formulas that added to the efficacy of prayer. Some older women had a secret knowledge of medicinal herbs, in which indeed there might be some pragmatic value but which was blended with the mysterious and the occult. Bad magic was used to cause harm; it taught the black arts; it gave force to curses; it often involved a compact with the devil; it was what made witches so fearsome. By 1700 such ideas were subsiding. Judges who were trained to evaluate empirical evidence no longer believed that such powers existed, and so would no longer preside at witchcraft trials. The same may be said of belief in prophecies and oracles: in the elite culture only those recorded in the Bible retained any credibility, but there was still a popular acceptance of recent prophecies and foretellings of the future.

Popular culture continued to express itself also in fairs and carnivals. For men and women who rarely traveled and lived limited lives, these were exciting events that occurred only at certain times of the year and to which people flocked from miles around. At the fairs one could buy things that local shops and the wandering peddlers could not supply. There would be puppet shows, jugglers, and acrobats. There were conjurers who refused to admit like modern magicians that they were using merely natural means. A mountebank was someone who mounted a platform (*banco* in Italian) where he sold questionable remedies for various ills while keeping up a patter of jokes and stories, often accompanied by a clown. Blind singers and traveling musicians entertained the throngs, and for the tougher minded there were cockfights and bear baiting. In such a hubbub itinerant preachers might denounce the vanities of this world or throw doubt on the wisdom of bishops and lawyers.

Carnival went on for several weeks preceding Lent. The word itself, from the Italian *carne vale,* meant "farewell to meat," from which good Christians were to abstain during the 40-day Lenten fast; in France it climaxed in the Mardi Gras ("fat Tuesday"). It persisted in Protestant countries also. It was a time for big eating and heavy drinking, for general merrymaking and foolery, and for playful inversions of the normal social hierarchies and cultural solemnities. Comical processions marched through the streets. Farces were performed and mock sermons were delivered. Young men showed their strength in

THE KERMESSE OF ST. GEORGE
by Pieter Bruegel, the Younger (Flemish, 1564–1638)
Festivals and popular carnivals often altered the normal patterns of daily work in European towns throughout the early modern era. Bruegel's painting conveys his interest in the social lives of common people. It portrays an early seventeenth-century kermesse or festival in the town square of a small Flemish village, but the eating, drinking, dancing, banners, and playful conversations were typical of popular feast days in all parts of Europe during this era.
(©Fine Art Photographic/Getty Images)

tugs-of-war, footraces, and a rough-and-tumble kind of football. A common theme was what was called in England "the world turned upside down." Men and women put on each other's clothing. Horses were made to move backward with the rider facing the tail. Little street dramas showed the servant giving orders to the master, the judge sitting in the stocks, the pupil beating the teacher, or the husband holding the baby while the wife clutched a gun. In general, the carnival was a time for defying custom and ridiculing authority. It is hard to know how much such outbursts were expressions of genuine resentments and how much they were only a form of play. They could, indeed, be both.

In 1600 people of all classes took part in these festive activities. In the following century, as both the Protestant and the Catholic Reformations extended their influences, the clergy undertook to purge such public events of what they considered excesses, and the civil authorities in the growing state governments began to frown on them as incitements to subversion. By 1700 the people of elite culture, the wealthy, the fashionable, and the educated, were more inclined to stay away; or they attended only as spectators to be amused at the simple pleasures of the common people. In the eighteenth century, as the various elites took to more formal manners and to neoclassicism in literature and the arts, the gulf between the elite and popular cultures widened. The clergy campaigned against the belief in magic and tried to restrain the faithful in the matter of pilgrimages and veneration of dubious local saints. As the medical profession developed, the popular healers and venders of mysterious nostrums were seen as charlatans and quacks. As scientific and other knowledge increased among educated elites, those who lacked such knowledge appeared to be simply superstitious or ignorant. It may be said both that the elites withdrew from the popular culture and that the people as a whole had not yet been brought into the education and science of an evolving elite culture. In any case, class distinctions became sharper than ever. But nothing ever stands still, and before the year 1800 there were persons in the elite culture who were beginning to "rediscover" the people, to collect ballads and fairy tales, and to lay a cultural foundation for what nineteenth-century nationalists would call "folklore."

32.   THE GLOBAL ECONOMY
OF THE EIGHTEENTH CENTURY

The opening of the Atlantic in the sixteenth century, it will be recalled, had reoriented Europe. In an age of oceanic communications western Europe became a center from which America, Asia, and Africa could all be reached. A global economy had been created. The first to profit from it had been the Portuguese and Spanish, and they retained their monopoly through most of the sixteenth century; but the gradual decline of the Portuguese and Spanish paved the way for the triumph of the British, the French, and the Dutch. In the eighteenth century the most important economic development was the expansion of the global economy and the fact that Europe became incomparably wealthier than any other part of the world.

Commerce and Industry in the Eighteenth Century

The increase of wealth was brought about by the methods of commercial capitalism and handicraft industry. Though the Industrial Revolution in England is usually dated from 1760 or 1780, it was not until the nineteenth century that the use of steam engines and power-driven machinery, and the growth of large factories and great manufacturing cities, brought about the conditions of modern industrialism. The economic system of the eighteenth century, while it contained within itself the seeds of later industrialism, represented the flowering of the older merchant capitalism, domestic industry, and mercantilist government policies that had grown up since the sixteenth century.

Rural industry

Most people in the eighteenth century lived in the country. Agriculture was still the greatest single industry and source of wealth. Cities remained small. London and Paris, the largest of Europe, each had a population of 600,000 or 700,000, but the next largest cities did not much exceed 200,000, and in all Europe at the time of the French Revolution in 1789 there were only 50 cities with as many as 50,000 people. Urbanization, however, was in itself no sign of economic advancement. Spain, Italy, and even the Balkan peninsula, according to an estimate made in the 1780s, each had more large cities (over 50,000) than did Great Britain. Urbanization did not equate with industry because most industry was carried on in the country, by peasants and part-time agricultural workers who worked for the

Most people who were "engaged in manufactures" in eighteenth-century Europe still worked in their own rural homes. This engraving from the early 1780s shows three women at work on cloth in an Irish cottage, where they are spinning and winding thread while another woman contributes to the domestic production by preparing a meal and watching a child.
(©SSPL/The Image Works)

merchant capitalists of the towns. Thus, while it is true to say that most people still lived in the country, it would be false to say that their lives and labors were devoted exclusively to agriculture. One English estimate, made in 1739, held that there were 4,250,000 persons "engaged in manufactures" in the British Isles, a figure that included women and children and comprised almost half the entire population. These people worked characteristically in their own cottages, employed as wage earners by merchant capitalists under the "domestic" system. Almost half of them were engaged in the weaving and processing of woolens. Others were in the copper, iron, lead, and tin manufactures; others in leather goods; much smaller were the paper, glass, porcelain, silk, and linen trades; and smallest of all, in 1739, was the manufacture of cotton cloth, which accounted for only about 100,000 workers. Nonagricultural occupations were thus already important and widespread in the preindustrial age.

Even with half its population engaged at least part of the time in manufactures, however, England was not yet the unrivaled manufacturing country that it was to become after 1800. England in the eighteenth century produced no more iron than Russia and no more manufactures than France. The population of England was still small; it began to grow rapidly about 1760, but as late as 1800 France was still twice as populous as England and Scotland together. France, though less intensively developed than England, with probably far less than half its people engaged in manufactures, nevertheless, because of its greater size, remained the chief industrial center of Europe.

Although foreign and colonial trade grew rapidly in the eighteenth century, it is probable that, in both Great Britain and France, the domestic or internal trade was greater in volume and occupied more people. Great Britain, with no internal tariffs, with an insignificant guild system, and with no monopolies allowed within the country except to inventors, was the largest area of internal free trade in Europe. France, or at least Colbert's Five Great Farms, offered an almost equal-sized free-trading internal market. A great deal of economic activity was therefore domestic, consisting of exchange between town and town or between region and region. The exact proportions between domestic and international trade cannot be known. But foreign trade was increasingly important for the largest business enterprises. International trade created the greatest commercial fortunes and the main accumulations of new capital. And it was the foreign trade that led to international rivalry and war.

The World Economy: The Dutch, British, and French

Trade

On the international economic scene a great part was still played by the Dutch. After the Peace of Utrecht the Dutch ceased to be a great political power; but their role in commerce, shipping, and finance remained undiminished, or diminished only when compared to the continuing commercial growth of France and Great Britain. They were still the middlemen and common carriers for other peoples. Their freight rates remained the lowest of Europe. They continued to grow rich on imports from the East Indies. To a large extent also, in the eighteenth century, the Dutch lived on their investments. The capital they had accumulated over 200 years they now lent out to French or British or other entrepreneurs. Dutch capital was to be found in every large commercial venture of Europe and was lent to governments far and wide. A third of the capital of the Bank of England in the mid-eighteenth century belonged to Dutch shareholders. The Bank of Amsterdam remained the chief clearinghouse and financial center of Europe. Its supremacy did not end until a French Revolutionary army invaded Holland in 1795.

East India companies

The Atlantic trade routes, leading to America, to Africa, and to Asia, attracted the merchants of many nationalities in Europe. A great many East India companies were established—usually to do business in America as well as the East, for the "Indies" at the beginning of the eighteenth century was still a general term for the vast regions overseas. Both the English and the French East India companies were reorganized, with an increased investment of capital, shortly after 1700. A number of others were established—by the Scots, the Swedes, the Danes, the imperial free city of Hamburg, the republic of Venice, Prussia, and the Austrian monarchy. But, with the exception of the Danish company that lasted some 60 years, they all failed after only a few years, either for insufficiency of capital or because they lacked strong diplomatic, military, and naval support. Their failure showed that, in the transoceanic trade, unassisted business enterprise was not enough. Merchants needed strong national backing to succeed in this sphere. Neither free city, nor small kingdom, nor tiny republic, nor the amorphous Austrian Empire provided a firm enough base to sustain a global trading company.

Commercial rivalry

It was the British and French who won out in the commercial rivalry of the eighteenth century. Britain and France were alike in having, besides a high level of industrial production at home, national-scale governments that could protect and advance, under mercantilist principles, the interests of their merchants in distant countries. For both peoples the eighteenth century—or the three-quarters of a century between the end of the War of the Spanish Succession in 1713 and the beginning of the French Revolution in 1789—was an age of spectacular enrichment and commercial expansion.

Although the trade figures are difficult to define precisely, French foreign and colonial trade may well have grown even more rapidly than the British in the years between the 1720s and the 1780s. In any event, by the 1780s, the two countries were about equal in their total foreign and colonial trade. The British in the 1780s enjoyed proportionately more of the trade with America and Asia; the French, more of the trade with the rest of Europe and the Middle East. The growing competition for global markets contributed to all of the colonial and commercial wars between Britain and France during the eighteenth century and on into the final, climactic struggle, and British triumph, in the time of Napoleon.

Asia, America, and Africa in the Global Economy

In the expanding global economy of the eighteenth century each continent played its special part. The European trade with Asia was subject to an ancient limitation. Asia was almost useless as a market for European manufactures. There was much that Europeans wanted from Asia but almost nothing that Asians wanted from early modern Europe. The peoples of Chinese, Indian, and Malay culture had elaborate civilizations with which they were content; Asian elites in this era lacked the global trading ambitions of European entrepreneurs, and the masses were so impoverished (more so even than in Europe) that they could buy nothing anyway. Europeans found that they could send little to Asia except gold. The trade of gold from Europe to Asia had gone on since ancient times, and even more gold and silver flowed to east Asia from European colonies in the Americas after the sixteenth century. Accumulating over time, the wealth from this trade became one source of the fabulous treasures of Eastern princes. To finance the swelling demand for Asian products it was necessary for Europeans constantly to replenish their stocks of gold. The British found an important new supply in Africa along the Gulf of Guinea, where the Royal African Company began to export gold from a region (the present Ghana) that was long called the Gold Coast. The word "guinea" became the name of a gold coin minted in England from 1663 to 1813 and long remained a fashionable way of saying 21 shillings.

What Europeans sought from Asia was still in part spices—pepper and ginger, cinnamon and cloves—now brought in mainly by the Dutch from their East India islands. But they wanted manufactured goods also. Asian technical skills were superior to eighteenth-century European technologies in several lucrative spheres of transnational commerce. It is enough to mention rugs, chinaware, and cotton cloth. The very names by which cotton fabrics are known in English and other European languages reveal the places from which they were thought to come. "Madras" and "calico" refer to the Indian cities of Madras and Calicut; "muslin," to the Arabic city of Mosul. "Gingham" comes from a Malay word meaning "striped"; "chintz," from a Hindustani word meaning "spotted." Most of the Eastern manufactures were increasingly imitated in the eighteenth century in Europe. Axminster and Aubusson carpets competed with Oriental rugs. In 1709 a German named Boettcher discovered a formula for making a vitreous and translucent substance comparable to the porcelain of China; this European "china," made at Sèvres, Dresden, and in England, soon competed successfully with the imported original.

Spices and Asian manufactures

Cotton fabrics were never produced in Europe at a price to compete with fabrics from India until after the introduction of power machinery, which began in England about 1780. Before that date the European demand for Indian cotton goods was so heavy that the woolen, linen, and silk interests became alarmed. They could produce nothing like the sheer muslins and bright calico prints that caught the public fancy. Many governments, seeking to protect the jobs and capital involved in the old European textile industries, simply forbade the import of Indian cottons altogether. But it was a time of many laws and little enforcement. The forbidden fabrics continued to come in, and the English writer Daniel Defoe observed in 1708 that, despite the laws, cottons were not only sought as clothing by all classes, but "crept into our houses, our closets and bedchambers; curtains, cushions, chairs and at last beds themselves were nothing but calicoes or Indian stuffs." Gradually, in the face of tariff protection for "infant industries" in Europe, and the rapid growth of European cotton manufactures, import of cottons and other manufactures from Asia declined. After about 1770 most of the imports of the British East India Company consisted of tea, which was brought from China.

The Americas, including the West Indies, bulked larger than Asia in the eighteenth-century trade of western Europe. The American trade was based mainly on sugar—a popular commodity that generated enormous profits for European traders throughout the eighteenth century. Sugar had long been known in the East, and in the European Middle Ages little bits of it had trickled through to delight the palates of lords and prelates. In the early modern era, however, the production and consumption of sugar were transformed. Europeans began to bring sugar cane into the Americas from South Asia and the Middle East in the sixteenth century, and after about 1650 sugar became the most important cash crop in Europe's Caribbean colonies. A whole new economic system arose in the West Indies over the next few decades. It was based on the "plantation." A plantation was an economic unit consisting of a considerable tract of land, a sizable investment of capital, often owned by absentees in France or England, and a force of impressed labor, supplied by enslaved black workers brought from Africa. Sugar, produced in quantity with cheap labor at low cost, proved to have an inexhaustible market.

Sugar and the plantation system

The eighteenth century was the golden age, economically speaking, of the West Indies. From its own islands alone, during the 80 years from 1713 to 1792, Great Britain imported a total of £162,000,000 worth of goods, almost all sugar; imports from India and China, in the same 80 years, amounted to only £104,000,000. The little islands of Jamaica, Barbados, St. Kitts, and others, as suppliers of Europe, not only dwarfed the whole mainland of British America but the whole mainland of Asia as well. For France, less well established than Britain on the American mainland and in Asia, the same economic pattern developed with even greater commercial force. France controlled the richest of all the Caribbean sugar colonies, Saint-Domingue, on the island that the English called Santo Domingo (which is now divided between Haiti and the Dominican Republic).

Slave trade

The plantation economy, first established in sugar and later in cotton (after 1800), brought Africa into the foreground. Slaves had been obtained in Black Africa from time immemorial, by the Roman Empire and later by the Muslim world, both of which, however, enslaved blacks and whites indiscriminately. After the European discovery of America, enslaved blacks were taken across the Atlantic by the Spanish and Portuguese to provide labor in places where disease and abuse had decimated the Native American populations. Dutch slavetraders also took enslaved Africans to Virginia in 1619, a year before the arrival of the first English Pilgrims in Massachusetts. But slavery in the Americas before 1650 may be described as less systematic. With the rise of the plantation economy after 1650, and especially after 1700, it became a fundamental economic institution. Slavery now formed the labor supply of a very substantial and heavily capitalized branch of world production. About 920,000 blacks were landed from Africa on the island of Jamaica alone between 1700 and 1800; and roughly 800,000 enslaved people were brought to the French colony of Saint-Domingue. The eighteenth century thus became the most active era in the long history of the Atlantic slave trade. Seeking the steady flow of profits that came mostly from an insatiable demand for slave labor on Caribbean and Brazilian plantations, European slave traders moved more than 5 million enslaved Africans to the Americas during the 100 years after 1700. It is certain that, until well after 1800, far more Africans than Europeans made the voyage to the Americas; and these manacled, disoriented, vulnerable human beings were transported everywhere in the most dehumanizing conditions of overcrowded slave ships.

The transatlantic slave trade in the eighteenth century was conducted mainly by English-speaking interests, principally in England but also in New England, followed as closely as they could manage it by the French. Yearly export of merchandise from Great Britain to Africa, used chiefly in exchange for slaves, increased tenfold between 1713 and 1792. As for merchandise coming into Britain from the British West Indies, virtually all produced by slaves, in 1790 it constituted almost a fourth of all British imports. If we add British imports from the American mainland, including what after 1776 became the United States, the importance of black slave labor to the British economic system will appear still greater, because a great part of exports from the mainland consisted of agricultural products, such as tobacco and indigo, produced in most places by slaves. The rapid growth of trade within the British Empire and the phenomenal rise of British capitalism in the eighteenth century were therefore based to a considerable extent on the enslavement of Africans. The town of Liverpool, an insignificant place on the Irish Sea in 1700, built itself up by the slave trade and the trade in slave-produced commodities to become a busy transatlantic commercial center, which in turn, as will be seen later, stimulated the "industrial revolution" in Manchester and other neighboring towns.

Slavery and British capitalism

The western European merchants, British, French, and Dutch, sold the products of America and Asia to their own peoples and to those of central and eastern Europe. Trade with Germany and Italy was fairly stable. With Russia it enormously increased. To cite the British record only, Britain imported 15 times as much from Russia in 1790 as in 1700, and sold the Russians 6 times as much. The Russian landlords, as they became more connected to Europe, desired Western manufactures and the colonial products such as sugar, tobacco, and tea that could be purchased only from western Europeans. They had grain, timber, and naval stores to offer in return. Similarly, landlords of Poland and north Germany, in the seventeenth and eighteenth centuries, found themselves increasingly able to move their agricultural products out through the Baltic and hence increasingly able to buy the products of western Europe, America, and Asia in return. Eastern European landlords now had another incentive to make their estates more productive. The early modern global trading system therefore began to affect all parts of Europe, including also the landlords and peasants in central and eastern Europe. The large landowners who sought more profits with which to purchase commodities and other goods coming from the Americas and western Europe helped to spread "big" agriculture into new areas, developing in eastern Europe a system not unlike the plantation economy of the New World. This expanding system of European trade and agriculture had many effects. It contributed, along with political causes, to reducing the bulk of the eastern European population to serfdom. It helped to bring western European culture to the upper classes of eastern Europe. And it helped to enrich the cities and merchants of western Europe.

Historical Documents
John Wesley, *Thoughts Upon Slavery* (1778)

European slave traders moved more than 5 million enslaved Africans to the Americas during the eighteenth century alone. These enslaved workers produced the sugar, cotton, and other commodities that generated great wealth for the expanding commercial classes of western Europe. At the same time, however, religious thinkers and political advocates of natural human rights increasingly condemned slavery as immoral and called for its abolition. The following excerpts from a pamphlet by the most prominent leader of the influential Methodist movement in England, John Wesley (1703-1791), shows how religious and political ideas fused in new critiques of slavery on both sides of the Atlantic—even as Europeans continued to expand the slave system into more places.

Who can reconcile this treatment of the Negroes . . . with either mercy or justice?

Where is the justice of inflicting the severest evils, on those who have done us no wrong? . . . Of tearing them from their native country, and depriving them of liberty itself? To which an Angolan, has the same natural right as an Englishman, and on which he sets as high a value? Yea where is the justice of taking away the lives of innocent, inoffensive men? . . .

I absolutely deny all slave-holding to be consistent with any degree of even natural justice. . . .

If therefore you have any regard to justice, (to say nothing of mercy, nor of the revealed law of GOD) render unto all their due. Give liberty to whom liberty is due, that is to every child of man, to every partaker of human nature. Let none serve you but by his own act and deed, by his own voluntary choice. —Away with all whips, all chains, all compulsion! Be gentle towards men. And see that you invariably do unto every one, as . . . he should do unto *you*. . . .

O thou GOD of love, thou who art loving to every man, . . . Thou who hast mingled of one blood, all the nations upon earth: Have compassion upon these outcasts. . . . Arise and help these that have no helper, whose blood is spilt upon the ground like water! . . . Stir them up to cry unto thee in the land of their captivity; . . . Savior of all, make them free.

John Wesley, *Thoughts Upon Slavery* (London, and reprinted in Philadelphia by Joseph Crushank, 1778), from the electronic edition, Academic Affairs Library, University of North Carolina at Chapel Hill (1999), pp. 34-35, 56-57.

The Wealth of Western Europe: Social Consequences

The wealth that accumulated along the Atlantic seaboard of Europe was, in short, by no means produced only by the efforts of western Europeans. All the world contributed to its formation. The natural resources of the Americas, the gold and people of Africa, the labor of enslaved workers on Caribbean islands, the resources and manufacturing skills of Asia, all alike went into producing the vastly increased volume of goods moving in world commerce. Europeans directed the movement. They supplied capital; they contributed technical and organizing abilities; and it was the economic demands of Europeans, at home in Europe and as traders abroad, that set increasing numbers of Indians to spinning cotton, Chinese to raising tea, Malays to gathering spices, and enslaved Africans to the tending of sugar cane. A few non-Europeans might benefit in the process—Indian or Chinese merchants "subsidized" by the East Indian companies, African chiefs who captured slaves from neighboring tribes and sold them to Europeans. But the profits of

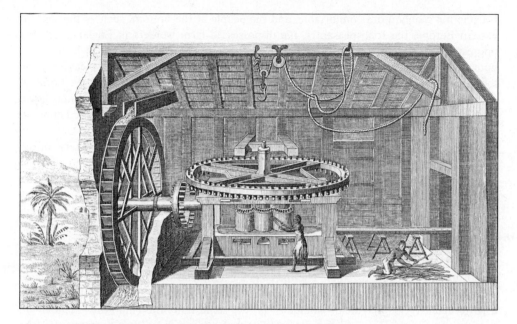

European traders and merchants gained much of their new wealth in the seventeenth and eighteenth centuries from commodities produced on plantations in the Americas and the Caribbean. This plantation economy depended on the labor of enslaved African workers such as the people in this illustration of a water-powered sugar mill in a French Caribbean colony. The image, which shows the processing of sugar cane, appeared in the famous French Encyclopedia that was published between 1751 and 1772. (©DEA PICTURE LIBRARY/Getty Images)

the world economy and the far-flung colonial empires really went to Europe. The new wealth, over and above what was necessary to keep the widely dispersed and polyglot labor force in being, and to pay other expenses, piled up in Britain, Holland, and France.

The new wealth was owned and managed by private persons. It accumulated within the system of private property and as part of the institutions of private enterprise or private capitalism. Governments were increasingly dependent on these private owners of property, for

Accumulation of private wealth

governments, in western Europe, had no important sources of revenue except loans and taxes derived from their peoples. When the owners of wealth gave their support, the government was strong and successful, as in England. When they withdrew support, the government collapsed, as it was to collapse in France in the Revolution of 1789.

In a technical sense there were many "capitalists" in western Europe, persons who had a little savings which they used to buy a parcel of land or a loom or entrusted to some other person to invest at interest. And in a general sense the new wealth was widely distributed; the standard of living rose in western Europe in the eighteenth century, in part because the declining price of popular commodities made such goods more accessible for most European consumers. Tea, for example, which cost as much as £10 a pound when introduced into England about 1650, was an article of common consumption a hundred years later. But wealth used to produce more wealth, that is, capital, was owned or controlled in significant amounts by relatively few persons. In the eighteenth century some people became unprecedentedly rich (including some who started quite poor, for it was a time of new commercial opportunities); the great intermediate layers of society became noticeably more comfortable; and the people at the bottom, such as the serfs of eastern Europe, the Irish peasantry, the dispossessed farm workers in England, and the poorest peasants and workers of France, were worse off than they had been before. The poor continued to live in hovels. The prosperous created for themselves a pleasant, comfortable social world that connoisseurs still admire, a new eighteenth-century world of well-ordered Georgian homes, closely cropped lawns and shrubs, furniture by Chippendale or à la Louis XV, coach-and-four, family portraits, high chandeliers, books bound in morocco, and a staff of servants "below stairs."

The merging of bourgeois and aristocratic wealth

Families enriched by commerce, especially the daughters, mixed and intermarried with older noble families who owned land. Women thus played an essential economic role in the carefully arranged marriages that both protected and increased the wealth of upper-class families. Landowners needed the capital that could be acquired through marriages with the daughters of wealthy traders; prosperous entrepreneurs sought the landed properties that might come into their families through marriages with women of the old aristocracy. But marriage was only one of the ways in which the old and new wealth of Europe came together. The merchants in England or France no sooner became prosperous than they bought themselves a landed estate. In France they might also purchase a government office or patent of nobility. At the same time, the landowning gentlemen, especially in England, no sooner increased their landed income than they invested the proceeds in commercial enterprise or government bonds. The two forms of property, bourgeois commerce and aristocratic land, tended to merge. The various propertied interests usually worked harmoniously together, but the unpropertied classes, the vast majority, could influence the government only by riot and tumult. The eighteenth century, though an era of rapid commercial expansion, was on the whole an age of considerable social stability in western Europe. It was the upheavals of the French Revolution that would eventually disrupt and transform much of the social and political order that had developed since the late seventeenth century through the fusion of commercial and landed wealth.

The foregoing might be illustrated from the lives of thousands of men and women. Two examples are enough, one English and one French. They show the working of the world economic system, the rise of the commercial class in western Europe, and the role of that class in the political life of the Western countries.

Thomas Pitt

Thomas Pitt, called "Diamond" Pitt, was born in 1653, the son of a parish clergyman in the Church of England. He went to India in 1674. Here he operated as an "interloper," trading in defiance of the legal monopoly of the East India Company. Returning to England, he was prosecuted by the company and fined £400 but was rich enough to buy the manor of Stratford and with it the borough of Old Sarum, a rotten borough that gave him a seat in the House of Commons without the trouble of an election. He soon returned to India, again as an interloper, where he competed so successfully with the company that it finally took him into its own employment. He traded on his own account, as well as for the company, and he defended the position of the company in Chennai (a city then called Madras) against the local ruler of the Carnatic, the coastal area around Chennai, buying him off with money.

In 1702, though Pitt's salary was only £300 a year, he purchased a 410-carat uncut diamond for £20,400. He bought it from an Indian merchant who had himself bought it from an English skipper, who in turn had stolen it from the slave who had found it in the mines and who had concealed it in a wound in his leg. Back in Europe, Pitt had his diamond cut at Amsterdam and sold it in 1717 to the regent of France for £135,000. The regent put it in the French crown; it was appraised at the time of the French Revolution

MR. RICHARD BULL AND HIS WIFE
by Arthur Devis
(English, 1712–1787)

The prosperity of the upper classes in eighteenth-century England supported the culture and comforts of the kinds of people who are represented in this painting. Expanding global trade provided a pleasant, comfortable life for increasingly wealthy European elites and a new market for good furniture, fine art, and portrait artists such as Arthur Devis.

(©DEA/A. DAGLI ORTI/Getty Images)

at £480,000. "Diamond" Pitt died in 1726. One of his daughters became the Countess of Stanhope and one of his sons became the Earl of Londonderry. Another son became father to the William Pitt who guided Britain through the Seven Years' War with France and who was raised to the peerage as the Earl of Chatham. The city of Pittsburgh was named for this Pitt, so that a fortune gained by unconventional or illicit means in India later gave its name to a frontier settlement in the interior of America. Chatham's younger son, the second William Pitt, became prime minister at 24. The younger Pitt guided Britain through its wars with revolutionary France and Napoleon, until his death in 1806 during the high tide of the Napoleonic Empire.

Jean-Joseph Laborde was born in 1724, of a bourgeois family in southern France, but his career showed how commercial wealth could *Jean-Joseph Laborde* transform a person's social position. He went to work for an uncle whose trading business connected French commerce with both Asia and the Americas. From the profits he built up vast plantations and slaveholdings in the colony of Saint-Domingue. His ships brought sugar to Europe and returned with prefabricated building materials, each piece carefully numbered, for his plantations and refineries in the West Indies. Wealth from the sugar trade enabled him to become one of the leading bankers in Paris. His daughter became the Countess de Noailles. He himself received the title of marquis, which he did not use. He bought manors and châteaux near Paris. As a real estate operator he developed that part of Paris, then suburban, now called the Chaussée d'Antin.

By 1760 Laborde was directing the king's tax collection system; and during the Seven Years' War he was sent by the French government to borrow money in Spain, where he was told that Spain would lend nothing to Louis XV but would gladly lend him personally 20,000,000 reals. In the War of American Independence Laborde raised 12,000,000 livres in gold for the government to help pay the French army and navy, thus contributing to the success of the American Revolution. He acted as investment agent for Voltaire, gave 24,000 livres a year to charity, and subscribed 400,000 livres in 1788 toward building new hospitals in Paris. In July 1789 he helped to finance the insurrection that led to the fall of the Bastille and the Revolution. His son, in June 1789, took the Oath of the Tennis Court, swearing to write a constitution for France. Despite his early support for the Revolution, Laborde himself was guillotined in 1794. His children later turned to scholarship and the arts.

33. WESTERN EUROPE AFTER THE PEACE OF UTRECHT, 1713–1740

Amid the social and economic transitions that were transforming early modern Europe's relations with the wider world, the major European states continued their struggles for international power and political influence within Europe itself. The evolving competition for global trade and profitable colonies, however, became an increasingly important factor in most European conflicts, even when such conflicts extended the now-traditional efforts to maintain a stable balance of power among the various continental monarchies. The Peace of Utrecht, it will be recalled, had registered the defeat of French ambitions in the wars of Louis XIV. The French move toward "universal monarchy" had been blocked. The European state system had been preserved. Europe was to consist of independent and sovereign states, all legally free and equal, continuously entering or leaving alliances along the principles of the balance of power. The peace settlement of 1713–1714 placed the Bourbon Philip V on the Spanish throne but gave most of Spain's European possessions, outside Spain itself, to the Austrian Habsburgs (see maps, pp. 199, 336). Great Britain, which had been consolidated during the wars as a combined kingdom of England and Scotland, took Newfoundland, Nova Scotia, and the Hudson Bay region from France and, taking Gibraltar and Minorca from Spain, became a naval power in the Mediterranean. The British also received trading rights in Spanish America, thus expanding their role in the Atlantic slave trade and enhancing their position as the most dynamic power in the rapidly developing transatlantic economic system.

Repairing the damages of war

Governments now turned to repairing the damages of war. Spain was somewhat rejuvenated by the French influence under its new Bourbon monarchy. The drift and decadence that had set in under the last Habsburgs were at least halted. The Spanish state was administratively strengthened. Its officials followed the absolutist government of Louis XIV as a model. The estates of the east-Spanish kingdoms, Aragon and Valencia, ceased to meet, going like the Estates General of France into the limbo of obsolete institutions. On the whole the French influence in eighteenth-century Spain was intangible. Nothing was changed in substance, but the old machinery functioned with more precision. Administrators were better trained and took a more constructive attitude toward government work; they became more aware of the world north of the Pyrenees and recovered confidence in their country's future. They tried also to tighten up the administration of their American Empire. More revenue officers and coast guards were introduced in the Caribbean, whose zeal led to repeated clashes with smugglers, mainly British. Friction along the Spanish-controlled coasts of the

American mainland, reinforced by Spanish dislike for British occupation of Gibraltar, kept Spain and Britain in a continual ferment of potential hostility.

The Dutch after Utrecht receded from the international political stage, though their alliance was always sought because of the huge shipping and financial resources they controlled. The Swiss also became important in banking and financial circles. A new commercial group in the Austrian Netherlands (the region that would later become Belgium) founded an overseas trading company in 1723 on the authority of their new Austrian ruler; this "Ostend Company" sent out six highly profitable voyages to China, but the commercial jealousy of the Dutch and British obliged the Austrian emperor to withdraw his support as a price for British recognition of his daughter's right to inherit the Austrian throne. The Ostend enterprise thus came to an end. The Scots began at about this time to play their remarkable role of energizing business affairs in many countries. Union with England in 1707 gave them access to the British Empire and to the numerous commercial advantages won by the English. John Law, the financial wizard of France, was a Scot, as was William Paterson, one of the chief founders of the Bank of England.

France and Britain after 1713

Our main attention falls on France and Britain. Though one was the victor and the other the vanquished in the wars that ended in 1713, and though one stood for royal absolutism and the other for parliamentary constitutionalism in government, their development in the years after Utrecht was in some ways surprisingly parallel. In both countries for some years the king was personally ineffective, and in both the various propertied interests therefore gained many advantages. Both pursued the commercial and colonial expansion described above. Both went through a short period of financial experimentation and frantic speculation in stocks, the financial bubble bursting in each case in 1720. Each was thereafter governed by a statesman, Cardinal Fleury in France and Robert Walpole in England, whose policy was to keep peace abroad and conciliate all interests at home. Fleury and Walpole held office for about two decades, toward the end of which the two countries again went to war. But the differences are at least as instructive as the parallels.

In France the new king was a child, Louis XV, the great-grandson of Louis XIV, and only five years old when his reign began in 1715. The government was entrusted to a regent, the Duke of Orleans, an elder cousin of the young king. Orleans, lacking the authority of a monarch, had to admit the aristocracy to a greater share of the power that nobles had lost during the long reign of Louis XIV. Most of the nobles had never liked the absolutist policies of Louis XIV, and there was much dissatisfaction with absolutism among all classes, because of the ruin and suffering brought by Louis XIV's wars.

The eighteenth century, for France, was a period in which absolutism was checked and balanced by organized privileged groups. Nobles won back many of the powers that Louis XIV had taken from them in the previous century, thereby achieving a kind of aristocratic resurgence.

The higher nobles, ousted by Louis XIV, now reappeared in the government. For a time Orleans worked through committees of noblemen, roughly corresponding to ministries, a system lauded by its backers as a revival of political freedom; but the committees proved so *French aristocratic resurgence* incompetent that they were soon abandoned. The old parlements of France, and especially the Parlement of Paris, which Louis XIV had reduced to silence, vigorously reasserted themselves after his death. The parlements were primarily law courts, originally composed of bourgeois judges. But Louis XIV and his predecessors, to raise money, had made the judgeships into offices to be sold; and they attached titles of nobility to increase the price. Hence in the time of the Regency the judges of the parlements had bought or inherited their seats and were almost all nobles. Because they owned their offices as a kind of private property, they could not be removed by the king. The Regent conceded much influence to the Parlement of Paris, utilizing it to modify the will of Louis XIV. The parlements thus broadened their position, claiming the right to assent to legislation and taxes, through refusing to enforce government measures that they considered contrary to the unwritten constitution or fundamental laws of France. They managed to exercise this right, off and on, from the days of the Regency until the great Revolution of 1789.

The English Parliament

In Great Britain the Parliament was very different from the French parlements, and the British aristocracy was more politically competent than the *noblesse* of France. Parliament proved an effective machine for the conduct of public business. The House of Lords was hereditary, with the large exception of the bishops, who were appointed by the government and made up about a quarter of the active members of the upper house. The House of Commons was not at all representative of the country according to modern ideas. Only the wealthy, or those patronized by the wealthy, could sit in it, and they were chosen by diverse and eccentric methods, in counties and towns, almost without regard to the size or wishes of the population. Some boroughs were owned outright, like the Old Sarum of the Pitt family. But through the machinations of bosses, or purchase of seats, all kinds of interests managed to get representatives into the Commons. Some members spoke for the "landed interest"; others for the "funded interest" (mainly government creditors); others for the "London interest," the "West India interest," the "East India interest," and others. All of the leading economic groups and politically significant social classes could expect to have influence in Parliament, and all therefore were willing to go through parliamentary channels. Parliament was corrupt, slow, and expensive, but it was effective. For Parliament was not only a roughly representative body; it had also acquired, in practice, the power to legislate.

Queen Anne, the last reigning Stuart, died in 1714. She was succeeded by George I, Elector of Hanover, as Parliament had previously arranged in the Act of Settlement of 1701. George I was the nearest relative of the Stuarts who was also a Protestant. A middle-aged German who spoke no English, he continued to spend much of his time in Germany, and he brought with him to England a retinue of German ministers and mistresses. He was never popular in England, where he was regarded as at best a political convenience. He was in no position to play a strong hand in English public life, and during his reign Parliament gained considerable independence from the crown.

The main problem was still whether the principles of the Revolution of 1688 should be maintained. The Whigs, who considered the revolution as their work, long remained a minority made up of a few great landowning noblemen, wealthy London merchants, lesser businesspeople, and nonconformists in religion. The Whigs generally controlled the House of Lords, but the House of Commons was more uncertain; at the time of the Peace of Utrecht its majority was Tory.

British Whigs and Tories

After 1714 the two parties tended to dissolve, and the terms "Whig" and "Tory" ceased to have much definite meaning. In general the government, and the Anglican bishops who were close to the government, remained "Whig." Men who were remote from the central government, or suspicious of its activities, formed a kind of country party quite different from the earlier Tories. Gentry and yeomen of the shires and byways were easily mobilized against the great noblemen and men of money who led the Whigs. In the established church the lesser clergy were sometimes critical of the Whig bishops. In Scotland also, the ancestral home of the Stuarts, many were disaffected with the new regime.

Tories and Scots made up a milieu after 1688 in which what would now be called counterrevolution might develop. Never enthusiastic for the "Whig wars" against France, critical of the mounting national debt that the wars created, distrustful of the business and moneyed interests, they began to look wistfully to the exiled Stuarts. After 1701, when James died in France, the Stuart claims devolved upon his son, who lived until 1766, scheming time and again to make himself king of England. His partisans were known as Jacobites, from *Jacobus,* the Latin for James. They claimed that he had a divine right to the monarchy and regarded him as "James III," whereas others called him the Pretender. The Jacobites felt that if he would give up his Catholic religion, he should be accepted as Britain's rightful king.

"James III"

The Whigs could not tolerate a return of the Stuarts. The restoration of "James III" and his divine-right partisans would undo the principles of the Glorious Revolution—limited monarchy, constitutionalism, parliamentary supremacy, the rule of law, the toleration of dissenting Protestants, in short all that was summarized and defended in the political writings of John Locke. Moreover, those who held stock in the Bank of England or who had lent their money to the government would be ruined, because "James III" would surely repudiate a debt contracted by his foes. The Whigs were bound to support the Hanoverian George I. And George I was bound to look for support in a strange country among the Whigs.

George lacked personal appeal even for his English friends. To his enemies he was ridiculous and repulsive. The successful establishment of his dynasty would ruin the hopes of Tories and Jacobites. In 1715 the Pretender landed in Scotland, gathered followers from the Highlands, and proclaimed a rebellion against George I. Civil war seemed to threaten. But the Jacobite leaders bungled, and many of their followers proved to be undecided. They were willing enough to toast the "king over the water" in protest against the Whigs but not willing in a show-

Threats of civil war

down to see the Stuarts, and all that went with them, again in possession of the crown of England. The Fifteen, as the revolt came to be called, petered out. But 30 years later came the Forty-five. In 1745, during war with France, the Pretender's son, "Bonnie Prince Charlie" or the "Young Pretender," again landed in Scotland and again proclaimed rebellion. This time, though almost no one in England rallied, the uprising was more successful. A Scottish force penetrated to within 80 miles of London and was driven back and crushed with the help of Hanoverian regiments rushed over from Germany. The British government set out to destroy Jacobitism in the Scottish Highlands. The social system of the Highlands was wiped out, the clans were broken up, and their lands were forcibly reorganized according to modern notions of property and of landlord and tenant.

The Jacobite uprisings confirmed the old reputation of England in the eyes of Europe, namely, as Voltaire said, that its government was as stormy as the seas that surrounded it. To partisans of monarchy on the Continent the uprisings showed the weaknesses of parliamentary government. But their ignominious collapse actually showed the growing strength of the parliamentary regime in England. The Jacobites left little permanent mark and soon passed into romantic legend.

The "Bubbles"

Meanwhile, immediately after the Peace of Utrecht, the problem of dealing with a large postwar government debt had to be faced in both England and France. Organized permanent public debt was new at the time. The possibilities and limitations of large-scale banking, paper money, and credit were not clearly seen. In France there was much amazement at the way in which England and Holland, though smaller and less wealthy than France,

Critics of John Law ridiculed the Scottish financier's plan to pay off the French government's debt with profits from the sale of shares in the "Mississippi Company." This early eighteenth-century Dutch cartoon, for example, portrayed Law as a salesman of bogus shares and showed naive investors falling toward ruin in distant waters.

(©Universal History Archive/Getty Images)

had been able to maximize their resources through banking and credit and even to finance the alliance that had eclipsed the Sun King. In addition there was much private demand for both lending and borrowing money. Private persons all over western Europe were looking for enterprises in which to invest their savings. And promoters and organizers, anticipating a profit in new lines of business, were looking for capital with which to work. Out of this whole situation grew the "South Sea bubble" in England and the "Mississippi bubble" in France. Both bubbles broke in 1720, and both had important long-range effects.

A close tie between government finance and private enterprise was usual at the time, under mercantilist ideas of government guidance of trade. In England, for example, a good deal of the government debt was held by trading companies organized for that purpose. The government would charter a company, strengthen it with a monopoly in a particular kind of business, and then receive from the company, after the stockholders had bought up the shares, a large sum of cash as a loan. Much of the British debt, contracted in the wars from 1689 to 1713, was held in this way by the Bank of England, founded in 1694; by the East India Company, reorganized in 1708 in such a way as to provide funds

Ties between government and private enterprise

for the government; and by the South Sea Company, founded in 1711. The bank enjoyed a legal monopoly over certain banking operations in London, the East India Company over trade with the East, the South Sea Company for exploiting the *asiento* and other commercial privileges extorted from Spain. The companies were owned by private investors. Savings drawn from trade and agriculture, put into shares in these companies, became available both for economic reinvestment and for use by the government in defraying the costs of war.

In 1716 the Prince Regent of France, the Duke of Orleans, became interested in the ideas of a Scottish financier, John Law, reputedly   *John Law* because Law had a remarkable mathematical system for gambling at cards. Law founded a much-needed French central bank. In the next year, 1717, he organized a *Compagnie d'Occident,* popularly called the Mississippi Company, which obtained a monopoly of trade with Louisiana, where it founded New Orleans in 1718. This company, under Law's management, soon absorbed the French East India, China, Senegal, and African companies. It now enjoyed a legal monopoly of all French colonial trade. Seeing this trade as a means to solve France's financial problems, the Regent authorized Law to assume the entire government debt. The Mississippi Company received from individuals their certificates of royal indebtedness or "bonds" and gave them shares of company stock in return. It proposed to pay dividends on these shares and to extinguish the debt from profits in the colonial trade and from a monopoly over the collection of all indirect taxes in France. The project carried with it a plan for drastic reform of the whole taxation system, to make taxes both more fair to the taxpayer and more lucrative to the government. Shares in the Mississippi Company were gobbled up by the public. There was a frenzy of speculation, a wild fear of not buying soon enough. Quotations rose to 18,000 livres a share. But the company rested only on unrealized projects. Shareholders began to fear for their money. They began to unload. The market broke sharply. Many found their life savings gone. Others lost ancestral estates on which they had borrowed in the hope of getting rich. Those, however, who had owned shares in the company before the rise, and who had resisted the speculative fever, lost nothing by the bursting of inflated prices and later enjoyed a gilt-edged commercial investment.

Much the same thing happened in England, where many believed that Law was about to provide a panacea for France. The South Sea Company, outbidding the Bank of England, took over a large fraction of the public debt by receiving government "bonds" from their owners in return for shares of its stock. The size and speed of profits to be made in Spanish America were greatly exaggerated, and the market value of South Sea shares rose rapidly for a time, reaching £1,050 for a share of £100 par value. Other schemes abounded in the passion for easy money. Promoters organized mining and textile companies, as well as others of more fanciful or bolder design—a   *South Sea bubble* company to bring live fish to market in tanks, an insurance company to insure female chastity, even a company "for an undertaking which shall in due time be revealed." Shares in such enterprises were snatched at mounting prices. But in September 1720 the South Sea stockholders began to sell, doubting whether operations would pay dividends commensurate to £1,000 a share. They dragged down the whole unstable structure. As in France, many people found that their savings or their inheritances had disappeared in the financial implosion of a speculative bubble.

Indignation in both countries was extreme. Both governments were implicated in the scandal. John Law fled to Brussels. The Regent was discredited; he resigned in 1723, and French affairs were afterward conducted by Cardinal Fleury. In England there was a change of ministers. Robert Walpole, a country gentleman of Whig persuasion who had long sat in the Commons and who had warned against the South Sea scheme from the beginning, became the principal minister to George I.

Britain recovered from the crisis more successfully than France. Law's bank, a useful institution, was dissolved in the reaction against him, and France lacked an adequate banking and credit system during the rest of the century. French investors developed a morbid fear of paper securities and a marked preference for putting their savings into land.

The "Bubble Act"

In England the same fears were felt. Parliament passed the "Bubble Act," forbidding all companies except those specifically chartered by the government to raise capital by the sale of stock. In both countries the development of joint-stock financing along the lines of the modern corporation was slowed down for over a century. Business enterprises continued to be typically owned by individuals and partnerships, which expanded by reinvestment of their own profits and so had another reason to keep profits up and wages down. But in England Walpole managed to save the South Sea Company, the East India Company, and the bank, all of which were temporarily discredited in the eyes of the public. England continued to perfect its financial machinery.

The credit of the two governments was also shaken by the bubbles. Much of the French war debt was repudiated in one way or another. Repudiation was in many cases morally justifiable, for many government creditors were unscrupulous war profiteers, but financially it was disastrous, for it discouraged honest people from lending their money to the state. Nor was much accomplished toward reform of the taxes. The nobles continued to evade taxes imposed on them by Louis XIV, John Law's plans for taxation evaporated with the rest of his project, and when in 1726 a finance minister tried to levy a 2 percent tax on all property, the vested interests, led by the Parlement of Paris, demolished this proposal also. Lacking an adequate revenue, facing opposition to every proposed tax increase, and repudiating its debts, the French monarchy had little credit. The con-

Credit and the national debt

ception of the public or national debt hardly developed in France in the eighteenth century. The debt was considered to be the king's debt, for which no one except a few ministers felt any responsibility. The Bourbon government in fact often borrowed through the church, the Provincial Estates, or the city of Paris, which lenders considered to be better financial risks than the king himself. The government was severely handicapped in its foreign policy and its wars. It could not fully tap the wealth of its own subjects or expanding global commerce.

In England none of the government debt was repudiated. Walpole managed to launch and sustain the system of the sinking fund, by which the government regularly set aside the wherewithal to pay interest and principal on its obligations. The credit of the British government became absolutely firm. The debt was considered a national debt, for which the British people themselves assumed the responsibility. Parliamentary government made this development possible. In France no one could tell what the king or his ministers might do, and hence the French were reluctant to trust them with their money. In England the people who had the money could also, through Parliament, determine the policies of state, decide what the money should be spent for, and levy enough taxes to maintain confidence in the debt. England's social elites nevertheless shared the common French aversion to taxes that would most affect their own interests, and the landowners who controlled the British Parliament, like those who controlled the Parlement of Paris, resisted direct taxation. The British government therefore drew two-thirds or more of its revenues from indirect taxes paid by the mass of the population. Yet British landowners,

Angry investors in London responded to the collapse of the South Sea Company in 1720 by seeking compensation for their lost money. As this illustration suggests, however, the unhappy shareholders could not recover their losses, and the South Sea Bubble destroyed the savings of English speculators in the same way that the Mississippi Bubble wiped out investments in France. The English banking system, however, recovered from this financial collapse more quickly than the French.
(©Culture Club/Getty Images)

even dukes, did pay significant amounts of taxes. There were no exemptions by class or rank, as in France. All propertied interests had a stake in the government. The wealth of the country stood behind the national debt. The national credit seemed inexhaustible. This gave the British a decisive financial advantage in all their wars with France from the founding of the Bank of England in 1694 to the fall of Napoleon 120 years later. And it was the political freedom and power of Parliament that gave Britain's government its economic strength.

Fleury in France; Walpole in England

Fleury was 73 years old when he took office in 1726 and 90 when he left it. He was thus not inclined to initiate programs for the distant future. Louis XV, as he came of age, proved to be indolent and selfish. Public affairs drifted, while France grew privately more wealthy, especially the commercial and bourgeois classes. Walpole likewise kept out of controversies. His motto was *quieta non movere,* "let sleeping dogs lie." He sought to win over the Tory squires to the Hanoverian and Whig regime by keeping the land taxes low. This policy was successful, and Jacobitism quieted down. Walpole supported the bank, the trading companies, and the financial interests, and they in turn supported him. It was a time of political calm, in which the lower classes were quiet and the upper classes were not quarreling; and it was therefore a favorable time for the development of parliamentary institutions.

Walpole and cabinet government

Walpole has been called the first prime minister and the architect of cabinet government, a system in which the prime minister and the ministers who head the cabinet departments are also members of the legislative body. He saw to it, by careful rigging, that a majority in the Commons always supported him. He avoided issues on which his majority might be lost. He thus began to acknowledge the principle of cabinet responsibility to a majority in Parliament, which was to become an important characteristic of cabinet government. And by selecting colleagues who agreed with him, and getting rid of those who did not, he advanced the idea of the cabinet as a body of ministers bound to each other and to the prime minister, obligated to follow the same policies and to stand or fall as a group. Thus Parliament was not only a representative or deliberative body, but also one that developed an effective executive power, without which neither representative government nor any government could survive.

To assure peace and quiet in domestic politics the best means was to avoid raising taxes. And the best way to avoid taxes was to avoid war. Fleury and Walpole both tried to keep their countries at peace. They were not in the long run successful. Fleury was drawn into the War of the Polish Succession in 1733. Walpole kept England out of war until 1739. He always had a war party to contend with, and the most bellicose were those interested in the American trade—the slave trade, the sugar plantations, and the illicit sale of goods in the Spanish Empire. The British official figures show that while trade with Europe in the eighteenth century was always less in war than in peace, trade with America always increased during war, except, indeed, during the War of American Independence.

In the 1730s there were constant complaints of indignities suffered by Britons on the coasts of Spain's American colonies. The war party produced a Captain Jenkins, who carried with him a small box containing a withered ear, which he said had been cut from his head by the outrageous Spaniards. Testifying in the House of Commons, where he "commended his soul to God and his cause to his country," he stirred up a commotion that led to war. So in 1739, after 25 years of peace, England plunged with wild enthusiasm into the War of Jenkins's Ear. "They are ringing the bells now," said Walpole; "they will soon be wringing their hands." The war soon merged into a wider conflict involving Europeans and others in all parts of the world. European wars could no longer be contained within Europe. The global economic and colonial systems that produced the expanding global trade also produced a series of global wars in which the European powers extended their conflicts across all of the distant territories and seas they sought to control.

34.   THE GREAT WAR OF THE MID-EIGHTEENTH CENTURY: THE PEACE OF PARIS, 1763

The fighting lasted until 1763, with an uneasy interlude between 1748 and 1756. It went by many names. The opening hostilities between England and Spain were called, by the English, the War of Jenkins's Ear. The struggle on the Continent in the 1740s over the Habsburg inheritance of the Austrian Empire was often known as the War of the Pragmatic Sanction. The Prussians spoke of the three "Silesian" wars. British colonials in America called the fighting of the 1740s King George's War, or used the term "French and Indian Wars," for the whole sporadic conflict. Other unnamed colonial struggles at the same time shook the peoples of India. Eventually these widely scattered conflicts came to be called by two names: the War of the Austrian Succession (for hostilities between

1740 and 1748) and the Seven Years' War (for the conflicts between 1756 and 1763). The two wars were really one. They involved the same two principal issues: the global duel of Britain and France for colonies, trade, and sea power, and the European duel of Prussia and Austria for territory and military power in central Europe.

Eighteenth-Century Warfare

Warfare at the time was in a kind of classical phase, which strongly affected the development of events. It was somewhat slow, formal, elaborate, and indecisive. The enlisted ranks of armies and navies were filled with men considered economically useless, picked up by recruiting officers among unwary loungers in taverns or on the wharves. All governments protected their productive population, peasants, mechanics, and bourgeois, preferring to keep them at home, at work, and paying taxes. Despite their diverse origins, the careers of soldiers and military officers changed in this era. They became a professional class apart from civilian life, enrolling for long terms of service, receiving regular wages, and going through extensive, systematic training. They lived in barracks or great forts and were dressed in bright uniforms (like the British "redcoats"), which, because camouflage was unnecessary, they wore even in battle. Weapons were not powerful; infantry was predominant and was armed in this era with the smooth-bore musket to which the bayonet could be attached. In war the troops depended on great supply depots built up beforehand, which were practically immovable with the transportation available, so that armies, at least in central and western Europe, rarely operated more than a few days' march from their bases. Soldiers fought methodically for pay. Generals hesitated to risk their troops, which took years to train and equip and were very expensive. Strategy took the form not of seeking out the enemy's main force to destroy it in battle but of maneuvering for advantages of position, applying a cumulative and subtle pressure somewhat as in a game of chess.

Little national feeling

There was little religious or national feeling in such wars, though new kinds of "patriotic" thought and identity began to emerge by the 1760s in England and France. The Prussian army recruited half or more of its enlisted personnel outside Prussia; the British army was largely made up of Hanoverian or other German regiments; even the French army had German units incorporated in it. Deserters from one side were enlisted by the other. War was waged between governments, or between the oligarchies and aristocracies that governments represented, not between whole peoples. It was fought for power, prestige, or calculated practical interests, not for ideologies, moral principles, world conquest, national survival, or ways of life. Popular nationalism had developed farthest in England, where "Rule Britannia" and "God Save the King," both expressing a low opinion of foreigners, became popular songs during these mid-eighteenth-century wars.

Civilians were little affected, except in India or the American wilderness where the methods of European military organization did not prevail. In Europe, a government aspiring to conquer a neighboring province did not wish to ruin or antagonize it beforehand. The fact that the western European struggle was largely naval kept it well outside civilian experience. Never had war been so contained within such parameters, certainly not in the religious wars of earlier times or in the national and "total" wars initiated later. This was one reason why governments went to war so easily. On the other hand governments also withdrew from war much more readily than in later times. Their treasuries might be exhausted, their trained soldiers used up; only practical or strategic questions were at stake; there was no war hysteria or pressure of mass opinion; the enemy of today might be the ally of tomorrow. Peace was almost as easy to make as war. Peace treaties were negotiated, not imposed. So the eighteenth century saw a series of wars and treaties and rearrangements of alliances, all arising over much the same issues and with exactly the same powers present at the end as at the beginning.

The War of the Austrian Succession, 1740–1748

Frederick II

The War of the Austrian Succession was started by the king of Prussia. Frederick II, or the "Great," was a young man of 28 when he became king in 1740. His youth had not been happy; he was temperamentally incompatible with his father. His tastes as a prince had run to playing the flute, corresponding with French authors, and writing prose and verse in the French language. His father, the sober, military-minded Frederick William I, thought him frivolous and dealt with him so clumsily that at the age of 18 he tried to escape from the kingdom. Caught and brought back, he was forced to witness the execution, by his father's order, of the friend and companion who had shared in his attempted flight. Frederick changed as the years passed from a jaunty youth to an aged cynic, equally undeceived by himself, his friends, or his enemies, and seeing no reason to expect much from human nature. Though his greatest reputation was made as a soldier, he retained his literary interests all his life, became a historian of merit, and is perhaps of all modern monarchs the only one who would have a respectable standing if considered only as a writer. An unabashed freethinker, like many others of his day, he considered all religions ridiculous and laughed at the divine right of kings; but he would have no nonsense about the rights of the house of Brandenburg, and he took a solemn view of the majesty of the state.

Frederick lost no time in showing a boldness that his father would have surely dreaded. He decided to conquer Silesia, and in December 1740, he invaded that province, a region adjoining Prussia, lying in the upper valley of the Oder, and belonging to the kingdom of Bohemia and hence to the Danubian Empire of the Habsburgs (see map, p. 220, panel 3). Frederick's invasion thus violated the Pragmatic Sanction that the Austrian emperor Charles VI had methodically negotiated throughout his long reign. The Pragmatic Sanction was the general agreement signed by the European powers, including Prussia, that had stipulated that all domains of the Austrian Habsburgs should be inherited integrally by the daughter of Charles VI, Maria Theresa. The issue was between negotiated agreements and force; and Frederick, in attacking Silesia, could invoke nothing better than "reason of state," the welfare and expansion of the state of which he was ruler.

The Pragmatic Sanction was now universally disregarded. All turned against Maria Theresa. Bavaria and Saxony put forward territorial claims. Spain, still hoping to revise the Peace of Utrecht, saw another chance to win back former Spanish holdings in Italy. The decisive intervention was that of France, which was torn between ambitions on the European continent and ambitions on the sea and beyond the seas. Economic and commercial advantage might dictate concentration on the transoceanic struggle with Britain. But the French nobles were less interested than the British aristocrats in commercial considerations. They were influential because they furnished practically all the army officers and diplomats. They saw Austria as the traditional enemy, Europe as the traditional field of valor, and the Austrian-controlled southern Netherlands as the traditional object for annexation to France. Cardinal Fleury, much against his will and judgment, found himself forced into war against the Habsburgs.

Maria Theresa

Maria Theresa was at this time a young woman of 23. She proved to be one of the most capable rulers ever produced by the house of

The young Frederick II of Prussia, who would later be called Frederick the Great, was more interested in music and literature than in the military and political tasks of a monarch—which he nevertheless pursued boldly after becoming king in 1740. This painting by Antoine Pesne portrays the "Crown Prince" in the year before he inherited the Prussian throne.

(©DEA PICTURE LIBRARY/ Getty Images)

Habsburg. She bore 16 children, and set a model of conscientious family living at a time of much indifference to such matters among the upper classes. She was as devout and as earnest as Frederick of Prussia was irreligious and seemingly flip. She dominated her husband and her grown sons as she did her kingdoms and her duchies. With practical sense and political talents, she reconstructed her empire without having any doctrinaire program, and she accomplished more in her methodical way than other rulers who pursued more spectacular projects of reform.

Soon after Frederick invaded Silesia, she gave birth to her first son, the future emperor Joseph II, in March 1741. She was preoccupied at the same time by the widening political crisis. Her dominions were assailed by half a dozen outside powers and her two kingdoms of Hungary and Bohemia (both of which had accepted the Pragmatic Sanction) were waiting to see if a break from the Habsburg Empire would best serve their interests. Facing these dangers from all directions, she traveled to Hungary, where she would be crowned with the crown of St. Stephen and rally essential support. She made a carefully arranged and dramatic appearance before the Hungarian political elite, implored them to defend her, and swore to uphold the liberties of the Hungarian nobles and the separate constitution of the kingdom of Hungary. Stories spread across Europe, telling how the young queen, by raising aloft the infant Joseph, who was to be heir to the throne, at a session of the Hungarian parliament, had thrown the Magyar leaders into paroxysms of chivalrous resolve. The story was not quite true, but it was true that she made an eloquent address to the Magyars and that she took her baby with her and proudly exhibited him. The Hungarian magnates pledged their "blood and life" and delivered 100,000 soldiers.

The war, as it worked out in Europe, was reminiscent of the struggles in the time of Louis XIV, or even of the Thirty Years' War now a century in the past. It was, again, a kind of civil struggle within the Holy Roman Empire, in which a league of German princes banded together against the monarchy of Vienna. This time the anti-Habsburg forces included the new kingdom of Prussia. It was, again, a collision of Bourbons and Habsburgs, in which the French pursued their old policy of maintaining division in Germany by supporting the German princes against the Habsburgs. The enduring aim of French policy was to keep the Germans divided into smaller, fragmented states and to prevent the expansion of Habsburg power in the extremely weak Holy Roman Empire. This time France had Spain on its side. Maria Theresa was supported only by Britain and Holland, which subsidized her financially but had inadequate land forces. The Franco-German-Spanish combination was highly successful. In 1742 Maria Theresa, hard pressed, accepted the proposals of Frederick for a separate peace. She temporarily granted him Silesia, and he temporarily slipped out of the war that he had been the first to enter. In 1745 the French won the battle of Fontenoy in the Austrian Netherlands, the greatest battle of the war. France and its allies seemed to be winning the land war in Europe.

Alliances in War of Austrian Succession

But the situation overseas offset the military situation in Europe. It was America that tilted the balance. The French fortress of Louisburg on Cape Breton Island was captured by an expedition of New Englanders in conjunction with the British navy. British warships drove French and Spanish shipping from the seas. The French West Indies were blockaded. The French government, in danger of losing the wealth and taxes drawn from the sugar and slave trades, announced its willingness to negotiate.

Peace of Aix-la-Chapelle

Peace was made at Aix-la-Chapelle in 1748. It was based on an Anglo-French agreement in which Maria Theresa was obliged to concur. Britain and France arranged their differences by a return to the prewar status quo. The British returned Louisburg to French control, despite the protests of the Americans, and relaxed their stranglehold on the Caribbean. The French returned to British control the Indian coastal city Madras (now Chennai), which they had captured, and gave up their recent gains in the Austrian Netherlands (now Belgium). The Atlantic powers recognized Frederick's annexation of Silesia, and the southern Netherlands were returned to Maria Theresa at the insistence of Britain and the Dutch. She and her ministers were very dissatisfied. They would infinitely have preferred to lose their territory in the southern Netherlands and keep Silesia. They were required, in the interest of a European or even intercontinental balance of power, to give up Silesia and to hold the Austrian Netherlands for the benefit of the Dutch, who wanted a territorial buffer against the French.

The war had been more decisive than the few readjustments of the map seemed to show. It proved the weakness of the French position, straddled as it was between Europe and the overseas world. Maintaining a huge army for use in Europe, the French could not, like Britain, concentrate upon the sea. On the other hand, because they were vulnerable on the sea, they could not hold their gains in Europe or expand into the southern Netherlands. The Austrians, though bitter, had reason for satisfaction. The war had been waged as a campaign to partition the Habsburg Empire. The Habsburg Empire still stood. Hungary had thrown in its lot with Vienna, a fact of much subsequent importance. Bohemia, which was almost lost, remained under Austrian control. In 1745 Maria Theresa got her husband elected Holy Roman Emperor as Francis I, a position for which, as a woman, she could not qualify. But the loss of Silesia was momentous. Silesia was as populous as the Dutch Republic, heavily German, and industrially the most advanced region east of the Elbe. Prussia's control of this valuable territory doubled its German

MARIA THERESA AND HER FAMILY
by Martin van Meytens (Austrian, 1695–1770)

Maria Theresa had an imposing public image in her dual roles as Queen in the Austrian house of Habsburg and mother in a large household of 16 children. This portrait of the Queen with her husband and many of her children shows her devotion to family life as well as the power she exercised in governing her empire.

(©DEA/MEYER/Getty Images)

population and more than doubled its resources. Prussia with Silesia was unquestionably a great power. Because Austria was still a great power, there were henceforth two great powers in the vague world known as "Germany," a situation that came to be known as the German dualism. But the transfer of Silesia made the Habsburg Empire less German, more Slavic and Hungarian, more Danubian and international. Silesia was the keystone of Germany. Frederick was determined to hold it; Maria Theresa was determined to win it back. A new war was therefore foreseeable in central Europe. As for Britain and France, the peace of Aix-la-Chapelle was clearly only a truce.

The next years passed in a busy diplomacy, leading to what is known as the "reversal of alliances" and the Diplomatic Revolution of 1756. The Austrians set themselves to checking the growth of Prussia. Maria Theresa's foreign minister, Count Kaunitz, perhaps the *The Diplomatic Revolution of 1756* most artful diplomat of the century, concluded that the rise of Prussia had revolutionized the balance of power. Kaunitz, dramatically reversing traditional policy, proposed an alliance between Austria and France—between the Habsburgs and the Bourbons. He encouraged the long-standing French aspirations for the Austrian Netherlands in return for French support in the destruction of Prussia. The overtures between Austria and France obliged Britain, Austria's former ally, to reconsider its position in Europe; the British had Hanover to protect and were favorably impressed by the Prussian army. An alliance of Great Britain and Prussia was concluded in January 1756. Meanwhile Kaunitz consummated his alliance with France. One consequence was to marry the future Louis XVI to one of Maria Theresa's daughters, Marie Antoinette, the "Austrian woman" of French Revolutionary fame. The Austrian alliance was never popular in France. Some French thought that the ruin of Prussia would only enhance the Austrian control of Germany and so undo the fundamental "Westphalia system." The French progressive thinkers, known as "philosophes," believed Austria to be priest-ridden and backward and were for ideological reasons admirers of the freethinking Frederick II. Dissatisfaction with its foreign policy was one reason for the growth of internal opposition to the Bourbon government.

A new global conflict that later came to be called the Seven Years' War broke out in 1756. Although it was a continuation of the preceding war in that Prussia fought Austria, and Britain fought France, the belligerents had all changed partners. Great Britain and Prussia were now allies, as were, more remarkably, the Bourbons and the Habsburgs. In addition, Austria had concluded a treaty with the Russian Empire for the annihilation of Prussia.

The Seven Years' War, 1756–1763: In Europe and America

The Seven Years' War began in America, but let us turn first to Europe, where the war was another in a series of wars of territorial partition. A league of powers had recently attempted to partition the Habsburg empire of Maria Theresa, and an earlier league had in fact partitioned the empires of Sweden and Spain. Now Austria, Russia, and France set out to partition the newly created kingdom of Prussia. Their aim was to relegate the Hohenzollerns to the territory of Brandenburg. Even with Silesia, Prussia had less than 6,000,000 people; each of its three principal enemies had 20,000,000 or more. But war was less an affair of peoples than of states and standing armies, and the Prussian state

Frederick's military triumphs	and Prussian army were the most efficient in Europe. Frederick fought brilliant campaigns, moved rapidly along interior lines, and eluded, surprised, and reattacked the badly coordinated armies opposed to him. He proved himself the great military genius of his day. But genius

was scarcely enough. Against three such powers, reinforced by Sweden and the German states, and with no ally except Great Britain (and Hanover) whose aid was almost entirely financial, the kingdom of Prussia by any reasonable estimate had no chance of survival. There were times when Frederick believed all to be lost, yet he went on fighting, and his strength of character in these years of adversity, as much as his ultimate triumph, later made him a hero and symbol for the Germans. His subjects, Junkers and even serfs, advanced in patriotic spirit under external pressure. The coalition tended to fall apart. The French lacked enthusiasm; they were fighting Britain, the Austrian alliance was unpopular, and Kaunitz would never plainly promise them the Austrian Netherlands. The Russians found that the more they moved westward the more they alarmed their Austrian allies. Frederick was left to deal only with the implacable Austrians, for whom he was more than a match. By the peace of Hubertusburg in 1763 Prussia retained Silesia and lost nothing.

Schönbrunn Palace, near Vienna, was the great palace of the Austrian Habsburgs. It was planned to compete with the vast palace of their French Bourbon rivals, but the plan was never completed because Maria Theresa (1740–1780) thought that the building seen here was adequate for her needs. (©DEA PICTURE LIBRARY/Getty Images)

For the rest, the Seven Years' War was a phase in the long global conflict between France and Great Britain. Its stakes were supremacy in the growing world economy, control of colonies, and command of the sea. The two empires had been left unchanged in 1748 by the peace of Aix-la-Chapelle. Both held possessions in India, in the West Indies, and on the American mainland (see maps, pp. 199, 314). In India both Britain and France possessed *British and French colonial interests* only disconnected commercial establishments on the coast, tiny economic and cultural specks on the giant body of India which always depended on Indian allies and commercial partners. Both countries also traded with the Chinese along the Pearl River Delta in South China. Both occupied colonial way stations on the route to Asia—the British in St. Helena and Ascension Island in the south Atlantic, the French in the more valuable islands of Mauritius and Reunion in the Indian Ocean. The French were active also on the coasts of Madagascar. The greatest way station, the Cape of Good Hope, belonged to the Dutch. In the West Indies the British plantations were mainly in Jamaica, Barbados, and some of the Leeward Islands; the French, in Saint-Domingue, Guadeloupe, and Martinique. All were supported by the booming Atlantic slave trade that was transporting millions of enslaved people from Africa.

On the American mainland the French had more territory and the British had more people. In the British colonies from Georgia to Nova Scotia lived perhaps 2 million Europeans, predominantly English but with strong infusions of Scots-Irish, Dutch, Germans, French, and Swedes. Philadelphia, with some 40,000 people, was as large as

CHRONOLOGY OF NOTABLE EVENTS, 1619–1763

1619	First enslaved Africans arrive in Virginia
1700–1780	Expansion of European plantation system in Caribbean sugar islands
1720	The "Mississippi bubble" in France and "South Sea bubble" in Britain
1740–1748	War of Austrian Succession in Europe
1740–1780	Queen Maria Theresa rules and expands the Austrian Empire
1740–1786	Frederick II (the Great) rules and expands the kingdom of Prussia
1756–1763	The Seven Years' War; expansion of British power in India and America

any city in England except London. Native Americans were decimated by disease or driven out of most Atlantic coastal lands. But the population in these areas continued to grow,

North American colonies

in part because of the expanding slave trade. About 275,000 enslaved Africans arrived in Britain's North American colonies before 1775, and by the late eighteenth century the African American population in these mainland territories had increased to more than 700,000 people.

Meanwhile, the number of Europeans grew to be almost a quarter as large as the population in the mother country. The European Americans, however, were provincial, locally minded, and incapable of concerted action. In 1754 the British government called a congress at Albany in New York, hoping that the colonies would assume some collective responsibility for the next war. The congress adopted an "Albany plan of union" drawn up by Benjamin Franklin, but the colonial legislatures declined to accept it, through fear of losing their separate identity. The colonials were willing, in a politically immature way, to rely on Britain for military action against France.

The French were still in possession of Louisburg on Cape Breton Island, a northern stronghold established by Louis XIV, located in the Gulf of St. Lawrence. It was designed for naval domination of the north Atlantic and to control access to the St. Lawrence River, the Great Lakes, and the vast region now called the Middle West. Through all this tract of country the French constantly came and went, but there were sizable French settlements only around New Orleans in the south and Quebec in the north. One source of French strength was that the French were more successful than the British in gaining the support of the Indians. This was probably because the French, being few in numbers, did not threaten to expropriate their lands and also because Catholics at this time were incomparably more active than Protestants in Christian missions among non-European peoples. The French were also active in the fur trade with Native Americans, an economic exchange that added important commercial components to French-Indian relations.

Mercantilist regulations

Both empires, French and British, were held together by mercantilist regulations framed mainly in the interest of the home countries. In some ways the British Empire was more liberal than the French; it allowed local self-government and permitted immigration from all parts of Europe. In other ways the British system was stricter. British subjects, for example, were required by the Navigation Acts to use British ships and seamen—English, Scottish, or colonial—whereas the French were freer to use the transport services of other nations. British sugar planters had to ship raw sugar to the home country, there to be refined and sold to Europe, whereas French planters were free to refine their sugar in the Caribbean islands. The mainland British colonials were forbidden to manufacture ironware and numerous other articles for sale; they were expected to buy such objects from England. Because the British sold little to the West Indies, where the enslaved population had no income with which to buy, the mainland colonies, though less valued as a source of wealth, were a far more important market for British goods. The North American colonials had prospered under the restrictive system, but they were beginning to find much of it irksome at the time of the Seven Years' War, and indeed evaded it when they could.

Fighting was endemic in the empires, even during years of peace in Europe. Nova Scotia was a trouble spot. French in population, it had been annexed by Britain at the Peace of Utrecht. Its proximity to Louisburg made it a scene of perpetual agitation. The British government in 1755, foreseeing another war with France, forced about 7,000 mostly French-speaking inhabitants to leave Acadia, originally a French colony and part of Nova Scotia. Although they were dispersed throughout Britain's North American colonies, some of these displaced people eventually migrated to Louisiana and preserved a distinctive identity in the French Cajun culture that developed there. But the great disputed area was the Alleghenies. British colonials were beginning to find their way westward through the mountains. French traders, soldiers, and empire builders were moving eastward toward the same mountains from points on the Mississippi and the Great Lakes. In 1749, at the request of Virginia and London capitalists, the British government chartered a land-exploitation company, the Ohio Company, to operate in territory claimed also by the French. The French built a fort at the point where the Ohio River is formed by the junction of two smaller rivers—Fort Duquesne, later called Pittsburgh. A force of colonials and British regular troops, commanded by General Braddock and colonial officers such as the young George Washington, started through the wilderness to dislodge the French. It was defeated in July 1755, but this frontier confrontation soon led to wider conflicts. A year later France and Britain declared war.

The British were brilliantly led by William Pitt, subsequently the Earl of Chatham, a man of wide vision and exceptional confidence. "I know that I can save the country," he said, "and I know that no one else can." He concentrated Britain's military campaigns on the navy and colonies, while subsidizing Frederick of Prussia to fight in Europe, so that England, as he put it, might win an empire on the plains of Germany. Only the enormous financial credit of the British government made such a policy feasible. In 1758 British forces finally took Fort Duquesne, and Louisburg fell again in the same year. Gaining entry to the St. Lawrence, the British moved upstream to Quebec, and in 1759 a force under General Wolfe, stealthily scaling the heights, appeared by surprise on the Plains of Abraham outside the fortress, forcing the garrison to accept a battle, which the British won. With the fall of Quebec no further French resistance was possible on the American mainland. The British also, with superior naval power, occupied Guadeloupe and Martinique in the Caribbean and French slavetrading outposts in Africa.

The Seven Years' War, 1756-1763: In India

Both British and French interests meanwhile profited from disturbed conditions in India. As large as Europe without Russia, India was a congested country of impoverished masses, speaking hundreds of languages and following many religions and subreligions, the two greatest being the Hindu and the Muslim. Waves of invasion through the northwest frontier since 1001 C.E. had produced a Muslim Empire, whose capital was at Delhi and which for a time held jurisdiction over most of the country. These Muslim emperors were known as Great Moguls. The greatest was Akbar, who ruled from 1556 to 1605, built roads, reformed the taxes, patronized the arts, and attempted to minimize religious differences among his peoples. The Muslim artistic culture flourished for a time after Akbar. One of his successors, Shah Jehan (1628–1658), built the beautiful Taj Mahal near Agra and at Delhi built the delicately carved alabaster palace of the Moguls, in which he placed the Peacock Throne made of solid gold and studded with gems.

Religious and political upheaval in India

But meanwhile there was restless opposition among the Hindus. The Sikhs, who had originated in the fifteenth century as a reform movement in Hinduism, went to war with the Mogul emperor in the seventeenth century. They became one of the most ferociously warlike of Indian peoples. Hindu princes in central India meanwhile formed a "Mahratta confederacy" against the Muslim emperor at Delhi. Matters were made worse when Aurungzeb, the last significant Mogul emperor (1658–1707), adopted repressive measures against the Hindus. After Aurungzeb, India fell into a political dissolution that made the country vulnerable to both internal rebellions and new interventions from the increasingly assertive Europeans. Many of the modern princely states originated or became autonomous at this time. Hindu princes rebelled against the Mogul. Muslims, beginning as governors or commanders under the Mogul, set up as rulers in their own right. Thus originated Hyderabad, which included the fabulous diamond mines of Golconda and whose ruler long was called the wealthiest man in the world. Princes and would-be princes fought with each other and with the emperor.

The situation in India resembled, on a larger and more multicultural scale, what had happened in early modern Europe in the Holy Roman Empire, where irreconcilable religious differences (of Catholics and Protestants) had also torn the country asunder, ambitious princes and city-states had won a chaotic independence, and foreign armies appeared repeatedly as invaders. India, like central Europe, suffered chronically from war, intrigue, and rival pretensions to territory; and in India, as in the Holy Roman Empire, outsiders and ambitious insiders benefited together.

The instability and violence in the interior had significant repercussions on the Indian coasts. Here handfuls of Europeans were established in the coastal cities. By the troubles in the interior the Indian authorities along the coasts were reduced, so to speak, to a size and power with which the Europeans could deal. The Europeans—British and French—were agents of their respective East India companies. These companies built forts, maintained soldiers, coined money, and entered into treaties with surrounding Indian powers, under charter of their home governments and with no one to deny them the exercise of such sovereign rights or political autonomy. Agents of the companies, like Indians themselves, ignored or respected the Mogul emperor as suited their own purpose. They were, at first, only one of the many contending forces in the flux and reflux of Indian affairs. Their presence in India showed the international reach of European companies, the worldwide competition between British and French interests, and the growing importance of India in the global economic system.

Intentions of the British and the French

Neither the British nor the French government, during the Seven Years' War, had any intention of territorial conquest in India, their policy in this respect differing radically from their colonial ambitions in America. Nor were the two trading companies pushing their agents toward imperialistic political interventions in South Asia. The company directors in London and Paris disapproved of fantastic schemes to intervene in Indian politics, insisted that their agents should attend to business only, and resented every penny and every sou not spent to bring in commercial profit. But it took a year or more to

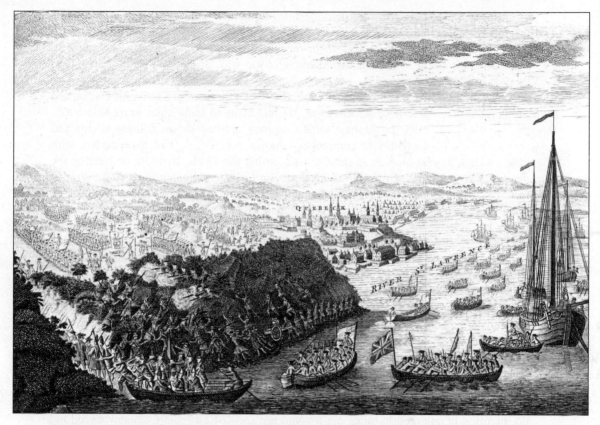

The battle of Quebec, depicted here in an English illustration of the British army's surprise approach to the Plains of Abraham, allowed Britain to gain control over most of North America and to increase its power in the expanding, global system of eighteenth-century trade.
(©MPI/Getty Images)

exchange messages between Europe and India, and company representatives in India, caught up in the Indian power struggles and overcome by the chance to make personal fortunes or by dreams of empire, acted very much on their own, committing their home offices without compunction. Involvement in Indian affairs was not exactly new. We have seen how "Diamond" Pitt, in 1702, purchased the goodwill of the local ruler of the Carnatic when he had threatened by military force to reduce the English traders at Madras (now Chennai) to submission.

The first European to exploit the possibilities of the changing situation in mid-eighteenth-century India was the Frenchman Joseph-François Dupleix, who believed that the funds sent out by the company in Paris to finance the Indian trade were insufficient. His idea seems to have been not empire-building but to make the company into a local territorial power in order that, from taxes and other political revenues, it might have more capital for its commercial operations. In any case, during the years of peace in Europe after 1748, Dupleix found himself with about 2,000 French troops in the Carnatic. He lent them out to neighboring local rulers in return for territorial concessions. He also began to drill Indian soldiers by European methods, thereby creating the first regiments of "sepoys"—Indian troops who served in the military forces of the European companies. Following a program of backing claimants to various Indian thrones, he built up a clientele of local rulers who now had specific obligations to Dupleix himself. He was very successful, for a small number of well-armed European troops or sepoys could overcome much larger, poorly armed Indian forces in pitched battle. But he was recalled to France in 1754, after his company became apprehensive of war with Britain and other trouble; and he died in disgrace.

British expansion in India

When war came in 1756, British interests in India were advanced chiefly by Robert Clive. He had come to India many years before as a clerk for the East India Company but had shown military talents and an ability to comprehend Indian politics. He had maneuvered, with little success, against Dupleix in the Carnatic during the 1740s. In 1756, on hearing the news of war in Europe, Clive shifted his attention to Bengal, hoping to drive the French from their trading stations there. The French were favored in Bengal by the local Muslim ruler, Suraja Dowla, who proceeded to anticipate Clive's arrival by expelling the British from Calcutta (the city now called Kolkata). Capturing the city, he shut up 146 Englishmen in a small room without windows—soon known in England as the "Black Hole of Calcutta"—and kept them there all night, during which most of them died of suffocation. Clive, soon arriving with a small force of British and sepoys, routed Suraja Dowla at the battle of Plassey in 1757. He put his own puppet on the Bengal throne and extorted huge reparations both for the company and for himself. Returning to England, he was received with mixed feelings; but he was given a new title (Baron Clive of Passy) and appointed the "governor" of Bengal. He strove in India to reduce the almost incredible corruption of company employees there, individuals who abandoned virtually all moral scruples to pursue irresistible chances for easy riches. Finally he committed suicide in 1774.

It was British sea power, more fundamentally than Clive's tactics, that assured the triumph of British over French ambitions in South Asia. The British government still had no intention of conquest in India, but it could not see its East India Company forced out by agents of the French company in collaboration with Indian princes. Naval forces were therefore dispatched to the Indian Ocean; and it was the British navy that made it possible for Clive to move quickly from Chennai to Kolkata. British ships also cut off the French posts in India from Europe and from each other. By the end of the war all the French establishments in India, as in Africa and America, were at the mercy of the British. The French overseas colonies lay prostrate, and France itself was again detached from the transoceanic trade on which much of its commercial economy rested. In 1761 France made an alliance with Spain, which was alarmed for the safety of its own American Empire after the British victories at Quebec and in the Caribbean. But the British also defeated Spain.

The Peace Settlement of 1763

The British navy and other armed forces had been spectacularly successful. Yet the peace treaty, signed at Paris in February 1763, five days before the Austro-Prussian peace of Hubertusburg, was by no means unfavorable to the defeated. The French Duke of Choiseul was a skillful and single-minded negotiator. The British, Pitt having fallen from office in 1761, were represented by a confused group of parliamentary favorites of the new king,

French concessions

George III. France ceded to Britain all French territory on the North American mainland east of the Mississippi. Canada thereby became British, and the European settlers in Britain's other thirteen mainland colonies were relieved of the French presence beyond the Alleghenies. To Spain, in return for aid in the last days of the war, France ceded all holdings west of the Mississippi and

Britain's imperial role in late eighteenth-century India is represented in this Indian miniature of a British officer's wife surrounded by Indian servants. The social hierarchies within the growing empire appear in this scene of domestic order and wealth, which dates from about 1785.
(©Werner Forman/Getty Images)

at its mouth, including New Orleans. France thereby virtually abandoned the North American continent. But these regions were still of minor commercial importance for European trading companies, and the French, in return for surrendering them, retained many economically more valuable establishments elsewhere. In the West Indies the British planters, and in England the powerful "West India interest," feared competition from the French sugar islands and wanted to exclude them from the protected economic system of the British Empire. France therefore received back Guadeloupe and Martinique, as well as most of its slavetrading stations in Africa; and the French still controlled the highly lucrative sugar plantations in Saint-Domingue (Santo Domingo). In India, the French remained in possession of their commercial installations—offices, warehouses, and docks— at Pondicherry (now Puducherry) and other cities. They were forbidden to erect fortifications or pursue political ambitions among Indian princes—a practice which neither the French nor the British government had hitherto much favored in any case.

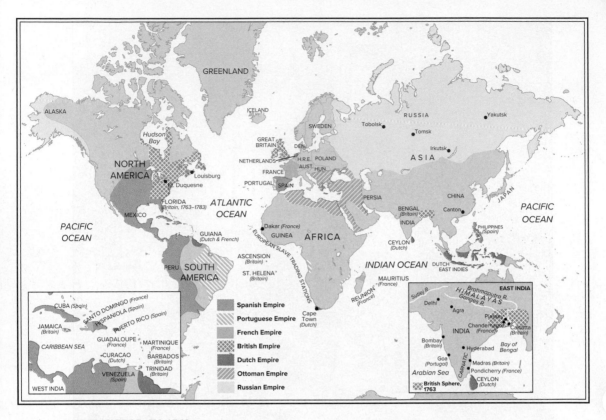

THE WORLD IN 1763

At the Peace of Paris of 1763 the British overseas empire triumphed over the French. The French ceded their holdings on the North American mainland east of the Mississippi to Britain, those west of the Mississippi to Spain. Britain also took Florida from Spain in 1763, but lost it, returning it to Spain in 1783, at the close of the War of American Independence. The French retained their sugar islands in the West Indies and their trading stations in India; they were stopped from empire-building but did not greatly suffer commercially from the Seven Years' War. The British proceeded to build their empire in India.

The treaties of Paris and Hubertusburg, closing the prolonged war of the midcentury, made the year 1763 a memorable turning point. Prussia confirmed its status as an emerging major power, which meant that the dualism of political power in Germany would continue. Austria and Prussia eyed each other as rivals.

Results of Seven Years War

Frederick's aggressive occupation of Silesia in 1740 was legalized and even given a new moral status in Prussia by the heroic defense that had proved necessary to retain the plunder. Frederick himself, from 1763 until his death in 1786, was a man of peace, philosophical and even benign. But the German crucible had boiled, and out of it had come a Prussia even more disposed by its escape from annihilation to glorify its army as the steel framework of its life.

The Anglo-French settlement was far-reaching and rather curious. Although the British won decisive victories everywhere in the global war, the French suffered more from political and military anxieties about imperial decline than from any kind of commercial calamity. French trade with America and Asia continued to grow as rapidly after the Seven Years' War as before it, and by 1785 it was double what it had been in 1755. For England the war also opened up new commercial channels. British trade with America and Asia probably tripled between 1755 and 1785. But the outstanding British gains were imperial and strategic. The European balance of power was preserved, the French had been kept out of the southern Netherlands, British colonial subjects in North America seemed secure, and Britain had again vindicated its command of the sea. British sea power implied, in turn, that British sea-borne commerce was safe in peace or war, while the seaborne commerce for the French, or of any others, depended ultimately on the political requirements of the British. But the French still had a few cards to play, and they would soon play them in the American and French revolutions.

For America and India the peace of 1763 was decisive in pushing the peoples of these two vast territories toward closer connections with the political and commercial institutions of the British Empire. America north of Mexico was to become part of an English-speaking world. In India the British govern- *Repercussions of* ment was drawn increasingly into a policy of territorial occupation; a *the settlement* British "paramount power" eventually emerged in place of the empire of the Moguls. British political rule in India stimulated and protected British business there, until in the greatest days of British prosperity India was one of the main pillars of the British economic system, and the road to India became in a real sense the lifeline of the British empire. But in 1763 this state of affairs was still in the future and was to be reached by many intermediate steps.

Suggested Further Readings can be found in the ebook, on Connect, or online at www.mhhe .com/kramer12e.

Chapter 8

THE AGE OF ENLIGHTENMENT

The eighteenth century, or at least the years of that century preceding the French Revolution of 1789, is commonly known in European history as the Age of Enlightenment. This broad term may simplify or distort the era's complex currents of cultural and political change, but no other name describes so many features of the time so well. Many Europeans strongly believed that they were living in a new, more enlightened age, and it is from their own evaluation of themselves that our term Age of Enlightenment is derived. Everywhere there was a feeling that Europeans had at last emerged from a long cultural twilight. The past was generally regarded as a time of barbarism or darkness in which people knew much less about the laws of nature and the value of rational analysis. The sense of progress was all but universal among the educated classes. It was the belief both of the forward-looking thinkers and writers known as the philosophes and of the forward-looking monarchs, the "enlightened despots," together with their ministers and officials.

The leading ideas of the Enlightenment—optimistic beliefs in the historical advance of reason, science, education, social reform, tolerance, and enlightened government—have been constant themes in the modern world. The Enlightenment, in short, remains a dynamic tradition in cultural and political life. Intellectual debates since the eighteenth century have almost always returned, explicitly or implicitly, to questions about the validity and legacy of Enlightenment conceptions of truth, knowledge, and progress. The Enlightenment has often been challenged or condemned by influential cultural movements (for example, romanticism, postmodernism, new or resurgent religions) and by modern political ideologies (for example, fascism, ethnic nationalisms). Yet the vehemence of its modern critics confirms the Enlightenment's exceptional, enduring importance in the cultures and politics of modern societies.

Chapter emblem: Detail from a portrait of Jean-Jacques Rousseau by David Martin (1737–1797) after Allan Ramsay (1713–1784). (National Gallery of Art)

Eighteenth-century critiques of existing regimes and cultural traditions drew increasingly on the ideas of the Enlightenment; indeed, such ideas were contributing by the end of the century to explosive political revolutions in America and Europe. In later centuries, Enlightenment ideas continued to generate opposition to unpopular governments or dominant cultural ideologies or hierarchical social systems, but the Enlightenment was also condemned in many cultures. For its advocates and critics alike, however, the "Age of Enlightenment" has always represented a decisive historical moment and cultural force in the development of "modernity."

35. THE PHILOSOPHES AND THE IDEAS OF ENLIGHTENMENT CULTURE

The Spirit of Progress and Improvement

The spirit of the eighteenth-century Enlightenment was drawn from the scientific and intellectual revolution of the seventeenth century. The Enlightenment carried over and popularized the ideas of Bacon and Descartes, of Bayle and Spinoza, and, above all, of Locke and Newton. It carried over the philosophy of natural law and of natural right. There had never been an age in which Europeans were so skeptical toward tradition, so confident in the powers of human reason and of science, so firmly convinced of the regularity and harmony of nature, and so deeply imbued with the sense of civilization's advance and progress.

Faith in progress

The idea of progress has often been described as the dominant or characteristic idea of European civilization in the modern era, or since the late seventeenth century. It is a belief, a kind of nonreligious faith, that the conditions of human life become better as time goes on, that in general each generation is better off than its predecessors and will contribute by its labor to an even better life for generations to come, and that in the long run all humankind will share in the same advance. All the elements of this belief had been present by 1700. It was after 1700, however, that the idea of progress became explicit. In the seventeenth century it had shown itself in a more rudimentary way in the sporadic intellectual dispute in England and France known as the quarrel of Ancients and Moderns (which, as noted earlier, also became part of the challenge to official theorists in Louis XIV's academies). The Ancients held that the works of the Greeks and Romans had never been surpassed. The Moderns, pointing to science, art, literature, and invention, declared that their own time was the best, that it was natural for people of their time to do better than the ancients because they came later and built upon their predecessors' achievements. The quarrel was never exactly settled, but a great many people in 1700 were Moderns.

Far-reaching also was the growing faith in the natural faculties of the human mind. Extreme skepticism, but not a skeptical outlook, was rejected. Educated persons in the eighteenth century were less likely to be superstitious, terrified by the unknown, or addicted to magic. The witchcraft mania abruptly died. Indeed all sense of the supernatural became dim for many Europeans. "Modern" people not only ceased to fear the devil but also to fear God. They thought of God less as a Father than as a First Cause of the physical universe. There was less sense of a personal God, or of the inscrutable imminence of divine Providence, or of the human need for saving grace. God was less the God of Love than the inconceivably intelligent Being who had made the amazing universe now discovered by human reason. The great symbol of the Christian God was the Cross, on which a divine being had suffered in human form. The symbol of divinity that occurred to people of scientific view was the Watchmaker. The intricacies of the physical universe were compared to the intricacies of a watch, and it was argued that just as a watch could not exist without a watchmaker, so the universe as discovered by Newton could not exist without a God who created it and set it moving by its mathematical laws. Among scientific-minded Europeans, "divine power" increasingly came to mean a kind of almighty intelligence.

Of course not everyone was primarily moved by such ideas. The first half of the eighteenth century was in fact also a time of continuing religious fervor, and new religious movements attracted deeply committed adherents throughout the whole century. Isaac Watts wrote many hymns that are still familiar in *Religious fervor* English-speaking churches; the great church music of J. S. Bach was *and Pietism* composed mainly in the 1720s; Handel's oratorio, *The Messiah,* was first performed in 1741; and it was at about this time that congregations first sang the *Adeste fideles* ("O Come, All Ye Faithful"), originally Catholic in inspiration but soon adopted by Protestants also. The Lutherans of Germany were stirred by the movement known as Pietism, which stressed the inner spiritual experience of ordinary persons as distinct from the doctrines taught and debated in theological faculties. The quest for an "inner light," or illumination of the soul rather than of the reason, was somewhat contrary to the main rationalist thrust of the Age of Enlightenment. A religious urge for improvement of the individual rather than of social institutions was hardly central to the main ideas of most Enlightenment-era thinkers, but such ideas were by no means merely conservative, for they were in general highly critical of the existing order.

Within the Church of England John Wesley, while a student at Oxford, joined a group of like-minded young men for prayer and med- *John Wesley and* itation. They engaged in good works to relieve the sufferings of prisoners *Methodism* and the poor, to whom they distributed food and clothing, while also teaching them how to read. Going outside the restrictive system of parishes, Wesley and others took to itinerant preaching, often to immense crowds in open fields. Wesley is said to have traveled 250,000 miles within Great Britain over a period of 50 years. He and George Whitfield, who shared his views, preached also in the English American colonies, where they helped to arouse the Great Awakening of the 1740s. Wesley contributed to a new popular understanding of natural rights and to a growing religious denunciation of the slave trade. Methodism and other such religious movements had a democratizing effect in stressing individual worth and spiritual consciousness independently of the established religious authorities. Indeed, the spokesmen for older churches dismissed such movements as "enthusiasm," which was then a word of reproach. By the time he died in 1791, Wesley had about half a million followers in what were called Methodist societies. Wesley himself tried to keep them within the Church of England, but separate Methodist churches were already founded in England and the United States.

In a way these expressions of religious feeling reflected differences between the popular and elite cultures that have already been described. While some of the elite joined in the new movements, it was on the whole the less comfortable social classes who did so. The official churches, Anglican, Lutheran, Catholic, did not wish to be disturbed by religious revivalism. Bishops were cultivated gentlemen of the age. But the most vehement intellectual leaders pushed churches and theological traditions aside as they promoted the progressive uses of human reason.

The science and new learning in this "age of reason," however, did not end the popular interest in magic or mystification. A Swiss pastor, J. C. Lavater, attracted attention with his supposed science of "physiognomy," by which a person's character could be read

John Wesley became the inspired leader of Methodism, a new religious movement in eighteenth-century England that attracted wide popular support, encouraged personal spiritual awakening, and condemned social injustices such as slavery. This image of Wesley preaching in 1742 shows how he read from the Bible at his religious services and how women participated very actively in the Methodist movement.
(Library of Congress, Prints & Photographs Division, Reproduction number LC-DIG-pga-09226 (digital file from original item) LC-USZC2-2716 (color film copy slide))

in the play of the facial features. An Austrian physician, F. A. Mesmer, created a stir in Paris by arranging séances where people were touched by a wand, or sat in tubs, to receive "animal magnetism" in the hope of curing various ills. His "mesmerism" was an early stage in the discovery of hypnosis, but it is significant that a committee of the Royal Academy of Sciences, after investigation, concluded that Mesmer's own theories to explain these strange phenomena were without foundation.

Freemasonry

More in the mainstream of the new intellectual culture was Freemasonry, which took form in England and soon spread to the Continent. The Masons were generally persons who held typical Enlightenment ideas, well disposed toward reason, progress, toleration, and humane reforms, and respectful toward God as architect of the universe; but they met secretly in lodges, in an atmosphere of mysterious rituals and occult knowledge. Men of all walks of life, nobles, clergy, and middle classes, belonged to the lodges (a few also allowed women to join). Freemasonry thus had the effect of bringing together persons of different social classes and religious views for self-improvement and the improvement of others. It aroused suspicion, however, because of its secrecy; and a small deviant offshoot, the Illuminati of south Germany, was considered so dangerous that the Bavarian government suppressed it in 1786. There were later some who insisted that the French Revolution had been caused by a secret conspiracy of Illuminati, philosophes, and other clandestine plotters, but this idea was never any more than the belief of a few frightened conservative critics. The word

Illuminati meant "the enlightened ones," but the notion of secrecy was foreign to the Enlightenment, which relied above all else on publicity and the reading public.

The Philosophes

Philosophe is simply French for philosopher, but to be "philosophical" in the eighteenth century meant to approach any subject in a critical and inquiring spirit. The French word is used in English to denote a group of writers who were not philosophers in the sense of treating ultimate questions of knowledge or existence. They were social or literary critics, popularizers, and publicists. Most philosophes were men, but many women also participated in Enlightenment culture. The French writer Emilie du Châtelet, for example, translated Newton and explained the significance of the new theories in her scientific essays. Though often learned, the philosophes wrote to gain attention, and it was the philosophes who spread the ideas of the Enlightenment across Europe and the Atlantic world. Formerly authors had generally been persons of leisure, or talented protégés of aristocratic or royal patrons, or professors or clerics supported by the income from religious foundations. In the Age of Enlightenment a great many were freelancers, grubstreeters, or journalists. They wrote for "the publick."

The reading public had greatly expanded; by the 1780s in France, literacy rates had risen to 47 percent among men and 27 percent among women. The educated middle class, commercial and professional, was *The reading public* much larger than ever before. Women readers formed a growing audience for novels and literary journals, country gentlemen sought new scientific advice on agriculture, and even noblemen wished to keep informed. Newspapers and magazines multiplied, and people who could not read them at home could read them in coffeehouses or in reading rooms organized for that purpose. There was a great demand also for dictionaries, encyclopedias, and surveys of all fields of knowledge. The new readers wanted matters made interesting and clear. They appreciated wit and lightness of touch. From such a public, literature itself greatly benefited.

The style of the eighteenth century became admirably fluent, clear, and exact, neither ponderous on the one hand nor frothy on the other. Such writings attracted new readers in every country, from the interior of Europe to the America of Benjamin Franklin. People began to talk of "public opinion" as a kind of critical tribunal that judged the significance of new books and established or destroyed the reputations of ambitious authors. This new public opinion, the French writer Malesherbes explained, was an independent social force "that all powers respect, that appreciates all talents, that pronounces on all people of merit." Critical reviews of literature, art, and music provoked debates in newspapers, journals, and coffeehouses, all of which contributed to an expanding public sphere beyond the personal world of private households and outside the official world of government institutions. The bourgeois middle class was becoming not only educated but also thoughtful and critical. But the expanding public sphere was not limited to the ideas or cultural preoccupations of a single social class.

The writings of the day were nevertheless affected by social conditions and by the cultural context that constrained their publication. They were all written under censorship. The theory of censorship was to protect people from harmful ideas as they were protected from shoddy merchandise or dishonest weights and *Censorship* measures. In England the censorship was so mild as to have little effect. Other countries, such as Spain, had a powerful censorship. France, the center of the Enlightenment, had both a complicated censorship and a large reading and writing public.

The church, the Parlement of Paris, the royal officials, and the printers' guilds all had a hand in the censoring of books. French censorship, however, was loosely administered, and after 1750 writers were little disturbed by it. It cannot be compared to the repressive censorship of more recent authoritarian governments. Yet in one way it had an unfavorable effect on French thought and letters. It discouraged writers from openly or explicitly addressing concrete public questions. Legally forbidden to criticize church or state, they threw their criticisms on a more abstract level. Barred from attacking matters in particular, they tended to attack matters in general. Or they talked of the customs of the Persians and the Iroquois but not the French. Their works became full of double meanings, sly digs, innuendoes, and jokes by which authors, if questioned, could declare that they did not mean what all the world knew they did mean. As for readers, they developed a taste for forbidden books, which were always easy enough to obtain through illicit channels and foreign booksellers.

Paris: the heart of the Enlightenment

Paris was the heart of the movement. Here, in the town houses of the well-to-do, literary and social celebrities gathered for literate conversation. It might occasionally happen that a notable philosophe was also wealthy; such was the case of Helvétius, who not only wrote books *On the Mind* and *On Man* but also gave grand entertainments at which such matters were discussed. Mainly, however, this mingling of people and ideas went on in salons conducted by women who became famous as hostesses, or salonnières, and who played a crucial mediating role in what came to be called the "Republic of Letters." Madame de Geoffrin, for example, for a period of 25 years beginning about 1750, organized conversations of artists and writers at dinner, sometimes helped them financially, and introduced them to persons of influence in high society or in government. She welcomed visiting foreigners also, such as Horace Walpole and David Hume from England and young Stanislas Poniatowski before he became king of Poland. Because other women held similar salons, philosophes and other writers had frequent opportunity to meet and exchange ideas.

Salons became well-organized meeting places at which authors introduced new works to critical readers, salonnières read letters from travelers or distant correspondents, and lively conversation spread the reputations of aspiring philosophes. The leading salonnières gave careful attention to the intellectual themes and social continuities of their salons. Suzanne Necker, whose salon met on Friday afternoons during the 1770s and 1780s, prepared for her weekly conversations by listing in her journal the ideas and books that

Women and salons

she wanted to discuss. Julie de Lespinasse provided opportunities for almost constant discussion at her Parisian home, where she received visitors every evening of the week for 12 years. "Her great art," wrote one admirer, "was to show to advantage the minds of others, and she enjoyed doing that more than revealing her own." Salons and salonnières promoted the ideals of a cosmopolitan Republic of Letters in which talent and creativity counted for more than noble lineage; and though women lost much of their cultural influence after the 1780s, some salons of this kind survived the Revolution. In 1795, after the Terror, the widows of two eminent philosophes, Helvétius and Condorcet, opened or reopened their salons in Paris for people of moderate republican or liberal sentiments. Sophie Condorcet became a writer herself and a translator of Adam Smith. Her salon remained a center of liberal opposition during the years of Napoleon. More short-lived was the salon of the even more famous Germaine de Staël, who also wrote widely read books and who, among her many other ideas, deplored the subordination of women that the Revolution had done little to change. These post-Revolutionary salons became social-cultural meeting places in which much of France's nineteenth-century liberalism would begin to emerge.

In Paris also, in the mid-eighteenth century, the most serious of all philosophe enterprises, the *Encyclopédie,* was published in 17 large volumes and completed over the years 1751 to 1772. Edited by Denis Diderot, it was a great compendium of scientific, technical, and histor-

Diderot's Encyclopédie

ical knowledge, carrying a strong undertone of criticism of existing society and institutions and epitomizing the skeptical, rational, and scientific spirit of the age. It was not the first encyclopedia, but it was the first to have a distinguished list of contributors or to be conceived as a positive force for social progress. Virtually all the French philosophes contributed—Voltaire, Montesquieu, Rousseau, d'Alembert (who assisted in the editing), Buffon, Turgot, Quesnay, and many others, all sometimes collectively called the Encyclopedists. Although edited in Paris, the *Encyclopédie* became very widely known and read. About 25,000 multivolumed sets were sold before the Revolution, about half of them outside France, because French had become an international language understood by educated persons all over Europe. Within France itself the *Encyclopédie* was read in all parts of the country and in the most influential ranks of society. At Besançon, for example, a city of about 28,000 inhabitants, 137 sets were sold to local residents, of whom 15

A READING OF VOLTAIRE'S TRAGEDY *L'ORPHELINE DE LA CHINE* IN THE SALON OF MADAME GEOFFRIN

by Anicet Charles Gabriel Lenommier (French, 1743–1824)

The salon of Madame de Geoffrin, depicted here by the artist Lemonnier, became one of the best-known meeting places for writers and artists in mid-eighteenth-century Paris. This imagined scene of someone reading from a work by Voltaire was painted early in the following century, but it shows the social style and enduring cultural reputation of famous salons and salonnières.

(©Heritage Images/Getty Images)

were members of the clergy, 53 were of the nobility, and 69 were lawyers, doctors, merchants, government officials, or others of what was called the Third Estate. The privileged groups whom the Encyclopedists most often criticized, that is, the clergy and the nobility, read the *Encyclopédie* or at least purchased it far out of proportion to their numbers in the population as a whole.

Men and women who considered themselves philosophes, or close to the philosophes in spirit, were found all over Europe. Frederick the Great was an eminent philosophe; not only was he the friend of Voltaire and host to a circle of literary and scientific men at Potsdam, but he also wrote epigrams, satires, and histories, as well as works on military science; and he had a gift of wit, a sharp tongue, and a certain impishness toward the traditional and the pompous. Catherine the Great, empress of Russia, was also a philosophe for much the same reason. Maria Theresa, of Austria, was not a philosophe; she was too religious and too little concerned with general ideas. Her son Joseph, on the other hand, as we shall see, proved to be virtually a philosophe enthroned. In England Bishop Warburton was considered by some of his friends as a philosophe; he held that the Church of England of his day, as a social institution, was exactly what pure reason would have invented. The Scottish skeptical philosopher David Hume also counted as a philosophe, as did Edward Gibbon, who shocked the pious by his attacks on Christianity in his famous *Decline and Fall of the Roman Empire.* Dr. Samuel Johnson was not a philosophe, though he was best known for a typical eighteenth-century project—the compilation of a new dictionary of the English language. Johnson worried over the supernatural, adhered to the established church, deflated pretentious authors, and even declared that Voltaire and Rousseau were evil men who should be sent "to the plantations." There were also Italian and German philosophes, like the Marquis di Beccaria, who condemned torture and sought to humanize the criminal law, or Baron Grimm, who sent a literary newsletter from Paris to his many subscribers.

Montesquieu, Voltaire, and Rousseau

Most famous of all philosophes were the French trio Montesquieu (1689-1755), Voltaire (1694-1778), and Rousseau (1712-1778). They differed vehemently with each other, but all were hailed as literary geniuses in their own day. All turned from pure literature to works of political commentary and social analysis. All thought that the existing state of society could be improved.

Montesquieu was a landed aristocrat, a seigneur or manorial lord in southwestern France. He inherited from his uncle a seat in the Parlement of Bordeaux and participated actively in that parlement after the death of Louis XIV. He was part of the noble resurgence that began about 1715 and continued on through the eighteenth century. Although he shared many of the ideas in the stream of aristocratic and antiabsolutist thought, he went beyond a mere self-centered class philosophy. In his great work, *The Spirit of Laws,*

Montesquieu's The Spirit of Laws published in 1748, he developed two principal ideas. One of his political arguments asserted that forms of government varied according to climate and circumstances. He claimed, for example, that despotism was suited to large empires in hot climates, and that democracy would work only in small city-states. His other great doctrine, aimed against royal absolutism in France (which he called "despotism"), strongly affirmed the need for a separation and balance of political powers. In France he believed that power should be divided between the king and a great many "intermediate bodies"—parlements, provincial estates, organized nobility,

This portrait of Voltaire (c. 1736) by Maurice-Quentin de La Tour suggests the playful, ironic style that made his works accessible and popular, even when he was attacking religious persecutions or the suppression of controversial ideas.
(©Photo 12/Getty Images)

chartered towns, and even the church. His position as a judge in parlement, a provincial, and a nobleman gave him good reasons to favor the first three, and his work in Bordeaux helped him to recognize the importance of the bourgeoisie in French towns; as for the church, he observed that, while he took no stock in its teachings, he thought it useful as a barrier to undue centralization of government. He greatly admired the English constitution as he understood it, believing that England carried over, more successfully than any other country, the feudal liberties of the early Middle Ages. He thought that in England the necessary separation and balance of powers was obtained by an ingenious mixture of monarchy, aristocracy, and democracy (king, lords, and commons) and by a separation of the functions of the executive, legislature, and judiciary. This doctrine had a wide influence in Europe and was also well known to the Americans who in 1787 wrote the Constitution of the United States. Montesquieu's own philosophe friends thought him too conservative and even tried to dissuade him from publishing his ideas. He was, indeed, technically a reactionary, favoring a scheme of things that antedated Louis XIV, and he was unusual among contemporaries in his admiration of the "barbarous" Middle Ages.

Voltaire was born in 1694 into a comfortable bourgeois family and christened François-Marie Arouet; "Voltaire," an invented name, is simply the most famous of all eighteenth-century pen names. Until he was over 40 he was known only as a clever writer of epigrams, tragedies in verse, and an epic. Thereafter he turned increasingly to philosophical and public questions. His strength throughout lay in the facility of his pen. He is the easiest of all great writers to read. He was always trenchant, logical, and incisive, sometimes

Voltaire and freedom of thought

scurrilous; mocking and sarcastic when he wished to be, equally a master of deft irony and of withering ridicule. However serious in his purpose, he achieved it by getting his readers to laugh.

In his youth Voltaire spent 11 months in the Bastille for what was considered to be impertinence to the Regent, who, however, in the next year rewarded him with a pension for one of his dramas. He was again arrested after a fracas with a nobleman, the Chevalier de Rohan, but he moved to England to avoid another imprisonment. He remained an incorrigible bourgeois, while never deeply objecting to the aristocracy on principle. Through his admirer Mme. de Pompadour (another bourgeois, though the king's favorite) he later became a gentleman of the bedchamber and royal historian to Louis XV. These functions he fulfilled *in absentia,* when at all, for Paris and Versailles were too unsafe for him. He was the personal friend of Frederick the Great, in whose household he lived for about two years at Potsdam. The two finally quarreled, for no stage was big enough to hold two such prima donnas for long. Voltaire made a fortune from his writings, pensions, speculations, and practical business sense. In his later years he purchased a manor at Ferney near the Swiss frontier. Here he became, as he said, the "hotel keeper of Europe," receiving the streams of distinguished admirers, favor hunters, and distressed persons who came to seek him out. He died at Paris in 1778, at the age of 84, by far the most famous man of letters in Europe. His collected writings fill over 70 volumes.

Voltaire was mainly interested in the freedom of thought. Like Montesquieu, he was an admirer of England. He spent three years in that country, where, in 1727, he witnessed the state funeral accorded to Sir Isaac Newton and his burial in Westminster Abbey. Voltaire's *Philosophical Letters on the English* (1733) and *Elements of the Philosophy of Newton* (1738) not only brought England increasingly before the consciousness of the rest of Europe but also popularized the new scientific ideas—the inductive philosophy of Bacon, the physics of Newton, and the psychology of Locke, whose doctrine that all true ideas arose from sense experience undercut the authority of religious belief. What Voltaire mainly admired in England was its religious liberty, its tolerance for diverse ideas and scientific inquiry, its relative freedom of the press, and its respect for men of letters like himself. Political liberty concerned him much less than it did Montesquieu. Louis XIV, whom Montesquieu and the neoaristocratic school viewed critically as the enemy of traditional liberties, was a hero for Voltaire. In opposition to the aristocratic critics, he wrote a laudatory *Age of Louis XIV* (1751), praising the Sun King for the splendor of art and literature in his reign. Voltaire likewise continued to respect the policies of Frederick the Great, though he quarreled with him personally. Frederick was in fact almost his ideal of the enlightened ruler, a man who sponsored the arts and sciences, recognized no religious authority, and granted toleration to all creeds, welcoming Protestants and Catholics on equal terms if only they would be socially useful.

After about 1740 Voltaire became more definitely the crusader, preaching the cause of religious toleration. He fought to clear the memory of Jean Calas, a Protestant who was tortured and put to death on the false charge of murdering a son to prevent his conversion to Catholicism. He wrote also to exonerate a youth named La Barre, who had been executed for defiling a wayside cross. *Écrasez l'infâme!* became the famous Voltairean war cry—"crush the infamous thing!" The *infâme* for him was bigotry, intolerance, and superstition and behind these the power of an organized clergy. He assaulted not only the Catholic Church but the whole traditional Christian view of the world as well. He argued for "natural religion" and "natural morality," holding that belief in God and the difference between good and evil arose from reason itself. This doctrine had in fact long been taught by the Catholic Church. But Voltaire insisted that no supernatural revelation

Historical Documents
Voltaire, *Letters on England* (1733)

Most eighteenth-century European philosophes believed that human societies could be improved when people drew upon reason and scientific knowledge to reform their social, political, and cultural institutions. They also argued for more tolerance of religious differences and for intellectual freedom. The French writer Voltaire (1694-1778), who lived as an exile in England for three years in the late 1720s, wrote an influential account of English culture that emphasized all of these themes and helped to shape the cultural aspirations of the philosophes. These excerpts from Voltaire's famous book suggest how his idealized descriptions of England became a literary strategy for promoting social reforms and religious tolerance in France.

Go into the London Stock Exchange . . . and you will see representatives from all nations gathered together for the utility of men. Here Jew, Mohammedan and Christian deal with each other as though they were all of the same faith, and only apply the word infidel to people who go bankrupt. . . .

If there were only one religion in England there would be danger of despotism, if there were two they would cut each other's throats, but there are thirty, and they live in peace and happiness. . . .

In England as a rule people think, and literature is more honored than in France. This advantage is a natural outcome of the form of their government. In London there are some eight hundred people with the right to speak in public and uphold the interests of the nation; about five or six thousand aspire to the same honour in their turn, all the rest set themselves up in judgement on these, and anybody can print what he thinks about public affairs. So the whole nation is obliged to study.

Voltaire, *Letters on England*, translated and with an introduction by Leonard Tancock (London: Penguin Books Ltd., 1980), pp. 41, 101.

was desirable or necessary because reason alone revealed essential truths and good human actions; belief in a special supernatural revelation, he argued, made people intolerant, stupid, and cruel.

Voltaire was also the first to present a purely secular conception of world history. In his *Essai sur les moeurs,* or "Universal History," he began with ancient China and surveyed the great civilizations in turn. Earlier writers of world history had put human events within a Christian framework. Following the Bible, they began with the Creation, proceeded to the Fall, recounted the rise of Israel, and so on. Voltaire put Judeo-Christian history within a much broader world history and placed religious thought in a sociological framework. He represented Christianity and all other organized religions as social phenomena or mere human inventions. Spinoza had said as much; Voltaire's engaging literary style helped to spread these ideas through Europe.

In matters of politics and self-government Voltaire was neither a liberal nor a democrat. His opinion of the human race was about as low as his friend Frederick's. If only a government was enlightened, he

Voltaire on politics

did not care how powerful it was. By an enlightened government he meant one that fought against sloth and stupidity, kept the clergy in a subordinate place, allowed freedom of thought and religion, encouraged the development of reason and science, and advanced the cause of material and technical progress. He had no developed political theory, but his ideal for large civilized countries approached that of enlightened or rational despotism. Believing that only a few could be enlightened, he thought that rational elites and kings should have the power to carry out their program against all opposition. To overcome ignorance, credulity, and priestcraft it was necessary for the state to be strong. What Voltaire most desired was liberty for the enlightened, or for people like himself.

Jean-Jacques Rousseau

Jean-Jacques Rousseau was very different. Born in Geneva in 1712, he was a Swiss, a Protestant, and almost of lower-class origin. He never felt at ease in France or in Parisian society. His mother died a few days after his birth, and he was neglected as a child. Running away from Geneva at age 16, he lived for years by odd jobs, such as copying music, and not until the age of 40 did he have any success as a writer. He was intellectually ambitious, but he viewed himself always as a social outsider. In addition, his personal relations with women were difficult and unstable; he finally settled down with an uneducated woman named Thérèse Levasseur and her mother. By Thérèse he had five children, all of whom he deposited at an orphanage. He had no social status, no money, and no sense of money, and after he became famous he lived largely by the generosity of his friends. He was pathetically and painfully maladjusted. He came to feel that he could trust no one, that those who tried to befriend him were deriding or betraying him behind his back. He condemned the cultural influence of French women, criticizing especially their prominent role in Parisian salons ("they do not know anything, although they judge everything"). He suffered from what would now be termed psychological complexes; possibly he was paranoid. He talked endlessly of his own virtue and innocence and complained bitterly that he was misunderstood.

But unbalanced though he was, he was possibly the most profound writer of the age and was certainly the most permanently influential. Rousseau felt, from his own experience, that in society as it existed a good person could not be happy. He therefore attacked society, declaring that it was artificial and corrupt. He even attacked reason, calling it a false guide when followed without feelings or emotions. He felt doubts about the social and cultural progress that gave satisfaction to his contemporaries. In

Rousseau's "discourses"

two "discourses," one on the *Arts and Sciences* (1750), the other on the *Origin of Inequality among Men* (1753), he argued that civilization was the source of much evil and that life in a "state of nature," were it only possible, would be much freer; and all people in such conditions would be far more equal. As Voltaire said, when Rousseau sent him a copy of his second discourse (Voltaire who relished civilization in every form), it made him "feel like going on all fours." To Rousseau the best traits of human character, such as kindness, unselfishness, honesty, and true understanding between different persons, were products of nature rather than the social progress of modern civilizations. Deep below reason, he sensed the presence of feeling. He delighted in the warmth of sympathy, the quick flash of intuition, the clear message of conscience. He was religious by temperament, for though he believed in no church, no clergy, and no revelation, he had a respect for the Bible, a reverent awe toward the cosmos, a love of solitary meditation, and a belief in a God who was not merely a "first cause" but also a God of love and beauty. Rousseau thus made it easier for serious-minded people to slip away from orthodoxy and all forms of churchly discipline. He was feared by the churches as the most dangerous of all "infidels" and was condemned both in Catholic France and Protestant Geneva.

In general, in most of his books, Rousseau, unlike so many of his contemporaries, gave the impression that impulse is more reliable than considered judgment, spontaneous feeling more to be trusted than critical thought. Mystical insights were for him more truthful than rational or clear ideas. He became the "man of feeling," the "child of nature," the forerunner of the coming age of romanticism, and an important source of all modern emphasis on the nonrational and the subconscious. He thus became an early, influential critic of the Enlightenment, even as he resembled other philosophes in his desire to change the existing social order.

In *The Social Contract* (1762), however, Rousseau seemed to contradict much of his famous sentiment for nature and to argue for the value of a well-organized government. In this book he held, somewhat like Hobbes, that the state of nature was a brutish condition without law or morality. In other works he had held that human evil was due to the evils of society. He now held that good people could be produced only by an improved society. Earlier thinkers, such as John Locke, for example, had thought of the "contract" as an agreement between a ruler and a people. Rousseau thought of it as an agreement among the people themselves. It was a social, not merely a political, contract. Organized civil society, that is, the community, rested upon it. The social contract was an understanding by which all individuals surrendered their natural liberty to each other, fused their individual wills into a combined general will, and agreed to accept the rulings of this general will as final. This general will was the sovereign; and true sovereign power, rightly understood, was "absolute," "sacred," and "inviolable." He preferred republics, but government institutions were secondary; kings, officials, or elected representatives were only delegates of a sovereign people. Rousseau devoted many difficult pages to explaining how the *real* general will could be known. It was not necessarily determined by vote of a majority. "What generalizes the will," he said, "is not the number of voices but the common interest that unites them." He said little of the mechanism of government and had no admiration for parliamentary institutions. He was concerned with something deeper. Maladjusted outsider that he was, he craved a commonwealth in which every person could feel that he or she belonged. He wished a state in which all persons had a sense of membership and participation.

The Social Contract

By these ideas Rousseau made himself the prophet of both democracy and nationalism. Indeed, in his *Considerations on Poland,* written at the request of Poles who were fighting against the partitions of their nation's territories by foreign powers, Rousseau applied the ideas of the social contract in more concrete form and became the first systematic theorist of a conscious and calculated nationalism. In writing *The Social Contract* he had in mind a small republican city-state like his native Geneva. But what he did, in effect, was to generalize and make applicable to large territories the psychology of small city republics—the sense of membership, of community and fellowship, of responsible citizenship and intimate participation in public affairs—in short, of a common and collective will. All modern states, democratic or undemocratic, strive to impart this sense of moral solidarity to their peoples. Whereas in democratic states the general will can in some way be identified with the sovereignty of the people, in dictatorships it becomes possible for individuals (or parties) to arrogate to themselves the right to serve as spokesmen and interpreters of the general will. Both totalitarians and democrats have regarded Rousseau as one of their prophets.

Rousseau's influence on his contemporaries spread also through his other writings, especially his theories of education in, *Émile* (1762) and his popular novel, *Julie, or the New Héloïse* (1760). His novels were widely read in all literate classes of society, by men and especially by women, who found an emotional resonance in characters such as the ill-fated Julie, and who made a kind of cult of Jean-Jacques. He was a literary master, able to evoke shades of thought and feeling that few writers had touched before. His literary writings helped to spread in the highest circles a new respect for the common person, a love of common things, an impulse of human pity and compassion, and a sense of the artifice or superficiality in aristocratic life. Women took to nursing their own babies, as Rousseau said they should. Men began describing the delicacy of their sentiments. Tears became the fashion. The queen, Marie Antoinette, built herself a village in the gardens at Versailles, where she pretended to be a simple milkmaid. In all this there was much that was shallow or contrived or completely disconnected from the lives of people in a real peasant village. Yet this new interest in the lives of lower-class persons became the wellspring of modern humanitarianism, the force leading to a new sense of human equality. Rousseau estranged the French upper classes from their own mode of life. He made many of them lose faith in their own superiority. That was his main direct contribution to the French Revolution, even more significant than his political theories about the general will.

Political Economists

Physiocrats

In France, somewhat apart from the philosophes, were the Physiocrats, whom their critics called "economists," a word originally thought to be mildly insulting. Many of the Physiocrats, unlike the philosophes, were close to the government as administrators or advisers. Quesnay was physician to Louis XV, Turgot was an experienced official who became minister to Louis XVI, and Dupont de Nemours, an associate of Turgot's, became the founder of the industrial family of the Du Ponts in the United States. Such advisers concerned themselves with fiscal and tax reform and with measures to increase the national wealth of France. They argued that agriculture, grain production, and efficient uses of the land provided essential economic foundations for an expanding national commerce. Moving away from earlier mercantilist strategies for government control of trade, they opposed guild regulations and price controls as impediments to the production and circulation of goods. The Physiocrats were the first to use the term laissez-faire ("let them do as they see fit") as a principle of economic activity; and some proposed that even the grain trade should operate without government interventions—a politically risky proposal that no French king would ever accept. They favored strong government, however, relying on it to overcome traditional obstacles and to provide inducements for the establishment of new industries.

Economics, or what was long called political economy, arose from these activities of the Physiocrats, from the somewhat similar work of "cameralists" in the German states, and from the collection and analysis of quantitative data, that is, the birth of statistics. Political economy thus became another example of the belief that scientific methods should be used to understand human societies as well as nature. Economic thinking flourished especially in Great Britain, and notably in Scotland, where Adam Smith's *The Wealth of Nations* appeared in 1776. By 1800, *The Wealth of Nations* had been translated into every western European language except Portuguese.

Adam Smith

Adam Smith's purpose, like that of the French Physiocrats, was to increase the national wealth by the reduction of barriers that hindered its growth. He undercut the premises of what we have called "the struggle for wealth and empire," because he argued that to build up a nation's wealth it was unnecessary to have an empire. He attacked most of the program of mercantilism that had evolved since the sixteenth century, and he expected that Britain's American colonies would soon become independent without loss to British trade. Where others looked to planning by an enlightened government, Adam Smith preferred to limit the functions of

JEAN-JACQUES ROUSSEAU
by David Martin (Scottish 1737–
1797) after Allan Ramsay (Scottish,
1713–1784)

**Some hints of the complexities of
Rousseau's personality and thought
(including his desire for the clothing
of a "natural" man) appear in this
portrait by a Scottish artist who studied with the portrait painter Allan
Ramsay.**

(National Gallery of Art)

government to defense, internal security, and the provision of reasonable laws and fair
law courts by which private differences could be adjudicated. For innovation and enterprise he counted more on private persons than on the state. He became the philosopher
of the free market, the prophet of free trade. If there was a shortage of a given commodity,
its price would rise and so stimulate producers to produce more, while also attracting new
persons into that line of production. If there was an excess, if more was produced than
purchasers would buy, both capital and labor would withdraw and gradually move into
another area where demand was stronger. Demand would increase with lower prices,
which depended on lower costs, which in turn depended on the specialization or division
of labor. His most famous example was that of the pin factory of his time, where each of
a dozen workers engaged in only one part of the process of manufacture, so that together
they produced far more pins than if each worker produced whole pins; the price of pins
then fell, and more pins could be used by more people. The same principle held in international trade; some countries or climates could produce an article more cheaply than
others, so that if each specialized and then exchanged with the others, all would have
more. Each nation could use its comparative advantage in certain spheres of production
or trade to compensate for economic weaknesses in other spheres and also to increase
its national wealth.

The motivation for all such production and exchange was to be the self-interest of
the participants. As he said, we rely for our meat not on the goodwill of the butcher but
on his concern for his own income. To those who might object that this was a system of
selfishness Adam Smith would reply (being a professor of moral philosophy at the University of Glasgow) that a free market system was at least realistic, describing how people

Historical Interpretations and Debates
Social Institutions and Culture in the Age of Enlightenment

Historians have increasingly moved beyond the analysis of Enlightenment-era intellectual debates to examine the social contexts in which writers exchanged ideas or tried to build their literary reputations. The Parisian salons, which were organized and led by women called "salonnières," became important meeting places for the philosophes, but historians disagree about the salons' intellectual and social significance. Some view the salons as a key site for the intellectual exchanges of an evolving Republic of Letters; others argue that salons and salonnières brought people together (including writers) mainly for elite social leisure. Dena Goodman and Antoine Lilti develop these arguments in their opposing views of Enlightenment-era salon culture.

Dena Goodman, *The Republic of Letters: A Cultural History of the French Enlightenment* (1994)

The philosophes adopted the salons as a center for their Republic of Letters and respected the women who led them as governors because they provided the republic with a basis of order. . . .

The function of salonnières was to maintain order in the Republic of Letters by enforcing the rules of polite conversation. The rules, and thus the governors, were necessary because eighteenth-century French intellectual practice was both militant and personal. . . .

The Parisian salon, in which seventeenth-century men of letters had learned to participate in a discourse that cut across social lines, became for the philosophes the central institution of their republic. . . .

The salonnière had always been crucial to the functioning of the salon; now she became crucial to the project of Enlightenment carried out in and through it. . . .

Philosophes and salonnières agreed that the salonnière achieved success by balancing and blending voices into a harmonious whole. . . . [T]he salonnière brought order to the variety of views expressed by her guests. . . .

When the philosophes rejected the academy and the university as the institutional bases for their Republic of Letters and instead adopted the Parisian salon . . . they brought with them the mentality and practices learned during their initiation into the culture against which they were trying to rebel. Salonnières helped to save them from themselves.

Antoine Lilti, *The World of the Salons: Sociability and Worldliness in Eighteenth-Century Paris* (2015)

Dena Goodman . . . argues that eighteenth-century salons were the central institution of the republic of letters, ruled by women and devoted to the critical project of the Enlightenment. . . . For Goodman, the salons of the eighteenth-century had nothing in common with their predecessors of the age of Louis XIII and Louis XIV, . . . which were products of aristocratic leisure. In the eighteenth century they were serious places, devoted to intellectual debate, in which the rules of politeness and a discreet governance by *salonnières* constituted the social grounding for the Enlightenment republic of letters, using an ideal of egalitarian sociability. . . .

However, using the notion of the republic of letters to think about the salons is misguided because it leads us to misinterpret both the historical significance of the salons and the social history of the Enlightenment. It induces considering salons as literary or intellectual venues, whereas they were, above all, the social spaces of elite leisure. . . .

[I]dentifying the salons with the republic of letters of the Enlightenment presupposes an ideological coherence and neglects the social dynamics. . . .

A focus on sociability allows for the study of the practices of conviviality among the urban elite. . . .

[E]ighteenth-century social elites redefined themselves through their practices of worldly sociability and . . . some men of letters of the Enlightenment participated in that same sociability, by attending the salons.

Sources: Goodman, Dena, *The Republic of Letters: A Cultural History of the French Enlightenment* Ithaca, NY: Cornell University Press, 1994, 91, 99, 101–102; Lilti, Antoine, *The World of the Salons: Sociability and Worldliness in Eighteenth-Century Paris*, translated by Lydia G. Cochrane. Oxford: Oxford University Press, 4–5, 8–9.

really behaved, and that a free market system was morally justified because it ultimately produced a maximum of both freedom and abundance. The mutual interaction of the enlightened self-interest of millions of persons would in the end, as if by an "invisible hand," he said, result in the highest welfare of all. Among problems that Smith minimized, or accepted as lesser evils, were the economic insecurity of individuals, the destabilizing political consequences of extreme differences in wealth, and the dangers of excessive dependence of a whole country on imports of essential goods such as food. If the visible hand of government continued to regulate the price of bread, for example, such actions showed how economic policies still had to fit within the broader political goals of governments that wanted to prevent rioting, ensure social peace, and retain popular support.

Main Currents of Enlightenment Thought

It is clear that the main currents of eighteenth-century thought in France and Europe were divergent and inconsistent. There was a general belief in progress, reason, science, and the advance of knowledge in European civilization, but there were also critics of every influential idea. Rousseau had his doubts about progress and praised the imagined conditions in a precivilized state of nature. Montesquieu thought the church useful but did not believe in religion; Rousseau believed in religion but saw no need for any church. Montesquieu was concerned about practical political liberty; Voltaire would surrender political liberty in return for guarantees of intellectual freedom; Rousseau wanted emancipation from the restraints of society and sought the freedom that consists in merging with nature and with one's fellows. Most philosophes were closest to Voltaire. They favored more tolerance for intellectual differences and more legal equality in European societies. It was not a very far-reaching conception of equality, but it meant equality of rights for persons of different religions, a reduction of privileges enjoyed by nobles but not by commoners, greater equality of status in law courts and in the payment of taxes, and more opportunity for middle-class persons to rise to positions of social or political importance.

France was the main center of the Enlightenment. French philosophes traveled all over Europe. Frederick II and Catherine II invited French thinkers to their courts. French was the language of the academies of St. Petersburg and Berlin. Frederick wrote his philosophical works in the French language. The upper classes of Europe shared a uniform cosmopolitan culture, and this culture was predominantly French. But Britain was important also. Hitherto somewhat on the fringes of the European consciousness, Britain now moved closer to the center. Montesquieu and Voltaire may be said to have "discovered" Britain for Europe. Through them the ideas of Bacon, Newton, and Locke, and the whole theory of British liberty, parliamentary government, and public debate became matters for general European discussion. We have seen, too, how Adam Smith's *The Wealth of Nations* was soon translated into many languages.

Although the Physiocrats and others had begun to advocate laissez-faire economic theories, the state was widely viewed as the main agent of social progress. Whether in the form of limited monarchy on the British model favored by Montesquieu, or of enlightened despotism preferred by Voltaire, or of the idealized republican commonwealth portrayed by Rousseau, the rightly ordered government was considered the best guarantee of social welfare. Even the political economists needed the state to shake people out of the habits of ages, sweep away a mass of local regulation, preserve law and order and the enforcement of contracts, and so assure the existence of a free market. But if they relied on the state, they were not nationalists in any later sense of the word. As "universalists," they believed in the unity of humankind under a natural law of right and reason and thus they carried over classical and Christian beliefs in a more secular framework. Although

Belief in universal ideas

they generally believed that different cultures and racial groups had reached very different levels of civilization in the eighteenth century, they supposed that all peoples would participate eventually in the same progress. No nation was thought to have a distinctive message or unique path to progress. French ideas enjoyed a wide currency, but no one thought of them as peculiarly French, arising from a French "national character." It was simply thought that the French at the time were in the vanguard of civilized, universalist thinking. Such was the idea of Condorcet, one of the later philosophes, a leading spokesman of the Enlightenment who became an active figure in the French Revolution, and also one of its victims, and who in 1794, while in hiding from his radical political enemies, wrote the great testament to the Enlightenment, his *Sketch for a Historical Picture of the Progress of the Human Mind.*

36. ENLIGHTENED DESPOTISM: FRANCE, AUSTRIA, PRUSSIA

The Meaning of Enlightened Despotism

Enlightened despotism is hard to define, because it grew out of earlier forms of absolutism that Louis XIV and Peter the Great had established in France and Russia. Characteristically, the enlightened despots drained marshes, built roads and bridges, codified the laws, repressed provincial autonomy and localism, curtailed the independence of church and nobles, and developed a trained and salaried state bureaucracy. Kings had done all these things before. Enlightened despots differed from their "unenlightened" predecessors mainly in attitude and tempo. They said little of a divine right to the throne. They might even not emphasize hereditary or dynastic family rights. They justified their authority on grounds of usefulness to society, calling themselves, as Frederick the Great did, the "first servant of the state."

The secular outlook

Enlightened despotism was secular; it claimed no mandate from heaven and recognized no special responsibility to God or church. The typical enlightened despot consequently favored toleration in religion, and this was an important new emphasis after about 1740; but here again there was precedent in the older absolutism, for the rulers of Prussia had been inclined toward toleration before Frederick, and even the French Bourbons had recognized a degree of religious liberty for almost a century following the Edict of Nantes in 1598. The secular outlook of the enlightened governments also shaped the common front they adopted against the Jesuits. High papalists, affirming the authority of a universal church in Rome and asserting themselves in other ways as the strongest religious order in the Catholic world, the Jesuits were distasteful to the enlightened monarchs. In the 1760s the order was banned in almost all Catholic countries. In 1773 the pope was persuaded to dissolve the Society of Jesus entirely. Governments in France, Austria, Spain, Portugal, and Naples confiscated Jesuit property and took over the Jesuit schools. Not until 1814 was the order reconstituted.

Enlightened despots wanted to be rational and reformist. The typical enlightened monarch set out to reconstruct the state by the use of reason. Sharing the widespread eighteenth-century view of the past as benighted, the new monarchs were impatient of all that was imbedded in social custom or claimed as a heritage from the past, such as systems of customary law and the rights and privileges of church, nobles, towns, guilds, provinces, assemblies of estates, or, in France, the judicial bodies called parlements. The complex network of such institutions was disparagingly referred to as "feudalism." Monarchs had long struggled against feudalism in this sense, but in the past they had usually compromised. The enlightened despot was less willing to compromise, and herein lay a difference in tempo. The new monarchs acted abruptly, desiring quicker results.

Enlightened despotism, in short, was an acceleration of the old centralizing institution of monarchy, which now put aside its quasi-sacred mantle and undertook to justify itself in the cold light of reason and secular usefulness. In theory even the dynastic claim was awkward, for it also rested on inheritance from the past. Under enlightened despotism the idea of the state itself was changing, from the older notion of an entity that belonged by a kind of sanctified property right to its ruler, to a newer notion of an abstract and impersonal authority that public officials exercised to promote or protect the interests of a whole country. The king was simply the highest public official or embodiment of the state's sovereign authority.

The roots of enlightened despotism

The trend to enlightened despotism after 1740 owed a great deal to writers and philosophes, but it arose also out of a very practical situation, namely, the great wars of the mid-eighteenth century. War, in modern history, has usually led to concentration and rationalizing of government power, and the wars of 1740–1748 and 1756–1763 were no exception. Under their impact even those governments that were not considered enlightened, notably those of Louis XV and Maria Theresa, and even the government of Great Britain, which was certainly not despotic within Britain itself, embarked on programs that all exemplified common centralizing patterns. They attempted to augment their revenues, devise new taxes, impose taxes on persons or regions hitherto more or less tax exempt, limit the autonomy of outlying political bodies, and centralize and renovate their respective political systems. The workings of enlightened despotism might be seen in many states, but the new policies had the most far-reaching influence in the larger Continental countries—France and Austria, Prussia and Russia—and in the rather different, yet not wholly different, course of events in the British Empire.

The Failure of Enlightened Despotism in France

It was in France that enlightened despotism had the least success. Louis XV, who had inherited the throne as a child in 1715 and lived until 1774, was by no means stupid; but he was indifferent to most serious questions, absorbed in the daily rounds at Versailles, disinclined to make trouble for people with whom he had personal contact, and interested in government only by fits and starts. His reputed remark, *après moi le déluge,* whether or not he really said it, sufficiently characterizes his personal attitude to conditions in France. Yet the French government was not unenlightened, and many capable officials carried on its affairs all through the century. These officials generally understood the government's basic problem. Most of the practical difficulties of the French monarchy could be traced to its methods of raising revenue. It derived some income from the sale of offices and privileges, which had the perverse effect of building up vested interests in the existing system. Among the government's actual taxes the most important was the *taille,* a kind of land tax, generally paid only by peasants. Nobles were exempt from it on principle, and

Flaws of tax collection

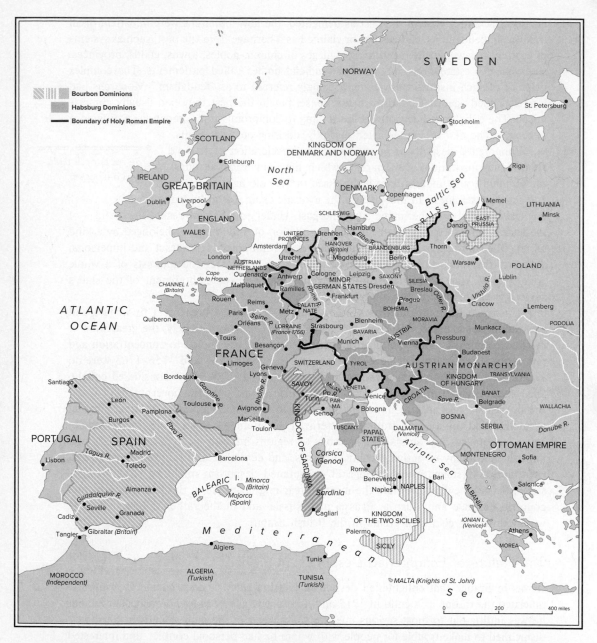

EUROPE, 1740

Boundaries show how territories were controlled by the various European states in 1740. There were now three Bourbon monarchies (France, Spain, and the Two Sicilies). The Austrian monarchy possessed most of what is now Belgium (then known as the Austrian Netherlands), and, in Italy, the duchy of Milan and grand duchy of Tuscany, where the Medici family had recently died out. Prussia expanded by acquiring Silesia in the war of the 1740s. The first partition of Poland in 1772 enlarged Prussia, Austria, and Russia. France acquired Lorraine in 1766 and Corsica in 1768. Otherwise there were no changes until the Revolutionary-Napoleonic wars of 1792-1814.

officeholders and bourgeois professional groups, for one reason or another, were often exempt also. In addition, the church, which owned between 5 and 10 percent of the land of the country, insisted that its property was not taxable by the state; it granted to the king a periodic "free gift" that, though sizable, was less than the government might have received from direct taxation. The consequence of the tax exemptions was that, although France itself was wealthy and prosperous, the government was chronically poor, because the social classes that enjoyed most of the wealth and prosperity did not pay taxes corresponding to their incomes.

Louis XIV, under pressure of war, had tried to tax everybody alike by creating new levies—the capitation or poll tax and the *dixième* or tenth, both of which were assessed in proportion to income; but these taxes had been widely evaded. A similar effort to tax higher incomes was made in 1726, but it too had failed. The propertied classes resisted taxation because they thought it degrading. France had succumbed to the pernicious principle that to pay direct taxes was the sure mark of inferior status. Nobles, churchmen, and the bourgeois professions also resisted taxation because they were kept out of the policymaking functions of government, and so they had no sense of political responsibility or control.

In the 1740s, under pressure of heavy war costs, the French monarchy introduced the *vingtième* or twentieth, which imposed a 5 percent tax on income from all forms of property and was to be paid irrespective of class status, provincial liberties, or previous exemptions of any kind. In practice, the *vingtième* amounted to less than 5 percent and fell only upon land, but it was paid by nobles and bourgeois alike and lasted until the Revolution. During the Seven Years' War the government tried to increase it, without success. A clamor arose from the Parlement of Paris, the provincial parlements, the estates of Brittany, and the church. All these institutions were now stronger than in the days of Louis XIV, and they could now cite Montesquieu to justify their opposition to the crown. The parlements ruled the tax increase to be incompatible with the laws of France, that is, unconstitutional; and the *pays d'états,* or provinces having assemblies of estates, declared that their historic liberties were being violated. After several years of wrangling, Louis XV decided to push the matter no further.

But after the Seven Years' War, burdened with war debts, the government sought to win effective central control by eliminating the parlements as a political force. In 1768 Louis XV called to the chancellorship a man named Maupeou, who simply abrogated the old parlements and set up new ones in their place. Maupeou had the sympathy of Voltaire and most of the philosophes. In the "Maupeou parlements" the judges had no property rights in their seats but became salaried officials appointed by the crown with assurances of secure tenure; and they were forbidden to reject government edicts or to pass on their constitutionality, being confined to purely judicial functions. Maupeou proposed to make the laws and judicial procedure more uniform throughout the whole country. Meanwhile, with the old parlements out of the way, the government tried again to tax the privileged and exempted groups.

The "Maupeou parlements"

But Louis XV died in 1774. His grandson and successor, Louis XVI, though more conscientious than his grandfather and possessed by a genuine desire to govern well, resembled Louis XV in that he lacked sustained will power and could not bear to offend the people who could get to see him personally. In any case he was only 20 in 1774. The kingdom resounded with outcries against Maupeou and his colleagues as minions of despotism and with demands for the immediate restoration of the old Parlement of Paris and all the others. Louis XVI, fearful

Louis XVI

of beginning his reign as a "despot," therefore recalled the old parlements and abolished those that Maupeou had established. The abortive Maupeou parlements represented the farthest step taken by enlightened despotism in France. It was arbitrary, high-handed, and despotic for Louis XV to destroy the old parlements, but it was certainly "enlightened" in the sense then connoted by the word, for the old parlements were strongholds of aristocracy and privilege and had for decades blocked programs of legal and financial reform.

Louis XVI, in recalling the old parlements in 1774, began his reign by pacifying the privileged classes. At the same time he appointed a reforming ministry. At its head was Turgot, a philosophe and a Physiocrat and a widely experienced government administrator. Turgot undertook to suppress the guilds and their privileged municipal monopolies in their several trades. He allowed greater freedom to the internal commerce in grain. He planned to abolish the royal *corvée* (a requirement that certain peasants labor on the roads a few days each year), replacing it by a money tax that would fall on all classes. He began to review the whole system of taxation and in religious matters was known even to favor the legal toleration of Protestants. The Parlement of Paris, supported by the Provincial Estates and the church, vociferously opposed him, and in 1776 he resigned. Enlightened despotism in France had failed. Louis XVI, by recalling the parlements, had made reform impossible. In 1778 France again went to war with Britain. The same cycle was repeated: war costs, debt, deficit, new projects of taxation, resistance to tax reform from the parlements and other semiautonomous bodies. In the 1780s the clashes led to revolution.

Austria: The Reforms of Maria Theresa (1740–1780) and of Joseph II (1780–1790)

For Maria Theresa the European war of the 1740s proved the extraordinary flimsiness of her empire and the Austrian monarchy. Her subjects did not show much inclination to remain united under her rule, even when threatened by invading armies. The empire was only a loose bundle of territories without common purpose or common will. The Pragmatic Sanction devised by Charles VI, it should be recalled, had been meant not only to guarantee the Habsburg inheritance against foreign attack but also to secure the assent of the several parts of the empire to remain united under the woman who became the reigning Habsburg monarch.

Internal consolidation of the empire

The war of the 1740s led to internal consolidation. The reign of Maria Theresa set the course of all later development of the Austrian Empire and hence of the many peoples who lived within its borders.

She was aided by a notable team of ministers, whose origin illustrated the nonnational character of the Habsburg system. Her most trusted adviser in foreign relations, the astute Kaunitz, was a Moravian; her main assistants in domestic affairs were a Silesian and a Bohemian-Czech. They worked smoothly with the German archduchess-queen and with German officials in Vienna. Their aim was to prevent dissolution of the monarchy by enlarging and guaranteeing the flow of taxes and soldiers. This involved breaking the local control of territorial nobles in their diets. Hungary, profoundly separatist, was left alone. But the Bohemian and Austrian provinces were welded together, and a unified state bureaucracy took the place of local self-government. Officials (following the form of mercantilist doctrine called cameralism in central Europe) planned to augment the economic strength of the empire by increasing production. They reduced the influence of the local guild monopolies; suppressed brigandage on the roads; and in 1775 created a tariff union of Bohemia, Moravia, and the Austrian duchies. This region became

The restoration of the traditional parlements at the beginning of the reign of Louis XVI was an important political victory for the privileged classes in French society, whose power had been challenged by the Maupeou ministry in the early 1770s. The restored Parlement of Paris, shown here at an extraordinary meeting with King Louis XVI in 1787, steadfastly refused to approve new taxes and blocked the development of enlightened despotism in France; but this resistance to new taxation also deepened a state financial crisis that led to the French Revolution.

(©Christophel Fine Art/Getty Images)

the largest area of free trade on the European continent, because even France was still divided by internal tariffs. Bohemia, industrially the most advanced part of the empire, benefited substantially; one of its cotton manufacturing plants, at the end of Maria Theresa's reign, employed 4,000 persons.

The great social fact, both in the Habsburg lands and in all eastern Europe, was the serfdom into which the rural masses had progressively fallen during the past 200 years. Serfdom meant that the peasant owed more to the landlord than to the state. The serf owed labor to the lord, often unspecified in amount or kind. The tendency, so long as the landlords ruled locally through their diets, was for the serf to do forced labor for six days a week on the lord's land. Maria Theresa, from humane motives and also from a desire to control the manpower from which her armies were recruited, launched a systematic attack on the institutions of serfdom, which meant also an attack on the landed aristocracy of the empire. The whole agricultural labor system of her territories was involved, so Maria Theresa proceeded with caution. Laws were passed against abuse of peasants by lords or their overseers. Other

Attacks on serfdom

laws regularized the labor obligations, requiring that they be publicly registered and usually limiting them to three days a week. The laws were often evaded. But the peasant was to some extent freed from arbitrary exactions of the lord. Maria Theresa accomplished more to alleviate serfdom than any other ruler of the eighteenth century in eastern Europe, with the single exception of her own son, Joseph II.

The great archduchess-queen died in 1780, having reigned for 40 years. Her son, who had been co-regent with his mother since 1765, had little patience with her cautious methods. Maria Theresa, though steady enough in aim, had always been content with partial measures. Instead of advertising her purposes by philosophical pronouncements, she disguised or understated them, never carrying matters to the point of arousing an unmanageable reaction or of uniting against her the vested interests that she undermined.

Joseph II: the "revolutionary emperor"

She watched and waited. Joseph II was more impatient. Though he thought the French philosophes frivolous, and Frederick of Prussia a clever cynic, he was himself a pure representative of the Age of Enlightenment, and it is in his brief reign of 10 years that the character and the limitations of enlightened despotism can best be seen. He was a solemn, earnest, good man, who sensed the misery and hopelessness of the lowest classes. He believed existing conditions to be bad, and he would not regulate or improve them; he would end them. Right and reason, in his mind, lay with the views which he himself adopted; upholders of the old order were self-seeking or mistaken and to yield to them would be to compromise with evil.

"The state," said Joseph, anticipating the later Philosophical Radicals in England, meant "the greatest good for the greatest number." He acted accordingly. His 10 years of rule passed in a quick succession of radical decrees. Maria Theresa had regulated serfdom. Joseph abolished it. His mother had collected taxes from nobles as well as peasants, though not equally. Joseph decreed absolute equality of taxation. He insisted on equal punishment for equal crimes whatever the class status of the offender; an aristocratic army officer, who had stolen 97,000 gulden, was exhibited in the pillory, and Count Podstacky, a forger, was made to sweep the streets of Vienna chained to common convicts. At the same time many legal punishments were made less physically cruel. Joseph granted complete liberty of the press. He ordered toleration of all religions, except for a few popular sects that he thought too ignorant to allow. He granted equal civil rights to the Jews, and equal duties, making Jews liable, for the first time in Europe, to service in the army. He even created Jewish nobles, an amazing phenomenon to those who believed in aristocratic "blood."

Joseph clashed openly and rudely with the pope. He demanded increased powers in the appointment and supervision of Catholic bishops, and he suppressed numerous monasteries, using their property to finance secular hospitals in Vienna, and thus laying the foundations for later Viennese excellence as a medical center. He attempted also to develop the empire economically and built up the port of Trieste, where he even established an East India Company, which soon failed because neither capital nor naval support was forthcoming from central Europe. His attempts to reach the sea commercially through the Austrian Netherlands like those of his grandfather at the time of the Ostend Company, were blocked by Dutch and British interests.

To force through his program Joseph had to centralize his state, like earlier rulers, except that he went further. Regional diets and aristocratic self-government fared even worse than under his mother. Where she had always sagaciously let Hungary go its own way, he applied most of his measures to Hungary also—what was right must be right everywhere. His ideal was a perfectly uniform and rational empire, with all irregularities smoothed out as if under a modern steamroller. He thought it reasonable to have a single language for administration and naturally chose German; this led to a program of Germanizing the Czechs, Poles, Magyars, and others, which in turn aroused their strong linguistic resistance. Using the German language, and pushing the emperor's program against regional and class opposition, was a hard-pressed, constantly growing, and increasingly disciplined body of officials. Bureaucracy became recognizably modern, with training courses, promotion schedules, retirement pensions, efficiency reports, and visits by inspectors. The clergy likewise were employed as representatives of the state to explain new laws to their parishioners and teach due respect for the government. To watch over the whole structure Joseph created a secret police, whose agents, soliciting the confidential aid of spies and informers, reported on the performance of government employees or on the ideas and actions of nobles, clergy, or others from whom trouble might be expected. The police state, so widely condemned in modern democratic societies, was first systematically built up under Joseph as an instrument of enlightenment and reform.

Joseph II, the "revolutionary emperor," anticipated much that was soon done in France by the Revolution and under Napoleon. He could not abide "feudalism" or "medievalism"; he personally detested the nobility and the church. But few of his reforms proved lasting. He died prematurely in 1790, at the age of 49, disillusioned and broken-hearted. Joseph was a revolutionist without a party or supporting political movement. He failed because *Limitations of Joseph's reforms* he could not be everywhere and do everything himself, and because he was opposed by the most powerful social groups in his empire. His reign demonstrated the limitations of a merely despotic enlightenment. It showed that a legally absolute ruler could not really do as he pleased. It suggested that drastic and abrupt reform could perhaps come only with a true revolution, on a wave of public opinion, and under the leadership of persons who shared in a coherent body of ideas.

Joseph was succeeded by his brother Leopold, one of the ablest rulers of the century, who for many years as grand duke of Tuscany had given that country the best government known in Italy for generations. Now, in 1790, Leopold was plagued by outcries from his sister, Marie Antoinette, caught in the turmoil of a real revolution in France. He refused to interfere in French affairs; in any case, he was busy dealing with the uproar left by Joseph. He abrogated most of Joseph's edicts, but he did not yield entirely. The nobles did not win back full powers in their diets. The peasants were not wholly consigned to the old serfdom; Joseph's efforts to provide them with land and to rid them of forced labor had to be given up, but they remained legally free to migrate, marry, or choose an occupation at will. Leopold died in 1792 and was followed by his son Francis II. Under Francis the aristocratic and clerical reaction gathered strength, terrified by the memory of the reform-minded Joseph II and by the spectacle of revolutionary France, with which Austria went to war soon after Leopold's death.

Prussia under Frederick the Great (1740–1786)

In Prussia, Frederick the Great continued to reign for 23 years after the close of the Seven Years' War in 1763. "Old Fritz," as he was called, spent the time peaceably, writing memoirs and histories, rehabilitating his shattered country, promoting agriculture and industry, replenishing his treasury, drilling his army, and assimilating both Silesia and the Polish lands that fell to him after the first partition of Poland in 1772. Frederick's fame as one of the most eminent of enlightened despots rests, however, not so much on his actual innovations as on his own intellectual gifts, which were considerable, and on the admiring publicity that he received from such literary friends as Voltaire. "My chief occupation," he wrote to Voltaire, "is to fight ignorance and prejudices in this country. . . . I must enlighten my people, cultivate their manners and morals, and make them as happy as human beings can be, or as happy as the means at my disposal permit." He did not conceive that sweeping changes were needed for happiness in Prussia. The country was docile; its Lutheran church had long been subordinate to the state, its relatively few burghers were largely dependents of the crown, and the independence of the Junker landlords, as expressed in provincial diets, had been curtailed by Frederick's predecessors. Frederick simplified and codified the many laws of the kingdom and made the law courts cheaper, more expeditious, and more honest. He kept up a wholesome and energetic tone in his civil service. He protected religious freedom, and he decreed, though he did not achieve, a modicum of elementary education for all children of all classes. Prussia under Frederick was attractive enough for some 300,000 immigrants to seek it out.

But society remained stratified in a way hardly known in the more western parts of Europe. Nobles, peasants, and burghers lived side by side in a kind of segregation. Each

Social stratification in Prussia

group paid different taxes and owed different duties to the state, and no person could buy property of the type owned by one of the other two groups. Property was legally classified, as well as persons; there was little movement from one social group to another. These policies served a specific military purpose. They preserved a distinct peasant class from which to draw soldiers and a distinct aristocratic class from which to draw officers. The peasants, except in the western extremities of the kingdom, were serfs holding patches of land on precarious terms with obligations to labor on the estates of the lords. They were considered the lord's "hereditary subjects" and were not free to leave the lord's estate, to marry, or to learn a trade except with his permission. Frederick in his early years considered steps to relieve the burden of serfdom. He did relieve it on his own manors, those belonging to the Prussian crown domain, which comprised a quarter of the area of the kingdom. But he did nothing for serfs belonging to the private landlords or Junkers. No king of Prussia could antagonize the Junker class, which commanded the army. On the other hand, even in Prussia, the existence of a monarchical state was of some advantage for the common person; the serf in Prussia was not so badly off as in adjoining areas—Poland, Livonia, Mecklenburg, or Swedish Pomerania—where the will of the landlords was the law of the land, and which therefore have been called Junker republics. In these countries owners sometimes sold their serfs as movable property or gambled or gave them away, breaking up families in the process, as Russian landlords might do with their serfs or American plantation owners with their slaves. Such abuses were unknown in Prussia.

Frederick's system was centralized not merely at Potsdam but in his own head. He himself attended to all business and made all important decisions. None of his ministers or generals ever achieved an independent reputation. As he said of his army, "no one reasons, everyone executes"—that is, no one reasoned except the king himself. Or again, as Frederick put it, if Newton had had to consult with Descartes he would never have discovered the law of universal gravitation. To have to take into account other people's ideas, or to entrust responsibilities to people less capable than himself, seemed to Frederick wasteful and anarchic. He died in 1786, after ruling 46 years and having trained no successors. Twenty years later Prussia was all but destroyed by Napoleon. It was not surprising that Napoleon's well-organized French army should defeat Prussia, but Europe was amazed, in 1806, to see Prussia collapse so totally and abruptly. It was then concluded in Prussia and elsewhere that government by a mastermind working in lofty and isolated superiority did not offer a viable state system under modern conditions.

37. ENLIGHTENED DESPOTISM: RUSSIA

The Russian Empire has long been out of sight in the preceding pages. There are reasons for its absence, for it played no part in the intellectual revolution of the seventeenth century, and its role in the early modern struggle for wealth and empire, which reached a climax in the Seven Years' War, was somewhat incidental. In the Age of Enlightenment the role of Russia was passive. Russian thinkers were unknown in western Europe, but western European thinkers were well known in Russia by the later eighteenth century. The French-dominated cosmopolitan culture of the European upper classes spread to the upper classes of Russia. The Russian court and aristocracy took over French as their common conversational language. With French (German was also known, and sometimes English, for the Russian aristocrats were remarkable linguists) all the ideas boiling up in western Europe streamed into Russia. The Enlightenment, if it did not affect Russia profoundly, affected it significantly. It extended the European influence so forcibly pushed forward by Peter and carried further the estrangement of the Russian upper classes from their own people and their own native scene.

Russia absorbs French culture

Russia after Peter the Great

Peter the Great died in 1725. To secure his revolution he had decreed that each tsar should name his successor, but he himself had named none and had put to death his own son Alexis to prevent social reaction. Peter's long reign was therefore followed by a period of political instability. Rival factions at court—a German party and a native Russian party—struggled for control over successive tsars, tsarinas, and short lived governments until a palace revolution in 1741 brought to the throne Peter the Great's daughter, Elizabeth, who managed to hold power until her death 21 years later. Russian military power expanded during her reign; and she entered into European diplomacy and joined in the Seven Years' War against Prussia, fearing that the continued growth of Prussia would endanger the new Russian position on the Baltic. Her nephew, Peter III, was almost immediately dethroned, and probably assassinated, by a group acting in the name of his young wife Catherine. The victorious coterie claimed that Peter III had been an incompetent, child-like tsar, who at the age of 24 still played with paper soldiers. Using such rumors to justify her rise to power, Catherine was proclaimed the Empress Catherine II and later came to be called "the Great." She enjoyed a long reign from 1762 to 1796, during which she acquired a somewhat exaggerated reputation as an enlightened despot.

The names of the tsars and tsarinas between Peter I and Catherine II are of slight importance, but their violent and rapid sequence tells a story. With no principle of succession, dynastic or other, the empire fell into a lawless struggle of parties, in which plots against ruling tsars alternated with palace revolutions upon their death. In all the confusion an underlying issue was always how Peter's European reform program would turn out. Although Russia's social elites were becoming more "European," most people in western Europe still viewed Russia as an alien and remote place on the distant frontier of European culture.

Catherine the Great (1762–1796): Domestic Program

Catherine the Great was a German woman of a small princely house of the Holy Roman Empire. She had gone to Russia at the age of 15 to be married. She had immediately cultivated the goodwill of the Russians, learned the language, and embraced the Orthodox church. Early in her married life, disgusted with her husband, she foresaw the chance of becoming empress herself. Like the other prominent woman ruler of this era in Europe, Maria Theresa, she approached political issues with a strong practical sense and great energy (though she did not share Maria Theresa's devotion to family life). Catherine's intellectual powers were as remarkable as her physical vigor; even after becoming empress she often got up at five in the morning, lit her own fire, and turned to her books, making a digest, for example, of Blackstone's *Commentaries on the Laws of England,* published in 1765. She corresponded with Voltaire and invited Diderot, editor of the *Encyclopédie,* to visit her at St. Petersburg, where, she reported, he thumped her so hard on the knee during their energetic conversations that she had to put a table between them. She bought Diderot's library, allowing him to keep it during his lifetime, and in other ways won international renown by her benefactions to the philosophes, whom she regarded as useful press agents for Russia.

Catherine's reforms

When she first came to power, she publicized an intention to introduce certain enlightened reforms. She summoned a great consultative assembly, called a Legislative Commission, which met in 1767. From its numerous proposals Catherine obtained a good deal of information on conditions in the country and concluded, from the profuse loyalty exhibited by the deputies, that though a usurper and a foreigner she possessed a strong hold upon Russia. She subsequently enacted reforms that included a new legal codification, restrictions on the use of torture, and a limited support of religious toleration, though she would not allow Old Believers to build their own chapels. Such innovations were enough to raise an admiring chorus from the philosophes, who saw in her, as they saw retrospectively in Peter the Great, the standard-bearer of an enlightened civilization among a backward people.

Whatever early ideas Catherine may conceivably have held on the fundamental subject of reforming serfdom in Russia did not last long after she became empress; and there was no consideration of reform after the great peasant insurrection of 1773, known as Pugachev's rebellion. The condition of the Russian serfs was deteriorating. Serf owners were increasingly selling them apart from the land, breaking up families, using them in mines or manufactures, disciplining and punishing them at will, or exiling them to Siberia. The serf population was restless, worked upon by the religious warnings of Old Believers and cherishing distorted popular memories of the mighty hero, Stephen Razin, who a century before had led an uprising against the landlords. Class antagonism, though latent, was profound, and it may have grown when the rough muzhik, in some places, heard the lord and his family talking French so as not to be understood by the servants or saw them wearing European clothes, reading European books, and adopting the manners of a foreign way of life.

Pugachev's rebellion

In 1773 a Don Cossack, Emelian Pugachev, a former soldier, appeared at the head of an insurrection in the Urals. Following an old Russian custom, he announced himself as the true tsar, Peter III (Catherine's deceased husband), now returned after long travels in Egypt and the Holy Land. He surrounded himself with his own imperial family, courtiers, and even a secretary of state, He issued an imperial manifesto proclaiming the end of serfdom, taxes, and military conscription. In the Urals and Volga regions, hundreds of thousands Tartars,

CATHERINE THE GREAT
by Alexander Roslin (Swedish, 1718–1793)

Catherine's forceful character and slightly whimsical smile are represented in this portrait, which was painted shortly after the powerful tsarina suppressed the great peasant rebellion of 1773–1774.

(©Heritage Images/Getty Images)

Kirghiz, Cossacks, agricultural serfs, servile workers in the Ural mines, fishermen in the rivers and in the Caspian Sea, flocked to Pugachev's banner. The great host surged through eastern Russia, burning and pillaging, killing priests and landlords. The upper classes in Moscow were terrified; 100,000 serfs lived in the city as domestic servants or industrial workers and their sympathies went out to Pugachev and his militant supporters. Armies sent against him were at first unsuccessful. But famine along the Volga in 1774 dispersed the rebels. Pugachev, betrayed by some of his own followers, was brought to Moscow in an iron cage. Catherine forbade the use of torture at his trial, but he was executed by the drawing and quartering of his body, a punishment, it should perhaps be noted, used at the time in western Europe in cases of flagrant treason.

Pugachev's rebellion was the most violent peasant uprising in the history of Russia, and the most formidable mass upheaval in Europe in the century before 1789. Catherine replied to it by repression. She conceded more powers to the landlords. The nobles shook off the last vestiges of the compulsory state service to which Peter had bound them. The peasants were henceforth the only bound or unfree class. As in Prussia, the state came more than ever to rest on an understanding between ruler and gentry, by which the gentry accepted the monarchy, with its laws, officials, army, and foreign policy, and received from it, in return, the assurance of full authority over the rural masses. Government reached down through the aristocracy and the scattered towns, but it stopped short at the manor; there the lord took over and was himself a kind of government in his own person. Under these conditions the number of serfs increased, and the load on each became heavier. Catherine's reign saw the culmination of Russian serfdom, which now ceased to differ in any important respect from the chattel slavery that controlled the lives of enslaved blacks in the Americas. One might read in the Moscow *Gazette* demeaning notices for the sale of human beings such as the following advertisements: "For sale, two plump coachmen; two girls 18 and 15 years, quick at manual work. Two barbers; one, 21, knows how to read and write and play a musical instrument; the other can do ladies' and gentlemen's hair."

Catherine the Great: Foreign Affairs

Territorially Catherine was one of the main builders of modern Russia. When she became tsarina in 1762, the empire reached to the Pacific and into central Asia, and it touched upon the Gulf of Riga and the Gulf of Finland on the Baltic, but westward from Moscow one could go only 200 miles before reaching Poland, and no one standing on Russian soil could see the waters of the Black Sea (see maps, pp. 236–237). Russia was separated from central Europe by a wide band of loosely organized domains, extending from the Baltic to the Black Sea and the Mediterranean and nominally belonging to the Polish and Turkish states. Poland was an old enemy, but in both Poland and the Ottoman Empire there were many Greek Orthodox Christians with whom Russians felt an ideological tie.

Territorial expansion

Catherine's supreme plan was to penetrate the entire area, Polish and Ottoman territories alike. In a war with the Ottoman Empire in 1772 she developed her "Greek project," in which "Greeks," that is, members of the Greek Orthodox Church, would replace Muslims as the dominant element throughout the Middle East. She defeated the Ottoman forces in the war, but was herself checked by the diplomatic pressures of the European balance of power. The result was the first partition of Poland—a seizure of land and people in which the monarchs of Prussia, Russia, and Austria began to divide up Polish territory between them. Frederick took Pomerelia, which he renamed West Prussia; Catherine took parts of Byelorussia; Maria Theresa occupied Galicia. Frederick digested his portion with relish, realizing an old dream of the Brandenburg house; Catherine swallowed hers with somewhat less appetite, because she had satisfactorily controlled the whole of Poland before; to Maria Theresa the dish was distasteful, and even shocking, but she could not see her neighbors go ahead without her, and she shared in the feast by suppressing her moral scruples. "She wept," said Frederick cynically, "but she kept on taking." Catherine, in 1774, signed a peace treaty with the defeated Turks. This treaty opened opportunities for Russian expansion around the Black Sea, where the Ottoman sultan ceded control of Tartar principalities on the north coast and where the Russians soon founded the seaport of Odessa.

Catherine had only delayed, not altered, her plans with respect to Ottoman Turkey. She decided to neutralize the opposition of Austria. She invited Joseph II to visit her in Russia, and the two sovereigns proceeded together on a tour of her newly won Black Sea provinces. Her long-time adviser and lover, Grigory Potemkin, accompanied Catherine on this tour, which included visits to numerous towns and fortresses that Potemkin had established in the Crimea. Although the Russians had actually made significant progress in developing the region, Potemkin's enemies claimed that the new towns were nothing but a facade—thus creating the famous phrase "Potemkin villages" to mean bogus evidence of a nonexistent prosperity. But Catherine achieved her main goal when Joseph II agreed to bring Austria into a war of conquest against the Ottoman Empire.

Emelian Pugachev, leader of the most violent, widespread peasant uprising in Russian history, was held in an iron cage before his trial and execution for treason.
(©Bettmann/Getty Images)

This war was interrupted by the French Revolution, however, and both governments reduced their commitments in the Balkans to await developments in western Europe. It became Catherine's policy to incite Austria and Prussia into a war with revolutionary France, in the name of monarchy and civilization, in order that she might have a free hand in the Polish-Turkish sphere. Meanwhile she contributed to a collective assault on the nationalist and reforming movement among the Poles. In 1793 she arranged with Prussia for the second partition, and in 1795, with both Prussia and Austria, for the third. She was the only ruler who lived to take part in all three partitions of Poland (which are described later in this chapter).

Her protestations of enlightenment tempt one to an ironic judgment of her career. Her foreign policy was purely expansionist and unscrupulous, and the net effect of her domestic policy, aside from a few reforms of detail, was to favor the half-Europeanized aristocracy

Catherine's reign evaluated

and to extend serfdom among the people. In her defense it may be observed that unscrupulous expansion was the accepted practice of the time, and that, domestically, probably no ruler could have corrected the eighteenth-century serf system or the social evils from which Russia suffered. If there was to be a Russian Empire, it had to be with the consent of the serf-owning gentry, which was the only articulate and politically significant class. As Catherine observed to Diderot on the subject of reforms: "You write only on paper, but I have to write on human skin, which is incomparably more irritable and ticklish."

She had reason to know how easily tsars and tsarinas could be unseated and even murdered and that the danger for tsars came not from the peasants but from cliques of army
officers and landlords.

Yet she remained attuned to western Europe. She never thought that Russian institutions should become a model for others. She continued to recognize the cultural standards
of the Enlightenment. In her later years she gave careful attention to her favorite grandson,
Alexander, closely supervising his education, which she planned on the western European
model. She gave him as a tutor the Swiss philosophe La Harpe, who filled his mind with
humane and liberal sentiments on the duties of princes. Trained by Catherine as a kind
of ideal ruler, Alexander I was destined to cut a wide circle in the affairs of Europe, to
help defeat Napoleon Bonaparte, to preach peace and freedom, and to suffer from the
same internal cultural divisions and frustrations by which European-educated Russians
were often afflicted.

The Limitations of Enlightened Despotism

Enlightened despotism, seen in retrospect, foreshadowed an age of revolutionary changes
and even signified a preliminary effort to revolutionize society by authoritative action from
above. People were told by their own governments that reforms were needed, that many
privileges, special liberties, or tax exemptions were bad, that the past was a source of
confusion, injustice, or inefficiency in the present. The state rose up as more completely
sovereign, whether acting frankly in its own interest or claiming to act in the interest of
its people. All old and established rights were brought into question—rights of kingdoms
and provinces, orders and classes, legal bodies and corporate groups. Enlightened despotism overrode or exterminated the Society of Jesus, the Parlement of Paris, the autonomy
of Bohemia, and the independence of Poland. Customary and common law was pushed
aside by authoritative legal codes. Governments, by opposing the special powers of the
church and the nobility tended to make all persons into uniform and equal subjects. To this
extent enlightened despotism favored equality before the law. But it could go only a certain
distance in this direction. The king was after all a hereditary aristocrat himself, and no
government can be revolutionary to the point of breaking up its own foundations.

Even before the French Revolution enlightened despotism had run its course.
Everywhere the "despots," for reasons of politics if not of principle, had reached a point
beyond which they could not go. In France Louis XVI had appeased the privileged classes;
in the Austrian Empire Joseph's failure to appease them threw them into open revolt; in
Prussia and in Russia the brilliant reigns of Frederick and Catherine actually increased the
power of landlordism for most people in the countryside. Almost everywhere there was an
aristocratic and even feudal resurgence. Religion also was renewing itself in many places.
Many were again saying that kingship was in a sense divine, and a new alliance was forming
between "the throne and the altar." The French Revolution, by terrifying the old vested
interests, was to accelerate and embitter an aristocratic and monarchical reaction that had
already begun. Monarchy in Europe, ever since the Middle Ages, had generally been a
centralizing but progressive institution that set itself against the feudal and ecclesiastical
powers. Enlightened despotism was the culmination of the historic development of European monarchies. After the enlightened despots, and after the French Revolution, monarchy
became on the whole nostalgic and backward-looking, supported most ardently by the
churches and aristocracies that it had once tried to subdue and least of all by those who
felt in themselves the surge of progress and a more enlightened future.

38.   THE PARTITIONS OF POLAND

The fate of eighteenth-century Poland has been mentioned as a consequence of the growing power of the newer Central European monarchies, but the partitions of Polish territories also illustrate the assumptions and practices of the so-called enlightened despots. Apart from the still somewhat non-European state of Russia, Poland in the eighteenth century was by far the largest state in Europe. It reached at the beginning of the century from the Baltic almost to the Black Sea and extended eastward for 800 miles across the north-European plain. But it was the classic example, along with the Holy Roman Empire, of an older political structure that failed to develop modern, centralizing government institutions (see maps, pp. 205, 206). It fell into ever deeper anarchy and confusion. Without army, revenues, or administration and internally divided among parties forever at cross-purposes, the country was a perpetual theater for foreign diplomatic maneuvering and was finally absorbed into the territories of its growing neighbors.

The Polish kings were chosen in elections that became an object of regular international interference. A movement for reform therefore began to gather strength after the 1730s, and Polish patriots sought to do away with the *liberum veto* and other elements in the constitution that made government impossible. The reformers were repeatedly frustrated, however, by the influence of Catherine the Great and other foreign rulers who preferred a Poland in which they could intervene at will. Catherine's candidate for the Polish throne, Stanislas Poniatowski,   *Interference in Polish elections*
won an election in 1763, thereby giving her new influence over Poland's domestic affairs. She declared herself protector of the Polish liberties. It was to the Russian advantage to maintain the existing state of affairs in Poland rather than to divide the country with neighbors who might exclude Russian influence from their own spheres. The Prussian government, which was eager to join the old duchy of Prussia with its other territories in the east, developed a greater interest in dividing Poland as a means to enhance its own strategic position.

The opportunity for Prussia presented itself in 1772, when Russia's war with Ottoman Turkey destabilized the situation in eastern Europe. The Russian victories in this war were so overwhelming that both Austrians and Prussians feared an enduring Russian disruption of the balance of power. The Prussians therefore came forward with a proposal to prevent an Austro-Russian war and to preserve the balance in eastern Europe by leaving the Ottoman Empire more or less intact. Looking for an alternative to Russian expansion into Ottoman lands, the Prussians proposed that all three European powers should annex territory from Poland instead. The proposition was accepted by all three parties.

Poland was thus sacrificed. By the first partition in 1772, its outer territories were cut away. Russia took an eastern slice around the city of Vitebsk. Austria took a southern slice, the region known as Galicia. Prussia realized its territorial ambitions by taking the Pomerelian borderland in West Prussia and creating   *Three partitions of Poland*
a solid Prussian block from the Elbe to the borders of Lithuania (see map, p. 220, panel 4). The partition sobered the Poles, who renewed their efforts at a national revival, hoping to create an effective sovereignty that could secure the country against outsiders. But the Polish movement lacked deep popular strength, for it was confined mainly to nobles, whose conflicts had brought the country to ruin. The mass of the serf population and the numerous Jewish communities did not much care at this time whether they were governed by Poles, Russians, or Germans.

Nevertheless, beginning in 1788, a reform party gathered strength. One of its members was King Stanislas Poniatowski himself, who had begun his reign as a protégé of the Russian empress. The reformers produced a new constitution in 1791. It made the Polish kingship hereditary, thus strengthening the executive government, and it reduced the powers of the great magnates while giving political rights to many burghers in the towns. By this time, however, the governments of eastern Europe were afraid of the French Revolution. Denouncing the Polish reformers as French-inspired Jacobins, Catherine the Great said she would "fight Jacobinism and beat it in Poland." In collusion with a few disgruntled Polish noblemen she sent an army into Poland and destroyed the constitution of 1791. In agreement with Prussia she then carried out the Second Partition in 1793. In 1794 Thaddeus Kosciusko led a more revolutionary political movement, which included even a proposed abolition of serfdom. Although it received no aid from the revolutionaries then governing France, it was crushed in the general European counterrevolution when Russian and Prussian armies again invaded Poland, defeated Kosciusko, and in a Third Partition in 1795 divided what remained of the country among themselves and Austria. Poland as a political entity ceased to exist (see map, p. 351, panel 2).

Many advanced thinkers of the day praised the partitions of Poland as a triumph of enlightened rulers, putting an end to an old nuisance. The three partitioning powers justified their conduct on various grounds and even took pride in it as an enlightened diplomatic achievement by which they had prevented war among themselves. It was argued also that the partitions of Poland put an end to an old cause of international rivalry and war, replacing anarchy with more stable governments in a large area of eastern Europe. It is a fact that Poland had been scarcely more independent before the partitions than after. It is to be noted also, though nationalist arguments were not used at the time, that on national grounds the Poles themselves had no claim to large parts of the old Poland. The regions taken by Russia were inhabited overwhelmingly by Byelorussians and Ukrainians, among whom the Poles were mainly a landlord class. Russia, even after the third partition, reached only to the true ethnic border of Poland. But later, after the fall of Napoleon, by general international agreement, the Russian sphere was extended deep into the territory inhabited by Poles.

The partitions of Poland, however extenuated, were nevertheless a great shock to the old system of Europe. Edmund Burke, in England, prophetically saw in the first partition the crumbling of the old international order. His diagnosis was a shrewd assessment of Europe's changing system of state power. The principle of the balance of power had been historically invoked to preserve the independence of European states and to secure weak or small countries against universal monarchy. It was now used to destroy the independence of a weak but ancient kingdom. Poland was not the first European kingdom to be partitioned, but it was the first to be partitioned without war and the first to disappear totally. That Poland was partitioned without war, a source of great satisfaction to the partitioning powers, was still a very unsettling fact. It was alarming for a huge state to vanish simply by cold diplomatic calculation. It seemed that no established rights were safe even in peacetime. The partitions of Poland showed that in a world where great powers had arisen through control of a modern state apparatus it was dangerous not to be strong. They suggested that any area failing to develop a sovereign state capable of keeping out foreign infiltration, and so situated as to be within the reach of the great powers of Europe, was unlikely to retain its independence. In this way the history of eighteenth-century Poland anticipated, for example, the partitions of Africa a century later, when Africa too, lacking strong governments, was almost totally divided, without war, among half a dozen states of Europe.

Debate over the partitions

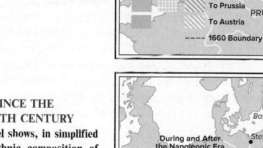

POLAND SINCE THE EIGHTEENTH CENTURY

The top panel shows, in simplified form, the ethnic composition of the area included in the Poland of 1772. In addition to languages shown, Yiddish was spoken by the large scattered Jewish population. The line set in 1795 as the western boundary of Russia persists through later changes. It reappears as the eastern border of Napoleon's Grand Duchy and of Congress Poland. After the First World War the victorious Allies contemplated much this same line as Poland's eastern frontier (the dotted line in the fourth panel, known as the Curzon Line); but the Poles in 1920–1921 conquered territory farther east. After the Second World War the Russians pushed the Poles back to the same basic line, but compensated Poland with territory taken from Germany, as far west as the river Oder and its tributary, the Neisse. The position of Warsaw in each panel shows how Poland has been shoved westward.

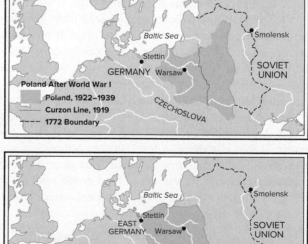

Moreover the partitions of Poland, while maintaining a balance of power in eastern Europe, profoundly changed the balance of Europe as a whole. The disappearance of Poland was a blow to France, which had long used Poland, as it had used Hungary and Turkey, as an outpost of French influence in eastern Europe. The three eastern powers expanded their territory, while France enjoyed henceforth no permanent growth. Eastern Europe bulked larger than ever before in the affairs of Europe. Prussia, Russia, and the Austrian Empire became contiguous. Although they had drawn somewhat differently on western European methods of statecraft and military organization to build their power, they had a common interest and objective in eastern Europe: the repression of Polish resistance to their rule. Polish resistance, dating from before the partitions and continuing thereafter, became the earliest example of modern revolutionary nationalism in Europe.

The independence of Poland, and of other submerged nationalities, later attracted wide support in western Europe, while the three great monarchies of eastern Europe were drawn together in common opposition to national liberation; this fact, plus the fact that the eastern monarchies were primarily landlord states, accentuated the political and social division of Europe in the nineteenth century between a western Europe that inclined to be liberal and an eastern Europe that inclined to be reactionary. The subsequent political divergence of western and eastern Europe might therefore be compared to the earlier north–south religious divergence of Protestant and Catholic states, in that both the political and the religious differences contributed to the fragmentation of Europe and to the emerging nationalisms that would later shape the major, modern European conflicts. The first great political assault on the older social order and political system in eighteenth-century Europe, however, came from the enlightened despots who destroyed the kingdom of Poland.

39.   NEW STIRRINGS: THE BRITISH REFORM MOVEMENT

It was not only by monarchs and their ministers that the older privileged, feudal, and ecclesiastical interests were threatened. Beginning about 1760 they were challenged also by broader-based political and social groups. Growing out of the Enlightenment, and out of the failure of governments to cope with grave social and fiscal problems, a new era of revolutionary disturbance was about to open. It was marked above all by the great French Revolution of 1789, but the American Revolution of 1776 was also of international importance. In Great Britain, too, the long-drawn-out movement for parliamentary reform that began in the 1760s was in effect revolutionary in character, though nonviolent, because it questioned the foundations of traditional English government and society. In addition, in the last third of the eighteenth century, there was revolutionary agitation in Switzerland, in the Austrian Netherlands, and Holland, in Ireland, Poland, Hungary, and Italy, and in lesser degree elsewhere. After 1800 revolutionary ferment was increasingly evident in Germany, Spain, and Latin America. This general wave of revolution in Europe and the Atlantic world may be said not to have ended until the revolutions of 1848 or even until the later consolidation of modern national states around 1870.

Onset of an Age of "Democratic Revolution"

Age of "Democratic Revolution"

For the whole period the term "Atlantic Revolution" has sometimes been used, because countries on both sides of the Atlantic were affected. It has been called also an age of "Democratic Revolution," because in all the diversity of these upheavals, from the American Revolution to those of the mid-nineteenth century, certain principles of modern democratic societies were affirmed in one way or another. In this view, the particular revolutions, attempted revolutions, or basic reform movements are seen as aspects of one great revolutionary wave by which virtually the whole area of Western civilization was transformed. There is also another view of this revolutionary age, namely, that each country presented a special case, which can be misunderstood if specific national events are described only as part of a vague general international turmoil. Thus the American Revolution, it is argued, was essentially a movement for independence, conservative in its objectives, and entirely different from the French Revolution, in which a thorough renovation of all society and ideas was contemplated; and both were utterly different from what happened in England, where there was no revolution at all. It need only be stressed here, however, that the American revolutionaries, the French Jacobins, the United Irish, the Dutch Patriots, and similar groups, though differing from each other, shared much in common that can only be characterized as revolutionary and as contributing to a revolutionary age in the Atlantic world.

It is important to see in what ways the movement that began about 1760 was and was not "democratic." It did not generally demand universal suffrage, though a handful of persons in England made such demands as early as the 1770s and some of the American states practiced an almost universal male suffrage after 1776, as did the more militant French revolutionaries in 1792. It did not aim at a welfare state, nor question the right of property, though there were signs pointing in these directions in the most extreme wing of the French Revolution. It did not generally promote equal rights for women or the abolition of slavery, though some women and early abolitionists strongly asserted that the "rights of man" should apply equally to women and enslaved people—and slavery was (temporarily) abolished in the French colonies in 1794. It was not especially directed against monarchy as such. The quarrel of the colonial Americans was primarily with the British Parliament, not the king; the French proclaimed a republic by default in 1792, three years after their revolution began; the revolutionary Poles after 1788 tried to strengthen their king's position, not weaken it; and revolutionary groups could come into action where no monarchy existed at all, as in the Dutch provinces before the French Revolution, and the Swiss cantons, the Venetian Republic, or again in Holland, under French influence after 1795. Indeed the first revolutionary outbreak of the period occurred in 1768 at Geneva, a very nonmonarchical small city-republic, ruled by a close-knit circle of hereditary patricians. Royal power, where it existed, became the victim of revolutionaries only where it was used to support various privileged social groups.

The revolutionary movement announced itself everywhere as a demand for "liberty and equality." It favored declarations of rights and explicit written constitutions. It proclaimed the sovereignty of the people, or "nation," and it formulated the idea of national citizenship. In this context the "people" were essentially classless; it was a legal term, signifying not government but the community over which public authority was exercised and from which government itself was in principle derived. To say that citizens were equal meant originally that there was no difference between noble and commoner—a radical idea in societies that had always made legal distinctions between persons in different social categories. To say that the people were sovereign meant that neither the king, nor the British Parliament, nor any group of nobles, patricians, regents, or other elite possessed power of government in their own right; that all public officers were removable and exercised a delegated authority within limits defined by the constitution. Nobody (in theory) could act or exercise power "above the law." There must be no magistrate above the people, no self-perpetuation in

Liberty and equality

office, no rank derived from birth and acknowledged in the law. Social distinctions, as the French said in their Declaration of Rights of 1789, were to be based only "on common utility." Elites of talent or function there might be, but none of birth, privilege, or estate. "Aristocracy" in every form must be shunned. In representative bodies, there could be no special representation for special groups; representatives should be elected by frequent elections, not indeed by universal suffrage, but by a body of voters, however defined, in which each voter should count for one in a system of equal representation. Representation by numbers, with majority rule, replaced the older idea of representation of social classes, privileged towns, or other corporate groups. Women, specific racial groups, and enslaved persons, however, were excluded from voting, public offices, and political participation in legislative institutions.

Everything associated with absolutism, feudalism, or inherited rights (except the rights of property and the denial of rights because of gender or birth into slavery) was repudiated. Likewise rejected was any connection between religion and citizenship, or civil rights. The Democratic Revolution undermined the special position of the Catholic Church in France, the Anglican in England and Ireland, and the Dutch Reformed in the United Provinces. This was also the great period of what has been called Jewish "emancipation," which gave Jews political and social rights that had been denied to them throughout the Middle Ages and early modern era. The whole idea that government, or any human authority, was somehow willed by God and protected by religion faded away. A general liberty of opinion on all subjects was countenanced, in the belief that it was necessary to progress. Here again the secularism of the Enlightenment was carried from science and philosophy into many of the new political and cultural institutions that emerged during this era of revolutionary change.

On the whole, the Democratic Revolution was a middle-class movement, and indeed the term "bourgeois revolution" was later invented to describe it, though "bourgeois" refers to cultural values as well as to a broadly defined social-economic class. Many of its leaders in Europe were in fact nobles who were willing to forgo the historic privileges of nobility; and many of its active supporters were of the poorer classes, especially in the great French Revolution. But the middle classes were the great beneficiaries, and new middle-class or bourgeois societies generally emerged from the revolutionary upheavals. Persons of noble ancestry continued to exist after the storm was over, but the social and political world of noble hierarchies was gone. Nobles henceforth either took part in various activities on much the same terms as others or retreated into exclusive drawing rooms to enjoy their aristocratic distinctions in private. The main drive of the working classes was still to come.

The English-Speaking Countries: Parliament and Reform

If the American Revolution was the first act of a larger social and political drama, it must be understood also in connection with the broader British world of which the American colonies formed a part. The British Empire in the middle of the century was decentralized and composite. Thirty-one governments were directly subordinate to Westminster, ranging from the separate kingdom of Ireland through all the crown and charter colonies to the various political establishments maintained in Asia by the East India Company. The whole empire, with about 15,000,000 people of all colors in 1750, was less populous than France or the Austrian monarchy. The whole tract of the American mainland from Georgia to Nova Scotia compared in the number of its European or white population with Ireland or Scotland—or with Brittany or Bohemia—a figure of about 2,000,000 being roughly applicable in each case.

Britain had its own way of passing through the Age of Enlightenment. There was general contentment with the arrangements that followed the English Revolution of 1688—it has often been remarked that nothing is so conservative as a successful revolution. British thought generally lacked the asperity of thought on the Continent. The writers who most resembled French philosophes, such as the Scottish philosopher David Hume and the English historian Edward Gibbon, were moderate in their political ideas. The prevailing mood, however, was one of complacency, a self-satisfaction in the glories of the unwritten British constitution by which Englishmen enjoyed liberties unknown on the Continent.

In Britain, Parliament was as supreme as the monarchs in most Continental countries. The British Parliament was indeed more sovereign than any European ruler, because less that could be called "feudalism" remained in England than on the Continent. Nor was there any political despotism in England, enlightened or otherwise. The young George III, who inherited the throne in 1760, did feel himself to be a "patriot king." He did wish to heighten the influence of the crown and to overcome the factionalism of parties. But it was through Parliament that he had to work. He had to descend into the political arena himself, buy up or otherwise control votes in the Commons, grant pensions and favors, and make promises and deals with parliamentary politicians. What he did in effect was to create a new faction, the "king's friends." This faction was in power during the ministry of Lord North from 1770 to 1782. It is worth noting that all factions were factions of Whigs, that the Tory Party was practically defunct, that Britain did not yet have a two-party system, and that the word "Tory," as it came to be used by American revolutionaries, was little more than a term of abuse.

The monarchy in Great Britain

While Parliament was supreme, and constitutional questions apparently settled, there were nevertheless numerous undercurrents of discontent. These were expressed, because the press was freer in England than elsewhere, in many books and pamphlets that were read in the American colonies and helped to form the psychology of the American Revolution. There was, for example, a school of Anglo-Irish Protestant writers who argued that because Ireland was in any case a separate kingdom, with its own parliament, it ought to be less dependent on the central government at Westminster. The possibility of a similar separate state remaining within the British Empire, was one of the alternatives considered by Americans before they settled on independence. In England there was the considerable body of Dissenters, or Protestants not accepting the Church of England, who had enjoyed religious toleration since 1689 but continued to labor (until 1828) under various forms of political exclusion. They overlapped with two other amorphous groups, a small number of "commonwealthmen" and a larger number of parliamentary reformers. The commonwealthmen, increasingly eccentric and largely ignored, looked back nostalgically to the Puritan Revolution and the republican era of Oliver Cromwell. They kept alive memories of the Levellers and ideals of equality, well mixed with a pseudo-history of a simple Anglo-Saxon England that had been crushed by the despotism of the Norman Conquest. They had less influence in England than in the American colonies and especially New England, whose origins were closely connected to the Puritan Revolution. The parliamentary reformers were a more diverse and influential group. They were condemned in the eighteenth century to repeated frustration; not until the First Reform Bill of 1832 did they begin to accomplish their goals.

English discontent

The very power of Parliament meant that political leaders had to take strong measures to assure its votes—measures that were generally

Parliamentary politics

denounced by their critics as corruption. Control of Parliament, and especially of the House of Commons, was sustained by various devices, such as patronage or the giving of government jobs (called "places"), or awarding contracts, or having infrequent general elections (every seven years after 1716); or the fact that in many constituencies there were no real elections at all. The distribution of seats in the Commons bore no relation to numbers of inhabitants. A town having the right to send members to Parliament was called a "borough," but no new borough was created after 1688 (or until 1832). Thus localities that had been important in the medieval or Tudor periods were represented, but towns that had grown up recently, such as Manchester and Birmingham, were not. A few boroughs were populous and democratic, but many had few inhabitants or none, so that influential "borough mongers" decided who should represent them in Parliament.

Agitation for political reform

The reform movement began in England before the American Revolution, with which it was closely associated. The first agitation for reform centered about John Wilkes, a journalist and member of Parliament who vehemently attacked the policies of King George III. He was vindicated when the courts pronounced the arrest of his publisher illegal, but the king's supporters expelled him from the House of Commons. Wilkes became a political hero, however, and was later reelected three times to the House, which refused to seat him. A whirl of protests, public meetings, and petitions supported him against the exclusionary actions of Parliament. His followers in 1769 founded the Supporters of the Bill of Rights, the first of many societies dedicated to parliamentary reform. His case raised the question of whether the House of Commons should be dependent on the electorate and on the propriety of public agitation "out of doors" on political questions. It was in this connection, also, that debates in Parliament for the first time came to be reported in the London press. Parliament stood on the eve of a long transition, by which it was to be converted from a select body meeting in private to a modern representative institution answerable to the public and its constituents. Wilkes himself finally regained his parliamentary seat in 1774 and soon introduced the first of many reform bills, none of which passed for over half a century.

Meanwhile, the important Whig leaders, who had previously managed Parliament by manipulating elections in lightly populated boroughs, began to sense corruption in such methods after control passed to George III and his "friends." Their most eloquent spokes-

Edmund Burke

man was Edmund Burke (1729–1797), who would become an influential founder of philosophical conservatism. Other reformers called for more frequent elections, annual parliaments, a wider and more equal or even universal male suffrage, with dissolution of some boroughs in which no one was really represented. Burke favored none of these things; in fact he came strenuously to oppose them. He was more concerned that the House of Commons should be independent and responsible than that it should be mathematically representative. He thought that the landowning interest should govern. But he supported parliamentary reform by pleading for a strong sense of party in opposition to royal encroachments, and he argued that members of Parliament should follow their own best judgment of the country's interests, bound neither by the king on the one hand nor by their own constituents on the other. Like other reformers, he objected to "placemen," or jobholders dependent on their ministerial patrons, and he objected to the use made, for political purposes, of a bewildering array of pensions, sinecures, honorific appointments, and ornamental offices, ranks, and titles. In his Economical Reform of 1782, which curtailed crown patronage, he got many of these abolished.

FRANCES SUSANNA, LADY DE DUNSTANVILLE
by Thomas Gainsborough
(English, 1727–1788)
High social status is evident in this portrayal of a young English woman who was the wife of a wealthy member of Parliament. The wealth and status of her social class are apparent in her jewelry, her elegant gown, and her feather. Her hands and the background trees suggest a life of leisure and rural virtues. This is the way that English aristocrats of the eighteenth century liked to imagine themselves and to be portrayed for posterity.
(Source: National Gallery of Art)

The reform movement evolved and took on new strength at the time of the French Revolution, spreading then to more popular levels, as members of the skilled artisan class responded to events in France by demanding a more adequate "representation of the people" in England. They then had upper-class support from Charles James Fox and a minority of the Whigs. But conservatism (as described in Burke's critiques of the French Revolution), satisfaction with the British constitution, and a new patriotism that arose during the wars against revolutionary France all raised an impassable barrier. Reform was delayed for another generation.

After the American Revolution, which was a kind of political civil war within the English-speaking world, the English reformers generally blamed the trouble with America on King George III. This was less than fair, because Parliament on the American question was never dragooned by the king. The most ardent reformers later argued that if Parliament had been truly representative of the British people, the Americans would not have been driven to independence. This seems unlikely. In any case, reformers of various kinds, from Wilkes to Burke, were sympathetic to the complaints of the American colonials after 1763. There was much political correspondence across the Atlantic. Wilkes was a hero in Boston as well as London. Burke pleaded for conciliation with the colonies in a famous speech of 1775. His very insistence on the powers and dignity of Parliament, however, made it hard for him to find a workable solution; and after the colonies became independent, he showed no interest in the political ideas of the new American states. It was the more radical reformers in England, as in Scotland and Ireland, who most consistently favored the Americans, both before and after independence. They of course had no power. On the American

Reformers' influence in American colonies

Edmund Burke's insistence on the political and social value of inherited traditions made him a key figure in the emergence of modern conservatism. Although he favored an independent Parliament in Britain, he wrote a famous critique of the revolution that abolished traditional royal prerogatives in France. He appears here in an engraving from the 1770s, after a painting by Sir Joshua Reynolds.
(©Hulton Archive/Getty Images)

side, for a decade before independence, the increasingly discontented colonials, reading English books and pamphlets and reports of speeches, heard George III denounced for despotism and Parliament accused of incorrigible corruption. All this seemed to confirm what Americans had long been reading in the works of English Dissenters or old commonwealthmen, now on the fringes of English society but sure of a receptive audience in the American colonies. The result was to make Americans suspicious of all actions by the British government, to sense tyranny everywhere, to magnify such things as the Stamp Act into a kind of plot against American liberties.

The real drift in England in the eighteenth century, however, despite the chronic criticism of Parliament, was for Parliament to extend its powers in a general centralization

British centralization

of the empire. The British government faced somewhat the same problems as centralizing governments on the Continent. All had to deal with the issues raised by the great war of the midcentury, in its two phases of the Austrian Succession and Seven Years' War. Governments everywhere responded to the financial and military costs of these wars by trying to increase their own central power. We have seen how the French government, in attempting to tap new sources of revenue, tried to encroach on the liberties of Brittany and other provinces and to subordinate the bodies that in France were called parlements. We have likewise seen how the Habsburg government, also in an effort to raise more taxes, repressed local self-government in the empire and consolidated power in a more centralized bureaucracy. The same tendency showed itself in the British system. The Habsburg revocation of a constitutional charter in Bohemia in 1749 had its parallel in the revocation of the charter of Massachusetts in 1774. The disputes of the French king with the estates of Brittany or Languedoc had their parallel in the disputes of the British Parliament with the provincial assemblies of Virginia or New York. And the French government's unsuccessful attempts to collect more taxes from recalcitrant provincial nobles resembled the stymied British attempts to collect more revenue from their colonial subjects in North America.

Scotland, Ireland, India

The British also faced problems nearer home. Scotland proved a source of weakness in the War of the Austrian Succession. The Lowlanders were loyal enough, but the Highlanders revolted with French assistance in the Jacobite rising of 1745 and threatened the British government

British rule in Scotland

as it was locked in the struggle with France. The Highlands had never really been under any government, even under the old Scottish monarchy before the union of 1707 with England. Men in the Highlands looked to the heads of their clans to tell them whom and when to fight. A few leaders could throw the whole region to the Stuarts or the French. The British government, after 1745, proceeded to make its sovereignty effective in the Highlands. Troops were quartered there for years. Roads were pushed across the moors and through the glens. Law courts enforced the law of the Scottish Lowlands. Revenue officers collected funds for the treasury of Great Britain. The heads of the Scottish clans lost their old quasi-feudal jurisdiction. Fighting Highlanders were incorporated into newly formed Highland regiments of the British army, under the usual discipline imposed by the modern state on its fighting forces. For 30 years the Scots were forbidden to wear the kilt or play the bagpipes.

In Ireland the process of centralization worked itself out more slowly. Ireland had been subjected to new repression after the English Revolution of 1688, in part because of Irish involvement with the

The British in Ireland

anti-revolutionary forces. A French army had landed in Ireland, supported the deposed James II, and lost the decisive battle of the Boyne in 1690. The new English constitutional arrangements, the Hanoverian succession, the Protestant ascendancy, the church and the land settlement in Ireland, together with the prosperity of British commerce, were thus all secured by the continuing subordination of the smaller island. The native or Catholic Irish remained generally pro-French. The Presbyterian Irish disliked both the French and popery, but they were alienated from England also; many in fact emigrated to America in the generation before the American Revolution. Ireland remained quiet in the midcentury wars. When the trouble began between the British Parliament and the American colonies, the Presbyterian Irish generally took the American side. They were greatly stirred by the example of American independence. Thousands formed themselves into Volunteer Companies; they wore uniforms, armed, and drilled; they demanded both internal reform of the Irish parliament (which was even less representative than the British) and greater autonomy for the Irish parliament as against the central government at Westminster.

Faced with these demands, and fearing a French invasion of Ireland during the War of American Independence, the British government made concessions. It allowed an increase of power to the Irish parliament at Dublin. But from the English parliament Catholics were still excluded. In the next war between France and Great Britain, which began in 1793, many Irish felt a warm sympathy for the French Revolution. Catholics and Presbyterians, at last combining, formed a network of United Irish societies throughout the whole island. They sought French aid, but the French were never able to land a promised army. Even without French military support, the United Irish rose in 1798 to drive out the English and establish an independent republic. The British, suppressing the rebellion, now turned to centralization. The separate kingdom of Ireland, and the Irish parliament, ceased to exist. The Irish were thereafter represented in the imperial Parliament at Westminster. These provisions were incorporated in the Act of Union of 1801, creating the United Kingdom of Great Britain and Ireland, which Irish nationalists vehemently disliked but which lasted until 1922.

CHRONOLOGY OF NOTABLE EVENTS, 1733–1795

1733	Voltaire publishes *Philosophical Letters on the English*
1741	Montesquieu publishes *The Spirit of Laws*
1751–1772	Publication of the *Encyclopédie* in Paris
1753	Jean-Jacques Rousseau publishes *Origin of Inequality among Men*
1762	Rousseau publishes *The Social Contract* and *Émile*
1762–1796	Tsarina Catherine the Great reigns as enlightened despot in Russia
1769	Emergence of Reform Movement in British Parliament
1772	Prussia, Austria, and Russia impose the First Partition of Poland
1773	Emelian Pugachev leads a rebellion of the lower classes in Russia
1774–1792	King Louis XVI reigns in France
1776	Adam Smith publishes *The Wealth of Nations*
1776–1783	Revolutionary War leads to American independence from Britain
1780–1790	Emperor Joseph II introduces "enlightened" reforms in Austria
1784	Britain creates the India Office to manage British interests in India
1787	Written Constitution establishes new government in the United States
1793, 1795	Second and Third Partitions of Poland destroy the Polish state

Intervention in India

British establishments in India also faced new interventions from the centralizing imperial policies of Parliament. At the close of the Seven Years' War the various British posts in and around Mumbai, Chennai, and Kolkata (cities long known to the English as Bombay, Madras, and Calcutta) were unconnected with each other and subordinate only to the board of directors of the East India Company in London. Company employees interfered at will in the wars and politics of the Indian states and enriched themselves by such means as they could, which included graft, trickery, intimidation, rapine, and extortion. In 1773 the ministry of Lord North passed a Regulating Act, of which the main purpose was to regulate and restrict the often illegal actions of British subjects in India, whom no Indian government could control. The company was left with its trading activities, but its political activities were brought under parliamentary supervision. The act gathered all the British establishments under a single governor general, set up a new supreme court with British judges at Kolkata, and required the company to submit its correspondence on political matters for review by the ministers of His Majesty's Government. Warren Hastings became the first British governor general in India. He was so high-handed with some of the Indian princes, and made so many enemies among jealous English residents in Bengal, that he was denounced at home, impeached, and subjected to a trial that dragged on for seven years in the House of Lords. He was finally acquitted. After Clive, whose interventions had rapidly expanded British power there during the 1750s, Hastings was the main author of British supremacy in India. Meanwhile, in 1784 an India office was created in the British ministry at home. The governor general henceforth ruled the growing British sphere in India almost as an absolute monarch but only as the agent of the ministry and Parliament of Great Britain.

Thus the trend in the British world was to centralization. Despite the flutter of royalism under George III, the increasing centralization of all British territories developed under the authority of Parliament. What was happening in empire affairs, as in domestic politics in England, was a continuing application of the principles of 1689. The parliamentary sovereignty established in 1689 was now, after the middle of the eighteenth century, being applied to regions where it had heretofore had little effect. And it was against the centralizing authority of the British Parliament that the Americans primarily rebelled.

40. THE AMERICAN REVOLUTION

Background to the Revolution

The behavior of the Americans in the Seven Years' War, as viewed by the British government, left much to be desired. The several colonial legislatures rejected the Albany Plan of Union drafted by Franklin and commended to them by British officials. During the war it was the British regular army and navy, financed by taxes and loans in Great Britain, that drove the French out of North America. The war effort of the Anglo-Americans was desultory at best. After the defeat of the French the colonials had still to reckon with the Indians of the interior, who preferred French rule to that of the British and British-colonial governments that began to extend their control into western Indian lands. Many tribes joined in an uprising led by Pontiac, a western chief, and they carried their attacks on colonial and British outposts as far eastward as the Pennsylvania and Virginia frontiers. Again, the colonials proved unable to deal with a problem vital to their own future, and peace was brought about by officials and army units taking their orders from Great Britain.

The British government now tried to make the colonials pay a larger share toward the expenses of the empire. The colonials had hitherto paid only local taxes. They were liable to customs duties, of which the proceeds went in principle to Great Britain; but these duties were levied to enforce the Acts of Trade and Navigation and to direct the flow of commerce, not to raise revenue; and they were seldom paid, because the Acts of Trade and Navigation were persistently ignored. American merchants, for example, commonly imported sugar from the French West Indies, contrary to law, and even shipped in return the iron wares that it was against the law for Americans to manufacture for export. The colonials in practice paid only such taxes as were approved by their own local legislature for local purposes. The Americans in effect enjoyed a degree of tax exemption within the empire, and it was against this form of provincial privilege that Parliament began to move.

By the Revenue Act of 1764 (the "Sugar" Act), the British ministry, while reducing and liberalizing the customs duties payable in America, entered upon a program of actual and systematic collection. In the following year the ministry attempted to extend to British subjects in America a tax peaceably accepted by those in Great Britain and commonplace in most of Europe. This imposed on all uses of paper, as in newspapers and commercial and legal documents, the payment of a fee that was certified by the affixing of a stamp. The Stamp Act aroused violent and concerted resistance in the colonies, especially among the businessmen, lawyers, and editors who were the most articulate class. It therefore was repealed in 1766. In 1767 Parliament, clumsily casting about to find a tax acceptable to the Americans, hit upon the "Townshend duties," which taxed colonial imports of paper,

Colonial resistance to new taxes

paint, lead, and tea. Another outcry went up, and the Townshend duties were repealed, except the one on tea, which was kept as a token of the sovereign power of Parliament to tax all persons in the empire.

Debate over representation

The colonials had proved stubborn; and they had argued that Parliament had no authority to tax them because they were not represented in it. The British replied that Parliament represented America as much as it represented Great Britain. If Philadelphia sent no actually elected deputies to the Commons, so this argument ran, neither did Manchester in England. Both places enjoyed a kind of "virtual representation," because members of the Commons did not merely speak for local constituencies but made themselves responsible for imperial interests as a whole. To this many Americans retorted that if Manchester was not really represented it ought to be, which was of course also the belief of the English reformers. Meanwhile the strictly Anglo-American question subsided after the repeal of the Stamp Act and the Townshend program. There had been no clarification of principle on either side. But in practice the Americans had resisted significant taxation, and Parliament had refrained from making any drastic use of its sovereign power.

The Boston Tea Party

The calm was shattered in 1773 by an event that proved, to the more dissatisfied Americans, the disadvantages of belonging to a global economic system in which the main policies were made on the other side of the ocean. The East India Company was in difficulties. It had a great surplus of Chinese tea, and in any case it wanted new commercial privileges in return for the political privileges that it was losing in India by the Regulating Act of 1773. In the past the company had been required to sell its wares at public auction in London; other merchants had handled distribution from that point on. Now, in 1773, Parliament granted the company the exclusive right to sell tea through its own agents in America to American local dealers. Tea was a large item of business in the commercial capitalism of the time. The colonial consumer might pay less for it, but the intermediary American merchant would be shut out. The company's tea was boycotted in all American ports. In Boston, to prevent its forcible landing, a party of disguised men invaded the tea ships and dumped the chests into the harbor. To this act of vandalism the British government replied by measures far out of proportion to the offense. It "closed" the port of Boston, thus threatening the city with economic ruin. It virtually rescinded the charter of Massachusetts, forbidding certain local elections and the holding of town meetings.

The Quebec Act

And at the same time, in 1774, apparently by coincidence, Parliament enacted the Quebec Act. The wisest piece of British legislation in these troubled years, the Quebec Act provided a government for the newly conquered Canadian French, granting them security in their French civil law and Catholic religion and laying foundations for the British Empire that was to come. But the act defined the boundaries of Quebec somewhat as the French themselves would have defined them, including in them all territory north of the Ohio River—the present states of Wisconsin, Michigan, Illinois, Indiana, and Ohio. In the view of British legislators these boundaries were perfectly reasonable, because the few Europeans in the area were French, and since, in the age before canals or railways, the obvious means of reaching the whole region was by way of the St. Lawrence valley and the Lakes. But to the Americans the Quebec Act was a pro-French and pro-Catholic outrage, and at a time when the powers of juries and assemblies in the old colonies were threatened, it was disquieting that the Quebec Act made no mention of such representative institutions for the new northern province. It was lumped with the closing of an American port and the destruction of the Massachusetts government as one of the "Intolerable Acts" to be resisted.

MERCY OTIS WARREN
by John Singleton Copley (American, then English, 1737–1815)

This painting portrays an important writer and political activist in colonial Massachusetts. Mercy Otis Warren could not hold political offices, but she came from the kind of middle-class family that produced many leaders in the American and French Revolutions. Although this portrait dates from an earlier decade (c. 1763), it conveys the social position and values of a woman whose clothing and lack of expensive jewelry suggest her differences from the English aristocracy. Warren became an active opponent of British imperial policies and an influential author, but Copley disliked the rising revolutionary agitation in America and emigrated permanently to England in 1774.

(©Art Reserve/Alamy Stock Photo)

And indeed the implications of parliamentary sovereignty and centralized planning were now apparent. It was no longer merely an affair of taxation. A government that had to take account of the East India Company, the French Canadians, and the British taxpayers, even if more prudent and enlightened than Lord North's ministry of 1774, could not possibly at the same time have satisfied the Americans of the thirteen seaboard colonies. These Americans, since 1763 no longer afraid of the French Empire, were less inclined to forgo their own interests in order to remain under British protection or control. British policies had aroused antagonism in the coastal towns and in the backwoods, among wealthy land speculators and poor squatter frontiersmen, among merchants and the workers who depended on the business of merchants. The freedom of Americans to determine their own political life was in question. Yet there were few in 1774, or even later, prepared to face the thought of independence from the British Empire.

The War of American Independence

After the "Intolerable Acts," self-authorized groups met in the several colonies and sent delegates to a "continental congress" in Philadelphia. This body adopted a boycott of British goods, to be enforced on unwilling Americans by local organizers of resistance. Fighting began in the next year, 1775, when the British commander at Boston sent a detachment to seize unauthorized stores of weapons at Concord. On the way, at Lexington, in a brush between soldiers and partisans, or "minutemen," someone fired the

The "shot heard
round the world"

"shot heard round the world." The Second Continental Congress, meeting a few weeks later, proceeded to raise an American army, appointed George Washington as the commanding general of its troops, dispatched an expedition to force Quebec into the revolutionary union, and entered into overtures with Bourbon France.

The Congress was still reluctant to repudiate the tie with Britain. But passions grew fierce in consequence of the fighting. Radicals convinced moderates that the choice now lay between independence and enslavement. It appeared that the French, naturally uninterested in a reconciliation of British subjects, would give help if the avowed aim of American rebels was to dismember the British Empire. In January 1776 Thomas Paine, in his pamphlet *Common Sense,* made his debut as a kind of international revolutionary; he was to figure in the French Revolution and to work for revolution in England. He had come from England less than two years before, and he detested English society for its injustices. Eloquent and vitriolic, *Common Sense* identified the independence of the American colonies with the cause of liberty for all humankind. It pitted freedom against tyranny in the person of "the royal brute of Great Britain." It was "repugnant to reason," said Paine, "to suppose that this Continent can long remain subject to any external power. . . . There is something absurd in supposing a Continent to be perpetually governed by an island." *Common Sense* was read everywhere in the colonies, and its slashing arguments unquestionably spread a sense of proud isolation from the Old World. Such ideas also gained wide support in the Continental Congress, where Thomas Jefferson and other members of a special committee began drafting a theoretical and historical justification for America's separation from Britain. Like Paine, the authors linked their specific grievances to broad Enlightenment claims for universal human rights, thus giving the widest possible significance to the armed rebellion of some sparsely settled colonies in Britain's far-flung eighteenth-century empire. On July 4, 1776, the Congress adopted the Declaration of Independence, by which the United States assumed its separate and equal station among the powers of the earth.

Role of the
European powers

The War of American Independence thereupon turned into another European struggle for empire. France remained ostensibly noninterventionist for two more years, but meanwhile the French government secretly poured munitions into the colonies through an especially rigged-up commercial concern. Nine-tenths of the arms used by the Americans at the battle of Saratoga came from France. After the American victory in this battle the French government concluded, in 1778, that the insurgents were a good political risk, recognized them, signed an alliance with them, and declared war on Great Britain. Spain soon followed, hoping to drive the British from Gibraltar and deciding that its overseas empire was more threatened by a restoration of British supremacy in North America than by the disturbing example of an independent American republic. The Dutch were drawn into hostilities through their trade with the Americans, which flowed mostly by way of the Dutch West Indies. Other powers—Russia, Sweden, Denmark, Prussia, Portugal, and Turkey—irked at British employment of blockade and sea power in time of war, formed an "Armed Neutrality" to protect their commerce from dictation by the British fleet. The French, in a brief revival of their own sea power, landed an expeditionary force of 6,000 soldiers in Rhode Island. The Americans suffered from the internal differences inseparable from all revolutions and were in any case still unable to govern themselves to any effect, meeting with the old difficulties in raising both troops and money. It was therefore the participation of regiments of the French army, in conjunction with squadrons of the French fleet, that made possible the defeat of the armed forces of the British Empire and so persuaded the British government to recognize the

independence of the United States. By the peace treaty of 1783, though the British were still in possession of New York and Savannah and though the governments befriending the Americans would just as soon have confined them east of the mountains, the new republic obtained territory as far west as the Mississippi. Canada remained British. It now received an English-speaking population of more than 60,000 refugee American "Loyalists" who wanted to remain in the British Empire.

Significance of the American Revolution in the Atlantic World

The upheaval in America was a revolution in the Atlantic world as well as a war of independence. The Declaration of Independence was more than an announcement of secession from the empire; it was a justification of rebellion against established authority.

The Declaration of Independence

Curiously, although the American quarrel had been with the Parliament, the Declaration arraigned no one but the British king. One reason was that the Congress, not recognizing the authority of Parliament, could separate from Great Britain only by a denunciation of the British crown; another reason was that the cry of "tyrant" made a more popular and flaming issue. Boldly voicing the natural right philosophy of the age, the Declaration held as "self-evident"—that is, as evident to all reasonable people—that "all men are created equal, that they are endowed by their Creator with certain unalienable rights, that among these are life, liberty, and the pursuit of happiness." These electrifying words leaped inward into America and outward to Europe and the wider world.

Advances and limitations of equality

In the new states democratic equality made many advances. It was subject, however, to a great limitation, in that it long applied only to white males of European origin. It was more than a century before women received the vote. American Indians were relatively few in number, and the colonizing Europeans had already pushed most of them out of the coastal lands; but the black population at the time of the Revolution comprised about a fifth of the emerging nation's whole population. Many American whites of the revolutionary generation were indeed troubled by the institution of slavery. It was abolished outright in Massachusetts, and all states north of Maryland took steps toward its gradual extinction in the following decades. But application of the principles of liberty and equality without regard to race or gender went far beyond the political and cultural assumptions of even the most enlightened white Americans at the time. In the South, all censuses from 1790 to 1850 showed a third of the population to be slaves. For enslaved African Americans, the "self-evident" and "unalienable rights" would be blocked by a kind of internal white political truce until slavery was finally abolished in the American Civil War—a social upheaval that might well be described as the final, violent phase of a long revolutionary struggle that was first announced, in 1776, in America's Declaration of Independence. Meanwhile, in the North, free blacks found that in fact, and often in law, they were debarred from voting, from adequate schooling, and from the widening opportunities in which white Americans saw the essence of their national life and their superiority to Europe.

Democratization

For the white male population, however, the Revolution had a democratizing effect in many ways. Lawyers, landowners, and business-men who led the movement against Britain needed popular support, and to obtain it they were willing to make promises and concessions to the lower classes. Or the popular elements, workmen and mechanics, farmers and frontiersmen, often dis-sidents in religion, extorted concessions by force or threats. There was a good deal of

violence, as in all revolutions; the new states confiscated property from the counterrevolutionaries, called Tories, some of whom were tarred and feathered by infuriated mobs. The dissolution of the old colonial governments threw open all political questions. In some states more men became qualified to vote. In some, governors and senators were now popularly elected, in addition to the lower houses of the legislatures as in colonial times. The principle was adopted, still unknown to the parliamentary bodies of Europe, that each member of a legislative assembly should represent about the same number of citizens. Primogeniture and entail, which landed families aspiring to an aristocratic mode of life sometimes favored, went down before the demands of democrats and small property owners. Tithes were done away with, and the established churches—Anglican in the South, Congregationalist in New England—lost their privileged position in varying degree. But the Revolution was not socially as profound as the revolution soon to come in France, or as the revolution in Russia in 1917. Property changed hands, but the law of property was modified only in detail. There had been no such thing in British America as a native nobleman or even a bishop; clergy and aristocracy had been incomparably less ingrained in American than in European society, and the rebellion against them was thus less devastating in its effect.

Influence of Enlightenment thinkers

The main importance of the American Revolution remained political and even constitutional in a strict sense. The American leaders were themselves part of the wider Age of Enlightenment, sharing fully

Thomas Paine (1737-1809) lived in England until he arrived in Philadelphia in 1774. He published his *Common Sense* anonymously two years later, after the armed conflict had begun. Widely read, it helped persuade Americans to fight for complete independence from Britain.

in its humane and secular spirit. But Montesquieu was the only non-British thinker who significantly influenced America's political elite, and Montesquieu owed his popularity to his philosophizing upon English institutions. The Americans drew heavily on the writings of John Locke, but their cast of mind went back before Locke to the English Puritan movement of the first half of the seventeenth century. Their thought was formed not only by Locke's ideas of human nature and government, but, as already noted, by the dissenting literature and the neorepublican writings that had never quite died out in England. The realities of life for five generations in America had sharpened the old insistence upon personal liberty and equality. When the dispute with Britain came to a head, the Americans found themselves arguing for the historic and chartered rights of the English as well as the timeless and universal rights of man, both of which were invoked in the colonies to challenge the British imposition of parliamentary sovereignty. The Americans came to believe, more than any other people, that government should possess limited powers and operate only within the terms of a fixed and written constitutional document.

All of the 13 new states quickly produced or reaffirmed written constitutions, and each enshrined virtually the same principles. All asserted the central idea in the great Declaration, that it was to protect "unalienable" rights that governments were instituted among men and that whenever government became destructive to this end the people had a right to "institute new government" for their safety and happiness. All the constitutions undertook to limit government by a separation of executive, legislative, and judicial powers. Most appended a bill of rights, stating the natural rights of the citizens and the actions that no government might justly take. None of the constitutions were as yet fully democratic. Even the most liberal constitutions gave some advantage in public affairs to the owners of property and excluded women from voting and holding government offices; and many, as noted earlier, would long protect slavery.

Despite the clear limits on democratic participation, the early state constitutions and later national constitution affirmed numerous Enlightenment ideas and also helped to shape the new concept of federalism. Federalism, or the allocation of power between central and outlying governments, went along with the idea of written constitutions as a principal offering of the Americans to the wider world history of political theories and institutions. Like constitutionalism, federalism developed in the atmosphere of protest against a centralized sovereign power. It was a hard idea for Americans to work out, and until 1789 the states maintained only a loose affiliation in the Articles of Confederation. The United States was a union of 13 independent republics. Disadvantages in this scheme becoming apparent, a constitutional convention met at Philadelphia in 1787 and drew up the constitution that is today the world's oldest written instrument of government still in operation. In it the United States was conceived not merely as a league of states but as a union in which individuals were citizens of the United States of America for some purposes and of their particular states for others. Persons, not states, composed the federal republic, and the laws of the United States fell not merely on the states but on the people.

Constitutionalism and federalism

The international consequences of the American Revolution can hardly be overstated. By overburdening the French treasury, the American war became a direct cause of the French Revolution. Beyond that, it ushered in the age of predominantly liberal or democratic revolution that lasted through the European revolutions of 1848 and even into later struggles for national independence or unity. The American doctrine, like most thought in the Age of Enlightenment, was expressed in universal terms of "man" and "nature." All peoples regardless of their own history could apply it to themselves, because as

Alexander Hamilton once put it in his youth, "the sacred rights of man are not to be rummaged for among old parchments or musty records. They are written, as with a sun-beam, in the whole volume of human nature, by the hand of Divinity itself, and can never be erased or obscured by mortal power." The Americans, in freeing themselves, had done what all peoples ought to do to affirm the "rights of man."

Significance of American Revolution

The revolt in America offered a dramatic judgment on the old colonial system, convincing some, in England and elsewhere, that the empires for which they had long been struggling were hardly worth acquiring, because colonies in time, in the words of Turgot, fell away from the mother country "like ripe fruit." The idea spread, because trade between Britain and America continued to prosper, that one could do business with a country without exerting political influence or control, and this idea became fundamental to the coming movement of economic liberalism and free trade. By coincidence, the book that became the gospel of the free trade movement, Adam Smith's *The Wealth of Nations*, was published in England in the year 1776. The American example was pointed to by other peoples wishing to throw off colonial status—first by the Latin Americans, then by the peoples of the older British dominions, and, finally, in the twentieth century, by those of Asia and Africa also. In Europe, the American example encouraged the type of nationalism in which subjugated nations aspired to be free. And within the former British-American colonies the Revolution did much to determine the spirit and method by which the new nation spread across the North American continent and the ideas by which the United States, when it became a leading power a century and a half later, would explain and justify its national actions in the modern world.

More immediately, the American example was not lost on the many Europeans who sojourned in the new states during and after the war. Of these the French Marquis de Lafayette was the most famous, but there were many others: Thomas Paine, who returned to Europe in 1787; the future French revolutionist Brissot; the future Polish national leader Kosciusko; the future marshals of Napoleon, Jourdan and Berthier; the future reformer of the Prussian army Gneisenau. Numerous Americans also went to Europe, notably the aging Benjamin Franklin, who in the 1780s was incredibly lionized in the fashionable and literary world of Paris. People and ideas thus flowed in both directions across the Atlantic.

Vindication of Enlightenment ideas

The establishment of the United States was taken in Europe to prove that many ideas of the Enlightenment were practicable. Rational-ists declared that here was a people, free of past errors and supersti-tions, who showed how enlightened beings could plan their own affairs. Rousseauists saw in America the very paradise of natural equality, unspoiled innocence, and patriotic virtue. But nothing so much impressed Europeans, and especially the French, as the spectacle of the Americans meeting in solemn conclave to draft their state consti-tutions. These, along with the Declaration of Independence, were translated and published in 1778 by a French nobleman, the Duke de la Rochefoucauld. They were endlessly and excitedly discussed as Europeans projected their own ideas or traditions onto a place that they did not really know. Constitutionalism, federalism, and limited government were not new ideas in Europe. They came out of the Middle Ages and were currently set forth in many quarters, for example, in Hungary, the Holy Roman Empire, and the Parlement of Paris. But in their prevailing form, and even in the philosophy of Montesquieu, they were associated with feudalism and aristocracy. The American Revolution made such ideas progressive. The American influence, added to the force of developments in Europe, made

DECLARATION OF INDEPENDENCE
by John Trumbull (American, 1756–1843)

Trumbull's painting shows the committee that presented America's Declaration of Independence to the Continental Congress in 1776. Although Franklin and Adams are standing with the committee, Thomas Jefferson is presenting the document. Trumbull met often with Jefferson in Paris when he was at work on this painting in the late 1780s, and the picture conveys a Jeffersonian view of the event it portrays.

(Ormsby, Waterman Lilly, 1834–190/Library of Congress Prints and Photographs Division [LC-DIG pga-02322])

the thought of the later Enlightenment more democratic. The United States replaced England as the model country of advanced thinkers. On the Continent there was less passive trust in the enlightened despotism of the official state and more confidence in the idea of enlightened self-government.

The American constitutions seemed to offer a practical demonstration of the social contract. They offered Europeans an idealized image of men in a state of nature, having cast off their old government, deliberately sitting down to contrive a new one, weighing and judging each branch of government on its merits, assigning due powers to legislature, executive, and judiciary, declaring that all government was created by the people and in possession of a merely delegated authority, and listing specifically the inalienable human rights—inalienable in that they could not conceivably be taken away, because all persons possessed them even if denied them by force. And these rights were the very same rights that many eighteenth-century Europeans wanted for themselves—freedom of religion, freedom of press, freedom of assembly, freedom from arbitrary arrest at the discretion of officials. And they were all based on the rigorous principle of equality before the law. The American example crystallized and made tangible the ideas that were strongly blowing in Europe, and the American example was one reason why the French, in 1789, began their revolution with a declaration of human rights and with the drafting of a written constitution.

And more deeply still, America became a kind of mirage or ideal vision for Europe, land of open opportunity and of new beginnings, free from the load of history and of the past, wistfully addressed by Goethe:

> *America, thou hast it better*
> *Than has our Continent, the old one.*

It is evident that this was only part of the picture. The United States, as its later history was to show, bore a heavy load of inherited burdens and unsolved problems, especially slavery and pervasive racial discrimination. The new American nation had emerged from the complex cross-cultural encounters of the previous two centuries and from the wider history of the early modern Atlantic World—to which it remained deeply connected through its religions and politics, its international trade, and its diverse African, Indian, and European populations. But in a general way, until new revolutionary and radical social movements set in a century later, America stood for many Europeans as a kind of utopian opportunity for common people, a "new world" not only for the millions who emigrated to it but for other millions who stayed at home, who often wished that their own countries might become more like it, and many of whom might even have agreed with Abraham Lincoln in calling it "the last best hope of earth."

Suggested Further Readings can be found in the ebook, on Connect, or online at www.mhhe .com/kramer12e.

Chapter 9

THE FRENCH REVOLUTION

In 1789 France fell into revolution, and the world has never since been the same. The French Revolution was by far the most momentous upheaval of the whole revolutionary age. It replaced the "old regime" with a new kind of "modern society," and at its extreme phase it became very radical, so much so that later revolutionary movements often looked back to it as a predecessor. The ideas of the French Revolution, spreading far beyond France itself, decisively influenced the subsequent development of political parties and ideological conflicts throughout much of Europe and elsewhere; indeed, the Revolution still provokes highly charged debates about the characteristics or consequences of social reform, political radicalism, and revolutionary violence.

At the time, in the age of the Democratic or Atlantic Revolution from the 1760s to the 1860s, the role of France was decisive. Even the Americans, without French military intervention, would hardly have won such a clear settlement from England or been so free to set up the new states and new constitutions that have just been described. And while revolutionary disturbances in Ireland and Poland, or among the Dutch, Italians, and others, were by no means caused by the French example, it was the presence or absence of French aid that usually determined whatever successes they achieved. The Revolution in France also contributed to other revolutions in the wider Atlantic world. The great slave uprising in the French colony at Saint-Domingue, which began in 1791 and led eventually to the creation of the independent Republic of Haiti, was inspired in part by reports of the recently declared "rights of man" in France; and later French military interventions in Spain and Portugal set off, somewhat indirectly, the revolutionary movements that swept across Latin America after 1808. Few revolutions, in short, have ever generated such far-reaching historical upheavals.

Chapter emblem: Detail from *The Tennis Court Oath* by Jacques-Louis David (1748–1825). (©Print Collector/Getty Images)

The French Revolution, unlike the Russian or Chinese revolutions of the twentieth century, occurred in what was in many ways the most advanced country of the day. France was the center of the intellectual movement of the Enlightenment. French science then led the world. French books were read everywhere, and the newspapers and political journals that became very numerous after 1789 carried a message that hardly needed translation. French was an international language for educated and aristocratic people in most European countries. France was also, potentially before 1789 and actually after 1793, the most powerful country in Europe. It may have been the wealthiest, though not per capita. With a population of 24,000,000 the French were the most numerous of all European peoples under a single government. Even Russia was hardly more populous until after the partitions of Poland. The Germans were divided, the subjects of the Habsburgs were of diverse nationalities, and the English and Scots together numbered at this time only 10,000,000. Paris, though smaller than London, was over twice as large as Vienna or Amsterdam. French exports to Europe were larger than those of Great Britain. It is said that half the goldpieces circulating in Europe were French. Europeans in the eighteenth century were in the habit of taking ideas from France; they were therefore, depending on their social position, the more excited, encouraged, alarmed, or horrified when revolution broke out in that country.

41.　SOCIAL AND CULTURAL BACKGROUNDS

The Old Regime: The Three Estates

We have noted the hierarchical organization of the social and political institutions of the monarchical Old Regime, as the prerevolutionary French society came to be called after it disappeared, and we have seen that enlightened despotism failed to alter these institutions in any fundamental way. The essential fact about the Old Regime was that it was still legally aristocratic and in some ways feudal. Everyone belonged legally to an "estate" or "order" of society. The First Estate was the clergy, the Second Estate was the nobility, and the Third Estate included everyone else—from the wealthiest business and professional classes to the poorest peasants and city workers. These categories were important in that the individual's legal rights and personal prestige depended on the category to which he or she belonged. Politically, the estates were obsolescent; not since 1614 had they assembled in an Estates General of the whole kingdom, though in some provinces they had continued to meet as provincial bodies. Socially, they were obsolescent also, for the three-fold legal division no longer corresponded to the real distribution of social influence, property, or productive activity among the French people.

Conditions in the church and the position of the clergy have sometimes been much exaggerated as a cause of the French Revolution. The church in France

The church

levied a tithe on all agricultural products, but so did the church in England; the French bishops often played a part in government affairs, but so did bishops in England through the House of Lords. The French bishoprics of 1789 were no wealthier than those of the Church of England were found to be when investigated 40 years later. In actual numbers, in the secular atmosphere of the Age of Enlightenment, the clergy, especially the monastic orders, had greatly declined, so that by 1789 there were probably not more than 100,000 Catholic clergy of all types in the entire population. But if some past historians overemphasized the importance of the clergy, still it must be said that the church was deeply involved in the prevailing social system. For one thing, church bodies—bishoprics, abbeys, convents, schools, and other religious

This image of French peasants shows how farmers prepared their fields and planted seeds during the 1760s, when the picture was published in a French book. The agrarian system shaped property rights and social hierarchies as well as the supply of food in French cities—all of which created resentments or fears that contributed to the coming of the French Revolution.

(©ARPL/HIP/The Image Works)

foundations—owned between 5 and 10 percent of the land of the country, which meant that collectively the church was the greatest of all landowners. Moreover, the income from church properties, like all income, was divided very unequally, and much of it found its way into the hands of the aristocratic occupants of the higher ecclesiastical offices.

The noble order, which in 1789 comprised about 400,000 persons, including women and children, had enjoyed a great resurgence since the death of Louis XIV in 1715. Distinguished government service, higher church offices, army, parlements, and most other public and semipublic honors were almost monopolized by the nobility in the time of Louis XVI, who, it will be recalled, had mounted the throne in 1774 and had abandoned recent attempts to break the nobility's power in the traditional parlements. Repeatedly, through parlements, Provincial Estates, or the assembly of the clergy dominated by the noble bishops, the aristocracy had blocked royal plans for taxation and shown a desire to control the policies of state. At the same time the bourgeoisie, or upper crust of the Third Estate, had never been so influential. Although the bourgeoisie was an amorphous social category (indeed, some historians argue that "bourgeois" refers to a class that never had a real social identity), the number of French merchants, lawyers, and other professional groups clearly grew over the course of the eighteenth century. The fivefold increase of French foreign trade between 1713 and 1789 suggests the growth of the merchant class and of the legal and governmental classes associated with it. As members of the growing merchant and professional groups became economically stronger, more widely read, and more self-confident, they

The nobility

resented the distinctions and privileges that enhanced the status of nobles. Some of these were financial: nobles were exempt on principle from the most important direct tax, the taille, whereas bourgeois persons obtained exemption with more effort; but so many bourgeois persons enjoyed tax privileges that purely monetary self-interest was not primary in their psychology. The higher echelons of the non-noble social elite resented the nobles for their sense of superiority and their social arrogance. What had formerly been customary respect was now felt as humiliation. Many otherwise successful and wealthy people felt that they were being shut out from office and honors and that the nobles were seeking more power in government as a class. The Revolution thus began in the social and political collision of two moving objects: an assertive nobility that sought to protect its privileges and an expanding, assertive bourgeoisie that resented the nobles' protected status.

The common people, below the commercial and professional families in the Third Estate, were probably as well off as in most countries. But they were not well off compared with the upper classes. Wage earners had by no means shared in the eighteenth-century wave of business prosperity. Between the 1730s and the 1780s the prices of consumers' goods rose about 65 percent, whereas wages rose only 22 percent. Persons dependent on wages were therefore badly pinched, but they were less numerous than today, for in the country there were many small farmers and in the towns many small craftsmen who made a living not by wages but by selling the product of their own labor at market prices. Yet in both town and country there was a significant wage-earning population, which was to play a decisive part in the Revolution.

The Third Estate

The Agrarian System of the Old Regime

Over four-fifths of the people lived on agrarian lands and in rural villages. The agrarian system had evolved so that there was no serfdom in France as it was known in eastern Europe. The peasant owed no labor to the lord—except a few token services in some cases. The peasants worked for themselves, either on their own land or on rented land; or they worked as sharecroppers; or they hired themselves out to the lord or to another peasant.

The manor, however, still retained certain surviving features of the feudal age. The noble owner of a manor enjoyed "hunting rights," or the privilege of keeping game preserves and of hunting on his own and the peasants' land. He usually had a monopoly over the village mill, bakeshop, or wine press, for the use of which he collected fees called *banalités*. He possessed certain vestigial powers of jurisdiction in the manorial court and certain local police powers, from which fees and fines were collected. These seigneurial privileges were of course the survivals of a day when the local manor had been a unit of government and the noble had performed the functions of government, an age that had long passed with the development of the centralized modern state.

Survival of feudal privileges

There was another special feature to the property system of the Old Regime. Every owner of a manor (there were some bourgeois and even wealthy peasants who had purchased manors) possessed what was called a right of "eminent property" with respect to all land located in the manorial village. This meant that lesser landowners within the manor owned their land in that they could freely buy, sell, lease, and inherit or bequeath it; but they owed to the owner of the manor, in recognition of his "eminent property" rights, certain rents, payable annually, as well as transfer fees that were payable whenever the land changed owners by sale or death. Subject to these eminent property rights, landowner-ship was fairly widespread. Peasants directly owned about two-fifths of the soil of the country; bourgeois owners held a little under a fifth. The nobility owned perhaps a little over a fifth and the church owned somewhat under a tenth, the remainder being crown lands, wastelands, or commons. Finally, all property rights were subject also to certain "collective" rights by which villagers might cut firewood, run their pigs in the commons, or pasture cattle on land belonging to other owners after the crops were in, which they could easily do because there were usually no fences or enclosures.

All this may seem rather complex, but it is important to realize that property is a changing institution. Even today, in industrialized countries, a high proportion of all property is in land, including natural resources in and below the soil. In the eighteenth century property meant land even more than it does today. The bourgeois class, whose wealth was so largely in ships, merchandise, or commercial paper, also invested heavily in land, and in 1789 they owned almost as much land in France as the nobility and more than the church. The Revolution *Property ownership* transformed the law of property by freeing the private ownership of land from all the traditional and indirect encumbrances described—manorial fees, eminent property rights, communal village agricultural practices, and church tithes. It also was to abolish other older forms of property, such as property in public office or in masterships in the guilds, which had worked to the advantage mainly of closed and privileged groups. In final effect the Revolution defined and established the institutions of private property in the modern sense and therefore brought the greatest economic benefits to the land-owning peasants and the bourgeoisie.

The peasants not only owned two-fifths of the soil but also worked almost all of it on their own initiative and risk. In effect, the land owned by the nobility, the church, the bourgeoisie, and the crown was divided up and leased to peasants in small parcels. France was thus already mainly a country of small farmers. There was no "big agriculture" as in England, eastern Europe, or the plantations of America. The manorial lord performed no economic function. He lived (there were of course exceptions) not by managing an estate and selling his own crops and cattle but by receiving innumerable dues and fees. During the eighteenth century, in connection with the general aristocratic resurgence, there was an economic change that has often been called *The "feudal reaction"* the "feudal reaction." Manorial lords, faced with rising living costs and acquiring higher living standards because of the general material progress, collected their dues more rigorously or revived old ones that had fallen into disuse. Leases and sharecropping arrangements also became less favorable to the peasants. The farmers, like the wage earners, were under a steadily increasing pressure. At the same time the peasants resented the "feudal dues" more than ever because they often regarded themselves as the real owners of the land and viewed the lord as a gentleman of the neighborhood who for no reason enjoyed a special income and a status different from their own. Resentments arose because many of the fees and obligations in the property system no longer bore any relation to real economic usefulness or activity.

The political unity of France, achieved over the centuries by the monarchy, was likewise a fundamental prerequisite, and even a cause, of the Revolution. Whatever social conditions might have existed, they could give rise to nationwide public opinion, nationwide agitation, nationwide policies, and nationwide legislation only in a country already politically unified as a nation. These conditions were lacking in central Europe. In France a centralized French state existed. Reformers did not have to create it but only capture and remodel it. The French in the eighteenth century already had developed the sense of membership in a political entity called France. The Revolution saw a tremendous stirring or expansion of this sense of membership and of fraternity, turning it into a passion for citizenship, civic rights, voting powers, and the use of the state and its sovereignty for the public advantage; but at the very outbreak of the Revolution people could salute each other as *citoyen* or *citoyenne* and shout *vive la nation!*

Political Culture and Public Opinion after 1770

The social and economic resentments that existed among ambitious people in French cities and among peasants in the French countryside could finally explode in a revolutionary upheaval because eighteenth-century writers had created a culture that encouraged political and social criticism. Educated persons in the Third Estate could draw on Enlightenment conceptions of reason, natural rights, and historical progress to complain about the irrationality of ancient privileges or the injustice of noble prerogatives. Enlightenment thought provided a language in which people could now describe their dissatisfactions with the obstacles that stymied professional or economic ambitions.

The Revolution and the Enlightenment

It has been argued that the famous works of the French philosophes led directly to the revolutionary events of 1789; it was the "fault" of Voltaire, critics explained; it was the "fault" of Rousseau. Many who supported the Revolution also made such claims for its intellectual origins, so that the history of the French Revolution has always been linked in complex ways with the legacy of the Enlightenment. Yet most historians now argue that the connections between the philosophes and the Revolution were by no means as direct as people once imagined. The philosophes themselves favored enlightened social reforms, but they were not revolutionaries and, except perhaps for Rousseau, they rarely promoted the political rights of the lower classes. Their most important publications, including the famous *Encyclopédie,* often attracted more readers among the nobility than among the middle classes. Political theory was far less popular than novels or social satires; there was an enormous audience for Rousseau's *Julie, or the New Héloise,* for example, but few persons read *The Social Contract.* The notion that great Enlightenment writers caused the French Revolution is therefore an inadequate explanation for what happened (much as claims that bourgeois economic interests caused the Revolution are also inadequate). It is nevertheless true that the Enlightenment contributed widely to new forms of criticism, public debate, and public opinion, most of which challenged the traditional authority of the French king and nobles.

The last two decades of the Old Regime were filled with intense political controversy as the monarchy sought unsuccessfully to suppress the traditional French parlements, as successive ministries sought to raise new revenues, as French journals reported on the new American state constitutions, and as pamphleteers increasingly attacked the officials and courtiers at Versailles. The critical spirit that had developed in salons, coffeehouses, and literary arguments spread rapidly into a developing public sphere of political debate. The new political pamphlets were scarcely concerned with the subtle nuances of political theory; in fact, many consisted of little more than scandalous rumors of sexual misconduct or financial corruption in the affairs of the royal family and government ministries. Stories of corruption in high places stripped away the once sacred image of the monarchy, the church, and the social hierarchy. At the same time, the reading public developed an interest in scandalous legal cases that pitted members of the aristocracy against aggrieved persons of the Third Estate or that revealed immorality and decadence among ancient noble families. Lawyers could publish their legal briefs without securing the approval of government censors, and, using this freedom, they bolstered their legal arguments with

Critical spirit

appeals to popular sentiment or natural rights. The injustice of inherited privilege thus became a recurring theme in the scandalous stories of social and personal disputes that French lawyers carried from French courtrooms to the tribunal of public opinion.

By 1789, in France, educated persons in all social classes were coming to believe what Voltaire had said after the famous Calas Affair in the 1760s: "Opinion governs the world." Campaigns to influence public opinion became a powerful political force in French society during the last decades of the Old Regime, and most such campaigns appealed for public support in the name of reason, rights, or justice. In these ways, the critical thought of Enlightenment culture entered into bitter political conflicts that led finally and unexpectedly to the Revolution.

42.   THE REVOLUTION AND THE REORGANIZATION OF FRANCE

The Financial Crisis

The Revolution was precipitated by a financial collapse of the government. What overburdened the government was by no means the costly magnificence of the court of Versailles. Only 5 percent of public expenditures in 1788 was devoted to the upkeep of the entire royal establishment. What overburdened all governments was war costs, both current upkeep of armies and navies and the burden of public debt, which in all countries was due almost totally to the high costs of past wars. In 1788 the French government devoted about a quarter of its annual expenditure to maintenance of the armed forces and about half to the payment of its debts. British expenditures showed almost the same distribution. The French debt stood at almost 4 billion livres. It had been greatly swollen by the War of American Independence. Yet it was only half as great as the national debt of Great Britain, and less than a fifth as heavy per capita. It was less than the debt of the Dutch Republic. It was apparently no greater than the debt left by Louis XIV three-quarters of a century before. At that time the debt had been lightened by repudiation. No responsible French official in the 1780s even considered repudiation, a sure sign of the late eighteenth-century expansion and public influence of the well-to-do classes, who were the main government creditors.

Yet the debt could not be carried, for the simple reason that revenues fell short of necessary expenditures. This in turn was not due to national poverty but to the tax exemptions and tax evasions of privileged elements and to complications in the fiscal system, or lack of system, by which much of what taxpayers paid never came into the hands of the Treasury. We 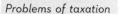 *Problems of taxation* have already described how the most important tax, the taille, was generally paid only by the peasants—the nobles being exempt by virtue of their class privilege, and officeholders and other wealthy persons obtaining exemption in various ways. The church too insisted that its property was not taxable by the state; and its periodic "free gift" to the king, though substantial, was less than might have been obtained from direct taxation of the church's land. Thus, although the country itself was prosperous, the government treasury was empty. The social classes that enjoyed most of the wealth of the country did not pay taxes corresponding to their income—and, even worse, they resisted taxation as a sign of inferior status.

A long series of responsible persons—Louis XIV himself, John Law, Maupeou, Turgot— had seen the need for taxing the privileged classes. Jacques Necker, a Swiss banker who

The French government's financial crisis in the 1780s led these two ministers, Charles Alexandre de Calonne and the archbishop Loménie de Brienne (on the right), to propose new taxation plans, but neither a special Assembly of Notables nor the Parlement of Paris would accept their proposals. The failure to enact tax reforms forced Louis XVI to convene the long-inactive Estates General, which would give members of the Third Estate new opportunities for political action.

(©Print Collector/Getty Images)

became director of the finances in 1777, made moves in the same direction and, like his predecessors, was dismissed. His successor, Calonne, as the crisis mounted, came to even more revolutionary conclusions. In 1786 he produced a program in which enlightened despotism was tempered by a modest resort to representative institutions. He proposed, in place of the taille, a general tax to fall on all landowners without exemption, a lightening of indirect taxes and abolition of internal tariffs to stimulate economic production, and a confiscation of some properties of the church. He also sought to give the propertied elements a greater interest in the government by proposing the establishment of provincial assemblies in which all landowners should be represented without regard to estate or order.

Resistance of the nobles

Calonne's program, if carried out, might have solved the fiscal problem and averted the Revolution. But it struck not only at noble privileges in taxation but also at the threefold hierarchic organization of society. Knowing from experience that the Parlement of Paris would never accept it, Calonne in 1787 convened an "assembly of notables," hoping to win its endorsement of his ideas. The notables insisted on concessions in return, for they wished to share in control of the government. A deadlock followed; the king dismissed Calonne and appointed as his successor Loménie de Brienne, the worldly-wise archbishop of Toulouse. Brienne tried to push the same program through the Parlement of Paris. The Parlement rejected it, declaring that only the three estates of the realm, assembled in an Estates General, had authority to consent to new taxes. Brienne and Louis XVI at first refused, believing that the Estates General, if convened, would be dominated by the nobility. Like Maupeou and Louis XV, Brienne and Louis XVI tried to break the parlements, replacing them with a modernized judicial system in which the law courts should have no influence over financial policies. This led to a veritable revolt of the nobles. All the parlements and Provincial Estates resisted; army officers refused to serve; the intendants hesitated to act; and noblemen began to organize political clubs and committees of correspondence. With his government brought to a standstill, and unable to borrow money or collect taxes, Louis XVI on July 5, 1788, promised to call the Estates General for the following May. The various Estates were invited to elect representatives and also to draw up lists of their grievances.

From Estates General to National Assembly

Because no Estates General had met in over a century and a half, the king asked for proposals on how such an assembly should be organized under modern conditions. This led to an outburst of public discussion, which soon expanded far beyond all previous campaigns to influence public opinion. Hundreds of political pamphlets appeared, many of them demanding a change in the old system by which the three estates sat in separate chambers, each chamber voting as a unit. This voting system was widely criticized because it meant, in practice, that the chamber of the Third Estate was always outnumbered. But in September 1788 the Parlement of Paris, restored to its functions, ruled that the Estates General should meet and vote as in 1614, in three separate orders.

The nobility, through the Parlement, thus revealed its aim. It had forced the summoning of the Estates General to protect and enhance its own political influence, and in this way the French nobility initiated the Revolution. The Revolution began as another victory in the aristo-cratic resurgence against the earlier absolutism of the king. The nobles actually had a liberal program: they demanded constitutional government, guarantees of personal liberty for all, freedom of speech and press, freedom from arbitrary arrest and confinement. Many now were even prepared to give up special privileges in taxation; this might have worked itself out in time. But in return they hoped to become the preponderant political element in the state. It was their idea not merely to have the Estates General meet in 1789 but for France to be henceforth governed through the Estates General, a supreme body in three chambers—one for nobles, one for a clergy in which the higher officers were also nobles, and one for the Third Estate.

The aims of the nobility

This was precisely what the Third Estate wished to avoid. Lawyers, bankers, business owners, government creditors, shopkeepers, artisans, working people, and peasants had no desire to be governed by lords temporal and spiritual. Their hopes for a new, more equitable political and legal system formed by the philosophy of the Enlightenment, stirred by the revolution in America, rose to the utmost excitement when "good king Louis" called the Estates General. The ruling of the Parlement of Paris in September 1788 thus came to them as a slap in the face—an unprovoked class insult. The whole Third Estate turned on the nobility with detestation and distrust. The Abbé Sieyès in January 1789 published his famous pamphlet *What Is the Third Estate?*, declaring that the nobility was a useless caste that could be abolished without loss, that the Third Estate was the one necessary element of society, that it was identical with the nation, and that the people of the Third Estate thus embodied (or should embody) the sovereignty of the French nation. Through Sieyès the ideas of Rousseau's *The Social Contract* entered the thought of the Revolution. At the same time, even before the Estates General actually met, and not from the books of philosophes so much as from actual events and conditions, nobles and commoners viewed

The Third Estate reacts

Convoked for the first time in 175 years, the Estates General met in a large hall at Versailles in May 1789. This picture shows Louis XVI seated on his throne, with deputies of the clergy seated on his right, those of the nobility on his left, and those of the Third Estate facing him at the other end of the hall.
(©Print Collector/Getty Images)

each other with fear and suspicion. The Third Estate, which had at first supported the nobles against the "despotism" of the king's ministers, now ascribed to the former the worst possible motives. Bourgeois critics vehemently rejected the political program and ambitions of the nobility. Class antagonism poisoned the Revolution at the outset and threw many articulate members of the Third Estate into a radical and destructive mood.

The Estates General met as planned in May 1789 at Versailles. The Third Estate, most of whose representatives were lawyers, would not accept the division of the orders into three separate chambers. It insisted that deputies of all three orders should sit as a single house and vote as individuals; this procedure would give an advantage to the Third Estate, because the king had granted it as many deputies as the other two orders combined. For six weeks a deadlock was maintained. On June 13 a few priests, leaving the chamber of the First Estate, came over and sat with the Third. They were greeted with jubilation. On June 17 the Third Estate declared itself the "National Assembly." Louis XVI, under pressure from the nobles, closed the hall in which it met. The members found a neighboring indoor tennis court and there, milling about in a babel of confusion and apprehension, swore and signed the Oath of the Tennis Court on June 20, 1789, affirming that wherever they gathered, they were the actually existing National Assembly and that they would not disband until they had drafted a constitution. This was a revolutionary step, for it assumed virtually sovereign power for a body that had no legal authority. The king ordered members of the three estates to sit in their separate houses, though he now presented a reforming program of his own, too late to win the confidence of the disaffected and in any case continuing the organization of French society in legal classes.

The self-entitled National Assembly refused to back down. The king faltered, failed to enforce his commands promptly, and allowed the Assembly to remain in being. In the following days, at the end of June, he summoned about 18,000 soldiers to Versailles.

What had happened was that the king of France, in the dispute raging between nobles and commoners, chose the nobles. It was traditional in France for the king to oppose and reduce the autonomous powers of the nobility. For centuries the French monarchy had drawn strength from the support of urban or bourgeois social groups. All through the eighteenth century the royal ministers had carried on the struggle against the privileged interests. Only a year before, Louis XVI had been almost at war with his rebellious aristocracy. In 1789 he failed to assert himself. He lost control over the Estates General, exerted no leadership, offered no program until it was too late, and provided no symbol behind which parties could rally. He failed to make use of the profound loyalty to himself felt by the bourgeoisie and common people, who yearned for nothing so much as a king who would stand up for them, as in past times, against an aristocracy of birth and status. He tried instead, at first, to compromise and postpone a crisis; then he found himself in the position of having issued orders that the Third Estate boldly defied; and in this complex political predicament he yielded to his wife Marie Antoinette, to his brothers, and to the court nobles, all of whom told him that his dignity and authority were being undermined. At the end of June Louis XVI undoubtedly intended to dissolve the Estates General by military force. But what the Third Estate most feared was a future in which the king would support the nobles as they sought to control the government of the country. There was now no going back; the revolt of the Third Estate had allied Louis XVI with the nobles, and the Third Estate now feared the nobles more than ever, believing with good reason that they now had the king in their hands.

Louis XVI supports the nobles

The Lower Classes in Action

The country meanwhile was falling into social dissolution, as the lower classes, below the bourgeoisie, moved into open rebellion against their economic and social conditions. For them too the convocation of the Estates General had seemed to herald a new era. The grievances of ages, and those that existed equally in other countries than France, rose to the surface. Short-run conditions were bad. The harvest of 1788 had been poor; the price of bread, by July 1789, was higher than at any time since the death of Louis XIV. It was also a time of widening economic depression; the rapid growth of trade since the American war had suddenly halted, so that wages fell and unemployment spread while scarcity drove food prices up. The government, paralyzed at the center, could not take its customary action to relieve the problem of food shortages. The masses were restless everywhere. Labor trouble broke out; in April a riot of workers devastated a wallpaper factory in Paris. In the rural districts there was much disorder. Peasants were declaring that they would pay no more manorial dues and were refusing to pay taxes. In the best of times the countryside was troubled by vagrants, beggars, and smugglers who flourished along the many tariff frontiers. Now the business depression reduced the income of honest peasants who engaged in weaving or other domestic industries in their homes; unemployment and indigence spread in the country; people were uprooted; and the result was to raise the number of vagrants to terrifying proportions. It was believed, because nothing was too bad to believe of the aristocrats (though it was not true), that they were secretly recruiting these "brigands" for their own purposes to intimidate the Third Estate. The economic and social crises thus provoked widespread fear and became acutely political.

THE TENNIS COURT OATH
by Jacques-Louis David (French, 1748–1825)
**This famous picture portrays the momentous decision by members of the Third Estate to continue
meeting as the National Assembly of France until they had written a new constitution. The deputies
swore their oath at an indoor tennis court because the king had closed the hall in which they had been
holding their sessions.**
(©Print Collector/Getty Images)

People in the towns feared that they would be swamped by beggars and desperadoes.
This was true even of Paris, the largest city in Europe except London. The Parisians were
also alarmed by the concentration of troops about Versailles. They began to arm in self-
defense. All classes of the Third Estate took part. Crowds roamed the city, looking for

> *The storming of the
> Bastille*

weapons in arsenals and public buildings. On July 14 they came to the
Bastille, a stronghold built in the Middle Ages to overawe the city, like
the Tower of London in England. It was used as a place of detention
for persons with enough influence to escape the common jails but was
otherwise in normal times considered harmless; in fact there were few
prisoners in the fortress, and there had been talk, some years before, of tearing it down
to make room for a public park. Now, in the general turbulence, the governor had placed
cannons in the embrasures. The crowd requested him to remove his cannons and to
furnish them with arms. He refused. Through a series of misunderstandings, reinforced
by the vehemence of a few firebrands, the crowd turned into a mob, which violently
assaulted the fortress and which, when helped by a few trained soldiers and artillery
pieces, persuaded the governor to surrender. The mob, enraged by the death of 98 of its
members, streamed in and murdered 6 soldiers of the garrison in cold blood. The governor
was also murdered while under escort to the Town Hall. A few other officials met the
same fate. Their heads were cut off, stuck on the ends of pikes, and paraded about the

city. While all this happened, the regular army units on the outskirts of Paris did not stir; their reliability was open to question and the authorities were in any case unaccustomed to firing on the people.

The capture of the Bastille, though not so intended, had the effect of saving the Assembly at Versailles. The king, not knowing what to do, accepted the new situation in Paris. He recognized a citizens' committee, which had formed there, as the new municipal government. He sent away the troops that he had summoned and commanded the recalcitrants among nobles and clergy to join in the National Assembly. In Paris and other cities a new national guard was established to keep order. The Assembly appointed the Marquis de Lafayette, who had returned from the American Revolution as "the hero of two worlds," to command the guard in Paris. For insignia Lafayette combined the colors of the city of Paris, red and blue, with the white of the house of Bourbon. The French tricolor, emblem of the Revolution and the new sovereign nation, thus originated in this symbolic fusion of the old and new.

In the rural districts matters went from bad to worse. Vague insecurity rose to the proportions of a general panic in the Great Fear of 1789, which spread over the country late in July in the wake of travelers, postal couriers, and others. The cry was relayed from point to point that "the brigands were coming." Peasants, armed to protect their homes and crops

The Great Fear of 1789

and mobilized by shared fears of imagined dangers, turned their attention to the manor houses, burning them in some cases and in others simply destroying the manorial archives in which fees and dues were recorded. The Great Fear became part of a general agrarian insurrection, in which peasants, far from being motivated simply by wild alarms, knew perfectly well what they were doing. They intended to destroy the manorial regime by force.

The Initial Reforms of the National Assembly

The Assembly at Versailles could restore social order only by meeting the demands of the peasants, but to wipe out all manorial payments would deprive the landed aristocracy of much of its income; and many bourgeois also owned manors. There was thus much perplexity as the new Assembly considered possible responses to the rural upheaval. A small group of deputies prepared a surprise move in the Assembly, choosing an evening session from which many would be absent. Hence came the "night of August 4." A few liberal noblemen, by prearrangement, arose and surrendered their hunting rights, their *banalités,* their rights in manorial courts, and feudal and seigneurial privileges generally. What was left of serfdom and all personal servitude was declared ended. Tithes were abolished. Other deputies repudiated the special privileges of their provinces. All personal tax privileges were given up. On the main matter, the dues arising from eminent property in the manors, a compromise was adopted. These dues were all abolished but compensation was to be paid by the peasants to the former owners. The compensation was in most cases never paid. Eventually, in 1793, in the radical phase of the Revolution, the provision for compensation was repealed. In the end French peasant landowners rid themselves of their manorial obligations without cost to themselves. This was in contrast to what later happened in most other countries, where peasants, when liberated from manorial obligations, either lost part of their land or were burdened with installment payments lasting many years.

In a decree summarizing the resolutions of August 4 the Assembly declared flatly that "feudalism is abolished." With legal privilege replaced by legal equality, it proceeded to map the principles of the new order. On August 26, 1789, it issued the Declaration of the Rights of Man and Citizen.

PRISE DE LA BASTILLE,
le 14 Juillet 1789.

The capture of the Bastille—the prison-fortress that became a symbol of Old Regime repression—marked the dramatic entry of the Parisian crowd into the rapidly evolving Revolution. Violence in the streets of Paris in July 1789 saved the National Assembly from the king's intention to dissolve it.
(Library of Congress Prints & Photographs Division [LC-USZ62-10833])

The Declaration of the Rights of Man and Citizen

The Declaration of 1789 consisted of 17 articles that affirmed the general principles of the new state, which were essentially the rule of law, the equality of individual citizenship, and the collective national sovereignty of the people. "Men are born and remain," declared Article I, "free and equal in rights." Man's natural rights were held to be "liberty, property, security, and resistance to oppression." Freedom of thought and religion was guaranteed; no one might be arrested or punished except by process of law; all persons were declared eligible for any public office for which they met the requirements. Liberty was defined as the freedom to do anything not injurious to others, which in turn was to be determined only by law. Law must fall equally upon all persons. Law was the expression of the general will, to be made by all citizens or their representatives. The only sovereign was the nation itself, and all public officials and armed forces acted only in its name. Taxes might be raised only by common consent, all public servants were accountable for their conduct in office, and the powers of government were to be separated among different branches. Finally, the state might for public purposes, and under law, confiscate the property of private persons, but only with fair compensation. The Declaration, printed in thousands of leaflets, pamphlets, and books, read aloud in public places, or framed and hung on walls, became the catechism of the Revolution in France. When translated into other languages it soon carried the same message to all of Europe. Thomas Paine's

Although women gained some new rights during the French Revolution, they were denied the right to vote or to hold public office; and women's political clubs were eventually disbanded. Olympe de Gouges, who is portrayed here in a later engraving, challenged such exclusions in her *Declaration of the Rights of Woman* (1791) and other writings, thereby provoking strong opposition from revolutionary leaders. She was charged with sedition and put to death during the Terror in 1793.
(©Kean Collection/Getty Images)

book *The Rights of Man,* published in 1791 to defend the French Revolution, gave the phrase a powerful impact in English.

The "rights of man" had become a motto or watchword for potentially revolutionary ideas well before 1789. The thinkers of the Enlightenment had used it, and during the American Revolution even Alexander Hamilton had spoken of "the sacred rights of man" with enthusiasm. "Man" in this sense was meant to apply abstractly to the rights of all people, regardless of nationality, race, or sex. In French as in English the word "man" was used to designate all human beings, and the Declaration of 1789 was not intended to refer to males alone. In German, for example, where a distinction is made between *Mensch* as a human being and *Mann* as an adult male, the "rights of man" was always translated as *Menschenrechte.* Similarly the word "citizen" in its general sense applied to women, as is shown by the frequency of the feminine *citoyenne* during the Revolution, in which a great many women were very active. But when it came to the exercise of specific legal rights the Revolutionaries went no farther than contemporary opinion. Thus they assigned the right to vote and hold office only to men, and in most matters of property, family law, and education it was the boys and men who benefited most. Very few persons at the time argued for full legal and political equality between the sexes.

One of them, however, was Olympe de Gouges, a woman who had gained prominence as a writer of plays and pamphlets and who, in 1791, published *The Declaration of the Rights of Woman and the Female Citizen.* Following the official Declaration in each of its 17 articles, she applied them to women explicitly in each case, and she asserted also, in addition, the right of women to divorce under certain conditions, to control property

The Rights of Woman

in marriage, and to have equal access with men to higher education, civilian careers, and public employment. Mary Wollstonecraft in England published a similar *Vindication of the Rights of Woman* in 1792. In France some of the secondary figures in the Revolution, and some of the teachers in boys' schools, thought that women should have greater opportunities at least in education. And there were in fact a few reforms that improved the social rights of women. The revolutionary government redefined marriage as a civil contract and legalized divorce in 1792, thereby enabling women to leave abusive or unhappy marriages (until divorce was banned again in 1816). Inheritance laws were also changed in ways that gave women the legal right to equal inheritance of their family's property.

Historical Documents

Olympe de Gouges, *Declaration of the Rights of Woman and the Female Citizen* (1791)

The revolutionary National Assembly defined France's new political principles in its "Declaration of the Rights of Man and Citizen" of 1789. The Declaration's 17 articles affirmed that human beings were born "free and equal" and that the nation was the source of all sovereign power, but the new political institutions and electoral processes excluded women. Olympe de Gouges (1748-1793), who had previously written plays and pamphlets, asserted that women had the same rights as men. She summarized her arguments in a new Declaration that revised the Assembly's general principles and 17 articles by explicitly extending each essential right to women, as in the following excerpts. De Gouges was charged with anti-revolutionary sedition and executed on the guillotine in 1793.

Preamble

Mothers, daughters, sisters, female representatives of the nation ask to be constituted as a national assembly. Considering that ignorance, neglect, or contempt for the rights of woman are the sole causes of public misfortunes and governmental corruption, they have resolved to set forth in a solemn declaration the natural, inalienable, and sacred rights of woman. . . .

1. Woman is born free and remains equal to man in rights. Social distinctions may be based only on common utility.
2. The purpose of all political association is the preservation of the natural and imprescriptible rights of woman and man. These rights are liberty, property, security, and especially resistance to oppression. . . .

Postscript

Women, wake up; the tocsin of reason sounds throughout the universe; recognize your rights. The powerful empire of nature is no longer surrounded by prejudice, fanaticism, superstition, and lies. The torch of truth has dispersed all the clouds of folly and usurpation. . . .

Oh women! Women, when will you cease to be blind? What advantages have you gathered in the Revolution? A scorn more marked, a disdain more conspicuous. . . . Whatever the barriers set up against you, it is in your power to overcome them; you only have to want it. . . . [A]nd since national education is an issue at this moment, let us see if our wise legislators will think sanely about the education of women.

Olympe de Gouges, "Declaration of the Rights of Women," *The French Revolution and Human Rights: A Brief Documentary History*, translated, edited, and with an introduction by Lynn Hunt (Boston: Bedford/ St. Martin's, 1996), pp. 124–127.

Exclusion of women

But among the leaders of the Revolution, only Condorcet argued for legal equality of the sexes. Intent on political change, the revolutionaries thought that politics, government, law, and war were a masculine business, for which only boys and young men needed to be educated or prepared. The Revolution generally reduced or restricted the cultural and political influence that some women had exercised in the elite circles of Old Regime society. The new political order, as most revolutionaries defined it, was to develop through "manly" opposition to the "feminine" corruptions of the Old Regime court and social hierarchies. "Women are disposed . . . to an over-excitation which would be deadly in public affairs," one revolutionary deputy argued in a typical justification for excluding women from government institutions. Such assumptions led to restrictions on the rights of women to petition or

**A WOMAN OF THE
REVOLUTION
by Jacques-Louis David (French,
1748–1825)**

**David's portrait of a lower-class
French woman in 1795 suggests
the determination of the women
who joined the revolutionary Parisian crowds and clubs during the
French Revolution; and the painting conveys in a more general way
the revolutionary challenge to traditional social and legal privileges.**

(©Christophel Fine Art/Getty Images)

gather in political meetings; finally, in 1793, the revolutionary government closed all
women's political clubs—even though many women had been among the Revolution's
earliest and most active supporters.

Shortly after adoption of the Declaration of the Rights of Man the Revolutionary leadership fell into multiple factions. In September 1789 the Assembly began the actual planning
of the new government. Some wanted a strong veto power for the king and a legislative body
in two houses, as in England. Others, the "patriots," wanted only a delaying veto for the
king and a legislative body of one chamber. Here again, it was suspicion of the nobles that
proved decisive. The "patriots" were afraid that an upper chamber would bring back the
nobility as a collective force, and they were afraid to make the king constitutionally strong
by giving him a full veto, because they believed him to be in sympathy with the nobles. His
brother, the Count of Artois, followed by many aristocrats, had already emigrated to foreign
parts and, along with these other émigrés, was preparing to agitate against the Revolution
with all the governments of Europe. The patriot party would concede nothing; the more
conservative party could gain nothing. The debate was interrupted again, as in July, by
insurrection and violence. On October 4, a crowd of market women and revolutionary
militants, followed by the revolutionary Paris national guard, took the road from Paris to
Versailles. Besieging and invading the château, they forced Louis XVI and his family to take
up residence in Paris, where he could be watched. The National Assembly also moved to
Paris, where it too soon fell under the influence of radical elements in the city. The champions of a one-chamber legislative body and of a suspensive veto for the king won out.

The more conservative revolutionaries, if such they may be called, disillusioned at
seeing constitutional questions settled by mobs, began to drop out of the Assembly. Men

who on June 20 had bravely sworn the Oath of the Tennis Court now felt that the Revolution was falling into unworthy hands. Some even emigrated, forming a second wave of émigrés that would have nothing to do with the first. The counterrevolution gathered strength.

But those who wanted still to go forward, and they were many, began to organize in clubs. Most important of all was the Society of Friends of the Constitution, called the

The Jacobins

Jacobin club for short, since it met in an old Jacobin monastery in Paris. The dues were at first so high that only wealthier persons could belong; the dues were later lowered but never enough to include people of the poorest classes, who therefore formed clubs of their own. The most advanced members of the Assembly were Jacobins, who used the club as a caucus in which to discuss their policies and develop their plans. They remained a middle-class group even during the later and more radical phase of the Revolution, and numerous women participated in their meetings. Madame Rosalie Jullien, for example, who was as dedicated a revolutionary as her husband and son, attended a meeting of the Paris Jacobin club on August 5, 1792. Tell your friends in the provinces, she wrote to her husband, that these Jacobins are "the flower of the Paris bourgeoisie, to judge by the fancy jackets they wear. There were also two or three hundred women present, dressed as if for the theater, who made an impression by their proud attitude and forceful speech."

Constitutional Changes

In the two years from October 1789 to September 1791 the National Assembly (or the Constituent Assembly, as it had come to be called because it was preparing a constitution) continued its work of simultaneously governing the country, devising a written constitution, and destroying in detail the institutions of the Old Regime. The Assembly soon discarded most of the political and legal institutions that had governed French affairs for centuries—the old monarchical ministries, the organization of government bureaus, the taxes and tax exemptions, the private ownership of government positions, the titles of nobility, the parlements, the hundreds of regional systems of law, the internal tariffs, the provinces, and the urban municipalities. Contemporaries such as Edmund Burke were appalled at the thoroughness with which the French seemed determined to eradicate their national institutions. Why, asked Burke, should the French fanatics cut to pieces the living body of Normandy or Provence? The truth is that the provinces, like everything else, formed part of the whole system of special privilege and unequal rights. All had to disappear if the hope of equal citizenship under national sovereignty was to be attained. In place of the provinces the Constituent Assembly divided France into 83 equal "departments." In place of the old towns, with their quaint old magistrates, it introduced a uniform municipal organization, all towns henceforth having the same form of government, varying only according to size. All local officials, even prosecuting attorneys and tax collectors, were elected locally. Administratively the country was decentralized in reaction against the bureaucracy of the Old Regime. No one outside Paris now really acted for the central government, and local communities enforced the national legislation, or declined to enforce it, as they chose. This proved ruinous when war came, and although the departments created by the Constituent Assembly still exist, it became common in France after the Revolution, as it was before, to keep local officials under strong control by ministers in Paris.

The Constitution of 1791

Under the constitution that was prepared, sometimes called the Constitution of 1791 because it went into effect at that date, the sovereign power of the nation was to be exercised by a unicameral elected

The three men at an anvil are a noble, a cleric, and a commoner hammering out a new constitution together. At the beginning of the Revolution, most people expected the three estates to fraternize in the redefined French nation.
(©Editorial Image Provider/Getty Images)

assembly called the Legislative Assembly. The king was given only a suspensive veto power by which legislation desired by the Assembly could be postponed. In general, the executive branch, that is, king and ministers, was kept weak, partly in reaction against "ministerial despotism," partly from a well-founded distrust of Louis XVI. In June 1791 Louis attempted to escape from the kingdom, join with émigré noblemen abroad, and seek help from foreign powers. He left behind him a written message in which he explicitly repudiated the Revolution. Arrested at Varennes in eastern France, he was brought back to Paris and forced to accept his status as a constitutional monarch. The hostile attitude of Louis XVI greatly disoriented the Revolution, for it made impossible the creation of a strong executive power and left the country to be ruled by a debating society, which under revolutionary conditions contained more than the usual number of hotheads.

Not all this machinery of state was democratic. As noted above, women did not receive the right to vote or hold public office; and in the granting of political rights to men the abstract principles of the great Declaration were seriously modified for practical reasons. Because most people were illiterate, it was thought that they could have no reasonable political views; and it was assumed that persons such as domestic servants or shop assistants would merely follow the political views of their employers. The Constituent Assembly therefore distinguished in the new constitution between "active" and "passive" citizens. Both had the same civil rights, but only active citizens had the right to vote. These active citizens chose "electors" on the basis of one elector for every hundred active citizens. The electors convened in the chief town of their new department and there chose deputies to the national legislature as well as certain local officials. Males over 25 years of age, and wealthy enough to pay a small direct tax, qualified as active citizens; well over half the adult male population could so qualify. Of these, men paying a somewhat higher tax qualified as electors; even so, almost half the adult males qualified for this role. In practice, what limited the number of available electors was that, to function as such, a man had to have enough education, interest, and leisure to attend an electoral assembly at a distance from home and remain in attendance for several days. In any case, only about 50,000 persons served as electors in 1790-1791 because a proportion of one for every hundred active citizens yielded that figure.

Economic and Cultural Policies

Economic policies favored the middle rather than the lowest classes. The public debt had precipitated the Revolution, but the revolutionary leaders, even the most extreme Jacobins, never disowned the debt of the Old Regime. The reason is that the bourgeois class, on the whole, were the people to whom the money was owed. To secure the debt, and to pay current expenses of government, because tax collections had become very sporadic, the Constituent Assembly as early as November 1789 resorted to a device by no means new in Europe, though never before used on so extensive a scale. It confiscated all the property of the church. Against this property, it issued negotiable instruments called *assignats,* first regarded as bonds and issued only in large denominations, later regarded as currency and issued in small bills. Holders of *assignats* could use them, or any money, to buy parcels of the former church lands. None of the confiscated land was given away; all was in fact sold, because the interest of the government was fiscal rather than social. The peasants, even when they had the money, could not easily buy land because the lands were sold at distant auctions or in large undivided blocks. The peasants were disgruntled, though they did acquire a good deal of the former church lands through middlemen. Peasant landowners were likewise expected, until 1793, to pay compensation for many of their old manorial fees. And the landless peasants actively opposed some of the revolutionary changes when the government, with its modern ideas, encouraged the dividing up of the village commons and extinction of various collective village rights in the interest of individual private property.

Assignats

The revolutionary leadership favored free economic individualism. It had had enough, under the Old Regime, of government regulation over the sale or quality of goods and of privileged companies and other economic monopolies. Reforming economic thought at the time in France and in Britain, where Adam Smith had published his epoch-making *The Wealth of Nations* in 1776, held that organized special interests were bad for society and that all prices and wages should be determined by free arrangement between the individuals concerned. The more prominent leaders of the French Revolution believed firmly in this freedom from control. The Constituent Assembly thus abolished the guilds, which were mainly monopolistic organizations of small businessmen or master craftsmen, interested in keeping up prices for certain goods or services and averse to new machinery or new methods.

There was also in France what we would now call an organized labor movement. Because the masterships in the guilds were practically hereditary (as a form of property and privilege), the journeymen had formed their own associations, or trade unions, called *compagnonnages,* outside the guilds. Many trades were so organized—the carpenters, plasterers, paper workers, hatters, saddlers, cutlers, nail makers, carters, tanners, locksmiths, and glassworkers. Some were organized nationally; some, only locally. All these journeymen's unions had been illegal under the Old Regime, but they had flourished nevertheless. They collected dues and maintained officers. They often dealt collectively with the guild masters or other employers, requiring the payment of a stipulated wage or change of working conditions. Sometimes they even imposed closed shops. Organized strikes were quite common. The labor troubles of 1789 continued on into the Revolution. Business fell off in the atmosphere of disorder. In 1791 there was another wave of strikes. The Assembly, in the Le

Banning labor organizations

The revolutionary government used paper money to finance its policies. The notes were called *assignats* because they were assigned to, or secured by, real estate confiscated during the Revolution, mostly from the church. Inflation rose rapidly after 1794, so that even notes with denominations as high as 10,000 livres, as shown in this picture, became worthless. The assignats were therefore abolished, and a new, more stable French currency came into use in 1796.

(©Heritage Images/Getty Images)

Chapelier law of that year, renewed the old prohibitions of the *compagnonnages*. The same law restated the abolition of the guilds and forbade the organization of special economic interests of any kind. All trades, it declared, were free for all to enter. All persons, without belonging to any organization, had the right to work at any occupation or business they might choose. All wages were to be settled privately by the worker and his or her employer. This was not at all what the workers, at that time or any other, really wanted. Nevertheless the provisions of the Le Chapelier law remained a part of French law for three-quarters of a century. The embryonic trade unions continued to exist secretly, though with more difficulty than under the hit-and-miss law enforcement of the Old Regime.

Meanwhile, revolutionary activists set about transforming the symbols, rituals, dress, and holidays of Old Regime society. Seeking to break from the hierarchies and privileges of the past, they developed a new political culture that would be symbolized by a new tricolor flag, new forms of democratic language, new clothing, new festivals, and new public monuments. The art and imagery of the traditional monarchy and church rapidly disappeared from public life. Great festivals of national unity were organized, beginning with the famous "Festival of the Federation," which brought together a vast crowd in Paris to mark the first anniversary of the assault on the Bastille (July 14, 1790), to celebrate the new liberties of the French people, and to create new rituals for what would eventually become the French national holiday.

A revolutionary political culture

Supporters of the Revolution planted "liberty trees" in towns throughout France, and they began to wear "liberty caps" and tricolor cockades to show their political allegiances. Later revolutionary governments encouraged new artwork in which the nation came to be represented by a female symbol of liberty, Marianne. Statues of Marianne offered alternatives to traditional Catholic icons of the Virgin Mary and gave illiterate persons new visual images by which they could understand that national sovereignty and liberty had replaced the king and church at the symbolic center of French political life. A profusion of revolutionary plays, novels, and songs conveyed the same message. By promoting the new political ideas and symbols in every sphere of daily life, the French Revolution created a new national identity and "nationalized" the French people through the use of cultural rituals that would later become common in other national movements of the modern world.

The Quarrel with the Church

Most fatefully of all, the Constituent Assembly quarreled with the Catholic Church. The confiscation of church properties came as a shock to the clergy. The village priests, whose support had made possible the revolt of the Third Estate, now found that the very buildings in which they worshipped with their parishioners on Sunday belonged to the "nation." The loss of income-producing properties undercut the religious orders and ruined the schools, in which thousands of boys had received free education before the Revolution. Yet it was not on the question of material wealth that the church and the Revolution came to blows. Members of the Constituent Assembly took the view of the church that the great monarchies had taken before them. The idea of separation of church and state was far from their minds. They regarded the church as a form of public authority and as such subordinate to the sovereign power. They frankly argued that the poor needed religion if they were to respect the property of the more wealthy. In any case, having deprived the church of its own income, they had to provide for its maintenance. For the schools many generous and democratic projects of state-sponsored education were drawn up, though under the troubled conditions of the times little was accomplished. For the clergy the new program was mapped out in the Civil Constitution of the Clergy of 1790.

The Civil Constitution of the Clergy

This document went far toward setting up a French national church. Under its provisions the parish priests and bishops were elected, the latter by the same 50,000 electors who chose other important public officials. Protestants, Jews, and agnostics could legally take part in the elections, purely on the ground of citizenship and property qualifications. Archbishoprics were abolished, and all the borders of existing bishoprics were redrawn, so that one would be coterminous with each of the 83 departments. Bishops were allowed merely to notify the pope of their elevation; they were forbidden to acknowledge any papal authority on their assumption of office, and no papal letter or decree was to be published or enforced in France except with government permission. All clergy received salaries from the state; the average income of bishops was somewhat reduced and that of parish clergymen was raised. Sinecures, plural holdings, and other abuses by which the church had supported noble families were done away with. The Constituent Assembly (independently of the Civil Constitution) also prohibited the taking of religious vows and dissolved all monastic houses.

Some of these church reforms were not in principle alarmingly new, because before the Revolution the civil authority of the king had designated the French bishops and passed judgement on the admission of papal documents into France. French bishops, in the old spirit of the "Gallican liberties," had traditionally resisted papal power in France. Many members of the clergy were now willing to accept something like the Civil Constitution if allowed to produce it on their own authority. The Assembly refused to concede so much jurisdiction to the Gallican Church and applied instead to the pope, hoping to force its plans upon the French clergy by invoking the authority of the Vatican. But the

The revolutionaries created rituals and symbols to celebrate the new nation they were trying to establish. The great festival of the Federation in Paris on July 14, 1790, shown here, assembled the king, the National Guard, and a huge crowd in a symbolic expression of the national unity and national liberties that the new political institutions were supposed to protect.
(©Christophel Fine Art/Getty Images)

Vatican pronounced the Civil Constitution a wanton usurpation of power over the Catholic Church. Unfortunately, the pope also went further, condemning the whole Revolution and all its works. The Constituent Assembly retorted by requiring all French clergy to swear an oath of loyalty to the constitution, including the Civil Constitution of the Clergy. Half took the oath and half refused it, the latter half including all but seven of the bishops. One of the seven willing to accept the new arrangements was Talleyrand, soon to be famous as foreign minister of numerous French governments.

There were now two churches in France, one clandestine, the other official, one maintained by voluntary offerings or by funds smuggled in from abroad, the other financed and sponsored by the government. The former, comprising the nonjuring, unsworn, or "refractory" clergy, turned violently counterrevolutionary. To protect themselves from the Revolution they insisted, with an emphasis quite new in France, on the universal religious supremacy of the Roman pontiff. They denounced the "constitutional" clergy as schismatics who spurned the pope and as mere careerists willing to hold jobs on the government's terms. The constitutional clergy, those taking the oath and upholding the Civil Constitution, considered themselves to be patriots and defenders of the universal rights of man; and they insisted that the Gallican Church had always enjoyed a degree of liberty from Rome. The Catholic laity were terrified and puzzled. Many were sufficiently attached to the Revolution to prefer the constitutional clergy but to do so meant to defy the pope, and Catholics who persisted in defying the pope were on the whole those least zealous in their religion. The constitutional clergy therefore stood on shaky foundations. Many of their followers, under stress of the times, eventually turned against Christianity itself.

Constitutional and refractory clergy

Good Catholics tended to favor the refractory clergy. The outstanding example was the king himself. He personally used the services of refractory priests, and thus gave a new reason for the revolutionaries to distrust him. Whatever chance there was that Louis XVI might go along with the Revolution now disappeared, for he concluded that he could do so only by endangering his immortal soul. Former aristocrats also preferred the refractory clergy. They now put aside the Voltairean levities of the Age of Enlightenment, and the "best people" began to exhibit a new piety in religious matters. The peasants, who found little in the Revolution to interest them after their own insurrection of 1789 and the consequent abolition of the manorial regime, also favored the old-fashioned or refractory clergy. Much the same was true of the urban working-class families, in which both men and women might shout against priests and yet want to be sure that their marriages were valid and their children were properly baptized. The Constituent Assembly, and its successors, could never finally decide what to do. Sometimes they shut their eyes at the intrigues of refractory clergy, in which case the constitutional clergy then became fearful. Sometimes they hunted out and persecuted the refractories; in that case they only stirred the passions of the most devoutly religious persons and social groups.

The Civil Constitution of the Clergy has been called the greatest tactical blunder of the Revolution. Certainly its consequences were unfortunate in the extreme, and they spread to much of Europe. In the nineteenth century the Catholic Church became officially anti-democratic and antiliberal; and democrats and liberals in most cases became outspokenly anticlerical. The main beneficiary was the papacy. The French Catholic Church, which had clung for ages to its Gallican liberties, was thrown by the Revolution into the arms of the pope. These were steps in the process, leading through the proclamation of papal infallibility in 1870, by which the affairs of the modern Catholic Church became increasingly centralized at the Vatican.

With the proclamation of the constitution in September 1791, the Constituent Assembly disbanded. Before dissolving, it ruled that none of its members might sit in the forthcoming Legislative Assembly. This body was therefore made up of men who still wished to make their mark in the Revolution. The new regime went into effect in October 1791. It was a constitutional monarchy in which a unicameral Legislative Assembly confronted a king unconverted to the new order. Designed as a permanent system for the modern governance of France and for the protection of the rights of man, it was to collapse in 10 months, in August 1792, as a result of popular insurrection four months after France became involved in war. A group of Jacobins, known as Girondins, for a time became the left or advanced party of the Revolution and in the Legislative Assembly they led France into war.

43. THE REVOLUTION AND EUROPE: THE WAR AND THE "SECOND" REVOLUTION, 1792

The International Impact of the Revolution

The European governments were long reluctant to become involved with France. They were under considerable pressure from all sides. On the one hand, pro-French and pro-revolutionary groups appeared immediately in many quarters. The doctrines of the French Revolution, as of the American, were highly exportable: they took the form of a universal philosophy, proclaiming the rights of man regardless of time or place, race or nation.

Moreover, depending on what one was looking for, one might see in the first disturbances in France a revolt of either the nobility, the bourgeoisie, the common people, or the entire nation. In Poland those who were trying to reorganize the country against further partition hailed the French example. The Hungarian landlords also pointed to it in their reaction against Joseph II. In England, for a time, those who controlled Parliament complacently believed that the French were attempting to imitate them.

But it was the excluded classes of European society who were most inspired. The hard-pressed Silesian weavers were said to hope that "the French would come." Strikes broke out at Hamburg, and peasants rebelled elsewhere. One English diplomat found that even the Prussian army had "a strong taint of democracy among officers and men." In *Inspiration of the Revolution*

England the newly developing "radicals," men like Thomas Paine and Dr. Richard Price, who wished a thorough overhauling of Parliament and the established church, entered into correspondence with the Assembly in Paris. Business leaders of importance, including Watt and Boulton, the pioneers of the steam engine, were likewise pro-French because they had no representation in the House of Commons. The Irish too were excited and presently revolted. Everywhere the young were aroused, the young Hegel in Germany or the young Wordsworth in England, who later recalled the sense of a new era that had captivated so many spirits in 1789:

> Bliss was it in that dawn to be alive,
> But to be young was very heaven!

On the other hand the anti-Revolutionary movement gathered strength. Edmund Burke, frightened by the French proclivities of English radicals, published as early as 1790 his *Reflections on the* *Anti-Revolutionary sentiment*

Revolution in France. For France, he predicted anarchy and dictatorship. For England, he sternly advised the English to accept a slow adaptation of their own English liberties. For all the world, he denounced a political philosophy that rested on abstract principles of right and wrong, declaring that every people must be shaped by its own national circumstances, national history, and national character. He drew an eloquent reply and a defense of France from Thomas Paine in *The Rights of Man*—an influential book that argued for the universality of inalienable human rights. Burke soon began to preach the necessity of war, urging a permanent ideological struggle against French barbarism and violence. His *Reflections* was translated and read throughout Europe, becoming in the long run an important work in the emergence of modern conservative thought. In the short run it fell on willing ears. The king of Sweden, Gustavus III, offered to lead a monarchist crusade. In Russia Empress Catherine was appalled; she forbade further translations of her erstwhile friend Voltaire, she called the French "vile riffraff" and "brutish cannibals," and she packed off to Siberia a Russian named Radischev, who in his *Voyage from St. Petersburg to Moscow* pointed out the evils of serfdom. The foreign fears were heightened by plaintive messages from Louis XVI and Marie Antoinette and by the angry émigrés who were constantly leaving France and who were led as early as July 1789 by the king's own brother, the Count of Artois. The first émigrés were almost all nobles, and they settled in various parts of Europe where they could use their international aristocratic connections to preach a kind of holy war against the evils of revolution. They bemoaned the sad plight of the king, but what they most wanted was to get back their manorial incomes and other rights. Extremists among the émigrés even hinted that Louis XVI himself was a dangerous revolutionary and much preferred his brother, the unyielding Count of Artois.

In short, Europe was soon split by a division that overran all frontiers. The same was true also in the wider Atlantic world. In the United States the rising party of Jefferson was branded as Jacobin and pro-French, that of Hamilton as aristocratic and pro-British, while pro-revolutionary and anti-revolutionary groups fell into violent conflicts within the French Caribbean colony at Saint-Domingue. A new interest in independence began to spread among some Latin Americans, including the Venezuelan Francisco de Miranda, who became a general in the French army. In all countries of the European world, though least of all in eastern and southern Europe, there were revolutionary or pro-French elements that were feared by their own governments. In all countries, including France, there were implacable enemies of the French Revolution. In all countries there were people whose political ideas and local conflicts increasingly expressed their strong support or deep hostility for the revolutionary changes in France. There had been no such situation since the Protestant Reformation, nor was there anything like it again until after the Russian Revolution of the twentieth century.

The Coming of the War, April 1792

Yet the European governments were slow to move. Catherine had no intention of becoming involved in western Europe. She only wished to involve her neighbors. William Pitt, the British prime minister, resisted the war cries of Burke. Pitt had failed to carry a plan for reform of Parliament and was now concentrating on a policy of orderly finance and systematic economy. His domestic program would be ruined by war. He insisted that the internal affairs of France were of no concern to the British government. The key position was occupied by the Habsburg emperor, Leopold II, brother to the French queen. Leopold at first answered Marie Antoinette's pleas for help by telling her to adjust herself to conditions in France. He resisted the furious demands of the émigrés, whom he understood perfectly, having inherited from Joseph II a fractious aristocracy himself.

Still, the new French government was a disturbing phenomenon. It openly encouraged malcontents all over Europe. It showed a tendency to settle international affairs by unilateral action. For example, it annexed Avignon at the request of local revolutionaries but without the consent of its historic sovereign, the pope. Or again, in Alsace there had been much overlapping jurisdiction between France and Germany ever since the Peace of Westphalia in 1648 (see maps, pp. 148–149, 191, 336). The Constituent Assembly abolished traditional manorial dues in Alsace as elsewhere in France. To German princes who had long held rights to these payments in Alsace the Assembly offered compensation, but it did not ask their consent. Moreover, after the arrest of Louis XVI at Varennes, after his attempted flight in June 1791, it became impossible to deny that the French king and queen were prisoners of the revolutionaries.

The Declaration of Pillnitz

In August 1791 Leopold met with the king of Prussia at Pillnitz in Saxony. The resulting Declaration of Pillnitz rested on a famous *if:* Leopold would take military steps to restore order in France if all the other powers would join him. Knowing the attitude of Pitt, he believed that such an agreement could never materialize, but the French émigrés received the Declaration with delight. They used it as an open threat to their enemies in France, announcing that they would soon return alongside the forces of civilized Europe to punish the guilty and right the wrongs that had been done to them.

In France the upholders of the Revolution were alarmed. They were ignorant of what Leopold's "if" really meant and took the dire menaces of the émigrés at their face value. The Declaration of Pillnitz, far from cowing the French, enraged them against all the crowned heads of Europe. It gave a political advantage to the then dominant faction of Jacobins, known to history as the Girondins. These included the philosophe Condorcet, the humanitarian lawyer Brissot, and the civil servant Roland and his more famous wife, Madame Roland, whose house became a meeting place for the group. They attracted many foreigners also, such as Thomas Paine and the German Anacharsis Cloots, the "representative of the human race." In December 1791 a deputation of English radicals, led by James Watt, son of the inventor of the steam engine, received a wild ovation at the Paris Jacobin club.

The Girondins became the party of international revolution. They declared that the Revolution could never be secure in France until it spread to the world. In their view, once war had come, the peoples of states at war with France would not support their own governments. There was reason for this belief, because revolutionary elements antedating the French Revolution *France goes to war* already existed in both the Dutch and the Austrian Netherlands, and to a lesser degree in parts of Switzerland, Poland, and elsewhere. Some Girondins therefore contemplated a war in which French armies should enter neighboring countries, unite with local revolutionaries, overthrow the established governments, and set up a federation of republics. War was also favored by a very different group, led by Lafayette, which wished to curb the Revolution by holding it at the moderate political limits of constitutional monarchy. This group mistakenly believed that war might restore the much damaged popularity of Louis XVI, unite the country under the new government, and make it possible to put down the continuing Jacobin agitation. As the war spirit boiled up in France, the Emperor Leopold II died. He was succeeded by Francis II, a man much more inclined than Leopold to yield to the anti-revolutionary clamors of the aristocratic exiles. Francis resumed negotiations with Prussia. In France all who dreaded a return of the Old Regime listened more readily to the Girondins. Among the Jacobins as a whole, only a few, generally a handful of radical democrats, opposed the war. On April 20, 1792, without serious opposition, the Assembly declared war on "the king of Hungary and Bohemia," that is, the Austrian monarchy.

The "Second" Revolution: August 10, 1792

The war intensified the existing unrest and dissatisfaction of the unpropertied classes. Both peasants and urban workers felt that the Constituent and the Legislative Assembly had served the propertied interests and had done little for them. Peasants were dissatisfied with the inadequate measures taken to facilitate land distribution; workers felt especially the pinch of soaring prices, which by 1792 had greatly risen. Gold had been taken out of the country by the émigrés; paper money, the *assignats,* was almost the sole currency, and the future of the government was so uncertain that it steadily lost value. Peasants concealed their food products rather than sell them for depreciating paper. Actual scarcity combined with the falling value of money to *Economic* drive up the cost of living. The lowest income groups suffered the most. *dissatisfaction* But dissatisfied though they were, when the war began they were threatened with a return of the émigrés and a vindictive restoration of the Old Regime, which at least for the peasants would be the worst of all possible eventualities. The lower-income workers—peasants, artisans, mechanics, shopkeepers, wage laborers— rallied to the Revolution but not to the revolutionary government in power. The Legislative Assembly and the constitutional monarchy lacked the confidence of large elements of the population.

In addition, the war at first went very unfavorably for the French. Prussia joined immediately with Austria, and by the summer of 1792 the two powers were on the point of invading France. They issued a proclamation to the French people, the Brunswick Manifesto of July 25 declaring that if any harm befell the French king and queen the Austro-Prussian forces, upon their arrival in Paris, would exact the most severe retribution from the inhabitants of that city. Such menaces, compounding the military emergency, only played into the hands of the most violent activists. Masses of the French people, roused and guided by a more radical faction of Jacobin leaders, notably Robespierre, Danton, and the vitriolic journalist Marat, burst out in a passion of patriotic excitement. They turned against the king because he was identified with the foreign powers at war with France and also because, in France itself, those who still supported him were using the monarchy as defense against the lower classes. Republicanism in France was partly a rather sudden historical accident, in that France was at war under a king who could not be trusted, and partly a kind of popular lower-class movement against the traditional nobility, in which, however, many bourgeois revolutionaries shared.

Feeling ran high during the summer of 1792. Recruits streamed into Paris from all quarters on their way to the frontiers. One detachment, from Marseilles, brought with them a new marching song, known ever since as the *Marseillaise,* a fierce call to war upon

Agitation and violence in Paris

tyranny. The transient provincials stirred up the agitation in Paris. On August 10, 1792, the working-class quarters of the city rose in revolt, supported by the recruits from Marseilles and elsewhere. They stormed the Tuileries against resistance by the Swiss Guard, many of whom were massacred, and seized and imprisoned the king and the royal family. A revolutionary municipal government, or "Commune," was set up in Paris. Usurping the powers of the Legislative Assembly, it forced the abrogation of the constitution and the election, by universal male suffrage, of a Constitutional Convention that was to govern France and prepare a new and more democratic constitution. The very word Convention was used in recollection of the American Constitutional Convention in 1787. Meanwhile hysteria, anarchy, and terror reigned in Paris; mobs of insurrectionary volunteers,

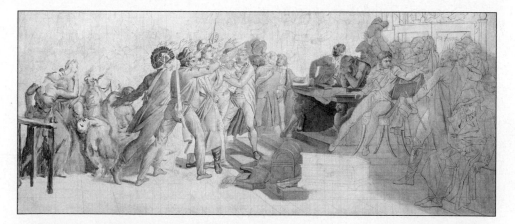

A Parisian crowd attacked the royal palace in the Tuileries on August 10, 1792, killing many of the king's guards, taking Louis XVI and his family as prisoners, and launching the most radical phase of the French Revolution. This sketch by François Gérard, a protégé of Jacques-Louis David, portrayed the intensity of a violent upheaval that shattered the recently established constitutional monarchy.
(©LACMA - Los Angeles County Museum of Art)

declaring that they would not fight enemies on the frontiers until they had disposed of enemies in Paris, dragged about 1,100 persons—common criminals, refractory priests, and other alleged counterrevolutionaries—from the prisons of the city and killed them after drumhead trials, in brutal executions known as the "September massacres."

For nearly three years, since October 1789, there had been an abatement of popular violence. Now the coming of the war and the dissatisfaction of the lower classes with the recent course of events had led to new explosions. The insurrection of August 10, 1792, the "second" French Revolution, initiated the most radical and violent phase of the Revolution.

44.   THE EMERGENCY REPUBLIC, 1792–1795:
THE TERROR

The National Convention

The National Convention met on September 20, 1792; it was to sit for three years. It immediately proclaimed the beginning of a new era: Year I of the French Republic. The disorganized French armies, also on September 20, won a great moral victory in the "cannonade of Valmy," a battle that was hardly more than an artillery duel, but which induced the Prussian commander to give up his march on Paris. The French soon occupied the Austrian Netherlands (modern Belgium), the Savoy region near the Swiss-Italian border (which belonged to the king of Sardinia, who had joined with the Austrians), and Mainz and other cities on the German Left Bank of the Rhine. Revolutionary sympathizers in these places appealed for French aid. The National Convention decreed assistance to "all peoples wishing to recover their liberty." It also ordered that French generals, in the occupied areas, should dissolve the old governments; confiscate government and church property; abolish tithes, hunting rights, and seigneurial dues; and set up provisional administrations. Thus revolution spread in the wake of the successful French armies.

Spread of the Revolution

The British and Dutch now prepared to resist. Pitt, still insisting that the French might have any domestic regime that they chose, declared that Great Britain could not tolerate the French occupation of the nearby Austrian Netherlands. The British and Dutch began conversations with Prussia and Austria, and the French declared war on them on February 1, 1793. Within a few weeks the Republic had annexed Savoy and Nice, as well as the Austrian Netherlands, and had much of the German Rhineland under its military government (see map, p. 414). Meanwhile, in eastern Europe, while denouncing the rapacity of the French Jacobins, the rulers of Russia and Prussia, as we have seen, came to an arrangement of their own, each appropriating a portion of Poland in the second partition in January 1793. The Austrians, excluded from this second partition, became anxious about their interests in eastern Europe. The infant French Republic, now at war with all Europe, was saved by the weakness of the Coalition, for Britain and Holland had no land forces of consequence and Prussia and Austria were too jealous of each other, and too preoccupied with Poland, to commit the bulk of their armies against France.

In the Convention all the leaders were Jacobins, but the Jacobins were again splitting. The Girondins were no longer the most advanced revolutionary group as they had been in the earlier Legislative Assembly. Beside the Girondins appeared a new group, whose members preferred to sit in the highest seats in the hall, and therefore were dubbed the "Mountain" in the political language of the day. The leading Girondins came from the great provincial cities; the leading

The Jacobins split

Montagnards, though mostly of provincial birth, represented Paris and owed most of their political strength to the radical and popular elements in that city.

These popular revolutionists, outside the Convention, proudly called themselves "sans-culottes," because they wore the workingman's long trousers, not the knee breeches or *culottes* of the middle and upper classes. They were the working class of a preindustrial age, shopkeepers and shop assistants, skilled artisans in various trades, including some who were owners of small manufacturing or handicraft enterprises. For two years their militancy and their activism pressed the Revolution forward. They demanded a broader equality that would be meaningful for people like themselves, they called for a mighty effort against foreign powers that presumed to intervene in the French Revolution, and they denounced the now deposed king and queen (correctly enough) for collusion with the Austrian enemy. The sans-culottes feared that the Convention might be too moderate. They favored direct democracy in their neighborhood clubs and assemblies, together with a mass rising if necessary against the Convention itself. The Girondins in the Convention began to dismiss these popular militants as anarchists. The group known as the Mountain was more willing to work with them, so long at least as the emergency lasted.

The execution of the king

The Convention put Louis XVI on trial for treason in December 1792. On January 15 it unanimously pronounced him guilty, but on the next day, out of 721 deputies present, only 361 voted for immediate execution, a majority of one. Louis XVI died on the guillotine forthwith. The 361 deputies were henceforth branded for life as regicides; never could they allow, in safety to themselves, a restoration of the Bourbon monarchy in France. The other 360 deputies were not similarly compromised; their rivals called them Girondins, "moderatists," or counterrevolutionaries. All who still wanted more from the Revolution, or who feared that the slightest wavering would bring the Allies and the émigrés into France, now looked to the Mountain wing of the Jacobins.

Background to the Terror

In April 1793 the most prominent French general, Dumouriez, who had won the victories in the Austrian Netherlands five months before, defected to Austria. The Allied armies now drove the French out of this strategic borderland territory and again threatened to invade France. Counterrevolutionaries in France exulted. From the revolutionaries went up the cry, "We are betrayed!" Prices continued to rise, the currency fell, food was harder to obtain, and the working classes were increasingly restless. The sans-culottes demanded price controls, currency controls, rationing, legislation against the hoarding of food, and requisitioning to enforce the circulation of goods. They denounced bourgeois traders as profiteers and exploiters of the people. While the Girondins resisted, the Mountain went along with the sans-culottes, partly from sympathy with their ideas, partly to win mass support for the war, and partly as a maneuver against the Girondins. On May 31, 1793, the Commune of Paris, under pressure from the sans-culottes, assembled a host of demonstrators and insurrectionists who invaded the Convention and forced the arrest of the Girondin leaders. Other Girondins fled into hiding, including Condorcet, who wrote his famous book, *Sketch for a Historical Picture of the Progress of the Human Mind*, before he was captured and put in prison, where he soon died.

The Mountain now ruled in the Convention, but the Convention itself ruled very little. Not only were the foreign armies and the émigrés bent on destroying the Convention as a band of regicides and social incendiaries, but the authority of the Convention was also widely repudiated within France itself. In the west, in the Vendée, the peasants had revolted against military conscription, and their spreading rebellion was strongly encouraged by refractory priests, British agents, and royalist emissaries of the Count of Artois. The great provincial cities, Lyons, Bordeaux, Marseilles, and others, had also rebelled, especially after the fugitive Girondins reached them. These "federalist" rebels demanded a more federal or decentralized republic. Like the Vendéans, with whom they had no connection, they objected to the ascendancy of Paris, having been accustomed to more regional independence under the Old Regime. These rebellions became counterrevolutionary, because all sorts of foreigners, royalists, émigrés, and clericals streamed in to assist them.

The Convention had to defend itself against extremists of the Left as well. To the mass action of the sans-culottes were now added the voices of even more excited militants called *enragés*. Various organizers, enthusiasts, and neighborhood agitators declared that parliamentary

The Convention under attack

methods were useless. Generally they were men outside the Convention—and also women, for women were particularly sensitive to the crisis of food shortage and soaring prices, and an organization of Revolutionary Republican Women helped to mobilize the sans-culottes in 1793 (until the suppression of women's political clubs). All such activists worked through units of local government in Paris and elsewhere as well as in thousands of popular societies and provincial clubs throughout the whole country. They also formed "revolutionary armies," semimilitary bands that scoured the rural areas for food, denounced suspects, and preached revolution.

A wave of popular violence in Paris in 1792 led to the proclamation of a new French republic. Angry crowds pulled down the symbols of the monarchical old regime, including this statue of Louis XIV.
(©Time Life Pictures/Getty Images)

Although no single leader ever controlled the Revolutionary Convention in 1793–94, Maximilien Robespierre, pictured here during the first year of the Revolution, became the most influential Jacobin leader, the determined advocate for a republic of virtuous citizens, and a key member of the Convention's Committee of Public Safety during the "Reign of Terror."
(Library of Congress Prints and Photographs Division [LC-USZC2-3607])

As for the Convention, while it cannot be said to have had any commanding leaders, the program it followed for about a year was on the whole that of Maximilien Robespierre, himself a Jacobin but not one to go along forever with popular revolution or anarchy. Robespierre is one of the most argued about and least understood figures in history. Persons accustomed to stable conditions and governing institutions condemn him as a bloodthirsty fanatic, dictator, and demagogue. Others have considered him an idealist, a visionary, and an ardent patriot whose goals and ideals were at least avowedly democratic. All agree on his personal honesty and integrity and on his revolutionary zeal. He was by origin a lawyer from northern France, educated with the aid of scholarships in Paris. He had been elected in 1789 to sit for the Third Estate in the Estates General, and in the ensuing Constituent Assembly played a minor role, though calling attention to himself by his views against capital punishment and in favor of universal suffrage. During the time when he could not serve in the Legislative Assembly, in 1791–1792, he continued to agitate for democracy and vainly pleaded against the declaration of war. In the Convention, which was elected in September 1792 and which was to write a new republican constitution, he represented a Paris constituency. He became a prominent member of the Mountain and welcomed the purge of the Girondins. He had always kept free of the bribery and graft in which some others became involved and for this reason was known as the Incorruptible. He was a great believer in the importance of "virtue," a term that the philosophes had used in a specialized way. Both Montesquieu and Rousseau, for example, had held that republics depended upon virtue, or unselfish public spirit and civic zeal, to which was added, under Rousseauist influence, a somewhat sentimentalized idea of personal uprightness and purity of life. Robespierre was determined, in 1793 and 1794, to bring about a democratic republic made up of good, virtuous, and honest citizens.

Robespierre

The Program of the Convention, 1793–1794: The Terror

The program of the Convention, which Robespierre helped to form, was to repress anarchy, civil strife, and counterrevolution at home and to win the war by a great national mobilization of the country's people and resources. It would prepare a democratic constitution and initiate legislation for the lower classes, but it would not yield to the Paris Commune and other agencies of direct revolutionary action. To conduct the government, the Convention granted wide powers to a Committee of Public Safety, a group of 12 members of the Convention who were reelected every month. Robespierre was an influential member; others were the youthful St. Just, the militant lawyer Couthon, and the army officer Carnot, "organizer of victory."

To repress the "counterrevolution," the Convention and the Committee of Public Safety set up what is popularly known as the "Reign of Terror." Revolutionary courts were instituted as an alternative to the lynch law of the September massacres. A Committee of General Security was created as a kind of supreme political police. Designed to protect the Revolutionary Republic from its internal enemies, the Terror struck at those who were in league against the Republic and at those who were merely suspected of hostile activities. Its victims ranged from Marie Antoinette and other royalists to numerous early supporters of the Revolution, including the Girondin leaders and women such as Olympe de Gouges. Before the year 1793–1794 was over, some of the old Jacobins of the Mountain who had helped inaugurate the Terror also went to the guillotine.

The "Reign of Terror"

Many thousands of people died in France at the height of the Revolution. Most deaths were in places that had openly revolted against the Convention, as in the Vendée in western France. Some resulted from acts of private vengeance. But if the Terror is understood to mean the official program of the government, which at one time decreed "terror the order of the day," the number who died in it was not large by the brutal standards of the twentieth century, in which dictatorial governments attempted to wipe out not only their political opponents but whole social classes or ethnic groups. About 40,000 persons perished in the Terror thus defined, and many more were temporarily imprisoned. The guillotine became the dreaded symbol of the Terror, especially in Paris, but more persons were actually put to death by other methods. About 8 percent of the victims of the official Terror were nobles, but nobles as a class were not molested unless suspected of political agitation; 14 percent of the victims were classifiable as bourgeois, mainly of the rebellious southern cities; 6 percent were clergy, while no less than 70 percent were of the peasant and laboring classes. A democratic republic, founded on the Declaration of the Rights of Man, was in theory to be established after the Terror and the various military campaigns had saved the Revolution from its internal and external enemies. Meanwhile, however, in 1793–1794, the Terror evolved into a kind of self-perpetuating revolutionary violence that was inhumane, expansive, irrational, and in some places a method for mass killings, as at Nantes, where 2,000 persons were loaded on barges and deliberately drowned. The Terror left long memories in France and created much of the enduring antipathy to the Revolution and to republicanism.

Victims of the Terror

To conduct the government in the midst of the war emergency the Committee of Public Safety operated as a joint dictatorship and war cabinet. It prepared and guided legislation through the Convention. It gained control over the "representatives on mission," who were members of the Convention on duty with the armies and in the insurgent areas of France. It established the *Bulletin des loix,* so that all persons might know what laws they were supposed to enforce or to obey. It centralized the administration, converting the swarm of locally elected officials left over from the Constituent Assembly (who were royalists in some places, wild extremists in others) into centrally appointed "national agents" named by the Committee of Public Safety.

The Committee of Public Safety

To win the war the Committee proclaimed the *levée en masse,* calling on all able-bodied men to join the army and all other French citizens to serve the revolutionary nation in whatever ways they could. It recruited scientists to work on armaments and munitions. The most prominent French scientists of the day worked for or were protected by the government of the Terror, though one, Lavoisier, "father of modern chemistry,"

*Mobilizing for
total war*

was guillotined in 1794 because he had been involved in tax farming before 1789. For military reasons also the Committee instituted economic controls, which at the same time met the demands of the *enragés* and other working-class spokesmen. The value of the *assignats* ceased to fall during the year of the Terror. Thus the government protected both its own purchasing power and that of the masses. It did so by controlling the export of gold, by confiscating specie and foreign currency from French citizens, to whom it paid assignats in return, and by legislation against hoarding or the withholding of goods from the market. Food and supplies for the armies, and for civilians in the towns, were raised and allocated by a system of requisitions, centralized in a Subsistence Commission under the Committee of Public Safety. A "general maximum" set ceilings for prices and wages. It helped to check inflation during the crisis, but it did not work very well; the Committee believed, in principle, in a free market economy and lacked the technical and administrative machinery to enforce thorough controls. By 1794 it was giving freer rein to private enterprise and to the peasants to encourage production. It tried also to hold down wages and in that respect lost the adherence of many working-class leaders.

In June 1793 the Committee produced, and the Convention adopted, a republican constitution that provided for universal male suffrage. But the new constitution was suspended indefinitely, and the government was declared "revolutionary until the peace," "revolutionary" meaning extraconstitutional or of an emergency character. In other ways the Committee showed intentions of legislating on behalf of the lower economic classes. The price controls and other economic regulations answered the demands of the sansculottes. The last of the manorial regime was done away with; the peasants were relieved of having to pay compensation for the obligations that had been abolished at the opening of the Revolution. The Committee busied itself also with measures of public improvement. It issued pamphlets to teach farmers to improve their crops, selected promising youths to receive instruction in useful trades, opened a military school for boys of all classes, even the humblest, and certainly intended to introduce universal elementary education.

It was also at this time, in 1794, that the National Convention decreed the abolition of slavery in the French colonies, meaning chiefly Saint-Domingue, the modern Haiti, the richest of all the sugar islands in the Caribbean. Free blacks in the colonies had already received civic rights earlier in the Revolution; and the enslaved black plantation workers had in fact already liberated themselves in a massive rebellion that spread across Saint-Domingue in 1791. The revolutionary government in Paris sent new representatives to manage affairs in the colony, but these commissioners needed the support of emancipated black fighters to suppress both the counterrevolutionary white colonists and the English forces that invaded the island in the fall of 1793. The Jacobin commissioners therefore abolished slavery in Saint-Domingue even before the National Convention acted to abolish slavery in the wider French Empire. The revolution in Saint-Domingue and the expulsion of foreign armies thus depended on increasingly autonomous black military commanders, one of whom was the once-enslaved Toussaint Louverture. In the months after the revolutionary government's official abolition of slavery, Louverture became a general in the French army that drove the Spanish and British from Saint-Domingue.

*Slavery abolished in
French colonies*

Amid the ensuing political and military conflicts Louverture became France's governor-general in the colony, but his new government soon broke away from all French control. Under pressure from the slave-owning and commercial interests (and the European demand for sugar) the government of Napoleon in 1802 reestablished slavery in the French colonies and sent about 40,000 troops to reassert French authority in Saint-Domingue.

Toussaint Louverture, pictured here with a sword and documents to symbolize his independence, served in the French military forces in Saint-Domingue during the Revolution and later led the political and military movement that ultimately established a new Republic of Haiti in 1804. Although Louverture was eventually captured and taken to a prison in France (where he died in 1803), the French defeat in Haiti made Napoleon abandon plans for a revived American empire and sell Louisiana to the United States.
(©Time Life Pictures/Getty Images)

The French captured Louverture and took him to France, where he died in prison. Other military leaders launched a new campaign for independence, however, and the French army was unable to defeat the armed rebellion of the mobilized black population. Most of the French troops on the island died in the fighting or perished of yellow fever, and the few survivors abandoned their operations late in 1803—becoming the first Napoleonic army to suffer a decisive military defeat after Bonaparte seized political power in 1799. Haitian leaders, in 1804, established an independent Republic of Haiti, which also became the Atlantic world's first postcolonial nation to abolish slavery. An unexpected consequence of the French defeat in Haiti was that Napoleon sold the remaining French possessions on the North American mainland ("Louisiana") to the United States in 1803. Slavery was not effectively abolished in the French colonies until a later revolution in 1848.

War for Haitian independence

Meanwhile, at the climax of the Revolution within France itself, in 1793–1794, the Committee of Public Safety sought to concentrate and manage all revolutionary initiatives through its own actions. It had no patience with unauthorized revolutionary violence. With its own plan for a democratic program, it disapproved of the turbulent democracy of popular clubs and local assemblies. In the fall of 1793, at the time of its prohibition of revolutionary women's organizations, the Committee arrested the leading *enragés*. Extreme revolutionary demands were expressed by Jacques Hébert, a journalist and officer of the Paris Commune. Robespierre called such people "ultra revolutionaries." They were a large and indefinable group and included many radical members of the Convention.

They indiscriminately denounced merchants and other bourgeois groups. They were the party of extreme Terror; an Hébertist brought about the mass drownings at Nantes. Believing all religion to be counterrevolutionary, they launched the movement of Dechristianization and strongly supported the creation of a new republican calendar. The Convention adopted this calendar as part of its campaign to strengthen popular allegiance to the republic and to establish a new national organization of daily life that would replace the Christian cycle of Sundays, saints' days, and holidays such as Christmas and Easter. The new calendar thus counted years from the founding of the French Republic, divided each year into new months of 30 days each, and even abolished the week, which it replaced with the 10-day décade.[1]

The Revolution and religion

Dechristianization also contributed to the development of the cult of reason, which sprang up all over France at the end of 1793. In Paris the Commune put on ceremonies in the cathedral of Notre Dame, in which Reason was impersonated by an actress. But Dechristianization was severely frowned upon by Robespierre. He believed that it would alienate the masses from the Republic and ruin such sympathy as was still felt for the Revolution abroad. The Committee of Public Safety, therefore, ordered the toleration of peaceable Catholics, and in June 1794 Robespierre introduced the cult of the Supreme Being, a deistic natural religion, in which the Republic was declared to recognize the existence of God and the immortality of the soul. Robespierre hoped that both Catholics and agnostic anticlericals could become reconciled on this ground. But Catholics were now beyond reconciliation, and the freethinkers, appealing to the tradition of Voltaire, regarded Robespierre as a reactionary mystery monger and would become instrumental in bringing about his fall.

Meanwhile the Committee proceeded relentlessly against the Hébertists, whose main champions it sent to the guillotine in March 1794. The paramilitary "revolutionary armies" were suppressed. The extreme Terrorists were recalled from the provinces. The revolutionary Paris Commune was destroyed. Robespierre filled the municipal offices of Paris with his own appointees. This Robespierrist commune disapproved of strikes and tried to hold down wages, on the plea of military necessity; it failed to win over the ex-Hébertists and working-class leaders, who became disillusioned with the Revolution and dismissed it as a movement that no longer served their interests. Probably to prevent just such a conclusion, and to avoid the appearance of deviation to the Right, Robespierre and the Committee, after liquidating the left-wing Hébertists, also liquidated certain right-wing members of the Mountain who were known as Dantonists. Danton and his followers were accused of financial dishonesty and of dealing with counterrevolutionaries; the charges contained some truth but were not the main reason for the executions.

By the spring of 1794 the French Republic possessed an army of 800,000 men, the largest ever raised up to that time by a European power. It was a national army representing a people in arms, commanded by officers who had been promoted rapidly on grounds of merit and composed of troops who felt themselves to be citizens fighting for their own cause. Its intense political-mindedness made it the more formidable and contrasted strongly with the political indifference of the opposing troops, some of whom were in fact serfs and none of whom had a comparable sense of membership in their own government systems. The Allied governments, each pursuing its own ends and still distracted by their

---

[1]Though not adopted until October 1793, the revolutionary calendar dated the Year I of the French Republic from September 22, 1792. The names of the months, in order and corresponding to the seasons of the year, were Vendémiaire, Brumaire, Frimaire (autumn); Nivôse, Pluviôse, Ventôse (winter); Germinal, Floréal, Prairial (spring); Messidor, Thermidor, Fructidor (summer).

ambitions in Poland, where the third partition was impending, could not combine their forces against France. In June 1794 the French won the battle of Fleurus, thereby ending the long-held Austrian control of the southern Netherlands. The Republican hosts again streamed into the Low Countries; in six months their calvary rode into Amsterdam on the ice. A revolutionary Batavian Republic soon replaced the old Dutch provinces; but the opposite was occurring at this time in eastern Europe, where Russian and Prussian armies stamped out the attempted revolution that Kosciusko led in Poland. All Polish lands and people were finally merged into the eastern European empires in 1795.

*Revolutionary
military victories*

Military success made the French less willing to put up with the dictatorial rule and economic regimentation of the Terror. Robespierre and the Committee of Public Safety had antagonized all significant parties. The working-class radicals of Paris would no longer support him, and after the death of Danton the National Convention was afraid of its own ruling committee. A group in the Convention obtained the "outlawing" of Robespierre on 9 Thermidor (July 27, 1794);

Fall of Robespierre

The French army won a great victory at the battle of Fleurus in June 1794, thus opening the way for republican troops to enter the Low Countries and easing the external threats that had pushed the Revolution toward internal repression and the Terror. This picture shows how the French used a balloon to observe enemy forces during the battle, but the results must have been disappointing, because balloons were not thereafter used by either side.

(©DEA PICTURE LIBRARY/Getty Images)

he was guillotined with some of his associates on the following day. Many who turned against Robespierre believed they were pushing the Revolution farther forward, as in destroying the Girondins the year before. Others thought, or said, that they were stopping a dictator and a tyrant. All agreed, to absolve themselves, in heaping all blame for the recent revolutionary excesses upon Robespierre. The idea that Robespierre was an ogre originated more with his former colleagues than with conservatives of the time.

The Thermidorian Reaction

The fall of Robespierre stunned the country, but its effects manifested themselves during the following months as the "Thermidorian reaction." The Terror subsided. The Convention reduced the powers of the Committee of Public Safety, and it closed the Jacobin club. Price controls and other regulations were removed. Inflation resumed its course, prices again rose, and the disoriented and leaderless working classes suffered more than ever. Sporadic uprisings broke out, of which the greatest was the insurrection of Prairial

The guillotine was used during the most radical phase of the Revolution to execute persons judged to be enemies of the republic. First adopted as a more humane way of inflicting capital punishment, it became a permanent symbol of revolutionary violence, and it claimed victims from every faction of the Revolution itself. This picture illustrates the execution of Robespierre and four others who were denounced as conspirators against liberty and sent to the guillotine in July 1794.

(©Bettmann/Getty Images)

Historical Interpretations and Debates
The Political and Social Significance of the French Revolution

Historians have proposed numerous and often conflicting political, economic, social, and cultural explanations to describe the historical significance of the French Revolution—though most agree that the Revolution contributed decisively to the emergence of modern European institutions and ideas. The influential interpretations of Albert Soboul and Lynn Hunt exemplify different economic and political explanations for the historical meaning of the Revolution and suggest why the debate about the French Revolution never ends.

Albert Soboul, *The Parisian Sans-Culottes and the French Revolution, 1793-4* (1959)

We need to remember that the Revolution was fundamentally a struggle between the European aristocracy and the Third Estate as a whole. In this struggle, it is hardly surprising that the French bourgeoisie should have played the leading role. The Revolutionary Government, founded upon an alliance between the Montagnard bourgeoisie and the Parisian sans-culotterie, had been given the task of defending the Revolution against the aristocracy both within France and beyond her borders. . . .

Without the Parisian sans-culotterie, the bourgeoisie could not have triumphed in so radical a fashion. . . .

The success of the popular movement . . . led to the organization of the Terror which struck such an irreparable blow to the old social order. The upper bourgeoisie of the *ancien régime,* founded on commercial capital and linked in some ways with the old social and political system of the feudal aristocracy, failed to survive the upheaval . . . The Terror had cleared the way for the introduction of new relationships of production. In the capitalist society born of the Revolution, industry was destined to dominate commerce: the function of commercial capital, against which the sans-culottes had fought so bitterly in the Year II, would be subordinated henceforth to the sole productive form of capital—industrial capital.

Lynn Hunt, *Politics, Culture, and Class in the French Revolution* (1984)

The Revolution showed how much everything depended on politics. . . . The structure of the polity changed under the impact of increasing political participation and popular mobilization; political language, political ritual, and political organization all took on new forms and meanings. . . .

Revolutionary political culture cannot be deduced from social structures, social conflicts, or the social identity of revolutionaries. Political practices were not simply the expression of "underlying" economic and social interests. Through their language, images, and daily political activities, revolutionaries worked to reconstitute society and social relations. . . .

The chief accomplishment of the French Revolution was the institution of a dramatically new political culture. The revolution did not startle its contemporaries because it laid the foundations for capitalist development or political modernization. . . . Revolution in France contributed little to economic growth or to political stabilization. What it did establish, however, was the mobilizing potential of democratic republicanism and the compelling intensity of revolutionary change. The language of national regeneration, the gestures of equality and fraternity, and the rituals of republicanism were not soon forgotten. Democracy, terror, Jacobinism, and the police state all became recurrent features of political life.

Sources: Albert Soboul, *The Parisian Sans-Culottes and the French Revolution, 1793-4*, translated by Gwynne Lewis (Oxford: Oxford University Press, 1964), pp. 249, 260-261; Lynn Hunt, *Politics, Culture, and Class in the French Revolution* (Berkeley: University of California Press, 1984), pp. 2, 12, 15.

in the Year III (May 1795), when a mob all but dispersed the Convention by force. Troops were called to Paris for the first time since 1789. Insurrectionists in the working-class quarters threw up barricades in the streets. The army prevailed without much bloodshed, but the Convention arrested, imprisoned, or deported 10,000 of the insurgents. A few organizers were guillotined. The affair of Prairial gave a foretaste of modern social revolution.

The triumphant element after 1794 consisted mostly of the bourgeois or professional classes of the former Third Estate, which had guided the Revolution since the Constituent Assembly and had not been really unseated even during the Terror. It was not mainly a bourgeoisie of modern capitalists, eager to make a financial profit by developing new

Politics and society after Thermidor

factories or machinery. The main political victors after Thermidor were bourgeois in an older social sense, those who had not been nobles before 1789 yet had held secure positions under the Old Regime, many of them lawyers or officeholders and often drawing income from the ownership of land. There were also new elements produced by the Revolution itself, parvenus and *nouveaux riches,* who had made money by wartime government contracts or had profited by inflation or by buying up former church lands at bargain prices. Such people, often joined by former aristocrats, and in reaction against Robespierrist virtue, set an extravagant and ostentatious style of living that gave a bad name to the new order. They also unleashed a "white terror" in which many ex-Jacobins were simply murdered.

But the Thermidorians, disreputable though a few of them were, had not lost faith in the Revolution. Democracy they associated with red terror and mob rule, but they still believed in individual legal rights and in a written constitution. Conditions were rather adverse, for the country was still unsettled, and although the Convention made a separate peace with Spain and Prussia, France remained at war with Great Britain and the Habsburg Empire. But the members of the Convention were still determined to make another attempt at constitutional government. They set aside the democratic constitution written in 1793 (and never used) and produced the Constitution of the Year III, which went into effect at the end of 1795.

45.   THE CONSTITUTIONAL REPUBLIC: THE DIRECTORY, 1795–1799

The Weakness of the Directory

The first formally constituted French Republic, known as the Directory, lasted only four years. It was politically weak and vulnerable because it rested on an extremely narrow social base and it presupposed certain military conquests. The new constitution applied not only to France but also to the southern Netherlands (territory that would become Belgium after 1830), which was now regarded as incorporated constitutionally into the French Republic. The Habsburgs had not yet ceded this land to France, nor had the

The constitution of 1795

British agreed to accept French occupation, so the constitution of 1795 committed the republic to a program of successful military and political expansion. At the same time it restricted the politically active class. It gave almost all adult males the vote, but they voted only for electors. Persons chosen as electors were usually men of some means, able to give their time and willing to take part in public life; this in effect meant men of the upper middle class, because the old nobility was disaffected. The electors chose all important department officials and also the members of the national Legislative Assembly, which was now divided into two chambers. The lower chamber was called the Council of Five Hundred; the upper, composed of 250 members, the Council of Ancients—"ancients" being those over 40. The chambers chose the executive, which was called the Directory (from which the whole regime took its name) and was made up of five Directors.

The government was thus constitutionally in the hands of substantial property owners, but its real base was narrower still. In the reaction after Thermidor many people began to consider restoring the monarchy. The Convention, to protect its own members, had ruled that two-thirds of the men initially elected to the Council of Five Hundred and Council of Ancients must be ex-members of the Convention. This interference with the freedom of the elections provoked serious disturbances in Paris, instigated mainly by royalists. The Convention, having now accustomed itself to using the army, instructed a young general named Bonaparte, who happened to be in Paris, to put down the royalist mob. He did so with a "whiff of grapeshot." The new constitutional republic thus made itself dependent on military protection at the outset.

The regime had enemies to both Right and Left. On the Right, undisguised royalists agitated in Paris and even in the two councils; and they were in continuous touch with the late king's brother, the Count of Provence, whom they regarded as Louis XVIII (Louis XVI's son, who died in prison, was counted as Louis XVII). Louis XVIII had installed himself at Verona in Italy, where he headed a propaganda agency financed largely by British money. The worst obstacle to the resurgence of royalism in France was Louis XVIII himself. In 1795, on assuming the title, he had issued a Declaration of Verona, in which he announced his intention to restore the Old Regime and punish all involved in the Revolution back to 1789. It has been said, correctly enough in this connection, that the Bourbons "learned nothing and forgot nothing." Had Louis XVIII offered in 1795 what he offered in 1814, it is quite conceivable that his partisans in France might have brought about his restoration and terminated the war. As it was, the majority of the French adhered not exactly to the republic as set up in 1795, but to any system that would shut out the Bourbons and privileged nobility, prevent a reimposition of the manorial system, and secure the new landowners, peasant and bourgeois, in the possession of the church properties that they had purchased.

The Left was made up of persons from various levels of society who still favored the more democratic ideas expressed earlier in the Revolution. Some of them thought that the fall of Robespierre had been a great misfortune. A tiny group of extremists formed the Conspiracy of Equals, organized in 1796 by "Gracchus" Babeuf. His intention was to overthrow the Directory and replace it with a dictatorial government in which private property would be abolished and equality would be decreed. For these ideas, and for his activist program, he has been regarded as a political precursor to modern communism. The Directory repressed the Conspiracy of Equals without difficulty and guillotined Babeuf. Meanwhile it did nothing to relieve the distress of the lower classes, who showed little inclination to follow Babeuf even though they suffered from the ravages of scarcity and inflation.

The Political Crisis of 1797

In March 1797 occurred the first really free election ever held in France under republican auspices. The successful candidates were for the most part constitutional monarchists or at least vaguely royalist. A change of the balance within the Five Hundred and the Ancients, in favor of royalism, seemed to be impending. This was precisely what most of the republicans of 1793, including the regicides, could not endure, even though they had to violate the constitution to prevent it. Nor was it endurable, for other reasons, to General Napoleon Bonaparte.

Napoleon Bonaparte

Bonaparte was born in 1769 into the minor nobility of Corsica, shortly after the annexation of Corsica to France. He had studied in French military schools and been commissioned in the Bourbon army but would never have reached high rank under the conditions of the Old Regime. In 1793 he was a fervent young Jacobin officer who had served the revolutionary cause by driving the British from Toulon and who was consequently made a brigadier general by the government of the Terror. In 1795, as noted, he rendered valuable service to the Convention by breaking up a demonstration of royalists. In 1796 he received command of an army, with which, in two brilliant campaigns, he crossed the Alps and drove the Austrians from north Italy. Like other generals he soon became independent from the government in Paris, which was financially too harassed to pay his troops or to supply him. He lived by local requisitions in Italy, became self-supporting, and in fact made the civilian government in Paris dependent on him.

He developed a foreign policy of his own. Many Italians had become dissatisfied with their old governments, so that the arrival of the French republican armies threw north Italy into turmoil. Combining with some of the Italian revolutionaries, Bonaparte established a "Cisalpine" Republic in the Po Valley, modeled on the French system, with Milan as its capital. Where the Directory, on the whole, had originally meant to return Milan to the Austrians in compensation for Austrian recognition of the French conquest of the Austrian Netherlands, Bonaparte insisted that France hold its position in both the Netherlands and Italy. He therefore needed expansionist republicans in the government in Paris and was perturbed by the royalist victories in the elections of 1797.

The Austrians negotiated with Bonaparte because they had been beaten by him in battle. The British also, in conferences with the French at Lille, discussed peace in 1796 and 1797. The war had gone badly for England; a party of Whigs led by Charles James Fox had always openly disapproved it, and the pro-French and republican radicals were so active that the government suspended habeas corpus in 1794, and thereafter imprisoned political agitators at its discretion. Crops were bad and bread was scarce and costly. England too suffered from inflation, for Pitt at first financed the war by extensive loans, and a good deal of gold had been shipped to the Continent to finance the Allied armies. The Austrians, Britain's only remaining ally, had nevertheless been routed by Bonaparte, and at the moment the British could subsidize them no further. The British had every reason to make peace.

Prospects for peace

Prospects for peace therefore seemed good in the summer of 1797, but, as always, it would be peace upon certain conditions. It was the royalists in France that were the peace party, because a restored king could easily return the conquests of the republic and would in any case abandon the new republics in Holland and the Po Valley. The republicans in the French government could make peace with difficulty, if at all. They were constitutionally bound to retain the southern Netherlands. They were losing control of their own generals. Nor could the supreme question be evaded: Was peace dear enough to purchase by a return of the Old Regime, such as Louis XVIII had himself promised?

The coup d'état of Fructidor

The coup d'état of Fructidor (September 4, 1797) was a forceful attempt to resolve all these internal and external issues. It was the turning point for France's constitutional republic, and it became a decisive event for all Europe. The Directory asked for help from Bonaparte,

---

CHRONOLOGY OF NOTABLE EVENTS, 1789–1804

May 1789	Estates General convenes at Versailles
June 1789	The Third Estate declares itself to be the National Assembly
July 1789	Crowd assaults and captures the Bastille fortress in Paris
August 1789	National Assembly issues "Declaration of the Rights of Man and Citizen" and abolishes "feudal privileges"
September 1791	New French Constitution establishes a constitutional monarchy
April 1791	France declares war on Austria and Prussia
September 1792	New National Convention meets in Paris; France becomes a republic
January 1793	King Louis XVI is executed in Paris
1793–1794	The Radical Revolution and the Reign of Terror
July 1794	Robespierre and his Jacobin allies are executed
1795–1799	Republic called "the Directory" governs France and sends armies to spread revolutionary republicanism in Europe
November 1799	Napoleon Bonaparte seizes power in a coup d'état
1799–1804	Napoleon is "First Consul" in French government called the Consulate; laws are codified in the Napoleonic codes
1801	Napoleon's Concordat with the Roman Catholic Church
1803–1804	Independent Republic of Haiti is established after French forces are defeated in Saint-Domingue
1804	France becomes an empire under Emperor Napoleon I

---

who sent one of his generals, Augereau, to Paris. While Augereau stood by with a force of soldiers, the councils annulled most of the elections of the preceding spring. On the whole, it was the old republicans of the Convention who secured themselves in power. Their justification was that they were defending the revolution, keeping out Louis XVIII and the Old Regime. But to do so they had violated their own constitution and quashed the first free election ever held in a constitutional French republic. And they had become more than ever dependent on the army.

After the coup d'état the "Fructidorian" government broke off negotiations with England. With Austria it signed the treaty of Campo Formio on October 17, 1797, incorporating Bonaparte's ideas. By the new treaty Austria recognized the French annexation of the former Austrian Netherlands, the French right to incorporate the Left Bank of the Rhine, and the French-dominated Cisalpine Republic in Italy. In return, Bonaparte allowed the Austrians to annex Venice and most of mainland Venetia.

In the following months, under French auspices, revolutionary republicanism spread rapidly through much of Italy, creating new republics with classical names. The old patrician republic of Genoa turned into a Ligurian Republic on the French model. At Rome the pope was deposed from his temporal power and a Roman Republic was established. In southern Italy a Neapolitan Republic, also called Parthenopean, was set up. In Switzerland at the same time, Swiss reformers cooperated with the French to create a new Helvetic Republic.

Revolutionary republicanism spreads

THE FRENCH REPUBLIC AND ITS SATELLITES, 1798–1799

By 1799 the French Republic had annexed the former Austrian Netherlands and the small German bishoprics and principalities west of the Rhine, and had created, with the aid of native sympathizers, a string of lesser revolutionary republics in the Dutch Netherlands, Switzerland, and most of Italy. With the treaty of Campo Formio between France and Austria in 1797, the Holy Roman Empire began to disintegrate, for the German princes of the Left Bank of the Rhine, who were dispossessed when their territories went to France, began to be compensated with territory of the church-states of the Holy Roman Empire. These developments were carried further in the following decade by Napoleon (see map, p. 433).

The Left Bank of the Rhine, in the atomistic Holy Roman Empire, was occupied by a great many German princes who now had to vacate their lands. The treaty of Campo Formio provided that they be compensated by church territories in Germany east of the Rhine and that France have a hand in this territorial reconstruction of Germany. The German princes turned greedy eyes on the German bishops and abbots, and the almost 1,000-year-old empire, hardly more than a solemn political abstraction since the Peace of Westphalia, sank to the level of a land rush or real estate speculation.

The Coup d'État of 1799: Bonaparte

After Fructidor the idea of maintaining the republic as a free or constitutional government was given up. There were more uprisings, more quashed elections, more purgings both to Left and Right. The Directory turned into an ineffective dictatorship. It repudiated most of the assignats and the debt but failed to restore financial confidence or stability. Guerrilla activity flared up again in the Vendée and other parts of western France. The religious schism became more acute; the Directory had to take severe measures toward the refractory clergy.

Meanwhile Bonaparte waited for the situation to ripen. Returning from Italy a conquering hero, he was assigned to command the army in training to invade England. He concluded that invasion was premature and decided to strike indirectly at England, by threatening India in a spectacular invasion of Egypt. In 1798, outwitting the British fleet, he landed a French army at the mouth of the Nile. Egypt was part of the Ottoman Empire, and the French occupation of Egyptian territories alarmed the Russians, who had their own designs on the Middle East. The Austrians objected to the French rearrangement of Germany. A year and a half after the treaty of Campo Formio, Austria, Russia, and Great Britain formed an alliance known as the Second Coalition. The French Republic was again involved in a general war. And the war went unfavorably, for in August 1798 the British fleet cut off the French army in Egypt by winning the battle of the Nile (or Aboukir), in October the people of Cairo rose in revolt against the French occupation of Egypt, and by 1799 Russian forces, under Marshal Suvorov, were operating as far west as Switzerland and north Italy, where the Cisalpine Republic went down in ruin.

Recognizing the obstacles to his ambitions in the Middle East as well as the multiple threats to France's revolutionary Republic, General Bonaparte decided that he could best pursue his own interests in Paris. He therefore abandoned his army in Egypt, slipped through the British fleet, and reappeared unexpectedly in France, where he found that certain civilian leaders in the Directory were planning a change. They included Sieyès, of whom little had been heard since he wrote *What Is the Third Estate?* in 1789, but who had sat in the Convention and voted for the death of Louis XVI. Sieyès' formula was now "confidence from below, authority from above"—what he now wanted of the people was acquiescence, and of the government, power to act. This group was looking about for a general, and their choice fell on the sensational young Bonaparte, who was still only 30. Dictatorship by an army officer was repugnant to most republicans of the Five Hundred and the Ancients. Bonaparte, Sieyès, and their followers therefore resorted to force, executing the coup d'état of Brumaire (November 9, 1799), in which armed soldiers drove the legislators from the chambers. They proclaimed a new form of the republic, which Bonaparte entitled the Consulate. It was headed by three consuls, with Bonaparte as the First Consul.

The Directory turns to Bonaparte

46.   THE AUTHORITARIAN REPUBLIC: THE CONSULATE, 1799–1804

The next chapter takes up the affairs of Europe as a whole in the time of Napoleon Bonaparte, the purpose at present being only to tell how he closed, in a way, the Revolution in France.

It happened that the French Republic, in falling into the hands of a general, fell also to a man whom many of his contemporaries and some later historians viewed as a "genius" or "great man" in European history. Bonaparte was a short man who would never have looked impressive in civilian clothing. His manners were rather coarse; he lost his temper, cheated at cards, and pinched people by the ear in a kind of formidable play—he was no "gentleman." A child of the Enlightenment and the Revolution, he was entirely emancipated not only from customary ideas but from moral scruples as well. He regarded the world as a flux to be formed by his own mind. He had an exalted belief in his own destinies, which became more mystical and exaggerated as the years went on. He claimed to follow his "star." His ideas of the good and the beautiful lacked nuance, but he was a man of extraordinary intellectual capacity, which impressed all with whom he came in contact. "Never speak unless you know you are the ablest man in the room," he once advised his stepson, on making him viceroy of Italy, a maxim that, if he followed it himself, still allowed him to do most of the talking. His interests ran to solid subjects, history, law, military science, public administration. His mind was tenacious and perfectly orderly; he once declared that it was like a chest of drawers, which he could open or close at will, forgetting any subject when its drawer was closed and finding it ready with all necessary detail when its drawer was opened. He had all the masterful qualities associated with leadership; he could dazzle and captivate those who had any inclination to follow him at all. Some of the most humane men of the day, including Goethe and Beethoven in Germany, and Lazare Carnot among the former revolutionary leaders, at first looked on him with high approval. He inspired confidence by his crisp speech, rapid decisions, and quick grasp of complex problems when they were newly presented to him. He was, or seemed, just what many people in France were looking for after ten years of upheaval.

Napoleon's "genius"

Under the Consulate France reverted to a form of enlightened despotism, and Bonaparte may be thought of as the last and most eminent of the enlightened despots. Despotic the new regime undoubtedly was from the start. Self-government through elected bodies was ruthlessly pushed aside. Bonaparte delighted in affirming the sovereignty of the people; but to his mind the people were a sovereign, like Voltaire's God, who somehow created the world but never thereafter interfered in it. He clearly saw that a government's authority was greater when it was held to represent the entire nation. In the weeks after the Brumaire coup he assured himself of a popular mandate by devising a written constitution and submitting it to a general "plebiscite." The voters could take it—or nothing. They took it by a majority officially reported as 3,011,007 to 1,562.

Bonaparte as First Consul

The new constitution set up a make-believe of parliamentary institutions. It provided for universal male suffrage, but the citizens merely chose "notables" who were then appointed by the government itself to public position. The notables had no powers of their own. They were merely available for appointment to office. They might sit in a Legislative Body, where they could neither initiate nor discuss legislation but only mutely reject or enact it. There was also a Tribunate that discussed public policies but had no enacting powers. There was a Conservative Senate, which had rights of appointment of notables to office ("patronage"

After repeatedly winning battles against all the powers of Europe, Napoleon developed even more grandiose ideas of himself and the imperial power of France. This painting was completed in 1806 by Jacques-Louis David, the aging revolutionary whose work had once portrayed the Tennis Court Oath and the faces of common people in Paris. Here he presents an idealized image of Napoleon as a young republican hero who crossed the Alps in 1800 to defeat the Austrians at the battle of Marengo.

(©John Parrot/Stocktrek Images/Getty Images)

in American terms) and in which numerous storm-tossed regicides found a haven. The main agency in the new government was the Council of State, imitated from the Old Regime; it prepared the significant legislation, often under the presidency of the First Consul himself, who always gave the impression that he understood everything. The First Consul made all the decisions and ran the state. The regime did not openly represent anybody, and that was its strength, for it provoked the less opposition. In any case, the political machinery just described fell rapidly into disuse.

Bonaparte entrenched himself also by promising and obtaining peace. The military problem at the close of 1799 was much simplified by the attitude of the Russians, who in effect withdrew from the war with France. In the Italian theater Bonaparte had to deal only with the Austrians, whom he again defeated, by again crossing the Alps, at the battle of Marengo in June 1800. In February 1801 the Austrians signed the treaty of Lunéville, in which the terms of Campo Formio were confirmed. A year later, in March 1802, peace was made even with Britain.

Peace was made also at home. Bonaparte kept internal order, partly by a secret political police but especially through a powerful and centralized administrative machine in which a "prefect," under direct orders of the minister of the interior, ruled firmly over each of the regional departments that the Constituent Assembly had created early in the Revolution. The new government put down the guerrillas in the west. Its laws and taxes were imposed on Brittany and the Vendée, and a new peace settled down on the factions left by the Revolution. Bonaparte offered a general amnesty and invited back to France, with a few exceptions, exiles of all stripes, from the first aristocratic émigrés to the refugees and deportees of the republican coups d'état. Requiring only that they work for him and stop quarreling with each other, he picked reasonable men from all camps. His Second Consul was Cambacérès, a regicide of the Terror; his Third Consul was Lebrun, who had been Maupeou's colleague in the days of Louis XV. Fouché emerged as minister of police; he had been an Hébertist and extreme terrorist in 1793 and had done as much as anyone to bring about the fall of Robespierre. Before 1789 he had been an obscure bourgeois professor of physics. Talleyrand reappeared as minister of foreign affairs; he had spent the Terror in safe seclusion in the United States, and his principles, if he had any, were those of constitutional monarchy. Before 1789 he had been a bishop, and he descended from an old and famous aristocratic lineage—no one who had not known the Old Regime, he once said, could realize how pleasant it had been. Men of this kind were now willing, for a few years beginning in 1800, to forget the past and work in common toward the future.

Disturbers of the new order the First Consul ruthlessly put down. Indeed, he concocted alarms to make himself more welcome as a pillar of order. On Christmas Eve, 1800, on the way to the opera, he was nearly killed by a bomb, or "infernal machine," as people then called such bombs. It had been set by royalists, but Bonaparte represented it as the work of Jacobin conspiracy, being most afraid at the moment of some of the old republicans; and over 100 former Jacobins were deported. Contrariwise, in 1804, he greatly exaggerated certain royalist plots against him, invaded the independent state of Baden, and there arrested the Duke of Enghien, who was related to the Bourbons. Though he knew Enghien to be innocent, he had him shot. His purpose now was to please the old Jacobins by staining his own hands with Bourbon blood; Fouché and the regicides concluded that they were secure so long as Bonaparte was in power.

The Settlement with the Church; Other Reforms

For all but the most convinced royalists and republicans, reconciliation was made easier by the establishment of peace with the church. Bonaparte himself was a pure eighteenth-century rationalist. He regarded religion merely as a social convenience or as a useful component of political order. But a Catholic revival was in full swing, and he saw its importance. The refractory clergy, those who never accepted the Revolution's Civil Constitution of the Clergy, were the spiritual force animating all forms of counterrevolution.

Concordat with the Vatican

"Fifty émigré bishops, paid by England," he once said, "lead the French clergy today. Their influence must be destroyed. For this we need the authority of the pope." Ignoring the horrified outcries of the old Jacobins, in 1801 he signed a concordat with the Vatican.

Both parties gained from the settlement. The autonomy of the prerevolutionary Gallican Church came to an end. The pope received the right to depose French bishops, because before the schism could be healed both constitutional and refractory bishops had to be obliged to resign. The constitutional or pro-revolutionary clergy came under the discipline of the Holy See. Publicity of Catholic worship, in such forms as processions in the streets, was again allowed. Church seminaries were again permitted. But Bonaparte and the heirs of the Revolution gained even more. The pope, by signing the concordat, virtually recognized the Republic. The Vatican agreed to raise no question over the former tithes and the former church lands. The new owners of former church properties thus obtained clear titles. Nor was there any further question of Avignon, an enclave within France, formerly papal, annexed to France in 1791. Nor were the papal negotiators able to undermine religious toleration; all that Bonaparte would concede was a clause that was purely factual, and hence harmless, stating that Catholicism was the religion of the majority of the French people. The clergy, in compensation for loss of their tithes and property, were assured of receiving salaries from the state. But Bonaparte, to dispel the notion of an established church, put Protestant ministers of all denominations on the state payroll also. He thus checkmated the Vatican on important points. At the same time, simply by signing an agreement with Rome, he disarmed the counterrevolution. It could no longer be said that the Republic was godless. Good relations did not, indeed, last very long, for Bonaparte and the papacy were soon at odds. But the terms of the concordat proved lasting.

With peace and order established, the constructive work of the Consulate turned to the fields of law and administration. The First Consul and his advisers combined what they conceived to be the best of the Revolution and of the Old Regime. The modern state took on clearer form. It was the reverse of everything feudal. All public authority was concentrated in officially employed agents of govern-   *Consulate reforms* ment, no person was under any legal authority except that of the state, and the authority of government fell on all persons alike. There were no more estates, legal classes, privileges, local liberties, hereditary offices, guilds, or manors. Judges, officials, and army officers received specified salaries. Neither military commissions nor civil offices could be bought and sold. Citizens were to rise in government service according to their abilities rather than their wealth or privileged birth.

This was the doctrine of "careers open to talent"; it was what the ambitious professional classes of the Third Estate had wanted before the   *"Careers open to talent"* Revolution, and a few persons of quite humble birth profited also. For sons of the old aristocracy, it meant that family pedigree was not enough; they must also show individual capacity to obtain employment. Qualification came to depend increasingly on education, and the secondary and higher schools were reorganized in these years, with a view to preparing young men for government service and the learned professions. Scholarships were provided, but it was mainly the upper middle class that benefited. Education, in fact, in France and in Europe generally, came to be an important determinant of social standing, with one system for those who could spend a dozen or more years at school, and another for those who were to enter the work force at the age of 12 or 14. Meanwhile, French intellectual life was strictly regulated and censored. When a few professors at the National Institute began to question certain government policies, for example, Bonaparte suppressed both their writings and the section of the Institute in which they worked; and when the liberal critic Germaine de Staël published books that displeased the First Consul, she was sent off to exile in Switzerland. Creative, critical intellectual debate thus became impossible in France during these years, though Bonaparte satisfied many of the popular demands for education and professional advancement.

Another deep demand of the French people, deeper than the demand for the vote, was for more reason, order, and economy in public finance and taxation. The Consulate gave these also. There were no tax exemptions because of birth, status, or special arrangement. Everyone was supposed to pay, so that no disgrace attached to payment, and there was less evasion. In principle these changes had been introduced in 1789; after 1799 they began to work. For the first time in ten years the government really collected the taxes that it levied and so could rationally plan its financial affairs. Accounting methods were improved, so there was a new order in both the receipt and the expenditure of government revenues. The revolutionary uncertainties over the value of money gradually dissipated. Because the Directory had shouldered the odium of repudiating the paper money and government debt, the Consulate was able to establish a sound currency and public credit. To assist in government financing, one of the banks of the Old Regime was revived and established as the Bank of France.

Like all enlightened despots, Bonaparte codified the laws, and of all law codes since the Romans the Napoleonic codes became the most   *The Napoleonic codes* famous. To the 300 legal systems of the Old Regime and the mass of royal ordinances were now added the thousands of laws enacted but seldom implemented by the revolutionary assemblies. Five codes emerged—the Civil Code (often called simply the Code Napoleon), the codes of civil and of criminal procedure, and the commercial and penal codes. The codes made France legally and judicially uniform. They assured legal equality; all French citizens had the same civil rights. They formulated the new law of property and set forth the law of contracts, debts, leases, stock companies, and similar matters in such a way as to create the legal framework for an economy of private enterprise. They repeated the ban of all previous regimes on organized labor unions and were severe with individual workers, their word not being acceptable in court against that of the employer—a significant departure from equality before the law. The criminal code was somewhat freer in giving the government the means to detect crime than in granting the individual the means of defense against legal charges. As for the family, the codes recognized civil marriage and divorce but left the wife with very restricted powers over property and the father with extensive authority over minor children; the legal system codified a paternalistic view of all family relations. The codes reflected much of French life under the Old Regime. They also helped to establish some of the most enduring aspects of modern French society: socially bourgeois, legally egalitarian, and administratively bureaucratic.

In France, with the Consulate, the Revolution was over. If its highest hopes had not been accomplished, many of the worst inequities and inefficiencies of the Old Regime had at least been cured. The beneficiaries of the Revolution felt secure. Even former aristocrats were beginning to accept the new system. The working-class movement, repeatedly frustrated under all the revolutionary regimes, now vanished from the political scene to reappear as a new socialism 30 years later. What the Third Estate had most wanted in 1789 was now both codified and enforced, with the exception of parliamentary government, which after ten years of turmoil many people were temporarily willing to forgo. Moreover, in 1802, the French Republic was at peace in Europe with the papacy, Great Britain, and all Continental powers, though a French army was still at war in Saint-Domingue. France reached to the Rhine and had dependent republics in Holland and

From Consulate to empire

Italy. So popular was the First Consul that in 1802, by another plebiscite, he had himself elected consul for life. A new constitution, in 1804, again ratified by plebiscite, declared that "the government of the republic is entrusted to an emperor." The Consulate became the empire, and Bonaparte emerged as Napoleon I, Emperor of the French.

But France, no longer revolutionary at home, was a revolutionary force outside its borders. Napoleon became a terror to the patricians of Europe. They called him the "Jacobin." And the France that he ruled, and used as his arsenal, was an incomparably formidable state. Even before the Revolution it had been the most populous in Europe, perhaps the most wealthy, in the front rank of scientific enterprise and intellectual leadership. Now all the old barriers of privilege, tax exemption, localism, and caste exclusiveness had disappeared. The new France could tap the wealth of its citizens and put able men into positions without inquiring into their origins. Every private, boasted Napoleon, carried a marshal's baton in his knapsack. The French looked with disdain on their caste-ridden adversaries. The principle of civic equality proved not only to have the appeal of justice, but also to be politically useful, and the resources of France were hurled against Europe with a force that for many years no other nation or balance of powers could successfully oppose.

Suggested Further Readings can be found in the ebook, on Connect, or online at www.mhhe .com/kramer12e.

Chapter **10**

NAPOLEONIC EUROPE

The repercussions of the French Revolution had spread throughout Europe since the fall of the Bastille, and even more definitely after the outbreak of war in 1792 and the ensuing victories of the French republican armies. They became even more evident after the republican General Bonaparte turned into Napoleon I, Emperor of the French, King of Italy, and Protector of the Confederation of the Rhine. Napoleon surpassed all previous European rulers in imposing a broad political unity on the European continent. Although his imperial power collapsed in less than 15 years, his military campaigns and political ascendancy transformed both international relations in Europe and the internal development of the various European peoples. The French impact on other nations, though based on military success, represented more than mere forcible subjugation. Many of the legal and social innovations that came to France through revolution were brought to other countries in the early nineteenth century by administrative decree and by collaborating local leaders. There were Germans, Italians, Dutch, and Poles who worked with the French emperor to introduce the changes that he demanded, and that they themselves often desired. In Prussia it was the resistance to Napoleon that gave the incentive to internal reorganization and fostered the emergence of a new German nationalism. Whether by collaboration or resistance, Europe was transformed.

It is convenient to think of the fighting from 1792 to 1814 as the first modern "total war" or as a world war. It affected not only all of Europe but also places as far away as Latin America, where the wars of independence began, or the interior of North America, where the United States purchased Louisiana in 1803 and attempted a conquest of Canada in the War of 1812. But it is important to realize that this world war was actually a series of wars, most of them quite short and distinct. Only Great Britain remained continually at war with France, except for about a year of peace in 1802–1803. Never were the four great European powers, Britain, Austria, Russia, and Prussia, simultaneously waging war against France until 1813.

Chapter emblem: Detail from a nineteenth-century illustration of Napoleon and Tsar Alexander I meeting on the Niemen River in 1807. (Rare Book Collection, Wilson Special Collections Library, University of North Carolina, Chapel Hill)

The history of the Napoleonic period would be much simpler if the European governments had fought merely to protect themselves against the aggressive French. Each, however, in its way, was as dynamic and expansive as Napoleon himself. For some generations Great Britain had been building a global commercial empire, Russia had been pushing upon Poland and Turkey, and Prussia had been consolidating its territories and striving for leadership in north Germany. Austria was less aggressive, but the Austrians were not without their own dreams of ascendancy in Germany, the Balkans, and the Adriatic. None of these ambitions ceased during the Napoleonic years. Governments, in pursuit of their own expansive aims, were quite as willing to ally with Napoleon as to fight him. Only gradually, and under repeated provocation, did they conclude that their main interest was to dispose of the French emperor entirely.

47.   THE FORMATION OF THE FRENCH IMPERIAL SYSTEM

The Collapse of the First and Second Coalitions, 1792-1802

The conflicting purposes of the major European powers had been apparent from almost the beginning of the French Revolution. Leopold of Austria, in issuing the Declaration of Pillnitz in 1791, had believed a general European coalition against France to be impossible. When war began in 1792, the Austrians and Prussians kept their main forces in eastern Europe, more afraid of each other and of Russia, in the matter of Poland, than of the French revolutionary republic. Indeed, the main accomplishment of the First Coalition was the partition of Poland and the dissolution of the Polish state.

The First Coalition disintegrates

In 1795 the French broke up the coalition. The British withdrew their army from the Continent. Prussia and Spain each made a separate peace with France. Indeed, Bourbon Spain—acting for reasons of strategic self-interest that ignored all ideology or principle—formed an alliance with the French republic that had guillotined Louis XVI and kept Louis XVIII from his monarchic rights. Spain simply reverted to an earlier eighteenth-century pattern in allying with France because of hostility to Great Britain, whose possession of Gibraltar, naval influence in the Mediterranean, and attitude toward the Spanish Empire were disquieting to the Spanish government. When Austria signed the peace of Campo Formio in 1797, the First Coalition was totally dissipated, only British naval forces remaining engaged with the French.

The Second Coalition of 1799 fared no better. After the British fleet defeated the French at the battle of the Nile, cutting off the French army in Egypt, the Russians saw their ambitions in the Mediterranean blocked mainly by the British and withdrew Suvorov's army from western Europe. Austria's acceptance of the peace of Lunéville in 1801 dissolved the Second Coalition, and in 1802 Great Britain signed the peace of Amiens. For the only time between 1792 and 1814 no European power was at war with another.

Peace Interim, 1802-1803

Never had a peace been so advantageous to France as the peace of 1802. But Bonaparte's ambitions gave it no chance to endure. He used peace as he did war to advance his interests. Seeking to reestablish slavery in the French Caribbean islands, Bonaparte dispatched a sizable army to Saint-Domingue, where (as noted earlier) the French forces suffered a major defeat and the Republic of Haiti emerged as a new independent state. Although he had wanted to suppress Toussaint Louverture and reassert imperial power over a colonial population that was slipping away from French control, Bonaparte sent this army with the additional and wider goal of reviving France's colonial empire in America. Spain had ceded Louisiana back to France in 1800, giving the French a base for expanding their

The war for Haitian independence was a brutal conflict that caused very high casualties on both sides. It led to the complete French withdrawal from their longtime colony of Saint-Domingue and the creation of the Republic of Haiti in 1804. Napoleon's failure to repress a guerrilla-style military resistance, as depicted in this image of a Haitian battle with French troops, became a prelude to future failures in a similar war in Spain.

(©Bettmann/Getty Images)

influence in the Caribbean, but this plan collapsed when France failed to defeat the revolutionary movement in Saint-Domingue. Bonaparte therefore decided to sell the Louisiana territories to the United States; and the Haitian Revolution, which prevented the restoration of slavery in a long-held French colony and created a new national state, also contributed directly to a vast expansion of the new republic in North America. Meanwhile, within the French-dominated territories of continental Europe, Bonaparte reorganized the Helvetic Republic, making himself "mediator" of the Confederation of Switzerland. He reorganized Germany; that is to say, he and his agents closely watched the rearrangement of territory that the Germans themselves had been carrying out since 1797.

By the treaty of Campo Formio, it will be recalled, German princes of the Left Bank of the Rhine, expropriated by the annexation of their dominions to the French Republic, were to receive new territories on the Right Bank. The result was a scramble that later patriotic German historians called the "shame of the princes." The German rulers, far from opposing Bonaparte or upholding any national interests, competed desperately for the acquisition of various German territories, each bribing and fawning upon the French to win French support against other Germans (Talleyrand made over 10 million francs in this process). The Holy Roman Empire was fatally mauled by the Germans themselves. Most of its

The "shame of the princes"

ecclesiastical principalities and 45 out of its 51 free cities disappeared, annexed by their larger neighbors. The number of states in the Holy Roman Empire was greatly reduced, but Prussia, Bavaria, Württemberg, and Baden consolidated and enlarged themselves. These arrangements were ratified in February 1803 by the diet of the empire. The enlarged German states now depended on Bonaparte for the maintenance of their newly enhanced position.

Formation of the Third Coalition in 1805

Britain and France went to war again in 1803. Bonaparte, his communications with America menaced by the British navy, and his army in Haiti decimated by disease and by the military campaigns of the Haitian independence movement, had suspended his ideas for re-creating an American empire. In May 1804, however, he pronounced himself to be Emperor Napoleon of the French to ensure the hereditary permanency of his imperial system in Europe, though at the time he had no heir. Francis II of Austria, seeing the Holy Roman Empire in ruins, promulgated the Austrian Empire in August 1804. He thus advanced the long process of integrating the Danubian monarchy. In 1805 Austria signed an alliance with Great Britain;

Tsar Alexander I

and the Third Coalition was soon completed by the accession of the Russian Tsar Alexander I, who, after Napoleon himself, was to become the most prominent figure on the early nineteenth-century European stage. Alexander was the grandson of Catherine the Great, educated by her to be a kind of enlightened despot on the eighteenth-century model. The Swiss tutor of his boyhood, La Harpe, later turned up as a pro-French revolutionary in the Helvetic Republic of 1798. Alexander became tsar in 1801, at the age of 24, through a palace revolution that implicated him in the murder of his father Paul. He still corresponded with La Harpe, and he surrounded himself with a circle of liberal young men of various nationalities, of whom the most influential was the young Polish diplomat, Adam Jerzy Czartoryski. Alexander regarded the still recent partitions of Poland as a crime. Encouraged by Czartoryski, he wished to restore the unity of Poland with himself as a constitutional king. In Germany many who had first warmed to the French Revolution, but had become disillusioned, began to hail the new liberal tsar as the protector of Germany and hope of the future. Alexander perceived himself as a rival to Napoleon in guiding the destinies of Europe in an age of change. Moralistic and self-righteous, he puzzled and disturbed the statesmen of Europe, who generally saw, behind his humane utterances, either an enthroned leader of all the "Jacobins" of Europe or the familiar specter of Russian aggrandizement.

Yet Alexander, more than his contemporaries, formed a conception of international peace and collective security. He declared that the issue in Europe was clearly between law and force—between an international society in which the rights of each member were secured by international agreement and organization and a society in which all trembled before the rule of cynicism and conquest embodied in the French imperial usurper.

Alexander was therefore ready to enter a Third Coalition with Great Britain. Picturing himself as a future arbiter of Poland and central Europe, and with secret designs on the Ottoman Empire and the Mediterranean, he signed a treaty with England in April 1805. The British agreed to pay Russia £1,250,000 for each 100,000 soldiers that the Russians raised.

The Third Coalition, 1805–1807: The Peace of Tilsit

Napoleon meanwhile, since the resumption of hostilities in 1803, had been making preparations to invade England. He concentrated large forces on the Channel coast, together with thousands of boats and barges in which he gave the troops amphibious training in embarkation and debarkation. He reasoned that if his own fleet could divert or cripple the British fleet for a few days he could place enough soldiers on the defenseless island to force its capitulation. The British, sensing mortal danger, lined their coasts with look-outs and signal beacons and set to drilling a home guard. Their main defense was twofold: the Austro-Russian armies on the continent and the British fleet under Lord Nelson. The Russian and Austrian armies moved westward in the summer of 1805. In August Napoleon relieved the pressure upon England, shifting seven army corps from the Channel to the upper Danube. On October 15 he surrounded an Austrian force of 50,000 men at Ulm in Bavaria, forcing it to surrender without resistance. On October 21 Lord Nelson, off Cape Trafalgar on the Spanish coast, caught and annihilated the main body of the combined fleets of France and Spain.

The battle of Trafalgar established the supremacy of the British navy for over a century—but only on the proviso that Napoleon be prevented from controlling most of Europe, which could furnish an ample base for eventual construction of a greater navy than the British.

British victory at Trafalgar

And to control Europe was precisely what Napoleon proceeded to do. Moving east from Ulm he came upon the Russian and Austrian armies in Moravia, where on December 2 he won the great victory of Austerlitz. The broken Russian army withdrew into Poland, and Austria made peace. By the treaty of Pressburg Napoleon took Venetia from the Austrians, to whom he had given it in 1797, and annexed it to his kingdom of Italy (the former Cisalpine and Italian Republic), which now included much of Italy north of Rome. Venice and Trieste soon resounded with the hammers of shipwrights rebuilding the Napoleonic fleet. In Germany, early in 1806, the French emperor raised Bavaria and Württemberg to the stature of kingdoms and Baden to a grand duchy. The Holy Roman Empire was finally, formally, and irrevocably dissolved. In its place Napoleon began to gather his German client states into a new kind of Germanic federation, the Confederation of the Rhine, of which he made himself the "protector."

Prussia, at peace with France for ten years, had declined to join the Third Coalition. But as Napoleon's program for controlling Germany became clear after Austerlitz, the war party in Prussia became irresistible, and the Prussian government now went to war with the French unaided and alone. The French smashed the famous Prussian army at the battles of Jena and Auerstädt in October 1806. The French cavalry galloped all over north Germany

The Third Coalition collapses

unopposed. The Prussian king and his government took refuge in the east, at Königsberg, where the tsar and the re-forming Russian army might protect them. But the terrible Corsican pursued the Russians also. Marching through western Poland and into East Prussia, he met the Russian army first at the sanguinary but indecisive battle of Eylau and then defeated it on June 14, 1807, at Friedland. Alexander I was unwilling to continue the war by retreating into Russia. He was unsure of his own resources; if the country were invaded, there might be a revolt of the nobles or even of the serfs—for people still remembered the great serf rebellion of the 1770s. Alexander feared also merely playing the game of the British. He put aside his war aims of 1804 and signified his willingness to negotiate with Napoleon. The Third Coalition had gone the way of the two before it.

The Emperor of the French and the Autocrat of All the Russias met privately on a raft in the Niemen River, not far from the border between Prussia and Russia, the very easternmost frontier of modern or "civilized" Europe, as the triumphant Napoleon glee-fully imagined it. The hapless Prussian king, Frederick William III, paced nervously on the bank while the two imperial rulers discussed their visions for the whole European continent. Bonaparte turned all his charm upon Alexander, denouncing England as the author of all the troubles of Europe and setting before Alexander an imagined boundless destiny as Emperor of the East, intimating that Russia's future lay toward Turkey, Persia, Afghanistan, and India. The result of their conversations was the treaty of Tilsit of July 1807, in many ways the high point of Napoleon's success. The French and Russian empires became allies, mainly against Great Britain. Ostensibly this alliance lasted for five years. Alexander accepted Napoleon as a kind of Emperor of the West. As for Prussia, Napoleon continued to occupy Berlin with French troops, and he took away all Prussian territories west of the Elbe, combining them with others taken from Hanover to make a new kingdom of Westphalia, which became part of his Confederation of the Rhine.

The Treaty of Tilsit

The Continental System and the War in Spain

Hardly had the "peace of the continent" been reestablished on the foundation of a Franco-Russian alliance when Napoleon began to have serious trouble. He was bent on subduing the British who, secure on their island, seemed beyond his reach. Since the French naval disaster at Trafalgar, there was no possibility of invading England in the foreseeable future. Napoleon therefore turned to economic warfare. He would fight sea power with land power, using his political control of the Continent to shut out British goods and to block shipping to Britain from all European ports. He would destroy the British trade in exports to Europe, both exports of British products and the profitable British reexport of goods from America and Asia. The overall strategy, as Napoleon planned it, was to ruin British commercial firms and cause a violent business depression, marked by overloaded warehouses, unemployment, a fall of the currency, rising prices, and revolutionary agitation. The British government, which would simultaneously be losing revenues from its customs duties, would thus find itself unable to carry the enormous national debt, or to borrow additional funds from its subjects, or to continue its financial subsidies to the military powers of Europe. At Berlin, in 1806, after the battle of Jena, Napoleon issued the Berlin Decree, forbidding the importation of British goods into any part of Europe allied with or dependent on himself. He in that way formally established the Continental System.

Economic warfare

To make the Continental System effective Napoleon believed that it must extend to all continental Europe without exception. By the treaty of Tilsit, in 1807, he required both Russia and Prussia to adhere to it. They agreed to exclude all British goods; in fact, in the following months Russia, Prussia, and Austria all declared war on Great Britain. Napoleon then ordered two neutral states, Denmark and Portugal, to adhere to his exclusionary commercial system. Denmark was an important entrepôt for all central Europe, and the British, fearing Danish compliance, dispatched a fleet to Copenhagen, bombarded the city for four days, and took captive the Danish fleet. The outraged Danes allied with Napoleon and joined the Continental System. Portugal, long a satellite of Britain, refused compliance; Napoleon invaded it. To control the whole European coastline from St. Petersburg around to Trieste he now had only to control the ports of Spain. By a series of deceptions he got both the Bourbon Charles IV and his son Ferdinand to abdicate the Spanish throne, whereupon the young Ferdinand was imprisoned in France. He then made his own brother Joseph king of Spain in 1808 and reinforced him with a large French army.

He thus involved himself in an Iberian entanglement from which he never escaped. The Spanish regarded the Napoleonic soldiers as godless villains who desecrated churches. Fierce guerrillas took the field. Cruelties of one side were answered by atrocities of the other. The British sent an expeditionary force of their small regular army, eventually under the Duke of Wellington, to sustain the Spanish guerrillas; the resulting Peninsular War dragged on for five years. But from the beginning the affair went badly for Napoleon. In July 1808

This meeting between Napoleon and Russia's Alexander I on the Niemen River produced an alliance and an agreement on the Continental System. The new system was aimed against the British, but Alexander soon disliked the restrictions on Anglo-Russian commerce. His withdrawal from the Continental System provoked Napoleon's disastrous invasion of Russia in 1812.

(Rare Book Collection, Wilson Special Collections Library, University of North Carolina, Chapel Hill)

a French general, for the first time since the Revolution, surrendered an entire army corps, which had been surrounded and forced to capitulate at Bailén. In August another French force surrendered to the British army in Portugal. And these events raised hopes in the rest of Europe.

The Peninsular War in Spain

An anti-French movement swept over Germany. It was felt strongly in Austria, where the Habsburg government, undaunted by three defeats and hoping to lead a general German national resistance, prepared for a fourth time since 1792 to go to war with France.

The Austrian War of Liberation, 1809

Napoleon convened a general congress of European leaders at Erfurt in Saxony in September 1808. His main purpose was to talk with his ally of a year, Alexander; but he assembled numerous dependent monarchs as well, by whose presence he hoped to overawe the tsar. He even had Talma, the leading actor of the day, play in the theater of Erfurt before "a parterre of kings." Alexander was unimpressed. He was hurt in a sensitive spot because Napoleon had recently made moves without Russian involvement to re-create a Polish state, setting up what was called the Grand Duchy of Warsaw. This was not the kind of Polish state that Alexander had envisioned, and he had also found Napoleon unwilling, despite the grandiose language of Tilsit, really to support his expansion into the Balkans. In addition, Alexander

Talleyrand

was taken aside by Talleyrand, Napoleon's foreign minister. Talleyrand had concluded that Napoleon was overreaching himself and said so confidentially to the tsar, advising him to wait for future opportunities. Talleyrand thus betrayed the man whom he ostensibly served and prepared a safe place for himself in the event of Napoleon's fall; but he acted also as an aristocrat of the prenationalistic Old Regime, seeing his own country as only one part of the whole of Europe, believing a balance among the several parts to be necessary and holding that peace would be possible only when the exaggerated reach of French power would be reduced. For France and Russia, the two strongest states, to combine against all other states was contrary to all principles of the older diplomacy.

Austria proclaimed a war of liberation in April 1809. Napoleon advanced rapidly along the familiar route to Vienna. The German princes, indebted to the French, declined to join in a general German war against him. Alexander stood watchfully on the sidelines. Napoleon won the battle of Wagram in July. In October Austria made peace. The short war of 1809 was over. The Danubian monarchy, by no means as fragile as it seemed, survived a fourth defeat at the hands of the French without internal revolution or disloyalty to the Habsburg house. From it, in punishment, Napoleon took part of Austrian Poland to enlarge the Grand Duchy of Warsaw; and he took parts of Austrian-controlled Dalmatia, Slovenia, and Croatia to establish a new creation that Napoleon called the Illyrian Provinces (see map, p. 433).

Napoleon at His Peak, 1809–1811

| Metternich |

The next two years saw the Napoleonic Empire at its peak. In Austria after the defeat of 1809 the conduct of foreign affairs fell to Clemens von Metternich, who was to remain the Austrian foreign minister for 40 years. He was a German from west of the Rhine, whose ancestral territories had been annexed to the French Republic, but he had entered the Austrian service and even married the granddaughter of Kaunitz, the old model of diplomatic savoir-faire, of which Metternich now became a model himself. Austria had been repeatedly humiliated and even partitioned by Napoleon, but Metternich was not inclined to conduct diplomacy by grudges. Believing that Russia was the really permanent problem for a state situated in the Danube valley, Metternich thought it wise to renew good relations with France. He was quite willing to go along with Napoleon, whom he knew personally, having been Austrian ambassador to Paris before the short war of 1809.

The French emperor, who in 1809 was exactly 40, was increasingly concerned by the fact that he was childless. He had made an empire that he pronounced hereditary. Yet he had no heir. Between him and his wife Josephine whom he had married in youth, and who was six years his senior, there had long since ceased to be affection or even fidelity on either side. He divorced her in 1809, though she protested that Napoleon's childlessness was not her fault (she had two children by a first husband). He intended to marry a younger woman who might bear him offspring. He intended also to make a spectacular marriage, to extort for himself, a self-made Corsican army officer, the highest and most exclusive recognition that aristocratic Europe could bestow. Tactful inquiries at St. Petersburg concerning the availability of Alexander's sister were tactfully rebuffed; the tsar intimated that his mother would never allow it. The Russian alliance again showed its limitations. Napoleon was thus thrown into the arms of Metternich—and of Marie Louise, the 18-year-old daughter of the Austrian emperor and niece of another Austrian woman, Marie Antoinette. They were married in 1810. In a year she bore him a son, whom he entitled the King of Rome.

Napoleon assumed ever more pompous airs of imperial majesty. He was now, by marriage, the nephew of Louis XVI. He showed more consideration to French noblemen of the Old Regime—only they, he said, knew really how to serve. He surrounded himself with a newly made hereditary Napoleonic nobility, hoping that the new families, as time

THE THIRD OF MAY 1808
by Francisco de Goya (Spanish, 1746–1828)

Facing steadfast resistance to their military occupation of Spain, the French army committed atrocities such as the brutal scene that Goya portrayed in this image of the Peninsular War.

(©PHAS/Getty Images)

went on, would bind their own fortunes to the house of Bonaparte. The marshals became dukes and princes; Talleyrand became the Prince of Benevento; and the bourgeois Fouché, an Hébertist radical in 1793 and more latterly a police official, was now solemnly addressed as the Duke of Otranto. In foreign affairs also older diplomatic relations seemed to be reappearing. With the significant exception of Great Britain, all the powers of the successive coalitions were allied with the French, and the Son of the Revolution now gravely referred to the emperor of Austria as "my father."

48.   THE GRAND EMPIRE: SPREAD OF THE REVOLUTION

The Organization of the Napoleonic Empire

Territorially Napoleon's influence enjoyed its farthest reach in 1810 and 1811, when it included the entire European mainland except the Balkan peninsula. The Napoleonic domain was in two parts. Its core

The empire at its height

was the French Empire; then came thick layers of dependent states, which together with France comprised the Grand Empire. In addition, to the north and east were the "allied states" under their traditional governments—the three great powers, Prussia, Austria, and Russia, and also Denmark and Sweden. The allied states were at war with Great Britain, though not engaged in positive hostilities; their populations were supposed to do without British goods under the Continental System, but otherwise Napoleon had no direct lawful influence upon their internal affairs.

The French Empire, as successor to the French Republic, included the southern Netherlands and the Left Bank of the Rhine. In addition, by 1810, it had developed two appendages that on a map looked like tentacles outstretched from it (see the map on p. 433). When he proclaimed France an empire and turned its dependent republics into kingdoms, Napoleon had set up his brother Louis as king of Holland; but Louis had shown such a tendency to ingratiate himself with the Dutch, and such a willingness to let Dutch businessmen trade secretly with the British, that Napoleon dethroned him and incorporated Holland into the French Empire. In his endless war upon British goods, Napoleon found it useful to exert more direct control over the ports of Bremen, Hamburg, Lübeck, Genoa, and Leghorn; he therefore annexed directly to the French Empire the German coast as far as the western Baltic, and the Italian coast far enough to include Rome, which he desired for its imperial rather than its commercial value. Harking back to traditions as old as Charlemagne, he considered Rome the second city of his empire, as he affirmed when entitled his son the King of Rome. When Pope Pius VII protested the French annexation of papal lands, Napoleon took him prisoner and interned him in France, where he remained until 1814. The whole French Empire, from Lübeck to Rome, was governed directly by departmental prefects who reported to Paris, and the 83 departments of France, created by the Constituent Assembly, had risen to 130 by 1810.

The dependent states, forming with France the Grand Empire, were of different kinds. The Swiss federation remained republican in form. The Illyrian Provinces, which included Trieste and the Dalmatian coast, were administered in their brief two years almost like departments of France. In Poland, because the Russians objected to a revived kingdom of Poland, Napoleon called his creation the Grand Duchy of Warsaw. Among the most important of the dependent states in the Grand Empire were the German states organized into the Confederation of the Rhine. Too modestly named, the Confederation included all Germany between what the French annexed on the west and what Prussia and Austria retained on the east. It was a league of all the German princes in this region who were regarded as sovereign and who now numbered only about 20, the most important being the four newly made kings of Saxony, Bavaria, Württemberg, and Westphalia. Westphalia was an entirely new and synthetic state, made up of Hanoverian and Prussian territories and of various small parts of the old Germany. Its king was Napoleon's youngest brother, Jerome.

Napoleon liked to use his family as a means of rule. The Corsican clan became the Bonaparte dynasty. His brother Joseph from 1804 to 1808 functioned as king of Naples and after 1808 as king of Spain. Louis Bonaparte was for six years king of Holland; Jerome was king of Westphalia. Sister Caroline became queen of Naples after brother Joseph's transfer to Spain; for Napoleon, running out of brothers (having quarreled with his remaining brother, Lucien), gave the throne of Naples to his brother-in-law, Joachim Murat, a cavalry officer who was Caroline's husband. In the "Kingdom of Italy," which in 1810 included Lombardy, Venetia, and most of the former papal states, Napoleon himself retained the title of king, but set up his stepson, Eugène Beauharnais (Josephine's son) as viceroy. The mother of the Bonapartes, Letitia, who had brought up all these children under very different circumstances in Corsica, was suitably installed at the imperial court as Madame Mère. According to legend she kept repeating to herself, "If only it lasts!"; she outlived Napoleon by 15 years.

Napoleon and the Spread of the Revolution

In all the states of the Grand Empire the same course of events tended to repeat itself. First came the stage of military conquest and occupation by French troops. Then came the establishment of a native satellite government with the support of local persons who were willing to collaborate with the French and who helped in the drafting of a constitution specifying the powers of the new government and regularizing its relationships with France. In some areas these two stages had been accomplished under the republican governments before Napoleon came to power. In some regions no more than these two stages really occurred, notably in Spain and the Grand Duchy of Warsaw.

Stages of French occupation

The third stage of French influence was one of sweeping internal reform and reorganization, modeled on Bonaparte's program for France and hence derivatively on the French Revolution. The former Austrian Netherlands and the German territories west of the Rhine underwent this stage most thoroughly, because they were annexed directly to France for 20 years. Italy and much of Germany west of Prussia and Austria also experienced the third stage.

Napoleon considered himself a great reformer and man of the Enlightenment. He called his system "liberal," and though the word to him meant almost the reverse of what it later meant to nineteenth-century liberals, he was possibly the first to use it in a political sense.

Napoleon as reformer

He believed also in "constitutions"; not that he favored representative assemblies or limited government, but he wanted government to be rationally "constituted," that is, deliberately mapped out and planned, not merely inherited from the jumble of the past. Although his own methods of governing were authoritarian, he believed firmly in the rule of law. He insisted with the zeal of conviction on transplanting his Civil Code to the dependent states. He assumed that this code was based on the universal nature of justice and human relationships, and he believed that it must therefore be applicable to all countries with no more than minor adaptation. The idea that a country's laws must mirror its distinctive national character and history was foreign to his mind, for he carried over the rationalist and universalist outlook of the Age of Enlightenment. He thought that people everywhere wanted, and deserved, much the same thing. As he wrote to his brother Jerome, on making him king of Westphalia, "the peoples of Germany, as of France, Italy and Spain, want equality and liberal ideas. For some years now I have been managing the affairs of Europe, and I am convinced that the crowing of the privileged classes was everywhere disliked. Be a constitutional king."

The same plan of reform was initiated, with some variation, in all the dependent states from Spain to Poland and from the mouth of the Elbe to the Straits of Messina. The reforms were directed, in a word, against everything that still affirmed or protected the old "feudal" hierarchies. They established the legal equality of individual persons and gave governments more complete authority over their individual subjects. Legal classes were wiped out, as in France in 1789; the theory of a society made up of "estates of the realm" gave way to the theory of a society made up of legally equal individuals. The nobility lost its privileges in taxation, officeholding, and military command. Careers were "opened to talent."

The manorial system, bulwark of the old aristocracy, was virtually liquidated wherever French influence became predominant. Lords lost all legal jurisdiction over their peasants; peasants became subjects of the state, personally free to move, migrate, or marry, and able to bring suit in the courts of law. The manorial fees, along with tithes, were generally abolished, as in France in 1789. In France the peasants mostly escaped from these burdens without having to pay compensation, in part because they had themselves risen in rebellion in 1789 and in part because France passed through a radical popular revolution in 1793. In other parts of the Grand Empire, however, the peasants were required to pay indemnities, and the former feudal class continued to receive income from its abolished rights. Only in the southern (Belgian) Netherlands and the Rhineland, incorporated into France under the republic, did the manorial regime disappear without compensation as in France, leaving a numerous entrenched class of small landowning farmers. East of the Rhine Napoleon had to compromise with the aristocracy that he assailed. In Poland, the only country in the Grand Empire where a thoroughgoing serfdom had prevailed, the peasants received legal freedom during the French occupation; but the Polish landlords remained economically unharmed, because they owned all the land. Napoleon had to conciliate them, for there was no other effective class in Poland to which he could look for support. In general, outside of France, the assault upon feudal traditions was not socially as revolutionary as it had been in France. The lord was gone, but the landlord remained.

Everywhere in the Grand Empire the church lost its position as a public authority alongside the state. Church courts were abolished or restricted; the Inquisition was outlawed in Spain. Tithes were done away with, church property was confiscated, and monastic orders were dissolved or severely regulated. Toleration became the law; Catholics, Protestants, Jews, Muslims, and unbelievers received the same civil rights. The state was to be based not on the idea of religious community but on the idea of territorial residence. With the nobility, or on economic matters, Napoleon would compromise; but he would not compromise with the Catholic clergy on the principle of a secular state. Even in Spain he insisted on the fundamental secularism of his system, a sure indication that he was not motivated by expediency only, because it was largely his antireligious program that provoked the Spanish populace to rebellion.

Guilds were generally abolished or reduced to empty forms, and the individual's right to work was generally proclaimed. Peasants, gaining legal freedom, might learn and enter any trade they chose. The old town oligarchies and bourgeois patriciates were broken up. Towns and provinces lost their antique liberties and came under the general legislation of the whole governing state. Internal tariffs were removed, and free trade within state frontiers was encouraged. Some countries shifted to a decimal system of money; and the heterogeneous weights and measures that had originated in the Middle Ages, and of which the Anglo-American bushels, yards, ounces, and pints are living survivals, yielded to the Cartesian regularities of the metric system. Ancient and diverse legal systems gave way to the Napoleonic codes. Law courts were separated from the administration. Hereditary office and the sale of office disappeared. Officials received salaries large enough to shield them from the temptations of corruption. Kings were put on civil lists, with their personal expenses separated from those of the government. Taxes and finances were modernized. The common tax became a land tax, paid by every landowner; and governments knew how much land each owner really possessed, for they developed systematic methods of appraisal and assessment. Tax farming was replaced by direct collection. New methods of accounting and of collecting statistics were introduced.

NAPOLEONIC EUROPE, 1810

Napoleon extended the sphere of French power well beyond the earlier expansion of the French Republic. By 1810 he dominated the whole continent except Portugal and the Balkan peninsula. Russia, Prussia, and Austria had been forced into alliance with him, and he had made his brothers kings of Spain, Holland, and Westphalia; his brother-in-law king of Naples; and his stepson viceroy of Italy. The old Holy Roman Empire disappeared into other states, including Napoleon's Confederation of the Rhine. In Poland, Napoleon undid part of the late eighteenth-century partitions by setting up the Grand Duchy of Warsaw.

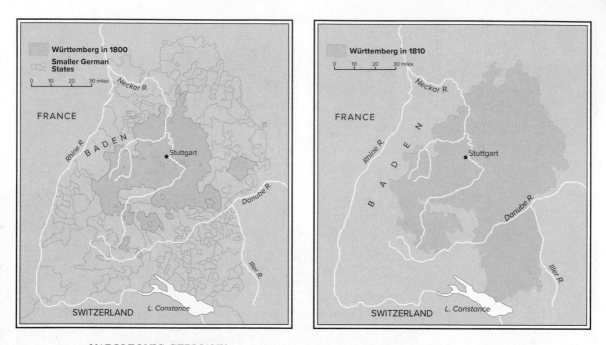

NAPOLEONIC GERMANY

In the panel at the left are shown, by shading, territories of the Duchy of Württemberg in 1800. Note how Württemberg had "islands" of territory embedded within other states and how "holes" or enclaves formed by smaller states were enclosed within the core territories of Württemberg. Note, too, how Württemberg, itself only 50 miles wide, was surrounded by a mosaic of tiny jurisdictions— free cities, counties, duchies, principalities, abbacies, commanderies, bishoprics, arch-bishoprics, etc.—all "independent" within the Holy Roman Empire. The right-hand panel shows the Kingdom of Württemberg as consolidated and enlarged in the time of Napoleon. Similar consolidations all over Germany greatly reduced the number of states and added to the efficiency of law and government.

In general, in all countries of the Grand Empire, some of the main principles of the French Revolution were introduced under Napoleon, with the notable exception that there

Support for Napoleon

was no self-government through elected legislative bodies. In all countries Napoleon found numerous persons who were willing to support him, mainly among people in the commercial and professional classes, who were generally aware of Enlightenment writers, often anticlerical, desirous of more equality with the nobility, and eager to break down the old localisms that interfered with trade and the exchange of ideas. He found supporters also among many progressive nobles and, in the Confederation of the Rhine, among the German rulers. His program appealed to some people everywhere, and in all parts of the Grand Empire the Napoleonic reforms were executed mainly by local leaders. Repression went with it, though hardly on the same scale as the repressions of later dictatorships. There were no vast internment camps, and Fouché's police were engaged more in spying and submitting reports than in the brutalizing of the disaffected. The execution of a single Bavarian bookseller, named Palm, became a famous outrage.

In short, there was at first a good deal of pro-Napoleonic feeling in the Grand Empire. Outside the Rhineland and the territories that would later become Belgium, the French influence struck deepest in north Italy, where there were no native monarchist traditions and where the old Italian city-states had produced a strong and often anticlerical burgher class. In south Germany also the French influence was profound. The French system had the least appeal in

Spain, where Catholic royalist sentiment produced a kind of counterrevolutionary movement of independence. Nor did it appeal to agrarian eastern Europe, the land of lord and serf. Yet even in Prussia, as will be seen, the state was remodeled along French lines. In Russia, during the Tilsit alliance, Alexander gave his backing to a pro-French reforming minister, Speranski. The Napoleonic influence was pervasive because it carried over the older movement of enlightened despotism and seemed to confer the advantages of the French Revolution without the violence and the disorder. Napoleon, it seemed to Goethe, "was the expression of all that was reasonable, legitimate and European in the revolutionary movement."

But Napoleon's reforms were also weapons of war. All the dependent states were required to supply Napoleon with money and soldiers. Germans, Dutch, Italians, Poles, and even Spaniards fought in his armies. In addition, the dependent states defrayed much of the cost of the French army, most of which was stationed outside France. This meant that taxes in France could remain low, to the general satisfaction of the propertied interests that had emerged or benefited from the Revolution.

49. THE CONTINENTAL SYSTEM: BRITAIN AND EUROPE

Beyond the tributary states of the Grand Empire lay the countries nominally independent, joined under Napoleon in the Continental System. Napoleon thought of his allies as at best subordinate partners in a common project. The great project was to crush Great Britain, and it was for this purpose that the Continental System had been established. But the crushing of Britain became in Napoleon's mind a means to a further end, the unification and mastery of all of Europe. This in turn, had he achieved it, would doubtless have merely opened the way to other campaigns to expand his empire.

Germaine de Staël was an influential leader of the liberal opposition to Napoleon's repressive cultural policies. She was forced to live in exile in Switzerland, but both her writings and the refuge of her Swiss home provided crucial support for Napoleon's critics.

(©Photos.com/Getty Images)

Historical Documents
Germaine de Staël, *Ten Years' Exile* (1810–1813)

Germaine de Staël (1766–1817) was a steadfast critic of Napoleon's authoritarian political regime, military ambitions, and repression of cultural dissent. Angered by her criticisms and by the assertiveness of such an independent-minded woman, Napoleon forced her to live as an exile in Switzerland. Her chateau—known as Coppet—became a gathering place for European writers who shared the views that de Staël summarized in this critique of Napoleon's self-centered, cynical approach to all political and cultural issues. These excerpts are from her memoir about exile, which de Staël's son published in London after her death.

The greatest grievance which the Emperor Napoleon has against me is the respect which I have always entertained for real liberty. These sentiments have been in a manner transmitted to me as an inheritance, and adopted as my own, ever since I have been able to reflect on the lofty ideas from which they are derived, and the noble actions which they inspire. . . .

[Napoleon] believes in the sincerity of no one's opinions; he considers every kind of morality as nothing more than a form, . . . so if any one says that he is a lover of liberty—that he believes in God—that he prefers his conscience to his interest, Bonaparte considers such professions only as an adherence to custom, or as the regular means of forwarding ambitious views or selfish calculations. The only class of human beings whom he cannot well comprehend, are those who are sincerely attached to an opinion, whatever be the consequences of it. . . .

What particularly characterizes the government of Bonaparte, is his profound contempt for the intellectual riches of human nature; virtue, mental dignity, religion, [and] enthusiasm, . . . [which] in his eyes, [are] the eternal enemies of the continent; . . . he would reduce man to force and cunning, and designate everything else as folly or stupidity.

Madame de Staël, *Ten Years' Exile; Memoirs of That Interesting Period of the Life of the Baroness De Stael-Holstein, Written by Herself, during the Years 1810, 1811, 1812, and 1813, Published from the Original Manuscript, by Her Son,* translated from the French (London: Howlett & Brimmer, 1821), pp. 2–5, 16–17.

Continental unity

At the point where he stood in 1807 or 1810 the unification of continental Europe seemed a not impossible objective. He cast about for an ideology to inspire both his Grand Empire and his allies. He held out the cosmopolitan doctrines of the eighteenth century, spoke endlessly of the enlightenment of the age, and urged all peoples to work with him against the medievalism, ignorance, and obscurantism by which they were surrounded. Although he disliked and even suppressed the creative work of writers such as his vehement critic Germaine de Staël, Napoleon encouraged innovative scientific research and rewarded the scientists who pursued it. Among his favored scientists, for example, he strongly supported the chemist Claude Berthollet and the mathematician Gaspard Monge—both of whom he rewarded with aristocratic titles and well-paid positions in his carefully selected French Senate. Napoleon viewed science as the essential, rational foundation of modern knowledge. And while appealing to ideas of modernity or progress he dwelt also on the grandeur of Roman times. The Roman inspiration appeared in the arts he supported and in the architecture that expressed Napoleon's conception of imperial glory. The massive "empire" furniture, the heroic canvases of David, the church of the Madeleine in Paris (resembling a classical temple and called a Temple of Glory), and the Arch of Triumph in the same city (begun in 1806) all evoked the atmosphere of far-spreading imperial majesty and unity in which Napoleon would have liked the peoples of Europe to live. In addition, to arouse an all-European feeling, Napoleon encouraged the latent hostility to Great Britain. The British, in winning much of the eighteenth-century struggle for wealth and empire, had made themselves disliked in many quarters. There was much envy for Britain's commercial success, and many Europeans resented the high-handedness by which this success had been won and maintained. It was widely believed that the British were really using their sea power to win a larger permanent share of the world's seaborne commerce for themselves. Nor, in truth, was this belief mistaken.

British Blockade and Napoleon's Continental System

The British, in the Revolutionary and Napoleonic wars, when they declared France and its allies in a state of blockade, did not expect either to starve them or to deprive them of necessary materials of war. Western Europe was still self-sufficient in food, and armaments were to a large extent produced locally from simple materials like iron, copper, and saltpeter. Europe required almost nothing indispensable from overseas. The chief aim of the British blockade was not, therefore, to keep imports out of enemy countries. The goal was to keep the trade in such imports out of French or European control and thereby kill off enemy commerce and shipping. In the short run the British sought to weaken the war-making powers of the enemy government by undermining its revenues and its navy; and in the long run they wanted to weaken the enemy's commercial position in world markets. Economic warfare was trade warfare. The British were willing enough to have British goods pass through to Europe either by smuggling or by the mediation of neutrals.

As early as 1793 the French republicans had denounced England as the "modern Carthage," a ruthless mercantile and profit-seeking power that aspired to enslave Europe to its financial and commercial system. With the wars, the British in fact obtained a monopoly over *Anti-British sentiments* the shipment of overseas commodities into Europe. At the same time, being relatively advanced in the new techniques of industrial production, they could produce cotton cloth and certain other articles, by power machinery, more cheaply than other peoples of Europe. Britain thus threatened to monopolize the European market for such manufactured goods. There was much feeling against the modern Carthage, especially among the European commercial classes who were in competition with it. The upper classes were perhaps less hostile, not caring where the goods that they consumed had originated, but aristocracies and governments were susceptible to the argument that Britain was a money power, a "nation of shopkeepers" as Napoleon put it, which fought its wars with pounds sterling instead of blood and was always in search of dupes in Europe.

It was on all these feelings that Napoleon played, reiterating time and again that England was Europe's real enemy and that Europeans would never be prosperous or economically independent until they removed the incubus of British "monopoly." To prevent the flow of goods into Britain was no more the purpose of the Continental System than to prevent the flow of goods into France was the purpose of the British blockade. The purpose of each was to destroy the enemy's commerce, credit, and public revenues by the destruction of its exports—and also to build up markets for their own national economies.

To destroy British exports Napoleon prohibited, by the Berlin *Trade warfare* Decree of 1806, the importation of British goods into the continent of Europe. Goods were counted as British if they came from either British or British colonial origins, even if they were brought to Europe in neutral ships as the property of neutrals.

The British, in response, ruled by an "order in council" of November 1807 that neutrals might enter Napoleonic ports only if they first stopped in Great Britain, where the regulations were such as to encourage their loading with British goods. The British thus tried to move their exports into enemy territory through neutral channels, which was precisely what Napoleon intended to prevent. He announced, by the Milan Decree of December 1807, that any neutral vessel that had stopped at a British port, or submitted to search by a British warship at sea, would be confiscated upon its appearance in a Continental harbor.

With all Europe at war, virtually the only major trading neutral nation was the United States, which could now trade with neither England nor Europe except by violating the regulations of one belligerent or the other. It would thus become liable to reprisals, and hence to involvement in war. President Jefferson, to avoid war, attempted a self-imposed policy of commercial isolation that proved so ruinous to American foreign trade that the United States government took steps to renew trade relations with whichever belligerent first removed its controls over neutral commerce. Napoleon offered to do so, on the condition that the United States would defend itself against the enforcement of British controls. At the same time an expansionist party among the Americans, ambitious to annex Canada, believed that with the British army engaged in Spain the time was ripe to

The War of 1812

complete the War of Independence by driving Britain from the North American mainland. The result was the Anglo-American War of 1812, which brought the new American nation into the wider conflict of the Atlantic world but had few results, except to demonstrate the inefficiency of military institutions in the new republic.

But Napoleon's Continental System was more than a device for destroying the export trade of Great Britain. It was also a scheme for developing the economy of continental Europe, around France as its main center. The Continental System, if successful, would replace the national economies with an integrated economy for the Continent as a whole. It would create the commercial framework for a more unified European civilization. And it would ruin the British sea power and commercial monopoly; for a unified Europe, Napoleon thought, would itself soon take to the sea.

The Failure of the Continental System

But the Continental System failed; it was worse than a failure, for it caused widespread antagonism to the Napoleonic regime. The dream of a united Europe, under French rule, was not sufficiently attractive to inspire the necessary sacrifice—even a sacrifice more of comforts than of necessities. As Napoleon impatiently said, one would suppose that the destinies of Europe turned upon a barrel of sugar. It was true, as he and his propagandists insisted, that Britain monopolized the sale of sugar, tobacco, and other overseas goods, but people preferred to deal clandestinely with the British rather than go without them. The irrepressible desire for American commodities destroyed the Continental System.

British manufactures were somewhat easier than colonial goods to replace. Raw cotton was brought by land from the Middle East through the Balkans, and the cotton manufacturers of France, Saxony, Switzerland, and north Italy were stimulated by the relief from British competition. There was a great expansion of Danish woolens and German hardware. The cultivation of sugar beets, to replace cane sugar, spread in France, central Europe, Holland, and even Russia. Thus infant industries and investments were built up that, after Napoleon's fall, clamored for tariff protection. In general, the European industrial interests were well disposed toward the Continental System.

Construction on the Arch of Triumph began in 1806, but it was not completed until 1836. It became a monument of French nationalism, symbolizing both the Republic and the Empire. The continuous band of bas reliefs above the curve of the arch represented 172 French battles since Valmy in 1792. (©Hulton Archive/Getty Images)

Yet they could never adequately replace the British in supplying the market. One obstacle was transportation. Much trading between parts of the Continent had always been by sea; this coastal traffic was now blocked by the British. Land routes were increasingly used, and improved roads were built through the Simplon and Mont Cenis passes in the Alps. No less than 17,000 wheeled vehicles crossed the Mont Cenis pass in 1810. But land transport, at best, was no substitute for the sea. Without railroads, introduced some 30 years later, a purely Continental modern economy could not be maintained; and transoceanic trade had in any case already shown that the political plan for a land-based commercial system would likely become a historical anachronism in modern European societies.

Consequences of the Continental System

Another obstacle was tariffs. The idea of a Continental tariff union was put forward by some of his subordinates, but Napoleon never adopted it. The dependent states remained insistent on their ostensible sovereignty. Each had widened its trading area by demolishing former internal tariffs; but Europeans could not yet view their continent as a unified commercial system, and each state kept a tariff against the others. The kingdoms of Italy and Naples enjoyed no free trade with each other nor did the German states of the Confederation of the Rhine. France remained protectionist; and when Napoleon annexed Holland and parts of Italy to France, he kept them outside the French customs. At the same time Napoleon forbade the satellite states to raise high tariffs against France. France was his base, and he meant to favor French industry, which was much crippled by its loss of its Middle Eastern and American markets.

Napoleon used architecture to show that Paris was the capital of modern Europe and that his empire replicated the imperial grandeur of ancient Rome. He built this multicolumned Madeleine to be a Temple of Glory, but after his fall from power it became a church.
(©Apic/RETIRED/Getty Images)

Economic stagnation   Shippers, shipbuilders, and dealers in overseas goods, a powerful element of the older bourgeoisie, were ruined by the Continental System. The French ports were idle and their populations were distressed and disgruntled. The same problems befell all ports of Europe where the blockade was strictly enforced; at Trieste, total annual tonnage fell from 208,000 in 1807 to 60,000 in 1812. Eastern Europe was especially hard hit. In western Europe there was some stimulus to new manufactures. Eastern Europe, long dependent on western Europe for manufactured goods, could no longer obtain them from England legally, nor from France, Germany, or Bohemia because of the difficulties of land transport and the British control of the Baltic. Nor could the landowners of Prussia, Poland, and Russia market their produce. The aristocracy of eastern Europe, which was the principal spending and importing class, had additional reason to dislike the French and to sympathize with the British.

As a war measure against Britain the Continental System also failed. British trade with Europe was significantly reduced, but the loss was made up elsewhere because of British control of the sea. Exports to Latin America rose from £300,000 in 1805 to £6,300,000 in 1809. Here again the existence of the overseas world frustrated the Continental System. Despite the System, export of British cotton goods, rising on a continuous tide of the rapidly developing Industrial Revolution, more than doubled in four years from 1805 to 1809. And while part of the increase was due to mere inflation and rising prices, it is estimated that the annual income of the British people more than doubled in the Revolutionary and Napoleonic wars, growing from £140,000,000 in 1792 to £335,000,000 in 1814. Napoleon's Continental System, in short, could never match or constrain the expanding global systems of international trade and commerce.

50.   THE NATIONAL MOVEMENTS AND NEW NATIONALIST CULTURES

The Resistance to Napoleon: Nationalism

From the beginning, as far back as 1792, the French met with resistance as well as collaboration in the countries they occupied. There was resentment when the invading armies plundered and laid requisitions upon the occupied countries; and there was anger when local populations were required to pay tribute in men and money and to adopt policies that were dictated by representatives of the French government. Europeans began to feel that Napoleon was employing them merely as tools against England. And in all countries, including France itself, people grew tired of the peace that was no peace, the wars and rumors of war, the conscription and the taxes, the loss of lives and local liberties, the increasingly bureaucratic governments, and Napoleon's insatiable appetite for power and self-exaltation. Movements of protest and independence showed themselves within the Napoleonic imperial structure and within the dependent states. Even the emperor's proconsuls tried to gain the support of local opinion, as when Louis Bonaparte, king of Holland, tried to defend Dutch interests against Napoleon's demands, or when Murat, king of Naples, appealed to Italian sentiment to secure his own throne.

Nationalism developed as a movement of resistance against the forcible internationalism of the Napoleonic Empire. Because the international system was essentially French, the nationalistic movements were anti-French; and because Napoleon was an autocrat, they were antiautocratic. The nationalism of the period was a mixture of the conservative and the liberal. Some nationalists, predominantly conservative, insisted on the value of their own unique institutions, customs, folkways, and historical development, which they feared might be obliterated under the French and Napoleonic system. Others, or indeed the same persons, insisted on more self-determination, more participation in government, more representative institutions, and more freedom for individuals against the bureaucratic interference of the state. Both conservative and liberal nationalists rose up against Napoleon, destroyed him, outlasted him, and shaped the history of the following generations.

Anti-French nationalism

Nationalism was thus very complex and appeared in different countries in different ways. In England a profound national solidarity developed as people of different social classes stood shoulder to shoulder against "Boney"; and ideas of reforming Parliament or tampering with historic English liberties were resolutely put aside. It is possible that the Napoleonic wars helped England through a very difficult social crisis, for the Industrial Revolution was causing dislocation, misery, unemployment, and even revolutionary agitation among a small minority, all of which were eclipsed by the patriotic need for resistance to Bonaparte. In Spain, nationalism took the form of implacable resistance to the French armies that desolated the land. Some Spanish nationalists were liberal; a bourgeois group at Cádiz, rebelling against the French regime, proclaimed the liberal Spanish constitution of 1812, modeled on the French constitution of 1791. But Spanish nationalism drew its greatest strength from sentiments that were counterrevolutionary, aiming to restore the clergy and the Bourbons. In Italy the Napoleonic regime was better liked and national feeling was less anti-French than in Spain. Commercial groups in the Italian cities generally prized the efficiency and enlightenment of French methods and often shared in the anticlericalism of the French Revolution. The French regime, which lasted in Italy from 1796 to 1814, broke the habit of loyalty to the various duchies, oligarchic republics, papal states, and foreign dynasties by which Italy had long been ruled. Napoleon never unified Italy, but he consolidated it into only three parts, and the French influence brought the emerging desire for a politically united Italy within the bounds of reasonable aspiration. Among the Poles, Napoleon positively encouraged national feeling. He repeatedly told them that they might win a restored and united Poland by faithfully fighting in his cause. A few Polish nationalists, like the aging patriot Kosciusko, never trusted Napoleon, and some others, like Czartoryski, looked rather to the Russian tsar for a restoration of the Polish kingdom; but in general the Poles, for their own national reasons, were exceptionally devoted to the emperor of the French and long lamented his passing.

The Movement of Thought in Napoleonic Germany

The national movement in Germany

By far the most momentous new national movement developed in Germany. The Germans rebelled not only against the Napoleonic rule but also against the century-old ascendancy of French civilization. They rebelled not only against the French armies but also against much of the philosophy of the Age of Enlightenment. The years of the French Revolution and Napoleon were for Germany the years of great cultural efflorescence, the years of Beethoven, Goethe, and Schiller, of Herder, Kant, Fichte, Hegel, Schleiermacher, and many others. German ideas fell in with all the ferment of the new cultural movement known as "romanticism," which was everywhere challenging the "dry abstractions" of the Age of Reason and shaping the new themes of literature, music, art, and historical research. Romanticism contributed to a growing German critique of eighteenth-century French culture, and German influence spread into the culture and politics of other European societies. In the nineteenth century the Germans came to be widely regarded as intellectual leaders, somewhat as the French had been in the century before. And many of the distinctive features of German thought were somehow connected with the broader anti-Enlightenment themes of both nationalism and romantic philosophy.

Formerly, especially in the century following the Peace of Westphalia in 1648, the Germans had been less nationally minded than other western European peoples. They prided themselves on their world citizenship or cosmopolitan outlook. Looking out from the small states in which most Germans lived, they were conscious of Europe, conscious of other countries, but hardly conscious of Germany. The Holy Roman Empire was neither a forceful political power nor the public embodiment of a well-defined national culture. The German world had no tangible frontiers; the area of German speech simply faded out into Alsace or the Austrian Netherlands, or into Poland, Bohemia, or the upper Balkans. "Germany" had not yet taken on a coherent cultural or political existence. The upper classes, becoming contemptuous of much that was German, adopted French fashions, dress, etiquette, manners, ideas, and language, regarding them as an international norm of civilized living. Frederick the Great hired French tax collectors and wrote his own books in French.

Nationalism grew rapidly as people throughout Europe increasingly questioned and resisted Napoleon's expansionist, imperial policies. This cartoon depiction of an angry fighter attacking Napoleon expresses the British pride in their successful national resistance to every French plan for invading Great Britain. (©Henry Guttmann/Getty Images)

About 1780 signs of a change set in. Even Frederick, in his later years, predicted a golden age of German literature, proudly declaring that Germans could do what other nations had done. In 1784 appeared a book by J. G. Herder called *Ideas on the Philosophy of the History of Mankind.* Herder was a Protestant pastor and theologian who had once lived in Paris and found the French somewhat frivolous. He concluded that imitation of foreign ways made people shallow and artificial. He declared that German ways were indeed different from French but not any less wor- *Herder's cultural* thy of respect. All true culture or civilization, he held, must arise from *nationalism* native roots. It must arise also from the life of the common people, the *Volk,* not from the cosmopolitan and artificial life of the upper classes. Each group of people who shared the same language, Herder argued, also shared their own distinctive attitudes, spirit, or genius. A sound civilization must express its own national character or *Volksgeist.* Herder did not believe the nations to be in conflict; quite the contrary, he simply insisted that they were different. He did not believe German culture to be the best; many other peoples, notably the Slavs, would therefore find his ideas applicable to their own nationalist needs. His philosophy of history, however, was very different from that of Voltaire and the philosophes, who had expected all people to progress along the same path of reason and enlightenment toward a similar civilization. Herder thought that all peoples should develop their own genius in their own way, each slowly unfolding with a kind of plantlike growth, avoiding sudden change or distortion by outside influence, and all ultimately reflecting, in their endless diversity, the infinite richness of humanity and of God.

The idea of the *Volksgeist* soon passed to other countries in the general movement of romantic thought. Like much else in romanticism, it emphasized genius or intuition rather than reason. It stressed the differences rather than the similarity of mankind. It broke down that sense of human similarity or universality that had been characteristic of the Age of Enlightenment, and that revealed itself in French and American doctrines of the rights of man, or again in the law codes of Napoleon. In the past it had been usually thought that whatever was truly good was good for all peoples. Good poetry, for example, adhered to certain classical principles or rules of composition, which were the same for all writers from the Greeks on down. Now, according to Herder and to romantics in all countries, good poetry was the poetry that expressed an inner genius, either an individual genius or the unique genius of a people—there were no more rigid, classical rules. Good and just laws, according to the older philosophy of natural law, somehow corresponded to a standard of justice that was the same for all people. But now, according to Herder and the romantic school of jurisprudence, good laws were those that reflected local conditions or national idiosyncrasies. Here again there were no rules, except possibly the rule that each nation should follow its own cultural path.

Herder's philosophy set forth a cultural nationalism, without a political message, but the French Revolution made the Germans more aware of national political questions and acutely conscious of the state. It showed what a people could do with a powerful state, once they took it over and used it for their own purposes. For one thing, the French had raised themselves to the dignity of citizenship; they had become free individuals, responsible for themselves, taking part in the affairs of their country. For another, because they had a unified state that included all French people, and one in which a whole nation surged with a new sense of freedom, they were able to rise above all the other nations of Europe.

German political aspirations

Many in Germany were beginning to feel humiliation at the paternalism of their governments. The futilities of the Holy Roman Empire, which had made Germany for centuries the battlefield of Europe, now filled them with shame and indignation. They saw with disgust how their German princes, forever squabbling with each other for control over German subjects, disgraced themselves before the French to promote their own interests. The national awakening in Germany, which set in strongly after 1800, was therefore directed not only against Napoleon and the French but also against the German rulers and many of the half-Frenchified German upper classes. It was democratic in that it stressed the superior virtue of the common people.

Many Germans became fascinated by the idea of political and national greatness, precisely because they had neither. A great national German state, expressing the deep moral will and distinctive culture of the German people, seemed to offer solutions to both their political and cultural problems. It would give moral dignity to the individual German, solve the vexatious question of the selfish petty princes, protect the deep German *Volksgeist* from violation, and secure the Germans from subjection to outside powers. The nationalist philosophy remained somewhat vague, because in practice there was little that one could do. "Father" Jahn organized a kind of youth movement and led young men on open-air expeditions into the country, where they made fun of aristocrats in French costume. He taught them to be suspicious of foreigners, Jews, and internationalists, and indeed of everything that might corrupt the purity of the German *Volk*. Most

Germans thought him too extreme. Others collected wonderful stories of the rich medieval German past. There was an anonymous anti-French work, *Germany in Its Deep Humiliation,* for selling which the publisher Palm was put to death. Others founded the Moral and Scientific Union, generally known as the *Tugendbund* or league of virtue or manliness, whose members, by developing their own moral character, were to contribute to the future of Germany.

The career of J. G. Fichte illustrates the course of German thought in these years. Fichte was a moral and metaphysical philosopher, a professor at the University of Jena. His doctrine that the inner spirit of the individual creates its own moral universe was much admired in many countries. In America, for example, it entered into the transcendental philosophy of Ralph Waldo Emerson. During his early philosophical career, Fichte expressed little interest in a specific national feeling. He enthusiastically approved of the French Revolution, as did many other German intellectuals at the time. In 1793, with the Revolution at its height, Fichte published a laudatory tract on the French Republic. He saw it as an emancipation of the human spirit, a step upward in the elevation of human dignity and moral stature. He accepted the idea of the Terror, that of "forcing men to be free," and he shared Rousseau's conception of the state as the embodiment of the sovereign will of a people. He came to see the state as the means of human salvation. When the French conquered Germany Fichte became intensely and self-consciously German. Responding to the French occupation, he took over the idea of the *Volksgeist:* not only did the individual spirit create its own moral universe, but the spirit of a people created a kind of moral universe as well, manifested in its language, history, arts, folk-ways, customs, institutions, and ideas.

Fichte and the German national spirit

At Berlin, in 1808, Fichte delivered a series of *Addresses to the German Nation,* declaring that there was an ineradicable German spirit, a primordial and immutable national character, more noble than that of other peoples (thus going beyond Herder), to be kept pure at all costs from all outside influence, either international or French. The German spirit, he held, had always been profoundly different from that of France and western Europe. Germany had never yet really achieved the national or international stature that such a noble, creative people should attain, but Fichte confidently affirmed that the Germans would eventually play a great role in world history. The commander of the French army then occupying the city thought the lectures too academic to be worth suppression. They attracted only small audiences; but his published lectures provided an enduring philosophical argument for German nationalism, and many Germans later regarded him as a national hero.

Reforms in Prussia

Politically, the revolt against the French led to major transformations in Prussia and the Prussian state. After the death of Frederick the Great in 1786 Prussia had fallen into a period of satisfied inertia, such as is likely to follow upon rapid growth or spectacular success. Then in 1806, at Jena-Auerstädt, the kingdom collapsed in a single battle. Its western and most of its Polish territories were taken away. It was relegated by Napoleon to its old holdings east of the Elbe River. Even here the French remained in occupation, for Napoleon stationed his Ninth Corps in Berlin. But in the eyes of German nationalists Prussia had a moral advantage. Of all the German states it was the least compromised by collaboration with the French. Toward Prussia, as toward a haven, German patriots therefore made their way. Prussia, east of the Elbe, formerly the least German of German

CHRONOLOGY OF NOTABLE EVENTS, 1799–1815

1799–1801	Second Coalition (Austria, Russia, Britain) wages war with France
1803	Napoleon's army is defeated in Haiti and France sells Louisiana to the United States
1805–1807	Third Coalition (Austria, Russia, Britain) wages war with France
1806	Napoleon defeats Prussian armies and occupies Berlin
1806–1825	Latin American countries pursue successful campaigns for national independence from Spain and Portugal
1807	Treaty of Tilsit creates French-Russian alliance; Napoleon expands the "Continental System" to exclude trade with Britain
1808–1814	Peninsular War leads to French defeats in Spain
1810	Napoleon marries Marie Louise, daughter of Austrian Emperor
1812	Napoleon's "Grand Army" invades Russia and is destroyed in winter retreat
1813	French army loses decisive battle of Leipzig in Germany
1814	Abdication of Napoleon and restoration of Bourbon monarchy in France
1814–1815	Congress of Vienna reorganizes the political order in Europe
1815	Napoleon returns to power for the Hundred Days; final defeat at the battle of Waterloo

lands, became the center of an all-German movement for national freedom. The German responses to French imperial expansion during the years after Jena thus increased Prussian influence throughout Germany; but neither Fichte nor Hegel, Gneisenau nor Scharnhorst, Stein nor Hardenberg, all of whom contributed to the rebuilding of Prussia and to a deepening German identity within Prussia, was a native Prussian.

The reform movement in Prussia

The main problem for Prussia was military, because Napoleon could be overthrown only by military force. And as always in Prussia, the requirements of the army strongly influenced the evolution of the state. The problem was conceived to be one of morale and personnel. The old Prussia of Frederick, which had fallen ingloriously, had been mechanical, arbitrary, soulless. Its people had lacked the sense of membership in the state, and in the army its soldiers had held no hope of promotion and felt no patriotic spirit. To produce this spirit was the aim of the army reformers Gneisenau and Scharnhorst. Gneisenau was a Saxon who had served in one of the British "Hessian" regiments in the War of American Independence, during which he had observed the military value of patriotic feeling in the American soldiers. He was also a close observer of the consequences of the French Revolution, which, he said, had "set in action the national energy of the entire French people, putting the different classes on an equal social and fiscal basis." If Prussia was to strengthen itself against France, or indeed to avoid a future revolution within Prussia itself, it must find a means to inspire similar feelings of participation among its own people and to allow capable individuals to fill important positions in the army and government without regard to their social status.

The reconstruction of the state, prerequisite to the reconstruction of the army, was initiated by Baron Stein and continued by his successor, Hardenberg. Like Metternich,

Stein came from western Germany, and he was long hostile to what he considered a barely civilized Prussia, but he finally turned to the Prussian state as the best hope to lead Germany as a whole into the future. Deeply committed to the philosophy of Kant and Fichte, he emphasized the concepts of duty, service, moral character, and responsibility. He thought that the common people must be awakened to moral life and raised from a brutalized servility to the level of self-determination and membership in the community. This, he believed, required an equality more of duties than of rights.

Under Stein the old caste structure of Prussia became somewhat less rigid. Property became interchangeable between social classes, and soldiers of all classes could now serve as officers in the army. The burghers, to develop a sense of citizenship and participation in the state, were given extensive freedom of self-government in the cities; the municipal systems of Prussia, and later of Germany, became a model for much of Europe in the following century.

Stein's most famous work was the "abolition of serfdom." It was impossible to strengthen Prussia for a war of liberation against the French by introducing radical reforms that would antagonize the Junkers who commanded the army. Stein's ordinance of 1807 thus abolished only the "hereditary subjection" of peasants to their manorial lords. It gave peasants the right to move and migrate, marry, and take up trades without the lord's approval. If, however, they remained on the land, they were still subject to all the old services of forced labor in the fields of the lord. Peasants who held small plots of land as "tenures" from their lords continued to be liable for the old dues and fees. By an edict of 1810, they might convert this traditional tenure into their own private property, getting rid of the manorial obligations, but only on the condition that one-third of the land held should become the private property of the lord. In the following decades many such conversions took place; as a result, the estates of the Junkers grew considerably larger. The reforms in Prussia gave new legal status and freedom of movement to the mass of the population, thereby laying the foundation for a modern state and modern economy. The peasants tended to become mere hired agricultural laborers, however, and the social position of the landowning Junkers was heightened, not reduced; but Prussia avoided a political revolution. Stein himself, because Napoleon feared him, was obliged to go into exile in 1808, but his reforms endured.

51. THE OVERTHROW OF NAPOLEON: THE CONGRESS OF VIENNA

The situation at the close of 1811 may be summarized as follows. Napoleon had the mainland of Europe in his grip. Russia and Turkey were at war on the Danube, but otherwise there was no war except in Spain, *Europe in 1811* where four years of fighting had blocked the consolidation of French control. The Continental System was working badly. Britain was hurt by it only in that, without it, British exports to Europe would have risen rapidly in these years. Well launched in the economic growth of the Industrial Revolution, Britain was amassing a vast store of national wealth that could be used to assist European governments financially against Napoleon. The peoples of Europe were growing restless, dreaming increasingly of national freedom. In Germany especially, many were looking for an opportunity to rise in a war of independence. But Napoleon could be overthrown only by the destruction of his army, over which neither British wealth nor British sea power, nor the European patriots and nationalists, nor the Prussian nor the Austrian armed forces were able to prevail. All eyes turned to

Russia. Alexander I had long been dissatisfied with his French alliance. He had obtained from it nothing but the annexation of Finland in 1809. He received no assistance from France in his war with Ottoman Turkey; and he had to tolerate the existence of a French-oriented Poland at his very door. The articulate classes in Russia, namely, the landowners and serf owners, denounced the French alliance and demanded a resumption of open trade relations with England. An international clientele of émigrés and anti-Bonapartists, including Baron Stein, also gradually congregated at St. Petersburg, where they poured into the tsar's ears the welcome message that Europe looked to him for its salvation.

The Russian Campaign and the War of Liberation

On December 31, 1810, Russia formally withdrew from the Continental System. Anglo-Russian commercial relations were resumed. Napoleon resolved to crush the tsar. He concentrated the Grand Army in eastern Germany and Poland, a vast force of 700,000 men, the largest European army ever assembled up to that time for a single military operation. It was an all-European host. Hardly more than a third was French; another third was German, from German regions annexed to France, from the states of the Confederation of the Rhine, and with token forces from Prussia and Austria; and the remaining third was drawn from all other nationalities of the Grand Empire, including 90,000 Poles. Napoleon at first hoped to meet the Russians in Poland or Prussia. This time, however, they decided to fight on their own ground, and they needed in any case to delay until their forces on the lower Danube could be recalled. In June 1812 Napoleon led the Grand Army into Russia.

He intended a short, sharp war, such as most of his wars had been in the past, and carried with him only three weeks' supplies. But from the beginning everything went wrong. It was Napoleon's principle to force a decisive battle; but the Russian army kept withdrawing toward the east. It was his principle to live on the country, so as to reduce the need for supply trains; but the Russians destroyed as they retreated, and in any case, in Russia, even in the summer, it was hard to find sustenance for so many men and horses. Finally, not far from Moscow, Napoleon was able to join battle with the main Russian force at Borodino. Here again everything miscarried. It was his principle always to outnumber the enemy at the decisive spot, but the Grand Army had left so many detachments along its line of march that at Borodino the Russians outnumbered it. It was Napoleon's principle to concentrate his artillery, but here he scattered it instead. His principle was to throw in his last reserves at the critical moment, but at Borodino, so far from home, he refused the risk of ordering the Old Guard into action. Napoleon won the battle, at a cost of 30,000 men, as against 50,000 lost by the Russians; but the Russian army was able to withdraw in good order.

On September 14, 1812, the French emperor entered Moscow. Almost immediately the city was destroyed by a great fire that Russian forces had probably set alight as they retreated into the countryside. Napoleon found himself camping in a ruin, with troops strewn along a vulnerable line all the way back to Poland, and with a hostile army maneuvering near at hand. Baffled, he tried to negotiate with Alexander, who refused all overtures. After five weeks, not knowing what to do and fearful of remaining isolated in Moscow over the winter, Napoleon ordered a retreat. Prevented by the Russians from taking a more southerly route, the Grand Army retired by the same way it had come, but it could no longer live off the land. The cold weather set in early and was unusually severe. For a century after 1812 the retreat from Moscow remained the last word in military horror. Men froze

The retreat from Moscow

and starved, horses slipped and died, vehicles could not be moved, and equipment was abandoned. Discipline broke down toward the end; the army dissolved into a horde of starving, disoriented fugitives, speaking a babel of languages, harassed by bands of Russian irregulars, picking their way on foot over ice and snow, most of the time in the dark, for the nights are long in these latitudes in December. Of 611,000 who entered Russia 400,000 died of battle wounds, starvation, and exposure, and 100,000 were taken prisoner. The Grand Army no longer existed.

Now at last all the anti-Napoleon forces rushed together. The Russians pushed westward into central Europe. The Prussian and Austrian governments, which in 1812 had half-heartedly supplied troops for the invasion of Russia, switched over in 1813 and joined the tsar. Throughout Germany, the patriots, often half-trained boys, marched off in the War of Liberation, though it was the professional armies of the German states that made the difference. In Spain Wellington at last pushed rapidly forward; in June 1813 he crossed the Pyrenees into France. The British government, in three years from 1813 to 1815, poured £32,000,000 as subsidies into Europe, more than half of all the funds granted during the 22 years of the wars. An incongruous alliance of British capitalism and eastern European agrarian feudalism, of the British navy and the Russian army, of Spanish clericalism and German nationalism, of divine-right monarchies and newly aroused democrats and liberals, combined at last to bring the Man of Destiny to the ground.

Napoleon, who had left his army in Russia in December 1812 and rushed across Europe to Paris by sleigh and coach in the remarkable time of 13 days, raised a new army in France in the early months of 1813. But it was untrained and unsteady, and he himself had lost some of his genius for command. His new army was smashed in October at the battle of Leipzig, known to the Germans as the Battle of the Nations, the greatest battle in number of men engaged ever fought until the twentieth century. The allies drove Napoleon back upon France. But the closer they came to defeating him the more they began to fear and distrust each other.

The Battle of the Nations

The Restoration of the Bourbons

The coalition already showed signs of splitting. Should the allies, together or singly, negotiate with Napoleon? How strong should the France of the future be? What should be its new frontiers? What form of government should it have? There was no agreement on these questions. Alexander wanted to dethrone Napoleon and dictate peace in Paris, in dramatic retribution for the destruction of Moscow. He had a scheme for giving the French throne to Bernadotte, a former French marshal, now crown prince of Sweden, who as king of France would depend on Russian support. Metternich preferred to keep Napoleon or his son as French emperor, after clearing the French out of central Europe; for a Bonaparte dynasty in a reduced France would be dependent on Austria. The British, with an eye on one of their main strategic concerns, declared that the French must get out of the southern Netherlands and that Napoleon must go; they held that the French might then choose their own government but believed a restoration of the Bourbons to be the best solution. The Continental monarchies in Austria, Prussia, and Russia had no concern for the Bourbons, and both Alexander and Metternich, if they could make France dependent respectively on themselves, were willing to see it remain strong even to the extent of including territories in the southern Netherlands.

The British foreign minister, Viscount Castlereagh, arrived on the Continent for consultations in January 1814. He held a number of strong cards. For one thing, Napoleon continued to fight, and the allies therefore continued to ask for British financial aid.

The French army's retreat from Russia in 1812 shattered Napoleon's image of military invincibility and brought the anti-Napoleonic forces together for a decisive victory in the following year. This French painting portrays the misery that gave the retreat of 1812 its lasting reputation for military horror. (©Popperfoto/Getty Images)

Castlereagh skillfully used the promise of British subsidies to win acceptance of Britain's war aims. In addition, he found a common ground for agreement with Metternich, both Britain and Austria fearing the domination of Europe by Russia. Castlereagh's first great problem was to hold the alliance together, for without Continental allies the British could not defeat France. He succeeded, on March 9, 1814, in getting Russia, Prussia, Austria,

The Quadruple Alliance

and Great Britain to sign the treaty of Chaumont. Each power bound itself for 20 years to a Quadruple Alliance against France, and each agreed to provide 150,000 soldiers to enforce such peace terms as might be arrived at. For the first time since 1792 a solid coalition of the four great powers now existed against France. Three weeks later the allies entered Paris, and on April 4 Napoleon abdicated at Fontainebleau.

He was forced to this step by lack of support in France itself. Twenty years before, in 1793 and 1794, France had fought off the combined powers of Europe—minus Russia. It could not and would not do so in 1814. The country cried for peace. Even the imperial marshals advised the emperor's abdication. But what was to follow him? For 25 years the French had lived under one revolutionary or activist regime after another. Now they were divided. Some wanted a republic; others wished to retain the empire under Napoleon's infant son; still others desired a constitutional monarchy; and there were even those who longed for the old regime. Talleyrand stepped into the breach. The "legitimate" king, he said, Louis XVIII, was the man who would provoke the least factionalism and opposition. The monarchical powers, likewise, had by this time concluded in favor of the Bourbons. A Bourbon king would be peaceable, under no impulse to win back the conquests of the republic and empire. He would also, as the native and rightful king of France, need no foreign support to bolster him, so that the control of France would not arise as an issue to divide the victorious powers.

The Bourbon dynasty was thus restored. Louis XVIII, ignored and disregarded for a whole generation, both by most people in France and by the governments of Europe, returned to the throne of his brother and his Bourbon forefathers. He issued a "constitutional charter," partly *The Bourbons restored* at the insistence of the liberal tsar and partly because, having actually learned from his long exile, he sought the support of influential people in France. The charter of 1814 made no concession to the principle of popular or national sovereignty. It was represented as the gracious gift of a theoretically absolute king. But in practice it granted what most of the French wanted. It promised legal equality, eligibility of all to public office without regard to class, and a parliamentary government in two chambers. It recognized the Napoleonic law codes, the Napoleonic settlement with the church, and the redistribution of property effected during the Revolution. It carried over the abolition of all feudal privileges and manorial rights. It confined the vote, to be sure, to a very few large land-owners; but for the time being, except for a few irreconcilables, France settled down to enjoy the blessings of a chastened revolution—and peace.

The Settlement before the Vienna Congress

It was with the government of the restored Bourbons that the powers, on May 30, 1814, signed a peace treaty. This document, the "first" Treaty of Paris, confined France to its prewar boundaries of 1792. The allied statesmen disregarded popular cries for vengeance and punishment, imposed no indemnity or reparations, and even allowed the works of art gathered from Europe during the wars to remain in Paris. It was not the desire of the victors to handicap the restored French monarchy on which they now placed their hopes. Napoleon meanwhile was exiled to the island of Elba on the Italian coast.

To deal with other postwar questions, the powers had agreed, before signing the Alliance of Chaumont, to hold an international congress at Vienna after defeating Napoleon. Both Russia and Great Britain, however, before consenting to a general conference, specified certain matters that they would decide for themselves as not susceptible to international consideration. The Russians refused to discuss Turkey and the Balkans; they retained Bessarabia as the prize of their recent war with the Turks. They also kept Finland, as an autonomous constitutional grand duchy, as well as certain conquests in the Caucasus almost unknown to Europe, namely Georgia and Azerbaijan. The British refused any discussion of the freedom of the seas and also barred all questions about colonial and overseas territories. The British government simply announced which of its colonial and insular conquests it would keep and which it would return. The revolts against the Spanish empire in Latin America were left to run their course.

In Europe, the British remained in possession of Malta, the Ionian Islands, and the island of Heligoland in the North Sea; in America, they kept St. Lucia, Trinidad, and Tobago in the West Indies. Of former French possessions, the British kept the island of Mauritius in the Indian Ocean. Of former Dutch territories, they kept the Cape of Good Hope and Ceylon, but returned the Netherlands Indies. During the Revolutionary and

Napoleonic wars in Europe the British had also made extensive conquests in India, bringing much of the Deccan and the upper Ganges Valley under their rule. The British emerged, in 1814, as the controlling European power in both India and the Indian Ocean.

Indeed, of all the colonial empires founded by Europeans in the sixteenth and seventeenth centuries, only the British now remained as a growing and dynamic system. The old French, Spanish, and Portuguese empires were struggling against revolutionary movements and declining to much-reduced political and territorial versions of their former selves; the Dutch still held vast establishments in the East Indies, but all the intermediate positions—the Cape, Ceylon, Mauritius, Singapore—would soon be controlled by Britain. Nor, after 1814, did any people except the British have a significant navy. With Napoleon and the Continental System defeated, with the Industrial Revolution bringing power machinery to the manufacturers of England, with no rival left in the contest for overseas dominion, and with a virtual monopoly of naval power, whose use they studiously kept free from international regulation, the British embarked on their century of world leadership, which may be said to have lasted from 1814 to 1914.

The Congress of Vienna, 1814–1815

The Congress of Vienna assembled in September 1814. Never had such a brilliant gathering been seen. All the states of Europe sent representatives; and many defunct states, such as the formerly sovereign princes and ecclesiastics of the late Holy Roman Empire, sent lobbyists to urge their restoration. But procedure was so arranged that all important matters were decided by the four triumphant Great Powers. Indeed it was at the Congress of Vienna that the terms "great" and "small" powers entered clearly into the diplomatic vocabulary. Europe was at peace with the late enemy, but France was represented at the Congress, by none other than Talleyrand, now minister to Louis XVIII. Castlereagh, Metternich, and Alexander spoke for their respective countries; Prussia was represented by Hardenberg. Although they were all aristocrats of the Old Regime, they by no means desired to restore the territorial boundaries of the era before the wars. They did desire, as they put it, to restore the "liberties of Europe," meaning the freedom of European states from domination by a single power; and it was hoped that a proper balance of power would also produce a lasting peace.

The chief menace to peace, and most likely claimant for the domination of Europe, seemed to be the late troublemaker, France. The Congress of Vienna, without much disagreement, erected a barrier of strong states along the French eastern frontier. The historic Dutch Republic, extinct since 1795, was revived as the kingdom of the Netherlands, with the house of Orange as a hereditary monarchy; to it was added the old Austrian Netherlands with which Austria had long been willing to part (sixteen years later this region would become the independent kingdom of Belgium). It was hoped that the enlarged kingdom in the Netherlands would be strong enough to discourage the perennial French drive into the Low Countries. On the south, the kingdom of Sardinia, or Piedmont, was restored and strengthened by the incorporation of Genoa. Behind the Netherlands and Piedmont, and further to discourage a renewal of French pressure upon Germany and Italy, two great powers were installed. Almost all the German left bank of the Rhine was ceded to Prussia; and in Italy, again as a kind of secondary barrier against France, the Austrians were firmly installed. They not only took back Tuscany and Milan, which they had held before 1796, but also annexed the extinct republic of Venice. The Austrian Empire now

The Congress of Vienna combined complex diplomatic negotiations with the cultural elegance of traditional elites. This picture shows the social status of the diplomats who sought to establish peace and order in Europe after 25 years of revolution and warfare.
(©Bildagentur-online/Getty Images)

included a Lombardo-Venetian kingdom in north Italy, which lasted for almost half a century. In the rest of Italy the Congress recognized the restoration of the pope in the papal states and of former rulers in the smaller duchies; but it did not insist on a restoration of the Bourbons in the kingdom of Naples. There Napoleon's brother-in-law Murat, with support from Metternich, managed for a time to retain his throne. The Bourbon and Braganza rulers restored themselves in Spain and Portugal, respectively, and were recognized by the Congress as the reigning royal families in the Iberian states.

As for Germany, the Congress substantially confirmed the French and Napoleonic reorganization of the defunct Holy Roman Empire. The kings of Bavaria, Württemberg, and Saxony kept the royal crowns that Napoleon had bestowed on them. The king of England, George III, was now recognized as king, not "elector," of Hanover. The German states, 39 in number, including Prussia and Austria, were joined in a loose confederation in which the members remained virtually sovereign. The Congress ignored the yearnings of German nationalists for a great unified Fatherland; Metternich especially feared nationalistic agitation; and in any case the nationalists themselves had no practical answer to concrete questions, such as the government and frontiers that a united Germany should have.

Germany remains divided

Finally, there was the question of Poland, which almost brought the Congress to disaster. The fall of Napoleon's Grand Duchy of Warsaw had given Alexander an opportunity to reassert his long-held plan for undoing the crime of the Polish partitions and reconstituting a Polish kingdom—with himself as the constitutional king. He sought to achieve this goal by allowing Prussia to absorb the kingdom of Saxony, but both Metternich and Castlereagh vehemently opposed this plan. The Austrians feared the expansion of their two main rivals in central Europe, and the British had not fought the French emperor to help the Russian tsar extend his power over other European peoples and territories. After prolonged negotiations, the strategic interventions of Talleyrand, and the threat of a possible war among the recent allies, the contending factions reached a compromise.

Congress Poland

The Congress created a new, somewhat smaller Polish kingdom that would be remembered in history simply as "Congress Poland." Alexander gave the new state a constitution and became its king, but this new kingdom (which comprised roughly the same area as Napoleon's Grand Duchy) survived as a political entity for only 15 years. Prussia, for its part, received about two-fifths of Saxony, but the enduring addition of both Saxon and Rhineland territories brought the Prussian monarchy into the most economically advanced regions of Germany and to the borders of France. The net effect of the Napoleonic wars and the peace settlement was thus to shift the center of gravity of both Russia and Prussia farther west (see maps, pp. 220–221, 236–237).

The main political work of the Congress was completed with the agreements on Poland and Saxony, but at this point the whole settlement was unexpectedly brought into jeopardy by the reappearance of Napoleon.

The Hundred Days and Their Aftermath

Napoleon escaped from Elba, landed in France on March 1, 1815, and again proclaimed the empire. In the year since the restoration of the Bourbon monarchy discontent had been spreading in France. Louis XVIII proved to be a sensible man, but a swarm of unreasonable and vindictive émigrés had come back with him. Reaction and a "white terror" were raging through the country. Most adherents of the Revolution therefore rallied to the emperor on his dramatic reappearance. Napoleon reached Paris, regained control over the government and army, and soon led an army into the southern territory of the just-established United Kingdom of the Netherlands. To the victors of the year before, and to most of Europe, it seemed that the Revolution was again stirring, that the old horror of toppling thrones and recurring warfare might not after all be ended. The anti-French allies reassembled their troops and met Napoleon's army at Waterloo, where the Duke of Wellington led a coalition of British and Prussian forces to a great victory. Napoleon again abdicated and was again exiled, this time to distant St. Helena in the south Atlantic. A new peace treaty was made with France, the "second" Treaty of Paris. It was more severe than the first, because the French seemed to have shown themselves incorrigible and unrepentant. The new treaty imposed minor changes on the frontiers, forced the French to pay an indemnity of 700,000,000 francs over five years, and placed a French-financed European army of occupation in northeastern France

The effect of the Hundred Days, as the episode following Napoleon's return from Elba is called, was to renew the dread of revolution, war, and aggression. Britain, Russia, Austria, and Prussia, after being almost at war with each other over Poland and Saxony in January, again joined forces to get rid of the apparition from Elba, and, in November 1815, they solemnly reconfirmed the Quadruple Alliance of Chaumont, adding a provision that no Bonaparte should ever govern France. They agreed also to hold future congresses to review the political situation and enforce the peace. No change was made in the arrangements agreed to at Vienna, except that Murat, who fought for Napoleon during the Hundred Days, was captured and shot, and an extremely unenlight- ened Bourbon monarchy was restored in Naples. In addition to the Quadruple Alliance of the Great Powers, Alexander devised a vaguer scheme that he called the Holy Alliance. The tsar proposed that all

Monarchical alliances

European monarchs sign a statement by which they promised to uphold Christian prin- ciples of charity and peace. All signed except the pope, the sultan of the Ottoman Empire, and the prince regent of Great Britain. The Holy Alliance was probably sincerely meant by Alexander as a condemnation of violence. Other leaders who signed it were skeptical about mixing Christianity with politics, but it soon came to signify, in the minds of lib- erals, a kind of unholy alliance of monarchies against liberty and progress.

The Peace of Vienna, including generally the Treaty of Vienna itself, the treaties of Paris, and the British and colonial settlement, was

The Peace of Vienna

the most far-reaching diplomatic agreement between the Peace of West- phalia of 1648 and the Peace of Paris, which closed the First World War in 1919. It had its strong points and its weak ones. It produced a minimum of resentment in France, where most people were willing to accept the new arrangements. It ended almost two centuries of European conflicts over the control of colonial territories in Asia and the Americas; for 60 or 70 years no colonial empire seriously challenged the British. Two other causes of friction in the eighteenth century—the control of Poland and the Austro- Prussian dualism in Germany—were smoothed over for 50 years. The Vienna treaty was not illiberal in its day; it was by no means entirely reactionary, for the Congress showed little desire to restore the state of affairs in existence before the wars. The conservative reaction that gathered strength after 1815 was not written into the treaty itself.

But the treaty gave no satisfaction to nationalists and democrats. It was a disappoint- ment even to many liberals, especially in Germany. The peacemakers were in fact hostile both to nationalism and to democracy, the potent forces of the coming century; they regarded them, with reason, as leading to revolution and war. The problem to which they addressed themselves was to restore a more traditional balance of power, the "liberties of Europe," and to make a lasting peace. In this they were successful. They restored the European state system, a system in which a number of sovereign and independent states existed without fear of conquest or domination. And the peace they made, though some details broke down in 1830 and others in 1848, on the whole subsisted for half a century; and not for a full century, not until 1914, was there a war within Europe that lasted longer than a few months or in which all the great powers were again involved.

The Peace of Vienna thus brought to a close the great political and military upheavals that had spread across Europe in the wake of the French Revolution. Yet even the most conservative diplomats at Vienna recognized that the revolutionary events and legacy would not simply vanish from European culture or history; indeed the Holy Alliance and the vigilance of the conservative European states after 1815 showed how deeply the French Revolution

Legacy of the Revolution

had affected all of Europe and those places outside Europe where revolutionary ideas had become popular and influential. The Latin American struggle for independence from Spain, for example, continued to draw on the new conceptions of national sovereignty

EUROPE, 1815

Boundaries show the political arrangements that emerged from the Congress of Vienna. France was reduced to the borders it had in 1789. Prussia was firmly installed on both banks of the Rhine, but South Germany remained as reorganized by Napoleon. Poland was again partitioned, with a larger share than in 1795 going to Russia—which also acquired Finland and Bessarabia. The Austrians added Venetia to what they had held before 1796. The union of the Dutch and Belgian Netherlands lasted only until 1831, when the kingdom of Belgium was established. Otherwise, the boundaries of 1815 lasted until the Italian war of 1859, which led to the unification of Italy.

and continued to spread across the New World while diplomats in Vienna were working to restore stability and order in Europe.

The French Revolution and the Napoleonic Empire had demonstrated how a new, more open system of social and professional advancement enabled a nation to exercise power more effectively than any of the traditional, monarchical states. The revolutionary regimes had introduced new methods for mobilizing national economic resources, military forces, and large populations, all of which would reappear in the national mobilizations of other modern states. The Revolution and Napoleon, in short, gave the modern world new models of political organization and authoritarian rule. At the same time, however, the famous revolutionary events also helped to spread new conceptions of human rights, political participation, democratic government, and economic organization that would remain powerful cultural ideals throughout Europe and much of the modern world; and the popular ideology of nationalism, which developed among both supporters and opponents of the French Revolution and Napoleon, rapidly became one of the most pervasive political and cultural forces in modern world history.

All of these ideas helped to produce and reshape the characteristic institutions of modern societies. They continued to attract fervent supporters after the Congress of Vienna and after all other attempts to defend or revive the old order. The French Revolution and the Napoleonic wars, for all their turmoil and terrible destructive violence, created a lasting political and cultural legacy that has influenced modern nations almost everywhere, even down to the twenty-first century.

Suggested Further Readings can be found in the ebook, on Connect, or online at www.mhhe .com/kramer12e.

Chapter 11

INDUSTRIES, IDEAS, AND THE STRUGGLE FOR REFORM, 1815–1848

In the period of some 30 years preceding 1815 two "revolutions" had been taking place. One was the upheaval associated with the French Revolution and the Napoleonic Empire. This revolution altered traditional social hierarchies and produced other social changes, but its explicit goals focused mainly on political reforms such as the reorganization of government, public power and authority, public finance, taxation, administration, law, individual rights, and the legal position of social classes. The other revolution, a revolution in a more metaphorical sense, was primarily economic, having to do with the production of wealth, the techniques of manufacture, the exploitation of natural resources, the development of new technologies, the formation of capital, and the distribution of products to consumers. The political and the economic revolutions in these years went on somewhat independently of each other. Until 1815 the political revolution affected mainly the Continent, while the economic revolution was most active in England. The Continent, while evolving politically, remained economically less advanced than England, which was transforming itself economically even as it remained conservative in other respects. Hence it has been possible to deal with the political significance of the French Revolution and its Napoleonic sequel without much discussion of the Industrial Revolution, as historians have always described the economic changes then occurring in England.

It may be (the matter is arguable) that the Industrial Revolution was more important than the French Revolution or any other change in the social and political history of human societies. In a telescopic view of world history the two biggest changes experienced by the human race in the past 10,000 years may have been the agricultural or Neolithic revolution, which, beginning about 8000 B.C.E., ushered in the first civilizations, and the Industrial Revolution, which ushered in the modern global civilization of the last two

Chapter emblem: Detail from an illustration of a cotton mill in Lancashire, England, during the early 1830s (©Mary Evans Picture Library/The Image Works)

Political and economic factors

centuries. Historians disagree about the specific social and cultural effects of this modern, global transition, but they recognize that the economic and political changes, the Industrial Revolution, and the other revolutions in governments and social institutions have constantly overlapped or converged in modern societies. The Industrial Revolution occurred first in England, becoming evident by about 1780, because of certain political characteristics of English society, because earlier commercial and naval successes had expanded England's access to world markets, and because English social life offered rewards to the individual for new forms of risk-taking and innovation. Nor can the effects of political and economic revolution, in England or elsewhere, be kept apart for the years after 1815.

With the defeat of Napoleon and signing of the peace treaty at Vienna in 1815, it seemed that the French Revolution was at last over. European conservatism had triumphed; because it restored European monarchies and frankly opposed the new "French ideas," it can appropriately be called a political "reaction." But the processes of industrialization, as they accelerated in England and spread to the Continent, worked against the politically conservative settlement. Industrialization greatly enlarged both the business and wage-earning classes, and made it harder for monarchs and landed aristocrats to maintain their control over public power. Industrial development in the nineteenth century was often called "progress," and economic progress led to a steady growth of the social groups that would challenge and overturn the political reaction. Spreading across Europe in the nineteenth century, industrialization transformed social, cultural, religious, and political traditions that conservatives did not want to change.

Industrial society arose in England, western Europe, and the United States in the nineteenth century, within the system known as capitalism. In the twentieth century, after the Russian Revolution in 1917, other industrial societies were created in which capitalism was vehemently rejected. Industrialism and capitalism are therefore by no means the same. Yet all industrial societies use capital, which is defined as wealth that is not consumed but is used to produce more wealth, or future wealth. An automobile is a consumer's good; the automobile factory is the capital. What distinguishes a capitalist from a noncapitalist society is not the existence of capital but the ways in which the capital is controlled. The distinctions sometimes become blurred because modern states have played an active role in most spheres of economic activity and because many privately owned economic enterprises have developed through government protection, support, or expenditures. But the systemic differences in the social and political control of capital have always carried wide-ranging consequences, and they have shaped many of the key divergences in modern European societies. In one form of society the control of capital is through private ownership, or institutions of private property, by which capital is owned by individuals, families, or corporations that are in turn owned by shareholders—in any case not by the state. In such societies, though ownership may be widespread, most capital is controlled by relatively few people, responding to market forces. In the other form of society productive capital in principle belongs to the public and is in effect owned and controlled by the state or its agencies; such societies usually call themselves socialist, because the first socialists rejected the principle of private ownership of the means of production, that is, of capital. In these societies the control of capital, or decisions on saving, investment, and production, are also in the hands of relatively few under some form of government management and plan.

Industrialism and capitalism

In Europe the institutions of secure private property had developed gradually since the Middle Ages, and much that happened in the French Revolution was designed to protect such property from the demands of the state. Possession of property was viewed as the basis of personal independence and political liberty, and the expectation of keeping future profits inspired, in some, a willingness to commit their capital to new and uncertain ventures. It made possible an entrepreneurial spirit. There had been a commercial capitalism in Europe at least since the sixteenth century. Industrialization in western Europe therefore developed through capitalist institutions. Countries outside the western European orbit, and industrializing later, faced a different problem. Those countries in which little capital had accumulated from the trade and agriculture of previous generations, and that had few owners of capital or few commercial enterprises, generally lacked the resources to industrialize by European methods. Such countries also often lacked the various political, social, legal, and organizational features that were as important as the economic in fostering industrial development. When these countries set out somewhat later to achieve industrialization, they frequently placed more of their economic planning, decision making, and financial management under direct state control.

In the short run, within a few years, the Industrial Revolution in western Europe favored the liberal, modernizing principles and legal rights proclaimed in the French Revolution. In the middle run, or in half a century, it made Europe overwhelmingly more powerful than other parts of the world, leading to a worldwide European ascendancy in the form of imperialism. In the still longer run, by the twentieth century, the European empires provoked anticolonial and anti-European political movements that challenged Europe's global ascendancy by trying to industrialize in self-protection or to improve the economic conditions of their own peoples or to catch up with the political centralization of the modern European states. The leaders of such movements often affirmed their national and economic identities, in part, by denouncing the capitalism of the European imperial powers. Among these later industrializing societies the Soviet Union, until its dissolution in 1991, and the People's Republic of China, from 1949 into the twenty-first century, would become the most influential proponents of a state-managed industrial revolution. Since the 1990s, the former socialist states in eastern Europe, Asia, and elsewhere have continued to manage their economies in various ways (as, indeed, governments in capitalist societies also seek to manage economic policies). Yet, the twentieth-century socialist or communist systems of comprehensive government control have given way in most places to hybrid economies with active stock exchanges and much private ownership of property, capital, and industrial production.

Socialist industrial systems

52. THE INDUSTRIAL REVOLUTION IN BRITAIN

On the whole, from the beginning of history until about 1800, the human work of the world was done with hand tools. Since then it has been increasingly done by machines. Before about 1800 power was supplied by human or animal muscle, reinforced by levers or pulleys, and supplemented by the force of running water or moving air. Since then power has been supplied by the human manipulation of forms of energy found in steam, electricity, the combustion of gases, sunlight, and the atom. The far-reaching transition from hand tools to power machinery launched the vast technological and economic process that is called the Industrial Revolution. Its beginning cannot be dated exactly. It grew gradually out of the technical practices of earlier times. It is still going on, for in some countries industrialization began only recently, and even in the most highly developed countries it is always evolving and making advances. But the first country to be profoundly affected by industrialization was Great Britain, where its effects became manifest in the half-century following 1780.

It seems likely, despite the emphasis placed on revolutionary upheavals by historians, that people are habitually quite conservative. Working people do not put off their old way of life, move to strange and overcrowded towns, migrate to other countries, or enter the deadly rounds of mine and factory except under strong incentive. Well-to-do people, living in comfort on assured incomes, do not readily risk their wealth in new and untried ventures. The shift to modern machine production caused and required a new mobility of workers and wealth within and between all industrializing countries. This movement of people and money was also connected to other political and cultural transitions, however, and the new mobility in eighteenth-century England developed from wider social changes as well as the new system of factory production.

The Agricultural Revolution in Britain

The English Revolution of 1688, confirming the ascendancy of Parliament over the king, meant in economic terms the ascendancy of the more well-to-do property-owning classes. Among these the landowners were by far the most important, though they counted the great London merchants among their allies. For a century and a half, from 1688 to 1832, the British government was substantially in the hands of these landowners—the "squirearchy" or "gentlemen of England." The result was a thorough transformation of English farming, an Agricultural Revolution without which the Industrial Revolution could not have occurred.

Many landowners, seeking to increase their money incomes, began experimenting with improved methods of cultivation and stock raising.

Agricultural experimentation

They made more use of fertilizers such as animal manure; they introduced useful implements such as the horse-hoe and the new seed drill, which was invented by Jethro Tull in the early eighteenth century; they brought in new crops, such as turnips, and a more scientific system of crop rotation; and they attempted to breed larger sheep and fatter cattle. Landlords who wanted to introduce such changes needed and sought full control over their land. They saw only a barrier to progress in the old village system of open fields, common lands, and semicollective methods of cultivation. Agrarian improvements also required an investment of capital, which was impossible so long as the soil was tilled by numerous poor and custom-bound small farmers.

The old common rights of the villagers were part of the English common law. Only an act of Parliament could modify or extinguish these traditional rights, but the great landowners who controlled Parliament were able to pass hundreds of "enclosure acts,"

The enclosure acts

authorizing the enclosure, by fences, walls, or hedges, of the old common lands and unfenced open fields. Land thus came under a strict regime of private ownership and individual management; and many small owners sold their lands to the larger landholders who now controlled the enclosed fields. Ownership of land in England, more than anywhere else in central or western Europe, became concentrated in the hands of a relatively small class of wealthy landlords, who leased it out in large blocks to a relatively small class of substantial farmers. This development, though in progress throughout the eighteenth century, reached its height during the Napoleonic wars.

One result was greatly to raise the productivity of land and of farm labor. Fatter cattle yielded more meat; more assiduous cultivation yielded more cereals. The food supply of England increased, while a smaller percentage of the population was needed to produce it. Labor was thus released for other pursuits, so that many English country people became wage earners, working for the farmers and landlords, or spinning or weaving in their

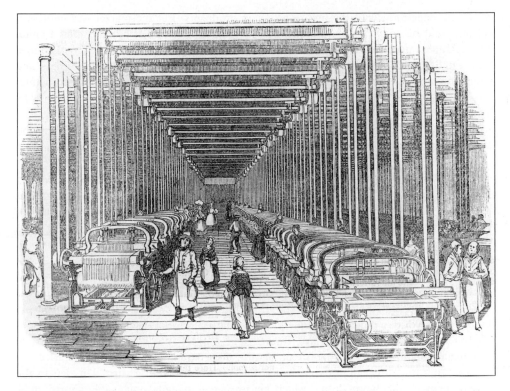

The construction of cotton mills led to a rapid increase in the production of textiles and brought large numbers of workers together in new cities. This illustration of an English cotton mill in the early 1830s shows the technology of industrialization and the women workers who moved from older cottage industries into the new factories.

(©Mary Evans Picture Library/The Image Works)

cottages for merchants in the towns. English working men and women were therefore already dependent on daily wages long before the coming of the factory and the machine. Working people became mobile; they would go where the jobs were, or where the wages were slightly higher. They also became available for new kinds of work because fewer of them were needed on the land to produce food. Such conditions hardly existed except in Great Britain. On the Continent agricultural methods were less productive, and the rural workers were more established on the soil, whether by institutions of serfdom as in eastern Europe or by the possession of property or firm leaseholds as in France.

Industrialism in Britain: Incentives and Inventions

Meanwhile, as the eighteenth-century Agricultural Revolution ran its course, the British had conquered a colonial empire, staked out markets all over the Americas and Europe, built up a huge mercantile marine, and won command of the sea. British merchants could sell more, if only more could be produced. They had customers and ships, and they could also obtain the capital with which to finance new ideas. The profit motive prompted a continuing search for more rapid methods of production. The old English staple export, woolen cloth, could be marketed indefinitely if only more could be woven. The possibilities in cotton cloth were enormous. The taste of Europeans for cottons had been already formed by imports from Asia. Using hand methods, Europeans could not produce cotton cloth in competition with the lower-cost Asian producers. But the market was endless if cotton could be spun, woven, and printed with less labor, that is, by machines. Capital was available, mobile, and fluid because of the rise of banking, credit, and stock companies. Funds could be shifted from one enterprise to another. Wealthy landowners and merchants could divert some of their profits to industry. If an invention proved a total loss, as sometimes happened, or if it required years of development before producing any income, the investment could still be afforded. Only a country already wealthy from commerce and agriculture could have been the first to initiate the machine age. England was such a country.

Inventions in the textile industry

These economic conditions induced a series of successful inventions in the textile industry. In 1733 a man named John Kay invented the fly shuttle, by which only one person instead of two was needed to weave cloth on a loom. The resulting increase in the output of weaving set up a strong demand for yarn. This was met in the 1760s by the invention of the spinning jenny, a kind of mechanized spinning wheel that enabled workers to increase their production of yarn. The new shuttles and jennies were first operated by hand and used by domestic workers in their homes. But in 1769 Richard Arkwright patented the water frame, a device for the multiple spinning of many threads. At first it was operated by water power, but in the 1780s Arkwright introduced the steam engine to drive his spinning machinery. Requiring a considerable installation of heavy equipment, he gathered his engines, frames, and workers into large and usually dismal buildings, called mills by the English, or factories in subsequent American usage. Mechanical spinning now for a time overwhelmed the hand weavers with yarn. This led to the development of the power loom, which became economically practicable shortly after 1800. Weaving as well as spinning therefore took place increasingly in factories. These improvements in the finishing process put a heavy strain on the production of raw cotton. An ingenious Connecticut inventor, Eli Whitney, while employed as a children's tutor on a Georgia plantation in 1793, produced a cotton gin, which by speeding up the removal of seeds greatly increased the output of cotton. The gin soon spread through the American South, where the almost decaying plantation economy was abruptly revived, creating a new demand for enslaved labor and becoming an adjunct to the Industrial Revolution in England. British imports of raw cotton multiplied fivefold in the 30 years following 1790. In value of manufactures, cotton cloth rose from ninth to first place among British industries in the same years. By 1820 it made up almost half of all British exports.

The steam engine

The steam engine, applied to the cotton mills in the 1780s, had for a century been going through a development of its own. Scientific and technical experiments with steam pressures had been fairly common in the seventeenth century, but what gave the economic impetus to invention was the gradual dwindling of Europe's primeval stocks of timber. The wood shortage became acute in England about 1700, so that it was more difficult to obtain the charcoal needed in smelting iron, and smelters turned increasingly to coal. Deeper coal shafts could not be sunk until someone devised better methods of pumping out water. About 1702 Thomas Newcomen built the first economically significant steam engine, which was soon widely used to drive pumps in the coal mines. However, it consumed so much fuel in proportion to power delivered that it could generally be used only in the coal fields themselves. In 1763 James Watt, a technician at the University of Glasgow, began to make improvements on Newcomen's engine. He formed a business partnership with Matthew Boulton, who was originally a manufacturer of toys, buttons, and shoe buckles. Boulton provided the funds to finance Watt's costly experiments, handmade

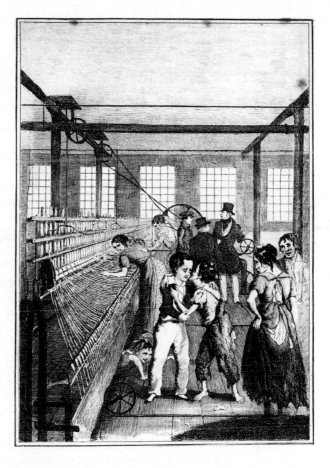

The factory owners in early nineteenth-century Britain often employed children to work on the spinning machines (called mules). The women and children in this illustration show the kind of workers who were drawn into the textile factories and why social reformers soon began to call for legal restrictions on child labor.

(©Print Collector/Getty Images)

equipment, and slowly germinating ideas. Their partnership exemplified the evolving connections between entrepreneurial inventors and wealthy investors; and by the 1780s the highly successful firm of Boulton and Watt was manufacturing steam engines both for British use and for the export trade.

Soon after 1800 the steam engine was successfully used to propel river boats, notably in New York on the Hudson River in 1807, by Robert Fulton, who employed an imported Boulton and Watt engine. Experiments with steam power for land transportation began at the same time. Just as Newcomen's engine had been put to practical uses in the coal fields of England a century before, so now it was in the coal fields that Watt's engine first became a locomotive. Well before 1800 the mines had taken to using railways, on which wagons with flanged wheels, drawn by horses, carried coal to canals or to the sea. In the 1820s steam engines were successfully placed on moving vehicles. The first fully satisfactory loco-

Transportation

motive was George Stephenson's *Rocket,* which in 1829, on the newly built Liverpool and Manchester Railway, not only reached an impressive speed of 16 miles per hour but met more important safety tests as well. By the 1840s the era of railroad construction was under way in both Europe and the United States.

The Industrial Revolution in Great Britain in its early phase, down to 1830 or 1840, took place principally in the manufacture of textiles, with accompanying developments in the exploitation of iron and coal. The early factories were mostly textile factories, and indeed mainly cotton mills; for cotton was an entirely new industry in Europe and hence easily mechanized, whereas the long established woolen trade, in which both employers and workers hesitated to abandon their customary ways, was mechanized more slowly. The suddenness of the change must not be exaggerated. It is often said that the Industrial Revolution was not a revolution at all. As late as the 1830s only a small fraction of the British working people were employed in factories. But the factory and the factory system were even then regarded as the coming mode of production, destined to grow and expand and symbolize the irresistible march of progress.

Some Social Consequences of Industrialism in Britain

The Britain that emerged fundamentally unscathed and in fact strengthened from the wars with Napoleon was no longer the sparsely populated "merrie England" of days of yore. The island was becoming crowded with people, as was the smaller island of Ireland. The combined population of Great Britain and Ireland tripled in the century from 1750 to 1850, rising from about 10 million in 1750 to about 30 million in 1850. The growth was distributed very unevenly. Formerly, in England, most people had lived in the south. But the coal and iron, and hence the steam power, lay in the Midlands and the north. Here whole new cities rose seemingly out of nowhere. In 1785 it was estimated that in England and Scotland, outside of London, there were only three cities with more than 50,000 people. Seventy years later, the span of one lifetime, there were 31 British cities of this size.

Manchester

Preeminent among them was Manchester in Lancashire, the first and most famous of the new industrial cities. Manchester, before the coming of the cotton mills, was a rather large market town. Though very ancient, it had not been significant enough to be recognized as a borough for representation in Parliament. Locally it was organized as a manor. Not until 1845 did the inhabitants extinguish the manorial rights, buying them out at that time from the last lord. In population Manchester grew from 25,000 in 1772 to 455,000 in 1851. But until 1835 there was no regular procedure in England for the incorporation of cities. Urban organization was more backward than in Prussia or France. Unless it had inherited its legal status from the Middle Ages, a city had no legal existence. It lacked proper officials and adequate tax-raising and lawmaking powers. It was therefore difficult for Manchester and the other new factory towns to deal with problems of rapid urbanization, such as provision for police protection, water and sewers, or the disposal of garbage.

The new urban agglomerations were drab places, blackened with the heavy soot of the early coal age, settling alike on the mills and the workers' quarters, which were dark at best, for the climate of the Midlands is not sunny. Housing for workers was hastily built, closely packed, and always in short supply, as in all rapidly growing communities. Entire families lived in single rooms, and family life in such conditions tended to disintegrate. A police officer in Glasgow observed that there were whole blocks of tenements in the city, each swarming with a thousand ragged children who had first names only, usually nicknames—like animals, as he put it.

Unskilled labor

The distressing feature of the new factories was that for the most part they required unskilled labor only. Skilled workers found themselves degraded in status. Hand weavers and spinners, thrown out of work by the new machines, either languished in misery or went off to a factory to find a less skilled job. The factories paid good wages by the standards for unskilled labor at the time. But these standards were very low, too low to allow a man to

The invention of the steam locomotive and the development of new railways contributed to early nineteenth-century industrialization. This train was coming into London on one of the rail lines that began to connect smaller industrial cities to the commercial life of the British capital in the 1830s.
(©Science & Society Picture Library/Getty Images)

support his wife and children. This had generally been true for unskilled labor, in England and elsewhere, under earlier economic systems also. In the new factories, however, the work was so mechanical that children as young as 6 years old were often preferred. Women, too, worked for less and were often more adept at handling a bobbin, which brought many women spinners from the older, displaced "cottage industries" into the new industrial working class.

The people who found jobs in the new factories—men, women, children—often worked 14 hours a day or occasionally even more; and though such hours were familiar to persons who had worked on farms, or at domestic industry in rural households, they became more tedious and oppressive in the more regimented working conditions in the mills. Holidays were few, except for the unwelcome leisure of unemployment, which was a common scourge, because the short-run ups and downs of business were very erratic. A day without work produced nothing to live on, but even where the daily wage was relatively attractive, the worker's real income was chronically insufficient. Workers in the factories, as in the mines, were almost entirely unorganized. They were a mass of recently assembled humanity without traditions or common ties. They bargained individually with their employers who, usually small business people themselves, faced ferocious competition with others. The employers were often in debt for the equipment in their own factories, or they were determined to save money in order to purchase more, and so they held their wages bill to the lowest possible figure.

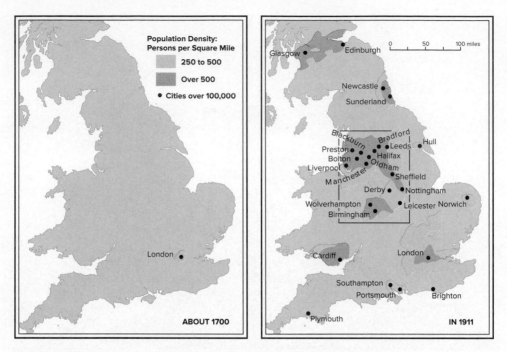

BRITAIN BEFORE AND AFTER THE INDUSTRIAL REVOLUTION
In 1700 England, Scotland, and Wales had only one city with a population of more than 100,000.
In 1911 they had nearly 30, most of which were located in the industrialized Midlands (the area within
the small rectangle).

The cotton lords

The factory owners, the new "cotton lords," were the first industrial capitalists. They were often self-made men, who owed their position
to their own intelligence, persistence, and foresight rather than to an
aristocratic birth. They lived in comfort without ostentation or luxury, saving from each
year's income to build up their factories and their machines. Hard-working themselves,
they thought that landed gentlemen were usually idlers and that the poor tended to be
lazy, but most factory owners were neither brutal nor knowingly hard-hearted. They gave
to charitable and philanthropic causes. They believed that they did the poor a favor by
furnishing them with work and by seeing to it that they worked diligently and productively.
Most of them disapproved of public regulation of their business, though a few, driven by
competition to expedients that they did not like, such as the employment of small children,
would have accepted some regulation that fell on all competitors equally. It was a cotton
magnate, the elder Robert Peel, who in 1802 pushed the first Factory Act through
Parliament. This act purported to regulate the conditions in which pauper children were
employed in the textile mills, but it was a dead letter from the beginning, because it provided no adequate body of factory inspectors. The English at this time, alone among the
leading European peoples, had no class of trained, paid, and professional government
administrators; nor did they yet want such a class, preferring self-government and local
initiative. To have inspectors for one's affairs smacked of Continental bureaucracy. The
new English industrialists wanted to be left alone to manage their factories and workers
without government interventions. They considered it unnatural to interfere with business
and believed that, if allowed to follow their own judgment, they would assure the future
prosperity and progress of the country.

Classical Economics: "Laissez-Faire" and the Free Market Economy

The industrialists were strengthened in these beliefs by the emerging science of political economy. In 1776 Adam Smith published his epochal *The Wealth of Nations,* which criticized the regulatory and monopolistic economic practices of the older mercantilism. Smith urged, though with moderation, that certain "natural laws" of production and exchange be allowed to work freely in economic markets, and these themes were further developed by early nineteenth-century theorists such as Thomas R. Malthus, David Ricardo, and the so-called Manchester School. Their doctrine was dubbed (by its opponents) laissez-faire and in its elaborated form is still called classical economics. It held, basically, that there is a world of economic relationships autonomous and separable from government or politics. It is the world of the free market, and this market is regulated within itself by certain natural laws, such as the law of supply and demand. All persons should follow their own enlightened self-interest; all know their own interests better than anyone else; and the sum total of individual interests will add up to the general welfare and liberty of all. The market itself, as the Manchester School theorists described it, will resolve the economic crises or imbalances that arise in the recurring cycles of production and trade and supply and demand. Government therefore should do as little as possible; it should confine itself to preserving security of life and property and to providing reasonable laws and reliable courts, thus ensuring the efficient discharge of private contracts, debts, and obligations. Not only business but education, charity, and personal matters generally should be left to private initiative. There should be no tariffs; free trade should reign everywhere, for the economic system is worldwide, unaffected by political barriers or national differences.

Self-interest and free trade

As for workers, according to classical economists before about 1850, they should not expect to make more than a bare minimum living; an "iron law of wages," the economists argued, shows that as soon as workers receive more than a subsistence wage they have more children, who eat up the excess, so that they reduce themselves again to a subsistence level. Workers, if discontented, should see the folly of changing the economic system, for this *is* the system, the natural system—there is no other. Political economy as taught by the Manchester School was not without reason called the "dismal science."

Working people's experiences

For working people in England the Industrial Revolution was a hard experience. It should be remembered, however, that neither low wages, nor the 14-hour day, nor the labor of women and children, nor the ravages of unemployment were anything new. All had existed for centuries, in England and western Europe, as agricultural and commercial capitalism replaced the more self-sufficient economies of the Middle Ages. Economic insecurity was thus a long-existing social experience for most people in premodern Europe. The factory towns were in some ways better places than the impoverished rural villages from which many of their people came. Factory routine was psychologically deadening, but the textile mills were not always worse than the domestic sweatshops in which manufacturing processes had previously taken place. The concentration of working people in city and factory eventually opened the way to improvement in their condition. It made their misery apparent; philanthropic sentiment gradually arose among the more fortunate. Gathered in cities, workers obtained more knowledge of the world. Mingling and talking together, they developed a sense of solidarity, class interest, common political aims, and new social identities; and in time they became organized, establishing labor unions by which to obtain a larger share of the national income.

Historical Interpretations and Debates
Women and the Industrial Revolution

Historians agree that the transition to large-scale industrial production during the nineteenth century became one of the most far-reaching transformations in human history, but they often disagree about how industrialization changed social hierarchies, family life, and the economic positions of different social classes. Among numerous other changes, the Industrial Revolution altered traditional patterns of work and domestic life for both women and men, so that the new factory system helped to reshape the meaning of masculinity, womanhood, and the gendered division of labor. Compare the interpretations that Louise A. Tilly and Joan W. Scott and Sonya O. Rose develop in their accounts of how industrialization influenced nineteenth-century European women and ideas about gender.

Louise A. Tilly and Joan W. Scott, *Women, Work, and Family* (1987)

Under the [pre-industrial] family wage economy married women performed several roles for their families. They often contributed wages to the family fund, they managed the household, and they bore and cared for children. With industrialization, however, the demands of wage labor increasingly conflicted with women's domestic activities. . . . Industrial jobs required specialization and a full-time commitment to work, usually in a specific location away from home. While under the domestic mode of production women combined market-oriented activities and domestic work, the industrial mode of production precluded an easy reconciliation of married women's activities. The resolution of the conflict [in nineteenth-century England and France] was for married women not to work unless family finances urgently required it. . . .

In general, married women tended to be found in largest numbers in the least industrialized sectors of the labor force, in those areas where the least separation existed between home and workplace and where women could control the rhythm of their work. . . .

Married women were thus clustered in those jobs which were temporary and episodic, which corresponded to their less certain commitment to wage earning. These jobs were also low-paying, exploiting the usually desperate need that drove a married woman to seek employment and the fact that she had neither the skill nor the organizational support which might command higher wages.

Sonya O. Rose, *Limited Livelihoods: Gender and Class in Nineteenth-Century England* (1992)

Gender distinctions were woven into the fabric of industrial capitalism, and the development of industrial capitalism had an impact on what it meant to be a man and what it meant to be a woman. . . .

Gender distinctions . . . were articulated in an ideology of family life that portrayed men as those who were answerable for the economic well-being of the family and women as those charged with the care of children and the upkeep of the household. These representations were embedded in employer hiring and managerial practices. . . . However, the representations belied the extent to which most men were frequently economically dependent on their wives and children and most married women frequently combined their domestic responsibilities with economic contributions to their households. Single and widowed women had to be self-supporting or the sole support of others, or they had to make substantial economic contributions to the households in which they lived. Because women as a category were low-waged workers and primarily were hired to do work defined as unskilled, women without men were forced to subsist on earnings that did not cover the costs of maintaining themselves. . . .

The language of gender . . . constituted the labor market as a domain in which jobs were designed for men. Women's employment, especially the employment of married women and women with children, became problematic.

Sources: Louise A. Tilly and Joan W. Scott, *Women, Work, and Family* (New York: Methuen, 1987), pp. 123–124, 126; Sonya O. Rose, *Limited Livelihoods: Gender and Class in Nineteenth-Century England* (Berkeley: University of California Press, 1992), pp. 185–186.

Britain after the fall of Napoleon became the workshop of the world. Though factories using steam power also sprang up in France, Belgium, New England, and elsewhere, it was really not until after 1870 that Great Britain faced major industrial competition from abroad. The British had a virtual monopoly in textiles and machine tools. The English Midlands and Scottish Lowlands shipped cotton thread and steam engines to all the world. British capital was exported to all countries, where it helped to bring new enterprises into being and to develop the infrastructure for new industrializing economies. London became the world's clearinghouse and financial center. Progressive people in other lands looked to Britain as their model, hoping to learn from its advanced industrial methods, and to imitate its parliamentary political system.

53.   THE ADVENT OF THE "ISMS"

The combined forces of industrialization and of the French Revolution led after 1815 to a proliferation of new doctrines and movements, most of which contributed to a general European revolution in 1848. As for the 33 years from 1815 to 1848, there is no better way of grasping their long-run meaning than to reflect on the number of enduring "isms" that arose at that time. The "isms" developed as more or less systematic attempts to describe coherent sets of political, cultural, or social beliefs; and the advocates of each "ism" usually organized groups or public "movements" that sought to implement their ideas by changing political institutions or by transforming certain aspects of modern social and cultural life.

Words for the different "isms" appeared at various times in each European language, and the English usage of such terms often followed their earlier emergence in other places. Insofar as is known, however, the word "liberalism" first appeared in the English language in 1819, "radicalism" in 1820, "socialism" in 1832, "conservatism" in 1835. The 1830s first saw "individualism," "constitutionalism," "humanitarianism," "feminism," and "monarchism." "Nationalism" and "communism" date from the 1840s. Not until the 1850s did the English-speaking world use the word "capitalism" (French *capitalisme* is much older); and not until even later did people hear of "Marxism," though the doctrines of Marx grew out of and reflected the troubled times of the 1840s.

The rapid coinage of new "isms" does not in every case mean that the ideas they conveyed were new. Many of them had their origin in the Enlightenment, if not before. People had loved liberty before talking of liberalism, and they had been conservative without defining their ideas as conservatism. The appearance of so many "isms" shows rather that people were making their ideas more systematic. To the philosophy of the Enlightenment were now added an intense activism and partisanship generated during the French Revolution. People were obliged to reconsider and analyze society as a whole—and to compete for influence in the expanding public sphere of modern national states. An "ism" (excluding such words as hypnotism or favoritism) may therefore be defined as the conscious espousal of a specific doctrine in competition with other doctrines. Many of the new "isms" drew on the analytical themes of the emerging social sciences, and they often developed institutions in which intellectuals could carry their ideas to other social groups and wider social movements. New knowledge became linked to new forms of social and political action. Without the "isms" created in the 30-odd years after the peace of Vienna it is impossible to understand or even talk about the history of the world since that event, so that a brief characterization of some of the most important is in order.

Romanticism

One of the most influential "isms" was not explicitly political. It was called "romanticism," a word first used in English in the 1840s to describe a movement then half a century old. Romanticism was primarily a theory of literature and the arts. Its great exponents included William Wordsworth, Lord Byron, Percy Bysshe Shelley, and Mary Wollstonecraft Shelley in England; Victor Hugo, René Chateaubriand, and George Sand in France; and Friedrich von Schiller, Friedrich Schlegel, and many others in Germany. As a theory of art it raised basic questions about the nature of human knowledge, the importance of various human senses or faculties, the relation of thought and feeling, the meaning of the past and of time itself, and the processes of artistic creativity. Romanticism rejected the emphasis on classical rules and rational order that had shaped aesthetic theory during much of the eighteenth century. Romantics celebrated the idiosyncratic visions of creative individuals rather than the symmetries of classical art and literature. They helped produce the modern image of defiant artistic rebels. Representing a new way of sensing all human experience, romanticism affected much thinking on social and public questions as well as the early nineteenth-century debates about culture and the arts.

Love of the unclassifiable

Possibly the most fundamental romantic attitude was a love of the unclassifiable—of moods or impressions, scenes or stories, sights or sounds or things concretely experienced, personal idiosyncrasies or peculiar customs that the intellect could never classify, box up, explain away, or reduce to an abstract generalization. The romantics, characteristically, insisted on the value of feeling and nonrational experiences as well as of reason. They were aware of the importance of the subconscious. They were likely to suspect a perfectly lucid idea as somehow superficial. They loved the mysterious, the unknown, the half-seen figures on the far horizon. Hence romanticism contributed to a new interest in unfamiliar, distant societies and in strange, distant historical epochs. Where the philosophes of the Enlightenment had deplored the Middle Ages as a time of intellectual error, the romantic generation looked back upon them with respect and even nostalgia, finding in them a fascination, a colorfulness, or a spiritual depth that they missed in their own time. The "Gothic," which rationalists thought barbarous, had a strong appeal for romantics. A Gothic Revival emerged in the arts, of which one example was the British Parliament buildings, which were rebuilt in this architectural style during the 1840s.

Creative genius

In medieval art and institutions, as in the art and institutions of every age and people, the romantics saw the expression of an inner genius. The idea of original or creative genius was in fact another of the most fundamental romantic beliefs. A genius was a dynamic spirit that no rules could hem in, one that no analysis or classification could ever fully explain. Genius, it was thought, made its own rules and laws. The genius might be that of the individual person, such as the artist, writer, or Napoleonic mover of the world. It might be the genius or spirit of an age. Or it might be the genius of a people or nation, the *Volksgeist* of Herder, an inherent national character making each people grow in its own distinctive way, which could be known only by a study of its history; romanticism thus merged in many places with new forms of nationalism. Here again romanticism gave a new impetus to study of the past. Politically, romantics could be found in all camps, conservative, liberal, and radical, but the emphasis on individual creativity led most romantics toward a critical view of rigid social and cultural hierarchies. Romanticism thus added cultural and emotional passions to the more political "isms" that evolved rapidly after 1815.

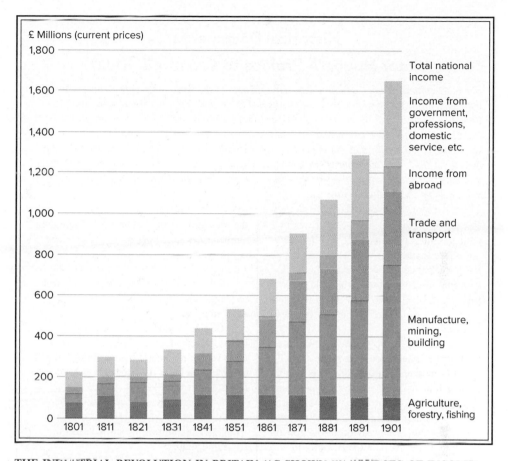

THE INDUSTRIAL REVOLUTION IN BRITAIN (AS SHOWN BY SOURCES OF INCOME)
British national income grew about eightfold in the nineteenth century. Income derived from agriculture, forestry, and the like remained about the same, but the income from these activities sank from one-third to one-sixteenth of all income. By 1851 half the national income came from manufacturing, trade, and transportation, and by 1901 three-quarters came from these sources. The category "income from abroad" refers to interest and dividends on loans and investments outside Great Britain, which grew rapidly after the 1850s.

Source: Adapted from P. Deane and W.A. Cole, *British Economic Growth* (Cambridge, England: Cambridge University Press, second edition, 1967), pp. 166–167.

Classical Liberalism

The first Liberals, calling themselves by that name (though Napoleon used that word for his own system), arose in Spain among opponents of the Napoleonic occupation who also sought reforms within Spanish political institutions. The word passed to France, where it denoted opposition to royalism after the restoration of the Bourbons in 1814 and where it gained intellectual influence through the work of liberal writers such as Benjamin Constant. In England, many Whigs became increasingly liberal, as did even a few Tories. Liberal political theorists also had influence in England, most notably in the writings of John Stuart Mill, and a new Liberal Party became an important force in British politics during the 1850s. Nineteenth-century, or "classical," liberalism varied from country to country, but it showed many basic similarities, including an emphasis on the rights and liberties that individuals should possess in every well-ordered, modern society.

Historical Documents
Victor Hugo, "A Preface to *Cromwell*," (1827)

Romantic cultural themes spread widely across Europe in the early nineteenth century, gaining particular influence among writers and artists in Britain and Germany. There were also Romantic authors such as Victor Hugo (1802-1885) in France. Like other Romantics of this era, Hugo rejected the classical literary guidelines as he wrote about mysterious settings, historical events, social rebels, and marginalized people. He also wrote a Romantic manifesto in the preface for his long play about Oliver Cromwell, which was never performed during his lifetime. The following excerpts from this preface express typical Romantic desires to break with tradition and celebrate the creative genius.

The Greek theatre, restricted as it was to a national and religious object, was much more free than ours. . . . The reason is that the [Greek theatre] . . . obeys only the laws that are suited to it, while the other [French theatre] takes upon itself conditions of existence which are absolutely foreign to its essence. . . .

But still the same refrain is repeated . . . : "Follow the rules! Copy the models! . . ."

Let us then speak boldly. The time for it has come, and it would be strange if, in this age, liberty, like the light, should penetrate everywhere except to the one place where freedom is most natural—the domain of thought. Let us take the hammer to

theories and poetic systems. . . . There are neither rules nor models; or, rather, there are no other rules than the general laws of nature, which soar above the whole field of art, and the special rules which result from the conditions appropriate to the subject of each composition. . . .

Genius, which divines rather than learns, devises for each work the general rules from the general plan of things, the special rules from the separate *ensemble* of the subject treated. . . .

The poet—let us insist on this point—should take counsel therefore only of nature, truth, and inspiration which is itself both truth and nature.

Victor Hugo, "The Preface to *Cromwell*," in *The Harvard Classics*, ed. by Charles W. Eliot, *Prefaces and Prologues to Famous Books* (New York: P.F. Collier & Son, 1910), pp. 377, 382-384.

Liberal beliefs

Liberals were generally persons of the business and professional classes, together with enterprising landowners wishing to improve their estates. They believed in what was modern, enlightened, efficient, reasonable, and fair. They had confidence in the human capacity for self-government and self-control. They set a high value on parliamentary or representative government, working through reasonable discussion and legislation, with responsible ministries and an impartial and law-abiding administration. Liberals thus demanded full publicity for all actions of government, and to ensure such publicity they insisted on freedom of the press and free rights of assembly. All these political advantages they thought most likely to be realized under a good constitutional monarchy. Outside England they favored explicit written constitutions. They were not democrats; they generally opposed giving every man the vote, fearing the excesses of mob rule or of irrational political action. Only as the nineteenth century progressed did liberals gradually and reluctantly come to accept the idea of universal male suffrage. Many continued to oppose female suffrage, though some liberals such as John Stuart Mill argued that women should have the same voting rights as men. Liberals subscribed to the doctrines of the "rights of man" as set forth in the American

NEW HOUSES OF PARLIAMENT.

The new British Houses of Parliament were built during the 1840s. They became a prominent example of the Gothic revival in architecture and of the early nineteenth-century romantic fascination with the Middle Ages.

(©Hulton Archive/Getty Images)

and French revolutions, but with a clear emphasis on the right of property, and in their economic views they typically followed the British Manchester School or the French economist J. B. Say. They favored laissez-faire capitalism and free markets, remained suspicious of government interventions to regulate business, wanted to get rid of the guild system where it still existed, and disapproved of attempts by the new industrial laborers to organize unions.

Internationally they advocated freedom of trade, to be accomplished by the lowering or complete abolition of tariffs, so that all countries might exchange their products easily with each other and with industrial England. In this way, they thought, each country would produce what it was best able to sell in international markets and so best increase its wealth and standards of living. From the growth of wealth, production, invention, and scientific progress they believed that the general progress of humanity would ensue. They generally frowned upon the established churches and landed aristocracies as obstacles to advancement. They believed in the spread of tolerance and education. They were also profoundly civilian in attitude, disliking wars, conquerors, army officers, standing armies, and military expenditures. They wanted orderly change through legislative processes. They shrank before the idea of revolution; and liberals on the Continent usually admired Great Britain, even as they set about creating their own distinctive national institutions.

Radicalism, Republicanism, Socialism

Radicalism, at least as a word, originated in England, where about 1820 the Philosophical Radicals proudly applied the term to themselves. These early Radicals included not only the few working-class leaders who were beginning to emerge but also many of the new industrial capitalists, who were still unrepresented in Parliament. They took up where such English "Jacobins" as Thomas Paine had left off a generation earlier, before the long crisis of the French wars had discredited all radicalism as pro-French. The main goal of Philosophical Radicalism, as its advocates described it, was to extend many of the liberal claims for individual rights to much wider segments of the population.

The Philosophical Radicals were a good deal like the rationalist French philosophes before the Revolution. They were followers of an elderly sage, Jeremy Bentham, who in prolific writings from 1776 to 1832 undertook to reform the English criminal and civil law, church, Parliament, and constitution. The English Radicals professed to deduce the right form of institutions from the fundamental traits of human nature and psychology. They impatiently waved aside all arguments based on history, usage, or custom. They wanted to go to the roots of social and political life. ("Radical" is from the Latin word for "root.") They wanted a total reconstruction of laws, courts, prisons, poor relief, municipal organization, rotten boroughs, and fox-hunting clergy. Their demand for the reform

Demands for radical reforms

of Parliament was vehement and insistent. They detested the Church of England, the peerage, and the squirearchy. Many radicals would just as soon abolish royalty also; not until the long reign of Queen Victoria (1837–1901) did the British monarchy become undeniably popular in all quarters. Above all, radicalism was democratic; it demanded a vote for every adult Englishman. After the Reform Bill of 1832 the industrial capitalists generally turned into liberals, but the working-class leaders remained radical democrats, as will be seen.

Republican ideals

On the Continent radicalism was represented by militant republicanism. The years of the First French Republic in the 1790s, which to liberals and conservatives signified horrors associated with the Reign of Terror, were for the republicans years of hope and progress, cut short by forces of reaction. Republicans were a minority even in France; elsewhere, as in Italy and Germany, they were fewer still, though they existed. Mostly the republicans were drawn from intelligentsia such as students and writers, from working-class leaders protesting social injustice, and from elderly veterans, or the descendants of veterans, to whom the Republic of '93, with its wars and its glory, was a living thing. Because of police repression, republicans often joined together in secret societies. They looked forward to future revolutionary upheavals, by which they believed that the cause of liberty, equality, and fraternity would be advanced. Strong proponents of political equality, they were democrats demanding universal male suffrage. They favored parliamentary government but were much less concerned with its successful or methodical operation than were the liberals. Most republicans were bitterly anticlerical. Remembering the internecine struggle between the church and the republic during the French Revolution, and still facing the political influence of the Catholic clergy (for republicanism was most common in Catholic countries), they regarded the Catholic Church as the implacable enemy of reason and liberty. Opposed to monarchy of any kind, even to constitutional monarchy, intensely hostile to church and aristocracy, conscious heirs of the great French Revolution, organized in national and international secret societies, not averse to overthrowing existing regimes by force, the more militant republicans were considered by most other people, including the liberals, to be little better than anarchists.

Republicanism shaded off into socialism. Socialists generally shared the political attitudes of republicanism but added other views besides. The early socialists, those before the Revolution of 1848, were

Socialist views

of many kinds, but all had certain ideas in common. All of them regarded the existing economic system and distribution of wealth as aimless, chaotic, and outrageously unjust. All thought it improper for owners of wealth to have so much economic power—to give or deny work to the worker, to set wages and hours in their own interests, to guide all the labors of society in the interests of private profit. All therefore questioned the value of private enterprise, favoring some degree of communal ownership of productive assets— banks, factories, machines, land, and transportation. All disliked competition as a governing economic or social principle and set forth principles of harmony, cooperation or association instead. All flatly and absolutely rejected the laissez-faire of the liberals and the political economists. Where the latter thought mainly of increasing production, without much concern over distribution, the early socialists thought mainly of a fairer or more equal distribution of income among all useful members of society. They believed that further steps toward social and economic equality would take people beyond (or help them actually achieve) the civil and legal equality that the French Revolution had so famously affirmed.

One of the first socialists was also one of the first cotton lords, Robert Owen (1771–1858) of Manchester and the Scottish Lowlands. Appalled at the condition of the mill-hands, he created a kind of model community for his own employees, paying high wages, reducing hours, sternly correcting vice and drunkenness, building schools and housing and company stores for the cheap sale of workers' necessities. From such paternalistic capitalism in his early years he passed on to a lifelong campaign for social reforms, in which he was somewhat handicapped, not only by the opposition of industrialists, but also by his unpopular radicalism in matters of religion.

Most of the early socialists were French, spurred onward by the sense of an uncompleted revolution. One was a nobleman, the Count de Saint-Simon (1760–1825), who had fought in the War of American Independence, accepted the French Revolution, and in his later years

Saint-Simonians and Fourier

wrote many books on social problems. He and his followers, who called themselves not socialists but Saint-Simonians, were among the first clear exponents of a planned society. They advocated the public ownership of industrial equipment and other capital, with control vested in the hands of great captains of industry or social engineers, who should plan vast projects like the digging of a canal at Suez, and in general coordinate the labor and resources of society to productive ends. Of a different type was Charles Fourier (1772–1837), a somewhat doctrinaire thinker who subjected all social institutions to a sweeping condemnation. His positive program took the form of proposing that society be organized in small communal units that he termed "phalansteries." Each of these he conceived to contain 1,620 persons, each doing the work suited to his or her natural inclination. Among the practical French no phalanstery was ever successfully organized. A number were established in the United States, still the land of Europe's utopian dream; the best known, because it was operated by literary people, was the Brook Farm "movement" in Massachusetts, which ran through a troubled existence of five years from 1842

MARY WOLLSTONECRAFT
Engraving after a portrait by John Opie
(English, 1761–1807)

Mary Wollstonecraft was the most influential English advocate for women's rights in the revolutionary era of the 1790s. Her writings emphasized that women should have equal opportunities for a rational education, which would prepare them to participate more equally with men in modern public life and professional work.

(Library of Congress, Prints & Photographs Division, Reproduction number LC-USZ62-64309)

to 1847. Robert Owen also, in 1825, had founded an experimental colony in America, at New Harmony, Indiana, on the then remote banks of the Wabash River; it, too, lasted only about five years. Such schemes, as their critics pointed out, presupposed the withdrawal of select spirits to live by themselves and really had little to say about the broader, interconnected social problems of the modern industrial age.

The French working classes

Politically the most significant form of socialism before 1848 was the movement stirring among the working classes of France, a compound of revolutionary republicanism and socialism. The politically minded Paris workers had been republican since 1792. For them the Revolution was not finished but only momentarily interrupted. Reduced to political impotence during the early nineteenth century, discriminated against in the law courts, obliged to carry identity papers signed by their employers, and goaded by the pressures of industrialization as new factories spread across France, they developed a deep hostility to the wealthier, property-owning classes. They found a spokesman in the Paris journalist Louis Blanc, editor of the *Revue de progrès* and author of *The Organization of Work* (1839), one of the most constructive of the early socialist writings. He proposed a system of "social workshops," or state-supported manufacturing centers, in which the workers should labor by and for themselves without the intervention of private capitalists. Of this kind of socialism we shall hear more.

As for communism, it was at this time an emerging synonym for socialism. A small group of German revolutionaries, mainly exiles in France, took the name for themselves in the 1840s. They would have been historically forgotten had they not included Karl Marx and Friedrich Engels among their members. Marx and Engels consciously used the word when they wrote *The Communist Manifesto* in 1848 and whenever they wanted to differentiate their variety of socialism from that of such utopians as Saint-Simon, Fourier, and Owen. But the word *communism* went out of general use after 1848, to be revived after the Russian Revolution of 1917, at which time it received a somewhat new meaning.

Feminism

Feminism emerged as a new political and cultural movement in the early nineteenth century, though the term itself did not appear until some women in France began to refer to themselves as "feminists" during the 1830s. There were several strands of feminism, as there were several strands of all significant "isms," but most feminists shared various ideas with liberals, radicals, or socialists—especially the belief in the fundamental rights of every person. Feminism sought to expand the rights of women in both public and private life. Drawing on the legacy of the French Revolution and its conceptions of human rights, feminists argued that the rights of man existed also for women (much as republicans and socialists claimed that such rights must also exist for poor people and workers). Some feminists, extending the arguments of Mary Wollstonecraft's influential book, *A Vindication of the Rights of Woman* (1792), worked mainly to secure new voting and civil rights for women. Other feminists, though they might also support the quest for voting rights, worked mainly to reform the laws that regulated family life or to advance the rights of women in education, cultural life, and the economy. Both the political and social strands of early nineteenth-century feminism drew on Enlightenment ideas about human rights, reform, education, and progress, so that feminism resembled republicanism, radicalism, and socialism in its links to eighteenth-century predecessors, including French writers such as Condorcet and Olympe de Gouges.

The writers and activists who sought new political rights for women tended to be "egalitarian" feminists; that is, they stressed the ways in which women and men shared the use of reason and universal human rights. Despite the obvious connection to themes of the French Revolution, the campaign for women's political rights developed more rapidly in early nineteenth-century Britain and America. These national differences may have reflected the fact that male voting rights became more widespread in Britain and America before 1848; or the different feminisms may have developed because French republicanism had become hostile to female political activities during the later stages of the French Revolution, and because the Napoleonic Code had given French women a subordinate position in the patriarchical legal system that regulated family relations. In any case, early French feminists tended to focus on the social, cultural, or legal rights of women rather than on campaigns to win the vote.

Egalitarian feminism

The first nineteenth-century advocates for women's rights in England were Philosophical Radicals and followers of the socialist leader Robert Owen. The socialists Anne Wheeler and William Thompson, for example, published an important statement of the new feminist themes in their *Appeal on Behalf of Women* (1825), which traced the inferior status of women to flaws in the economic system. Similar arguments appeared also in the writings of Owen himself and in the publications of his feminist friend, the Scottish writer Frances Wright. But the most influential English argument for women's political rights emerged in the works of the liberal writers Harriet Taylor and John Stuart Mill, who worked together as close intellectual partners for more than 20 years (they ultimately married after the death of her first husband). Beginning in the 1830s, Taylor and Mill produced important works on the social, legal, and political inequalities that women faced in even the most advanced modern societies. Their collaboration led finally to Mill's famous book, *The Subjection of Women* (1869), in which Mill referred to the decisive influence of Taylor's ideas, though she had died before its publication. Mill built his case for women's political and social rights on the claim that women were inherently equal to men (hence entitled to the same

English feminists

The Saint-Simonian movement in France produced early feminist publications and also helped to launch a new social analysis of the restrictions on women's rights. This portrayal of a Saint-Simonian woman is entitled "The Free Woman," and the placement of her left foot conveys a challenge to French laws. (©Universal History Archive/Getty Images)

La Femme libre.

rights) and on the utilitarian argument that society would greatly benefit from the increased participation of women in public life. Translated into all the major European languages, his book had much subsequent influence on feminist campaigns for the political and legal rights of women in other nations as well as in England. Meanwhile, American women launched their own campaign for voting rights at a convention in Seneca Falls, New York, where leaders such as Elizabeth Cady Stanton declared, in 1848, that women were entitled to vote because they were "created equal" with men.

French feminism

Feminists also entered public life on the Continent during the 1830s and 1840s, especially in France. Socialists such as Saint-Simon and Fourier gave critical attention to the history of the family, thereby encouraging their followers to develop a social analysis of traditional restrictions on the rights of women. Women activists in the Saint-Simonian groups of the 1830s established journals whose titles asserted new feminist identities: *The Free Woman* and *The New Woman*. A new generation of women writers also began to extend the earlier work of Germaine de Staël, who had argued that "it is useful to society's enlightenment and happiness that women should carefully develop their intelligence and their reason." All feminists advocated better education for young women, reforms in property and divorce laws to enhance women's independence, and the right of women to participate in public debates. Many feminists in France, however, moved away from the egalitarian arguments for women's rights by stressing certain differences between men and women. The special responsibilities of motherhood, for example, gave women a distinctive, essential task in educating the rising generation, but only well-educated, competent women could raise intelligent, well-educated children. Feminists thus strongly supported the creation of new schools for girls and began seeking women's access to higher education (public secondary schools for girls were not established in France until the 1880s).

In addition to the campaigns for education and legal reforms, many feminists wrote books that described the social lives of women or asserted their claims for a place in public life. The travel writings of Flora Tristan (1803–1844), for instance, examined the social constraints that women faced in both South America and Europe. Another French writer of Tristan's generation, George Sand (1804–1876), became the most influential literary woman of the 1840s. Her many novels and essays often portrayed independent women, but her personal life was almost as famous and controversial as her books. Critics mocked her for wearing male clothing, smoking cigars, and living with men outside marriage; yet Sand also won the admiring support of readers throughout Europe, many of whom saw her as a model for new forms of female cultural and political expression. She therefore became a famous symbol for both supporters and enemies of the new feminism; indeed, the term "George Sandism" was used to condemn women whose behavior seemed radical or unconventional. Such hostility indicates how feminism had become one of the expanding postrevolutionary "isms," though the political campaign for women's voting rights and other legal reforms would not achieve its main objectives until the twentieth century.

Nationalism: Western Europe

Nationalism first arose in many places as part of the general reaction against the international Napoleonic system, but it also drew its strength from specific cultural and political traditions in each country. It was the most pervasive and the least crystallized of the new "isms," in part because it usually overlapped with various forms of romanticism, republicanism, or liberalism. In western Europe—Britain, France, or Spain—where national unity already existed, nationalism was not a doctrine for nation-building so much as a set of political and cultural beliefs, easily aroused when national interests were questioned but normally taken for granted. Elsewhere—in Italy, Germany, Poland, the Austrian and Turkish empires—where peoples of the same nationality were politically divided or subject to foreign rule, nationalism became a deliberate and conscious program for political action. The influential examples of Great Britain and France, successful and flourishing because they were unified nations, helped to stimulate the ambitions of other peoples to become unified nations too. The period after 1815 was in Germany a time of rising agitation over the national question; in Italy, of the Risorgimento or "resurgence"; in eastern Europe, of the Slavic Revival.

The movement was led by intellectuals, who often found it necessary to instill in their compatriots the very idea of nationality itself. They seized upon Herder's conception of the *Volksgeist,* or

Volksgeist

national spirit, applying its emphasis on national differences to their own people. Usually they began with a cultural nationalism, holding that each people had a language, history, world view, and culture of its own, which must be preserved and perfected. They then usually passed on to a political nationalism, holding that to preserve this national culture, and to protect the inherent rights and freedom of its individual members, each nation should create for itself an independent sovereign state. Nationalism thus fused culture and politics to affirm the enduring existence of transcendent national identities, most of which took on the emotional meaning or intensity of a deeply felt religious faith. Rejecting the older dynastic state system that had regularly transferred territories and people among

This caricature of George Sand, which appeared in a lithograph by Alcide Lorentz in 1842, mocks the famous author for her apparently "masculine" actions. Dressed in pants, holding a cigarette, and surrounded by her writings and political concerns, Sand is ridiculed in both the image and in a sarcastic caption—which alludes to her claim that genius "has no sex." (©Iberfoto/The Image Works)

royal families, nationalists argued that governing authorities should be of the same nationality and language as those they governed. All persons who shared a national culture and national language should therefore be encompassed within the same state, and all should be granted the legal rights of national citizenship.

Because such ideas could not be fully realized without the overthrow of every government in Europe east of France, thoroughgoing nationalism was inherently revolutionary. Outspoken nationalists were therefore persecuted by the authorities, which drove them everywhere into secret nationalist societies. The Carbonari, organized in Italy in the time of Napoleon, was the best known, but there were many others—like the *Veri Italiani*, the Apophasimenes, and the Sublime and Perfect Masters. In some regions Masonic lodges might serve the same purpose. Nationalism often merged with liberalism, socialism, or revolutionary republicanism in an undifferentiated way. Members of the secret nationalist societies were initiated by a complex ritual intended to impress upon them the dire consequences of betraying the group's secrets. They used special grips and passwords and adopted revolutionary names to conceal their identity and baffle the police. They were usually so organized that the ordinary member knew the identity of only a few others, and never of the higher-ups, so that those arrested could reveal nothing important. The societies circulated forbidden literature and generally sought to generate a revolutionary ferment. Conservatives dreaded them, but they were not really dangerous to any government that enjoyed the support of its people.

Secret societies

Best known of the nationalist philosophers in western Europe was the Italian Joseph Mazzini (1805–1872), who spent most of his adult life in exile in France and England. In his youth he joined the Carbonari, but in 1831 he founded a society of his own, called Young Italy, and he edited and smuggled into Italy copies of a journal of the same name. Young Italy was soon imitated by other societies of similar aim, such as Young Germany. In 1834 Mazzini tried unsuccessfully to bring about an uprising against the kingdom of Sardinia, which he viewed as a key obstacle to the unification of Italy. Undeterred by the total failure of this plan, he continued to organize, to conspire, and to write. For Mazzini nationality and revolution were a holy cause in which the most generous and humane qualities were to find expression; and his most widely read book, *The Duties of Man,* placed duty to the nation intermediate between duty to family and to God.

Mazzini

To many Germans, divided and politically frustrated, nationality became the most important component of collective and personal identities. Nationalism therefore had a very wide influence on German culture, entering everything from folklore to metaphysics. *Grimm's Fairy Tales,* for example, was first published in 1812. It was the work of the two Grimm brothers, founders of the modern science of comparative linguistics, who traveled about Germany to study the popular dialects and in doing so collected the folktales that for generations had been current among the common people. They hoped in this way to find the ancient, indigenous "spirit" of Germany, deep and unspoiled in the bosom of the *Volk*—a theme that had emerged previously in the philosophical writings of Herder. A similar preoccupation with nationhood revealed itself in the philosophy of Hegel (1770–1831), possibly the most extraordinary of all nineteenth-century thinkers.

To Hegel, witnessing the spectacle of the Napoleonic years, it was evident that for a people to enjoy freedom, order, or dignity it must possess a potent and independent state. The state, for him, became the institutional embodiment of reason and liberty—the "march of God through the world," as he put it, meaning not an expansion in space through vulgar conquest, but an expansion of the "Idea" of freedom as it advanced through time and through the conflicts of human history. Hegel conceived of reality itself as a process of endless change, a development having an inner logic and necessary sequence of its own. He thus broke with the more static or mechanical philosophy of the eighteenth century, with its fixed categories of unchangeable right and wrong. He became a philosopher of history, in which he saw the unfolding of a "Universal Spirit" or Idea across time, and he linked this evolving Spirit in complex ways to reason and freedom. He held that change came about through a historical "dialectic," or irresistible tendency of the Universal Spirit and the human mind to move forward by the creation of opposing ideas and the conflicts that such oppositions caused. A given state of affairs (the *thesis*) would in this view inevitably produce the conception of an opposite state of affairs (the *antithesis*), which would be followed by a reconciliation and fusion of the two (the *synthesis*). This new synthesis became the starting point for a new "thesis" in the next stage of dialectical change. Thus, for example, the very disunity of Germany, by producing the opposing idea of unity, would ultimately lead toward the creation of a more unified German state.

Hegel's philosophy

The Hegelian dialectic was soon to be appropriated by Karl Marx to new uses, but meanwhile Hegel's philosophy, with other currents in Germany, made the study of history more philosophically meaningful than it had ever been before. History, the study of change across time, seemed to be the very key with which to unlock the true significance

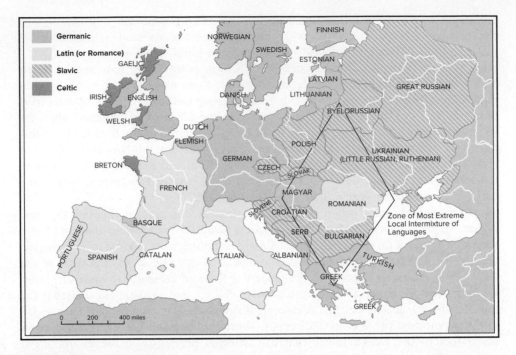

LANGUAGES OF EUROPE

National movements in modern Europe often referred to the distinctive languages of various national groups, but there are only three main European language families: Germanic, Latin, and Slavic. The map shows language areas in the early twentieth century. It does not show the overlap of adjoining languages, bilingual areas, or the existence of small language "pockets" such as Turkish in the Balkans, Greek in Asia Minor, Yiddish in Poland, or German in scattered parts of eastern Europe. In the extreme northwest is the "Celtic fringe," to which the Breton, Welsh, and Gaelic languages were pushed back in the early Middle Ages. For the area within the diamond-shaped zone no map on this scale can give a realistic idea of the overlapping languages. During the Second World War and its aftermath, however, many language pockets in eastern Europe were wiped out through exchange, transportation, or destruction of peoples.

of the world; it could show the unfolding of the Universal Spirit in specific times and places, and each historical era became important as a phase in the progress toward freedom and reason. Historical studies were stimulated, and the German universities became centers of historical learning, attracting scholars from many countries. Most eminent of the German historians was Leopold von Ranke (1795–1886), founder of the "scientific" school of historical writing. Ranke, too, though intellectually scrupulous to the last degree, owed much of his incentive to his national feeling. His first historical work was a study of the *Latin and Teutonic Peoples;* and one of his main ideas, throughout his long life, was that Europe owed its unique greatness to the coexistence and interplay of several distinct nations, which had always resisted the attempts of any one nation to control the whole. By the latter Ranke really meant France—the France of Louis XIV and Napoleon. The Germans, said Ranke in 1830, had a mission from God to develop a culture and a political system that differed from those of the French. They were destined to "create the pure German state corresponding to the genius of the nation." Ranke thus doubted that the constitutional, parliamentary, and individualist principles of other national liberalisms were suited to the national character of Germany.

In economics Friedrich List, in his *National System of Political Economy* (1840), held that political economy as taught in England was suited only to England. Economic theories were not abstract truths but a body of ideas developed in a certain historical stage in a certain country. List thus became a founder of the historical or institutional school of economics. The doctrine of free trade, he said, was a self-interested English idea because it was designed to make England the world's industrial center by keeping other countries in the status of suppliers of raw materials and food. But any country, he held, if it was to be civilized and develop its own national culture, must have cities, factories, industries, and capital of its own. It must therefore put up high tariffs (at least temporarily) for protection. List, it should be remarked, had developed his ideas during a sojourn in the United States, where he saw that Henry Clay's "American system" was in fact a national system of political economy.

List's economics

Nationalism: Eastern Europe

New nationalist movements emerged in eastern Europe as the region's diverse linguistic communities became more aware of their distinctive cultural histories. The Poles and the Magyars had long been active political nationalists, the Poles wishing to undo the eighteenth-century partitions of Polish territories and reestablish their Polish state, the Magyars insisting on autonomy for their kingdom of Hungary within the Habsburg Empire. But for the most part eastern European national identities had rarely gained much recognition or influence. Centuries of imperial political development had tended to submerge the Czechs, Slovaks, Ruthenians, Romanians, Serbs, Croats, Slovenes—and even the Poles and Magyars in lesser degree. Their upper classes spoke German or French and looked to Vienna or to Paris for their ideas. The native languages had remained peasant languages, barely known outside the isolated peasant cultures in which they were spoken. It seemed that many of these languages would disappear.

But early in the nineteenth century the new nationalist intellectuals began to demand the preservation of their historic cultures. They collected folktales and ballads; they studied the languages, composing grammars and dictionaries, often for the first time; and they took to writing books in their mother tongues. They urged their own educated social classes to give up foreign ways. They wrote histories showing the famous exploits of their several peoples in the Middle Ages. A new nationalism stirred the Magyars; in 1837 a national Hungarian theater was established at Budapest. In what was to become Romania a former Transylvanian peasant youth named George Lazar began as early as 1816 to teach at Bucharest. He lectured in Romanian (to the surprise of the upper classes, who preferred Greek), telling how Romania had a distinguished history back to the Roman emperor Trajan. As for the Greeks, they entertained visions of restoring the medieval Greek Empire (known to western Europeans as the Byzantine Empire) in which persons of Greek language or Greek Orthodox religion should become the predominant people of the Balkans.

Preservation of historic cultures

The most far-reaching of the East European movements was the Slavic Revival. The Slavs included the Russians, Poles, Ukrainians, Byelorussians, and Ruthenians; the Czechs and Slovaks; and the South Slavs, consisting of the Slovenes, Croats, Serbs, and Bulgars. All branches of the Slavs began to develop new nationalisms. In 1814, for example, the Serb Vuk Karajich published a grammar of his native tongue and a collection of *Popular Songs and Epics of the Serbs;* he worked out a Serbian alphabet and declared that the dialect spoken in the city of Ragusa (now Dubrovnik) should become the literary language of all South Slavs. In 1836

The Slavic Revival

the Czech historian Francis Palacky published the first volume of his *History of Bohemia,* designed to give the Czechs a new pride in their national past. He first wrote his book in German, the common reading language of educated Czechs. But he soon recast it into Czech, significantly reentitling it a *History of the Czech People.* Among Poles the poet and revolutionary Adam Mickiewicz became the most prominent advocate for a new cultural nationalism. Arrested by the Russians in 1823 for membership in a secret society, he was later allowed by the tsarist government to pass into western Europe. From 1840 to 1844 he taught Slavic literature in Paris at the Collège de France, using his lecture platform as a rostrum to deliver eloquent pleas for the liberation of all peoples and the overthrow of autocracy. He wrote epic poems on Polish historical themes and remained politically active among the revolutionary Polish exiles settled in France.

Russia itself, which Poles and Czechs regarded as backward, was slower to develop a pronounced national sense. Under Tsar Alexander I a Western or European orientation prevailed, but in Alexander's last years and after his death in 1825, the

Russian Slavophilism

doctrines of Slavophilism began to spread. Russian Slavophilism, or the idea that Russia possessed a distinctive way of life, different from and not to be corrupted by that of Europe, became a Russian affirmation of the fundamental idea of the *Volksgeist.* Such views in Russia were at least as old as the opposition to the reforms of Peter the Great. In the nationalistic nineteenth century they crystallized more systematically into an "ism," and they tended to merge into Pan-Slavism, which made substantially the same assertions for the Slavic peoples as a whole. But Pan-Slavism, before 1848, was no more than embryonic.

Other "Isms"

Romanticism, liberalism, radical republicanism, socialism, feminism, and nationalism were the political and cultural forces driving many of the new European political and cultural conflicts in the era between 1815 and 1848. Of other "isms"

Conservatism

less need be said. Conservatism remained strong. Politically, on the Continent, conservatism upheld the institutions of absolute monarchy, aristocracy, and church and thus opposed the constitutional and representative government sought by liberals. As a political philosophy, conservatism built upon the ideas of Edmund Burke, who had rejected the Enlightenment theories of universal natural rights. Burke held that every people must change its institutions by the gradual evolution of its own traditions and that no people could suddenly realize in the present any freedoms not already well prepared for in the past. This doctrine lacked appeal for those to whom the past had been a series of misfortunes, but it gained support among others who sought to define and defend long-established social or political practices. Conservatism sometimes passed into nationalism, because it stressed the firmness and continuity of national character. But nationalists at this time were more often liberals or republicans. Monarchism was conservative and even reactionary. Gone was the enlightened despotism of the previous century, when kings had boldly irritated their nobles and defied their churches. After the thunders of the French Revolution aristocracy and monarchy huddled together, and their new watchword was to maintain "the throne and the altar."

Deeper than other "isms," a feeling shared in varying ways by people of all parties, was the profound current of humanitarianism. It

Humanitarianism

consisted in a heightened concern about the cruelty inflicted upon others. Here the thought of the Age of Enlightenment suffered no reversal. Torture was gone, and even conservative monarchical governments showed no inclination to restore it. Conditions in prisons, hospitals, insane asylums, and orphanages attracted new humanitarian attention and gradually improved. Humanitarian activists sought to change the miserable social position of pauper children, chimney sweeps, women in the mines, and enslaved people in the Americas. Russian serf owners and American slave owners began to show psychological signs of moral doubt. To degrade human beings, use them as work animals, torture them, confine them unjustly, hold them as hostages for others, abuse their bodies, tear apart their families, and punish their relatives were increasingly regarded by Europeans as foreign to modern, enlightened civilizations. The Christian sense of the inviolability of the human person was now again, in a more secular, mundane way, beginning to relieve the sufferings of humanity.

54.   THE LEAKING DAM AND THE FLOOD: DOMESTIC

It is now time to look more specifically at the most influential political reactions and reform movements that emerged after the European peace settlement of 1814–1815. The governments that defeated Napoleon wanted to assure themselves above all else that the disturbances of the past 25 years would not be renewed. In France the restored Bourbon king, Louis XVIII, aspired to keep his throne for himself and his successors. In Great Britain the conservative governing class hoped to preserve the old England that they had so valiantly saved from the clutches of Bonaparte. In Germany, Austria, Italy, and central Europe the chief aim of Metternich, who for another 33 years remained the dominant political figure in these regions, was to maintain a system in which the prestige of the Habsburg dynasty should be supreme. The aims of the tsar, Alexander, were less clear. He was feared by representatives of the other powers as a dreamer, a self-chosen world savior, a man who said he wanted to bring Christianity into politics, and even a liberal. It became one of Metternich's chief hopes to convert Alexander to a firm conservatism.

The arrangements made by the victorious powers were in some ways moderate, at least when considered as responses to the provocations they had undergone in the Napoleonic wars. Partly by the tsar's insistence written constitutions existed after 1814 in France and in Russian or "Congress" Poland. Some of the rulers of south German states allowed a measure of representative government. Even the king of Prussia promised a representative assembly for his kingdom, though the promise was not kept. But it was difficult to maintain any kind of social or political stability. The forces of the political right and the privileged classes (or in France the former privileged classes) denounced all signs of liberalism as dangerous concessions to revolution. Those of the political left— liberals, nationalists, republicans—regarded the newly installed regimes as hopelessly reactionary. Statesmen were jittery on the subject of revolution. They therefore met every sign of agitation with attempts at repression, which, though they might drive agitation temporarily underground, really only made it worse by creating additional grievances. A vicious circle was set endlessly revolving.

Reaction after 1815: France, Poland

In France Louis XVIII began his reign in 1814 with an amnesty to the regicides of 1793. But the regicides, like all republicans, found the France of 1814 an uncomfortable place, exposed as they were to the unofficial vengeance of counterrevolutionaries, and most of them

The "white terror"

King Charles X sought to restore the political principles and practices of the prerevolutionary French monarchy. His coronation in 1824, as portrayed here, thus re-created traditional royal pomp and symbols, but his attempts to repress liberal constitutionalism led to a new revolution and his abdication of power in 1830.

(©Time Life Pictures/Getty Images)

had rallied to Napoleon when he returned from Elba. This exasperated the royalist counterrevolutionaries beyond all measure. A brutal "white terror" broke out after the Bourbon monarchy regained power in 1815. Upper-class youths murdered Bonapartists and republicans; Catholic mobs seized and killed Protestants at Marseilles and Toulouse. The Chamber of Deputies chosen in 1815 (by the tiny electorate of 100,000 well-to-do landowners) proved to be more reactionary and royalist than the king. The king himself could not control the mounting frenzy of reaction, which he was sensible enough to realize would only infuriate the revolutionary element still further, as in fact happened. In 1820 a fanatical workingman assassinated the king's nephew, the Duke de Berry. Those who said that all partisans of the French Revolution were criminal extremists seemed to be justified. The reaction deepened and continued after Louis XVIII died in 1824. The new king was his brother, Charles X, the father of the recently murdered Duke de Berry and the longtime leader of the most extreme anti-revolutionary exiles. As the Count of Artois, youngest brother of Louis XVI, he had been among the first to emigrate in 1789. He was the favorite Bourbon among the most obstinate ex-seigneurs, nobles, and churchmen. Regarding himself as hereditary absolute monarch by the grace of God, he had himself crowned at Reims with all the romantic pomp of ages past, and proceeded to stamp out not only revolutionary republicanism but liberalism and constitutionalism as well.

In Poland, it will be recalled, the Vienna settlement created a constitutional kingdom, with the Russian tsar Alexander as king, joined in merely personal union with the Russian Empire. The new machinery did not work very well. The Polish constitution provided for an elected diet, a wide suffrage by the standards of the day, the Napoleonic civil code, freedom of press and religion, and exclusive use of the Polish language. But the Poles discovered that Alexander, though favoring liberty in the abstract, did not like to have anyone disagree with him. They could make little use of their much touted freedom in any actual legislation. The elected diet could not get along with Alexander's viceroy, who was a Russian. In Russia the serf-owning aristocracy viewed Alexander's idea of a constitutional kingdom in Poland with a jaundiced eye. They wanted no experimentation with liberty on the very borders of Russia.

The Poles themselves played into the hands of their Russian enemies, in part because the Poles were among the first central European peoples *Polish ambitions* to develop strong nationalist aspirations. They were dissatisfied with the boundaries accorded to Congress Poland, and they dreamed of the vast kingdom that had existed before the First Partition in 1772. At the University of Vilna professors and students began to join secret societies. Some members of these societies were nationalist revolutionaries who wanted to drive out Alexander, reunite with Prussian and Austrian Poland, and reconstitute an independent Polish state. It was in the discovery and breaking up of one such society that Adam Mickiewicz was arrested in 1823. Reaction and repression now struck the University of Vilna.

Reaction after 1815: The German States, Britain

In Germany those who had felt national stirrings during the Wars of Liberation were disillusioned by the peace treaty, which maintained the several German principalities about as Napoleon had left them and purposely united them only in a loose federation, or Bund. National ideas were most common in the numerous universities, where students and professors were more susceptible than most people to the doctrines of an eternal *Volksgeist* and a far-flung *Deutschtum*. National ideas tended to glorify the German common people and thus carried with them a kind of democratic opposition to aristocrats, princes, and kings. Students in many of the universities in 1815 formed college clubs, called collectively the *Burschenschaft,* which, as centers of serious political discussion, were to replace the older clubs devoted to drinking and dueling. The *Burschenschaft,* a kind of German youth movement, held a nationwide congress at Wartburg in 1817. Students listened to rousing speeches by patriotic professors, marched about in "Teutonic" costume, and burned a few reactionary books. This undergraduate performance posed no immediate threat to any established state, but the nervous governments took alarm. In 1819 a theology student assassinated the German writer Kotzebue, known as an informer in the service of the tsar.

Metternich now chose to intervene. He had no authority in Germany except in that Austria was a member of the Germanic *Metternich intervenes* federation. He regarded all these manifestations of German national spirit, or of any demand for a more solidly unified Germany, as a threat to the favorable position of the Austrian Empire and to the whole balance of state power in Europe. He called a conference of the principal German states at Carlsbad in Bohemia; the frightened conferees adopted certain resolutions, proposed by Metternich, which were soon enacted by the diet of the Bund. These Carlsbad Decrees (1819) dissolved the *Burschenschaft* and the equally nationalistic gymnastic clubs (some of whose members thereupon

German students celebrated their conception of German nationhood at a festival in 1817. Gathering near a castle at Wartburg where Martin Luther had once lived, they commemorated the beginning of the Protestant Reformation in 1517 and also burned books that were deemed hostile to German liberty.

(©akg-images/Newscom)

joined secret societies). They provided for government officials to be placed in the universities and for censors to control the contents of books and the periodical and newspaper press. The Carlsbad Decrees remained in force for many years, and they imposed an effective check on the growth of liberal and nationalist ideas in Germany.

Economic crisis spurs radicalism

Nor did Great Britain escape the post-1815 cycles of agitation and repression. As elsewhere, radicalism produced reaction and vice versa. Britain after Waterloo was a country devoted to its old traditions but also afflicted by the most advanced social problems of a rapidly developing industrial economy. In 1815, at the close of the Napoleonic wars, the landed classes feared an inrush of imported agricultural products and consequent collapse of farm prices and rentals. The landowning gentry who controlled Parliament enacted a new Corn Law, raising the protective tariff to the point where import of grain became impossible unless prices were very high. Landlords and their farmers benefited, but wage earners and industrial workers found the price of breadstuffs soaring out of reach. At the same time there was a postwar depression in industry. Wages fell and many were thrown out of work. These conditions contributed to the spread of a resurgent political radicalism, which now called for a drastic reform of the House of Commons in order that thereafter a radical program of social and economic legislation might be enacted.

A riot broke out in London in December 1816. In the following February the Prince Regent was attacked in his carriage. The government suspended habeas corpus and employed *agents provocateurs* to obtain evidence against the agitators. Industrialists of Manchester and the new factory towns, determined to force through the reform of parliamentary representation, took the chance offered by the distress of the working classes to organize mass meetings of protest. At sprawling Manchester 80,000 people staged an enormous demonstration at St. Peter's Fields in 1819; they demanded universal male suffrage, annual election of the House of Commons, and the repeal of the Corn Laws. Although perfectly orderly they were fired upon by soldiers; 11 persons were killed and about 400 were wounded, including 113 women. Radicals called this episode the Peterloo massacre in derisive comparison with the battle of Waterloo.

The Peterloo massacre

The frightened government thanked the soldiers for their brave upholding of the social order. Parliament rushed through the Six Acts (1819), which out-lawed "seditious and blasphemous" literature, put a heavy stamp tax on newspapers, authorized the search of private houses for arms, and rigidly restricted the right of public meeting. A group of revolutionaries thereupon plotted to assassinate the whole cabinet at a dinner; they were caught in Cato Street in London in 1820—whence the name "Cato Street Conspiracy." Five of them were hanged. Meanwhile, for publishing the writings of Thomas Paine, Richard Carlisle spent seven years in prison.

"Our example," wrote the Duke of Wellington to a Continental correspondent in 1819, "will be of value in France and Germany, and it is to be hoped that the world will escape from the general revolution with which we all seem to be threatened."

In summary, the various European governments promoted reactionary policies everywhere they could reach in the years following the peace of 1815. The reaction was due only in part to memories of the French Revolution. It was due even more to the living fear of revolution in the present. This fear, though exaggerated, was no mere hallucination. Sensing the rising flood, the established interests desperately built new barriers against it in every country. The same is true of international politics at the time.

55. THE LEAKING DAM AND THE FLOOD: INTERNATIONAL

At the Congress of Vienna in 1814–1815 the powers agreed to hold meetings in the future to enforce the treaty and take up new issues as they arose. A number of congresses of the Great Powers resulted, which are significant as an early experimental step toward international regulation of European affairs. The congresses resembled, in a tentative and partial way, the League of Nations that arose after the First World War of 1914–1918, or the United Nations that followed after the war of 1939–1945, or the regular meetings of political leaders as the European Union evolved in the early twenty-first century. The powers had also, in 1815, in alarm after the return of Napoleon, subscribed to Alexander I's Holy Alliance, which became the popular term for the collaboration of the European states in the congresses. The Holy Alliance, on the face of it a statement of Christian purpose and international concord, gradually became an alliance for the suppression of revolutionary and even liberal activity, following in that respect the trend of the governments that had created it.

The Congress of Aix-la-Chapelle, 1818

The first general postwar assemblage of the powers took place at the Congress of Aix-la-Chapelle (or Aachen) in 1818. The principal item on the agenda was to withdraw the allied army of occupation from France. The French argued that Louis XVIII would

The "Peterloo massacre" of 1819 was condemned in this caricature by the English artist George Cruikshank. A peaceable crowd gathered in St. Peter's Fields, Manchester, to demand political reforms and repeal of the Corn Laws (which placed high tariffs on imported grains), but a militia of part-time soldiers opened fire on the protesters, causing numerous casualties. The British government responded by commending the soldiers and passing new restrictions on public meetings.

(©George Cruikshank/The Bridgeman Art Library/Getty Images)

never be popular in France so long as he was supported by a foreign army. The other powers, because they all wanted the French to accept the restored Bourbons, withdrew their military forces without disagreement. They arranged also to have private bankers take over the French reparations debt (the 700 million francs imposed by the second Treaty of Paris); the bankers paid the allied governments, and the French in due time paid the bankers.

Alexander's internationalism

Tsar Alexander was still the most advanced internationalist of the day. He suggested at Aix-la-Chapelle a kind of permanent European union and even proposed the maintenance of international military forces to safeguard recognized states against changes by violence. Governments if thus reassured against revolution, he argued, would more willingly grant constitutional and liberal reforms. But the others demurred, especially the British foreign minister Lord Castlereagh. The British declared themselves willing to make international commitments against specified contingencies, such as a revival of aggression on the part of France. But they would assume no obligations to act upon unforeseeable future events. They reserved the right of independent judgment in foreign policy.

Concretely, the congress addressed itself to the problems of the Atlantic slave trade and of the recurring attacks on commercial shipping by Barbary pirates in the Mediterranean Sea. It was unanimously agreed that both should be suppressed. (Britain had abolished the slave trade within the British Empire in 1807.) To suppress the slave trade and piracy, however, required strong naval forces, which only the British possessed in adequate amount, and it meant also that naval captains must be authorized to stop and search vessels at sea. The Continental states, always touchy on the subject of British sea power, refused to countenance any such uses of the British fleet. They feared for the freedom of the seas. As for the British, they would not even discuss placing British warships in an international naval pool or putting British squadrons under the authority of an international body. Nothing therefore was done; the slave trade continued in much of the Atlantic world, booming illicitly with the endless demand for cotton and other commodities; and the Barbary pirates were not removed from the Mediterranean until the French launched a colonizing invasion of Algeria in the early 1830s and took military control of this region along the North African coast. The growth of international institutions was therefore blocked by the separate interests of the sovereign states.

Revolution in Southern Europe: The Congress of Troppau, 1820

Scarcely had the Congress of Aix-la-Chapelle disbanded when revolutionary agitation came to a crisis in southern Europe. It was not that revolutionary or liberal sentiment was stronger here than in the north, but rather that the anti-revolutionary governments of Spain, Naples, and the Ottoman Empire, were more inefficient and disorganized. Many of the revolutionaries were hardly more than middle-class liberals; indeed, the Spaniards, as we have noted, were the first to use the word "liberal" in this modern political sense. Many of them had at first accepted the Napoleonic occupation of Spain as a progressive development but had then turned against it and proclaimed a new constitution in 1812, modeled on the French revolutionary constitution of 1789–1791. After Napoleon's final defeat they attempted to force the restored Bourbon kings of Spain and Naples to adopt this constitution of 1812.

Revolution in Spain and Naples

In 1820 the governments of both Spain and Naples collapsed with remarkable ease before the demonstrations of revolutionaries. The kings of both countries reluctantly took oaths to the Spanish constitution of 1812. But Metternich saw the insurrections as the first symptoms of a revolutionary seizure against which Europe should be quarantined. It was a fact that revolutionary agitation was international, easily leaping across frontiers, because of the operations of secret societies and of political exiles and because in any case the same ideas had spread in all countries after the French Revolution. Metternich considered Italy in particular to be within the legitimate sphere of influence of the Austrian Empire. He therefore called a meeting of the Great Powers at Troppau in the Austrian-controlled region in Silesia, hoping to use the authority of an international congress to put down the revolution in Naples. The governments of Great Britain and France, not eager to play Austria's game, sent only observers to the congress. Metternich's main problem was, as usual, Alexander. What would be the attitude of the liberal tsar, the friend and patron of constitutions, toward the idea of a constitutional monarchy in Naples? At an inn in Troppau Metternich and Alexander met alone, and there held a momentous interview over the teacups. Metternich reviewed the horrors of revolutionism, the unwisdom of granting any concessions lest revolutionaries be encouraged. Alexander was already somewhat disillusioned by the ungrateful feelings of the Poles, and the upheaval in Naples posed a new threat to his view of royal authority. He had always believed that constitutions should be granted by legitimate sovereigns, not extorted from them by revolutionaries, as had happened in Naples. He allowed himself to be persuaded by Metternich. He declared that he had always been wrong and that Metternich had always been right; and he announced himself ready to follow Metternich's political judgment.

Thus fortified, Metternich drew up a document, the protocol of Troppau, for consideration and acceptance by the five Great Powers. It held that all recognized European states should be protected by collective international action, in the interests of general peace and stability, from internal changes brought about by force. It was a statement of collective security against revolution. Neither France nor Great Britain accepted it. The British Tories did not object to the repression of the revolution in Naples, but they rejected the principle of a binding international collaboration. Metternich could get only Russia and Prussia to endorse his protocol, in addition to Austria. These three, acting as the Congress of Troppau, authorized Metternich to dispatch an Austrian army into Naples. He did so; the Neapolitan revolutionaries were arrested or put to flight; the incompetent and brutal Ferdinand I was restored as "absolute" king; the demon of revolution was

	seemingly exorcised. But the Congress of Troppau, ostensibly a
A gap opens between East and West	Europewide international body, had in effect functioned as an antirevolutionary alliance of Austria, Russia, and Prussia. A gap had opened between the three Eastern autocracies and the two Western powers— even when the latter consisted of Tories and Bourbons.

Spain and the Middle East: The Congress of Verona, 1822

Thousands of revolutionaries and liberals fled from the political terror raging in Italy. Many went to Spain, now dreaded by conservatives as the main seat of revolutionary infection. The Middle East also seemed about to ignite in conflagration. Alexander Ypsilanti, a Greek who had spent his adult life in the military service of Russia, in 1821 led a band of armed followers from Russia into Romania (then still a part of Ottoman Turkey), hoping that all Greeks and pro-Greeks in the Ottoman Empire would join him. He expected Russian support, because Russia had long wanted to use Greek Christians in a campaign to weaken its imperial rival in the regions around the Black Sea. The possibility of an Ottoman Turkish Empire converted into a Greek empire and dependent on Russia was naturally unpleasant to Metternich. To deal with all these matters an international congress convened at Verona in 1822.

Alexander, in shifting from liberal to reactionary views, had not changed his belief in the need for concerted international action. Had pure power politics determined his

	decisions, he would doubtless have favored Ypsilanti's Grecophile
Ypsilanti refused support	revolution. But he stood by the principle of international solidarity against revolutionary violence. He refused to support Ypsilanti, who found less enthusiasm for Greek culture among the Romanians and Balkan peoples than he had expected and was soon defeated by the

Turks. As for intervention to repress the uprising in Greece itself, the question did not arise, because the Ottoman government proved quite able for a time to handle the matter without assistance.

The question of the revolution in Spain was settled by foreign intervention. The Bourbon regime in France had no taste for a Spain in which revolutionaries, republicans, political exiles, and members of secret societies might be harbored. The French government proposed to the Congress of Verona that it be authorized to dispatch an army across the Pyrenees. The Congress welcomed the offer, and despite many dire predictions of ruin, arising from memories of Napoleon's Spanish disaster, a French army of 200,000 men moved into Spain in 1823. The campaign proved to be a military promenade through a cheering country. Spanish liberals, constitutionalists, or revolutionaries were a helpless minority. The mass of the people saw the invasion as a deliverance from radicals and heretics and as a welcome restoration of church and king. Ferdinand VII, unscrupulous and narrow-minded, repudiated his constitutional oath and let the most reactionary Spaniards have their way. The revolutionaries were savagely persecuted, exiled, or jailed.

The French invade Spain

Latin American Independence

The Napoleonic wars and later political disturbances in Europe had wide-ranging repercussions in all parts of America, where the European powers still controlled most of their long-held colonial empires. While Great Britain was engaged against Napoleon, the United States fought the inconclusive War of 1812 against its former mother country, and a few years later, after minor military operations, obtained the cession of Florida from Spain. During these same years, new movements for national independence emerged in Latin America and used the turmoil in Europe as an opportunity to break free from the weakening Portuguese and Spanish empires. The Portuguese royal family, to escape Napoleon, had taken refuge in its Brazilian Empire, becoming the only European monarchy ever to be based in one of its colonies. When the dynasty was restored to power at Lisbon, however, one of its members refused to leave Brazil, which emerged as a new "empire" independent of Portugal; in 1889 the imperial regime gave way to a new Brazilian republic.

Spanish America reached over the enormous area from San Francisco to Buenos Aires. Here, too, the thought of the Enlightenment, the news of the American and French revolutions, the Napoleonic occupation of Spain, the French imprisonment of the Spanish king, and the eventual restoration in 1814 of the Bourbon Ferdinand VII to the Spanish throne all had their effects. The British had been commercially active in Spanish America for over a century, and during the Napoleonic wars they had increased their exports to the Spanish Empire by twentyfold. There were thus business interests in Spanish America that resisted any return to the old Spanish imperial system of trade controls. More fundamental was the political and social resentment that Creoles felt for the peninsulars. The Creoles were the white population of Spanish descent born in America, and they found their ambitions blocked by the peninsulars who were sent out from Spain to occupy the highest offices in the empire. In many places most of the people were native Indians or mestizos of mixed Spanish and Indian origin, often living in depressed economic conditions and far from the capital cities. The movement for independence in most of Latin America therefore lacked the more widespread popular character that it had developed in the British colonies that became the United States. It was mainly led by Creoles who were active in municipal governments in the towns, though to achieve their political goals the Creole leaders sometimes recruited supporters from other racial and social groups. At times, the movement for independence also recruited some very conservative elements among large landowners and high churchmen. But the important leaders, such as Simón Bolívar and José de San Martín, were men who had spent years in Europe and preferred the new constitutional principles of republicanism. In the end, despite their success in gaining independence, they were generally unable to realize their other political aspirations for their new countries. The dissensions that long continued to afflict Spanish America were all present within the independence movement itself.

Motives for revolt

Simón Bolívar (1783–1830) was known as "The Liberator" for his leadership of the South American revolutionary movements. He had lived in Europe, where he was strongly influenced by the political ideas of the French Revolution. Although his revolutionary campaigns secured the independence of several new nations, Bolívar's attempts to establish stable, constitutional governments were generally stymied during the 1820s.
(©Hulton Archive/Getty Images)

Because of its vast extent, over 6,000 miles interrupted by mountain barriers, there could be less unity in the liberation of Spanish America than had been possible, however difficult, in the North American rebellion against England. There could be no Continental Congress such as had met in Philadelphia in 1774. Revolts took place separately within the great vice-royalties: New Spain (Mexico), New Granada (Colombia and Venezuela), Peru (including Ecuador and most of Bolivia and Chile), and La Plata (Argentina, with claims over what are now Uruguay and Paraguay).

The first revolts were against Joseph Bonaparte after Napoleon made him king of Spain in 1808. The rebels actually began their new political movements by proclaiming their loyalty to the deposed Ferdinand VII, who, however, when restored in 1814, refused to make any concessions to American demands, so that revolutionary sentiment turned against him also. There followed a series of disconnected struggles between those fighting for independence (with or without much internal change) and combinations of officials, army officers, landowners, and churchmen who remained loyal to the Spanish crown. Bolívar became the liberator of Venezuela and Colombia. San Martín became the liberator of Argentina and Chile, and both combined in the liberation of Peru. In Mexico, by way of exception, there was a true mass rising of Indians and mestizos, which was put down by the middle- and upper-class Creole leaders. This conservative repression of a more popular revolutionary movement led to a long period of turmoil in the newly independent Mexican state, but Mexico was also the first postcolonial nation after Haiti to abolish slavery (1829); and it was by no means the only postcolonial society to face the problems of internal conflicts, violence, or civil war. The United States soon plunged into its own bitter civil war because of disputes over slavery and other divisive political problems. Meanwhile, much of Spanish America struggled with shifting national boundaries, regional conflicts, attempted conquests, and various secessions. The political map of South and Central America did not settle into its present form until later in the nineteenth century. The transition from European colonial systems to the modern national states of the Americas was therefore often as complicated or as violent as the later postcolonial and national transitions out of the twentieth-century European empires in Asia and Africa.

In addition to the recurring conflicts among themselves, the emerging Latin American nations remained vulnerable to the imperial interventions of outside powers. Let us return to the congress of European powers meeting in Verona in 1822. At the very time when a French army suppressed the revolution in Spain, the revolutionaries in Spanish America were declaring their independence. At Verona, Tsar Alexander urged the Congress to mediate between Spain and its colonies. This was a euphemistic way of suggesting military intervention in Spanish America, following the principle of repressing revolutions that had been announced at Troppau. The British objected. Even the Tory government favored revolutions that might break up the Spanish Empire into independent states, with which free trade treaties might be negotiated. Without at least benevolent neutrality from the British fleet no armed force could sail to America. The Spanish Americans therefore maintained their independence, thanks in part to the transatlantic influence of British sea power.

British favor Spanish-American independence

The new republics also received strong moral support from the United States, which now declared its opposition to European colonial interventions in the Americas. In December 1823 President James Monroe, in a message to Congress, announced the "Monroe Doctrine." It stated that attempts by European powers to return parts of America to colonial status would be viewed as an unfriendly act by the United States. The British foreign minister George Canning (who had just succeeded Castlereagh) had at first proposed a joint statement by Great Britain and the United States against the eastern European powers on the Spanish-American question. President Monroe, at the advice of his secretary of state, John Quincy Adams, decided instead to make a unilateral statement in the form of a message to Congress. They intended to aim their "doctrine" at Great Britain as well as the Continental states, because Britain, with its command of the sea, was in fact the only European power that could actually threaten the independence of American states at this time. Canning, having no such threats in mind, and concerned more with the Congress of Verona, accepted the new international assertiveness from the United States. The Monroe Doctrine, at its inception, was thus a kind of counterblast to the Metternich doctrine of the protocol of Troppau. Where the latter announced a European principle of intervention against revolutions, the Monroe Doctrine announced that revolutions in America, if they resulted in regimes recognized by the United States, were outside the attention or control of European powers. In any case, the efficacy of the Monroe Doctrine long depended on the tacit cooperation of the British fleet.

The Monroe Doctrine

Over 300 years of European colonial empires in America thus came to an end, with few exceptions, in the half-century after 1776. One exception was Canada, where membership in the British Empire was voluntary, at least for the English-speaking inhabitants, and where both the English and French Canadians resisted threats of annexation by the United States. The other exceptions were in the West Indies, where Haiti was independent, but where the smaller islands remained British, French, or Dutch; and the large islands of Cuba and Puerto Rico remained Spanish until the United States expanded its own imperial ambitions in the Spanish-American War of 1898.

The End of the Congress System

After the Congress of Verona no more such meetings were held. The attempt at a formal international regulation of European affairs was given up. In the broadest retrospect, the congresses failed to make progress toward an international order because, especially after Alexander's conversion to Metternich's conservatism, they came to stand for nothing except preservation of the status quo. They made no attempt at accommodation with the new forces that were shaping Europe, so they could not evolve into a modern transnational system for managing conflicts or social change. It was not the policy of these congresses to forestall revolution by demanding that governments institute reforms. They simply repressed or punished all revolutionary agitation. They propped up governments that could not stand on their own feet.

In any case the congresses never succeeded in subordinating the separate interests of the Great Powers. Perhaps Alexander's repudiation of Ypsilanti was a sacrifice of Russian advantage to international principle; but when the Austrian government intervened to crush the revolution in Naples, and when the French government crushed the revolution in Spain, though in both cases they acted with an international mandate, each was really promoting what it conceived to be its own interests. The interest of Great Britain was to pull away from the system entirely and to stand aloof from permanent international commitments. British leaders such as Castlereagh and Canning sought to preserve the free exercise of sea power and foreign policy, and they were more willing to take a benevolent view toward revolution in other countries. Because France gradually pulled away also, the

Liberalism advances

Holy Alliance became no more than a counterrevolutionary league of the three East European autocracies. The cause of liberalism in Europe was thus advanced by the collapse of this highly conservative international system. At the same time, however, the collapse of this international system opened the way to the uncontrolled nationalism of the sovereign states. "Things are getting back to a wholesome state again," wrote George Canning in 1822. "Every nation for itself and God for us all!"

Russia: The Decembrist Revolt, 1825

Alexander I, "the man who defeated Napoleon," the ruler who had led his armies from Moscow to Paris, who had frightened European diplomats by the Russian shadow that he threw over the Continent, and who yet in his way had been the great pillar of constitutional liberalism and international order, died in 1825. His death was the signal for revolution in Russia. Officers of the Russian army, during the campaigns of 1812–1815 in Europe, had become acquainted with many unsettling ideas. Secret societies were formed even in the Russian officer corps; their members held all sorts of conflicting ideas, some wanting a constitutional tsardom in Russia, some demanding a republic, some even dreaming of an emancipation of the serfs. When Alexander died it was for a time uncertain which of his two brothers, Constantine or Nicholas, should succeed him. The restless coteries in the army preferred Constantine, who was the older brother and who was thought to be more favorable to innovations in the state. In December 1825 they proclaimed Constantine at St. Petersburg, having their soldiers shout "Constantine and Constitution!"

Constantine and Nicholas

But the fact was that Constantine had already renounced his claims in favor of Nicholas, who was thus the rightful heir. The uprising, known as the Decembrist revolt, was soon put down. Five of the mutinous officers were hanged; many others were condemned to forced labor or interned in Siberia. The Decembrist revolt was the first manifestation of the modern revolutionary movement in Russia—of a revolutionary movement inspired by an ideological program, as distinguished from the elemental mass upheavals of Pugachev or Stephen Razin in earlier times. But the immediate effect of the Decembrist revolt was to clamp repression upon Russia more firmly. Nicholas I (1825–1855) maintained an unconditional and despotic autocracy.

Ten years after the defeat of Napoleon the new forces issuing from the French Revolution seemed to be routed, and reaction, repression, and political immobility seemed to prevail everywhere in Europe. A massive, conservative dam had sprung some political and social leaks, but during most of the 1820s it seemed to be containing the flood.

56. THE BREAKTHROUGH OF LIBERALISM IN THE WEST: REVOLUTIONS OF 1830–1832

The reactionary dam broke open in 1830, and in western Europe the stream thereafter never stopped. The seepage, indeed, had already begun. By 1825 Spanish America was independent; the British and the French had pulled away from the congress system; and the Greek nationalist movement against the Turks had become a popular liberal cause across all of western Europe.

With the defeat of Ypsilanti in 1821 the Greek nationalists turned somewhat away from the idea of a neo-Greek empire and began promoting the idea of independence for Greece proper, the islands and peninsulas where Greek was the predominant language. Tsar Nicholas was more willing than Alexander to assist this movement. The governments of Great Britain and France were not inclined to let Russia stand as the only champion of Balkan peoples. Moreover, liberals in the West thought of the embattled Greeks as ancient Athenians fighting the modern despotism of an unenlightened Ottoman Turkish Empire.

The result of these converging interests and ideas was a joint Anglo-French-Russian naval intervention, which destroyed the Turkish fleet off the Greek coast at Navarino Bay in 1827. Russia again, as often in the past, sent armies into the Balkans. A Russo-Turkish war and a great Middle Eastern crisis followed, in the course of which the rival powers agreed in 1829 to recognize Greece as an independent kingdom. The Balkan states of Serbia, Wallachia, and Moldavia were also recognized as autonomous principalities within the badly shaken Ottoman Empire (see map p. 675). From the same crisis Egypt emerged as an autonomous region under Mehemet Ali and in time became a center of Arabic nationalism, which reduced Ottoman power in the south just as Balkan nationalism did in the north.

France, 1824–1830: The July Revolution, 1830

It was in 1830, beginning in France, that a new wave of revolutionary upheavals began and the wall of reaction really collapsed. The post-Napoleonic political arrangements broke down in much of western and eastern Europe. Charles X became king of France in 1824. In the next year the legislative chambers voted an indemnity, in the form of perpetual annuities totaling 30 million francs a year, to those who as émigrés thirty-odd years before had lost their property to confiscations by the revolutionary state. Catholic clergy began to take over classrooms in the schools. A law pronounced the death penalty for sacrilege committed in church buildings. But the France of the restored Bourbons still had a mostly free public sphere for political and cultural debates; and against these apparent efforts to revive the Old Regime a strong opposition developed in the newspapers and in the chambers. In March 1830 the Chamber of Deputies, in which the bankers Laffitte and Casimier-Périer led the "leftist" opposition, passed a vote of no confidence in the government. The king, as was his legal right, dissolved the Chamber and called for new elections. The elections produced clear majorities for those who repudiated the king's policies. He replied on July 26, 1830, with four ordinances issued on his own authority. One dissolved the newly elected Chamber before it had ever met; another imposed censorship on the press; the third so amended the suffrage as to reduce the voting power of bankers, merchants, and industrialists and to concentrate it in the hands of the old-fashioned aristocracy; the fourth called for an election on the new basis.

These July Ordinances provoked on the very next day the July Revolution. The bourgeois liberals were enraged by their brazen ouster from political life. But it was the republicans—the nucleus of revolutionary workers, students, and intelligentsia in Paris—who actually moved. For three days, from July 27 to 29, barricades were erected in the city, behind which a

| swarming populace defied the army and the police. Some of the protestors |
| **Charles X abdicates** |

swarming populace defied the army and the police. Some of the protestors were killed, but most of the army refused to fire. Charles X, in no mood to be made captive by a revolution like his long-dead brother Louis XVI, precipitately abdicated and headed for England.

A few of the leaders now wished to proclaim a democratic republic. Working people hoped for better conditions of employment. The political liberals, however, supported by bankers, industrialists, various journalists, and intellectuals, had other aims. They had been satisfied in general with the constitutional charter of 1814; it was only to the policies and personnel of the government that they had objected, and they wished now to continue with constitutional monarchy, somewhat liberalized, and with a king whom they could trust. A solution to the deadlock was found by Lafayette, the aging hero of the American and the French revolutions, who became commander of the reorganized National Guard and a popular symbol of national unity. Lafayette brought the Duke of Orleans onto the balcony of the Paris Hôtel de Ville, embraced him before a great concourse of people, and offered him as the answer to France's need. The duke was a collateral relative of the Bourbons; he had also, as a young man, served in the republican army of 1792 and had later lived for a time as an exile in the United States. The militant republicans accepted him, willing to see what would develop; and the Chamber of Deputies on August 7 offered him the throne, on condition that he observe faithfully the constitutional charter of 1814. He reigned, until 1848, under the title of Louis Philippe, king of the French.

The regime of Louis Philippe, called the Orléanist, bourgeois, or

The July Monarchy

July Monarchy, was viewed very differently by different groups in France and in Europe. To the other states of Europe and to the clergy and legitimists within France, it seemed shockingly revolutionary. The new king owed his throne to an insurrection, to a bargain made with republicans, and to promises made to the Chamber of Deputies. He called himself not king of France but king of the French, and he flew the tricolor flag of the Revolution in place of the Bourbon lily. He cultivated a popular manner, wore sober dark clothing (the ancestor of the modern business suit), and carried an umbrella. Though in private he worked stubbornly to maintain his royal position, in public he adhered scrupulously to the constitution.

The constitution remained substantially what it had been in 1814. The main political change was one of tone; there would be no more absolutism, with its notion that constitutional guarantees could be abrogated by a reigning prince. Legally the main change was that the Chamber of Peers ceased to be hereditary, to the chagrin of the old nobility, and that the Chamber of Deputies was to be elected by a somewhat enlarged body of voters. Where before 1830 there had been 100,000 voters, there were now about 200,000. The right to vote was still based on the ownership of a considerable quantity of real estate. About one-thirtieth of the adult male population (the top thirtieth in the possession of real property) now elected the Chamber of Deputies. The beneficiaries of the new system were the upper bourgeoisie—the bankers, merchants, and industrialists. The big property owners constituted the *pays légal,* the "legal country," and to them the July Monarchy was the consummation and stopping place of political progress. To others, and especially to the radical democrats, it proved as the years passed to be a disillusionment and an annoyance to which they would respond with new forms of political agitation.

Revolutions of 1830: Belgium and Poland

The immediate effect of the three-day Paris revolution of 1830 was to set off a series of similar explosions throughout Europe, most notably in Belgium and Poland. These in turn, coming after the collapse of the Bourbons in France, brought the whole peace settlement of 1815 into jeopardy. It will be recalled that the Congress of Vienna had joined Belgium with the Dutch Netherlands to create a strong buffer state against a resurgent France and had also done what it could to prevent direct Russian intervention in central Europe by way of Poland. Both these arrangements were now undone.

The Dutch-Belgium union proved economically beneficial, for Belgian industry complemented the commercial and shipping activity of the Dutch, but politically it worked poorly, especially because the Dutch king had absolutist and centralizing ideas. The Belgians, though | *Rejection of the Dutch-Belgian union*

they had never been independent, had always stood stiffly for their local liberties under former Austrian rulers (and Spanish before them); now they did the same against the Dutch. The Catholic Belgians disliked Dutch Protestantism; those Belgians who spoke French (the Walloons) objected to regulations requiring the use of Dutch. About a month after the July Revolution in Paris disturbances broke out in Brussels. The leaders asked only for local Belgian self-government, but when the king took arms against them, they went on to proclaim political independence. A Belgian National Assembly met and drafted a constitution.

Nicholas of Russia wished to send troops to stamp out the Belgian uprising. But he could not get his forces safely through Poland. In Poland, too, in 1830, a revolution broke out. The Polish nationalists | *Revolution in Poland*

saw in the fall of the French Bourbons a timely moment for them to strike. They objected also to the appearance of Russian troops bound presumably to suppress freedom in western Europe. One incident led to another, until in January 1831 the Polish diet proclaimed the dethronement of the Polish king (i.e., Nicholas), who thereupon sent in a large army. The Poles, outnumbered and divided among themselves, could not put up a successful resistance. They obtained no support from the West. The British government was unsettled by agitation at home. The French government, newly installed under Louis Philippe, had no wish to appear disturbingly revolutionary, and in any case feared the Polish agents who sought its backing as international firebrands and republicans. The Polish revolution was therefore crushed. Congress Poland disappeared; its constitution was abrogated, and it was merged into the Russian Empire. Thousands of Polish exiles settled in western Europe, where they became familiar figures in republican circles. In Poland the engines of repression rolled. The tsar's government sent thousands of Poles to Siberia, began to

LIBERTY LEADING THE PEOPLE
by Eugène Delacroix (French, 1798–1863)

Delacroix, a founder of the romantic school in nineteenth-century French art, painted this picture soon after the July Revolution in Paris in 1830. It well illustrates the idealistic conception of revolution that prevailed among revolutionaries before 1848. Revolution is shown as a noble and moral act on behalf of the abstract ideals of liberty. The figures express determination and courage but show no sign of hatred or even anger. They are not a class; they are the people, affirming the rights of man. Liberty, holding the tricolor aloft, is a composed and even rational goddess.

(©Christophel Fine Art/Getty Images)

Russify the eastern border, and closed the universities of Warsaw and Vilna. Because the Polish revolution prevented the tsar from moving toward a possible intervention in Belgium, it may be said that the sacrifice of the Poles contributed to the success of the West European revolution of 1830, as it had to that of the French Revolution of 1789–1795.

It was true enough, as Nicholas maintained, that an independent Belgium presented new international problems. Belgium for 20 years before 1815 had been part of France. A few Belgians now favored reunion with it, and in France the republican left, which regarded the Vienna treaty as an insult to the French nation, saw an opportunity to win back this first and dearest conquest of the First Republic. In 1831, by a small majority, the Belgian National Assembly elected as their king the son of Louis Philippe, who, however, not wishing trouble with the British, forbade his son to accept it. The Belgians thereupon elected Leopold of Saxe-Coburg, a German princeling who had married into the British royal family and become a British subject. He was in fact the uncle of a

12-year-old girl who was to be Queen Victoria. The British negotiated with Talleyrand, sent over by the French government (it was his last public service); and the result was a treaty setting up Belgium as a perpetually neutral state, incapable of forming alliances and guaranteed against invasion by all five of the Great Powers. The aim intended by the Treaty of Vienna, to prevent the annexation of Belgium to France, was thus again realized in a new way. Internally Belgium settled down to a stable parliamentary system, somewhat more democratic than the July Monarchy in France but fundamentally offering the same type of bourgeois and liberal rule.

Reform in Great Britain

The three-day Paris revolution of 1830 had direct repercussions across the Channel. The quick results following on working-class insurrection gave radical leaders in England the idea that threats of violence might be useful. On the other hand, the ease and speed with which the French bourgeoisie gained the upper hand reassured the British middle classes, who concluded that they might unsparingly embarrass the government without courting a mass upheaval.

    The Tory regime in England had in fact already begun to loosen up. A group of more liberal Tory leaders came forward in the 1820s, notably George Canning, the foreign minister, and Robert Peel, son of one of the first cotton manufacturers. This group was sensitive to the needs of British business and to the liberal doctrines of free trade. They reduced tariffs and liberalized the old Navigation Acts, permitting British colonies to trade with countries other than Britain. The Liberal Tories also undermined the legal position of the Church of England, forwarding the conception of a secular state, though such was hardly their purpose. They repealed the old laws (which dated from the seventeenth century) forbidding dissenting Protestants to hold public office except through a legal fiction by which they pretended to be Anglicans. They even allowed the Test Act of 1673 to be repealed and Catholic Emancipation to be adopted. Catholics in Great Britain and Ireland received the same rights as others. Capital punishment was abolished for about a hundred offenses. A professional police force was introduced in place of the old-fashioned and ineffectual local constables. (It is after Robert Peel that London policemen came to be called "bobbies.") The new police were expected to handle protest meetings, angry crowds, or occasional riots without having to call for military assistance.

The Tory regime

    Despite their willingness to introduce moderate reforms, the Liberal Tories could not challenge or change the two key pillars of Tory power. They could not question the Corn Laws, and they could not change the elite membership in the House of Commons. By the Corn Laws, which set the tariff on imported grain, a tariff raised to new heights in 1815, the gentlemen of England protected their rent rolls; and by the existing structure of the House of Commons they governed the country, expecting the working class and the business interests to look to them as natural leaders.

    Never in 500 years of its history had the Commons been so unrepresentative. No new borough had been created since the Revolution of 1688. The boroughs, or urban centers having the right to elect members of Parliament, were heavily concentrated in southern England. Although the Industrial Revolution was shifting population noticeably to the north, the new factory towns were not represented in Parliament. Rural areas with small populations thus had far more political influence than the densely populated industrial cities. In a few boroughs real elections took place, but in some of them it was the town

Problems of representation

corporation, and in others the owners of certain pieces of real estate, that had the right to name members of Parliament. Many boroughs were entirely dominated by influential persons called borough-mongers by their critics. As for the rural districts, the "forty-shilling freeholders" chose two members of Parliament for each county, in a convivial assembly much influenced by the gentlefolk. It was estimated about 1820 that fewer than 500 men, most of them members of the House of Lords, really selected a majority of the House of Commons.

Some two dozen bills to reform the voting system for the House of Commons were introduced in the half-century preceding 1830. They all failed to pass. In 1830, after the Paris revolution, the minority Whig party again raised the issue of electoral reform. The Tory prime minister, the Duke of Wellington, the victor of Waterloo and a most extreme conservative, so immoderately defended the existing system that he lost the confidence even of some of his own followers. The existing methods of election in England, he declared, were more perfect than any that human intelligence could contrive at a single stroke. After this outburst a Whig ministry took over the government. It introduced a reform bill. The House of Commons rejected it. The Whig ministry thereupon resigned, but the Tories, fearing popular violence, refused to take the responsibility for forming a cabinet. The Whigs resumed office and again introduced their reform bill. This time it passed the Commons but failed in the House of Lords. An angry roar went up over the country. Crowds milled in the London streets, rioters for several days were in control at Bristol, and violent protesters destroyed property in other English towns. Only the passage of the reform bill, it seemed, could prevent an actual revolution. Using this argument, the Whigs got the king to promise to create enough new peers to change the majority in the House of Lords. The Lords yielded rather than be swamped, and in April 1832 the bill became law.

The Reform Bill of 1832

The Reform Bill of 1832 was a very English measure. It adapted the traditional English system rather than the newer ideas of the French Revolution. On the Continent, constitutional political systems in countries such as France rested on the idea that each representative should represent roughly the same number of voters and that voters should qualify to vote by a uniform qualification, usually the payment of a stated amount of property taxes. The British held to the idea that members of the House of Commons represented boroughs and counties, in general without regard to size of population (with exceptions). In other words, no attempt was made to create equal electoral districts, and the vote was still distributed in the reformed boroughs and counties on the basis of economic status, reliability, and permanence rather than on the basis of population. The total effect on the size of the electorate was to raise the number of voters in the British Isles from about 500,000 to about 813,000.

The most important change was not the increased size of the electorate but its redistribution by region and by class. The Reform Bill reallocated the seats in the House of Commons, moving more than 140 parliamentary seats from small, older boroughs to the new industrial towns. Many previously excluded middle-class men in the growing northern cities gained the right to vote—factory owners and businessmen and their principal employees, doctors, lawyers, brokers, merchants, and newspaper people, relatives and connections of the well-to-do.

The ambiguous impact of reform

The Reform Bill of 1832 was more sweeping than the Whigs would have favored except for their fear of revolution. Whether Great Britain in 1830 was in danger of any real revolution can never be known. A distressed mass of workers was led by an irate manufacturing class that was unwilling to tolerate any longer its exclusion from political life, yet neither the workers nor the industrialists turned toward a violent revolution. The reason probably lies first of all in the existence of the historic institution of Parliament, which, erratic though it was before the Reform Bill, provided the means by which social changes could be legally accomplished and continued, in principle, to enjoy universal respect. Conservatives, driven to the wall, would yield; they could allow a revision of the suffrage because they could expect to remain themselves in public life. Radicals, using enough violence to scare the established interest, did not thereafter face a blank wall; they could expect, once the breach was made, to widen the suffrage, further democratize Parliament, and advance their social and economic program by orderly legislation.

Britain after 1832

But the British Reform Bill of 1832 was in its way a political revolution. The new business interests, created by industrialization, now took their place alongside the old aristocracy in the governing elite of the country. The aristocratic Whigs who had carried the Reform Bill gradually merged with formerly radical industrialists and with a few Liberal Tories to form the new Liberal Party. The main body of the Tories, joined by a few old Whigs and even a few former radicals, gradually turned into the Conservative Party. These two parties alternated in power at short intervals from 1832 to the First World War, this being the classic period in Great Britain of the Liberal-Conservative two-party system and a period in which numerous political and social reforms would be enacted.

In 1833 slavery was abolished in the British Empire. In 1834 a new Poor Law was adopted. In 1835 the Municipal Corporations Act, second only to the Reform Bill in basic importance, modernized the local government of English cities; it broke up the old local oli-

Social and political reforms

garchies and brought in uniform electoral and administrative machinery, enabling city dwellers to grapple more effectively with the problems of urban life. In 1836 the House of Commons allowed the newspapers to report how its members voted—a democratizing step toward more publicity of government proceedings. Meanwhile an ecclesiastical commission reviewed the affairs of the Church of England; financial and administrative irregularities were corrected, together with the grosser inequalities between the income of upper and lower clergy, all of which had long made the church a kind of closed preserve for the landed gentry.

The conservative Tories, thus assaulted in their traditional strongholds of local government and the established church, carried a counteroffensive into the strongholds of the new liberal manufacturing class, namely, the factories and the mines. Tories whose own wealth still depended on ownership of land became champions of the indus-

The Tory counteroffensive

trial workers. Landed gentlemen, of whom the most famous was Lord Ashley, later seventh Earl of Shaftesbury, took the lead in publicizing the social evils of a rapid and even ruthless industrialization. They received some support from a few humanitarian industrialists; indeed, the early legislation tended to follow practices already established by the best or strongest business firms. A Factory Act of 1833 forbade the labor of children less than 9 years old in the textile mills. It was the first effective legislation on child labor because it provided for paid inspectors and procedures for enforcement. An act of 1842 initiated significant regulation in the coal mines; the employment underground of women and girls, and of boys under 10, was forbidden.

CHRONOLOGY OF NOTABLE EVENTS, 1780–1869

1780s	Mechanical spinning of cotton spreads across England
1792	Mary Wollstonecraft publishes *A Vindication of the Rights of Woman*
1807	Robert Fulton uses the steam engine to propel river boats
1819	"Peterloo massacre" suppresses protesting English workers in Manchester
1819	Metternich's "Carlsbad Decrees" suppress the German nationalist movement
1820	Congress of Troppau calls for international action against all revolutions
1823	Monroe Doctrine opposes European intervention in Latin America
1825	Decembrist Revolt of military officers is put down in Russia
1829	Steam locomotive is tested safely in England
1830	July Revolution in France forces abdication of Charles X; Louis-Philippe becomes "king of the French"
1831	Russia suppresses national movement in Poland
1832	Reform Bill widens British suffrage; alters representation in Parliament
1839	Louis Blanc's *The Organization of Work* promotes new socialist ideas
1846	Repeal of Corn Laws marks ascendancy of British industrial interests
1869	John Stuart Mill argues for women's rights in *The Subjection of Women*

The greatest victory of the working classes came in 1847 with the Ten Hours Act, which limited the labor of women and children in all industrial establishments to 10 hours a day. Thereafter men commonly worked only 10 hours also, because the work of men, women, and young people was too closely coordinated in factories for the men to work alone. The Liberal John Bright, Quaker and cotton magnate, called the Ten Hours Act "a delusion practiced on the working classes." Many such industrialists believed that regulation of the hours of labor was contrary to the accepted principles of laissez-faire, economic law, the free market, freedom of trade, and individual liberty for employer and worker. Yet the Ten Hours Act stood, and British industry continued to prosper.

The Anti-Corn Law League

Gathering their strength, the Whig-liberal-radical combination established in 1838 an Anti–Corn Law League. Wage earners objected to the Corn Laws because the tariff on grain imports kept up the price of food. Industrial employers also objected to them because, in keeping up food prices, they drove up wages and the cost of industrial production in England, thus working to England's disadvantage in the export trade. Defenders of the Corn Laws argued that protection of agriculture was necessary to maintain the natural landowning aristocracy of the country, but they also sometimes used nationalist economic arguments, affirming that Britain should preserve an economic balance between industry and farming and avoid an overdependence on imported food. The issue became a straight contest between the industrialists, acting with working-class support, and the aristocratic and predominantly Tory landowning interest. The Anti-Corn Law League, whose headquarters were at Manchester, operated like a modern political party. It had plenty of money, supplied by large donations from manufacturers and small ones from laboring people. It sent lecturers on tour, agitated in the newspapers, organized open-air mass meetings, and issued a stream of polemical pamphlets. The pressure proved irresistible and received a final impetus from a famine in Ireland. It was a Tory government, headed by Sir Robert Peel, which in 1846 yielded before so vociferous a demand.

The repeal of the Corn Laws in 1846 stands as a symbol of the change that had come over England. It showed the revolutionary consequences of the Reform Bill of 1832. Industry was now a governing element in the country. Free trade was henceforth the rule. Great Britain, in return for the export of manufacturers, became deliberately dependent on imports for its very life. It was committed henceforth to a worldwide economic system in which tariffs would remain low or be abolished. The first to undergo the Industrial Revolution, possessing mechanical power and methods of mass production, the British could produce yarn and cloth, machine tools and railroad equipment, more efficiently and more cheaply than any other people. In Britain, the early industrial workshop of the world, people would pour increasingly into mine, factory, and city; live by selling manufactures, coal, shipping, and financial services to other people in far-flung global markets; and obtain raw cotton, rare ores, meat, cereals, and thousands of lesser but still vital necessities from the whole world in exchange. The welfare of Britain depended on the maintenance of a freely exchanging global economic system and, as always, on the British navy's control of the sea.

57.   TRIUMPH OF THE WEST EUROPEAN BOURGEOISIE

In general, the decades following 1830 may be thought of as a kind of golden age of the western European bourgeoisie, or what in English would be called the upper middle class. In the older meaning, in French, a *bourgeois* had been a townsperson who was not of the nobility but enjoyed an income from business, a profession, or the ownership of property. After the French Revolution, and even more after 1830, the word took on new meanings, not all of them consistent. Artists, literary people, and old-line aristocrats might disdain the bourgeois as a person of uncultivated tastes, supposedly interested only in making money. From another point of view, shared by social theorists and working-class leaders, the bourgeois was someone who could hire the labor of other people for business enterprises, recreational activities, or household service. In a word, the bourgeois was the employer. The nineteenth-century bourgeoisie and aristocracy tended to become more alike in their daily pursuits and style of life, and to draw income from the possession of income-producing property or capital. The bourgeoisie, formerly identified in contrast to the nobility, was now identified in contrast to the working class, that is, those whose whole income depended on daily labor in shops, offices, farms, factories, or mines.

The reigning liberal doctrine was the "stake in society" theory; those who govern should have something to lose. In the France of the July Monarchy (1830–1848), only about one adult male in 30 had the vote. In the Britain of the first Reform Bill (1832–1867), one man in eight could vote for a member of the House of Commons. In France only the most well-to-do were enfranchised; in Britain, virtually the whole middle class, which, however, long supported members of the aristocracy for the highest public positions. In Britain the continuation of the Tory landed interest in politics somewhat blunted the edge of capitalist and managerial rule, resulting in the passage of significant legislation for the protection of industrial labor. In France the aristocratic landed interest, already weaker and less public spirited than in England, lost most of its influence after the Revolution of 1830, and less was done to relieve the condition of labor.

"Stake in society" theory

The bourgeois age left its mark on Europe in many ways. For one thing, western Europe continued to accumulate capital and build up its industrial plant. National income was constantly rising, but a relatively small share went to the laboring class and a relatively large share went to owners of capital. This meant that less was spent on consumers' goods—housing, clothing, food, recreation—and that more was saved and available for reinvestment. New stock companies were constantly formed, and the law of corporations was amended, allowing for the extension of corporate enterprise to new fields. The factory system spread from Britain to the Continent and within Britain from the textile industry to other lines of production. The output of iron, a good index to economic advancement in this phase of industrialism, rose about 300 percent in Great Britain between 1830 and 1848 and about 65 percent in France between 1830 and 1845. (All the German states combined, at the latter date, produced about a tenth as much iron as Great Britain and less than half as much as France.) Railroad building began in earnest after 1840. In 1840 Samuel Cunard put four steamships into regular transatlantic service. Much capital was exported; as early as 1839 an American estimated that Europeans (mainly British) owned $200,000,000 worth of stocks in American companies. Such investments financed the purchase of British and other goods and helped to rivet together a world economic system, in which western Europe and especially England took the lead, with other regions remaining in a somewhat subordinate status.

The Frustration and Challenge of Labor

The bourgeois age had the effect also of estranging the world of labor. The state in Britain and France was as near as it has ever been to what Karl Marx was soon to call it—a committee of the bourgeois class. Republicans in France, radical democrats in Britain, felt cheated and imposed upon in the 1830s and 1840s. They had in each country forced through a virtual revolution by their insurrections and demonstrations and then in each country had been left without the vote. Some lost interest in representative institutions. Excluded from government, they were tempted to seek political ends through extragovernmental, which is to say revolutionary or utopian, channels. Social and economic reforms seemed to the average worker far more important, as a final aim, than mere governmental innovations. Workers were told by respected economists that they could not hope to change the fundamental processes of the economic system in their own favor. They were tempted, therefore, to destroy the system and to replace it utterly with some new system conceived mainly in the minds of thinkers. They were told by the Manchester School, and by its equivalent in France, that the income of labor was set by ineluctable natural laws, that it was best and indeed necessary for wages to remain low, and that the way to rise in the world was to get out of the laboring class altogether, by becoming the owner of a profitable business and leaving working people about where they were.

The labor market

The reigning doctrine emphasized the conception of a labor market. The worker sold labor; the employer bought it. The price of labor, or wage, was to be agreed upon by the two individual parties. The price would naturally fluctuate according to changes in supply and demand. When a great deal of a certain kind of labor was required, the wage would go up until new persons moved into the market offering more labor of this type, with the result that something like the old wage would again be established. When no labor was needed, none should be hired, and persons who could not sell labor might then subsist for a time by poor relief.

LE VENTRE LÉGISLATIF.

THE LEGISLATIVE BELLY
by Honoré Daumier (French, 1808–1879)

The French Revolution of 1830, romanticized at first by Delacroix and most European liberals, was followed by a period of moneymaking, economic development, and corruption, made famous by the novels of Honoré de Balzac and the graphic art of Daumier. It was also an era in which bourgeois social groups gained a more dominant position in French political culture, as Daumier suggests in this satirical portrait of self-satisfied legislators at the Chamber of Deputies in 1834. Daumier's images often criticized the self-serving public policies of the social and political elites who governed an increasingly commercialized French society.

(National Gallery of Art)

The new British Poor Law of 1834 was especially repugnant to the British working class. It corrected crying evils of the old poor laws that had left millions of people in habitual poverty but did nothing constructive to relieve productive workers suffering from the poverty of occasional or cyclical unemployment. The new law followed the stern precepts of the dismal science; its main principle was to safeguard the labor market by making relief more unpleasant than any job. It granted relief only to persons willing to enter a workhouse, or poorhouse; and in these establishments the sexes were segregated and life was in other ways made noticeably less attractive than in the outside world. The Poor Law thus viewed impoverished people with suspicion and imposed confinement on those who accepted its meager benefits. Workers condemned the law as an abomination. They called the workhouses "bastilles" and resented the whole conception of a labor market, in which labor was to be bought and sold (or remain unsold) like any other commodity. The fluctuating, cyclical labor market contributed to the social instability of working-class families and

The Poor Law of 1834

may also have created new tensions between women and men. Court records from early nineteenth-century England suggest that violent family disputes became more common when women earned significant portions of the working family's household income or found work more readily than their unemployed husbands; such situations challenged the traditional relations in English family life, though women almost always received lower wages than men.

In the long run the condition of the workers would gradually improve through an increase in productivity. Meanwhile the friends of the working class offered two means of escape. One was to improve the bargaining position of individual workers in the market. This led to the formation of labor unions that could represent whole groups of workers through collective bargaining with employers. Such unions, illegal in France, were barely legal in Great Britain after 1825, though it was still illegal in both countries to strike. The other means of escape was to repudiate the whole idea of a market economy and of the capitalist system. It was to conceive of a system in which goods were to be produced for use, not for sale; and in which working people should be compensated according to their need, not according to the requirements of an employer. This theory became the basis of most forms of nineteenth-century socialism.

Socialism and Chartism

Socialism emerged as one of the numerous early nineteenth-century "isms," but it only began to spread rapidly among the working classes after 1830. In France it blended with revolutionary republicanism. There was a revival of interest in the great Revolution and the democratic Republic of 1793. Cheap reprints of the writings of Robespierre began to circulate in the working-class quarters of Paris. Robespierre was now seen as a people's hero. The socialist Louis Blanc, for example, who in 1839 published his *Organization of Work* recommending the formation of social workshops, also wrote a long history of the French Revolution, in which he pointed out the egalitarian ideals that had inspired the National Convention in 1793. In Britain, as befitted the different political history of the country, socialistic ideas blended in with the wider movement for further parliamentary reform. This was advanced by the working-class group known as the Chartists, from the People's Charter that they drafted in 1838.

Chartism was far more of a mass movement than the French socialism of the day. Only a few Chartists were clearly socialists in their own minds. But all were anticapitalistic. All could agree that the first step toward social reform must be to win working-class representation in Parliament. The Charter of 1838 consisted of six points. It demanded (1) the annual election of the House of Commons by (2) universal suffrage for all adult males, through (3) a secret ballot and (4) equal electoral districts; and it called for (5) abolition of the property qualifications for membership in the House of Commons, which had long assured that only gentlemen of independent income could serve in Parliament, and urged instead (6) the payment of salaries to the elected members of Parliament, in order that people of small means might serve. A convention composed of delegates sent by labor unions, mass meetings, and radical societies all over the country met in London in 1839. Convention was an ominous word, with French revolutionary and even terrorist overtones; some members of this British convention regarded it as the body really representing the people and favored armed violence and a general strike, while others stood only for moral pressure upon Parliament.

The Charter of 1838

The newly organized London police await the arrival of a Chartist procession in the 1840s. The British government introduced a more disciplined police force to avoid incidents such as the Peterloo massacre and to manage the mass demonstrations of groups such as the Chartists, who campaigned (unsuccessfully) for more democratic electoral laws.

(©Hulton Archive/Getty Images)

A petition bearing over a million signatures, urging acceptance of the Charter, was submitted to the House of Commons. The petition was rejected, whereupon the movement's more revolutionary wing, or "physical force" Chartists, precipitated a wave of riots that were effectively quelled by the authorities. In 1842 the petition was again

Petitions and the defeat of the Chartists

submitted. This time, according to the best estimate, it was signed by 3,317,702 persons. Because the entire population of Great Britain in this period was about 19 million, it is clear that the Charter, whatever the exact number of signatures, commanded the explicit adherence of half the adult males of the country. The House of Commons nevertheless again rejected the petition by 287 votes to 49. It was feared that political democracy would threaten property rights and the whole economic system of British society. The Chartist movement gradually died down in the face of firm opposition by the government and the business classes and was weakened by mutual fears and disagreements among its own supporters. It had not been entirely fruitless; for without popular agitation and the publicizing of working-class grievances, the Mines Act of 1842 and the Ten Hours Act of 1847 might not have been enacted. These measures in turn alleviated the distress of industrial workers and kept alive a degree of confidence in the future of the capitalist industrial economic system. Chartism revived briefly in 1848, but in general, in the 1840s, British working people turned from overt political agitation to the forming and strengthening of labor unions by which they could deal directly with employers without having to appeal to the government. Not until 1867 was the suffrage extended in Great Britain, and it took about 80 years to realize the full program of the Charter of 1838, except for the annual election of Parliament, for which there soon ceased to be any demand.

The history of Europe between 1815 and 1848 cannot be described as the era of a single dominant ideology or social system. Among all the "isms" and social forces set free by the French and Industrial revolutions—liberalism, conservatism, nationalism, republicanism, socialism, feminism, free market capitalism, democracy—no stabilization had been achieved. No international system had been created; Europe had instead fallen increasingly into two polarized political and social camps, which represented the geographical, economic, and ideological divisions in nineteenth-century European societies. In general, the political and economic ideas of classical liberalism advanced most rapidly in the nations of western Europe, whereas eastern Europe remained more agrarian and mostly dominated by three autocratic monarchies. Western Europe generally adhered more closely to the principles of nationality and national sovereignty; governments in central and eastern Europe still opposed them. The countries of northwestern Europe were growing collectively richer, more industrialized, more liberal, more bourgeois. Middle-class people in Germany, central Europe, and Italy (as well as in Spain and Portugal) did not usually enjoy the political or social influence that they increasingly enjoyed in Great Britain or France. But the industrializing societies in northwestern Europe had not solved their social problem; their whole material civilization depended upon a restless and sorely tried working class. Everywhere there was repression, in varying degree, and everywhere apprehension, more in some places than in others; but there was also confidence in the progress of an industrial and scientific society, and political faith in the unfinished liberal program of the rights of individuals. The result was the general European Revolution of 1848.

Suggested Further Readings can be found in the ebook, on Connect, or online at www.mhhe.com/kramer12e.

Chapter 12

REVOLUTIONS AND THE REIMPOSITION OF ORDER, 1848–1870

Fears haunting the established classes of Europe for 30 years came true in 1848. Governments collapsed all over the Continent. Remembered horrors appeared again, as in a recurring dream, in much the same sequence as after 1789 only at a much faster rate of speed. Revolutionaries milled in the streets, kings fled, republics were declared, and within four years there was another Napoleon. Soon thereafter came a series of short wars.

Never before or since has Europe seen so truly universal an upheaval as in 1848. While the French Revolution of 1789 and the Russian Revolution of 1917 both had immediate international repercussions, in each of these cases a single country took the lead. There were large protests in many European countries in 1968, but governments did not fall; and the upheavals that overturned multiple communist regimes in 1989, though widespread, took place entirely in eastern Europe. In 1848 the revolutionary movements broke out spontaneously from Copenhagen to Palermo and from Paris to Budapest, challenging governments everywhere, destroying several well-established regimes, and creating new constitutions. Contemporaries sometimes attributed the universality of the phenomenon to the machinations of secret societies, and it is true that the faint beginnings of an international revolutionary movement existed before 1848; but the revolutionary plotters had little influence upon what actually happened, and the nearly simultaneous fall of governments is quite understandable from other causes. Many people in Europe sought substantially the same goals—constitutional government, the independence and unification of national groups, an end to serfdom and manorial restraints where they still existed. With some variation, there was a common body of ideas among politically conscious elements of all countries. Some of the powers that the new forces had to combat were themselves international, notably the Catholic Church and the far-spreading influence of

Chapter emblem: Detail from a nineteenth-century illustration of the 1848 uprising in Vienna. (©Bettmann/ Getty Images)

the Habsburgs, so that resistance to them arose independently in many places. In any case, only the Russian Empire and Great Britain escaped the European revolutionary convulsions of 1848, and the British received a very bad scare.

But the Revolutions of 1848, though they shook the whole Continent, lacked enduring political and social strength. They failed almost as rapidly as they succeeded. Their main consequence, at least in the short run, was to strengthen the more conservative forces that viewed all revolution with alarm. Revolutionary ideals soon succumbed to military repression. To some extent the European governments of the 1850s and 1860s, while hostile to revolution, satisfied some of the aims of 1848, notably in national unification and constitutional government with limited representation, but they did so in a mood of calculated realism that firmly reasserted their own authority. The repressed Revolutions of 1848 left a legacy of class fears and class conflict, in which prophets of a new society also became more realistic, as when Karl Marx, branding earlier forms of socialism as "utopian," offered his own views as hard-headed and "scientific." New "isms" arose in response to the evolving nineteenth-century political and cultural order, but power also remained firmly with the institutions and national ideologies of the various European states and their centralizing governments.

58.   PARIS: THE SPECTER OF SOCIAL REVOLUTION IN THE WEST

The July Monarchy in France was a platform of boards built over a volcano. Under it burned the repressed fires of the republicanism put down in 1830, which since 1830 had become steadily more socialistic.

Politics in the July Monarchy became increasingly separated from the changing social classes in French society. So few interests were represented in the Chamber of Deputies that the most basic social or political issues were seldom debated. Even most of the bourgeois class had no representation. Graft and corruption became more common as economic expansion favored stock swindles and fraud by business promoters and politicians in combination. A strong movement set in to give the vote to more people. Radicals wanted universal male suffrage and a republic, but liberals asked only for a broadening of voting rights within the existing constitutional monarchy. The king, Louis Philippe, and his prime minister, Guizot, instead of allying with the liberals against the radicals, resolutely opposed any change whatsoever.

The "February" Revolution in France

Reformers, against the king's expressed wishes, planned a great banquet in Paris for February 22, 1848, to be accompanied by demonstrations in the streets. The government on February 21 forbade all such meetings. That night barricades were built in the working-class quarters. Paving blocks, building stones, or large pieces of furniture were thrown together across the narrow streets and intersections of the old city, constituting a maze within which insurgents prepared to resist the authorities. The government called out the National Guard, which refused to move. The king now promised electoral reform, but republican firebrands took charge of the working-class elements, who demonstrated outside the house of Guizot. Someone shot at the guards placed around the house; the guards replied, killing 20 persons. The republican organizers put some of the corpses on a torch-lit cart and paraded them through the city, which soon began to erupt in an enormous riot. On February 24 Louis Philippe, like Charles X before him, abdicated and left immediately for England. The February Revolution of 1848, like the July Revolution of 1830, had unseated a monarch in three days.

The constitutional reformers hoped to carry on with Louis Philippe's young grandson as king, but the republicans, now aroused and armed, poured into the Chamber of Deputies and forced the proclamation of a new republic. Republican leaders set up a provisional government of 10 men, pending election by all France of a Constituent Assembly that would write a new constitution for the second French Republic. Seven of the 10 were "political" republicans, the most notable being the poet Lamartine.

Proclamation of the republic

Three were "social" republicans, the most notable being Louis Blanc. A huge crowd of workers appeared before the Hôtel de Ville, or city hall, demanding that France adopt the new socialist emblem—the red flag. They were dissuaded by the eloquence of Lamartine, and the tricolor remained the republican standard.

Louis Blanc urged the Provisional Government to push through a bold economic and social program without delay. But because the social republicans were in a minority in the Provisional Government

Louis Blanc

(though probably not among Paris republicans generally), Louis Blanc's ideas were very much watered down in the application. He wanted a Ministry of Progress to organize a network of "social workshops," a plan for state-supported and collectivist manufacturing establishments that he had proposed in his writings. The new government, however, would only create a more limited Labor Commission and a system of shops significantly entitled "national" rather than "social." The National Workshops, as they are always called in English (though "workshop" suggests something less significant than Louis Blanc had in mind), were established as a political concession to the social republicans, but no important industrial work was ever assigned them for fear that they would compete with private enterprise and disrupt the economic system. Indeed, the man placed in charge of them admitted that his purpose was to prove the fallacies of socialism. Meanwhile the Labor Commission was unable to win public acceptance for the 10-hour day, which the British Parliament had enacted the year before. One action of the Provisional Government, however, had permanent effect: the final abolition of slavery in the French colonies.

The National Workshops became in practice a kind of regional project for unemployment relief. Women were excluded from the workshops, but men of all trades, skilled and unskilled, were set to

The National Workshops

work digging on the roads and fortifications outside Paris. They were paid two francs a day. The number of legitimate unemployed workers increased rapidly, for 1847 had been a year of depression and the revolution prevented the return of business confidence. Other needy persons also presented themselves for remuneration, and soon there were too many men for the amount of work made available. From 25,000 enrolled in the workshops by the middle of March, the number climbed to 120,000 by mid-June, by which time there were also in Paris another 50,000 whom the bulging workshops could no longer accommodate. In June there were probably almost 200,000 essentially idle but able-bodied men in a city of about a million people.

The Constituent Assembly, elected in April by universal male suffrage throughout France, met on May 4. It immediately replaced the Provisional Government with a temporary executive board of its own. The main body of France, a land of provincial

LAMARTINE REJECTS THE RED FLAG AT THE HOTEL-DE-VILLE
by Henri Felix Philippoteaux (French, 1815–1884)

Conflicts between Parisian political activists and the police in February 1848 led quickly toward familiar patterns of revolutionary upheaval: crowds and barricades in the streets, abdication of a king (Louis Philippe left the country), and debates about France's national symbols. Philippoteaux's painting depicts a dramatic moment, when the poet Alphonse de Lamartine eloquently persuaded a Parisian crowd at the Hotel-de-Ville that a new French republic should keep the tricolor flag rather than adopt the red flag of the radical workers' movement.

(©Photo Josse/Leemage/Getty Images)

bourgeois and peasant landowners, was not socialist in the least. The temporary executive board, chosen by the Constituent Assembly in May, included no social republicans. All five of its members were known as outspoken enemies of Louis Blanc; the socialists could no longer expect even the grudging concessions that they had earlier obtained.

The battle lines were now drawn after only three months of revolution, somewhat as they had been drawn in 1792 after three years. Paris again stood for revolutionary actions in which the rest of the country was not prepared to share. Revolutionary leaders in Paris, in 1848 as in 1792, were unwilling to accept the processes of majority rule or slow parliamentary deliberation. But the crisis in 1848 differed from the events in 1792 because a larger proportion of the population were now wage earners. Under a system of predominantly merchant capitalism, in which machine industry and factory concentration were still just emerging, the workers were tormented by the same evils as the more industrialized working classes of England. Hours were if anything longer, and pay was less, in France than in Great Britain; insecurity and unemployment were at least as great; and many workers believed that a capitalist economy held no future for the laborer. In addition, where the English worker shrank from an actual assault on Parliament, the French worker was less deferential to elected assemblies. Too many regimes in France since 1789, including those preferred by the comfortable classes, had been based on insurrectionary violence for the French workers to feel much compunction over using it for their own ends.

The "June Days" of 1848

On the one hand stood the nationally elected Constituent Assembly, consisting mostly of bourgeois provincial representatives. On the other, the National Workshops had mobilized in Paris the most distressed elements of the working class. Tens of thousands had been brought together where they could talk, read journals, listen to speeches, and plan for common action. Agitators and organizers made use of the opportunity thus presented to them. Men in the workshops began to feel desperate, to sense that the social republic was slipping from them perhaps forever. On May 15 they attacked the Constituent Assembly, drove its members out of the hall, declared it dissolved, and set up a new provisional government of their own. They announced that a social revolution must follow the purely political revolution of February. But the National Guard, a kind of civilian militia, turned against the insurgents and restored the Constituent Assembly. The Assembly, to root out socialism, now prepared to get rid of the National Workshops. It offered those enrolled in them the alternatives of enlistment in the army, transfer to provincial workshops, or expulsion from Paris by force. The whole laboring class in the city began to resist. The government proclaimed martial law, the Assembly's civilian executive board resigned, and all power was given to General Cavaignac and the regular army.

Paris on the verge of revolution

There followed the "Bloody June Days"—June 24 to 26, 1848—three days during which a terrifying class war raged in Paris. Over 20,000 men from the workshops took to arms, and they were joined by thousands of men and women from the working-class districts of the city. Half or more of Paris became a labyrinth of barricades defended by determined men and equally resolute women. Military methods of the time made it possible for civilians to shoot it out openly with soldiers in the narrow streets; small arms were the main weapons, and armies still lacked the military advantage of armored vehicles. The soldiers found it a difficult operation, but after three days the outcome was in doubt no longer. Ten thousand persons had been killed or wounded. Eleven thousand insurgents were taken prisoner. The Assembly, refusing all clemency, decreed their immediate deportation to the colonies.

Class war

The June Days sent a shudder throughout France and Europe. Whether the battle in Paris had been a true class struggle, how large a portion of the laboring class had really participated (it was large in any case), how much they had fought for permanent objectives, and how much over the temporary issue of the workshops—all these were secondary questions. It was widely understood that a class war had in fact broken out in the capital of France. Militant workers confirmed their distrust and hatred of the bourgeois class; and many now believed that capitalism ultimately survived by shooting working-class men and women in the streets. People above the laboring class were thrown into a panic. They were sure that they had narrowly escaped a ghastly upheaval. The very ground of civilized living seemed to have quaked. After June 1848, wrote a Frenchwoman of the time, society was "a prey to a feeling of terror incomparable to anything since the invasion of Rome by the barbarians."

The revival of Chartist agitation

Nor were the political signs in England more reassuring for the upper classes. There the Chartist agitation for electoral reforms was revived by the February Revolution in Paris. "France is a Republic!" cried the Chartist Ernest Jones; the Chartist petition was again circulated and was soon said to have 6 million signatures. Another Chartist convention met, considered by its leaders to be the forerunner of a Constituent Assembly as in France. The violent minority was the most active; it began to gather arms and to drill. In London a revolutionary committee laid plans for systematic arson and organized men to break up the pavements for barricades. Meanwhile the petition, weighing 584 pounds, was carried in three cabs to the House of Commons, which estimated that it contained "only" 2 million signatures and again summarily rejected it. The revolutionary menace passed. One of the secret organizers in London proved to be a government spy; he revealed the whole plan at the critical moment, and the revolutionary committee was arrested on the day set for insurrection. Most Chartists had in any case refused to support the militants, but the truculent minority of radical workers and journalists had a deeper sense of envenomed class consciousness. The word "proletarian" was imported from France. "Every proletarian," wrote the Chartist editor of *Red Revolution,* "who does not see and feel that he belongs to an enslaved and degraded class is a *fool.*"

The specter of social revolution thus hung over western Europe in the summer of 1848, though in all probability there could have been no successful socialist revolution at the time. But the specter was there, and it spread a sinking fear among all who had wealth or social positions to lose. This fear shaped the whole subsequent course of the Second Republic in France and of the revolutionary movements that had by this time begun in other countries as well.

The Emergence of Louis Napoleon Bonaparte

In France, after the June Days, the Constituent Assembly (with General Cavaignac as a virtual dictator) set about drafting a republican constitution. It was decided, in view of the disturbances just passed, to create a strong executive power in the hands of a president to be elected by universal male suffrage. It was decided also to have this president elected immediately, even before the rest of the constitution was finished. Four candidates presented themselves: Lamartine, Cavaignac, Ledru-Rollin—and Louis Napoleon Bonaparte. The poet Lamartine stood for a somewhat vaguely moral and idealistic republic; Cavaignac, for a republic of disciplined order; Ledru-Rollin, for somewhat chastened social ideas. What Bonaparte stood for was not so clear. He was, however, elected by an avalanche of votes in December 1848, receiving over 5,400,000, compared to only 1,500,000 for Cavaignac, 370,000 for Ledru-Rollin, and a mere 18,000 for Lamartine.

Bonaparte's background

Thus entered upon the European stage the second Napoleon. Born in 1808, Louis Napoleon Bonaparte was the nephew of the great Napoleon. His father, Louis Bonaparte, was at the time of his birth the king of Holland. When Napoleon's own son died in 1832, Louis Napoleon assumed the headship of the Bonaparte family. He resolved to restore the glories of the Napoleonic Empire. With a handful of followers he tried to seize power at Strasbourg in 1836 and at Boulogne in 1840, leading what the following century would know as *Putsches.* Both failed ridiculously. Sentenced to life imprisonment in the fortress of Ham, he had escaped from it as recently as 1846 by simply walking off the grounds dressed as a stonemason. He professed advanced social and political ideas, and he wrote two books. *Napoleonic Ideas* claimed that his famous uncle had been misunderstood and checkmated by reactionary forces; his other book, *Extinction of Poverty,* was a somewhat anticapitalist tract like many others in this era of early industrial capitalism. But he was no friend of "anarchists," and in the spring of 1848, while still a refugee in England, he even joined a special constable force to oppose the Chartist agitation. He soon returned to France. Compromised neither by the June Days nor by their repression, he was supposed to be a friend of the common people and at the same time a believer in order; and his name was Napoleon Bonaparte.

For 20 years a groundswell had been stirring the popular mind. It is known as the Napoleonic Legend. Peasants put up pictures of the emperor in their cottages, fondly imagining that it had been Napoleon who gave them the free ownership of their land. The completion of the Arch of Triumph in 1836 drove home the memory of imperial glories, and in 1840 the remains of the emperor were brought from St. Helena and majestically interred at the Invalides on the banks of the Seine. All this happened in a country where most people had little political experience or political sense except what they had gained in revolution. When millions were suddenly, for the first time in their lives, asked to vote for a president in 1848, the name of Bonaparte was the only one they had ever heard of. "How should I not vote for this gentleman," said an old peasant, "I whose nose was frozen at Moscow?"

So Prince Louis Napoleon became president of the Second Republic, by an overwhelming popular mandate, in which an army officer was
his only faintly successful rival. He soon saw the way the wind was
blowing. The Constituent Assembly dissolved itself in May 1849 and

Louis Napoleon becomes president

was replaced by the Legislative Assembly. Although this new legislative body was established under the provisions of the new republican constitution and was elected by universal male suffrage, it was a strange assembly for a republic. Five hundred of the Second Republic's newly elected deputies, or two-thirds, were really monarchists, but they were divided into irreconcilable factions—the Legitimists, who favored the line of Charles X, and the Orléanists, who favored that of Louis Philippe. One-third of the deputies called themselves republicans. Of these, in turn, about 180 were socialists of one kind of another; and only about 70 were political or old-fashioned republicans to whom the main issue was the form of government rather than the form of the economy or society itself.

The president and the Assembly at first combined to conjure away the specter of socialism with which republicanism itself was now clearly associated. An abortive insurrection of June 1849 provided the chance. The Assembly, backed by the president, ousted 33 socialist deputies, suppressed public meetings, and imposed controls on the press. In 1850 it went so far as to rescind universal male suffrage, taking the vote away from about a third of the electorate—naturally the poorest and hence most socialistic third. The Falloux Law of 1850 put the schools at all levels of the education system under supervision of the Catholic clergy; for, as M. Falloux said in the Assembly, "lay teachers have made the principles of social revolution popular in the most distant villages," and it was necessary "to rally around religion to strengthen the foundations of society against those who want to divide up property." The French Republic, now actually
an antirepublican government, likewise intervened forcefully against the
revolutionary republic that Mazzini had established in the city of Rome.
French military forces were sent to Rome to protect the pope; they
remained there 20 years.

Antirepublican government

Bonaparte knew that his repression of the socialists made him virtually indispensable for the conservatives. They were so sharply divided between two sets of monarchists—Legitimist and Orléanist—that each would accept any antisocialist regime rather than yield to the other. Bonaparte's problem was to win over the radicals. He did so by urging in 1851 the restoration of universal suffrage, which he had himself helped repeal in 1850. He now posed as the people's friend, the one man in public life who trusted the common man and stood against those he portrayed as greedy plutocrats in the Legislative Assembly. He put his lieutenants in as ministers of war and of the interior, thus controlling the army, the bureaucracy, and the police. On December 2, 1851, the anniversary of his uncle's famous victory at the battle of Austerlitz, he sprang a well-organized coup d'état. Placards appeared all over Paris. They declared the Assembly dissolved and the vote for every adult Frenchman reinstated. When members of the Assembly tried to meet, they were attacked, dispersed, or arrested by the soldiers. The country did not submit without fighting. One hundred and fifty persons were killed in Paris, and throughout France probably 100,000 were put under arrest. But on December 20 the voters elected Louis Napoleon president for a term of 10 years, by a vote officially stated as 7,439,216 to 646,737. A year later the new Bonaparte proclaimed the empire, with himself as emperor of the French. Remembering Napoleon's son, who had died, he called himself Napoleon III.

French republicans had lost more than the political institutions of the Second Republic. The republic as republicans understood it, an egalitarian, anticlerical regime with socialist or at least antibourgeois tendencies, had been dead since June 1848. Feeble

The demise of parliamentary government

anyway, it was killed by its reputation for radicalism. Liberalism and constitutionalism were dead also, at least in the political institutions by which the new Napoleon now governed France. Republicans and monarchists were all pushed aside, and for the first time since 1815 France ceased to have any significant parliamentary life.

59.   VIENNA: THE NATIONALIST REVOLUTIONS IN CENTRAL EUROPE AND ITALY

The Austrian Empire in 1848

The Austrian Empire of the Habsburgs, with its capital at Vienna, was in 1848 the most populous European state except Russia. Its peoples, living principally in the three major geographical divisions of the empire (Austria, Bohemia, and Hungary) were of about a dozen recognizably different nationalities or language groups—Germans, Czechs, Magyars, Poles, Ruthenians, Slovaks, Serbs, Croats, Slovenes, Dalmatians, Romanians, and Italians (see map, p. 484). In some parts of the empire the nationalities lived in solid blocks, but in many regions two or more were interlaced together, the language changing from village to village, or even from house to house, in a way quite unknown in western Europe.

Germans were the most numerous national group. They occupied all of Austria proper and considerable parts of Bohemia and were scattered also in small pockets throughout Hungary. The Czechs occupied Bohemia and the adjoining Moravia. The

The diversity of the empire

Magyars were the dominant group in the historic kingdom of Hungary, which contained a mixture of nationalities with a considerable number of Slavic peoples. Two of the most economically advanced parts of Italy also belonged to the empire—Venetia, with its capital at Venice, and Lombardy, whose chief city was Milan.

The Czechs, Poles, Ruthenians, Slovaks, Serbs, Croats, Slovenes, and Dalmatians in the empire were all Slavs; that is, their languages were all related to one another and to the several forms of Russian. Neither the Magyars nor the Romanians were Slavs. The Magyars, as national sentiment grew, prided themselves on the uniqueness of their language in Europe, and the Romanians prided themselves on their linguistic affiliations with the Latin peoples of the West. Romanians, Magyars, and Germans formed a thick belt separating the South Slavs from those of the north. The peoples of the empire represented every cultural and economic level of nineteenth-century Europe. Vienna recognized no cultural or scientific peer except Paris, and Milan was a great center of trade. Bohemia had long had an important textile industry, which was beginning to be mechanized in the 1840s;

but 200 miles to the south a Croatian intellectual remarked, about the same time, that the first steam engine he ever saw was in a picture printed on a cotton handkerchief imported from Manchester.

Thus the empire that the Habsburgs ruled from Vienna included, according to political frontiers established 70 years later, in 1918, all of Austria, Hungary, and Czechoslovakia, with adjoining portions of Poland, Italy, Romania, and other territories in the Balkans. But the political authority of Vienna reached far beyond the borders of the empire. Austria since 1815 had been the most influ-

Vienna's authority and leadership

ential member of the German confederation, for Prussia in these years was content to look with deference upon the Habsburgs. The influence of Vienna was felt throughout Germany in many ways, as in the enactment and enforcement of Metternich's repressive Carlsbad Decrees described in the last chapter. It reached also through the length of Italy. Lombardy and Venetia were part of the Austrian Empire. Tuscany, ostensibly independent, was governed by a Habsburg grand duke. The kingdom of Naples or the Two Sicilies, comprising all Italy south of Rome, was virtually a protectorate of Vienna. The papal states looked politically to Vienna for leadership, at least until 1846, when the College of Cardinals elected a liberal-minded pope, Pius IX—the one contingency upon which Metternich confessed he had failed to reckon. In all Italy there was only one state ruled by a native Italian dynasty and attempting any consistent independence of policy—the kingdom of Sardinia (called also Savoy or Piedmont) tucked away in the northwest corner around Turin. Italy, said Metternich blandly, was only a "geographical expression," a mere regional name. He might have said the same of Poland, or even of Germany, though Germany was tenuously joined in the Bund, or loose confederation, of 1815.

These peoples since the turn of the century had all began to identify the distinctive meanings of their own *Volksgeist* as they developed new cultural nationalisms; and among Germans, Italians, Poles, and Hungarians a good deal of political agitation and liberal reformism had been at work. Metternich, in Vienna, had discouraged such manifestations for over 30 years, ominously predicting that if allowed to break out they would produce the *bellum omnium contra omnes*—"the war of all against all." As a prophet he was not wholly mistaken, but if it is the business of statesmanship to control events rather than merely to prophesy them, it cannot be said that Metternich's Austrian regime was very successful. The fundamental political problem of the century, the bringing of peoples into some kind of mutual relationship with their governments—a political aspiration that drew on diverse strands of nationalism, liberalism, constitutionalism, and democracy—was evaded by the responsible authorities of central Europe. Metternich believed that a reigning royal family, with an official bureaucracy, should rule benevolently over peoples with whom it need have no connection and who need have no national connection with each other. Such ideas could be found everywhere among the governing elites in eighteenth-century Europe. They dated from before the French Revolution, and they were best suited to the agricultural, locally oriented societies that by 1848 were giving way to cities, cultural nationalisms, and new commercial institutions.

The March Days

In March 1848 most of the political institutions in central Europe collapsed with incredible swiftness. At that time the diet of Hungary had been sitting for some months, considering constitutional reforms and, as usual, debating further means of keeping German influence out of Hungary. Then came news of the February Revolution in Paris. The radical party

The Revolution of 1848 spread rapidly across the European continent, provoking an uprising in Vienna by mid-March. Workers, students, and even soldiers joined together to erect barricades and resist the king's loyal troops. This nineteenth-century image of the Viennese crowd, however, suggests the tensions within a movement that rallied behind a banner for "King, Freedom, and Fatherland."

(©Bettmann/Getty Images)

in the Hungarian diet was aroused. Its leader, Louis Kossuth, on March 3 made an impassioned speech on the virtues of liberty. This speech was immediately printed in German and read in Vienna, where restlessness was also heightened by the news from Paris. On March 13 workers and students rose in insurrection in Vienna, erected barricades, fought off soldiers, and invaded the imperial palace. The Habsburgs, terrified by the violence and responding to the popular outcry against their principal minister, asked Metternich to resign. To the amazement of both liberals and conservatives throughout Europe, the long-powerful leader and symbol of central Europe's conservative, post-1815 international system fled Vienna in disguise for a safe refuge in England.

Metternich's fall

The fall of Metternich proved that the Vienna government was completely disoriented. Revolution swept through the empire and through all Italy and Germany. On March 15 rioting began in Berlin; the king of Prussia promised a constitution. The lesser German governments collapsed in sequence. On the last day of March a pre-Parliament met to arrange the calling of an all-German national assembly. In Hungary, now mobilized by Kossuth's national party, the diet on March 15 enacted the March Laws, by which Hungary sought complete constitutional separatism within the empire, while still recognizing the Habsburg house. The harassed Emperor Ferdinand a few days later granted substantially the same status to Bohemia. At Milan between March 18 and 22 the populace drove out the Austrian garrison. Venice proclaimed itself an independent republic. Tuscany drove out its grand duke and also established a republic. Charles Albert was king of Sardinia, a kingdom also called Piedmont because its capital Turin and much of its territory apart from the island of Sardinia lay in northwest Italy at the foot of the Alps. Stimulated by events in Paris,

Historical Documents
Louis Kossuth, "On Nationalities" (1851)

The Revolutions of 1848 mobilized new nationalists throughout central Europe and especially within the Austrian Empire. The national movement in Hungary, led by Louis Kossuth (1802-1894), asserted revolutionary claims for a complete constitutional separation from Austria's governing institutions, but Habsburg imperial forces soon regained control. Like many other liberal nationalists, Kossuth fled to the United States. Traveling widely in America, Kossuth advocated European nationalist ideas, as in this speech at a banquet for newspaper writers in New York City. The following excerpts convey Kossuth's commitment to a transnational European movement of liberal nationalism—which was suppressed everywhere after 1848.

No word has been more misrepresented than the word Nationality. . . .

It is not language only. [It is a] community of interests, of rights, of duties, of history, but chiefly [a] community of institutions; by which a population, varying perhaps in tongue and race, is bound together . . . in the towns, which are the centres and home of commerce and industry:—besides these, . . . the soil, the dust of which is mingled with the mortal remains of those ancestors who bled . . . for the same interests, the common inheritance of glory and of woe, the community of laws and institutions, common freedom or common oppression:—all this enters into the complex idea of Nationality.

[In Hungary] we struggled for civil, political, social, and religious freedom, common to all, against Austrian despotism. We struggled for the great principle of *self-government against centralization*. . . .

We want Republican institutions, so founded on self-government everywhere, that the people themselves may be sovereign everywhere. This is the cause . . . of oppressed Europe. It is the cause of Germany, bleeding under some thirty petty tyrants. . . . It is the cause of fair, but unfortunate Italy. . . . We have a common enemy; so we are brothers in arms for freedom and independence. I know . . . there is no hope for Italy, but in that great republican party, at the head of which Mazzini stands . . . [and which] wills that Italy be free and republican.

Louis Kossuth, "On Nationalities," in *Select Speeches of Kossuth*, condensed and abridged with Kossuth's express sanction by Francis W. Newman (New York: C. S. Francis, 1854), pp. 62-63, 70-71.

Charles Albert had granted a constitution to his small country. He now declared war on Austria on March 23 and invaded Lombardy-Venetia, hoping to bring that area under his house of Savoy. Italian troops streamed up from Tuscany, from Naples (where revolution had broken out as early as January), and even from the papal states (the new pope had expressed some earlier sympathy with liberal aims) to join in an all-Italian war against the seemingly helpless Austrian government.

Thus in the brief span of these phenomenal March Days in 1848 the whole political structure based on Vienna went to pieces. The Austrian Empire had fallen into its main components, Prussia had yielded to revolutionaries, all Germany was preparing to unify itself, and war raged in Italy. Everywhere constitutions had been widely promised by stupefied governments, constitutional assemblies were meeting, and independent or autonomous nations struggled into existence. Patriots everywhere demanded liberal government and national freedom—written constitutions, representative assemblies, responsible ministries, a more or less extended suffrage, restrictions upon police action, jury trial, civil liberty, freedom of press and assembly. And where serfdom still existed—in Prussia, Galicia, Bohemia,

Hungary—the serfs' legal subservience to noble landowners was abolished. Although most peasants remained poor and vulnerable to economic hardships, the peasant masses became legally free from control by their local lords. This change in the legal status of peasants would become the most enduring and significant social consequence of the central European revolutions.

The Turning of the Tide after June

The revolution, as in France, surged forward until the month of June and then began to ebb in every country. The old governments had been stunned during the March Days, but not really broken. They merely awaited the opportunity to take back promises extorted by force. The pressure originally imposed by the revolutionaries could not be sustained. The eastern European revolutionary leaders lacked a strong social base. Middle-class, bourgeois, property-owning, and commercial interests were nowhere nearly as highly developed as in western Europe. The revolutionary leaders were to a large extent writers, editors, professors, and students—intellectuals rather than the representatives of powerful social and economic interests. In Vienna, Milan, and a few other cities the working class was numerous and socialist ideas were fairly common, but the workers were not as literate, organized, or politically conscious as in Paris or Great Britain. They were strong enough, however, to disquiet the middle classes; and especially after the specter of social revolution rose over western Europe, the middle-class and lower-class revolutionaries began to be afraid of each other. The liberated nationalities also began to disagree. The peasants, once emancipated, had no further interest in revolution. Nor did the peasants at this time have much awareness of the emerging belief in collective national identities; nationalism was primarily a doctrine of the educated middle classes or of the aristocratic landowning classes in Poland and Hungary. Because most army officers came from the old internationally minded aristocracy and most soldiers came from peasant families, the armies remained almost immune to nationalist aspirations. This attitude within the armies was decisive.

The tide first turned in Prague. The all-German national assembly met at Frankfurt in May. Representatives from Bohemia had been invited to come to Frankfurt, because many Germans had always lived in Bohemia and because Bohemia formed part of the confederation of 1815 and part of the Holy Roman Empire that had preceded it. Many of the Germans in Bohemia, the Sudeten Germans, were attracted to the Frankfurt Assembly, but the idea of belonging to a national German state, a Germany based on the principle that the inhabitants embodied a German nationality, did not appeal to the Czechs in Bohemia. They refused to go to the all-German congress at Frankfurt. Instead, they called an all-Slav congress of their own. At Prague, in June 1848, this first Pan-Slav Assembly met. Most of the delegates were from Slav communities within the Austrian Empire, but a few came from the Balkans and non-Austrian Poland.

The first Pan-Slav Assembly

The spirit of the Prague congress was that of the Slavic Revival described in the last chapter; the Czech historian Palacky was in fact one of its most active figures. The congress was profoundly anti-German, because the essence of the Slavic Revival was resistance to Germanization. But it was not profoundly anti-Austrian or anti-Habsburg. Although a few radicals questioned the value of the Austrian Empire, the great majority at the Prague congress were Austroslavs who held that the many Slavic peoples, pressed on two sides by the Russians and Germans, needed the Austrian Empire as a political frame within which to develop their own national life. The congress therefore demanded that the Slavic peoples be admitted as equals with the other nationalities in the Austrian Empire, enjoying local autonomy and constitutional guarantees.

EUROPEAN REVOLUTIONS, 1848

The map shows cities in which notable revolutionary upheavals occurred during 1848. Although opponents of the revolutionary agitation suspected an international conspiracy, the revolutions developed more or less spontaneously as urban populations took to the streets with demands for constitutional government, national independence, or new civil rights. It should be noted that the revolutions of 1848 erupted mainly in central and eastern Europe—a pattern that suggests the spreading influence of ideas that had appeared earlier in the American and French revolutions. But the failure of these revolutions led to a conservative resurgence that delayed or prevented the development of liberal, constitutional governments in most of central and eastern Europe

Victories of the Counterrevolution, June–December, 1848

But the Emperor Ferdinand, and the advisers on whom he chose to rely, would have nothing to do with the liberal national movements or with the restrictions they wanted to impose upon the powers of the centralizing state. All national movements were thus resisted. A Czech insurrection broke out in Prague on June 12, at the time when the Slav congress was sitting, but the local Austrian army commander bombarded and subdued the city, thereby reasserting Habsburg military control. The Slav congress dispersed, giving the Vienna government its first counterrevolutionary victory.

The counterrevolution also advanced rapidly in north Italy. Only Lombardy-Venetia, of all parts of the empire, had declared independence from the Habsburgs during the upheavals of March. The diminutive kingdom of Sardinia had lent support and had declared war on Austria. Italians from all over the peninsula had flocked in to fight; and until after the June Days in Paris it even seemed possible that republican France might intervene to befriend fellow revolutionaries as in 1796. But in France the radical revolution was suppressed. The Italians were left to themselves, and an Austrian army crushed the disparate revolutionary movement in late July. The Sardinian king, Charles Albert, retreated into his own country. Lombardy and Venetia were restored with savage vengeance to the Austrian Empire.

The Italians defeated

Magyar nationalism
The third victory of the counterrevolution came in September and October. The Hungarian radical party of Louis Kossuth was liberal and even democratic in many of its principles, but it was a Magyar nationalist party above all else. Triumphant in the March Days, it completely shook off the German connection. It moved the capital from Pressburg near the Austrian border to Budapest in the center of Hungary. It changed the official language of Hungary from Latin to Magyar. Less than half the people of Hungary were Magyars, and Magyar is a difficult language, quite alien to the Indo-European tongues of Europe. It soon became clear that the new liberal constitution was designed to benefit Magyars and that the Magyars intended to repress the national ambitions of all others with whom they shared the country. Slovaks, Romanians, Germans, Serbs, and Croats violently resisted, each group determined to keep its national identity unimpaired. The Croats, who had enjoyed certain liberties before the Magyar revolution, took the lead under Count Jellachich, the provincial governor of Croatia. In September Jellachich launched a civil war in Hungary, leading a force of Serbo-Croatians, supported by the whole non-Magyar half of the population. Half of Hungary, alarmed by Magyar nationalism, now looked to the Habsburgs and the empire to protect them. Emperor Ferdinand made Jellachich his military commander against the Magyars. Hungary dissolved into the war of all against all.

At Vienna the more clear-sighted revolutionaries, who had led the March rising, now saw that Jellachich's anti-Magyar army might soon be turned against them. They therefore rose in a second mass insurrection in October 1848. The emperor fled; never had the Viennese revolution gone so far. But it was already too late. The Austrian forces that had earlier subdued the revolution in Prague now arrived at Vienna, where the besieged radicals soon surrendered.

Vienna recaptured
With the recapture of Vienna the upholders of the old order took heart. Counterrevolutionary leaders—large estate holders, Catholic clergy, high-ranking army men—decided to clear the way by getting rid of the Emperor Ferdinand, considering that promises made in March by Ferdinand might be more easily repudiated by his successor. Ferdinand abdicated and on December 2, 1848, was succeeded by Francis Joseph, a boy of 18, destined to live until 1916 and to end his reign in a crisis even more shattering than the revolutionary year in which he had come to power.

Final Outburst and Repression, 1849

For a time in the first part of 1849 the revolution in many places seemed to blaze more fiercely than ever. Republican riots broke out in parts of Germany, and political violence in Rome forced Pope Pius IX to flee from the city. A radical Roman Republic was proclaimed under three Triumvirs, one of whom was the nationalist leader Mazzini, who hastened from England to take part in the republican upheaval. In north Italy Charles Albert of Sardinia again invaded Lombardy. In Hungary, after the revived Habsburg authorities repudiated the new Magyar constitution, the Magyars, led by the inflamed Kossuth, went on to declare absolute independence. But all these manifestations proved short-lived. German republicanism flickered out. A French army drove Mazzini and his republican allies from Rome, thereby restoring Pope Pius IX to his traditional powers. The Sardinian king was again defeated by an Austrian army, but in Hungary the Magyars put up a sustained resistance, which Austria's imperial army and the anti-Magyar native irregulars could not overcome. The Habsburg authorities now renewed the procedures of the Holy Alliance. The new Emperor Francis Joseph invited

Tsar Nicholas to intervene. In August 1849 over 100,000 Russian troops poured over the mountains into Hungary, defeated the Magyars, and laid the prostrate country at the feet of the court of Vienna.

The nationalist upheaval of 1848 in central Europe and Italy was now over. The Habsburgs had reasserted their imperial authority over Czech nationalists in Prague, Magyars in Hungary, Italian patriots in north Italy, and liberal revolutionists in Vienna itself. Reaction, or antirevolutionism, became the order of the day. Pius IX, the formerly "liberal pope," returned to the papal throne and rejected all of his earlier liberal ideas. The breach

Antirevolutionism

between liberalism and Roman Catholicism, which had opened wide in the first French Revolution, was made a yawning chasm by the revolutionary violence of Mazzini's Roman Republic and by the measures taken to repress it. Pius IX now reiterated the anathemas of his predecessors. He codified them in 1864 in the *Syllabus of Errors,* which warned all Catholics, on the authority of the Vatican, against everything that went under the names of liberalism, rationalism, socialism, and other modern "isms." The Catholic Church thus emerged from the mid-nineteenth-century revolutions (and the pope's own encounter with revolutionary violence in Rome) as a more steadfast opponent of the European agitation for social reform as well as the expanding movements for political and cultural nationalism. Facing this resolute opposition, many Italian nationalists became disillusioned with the firecracker methods of romantic republicans; and the more pragmatic nationalists concluded that Italy would be liberated from Austrian influence only by an old-fashioned war between established powers.

In the Austrian Empire the main policy was now to oppose all forms of popular self-expression with a more candid reliance on military force. Constitutionalism was to be rooted out, as well as all

The Bach system

Joseph Mazzini (1805–1872) led the short-lived republic in Rome during the Italian upheavals of 1849, but his new regime was soon suppressed by foreign powers and he retreated to the life of an exile in England. Although Mazzini's Romantic nationalism lost favor in Italy after about 1850, his writings and political activities gave him a prominent place in the intellectual life of London.

(©Time Life Pictures/Getty Images)

forms of anti-Habsburg nationalism. The regime came to be called the Bach system, after Alexander Bach, the minister of the interior. Under it, the government was rigidly centralized. Hungary lost the separate rights it had held before 1848. The ideal was to create a perfectly solid and unitary political system. Bach insisted on maintaining the recent emancipation of the peasants, which had converted the mass of the people from subjects of their landlords into subjects of the state. He drove through a reform of the legal system and law courts, created a free trading area of the whole empire with only a common external tariff, and subsidized the building of highways and railroads. The aim, as in France at the same time under Louis Napoleon, was to make people forget liberty in an overwhelming demonstration of administrative efficiency and material progress. But some, at that time, would not forget. A liberal said of the Bach system that it consisted of "a standing army of soldiers, a sitting army of officials, a kneeling army of priests, and a creeping army of informers."

60.   FRANKFURT AND BERLIN:
THE QUESTION OF A LIBERAL GERMANY

The German States

Meanwhile, from May 1848 to May 1849, the Frankfurt Assembly was sitting at the historic city on the Main. It was attempting to bring a unified German state into being, one that should also be liberal and constitutional, assuring civil rights to its citizens and possessing a government responsive to popular will as manifested in free elections and open parliamentary debate. The mid-nineteenth-century failure to produce a democratic Germany became one of the overshadowing facts of modern European history.

The convocation of the Frankfurt Assembly was made possible by the collapse of the existing German governments in the March Days of 1848. These governments, the 39 states recognized after the Congress of Vienna, enjoyed their political independence and formed the main obstacles in the way of unification. The German

Obstacles to unification

states resisted the surrender of sovereignty to a united Germany just as national states in later eras were to resist the surrender of sovereignty to a United Nations. In another way the German world was a miniature of the wider political world. It consisted of both great and small powers. Its great powers were Prussia and Austria. Austria was the miscellaneous empire described earlier. Prussia after 1815 included the Rhineland, the central regions around Berlin, West Prussia and Posen (acquired in the partitions of Poland), and historic East Prussia. The former Polish areas were inhabited by a mixture of Germans and Poles. Neither of these great powers would submit to the other or allow the other to dominate its lesser German neighbors.

German dualism

This German "dualism," or polarity between Berlin and Vienna, had become somewhat less intense under the common menace of the Napoleonic Empire. The whole German question had lain dormant insofar as the governments were concerned, nor did it agitate the old aristocracies. In Prussia the Junkers, the owners of great landed estates east of the Elbe, were singularly indifferent to the all-German dream. Their political feeling was not German but Prussian. They were satisfied with their dominant position in Prussia and could expect only to lose by absorption into Germany as a whole, for in Germany west of the Elbe the small peasant holding was the basis of society, and there was no landowning element corresponding to the Junkers. The rest of Germany looked upon Prussia as somewhat uncouth and eastern; but this feeling, too, had diminished in the time of Napoleon, when patriots from all over Germany enlisted in the Prussian service.

Berlin: Failure of the Revolution in Prussia

Prussia was illiberal but not backward. Frederick William III repeatedly evaded his promise to grant a modern constitution. His successor, Frederick William IV, who inherited the throne in 1840 and from whom much was at first expected by liberals, was equally determined not to share his authority with his subjects. At the same time the government, administratively speaking, was efficient, progressive, and fair. The universities and elementary school system surpassed those of western Europe. Literacy was higher than in England or France. The government followed in mercantilist traditions of evoking, planning, and supporting economic life. In 1818 it initiated a tariff union, at first with tiny states (or enclaves) wholly enclosed within Prussia. This tariff union, or *Zollverein,* was extended in the following decades to include almost all Germany.

On March 15, 1848, the rioting and street fighting that we have noted broke out in Berlin. For a time it seemed as if the army would master the situation. But the erratically conscientious king, Frederick William IV, called off the soldiers and allowed his subjects to elect the first all-Prussian legislative assembly. Thus though the army remained intact, and its Junker officers remained unconvinced, revolution proceeded superficially on its way. The new Prussian Assembly met in Berlin in May and proved surprisingly radical, because it was dominated by anti-Junker, lower-class extremists from East Prussia. These men supported Polish revolutionaries and exiles who sought the restoration of Polish freedom. Their main belief was that the fortress of reaction was tsarist Russia—that the whole structure of Junkerdom, landlordism, serf-owning, and repression of national freedom depended ultimately on the armed might of the tsarist empire. (The subsequent intervention of Russia in Hungary indicated the truth of their diagnosis.) Prussian radicals, like many elsewhere, hoped to smash the old Holy Alliance by raising an all-German or even European revolutionary war against Russia.

Radical Prussian Assembly

Meanwhile the radicals in Berlin supported demands for local self-government by the Poles of West Prussia and Posen. But in those areas Germans and Slavs had long lived side by side, and the Germans in Posen now refused to respect the authority of Polish officials. Prussian army units stationed in Posen supported the German element. As early as April 1848, a month after the "revolution," the army began to crush new pro-Polish institutions that had been set up in Posen. It was clear where the only real power lay. By the end of 1848, in Prussia as in Austria, the revolution was over. The king again changed his mind; and the old authorities, acting through the army, were again in control.

The Frankfurt Assembly

Meanwhile a similar story was enacted on the larger stage of Germany as a whole. The disabling of the old governments left a power vacuum. A self-appointed committee convoked a preliminary parliament, which in turn arranged for the election of an all-German assembly. Bypassing the existing sovereignties, voters throughout Germany sent delegates to Frankfurt to create a federated superstate. The strength and weakness of the resulting Frankfurt Assembly originated in the manner in which it was elected. The Assembly represented the moral sentiment of people at large, the liberal and national aspirations of many Germans. It stood for an idea, but the delegates had no power to issue orders or expect compliance. Superficially resembling the National Assembly that met in France in 1789, the German National Assembly at Frankfurt was really in a very different position. There was no preexisting national structure for it to work with. There was no all-German army or civil service for the Assembly to take over, as had happened after 1789 in revolutionary France. The Frankfurt Assembly, having no power of its own, became dependent on the power of the very sovereign states that it was attempting to supersede.

The Assembly met in May 1848 (thus convening in the same month as the more regional Prussian Assembly that met in Berlin). Its members were overwhelmingly professional people—professors, judges, lawyers, government administrators, clergy both Protestant and Catholic, and prominent businessmen. They wanted a liberal, self-governing, federally unified, and "democratic" though not egalitarian Germany. Their outlook was earnest, peaceable, and legalistic; they hoped to succeed by persuasion. Revolutionary violence was abhorrent to them. The example of the June Days in Paris, and the Chartist agitation in Great Britain, coinciding with the early weeks of the Frankfurt Assembly, increased the dread for radicalism and republicanism in Germany. The fate of Germany (and also the later history of Europe) lay in the fact that this German revolution came at a time when social revolutionaries had already begun to declare war on the bourgeoisie and the bourgeoisie was already afraid of the lower classes. It was the worker or artisan, not the professor or respectable merchant, who in unsettled times had actually seized firearms and shouted revolutionary utterances in the streets. Without lower-class insurrection not even middle-class revolutions have been successful. The combination that came together in France between 1789 and 1794, an unwilling and divergent combination of bourgeois and lower-class revolutionaries, could not develop in Germany in 1848. One form of revolutionary power—controlled popular turbulence—the Germans of the Frankfurt

An untimely revolution

Assembly would not or could not use. Quite the contrary: when radical riots broke out in Frankfurt itself in September 1848, the Assembly undertook to repress them. Having no force of its own, it appealed to the Prussian army. The Prussian army put down the riots, and thereafter the Assembly met under its protection.

But the most troublesome question facing the Frankfurt Assembly was not social but national. What, after all, was this "Germany" that so far existed only in the mind? The

Questions of territory

Assembly at Frankfurt, eager to create a modern German government that would represent and protect a modern national culture, could not propose a German state that would be smaller than the shadow Germany that they so much deplored. Most members of the Assembly were therefore Great Germans; they thought that the Germany for

which they were writing a constitution should include the Austrian lands, except Hungary. This would mean that the federal crown must be offered to the Habsburgs. Others, at first a minority, were Little Germans; they thought that Austria should be excluded and that the new Germany should comprise the smaller states and the entire kingdom of Prussia. In that case the king of Prussia would become the federal emperor.

The desire of the Frankfurt Assembly to retain non-German peoples in the new Germany, at a time when these peoples also were asserting national ambitions, was

Dependence on Austrian and Prussian armies

another reason for its fatal dependency upon the Austrian and Prussian armies. The Frankfurt Assembly applauded when an Austrian army broke the Czech revolution and when Prussian forces put down the Poles in Posen. On this matter the National Assembly at Frankfurt and the Prussian Assembly at Berlin did not agree. The men of Frankfurt, thinking the Prussian revolutionary assembly was too radical and pro-Polish, in effect supported the Prussian army and the Junkers against the Berlin revolution, without which the Frankfurt Assembly itself never could have existed. The Assembly, in short, turned against the revolutionary movement in Berlin and lost its earlier base of popular support. When radical riots later broke out against the Junkers, the tsar, and the Frankfurt Assembly itself, the Assembly acknowledged its weak position by calling in Prussian forces for its own protection.

The Failure of the Frankfurt Assembly

By the end of 1848 the nationalists had checkmated each other. Everywhere in central Europe, from Denmark to Naples and from the Rhineland to Romania, the awakening nationalities had failed to respect each other's aspirations; and by quarreling with each other they had hastened the return of the old absolutist and nonnational order. At Berlin and at Vienna the counterrevolution, backed by the army, was in the saddle. At this very time, in December 1848, the Frankfurt Assembly at last issued a Declaration of the Rights of the German People. It was a humane and high-minded document, announcing numerous individual rights, civil liberties, and constitutional guarantees, much along the line of the French and American declarations of the eighteenth century, but with one significant difference—the French and Americans spoke of the rights of man, while even the liberal Germans spoke of the rights of Germans. In April 1849, the Frankfurt Assembly completed its constitution. It was now clear that Austria must be excluded, for the simple reason that the restored Habsburg government refused to come in. The Little Germans in the Assembly therefore had their way. The hereditary headship of a new German Empire, a constitutional and federal union of German states minus Austria, was now offered to Frederick William IV, the king of Prussia.

Frederick William was tempted. The Prussian army officers and East Elbian landlords were not. They had no wish to lose Prussia in Germany. The king himself had his scruples. If he took the proffered crown, he would still have to impose himself by force on the lesser states, which the Frankfurt Assembly did not represent and which were in fact still the actual powers in the country. He could also expect trouble with Austria. He did not want war. Nor was it proper for an heir to the Hohenzollerns to accept a throne with constitutional limitations and representing the revolutionary conception of the sovereignty of the people. Declaring that he could not "pick up a crown from the gutter," he turned it down. It would have to be offered freely by his equals, the sovereign princes of Germany.

Frederick William tempted

Thus all the work of the Frankfurt Assembly went for nothing. Most members of the Assembly, having never dreamed of using violence in the first place, concluded that they were beaten and went home. A handful of radicals remained at Frankfurt, promulgated the constitution on their own authority, urged revolutionary outbreaks, and called for elections. Riots broke out in various places. The Prussian army put them down—in Saxony, in Bavaria, in Baden. The same army drove the rump Assembly out of Frankfurt, and that was the end of it.

The failure of liberal nationalism

In summary, liberal nationalism failed to produce a unified constitutional German state in 1848, and a less liberal kind of nationalism soon replaced it. The weakness and failures of German liberalism in 1848–1849 in the long run contributed to a complex estrangement between Germany and western Europe. The failed revolutions of 1848 also pushed thousands of disappointed German liberals and revolutionaries toward the

The Frankfurt Assembly that convened in May 1848 (as depicted in this nineteenth-century illustration) consisted mostly of professional people who feared the working classes almost as much as or more than they feared the political powers of kings and Prussian aristocrats. The members of the Assembly wrote a constitution and sought to create a constitutional monarchy for all Germany outside Austria. But the Prussian king would not accept this kind of constitutional appointment to royal power and the Frankfurt Assembly's national, democratic aspirations were blocked when the Assembly was dissolved in 1849.

(©akg-images/Newscom)

United States, where the stream of liberal immigrants came to be known as the "forty-eighters."

In Prussia itself the ingenious monarch now undertook to placate everybody by issuing a constitution of his own, one that should be peculiarly Prussian. It remained in effect from 1850 to 1918. The Constitution established a single parliament for all the miscellaneous regions of Prussia and divided the parliament into two chambers. The lower chamber was elected by universal male suffrage, but the system of elections in effect divided the population into three estates—the wealthy, the less wealthy, and the general run of the people. Those few big taxpayers who together contributed a third of the tax returns chose a third of the members of district electoral colleges, which in turn chose deputies to the Prussian lower house. In this way one large property owner had as much voting power as hundreds of working people. Large property in Prussia in 1850 still meant mainly the landed estates of the East Elbian Junkers, but as time went on, it came to include industrial property in the Rhineland also. The Junkers likewise were not harmed by the final liquidation of serfdom. They increased the acreage of their holdings, and the former servile agricultural workers turned into free wage earners economically dependent on the great landowners.

For 1850 the Prussian constitution was fairly progressive. If the mass of the people in Prussia could elect very few deputies, the mass of the British people, until 1867 or even 1884, could elect no deputies to Parliament at all. But the Prussian constitution remained in force until

The Prussian Constitution of 1850

1918. By the close of the nineteenth century, with democratic reforms advancing elsewhere, the electoral system in Prussia, by comparison, came to be more illiberal, giving the great landowners and industrialists an unusual position of electoral privilege within the state.

61. THE NEW EUROPEAN "ISMS":
REALISM, POSITIVISM, MARXISM

The revolutions of 1848 failed not only in Germany but also in Hungary, Italy, and France. The "springtime of peoples," as it was called, was followed by chilling blasts of winter. The dreams of half a century, visions of a humane nationalism, aspirations for liberalism without violence, ideals of a peaceful and democratic republican common-wealth, were all exploded. Everywhere the cry had been for constitutional government, but only in a few smaller states—Denmark, Holland, Belgium, Switzerland, Piedmont—was constitutional liberty more firmly secured by the revolutions of 1848. Everywhere the cry had been for the freedom of nations, to unify national groups or rid them of foreign rule; but nowhere was national liberty more advanced in 1850 than it had been two years before. France established universal male suffrage in 1848 and kept it permanently there-after (except for a brief reversion to a restricted suffrage in 1850–1851), but it did not establish a democracy; it settled into a kind of popular dictatorship under Louis Napoleon Bonaparte. One accomplishment, however, was real enough. The peasantry was emanci-pated in the German states and the Austrian Empire. Serfdom and manorial restraints were abolished, nor were they reimposed after the failure of the revo-lutions. This was the most fundamental accomplishment of the whole movement. The peasant masses of central Europe were thereafter free to move about, find new jobs, enter a labor market, take part in a money economy, receive and spend wages, migrate to growing cities—

New freedoms for peasants

or even go to the United States. But the peasants, once freed, showed little concern for constitutional or liberal ideas. Peasant emancipation, in fact, strengthened the forces of political counterrevolution.

The most immediate and far-reaching consequence of the 1848 revolutions, or of their failure, was a new kind of intellectual and political realism. Idealism and romanticism were discredited in European culture and politics. Revolutionaries became less optimistic; conservatives, more willing to exercise repression. It was now a point of pride to be real-istic, emancipated from illusions, willing to face facts as they were. The future, it was thought, would be determined by present realities rather than by imagining what ought to be. Industrialization went forward, with England still far in the lead, but now spreading across the Continent and initiating the momentous transformation of Germany. The 1850s were a period of rising prices and wages, thanks in part to the gold rush in California. There was more prosperity than in the 1840s; the propertied classes felt more secure, and labor leaders often turned from broad theories of society to the organizing of viable unions, especially in the skilled trades.

CHRONOLOGY OF NOTABLE EVENTS, 1848–1857

January 1848	Marx and Engels publish *The Communist Manifesto*
February 1848	Revolution in Paris; proclamation of the Second French Republic
March 1848	Revolutions in Vienna, Berlin, Bohemia, and Hungary; Metternich flees from Vienna to England; legal serfdom is abolished in central Europe
March 1848	Italians rise against Austrian rule in northern Italy
May 1848	Prussian Legislative Assembly meets in Berlin
May 1848	All-German Frankfurt Assembly convenes to draft constitution for a unified German state
June 1848	Thousands die in worker-army clashes in Paris
June–December 1848	Counterrevolutionary forces regain control of Austrian Empire: Bohemia, northern Italy, Hungary, Vienna
December 1848	Louis Napoleon Bonaparte is elected president of French Republic; Francis Joseph becomes emperor of Austrian Empire
April 1849	King Frederick William IV of Prussia rejects Frankfurt Assembly's constitution and offer of hereditary rule in a federal German state; Frankfurt Assembly is dissolved
1852	Louis Napoleon Bonaparte becomes "Emperor Napoleon III" and establishes Second French Empire
1853–1870	Baron Haussmann supervises the modern rebuilding of Paris
1857	Gustave Flaubert publishes *Madame Bovary*

Materialism, Realism, Positivism

The mid-nineteenth-century intellectual themes appeared in a new philosophical emphasis on materialism, holding that everything mental, spiritual, or ideal was an outgrowth of physical or physiological forces. In literature and the arts the new themes contributed to descriptions or portrayals of the social world that came to be called realism. Writers and painters broke away from romanticism, which they said colored things out of all relation to the real facts. The "realists" attempted to represent and reproduce life as they found it, without intimation of a better or nobler world. The French writer Gustave Flaubert, for example, wrote meticulous descriptions of a provincial woman's tedious, unhappy marriage in his famous novel *Madame Bovary* (1857), a book that both mocked the illusions of romantic literature and showed the new artistic desire for a precise, unsentimental literary language. More people in this era came to trust science, not merely for an understanding of nature but for insights into the true meaning of human life and social relations. In religion the movement was toward skepticism, renewing skeptical trends of the eighteenth century, which had been somewhat interrupted during the intervening period of romanticism. It was variously held, not by all but by many intellectuals and other persons in the urban professional classes, that religion was unscientific and hence not to be taken seriously; or that it was a mere historical growth among peoples in certain stages of development and hence irrelevant to modern civilization; or that one ought to go to church and lead a decent life, without taking the priest or clergyman too seriously, because religion was necessary to preserve the social order against radicalism and anarchy. To this idea the radical or working-class counterpart was the claim that religion was a bourgeois invention to delude the people.

"Positivism" was another term used to describe the new attitude. It originated with the French philosopher Auguste Comte, who had begun to publish his numerous volumes on *Positive Philosophy* as long

Auguste Comte

ago as 1830 and was still writing in the 1850s. He saw human history as a series of three stages, the theological, the metaphysical, and the scientific. The French revolutions of 1789 and 1848 suffered, in his view, from an excess of metaphysical abstractions, empty words, and unverifiable high-flying principles. According to Comte, those who worked for the improvement of society must adopt a strictly scientific outlook, and he set out to promote this outlook by producing an elaborate classification of the sciences, of which the highest would be the science of society, for which he coined the word "sociology." This new science would build upon the systematic observation of actual "positive" facts to develop broad scientific laws of social progress. Comte himself, and his closest disciples, envisaged a final scientific Religion of Humanity, which, stripped of archaic theological and metaphysical concerns, would serve as the basis for a better world in the future. More generally, however, positivism came to mean an insistence on verifiable facts, an avoidance of wishful thinking, a questioning of all assumptions, and a dislike of unprovable generalizations. Positivism in a broad sense, both in its demand for observation of facts and testing of ideas, and in its aspiration to be humanly useful, contributed to the growth of the social sciences as a branch of learning and as an intellectual foundation for the expanding belief in historical progress.

In politics the new emphasis on realism came to be known by the German term *Realpolitik*. This simply meant a "politics of reality." In domestic affairs it meant that people should give up utopian

Realpolitik

dreams, such as had caused the revolutionary debacle of 1848, and content themselves with the blessings of an orderly, honest, hard-working government. For radicals it meant that people should stop imagining that the new society would result from goodness or the love of justice and that social reformers must resort to the strategic methods of politics—power and calculation. In international affairs *Realpolitik* meant that governments should not be guided by ideology, or by any system of "natural" enemies or "natural" allies, or by any desire to defend or promote any particular view of the world; but that they should follow their own practical or strategic interests, meet facts and actual situations as they arose, make any alliances that seemed useful, disregard ethical theories and scruples, and use any practical means to achieve their ends. The same persons who before 1848 had been not ashamed to express pacifist and cosmopolitan hopes now dismissed such ideas as a little softheaded. War, which governments had successfully tried to prevent since the final overthrow of Napoleon in 1815, was accepted in the 1850s as a strategic option that was sometimes needed to achieve a political purpose. It was not especially glorious; it was not an end in itself; it was simply one of the tools of realistic statesmanship. *Realpolitik* was by no means confined to Germany or even to the leaders of European governments, despite its German name and despite the fact that the famous German chancellor Bismarck became its most famous practitioner. Two other *Realpolitik* thinkers, each in his own way, were Karl Marx and Louis Napoleon Bonaparte.

Early Marxism

Karl Marx and Friedrich Engels were among the disappointed revolutionaries of 1848. Marx (1818–1883) was the son of a lawyer in the Prussian Rhineland. He studied law and philosophy at several German universities and received a doctoral degree in 1841. Unable to find an academic job, Marx associated with radical German intellectuals, began writing for left-wing journals, and soon moved to Paris with other Germans who wanted to produce philosophical publications in the historic birthplace of modern revolutions. Engels (1820–1893), the son of a well-to-do German textile manufacturer, was sent as a young man to Manchester in England where his father owned a factory, to learn the business and then manage it. Marx and Engels met in Paris in 1844. The French government forced Marx to leave Paris early in the following year, but Marx and Engels would continue a close intellectual and political collaboration over the next 40 years, mostly in England.

In 1847 they joined the Communist League, a tiny secret group of revolutionaries, mainly Germans in exile in the more liberal cities of western Europe. The word "communist" then had only a vague meaning, and the League, as Engels later recalled, was at first "not actually much more than the German branch of the French secret societies." It agitated like other societies during the revolutions of 1848 and issued a set of "Demands of the Communist Party in Germany," which urged a unified indivisible German republic; democratic suffrage; universal free education; arming of the people; a progressive income tax; limitations upon inheritance; state ownership of banks, railroads, canals, mines, and the like; and a degree of large-scale, scientific, collectivized agriculture. It was such obscurely voiced radicalism that alarmed the Frankfurt Assembly. With the triumph of counterrevolution in Germany the Communist League was crushed.

The Communist League

It was for this League that Marx and Engels wrote their *Communist Manifesto,* which was published in January 1848. But there was as yet no Marxism, and Marxism played no role in the revolutions of 1848; it would not really emerge as a historical force in European societies until the 1870s. Meanwhile, with the failure of the revolutions, Engels returned to his factory at Manchester. Marx also settled in England, spending the rest of his life in London, where, after long labors in the library of the British Museum, he finally produced his huge work called *Capital,* of which the first volume was published in German in 1867. The final two volumes were edited by Engels and published after Marx's death.

Sources and Content of Marxism

Marxism may be said to have had three sources or to have merged three national streams of early nineteenth-century European history: German philosophy, French revolutionism, and the British Industrial Revolution. As a student in Germany, and for a while thereafter, Marx mingled with a group known as Young Hegelians, who were actually critics of Hegel in that they expected the course of history to lead to a free and democratic society, instead of to the existing Prussian state as Hegel had maintained. Like democrats and republicans in other countries, they believed that the promise of the French Revolution had not yet been fulfilled, because social and economic equality as well as a true political equality should follow the civil and legal equality already won. In keeping with the general movement of

The Young Hegelians

A BURIAL AT ORNANS
by Gustave Courbet (French, 1819–1877)

A new realism emerged in many spheres of European culture after the failure of the revolutions in 1848. The artist Courbet in fact began to use the term "realism" in this period to describe his work, which frequently depicted ordinary people and peasants on monumental canvasses. Paintings such as this portrayal of a funeral in the French countryside disturbed many nineteenth-century critics because Courbet painted images of the lower classes and also because he refused to romanticize his subjects or to portray common people in sentimental poses.

(©DEA/G. DAGLI ORTI/Getty Images)

romanticism, the Young (or left) Hegelians hoped for a more personal emancipation from the trammels of society, government, and religion.

In the mid-1840s, elaborating on Hegel, Marx developed the idea of the alienation of labor, a social experience and state of mind produced when human beings in the historic process of mechanization become estranged from the objects on which they work. This alienation, as Marx described it, was a distinctive feature of modern capitalist societies. The economic system of wage labor and private ownership of the means of production kept workers from identifying with or benefiting from the products of their labor. In fact, Marx argued, the wealth (or capital) that workers produced was regularly used against them in the social and political institutions of capitalist societies. It followed that true freedom would become possible only when private production of industrial goods was abolished. Some of the early writings in which these ideas were worked out in the 1840s were not published until a century later. They then led to a wide-ranging reconsideration of Marxism, in which the early Marx was seen more as a social analyst, "left" Hegelian philosopher or critical historian than as a revolutionary. But Marx's early writings had little impact on the growth of Marxism as a program for revolutionary socialism in the nineteenth century.

Engels and British industrialism

Engels, engaged in the Manchester cotton industry, possessed a personal knowledge of the new industrial and factory system in England. In 1844 he published a revealing book, *The Condition of the Working Classes in England.* He drew from his observations much the same conclusions that Marx drew from philosophical analysis and historical

Workers in Manchester came to be known as some of the most impoverished in the new industrial age, partly because writers such as Friedrich Engels focused on the city in their critiques of the capitalist economy. This image of a demoralized worker was published in Elizabeth Gaskell's novel *Mary Barton* (1848), a popular work that portrayed the miseries of the heroine's unhappy working-class father in Manchester.

(©Lebrecht/The Image Works)

study. The depressed condition of labor was an actual fact. It was a fact that labor received a relatively small portion of the national income and that much of the product of society was being reinvested in stocks and industrial technologies, which belonged as private property to private persons. Government and parliamentary institutions, also as a matter of fact, were in the hands of the well-to-do in both Great Britain and France. Religion was commonly viewed as necessary for keeping the lower classes in order, but such views did not encourage the kinds of reform movements that religious groups had often led in other centuries and in other cultures. The churches at the time actually took little interest in problems of the workers. The family, as an institution, was indeed disintegrating among laboring people in the cities, through exploitation of women and children and the overcrowding in inadequate and unsanitary living quarters.

Much of this was seized upon and dramatized in *The Communist Manifesto* as a summons to revolution. The outbreak of revolution in France in February 1848, and its rapid spread to other countries, confirmed Marx and Engels in their beliefs. They interpreted the actual class war that shook Paris in the June Days as a manifestation of a universal class struggle, in which the workers or proletariat would rise against the owners of capital, the bourgeoisie.

The Communist Manifesto

As a call to action, *The Communist Manifesto* was meant to be inflammatory. It went beyond facts to denunciation and exhortation. It said that workers were deprived of the wealth they had themselves created. It called the state a committee of the bourgeoisie for the exploitation of the people. Religion was a drug to keep the worker quietly dreaming upon imaginary heavenly rewards. The women and children in working-class families had been brutalized by the bourgeoisie, and many women were forced into prostitution. It seemed to Marx and Engels that uprooted workers should be loyal to nothing—except their own class. Even the worker's native country, in their view, had become meaningless. The proletarian had no country. Workers everywhere had the same problems and faced everywhere the same enemy. Therefore "let the ruling classes tremble at a communist revolution. The proletarians have nothing to lose but their chains. They have a world to win. Workingmen of all countries, unite!" So closed the *Manifesto*.

But Marx was more interested in revolutionary theory than daily political activity. His mature thought was a system for producing revolution, but it showed how revolution would necessarily come by operation of vast historical forces.

It was from English sources that Marx developed much of his economic theory, as expounded at length in *Capital*. From British political economy and the influential "Manchester School" of economic writers he adopted the subsistence theory of wages, or Iron Law (which most

British political economy

economists soon abandoned because wages did in fact begin to rise). This theory held that the average worker could never obtain more than a minimum living standard—of which the corollary, for those who wished to draw it, was that the existing economic system held out no better future for the laboring class as a class. Marx likewise took from British economists the labor theory of value, holding that the value of any human-made object depended ultimately on the amount of labor put into it—capital being regarded as the stored up labor of former times. Most economists, it must be said, soon discarded the theory that economic value is produced by the input of labor alone. Marx drew upon the labor theory, however, to develop his doctrine of surplus value, which, to simplify, meant in effect that workers were being robbed because they received in wages only a fraction of the value of the products that their labor produced. This difference, or surplus value, was expropriated by the capitalist owners of the factories. Workers in this system, as Marx described them, would never receive wages that were equivalent to what they produced, which meant that capitalism was constantly menaced by the overproduction of goods that people could not afford to buy. Capitalist economies thus faced recurring crises and depressions that forced the factory owners to search constantly for new and growing markets, but the structural causes of these crises did not disappear. It was the depression of 1847, according to Marx, that had precipitated the revolutions of 1848; and with every such depression during the rest of his lifetime Marx hoped that the day of the great social revolution was drawing nearer.

What brought all these economic observations together in a unified doctrine was the philosophy of dialectical materialism. By dialectic, Marx meant what the German philosopher Hegel had meant, that all things are in movement and in evolution and that all change comes through the clash of antagonistic forces and ideas. The implications of the dialectic,

Dialectical materialism

for both Hegel and Marx, were that all history is a process of development in which events unfold in a clear historical direction; that every event happens for good and sufficient reasons; and that history—though not exactly predetermined—is always shaped by impersonal forces and deep structural changes rather than by individuals or chance events.

Marx differed from Hegel in one vital respect. Whereas Hegel emphasized the primacy of ideas in social change, Marx gave emphasis to the primacy of material conditions, or the relations of production, which included technology, inventions, natural resources, and property systems. These material realities create the social world in which people live. It is the relations of production that determine the most widely accepted or dominant religions, philosophies, governments, laws, and moral values in specific societies. To believe that ideas cause the changes in social and political history was, in Marx's view, Hegel's most significant error. Hegel had thought, for example, that the mind conceives the idea of freedom, which it then realizes in the Greek city-state, in Christianity, in the French Revolution, and in the kingdom of Prussia. Not at all, according to Marx: the idea of freedom, or any other idea, was generated by specific economic and social conditions. Conditions were the roots; ideas, the trees. Hegel had held the ideas to be the roots and the resulting actual conditions to be the trees. Or as Marx and Engels said, they found Hegel standing on his head and set him on his feet again.

Historical development

In the picture of historical development offered by Marx material conditions, or the relations of production, give rise to economic classes. Agrarian conditions produce a landholding or feudal class, but with changes in trade routes, money, and productive techniques a new commercial or bourgeois class arises. Each class, feudal and bourgeois, develops an ideology suited to its economic and political needs. The two classes inevitably clash. Bourgeois revolutions against feudal interests break out when bourgeois economic development becomes increasingly constrained by the political power of the older feudal or aristocratic class—as in England in 1642, in France in 1789, in Germany in 1848, though the bourgeois revolution in Germany proved abortive.

Meanwhile, as the bourgeois class develops, it inevitably calls another class into being, its dialectical antithesis, the proletariat. The bourgeois is defined as the private owner of capital, the proletarian as the wage worker who possesses nothing but his or her own hands. The more a country becomes industrialized and bourgeois, the more it also develops a proletarian laboring class. Under competitive conditions, the bourgeois tend to devour and absorb each other; ownership of the factories, mines, machines, and railroads (capital) becomes concentrated into very few hands. Others sink into the proletariat. In the end the proletarianized mass simply takes over from the remaining bourgeois. It "expropriates the expropriators," and a social revolution abolishes private property as the ownership system for the means of production.

Marx assumed that this revolution would create a classless society, because social classes arose from economic differences that would disappear. The state and religion, being outgrowths of bourgeois interests, would also disappear. For a time, until all vestiges of bourgeois interests had been rooted out, or until the danger of counterrevolution against socialism had been overcome, there would be a "dictatorship of the proletariat." After that the state would "wither away," because there would no longer be an exploiting class that required it.

Class war between bourgeois and proletariat

In the meantime, bourgeois and proletarian were locked in a universal struggle. Marx wanted workers always to recognize that the employer was their class enemy and that government, law, morality, and religion were merely so much artillery directed against them. Workers must never let themselves be fooled; they must learn how to detect the class interest underlying the most exalted institutions and beliefs, but they would be helped by intellectuals who could explain the strategies of their economic enemies.

Worker solidarity

Given this enduring class struggle, Marx argued that it would be dangerous for labor unions merely to obtain better wages or hours by negotiation with employers, for by such little gains the war itself might be forgotten. It would likewise be dangerous, and even treasonous, for workers to put faith in democratic machinery or "social legislation," for the state's laws would continue to express the will of the stronger class; "right" and "justice" were thin emanations of class interest. We must hold, wrote Marx in 1875, to "the realistic outlook

Karl Marx as he appeared near the end of his life. By the time he sat for this photograph in the early 1880s, he had been living in London for about 30 years, but he had developed many of his social and historical theories while living on the European continent in the political, economic, and revolutionary context of the 1840s.
(©English School/Getty Images)

which has cost so much effort to instill into the party, but which has now taken root in it"; and it was by such claims to realism or a "realistic outlook" that Marx sought to separate communism from earlier socialist theories. Marx's many critics have long argued, however, that his own theories (though claiming a new realism) actually proposed inadequate or unrealistic accounts of human history as well as the future development of industrial societies.

The Significance of Marxism: Its Strength and Weaknesses

The original Marxism was a hard doctrine, with both advantages and handicaps in the winning of adherents. One of its advantages was its claim to be scientific. Marx classified earlier and rival forms of socialism as utopian: they rested on moral indignation, and their formula for reforming society was for human beings to become more just, or for the upper classes to enact reforms as they became more responsive or sympathetic to the needs of the lower classes. His own doctrine, Marx insisted, had nothing to do with ethical ideas; it was purely scientific, resting upon the study of actual facts and real processes, and it showed that socialism would be a historical continuation rather than a miraculous reversal of what was already taking place. He also considered it utopian and unscientific to describe the future socialist society in any detail. It would be classless, with neither bourgeois nor proletarian; but to lay any specific plans would be idle dreaming.

Marxism thus brought together ideas that were scientific, historical, philosophical, political, and apocalyptic. The upper classes feared and condemned Marxist ideas throughout Europe, but some elements of Marxism also reduced its attraction among the lower

*Conflicting
working-class values*

classes. The working people of Europe were not really in the frame of mind of an army in battle. They hesitated to subordinate all else to the distant prospect of a class revolution. They were not exclusively class-people, nor did they behave as such. They still held to religious beliefs or to a political faith in natural rights that could not portray morality as simply a class weapon or right and justice as bourgeois deceptions. Increasingly, they had national loyalties to their own countries, and they were not inclined to identify emotionally with a world proletariat in an unrelenting struggle against their own neighbors.

The cure for the revolutionism of 1848 proved in time to be the admission of the laboring classes to a fuller membership in economic and political institutions. Wages generally rose after 1850, labor unions were organized, and by 1870 in the principal European countries the workingman very generally had gained the right to vote. Through their unions, workers were often able to get better wages and working conditions by direct pressure upon employers. Having the vote, they gradually formed working-class parties and sought to advance their interests through the state. Marx's dismissive term for these maneuvers was "opportunism," but such political campaigns gained increasing support among workers, most of whom wanted to better themselves by dealing with employers and by obtaining social reforms through existing

Opportunism

government institutions rather than by waging class war. From Marxism the European working class absorbed much, including a watchful hostility to employers and a sense of working-class solidarity; but on the whole, as Marxism spread at the close of the nineteenth century, it ceased to be really revolutionary. Had the old Europe not gone to pieces in the twentieth-century wars, and had Marxism not been revived by Lenin and transplanted to Russia, it is probable that Marx's ideas would have been gradually domesticated into the general body of European thought and that much less would have been said about them in later years in Europe or elsewhere.

62.   BONAPARTISM: THE SECOND FRENCH EMPIRE, 1852–1870

The new realism in European culture after 1848 extended also to the exercise of post-revolutionary political power. We have seen how Louis Napoleon Bonaparte, elected president of the French Republic in 1848, soon made himself Emperor of the French with the title of Napoleon III. Those willing to fight for the parliamentary and liberal institutions that he crushed were silenced. He became chief of state and then Emperor (in 1852) on a wave of popular acclaim.

Political Institutions of the Second Empire

Napoleon III, like Napoleon I, came to power because of the fear of radicalism in a discredited republic. Otherwise he bore little resemblance to his famous uncle. He was not a professional soldier or a great organizer. When he became president of the republic at the age of 40 he had been an adventurer and a conspirator, but he undoubtedly felt more concern than Napoleon I for the plight of the working classes. Where Napoleon I had been disdainful of public opinion, his nephew recognized it as an opportunity, not a nuisance; and he appealed to the masses by giving them the vote (however useless), by promises of prosperity, and by pageantry. He understood perfectly that a single leader exerts more magnetism than an elected assembly. And he knew that a Europe still shuddering over the June Days was hoping desperately for order in France.

He gloried in modern progress. Napoleon III boldly offered himself as the strong leader who would move France toward a brave new
world. Like his uncle, he announced that he embodied the sovereignty
of the people. He said that he had found a solution to the problem of
mass democracy. In all the other great Continental states and in Great Britain, in 1852,
universal suffrage was thought to be incompatible with intelligent government and
economic prosperity. Napoleon III claimed to put them together. Like Marx and other
realists after 1848 he held that elected parliamentary bodies, far from representing an
abstract "people," only accentuated class divisions within a country. He declared that the
regime of the restored Bourbons and the July Monarchy had been dominated by special
interests; that the republic of 1848 had fallen into the hands of a distrustful assembly that
robbed the laboring man of his vote; and that France would find in the empire the
permanent, popular, and modern system for which it had been vainly searching since
1789. He affirmed that he stood above classes and would govern equally in the interests
of all. In any case, like many other political leaders after 1848, he held that forms of
government were less important than economic and social realities.

Napoleon III's view of progress

The political institutions of the Second Empire were therefore
authoritarian, modeled on those of the Consulate of the first Bonaparte. There was a Council of State, composed of experts who drafted
legislation and advised on technical matters. There was also an appointive Senate and a Legislative Body, which was elected by universal male suffrage in carefully
managed elections. But the Legislative Body had no real power to make laws, set the
budget, or control the army. Parliamentary life was reduced almost to absolute zero.

Authoritarian political institutions

To captivate public attention and glorify the Napoleonic name the new emperor set
up a sumptuous court at the Tuileries. Balked in the ambition to marry into one of the
great dynasties, Napoleon III chose as his empress a young Spanish noblewoman, Eugénie,
who was destined to outlive the empire by 50 years, dying in 1920. It was said to be a
love match—a sure sign of popularized royalty. The court life of the empire was brilliant
and showy beyond anything known at the time in St. Petersburg or Vienna, and the
pageantry was expanded into the embellishment of the city of Paris. Baron Haussmann,
who served as Napoleon III's creative, strong-willed city planner for major renovations in
the French capital, gave Paris much of the appearance that it has today. He built roomy
railway stations with broad approaches, and he constructed a system of boulevards and
public squares offering long vistas ending in fine buildings or monuments, as at the Place
de l'Opéra. He also modernized the sewers and the water supply. The building program,
like the expensive court, had the additional advantage of stimulating business and employment. And the cutting of wide avenues through the crooked streets and congested old
houses would permit easier military operations against insurrectionists entrenched behind
barricades, should the events of 1848 ever be repeated.

Economic Developments under the Empire

It was as a great social engineer that Napoleon III preferred to be known. In his youth
he had tried to understand the riddle of modern industrialism, and now, as emperor, he
found some of his main backers in former Saint-Simonians, who called him their "socialist
emperor." Saint-Simon, it may be recalled, had been among the first to conceive of a
centrally planned industrial system. But the Saint-Simonians of the 1850s shared the new
desire to be realistic, and their most significant triumph was the invention of investment
banking, by which they hoped to guide economic growth through the concentration of

financial resources. They founded a novel kind of French banking institution, the *Crédit Mobilier,* which raised funds by selling its shares to the public, and with the funds thus obtained bought stock in such new industrial enterprises as it wished to develop. France entered a new phase of rapid economic development through a distinctive French version of the Industrial Revolution.

Expansion

The times were exceedingly favorable for expansion, for the discovery of gold in California in 1849, and in Australia soon afterward, together with the newly organized credit facilities, brought a substantial increase in the European money supply, which had a mildly inflationary effect. The steady rise of prices encouraged the expansion of new companies and the investment of capital. Railway mileage, increasing everywhere in the Western world, increased in France from 3,000 to 16,000 kilometers in the 1850s. The demand for rolling stock, iron rails, auxiliary equipment, and building materials for stations and freight houses kept the mines and factories busy. The railway network was rationalized, 55 small lines in France being merged into six big regional trunks. Iron steamboats replaced wooden sailing ships. Between 1859 and 1869 a French company built the Suez Canal, which it continued to own for almost a century, though the British government after 1875 was the principal stockholder.

Large French corporations made their appearance, in railroads and banking first of all. In 1863 the law granted the right of "limited liability," by which a stockholder could not lose more than the par value of the stock, however insolvent or debt-burdened the corporation might become. This encouraged investment by persons of both smaller and larger means in enterprises of which they knew very little; thus the wealth and savings of the country were more effectively mobilized and put to work. The Stock Exchange boomed. Financiers—those whose business was to handle money, credit, and securities—assumed a new eminence in the capitalistic world as more investors bought shares in the new industrial companies. Many people became very rich, richer perhaps than anyone had ever been in France before.

The emperor aspired also to do something for the working class, within the limits of the existing system. Jobs were plentiful and wages were good, by the ideas of the day, at least until the temporary depression of 1857. The emperor had a plan, as did some of the Saint-Simonians, for organizing forces of workers in military fashion and setting them to clear and develop uncultivated land. Not much was done in this direction. More was accomplished in the humanitarian relief of suffering. Hospitals and asylums were established, and free medicines were distributed. The outlines of a social-welfare state began somewhat vaguely to appear. Meanwhile the workers were building up unions. All combinations of workers had been prohibited during the French Revolution, a prohibition that was deemed to be still in force until the ambiguous legal position of labor unions began to change. In 1864 it even became legal for organized workers to go on strike. Large labor units, or unions, and large business units, or corporations, were thus legalized at the same time. Napoleon III hardly did enough for labor to rank as a working-class hero, but he did enough to be suspected as "socialistic" by many middle-class people of the day.

Napoleon's "socialistic" initiatives

Later authoritarian regimes, bent like the Second Empire on a program of economic development, were usually highly protectionist, but Napoleon III believed in freedom of international trade. He had a project for a tariff union with Belgium, which some Belgians also supported. Belgium was already well industrialized, and a Franco-Belgium

Napoleon III's ambitious plan to rebuild the city of Paris became one of the great urban projects of modern times. Organized by the strong-willed Baron Haussmann, the systematic, controversial reconstruction of Parisian streets, parks, buildings, sewers, and monuments transformed the city and produced an aesthetic grandeur that has drawn visitors ever since. This illustration from a London newspaper in the 1860s shows work crews and equipment at a demolition site on the Left Bank of the Seine.

(©Popperfoto/Getty Images)

union, especially because Belgium had the coal that France lacked, would have formed a trading area of very great strength. The plan was blocked by private interests in both countries, however, and strongly opposed by both Great Britain and the German *Zollverein*. The emperor then turned to an all-around reduction of import duties. Since the repeal of the Corn Laws in 1846 the free traders were in power in England. They were eager to abolish trade barriers between Britain and France. Napoleon III, overriding unusual opposition in his Legislative Body, concluded a free trade treaty with Great Britain in 1860. He set aside 40 million francs of government funds to assist French manufacturers in making adjustments to British competition; but this sum was never spent in full, which suggests that French industry was generally able to compete successfully with the more intensively mechanized industry of Britain. The Anglo-French treaty was accompanied by lesser trade agreements with other countries. It looked, in the 1860s, as if Europe might actually be about to enter a new era of economic cooperation and free trade.

Free trade treaty with Britain

Internal Difficulties and War

But by 1860 the empire was running into trouble. It took a few years to overcome the depression of 1857. By his policy of free trade the emperor made enemies among certain industrialists. The Catholics objected to his intervention in Italy, where he briefly joined an anti-Austrian military campaign in 1859. After 1860 opposition mounted. The emperor granted more leeway to the long-subservient Legislative Body. The 1860s are called the decade of the Liberal Empire—all such terms being relative. The empire might have evolved through these internal changes, but Louis Napoleon actually ruined himself by war before internal reforms could have much effect. His empire evaporated on the battlefield in 1870, but he was at war long before that.

"The empire means peace," he had assured his audiences in 1852. Yet war is after all a supreme form of pageantry (or was then), France was the strongest country in Europe, and the emperor's name was Napoleon. Less than a year and a half after the proclamation of the empire France was at war with a European state for the first time since Waterloo. The enemy was Russia, and the war was fought mainly on the Crimean Peninsula along the north coast of the Black Sea. Although Napoleon III did not alone instigate the Crimean War, this conflict showed his inclination to send French armies abroad. In 1859 the new Napoleon was fighting in Italy, from 1862 to 1867 in Mexico, and in 1870 in France itself, in a war with Prussia that he could easily have avoided. These wars were limited in scope and duration (as compared to the huge Napoleonic wars in the early nineteenth century), but they formed part of the wider European struggles for international influence, which are discussed in the next chapter.

It is enough to say here that in 1870 the Second Empire went the way of the First, into the limbo of governments tried and discarded by the French. It had lasted 18 years, exactly as long as the July Monarchy, and longer than any other regime known in France, up to that time, since the fall of the Bastille. Not until the twentieth century, when dictators sprouted all over Europe, did people begin to recognize that the authoritarian Louis Napoleon and his strongman uses of state power had been an anti-democratic omen of the future rather than a bizarre reincarnation of the past.

> *"The empire means peace"*

Suggested Further Readings can be found in the ebook, on Connect, or online at www.mhhe.com/kramer12e.

Chapter 13

THE CONSOLIDATION OF LARGE NATION-STATES, 1859–1871

The rise of nineteenth-century nationalism and the quest for unified national governments led to a remarkable consolidation of nation-states during the 12 years after 1859. Notable political unifications and reforms in Europe during this period included the formation of a new German empire, a unified kingdom of Italy, the Dual Monarchy of Austria-Hungary, and the introduction of drastic internal changes in tsarist Russia. Although this chapter focuses mainly on national consolidations within Europe, it should be noted that the unification of larger European states was part of a wider global pattern that included the triumph of central authority after a civil war in the United States, the creation of an independent, united Dominion of Canada, and the emergence of a modernizing government and economy in the empire of Japan. All these disparate events were influenced and advanced by the development of new technologies such as the railroad, steamship, and telegraph. The communication of ideas, exchange of goods, and movement of people over wide areas became more frequent and easier than ever before. New technologies and the rapid expansion of new industries strengthened the political power of nation-states, which gained increasing influence in the evolving social, economic, and cultural life of all modern societies.

63. BACKGROUNDS: THE IDEA OF THE NATION-STATE

Before 1860 there were two prominent, relatively coherent nation-states in Europe—Great Britain and France. Spain, united on the map, was internally so fragmented as to belong to a different category. Portugal, Switzerland, the Netherlands, and the Scandinavian

Chapter emblem: Painting by Anton von Werner of the Proclamation of the German Empire at Versailles in 1871. (©ullstein bild Dtl./Getty Images)

countries were nation-states, but small or peripheral in this era to the main national centers of European power. The characteristic political organizations were small states comprising fragments of a nation, such as were strewn across the middle of Europe—Hanover, Baden, Sardinia, Tuscany, or the Two Sicilies—and large sprawling empires made up of all sorts of peoples, distantly ruled from above by dynasties and bureaucracies, such as the Romanov, Habsburg, and Ottoman domains. Except for recent developments in the Americas the same mixture of small nonnational states and of large nonnational empires was to be found in most of the rest of the world.

Since the later nineteenth century a nation-state system has prevailed as the main form of governmental power, even where later international alliances and free trade agreements have expanded all kinds of transnational exchanges. The consolidation of large nations became a model for other peoples large and small. In time, in the following century, other large groups of people undertook to establish nation-states as they gained independence from European colonial empires in Asia, Africa, and the Middle East. Small and middle-sized populations increasingly thought of themselves as nations, entitled to their own political sovereignty and independence. Some of these sovereignties that emerged after 1945 comprised fewer people than a single modern city. The idea of the nation-state has thus served both to bring people together into larger units and to break them apart into smaller ones. In the nineteenth century, outside the disintegrating Ottoman Empire, from which Greece, Serbia, Bulgaria, and Romania became independent, and in which an Arab national movement also began to stir, the national idea served mainly to create larger units in place of small ones. The map of Europe from 1871 to 1918 was the simplest it has ever been before or since (see map, pp. 570–571).

Unity and disunity

This book has already had much to say about the idea of the nation-state and the emergence of modern nationalisms. Earlier chapters have described the ferment of national ideas and political movements stirred up by the French Revolution and by the Napoleonic domination of Europe, the nationalist agitation and repression of nationalism in the years after 1815, and the general failure to achieve popular nationalist aspirations in Germany, Italy, and central Europe in the Revolution of 1848. For many in the nineteenth century, nationalism became a kind of modern secular faith; and it spread throughout most of Europe, stimulating an emotion-laden desire for national unity, independence, and the creation of a national state that could embody and protect a distinctive national culture. For most devout nationalists, the nation represented higher truths as well as collective and personal aspirations for a better future life.

Characteristics of nation-states

A nation-state may be thought of as one in which supreme political authority somehow rests upon and represents the will and feeling of its inhabitants. There must be a people, not merely a swarm of human beings. As Louis Kossuth and other nationalists asserted in the revolutions of 1848, people must feel some common cultural and political identity and have the will to create a sovereign government. They must sense that they belong—that they are members of a community, participating somehow in a common social and cultural life, that the government is their government, and that outsiders are "foreign." The outsiders or foreigners are usually (though not always) those who speak a different language. The nation is usually (though not always) composed of persons sharing the same speech. A nation may also possess a belief in common descent or racial origin (however mistaken), or a sense of a common history (remembered as coherent and purposeful), a common future, a common religion, a common geographical home, or a common external menace. Nations take form in many ways. But the people in all nations are alike in feeling or imagining themselves to be communities, permanent communities in which individual persons, together with their children and their children's children, are committed to a collective destiny on earth. Such beliefs in a shared collective culture do not arise spontaneously in large populations. They develop over time and are sustained by the social networks in which individuals go about their daily lives. People learn to identify with their nations as they grow up in the families, schools, social organizations, religious institutions, and holiday rituals that shape a sense of selfhood in modern human societies.

In the nineteenth century governments found that they could not effectively rule or develop the full powers of state except by enlisting this sense of membership and support among their subjects. The consolidation of large nation-states had two distinguishable phases. Territorially, it meant the union of preexisting smaller states. Politically and psychologically it meant the creation of new ties between government and governed, the admission of new segments of the population to political life, through the expansion of education and through the creation or extension of liberal and representative institutions. This process of national integration and institution-building was repeated in widely disparate cultures, ranging from western Europe and tsarist Russia to Japan and the frontier societies of North America. Although there was considerable variation in the real power of the new political institutions and in the extent of actual self-government within the different nations, parliaments were set up for the new Italy, the new Germany, the new Japan, the new Canada; and there was eventually movement in Russia in the same direction. In Europe, some of the nationalist aims that the revolutionists had failed to achieve in 1848 were now brought about by the established authorities.

Consolidation and constitutionalism

They were brought about, however, only through a series of wars. To create an all-German or an all-Italian state, as the revolutions of 1848 had already shown, it was necessary to break the power of Austria, render Russia at least temporarily ineffective, and overthrow or intimidate those German and Italian governments that refused to surrender their sovereignty. For almost 40 years after 1815 there had been no war between established powers of Europe. Then in 1854 came the Crimean War; in 1859, the Italian War; in 1864, the Danish War; in 1866, the Austro-Prussian War; and in 1870, the Franco-Prussian War. Concurrently the Civil War in the United States maintained national unity by suppressing a secessionist movement for southern independence. After 1871, for 43 years there was again no war in Europe between the major European powers.

The Crimean War, 1854-1856

Before moving on to the first of the national consolidation movements, the Italian, we must examine the Crimean War, which, though seemingly remote to most Europeans, helped to make possible the success of the European national movements. Its chief political significance for Europe was that it seriously weakened both Austria and Russia, the two powers most bent on preserving the peace settlement of 1815 and on preventing national changes. The Crimean War also had significant cultural and social influences, however, because it became a new kind of modern national war in which telegraph communications kept the civilian populations of the western belligerent powers more immediately informed about distant military campaigns. It was the first war covered by newspaper correspondents and the first to be portrayed to noncombatants in the visual images of early photography; and it was the first war in which women, led by Britain's Florence Nightingale, established their position as army nurses.

Russian pressure

The pressure of Russia upon Ottoman Turkey was an old story. Every generation saw its Russo-Turkish war. In the last Russo-Turkish war, to go back no further than 1828–1829, Tsar Nicholas I protected the independence newly won by Greece and annexed the left bank of the mouth of the Danube. Now, in 1853, Nicholas again made demands upon the still large but weakened Ottoman Empire, moving in on the two Danubian principalities, Wallachia and Moldavia (later to be known as Romania), with military forces (see map, p. 675). The dispute this time ostensibly involved the protection of Christians in the Ottoman Empire, including the foreign Christians at Jerusalem and in Palestine. Over these Christians the French also claimed a certain protective jurisdiction. The French had for centuries been the western European people who were most engaged in the Middle East. They had often furnished money and advisers to the Ottoman sultan, they carried on a huge volume of trade, they staffed and financed Christian missions, and they often talked of building a Suez canal. Napoleon III thus had his own aspirations in the eastern Mediterranean, and he encouraged the Ottoman government to resist Russian claims to protect Christians within the Ottoman Empire. War between Russia and Turkey broke out late in 1853. In 1854 France joined the side of the Turks, as did Great Britain, whose settled policy was to uphold Ottoman Turkey and the Middle East against any Russian expansion. The two Western powers were soon joined by a small ally, the kingdom of Sardinia, better known because of its Italian mainland territory and seat of government as Piedmont. Sardinia had no visible interest in the issues in the Middle East, but it entered the war as a means to influence the Italian question.

The British fleet successfully blockaded Russia in both its Baltic and Black Sea outlets. French and British armies invaded Russia itself, landing in the Crimean Peninsula, to which all the important fighting was confined. The Austrian Empire had its own reasons to oppose Russian expansion into Ottoman territories; and the Austrians did not want Russia to conquer the Balkans, or to see Britain and France master the situation alone. Austria therefore, though still recovering from the recent upheaval of 1848–1849, mobilized its armed forces at a great effort to itself and occupied Wallachia and Moldavia, which the Russians evacuated under this threat of attack by a new enemy. Tsar Nicholas died in 1855, and his successor, Alexander II, sued for peace.

Peace in 1856

A congress of all the great powers made a peace treaty at Paris in 1856, pledging jointly to maintain the "integrity of the Ottoman Empire." The Russian tide ebbed a little. Russia ceded some territory to Moldavia and gave up its claim to the special protection of Christians in the Ottoman Empire. Moldavia and Wallachia (united as Romania in 1858), together with Serbia, were recognized as self-governing principalities under protection of the European powers. At the Congress of Paris European diplomacy seemed to be achieving a more harmonious international system.

But trouble was in the making. Napoleon III needed glory. The Italians wanted some kind of unified Italy. The Prussians, who had done nothing in the Crimean War and were only tardily invited to the Congress of Paris, feared that their status as a great power might be slipping away. Napoleon III, the Italian nationalists, and the Prussians all stood to gain by change. Change in central Europe and Italy meant a tearing up of the Treaty of Vienna of 1815, long guarded by Metternich and unsuccessfully challenged by the revolutionaries of 1848. Now, after the Crimean War, the forces opposing change were very weak. It was the Russian and Austrian empires that had stood firmly for the status quo. But these two powers, which had most seriously attempted to uphold the Vienna settlement, could do so no longer. The first proof came in Italy.

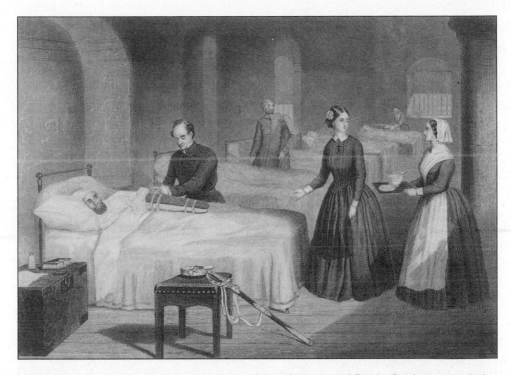

The Crimean War weakened the international position of Austria and Russia, but its most enduring effect on nations such as Britain may have come in the ways that wars were described in the popular press and in the new role of women nurses. Florence Nightingale arrived in the Crimea with 36 nurses and was at first opposed by army doctors. She is pictured here in one of the hospitals where she began to create the new military and social identity of the female nurse.

(©Time Life Pictures/Getty Images)

64. CAVOUR AND THE ITALIAN WAR OF 1859: THE UNIFICATION OF ITALY

Italian Nationalism: The Program of Cavour

In Italy there had long been about a dozen sizable states, together with a few very small ones. Several of them had dissolved in the wars of the French Revolution, and all had been reorganized, first by Napoleon and then by the Congress of Vienna. The governments of these states were generally content with their autonomy and independence. But the governments were remote from their peoples.

There was a widespread disgust in Italy with the existing authorities, and a growing desire for a liberal national state in which all Italy might be embodied and through which the Italian grandeur of ancient times and of the Renaissance might be resurrected. This sentiment, the dream of an Italian Risorgimento, or resurgence, had become very heated at the time of the French Revolution and Napoleon, and had then been transformed by the writings of Mazzini and other nationalists into an intensely moral campaign for Italian national unity. Mazzini had seen his hopes for a unified republican Italy elevated for a brief moment

Italian Risorgimento

Historical Interpretations and Debates
The Roots of Modern Nationalism

Nationalist movements gained wide influence during the nineteenth century by combining a popular belief in the distinctive cultural traits of different human communities with an equally popular claim that every such cultural group should have its own sovereign political state. Most historians of nationalism agree that these ideas spread widely in modern schools, newspapers, political parties, and government institutions. They frequently disagree, however, about the influence of modern social and economic changes on the rise of nationalism; and they propose different interpretations of the possible continuities between premodern cultures and modern national identities. Compare the views of Ernest Gellner and Anthony D. Smith as they analyze the social roots and premodern origins of modern nationalisms and national identities.

Ernest Gellner, *Nations and Nationalism* (2nd ed., 2006)

Contrary to popular and even scholarly belief, nationalism does not have very deep roots in the human psyche. . . . What is crucial for its genuine explanation is to identify its specific roots. . . .

The roots of nationalism in the distinctive structural requirements of industrial society are very deep indeed. This movement [toward nationalism] is the fruit neither of ideological aberration, nor of emotional excess. . . .

Universal literacy and a high level of numerical, technical and general sophistication are among [industrial society's] functional prerequisites. Its members are and must be mobile and ready to shift from one activity to another. . . . The educational system which guarantees this social achievement becomes large and is indispensable. . . .

[This] educational infrastructure is too large and costly for any organization other than the biggest one of all, the state. . . .

[State] and culture *must* now be linked, whereas in the past their connection was . . . often minimal. Now it is unavoidable. That is what nationalism is about, and why we live in an age of nationalism. . . .

But nationalism is *not* the awakening of an old, latent, dormant force, though that is how it does indeed present itself. It is in reality the consequence of a new form of [industrial] social organization, based on deeply internalized, education-dependent high cultures, each protected by its own state. . . .

Anthony D. Smith, *The Nation in History: Historiographical Debates about Ethnicity and Nationalism* (2000)

[I] stress the importance of treating the history of collective cultural identities and ideologies like nations and nationalism over long time spans. This is quite compatible with the evidence that nationalism is a modern ideological movement and that many nations are both recent and novel. But these modern nations are not created ex nihilo; they have premodern antecedents that require investigation in order to establish the basis on which they were formed. . . .

[The] central components of ethnic and national phenomena [are] both sociocultural and symbolic, rather than demographic or political. Apart from various symbols, like language, dress, emblems, rituals, and artifacts, these elements consist in memories, myths, values, and traditions and in the institutionalized practices that derive from them. . . .

[We] can begin to interpret the historical record of collective cultural identities and sentiments as predominantly one in which *ethnies* flourished alongside other collectivities in the ancient and medieval epochs of empires, city-states, and kingdoms. . . . Thus, in several cases we find elements of nationhood stretching back to the late medieval period. . . . We can still agree that nations, like nationalisms, are for the most part relatively recent. . . .

Ernest Gellner . . . *(contd. . . .)*	**Anthony D. Smith . . .** *(contd. . . .)*
Nations as a natural, God-given way of classifying men, as an inherent though long-delayed political destiny are a myth.	But this does not entail the acceptance of the modernists' further contention that nations are the products of modernity or modernization. . . . We cannot derive the identity, the location, or even the character of the units we term nations from the processes of modernization *tout court.*

Sources: Ernest Gellner, *Nations and Nationalism,* 2nd ed., introduction by John Breuilly (Ithaca, NY: Cornell University Press, 2006), pp. 34, 36–37, 46–47; Antony D. Smith, *The Nation in History: Historiographical Debates about Ethnicity and Nationalism* (Hanover, NH: University Press of New England, 2000), pp. 63, 69.

and then blasted in the general debacle of 1848. In the stormy events of 1848 the pope had vehemently rejected the radical romantic republicanism of Mazzini and Garibaldi and turned against the whole cause of Italian nationalism. The same events had shown that Austria could not be ousted from the Italian peninsula without the aid of an outside power.

These lessons were not lost on the prime minister of Piedmont, Camillo di Cavour, one of the shrewdest political tacticians of that or any age. Serving as prime minister for almost ten years after 1852, Cavour was a mid-century liberal who wanted Piedmont to be a model of modern progress, efficiency, and fair government that other Italians would admire. He worked hard to establish modern parliamentary practices in a constitutional monarchy under King Victor Emmanuel. He favored the building of railroads and docks, the improvement of agriculture, and emancipation of trade. He followed a strongly anti-clerical policy, cutting down the number of religious holidays, limiting the right of church bodies to own real estate, abolishing the church courts—all without negotiation with the Holy See. A liberal constitutional monarchist and a wealthy landowner in his own right, he had no sympathy for the revolutionary, romantic, and republican nationalism of Mazzini.

Cavour's "politics of reality"

Cavour shared in the new, post-1848 realism described in the last chapter. He did not idealize war but was willing to make war to unify Italy under the royal family of Savoy. With unruffled calculation he took Piedmont into the Crimean War, sending troops to Russia in the hope of winning a place at the peace table and raising the Italian question at the Congress of Paris. It was evident to him that against one great power one must pit another and that the only way to get Austria out of Italy was to use the French army. He therefore developed a master plan to provoke war with Austria, after having assured himself of French military support.

It was not difficult to persuade Napoleon III to collaborate. The Bonapartes looked upon Italy as their ancestral country, and Napoleon III, in his adventurous youth, had traveled in conspiratorial Italian circles and even participated in an Italian insurrection in 1831. Now, as emperor and as an apostle of modernity, he entertained a "doctrine of nationalities" that held the consolidation of nations to be a forward step at the existing stage of history. To fight reactionary Austria for the freedom of Italy would also mollify liberal opinion in France, which in other ways Napoleon was engaged in suppressing. Napoleon III therefore reached a secret agreement with Cavour. In April 1859, Cavour tricked Austria into a declaration of war. The French army poured over the Alps.

There were two battles, Magenta and Solferino, both won by the French and Pied-montese. But Napoleon III was now in a quandary. In Italy, with the defeat of the Austrians, revolutionary agitation broke out all over the peninsula, as it had a decade before—and the French emperor was no patron of popular revolution. The revolutionaries overthrew or denounced the existing governments and clamored for annexation to Pied-mont. In France, as elsewhere, the Catholics, fearful that the pope's temporal power would be lost, upbraided the emperor for his godless and unnecessary war. The French position was indeed odd, for while the bulk of the French army fought Austria in the north, a French military detachment was still stationed in Rome, sent there in 1849 to protect the pope against Italian republicanism. Napoleon III, in July 1859, at the height of his victo-ries, stupefied Cavour. He made a separate peace with the Austrians.

	The Franco-Austrian agreement gave Lombardy to Piedmont but left
Franco-Austrian agreement	Venetia within the Austrian Empire. It offered a compromise solution to the Italian question, in the form of a federal union of the existing Italian governments, to be presided over by the pope. This was not what Cavour

or the Piedmontese or the more fiery Italian patriots wanted. Revolution continued to spread across the northern Italian states. Tuscany, Modena, Parma, and Romagna drove out their old rulers. They were annexed to Piedmont, after plebiscites or general elections in these regions had shown overwhelming popular favor for this step. Because Romagna belonged to the papal states, the pope excommunicated the organizers of the new Italy. Undeterred, representatives of all north Italy except Venetia met at the Piedmontese capital of Turin in 1860 in the first parliament of the enlarged kingdom. The British government hailed these events with enthusiasm, and Napoleon III also recognized the expanded Piedmontese state, in return for the transfer to France of Nice and Savoy, where plebiscites disclosed enormous majorities for annexation to France.

The Completion of Italian Unity

There were now, in 1860, a north Italian kingdom, the papal states in the middle, and the kingdom of the Two Sicilies, ruled by a Bourbon king in Naples and still standing in the south. A Piedmontese republican, Giuseppe Garibaldi, brought the kingdom of the Two Sicilies to a revolutionary crisis. Somewhat like Lafayette, Garibaldi was a "hero of two worlds," who had fought for the independence of Uruguay, lived in the United States, and been one of the Triumvirs in the short-lived Roman Republic of 1849. He now orga-nized a group of about 1,150 personal followers—Garibaldi's Thousand, or the Red Shirts—for an armed expedition that he would lead from northern Italy to the kingdom of the Two Sicilies in the south. Garibaldi landed in Sicily and soon crossed to the mainland. Revolutionists hastened to join him, and the Bourbon government of the Two Sicilies, backward and corrupt, commanding little loyalty from its population, collapsed before this picturesque march into Naples.

Garibaldi now prepared to push from Naples up to Rome. Here, of course, he would meet not only the pope but also the French army, and the international scandal would

	reverberate far beyond Italy. Cavour, examining the new opportunities
Garibaldi's compromise	with his usual pragmatism, decided that so extreme a step must be averted, but he also saw that Garibaldi's successes must be used to advance the national cause. Garibaldi, though not all his followers, was

now ready to accept a monarchy as the best solution to the problem of Italian unification. The chief of the Red Shirts, the one-time foe of kings thus consented to ride in an open carriage with the king of Piedmont, Victor Emmanuel, through the streets of Naples amid

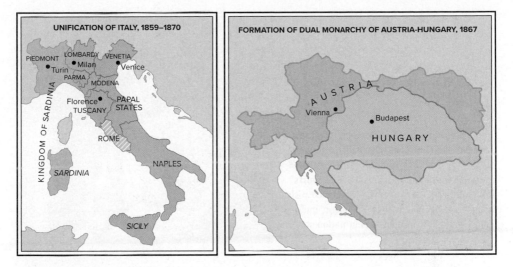

UNIFICATION OF ITALY, 1859–1870

FORMATION OF DUAL MONARCHY OF AUSTRIA-HUNGARY, 1867

NATION-BUILDING, 1859–1867

In the eight years after 1859 Italy was unified (except for the city of Rome, annexed in 1870), and the Habsburg government tried to solve its nationalities problem by creating the Dual Monarchy of Austria-Hungary. The maps show the political components of the new Italian nation-state and the two adjoining regions that formed the Habsburg-ruled Dual Monarchy in central Europe.

cheering thousands. Plebiscites held in the Two Sicilies showed an almost unanimous willingness to join with Piedmont. In the remainder of the papal states, except for Rome and its environs, plebiscites were held also, with the same result. A parliament representing all Italy except Rome and Venetia met in 1861, and the Kingdom of Italy was formally proclaimed, with Victor Emmanuel II as king "by grace of God and the will of the nation." Venetia was added in 1866, as a reward for Italian aid to Prussia in a war against Austria. Rome was annexed in 1870 after the withdrawal of French troops in the Franco-Prussian War of 1870.

So Italy was "made," as the phrase of the time expressed it. It had been made by the high-minded cultural nationalism of Mazzini, the audacity of Garibaldi, and the cold realism of Cavour. In the end, however, the Italians also achieved national unification through insurrections, armed violence, and the endorsement of popular votes.

Persistent Problems after Unification

Very little was settled or ended by unification. Even territorially, the more pronounced nationalists refused to believe that Italian unity was completed. They looked beyond to regions of mixed population where Italians were numerous or preponderant—to the Trentino, to Trieste, to certain Dalmatian islands, or to Nice and Savoy. They saw in these regions an *Italia irredenta,* "an unredeemed Italy," awaiting in its turn the day of incorporation. Irredentism even passed into the English language as a word signifying a vociferous demand, on nationalist grounds, for annexation of regions beyond one's own frontiers.

The occupation of Rome in 1870 by the Italian government further widened the rift between the church and the Italian national movement. The pope, deprived of territories the papacy had held for a thousand

Occupation of Rome

This photograph of Giuseppe Garibaldi suggests the confident, charismatic personal style that enabled him to lead a spirited group of Italian nationalists or "Red Shirts" into southern Italy, to form an alliance with King Victor Emmanuel of Piedmont, and to help establish a unified Italian nation-state.
(©Hulton Archive/Getty Images)

years, renewed his condemnations of Italian nationalists and chose to remain in lifelong seclusion in the Vatican. His successors followed the same policy until 1929. Hence good Italian patriots were bound to be anticlerical, and good Catholics were bound to look upon the Italian state with unfriendly eyes. The regional differences between northern and southern Italy did not disappear with unification. Many nationalists in the north still looked upon the agrarian south—the land of priest, landlord, and impoverished peasant—as disgracefully backward.

The new Italy was parliamentary but not democratic. At first the vote was only given to some 600,000 men in a country of almost 25 million people. Not until 1913 was the male suffrage significantly broadened (and women would not gain the right to vote until 1945). Meanwhile parliamentary life, confined to a few, was somewhat isolated from most of the population and frequently corrupt. But the political dream of ages was realized. Italy was one. The period of fragmentation and foreign rule that seemed so shameful to patriots, the long centuries that had elapsed since the Renaissance, were now terminated in the glories of a successful Risorgimento.

65.   THE FOUNDING OF A GERMAN EMPIRE AND THE DUAL MONARCHY OF AUSTRIA-HUNGARY

The major European powers had long enhanced their own strategic positions by keeping Germany divided into small, weak states that could never have much influence in diplomacy, warfare, or the expanding global economy. To play upon the divisions among the Germans, keeping them in rivalry with each other and dependent upon outside powers, had been the policy of France ever since the Reformation and of Russia since it entered into the affairs of Europe. To keep the Germanic world divided was in fact a kind of negative prerequisite to the development of early modern European history as we know it, for without it the economic and cultural leadership of Europe would hardly have become concentrated along the Atlantic seaboard; nor would a great military empire have arisen in Russia and spread along the Baltic and into Poland.

Gradually, as we have seen, the Germans became dissatisfied with their weak, fragmented position. They became increasingly nationalistic during and after the

Napoleonic wars. Many German thinkers held that Germany was different from both western and eastern Europe, destined someday to work out its own distinctive German way of life and political system. The Germans felt immeasurably superior to the Slavic peoples and cultures. German philosophy, as shown most clearly in Hegel, took on a certain characteristic tone. It tended to criticize modern individualism and to skip lightly over liberal conceptions of individual liberty; it also tended to glorify the state, the nation, and group loyalties. It emphasized the progressive evolution of history, which in the thought of Hegel, and after him Marx, became a vast impersonal force that was moving in clear directions and almost independent of human beings or human will. History was often said to ordain, require, condemn, justify, or excuse. What one did not like could be dismissed as a mere historical phase, opening into a quite different and more attractive future. What one wanted, in the present or future, could be described as historically necessary and bound to come.

The German States after 1848

In 1848 a series of revolutions had unseated the several governments of Germany. At the Frankfurt Assembly a group composed essentially of private citizens had tried to organize a united Germany by constitutional methods. They failed because they had no power. Hence after 1848 the Germans began to think in terms of power and to seek new methods for achieving national unity, though most Germans were also still attached emotionally to their various regional states. What happened in Italy, a revolutionary destruction of all the old governments except that of Piedmont, could not readily happen in Germany.

After the failures of the 1848 revolution the old German states were restored—Austria and Prussia, the kingdoms of Hanover, Saxony, Bavaria, and Württemberg, together with about 30 other states ranging in size down to the free cities of Hamburg and Frankfurt. The loose confederation of 1815, linking all these states together, was restored also (see map, p. 561). But within this framework great economic and social changes were occurring. Between 1850 and 1870 the output of both coal and iron in Germany multiplied sixfold. In 1850 Germany produced less iron than France; in 1870, more. Germany was rapidly gaining economic unity and overcoming the economic and social lag that had separated Germans from the fast-developing industrial and global commerce in northwestern Europe. The German cities were growing, bound together by railroad and telegraph, and requiring larger supporting areas to sustain their urban populations. Industrial capitalists and industrial workers were becoming more numerous. With the advantages of unity more obvious than ever, with the ideals of 1848 badly compromised, with a strong philosophical respect for the state and for power, and with a philosophical habit of accepting the successful event as the "judgment of history," the Germans were ripe for what happened. They did not unify themselves by their own exertions. They fell into the arms of Prussia.

Advantages of unity

Prussia in the 1860s: Bismarck

Prussia had always been the smallest and most precarious of the early modern great powers. Ruined by Napoleon, it had risen again. It owed its international influence and internal character to its army. Actually it had fought fewer wars than other great powers, but its army enabled Prussia to expand by conquest or diplomacy. The taking of Silesia in 1740 by force, the acquisition of parts of Poland in the partitions of the 1770s and 1790s, and the addition of the Rhineland in 1815 by diplomatic or international agreement were the highlights of Prussian growth. After 1850 those who controlled the destinies of Prussia were apprehensive. Their state had been shaken by revolution. In the Crimean War and at the Congress of Paris they were hardly more than spectators. It seemed as if the hard-won and still relatively recent position of Prussia might be waning.

Since 1815 the population of Prussia had grown from 11 to 18 million, but the size of the army had not changed. Merely to enforce existing principles of conscription would therefore almost double the army. But this would require increased financial appropriations. After 1850 Prussia had a parliament. It was a parliament, to be sure, dominated by men of wealth; but some of the wealthy Prussians, notably the industrialists of the Rhine-

Parliamentary politics

land, were liberals who wished the parliament to have control over government policies. These men did not like professional armies and considered the Prussian Junkers, from whom the officer corps was recruited, as their main rivals in the state. The parliament refused the necessary military appropriations. The king at this juncture, in 1862, appointed a new chief minister, Otto von Bismarck.

Bismarck

Bismarck was a Junker from old Brandenburg east of the Elbe. He cultivated the gruff manner of an honest country squire, though he was intellectually superior to the rather unsophisticated landlord class from which he sprang and for which he often felt an impatient contempt. He shared in many Junker ideas. He advocated, and even felt, a kind of stout Protestant piety. Although he cared for the world's opinion, it never deterred him in his actions; criticism and denunciation left him untouched. He was not a nationalist. He did not look upon all Germany as his Fatherland. He was a Prussian. His social affinities, as with the Junkers generally, lay to the East with corresponding landowning elements of the Baltic provinces and Russia. Western Europe, including most of Germany, he neither understood nor trusted; it seemed to him revolutionary, free-thinking, and materialistic. Parliamentary bodies he considered ignorant and irresponsible as organs of government. Individual liberty seemed to him disorderly selfishness. Liberalism, democracy, and socialism were repugnant to him. He preferred to stress duty, service, order, and the fear of God. The idea of forming a new German union developed only gradually in his mind and then as an adjunct to the strengthening of Prussia.

Bismarck thus had his predilections and even his principles. But no principle bound him; no ideology seemed to him an end in itself. He became the classic practitioner of *Realpolitik.* First he made wars; then he insisted upon peace. Enmities and alliances were to him only matters of passing convenience. The enemy of today might be the friend of tomorrow. Far from planning out a long train of events, then following it step by step to a grand consummation, he seems to have been practical and opportunistic, taking advantage of situations as they emerged and prepared to act in several different directions as events might suggest.

In 1862, as minister president, he set out to thwart the liberals in the Prussian parliament. For four years, from 1862 to 1866, Bismarck waged this constitutional struggle.

Constitutional struggle

The parliament refused to vote the proposed taxes. The government collected them anyway. The taxpayers paid them without protest—it was the orderly thing to do, and the collectors represented public authority.

The limitations of Prussian liberalism, the docility of the population, the respect for officialdom, the belief that the king and his ministers were wiser than the elected deputies—all clearly revealed themselves in this triumph of military policy over the theory of government by consent. The army was enlarged, reorganized, retrained, and reequipped. Bismarck fended off the showers of abuse from the liberal majority in the

Otto von Bismarck's pragmatic use of power and his successful campaign to create a unified German nation-state made him the most successful practitioner of *Realpolitik* in late nineteenth-century Europe. This photograph suggests the talent for well-focused observation that enabled Bismarck to see clearly what was at stake in the political and diplomatic conflicts of his generation.
(©Hulton Archive/Getty Images)

chamber. The liberals declared that the government's policy was flagrantly unconstitutional. The constitution, said Bismarck, could not have been meant to undermine the state. The government, said the liberals, was itself undermining Prussia, for the rest of Germany hoped to find in Prussia, as Italy had found in Piedmont, a model of political freedom. What the Germans admired in Prussia, replied Bismarck coldly, was not its liberalism but its power. He declared that the Prussian boundaries as set in 1815 were unsound, that Prussia must be prepared to seize favorable opportunities for further growth. And he added one of his most memorable utterances: "Not by speeches and majority votes are the great questions of the day decided—that was the great error of 1848 and 1849—but by blood and iron."

Bismarck's Wars: The Creation of the North German Confederation, 1867

A favorable opportunity for Prussian expansion soon emerged. The Danes, engaged in a process of national consolidation of their own, wished to make the duchy of Schleswig an integral part of Denmark. The population of Schleswig was part Dane and part German. The diet of the German confederation, unwilling to see Germans thus annexed outright to Denmark, called for an all-German war upon the Danes. Bismarck had no desire to support or strengthen the existing German confederation. He wanted not an all-German war but a Prussian war. To disguise his aims he acted jointly with Austria, a fellow member of the German confederation. In 1864 Prussia and Austria together went to war with Denmark, which they soon defeated. It was Bismarck's intention to annex both Schleswig and the duchy of Holstein to Prussia, gaining whatever other advantages might present themselves from future trouble with Austria. He arranged a provisional occupation of Schleswig by Prussia and of Holstein by Austria. Disputes soon arose over the kinds of policing problems that commonly afflict occupying forces.

Bismarck now proceeded to discredit and isolate Austria. Other European powers were preoccupied with their own domestic issues and not much concerned with Austrian interests in a regional territorial dispute, so Bismarck used strategic diplomatic negotiations to ensure that no foreign state would ally itself with Austria or intervene in German affairs. To weaken Austria within Germany, Bismarck presented himself as a "democrat." He proposed a reform of the German confederation, recommending that it have a popular chamber

Bismarck as "democrat"

elected by universal male suffrage. He calculated that the mass of the German people were wedded neither to the well-to-do capitalistic liberals, nor to the existing government structures of the German states, nor to the house of Habsburg. He would use "democracy" to undermine all established interests that stood in his way.

Meanwhile the occupying powers continued to quarrel over Schleswig-Holstein. Austria finally raised the matter formally in the German federal diet, one of whose functions was to prevent war between its members. Bismarck declared that the diet had no authority, accused the Austrians of aggression, and ordered the Prussian army to enter Holstein. The Austrians called for an all-German force to be sent against Prussia. The result was that Prussia, in 1866, was at war not only with Austria but also with most of the other German states. The Prussian army soon proved its superiority. Trained to an unprecedented precision, equipped with the new needle-gun, by which the infantryman could deliver five rounds a minute, brought into the zone of combat by an imaginative use of the new railroads, and skillfully commanded, the Prussian army overwhelmed the Austrians and defeated the other German states soon thereafter. The Austro-Prussian, or

Seven Weeks' War

Seven Weeks' War, was amazing in its brevity. Bismarck hastened to make peace before the other European powers could realize what had happened.

Prussia annexed outright, together with Schleswig-Holstein, the whole kingdom of Hanover, the duchies of Nassau and Hesse-Cassel, and the free city of Frankfurt. Here the old governments simply disappeared before the axe of the "red reactionary." The German federal union disappeared likewise. In its place, in 1867, Bismarck organized a North German Confederation, in which the newly enlarged Prussia joined with 21 other states, all of which combined it greatly outweighed. The German states south of the river Main—Austria, Bavaria, Baden, Württemberg, and Hesse-Darmstadt—remained outside the new organization, with no kind of union among themselves.

A new constitution

For the North German Confederation Bismarck produced a constitution. The new structure, though a federal one, was much stronger than the now defunct Confederation of 1815. The king of Prussia became its hereditary head. Ministers were responsible to him. There was a parliament with two chambers. The upper chamber, as in the United States, represented the states as such, though not equally. The lower chamber, or Reichstag, was deemed to represent the people and was elected by universal male suffrage. Such flirting with democracy seemed madness to both conservative Junker and liberal bourgeois. It was indeed a bold step, for only France at the time exemplified universal male suffrage in Europe on a large scale, and in the France of Napoleon III neither old-fashioned conservatives nor genuine liberals could take much satisfaction. As for Great Britain, where voting rights were extended in this same year, 1867, they were still given to fewer than half the adult male population. Bismarck sensed in the "masses" an ally of strong government against private interests. He negotiated even with the socialists, who had arisen with the industrialization of the past decade, and who, in Germany at this time, were mainly followers of Ferdinand Lassalle. The Lassallean socialists, unlike the Marxian, believed it possible to improve working-class conditions through the action of existing governments. To the great annoyance of Marx, then in England, the majority of the German socialists reached an understanding with Bismarck. In return for a democratic suffrage they agreed to accept the North German Confederation. Bismarck, for his part, by making use of democratic and socialist sentiment, won popular approval for his emerging empire.

THE GERMAN QUESTION, 1815–1871

From 1815 to 1866 there were 39 German states joined in the German Confederation (the largest states are shown here). The movement to create a unified Germany gave rise in this era to opposing nationalist groups: the Great Germans, who favored an all-German union that would include Austria; and the Little Germans, who were willing to exclude Austria and its empire from a new German nation-state. Bismarck was a Little German but a Great Prussian. He (1) enlarged Prussia by conquest in 1866; (2) joined Mecklenburg, Saxony, and other regions with Prussia in the North German Confederation of 1867; and (3) combined this Confederation with Bavaria, Württemberg, and other southern states to form the German Empire in 1871. He also (4) conquered Alsace-Lorraine from France; and (5) excluded Austria from the new German empire. These boundaries remained unchanged until 1918.

The Franco-Prussian War

The creation of the North German Federation greatly expanded Prussia's political influence, but the situation was not yet stable. The small south German states were left floating in empty space; they would sooner or later have to gravitate into some orbit or another, whether Austrian, Prussian, or French. In France there were angry criticisms of Napoleon III's foreign policy. France had sent troops to Mexico during the early 1860s and (with the collaboration of Mexican monarchists) had managed to place Napoleon's own chosen ruler—an Austrian archduke named Maximilian—on a precarious Mexican imperial throne. But this French-style empire lacked broad support, and a popular republican movement overthrew Maximilian's regime in 1867, soon after Napoleon III withdrew his military forces. Maximilian was executed, and the whole Mexican intervention became a transatlantic imperial fiasco. Meanwhile, a united Italy had been allowed to rise on France's borders. And now, contrary to all principles of French national interest observed by French governments for hundreds of years, a strong and independent power was being allowed to spread over virtually the whole of Germany. Everywhere people began to feel that war was inevitable between France and Prussia. Bismarck played on the fears of France among the leaders and populations in the south German states. South Germany, though in former times often a willing satellite of France, was now sufficiently nationalistic to consider such subservience to a foreign people disgraceful. To Bismarck it seemed that a war between Prussia and France would frighten the small south German states into a union with Prussia, leaving only Austria outside—which was what he wanted. To Napoleon III, or at least to some of his advisers, it seemed that such a war, if successful, would restore public approval of the Bonapartist Empire. The leaders of both Prussia and France were thus drawn toward war as a solution for various internal problems.

Meanwhile, in a totally unexpected chain of events, a revolution in Spain had driven the reigning queen into exile, and a Spanish provisional government invited Prince Leopold of Hohenzollern, a cousin of the king of Prussia to be constitutional king of Spain. Installing a member of the Prussian royal family as the head of government in Spain would clearly provoke strong opposition from France. Three times the Hohenzollern family refused the Spanish offer. Bismarck, who could not control such family decisions but who foresaw the possibility of a usable incident, deviously persuaded the Spanish to issue the invitation still a fourth time. On July 2, 1870, Paris heard that Prince Leopold had accepted. The French ambassador to Prussia, Benedetti, at the direction of his govern-

France thwarts new Spanish king

ment, met the king of Prussia at the bathing resort of Ems, where he formally demanded that Prince Leopold's acceptance be withdrawn. It was withdrawn, and the French seemed to have their way. Bismarck was disappointed.

The French government now went still further. It instructed Benedetti to approach the king again at Ems and demand that at no time in the future would any Hohenzollern ever become a candidate for the Spanish throne. The king politely declined any such commitment and telegraphed a full report of the conversation to Bismarck at Berlin. Bismarck, receiving the telegram, which became famous as the "Ems dispatch," saw a new opportunity, as he put it, to wave a red flag before the Gallic bull. He condensed the Ems telegram for publication, so reducing and abridging it that it seemed to newspaper readers as if a curt exchange had occurred at Ems, in which the Prussians believed that their king had been insulted and the French believed that their ambassador had been snubbed. In both countries the war party demanded satisfaction. On July 19, 1870, on these trivial grounds, and with the ostensible issue of the Spanish throne already settled, the

The French suffered a crushing defeat at Sedan in northeastern France during the brief Franco-Prussian War in 1870. Napoleon III was captured along with much of his army. French civilians fled from both the battle and advancing Prussian troops, as can be seen in this German engraving of terrified people crossing a dangerous, crowded bridge.
(©DEA/G. DAGLI ORTI/Getty Images)

irresponsible and decaying government of Napoleon III declared war on Prussia.

France's military isolation

Again the war was short. Again Bismarck had taken care to isolate his enemy in advance. The British generally viewed France as wrong to launch the war; and they had already been alarmed by the French operations in Mexico, which suggested an ambition to re-create a French American empire. The Italians had long been awaiting the chance to seize Rome; they did so in 1870, when the French withdrew their troops from Rome for use against Prussia. The Russians had been awaiting the chance to upset a clause of the Peace of 1856 that forbade them to keep naval vessels in the Black Sea. They did so in 1870.

The War of 1870, like the others of the time, failed to become a general European struggle. Prussia was supported by the south German states. France had no allies. The French army proved to be technically backward compared with the Prussian. War began on July 19; on September 2, after the battle of Sedan, the principal French army surrendered to the Germans. Napoleon III was himself taken prisoner. On September 4 an insurrection in Paris proclaimed the Third Republic. The Prussian and German forces moved into France and laid siege to the capital. Though the French armies dissolved, Paris refused to capitulate. For four months it was surrounded and besieged.

The German Empire, 1871

With their guns encircling Paris, the German rulers or their representatives assembled at Versailles. The château and gardens of Versailles, since Louis XVI's unceremonious departure in October 1789, had been little more than a vacant monument to a society long since dead. Here, in the most sumptuous room of the palace, the resplendent Hall of Mirrors, where the Sun King had once received the deferential approaches of German princes, Bismarck on January 18, 1871, arranged for the German Empire to be proclaimed. The king of Prussia received the hereditary title of German emperor. The other German rulers (excepting, to be sure, the ruler of Austria, and those whom Bismarck had himself dethroned) accepted his imperial authority. Ten days later the people of Paris, shivering, hungry, and helpless, opened their gates to the enemy. France had no government with which Bismarck could make peace. It was not at all clear what kind of government the country wanted.

Bismarck's demands

Bismarck insisted on the election of a French Constituent Assembly by universal suffrage. He demanded that France pay the German Empire a war indemnity of 5 billion gold francs (then an enormous and unprecedented sum) and cede to it the border region of Alsace and most of Lorraine. Though most Alsatians spoke German, most of them also felt themselves to be French, having shared in the general history of France since the seventeenth century. There was strong local protest at the transfer to Germany; thousands of Alsatians moved to other places within the new French Republic or to Algeria, and the French never reconciled themselves to this cold-blooded amputation of their frontier. The peace dictated by Bismarck was embodied in the treaty of Frankfurt of May 10, 1871. Thereafter, as will be seen, the French Constituent Assembly gradually proceeded to construct the Third Republic.

The strength of the German state

The consolidation of Germany transformed the face of Europe. It reversed the dictum not only of the Peace of Vienna but even of the Peace of Westphalia. The German Empire, no sooner born, was the strongest state on the continent of Europe. Rapidly industrialized after 1870, it became more potent still. Bismarck had astutely exploited the conflicting ambitions of other European states and used three short wars to bring about a German unification that most European governments had long sought at all costs to prevent. He outwitted everybody in turn, including the Germans. The united all-German state that issued from the nationalist movement was a Germany conquered by Prussia. Within the new empire Prussia directly controlled about two-thirds of the whole imperial territory. Before such unanswerable success the Prussian liberals capitulated, and the Prussian parliament passed an indemnity act; the gist of it was that Bismarck admitted to a certain high-handedness during the constitutional struggle but that the parliament legalized the disputed tax collections ex post facto, agreeing to forgive and forget, in view of the victory over Austria and its consequences. Thus liberalism gave way to a triumphant nationalism.

The German Empire received substantially the earlier constitution of the North German Confederation. It was a federation of monarchies, each based in theory on divine or hereditary right. At the same time, in the Reichstag elected by universal male suffrage, the empire rested on a kind of mass appeal and was in a sense democratic. Yet the country's ministers were responsible to the emperor and not to the elected chamber. Moreover, it was the rulers who joined their territories to the empire, not the peoples. There were no popular plebiscites as in Italy. Each state kept its own laws, government, and constitution. The people of Prussia, for example, remained for Prussian affairs under the rather illiberal constitution of 1850 with its three-class system of voting; in affairs of the Reich,

The new German Empire was officially proclaimed in January 1871 at the historic French palace in Versailles. King Wilhelm of Prussia became the German Emperor. This painting by Anton von Werner shows how Bismarck assembled military officers and representatives from all of the constituent German states in the famous "Hall of Mirrors"—a symbolic site of past French grandeur that made the German celebration all the more humiliating for the French.

(©ullstein bild Dtl./Getty Images)

or empire, however, they enjoyed an equal vote by universal suffrage. The emperor, who was also the king of Prussia, had legal control over the foreign and military policy of the empire. The German Empire in effect served as a mechanism to magnify the role of Prussia, the Prussian army, and the East Elbian Prussian aristocracy in world affairs.

The Habsburg Empire after 1848

Bismarck united Germany, but he also divided it, for he left about a sixth of the central European Germans outside his German Empire. These Germans of Austria and Bohemia had now to work out a common future with the dozen other nationalities in the Danubian domain. The clumsiness and limitations of the old Habsburg multinational empire are clear enough, but more impressive is its astonishing capacity to survive the recurring upheavals in central European societies. Having survived repeated attempts to dismember it during the eighteenth century, the Napoleonic wars, and the revolutions of 1848, the empire held together until the cataclysm of the First World War. But the events of the 1850s and 1860s greatly altered its character.

Habsburg resilience

The essential question, in a nationalist age, was how the Habsburg government would adapt to the challenges that emerged from the expanding campaigns for national self-expression. By Habsburg, in this period, one means primarily Francis Joseph, who as emperor from 1848 to 1916 reigned even longer than his famous contemporary, Queen Victoria. Francis Joseph, like many others, could never shake off his own tradition. Buffeted unmercifully by the waves of change and by central European nationalisms, he cordially disliked everything liberal, progressive, or modern. Personally, Francis Joseph was incapable of enlarged views, ambitious projects, bold decisions, or persevering action. And he lived in a pompous dream world, surrounded in the imperial court by great noblemen, high churchmen, and bespangled personages of the army.

Yet the government was not idle; it was, if anything, too fertile in devising new deals and new dispensations. Various expedients were tried after 1849, but none was tried long

German language and centralization

enough to see if it would work. For several years the ruling idea was centralization—to govern the empire through the German language and through efficient, Vienna-based, bureaucratic systems. The abolition of serfdom, as accomplished in 1848, would become permanent for all parts of the empire (this policy required strong official control over landlords to work in practice), and there would be more government support for the building of railroads and other forms of material progress. This Germanic and bureaucratic centralization was distasteful to the non-German nationalities, and especially to the Magyars. It is important to say Magyars, not Hungarians, because the Magyars composed less than half of the very mixed population within the then existing borders of Hungary. Nevertheless the Magyars, as the strongest of the non-German groups, and hence the most able to maintain a political system of their own, felt the Germanic influence as most oppressive.

The Compromise of 1867

In 1867 a compromise was worked out between the Germans of Austria-Bohemia and the Magyars of Hungary. It worked to the common disadvantage of the Slavs, who were

A Dual Monarchy

viewed as a backward, less civilized people by both the Germans and the Magyars. The compromise created a Dual Monarchy, of a kind unparalleled in Europe. West of the river Leith was the Empire of Austria; east of it was the Kingdom of Hungary. The two were now judged exactly equal. Each had its own constitution and its own parliament, to which the governing ministry in each country was henceforth to be responsible. The administrative language of Austria would be German; of Hungary, Magyar. Neither state could intervene in the other's affairs. The two countries were joined by the fact that the same Habsburg ruler should always be emperor in Austria and king in Hungary. Yet the union was not personal only; for, though there was no common parliament, delegates of the two parliaments were to meet together alternately in Vienna and Budapest, and there was to be a common ministry for finance, foreign affairs, and war. To this common ministry of Austria-Hungary both Austrians and Hungarians were to be appointed.

Both Austria and Hungary under the Dual Monarchy were in form constitutional parliamentary states, but neither was democratic. In Austria, after much juggling with voting systems, a true universal male suffrage was instituted in 1907. In Hungary, when the First World War came in 1914, still only a quarter of the adult male population had the vote. Socially, the great reform of 1848, the abolition of serfdom, was not allowed to move toward more upsetting political or economic conclusions. The owners of great landed estates, especially in Hungary (but also in parts of the Austrian Empire) remained the unquestionably dominant class. They were surrounded by landless peasants, an agrarian proletariat,

Hungary and Austria formed a political union under a Dual Monarchy and common government ministries after 1867, but most of the population continued to live a traditional agrarian life. This painting by the Hungarian artist Miklos Barabas, *The Arrival of the Bride* **(1856), portrays one of the enduring rituals of rural societies, which were often romanticized in nineteenth-century nationalism.**

(©DEA/G. DAGLI ORTI/Getty Images)

composed partly of lower classes of their own nationality and partly of other peasant peoples, like the Slovaks and Serbs, who in this era lacked an educated or wealthy class of their own. National and social questions therefore came together. For some nationalities, especially the Magyars,

National and social questions

a social and economic ascendancy was entangled with a national ascendancy. Landlordism became the basic social issue. A landowning class, increasingly educated in the knowledge and organizational methods of modern European cultures, faced a depressed peasant mass that was generally left out of the advancing civilization of the day.

66.   TSARIST RUSSIA: SOCIAL CHANGE AND THE LIMITS OF POLITICAL REFORM

Tsarist Russia after 1856

For Russia also the Crimean War set off a series of changes. The ungainly empire, an "enormous village" as it has been called, stretching from Poland to the Pacific, had proved unable to repel a localized attack by France and Great Britain, into which neither of the Western powers had put anything like its full resources. Alexander II (1855–1881), who became tsar during the war, was no liberal by nature or conviction. But he saw that something drastic must be done. The prestige of western Europe was at its height, because the most successful governments and advanced industrial economies had developed in the western European nation-states. The reforms in Russia therefore followed, at some distance, the European model.

Imperial Russia was a political organization very difficult to describe. Its own subjects did not know what to make of it. Some, called Westernizers in the mid-nineteenth century, believed Russia was destined to become more like western Europe. Others, the Slavophiles, believed Russia was entrusted with a special destiny of its own, which would only be weakened or perverted by using western Europe as a model for Russian development.

Autocracy of the tsar

That Russia differed from other regions of Europe, at least in degree, was doubted by nobody. The leading institution was the autocracy of the tsar. This was not exactly the absolutism known in earlier European monarchies. In Russia some very old European conceptions were missing, such as the idea that spiritual authority is independent of even the mightiest prince or the old feudal idea of reciprocal duties between king and subject or the premodern notion that specific groups of people have certain rights or claims for justice at the hands of power. The tsardom did not rule by law; it ran the country by ukase, police action, and the army. The tsars, since Peter and before, had built up their state very largely by importing and imposing European technical methods and technical experts, often against strong objection by native Russians of all classes. More than any state in Europe, the Russian Empire was a machine superimposed upon its people without organic connection—bureaucracy pure and simple. But as more Russians entered into contact with the other cultures of Europe many people acquired European ideas in which the autocracy was not interested— ideas of liberty and fraternity, of a just and classless society, of individual personality enriched by humane culture and moral freedom. Russians who began to espouse such ideas found themselves chronically critical of the government and of Russia itself. The government, massive though it seemed, was afraid of such people. Any idea arising outside official circles seemed pernicious, and the press and the universities were as a rule severely censored.

The severity of Russian serfdom

A second fundamental institution, which had grown up with the tsardom, was legalized bondage or serfdom. The majority of the population living on Russia's vast landed estates, in the households of wealthy landlords, or in rural villages were serfs dependent upon masters. Russian serfdom was more onerous than the serfdom that existed in east-central Europe until 1848. It resembled the slavery of the Americas in that serfs were "owned"; they could be bought and sold and used in occupations other than agriculture. Some serfs worked the soil, rendering unpaid labor service to the gentry. Others could be used by their owners in factories or mines or rented out for such purposes. Others were more independent, working as artisans or mechanics, and even traveling about or residing in the cities, but from their earnings they had to remit certain fees to the lord or return home when he called them. The owners had a certain paternalistic responsibility for their serfs, and in the villages the gentry constituted a kind of personal local government. The law, as in the American South, did little or nothing to interfere between gentry and their servile laborers so that the serfs' day-to-day fortunes depended on the personality or economic circumstances of their owners.

By the mid-nineteenth century most Russians agreed that serfdom must some day end. Serfdom was in any case ceasing to be profitable; some two-thirds of all the privately owned serfs (that is, those not belonging to the tsar or state) were mortgaged as security for loans at the time of Alexander II's accession. Increasingly serfdom was recognized as a bad system of labor relations, making the serfs illiterate and stolid drudges, without incentive, initiative, self-respect, or pride of workmanship, and also very poor soldiers for the army.

Educated Russians, full of ideas from western Europe, were estranged from the government, from the Orthodox Church, which was an arm of the tsar, and from the common people of their own country. They felt ill at ease in a nation of uneducated peasants and a pang of guilt at the virtual slavery on which their own position rested. Hence

Western ideas and education

arose another distinctive feature of nineteenth-century Russian life, the intelligentsia. In Russia it seemed that the experience of being educated, debating ideas, and reading books made the intelligentsia more self-conscious of themselves as a class apart. They were made up of students, university graduates, and persons who had a good deal of leisure to read. Such people, while not very free to think, were more free to think than to do almost anything else. The Russian intelligentsia tended to embrace sweeping reformist philosophies, and they believed that intellectuals should play a large role in society. They formed an exaggerated idea of how critical, oppositional thinkers could direct the course of historical change. Some, overwhelmed by the mammoth immobility of the tsardom and of serfdom, turned to revolutionary and even terroristic philosophies. This only made the bureaucrats more anxious and fearful, and the government more fitfully repressive.

The Emancipation Act of 1861 and Other Reforms

Alexander II, on becoming tsar in 1855, attempted to enlist the support of the liberals among the intelligentsia by implementing a whole series of significant reforms. He gave permission to travel outside Russia, eased the controls on the universities, and allowed the censorship to go relatively unenforced. Newspapers and journals were founded, and those written by Russian revolutionaries abroad, like the *Polar Star* of Alexander Herzen in London, circulated more freely within the country. The result was a great outburst of public opinion, which was agreed at least on one point: the necessity of emancipating the peasants. Alexander's father, Nicholas I, had been a noted reactionary, who abhorred European liberalism and organized a system of secret political police until then unparalleled in Europe for its arbitrary and inquisitorial methods. Yet even Nicholas I had taken serious measures to alleviate serfdom. Alexander II, basically conservative on Russian affairs, proceeded to set up a special branch of the government to study the question. The government did not wish to throw the whole labor system and economy of the country into chaos, nor to ruin the gentry class without which it could not govern at all. After many discussions, proposals, and memoranda, an imperial ukase of 1861 declared serfdom abolished and the peasants free.

By this great decree the peasants became legally free from the control of their former masters. They were henceforth subjects of the government, not subjects of their previous owners. It was hoped that they would be stirred by a new sense of human dignity. As one enthusiastic official put it shortly after emancipation: "The people are erect and transformed; the look, the walk, the speech, everything is changed." The gentry lost their old quasi-manorial jurisdiction over the villages. They could no longer exact forced and unpaid labor or receive fees arising from servitude.

It is important to realize what the Act of Emancipation did and did not do. Roughly (with great differences from region to region) it allocated about half the cultivated land to the gentry and half to the former serfs. The latter had to pay redemption money for the land they

Land allocation

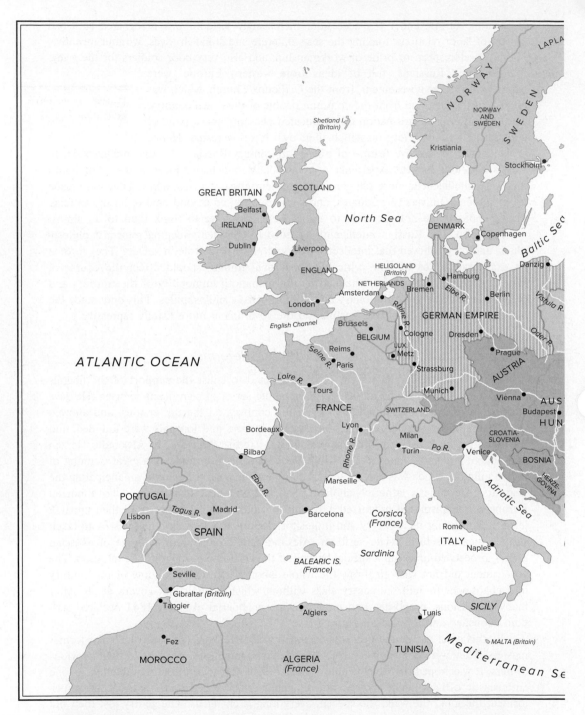

EUROPE, 1871

This map shows the existence of the newly unified German Empire and a unified Kingdom of Italy. The German domain was enlarged by the incorporation of Schleswig (in the neck of the Danish Peninsula) and the annexation from France of Alsace and parts of Lorraine (the regions around Strassburg and Metz on the map). From 1871 to 1914, Europe had fewer separate states than at any other time in its history. There were no further changes in national borders during this period except for the voluntary separation of Norway and Sweden in 1905 and various realignments in southeastern Europe as the Ottoman Empire withdrew from the Balkans.

received and for the fees that the gentry lost. The government actually paid the redemption money directly to the gentry at the time of emancipation, but the emancipated serfs were required to repay these funds to the government over many years and decades. The Russian aristocracy was thus far from weakened; in place of a kind of human property largely mortgaged anyway, they now had clear possession of roughly half the land, they received the redemption money, and they were rid of obligations to the peasants.

The peasants, on the other hand, now owned about half the arable land in their own right—a considerable amount by the standards of almost any European country. They did not, however, possess it according to the principles of private property or independent farming that had become prevalent in Europe. The peasant land, when redeemed, became the collective property of the ancient peasant village assembly, or *mir*. The village, as a unit, was responsible to the government for repayment of the redemption money and for collection of the necessary sums from its individual members. The village assembly, in default of collection, might require forced labor from the defaulter or a member of his family; and it could prevent peasants from moving away from the village, lest those remaining bear the whole burden of payment. It could (as in the past) assign and reassign certain lands to its members for tillage and otherwise supervise cultivation as a joint concern. To keep the village community intact, the government presently forbade the selling or mortgaging of land to persons outside the village. This tended to preserve the peasant society but also to discourage the investment of outside capital, with which equipment might be purchased, and so to retard agricultural improvement and the growth of wealth.

Inequality among peasants

Not all peasants within the village unit were equal. As in France before the Revolution, some had the right to work more land than others. Some were only day laborers. Others had rights of inheritance in the soil (for not all land was subject to reassignment by the commune) or rented additional parcels of land belonging to the gentry. These lands they worked by hiring other peasants for wages. None of the Russian peasants, however, after the emancipation, possessed full individual freedom of action. In their movements and obligations, as in their thoughts, they were restricted by their villages as they had once been restricted by their lords.

Alexander II proceeded to overhaul the legal system with reforms that brought the Russian system closer to the judicial practices in western European countries. A new system of local courts was needed to replace the lord's traditional jurisdiction over the peasants, but there was also a broader reform of the courts from bottom to top. The arbitrariness of authority and defenselessness of the subject were the long-established evils. They were greatly mitigated by an edict of 1864. Trials were made public, and private persons received the right to be represented in court by lawyers of their own choosing. All class distinctions in judicial matters were abolished, although in practice peasants continued to be subject to harsh disadvantages. A clear sequence of lower and higher courts was established. Requirements were laid down for the professional training of judges, who henceforth received stated salaries and were protected from administrative pressure. A system of juries on the English model was introduced.

A system of self-government

While thus attempting to establish a rule of law, the tsar also moved in the direction of allowing self-government. He hoped to win over the liberals and to shoulder the upper and middle classes with some degree of public responsibility. He created, again by an edict of 1864, a system of provincial and district councils called zemstvos. Elected by various elements, including the peasants, the zemstvos gradually went into operation and took up matters of education, medical relief, public welfare, food supply, and road maintenance in

The emancipation of the peasants in Russia transformed the legal status of the former serfs and opened opportunities for the development of more prosperous peasant communities. There was still much poverty in the Russian countryside after 1861, but the people who are drinking and playing music outside this rural Russian house seem to be part of a more prosperous post-emancipation peasant class.

(©Fotosearch/Getty Images)

their localities. Their great value was in developing civic sentiment among those who took part in them. Many liberals urged a representative body for all Russia, a Zemsky Sobor or Duma, which, however, Alexander II refused to concede. After 1864 his policy became more cautious, and he resisted the kinds of political institutions that contributed to the development of more liberal nation-states in other societies. A rebellion in Poland in 1863 inclined him to take advice from those who favored repression. He began to mollify the vested interests that had been disgruntled by the reforms and to whittle down some of the concessions already granted. But the essence of the reforms remained unaffected.

Revolutionism in Russia

The autocrat who thus undertook to liberalize Russia barely escaped assassination in 1866, had five shots fired at him in 1873, missed death by half an hour in 1880 when his imperial dining room was dynamited, and in 1881 was to be killed by a bomb. The revolutionaries were not pleased with the reforms, which if successful would merely strengthen the existing order. Some of the dissatisfied intelligentsia in the 1860s began to call themselves "nihilists": they believed in "nothing"—except science—and took a cynical view of the reforming tsar and his zemstvos. The peasants, saddled with heavy redemption payments, remained basically unsatisfied, and intellectuals toured the villages fanning this discontent. Revolutionaries developed a mystic conception of the revolutionary role of the Russian masses. Socialists, after the failure of socialism in Europe in the Revolution of 1848, came in many cases to believe, as Alexander Herzen wrote, that the true future of socialism lay in Russia, because of the very weakness of capitalism in Russia and the existence of a kind of collectivism already established in the village assemblies or communes.

Bakunin and anarchism

More radical than Herzen were the anarchist Bakunin and his disciple Nechaiev. In their *People's Justice* these two called for terrorism not only against tsarist officials but against liberals also. As they wrote in the *Catechism of a Revolutionist,* the true revolutionary "is devoured by one purpose, one thought, one passion—the revolution. . . . He has severed every link with the social order and with the entire civilized world. . . . Everything which promotes the success of the revolution is moral, everything which hinders it is immoral." Terrorism (which in that time generally meant assassination) was rejected by many of the revolutionaries, especially by those who in the 1870s took up the scientific socialism of Karl Marx. To Marx it did not seem that violence against some specific government officials would advance an inevitable historical or social process. But other groups, inspired by revolutionary theorists like Bakunin and Nechaiev, organized secret terrorist societies. One of these, the People's Will, determined to assassinate the tsar. In an autocratic state, they held, there was no other road to justice and freedom.

Alexander II, alarmed by this underground menace, which of course did not escape the attention of the police, again turned for support to the liberals. The liberals, who were themselves threatened by the revolutionaries, had become estranged from the government by its failure to follow through with the reforms of the early 1860s. Now, in 1880, to rally support, the tsar again relaxed the autocratic system. He abolished the dreaded secret police set up by his father, allowed the press to discuss most political subjects freely, and encouraged the zemstvos to do the same. Further to associate representatives of the public with the government, he proposed, not exactly a parliament, but two nationally elected commissions to sit with the council of state. He signed the edict to this effect on March 13, 1881, and on the same day was assassinated, not by a demented individual acting

CHRONOLOGY OF NOTABLE EVENTS, 1854–1871

1854–1856	France and Britain join with Ottoman Turkey to defeat Russia in the Crimean War
1861	Italians establish the unified Kingdom of Italy
1861	Tsar Alexander II abolishes serfdom in Russia
1861–1865	Civil War in the United States; federal union is upheld and slavery is abolished
1867	Austria and Hungary join together in a "Dual Monarchy" under the Habsburg ruler Francis Joseph
1867	Creation of the independent Dominion of Canada
1870	Prussia defeats France in brief war; Napoleon III abdicates and the French proclaim a Third French Republic
1871	King Wilhelm of Prussia becomes emperor in newly established German Empire

wildly and alone, but by the joint efforts of highly trained members of the terrorist society, the People's Will.

Alexander III, upon his father's death, abandoned the project for elected commissions and during his whole reign, from 1881 to 1894, reverted to a program of brutal resistance to liberals and revolutionaries alike. Although the new regime established by peasant emancipation, judicial reform, and the zemstvos was allowed to continue, the broader process of creating new political institutions for a more modern Russian state did not move forward in the late nineteenth century. How Russia finally received a parliament in 1905 is explained below in the chapter on the Russian Revolution. At present it is enough to emphasize that tsarist Russia, under Alexander II, shared in a transnational, reformist movement that was then at its height. The abolition of serfdom, putting both aristocrat and peasant more fully into a money economy, opened the way for capitalistic development within the empire. Between the two confining walls of autocracy and revolutionism—equally hard and unyielding—European ideas of law, liberty, and humanity began to spread in a tentative way; and the Russian government, with its own halting methods, began to move Russian society toward the political and legal consolidation that was developing more rapidly in the national states of western Europe.

Between autocracy and revolutionism

67. NATION-BUILDING IN THE WIDER ATLANTIC WORLD: THE UNITED STATES AND CANADA

The history of Europe, long interconnected with the history of other societies around the world, remained connected to the history of the new American nations that had gained their independence from European empires in the late eighteenth and early nineteenth centuries. European cultures were still influential in all parts of the Americas, and Europeans were much involved in the North American societies that emerged from earlier

English, French, and Spanish colonies. The United States steadily expanded its economic and political power during the nineteenth century, Canada moved gradually toward independence from Great Britain, and Mexico struggled to protect its sovereignty and lands against invasions from both the United States and European forces coming from France. This book mostly examines the societies, cultures, and states of Europe, but the significance of European nation-building becomes more apparent within the context of other developments in the transatlantic world. The European processes and models of national consolidation also influenced North America—where millions of Europeans continued to immigrate throughout the nineteenth century and where the growing populations were also constructing more unified national states.

Immigration, Civil War, and National Consolidation in the United States

The immigrants to the United States in this era (except for an uncounted, illegal importation of enslaved Africans) came almost entirely from Europe, and before 1860 most of the immigration flowed from Great Britain, Ireland, and Germany. Few concessions were made to the non-English immigrant populations. English was the language of the public schools, the police, law courts, local government, and public documents, all of which contributed to the nationalism and new national identity that spread across American society. The immigrants did not constitute minorities in the European sense. They generally learned to speak English, and they were more than willing to accept the eighteenth-century political traditions of republicanism, self-government, and individual liberty. Immigrants also embraced the popular belief in the social component of America's national creed, which confidently asserted that the future would be better in America than either the present or the past in Europe. Such ideas contributed to a collective affirmation of national destiny and unity among the nation's diverse social classes and immigrant communities.

Immigration

But at the same time the United States was falling to pieces, in large part because the Industrial Revolution in the Atlantic world had different effects on the U.S. North and South. The South became closely connected to the British economy, producing raw cotton for British textile mills and depending on an enslaved labor force to generate the exports that were the region's main economic product. In the North, the Industrial Revolution led to the building of factories, for which the manufacturers needed both tariff protection and new workers, many of whom were recent immigrants from Europe. Conflicts over free trade and tariffs thus became entangled with the issue of slavery; and the conflict over slavery became part of a larger debate about individual rights and liberty on both sides of the Atlantic. Over the course of the nineteenth century, slavery had come under increasing moral condemnation in both Europe and the Americas. It was abolished in the British colonies in 1833, in the French colonies in 1848, and in the Spanish American republics at different dates in the first half of the century. Similarly, legal serfdom was abolished in the Habsburg possessions in 1848 and in Russia in 1861. The slave system in the American South was increasingly out of step with the nineteenth-century liberal movement toward individual legal and political rights.

Northern and Southern economies

The westward expansion of the United States thus extended a conflict that France and Great Britain had once waged for control of lands beyond the Allegheny Mountains. Now the Northern and Southern states in the American republic competed to make the western territories either free or slave. In 1846 the United States made war upon Mexico by methods that anticipated the aggressive tactics Bismarck would soon use to expand the territories of Prussia. Many Northerners denounced the war as an act of Southern aggression, but the new conquests became permanent possessions of the United States. This territory, which extended from Texas to the Pacific coast, was more than half of the land in the entire Mexican Republic, and its conquest by the United States showed how European methods of national state expansion and consolidation were also used in North America.

Mexican-American War

The Mexican-American War further intensified the sectional conflict in the United States, especially after the first new state created in this vast new region of the country, California, joined the Union as a free state. The American opponents of slavery, the Abolitionists, were part of a transatlantic humanitarian movement; and their political goals somewhat resembled the aspirations of the radical democrats who came forward in Europe in 1848. Meanwhile, a growing sectionalism in the American South came to resemble the new nationalism felt by many peoples in Europe who were seeking to separate from larger empires or older monarchical states. Like the Magyar landowners of the Austrian empire, Southern white elites began to believe that their way of life could be best maintained by separation from a Union in which they were likely to become a permanent political minority. When the new, Northern-based Republican party was able to elect Abraham Lincoln as the American president in 1860, the advocates for Southern independence moved quickly to secede from the United States and to form the Confederate States of America. This secession set off a prolonged civil war, which attracted much attention among Europeans, in part because some of the battles were as large as the major battles in Europe during the Napoleonic wars, and in part because the war's outcome would affect the balance of power in the wider Atlantic world.

Secession of the American South

European governments, while never recognizing the Confederacy, were mostly partial to the South. The United States stood for principles still considered revolutionary in Europe, so that while the European working classes generally favored the North, the upper classes were willing enough to see the North American republic collapse into fragments. In this respect, Great Britain and France viewed the breakup of the United States as a strategic opportunity that they had formerly seen in the breakup of the Spanish Empire: an independent Confederate nation might provide convenient access to agricultural commodities that were needed in European factories, and it might open a new tariff-free market in which Europeans could sell their manufactured goods. The breakup of the United States might also offer new opportunities for European expansion in other parts of the Americas. It was, for example, during the American Civil War that Napoleon III sent a French army to Mexico and set up a kind of satellite empire under the Austrian archduke Maximilian. The most serious European attempt to challenge the Monroe Doctrine, violate the independence of a Latin American republic, and revive European colonialism thus occurred at the time when the United States was in dissolution.

European responses to American Civil War

But the North won the war and the Union was upheld; the Mexicans soon got rid of their unwanted European emperor; and Tsar Alexander II sold Alaska to the United States. More generally, the war ended the older idea that the United States was a Union or confederation from which member states might withdraw at will. The outcome of the American Civil War therefore settled a political argument about the meaning of the American republic, and the United States in the 1860s affirmed the increasingly popular view of the nation-state as it was

The Union upheld

Les negres affranchis colportant le décret d'affranchissement du président Lincoln.

The victories of Union armies during the American Civil War preserved the unity of the United States and also gave the national government the power to abolish slavery. This illustration from a French journal in 1863 provides a European image of newly freed people celebrating President Lincoln's Emancipation Proclamation and leaving the places where they had been enslaved. Lincoln's proclamation is posted on the side of the coach. The abolition of slavery became another example of how the consolidation of large nation-states took place on both sides of the Atlantic, and also brought about numerous social reforms.

(©Hulton Archive/Getty Images)

defined in Europe. The United States would be a national state, composed not of member states but of a unitary national people irrevocably bound together. This doctrine was now written explicitly into the Fourteenth Amendment of the Constitution, which pronounced all Americans to be citizens not of their several states but of the United States. Meanwhile, the Thirteenth Amendment abolished slavery everywhere in the country (without compensation to the former slaveholders) and linked the United States somewhat belatedly to the broader nineteenth-century European campaign to abolish slavery and serfdom. The Northern triumph in the Civil War thus ensured the continuing consolidation of a unified North American nation that could be counted among those countries such as Germany and Italy that were also unifying diverse territories under more centralized national governments during this same era.

The Union victory in the American Civil War expanded the influence of Northern industrialists and others who sought to advance the nation's internal economic development through manufacturing and finance. As in France under Napoleon III, there was a good deal of corruption, fraud, and irresponsible speculation, but industry boomed, the cities grew, and the American national state became more like other industrializing nations in Europe as it promoted the building of railroads, provided public lands for the creation of state-supported universities, and facilitated the growth of new business corporations. In short, the American Civil War, which might have reduced English-speaking America and its diverse regions into competing minor republics, resulted instead in the economic and political consolidation of a large nation-state, liberal and more democratic in its political principles, officially opposed to slavery, and committed to the expansion of a capitalist industrial economy. In all of these ways, the history of the United States in this era can be seen as part of the broader nineteenth-century history of nation-building, national territorial consolidations, and assertive nationalist ideologies throughout the Atlantic world.

Influence of business and finance

The Dominion of Canada: A New Model for Decolonization

North of the United States, at the time of the American Civil War, lay a vast territory that was still part of the British Empire and in varying degrees still dependent on Great Britain. Diverse and numerous indigenous peoples (or "First Nations") had lived on these lands for thousands of years, but the European population in this territory had originated in three great migration streams. One part was French, settled in the St. Lawrence Valley since the seventeenth century. A second part was made up of descendants of United Empire Loyalists, the old seaboard colonists who had fled from the United States after the American Revolution. A third part consisted of recent immigrants from Great Britain, men and women of the working classes who had left the home country to improve their lives in America.

European population

Although there were recurring tensions and conflicts between the Europeans and the indigenous peoples and between the French-speaking and English-speaking populations, the people in Canada had shown little inclination to separate from Great Britain. During the 1840s and 1850s, however, the British government moved toward a new system of self-government for its enormous North American colony. This transition drew on the recommendations of Lord Durham, a Whig political leader who had served as a governor in Canada and also written an influential report on Canadian affairs. Durham's Report was long regarded as one of the classic documents in the rise of the British Commonwealth of Nations—the international system that gradually evolved out of the modern British Empire. His recommendations included proposals for economic improvements such as the building of railroads, but Durham's Report also put forward new political plans. He urged the granting of virtual self-government for Canada (united in one great province of French- and English-speaking populations) and the introduction of the British system of "responsible government," in which the prime minister and cabinet should be responsible to and under the control of the elected assembly in the province. The British governor would become a kind of legal and ceremonial figure like the sovereign in Great Britain.

Lord Durham's Report

Self-government

Lord Durham's proposals were generally adopted, and Canada moved toward the autonomous governing of its internal affairs. The principle of responsible government was established by the late 1840s, so that the British governors of Canada allowed the elected assembly to adopt policies and appoint or remove ministers as it chose. This system became the foundation for an even more independent Canadian state that began to emerge while the Civil War was tearing apart the United States. In the face of this example (and despite the concerns of many French Canadians), the Canadian political elites decided to form a strong union in which all powers were to rest in the central government except those specifically assigned to the various provinces. A new federal constitution, drafted in Canada by Canadians, was passed by the British Parliament in 1867 as the British

British North America Act

North America Act, which constitutionally established the Dominion of Canada. The eastern maritime provinces (Nova Scotia, New Brunswick, and Prince Edward Island) joined Quebec and Ontario in the new Dominion. These political arrangements established a united country that facilitated rapid westward expansion to the Pacific Coast, and Canada became another example of the transatlantic movement toward modern national consolidation.

The Dominion of Canada, though at first not large in population, possessed from the beginning a significance beyond the mere number of its people. It was the first example of successful devolution, or granting of political liberty and independence, within one of the European colonial empires. It embodied principles that Edmund Burke and Benjamin Franklin had vainly recommended a century before to keep the thirteen colonies loyal to Great Britain. The Dominion after 1867 moved forward from independence in internal matters to independence in such external affairs as tariffs, diplomacy, and the decisions

Model for dominion status

of war and peace. Although Britain would continue to expand its empire in other parts of the world after 1870, its policies in Canada pioneered the development of a "dominion status" that became the precedent for other European "settler societies" that later gained political independence—Australia (1901), New Zealand (1907), and the Union of South Africa (1910). A similar model was also used in the 1920s, temporarily, in Ireland. By the middle of the twentieth century the same idea, or what may be called the Canadian idea, was also applied in various ways to the worldwide process of decolonization as the British Empire gave up control of its colonies in Asia and Africa, transferring power (as in Canada) to national and local political elites. Despite their often difficult and conflicted transitions to national independence, people in India, Pakistan, Sri Lanka, and the former British colonies in Africa chose to become postcolonial republics that would remain loosely and voluntarily joined together and to Great Britain in a Commonwealth of Nations.

More immediately, in America, the founding of the Canadian dominion stabilized relations between British North America and the United States. Both Canada and the United States regarded their long national border as final; and each of these expanding nations now set out to develop their national territories (a process that would include the displacement of indigenous peoples and new internal conflicts among the different regions of each nation). The withdrawal of British control from Canadian affairs also furthered the long-developing conception of an American continent entirely free from European political control, though the European model of state-building and national cultures would remain influential long after the departure of the last British colonial administrators.

The unifying North American nations therefore exemplified a wider process of national consolidation that spanned the Atlantic Ocean and spread across Europe to Russia (reaching also into Japan). It was an era in which emerging modern societies were revolutionized economically by the railroad and steamship and also revolutionized

politically by the consolidation of new national political institutions.
These states increasingly embodied certain liberal and constitutional
principles, or at least the machinery of representative government. But
the whole earth had also become an arena in which powerful national

*Power of national
states*

states sought to promote their economic and political interests with little respect for the
constitutional principles that were becoming important in domestic political institutions.
The most powerful European states in 1871 included Great Britain, Germany, France,
Austria-Hungary, and Russia. Britain had developed a new political mechanism for the
emergence of a postcolonial nation in Canada, but the main European powers were at
this time more interested in acquiring colonies than in promoting decolonization. Whether
the newly united Italian nation should be called a Great Power was not yet clear. All agreed
that the United States would eventually play a large role in international affairs, but it had
not yet become a major influence on the politics and economies of Europe.

Suggested Further Readings can be found in the ebook, on Connect, or online at www.mhhe
.com/kramer12e.

Chapter 14

EUROPE'S ECONOMIC AND POLITICAL ASCENDANCY, 1871–1914

Half a century elapsed between the period of national consolidation described in the last chapter and the outbreak of the First World War in 1914. In this half-century European nations achieved their greatest power in global politics, developed their leading role in the global economy, and also exerted their maximum influence upon peoples outside Europe.

For Europe and the European world the years 1871 to 1914 were marked by hitherto unparalleled material and industrial growth; international peace; domestic stability; the advance of constitutional, representative, and democratic government; and continued faith in science, reason, and progress. But in these very years, in politics, economics, philosophy, and the arts, there were also new trends that challenged or began to undermine the liberal premises and tenets of Europe's expansive political and cultural power. Meanwhile, a new wave of European imperialism spread across Africa and Asia, creating new colonial empires, new global economic connections, and new international and cultural conflicts. All of these developments contributed to and reflected the European ascendancy before 1914, and all produced a legacy that has decisively influenced the modern world down to our own time.

For purposes of historical analysis, we are separating the European ascendancy in this complex era into different thematic strands. This chapter therefore examines economic and political trends in Europe after 1871, the next describes new European social and cultural movements that became influential during this period, and the following chapter discusses the worldwide impact of European imperialism. By 1914, the institutions and ideas of modern European civilization were spreading across most of the world, but these same institutions and ideas were also facing new critical challenges from within Europe and from people on other continents who resented the European domination of their economies, governments, and cultures.

Chapter emblem: Detail from a photograph of Italian immigrants arriving in New York in 1908. (©Bettmann/Getty Images)

68. THE CONCEPT OF THE MODERN "CIVILIZED WORLD"

Materialistic and Nonmaterialistic Ideals

With the extension of the nation-state system Europe was more clearly divided among self-conscious political entities that jealously guarded their borders and sovereign interests. Its unity lay in a kind of modern historical convergence that was moving Europeans toward similar ways of social life and similar cultural beliefs (despite the growth of nationalism, which, on a deeper level, expressed commonly held assumptions about human societies). This convergence also developed in countries where large numbers of Europeans continued to immigrate, including the United States, Canada, Australia, and New Zealand. Europe and its social, cultural offshoots constituted what Europeans and North Americans increasingly called the "civilized world" or the "West." Other regions—mostly in Asia, Africa, and Latin America—were described by Europeans as "backward." Europeans and the descendants of Europeans in other regions of the world were thus extremely conscious and inordinately proud of their civilization in the half-century before 1914. They believed it to be the well-deserved outcome of centuries of progress. Viewing themselves as the most advanced branch of mankind in the most important areas of human endeavor, they assumed that all peoples should respect the same social ideals—that insofar as other peoples were unwilling or unable to adopt them, they were labeled "backward," and that insofar as they adopted European ways, they became "modern" and "civilized" in their turn. Such ideas shaped the ideology and practice of imperialism, which entered a dynamic new phase in the late nineteenth century.

The ideals of European civilization

The ideals of this European or "Western" civilization were in part materialistic. If Europeans and Westerners considered their civilization to be better in 1900 than in 1800, or better than the ways of non-Western peoples at the same time, it was because they took pride in having more wealth and a higher standard of living, which gave them more kinds of food and clothing, new household comforts, and better sanitary facilities. Europeans also saw clear signs of material progress in their modern ocean liners, railroads, streetcars, and telegraph systems; and after about 1880 they were beginning to use telephones and electric lights. But the ideal of civilization, as Europeans defined it, was by no means exclusively materialistic. Knowledge as such, correct or truthful knowledge, was held to be a civilized attainment—scientific knowledge of nature, in place of superstition or demonology; geographical knowledge, by which modern people were aware of the earth as a whole with its general contours and diverse inhabitants. The ideal was also profoundly moral, derived from Christianity, but now secularized and detached from religion. An Englishman, Isaac Taylor, in his *Ultimate Civilization,* published in 1860, defined this moral ideal by listing the contrasting "relics of barbarism" that he thought would ultimately disappear from human history—"Polygamy, Infanticide, Legalized Prostitution, Capricious Divorce, Sanguinary and Immoral Games, Infliction of Torture, Caste and Slavery." Several of these had been condemned and placed outside the approved customs of Europe at least since the coming of Christianity (though prostitution was more or less tolerated in almost all European societies). Torture had gone out of use by about 1800, even in the illiberal European states; and legalized caste and slavery were gradually abolished by Western countries over the course of the nineteenth century. But numerous non-Western cultures, as Taylor described them in 1860, still allowed or tolerated two or three of the "relics" that he placed beyond the realm of civilized behavior.

Apart from these cultural conceptions of modern civilization, there were (and are) certain other indices, more purely quantitative, that sociologists worked out to show the level of advancement of a given society. One of these was the death rate, or number of persons per thousand of population who died each year. In England, France, and Sweden the "true" death rate (or death rate regardless of the proportion of infants and old people, who are most susceptible to death) fell from about 25 (per 1,000 per year) before 1850, to 19 in 1914 and 18 in the 1930s. Indeed, before the Second World War, it stood seemingly stabilized at about 18 in all countries of northwestern Europe, the United States, and the British dominions. Death rates in countries not "modern" have usually run over 40 even in favorable times. A closely related index was infant mortality, which fell rapidly after 1870 in all countries affected by medical science. Thus a woman under more modern conditions had to go through pregnancy and childbirth less often to produce the same number of surviving children. Another index of improving conditions was life expectancy, or the age that a person, at birth, had an even chance of attaining. In England life expectancy at birth rose from 40 years in the 1840s to 59 in 1933 and to 80 by 2015. In India in 1931 it was less than 27 years. It had risen to about 68 by 2015. Still another index was the literacy rate, or proportion of persons above a certain age (such as ten) able to read and write. In northwestern Europe by 1900 the literacy rate approached 100, whereas in some countries of the world at that time it had still not risen very far above zero. A further basic index of social change could be found in the productivity of labor, or amount produced by one worker in a given expenditure of time. This is often difficult to compute, especially for earlier periods for which statistical data are lacking. In the 1930s, however, the productivity of a farmer in Denmark was over ten times that of a farmer in Albania. All northwestern Europe was above the European average in this respect with the exception of Ireland, whereas Ireland, Spain, Portugal, Italy and all eastern Europe fell below it.

Indices of advancement

Rising Standards of Living

The essence of civilized living or of a "good life" has doubtless always evolved in the intangibles, in the way in which people use their minds and in the attitudes they form toward others or toward the conditions and planning of their own lives. The intangibles, however, can carry quite different meanings for persons of different cultures or ideologies. On the quantitative criteria there is less disagreement. People in almost all societies wish to lower the death rate, raise the literacy rate, and increase the productivity of human exertion. Whatever we might say about the intangible qualities of a civilized society, if we apply quantitative or sociological indices alone, we can say that for about four decades after 1870 Europe was the political, economic, and cultural center of a modern civilization that was developing new material advantages, improving the standard of living, and expanding rapidly around the world.

The "Zones" of Modern Societies after 1870

It may be more accurate to say that a certain region of Europe was the real center of this expanding modern civilization, for there were really two Europes in the late nineteenth century, an inner zone and an outer. A Frenchman writing in the 1920s about the two Europes that had risen since 1870, called the inner zone the "Europe of steam," and bounded it by an imaginary line joining Glasgow, Stockholm, Danzig, Trieste, Florence, and Barcelona. It included not only Great Britain but Belgium, Germany, France, northern Italy, and the western portions of the Austrian Empire. Virtually all heavy European industry was located in this zone. Here the railway network was thickest. Here the wealth of Europe was concentrated, in the form both of a high living standard and of

TRAIN IN THE SNOW
by Claude Monet (French, 1840–1926)

Trains became one of the new symbols of modernity during the nineteenth century, but few artists saw them as appropriate subjects for paintings. Monet and other Impressionists, however, wanted to apply their artistic techniques to the familiar objects of everyday life, including the iron shapes of a passing locomotive. In this typical Impressionist rendering of modern technology, the solid mass of the train melts into the play of light and the indeterminate grays of a dull winter day.

(©Heritage Images/Getty Images)

accumulations of capital. Here likewise were almost all the laboratories and scientific activity of Europe. Here, in the same zone, lay the strength of constitutional and parliamentary government and of liberal, humanitarian, socialist, and reformist movements of many kinds. In this zone the death rate was low, life expectancy was high, conditions of health and sanitation were at their best, literacy was almost universal, productivity of labor was impressive. To the same zone, for practical purposes, belonged certain regions of large-scale European settlement overseas, including the post–Civil War United States.

The outer zone   The outer zone included most of Ireland, most of the Iberian and Italian peninsulas, and all Europe east of what was then Germany, Bohemia, and Austria proper. The outer zone was agricultural, though the productivity of agriculture, per farm worker or per acre, was far less than in the inner zone. The people were poorer, more illiterate, and more likely to die young. The wealthy were landlords, often absentees. Most people in the outer zone increasingly supported themselves after 1870 by selling grain, livestock, wool, or lumber to the more industrialized inner zone but they were too poor to purchase many manufactured products in return. To obtain capital, the outer-zone societies borrowed in London or Paris. Their social and political philosophies were characteristically imported from Germany or other western European cultures. They borrowed engineers and technicians from the first zone to build bridges and install telegraph systems, and they sent their youth to universities in the first zone to study medicine or other professions. Many areas of European settlement overseas, for example in Latin America and the agrarian parts of the United States, may also be thought of at that time as belonging to this outer zone.

Beyond the European world lay a third zone, the immense reaches of Asia and Africa, all viewed as "backward" by the standards or cultural assumptions of late nineteenth-century Europe, with the exception of modernizing Japan; and it was these areas of the world, after 1870, that became most widely colonized by Europe and most disrupted by the new imperialism of the major European powers. Much of the world's history since 1870 could be written as a recurring story of the economic and cultural relations or interactions among these three evolving zones. But it is necessary in all human matters to guard against formulas that are too simple and also to recognize the constant changes as well as continuities in the histories of all human societies.

69. BASIC DEMOGRAPHY: THE INCREASE OF EUROPE'S POPULATION

European and World Population Growth since 1650

All continents except Africa gained enormously in population in the three centuries following 1650, but it was Europe that grew the most. There is little doubt that the proportion of Europeans in the world's total, including those of European origin in other continents, reached its maximum for all time between 1850 and the Second World War (broad estimates for global population trends, beginning with 1650, are given in the table on p. 588).

The causes of the rise in population after 1650 cannot be positively known. Some of them obviously operated in Asia as well as Europe. In Europe the organized sovereign states, as established in the seventeenth century, put an end to a long period of civil wars, stopping the

Causes of demographic growth

chronic violence and marauding, with the accompanying insecurity of agriculture and family life, which were more deadly than wars fought between governments. Similarly, the Tokugawa shogunate (1600–1868) kept peace in Japan, and the Manchu or Qing dynasty (1644–1912) brought a long period of order in China. The British rule in India and the Dutch in Java greatly reduced the autonomous power of local rulers, but it also curbed internal violence and famines, thus helping populations to grow very rapidly. All such factors, which allowed more people to remain alive longer, also favored the stability of families and the birth and raising of children. Death rates could fall and birth rates could rise from similar causes. The great exception to the global rise of population was Africa, where the slave trade removed over 10 million people (and what would have been an even larger number of their descendants) in three or four centuries, and where slave raiding led to the disruption of African cultures. In the Americas the native Indians were devastated by diseases brought from Europe to which at first they had no immunity.

ESTIMATED POPULATION OF THE WORLD BY CONTINENTAL AREAS[*]

	Millions					
	1650	1750	1850	1900	1950	2000
Europe	100	150	263	396	547	727
United States and Canada	1	2	26	82	172	313
Australasia-Oceania	2	2	2	6	13	31
Predominantly "European"	103	154	291	484	732	1,071
Latin America	12	16	38	74	167	521
Africa	100	106	111	133	230	811
Asia	330	515	822	959	1,403	3,719
Predominantly "Non-European"	442	637	971	1,166	1,800	5,051
World Total	545	791	1,262	1,650	2,532	6,123

	Percentages					
Europe	18.3	19.1	20.8	24.0	21.6	11.9
United States and Canada	.2	.2	2.1	5.0	6.8	5.1
Australasia-Oceania	.4	.2	.2	.3	.5	.5
Predominantly "European"	18.9	19.5	23.1	29.3	28.9	17.5
Latin America	2.2	2.0	3.0	4.5	6.6	8.5
Africa	18.3	13.0	8.8	8.1	9.1	13.3
Asia	60.6	65.0	65.1	58.1	55.4	60.7
Predominantly "Non-European"	81.1	80.0	76.9	70.7	71.1	82.5
World Total	100.0	100.0	100.0	100.0	100.0	100.0

[*]This table is designed to show only the numbers and proportion of people living in predominantly "European" cultures (that is, descended from societies with European languages and traditions) and "non-European" cultures over the modern period. It reveals the rapid increase in the proportion of "Europeans" in this sense from 1750 to 1900, and a steady decline in the "European" proportion during the twentieth century. The estimates show general population patterns rather than precise numbers (which cannot really be known). Demographers often revise their estimates for the number of people in past societies, and this table, though a useful overview, is subject to serious reservations. The population of the former Soviet Union is divided between Europe and Asia, but millions of Russian "Europeans" have long lived in the Asian parts of the former U.S.S.R. It must also be remembered that the population of the United States consists of Africans, Asians, Latin Americans, and Native Americans as well as Europeans, that the people in Latin American countries now generally speak a European language and differ widely in their racial composition, and that there are well over 4 million persons of European origin in southern Africa. In short, the table has nothing to do with race, for there are many whites who do not live in "European" cultural zones and many nonwhite people in the Americas and elsewhere (including Europe) who participate fully in institutions and languages derived from Europe.

Sources: For 1650 to 1900, A. N. Carr-Sanders, *World Population* (Oxford: Oxford University Press, 1936); for 1750, 1850, and 1900, John D. Durand, "The Modern Expansion of World Population," in *Proceedings of the American Philosophical Society,* vol. 111 (1967); and for 1950 and 2000, United Nations, *World Populations Prospects, the 2010 Revision* (New York: United Nations, 2011), and Massimo Livi-Bacci, *A Concise History of World Population,* 6th ed. (Oxford: Wiley Blackwell, 2017).

Improved living conditions

In Europe, sooner than elsewhere, other causes of growth were at work beyond the maintenance of civil peace. They included liberation from certain endemic afflictions, beginning with the subsiding of bubonic plague in the seventeenth century and the use of vaccination against smallpox in the eighteenth. Agricultural improvement produced more food, notably in England after about 1750. The improvement of transportation by road, canal, and railroad made localized famine a thing of the past, because food could be moved into areas of temporary shortage. With the Industrial Revolution larger populations could subsist in Europe by importing food from overseas. In the cities of Europe and North America, by 1900, the supply of pure drinking water and facilities for the disposal of garbage and sewage were better than in the past.

Hence population grew for several generations more substantially in Europe and its offshoots than elsewhere. The approximate percentages in the table on page 588 show that Asia, by these estimates, increased less than threefold between 1650 and 1900, but Europe increased fourfold, and the total number of Europeans, including the descendants of those who migrated to other continents, multiplied fivefold. The ascendancy of European civilization in the two and a half centuries after 1650 was due in some measure to demographic growth. But while in 1900 the proportion of "Europeans" in all continents was approaching a third of the human race, after 1900 this proportion began to fall. By the early twenty-first century it could be projected that "Europeans" would constitute only a tenth of the human beings on the planet in the year 2100.

Stabilization of European Population

The stabilization and relative decline of the European population followed from a fall in the birth rate. As early as 1830 the birth rate began noticeably to drop in France, with the result that France, long the most populous European state, was surpassed in population by Germany about 1870, by the British Isles about 1895, and by Italy about 1930. France, once thought to be decadent for this reason, was in fact only the leading country in a changing population cycle through which other European countries also began to pass. The birth rate, which had fallen below 30 per hundred in France in the 1830s, fell to that level in Sweden in the 1880s; in England in the 1890s; and in Germany and the Netherlands between 1900 and 1910. After the Second World War there was a temporary rise, but by the early twenty-first century the birth rate was well below 15 per 1,000 in Europe, Japan, and North America, hardly sufficient to maintain existing population levels. In much of the rest of the world it was still well over 20 or even 30.

The reduced birth rate is not a mere dry statistical item, nor does it affect populations merely in the mass. It is one of the indices of a more modern industrialized civilization, first appearing in that inner European zone in which the other indices were also highest, and thence spreading outward in a kind of wave. Concretely, a low birth rate in the nineteenth century meant that families averaged from two to four children, where in former times, families might consist of ten children or even more. The low birth rate reflects the small family system, and few institutions were more fundamental to modern life. The principal means used to hold down the birth rate, or to limit the family, was the practice of contraception. But the true causes or reasons why parents wanted to limit their families were deeply embedded in the social patterns of modernizing societies.

Historical demographers have detected a "European family pattern" as far back as the seventeenth century. It was a pattern in which, in comparison to other societies, Europeans married later, and a larger number never married at all. Late marriage shortened the number of years during which a woman bore children and enabled young people to acquire skills or accumulate savings (as in tools and household goods) before setting up new families. Evidence indicating the use of various forms of contraception can be found in the eighteenth century among the upper classes, by study of the number and spacing of their children.

A European family pattern

The practice seems to have spread to other social classes during and after the French Revolution, in part because the new Napoleonic Code (1804) required that inheritances be divided among all sons and daughters. The French peasants, many of them owners of land, began to limit themselves to two or three children in order that all children (by inheritance, marriage, and dowries) might remain in the same economic and social position as their landowning parents. It was thus the quest for economic security and higher living standards that led to the reduced birth rate in France and subsequently in other parts of Europe.

<table>
<tr><td>Life in the city</td><td></td></tr>
</table>

In the great cities of the nineteenth century, in which standards of life for the working classes often collapsed, the effect might at first be a proliferation of offspring. But life in the city, under crowded conditions of housing, also set a premium on the small family. After about 1880 child labor became much less frequent among the working classes. When children ceased to earn part of the family income, parents tended to have fewer of them. About the same time governments in the advanced countries and nation-states began to require universal compulsory schooling. The number of years spent in education, and hence in economic dependency upon parents, grew longer and longer until it became common even for young adults to be still engaged in study. Each child represented many years of expense for its parents. The growing need for extensive education and the desire of parents to give their children every possible advantage in a competitive world were probably the most basic causes of voluntary limitation of the family. Hardly less basic was the desire to lighten the burdens upon mothers. The small family system, together with the decline of infant mortality, because they combined to free women from the interminable bearing and tending of infants, probably did more than anything else to improve the position of women in modern societies. Freed at least in part from the traditional cycles of pregnancy and child care, middle-class women were eventually able to pursue advanced education, new professions, and new kinds of social or political activities. The use of contraception also spread widely among the working class during the early twentieth century; demographic research in England, for example, suggests that almost 70 percent of working-class couples were using contraception by the 1930s (compared to fewer than 20 percent in 1900).

The effects of the small family system upon total population became manifest only slowly. More people lived on into the middle and older age groups, and the fall of the birth rate was gradual, so that in all the leading countries total numbers continued to rise, except in France, which hardly grew between 1900 and 1945. Despite several immense wars and other social disruptions, the persistent demographic pattern was superabundant increase. In five generations, between 1800 and 1950, a population of about 200 million "Europeans" grew into roughly 700 million "Europeans" around the globe. Because productivity increased even more rapidly, the standard of living for most of these "Europeans" rose in spite of the increase of numbers, and there was no general problem of overpopulation.

Growth of Cities and Urban Life

Where did so many people go? Some stayed in the rural areas where most people had always lived. Rural populations in the inner zone became more dense, turning to the more intensive agriculture of truck gardening or dairy farming, leaving products like wool and cereal grains to be raised elsewhere and then imported. But it is

THE GLEANERS
by Jean-Francois Millet (French, 1814–1875)

Although France, like other European countries, became a more urban society over the course of the nineteenth century, many French people still lived and worked in the countryside, as Millet showed in this painting of poor peasant women who gleaned the fields for a few stalks of grain.
(©Godong/Getty Images)

estimated that of every seven persons added to the western European population only one stayed on the land. Of the other six, one left Europe altogether and five went to the growing cities.

The nineteenth-century city was rapidly reshaped by railroads. The new railroad systems made it possible to concentrate manufacturing in large towns, to which bulky goods such as foods and fuel could now be moved in great volume. The growth of cities between 1850 and 1914 was phenomenal. In England two-thirds of the people lived in places of 20,000 or less in 1830; in 1914 two-thirds lived in places of 20,000 or more. Germany, the historic land of archaic towns carried over from the Middle Ages, rivaled England after 1870 in modern industrial urbanization. Whereas in 1840 only London and Paris had a million people, the same could be said by 1914 of other major European cities such as Berlin, Vienna, St. Petersburg, and Moscow. Some places, like the English Midlands and the Ruhr Valley in Germany, became a mass of contiguous smaller cities, vast urban agglomerations divided only by municipal lines.

The evolving demographic pattern in nineteenth-century European bourgeois families may be seen in this portrait of a Victorian-era English family sitting in their garden. The declining number of children eventually gave women more time and freedom for diverse activities because they were less tied to long cycles of pregnancies and childrearing.

(©General Photographic Agency/Getty Images)

Impact of urban life

The great cities set the tone of modern society. City life was impersonal and anonymous; people were uprooted, less tied to home or church than in the country. They lacked the country person's feeling of deference for aristocratic families. They lacked the sense of self-help characteristic of older rural communities. It was in the city that the daily newspaper press, which spread rapidly in the wake of the telegraph after 1850, found its most habitual readers. The so-called yellow or sensational press appeared about 1900. Articulate public opinion was formed in the cities, and city people were on the whole disrespectful of tradition and more receptive to new ideas, having in many cases deliberately altered their own lives by moving from the country or from smaller towns. It is hardly surprising that the new conditions of urban life fostered the spread of socialism among the industrial masses in

European cities. Some of the more vehement nationalisms that arose after 1870 were also stimulated by city life, for people felt increasingly detached from all institutions except the state. At the same time city life, by its greater facilities for schooling, reading, and discussion, made for a more informed, engaged, and enlightened public opinion.

Migration from Europe, 1850–1940

During the same period in which cities were growing, almost 60 million people left Europe altogether, of whom possibly a fifth sooner or later returned. This vast movement of people is called the Atlantic Migration because all crossed that ocean except those who moved to European settler societies in Africa, Australia, and New Zealand or from European to Asian Russia. It towers above all other European migrations in magnitude, and possibly

The Atlantic Migration

also in significance, for it was by this means that earlier colonial offshoots of Europe were transformed into new, larger societies that carried the very strong influence of European political, social, religious, and cultural traditions. All parts of Europe contributed to the migration, as shown in the table below, which comprises the years from 1850 to 1940. Before 1850 the mass movement had scarcely begun, though by that time over a million immigrants had entered the United States since the close of the Napoleonic wars. After 1940 the character of intercontinental migration was greatly transformed. In recent decades, since the Second World War, there have been large migrations into Europe from Africa, the Middle East, and Asia, and into the Americas from places outside Europe. But in the century before 1940 the migration of European peoples was a key force in the dissemination of European institutions and cultures.

It is hard to give accurate or precise figures for emigration from Europe. In the statistical sources the English, Scots, Welsh, and Irish are usually mixed within the broad category of the "British Isles." The Poles, Czechs, other Slavic peoples, Hungarians, East

EMIGRATION FROM EUROPE, 1850–1940

From:		
	British Isles	18,300,000
	Italy	10,200,000
	Russia	9,000,000
	Germany	5,000,000
	Spain	4,500,000
	Austria-Hungary	4,200,000
	Portugal	2,500,000
	Sweden	1,200,000
	Norway	750,000
	Denmark	470,000
	Finland	390,000
	France	390,000
	Switzerland	340,000
	Netherlands	210,000
	Belgium	150,000
		57,600,000

Source: William Woodruff, *Impact of Western Man: A Study of Europe's Role in the World Economy, 1750–1960* (New York: St. Martin's Press, 1966), p. 106.

European Jews, and others were not counted in such groups before the First World War; they were simply included among emigrants from the Russian, Austro-Hungarian, and German empires. Millions of Jews, Irish, Poles, and many thousands of others are therefore invisible in the figures, which also include several million Russians who moved from the European to Asian parts of Russia. It must be remembered that there were also many international migrations that did not involve Europeans. For a few years after 1850 enslaved Africans were still brought illegally to the United States and Brazil. Workers went from India to the West Indies and South Africa, and many Chinese settled in the United States and southeast Asia. With these limitations in the global data, the table on immigrant destinations shows the main patterns of *European* emigration in the 90 years preceding the Second World War.

The British and Irish went to the British dominions and the United States. The Italians divided between the United States and Latin America. Spaniards settled overwhelmingly in the Spanish American republics, and the Portuguese settled in Brazil. The Germans moved overwhelmingly to the United States, though some went to Argentina and Brazil. The extraordinary preponderance of the United States is apparent. At the same time, it should be noted that almost half of the European migration went to other countries around the world. The new countries received the following influxes of people:

IMMIGRATION INTO VARIOUS COUNTRIES, 1850–1940

To:		
	United States	32,300,000
	Asian Russia	7,000,000
	Argentina	6,600,000
	Brazil	4,700,000
	Canada	4,300,000
	Australia	2,900,000
	New Zealand	650,000
	Uruguay	600,000
	Cuba	600,000
	South Africa	250,000
	Mexico	250,000

Source: Woodruff, *Impact of Western Man,* p. 108.

Causes of the exodus

The exodus from Europe was due to a remarkable and temporary juxtaposition of causes. One fundamental cause, or precondition, was that before 1914 the new countries generally welcomed immigration. New workers were needed and wanted to farm the land, build houses, dig in the mines. This was least true of Australia and New Zealand, which preferred to limit themselves to English-speaking settlers and which also pioneered as social democracies, becoming models even before 1900 of legislation to protect the working classes. One result was that there was little desire for outsiders who could compete for jobs at low wages. A similar combination of national preferences and labor protectionism led to laws restricting immigration in the United States in 1921 and 1924. Thereafter immigrants could enter only under quotas. Immigrants from Asia were generally banned from entering the United States, and the European quotas were lowest for eastern and southern Europe, the areas from which most emigration had been coming.

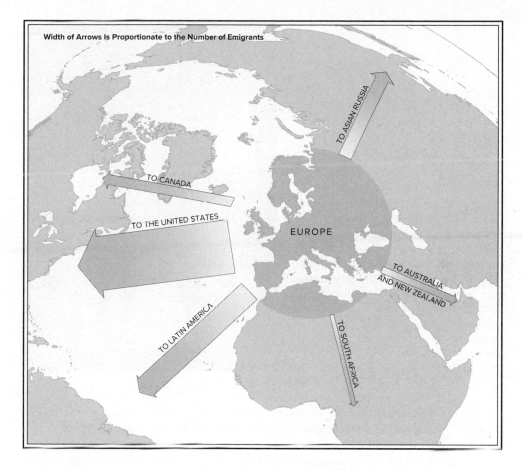

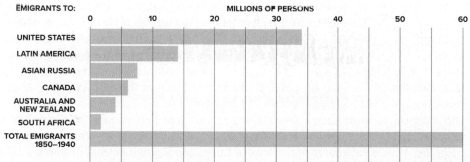

MIGRATION FROM EUROPE, 1850–1940

About 60 million people left Europe in the century preceding the Second World War, distributing themselves as shown in the diagram above. (See chart on p. 594.) About half went to the United States, but the migration of European peoples also built up "European" societies in other regions of the world. These expanding, overseas "European" societies included many non-European peoples and cultural histories, and they all developed new institutions and cultures that also differed from the evolving national cultures in Europe. They remained closely connected to Europe, however, because of enduring cultural influences and because they produced food and raw materials for European markets, borrowed European capital, and bought manufactured goods from European factories. The overseas "European" societies and migrations thus helped to support Europe's economic ascendancy and to expand the global economic system.

The mass migration of people is one of the distinctive social patterns of modern history, and such migrations have continually reshaped societies in all parts of the world. This Italian woman, Anna Schiacchitano, who arrived in New York with her children in 1908, was part of the vast emigration out of Europe that deeply affected the social and economic development of postcolonial nations in the Americas.

(©Bettmann/Getty Images)

In Europe there were many conditions propelling emigrants outward. Physically, the steamship made it easier and cheaper to cross the sea, and the new railroads helped people to get to the ports as well as to distribute themselves after landing in the new countries. Economically, people in the lower social classes could more easily afford a long journey. People migrated to improve their material circumstances; but some high points in the wave of emigration coincided with high points in the business cycle in Europe, when jobs in Europe were plentiful and wages were at their highest. There was also social flight in times of economic ruin or starvation, as in the emigration from Ireland after 1846. In the "great potato famine" of 1845–1849 nearly 1 million Irish died of starvation and disease, and more than 1.5 million emigrated to the United States in the next few years. After the revolutions of 1848 a certain number of Europeans also left Europe for political reasons, and, later on, to avoid compulsory military service. The best example of flight from segregation and discrimination, and from direct persecution in government-encouraged pogroms, was the emigration of the Jews of Russia and Russian Poland, of whom a million and a half moved to the United States in the 15 years preceding the First World War.

But perhaps the most basic historical factor in the whole European exodus was the underlying liberalism of the age. Never before (nor since) had people been legally so free

Freedom of movement

to move. Old laws requiring skilled workmen to stay in their own countries were repealed, as in England in 1824. The old semicommunal agricultural villages, with collective rights and obligations, holding individuals to their birthplaces and native groups, fell into disuse except in Russia. The disappearance of serfdom allowed the peasants of eastern Europe to change residences without obtaining a lord's permission. Governments permitted their subjects to emigrate, to take with them their savings of shillings, marks, kronen, or lire, and to change nationality by becoming naturalized in their new homes. The rise of personal liberty and social mobility in Europe, as well as the hope for more liberties and opportunities in America, made possible the great European emigration. This mass movement of people was all the more remarkable because it took place by private initiative and at private expense. The new national states did not initiate or organize the migration; individuals, families, and small local groups (to borrow the metaphor of one authority) simply detached themselves atom by atom from the mass of Europe, crossed the seas on their own, and reattached themselves atom by atom to the accumulating mass of the New World. The mass migrations of the late nineteenth century thus launched a worldwide movement of people that continues to the present day, grows in importance, and remains one of the most characteristic social patterns of modern world history.

70. THE WORLD ECONOMY
OF THE NINETEENTH CENTURY

How did the swelling population of Europeans manage to feed itself? How, in fact, did it not merely feed itself but enjoy an incomparably higher standard of living in 1900 than in 1800? The answers to such questions varied in the different regions of Europe, but the overall advance came through the new science, industry, transportation, and communications and also through the expansion of global trading systems. At the same time, Europeans were developing new business, financial, and labor organizations that contributed to a steady growth in economic productivity.

The "New Industrial Revolution"

The Industrial Revolution and the global economy entered upon a new phase, which is often called the "new" or "second" Industrial Revolution. The use of steam power, the growth of the textile and metallurgical industries, and the advent of the railroad had characterized the earlier era of industrialization. Now, after 1870, new sources of power were tapped, the already mechanized industries expanded, new industries appeared, and industry spread geographically.

The steam engine itself was refined and improved. By 1914 it still predominated over other power machinery, but electricity with its incomparable advantages came into use. The invention of the internal combustion (or gasoline) engine and the diesel engine gave the world automobiles, airplanes, and submarines in the two decades before 1914; the advent of the automotive and aviation industries made oil one of the most coveted natural resources. In the new chemical industries industrial research laboratories were replacing the individual inventor. Chemists discovered new fertilizers and from coal tar alone produced

Industrial advances

a bewildering array of new products ranging from artificial food flavors to high explosives. With explosives the first great tunnels were built, the Mount Cenis in 1873, the Simplon in 1906—both in the Alps; and great new canals, the Suez in 1869, the Kiel in 1895, the Panama in 1914. Chemistry made possible the production of synthetic fabrics like rayon, which revolutionized the textile industry. Electricity transformed all indoor and outdoor lighting, making cities both brighter and safer. There was a communications revolution too. The telephone appeared in the 1870s, and the Italian inventor Guglielmo Marconi helped to bring the continents closer together when he successfully transmitted wireless signals across the Atlantic in 1901. Motion pictures and the earliest radios were developed before 1914, leading soon to the production of new popular entertainments that crossed the traditional social and cultural boundaries of European societies. Medicine ran the alphabetical gamut from anesthetics to X-rays; yellow fever was overcome. Vastly improved processes for refining iron ore made possible a great expansion in the production of steel, the key product of the new industrial age; aluminum and other metal alloys were also produced through new industrial processes. Railroad mileage multiplied; the European network, including the Russian, increased from 140,000 miles in 1890 to 213,000 in 1914.

In this second phase of the Industrial Revolution machine industry spread geographically from Britain and Belgium, the only truly industrial countries in 1870, to France, Italy, Russia, Japan, and, most markedly, to Germany and the United States. In Europe industrial production was concentrated in the "inner zone." Three powers alone—Britain, Germany, and France—accounted in 1914 for more than seven-tenths of all European

The industrial powers

manufactures and produced over four-fifths of all European coal, steel, and machinery. Of the major European powers Germany was now forging ahead. To use steel alone as a criterion, in 1871 Germany was producing annually three-fifths as much steel as Britain; by 1900 it

was producing more, and by 1914 it was producing twice as much as Britain—but only half as much as the new industrial giant, the United States. By 1914 American steel output was greater than that of Germany, Britain, and France combined. Britain, the pioneer in mechanization, was being outstripped in both the Old World and the New. The three European powers increased their industrial production by about 50 percent in the two decades before 1914, but the United States had a far higher annual growth rate from 1870 to 1913, 4.3 percent as compared to the next leading powers, Germany with 2.9 percent, Britain with 2.2 percent, and France with 1.6 percent. By 1914 the United States had moved ahead of Europe in the mechanization of agriculture, in manufactures, and in coal and steel production, in which it was producing over two-fifths of the world's output. The Americans were pioneering also in assembly-line, conveyor-belt techniques for the mass production of automobiles and all kinds of consumer goods, thereby launching a twentieth-century industrial challenge to Europe's long-term dominance in the global economy.

Free Trade and the European "Balance of Payments"

It was Britain in the mid-nineteenth century, then the workshop of the world, that had inaugurated the movement toward free trade. It will be recalled that in 1846, by the repeal of the Corn Laws, the British embarked upon a systematic free trade policy, deliberately choosing to become dependent upon overseas imports for their food. France adopted free trade in 1860. Other countries soon followed. It is true that by 1880 there was a movement back to protective tariffs except in Britain, Holland, and Belgium. But the tariffs were impediments rather than barriers, and the economic system, until 1914, increasingly depended on the extreme mobility of goods across political frontiers. Politically, Europe was more than ever nationalistic; but economic activity, under generally liberal conditions in which business was supposed to be free from the political state, remained predominantly international and globe-encircling.

Broadly speaking, the great economic accomplishment of Europe before 1914 was to create a financial system by which the huge global imports into industrial Europe could be acquired and paid for. All European countries except Russia, Austria-Hungary, and the

Imports vs. exports

Balkan states imported more than they exported. It was the British again who led in this direction. Britain had been a predominantly importing country since the close of the eighteenth century. Despite

The Bessemer steel-making process enhanced the production of steel and rapidly became an important component of industrial expansion during the later decades of the nineteenth century. Its importance for Britain is suggested by this illustration of the future King Edward VII and Queen Alexandra, who are observing the new methods of steel production from box seats at a factory in Sheffield in 1875. (©Henry Guttmann/Getty Images)

the expanding export of cotton manufactures and other products of the Industrial Revolution, Britain consumed more goods from abroad than it sent out. Industrialization and urbanization in the nineteenth century confirmed the same situation. Between 1800 and 1900 the value of British exports multiplied eightfold, but the value of imports into Great Britain multiplied tenfold, and in the decade before 1914 the British had an import surplus of about three-quarters of a billion dollars a year. Great Britain and the industrial countries of Europe together (roughly Europe's inner zone), at the beginning of the twentieth century, were drawing in an import surplus, measured in dollars, of almost $2 billion every year (the dollar then representing far more goods than it came to represent later). The imports into Europe's inner zone consisted of raw materials for its industries and of food and amenities for its people.

How were the imports paid for? How did Europe continue to enjoy a favorable balance of payments despite an unfavorable balance of trade in commodities? Export of European manufactures paid for most imports, but not all. It was the so-called invisible exports that made up the difference, that is, shipping and insurance services rendered to foreigners, and interest on money lent out or invested, all bringing in foreign exchange and enhancing Britain's position in the global economy. An Argentine merchant in Buenos Aires, for example, to ship hides to Germany, might employ a British vessel; he would pay the freight charges in Argentine pesos, which might be credited to the account of the British shipowner in an Argentine bank; the British shipowner would sell the pesos to someone, in

Invisible exports

England or elsewhere in Europe, who needed them to buy Argentine meat. The far-flung British merchant marine thus earned global fees that helped to pay for the food and raw materials needed by Britain. To insure themselves against risks of every conceivable kind people all over the world turned to Lloyds of London. With the profits drawn from selling insurance the British could buy what they wished. Governments or business enterprises on other continents borrowed money in Europe, mainly in England, where the distribution of loans became another important income-producing export. The global interest payments on these loans flowed into European and British banks and helped to finance large quantities of imports. But the lending of money to foreigners was only part of a larger phenomenon, the export of capital.

The Export of European Capital

The migration of millions of Europeans had the effect of creating new European-style economies and societies that purchased manufactures from Europe and produced the food and other commodities that were needed in Europe. European nations could not have had such far-reaching international influence if they had exported people only, especially people of such small means as most emigrants were. Europe also exported the capital that enabled the new settlers in overseas societies to develop productive economies.

The export of capital meant that an older and wealthier country, instead of using its whole annual income to raise its own standard of living, or to add to its own capital by expanding or improving its houses, factories, machinery, mines, and transportation, diverted some of its income to expanding or improving the houses, factories, machinery, mines, and transportation of foreign countries. It meant that British, French, Dutch, Belgian, Swiss, and eventually German investors bought the stocks of foreign business enterprises and the bonds of foreign businesses and governments; or they organized companies of their own to operate in foreign countries; or their banks granted loans to banks in New York or Tokyo, which then lent the funds to local users.

Capital arose in Europe to some extent from the savings of quite small people, especially in France, where peasants and modest bourgeois families were notably thrifty. But most capital accumulated from savings by the well-to-do. The owners of a business, for example, instead of spending the company's income by paying higher wages, took a portion of it in profits or dividends, and instead of spending all this on their own living, reinvested part of it in domestic or foreign enterprises. The gap between rich and poor was thus one cause of the rapid accumulation of capital, though the accumulation of capital, in the nineteenth century, produced in turn a steady rise of living standards for the working classes. In a sense, however, the common people of western Europe, by forgoing the better housing, diet, education, or pleasures that a more democratic or consumer-oriented society might have provided for them, contributed by their productivity to the export of European capital. Workers benefited from the import of new foods or raw materials, but they also facilitated the financing and building up of other regions of the world.

Capital accumulation

The British were the chief exporters of capital, followed at some distance by the French, and at the close of the century by the Germans. As early as the 1840s half the annual increase of wealth in Great Britain was going into foreign investments. By 1914 the British had $20 billion in foreign investments, the French had about $8.7 billion, and the Germans had about $6 billion. A quarter of all the wealth owned by the inhabitants of Great Britain consisted in 1914 of their investments outside the country. Almost a sixth of the French national wealth lay in investments outside France. All three countries

CLASSIC LANDSCAPE
by Charles Sheeler (American, 1883–1965)

This landscape depicts an American plant of the Ford Motor Company in 1931, but it also symbolizes what has been called the second Industrial Revolution. In this phase of industrialization, electricity, the internal combustion engine, and the automobile were especially important, and industry spread far beyond its early centers in Britain and western Europe. The picture is "classic" in its clear delineation, its array of familiar mathematical forms, and the universality of its message. The plant seems rational and precise, but there are no human beings. It is as if the machine had a life of its own and could do without human hands.

(National Gallery of Art)

had given hostages to fortune, and fortune proved unkind, for in the First World War the British lost about a quarter of their foreign investments, the French lost about a third, and the Germans lost all.

These huge sums, pouring out from Europe's inner zone for a century before 1914, at first went mainly to finance the Americas and the less affluent regions of Europe. European capital was also invested in Asia and Africa, especially after the rapid expansion of Europe's colonial empires in the 1890s. No country except Great Britain completely built its railways with its own resources. In the United States the railway system was built very largely

*The recipients
of European capital*

with capital obtained from England. In central and eastern Europe British companies often constructed the first railways, then sold out to native operating companies or to governments that subsequently ran them. In the Argentine Republic the British not merely financed and built the railways, but long continued to operate and own them. In addition, up to 1914 the British sold about 75 million tons of coal a year to South America to keep the railways going, not to mention items for replacement and upkeep of equipment. Docks, warehouses, mines, plantations, processing and manufacturing establishments all over the world were similarly built up with capital drawn from Europe. European capital also helped emigrants in the new countries to develop public services and institutions that required major financial investments. In the United States, for example, state and local governments very commonly sold their bonds in Europe to build roads, pave streets, or construct school systems for the westward-moving population. A few of these American bonds proved a partial or total loss to European investors, but on the whole, by 1914, the United States had paid back a good deal of its indebtedness. Even so, in 1914, Americans still owed about $4 billion to Europeans—a sum three times as large as the national debt of the United States before the First World War. This kind of economic investment (along with the patterns of mass immigration) helps to explain how and why Europe remained deeply involved in distant nations that had long since declared their political independence from European colonial empires. European investors accumulated much wealth through the expanding, global financial system of the late nineteenth century, but this system also helped to develop new industries and infrastructures in faraway places that were virtually unknown to the people of Europe. The new money flowed into and out of European countries at the same time.

An International Money System: The Gold Standard

The international economy rested upon an international money system, based in turn upon the almost universal acceptance of the gold standard. England had adopted the gold standard in 1821, when the pound sterling was legally defined as the equivalent of 113 grains of fine gold. Western Europe and the United States adopted an exclusively gold standard in the 1870s. A person holding money in currencies that were deemed to be "civilized"—pounds, francs, dollars, marks, and the like—could turn it into gold at will, and a person holding gold could turn it into any of these same currencies. The national currencies were like so many different languages all expressing the same meaning. All had substantially the same value, and until 1914 the exchange rates between currencies remained highly stable. It was assumed that no modern industrial country's currency ever "fell"; such things might happen in a remote Latin American republic or in China, or in the French Revolution, but not in the world of modern progress and European affairs.

Currency exchange

The important currencies were all freely exchangeable. A French merchant selling silks to a German, and hence receiving German marks, could turn the marks into francs, pounds sterling, or dollars. That is, he was not obliged to buy from Germany or spend his money in Germany but could use the proceeds of his German sale to buy French, British, or American goods or services as he chose. Trade was multilateral. A country needing imports from another country, such as American cotton, did not have to sell to that country to obtain them; it could sell its own goods anywhere and then import according to its needs.

Effects of the gold standard

It was the acceptance of the gold standard, and the fact that all important countries possessed a sufficient share of gold to support their currencies, that made possible so fluid an interchange. At the same time the gold standard had less wholesome effects. It harmed the economies of countries that lacked gold. And it produced a gradual fall of prices, especially between 1870 and 1900, because (until the gold discoveries in South Africa, Australia, and Alaska in the 1890s) the world's production of gold lagged behind the expanding production of industrial and agricultural goods. Persistently declining prices were a hardship to those who habitually worked with borrowed money—many farmers, many businessmen, and debtor nations as a whole. A famous speech by William Jennings Bryan in the United States in 1896, declaring that mankind should not be crucified "upon this cross of gold," expressed a common, world-wide anger about a financial system that worked against the interests of indebted persons and indebted nations. But falling prices were an advantage to the wage-earning class, which generally improved its position in these years, and also to the wealthy, the owners and lenders of capital, the bankers and financiers, who so long as prices were falling were repaid in money of more value than that which they had lent.

The center of the global economic and financial system was London. The London banks prospered in consequence of the defeat of Napoleon, the older financial centers in Amsterdam having been ruined in the Revolutionary and Napoleonic wars. It may be recalled also that the victors in 1815 imposed upon France an indemnity of 700 million francs, which in 1818 was taken over by a syndicate of private bankers; the London banks played a leading part in this affair and so developed close connections with many government treasuries. In the Crimean War of 1854–1856, with England at war with Russia, the London banks floated loans for the Russian government—so independent were business and politics at the time. The early adoption of the gold standard in England meant that many people, British and foreign, kept their funds in the form of sterling on deposit in London, where quantities of available capital therefore accumulated. London became the apex of a financial pyramid that had the world for its base. It was the main center for the exchange of currencies, the clearinghouse of the world's debts, the depository from which all the world borrowed, the banker's bank, as well as the world's shipping center and the headquarters of many international corporations.

London at the center

A World Market: Unity, Competition—and Insecurity

Never had the earth been so unified economically, with each region playing specific roles in a global specialization. Western Europe, and in 1870 mainly Great Britain, was the world's industrial workshop. Other parts of the earth supplied its many needs. An English economist marveled in 1866 that Britain now had its granaries in Chicago and Odessa, its forests in Canada and the Baltic, its sheep farms in Australia, and its gold and silver mines in California and Peru, while drinking tea brought from China and coffee from East Indian plantations. The same could have been said of most of Europe's inner-zone nations by the time of the First World War.

A true global market had been created. Goods, services, commodities, money, capital, and people moved back and forth almost without regard to national boundaries. Articles were bought and sold at uniform world prices. Dealers in wheat, for example, followed prices in Minneapolis, Liverpool, Buenos Aires, and Danzig as reported by telegraph and cable from day to day. They bought where it was cheapest and sold where it was dearest. In this way the world's wheat supply was distributed roughly according to need or ability to pay. The worker of Milan, if the Italian crop was poor and prices were high, was fed from another source. On the other hand,

A true global market

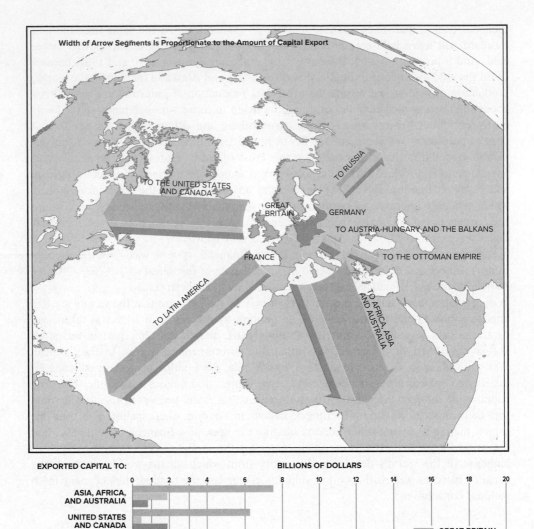

Width of Arrow Segments Is Proportionate to the Amount of Capital Export

TO RUSSIA

TO THE UNITED STATES AND CANADA

GREAT BRITAIN

GERMANY

TO AUSTRIA-HUNGARY AND THE BALKANS

FRANCE

TO THE OTTOMAN EMPIRE

TO LATIN AMERICA

TO AFRICA, ASIA AND AUSTRALIA

EXPORTED CAPITAL TO:	BILLIONS OF DOLLARS

0 1 2 3 4 6 8 10 12 14 16 18 20

ASIA, AFRICA, AND AUSTRALIA

UNITED STATES AND CANADA

LATIN AMERICA

RUSSIA

AUSTRIA-HUNGARY AND THE BALKANS

OTTOMAN EMPIRE

TOTAL EXPORTED CAPITAL TO 1914

GREAT BRITAIN
FRANCE
GERMANY

EXPORT OF EUROPEAN CAPITAL TO 1914

In 1914 the British, French, and Germans held upwards of $30 billion in foreign and colonial loans and investments, distributed as shown on the map. Dutch investments, especially in the West Indies, together with Swiss, Belgian, and Scandinavian holdings, would add several billion dollars more. Proceeds from such investments helped Europeans to pay for the excess of their imports over exports. British capital predominated in the overseas world, while the less-developed regions of eastern Europe and the Middle East were financed mainly from Germany and France. Much of the investment shown here was lost or expended in the First World War.

the Italian wheat grower would in this case feel the pinch of world competition. The world market, while it organized the world into a unified economic system, at the same time brought distant regions into competition for the first time. The producers of goods and commodities—whether entrepreneur, factory employee, farmer, or coffee planter—had no secure outlet for their products, as had generally been true in the past. They were in competition not only with persons across the street or down the road but also with other producers throughout the world. It was this worldwide system of production and consumption that established the modern economic foundation for what is now called "globalization."

The creation of an integrated world market, the financing and building up of countries outside of Europe, and the consequent feeding and support of Europe's increasing population were the great triumphs of the nineteenth-century system of unregulated capitalism. The system was intricate, with thousands and even millions of individuals and business firms supplying each other's wants without central planning. But it was extremely precarious, and the position of most people in this network of global economic exchanges was exceedingly vulnerable. Region competed against region and person against person. A fall of grain prices in the American Middle West, besides ruining a few speculators, might oblige German or Argentine wheat growers to sell at a price at which they could not live. Factory owners might be driven out of business if competitors successfully undersold them or if a new commodity made their own product obsolete. The workers, hired only when needed by an employer, faced unemployment when business slackened or when jobs disappeared because of labor-saving inventions.

The system went through cycles of boom and depression, the most notable example of the latter being the "long depression" that set in about 1873 and lasted to about 1893. The new global economy depended on expansion and on credit; but the declining prices of specific goods or commodities made it impossible for some people to pay their debts, so that credit collapsed; and sometimes expansion failed to keep pace with expectations, and anticipated profits proved to be losses. To combat the essential insecurity of private capitalism, governments, businesses, and workers resorted to all manner of devices. Against competition from other countries governments established protective tariffs; business enterprises entered into acquisitions and mergers, sometimes approaching monopolies. For the working classes governments adopted social insurance measures as protection against accidents, illness, and unemployment. Labor meanwhile turned increasingly to its own trade unions and socialist parties. All this signalized the gradual decline in the years after 1880 of nineteenth-century unregulated, laissez-faire capitalism.

Cycles of boom and depression

Changes in Organization: Big Business

A great change came over capitalism itself about 1880 or 1890. Formerly characterized by a large number of small units, small businesses run by individuals, partnerships, or small companies, it was increasingly characterized by large and impersonal corporations. The attractions of the "limited liability" corporation as a form of business organization and as a means of encouraging investment arose from laws enacted by most countries in the nineteenth century that limited the individual investor's personal loss in the event of a bankruptcy to the amount of his or her shares of stock in the enterprise. The corporation, in its modern form appearing first with the railroads, became the usual form of

The "limited liability" corporation

The new world markets and European colonial systems brought about a great expansion in the global production of commodities. During the decades before 1914, the colonized areas of Asia, Africa, and the West Indies exported vast shiploads of tea, coffee, sugar, cocoa, and other commodities to the more industrialized economies of Europe and North America. The Scottish entrepreneur Thomas Lipton, for example, established a highly profitable company that exported tea from the British colony of Ceylon (now Sri Lanka) to global markets. These women were working on a Lipton tea plantation in 1903. They thus participated, within colonial Ceylon and with very low wages, in a global trading system that was transforming agriculture and daily life throughout the modern world.

(©Print Collector/Getty Images)

organization for industry and commerce. As machinery grew more complicated, only a large pool of capital could finance it. And as corporations grew in size and number, relying on the sale of stock and the issue of bonds, the influence of banking and financial circles was enhanced. Financiers, using not so much their own money as the savings of others, had a new power to create or to destroy, to stimulate, discourage, or combine corporate enterprises in various industries. Industrial capitalism brought finance capitalism with it.

Corporate organization made it possible to concentrate diverse economic processes under unified management. In retail commerce, large department stores appeared after about 1870 in the United States and France, selling all kinds of goods that were formerly sold only in small shops and establishing a fixed price for each piece of merchandise. In industry, steel offers a good example of the new, large-scale enterprises. Steel became a big business when heavy blast furnaces were introduced. It was not economically safe for the steel business to rely for iron and coal on independent producers. Prices and supplies were often unstable or unpredictable. The steel works therefore began to operate mines of their own or to buy out or otherwise reduce coal and iron mines to subsidiary status. Some, to assure their markets, began to produce not merely steel but steel manufactures as well—steel ships, railway equipment, naval and military ordnance. Thus entire processes from mining to finished product became concentrated in a "vertical" integration.

Vertical integration

In addition to this vertical linking of raw materials and finished products, there was much new "horizontal" integration in which companies producing the same goods combined with each other to reduce competition and to protect themselves against fluctuations in prices and markets. Some fixed prices, some agreed to restrict production, and some divided up markets among themselves. They were called trusts in the United States; cartels, in Europe. They were common in the steel industry and in many other new industries at the close of the century, such as chemicals, aluminum, and oil. It was in the United States that such big business developed furthest, headed by "captains" of industry and "titans" of finance. Andrew Carnegie, by origin a poor Scottish immigrant boy, produced more steel than all England; but industrial production in Europe was also increasingly consolidated in large national and transnational cartels.

"Captains" of industry, "titans" of finance

Many of the new combinations were beneficial in making the ups and downs of business less erratic, and so providing more stable prices and more continuous and secure employment. Generally they reduced the costs of production; but whether the savings went into higher profits, higher wages, or lower prices depended on numerous factors. Some cartels were greedier than others or were confronted with only weakly organized or unorganized labor. In any case, for good or ill, decisions rested with management and finance. A new kind of private power had arisen, which its critics liked to call "feudal." Because no economic system had ever been so centralized up to that time, never in fact had so few people exercised so much economic power over so many. The middle class, with the rise of great corporations, came typically to consist of salaried employees; the salaried person might spend a lifetime with the same company, and feel toward it, in its disputes with labor or government, a loyalty not unlike that of a lord's retainer in feudal times. The laboring class was less amenable; labor attempted to organize unions capable of dealing with increasingly gigantic employers. It also after about 1880 played an increasingly decisive role in the politics of all advanced nations.

71. THE ADVANCE OF DEMOCRACY: THIRD FRENCH REPUBLIC, UNITED KINGDOM, GERMAN EMPIRE

In the years from 1815 to 1870 European political life had been marked by the rise of nationalism and by liberal agitation for constitutional government, representative assemblies, responsible ministries, and guarantees of individual liberties. In the years from 1871 to 1914 the most notable political development was the democratic extension of the vote to working-class men—the adoption of universal male suffrage, which in turn meant for the first time the creation of mass political parties and the need for political leaders to appeal to a wide electorate. Although there was growing agitation for voting rights for women in the decades before 1914, that reform would not be widely achieved until after the First World War (and, in some countries, after the Second World War). The extension of male suffrage and democratization often took place in a continuing monarchical and aristocratic framework, but almost everywhere in Europe by 1914 some machinery of democratic self-government was being introduced. In addition, to counter the growing strength of socialism after 1871, and for humanitarian reasons, governments were also assuming responsibility for the social and economic problems arising from industrialism. The welfare state in its modern form began to take shape.

France: The Establishment of the Third Republic

In France the democratic republic was not easily established, and its troubled early years left deep cleavages within the country. It will be recalled that in September 1870, when the empire of Napoleon III revealed its helplessness in the Franco-Prussian War, insurrectionaries in Paris, as in 1792 and 1848, again proclaimed the creation of a French Republic. A provisional government of national defense sought desperately to continue the war, but the cause was hopeless. By January 1871, a bitter siege of Paris came to an end and an armistice was signed. Bismarck, insisting that only a properly constituted government could make peace, permitted the election, by universal male suffrage, of a National Assembly that was to consider his peace terms and draft a constitution for the new French state. When the elections were held in February, it was found, as in 1848 (and, indeed, 1797), that republicanism was so distrusted by the French people as a whole, and most especially in the provinces and rural areas, that a free election brought monarchist elements into power. Republicanism was still thought to be violent—bellicose in its foreign policy, turbulent in its political workings, unfriendly to the church, and socialistic or at least egalitarian in its views of property and private wealth. The new Assembly contained only about 200 republicans out of more than 600 deputies.

But the Paris republicans, who had defended France when Napoleon III failed to do so, who for four months had been besieged, starved, and frozen by the Germans, and who still refused to make peace on the harsh terms imposed by Bismarck and about to be accepted by the Assembly, refused to recognize the latter's authority. A civil war broke out between the National Assembly, now sitting at Versailles, and the city of Paris, where a revolutionary municipal council or "Commune" was set up. Paris, so lately attacked by German soldiers, was soon attacked again by the French soldiers of the new National Assembly.

| *The Paris Commune* | The Paris Commune, which lasted from March to May 1871, seemed to be another explosion of social revolution. Actually, it was in essence a revival of the Jacobinism of 1793. It was fiercely patriotic and republican; anti-German; opposed to wealthy bourgeois, aristocrats, and clergy; in favor of government controls of prices, wages, and working conditions, but still not socialist in any sweeping or systematic way. Among its leaders, however, there were a few of the new international revolutionary socialists who saw a new Jacobin or democratic republic as a step toward a future socialist society. Marx in England, and others elsewhere, hopefully read into the Commune the impending doom of the bourgeoisie. This was precisely what more conservative elements feared. To many of the French middle and peasant class, and to people like them all over Europe, it seemed that the Communards were wild and savage destroyers

The Bon Marché department store in Paris became a well-known example of the new, large stores that began to displace smaller shops and independent merchants. The new commercial culture is evident in this late nineteenth-century illustration of the store's vast expanse, proliferation of merchandise, and affluent shoppers. Department stores provided a safe meeting place for women as well as lower prices for the many new products of the industrial era.

(©Fotosearch/Getty Images)

of nineteenth-century civilization. The fighting in Paris was atrocious beyond anything known in any preceding French revolution. The Communards, in final desperation, burned a number of public buildings and put to death the archbishop of Paris, whom they held as a hostage. The armed forces of the National Assembly, when finally triumphant, were determined to root out the inveterate revolutionism of Paris. Some 330,000 persons were denounced, 38,000 were arrested, 20,000 were put to death, and 7,500 were deported to the French-controlled island of New Caledonia in the South Pacific. The Third Republic was born in an atmosphere of class hate and social terror.

The form of government for the new regime still had to be established. The monarchist majority in the Assembly was itself evenly divided between those who favored a restoration of the Bourbon family and those who favored the Orléanist. The monarchists thus checkmated each other and, in effect, opened the way toward a new French Republic. Meanwhile, after extended discussion of various constitutional projects, the Assembly adopted in 1875 not a constitution, but certain constitutive laws. By a margin of one vote, a resolution indirectly amounting to the establishment of a republic was passed. The new laws provided for a president, a parliament in two chambers, and a council of ministers, or cabinet, headed by a premier. The two legislative bodies were to emerge from different electoral processes: the Senate was to be elected by a complicated and indirect system of election, the Chamber of Deputies, by universal, direct, male suffrage.

Within two years, in 1877, the role of the president, the ministers, and the parliament was further clarified as a result of an unsuccessful attempt by an early president, Marshal MacMahon, to dismiss a premier who had the backing of the Chamber. MacMahon proceeded to dissolve the Chamber and to hold new elections, but the example of Napoleon III's transformation of the Second Republic into an authoritarian regime was still fresh. The elections vindicated the principle of parliamentary primacy and of the responsibility of the premier and his cabinet to the legislature, especially to the more popularly elected lower house. The true executive in republican France for a long time was not the president, who became a ceremonial figure, but the premier and the cabinet, themselves held strictly to account by a majority of the legislature. Unfortunately, that majority, in a parliament where a dozen or so parties were represented, was always difficult to form and could be created only by unstable, shifting party alliances, coalitions, or blocs. No president, and indeed no premier, could henceforth dissolve the Chamber in order to hold new elections as could be done in Britain. Under the Third Republic the substantial machinery of state—ministries, prefectures, law courts, police, army, bureaucracy, all managed by highly centralized control—was actually carried over virtually untouched as in all upheavals since the time of Napoleon I. France in the nineteenth century, although volatile in appearance, in effect underwent less extensive governmental reorganization than any other leading country in Europe.

Parliamentary primacy

Troubles of the Third French Republic

Yet the Third Republic was precarious. The government had changed so often since 1789 that all forms of government seemed to be transitory. Questions that in other countries were questions about specific government policies or party programs became in France fundamental questions of regime—monarchy versus republic. Many people, especially those influenced by the upper classes, the Catholic clergy, and the professional army officers, continued to harbor a deep aversion to the republic. On the other hand, the unmerciful and vindictive repression of the Commune made many middle-class people

This barricade and its defenders suggest the revolutionary fervor of the Paris Commune, which controlled the French capital in the spring of 1871. The Commune was in many respects a revival of revolutionary Jacobinism rather than a precursor of social revolution, but it provoked intense fear and brutal repression from more conservative forces in French society. Revolutionary images of radical men and women in the Parisian streets—as seen in this photograph—made the Paris Commune a symbol of political idealism and martyrdom for many socialists and a symbol of dreadful social dangers for the middle and upper classes.

(©Keystone-France/Getty Images)

more sympathetic to the republicans. Many turned republican simply because no other form of government established itself or because it was the form of government that divided the country the least. As republicanism took in wider elements of society, it became less revolutionary and less fearsome. In 1879, for the first time, republicans won control of both houses of the government. In the 1880s their radicalism hardly went further than the founding of a democratic and compulsory school system at government expense and the passage of anticlerical legislation intended to curb church influence in education.

For over a quarter of a century, however, republicans had to defend the new republican institutions in order to ensure the survival of the regime itself. An initial crisis arose in 1886–1889, when General Boulanger gathered around him an incongruous following that included Bonapartists, monarchists, and aristocrats as well as various radical republicans who wished a war of revenge against Germany and even some workers who were disgruntled over their economic conditions. Boulanger became a popular figure and seemed for a moment about to seize power. But the menace collapsed in a

This photograph of Alfred Dreyfus shows the French army captain after he was found guilty of treason in 1894. Stripped of his army rank and deported to prison on an island near French Guiana, his unjust conviction sparked bitter debates in France, a surge of anti-Semitism, and protracted legal campaigns that ultimately led to his complete exoneration and return to the French army.

(©Hulton Archive/Getty Images)

comical failure as the general lost heart at the crucial hour and fled into exile. Meanwhile, in the 1880s and 1890s scandals and revelations of corruption in high republican circles provided ammunition for the antirepublicans. Moreover, the hope that unsympathetic French Catholics would rally to the republic, as urged by French prelates and by Pope Leo XIII in 1892, was shattered by the Dreyfus Affair, which in the late 1890s rocked the country and attracted wide attention outside France as well.

The Dreyfus Affair

In 1894 a French military court found Captain Alfred Dreyfus, a Jewish army officer, guilty of treason for leaking secret military documents to the German embassy in Paris. Dreyfus was deported to life imprisonment at Devil's Island, but evidence accumulated to show his innocence and to indicate the guilt of another officer, Major Esterhazy, an adventurer known to be riddled with gambling debts. But the army refused to reopen the case, unwilling to admit it had erred; a staff officer, Major Henry, even forged documents to confirm Dreyfus's guilt. Meanwhile anti-Semites, royalists, traditionalists, militarists, and most of the "best" people fought the reopening of the case, deeming it unpatriotic to shake the nation's confidence in the army and wishing also to disgrace the republican regime. The partisans of Dreyfus stubbornly upheld him, both because they believed in justice and because they wished to discredit their antirepublican adversaries. The country was deeply split into political and cultural factions that defended or attacked republicanism with arguments that repeated the bitter ideological conflicts of every French revolution since 1789. Finally, following a passionate pro-Dreyfus campaign by writers such as Émile Zola, Dreyfus was pardoned by the French president in 1899 and granted complete legal exoneration in 1906. In the aftermath of the affair,

---

Historical Documents
Émile Zola, *I Accuse [J'Accuse]* (1898)

The Dreyfus Affair led to bitter, polarizing divisions in the French Third Republic and exemplified wider European debates about national identities and human rights. Falsely accused and convicted of passing military secrets to Germany, Captain Alfred Dreyfus was sent to a prison in French Guiana. French military officials conspired to defend the verdict, despite evidence pointing to another officer's guilt. The case provoked a surge of anti-Semitic French nationalism, but it also elicited vehement defenses of French republicanism and "the rights of man" among pro-Dreyfus activists such as Émile Zola (1840-1902). Zola asserted Dreyfus's innocence in this famous newspaper article that accused the French army of hiding the truth and betraying the essential values of French republicanism. Dreyfus eventually received complete exoneration.

It is my duty to speak up. . . . [Dreyfus] pays for a crime he did not commit. . . .

Dreyfus's character, his financial situation, his lack of motives, the fact that he has never ceased to clamour his innocence—all these demonstrate that he has been a victim . . . of the clericalism that prevails in the military circles in which he moves, and of the hysterical hunt for "dirty Jews" that disgraces our times. . . .

It is a crime to poison the minds of humble, ordinary people, to whip reactionary and intolerant passions into a frenzy while sheltering behind the odious bastion of anti-Semitism. France, the great and liberal cradle of the rights of man, will die of anti-Semitism if it is not cured of it. It is a crime to play on patriotism to further the aims of hatred. . . .

Truth and justice—how ardently we have striven for them! And how distressing it is to see them slapped in the face, overlooked, forced to retreat! . . .

I have but one goal: that light be shed, in the name of mankind which has suffered so much and has the right to happiness. My ardent protest is merely a cry from my very soul.

Émile Zola, *The Dreyfus Affair, "J'Accuse" and Other Writings,* edited by Alain Pagès, translated by Eleanor Levieux (New Haven: Yale University Press, 1996), pp. 43, 46–47, 51, 53

---

leftist republicans and socialists held power in the Chamber of Deputies and gained revenge by blocking the promotions of antirepublican officers and by anticlerical legislation. In 1905, in a series of laic laws, they "separated" church and state, unilaterally ending the close relationship established under Napoleon's concordat a century earlier. All ties between church and state were severed, priests and bishops were no longer to be paid by the state, church property was taken over by the government, and Catholic laymen were to administer each parish. The Pope retaliated by excommunicating all deputies who had voted for these measures. Gradually compromises were worked out; some provisions were made less stringent, and tensions, if they did not disappear, at least eased.

The Strength and Weakness of the Republic

The Third Republic, when the First World War came in 1914, had lasted more than twice as long as any French regime since 1789. Born unwanted and accidentally, though it still had opponents, the republic now commanded the loyalty of the overwhelming mass of the French people. What it had done, since 1871, was to domesticate democratic republicanism in Europe. Republicanism, one of the most militant of revolutionary movements down to 1870, had been shown in France to be compatible with order, law, parliamentary government, economic prosperity, and a mutual tolerance between classes, to the extent at

Domesticating republicanism

least that they no longer butchered each other in the streets. Industrial workers were in many ways less well off than in England or Germany, but there were fewer of them. Despite its polarizing conflicts, republican France gradually came to be viewed as a more peaceful country, where painters, writers, scholars, and scientists flourished, where bankers, bourgeois and well-established farmers could freely pursue their economic interests, a country living comfortably and unhurriedly on the savings of generations, and one in which, in close-knit family groups, average men and women could plan securely for their own and their children's future.

But the comforts and values of bourgeois France were not those that would be needed for international leadership in the modern age of technology and industrial power. Though substantial economic progress was made, the country lagged behind Germany in industrial development. Politically, the fragmentation of political parties, itself a democratic reflection of a divided public opinion, and the distrust for historic reasons of a strong executive power led to the rise and fall of numerous short-lived ministries—no fewer than 50 in the years between 1871 and 1914. Ministerial instability was to be a chronic problem of the Third Republic both before and after 1914; continuity of government policy was, however, generally maintained because of stability in certain key ministries and because of the permanent civil service.

French labor often expressed an enduring social and political discontent. Although French workers benefited from some labor legislation in the two decades after 1890, they

The Radical Socialists

continued to seek a more egalitarian "social republic." Socialist representation in the Chamber grew, strengthening the antiroyalist factions in the French government. However, the most important single party of the republic, the Radicals, or Radical Socialists, were in actuality radical republicans—patriotic, anticlerical spokesmen for the small shopkeepers and the lesser propertied interests; they drew the line at the advanced social legislation that labor expected from them, and on occasion their leaders even took strong action to prevent unionization and to suppress strikes. Because some of these Radicals had started out as socialists, the distrust of French workers for all politicians and even for political processes was intensified. But the difficulties of the republic went deeper. The political energies of France's republican leaders had gone into liquidating the past, into curbing the political strength of the monarchists, the church, and the army; by the turn of the century, even before these older issues were fully resolved, the republic was compelled to meet the challenge of labor and to face other domestic and international pressures that were to try it sorely. The Third Republic would weather the crisis of the First World War but not that of the Second.

The British Constitutional Monarchy

The British constitutional monarchy in the half-century before 1914 was the great exemplar of orderly and peaceable domestic self-government through parliamentary methods. For over 60 years (1837–1901), spanning two-thirds of the nineteenth century, Queen Victoria reigned as a constitutional monarch and gave her name to a distinguished era of material progress, literary accomplishment, and political stability. The two major political parties, Liberal and Conservative, the heirs roughly of the Whigs and Tories, took form in the 1850s, the former producing its great leader in William E. Gladstone; the latter, a series of leaders of whom the most notable was Benjamin Disraeli.

The advance toward an egalitarian political democracy in Britain was more cautious and slower than in France. The Reform Bill of 1832 had granted the vote to about an eighth of the adult male population. The democratic Chartist agitation of the 1830s and 1840s attracted wide popular support but failed to produce further reforms in the electoral system. In 1867, however, in response to continued demand for a wider suffrage, the Second Reform Bill was passed, Conservatives as well as Liberals outdoing one another in an effort to satisfy the country and to win new political strength for their own party. The bill, adopted under Disraeli's Conservative ministry, extended the suffrage from about 1 million eligible voters to about 2 million, or over a third of the adult males in the United Kingdom, reaching down far enough in income levels to include most workers in the cities. Disraeli's colleague Lord Derby called it a "leap in the dark." In 1884, under Liberal auspices, the suffrage was again broadened, this time in the rural areas, adding some 2 million additional voters and enfranchising over three-fourths of all adult males in the country. Not until 1918 did Great Britain adopt universal male suffrage, as generally understood; and at that time the long campaign for women's political rights gained at least a partial victory when women over the age of 30 received the right to vote.

The extension of suffrage

The leadership of the country at the turn of the century was still in the hands of men from the upper and wealthier classes. Until 1911 the government paid no salaries to members of the House of Commons, who therefore, in both political parties, were usually gentlemen with private incomes, possessing the same family background and education. The two parties alternated in power at regular intervals, each indulgent toward the other, carrying over and developing rather than reversing the policies of its predecessor in office. Both parties sought support where they could find it, the Liberals leaning somewhat more on the industrial and commercial interests and the Conservatives relying more on the landed aristocracy; both sought and succeeded in winning their share of the new working-class vote.

The Liberals were usually the more willing to pioneer, the first of the four ministries of Gladstone being especially notable in this respect. Gladstone in this first ministry (1868–1874) developed the principle of state-supported public education under the Forster Education Act of 1870, introduced the secret ballot, formally legalized labor unions, promoted competitive examinations for civil service posts, reorganized the upper judiciary, eliminated the purchase and sale of commissions in the army (a form of property in office), and by abolishing religious tests enabled persons who were not members of the Church of England to graduate from Oxford and Cambridge. The Conservative Party, less sensitive to pressure from business interests for a laissez-faire policy in economic matters, took the initiative in promoting new labor legislation. Under Disraeli's second ministry (1874–1880), the existing acts regulating public sanitation and conditions in mines and factories were extended and codified, safety measures were enacted to protect sailors, and the first attempt to regulate housing conditions for the poorer classes was initiated. But the Liberals, it must be added, sought to protect the workers' interests too. In Gladstone's second ministry (1880–1885), for example, workers were assured of compensation for injuries not of their own responsibility, and Gladstone later campaigned to reduce labor hours and to extend employers' liability in accidents.

Liberals and Conservatives

British Political Changes after 1900

At the turn of the twentieth century, after the long era of Liberal and Conservative ministries, important changes began to transform British political culture. Labor emerged as an independent political force, the Labour Party itself being organized shortly after 1900. The rise of labor

Rise of British labor

had a deep impact upon the Liberal Party and indeed upon liberalism itself. The new Labour Party insisted that protective measures should be taken to counteract the poor health, low income, and economic insecurity of British workers. Facing this pressure from a politicized labor movement, the Liberals abandoned their traditional position of laissez-faire and sponsored a policy of government intervention and social legislation on behalf of working people. The Liberals, though they acted in part for humanitarian reasons, were aware that with the emergence of the Labour Party workers who customarily had voted for them might readily transfer their allegiance.

The Liberals, in control of the government from 1906 to 1916, with Herbert Asquith as prime minister and David Lloyd George as chancellor of the exchequer during most of this time, put through a spectacular program of social welfare. Sickness, accident, and old-age insurance, and a degree of unemployment insurance were adopted, and a moderate minimum wage law was enacted. Labor exchanges, or employment bureaus, were established throughout the country. Restrictions on strikes and other trade union activities were removed. To meet the costs of the new program as well as of other government expenditures, Lloyd George's budget of 1909 called for progressive income and inheritance taxes: wealthier taxpayers would be taxed at progressively higher rates. He was in effect advancing the then novel idea of using taxation to modify the social extremes

A war against poverty

of wealth and poverty. It was a "war budget," he said, intended "to wage war against poverty." Its fiscal measures were directed primarily at the landed aristocracy, and it aroused great opposition, especially in the House of Lords, where the contest over the budget led to a further constitutional curtailment of the power of the upper house. The Parliament Act of 1911 deprived the Lords of all veto power in money matters and of all but a two-year delaying veto on action of the Commons on other legislation. At this time, too, the government voted to pay salaries to members of the House of Commons, making it possible for workers and others without independent incomes to take seats in Parliament.

State intervention

The Liberal Party was embracing a program of positive state intervention in social and economic matters that the older liberalism, nurtured on the doctrines of laissez-faire and the Manchester School, would not have accepted. With the Liberals actively seeking the support of labor and altering much of their traditional program, the Conservatives in the twentieth century tended to become the party of industry as well as of landed wealth and to replace the Liberals as the champions of economic liberalism and laissez-faire. In the next generation, after the First World War, the Conservatives were to remain one of the two major parties of the country; the Liberals were to be far outstripped by the Labour Party.

Meanwhile, despite its gains, labor was not pacified. Real wages showed a tendency to fall after 1900, and great coal and railway strikes broke out in 1911 and 1912. The British capacity to survive crises without violence, while still conspicuous, was being strained. An even more serious threat came from Ireland.

The Irish Question

Britain suffered from one of the most bitter minorities conflicts in Europe—what the British called the Irish question. After 1801 Britain was known as the United Kingdom of Great Britain and Ireland. The British government had incorporated Ireland into the United Kingdom as a defensive measure against pro-French sympathies in Ireland during the wars of the French Revolution, but the Irish representatives who thereafter sat in Parliament were generally hostile to this incorporation and obstructionist in their tactics.

SUNDAY AFTERNOON ON THE ISLAND OF LA GRANDE JATTE
by Georges Seurat (French, 1859-1891)

This picture of sunny calm, painted in 1886, conveys the well-being that many prosperous Europeans enjoyed or imagined in the late nineteenth century. The people portrayed here seem to live in a peaceable world that is far removed from social conflicts and from a later age of speed and mechanical amusements. Technically, this is one of the most remarkable pictures ever painted. The artist created it without the use of lines by filling the canvas with thousands of minute dots of the primary colors, which blur and mix in the eye to produce the forms, hues, light, and shadows of nature.

(The Metropolitan Museum of Art, New York, Bequest of Sam A. Lewisohn, 1951)

The Irish had many substantial grievances, among which two were conspicuous. The Irish peasants were defenseless against their landlords, far more so, for example, than the French peasants before 1789; and the Irish people, though predominantly Catholic, were obliged to pay tithes to the established Church of Ireland (an Anglican sister church to the Church of England), which also owned a good deal of the land.

Gladstone, in his first ministry, disestablished the Church of Ireland. He also initiated measures to protect the Irish farm tenant. By 1900, under Conservative auspices, Irish tenants were being assisted by the British government to buy out their landlords—often English or Anglicized and absentee Irish landowners. The Irish also wanted home rule, or a parliament of their own. Gladstone, in trying *Home rule* to give it to them in 1886, split his Liberal Party, part of which went along with the Conservatives in opposing a political division of the British Isles. Home rule was finally granted to Ireland in 1914. But the Ulster Unionists, Protestants whose

Real wages for British workers tended to fall in first decade of the twentieth century, causing hardships for people such as these coal miners in Wales. Miners joined in strikes throughout Britain after 1910, contributing to economic and political crises that altered the older doctrines and policies of laissez-faire liberalism.

(©Topical Press Agency/Getty Images)

ancestors had moved into northern Ireland (mostly from Scotland) during the seventeenth century, objected vehemently to inclusion in an autonomous Ireland, in which they would be outnumbered by the Catholics of the south. The latter, however, insisted with equal vehemence on the inclusion of Ulster, not wishing to see a political division of Ireland.

The Ulster Unionists, backed by British Conservatives, started arming and drilling to resist the act of Parliament that authorized home rule. Great Britain, in 1914, was about to see a civil war on its own doorstep. It suffered from something like the insoluble nationalist disputes that afflicted Austria-Hungary. During the First World War home rule was suspended. After considerable violence on both sides Catholic Ireland—which for a time called itself Eire—received dominion status in 1922; but eventually this Irish dominion dissolved all ties with Britain and became the Republic of Ireland. Northern Ireland remained in the United Kingdom and was dominated by Protestants, so that its Catholic minority continued to be an alienated, discontented population within the British state. The "Irish question" thus remained one of modern Britain's unresolved issues, generating bitter resentments and violent conflicts during all of the twentieth century and beyond.

Bismarck and the German Empire, 1871–1890

The German Empire, as put together by Bismarck in 1871 with William I, king of Prussia, as Kaiser, was a federation of monarchies, a union of 25 German states, in which the weight of monarchical Prussia, the Prussian army, and the Prussian landed aristocracy was preponderant. It developed neither the strong constitutionalism of England nor the

CHRONOLOGY OF NOTABLE EVENTS, 1850–1914

1850–1940	About 60 million people migrate from Europe
1869	Opening of Suez Canal in Egypt facilitates global trade
1870s	Western Europe and United States adopt the "gold standard" for global currency exchanges
1871	The revolutionary Paris Commune is violently suppressed in France
1890	Kaiser William II dismisses Bismarck and begins to shape policies of the German Empire
1894–1899	Dreyfus Affair bitterly divides republican and antirepublican factions in France
c. 1900	European population reaches its highest percentage of world population
1906–1916	Liberal government in Britain introduces broad program of social welfare
1914	Opening of Panama Canal facilitates European trade in the Americas

recurring quest for democratic equality that was characteristic of France. To win popular support for his projects, Bismarck exploited existing democratic and socialist sentiment and provided that members of the Reichstag, the lower chamber, be elected by universal male suffrage. Remaining chancellor of the united empire for almost 20 years, from 1871 to 1890, he usually tried to have a majority in the Reichstag on his side, but he recognized no dependence on a majority in principle, holding to the doctrine that it was the emperor and his chancellor who were to govern the country. Moreover, in practice, the legislative powers of the lower house were severely restricted, and the upper chamber, representing the princes and not the people, and favored by the government, tended to be more important. Despite the nature of the empire Bismarck's unified Germany at first displeased the Prussian conservatives, the East Elbian Junker landlords. They opposed his democratic concessions and were horrified when in 1872 he undertook to abolish what was left of their manorial jurisdiction over their peasants.

Bismarck in the 1870s therefore leaned not on the Conservatives but on the National Liberals. With their aid he put through a number of economic and legal measures designed to consolidate the unity of the new empire. Bismarck's first serious conflict developed with the Catholic Church. At the very time that he was bent on subordinating all groups within the state to the sovereign power of the new empire, the church had spoken out. In 1864 in the *Syllabus of Errors,* the pope *The Catholic Church*
denounced the encroachment of all governments on educational and church affairs; in 1870 the new dogma of papal infallibility made it incumbent on Catholics to accept unreservedly the pope's pronouncements in matters of faith and morals. To defend Catholic interests and those of the south German states where Catholicism predominated, Catholic elements had organized the strong Center Party, which now upheld the church pronouncements. In 1871 Bismarck launched the *Kulturkampf,* or "battle for modern civilization," to reduce Catholic influence within the new German Empire." The Liberals joined in eagerly. Like nineteenth-century liberals elsewhere in Europe (Gladstone's campaign against Anglican privilege and the French laic laws have been noted), they were strongly anticlerical and disapproved of the influence of organized churches in public and private life. Laws were put through imposing restrictions upon Catholic worship and education, the Jesuits were expelled, and many Catholic bishops throughout Germany were arrested or went into exile. But Bismarck gradually concluded that the anti-Catholic legislation was fruitless, that he

had overestimated the danger to the state of organized Catholicism, and that he needed the support of the Center Party for other parts of his program. Meanwhile, the country's rapid and spectacular industrial expansion had stimulated the growth of the German working class, and to Bismarck's alarm, socialism was spreading.

The German Social Democratic Party had been founded in 1875 by a fusion of Marxian socialists and the reformist followers of Ferdinand Lassalle on an essentially moderate program that Marx had denounced. But even a moderate socialism was mistrusted by Bismarck. He shared in the European horror at the recent Paris Commune, he feared socialism as anarchy, and he knew that socialism was in any case inherently republican, which made it a potentially revolutionary movement in an empire of monarchies. Two radical attempts on the emperor's life (in neither case by Social Democrats) provided him with all the excuse he needed. In 1878, having already made peace with the Catholics, he set out to eradicate socialism. Antisocialist laws from 1878 to 1890 prohibited socialist meetings and socialist newspapers. For 12 years socialism was driven underground. But repression was not his only weapon; he turned also to another tactic. Bismarck sought to persuade the workers to place their faith in him and the German Empire rather than in the prophets of socialism. To that end, in the 1880s, he initiated an extensive program of social legislation. Workers were insured by the state against sickness, accident, and incapacity in old age. "Our democratic friends," said Bismarck, "will pipe in vain when the people see princes concerned with their well-being." In social insurance imperial Germany was, from whatever motives, years ahead of more democratic England, France, and the United States.

Repression of socialism

Bismarck failed to kill socialism. The number of socialists elected to the Reichstag was greater in 1890 than in 1878. It seems, however, that Bismarck by the later 1880s was more apprehensive than ever of a social revolution that would destroy his empire; and he contemplated new actions by which the Reichstag might be throttled. He never reached this point, however, because in 1890, at the age of 75, he was obliged by the new emperor, William II, to retire.

The German Empire after 1890: William II

William I died in 1888 and was succeeded by his son Frederick III, who had been married for many years to the eldest daughter of Britain's Queen Victoria. Incurably ill of cancer, he died some three months after his accession. Frederick's son, William II, the last king of Prussia and the last German Kaiser, began his reign (1888–1918) as a young man of 29, full of startling ideas about his personal power and privileges, somewhat in contrast to his father. He was also uncomfortable in the presence of an elder statesman who had made the German Empire, who had been his grandfather's aide and adviser, and whom he regarded partly with veneration and partly as an old fogy. William soon quarreled with Bismarck over continuation of the antisocialist laws and over matters of foreign affairs. When Bismarck forbade his ministers to meet with the emperor on policy matters unless he was present, William resolved that he, and not Bismarck, would rule the empire. In 1890 William ordered Bismarck to resign, "dropping the pilot," in the celebrated phrase. Under the four chancellors who succeeded Bismarck, it was William who dominated policy.

William II

After 1890 Germany embarked upon what was termed a "new course." In foreign affairs this meant a more aggressive and ambitious colonial, naval, and diplomatic policy. In domestic affairs it meant a more conciliatory attitude toward the laboring class. The

A "new course"

antisocialist laws were dropped, and the system of social security legislation was enlarged and codified. But no expansion of parliamentary democracy seemed possible. William II believed in the divinely ordained prerogatives of the house of Hohenzollern, and the empire still rested on the power of the federated princes, the Junkers, the army, and the new industrial magnates. But the Social Democrats, the Progressive Party, and other democratic forces were growing in strength. They demanded, for Prussia, a reform of the illiberal constitution of 1850, and for the Reich, real control over the federal chancellor by the majority party in the Reichstag. In the election of 1912 the Social Democrats reached a new high by polling 4.25 million votes, about one-third of the total, and by electing 110 members to the Reichstag, in which they now formed the largest single party; yet they were excluded from the highest posts of government. The imperial German political system, which Bismarck had created and which was now ruled by William II, was moving toward a constitutional crisis, but war came in 1914 and the political conflict was deferred.

Developments Elsewhere; General Observations

Of political developments in other European states before 1914, something has already been said in the preceding chapter. Italy had become a constitutional monarchy in the 1860s and completed its unification by the forceful seizure of Rome in 1870. Despite parliamentary reforms, Italian political life was charac- *Political scene* terized by unstable majorities and by opportunistic maneuvering and *in Italy* manipulation by moderate liberal political leaders who maintained themselves in office for long periods of time by shuffling and reshuffling political coalitions. The liberal leaders were anticlerical, and the quarrel with the papacy over the seizure of the papal territories remained unsettled. The popes refused to recognize the Italian kingdom and forbade Catholics to participate in its affairs or even to vote in elections. Catholics voted nonetheless and in 1907 bishops in each diocese were permitted to relax the ban, as they increasingly did.

Industry had begun to expand in northern cities such as Milan, and the government gradually moved to extend the franchise to the working classes. The narrow suffrage of 1861 was broadened, first in 1882, and then in 1912, when a new reform increased the number of eligible voters from 3 to 8 million, or virtually universal male suffrage. Because of illiteracy and political inertia not all of the newly enfranchised Italians hastened to exercise their voting privilege. The social problem remained serious, too, despite some modest labor legislation. Poverty and illiteracy, especially in the agrarian south, were widespread, and radical unrest appeared in the industrial cities. The first manifestations of an antiparliamentary ideology, chauvinistic nationalism, and explosive irrationalism appeared in the writings and political activism of literary men such as Gabriele d'Annunzio and Filippo Marinetti. The latter published in 1909 the manifesto of a radical new movement he called "Futurism," which vehemently condemned all artistic traditions, celebrated the speed of modern technologies, and portrayed human violence as a kind of creative action. Such ideas would soon spread into politics, bringing a new irrationalism to Italian political culture and destabilizing Italian parliamentary democracy.

In the Dual Monarchy of Austria-Hungary, created by the political compromise of 1867, Austria and Hungary were each in form consti- *Austria-Hungary* tutional parliamentary states. In theory, the Emperor-King Francis Joseph ruled through ministries responsible to the legislature in each state. However, in matters affecting the empire as a whole, such as foreign affairs and military questions, there was little parliamentary restraint on the emperor. Here he had virtually final

Kaiser William II's decision to remove Bismarck from his powerful position in Germany's government was widely described as "dropping the pilot" of the German Empire. This theme was conveyed by the British cartoonist John Tenniel, who portrayed William expelling Bismarck from the ship of state in this famous illustration for the British magazine *Punch*.

(©Spencer Arnold/Getty Images)

authority; moreover, in all matters he still had broad powers to govern by decree, which he exercised. As in Germany, the tide of socialism was held back both by repressive laws and by social insurance and benevolent legislation. The most serious problem in the empire remained the nationalist agitation by the various subject nationalities that were seeking more autonomy or their own sovereign states. This political agitation helped to deepen the new national self-consciousness among the Czechs and other Slavic peoples. Political democracy took a different course in Austria than in Hungary. In the former, partly as an effort to placate nationalist sentiment, universal male suffrage was introduced in 1907. In the latter the expansion of voting rights was bitterly and successfully resisted by the Magyars, who saw suffrage as a weapon that could be employed by the Slavs to contest and destroy the Magyar preponderance. Austria itself, despite the democratic suffrage, was ruled very much like the German Empire, with the legislature able to debate and criticize but not control policy.

Democratic advances

Of other countries it can be said that the political forms of democracy showed signs of advancing everywhere, though women were still generally excluded from voting and from all public offices. Universal male suffrage was adopted in Switzerland in 1874, in Belgium in 1893, in the Netherlands in 1896, and in the next few years in Norway and Sweden (Norway was peacefully separated in 1905 from Sweden). In southern Europe, besides Italy, universal male suffrage was introduced in Spain, Greece, Bulgaria, Serbia, and, after the revolt of 1908, in Ottoman Turkey. Even tsarist Russia, after the Revolution of 1905, received a Duma, or national parliament, elected on a wide franchise but on an indirect and undemocratic class basis and with narrow powers. Among states west of the Russian Empire, only Hungary and Romania had a highly restricted suffrage on the eve of the First World War. The vote for women progressed more slowly. Women gained voting rights before 1914 only in certain western states of the United States, in Australia, New Zealand, Finland, and Norway. Not until after the First World War did female suffrage begin to make significant advances, and women did not gain the right to vote in France and Italy until after the Second World War.

The progress of representative and democratic institutions did not mean an end to the rule of monarchs, landed aristocrats, and other minority interests. For one thing, with the exception of France and Switzerland, Europe remained monarchical. Second, despite the growing importance of parliaments, parliamentary control over political life was far from guaranteed; emperors and kings still ruled through their chancellors and prime ministers. Of the major world powers it was mainly within the United States, Britain, and France that democratic and popular control was something of a reality, though political rights were still generally granted only to white men. But the extension of the suffrage, by the relaxation of property qualifications, had a dynamic of its own and was altering the framework of politics everywhere; mass political parties, including socialist parties and confessional, or religious-oriented, parties were replacing the older narrow oligarchic political organizations, and support now had to be sought on a wider electoral basis. In almost all Europe, and in many of the outlying areas peopled by European descendants and immigrants, democracy was advancing, even within the older framework. By 1871, most European nations, with the notable exception of Russia, had written constitutions, guarantees of personal freedom, parliamentary and representative institutions, and limitations on absolutism; in the years between 1871 and 1914 the most significant new political development was the advance of male suffrage and the accompanying rise of new, mass-based political parties.

Expansion of the suffrage

The growing populations and economies of European nations thus created a social stability in which political institutions gradually became more democratic and more responsive to public opinion. Wealth and resources flowed into Europe from all parts of the world, so that the middle classes and even workers had more comforts and material goods than ever before—and more opportunities to participate in the political institutions of their various nations. Europe's dominant role in the global economy, the massive migration of European people, and the military power of European nation-states gave European civilization an extraordinary world influence in the decades after 1870.

During these same years, however, the growing power of industrial corporations and capitalist financial institutions as well as the traditional power of older European social hierarchies and cultural attitudes also provoked opposition, which appeared in popular political movements, as in socialism, and in criticisms of European imperialism. The critics eventually influenced many people outside Europe, gaining a following wherever European economic and cultural institutions had appeared. European critiques of Western capitalism, traditions, and ideas therefore became another aspect of Europe's global influence at the end of the nineteenth century.

Suggested Further Readings can be found in the ebook, on Connect, or online at www.mhhe .com/kramer12e.

Chapter 15

EUROPEAN SOCIETY AND CULTURE, 1871–1914

The belief in progress has been at the center of modern European thought since the Scientific Revolution of the seventeenth century. Although some romantic poets, conservatives, and socialists questioned the consequences of modern technologies and industry, most people in the nineteenth century assumed that progress was both inevitable and beneficial. Liberals were especially optimistic about progressive developments in all the main spheres of modern life: scientific knowledge, technological inventions, economic expansion, constitutional government, and protection for fundamental human rights. But the liberals were by no means alone in seeing the late nineteenth-century European ascendancy as the historical confirmation of human progress.

There were also many Europeans, however, who protested that whole groups of human beings were still denied the benefits of modern civilization, that workers were not receiving their rightful share of modern wealth, or that women were not entering their rightful place in modern political life. New political movements in these decades therefore sought to expand the economic and legal rights of workers and women, claiming that such reforms would advance the broader cause of social progress; and in fact the new political movements were often able to gain new rights or benefits for the groups they represented.

Meanwhile, science itself continued to produce advances in both the theoretical understanding of nature and the technological inventions that were transforming modern societies. Yet it was also at this time that various thinkers began to question the certitudes of scientific knowledge and to stress the limits of human reason, thus challenging many of the cultural assumptions that sustained the popular belief in human progress. These new trends in European intellectual life before 1914 began to erode some of the confidence in the progressive evolution of human history (at least among certain philosophers or artists) and to undermine the optimism of classical liberalism. The idea of progress remained a powerful theme in all modern cultures, but by the early twentieth century the limits and consequences of progress were also becoming subjects for historical reflection, artistic representation, and cultural debate.

Chapter emblem: Albert Einstein as he appeared after he had published scientific papers on the theory of relativity in 1905 and 1916. (©General Photographic Agency/Hulton Archive/Getty Images)

72.   THE ADVANCE OF DEMOCRACY: SOCIALISM, LABOR UNIONS, AND FEMINISM

The artisan and laboring classes had always been suspicious of "bourgeois" liberalism's optimistic view of free competition, unrestrained private enterprise, the Manchester School, laissez-faire, the laws of supply and demand, the free market for goods and labor,

Opponents of liberalism

and the idea of an economy independent of states and governments. These were the ideas of middle-class liberals, not of radical democrats. Popular leaders had opposed them in the French Revolution in 1793. The English Chartists had been outspokenly anticapitalistic, and on the

Continent the ideas of socialism had been spreading. In 1848 there was a strong movement among the working classes for a "social" republic, and, though the social revolution failed in 1848, the force of it was enough to terrify the possessing classes. With the advent of the ballot, workers pressed for social legislation and used their political power to gain a greater measure of social democracy.

But in addition, before and after obtaining the ballot, working people resorted to other devices for the improvement of their position. Against the owners of capital, who controlled the giving of jobs, workers advocated two principal lines of action. Some believed they could and should abolish the capitalist economic system; others believed they should bargain with their capitalist employers. The former view led to radical forms of socialism; the latter, to the formation of labor unions. Socialism, in logic, meant the extinction of the private employer as such, or at least to the dissolution of the larger capitalist corporations. Trade unionism, in logic, meant that the workers had every reason to keep their employers prospering in business in order that bargaining with them might produce better economic results. The working-class movement thus contained an internal conflict or contradiction that was never resolved in the nineteenth century and that would become even more divisive after the Russian Revolution in the early twentieth century.

Workers and intellectuals

Middle-class and educated people who took up the workers' cause, the intellectuals of the movement—Karl Marx, Friedrich Engels, Louis Blanc, Ferdinand Lassalle, and thousands of less famous names—tended more to socialism than to unionism. They thought of society as a whole, they saw the economy as a complex social system, and they

thought of future changes in long-run terms that allowed for whole historical epochs to come and go. Most actual workers, put to work at an early age, barely educated if at all, with the waking hours of their adult lives spent on manual jobs, were inclined to keep their attention more on the benefits of unionism than on the theories of socialism. To earn slightly more money every week beginning next week, to be spared the nervous strain and physical danger of constant exposure to unprotected machinery, to have 15 minutes more every day for lunch, were likely to seem more tangible and important than far-reaching but distant plans for a reconstructed society. The worker looked on the intellectual as an outsider, however welcome; the intellectual looked on the worker as shortsighted and timid, however much in need of help.

After the failures of 1848 the socialist and trade union movements diverged for a generation. The 1850s, compared with the hungry '40s, were a time of full employment, rising wages, and increasing prosperity for all classes. Workers set to organizing unions, socialist thinkers to perfecting their doctrines.

The Trade Union Movement and Rise of British Labor

Organizations of wage workers, or labor unions in the modern sense (as distinguished from medieval craft guilds), had long maintained a shadowy and sporadic existence. But they had always been extralegal, frowned upon or actually prohibited by governments. French revolutionaries in the Le Chapelier Act of 1791 and conservative British Tories in the Combination Act of 1799 had shared similar goals in forbidding workers to unite. It was the rise of bourgeois liberalism, so insensitive to the worker in most ways, that first gave legal freedom to labor unions. The British unions received a tacit recognition from the Liberal Tories in 1825 and explicit recognition from Gladstone's Liberal ministry in 1871. French unions were recognized by Napoleon III in 1864, then restrained in the reaction to the radical Commune, then fully legalized in 1884. In Germany Bismarck negotiated with labor leaders to find support against the vested interests that stood in his way.

The prosperity of the 1850s favored the formation of unions, for workers could always organize more easily when employers were most in need of their services. The craft union—or union of skilled workers in the same trade, such as carpenters—was at first the typical organization. It was most fully developed in England, where a "new model" unionism was introduced by the Amalgamated Society of Engineers (i.e., machinists) in 1851. It was the policy of the new model union officials to take the unions out of politics, to forget the semisocialism of the Chartists, to abandon Robert Owen's grandiose idea of "one big union" for all workers, and to concentrate on advancing the interests of each separate trade. The new leaders proposed to be reasonable with employers, avoid strikes, accumulate union funds, and build up their membership. This strategy was successful. The unions took root, and the two governing parties in England, reassured by the unexpected moderation of working-class representatives, combined to give the vote to town workers in 1867.

"New model" unionism

In the 1880s, and especially with a great London dock strike in 1889, which closed the port of London for the first time since the French Revolution, unions of unskilled workers began to form. Industrial unionism, or the joining in one union of all workers in one industry, such as coal or transportation, regardless of the skill or job of the individual worker, began to take shape at the same time. In some cases the older skilled unionists joined with unskilled laborers who worked beside them. By 1900 there were about 2,000,000 union members in Great Britain, compared with only 850,000 in Germany and 250,000 in France.

It was largely because British workers were so far advanced in trade unionism, and so successful in forcing collective bargaining upon their employers, that they were much slower than their Continental counterparts in forming a workers' political party. By the 1880s, when avowed socialists were already sitting in French, Belgian, and German parliaments, the only corresponding persons in Britain were a half-dozen "Lib-Labs," as they were called, laboring men elected on the Liberal ticket. The British Labour Party was formed at the turn of the century by the joint efforts of trade union officials and middle-class intellectuals. Where on the Continent the labor unions were often led, and even brought into being, by the socialist political parties, in Britain it was the labor unions that brought into being, and subsequently led, the Labour Party. The influence of British labor unions made the Labour Party less socialistic than working-class parties on the Continent. Its origin and rapid growth were due in large measure to a desire to defend the unions as established and respectable institutions.

The British Labour Party

A steady rise in the membership of labor unions transformed political life in all industrialized societies. This illustration of British miners voting to strike was published in an Italian newspaper, but it depicts the kind of worker activism that became common in most European nations and in other parts of the modern world during the early twentieth century.

(©DEA/A. DAGLI ORTI/Getty Images)

The Taff Vale decision

The unions were threatened in their very existence by a ruling of the British courts in 1901, the Taff Vale decision, which held a union financially responsible for business losses incurred by an employer during a strike. The shortest and most orderly strike, by exhausting a union's funds, might ruin the union. Opposition to the Taff Vale decision unified the unions and all other existing labor and socialist organizations and precipitated the formation of the modern Labour Party. In the election of 1906 the new Labour Party sent 29 members to Parliament, which thereupon overruled the Taff Vale decision by new legislation. The Labour Party also pushed the ruling Liberal Party to enact social legislation that gave workers new protections against illness, unemployment, and the post-employment vulnerabilities of old age (described in the previous chapter).

European Socialism after 1850

As for socialism, which had so frightened the middle and upper classes in 1848, it seemed in the 1850s to go into abeyance. Karl Marx, after issuing the *Communist Manifesto* with Engels in 1848, and agitating as a journalist in the German revolution of that year, withdrew to the secure haven offered by England, where, after years of painstaking research, he published the first volume of his *Capital* in 1867. This work, which later included two more volumes that were published after his death, gave economic details and new arguments to explain the broad ideas of the earlier *Communist Manifesto*. Marx lived for more than 30 years in London, but he scarcely mixed with the labor leaders then building up the English unions. He associated mainly with political exiles and temporary visitors of numerous nationalities, and the first volume of *Capital* was not even published in English until 1886.

In 1864 there took place in London the first meeting of the International Working Men's Association, commonly known as the First
International. It was sponsored by a heterogeneous group, including the
secretary of the British carpenters' union, Robert Applegarth; the aging

The First
International

Italian revolutionary, Mazzini; and Karl Marx. With the union officials absorbed in union
business, leadership in the Association gradually passed to Marx, who used it as a means
of publicizing the ideas about to appear in his *Capital.* At subsequent annual congresses in
other European cities Marx built up his position. He made the Mazzinians unwelcome, and
he denounced the German Lassalleans for their willingness to cooperate with Bismarck and
the German state. His sharpest struggle was with the Russian Bakunin. Drawing on his
experience in tsarist Russia, Bakunin viewed the state as the cause of the worker's afflictions;
he was hence an "anarchist," holding that the state should be attacked and abolished.
To Marx anarchism was abhorrent; the correct doctrine, in Marx's view, was that the state—
tsarist or bourgeois—was a product of economic conditions and a weapon of the propertied
interests, so that the true target for revolutionary action must be not the state but the
capitalist economic system. Marx drove Bakunin from the First International in 1872.

Meanwhile members of the First International watched with great
excitement as the Paris Commune emerged in 1871. They hoped that
the new revolutionary events in Paris might be the opening act of a
European working-class upheaval. Members of the International infil-

The Paris Commune

trated the Commune, and the connection between the two, though rather incidental, was
one reason why the French Provisional Government repressed the Commune with such
terrified ferocity. But the Commune actually destroyed the First International. Marx
praised the Commune as a stage in the international class war and even as a possible
example of what he was coming to call the "dictatorship of the proletariat." He thus
frightened away many possible followers. British trade unionists, for example, would never
support such revolutionary doctrines or violence. The First International faded out of
existence after 1872.

But in 1875, at a German workers' conference in Gotha, Marxian and Lassallean
socialists united to found the German Social Democratic Party, whose remarkable growth
thereafter, against Bismarck's attempts to stop it, has already been noted. Other socialist
parties soon sprouted in many European countries. In Belgium, highly industrialized,
a Belgian Socialist Party appeared in 1879. In the industrial regions of France some
workers were attracted to Jules Guesde, a self-taught worker, former Communard, and
now a rigid Marxist, who held it impossible to emancipate the working class by parliamentary compromises or piecemeal reforms; others followed Paul Brousse, who thought
workers could arrive at socialism through parliamentary methods; still others supported
Jean Jaurès, who eloquently linked social reform to the French revolutionary tradition
and the defense of republican institutions. Not until 1905 did the socialist groups in
France form a unified Socialist Party. In England, in 1881, H. M. Hyndman founded a
Social Democratic Federation with a more radical Marxist program; it never had more
than a handful of members. In 1883 two Russian exiles in Switzerland, Plekhanov and
Axelrod, recent converts to Marxism, founded the Russian Social Democratic Party, from
which the Russian communism of the following century would later
evolve. The socialist parties all came together to establish a new international league in 1889, known as the Second International, which
thereafter met every three years and lasted until 1914.

The Second
International

Revisionist and Revolutionary Socialism, 1880-1914

Marx died in 1883, but the new socialist parties of the 1880s were all Marxist in inspiration. Marxism or "scientific socialism," by the force of its social analysis, the mass of Marx's writings over 40 years, and an attitude of unyielding hostility to competing socialist doctrines, had gradually become the most influential form of systematic socialism. Strongest in Germany and France, Marxism was relatively less successful in Italy and Spain, where workers were less concentrated in large factories, generally less educated, and still unable to place their hopes in the ballot. Workers in southern Europe were more habituated to insurrectionism in the manner of Garibaldi, and they turned more frequently to the anarchism preached by Bakunin.

Marxism also attracted relatively little support from labor groups in England. The workers stood by their trade unions, and middle-class critics of capitalism followed the Fabian Society, established in 1883. The Fabians (so called from the ancient Roman general Fabius Cunctator, the "delayer," or strategist of gradual methods) were very

Fabian socialism in England

English and very un-Marxist. George Bernard Shaw, H. G. Wells, and Sidney and Beatrice Webb were among early members of the Society. For them socialism was the social and economic counterpart to political democracy, as well as its inevitable outcome. They believed that gradual and reasonable measures would in due time bring about a socialist state. Rejecting the idea that revolutionary violence would be needed to change the economic system, the Fabians argued that improvement of local government, or municipal ownership of such things as waterworks and electric lighting, were practical steps toward a more just society. The Fabians, like the trade union officials, were thus content with small and immediate satisfactions. They joined with the unions to form the Labour Party. At the same time, by patient and detailed research into economic realities, they provided a mass of practical information on which a legislative program could be based.

Parliamentary socialism on the Continent

The Marxist or Social Democratic parties on the Continent grew rapidly in the decades after 1870. Marxism turned into a less revolutionary "parliamentary socialism"—except indeed for the Russian Social Democratic Party, because Russia had no parliamentary government. The growth of socialist parties meant that true workers, and not merely intellectuals, were voting for socialist candidates for the Reichstag, Chamber of Deputies, or whatever the lower house of parliament might be called; and this in turn meant that the moderating influence of labor unions within the parties was increased. The workers and their union officials might in theory consider themselves locked in an enormous struggle with capital; but in practice their aim was to gain more for themselves out of their employers' business. They might believe in the internationalism of the workers' interests; but in practice, acting through the parliaments of their various national states, they would work for orderly legislation that benefited the workers of their own countries—social insurance, factory regulation, minimum wages, or maximum hours.

By the close of the nineteenth century it was becoming apparent that Marx's prediction of growing worker impoverishment (based initially on conditions of the 1840s) had not come true, at least not yet; the bourgeoisie was getting richer, but the proletarian was not getting poorer. Real wages—or what the wage earner's income would actually buy, even allowing for the losses due to unemployment—are estimated to have risen about 50 percent in the industrialized countries between 1870 and 1900. This increase was due to the greater productivity of labor through mechanization, the growth of the world economy, the accumulation of capital wealth, and the gradual fall in prices of food and other items that the workers had to buy.

Marxism began in the 1890s to undergo a movement of revisionism that responded to a changing social environment. Workers could now gain somewhat better wages and also vote for new political parties that gave them more public influence. The revisionists were led in France by Jean Jaurès, Socialist leader in the Chamber of Deputies, and in Germany by Eduard Bernstein, Social Democratic member of the Reichstag and author in 1898 of *Evolutionary Socialism,* an important tract setting forth the new views. The revisionists held that the class conflict might not be absolutely inevitable, that capitalism might be gradually transformed in the workers' interest, and that workers could now use the vote and their own political parties to improve their lives through democratic channels, without revolution and without any dictatorship of the proletariat. Most socialists or social democrats followed the revisionists. Repeatedly, but in vain, the Second International had to warn its component socialist parties against collaboration with the bourgeoisie.

The revisionists

This tendency to "opportunism" among socialist political leaders drove the really revolutionary spirits into new directions. Thus there arose revolutionary syndicalism, of which the main intellectual exponent was a Frenchman, Georges Sorel. "Syndicalism" is simply the French word for trade unionism (*syndicat,* a union), and the idea was that the workers' unions might themselves become the supreme authoritative institutions in society, replacing not only property and the market economy, but also government itself. The means to this end was to be a vast general strike, in which all workers in all industries would simultaneously stop work, thus paralyzing society and forcing acceptance of their will. Syndicalism made most headway where the unions were weakest, as in Italy, Spain, and France, because here the unions had the least to lose and the more sensational doctrines helped to attract members.

Syndicalism

Among orthodox Marxists there was also a revival of Marxist fundamentals in protest against revisionism. In Germany Karl Kautsky criticized the revisionists as compromisers who betrayed Marxism for petty-bourgeois ends. In 1904 he and other rigorists prevailed upon the Second International to condemn the political behavior of the French socialist Alexandre Millerand, who in 1899 had accepted a ministerial post in a French cabinet. Socialists might use parliaments as a forum, the Second International ruled, but socialists who entered the government itself were unpardonably identifying themselves with the enemy bourgeois state. Not until the First World War did socialists henceforth join the cabinet of any European country. In the Russian Social Democratic Party the issue of revisionism came to a head in 1903 at a party congress held in London—for the most prominent Russian Marxists were mainly exiles. Here a group led by the committed revolutionist V. I. Lenin demanded that revisionism be stamped out. Lenin won a majority, at the moment at least, and hence the uncompromising Marxists were called Bolsheviks (from the Russian word for majority), while the revisionist Russian Marxists, those willing to work with bourgeois liberals and democrats, were subsequently known as Mensheviks or the "minority" group. But in 1903 most European socialists viewed the Russian Marxists as marginal to their own national campaigns for social reform.

Orthodoxy vs. revisionism

In general, in Europe's inner zone, by the turn of the century, most people who called themselves Marxists were no longer actively revolutionary. As revolutionary republicanism had quieted down in the Third

Marxism transformed

French Republic, revolutionary Marxism also seemed to have quieted down into the milder doctrines of social democracy. What would have happened except for the coming of war in 1914 cannot be known; social revolutionism might have revived, because real wages no longer generally rose between 1900 and 1914, and considerable restlessness developed among workers in various industries, punctuated by great strikes. But in 1914 the European working class as a whole was not in a revolutionary mood. Workers still sought a greater measure of social justice, but the social agitation so feared or hoped for in 1848 had subsided. There seem to have been three principal reasons for the decline in revolutionary agitation. Capitalism had worked well enough to raise the workers' living standard above what they could remember of their parents' or grandparents' economic situation; workers had gained the right to vote, so they expected to benefit from new public policies rather than from the overthrow of their governments; and they had created political parties and increasingly powerful labor unions, all of which protected their interests and helped them acquire a larger share of the national income.

Feminism, 1880-1914

The campaign for women's rights also became more international and better organized during the same decades that the new workers' parties were spreading across Europe. Women received less pay than men for the work they performed in the new industrial economy, and in most places they still faced numerous restrictions on their rights to own property, participate in political meetings, vote in elections, and attend universities. The movement for women's rights therefore continued to promote the kind of reforms that feminists had been advocating since the early nineteenth century, including more access to education and the right to vote. Women's groups on the Continent tended to emphasize legal and social reforms rather than voting rights, whereas British and American feminists gave more attention to the campaign for women's suffrage. But activists in all industrialized societies were increasingly drawn to national and international organizations, in part because such groups created useful networks for spreading information and political ideas. American women such as Susan B. Anthony and Elizabeth Cady Stanton joined with European feminists to establish an International Council of Women in 1888, and the growing demand for women's rights crossed the borders of all modern nations.

Suffragettes seek the vote

Although some feminists worked to make birth control available to more women or to improve the conditions of women workers, the quest for voting rights attracted the most public attention, especially in the United States and Britain. New organizations such as the National American Woman Suffrage Association and, in Britain, the Women's Social and Political Union sponsored petitions, mass meetings, and protests that demanded equal voting rights in both local and national elections. The suffrage movement in Britain became especially militant after the British Parliament rejected every legislative proposal to grant women the vote—a pattern of official opposition that women had repeatedly challenged since the 1860s. Frustrated by the stubborn resistance of male politicians, the energetic leader of the Women's Social and Political Union, Emmeline Pankhurst, led a radical wing of the suffrage movement in a campaign of violent protests in the years before 1914. Pankhurst's supporters and allies disrupted sessions of Parliament, broke store windows, destroyed mailboxes, and damaged government buildings to protest the exclusion of women from British elections and political institutions. When arrested, the "suffragettes" went on hunger strikes, to which the police responded by painful forcible feedings.

The campaign for women's voting rights became increasingly militant as early twentieth-century leaders such as Emmeline Pankhurst urged activists to take direct action against government institutions and facilities. This photograph of Pankhurst was taken shortly before the First World War—a transformative event that would reshape the social roles of British women and lead finally to the enactment of female suffrage in 1918.

(Library of Congress, Prints and Photographs Division [LC-DIG-ggbain-12112])

The British campaign for women's voting rights often mobilized women for marches in the streets, public demonstrations, and confrontations with government officials. The protestors at this march in 1913 were following a woman who had been arrested at an earlier suffragist demonstration, and the presence of the police is an example of the close government surveillance that was part of every such event.

(©Hulton Archive/Getty Images)

Pankhurst and other suffragettes were widely ridiculed in the British press and Parliament, but their campaign attracted growing support during the First World War (when the militant protests were suspended), and, as noted earlier, British women over the age of 30 finally received the right to vote in 1918. The law was changed again in 1928, when the voting age for British women was lowered to 21. Meanwhile, women had also gained the right to vote in Germany, the United States, and other Western nations in the early years of this postwar era. The campaign for voting rights was only one component of modern feminism, however; and the movement to enhance women's rights in the economy, legal system, family, and education would develop new themes and new political strategies throughout the twentieth century.

73.   SCIENCE, PHILOSOPHY, THE ARTS, AND RELIGION

Faith in the powers of natural science has been characteristic of modern European society for over three centuries, but never was there a time when this faith spread to so many people or was held so firmly and with so few mental reservations as in the half-century preceding the First World War. Science created the foundation for the whole movement of industrialization; and if science gained wide popularity after about 1870, in that persons ignorant of science came to look upon it as an oracle of wisdom, it was because it manifested itself to everybody in the new wonders of daily life. Hardly had the world's more industrialized regions digested the railroad, the steamship, and the telegraph when a whole series of new inventions began to appear during the era of the second Industrial Revolution. In the 30 years following 1875 the number of patents tripled in the United States, quadrupled in Germany, and multiplied in all modern countries. The scientific and technical advance was as completely international (though confined mainly to the "inner zone") as any movement the world has ever seen. Never had the rush of scientific invention been so fundamentally useful, so helpful to the constructive labors and serious problems of mankind.

Changing conceptions in science

In more basic scientific thinking important changes set in about 1860 or 1870. Up to that time, generally speaking, the underlying ideas had been those set forth by Isaac Newton in the late seventeenth century. The law of universal gravitation reigned unquestioned, and with it, hardly less so, the geometry of Euclid and a physics that was basically mechanics. The ultimate nature of the universe was thought to be regular, orderly, predictable, and harmonious; it was also described as timeless, in that the passage of ages in the natural world brought no significant change or development. By the end of the era considered here, that is, by 1914, the old conceptions and certainties had begun to yield to a surge of new theories and knowledge in every field of scientific research.

The Impact of Evolution

Charles Darwin

In impact upon general thinking the greatest change came in the new emphasis upon biology and the life sciences. Here the great symbolic date is 1859, when Charles Darwin published *On the Origin of Species.* Evolution, after Darwin (1809–1882), became the most influential intellectual theme of the era. Evolutionary philosophies, holding that the way to understand anything was to understand its development, were not new in 1859. Hegel had introduced the evolutionary conception into modern metaphysics and into historical theories of human society. The idea of progress, taken over from the Age of Enlightenment, was also a kind of

Charles Darwin's *On the Origin of Species* (1859) set forth scientific arguments for the biological evolution of living organisms and provoked cultural debates far beyond the academic sphere of natural scientists. Darwin is portrayed here as an ageing scientific expert whose grandfatherly appearance scarcely suggests the intellectual revolution that he launched through his research and writings.
(Library of Congress, Prints & Photographs Division [LC-USZ61-104])

evolutionary philosophy; and the expanding activity in historical studies, under romantic and nationalist auspices, had made people think of human affairs in terms of a process that unfolded over time. In the world of natural science, the rise of geology after 1800 had opened the way to new evolutionary ideas about the surface of the earth, and venturesome biologists had begun to speculate on an evolutionary development of living forms. What Darwin did was to stamp evolution with the seal of science, marshaling the empirical evidence to support it and offering an explanation of how it worked. In 1871, in *The Descent of Man,* he applied the same hypotheses to human beings.

By evolution, Darwin meant that species are mutable; that no species is created to remain unchanged once and for all; and that all species of living organisms, plant and animal, microscopic or elephantine in dimensions, living or extinct, have developed by successive small changes from other species that went before them. An important corollary was that all life was interrelated and subject to the same laws. Another corollary was that the whole history of living things on earth, generally held by scientists in Darwin's time to be many millions of years, was a unified history unfolding continuously in a single complex process of evolution.

Darwin thought that species changed, not by any intelligent design or by a purposeful activity in the organism, but essentially by a kind of chance. Individual organisms, through the play of heredity, inherited slightly different characteristics, some more useful than others in getting food, fighting or fleeing predators, and producing offspring; and the organisms that had the most useful characteristics tended to survive, so that their characteristics were passed on to their progeny, until the whole species gradually changed. Certain phrases, not all of them invented by Darwin, summed up the theory. There was a "struggle for existence" resulting in the "survival of the fittest" through "natural selection" of the "most favored races"—races meaning not human races but the inherited strains within a species. The

"Survival of the fittest"

struggle for existence referred to the fact that in nature more individuals were born in each species than could live out a normal life span; the "fittest" were those individual specimens of a species having the most useful characteristics, such as fleetness in deer or ferocity in tigers; "natural" selection meant that the fittest survived without a preordained purpose or the interventions of a Creator; the "favored races" were simply the members of a species who had good survival powers in a complex natural environment.

Darwin's ideas precipitated a great outcry. Scientists rushed to defend him and churchmen attacked him. The biologist T. H. Huxley became the chief spokesman for Darwin—"Darwin's bulldog." He debated with, among others, the bishop of Oxford, Samuel Wilberforce, who denounced Darwin and his supporters for saying that human beings came from monkeys. It was feared that all grounds of human dignity, morality, and religion would collapse. Darwin himself remained complacent on this score. Under civilized conditions, he said, the social and cooperative virtues were useful characteristics assisting in survival, so that "we may expect that virtuous habits will grow stronger, becoming perhaps fixed by inheritance." Much of the outburst against Darwin was somewhat trivial, nor were those who attacked him generally noted for spiritual insight; yet they were not mistaken in sensing a profound danger.

That Darwinism said nothing of God, Providence, creative (or intelligent) design, or salvation was not surprising; no science ever did. That evolution did not square with the first chapter of Genesis was disturbing but not fatal; much of the Old Testament was already regarded as symbolic, at least outside fundamentalist religious circles. Even the idea that humans and animals were of one piece was not ruinous; the animal side of human nature had not escaped the notice of theologians. The novel and upsetting effects of evolutionary biology emerged most clearly in the changing conceptions of nature and in the implicit challenges to long-held ethical beliefs. Nature was no longer a harmony; it was a scene of struggle, "nature red in tooth and claw." Elimination of the weak was natural, and it might even be considered good insofar as it contributed to evolutionary development. Such conceptions of what was good or beneficial for evolutionary progress profoundly challenged traditional religious ideas about morality and virtue; indeed, the potential critique of Christian ethics posed a greater threat to religious values than the revision of the biblical account of creation. Darwin's theory asserted that there were no fixed species or perfected forms, but only an unending flux. Change was everlasting; and everything seemed relative to time, place, and environment. There were no higher norms of good and bad; a good organism was one that survived where others perished; adaptation replaced virtue; outside successful adaptation there was nothing "right." The test was, in short, success; the "fit" were those who survived; and here Darwinism merged with the new realism, or *Realpolitik,* and other social doctrines that were appearing in Europe at the same time from other causes.

Changing views of nature

Social Darwinism

Such at least were the implications if one generalized from science, carrying over scientific findings into human affairs, and the prestige of science was so great that this is precisely what many people wished to do. With the popularization of biological evolution, a school of social theorists known as Social Darwinists actively applied the ideas of the struggle for existence and survival of the fittest to human society. Social Darwinists were found all over Europe and the United States. Their doctrines were put to various political, cultural, and racist uses, to claim that European peoples or races were naturally superior to people of other races; or that the upper and middle classes deserved their social comforts and advantages because they had proved themselves "fitter" than the shiftless poor; or that big business in the nature of things had to take over smaller concerns; or that some states,

Historical Documents
Charles Darwin, *On the Origin of Species* (1859)

Charles Darwin's scientific account of how all plants and animals had evolved through the processes of natural selection attracted wide interest and debate during the late nineteenth century. Many Europeans accepted Darwin's evolutionary theories, and some also extended his ideas to human history in a "Social Darwinism" that celebrated the "survival of the fittest." Others denounced Darwin for demeaning human life, removing providential design from the natural world, and undermining religious beliefs. Darwin (1809-1882) himself, however, did not apply his theories to human social relations, and he believed that his research actually showed the beauty, grandeur, and complexity of all earthly life, as he noted in these concluding paragraphs of his famous book.

When I view all beings not as special creations, but as the lineal descendants of some few beings which lived long [ago] . . . , they seem to me to become ennobled. . . . And as natural selection works solely by and for the good of each being, all corporeal and mental endowments will tend to progress towards perfection.

It is interesting to contemplate an entangled bank, clothed with many plants of many kinds, with birds singing on the bushes, with various insects flitting about, and with worms crawling through the damp earth, and to reflect that these elaborately constructed forms, so different from each other, and dependent on each other in so complex a manner, have all been produced by [evolutionary] laws acting around us. . . .

Thus, from the war of nature, from famine and death, the most exalted object which we are capable of conceiving, namely, the production of the higher animals, directly follows. There is grandeur in this view of life, with its several powers, having been originally breathed by the Creator into a few forms or into one; and that, whilst this planet has gone cycling on according to the fixed law of gravity, from so simple a beginning endless forms most beautiful and most wonderful have been, and are being, evolved.

Charles Darwin, *On the Origin of Species* (London: John Murray, 1860), pp. 489-490.

such as the British or German Empires, were bound to rise, or that war was morally a fine thing, proving the virility and survival skills of those who fought. These ideas gave new meanings to national wars and to the claims for cultural or racial superiority that were used to justify late nineteenth-century European imperialism.

Genetics, Anthropology, and Psychology

Meanwhile Gregor Mendel (1822-1884), an Austrian monk patiently experimenting with the cross-pollination of garden peas in his Augustinian monastery, arrived at an explanation of how heredity operates and how hybridization can take place. Unlike Darwin, his findings,

Gregor Mendel

published in 1866, were ignored until 1900, when they were rediscovered and became the basis for the new science of genetics. Mendel's ideas foreshadowed the remarkable breakthroughs in the scientific study of heredity and control over genetic materials that began in the second half of the twentieth century and have continued into our own time.

Anthropologists gained public influence in this era by setting out to explain the physical and cultural characteristics of all branches of humankind. Physical anthropologists became interested in the several human "races," arguing, for example, that Europeans might be "favored" in the Darwinian sense, that is, superior in inheritance and survival value. Some European scientists and intellectuals also extended their racist categories to assert that the Nordics or Germans or Anglo-Saxons were superior among Europeans. The public became more race conscious than Europeans had ever been before. On the other hand the cultural anthropologists, surveying all manner of primitive or complex societies with scientific comparisons, seemed sometimes to teach a more deflating doctrine. Scientifically, it seemed, no culture or society was "better" than any other, all being adaptations to an environment, or merely a matter of custom—of the *mores,* as people said in careful distinction from "morals." The new anthropology thus contributed new cultural evidence to support a kind of relativism or skepticism—a negation of values, a belief that right and wrong were matters of social convention, psychological conditioning, mere opinion, or point of view. We are describing, let it be emphasized, not the history of science itself but the effects of science upon European cultures and beliefs at the time.

Anthropology and religion

The impact of anthropology was felt keenly in religion too. Sir James Frazer (1854–1941) in his multivolumed *The Golden Bough* demonstrated that some of the most sacred practices, rites, and ideas of Christianity were not unique among human religious traditions; similar rituals and beliefs could be found in numerous premodern societies, and, according to Frazer, only the thinnest of lines divided belief in magic from religion. Anthropology, like Darwinian evolution, could therefore undermine traditional religious beliefs, including a belief in either the uniqueness or the universal truth of European religions.

Psychology, as a science of human behavior, led to thoroughly upsetting implications about the very nature of human freedom and rationality. It was launched in the 1870s as a natural science by the German physiologist Wilhelm Wundt (1832–1920), who developed various new experimental techniques. The Russian Ivan Pavlov (1849–1936) conducted a famous series of experiments in which he "conditioned" dogs to salivate automatically at the ringing of a bell once they had become accustomed over a period of time to associate the sound with the serving of their food. Pavlov's observations were important. They implied that a great part of animal behavior, and presumably human behavior, could be explained on the basis of conditioned responses. In the case of human beings, their actions and responses to various situations were apparently conditioned or deeply shaped by earlier environments, training, and social experiences rather than by personal choices or conscious reasoning.

Sigmund Freud

Most significant of all the developments in the study of human behavior was the work of Sigmund Freud (1856–1939) and those influenced by him. Freud, a Viennese physician, founded psychoanalysis at the turn of the century. He came to believe that certain forms of emotional disturbance like hysteria were traceable to unconscious desires and painful earlier forgotten episodes of patients' lives. After first trying various techniques such as hypnosis, which he soon abandoned, he employed free association, or free recall. If patients could be helped to bring their suppressed desires or painful experiences into conscious recall, the symptoms of illness would often disappear.

From these beginnings Freud and his followers explored the role that the unconscious played in all human behavior, he himself stressing the sexual drive. In one of his most famous books, *The Interpretation of Dreams* (1900), he argued that the analysis of dreams provided the most direct access to a person's repressed memories and unconscious mind. In later books such as *Civilization and Its Discontents* (1930) Freud extended his account of unconscious drives and frustrations into the broader cultural spheres of religion, education, art, literature, and war, arguing that the deepest desires within the human mind were

Sigmund Freud's description of the unconscious mind reshaped modern conceptions of human psychology and influenced the arts, literature, and social theories as well as the medical treatment of mental illnesses. As this photograph suggests, however, the "revolutionary" Dr. Freud was also a typical member of his own cultural milieu—the professional class in early twentieth-century Vienna.

(©Mondadori Portfolio/Getty Images)

both repressed and expressed in the social customs and institutions of all societies. Freud and Freudian ideas had great influence on the social and behavioral sciences, and a good deal of the Freudian vocabulary later entered into everyday modern language and popular culture. Psychoanalysis gained transnational cultural influence by stressing that wide areas of human behavior came from drives or fears outside conscious control and by suggesting that human beings were not essentially rational creatures at all. Although Freud identified with the scientific traditions of the Enlightenment, his theory of the unconscious called into question the classical liberal and Enlightenment assumptions about how reasonable, free persons developed, explained, and acted upon their individual interests or beliefs.

The New Physics

The revolution in biology of the nineteenth century, together with the developments in psychology and anthropology, were soon to be matched and surpassed by the revolution in physics. In the late 1890s physics was on the threshold of a revolutionary transformation. Like Newtonian mechanics in the seventeenth century and Darwinian evolution in the nineteenth, the new physics represented one of the great scientific revolutions of all time. There was no single work comparable to Newton's *Principia* or Darwin's *On the Origin of Species* unless Albert Einstein's theory of relativity, propounded in a series of scientific papers in 1905 and 1916, might be considered as such. Instead there was a series of discoveries and findings, partly mathematical and then increasingly empirical, that

Einstein's theory of relativity

transformed scientific views of matter and energy. In Newtonian physics the atom, the basic unit of all matter, which the Greeks had hypothesized in ancient times, was like a hard, solid, unstructured billiard ball, permanent and unchanging; and matter and energy were separate and distinct.

But a series of discoveries profoundly altered this conception of matter in the early decades of the twentieth century. In 1896 the French scientist Antoine Henri Becquerel

The new theories that emerged in physics after 1900 transformed earlier Newtonian science and gave the young Albert Einstein an international reputation. This picture shows Einstein standing next to his personal books and papers in the 1920s, several years before he moved to the United States to escape the intolerance and repression in Nazi Germany.
(©General Photographic Agency/Hulton Archive/ Getty Images)

discovered radioactivity, observing that uranium emitted particles or rays of energy. In the years immediately following, from the observations and discoveries of the French scientists Pierre and Marie Curie and the Englishmen J. J. Thomson and Lord Rutherford, there emerged the notion that atoms were not simple but complex and, moreover, that various radioactive atoms were by nature unstable, releasing energy as they disintegrated. The German physicist Max Planck demonstrated in 1900 that energy was emitted or absorbed in specific and discrete units or bundles, each called a quantum; moreover, energy was not emitted smoothly and continuously as previously thought, nor was it as distinguishable from matter as once supposed. In 1913, the Danish physicist Niels Bohr postulated an atom consisting of a nucleus of protons surrounded by electrically charged units, called electrons, rotating around the nucleus, each in its orbit, like a minuscule solar system.

The study of radioactivity led scientists back toward an idea long rejected, the favored view of the alchemists, that matter was transmutable; in a way undreamed of even by the alchemists, it was convertible into energy. The German-born Jewish scientific genius

$$e = mc^2$$

Albert Einstein (1879-1955) expressed this conversion of matter into energy in a famous formula $e = mc^2$. The formula summarized his theory of relativity, which also carried the profoundly revolutionary notion that time, space, and motion were not absolute in character but were relative to the observer and the observer's own movement in space. In later years, in 1929 and in 1954, Einstein brought together into one common set of laws, as Newton formerly had done, a unified field theory, an explanation of gravitation, electromagnetism, and sub-atomic behavior. Einstein's theories were difficult for most people to understand, and many of his ideas remained controversial, but even non-scientists began to recognize that the new science was modifying much that had been taken for granted since Newton. The Newtonian world was being replaced by a four-dimensional world, a kind of space-time continuum; and in mathematics, non-Euclidian geometries were being developed.

It turned out, too, that neither cause and effect nor time and space nor Newton's law of universal gravitation meant very much in the subatomic world nor indeed in the cosmos when objects moved with the speed of light. It was impossible, as the German scientist Werner Heisenberg demonstrated a little later, in 1927, by his principle of uncertainty, or indeterminacy, to ascertain simultaneously both the position and the velocity of the indi-vidual electron. On these foundations established before the First World War there devel-oped the new science of nuclear physics and the tapping of the atom's energy. The atom and its world of subatomic particles were discovered to be even more complex than anyone had recognized before 1914. Despite the complexity of the scientific language and theories, new ideas about the "relativity" of human knowledge soon began to influence European art, philosophy, and literature—much as Newtonian physics had influenced nonscientific thought in the Enlightenment-era culture of the eighteenth century.

Trends in Philosophy and the Arts

Although some writers and artists resembled earlier Romantic thinkers in criticizing Enlightenment ideas or modern science, most European intellectuals in this period viewed science as the model for all forms of knowledge. They were drawn to positivism or to the belief that scientific methods provided the only "positive" knowledge of the world. Anything unknowable to science must therefore remain uncertain or unknowable forever—a doctrine called agnosticism, or the acknowledgment of the limits to what can be known about certain

Agnosticism

physical or metaphysical questions. The English sociologist Herbert Spencer (1820–1903) was one widely read popularizer of agnosticism who pictured a universe governed by the open-ended natural selection of Darwinian evolution. As Spencer described it, all philosophy could be unified, organized, and coordinated through the doctrine of evolution; this doctrine he applied not only to all living things but also to sociology, government, and economics as well. The evolution of society, he believed, was leading toward increasing freedom for the individual, the role of governments being merely to maintain freedom and justice; governments should therefore not interfere with natural social and economic processes, nor coddle the weak and unfit. Yet, like Darwin himself, Spencer believed that altruism, charity, and goodwill were useful as individual ethical virtues. He separated such virtues from religious traditions, however, by describing them as laudable products of evolutionary development.

These latter views of individual ethics were not shared by another of the serious writers of the age, also much influenced by evolutionary ideas, the German philosopher Friedrich Nietzsche (1844–1900). Drawing upon many intellectual currents of the century, Nietzsche was an unsystematic, radical thinker whose complex ideas often defied conventional cultural categories. It is evident, however, that he held a low opinion of modern, democratic

Friedrich Nietzsche

societies. From a background of evolutionary thinking he developed the concept of an Overman, a new kind of noble being who would create new ethical values and philosophical truths that would enable him to break away from constraining cultural traditions and also to dominate or dazzle the multitude. Qualities of humility, patience, helpfulness, hope, and love, in short the specifically Christian virtues, Nietzsche described as a slave morality concocted by the weak to disarm the strong. He drew sharp contrasts between the ethical traditions of Christianity and his own philosophical values, which emphasized aristocratic qualities of courage, love of danger, intellectual excellence, and personal independence. Indeed he argued that all humans, even philosophers, were driven more by their instincts and a "will to power" than by reason or rational thought.

Nietzsche therefore condemned the philosophical legacies of Plato and Kant as well as the main ideas of nineteenth-century liberalism and socialism. His critique of religion revived and revised some themes of classical paganism. Although Nietzsche was neither much read nor respected during his own lifetime, his writings soon attracted both German and international interest from readers who admired his frank, unyielding engagement with the unsettling ethical or philosophical implications of the new evolutionary ideas. More generally, his critical analysis of reason, rationality, and the belief in universal truths became widely influential among anti-Enlightenment thinkers before and after the First World War.

IA ORANA MARIA
by Paul Gauguin (French, 1848–1903)

Gauguin moved to Tahiti in the early 1890s, searching for non-European alternatives to the culture and art he had known in France. His portrayals of Tahitians often conveyed European ideas about the exoticism of colonized, non-European people, but his use of color and symbolic images influenced later avant-garde artists in Europe. Gauguin also continued to draw on (classical) European artistic themes. The title of this painting means "Hail Mary," an allusion to the biblical Annunciation in which the angel Gabriel told the Virgin Mary that she would give birth to a child.

(©The Metropolitan Museum of Art, New York, Bequest of Sam A. Lewisohn, 1951)

As in the sciences and philosophy, the new works of creative imagination—literature, drama and the fine arts—conveyed changing conceptions of truth, ethics, and social life. Some writers, like Emile Zola in France or Henrik Ibsen in Scandinavia, turned to the portrayal of social problems, producing a realistic literature that dealt with industrial strife, strikes, prostitution, divorce, or insanity. New psychological theories also appeared in literary works, especially in fictional portraits of troubled characters and irrational human behavior. The new novels and plays were indeed often truer to specific social or psychological experiences than the older forms of European literature. But some literary movements—for example, the symbolist poets in France—were experimenting with language in works that moved modern writing far away from the literal representation of social realities. In a sense the arts followed the intellectual developments of the age, reflecting, as they do today, diverse attitudes of relativism, irrationalism, social determinism, linguistic ambiguity, and interest in the operations of the unconscious mind. On the other hand, never had artist and society been so far apart. The French painter Paul Gauguin, an extreme case, fled to the South Seas, abandoned his family and modern European life, and reveled in vivid tropical colors (see Gauguin's painting *Ia Orana Maria* on this page). Others became absorbed in technicalities or mere capricious self-expression. Art at its extreme

**ROUEN CATHEDRAL,
WEST FAÇADE
by Claude Monet
(French, 1840–1926)**

A distinctive fascination with light can be seen in most Impressionist works, as in Claude Monet's paintings of the cathedral at Rouen. This view of the cathedral in the winter sunlight was one of a series that Monet painted in the 1890s, when he portrayed the different appearances and colors of the same objects in various shades of light at various times of the day.

(National Gallery of Art)

fringe became almost incomprehensible and the average person seemed deprived of a visual means (as old as the cave paintings of the Stone Age) of perceiving and enjoying the world.

The artistic movement known as Impressionism did not sever all links between painting and the external world, however, and the Impressionists became perhaps the most influential artists in late nineteenth-century Europe. Rising to prominence in the 1870s and 1880s, painters such as Claude Monet, Pierre-Auguste Renoir, Camille Pissaro, Berthe Morisot, and Mary Cassatt rejected traditional styles of academic painting in France and turned instead to the representation of everyday life and the colorful play of light in the natural world. In contrast to earlier painters who had worked in studios and depicted scenes from mythology, classical history, or exotic cultures, the Impressionists preferred to paint outdoors and to portray the streets or buildings of modern France, the daily activities of ordinary people, or the pleasures of a modern café. Monet was especially adept at representing the same object in various shades of light (see, for example, the *Rouen Cathedral* on this page), but all Impressionists used light and color rather than classical lines or themes to convey their "impressions" of the modern world. Most Impressionist painters were French and most were men, though women such as Morisot and the American-born Cassatt also produced innovative works, often portraying women

THE HARBOR AT LORIENT
by Berthe Morisot (French, 1841–1895)
The French painter Berthe Morisot was one of the first women to adopt the methods and perspectives of Impressionist art. This painting shows the movement's characteristic concern with the play of light and color in outdoor scenes. The portrayal of a young woman on a waterside wall was also typical of Morisot's particular interest in representing the experiences and memories of women.
(National Gallery of Art)

in the different phases of their lives (see Morisot's *The Harbor at Lorient* on this page and Cassatt's *The Boating Party* on p. 645)

Impressionism gradually gained international influence and became the aesthetic starting point for other artists, usually called Postimpressionists, who portrayed people and objects in novel and increasingly abstract forms and surprising colors. The works of Paul Cézanne are influential examples of the Postimpressionist art that pushed steadily beyond Impressionism in a continuing attempt to represent the artist's distinctive personal vision of human experience (see Cézanne's *Self-Portrait with Beret* on p. 646). By the early twentieth century, artists such as Pablo Picasso, Georges Braque, and Vasily Kandinsky were painting "Cubist" or "Abstract Expressionist" works that represented natural objects and the human body in highly abstract forms and splashes of color, most of which bore little or no resemblance to what scientists might have called objective reality (see Picasso's *Les Demoiselles d'Avignon* on p. 647).

After the First World War, and continuing throughout the twentieth century, the same trends of subjectivism in the arts attracted a wider, less-skeptical audience. People read books without punctuation (or with peculiar punctuation); listened to music called atonal, composed for effects of discord and dissonance; and studied intently abstract or "nonobjective" paintings and sculpture to which the artists themselves often refused to give titles. Although they frequently criticized modern industrial society, artists and their art also exemplified the specialization and division of labor in modern social and economic systems. Many artists were no longer creating art for common use or enjoyment (as, for example, in a Renaissance Italian city piazza). They were creative specialists plying their trade and pursuing their own concerns—like other modern specialists whose work was often incomprehensible to outsiders.

THE BOATING PARTY
by Mary Cassatt (American-born, lived in France, 1844–1926)

Cassatt lived and worked throughout her adult life in France. She developed her most distinctive works under the influence of both Impressionism and the traditions of Japanese art. She painted many pictures of mothers with their children, including this somewhat mysterious image of a man rowing a woman and child across a European lake.

(National Gallery of Art)

The Churches and the Modern Age

Religion had always been one of the most influential components of European societies, but like other cultural traditions it faced new challenges and critiques in the later nineteenth century. It was now a long time since almost everyone had looked to religion for social and intellectual guidance. But religion was more threatened after 1860 or 1870 than ever in the past, because never before had science, or philosophies drawing upon science, addressed themselves so directly to the nature of life and of human existence. Never before had so many of the fundamental premises of traditional religion been questioned or denied. Darwinian evolution challenged the value of Christian ethics as well as the traditional picture of Creation, and anthropologists questioned the uniqueness of the most sacred Christian tenets. There developed also the "higher" criticism of the Bible, an effort

Threats to religion

SELF-PORTRAIT WITH BERET
by Paul Cézanne (French, 1839–1906)
Cézanne went beyond early Impressionist art to develop a new emphasis on the shapes or contours of natural objects, buildings, and people. He also applied his innovative techniques to portraits of himself, striving to depict his identity as a painter through both the style and the content of such works.
(©Universal History Archive/Getty Images)

to apply to the Scriptures the techniques of scholarship long applied to secular documents, to incorporate archeological discoveries, and to reconstruct a naturalistic, historical account of ancient religious beliefs and traditions. This form of critical, textual analysis, going back at least to the seventeenth century, now drew on new methods of historical research and focused on both the Old Testament and the New. The Bible became for many scholars another object for comparative historical analysis rather than a sacred text. In the case of the Old Testament the patient scrutiny of style and language cast doubt on the validity of certain stories or prophecies; and in the New the inconsistencies or contrasts among the several Gospel sources were demonstrated by a new generation of scholars and critics. The German theologian David Friedrich Strauss (1808–1874), one such critical scholar, was the author of a widely discussed *Life of Jesus,* in which many

LES DEMOISELLES D'AVIGNON
by Pablo Picasso (Spanish, 1881–1973)

Picasso's portrayals of the human body in paintings such as this disorienting collective portrait of women in Avignon became the best-known works of early "Cubism." The Cubist painters portrayed objects from multiple perspectives and used abstract shapes or unexpected colors to convey the subjective visions of the artist rather than a realistic image of the external world.

(©Index/The Image Works; ©2018 Estate of Pablo Picasso/Artists Rights Society (ARS), New York)

miraculous and supernatural episodes were reverently but firmly explained away as myth. The sensitive French historian and man of letters Ernest Renan (1823–1892) in a somewhat similar vein wrote on Jesus and the origins of Christianity and on the life of ancient Israel, giving secular explanations for the oldest religious stories and beliefs. Moreover, the whole tenor of the time, its absorption in material and technological progress, kept many people away from church; and the wholesale uprooting, the movement from country to city, often broke religious ties.

The Protestant churches were less successful than the Catholic in protecting their membership from the disintegrating effects of the age. Church attendance among Protestants became increasingly casual, and the theological doctrines set forth in sermons seemed increasingly remote to science-minded, urban populations. Protestants traditionally trusted their own private judgment and regarded their clergy as their own agents, not as authoritative teachers placed above them. Protestants also had always set special emphasis on the Bible as the source of religious belief; and as doubts accumulated on the literal truth of Biblical narratives there seemed no other authoritative source on which to rely.

Challenges to Protestantism

Protestants tended to divide between fundamentalists and modernists. The fundamentalists, as they were called in the United States, sought to defend the literal word of Scripture, but their literal readings of the Bible clashed with some of the most indubitable findings of science. The modernists were willing enough to accept science and to interpret much of the Bible as allegory, but they often lost a strong sense of spirituality or urgent feeling of Christian truth. Most Protestant churches were slow to face the social problems and wholesale injustices produced by the economic system, though a group of "Christian socialists" had emerged by the early twentieth century in some Protestant denominations. Because both education and the care for orphans, sick, and mentally disturbed persons generally passed to the state, Protestant groups tended to be less involved in the relief of suffering and the upbringing of the young. European Protestantism, to the regret of many

Protestants, became increasingly a customary observance by people whose minds and social actions were elsewhere. Not until after the First World War could a strong Protestant revival be discerned, with a reaffirmation of basic doctrines by European theologians such as Karl Barth (1886-1968), and an ecumenical movement on the part of divergent Protestant churches to combine.

Catholicism resists

The Roman Catholic Church proved more resistant to the secularizing trends of the age. We have seen how Pope Pius IX (1846-1878), after being driven from Rome by republicans in 1848, gave up his inclinations to liberalism. In 1864, in the *Syllabus of Errors,* he denounced as erroneous a long list of widely current ideas, including the faith in rationalism and science, and he vigorously denied that the head of the church "should reconcile and align himself with progress, liberalism, and modern civilization." The *Syllabus* was a warning to Catholics, not a matter of dogma incumbent upon them to believe. In dogma, the Immaculate Conception of the Virgin Mary was announced as dogmatic truth in 1854; a century later, in 1950, the bodily assumption of Mary into heaven was proclaimed. Thus the Catholic Church reaffirmed in a skeptical scientific age, and against Christian modernists, its faith in the supernatural and miraculous.

Pius IX also convened a general church council, which met at the Vatican in 1870. It was the first such council since the Council of Trent some 300 years before. The Vatican Council proclaimed the dogma of papal infallibility, which holds that the pope, when speaking ex cathedra (that is, from his official position as head of the church) on matters of faith and morals, speaks with a final and supernatural authority that no Catholic may question or reject. The Vatican Council, and the acceptance of papal infallibility by Catholics, was the climax of centuries of development within the church. In brief, as the world grew more national, Catholicism became more international. As state sovereignty and secularism grew, Catholic clergy looked increasingly to the spiritual powers of Rome for protection against alien forces, including the rising influence of liberalism and socialism as well as the nationalism and centralizing power of modern nation-states. By 1870 the net effect was to throw Catholics into the arms of the Holy See. Ultramontanism, the unconditional acceptance of papal jurisdiction, prevailed over the old French Gallicanism and other national tendencies that had long existed within the Catholic Church as a counterbalance to the power of the popes.

In 1870, while the 600 prelates of the Vatican Council were sitting, the new Italian state unceremoniously entered and annexed the city of Rome. The pope's temporal power

Vatican City

thus disappeared. It is now widely agreed that the loss of local temporal interests ultimately enhanced the spiritual influence of the papacy on Catholics throughout the world. The popes long refused, however, to recognize the loss of Rome; and each pope in turn, from 1870 to 1929, adopted a policy of self-imprisonment in the Vatican grounds. By the Lateran treaty of 1929 the papacy finally recognized the Italian state, and Italy conceded the existence of a Vatican City about a square mile in area, as an independent state not legally within Italy at all. The papacy thus gained an enduring independence from national or secular authority and secured the requisite independence to lead the global Catholic Church.

Rerum Novarum

Pius IX's successor, Leo XIII (1878-1903), carried on the counteroffensive against irreligion and instituted a revival of medieval philosophy as represented by Thomas Aquinas. But Leo XIII is chiefly remembered for formulating Catholic social doctrine, especially in the encyclical *Rerum Novarum* ("of modern things") of 1891, to which subsequent pontiffs adhered, and from which various movements of Catholic socialism are derived. *Rerum Novarum* upheld private property as a natural right, within the limits of justice; but it found fault with capitalism for the poverty, insecurity, and even degradation in which many of the laboring classes were left. It declared that much in socialism was Christian in principle; but it criticized socialism insofar as (like Marxism) it was materialistic and antireligious. The pope therefore recommended that Catholics, if they wished, form socialist parties of their own and that Catholic workers form labor unions under Catholic auspices.

As for Judaism, the Jews were a small minority, but their condition had always been a kind of barometer reflecting changes in the atmosphere of tolerance as a whole. In the nineteenth century the basic trend was toward emancipation and assim-ilation. Science and secularism had the same challenging effects upon Orthodox Judaism as upon traditional Christianity. Reform Judaism grew up as the Jewish counterpart to modernism in other faiths. Secular Jews moved away from worship altogether. In society at large, the prevalence of liberalism allowed them to act as citizens and to enter business or the professions like everybody else, freed from old legal discriminations that had been imposed on them for centuries.

Jewish emancipation

Toward the end of the century two important new tendencies began to counter earlier trends that were leading to the assimilation of Jewish communities and individuals. One, a cultural and political nationalism, originated with Jews themselves, some of whom feared an assimilation that would lead to a loss of Jewish identity and perhaps even the disappearance of Judaism itself. The other countertendency, or barrier to assimilation, was the rise of a virulent new anti-Semitism, noticeable in many quarters by 1900. Racist theories, dislike for Jewish competitors in business and the professions, socialist scorn for Jewish capitalists like the Rothschilds, upper-class fears of Jewish revolutionists and Marxists, together with a growth of ethnic nationalism, which held that France should be purely French and Latin, Germany purely German and Nordic, or Russia purely Russian and Slav, all combined to raise an anti-Semitic hue and cry. In Russia there were fierce pogroms, or massacres of Jews. In France the Dreyfus case, which dragged on from 1894 to 1906, revealed unsuspected depths of anti-Semitic fury. Such hostility pushed many Jews toward a new or deeper sense of Jewish identity. The Hungarian-born Jewish journalist Theodor Herzl became one of the leading advocates for this resurgent religious and cultural identity. Appalled by the turbulence of the Dreyfus affair in civilized France, which he observed firsthand as a reporter for a Vienna newspaper, he founded modern, or political, Zionism when he organized the first international Zionist congress at Basel in 1897. Advocating many of the political and cultural ideas that shaped the popular nationalisms of this era, Zionists hoped to establish a Jewish state in Palestine, in which Jews from all the world might find refuge, although there had been no independent Jewish state there since ancient times.

The rise of anti-Semitism

Many Jews, wishing civic assimilation yet despairing of obtaining it, began to sympa-thize with the fusion of nationalism and religion in the Jewish nationalist movement, looking to Zionism and a Jewish renascence as a way to maintain their own dignity. Others insisted that Judaism was a religious faith, not a nationality by itself; that Jews and non-Jews within the same country shared in exactly the same nationality, citizenship, and political or social outlook. The American and French revolutions, the empire of Napoleon I, and the nineteenth-century liberals had all agreed that Jews should be inte-grated into national communities that affirmed Enlightenment ideas and traditions. But these traditions were often denounced by a new generation of European ethnic national-ists, whose anti-Semitism contributed to a threatening political environment in which Jews debated the opportunities as well as the obstacles for both civic assimilation and the expanding Zionist movement.

This is a photograph of the Jewish journalist Theodor Herzl (1860–1904), who responded to anti-Semitic ideologies in central Europe and the anti-Semitism of the Dreyfus Affair in France by launching a new Zionist movement in late nineteenth-century Europe. Herzl organized the first international Zionist Congress and called for the creation of a new Jewish state in Palestine, which was at this time part of the Ottoman Empire and occupied by a predominantly Arab population.
(©Three Lions/Getty Images)

74.   THE WANING OF CLASSICAL LIBERALISM

The net effect of the political, economic, cultural, and intellectual trends described above was twofold. There was a continued advance of much that was basic to classical liberalism and at the same time a weakening of the grounds on which liberalism had firmly rested ever since the seventeenth and eighteenth centuries. A third effect might be noted too. Even where the essentials of liberalism persisted, in program and doctrine it underwent important changes; liberalism persisted but the classical type of liberalism was gradually transformed.

Liberalism changed

Classical liberalism, the liberalism in its heyday in the nineteenth century, went back at least as far as John Locke in the seventeenth century and the philosophes of the eighteenth. It found its highest nineteenth-century expression in political philosophers such as John Stuart Mill and in the outlook of political leaders such as William Gladstone. Classical liberalism had as its deepest principle the liberty of the individual. Man, or each individual person of human-kind according to liberals, was or could become a freestanding being. "Man" meant for them any member of the human race, homo sapiens, though in practice, except for a few like Mill, they were usually thinking of adult males. The very principle of liberalism, however, with its stress on the autonomy of the individual, also contributed to the growing movement for women's rights.

The individual, in this view, was not simply formed by race, class, religion, nation, or state but was ultimately independent of all such collective identities. Individuals did not hold their ideas because they belonged to particular ethnic, social, or cultural groups. They were viewed as autonomous persons who were capable of the free use of reason or of thinking independently, apart from their own interests, prejudices, or unconscious

The rational individual

drives. And, because this was the nature of rational human behavior, people of different interests and cultures could reasonably and profitably discuss their differences, analyze public issues, make compromises, and reach solutions by peaceable agreement. It was because they

The English political writer John Stuart
Mill, who appears here in a photograph
from the early 1850s, was one of the most
influential advocates of classical liberalism.
By the last years of his career, however, he
had also become a prominent supporter of
political rights for women and of social
reforms that broke with some of the individualism in classical liberal theory.

(Library of Congress [LC-USZ62-2939])

thought all persons potentially reasonable that liberals strongly favored the expansion of
education and legal protections for free speech and a free press. They opposed all imposition of force upon the individual, from physical torture to mental indoctrination.

In religion, liberals thought each individual should adopt any faith or no faith as
he or she chose and that religious institutions should play little or no part in public
affairs. In politics, they thought that governments should be constitutional and limited
in power, with individuals governing themselves through their chosen representatives,
with issues discussed and decided by the use of intelligence, both by the voters in election campaigns and by elected deputies in parliamentary debate. The will of a majority,
or larger number of individuals, was taken as decisive, with the understanding that the
minority (or "loyal opposition") might become a majority in its turn as individuals
changed opinions and voted in free elections. At first distrustful of democracy, fearing
the excesses of popular rule, and eager to limit political power and the suffrage to the
propertied classes, in the course of the nineteenth century liberals came to accept the
democratic principle of universal male suffrage, if not yet the vote for women. In economics, liberals viewed the whole world as peopled by individuals doing business with
one another—buying and selling, borrowing and lending, hiring and firing—without interference from governments and without regard to religion or politics, both of which were
thought to impose superficial differences upon the underlying uniformity of mankind.
The practical or expected consequences of liberalism were toleration, constitutionalism,
laissez-faire government policies, free trade, and an international economic system. It
was thought that all peoples would eventually progress to these same ends, though the
era's pervasive racism and the social-political systems of imperialism blocked the actual
application of liberal principles to the non-European peoples who lived under European
rule in old and new colonial empires.

There never was a time, even in one country, when all liberal ideas were simultaneously triumphant. Pure liberalism, like most other cultural and political ideologies, has never existed except as a doctrine. Advancing in one way, liberalism would be impeded or reversed in another. On the whole, however, in the decades before 1914, European states and cultures adopted a predominantly liberal framework for their internal institutions. But signs of the wane of liberalism set in clearly after 1880; some, like the changing conceptions of human behavior, the new interest in the irrational and the rising anti-Semitism, have already been mentioned.

The Decline of Nineteenth-Century Liberalism: Economic Trends

The free economy produced many hardships. Workers tossed by the ups and downs of a labor market and producers caught in the uncertainties of a world commodity market clamored for protection against exposure. A severe depression in 1873 sent prices and wages into a global collapse, and the economy did not fully recover until 1893. European farmers, both small French farm owners and big Junker landlords in East Germany, demanded tariff protection; they could not compete with the American Middle West or the steppes of South Russia, both of which after 1870 poured their cereals at low prices into Europe. The revival of tariffs and decline of free trade, very marked in Europe about 1880, thus began with the protection of agricultural interests. Industry soon demanded the same favors. In Germany the Junkers and the rising Rhineland industrialists joined forces in 1879 to extort a tariff from Bismarck. The French in 1892 adopted a high tariff to shelter both manufacturing and agricultural interests. The United States, rapidly industrializing but still facing the competition of manufactured goods from Europe, also adopted protective tariffs beginning in the 1860s, the earliest of all.

The Industrial Revolution was now definitely at work in countries other than Great Britain. There was increasing resistance to free trade among Europeans who had long bought manufactures from England, selling only raw materials and foodstuffs in return.

A revival of List

Everywhere there was a revival of the arguments of the German economist Friedrich List, who a half-century before, in his *National System of Political Economy* (1840), had branded free trade as a system mainly advantageous to the British and declared that no country could become strong, independent, or even fully civilized if it remained an agrarian supplier of unfinished goods. With Germany, the United States, and Japan manufacturing for export, a nationalist competition for world markets set in, contributing also to the drive for colonies and the new imperialism described in the next chapter. The new imperialism itself was another sign of the waning of liberalism, which had been largely indifferent to colonies.

Economic nationalism

In all these respects the division between politics and economics, postulated by liberals, began to fade. A kind of neomercantilism arose, recalling the attempts of governments in the seventeenth and eighteenth centuries to subordinate economic activity to political ends. A better term for this later period is economic nationalism, which became noticeable by 1900 and which expressed national responses to the global trading system. Nations struggled to strengthen themselves by tariffs, by trade competition, and by internal regulation, without regard to the effect upon other nations. Workers and business entrepreneurs were now very much affected in purely economic matters by the nation to which they belonged and by the government or laws under which they lived. People in all social classes looked for new kinds of collective security.

CHRONOLOGY OF NOTABLE EVENTS, 1859–1920

1859	Charles Darwin publishes *On the Origin of Species;* "evolution" becomes a key theme in modern intellectual life
1880s–1890s	Claude Monet and other artists portray the nuances of light and color in Impressionist paintings
1889	European socialist parties establish the Second International
1897	Theodor Herzl organizes the first international Zionist congress
1900	Sigmund Freud develops his theory of the unconscious mind in *The Interpretation of Dreams*
1905	Albert Einstein introduces the theory of relativity in physics
1907	Pablo Picasso advances his new Cubist style of painting in works such as *Les Demoiselles d'Avignon*
1918–1920	Women gain the right to vote in Britain, Germany, and the United States

It was of course to protect themselves against insecurity and abuse as individuals that workers formed labor unions. It was likewise to protect themselves against the uncertainties of uncontrolled markets that business interests began to merge; to concentrate in large corporations; or to form monopolies, trusts, or cartels. The rise of big business and organized labor undermined the practice of individual competition and free markets to which the theories of classical liberalism had been closely attached. Organized labor, socialist parties, universal male suffrage, and a sensitivity to social distress all obliged political leaders to intervene increasingly in economic matters. Factory codes became more detailed and better enforced. Social insurance, initiated by Bismarck, spread to other countries. Governments regulated the purity of foods and drugs. The social service state developed, a state assuming new responsibilities for the social and economic welfare of the mass of its own subjects or citizens. The "new" liberalism on both sides of the Atlantic, that of the British Liberals during the David Lloyd George era, of the Republican President Theodore Roosevelt and the Democratic President Woodrow Wilson in the United States, accepted an enlarged role for government in social and economic matters. Both Roosevelt and Wilson, and others in Europe, sought also to reestablish economic competition by government action against monopolies and trusts. The new liberals were generally more favorably disposed toward workers and the disadvantaged classes than toward business; the improvement of the workers' lot was increasingly viewed as an extension of liberalism's traditional concern with the dignity and worth of the individual person. The social service state with an enlarged role for government, remote as it was from classical liberalism, was embraced by many new liberals as a mechanism for the advancement of individual interests. Unlike the socialists, who generally stressed the social identities of economic classes and the collective interests of workers, the new liberals still emphasized the autonomy of individual citizens—even as they argued that such citizens needed the assistance of government interventions for education, safer working conditions, and fair wages. Advocates of the older or classical liberalism, however, often opposed the growing power of governments and centralized authority and were apprehensive for individual liberties.

The "new" liberalism and social services

Intellectual and Other Currents

Challenges to
Liberalism

Liberalism, both old and new, was undermined also by many developments in the field of thought described earlier in this chapter—Darwinian
evolution, the new psychology, and trends in philosophy and the arts.
Paradoxically, this great age of science found new evidence to show
how the human being was not a rational animal. Darwinian theory implied that the human
species was merely a highly evolved organism whose faculties could be described basically
as successful adaptations to an environment. Psychology seemed to teach that what was
called reason was often only a rationalization to justify material wants or emotional and
unconscious needs, and that conscious reflection dominated only a narrow part of human
behavior. Ideas themselves were said to be the products of cultural conditioning or of
social power. There were English ideas or Anglo-Saxon ideas, or bourgeois or progressive
or reactionary ideas. In politics, some believed that parties or nations with conflicting
interests could never reasonably agree on a program common to both, because neither
could ever get beyond the limitations of its own outlook. It became common to dismiss
the arguments of an adversary without further thought and without any expectation that
analytical thought could overcome difficulties. This insidious "anti-intellectualism" was
destructive to liberal principles. If, because of prior conditioning, it was impossible to
change one's mind, then there was no hope of settling matters by persuasion.

From the view that the human being was not essentially a rational creature, which
in itself was only a scientific attempt at a better understanding of human behavior, it was
but a short step deliberately to reject reason and to celebrate the irrational; to stress the
will, intuition, impulse, and emotion; and to place a new value on violence and conflict.
A philosophy of "realism," a kind of unreasoning faith in the constructive value of struggle
and a tough-minded rejection of ideas and ideals, spread across much of Europe. It was
not new. Marxism, since the 1840s, had taught that class war, latent or open, was the
driving force of history. Now Nietzsche rejected the religious descriptions of ethical virtues
in favor of personal courage and daring; and the Social Darwinists glorified the successful
and the dominant in all phases of human activity as the most "fit" in a perpetual struggle
for existence. Other thinkers embraced a frank irrationalism. Georges Sorel, the philosopher of syndicalism, in his *Reflections on Violence* in 1908, declared that violence was an
essential form of collective social action and that workers should believe in the "myth" of
a future general strike and the collapse of bourgeois civilization, even though it was known
to be only a myth. The function of thought, in this concept of the social myth, was to
keep people agitated and ready for action, not to achieve any correspondence with rational
or objective truth. Such ideas soon passed into the fascism and other activist movements
of the twentieth century which played on human fears.

Thus, the end of the nineteenth century, the greatest age of peace in Europe's history,
abounded in philosophies glorifying struggle. People who had never heard a shot fired in
anger solemnly announced that world history moved forward by violence and antagonism.

The popularity
of struggle

They said not merely that struggle existed (which would have been a
purely factual statement) but that struggle was a positive good through
which historical progress was to be accomplished. The popularity of
struggle was due not only to historical theories but also in part to actual
historical events. People remembered that before 1871 certain political
and social questions had been settled by force, that the revolutionary movements in 1848
and in the Paris Commune of 1871 had been put down by the military, and that the
unity of Italy and Germany, as well as of the United States, had been confirmed by war.

These miners, who were on strike at a coal mine in northern France in 1906, represent the militancy of the early twentieth-century European labor movement. Demanding better wages, better working conditions, and a greater role in public life, labor became an important force in the political cultures of all major European states during this era.

(©Roger-Viollet/The Image Works)

In addition, after 1871, all continental European states maintained large standing armies, the largest ever supported until then in peacetime eras.

In economic and political matters, even in England, the homeland of classical liberalism, there were numerous signs between 1900 and 1914 that the older liberalism was on the wane. Joseph Chamberlain led an English movement to return to tariff protection (to repeal, so to speak, the repeal of the Corn Laws); the tariff was rejected, but the new protectionism was strong enough to disorient the Conservative Party in 1906. The Liberal Party abandoned its traditional laissez-faire policy in sponsoring the labor legislation of the years following 1906. The new Labour Party required its members in Parliament to vote as directed by the party, thus initiating a system of party solidarity, eventually copied by others, that hardened the lines of opposition, denied that individuals should freely change sides, and hence reduced the significance of parliamentary discussions. The Irish nationalists had long used unparliamentary methods; in 1914, when Parliament at last enacted Irish home rule, the anti-Irish and conservative interests prepared to resist parliamentary action by force. The English suffragettes, despairing of ever getting the right to vote resorted to the amazingly "un-English," violent political actions noted earlier. And in 1911 and 1912 great railway and coal strikes disclosed the rising power of organized labor outside of Parliament and Britain's other governing institutions.

The persistence of liberalism

Still, it is the persistence of liberalism rather than its wane that should be emphasized at the close of two chapters on the European ascendancy in the half-century before 1914. Tariffs existed, but goods still circulated freely in world trade. Nationalism was heightened, but there was nothing like totalitarianism. Racist ideas were widespread and influential, but they still had more influence on the peoples and policies in colonial empires than on government policies within Europe itself. Anti-Semitism was increasingly vocal; but all governments except the Russian protected the rights of Jews, and the years from 1848 to 1914 were in fact the great period of Jewish integration into general society. The laissez-faire state was disappearing, but social legislation continued the humanitarian strain that had always been an essential part of liberalism. A few radicals called for social revolutions, but social democrats and working people were overwhelmingly loyal to parliamentary procedures and to their existing states. Doctrinaires exalted the grim beauty of war, but all governments down to 1914 tried to prevent war on the continent of Europe among the great powers. And despite the skepticism of some radical philosophers, artists, and intellectuals, there was still a supreme popular faith in progress.

 Suggested Further Readings can be found in the ebook, on Connect, or online at www.mhhe .com/kramer12e.

Chapter 16

EUROPE'S COLONIAL EMPIRES AND GLOBAL DOMINANCE, 1871–1914

The economic, political, and cultural institutions and ideas of modern European societies, as described in the last two chapters, spread steadily across much of the world after about 1870. The large European nation-states, which were now equipped with the overwhelming new powers of science and industry, gained empires for themselves throughout the globe. The history of Europe became more closely involved than ever before in the interconnected history of the whole world.

For a while the most active of the imperialist nation-states were located in Europe, and the 40 years preceding the First World War can therefore be described as the era of Europe's most far-reaching global power and influence. With the rise of the United States the term "Western" came into use, signifying "European" cultures in an expanded sense. The rapid economic development of Japan made the term Western an inappropriate description for many aspects of "modernity" or "modernization," as did other later developments in the cultures and societies outside of Europe. "Modernizing" social changes were transforming almost all parts of the world by the early twentieth century. Somewhat later, in the decades after 1950, Europeans and other social analysts around the globe began to speak of "developed" countries, in comparison with which many regions were seen as "less developed" or "developing." There also came to be a broad category of nations that constituted a so-called Third World. This diffuse Third World had no *The "Third World"* specific geographical identity, but the term referred to developing countries that were outside the European-American and Soviet-Russian spheres of direct influence during the geopolitical conflicts of the later twentieth century. All such terms were somewhat imprecise, but they represented efforts to deal with the same complex historical reality, namely, a bifurcation between "modern" and "developing" societies, or between rich

Chapter emblem: British soldiers in southern Africa during the Boer War, 1899–1902. (©Fox Photos/ Getty images)

countries and poor ones, or between industrialized and less industrialized nations, or between powerful economies and weak economies.

For the first time in human history, by 1900, it was possible to speak of a world civilization. Although always retaining important differences in languages, culture, and social practices, all countries were increasingly drawn into a world economy and a world market. The attributes of political and economic modernity were much the same everywhere—modern science, modern weapons of warfare, machine industry, fast communications, public education, efficient taxation and law enforcement, and modern public health, sanitation, and medicine.

But not all peoples participated in this global evolution on equal terms. It was the Europeans, or those who were rapidly building European-style industrial economies on other continents, who reaped the greatest rewards. Elsewhere, small tribal or regional societies and massive old civilizations alike began to come apart, reacting to the pressures of modern economic and social changes. Scientific ideas changed ways of thinking everywhere, as they had in Europe. In India, China, or Africa local industries often suffered, and many people found it harder than ever to subsist even at a low level within the new global system. The building of railways in China, for example, threw boatmen, carters, and innkeepers out of work. In India, the hand spinners and weavers of cotton could not compete in their own villages with the machine-made products of Lancashire. In parts of Africa, tribal groups that had lived by owning herds of cattle, moving from place to place to obtain grazing lands, found European farmers or plantation owners or mine companies occupying their country and using European colonial laws to make them give up their migratory habits. Peoples of all races began to produce commodities for export—rubber, raw cotton, jute, petroleum, tin, gold—which exposed both workers and merchants to the rise and fall of world prices. A depression in one part of the global economy tended to become a world depression, dragging all down alike.

Imperialism, or the European colonialism of the late nineteenth century, may be somewhat narrowly defined as the government of one people by another. As a specific form of political control, European imperialism proved to be transitory, weakening and disappearing in this form after the Second World War. But the broader economic and cultural aspects of the colonial systems continued to influence "postcolonial" societies long after they regained their political independence. Imperialism and empire-building became a new nineteenth-century phase in the worldwide spread of the industrial and scientific civilization that had originated in Europe's "inner zone." That it was not the last phase of such expansion became clear as the twentieth century unfolded. The subordinated peoples, forcibly introduced to European economic and cultural systems by imperialism, came to see a need for modernizing and industrializing their own countries and for using the methods or resources of European science, technology, and capital; but they wished to get rid of imperialists, govern themselves, and control the conditions under which modernization and borrowing should take place. In opposition to European empires, subject peoples began to assert their own cultural identities and also to draw upon influential European ideas that were flowing throughout the modern world: ideas of liberty and democracy, and of an anticapitalism that passed easily into socialism. Many such ideas were derived from the French and American revolutions, or from Marxism, or from the whole modern history of Europe itself; but these ideas were also transformed or challenged as they entered into and interacted with the political and cultural traditions of other civilizations.

The present chapter deals only with the imperialist phase of this global transformation. By one of the ironies of history, the imperialist rivalries of the European powers, while representing Europe's global dominance, also contributed to the disaster of the First World War, and so to the collapse of such political and economic supremacy as Europe had enjoyed.

Imperialism

75.   IMPERIALISM: ITS NATURE AND CAUSES

European civilization had shown a strong tendency to expand since the early medieval era. In the Middle Ages Latin Christendom spread by conquest and conversion to include the whole area from Spain to Finland, and Christian crusaders had even for a time controlled territories amid the mostly Muslim lands of the Middle East. Then came the age of overseas discoveries and the founding of early modern colonial empires, whose expansion and conflicts affected the balance of power within Europe throughout the seventeenth and eighteenth centuries and whose most far-reaching consequences included large-scale European immigration and the gradual "Europeanization" of societies and cultures in most of the Americas. At the same time European culture spread among the upper classes of Russia. The final defeat of Napoleon in 1815, however, left only one of the old colonial empires standing in any strength, namely, the British. For 60 years after the Napoleonic wars there were no significant colonial rivalries among the major European powers. In many circles there was an indifference to overseas empires. Under principles of free trade, it was thought unnecessary to exercise political influence in areas in which one did business. During these years, however, the French took control of Algeria, the British strengthened their Indian Empire, the Dutch developed Java and the neighboring islands more intensively, and the Western powers "opened" Japan and began to move into the coastal territories of China. Among these various colonial interventions, the French occupation of Algeria may have had the most significant influence within a European society. The French army waged a series of brutal military campaigns in the 1830s and 1840s to suppress strong Muslim opposition to colonization; and a stream of immigrants began to flow from France into the Algerian towns and countryside that the army gradually brought under French control. Napoleon III viewed France's expansion across North Africa as another opportunity to demonstrate his own imperial grandeur, which he asserted in the course of two highly publicized trips to Algeria during the 1860s. But the French conquest of Algeria and the development of European colonies in Asia did not lead to overt imperial conflicts among Europeans, and there was no systematic imperial program, doctrine, or "ism."

Rather suddenly, about 1870 or 1880, colonial questions came again to the fore—driven in part by the rising power of the recently consolidated German Empire and French reactions to the loss of Alsace and Lorraine after the Franco-Prussian War. In the short space of two decades, by 1900, the advanced industrial countries partitioned most of the earth among themselves. A world map by 1900 showed their colonial possessions in some nine or ten colors, stretching widely across Asia, Africa, and islands in every ocean.

The New Imperialism

The new imperialism differed both economically and politically from the colonialism of earlier times. The older empires had been maritime and mercantile. European traders in India, Java, or south China had simply purchased the wares brought to them by local merchants or

New imperialism vs. old colonialism

commercial agents and as produced by the local organization of labor and by local technologies. They operated on a kind of cash-and-carry basis. European governments had few direct territorial ambitions in Asia beyond the protection of way stations and trading centers. To these generalizations America, the Philippines, and Australia had been exceptions. The societies in these areas of the world had neither native states that Europeans respected, nor native industries in which Europeans were interested. Europeans had therefore developed territorial claims, invested capital, brought in their own methods of production, and often imported enslaved labor, especially in the then-booming sugar islands of the West Indies.

The new imperialism changed the earlier patterns of European economic and political involvements in Asia and Africa. Europeans were no longer content simply to purchase what local workers and merchants provided. They wanted goods of a kind or in a quantity that preindustrial handicraft methods could not supply. They moved into the poorest and least industrialized countries more thoroughly. They invested capital in them, setting up mines, plantations, docks, warehouses, factories, refineries, railroads, river steamships, and banks. They built offices, homes, hotels, clubs, and cool mountain resorts for European officials and visitors. Taking over the productive economic life of the country, they transformed large elements of the local population into the wage employees of foreign owners and so introduced the class relations and problems of industrial Europe in a form accentuated by racial differences. Or they lent money to non-European rulers—the khedive of Egypt, the shah of Persia, the emperor of China—to enable them to hold up their tottering thrones or simply to live with more pleasure and magnificence than they could from their usual revenues. Europeans thus developed a huge financial stake in governments and economic enterprises outside their own nations and commercial networks within Europe.

To secure these investments, and for other reasons, in contrast to what had happened under the older colonialism, the Europeans now aspired to political and territorial

Political and territorial domination

domination. Some areas became outright colonies, directly governed by European states and their appointed government officials. Others became protectorates: here the native chief, sultan, bey, rajah, or prince was maintained and protected against internal upheaval or external conquest. A European "resident" or "commissioner" usually told him what to do, thereby safeguarding European interests through a kind of indirect rule. In other regions, as in China or Persia, where no single European state could make good its claims against the others, they arranged to divide the country into "spheres of influence," each European power having advisory privileges and investment and trade opportunities within its own sphere. The sphere of influence was the vaguest of all forms of imperial control; supposedly, it left the country independent, but each sphere of outside influence undermined the sovereignty or local power of the state in which it was established.

An enormous differential opened up, about 1875, between the power of European and non-European states. Queen Elizabeth had dealt with the Great Mogul of the Indian sub-continent with genuine respect, at least in part because his revenues in the early seventeenth century were some 20 times greater than those of the English monarchy. Even Napoleon had pretended to regard the shah of Persia as an equal. Then came the Industrial Revolution in Europe, iron and steel ships, heavier naval guns, and more accurate rifles. Democratic and nationalist movements produced large states and unified European peoples who gave service and financial support to their governments. Seemingly endless wealth, with modern administration, allowed European governments to tax, borrow, and spend without apparent limit. The modern nation-states loomed as enormous power complexes without precedent in the world's history. At the same time it so happened that all the principal non-European empires were internally divided or falling into political decay. They were receiving a minimum of support from their own subjects. As in the eighteenth century when the disintegration of the Mogul Empire had enabled the British to take over India, so in the nineteenth century the political weakness and vulnerabilities of the sultan of Turkey, the sultan of Zanzibar, the shah of Persia, the emperor of China, and the shogun of Japan made European intervention remarkably easy. Only the Japanese were

European access to colonial territories in the period of the "new imperialism" often depended on the construction of new railroads, which carried both people and goods into and out of the interior districts of the European colonies. This picture portrays the arrival of a locomotive that a team of elephants pulled into central India when a new railroad track was built in the region of Indore during the 1870s.
(©SSPL/Getty Images)

able to revolutionize their government in time to ward off imperialist penetration. Even the Japanese, however, were restricted by early treaties that controlled their tariff policies until after 1900.

So great was the difference in the sheer mechanics of power during this era that a mere show of force usually allowed the Europeans to impose their will. A garrison of only 75,000 troops long held India for the British. Numerous sporadic little wars were constantly fought—

Europeans impose their will

Afghan wars, Burmese wars, Zulu wars—which affected local populations but which passed unnoticed by Europeans in the home country. Such wars might be compared to the violent operations of the United States army against the Indians of the western plains, but they did not become national military mobilizations or total wars that affected most national citizens. The Spanish-American War of 1898 and the Boer War of 1899 were also wars of colonial type, fought between entirely unequal parties. Often a show of naval strength was enough to gain European control over a new territory. It was the classic age of the punitive bombardment. In 1856 the British consul at Guangzhou, to punish acts of violence against Europeans in southern China, called upon the local British admiral to bombard that Chinese city. In 1863 the British bombarded the Japanese province of Satsuma, and in 1864 an allied force including Americans bombarded Choshu—precipitating revolution in Japan. Similarly, Alexandria was bombarded in 1882 and Zanzibar in 1896. The usual consequence of such "gunboat diplomacy" was that the local ruler signed a treaty, reorganized the government, or accepted a European (usually British) adviser.

Incentives and Motives

Behind the new imperial aggressiveness lay many pressures and motives. The Europeans could not maintain for themselves the style of life to which they had become accustomed except by bringing the rest of the world and its resources within their economic orbit. But many other cultural and social concerns also drove Europeans into distant, unknown places. Catholic and Protestant groups sent growing numbers of missionaries to remote regions, where they sometimes got into trouble with the local people and where some missionaries were even killed. Public opinion in the home countries, soon learning of such events by ocean cable, might clamor for political action to suppress such outbreaks of anti-Christian violence. Similarly, scientists required geographical expeditions for their observations and discoveries. Wealthy Europeans traveled more, now that travel was so easy; they hunted tigers or elephants, or simply went to see the sights. It seemed only reasonable to Europeans at the close of the nineteenth century that all Europeans wherever they might choose to go should enjoy the personal security and the orderly legal procedures that colonial governments sought to provide for the Europeans who visited or lived in their overseas empires.

Raw materials

Economically, European life required material goods, many of which only tropical regions could supply. Even the working classes now drank tea or coffee every day. After the American Civil War Europe relied for its cotton increasingly on Africa and the East. Rubber and petroleum became staple needs. The lowly jute, which grew only in India, was used to make burlap, twine, carpets, and the millions of jute bags employed in commerce. The lordly coconut tree had innumerable common uses, which led to its intensive cultivation in the Dutch Indies. Various parts of it could be eaten, or manufactured into bags, brushes, cables, rope, sails, or doormats or converted into coconut oil, which in turn went into the making of candles, soap, margarine, and many other products.

Industrial countries also attempted to sell their own products, and the most fervent imperialists often emphasized the urgent necessity of finding new overseas markets. The rapid industrialization of Germany, the United States, Japan, and other countries, led to new economic competition among these countries and with Great Britain for foreign trade. A slow decline in prices after 1873 meant that a business firm had to sell more goods to turn over the same amount of money. The advanced industrial countries, as we have seen, responded to this commercial challenge by raising tariffs to keep out each other's products. It was therefore argued that each industrialized nation must develop a colonial empire, an area of "sheltered markets," as the phrase went in England, in which the home country would supply manufactured goods in return for raw materials. The idea was to create a large self-sufficient trading unit, embracing various climates and types of resources, protected if necessary from outside competition by tariffs, guaranteeing a mar-

Neomercantilism

ket for all its members and wealth and prosperity for the home country. This phase of imperialism is often called neomercantilism, because it revived in substance the mercantilism, or national economic systems, of the sixteenth to the eighteenth centuries.

The profit motive

Purely financial considerations also characterized the new European imperialism. Money invested in poorer, less industrialized countries by the close of the nineteenth century brought a higher rate of return than if invested in the more industrialized ones. For this there were many reasons, including the cheap cost of labor in non-European regions, the heavy and unsatisfied demand for non-European products in wealthier countries, and the greater risk of losses in areas where European ideas of law and order did not prevail. By 1900 western Europe

Europeans often described their colonial empires as systems that advanced a "civilizing mission." This "mission" consisted (in the European view) mainly of promoting European methods of education, commerce, labor, and legal justice, all of which provoked both resistance and adaptations among colonized peoples. This image portrays an African leader signing a treaty with French officials who would have been looking for French privileges and economic opportunities in the surrounding lands and in the community of people that was observing this event.

(©Prisma/UIG/Getty Images)

and the northeastern United States were equipped with their basic industrial apparatus. Their railway networks and first factories had become well-established. Opportunities for investment in these countries were more stable but less likely to produce the highest possible profits. At the same time, these countries were accumulating capital that was available for new investments. In the midcentury most exported capital was British-owned. By the close of the century more French, German, American, Dutch, Belgian, and Swiss investors were investing or lending outside their own borders. In 1850, most exported capital went to build up Europe, the United States, Canada, Australia, or Argentina. By 1900 more of it was going to undeveloped regions in other parts of the world. This capital was the property of individual small savers or of large banking combinations. Investors in Europe and North America preferred to see European political control over the parts of Asia, Africa, or Latin America in which their railroads, mines, plantations, government loans, or other investments were situated. Hence the profit motive, or desire to invest surplus capital, promoted imperialism.

This analysis was put forward by critics of the global economic system such as the English socialist J. A. Hobson, who wrote an influential book on imperialism in 1903, and later by Lenin, in his

Socialist critics

Imperialism, the Highest Stage of World Capitalism, written in 1916. They ascribed imperialism primarily to the economic need for profitable investments of surplus capital and condemned it on socialist grounds. Hobson argued that a change in the domestic economy of the industrialized nations would remove the main motive for imperialism: if more of the national income went to workers as wages, and less of it to capitalists as interest and dividends, or if wealthy people were more heavily taxed and the money used for social welfare, there would be no surplus of capital and no economic rationale for imperialism. Because the working class, if this were done, would also have more purchasing power, it would be less necessary to look endlessly for new markets outside the country. But the surplus capital explanation of imperialism was not entirely convincing. That investors and exporters were instrumental in the rise of imperialism was very true, and yet it was more doubtful that imperialism arose essentially from the capitalists' pressure to invest abroad. Perhaps even more basic was Europe's need for imports—only by enormous imports could Europe sustain its dense population, complex industry, and high standard of living. It was the demand for such imports—cotton, cocoa, coffee, copper, and the like drawn from the colonies—that made investment in the colonies financially profitable. Moreover, non-Europeans themselves often sought European capital, glad though the European lenders were to lend it at high rates. In 1890 this might mean merely that a shah or sultan wanted to build himself a new palace, but the need of non-Europeans for Western capital was basic, nor was it to decline in later times. Lastly, the imperialism of some countries, notably Russia and Italy, which had little capital and few modern-type capitalists of their own, could not reasonably be attributed to pressure for lucrative foreign investments.

For the British, however, the capitalistic incentive was of great importance. We have seen how the British, in 1914, had $20 billion invested outside Great Britain, a quarter of all their wealth. About half, or $10 billion, was invested in the British Empire. Only a tenth of French foreign investments was in French colonies. French investment in the colonial world in general, however, including Egypt, Suez, South Africa, and Asia in addition to the French colonies, amounted to about a fifth of all French foreign investments. Only an infinitesimal fraction of German foreign investment in 1914 was in German colonies, which were of slight economic value. A fifth of German foreign investments, however, was placed in Africa, Asia, and the Ottoman Empire. These sums are enough to suggest the economic pressures upon the European governments to assert political influence in Africa, Turkey, or China. In addition, French investors had in 1914 a huge stake in the Russian Empire.

Foreign economic interests in Russia

Russia, an imperial power with respect to adjoining countries in the Balkans and Asia, occupied an almost semicolonial status with respect to western Europe. The tsardom until its demise in 1917, not unlike the Ottoman sultanate or the Qing dynasty in China, increasingly depended on foreign loans, predominantly French. The French in 1914 had lent over $2 billion to Russia, more than to all colonial regions combined. For these huge outlays the motivation was at least as much political as economic. The French government urged French banks to buy Russian bonds. The aim was not merely to make a profit for bankers and small investors but to build up and hold together a military ally against Germany.

Politics went along with economics in the whole process of imperialist expansion. National security, both political and economic, was as important for the advocates of imperialism as the accumulation of private wealth. So, too, was the growing concern in many quarters over the economic security and welfare of the working classes.

Joseph Chamberlain

The ideas of the British statesman Joseph Chamberlain (1836–1914) illustrated how these motives entered into imperialist thinking.

Chamberlain, father of Neville Chamberlain, who was to be prime minister of Britain in the years just prior to the Second World War, began as a Birmingham manufacturer, the type of man who a generation before would have been a staunch free trader and upholder of laissez-faire. Discarding the old individualism, he came to believe that the national community should and could take better care of its members and that the British community (or empire) could advance the welfare of Britons. As mayor of Birmingham he introduced a kind of municipal socialism, including public ownership of utilities. As colonial secretary from 1895 to 1903, he preached Britain's need for "a great self-sustaining and self-protecting empire" in an age of rising international competition—a worldwide British trading area, developed by British capital, which would give a secure source of raw materials and food, markets for exports, and a steady level of profits, wages, and employment.

Chamberlain was thus concerned about the movement toward political independence in Canada, New Zealand, and the Australian Commonwealth. For these dominions he favored complete self-government, but he hoped that, once assured of their own political autonomy, they would reknit their ties with each other and with Great Britain. Britain and its dominions, in Chamberlain's view, should pool their resources for economic well-being as well as for military defense. The dominions had already levied tariffs against British manufacturers in order to build up their own. Chamberlain urged the dominions to charge a lower duty on British wares than on the same wares coming from foreign countries. In return, he even proposed that Great Britain adopt a protective tariff, so that it might then favor Canadian or Australian goods by offering them a lower rate. His plan was to bind the empire together through a kind of global tariff union, or system of "imperial preference." Because Britain imported mainly meat and cereals from the dominions, Chamberlain was obliged to recommend a tariff even upon these products—to "tax the people's food," repudiating the core principle of Free Trade upon which the British economy had rested for half a century. The proposal was rejected. Chamberlain died in 1914, his goal unaccomplished. But after the First World War the British Empire, or Commonwealth of Nations, followed closely the proposals he had mapped out.

Whether the economic welfare and security of the European working classes was advanced by imperialism is still debated. It is probable that the worker in western Europe did gain some economic benefits from imperialism. Socially conservative imperialists were joined in this belief by thinkers of the extreme Left. Marx himself, followed by Lenin, thought that the European worker obtained higher real wages through the inflow of low-priced colonial goods and commodities. To Marxists this was unfortunate, for it gave European workers a vested interest in imperialism, made the European proletariat "opportunistic" (i.e., unrevolutionary), and blocked the formation of a united world proletariat of all races.

Working classes and imperialism

Another imperialist argument much heard at the time held that European countries must acquire colonies to which surplus population could migrate without altogether abandoning the native land. It seemed unfortunate, for example, that so many Germans or Italians emigrating to the United States should be lost to the fatherland. This argument was purely specious. No European country after 1870 acquired any colony to which European families in any numbers wished to move. The millions who were still leaving Europe continued to go mainly to the Americas, where new European colonies could not be founded.

The competitive nature of the European state system introduced other almost exclusively political features to the new imperialism. The European states sought constantly to guard their security against each other. They wanted to keep some kind of balance among themselves, in the overseas world as in Europe. Hence, as in the scramble for Africa, one government often hurriedly annexed territory simply for fear that another might do so

This photograph of Indian servants bringing tea to British officials suggests the social hierarchy and the pattern of cross-cultural relations in colonial India at the end of the nineteenth century.
(©Popperfoto/Getty Images)

first. Or again, colonies came to have an intangible but momentous value in symbolism and prestige. To have colonies was a criterion of national greatness. It was the sign of having arrived as a Great Power. Britain and France had held colonies for centuries. Therefore the new powers that emerged after the 1860s—Germany, Italy, Japan, and the United States—came to believe they had to have colonies also.

Diplomacy and imperialism

Imperialism as Crusade

Imperialism arose from the commercial, industrial, financial, scientific, political, journalistic, intellectual, religious, and humanitarian impulses of Europe compounded together. It was a new outward expansion of the modern European states, economies, and cultures that had forcefully asserted their power and influence around the world for almost four centuries; and its advocates claimed that European colonialism would bring civilization and enlightenment to those who still sat in darkness. Faith in "modern civilization" had become a kind of substitute religion. Imperialism was its crusade.

So the British spoke of the White Man's Burden; the French, of their *mission civilisatrice;* the Germans, of diffusing *Kultur;* the Americans, of the "blessings of Anglo-Saxon protection." Social Darwinism and popular anthropology taught the racist doctrine that the white races were "fitter" or more gifted than the peoples of other races. Some imperialists gave less emphasis to "race" as a rationale for empires, turning instead to cultural justifications for the colonization of distant peoples and societies. They argued that the "backwardness" of non-European societies was due to historic, and hence temporary, causes but that for a long period into the future the more "civilized" Europeans must keep a guardianship over their darker protégés. The psychology of imperialism contained strands of idealism and humanitarianism as well as greed, and numerous Europeans went to the colonies to build schools or hospitals rather than railroads or mines. Young people of good family left the pleasant lands of Devonshire or Poitou to spend | *Trade missions* | long and lonely years in hot, isolated places, sustained by the thought that they were advancing the work of humanity. They saw their colonial labors as contributions to a humanitarian campaign to spread modern education; to put down slave raiding, torture, and famine; to combat degrading superstitions; to fight the diseases of neglect and filth; and to promote the ideas and institutions of legal justice (even though colonial legal systems did not treat the colonizers and native people in the same way). But these accomplishments, however real, went along all too obviously with European self-interest and were expressed with unbearable complacency and gross condescension to other cultures and the larger part of the global human population. As Rudyard Kipling wrote in 1899 (in his exhortation to Americans after their taking over of the Philippines):

> *Take up the White Man's burden—*
> *Send out the best ye breed—*
> *Go bind your sons to exile,*
> *To serve your captives' need;*
> *To wait in heavy harness,*
> *On fluttered folk and wild—*
> *Your new-caught sullen peoples,*
> *Half devil and half child.*

Responding to such demeaning ideas and to the imperial interventions that they encouraged, the colonized peoples in Asia and Africa would soon launch anticolonial movements that reshaped modern global history and also changed the views of imperialism within Europe itself. During the decades of new imperial expansion before 1914, however, people living in the newly colonized societies were generally unable to resist the European powers or to counter the popular fusion of nationalism and imperialism in most European cultures. Imperialism thus repeated similar themes and practices throughout the modern world, but we must now discuss some regional examples to see how the European ascendancy evolved somewhat differently in specific places, conflicts, and cross-cultural exchanges.

76.   THE DISSOLUTION OF THE OTTOMAN EMPIRE

The Ottoman Empire in the 1850s

Among all the diverse parts of the non-European world, the Ottoman, or Turkish, Empire was the nearest to Europe and the most directly connected to modern European history. The major European states had a long history of relations with the Ottoman Empire because of its geographical proximity and also because of its strategic dominance in the

Historical Interpretations and Debates
The Rationales and Paradoxes of Modern European Imperialism

Historians have often emphasized the economic and geo-political interests that contributed to the late nineteenth-century resurgence of European imperialism, but the cultural justifications for this "new imperialism" have also attracted historical attention in recent decades. Many Europeans believed that colonization brought humanitarian assistance and "civilizing progress" to non-European peoples, even as the imperial systems deprived them of political and economic independence. Compare the ways in which Antoinette M. Burton and Christopher L. Miller analyze the cultural presuppositions and paradoxes that emerged when British feminists and French liberals supported imperialism in Asia and Africa.

Antoinette M. Burton, "The White Woman's Burden: British Feminists and 'The Indian Woman,' 1865–1915" (1992)

[A] sense of national and racial superiority based on Britain's imperial status was an organizing principle of Victorian culture.

Middle-class Victorian feminists generally shared these assumptions. . . . Despite both their genuine concern for the condition of Indian women *and* the feminist reform activities of prominent Indian women during this period, many middle-class British feminists viewed the women of the East not as equals but as unfortunates in need of saving by their British feminist 'sisters.' . . .

Liberal bourgeois feminism in Britain contained a number of premises which made it . . . compatible with and easily fueled by an imperial ethos. First, both were grounded in the idea of superiority, rooted in the ostensibly feminine virtues of nurturing, child-care, and purity. . . .

Secondly, feminist argument, no less than imperial apologia, was preoccupied with race preservation, racial purity, and racial motherhood. . . .

Lastly, feminism, like imperialism, was structured around the idea of moral responsibility. . . . Feminism and female reform ideology virtually dictated the existence of dependent clients on whom to confer aid, comfort, and (hopefully) the status of having been saved. . . .

British women [therefore] felt they had a special responsibility toward Indian women. . . .

Christopher L. Miller, "Unfinished Business: Colonialism in Sub-Saharan Africa and the Ideals of the French Revolution" (1994)

[A] certain pattern of forced and dubious reconciliation [developed] between the ideals of the [French] Revolution and France's nationalistic and imperialistic tendencies. The pattern is clear: the ideals of the Revolution, by the very fact that they are taken to be immutable and immortal, are pressed into service as justifications for various policies of domination and exploitation . . . French colonialism passes [in the nineteenth century] for *the exportation of the ideals of 1789.*

This idea, as paradoxical as it may seem, served as the most compelling rationale for colonialism. . . . [T]he ideal of liberty, as it was translated into nineteenth-century contexts, became a banner of *liberalism* under which ardent republicans . . . advocated colonial conquest and rule. . . .

Because France embodies an ideal [of liberty], France can only do good by advancing its own self-interests in the world: idealism and nationalism will both be served. . . .

Once France is understood to be a force for moral good, and so long as France's ideals are not put into question, France can behave as it wants. . . .

A discourse of enlightenment and progress was the key to the success of colonialism; a misguided idealism, referring to either the *mission civilisatrice* or to national prestige, seems to have held the floor in the [French] debate on colonialism. . . .

Antoinette M. Burton ... *(contd. . . .)*	**Christopher L. Miller** ... *(contd. . . .)*
Historians must not lose sight of the fact that feminism(s) are and always will be as much quests for power as they are battles for rights. Nineteenth-century feminists sought empowerment by a variety of means—education, the vote, welfare legislation—not the least of which was by allying their cause with British imperial rule.	The French colonial system . . . built itself over a myth of the Revolution, while suppressing the truth that . . . you can't dominate and liberate at the same time.

Sources: Antoinette Burton, "The White Woman's Burden: British Feminists and 'The Indian Woman,' 1865-1915," in Nupur Chaudhuri and Margaret Strobel, eds., *Western Women and Imperialism: Complicity and Resistance* (Bloomington: Indiana University Press, 1992), pp. 137-139, 152; Christopher L. Miller, "Unfinished Business: Colonialism in Sub-Saharan Africa and the Ideals of the French Revolution," in Joseph Klaits and Michael H. Haltzel, eds., *The Global Ramifications of the French Revolution* (New York and Cambridge: Woodrow Wilson Center Press and Cambridge University Press, 1994), pp. 107, 112-113, 117, 126.

eastern Mediterranean. The empire still extended in the nineteenth century from Hungary and the Balkan Peninsula to the south Russian steppes and from French-controlled Algeria to the Persian Gulf. The empire was not at all like a modern (or imagined) European nation-state. Immense in extent, it was a complex social and political system within which people belonged to diverse and often overlapping religious communities. Most of its people were Muslim, including both orthodox Muslims and reformist sects such as the Druzes and the Wahhabis; some were Jews who had always lived in the Middle East; many were Christian, principally Greek Orthodox and Armenian, who had also always lived there. The Turks were the ruling class and Islam was the dominant religion. Only Muslims, for example, could serve in the army; non-Muslims were known as *raya,* the "flock" or "herd"—they paid the taxes. Persons holding different religious beliefs lived side by side, each under the laws, courts, and customs of his or her own religious group. Religious officials—patriarchs, bishops, rabbis, imams, ulemas—were responsible to the Turkish government for their own people, over whom therefore they had a great deal of authority.

Western Europeans had their own special rights. Roman Catholic clergy, living mainly in Palestine, looked to the pope in religion and to France for a mundane protector. European merchants enjoyed the regime of the "capitulations," or special rights granted by the Ottoman government in numerous treaties going back to the sixteenth century. By the capitulations Turkey could not levy a tariff

The capitulations

of more than 8 percent on imported goods. Europeans were exempt from most taxes. Cases involving two Europeans, civil or criminal, could be settled only in a court held by a European consul under European law. Disputes between a European and an Ottoman subject were settled in Turkish courts, but in the presence of a European observer.

The Ottoman Empire, in short, lacked the European idea of nationalism or national unity. European ideas of sovereignty and a uniform law for all its peoples were also absent, as was the idea of the secular state, or of law and citizenship separated from religion. More generally, the empire had fallen behind modern industrial nations in its scientific, mechanical, material, humanitarian, and administrative achievements.

Europeans began to call Ottoman Turkey the "sick man of Europe," and its declining power led to what European diplomats referred to as the "Eastern Question." Since the loss of Hungary in 1699 the Ottoman

The "sick man of Europe"

Empire had entered on a long process of territorial disintegration (see map, p. 675). The empire's survival over the following centuries was partly due to the competing interests of European states that wanted to preserve the European balance of power. But by the 1850s the empire was falling away at the edges. Russia had advanced in the Crimea and the Caucasus. Serbia was autonomous, Greece was independent, and Romania was recognized as a self-governing principality. The French occupied Algeria. A native Arab dynasty, the Sauds, of the Wahhabi reform sect, ruled over much of Arabia. A former Turkish governor of Egypt, Mehemet Ali, had established his family as hereditary rulers or "khedives" in the Nile Valley. Notwithstanding these changes, the Ottoman Empire in the 1850s was still huge. It encompassed not only the Turkish or Anatolian Peninsula, including Armenia and territories south of the Caucasus, but also the central portion of the Balkan Peninsula from Constantinople (as Istanbul was still generally called) to the Adriatic where many Christians of Slavic nationality lived, Tripoli (as Libya was then called) in North Africa, and the islands of Crete and Cyprus. Egypt and Arabia, though autonomous, were still under the nominal suzerainty of the sultan.

The Crimean War of 1854–1856 opened a new phase in Ottoman history as in that of Europe. We have seen how this war was followed by the consolidation of great nation-states in Europe and how the United States, Canada, and Japan consolidated or modernized themselves at the same time. Ottoman Turkish reformers tried to do the same between 1856 and 1876.

The Crimean War

In the Crimean War the Turks were on the winning side, but the war affected them as it affected Russia, the loser. Collaboration with the major European powers exposed the Ottoman Empire's military and political weakness and pointed to the need for better internal organization. The outcome of the war was taken to prove the superiority of the systems in England and France. It was therefore on western European lines that Turkish reformers wished to remodel. It was not merely that they wanted to defend themselves against another of the periodic wars with Russia. They wished also to avoid being periodically saved from Russia by the countries of western Europe, a process which if continued could lead only to French or British control of Turkey.

Attempts at Reform and Revival, 1856–1876

In 1856 the Ottoman government issued the Hatt-i Humayun, the most far-reaching Turkish reform edict of the century. Its purpose was to create an Ottoman national citizenship for all persons in the empire. It abolished the civil authority of religious hierarchs. Equality before the law was guaranteed, as was eligibility to public office without regard to religion. The army was opened to Christians and Muslims alike, and steps were even taken to include both in nonsegregated military units. The edict announced a reform of taxes, security of property for all, abolition of torture, and reform of prisons. It promised to combat the chronic evils of graft, bribery, and extortion by public officials.

For 20 years there were serious efforts to make the reform decree of 1856 a reality. European and liberal ideas circulated freely, gaining new influence in Ottoman society. Newspapers were founded. Writers called for a national Turkish revival, threw off the old Persian style in literature, composed histories of the Ottomans, and translated Enlightenment-era French authors such as Montesquieu and Rousseau. Foreign loans entered the country. Railroads connected Constantinople with cities on the Danube River. Abdul Aziz (1861–1876), the first sultan to travel to Europe, visited Vienna, London, and the great Paris world's fair of 1867. But powerful resistance developed against such

The Ottoman Sultan Abdul Hamid II came to power in alliance with a movement for constitutional reform, but he soon became an autocratic ruler who violently suppressed his political opponents, massacred ethnic minorities, and resisted the currents of modern social and cultural life that were coming into his empire from Europe. He is pictured here in his royal attire, sitting alone in the isolated style that characterized his long reign.

(©Stefano Bianchetti/Corbis/Getty Images)

radical changes. Also, the best efforts of the Turkish reformers miscarried. There were not yet enough Turks with the skills or experience in the technical work required, and there was too much dependence on borrowed money. In 1874 the Ottoman government, having recklessly overborrowed, repudiated half its debt.

A new and more determined reforming minister, Midhat Pasha, goaded by opposition and desperate at the weight of inertia, deposed Abdul Aziz in 1876, deposed the latter's nephew three months later,

Abdul Hamid II

and set up Abdul Hamid II as sultan. The new sultan at first briskly went along with the reform movement, proclaiming a new constitution in 1876. It declared the Ottoman Empire to be indivisible, and promised personal liberty, freedom of conscience, freedom of education and the press, and parliamentary government. The first Turkish parliament met in 1877. Its members addressed themselves to the project of political reform. But they reckoned without Abdul Hamid, who in 1877 revealed his true intentions. The sultan got rid of Midhat, packed off the parliament, and threw away the constitution.

Repression after 1876

Abdul Hamid reigned for 33 years, from 1876 to 1909. For all this time he lived in fear and isolation, fighting ferociously against modernizing forces that he did not accept or understand. The sultan feared that introducing the new science and constitutional forms of government might ruin the whole Ottoman system. He dreaded any moves to check his own whim or power. He was

Abdul Hamid's fears

thrown into a panic by Turkish reformers, who became increasingly driven to terrorist acts in the face of his opposition. Driven away by Abdul Hamid, some tens of thousands of Young Turks, the activists of the reform era before 1876, or their children and successors, lived in exile in Paris, London, or Geneva, plotting their return to Turkey and vengeance upon Abdul the Damned. The sultan was frightened also by agitation among his non-Turkish subjects. Nationalist Armenians, Bulgars, Macedonians, and Cretans defied and taunted the Ottoman authorities, which responded with the Bulgarian massacres of 1876 and the Armenian massacres of 1894. These horrible butcheries of thousands of peasants by Ottoman troops came as a shock to Europeans, who were becoming more critical of such violence within their own nation-states. Last, and with good reason, Abdul Hamid feared the imperialist European powers whose expansionist ambitions focused increasingly upon his dissolving empire.

A thoroughly reformed, consolidated, and modernized Ottoman Empire was far from what the European governments desired. They might wish for humanitarian reforms in Turkey, for more efficiency and honesty in Turkish government and finance, and even for a Turkish parliamentary system. Such demands were eloquently expressed by liberals like Gladstone in England. But no one in Europe wanted what Turkish reformers wanted, a reinvigorated Ottoman Empire that could deal with Europe politically as an equal.

The Russo-Turkish War of 1877–1878: The Congress of Berlin

In Russia, since the time of Catherine II in the eighteenth century, many had dreamed of installing Russian power on the shores of the Bosporus Strait. Constantinople they called Tsarigrad, the Imperial City, which (in their view) Orthodoxy was to liberate from the infidel. Crusading motives, in this nationalist and imperialist age, now reappeared anew in the form of Pan-Slavism. This doctrine was preached by some of Russia's leading nineteenth-century intellectuals, including the writer Nikolay Danilevsky, whose book *Russia and Europe,* published in 1869, predicted that Russia would enter into a long war with Europe. The war would be followed by the creation of a grand federation of the East that would bring Slavs, Greeks, Hungarians, and parts of Ottoman Turkey under Russian control. Danilevsky's theories of Pan-Slavism were patronized by the Russian government because they diverted attention from internal and revolutionary troubles. As for the Slav peoples of the Ottoman Empire, they were willing to use Russian Pan-Slavism as a means of combating their imperial Turkish rulers. Insurrection against the Ottoman Empire broke out in the Balkans during the mid-1870s. In 1877 Russia declared war, launching a military campaign against the Ottoman Empire for the sixth time in a hundred years.

Pan-Slavism

The British, who had fought Russia to protect Ottoman interests in 1854, were prepared to do so again. A number of recent developments added to their apprehension. The Suez Canal was completed in 1869, and the Canal's location within the Ottoman Empire restored the Middle East to its ancient position as a crossroads of world trade. In 1874 Benjamin Disraeli, a Conservative and an imperialist, became prime minister of Great Britain. By a sudden coup in the following year he was able to buy up, from the almost bankrupt ruling khedive of Egypt, 44 percent of the shares of the Suez Canal Company. In 1876, in a dramatic affirmation of imperial splendor, he had Queen Victoria take the title of empress of India. British commercial and financial interests in India and the Far East were growing, and the Suez Canal, of which the British government was now the principal stockholder, was becoming the economic lifeline of the empire. But the Ottoman state, and hence the whole Middle East, was now in danger of collapsing as the Russian armies advanced rapidly through the Balkans, reached Constantinople, and forced the Turks to sign a treaty in 1878, the treaty of San Stefano. By this treaty Turkey ceded to Russia

The treaty of San Stefano

strategic territory on the south side of the Caucasus Mountains, gave full independence to Serbia and Romania, promised reforms in Bosnia, and granted autonomy to a new Bulgarian state, whose boundaries were to be very generously drawn and which was expected to fall under Russian domination. England seethed with a popular clamor for war against Russia. The outcry gave the word "jingoism" to the language:

> *We don't want to fight, but by jingo, if we do,*
> *We've got the men, we've got the ships, we've*
> *got the money too.*

It now appeared that the Ottoman Empire's inability to fend off foreigners from its borders would precipitate at least an Anglo-Russian and possibly a general European war. But war was averted by diplomacy. Seeking to avert the extension of Russian influence in the eastern Mediterranean, Bismarck assembled a congress of all the European great powers at Berlin in 1878. Once again Europe attempted to assert itself as a unity, to restore life to the much-battered Concert of Europe by dealing collectively with the common problem presented by the Eastern Question. The congress in effect initiated a partition of the Ottoman domain, thereby keeping peace in Europe at the expense of the Ottoman government in Turkey. The European desire to maintain a balance of power now both protected and dismembered the Ottoman Empire at the same time.

Weakness of Ottoman Empire

The Russians were persuaded at Berlin to give up the recent treaty of San Stefano, but they held on to the territory they had gained below the Caucasus Mountains and confirmed the independence of the Serbs and Romanians. Montenegro, too, was recognized as an independent state. Bulgaria was divided into three zones with varying degrees of autonomy, all still nominally within the Ottoman Empire. At the same time, Austria-Hungary gained a new role in the Balkans. It was authorized by the congress to "occupy and administer" Bosnia (but not annex it) in compensation for the spread of Russian influence along the borders of the Ottoman Empire. The Ottoman government also ceded Cyprus to Britain, thereby giving the British a large island from which they could further ensure the security of the Suez Canal. The French were told that they might expand from Algeria into Tunisia. To the Italians (who counted least) it was more vaguely hinted that they might later be allowed to expand across the Adriatic into Albania. As Bismarck put it, "the Italians have such a large appetite and such poor teeth." Germany took nothing. Bismarck said he was the "honest broker" with no interest except in European peace.

The treaty of Berlin in 1878 dispelled the immediate threat of war. It expanded the western European presence in the Mediterranean and reduced the territories of the Ottoman Empire, but it left many continuing problems that would contribute to the causes of the First World War 36 years later. Neither the Balkan nationalists nor the Russian Pan-Slavs were satisfied. All politically minded Turks, both the reactionaries like Abdul Hamid and the revolutionary Young Turks in exile, were indignant that peace had been made by further dismemberment of their empire. The demonstrated weakness of Ottoman Turkey was a constant temptation to all of the European powers. In the years before 1914 the German government gained new influence within the Ottoman Empire. Germans and German capital entered Turkey, projecting, and partially completing, a great Berlin to Bagdad railway to be accompanied by the exploitation of Middle Eastern resources. The railroad was all but completed before 1914 despite the protests and representations of the Russians, the French, and particularly the British, who saw it as a direct threat to their empire in India.

The continuing Turkish problem

The Suez Canal, which was completed in 1869, quickly became Britain's all-important lifeline to its Asian Empire and a busy crossing point for the expanding global economy. This picture shows the ship of Edward, Prince of Wales, entering the canal in 1875, when the prince was en route to India.
(©Otto Herschan/Getty Images)

Egypt and North Africa

For Egypt, technically autonomous within the Ottoman Empire, the 1850s and 1860s were a time of reform, economic development, and deepening connections with Europe. The Egyptian government modernized its administration, court system, and property law, cooperated with the French in building the Suez Canal, encouraged shipping on the Red Sea, and let British and French interests construct railroads. Between 1861 and 1865, while the American South was unable to export raw cotton to Europe, the annual export of Egyptian cotton rose from 60 million to 250 million pounds. Egypt more than Turkey was drawn into the world market, and the khedive of Egypt became more interested in European culture. The khedive Ismail built a new opera house in Cairo, where, in 1871, two years after the opening of the Suez Canal, Verdi's *Aïda,* written at the khedive's request, was resoundingly performed for the first time.

Such improvements cost a good deal of money, borrowed in England and France. The Egyptian government was soon in financial straits, only temporarily relieved by the sale of canal shares to Disraeli. By 1879 matters reached the point where European banking interests forced the abdication of Ismail and his replacement by khedive Tewfik, who also became thoroughly enmeshed by his creditors. This led to nationalistic protests within Egypt, headed by Colonel Ahmed Urabi. In a pattern later repeated in many parts of the colonial world, the nationalists opposed both the foreigners and their own government, charging it with being a mere front for European interests. Urabi's movement, an early expression of Arab nationalism, led in 1882 to riots in Alexandria, to which a British naval squadron responded by bombarding the city. British troops disembarked soon thereafter at Suez and Alexandria, defeated Urabi, and took Tewfik under their protection. The military intervention of 1882 was said by the British to be temporary, but British troops remained there for a long time, through two world wars and well into the twentieth century, not leaving until 1956.

British intervention

Egypt thus became a British "protectorate," which would become a common form of European imperial control. The British protected the khedive from discontent within his own country, from the claims of the Ottoman court, and from the rival attentions of other European powers.

Egypt as protectorate

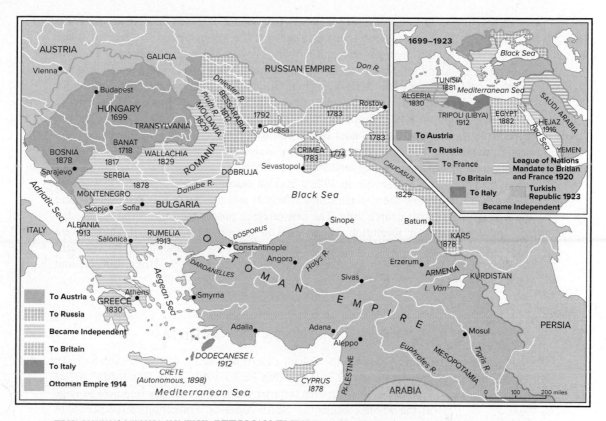

THE DISSOLUTION OF THE OTTOMAN EMPIRE, 1699–1914

Beginning in 1699, with the loss of Hungary to the Austrian Habsburgs, the Ottoman Empire entered upon a long process of territorial disintegration. Dates shown are those at which territories dropped away. In general, regions lost before 1815 were annexed directly by Austria and Russia. European territories lost in the nineteenth century emerged as independent states, owing to the rise of nationalism and rivalries among the great European powers. In the Arab world, reaching from Algeria to the Persian Gulf, regions lost before the First World War were absorbed into European colonial empires; those lost at the end of the First World War were mostly assigned to France and Britain as mandates, but after the Second World War these regions became independent Arab states and the Republic of Israel. A Turkish nationalist movement blocked European attempts to partition Turkey after the First World War, and in 1923 the Turks established the Turkish Republic.

The French strenuously objected when the British stayed on so long in Egypt. The French had long made the greatest investments in the Middle East, and persons in that region who were interested in European cultures overwhelmingly preferred French language and culture to English. The French, harboring deep suspicion of British designs in Egypt, compensated themselves by building a North African empire farther west. They continued to expand their control of Algeria, assumed a protectorate over Tunisia, and began to penetrate Morocco. Upon these latter French advances the British, and soon the Germans, looked with unmitigated disfavor. Rivalry for the spoils of the Ottoman Empire thus created enmity among the Great Powers of Europe and constituted a fertile source of the war scares, fears, and diplomatic maneuvers that preceded the First World War.

The dissolution of the Ottoman Empire became indistinguishable from the whole chronic international crisis before 1914. It is enough to say here, to keep the fate of the

Ottoman Empire in focus, that Abdul Hamid's repressive, defensive policies came to nothing and that the Young Turks won control of the Ottoman government in 1908. They forced the restoration of the constitution of 1876 and introduced many reforms. Finally, when all Europe became involved in war in 1914, Russia again declared war on Ottoman Turkey, and the Turks came into the war on the side of Germany, whose political and economic influence in the empire had been steadily growing. During the war, with British aid, the Arabs detached themselves from the empire and fell under British control before eventually becoming independent Arab states in the early 1930s. Egypt, too, ended all connections with the Ottoman Empire and moved toward independence from Britain's "protectorate" (though British troops remained in the country). In 1923 a Turkish republic was proclaimed. It was confined to Constantinople (henceforth called Istanbul) and the Anatolian Peninsula, where the bulk of the Turkish people lived. The new republic proceeded to undergo a thorough nationalist and secular revolution. Other areas of the pre-1914 Ottoman Empire were divided into various territorial "mandates" and states, whose instabilities and subsequent conflicts would have far-reaching effects in the Middle East, North Africa, Europe, and the wider world down to the twenty-first century.

77.   THE EUROPEAN PARTITION OF AFRICA

South of Mediterranean Africa lay the Sahara desert, and south of that lay sub-Saharan Africa, of which Europeans knew so little that they called it the "Dark Continent." Africa is so enormous that even the part south of the Sahara is almost as large as the whole continent of North America. For centuries the people of Europe knew only the African coasts—the Gold Coast, Ivory Coast, Slave Coast—where shackled processions of captive, enslaved people had been transported along with natural resources such as gold or ivory and sold to European traders. The great African rivers, including the Nile, Niger, and Congo, flowed from unknown hinterlands that were a subject of much European speculation. The people of sub-Saharan Africa were generally black, but (like all other racially described peoples) they were highly diverse in their physiques, cultures, and languages. They had been working with iron for more than 2,000 years, and they were adept in many arts, such as bronze sculpture, gold artifacts, weaving, basketry, and the making of ceremonial masks with strikingly symbolic or abstract patterns. Along the northern fringe some had converted to Islam, but mostly they adhered to other traditional religions that had emerged and evolved within the diverse cultural histories of African societies.

They lived mainly in villages in tribal communities, engaged in agriculture or moving herds of cattle from place to place. But great cities or agglomerations had also arisen, from Timbuktu in the north with its old caravan trade across the Sahara, to the vast complex of buildings at Zimbabwe in the south, which was already in ruins when the Europeans first saw it. There had also been extensive kingdoms whose memory was preserved, in the absence of writing, by specially trained narrators from one generation to the next. But these kingdoms had disappeared or declined by the nineteenth century. They had been weakened by intertribal wars, by the slave trade that set Africans against one another to satisfy the demand of outsiders, or by demographic causes that are now difficult to trace. Hence Africa, somewhat like the Ottoman Empire and China, met the assault of the Europeans at a time when its powers of resistance were reduced. Before the mid-nineteenth century there were no permanently resident non-African communities south of the Sahara except for some Arabs who had been on the east coast since the seventh century and the Europeans who had been at the Cape of Good Hope since 1652. In the Union of South Africa, when it was established in 1910, some 1.1 million whites lived among about 5 million blacks.

The Opening of Africa

Missionaries, explorers, and individual adventurers first opened this world to Europe without much assistance or interest from national governments. The historic pair, Livingstone and Stanley, well illustrate the drift of early European activities in sub-Saharan Africa. Before the

Livingstone and Stanley

new imperialist age, in 1841, the Scot David Livingstone arrived in southeast Africa as a medical missionary. He gave himself to humanitarian and religious work, with some occasional trading and much travel and exploration, but without political or economic aims. Exploring the Zambesi River, he was the first white man to look upon the Victoria Falls. Fully at home in inner Africa, safe and on friendly terms with the people who lived there, he was quite content to be left alone. But the invasive forces of modern civilization sought him out. Word spread in Europe and America that Dr. Livingstone was lost. The *New York Herald,* to manufacture news, sent the roving journalist H. M. Stanley to find him, which he did in 1871. Livingstone soon died, deeply honored by the Africans among whom he worked. Stanley was a man of the new era. Seeing vast economic possibilities in Africa, he went to Europe to solicit backers. In 1878 he found someone with the same ideas, who happened to be a king, Leopold II, king of the Belgians.

Leopold, for all his royalty, was at heart a commercial promoter. East Asia and North Africa had earlier attracted his fancy, but it was the central African basin of the Congo that he decided to develop. Stanley was exactly the man he needed, and the two founded at Brussels, with a few financiers, an International Congo Association in 1878. It was a purely private enterprise; the Belgian government and people had nothing to do with it. Europeans considered all Africa inland from the coasts to be, like America in the time of Columbus, a *terra nullius,* without government and claimed by nobody, wide open to the first Europeans or other outsiders who might arrive. Stanley, returning to the Congo in 1882, soon concluded treaties with over 500 chiefs, who received a few trinkets or a few yards of cloth for putting their marks on his mysterious European papers and accepting the blue-and-gold flag of the Congo Association.

Because sub-Saharan Africa still lacked the clearly mapped boundaries of delineated internal frontiers, no one could tell how much territory the Association might soon cover by these methods. The German explorer Karl Peters, working inland from Zanzibar, was also signing treaties with the chiefs of East Africa. The Frenchman Brazza, departing from the west coast and distributing the tricolor in every village, was claiming territory on the Congo River that was larger than all of France. The Portuguese meanwhile aspired to join their long-held coastal colonies of Angola and Mozambique into a trans-African empire, for which they sought a generous portion of the interior. Britain supported Portugal. In every case the home governments in Europe still hesitated to deepen their involvement in African lands and cultures that remained almost totally unknown to even the most adventurous European travelers. But the governments were pushed on by small organized minorities of colonizing enthusiasts, and they faced the probability that if they missed the moment for colonization it would be too late.

Bismarck personally thought African colonies were economically and politically absurd, but he was sensitive to the new political pressures. He therefore assembled another international conference at Berlin in 1885, seeking to bring the rapid European expansion into Africa under international regulation. Most European states, as well as the United States, attended. The Berlin conference had two goals: to set up the territories of the Congo Association as an international state, under international auspices and restrictions; and to draft a code governing the way in which European powers wishing to acquire African territory should proceed.

The Berlin conference of 1885

The Congo Free State, which in 1885 took the place of the International Congo Association, emerged as an international creation that also embodied in some ways what became known in the next century as international mandates or international (European-controlled) trusteeships for non-European peoples. The Berlin conference specified that the new state should not be the colony of any power, including Belgium, but delegated its administration to Leopold. It drew the boundaries, making the Congo Free State almost as large as the United States east of the Mississippi, and it added certain specific provisions: the Congo River was internationalized, persons of all nationalities should be free to do business in the Congo state, there should be no tariff levied on imports, and the slave trade should be suppressed. Leopold in 1889 reassembled the signatory powers in a second conference, held at Brussels. The Brussels conference took further steps to root out the slave trade, which remained a stubborn though declining evil, because the Muslim societies lagged behind Europe and the Americas in abolishing slavery. The Brussels conference also undertook to protect the rights of the local people, correct certain glaring abuses, and reduce the traffic in liquor and firearms.

But all this effort at internationalism failed because Europe had no international machinery by which the hard daily work of enforcing general agreements could be carried out. Although slavery was banned, Leopold went his own way in the Congo. His determination to make it commercially profitable for his own benefit led him to unconscionable abuses. Europe and America demanded rubber, and the rubber trees of the Congo were at the time one of the world's few sources of supply. The workers in the Congo rubber industry, afflicted by diseases and overwork in a hot lowland equatorial climate, could be made to fulfill assigned quotas of rubber sap only by inhumanly severe coercion. Leopold and his agents, some of whom were African, and the managers of the concessions he leased out extorted forced labor from the native population, compelling them to meet impossible quotas under brutal conditions in which hundreds of thousands died within two decades. The rubber trees meanwhile were destroyed without any plans for replacement.

The Belgian Congo

Leopold, by ravaging its resources and virtually enslaving its people, was able to draw from the Congo a personal fortune. He nevertheless could not make the entire enterprise profitable and needed more investment capital for further development. He therefore borrowed from his own government in 1889 and 1895 in return for giving the government the right to annex the Congo in 1901. The Belgian parliament turned down the opportunity that year, but beginning in 1904 public outrage mounted after European press revelations of the scandalous atrocities in the Congo. A concerted campaign compelled the Belgian government in 1908 to take the Congo over from Leopold, who died the following year. The Congo Free State became the Belgian Congo, a Belgian colony. Under the Belgian government's administration the worst excesses of forced labor and other abuses the Congo were ended, even though the colony continued to attract investments from Europeans and other outsiders.

The Berlin conference of 1885 had also laid down certain rules for imperial claims of African territories—a European power with holdings on the coast had prior rights in

BEATING RUBBER AND BEATING TIME—TO THE TUNE OF AN OLD LOVE-SONG.

DRAWN BY NORMAN H. HARDY.

THE RUBBER INDUSTRY IN THE BELGIAN CONGO: THUMPING RUBBER TO REMOVE PARTICLES OF WOOD AND FIBRE.

Workers in the Congo were forced to remove particles of wood and fiber from the rubber that was harvested for export to Europe and America. This picture of workers in one of the most deadly colonial enterprises was published in 1909. It shows the tedious physical labor in the rubber industry, but like many Western images of Africans in the era of European colonialism it also conveys an outsider's view of contentment rather than the miseries of actual working conditions.

(©Mary Evans Picture Library/The Image Works)

the hinterland; occupation must not be on paper only through drawing lines on a map, but must consist in real occupation by administrators or troops; and each power must give proper notice to the others as to what territories it considered its own. A wild scramble for "real occupation" quickly followed. In 15 years almost the entire continent was "occupied" by the various European nations. The sole exceptions were Ethiopia, and, technically, Liberia, founded in 1822 as a colony for emancipated American slaves and virtually a protectorate of the United States.

Everywhere a variant of the same process was repeated. First would appear a handful of white men, bringing their inevitable treaties—sometimes printed forms. To get what they wanted, the Europeans commonly had to ascribe powers to a tribal chief that by the customs of the tribal community he did not possess—powers to convey sovereignty, sell land, or grant mining concessions. Thus the Africans were baffled at the outset by the imposition of unfamiliar European legal conceptions. Then the Europeans would build up the position of the chief to whom they had ascribed new powers. This enhancement of a local leader's position was essential for the colonizing process because the Europeans themselves had no influence over the people. The collaboration with tribal chiefs led to the widespread system of "indirect rule,"

"Indirect rule"

by which colonial authorities acted through and expanded the existing social and political hierarchies. There were many things that only the chief could arrange, such as security for isolated Europeans, porter services, or gangs of workmen to build roads or railroads.

Labor was the overwhelming problem. For pure slavery Europeans now had an abhorrence, and they abolished it wherever they could. But the Africans, so long as they lived

The labor problem

within the traditional social customs and values of their own communities, did not react to European economic plans like the free wage earner postulated in European business and commercial theories. They had little expectation of individual gain and almost no use for money. They thus seemed to work only sporadically by European standards, disdaining the continuous and tedious labor that Europeans wanted them to perform. The result was that Europeans all over Africa resorted to forced labor, thereby disrupting the social communities that most Africans valued more than the very low wages of European companies. For road building, colonial officials forced workers to contribute their labor to construction systems that resembled the French *corvée* before the Revolution. A local chief would often be required to supply a quota of able-bodied men for a certain length of time, and frequently he did so gladly to raise his own importance and rewards in the European-managed economic system. More indirect methods were also used. The colonial government might levy a hut tax or a poll tax, payable only in money, for which the African would have to seek a job. Or the new government, once installed, might allocate so much land to Europeans as private property (another foreign conception) that the local tribe could no longer subsist on the lands that remained to it. Or the whole tribe might be moved to a reservation, like the displacement of Indians in the United States. In any case, while the women tilled the fields or tended the stock at home, the men would move away from their communities to take jobs under European control for infinitesimal pay. The men then lived in compounds, far from family and tribal kindred; they became demoralized; and the labor they gave, untrained and unwilling, would scarcely have been tolerated in more industrialized societies. In these circumstances everything was done to uproot the Africans, and little was done to benefit them or to protect the social systems in which they had lived before the Europeans arrived.

Conditions began to improve in the twentieth century as a more professional or enlightened colonial administration was gradually built up. Some colonial officials even came to serve as buffers or protectors of the local peoples against social abuses or the intruding white man's economic interests. Throughout the colonial era many European officials believed that part of the ethos of imperialism was to put down slavery, tribal warfare, superstition, disease, and illiteracy. Slowly a "Europeanized" class of Africans developed in the various colonial societies—chiefs and the sons of chiefs, Catholic priests and Protestant ministers, warehouse clerks and government employees. Young men from Nigeria or Uganda went away to study at Oxford, the University of Paris, or universities in the United States. These students increasingly resented both the exploitation and paternalism of the colonial systems. They showed signs of turning nationalistic, like their counterparts in the Ottoman Empire and Asia. Although they usually wanted to develop the economies, infrastructures, and schools in their own societies, they wanted such developments to evolve at a pace and for a purpose of their own, and with methods that recognized the value of their own cultural traditions. As the twentieth century progressed, nationalism in Africa grew more vocal, more intense, and more forceful in challenging the European powers.

PRECOLONIAL AFRICA: SITES AND PEOPLES
This map shows Africa before colonization by the Europeans in the nineteenth century. It does not refer to a particular date or to particular kingdoms that the Europeans displaced. Names in blue designate important ancient or medieval centers, such as the Ghana and Mali empires, which no longer existed in modern times. Even the most extensive African kingdoms had indefinite and shifting boundaries, which cannot be readily indicated on a map. "Bantu," as used in the phrase "Bantu peoples," refers to a large group of languages spoken from north of the Congo River to the southern African Coast. Concentrations of other language groups and peoples are also shown.

Friction and Rivalry between the European Powers

Meanwhile, in the 15 years from 1885 to 1900, the Europeans in Africa came dangerously near to open blows. The Portuguese annexed huge domains in Angola and Mozambique. The Italians took over two barren tracts, Italian Somaliland and Eritrea on the Red Sea. They then moved inland in quest of more colonies in Ethiopia and around the headwaters of the Nile. Some 80,000 Ethiopians, however, defeated and routed 20,000 Italians in pitched

The colonial rivalry in Africa

African workers built the new European-owned mines that began sending valuable minerals around the world. The laborers in this picture are digging a new gold mine in southern Africa in the late 1880s.
(©Robert Harris/Hulton Archive/Getty Images)

battle at Adowa in 1896. It was the first time that Africans successfully defended themselves against the forces of a European imperialist nation, and it discouraged invasion of Ethiopia by the Italians (or other Europeans) for 40 years. Italy and Portugal, like the Congo Free State and Spain (which retained a few vestiges of former days), were able to enjoy sizable holdings in Africa because of mutual fears among the principal contenders. The principal contenders were Great Britain, France, and Germany. Each preferred to have territory held by a minor power rather than by one of its significant rivals.

The Germans were latecomers in the African colonial race, which Bismarck entered with reluctance. By the 1880s all the usual imperialist arguments were heard in Germany, though most of them, such as the need for new markets, for emigration to overseas territories, or for the investment of capital, had little or no relevance for German interventions in tropical Africa. The Germans nevertheless established colonies in an eastern coastal region that came to be called German East Africa and in the Cameroons and Togo on the west coast, along with a desert area that became known as German Southwest Africa (where they ruthlessly suppressed the resistance of the Herero people). It did not escape the notice of German imperial planners that someday the Congo and the Portuguese colonies might be joined with their colonies in a solid German belt across the African heartland. The French controlled most of West Africa, from Algeria across the Sahara and the Sudan to various points on the Guinea coast. They also occupied Obok on the Red Sea, and after the Italian defeat in 1896 their influence in Ethiopia grew. French planners therefore dreamed of a solid French belt across Africa from Dakar to the Gulf of Aden. The French government in 1898 dispatched Captain J. B. Marchand with a small party eastward from Lake Chad to hoist the tricolor far away on the upper Nile, in the southern part of the Sudan, which no European power had as yet "effectively" occupied.

The two presumptive east-and-west belts, German and French, were cut (presumptively) by a north-and-south belt, projected in the British imperial imagination as an "Africa British from the Cape to Cairo." From the Cape of Good Hope Cecil Rhodes pushed northward into what was later called Rhodesia (now Zimbabwe). Kenya and Uganda in the mid-continent were already under British control. In Egypt, a British protectorate since 1882, the British began to support old Egyptian claims to the upper Nile. The first venture proved a disaster when in 1885 a British general popularly known as "Chinese Gordon" for previous military successes in China, leading an Egyptian force, was killed by Muslim troops at Khartoum. In the following decade British opinion turned imperialist in earnest. Another British officer, General Kitchener (with a young man named Winston Churchill under his command), again started southward up the Nile and defeated the local Muslims in 1898 at Omdurman. He then pushed on further upstream. At Fashoda he met Marchand, who had moved his small French force into this area on the White Nile tributary of the great river.

The ensuing Fashoda crisis brought Britain and France to the verge of war. Already at odds over Egypt and Morocco, the two governments used the encounter at Fashoda to force a showdown. It was a test of strength, not only for their respective plans for all Africa but also for their relative position in all imperialist and international issues. Both at first refused to yield. The British virtually threatened to fight. The French, fearful of their insecurity against Germany in Europe, at last decided not to take the risk. They backed down and recalled Marchand's expedition from Fashoda. A wave of hatred for the British swept over France.

The Fashoda crisis

The British no sooner won this Pyrrhic victory than they became involved in a major conflict at the other end of the African continent. In 1890 Cecil Rhodes had become prime minister of the Cape Colony. He was a principal sponsor of the Cape-to-Cairo imperial dream. Two small independent neighboring republics, the Transvaal and the Orange Free State, stood in the way of his plan for British imperial expansion. Their people were Afrikaners—descendants of the Dutch who had originally settled the Cape in the seventeenth century. After 1815, when England annexed the Cape of Good Hope, they had made the "great trek" into the interior territory of the Transvaal to escape from British rule. The Boers, as the English called them (from the Dutch word for farmer), were simple, obstinate, and old-fashioned. They had strongly opposed the British abolition of slavery, and they disliked fortune hunters, footloose adventurers, mining-camp people, and other outsiders.

The discovery of diamonds and gold in the Transvaal brought the issue of outsiders to a head. British capital and British people poured in. The Boers in the Transvaal refused to pass legislation needed by the mining corporations and their employees. In 1895 Rhodes, attempting to precipitate revolution in the Transvaal, sent a party of armed irregulars, under Dr. Jameson, a physician-turned-colonial administrator, over its borders. This Jameson Raid was a failure, but in Europe a great cry went up against British bullying of a small inoffensive republic. The German emperor, William II, dispatched a famous telegram to Paul Kruger, president of the Transvaal, congratulating him on his driving off the invaders "without having to call for the support of friendly powers," that is, Germany. Three years later, in 1899, the British Empire went to war with the two small republics. The South African (or Boer) War lasted until 1902 and provoked strong opposition within Britain as the human and financial costs steadily mounted. The British army sent 300,000 troops, who became bogged down in a guerilla war against elusive Boer fighters. Facing an irregular adversary, the British resorted to brutal "search and destroy" tactics that ravaged the country. They also gathered about 120,000 Boer women and children in concentration camps (a term that came into common usage during this war), where at least 20,000 people died after suffering in the harsh conditions of this confinement. The Boers were

The South African War

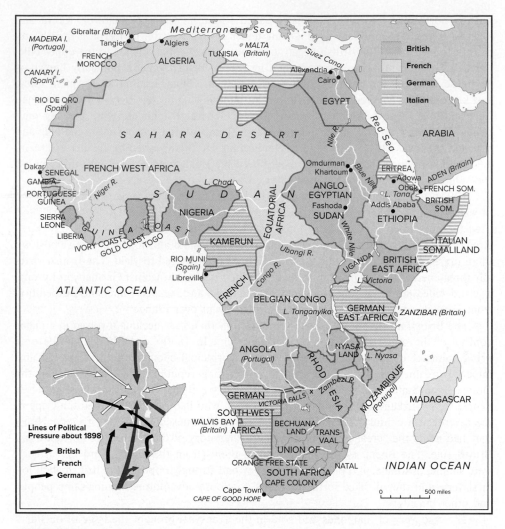

AFRICA, 1914

The map shows the recognized colonial holdings of European nations in 1914. The insert suggests the general directions of European expansion about 1898. These expansionary pressures led to the Fashoda crisis in 1898 and the Boer War in 1899. In 1898 the British and German governments held secret discussions on the possible partitioning of the Portuguese colonies, but no such partitioning took place because the British greatly preferred to have the Portuguese colonies remain in the hands of Portugal.

eventually subdued and brought within the British system, but their two republics were allowed to retain their self-governing institutions. In 1910 the Transvaal and the Orange Free State were combined with Cape Colony and Natal to form the Union of South Africa, which received semi-independent status along the lines of the Dominion of Canada.

The Fashoda crisis and the Boer War, coming in rapid succession, revealed to the British the bottomless depths of their unpopularity in Europe. All European governments and peoples were pro-Boer; only the United States, involved at the time in a similar military conquest of the Philippines, showed any sympathy for the British. The British, after the Boer War, began to rethink their international position, as will soon be seen.

The British military campaign against the Transvaal and the Orange Free State between 1899 and 1902 was widely condemned, in part because it was waged against descendants of seventeenth-century Dutch settlers (the Afrikaners or Boers) in South Africa; the suppression of black Africans never evoked the same criticisms within Europe. This picture of British soldiers crossing a river suggests the scale and costs of the Boer War, which became especially notorious when the British interned Afrikaner women and children in concentration camps, where thousands perished.

(©Fox Photos/Getty Images)

As in the case of the Ottoman Empire, imperial rivalries between the Great Powers over the spoils of Africa embittered European international relations and helped prepare the way for the First World War. In Africa as a whole, there was little territorial change after the Boer War, although in 1911 Italy took Libya from the Ottoman Empire. In 1914 the Germans were blocked from access to their short-lived empire. Had the Germans won the First World War, the map of Africa would probably have been greatly revised, but because they lost it, the only change was to assign the German colonies, under international mandate, to the French, British, and Belgians. With this change, and except for Italy's ephemeral conquest of Ethiopia in 1935, the political map of Africa remained divided by the lines that the European powers had drawn during the brief years of colonial partition—until the spectacular and rapid end of the European empires after the Second World War.

Embittered international relations

78.   IMPERIALISM IN ASIA: THE DUTCH, THE BRITISH, AND THE RUSSIANS

The Dutch East Indies and British India

British India and the Dutch East Indies, in the half-century before the First World War, became what the Europeans envisioned when they imagined their "ideal colonies." They illustrated the kind of empire that all imperialists would have wished to have, and a glance at them suggests the goal toward which European imperialism was moving and the system that it was trying to create.

Export surplus

Whereas all countries of western Europe showed a surplus of imports, receiving more goods from the rest of the world than they sent out, India and the Dutch East Indies invariably, year after year and decade after decade, showed a surplus of exports, sending out far more goods than they took in. This export surplus was the hallmark of a profitable colonial area, geared closely into the world market, with low purchasing power for the native population and kept going by foreign investment and management. Both regions, in addition, were so large as to have a good deal of internal business—commerce, insurance, banking, transportation—which never appeared in the statistics for world trade, but which, being dominated by Europeans, added immeasurably to their profits. Both had rich and varied natural resources, tropical in character, so that they never competed with the products of Europe—though India even before 1914 was beginning to develop various modern industries. In both regions the colonized people rapidly learned and adapted the methods of modern economic and bureaucratic institutions. But they were divided by religion and language, so that, once conquered, they were relatively easy for Europeans to govern because they could not easily come together in a united political movement.

Neither region before the First World War had any self-government at the highest levels. Both were ruled by a civil service, honest and high-minded by its own lights, in

European colonial rule

which the most influential and best-paying positions were reserved for Europeans. Hence upper-class families in England and the Netherlands valued their empires as fields of opportunity for their sons—somewhat as they had formerly valued an established church. In both India and Indonesia (as the Dutch colony began to be named by anti-Dutch nationalists in the early twentieth century) the governments were more or less benevolent despotisms, which, by curbing warfare, plague, and famine, at least allowed the population to grow in numbers. Java, with 5 million people in 1815, had 48 million in 1942. India's population in the same years grew from less than 200 million to almost 400 million. Finally, as the last virtue of a European-defined perfect colony, no foreign power directly challenged the British in India or the Dutch in their islands.

The Dutch in 1815 occupied little more than the island of Java itself. In the following decades the British moved into Singapore, the Malay Peninsula, and north Borneo, and made claims to Sumatra. The French in the 1860s entered Indochina. The Germans in the 1880s annexed eastern New Guinea and the Marshall and Solomon islands. Ultimately it was the mutual jealousy of these three European powers that preserved the Dutch position.

The Dutch also took the initiative themselves. To forestall occupation by other Europeans, and to put down native pirates and find raw materials for global exports, the Dutch spread their rule over the whole 3,000-mile extent of the archipelago. They created

The "culture system"

an empire in place of the old chain of coastal trading posts and suppressed internal revolts in 1830, 1849, and 1888; not till the twentieth century was northern Sumatra or the interior of Celebes brought under control. For some decades the Dutch exploited their huge empire by a kind of forced labor, the "culture system," in which the authorities required farmers to deliver, as a kind of tax, stated amounts of specific crops, such as sugar or coffee. After 1870 a freer system was introduced. The Dutch also, as an important matter of policy, favored instruction in the Malay and Javanese languages, not in Dutch. This preserved the cultures of colonized peoples from the disintegration or loss of cultural memories that could result from the imposition of European schooling, but at the same time it meant that the more radical or destabilizing European ideas of nationalism and democracy entered more slowly.

In India in 1857, the British faced a dangerous rebellion, which they commonly called the "Indian Mutiny", as if it had simply been a revolt of undisciplined soldiers. The British army in India, with its

The "Indian Mutiny"

"sepoys" (native Indian troops), was the only organization through which Indians could exert any collective pressure. The proportion of sepoys in Britain's Indian army was high in 1857 (about five-sixths) because units from Britain itself had been withdrawn for the Crimean War and for action in China. Many Indians outside the army had been unhappy with British policies for decades. Rulers had been conquered and dethroned. Landowners had lost their property and been replaced by new owners more friendly to the British. Religious sentiments were inflamed. The British too obviously regarded Indian beliefs as wrong or even repulsive; they had outlawed suttee, or widow burning, the ancient Hindu practice of a widow burning herself to death on the funeral pyre of her deceased husband; suppressed the Thugs, a small sect of holy assassins; and one British officer even declared that in ten years the government would abolish caste. Many Hindus therefore saw the British as dangerous opponents of their ancient religious traditions. Meanwhile, the Muslims were mobilized by Wahhabi fundamentalism, a popular reform movement that sought to purify and defend the religious practices of Islam. Mysterious propaganda circulated among the sepoys, announcing to Muslim soldiers that certain newly issued cartridges were greased with the fat of a pig and to Hindus that the same cartridges were greased with the fat of a cow. Because for Hindus the cow was sacred, and for Muslims to touch pork was profane, there was much agitation among soldiers from both of India's main religious groups. The sepoys launched an uprising in the Ganges Valley; and with them the other injured interests, including the fading Great Mogul and his court, also rose against the British.

The British put down the rebellion with much brutality, aided by the fact that western and southern India took no part in it. But the uprising persuaded the British to develop a radically new course of policy, pursued basically until the end of the Indian Empire almost a century later. The British East India Company

British rule in India

and the Mogul Empire were both finally and forever done away with. British authorities ruled directly, but the British concluded that they must rule India with and through the Indians themselves, not against them. This in practice meant a collaboration between the imperial power and the Indian upper classes. The British began to shelter Indian vested interests. They supported the Indian landlords and became more indulgent toward Indian "superstition." Where before 1857, when they conquered an Indian state, they had simply abolished it and incorporated its territories, after the great uprising or Mutiny they kept the remaining Indian states as protectorates. States existing in 1857, such as Hyderabad and Kashmir and over 200 others, with their galaxy of rajahs and maharajahs, carried on to the end of British rule in 1947. It was largely to provide a fitting summit for this mountain of Indian royalty that Queen Victoria was proclaimed empress of India in 1877.

India had been a considerable manufacturing country by preindustrial standards, Indian merchants had long managed important commercial activities throughout the Indian Ocean, and before 1800 Indian exports to Europe had included many textiles and other finished goods. The flourishing, premodern production of Indian goods and textiles mostly collapsed, however, as Britain used its growing imperial power to support British industries and to push the Indian economy toward agriculture. "India," observed a British expert in 1837, "can never again be a great manufacturing country, but by cultivating her connection with England she may be one of the greatest agricultural countries in the world." Free trade (made possible by military superiority, usually overlooked by the

The great Sepoy Rebellion in 1857 among local troops in India shook the British Empire more profoundly than any other event of the nineteenth century. Although the Indian Mutiny (as the British called it) was eventually suppressed, this illustration suggests why the violence and brutality left bitter memories on all sides and why the British soon restructured the whole system by which they governed Indian society.

(©Hulton Archive/Getty Images)

economists) turned Britain into the world's workshop and India into a supplier of raw materials. Indian exports in the latter part of the nineteenth century consisted increasingly of raw cotton, tea, jute, oilseeds, indigo, and wheat. The British shipped their manufactures to India in return. Business in India boomed; India came to have the densest railway network outside of Europe and North America. Although this commercial development was important, it should also be noted, as a commentary on European trade with colonies and poorer countries, that Britain in 1914 did far more trading with the 6 million people of Australia and New Zealand than with the 315 million impoverished people of India.

The British, in contrast to the Dutch, decided in 1835 to favor educational instruction in English, not in the native languages. The historian T. B. Macaulay, one of the members of a government commission that made this recommendation, branded the Indian languages as vehicles of barbarous and unenlightened ideas—a bar to progress. The British also, after the great Sepoy Rebellion, admitted Indians to the civil service and to governors' councils—sparingly indeed, but more than the Dutch in Indonesia. There were also

This photograph of the future Indian national leader Jawaharlal Nehru indicates the kind of British education that many young Indians received during the imperial era. Nehru studied at Harrow School (where this picture was taken about 1905) and at Cambridge University before joining Gandhi in the independence movement during the 1920s. He later served as the first prime minister of independent India from 1947 until his death in 1964.
(©Hulton Archive/Getty Images)

many Indian businessmen. A class of "hybrid" Indian intellectuals and government workers spoke perfect English, often after completing their education in England. They demanded more of a role in the public affairs and governance of their country. In 1885 the predominantly Hindu Indian National Congress was organized; in 1906, the All-India Muslim League. Muslim separatism, while favored by the British and sometimes even blamed upon them, expressed long-existing

Indian nationalism

religious identities, but these identities now became linked to new nationalist political movements. Nationalism spread. It became increasingly anti-British; and radical nationalism turned also against the Indian princes, capitalists, and businessmen, as accomplices in imperialism, and so the new nationalism often took on the critical economic themes of early twentieth-century socialism. In the period of the First World War, under nationalist pressure, the British granted more representation to Indians, especially in provincial affairs. But the movement toward self-rule was never fast enough to overcome the basic anti-British feeling of the Indian peoples, and Indian nationalism grew rapidly after the First World War.

Conflict of Russian and British Interests

While no outside power yet threatened the British in India, Britain's government leaders discerned in the northern sky a large and threatening new cloud. The Russian Empire had occupied northern Asia since the seventeenth century. About 1850 Russian pressure

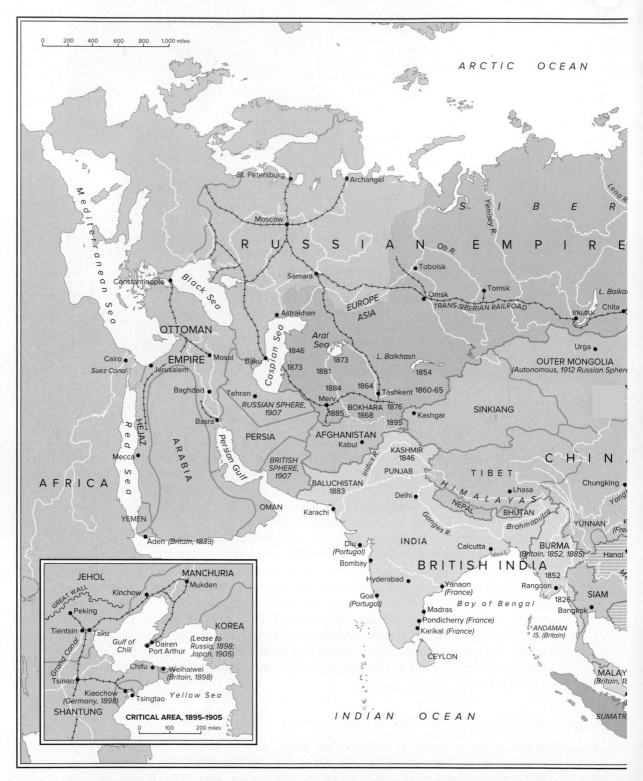

0   200   400   600   800   1,000 miles

ARCTIC OCEAN

St. Petersburg
Archangel
Moscow
S I B E R
Yenisey R.
Lena R.
R U S S I A N   E M P I R E
Ob R.
Tobolsk
Samara
Omsk
Tomsk
L. Baikal
Astrakhan
EUROPE
ASIA
TRANS-SIBERIAN RAILROAD
Irkutsk
Chita
Constantinople
Black Sea
Mediterranean Sea
Aral Sea
Caspian Sea
1846
1873
1873
1881
L. Balkhash
1854
Urga
Cairo
OTTOMAN
Mosul
Baku
EMPIRE
Suez Canal
Jerusalem
Baghdad
Tehran
1884
1864
Tashkent
1860-65
OUTER MONGOLIA
(Autonomous, 1912 Russian Sphere)
Merv
RUSSIAN SPHERE,
1907
BOKHARA
1876
1868
1895
SINKIANG
Basra
1885
Kashgar
Red Sea
HEJAZ
Persian Gulf
PERSIA
AFGHANISTAN
Kabul
C H I N A
Mecca
ARABIA
BRITISH
SPHERE,
1907
KASHMIR
1846
Indus R.
Chungking
Yang
AFRICA
OMAN
BALUCHISTAN
1883
PUNJAB
Delhi
NEPAL
TIBET
HIMALAYAS
Lhasa
BHUTAN
YÜNNAN
K
(Fre
YEMEN
Karachi
Ganges R.
Brahmaputra
Aden (Britain, 1839)
Diu
(Portugal)
Bombay
Hyderabad
INDIA
Calcutta
BRITISH INDIA
BURMA
(Britain, 1852, 1885)
Hanoi
Me
Goa
(Portugal)
Yanaon
(France)
Bay of Bengal
1852
Rangoon
SIAM
Madras
Pondicherry (France)
Karikal (France)
ANDAMAN
IS. (Britain)
1826
Bangkok
CEYLON
MALAY
(Britain, 18
INDIAN   OCEAN
SUMATRA

JEHOL
MANCHURIA
GREAT WALL
Kinchow
Mukden
Peking
KOREA
(Lease to
Russia, 1898;
Japan, 1905)
Tientsin
Taku
Gulf of
Chili
Dairen
Port Arthur
Grand Canal
Chifu
Weihaiwei
(Britain, 1898)
Tsinan
Tsingtao
Yellow Sea
Kiaochow
(Germany, 1898)
SHANTUNG
CRITICAL AREA, 1895–1905
0   100   200 miles

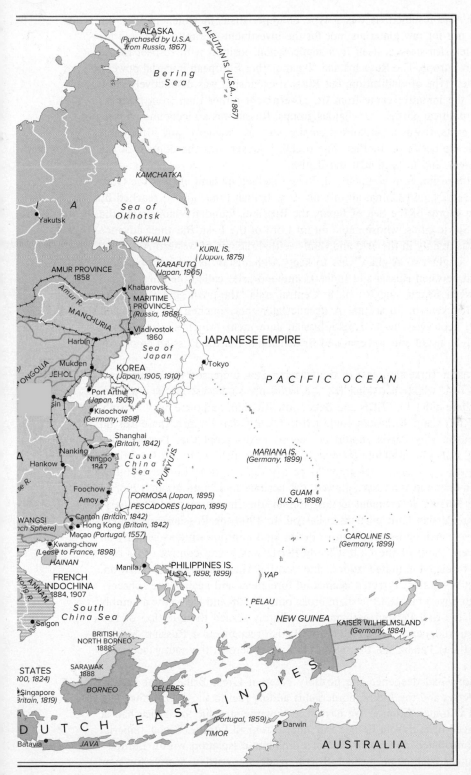

ALASKA
(Purchased by U.S.A.
from Russia, 1867)

ALEUTIAN IS. (U.S.A., 1867)

Bering Sea

KAMCHATKA

Sea of Okhotsk

Yakutsk

SAKHALIN

*KURIL IS.
(Japan, 1875)*

KARAFUTO
(Japan, 1905)

AMUR PROVINCE
1858

Khabarovsk

Amur R.

MANCHURIA

MARITIME
PROVINCE
(Russia, 1868)

Vladivostok
1860

Sea of Japan

JAPANESE EMPIRE

Harbin

Mukden

MONGOLIA

JEHOL

KOREA
(Japan, 1905, 1910)

Tokyo

PACIFIC OCEAN

Port Arthur
(Japan, 1905)

sin

Kiaochow
(Germany, 1898)

Shanghai
(Britain, 1842)

Nanking

Hankow

Ningpo
1842?

East China Sea

RYUKYUS

*MARIANA IS.
(Germany, 1899)*

Foochow

Amoy

FORMOSA (Japan, 1895)

PESCADORES (Japan, 1895)

*GUAM
(U.S.A., 1898)*

WANGSI
ch Sphere)

Canton (Britain, 1842)

Hong Kong (Britain, 1842)

Macao (Portugal, 1557)

Kwang-chow
(Lease to France, 1898)

HAINAN

*CAROLINE IS.
(Germany, 1899)*

PHILIPPINES IS.
(U.S.A., 1898, 1899)

Manila

YAP

FRENCH
INDOCHINA
1884, 1907

ANNAM

South China Sea

PELAU

NEW GUINEA

KAISER WILHELMSLAND
(Germany, 1884)

Saigon

BRITISH
NORTH BORNEO
1888

STATES
800, 1824)

SARAWAK
1888

BORNEO

CELEBES

Singapore
Britain, 1819)

D U T C H   E A S T   I N D I E S

(Portugal, 1859)

Darwin

TIMOR

AUSTRALIA

Batavia

JAVA

IMPERIALISM IN ASIA, 1840–1914

The map shows boundaries and possessions as they appeared in 1914. During these years the British and Dutch filled out their holdings in India and the East Indies; and Britain moved into Burma. The Russians pressed southward from Siberia into Central Asia, founded Vladivostok in 1860, and entered Manchuria at the close of the century. The French built their empire in Indochina and the United States took control of the Philippines. The Germans, as latecomers, were confined to miscellaneous parts of the western Pacific. The Japanese won control of Korea and the island of Formosa (now Taiwan). Meanwhile all of the imperial powers obtained special rights and concessions in the coastal cities and other regions of China.

on inner or central Asia resumed. It was a type of imperialism in which neither the demand for markets nor for raw materials, nor for the investment of capital, counted for much. In these matters Russia was itself in a semicolonial position with respect to the economies of western Europe. The Russians had, like the other European imperial powers, a desire to spread their type of civilization; but Russian expansion was distinctively political in that most of the initiative came from the government rather than from business interests, nationalist political parties, or religious groups. Russia was an icebound empire, craving warm-water ports. It was a landlocked empire, so that whichever way it turned it had to move toward one ocean or another. The ocean, however, was the domain of the major European powers, and in particular the British.

In the wide realm of imperial competition, Russia pushed by land against the Ottoman Empire, Persia, India, and China, all of which the British (and others) reached by sea. In 1860, on the shores of the Sea of Japan, the Russians founded Vladivostok, the farthest-flung of all Slavic cities, whose name meant Lord of the East. But their advance in the midcentury was mainly in the arid and thinly settled regions of western Asia. The British had already fought two Afghan wars to keep Afghanistan as a kind of uncontrolled no-man's land between Russia and India. Contemporaries called the political and military rivalry between Britain and Russia in Central Asia "the great game." In 1864 the Russians took Tashkent in Turkestan. A decade later they touched the borders of India itself but were kept away by an Anglo-Russian agreement, which allotted a long tongue of land to Afghanistan and so separated British India and the Russian empire by 20 miles.

Russian advances in Turkestan, east of the Caspian Sea, increased the pressure on Persia, which had long felt the same pressure west of the Caspian, where cities like Tiflis and Baku, now Russian, had once been Persian. If Tiflis and Turkestan could fall to the Russian Empire, there was no reason why Persia should not do so next—except that Persia had a seacoast and so might also be available for occupancy by the British. In 1864 a British company completed the first Persian telegraph as part of the line from Europe to India. Other British investments and interests followed. Oil became important about 1900. In 1890, to bolster the Persian government against Russia, the British granted it a loan—taking the customs in Persian Gulf ports as collateral. In 1900 the Russian government granted the same favor, making its own loan to Persia, and appropriating as security all Persian customs except those of the Gulf. Clearly Persia was losing control of its own affairs, falling into foreign-dominated zones, and turning ripe for imperial partition. A Persian nationalist revolution, directed against all foreigners and against the subservient government of the shah, broke out in 1905 and led to the assembly of the first Persian parliament but hardly settled the question of Persian independence. In 1907 the British recognized a Russian "sphere of influence" in northern Persia; the Russians, a British sphere in the south (see map, pp. 690–691).

Imperial ambitions had deepened the hostility between Great Britain and Russia, with disputes over Persia and the Indian borderlands adding fuel to the quarrel they had long waged over the Ottoman Empire. We have seen how the struggle for Africa had at the same time estranged Britain from France and indeed from all Europe. Global imperial rivalries therefore contributed directly to Britain's diplomatic isolation within Europe—an international danger that soon pushed British leaders toward a search for new alliances.

Foreign interests in Persia

Spheres of influence

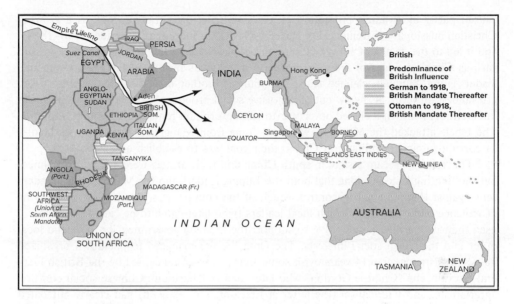

"THE BRITISH LAKE," 1918

This map shows the most important parts of the British Empire except for Canada, the Caribbean islands, and the United Kingdom itself. All shores of the Indian Ocean are shown to be British, except for French Madagascar; the politically weak Portuguese, Italian, and Dutch colonies; and the Arabian and Persian coasts, in which British influence was strong. It is easy to see why the Mediterranean and Suez Canal, leading from Europe into the Indian Ocean, were called the lifeline of the British Empire.

79.   IMPERIALISM IN ASIA: CHINA AND EUROPE

China before European Interventions

In this era of new European imperial rivalries, the biggest bone of imperialist contention was China. On this bone every Great Power without exception tried to bite. The Manchu, or Qing (formerly transliterated, and still pronounced, as Ch'ing), dynasty (1644–1912) held a suzerainty over the whole area affected by Chinese civilization, from the mouth of the Amur River (as far north as Labrador) to Burma and Indochina (as far south as Panama), and from the ocean westward into Mongolia and Tibet. In the old Chinese view China was the Middle Kingdom, the civilized center of the world surrounded by less enlightened peoples. The Europeans were outlandish barbarians. A few had trickled through to China since the European Middle Ages. But the Chinese people persistently wanted little or nothing to do with them.

China was moving into an upheaval even before European influence gained any importance. For about 4,000 years the country had seen dynasties come and go in long cycles. The Qing dynasty in the nineteenth century was showing the signs of a dynastic cycle nearing its end. It was failing to preserve order or to curb extortion. About 1800 a White Lotus Society revolted and was suppressed. In 1813 a Heavenly Reason Society attempted to seize Peking (now Beijing). In the 1850s a Muslim rebellion set up a temporary independent state in the southwest. Greatest of all the upheavals was the Taiping Rebellion, which was

The Taiping Rebellion

caused partly by Britain's promotion of a destabilizing drug trade as well as a growing Christian missionary movement. The Rebellion lasted for more than a decade (1850–1864), and it led to the deaths of at least 20 million people. Some of the Taiping rebels expressed various Christian ideas or recruited converts in religious meetings, and the movement's leader, Hong Xiuquan, claimed to be the younger brother of Jesus. The rebellion's key grievances, however, also grew out of pervasive social problems (exacerbated by European interventions), which included poverty, extortion, exorbitant rents, and absentee landlords. The rebels attacked the Manchus, who had come from Manchuria two centuries before, as corrupt foreigners ruling over China; their goal was to establish a new dynasty.

The Taipings set up a state in south China and their armies were at first disciplined, but the fighting lasted so long that both the Taiping leaders and the Manchu commanders sent against them got out of control. Much of the country was plunged into conditions of violence and disorder in which local leaders (who later came to be called "war lords") used their own armed forces either to support the Manchu government or to defend local order and their own social interests. The Qing Empire managed to put down organized Taiping resistance after 14 years, with some European assistance, led by the British General Gordon, the "Chinese Gordon" who later died at Khartoum. Chinese social conflict, agrarianism, and nationalism (the latter at first only anti-Manchu) had clearly antedated the impact of European imperialism—though the imperialist interventions also brought new conflicts and added new complexities to earlier social divisions.

This was the internally divided and distracted China in which Europeans began to intervene forcefully after about 1840. It became their policy to extort concessions from the Manchu Empire but at the same time to defend the Qing dynasty against internal opposition, as was shown in the European response to the Taiping Rebellion. Europeans supported the Qing emperors because they needed a Chinese government with which they could make treaties, legalizing their claims and binding upon the whole country.

The Expansion of European Influence in China

The modern phase of Chinese relations with Europe was inauspiciously opened by the Opium War of 1839–1841. We have already observed how, though Europeans wanted Chinese products, the Chinese had no interest in buying European products in return. Trade therefore was difficult, and the British East India Company had for decades solved the problem of getting Chinese tea for Europe by shipping Indian-grown opium in return, because opium was one available commodity for which Chinese demand existed or for which demand could be developed. When the Chinese government attempted to control this deadly and socially devastating inflow of opium, the British government went to war to protect their free trade of opium and other products. Fifteen years later, in 1857, Britain and France combined in a second war upon China to force the Chinese to receive their diplomats and deal with their traders. The Chinese continued to resist, whereupon 17,000 French and British soldiers entered Beijing and deliberately burned the emperor's very extensive Summer Palace, an appalling act of vandalism from which soldiers brought back enough stolen cultural objects—vases, tapestries, porcelain, enamels, jades, wood carvings— to set a fashion in Europe and America for Chinese art.

From the first of these wars arose the treaty of Nanking (1842); from the second, the treaties of Tientsin (1857), whose terms were soon duplicated in still other treaties signed by China with other European powers and with the United States. The resulting complex of interlocking agreements imposed restrictions on China or conferred rights upon foreigners and came to

The treaty system

be known as the "treaty system." To the British in 1842 the Chinese ceded the island of Hong Kong outright and somewhat later granted adjoining territories on a long lease. They opened over a dozen cities, including Shanghai and Canton (now called Guangzhou), to Europeans as "treaty ports." In these cities Europeans were allowed to make settlements of their own, immune to all Chinese law. Europeans traveling in the Chinese Empire remained subject only to their own governments, and European and American gunboats began to police the Yangtse River. The Chinese likewise paid large war indemnities, though they suffered most of the damages in every conflict. They agreed to the continuing import of opium and also agreed to levy no import duty over 5 percent; China thus became a free trade market for European products. To administer and collect the customs a staff of European experts was introduced. Money from the customs, collected with a new efficiency on a swelling volume of imports, went in part to the British and French in payment of the indemnities, but part remained with the Qing government, which, as noted, the Europeans had no desire to overthrow.

Annexations and Concessions

While China was thus permeated at the center by the extraterritorial and other insidious privileges for Europeans, whole blocks of its territory were cut away at the outer rim. The Russians moved down the Amur River, established their Maritime Province, and founded Vladivostok in 1860. The Japanese, now adapting to the methods of the Europeans in such matters, in 1876 recognized the independence of Korea. The British annexed Burma in 1886. The French in 1883 assumed a protectorate over Annam despite Chinese protests; they soon combined five areas—Annam, Cochin China, Tonkin, Laos, and Cambodia—into French Indochina. (The first three were known also as Vietnam, a word not familiar in most of the world until after the Second World War.) These outlying territories had never, it is true, been integral parts of China proper; but they had long maintained their most important political and cultural relations with China and had also paid tribute to the Chinese emperor.

Japan now joined with the European powers in developing new imperialist ambitions, which became apparent in 1894 when the Japanese went to war with China over disputes in Korea. The Japanese soon won, equipped as they were with modern weapons, training, and organization. They obliged the Chinese to sign the treaty of Shimonoseki in 1895, by which China ceded Formosa and the Liaotung Peninsula to Japan and recognized Korea as an independent state. The Liaotung was a tongue of land reaching down from Manchuria to the sea; at its tip was Port Arthur. Manchuria was the northeastern part of China itself. This sudden Japanese triumph precipitated a kind of upheaval among the Europeans who had been expanding their power and presence in east Asia. No one had realized how strong Japan had become. Europeans were astounded that a people who were not "European" in their culture or race should show such aptitude for modern war and diplomacy; and it appeared that Japan now had designs on Manchuria.

Japanese imperialism

It so happened that Russia, not long before, in 1891, had begun to build the Trans-Siberian Railway, whose eastern terminus was to be Vladivostok, the "Lord of the East." Manchuria extended northward between central Siberia and Vladivostok. The Russians, whether or not they ever dominated Manchuria themselves, could not allow its domination by another Great Power. It happened also that Germany was at this time looking for a chance to enter the Far Eastern arena, and that France had formed an alliance with Russia, whose good will it was eager

"Lord of the East"

CHRONOLOGY OF NOTABLE EVENTS, 1850–1906

1850–1864	Taiping Rebellion in China is suppressed by Qing dynasty; up to 20 million die
1856	Ottoman Empire launches reforms to modernize the legal and military system
1857	Uprising of sepoy troops in India, which Britain calls the "Indian Mutiny," leads to reforms in the imperial administration
1876	Abdul Hamid takes power as sultan in Ottoman Empire; repressive regime lasts for 33 years
1877–1878	Russo-Turkish War leads to Russian gains in the Balkans
1885	Berlin Conference sets European terms for imperial control of Africa
1885	Hindu Indian National Congress is organized to challenge British power in India
1894–1895	Japan goes to war with China and takes Formosa (later called Taiwan)
1898	French and English forces come to brink of imperial conflict at Fashoda in Sudan—the "Fashoda Crisis"
1899	Chinese revolt against European powers, the "Boxer Uprising," is suppressed by European forces
1899–1902	The Boer War enables Britain to consolidate power in South Africa
1904–1905	Japan defeats Russia in Russo-Japanese War and expands into Manchuria
1906	All-India Muslim League is organized to promote Indian nationalism and Muslim rights within Britain's largest Asian colony

to retain. Russia, Germany, and France joined together in demanding that Japan give up the Liaotung Peninsula. The Japanese hesitated; they were indignant, but they yielded to the European demands. The Liaotung Peninsula went back to China.

In China many alert people were humiliated at the defeat by the Japanese whom they had despised. The Chinese government, at last facing the inevitable, began to plan for a program of rapid modernization and reform, which led to even deeper European involvement in Chinese affairs. Huge loans were obtained from Europe—the customs being pawned as security, following a pattern already well established in Turkey, Persia, and Santo Domingo. But the European powers did not wish China to become consolidated too soon. Nor had they forgotten the sudden apparition of Japan. The result was a frantic European scramble for further Chinese concessions in 1898.

It seemed in 1898 as if the Chinese Empire in its turn would be partitioned. The Germans extorted a 99-year lease on Kiaochow (now Jiaozhou) Bay, plus exclusive rights in the Shantung (now Shandong) Peninsula. The Russians took a lease on the Liaotung (now Liaodong) Peninsula from which they had just excluded Japan; they thus obtained Port Arthur and rights to build railroads in Manchuria to interlock with their Trans-Siberian system. The French took Kwangchow (now Guangzhou) in the south and the British gained control of the northeastern port city Weihaiewei (now Weihai), in addition

The Open Door

to confirming their sphere of influence in the Yangtse Valley. The United States, fearing that all China might soon be parceled out into exclusive spheres, announced its policy of the Open Door. The idea of the Open Door was that China should remain territorially intact and independent and that powers having special concessions or spheres of influence should maintain the

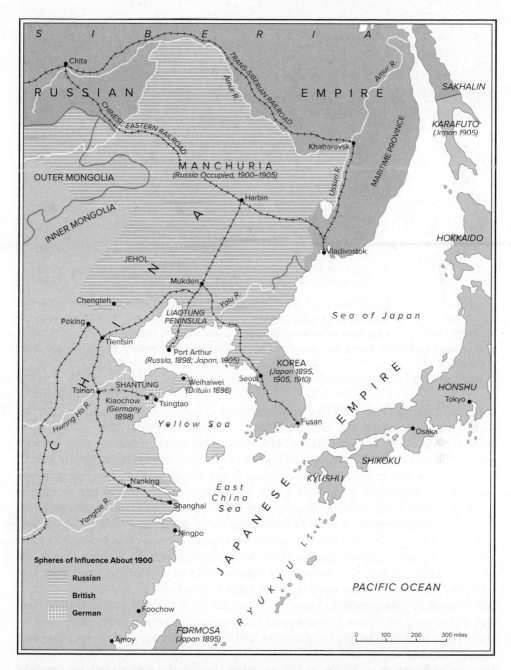

NORTHEAST CHINA AND ADJOINING REGIONS IN THE ERA OF IMPERIALISM

Manchuria became an object of dispute among China, to which it belonged historically, Russia, and Japan. It was dominated by the Russians from 1898 to 1905, by the Japanese from 1905 to 1945, and again by the Russians from 1945 to 1950, when they transferred it to the People's Republic of China. Korea was dominated by Japan from about 1895 (and formally annexed by Japan in 1910) until the end of the Second World War. It was then divided into Russian and American occupation zones. After the Korean War (1950–1953) it remained divided into two independent states, North Korea under a Communist regime and a Western-supported South Korea.

Chinese resentments against their government's concessions to foreign imperialist powers erupted in the violence of the so-called Boxer Uprising in 1899. This Chinese illustration, which shows European prisoners being held in humiliating positions by their Chinese captors, conveys the anger that fueled new national movements during this era of widespread European interventions in Chinese economic and political life.

(©Archiv Gerstenberg/ullstein bild/Getty Images)

5 percent Chinese tariff and allow businessmen of all nations to trade without discrimination. The British supported the Open Door as a means of discouraging actual annexations by neighboring Japan or Russia. The Open Door was a program not so much of leaving China to the Chinese as of assuring that all outsiders should find it literally "open."

If readers will imagine what the United States would be like if foreign warships patrolled the Mississippi as far as St. Louis; if foreigners came and went throughout the country without being under its laws; if New York, New Orleans, and other cities contained foreign settlements outside its jurisdiction but in which all banking and management were concentrated; if foreigners determined the tariff policy, collected the proceeds, and remitted much of the money to their own governments; if the western part of the city of Washington had been burned (the Summer Palace), Long Island and California had been annexed to distant empires (Hong Kong and Indochina), and all New England was coveted by two immediate neighbors (Manchuria); if the national authorities were half in collusion with these foreigners and half victimized by them; and if large areas of the country were prey to bandits, guerrillas, and revolutionary secret societies conspiring against the helpless government and occasionally murdering some of the foreigners—then they can understand how observant Chinese felt at the end of the nineteenth century, why European interventions were increasingly resented throughout Asia, and why the term "imperialism" came to be held in abomination by so many of the world's peoples.

One Chinese secret society, its name somewhat literally translated as the Order of Literary Patriotic Harmonious Fists, dubbed the Boxers by hostile foreigners, launched

---

The Boxer Uprising

an insurrection in 1899. The Boxers pulled up railway tracks, fell upon Chinese Christians, besieged the foreign legations, and killed about 300 foreigners, including numerous Christian missionaries. The European powers, joined by Japan and the United States, sent a combined international force against the insurgents, who were put down. The victors imposed still more severe controls on the Chinese government and inflicted an indemnity of $330 million that was to be divided among the foreign powers that had contributed troops to the anti-Boxer campaign. On the other hand, as a consequence of the Boxer Uprising, the Qing officials strove desperately to strengthen themselves by modernizing the country. Meanwhile, a new revolutionary movement, aiming at expulsion of Manchus and foreigners alike, began to spread rapidly throughout China, especially in the south, under the leadership of Sun Yat-sen.

80.   THE RUSSO-JAPANESE WAR AND ITS CONSEQUENCES

Russia and Japan increasingly opposed each other's intrigues in Manchuria and Korea. The Japanese felt a need for supplying their new factories with raw materials and markets on the Asian mainland, for employment for their modern army and navy and for recognition as a Great Power—a status that nations could attain in this era only by controlling an overseas empire. The Russian government needed an atmosphere of crisis and expansion to stifle criticism of tsarism at home; it could not abide the presence of a strong power directly on its East Asian frontier; it could use Manchuria and Korea to strengthen the exposed outpost of Vladivostok, which was somewhat squeezed against the sea and landlocked by Japanese waters. The Russians had obtained a concession from China to build the Chinese Eastern Railway to Vladivostok across the heart of Manchuria. A railway, in Manchuria, implied special zones, railway guards, mining and timber rights, and other auxiliary activities. The Japanese saw the fruits of their successful war of 1895 against China greedily enjoyed by their rival. In 1902 Japan signed a military alliance with Great Britain. We have seen how the British were alarmed by their diplomatic isolation after Fashoda and the Boer War and how for many years they had been expecting to have trouble with Russia. The Anglo-Japanese military alliance became one of the British responses to their international isolation, and the alliance lasted 20 years.

Russo-Japanese rivalry

War between Japan and Russia broke out in 1904, beginning with a Japanese naval attack on Russian installations at Port Arthur. Both sides sent large armies into Manchuria. The decisive battle of Mukden (which was fought for control of the important Manchurian city now called Shenyang) engaged more troops than any previous battle in human history—624,000 men. Military observers were present from all the major powers, anxiously trying to learn what the next war in Europe might be like. The Russians sent their Baltic fleet around three continents to the Far East, but to the world's amazement the Russian fleet was met and destroyed at Tsushima Strait by the new and untested navy of Japan. Russian communications by sea were thereby broken, and because the Trans-Siberian Railway was unfinished and because the Japanese also won the battle of Mukden, Russia was beaten.

At this point the president of the United States, Theodore Roosevelt, stepped upon the scene. With a new colonial outpost in the Philippines and a growing interest in China, it was to the American advantage to have neither side win too overwhelming a victory in the Far East. The most imperially minded of all American presidents offered his mediation, and plenipotentiaries of the two powers met at Portsmouth, New Hampshire. By the treaty of Portsmouth in 1905, Japan recovered from Russia what it had won and lost in 1895, namely Port Arthur and the Liaotung Peninsula; a preferred position in Manchuria, which

The treaty of Portsmouth

The Japanese victory over the Russians in the battle of Mukden, which is portrayed here, showed the world that Japan had become a major military and industrial power in east Asia. The battle lasted for eighteen days in February and March of 1905, ending with a decisive Japanese triumph that surprised European observers, gained symbolic importance in the rise of twentieth-century Japanese nationalism, and made the Russo-Japanese War a transitional event in modern Russian and global history.
(©Culture Club/Getty Images)

remained nominally Chinese; and a protectorate in Korea, which remained nominally independent until it was annexed by Japan in 1910. Japan also received from Russia the southern half of the island of Sakhalin. Much of what Russia lost to Japan in 1905 was regained 40 years later at the end of the Second World War.

The Russo-Japanese War was the first war between Great Powers since 1870. It was the first war fought under conditions of developed industrialism. It was the first actual war between modern powers to be caused by imperial competition in the exploitation of less developed countries. Most significant of all, in a period of intense concern with "race," it was widely noted that a nation of nonwhite people had defeated a nation of white people. The only other such defeat of a modern European nation was the Ethiopian rout of the Italians at Adowa in 1896, but now an Asian nation had shown that it could learn and play, in less than half a century, the geopolitical game of the Europeans.

The Japanese victory set off long chains of repercussions in at least three different directions. First, the Russian government, frustrated in its foreign policy in East Asia, shifted its attention back to Europe, where it resumed an active role in the affairs of the Balkans. This contributed to a series of international crises in Europe that led to the First World War. Second, the tsarist government was so weakened by the war, both in prestige and in actual

military strength, and opinion in Russia was so disgusted at the clumsiness and incompetency with which the war had been handled, that the various underground movements were able to come to the surface, producing the Russian Revolution of 1905. This in turn was a prelude to the great Russian Revolution of 1917, of which Soviet communism was the outcome. Third, news of Japan's victory over Russia electrified those who heard of it throughout the non-European world. The fact that Japan was itself an imperialist power was overlooked in the excited realization that the Japanese people were gaining the kind of international power and influence that had long given the European nations an apparently unstoppable ascendancy. Only half a century earlier the Japanese, too, had been deemed "backward"—defenseless, bombarded, and bulldozed by the Europeans. Now Japan had achieved the status of a Great Power that could sign military alliances with Great Britain and defeat the armed forces of the Russian Empire.

The moral was clear. Everywhere leaders of subjugated peoples concluded, from the Japanese precedent, that they must bring European science and industry to their own countries, but that they must do it, as the Japanese had done, by ending European political control of Asian or African colonies, supervising the process of modernization themselves, and preserving their own distinctive cultures. New "hybrid elites" in colonized societies combined their growing knowledge of European culture with a growing pride in their own cultural traditions, thereby creating the new nationalisms that would become a major, worldwide legacy of modern European imperialism. Nationalist revolutions began in Persia in 1905; in Turkey in 1908; in China in 1911. In India and Indonesia many were stirred by the Japanese achievement. In the face of rising agitation, the British admitted an Indian to the Viceroy's Council in 1909, and in 1916 the Dutch created a People's Council, to include Indonesian members, in the Dutch East Indies. The self-assertion of Asians was to grow in intensity after the First World War, when the limits of European power became increasingly evident.

The Japanese victory and Russian defeat can therefore be seen as starting points for three mighty developments: the First World War, the Russian Revolution, and the Revolt of Asia against European imperialism. These far-reaching upheavals all contributed to the weakening of Europe's influence in modern global history. They gradually put an end to

Europe's global ascendancy and undermined confident ideas about the inevitable progress and expansion of European civilization. Each of these transitional events would alter Europe's long-dominant international position and help to make the world of the twentieth century far different from that of the nineteenth. But Europeans could not have imagined, in 1905, that the Russo-Japanese War might be a first step toward great conflicts that would soon transform Europe's imperial role in the wider non-European world.

Suggested Further Readings can be found in the ebook, on Connect, or online at www.mhhe .com/kramer12e.

Chapter 17

THE FIRST WORLD WAR

Somewhere before 1914 Europe went off the historical track that was supposed to lead its peoples toward a better future. At the beginning of the twentieth century, most Europeans believed they were heading for a kind of high historical plateau, full of a benign progress and more abundant civilization, in which the benefits of modern science and invention would be more widely diffused and even competitive struggle would work out somehow for the best. Instead, Europeans stumbled in 1914 into disaster. It is not easy to see exactly where Europe went astray or when the First World War became inevitable, or (because the human mind cannot discern or predict historical inevitability) so overwhelmingly probable that only the most Olympian statesmanship could have avoided it.

But no such statesmanship appeared, and Europe fell into a deadly, grinding war that consumed much of its wealth, killed millions of its young men, and ultimately weakened or even destroyed much of its power and influence around the world. The Great War of 1914–1918, in short, became one of the decisive events in modern European and global history. Like other such upheavals—the Protestant Reformation, for example, or the French Revolution—this vast clash of opposing forces spread across all the traditional boundaries of Europe, shattering empires and cultural beliefs that had seemed as indestructible as the earlier unity of the Roman Catholic Church or the enduring power of "old regime" monarchies.

81. THE INTERNATIONAL ANARCHY

The great political questions in mid-nineteenth-century Europe had been settled by force. The German Empire was the strongest and most obvious of the new political structures that had emerged through the use of armed power, but all of the major European states had concluded

Chapter emblem: Soldier in the trenches near Passchendaele, Belgium, in 1917. (©Fotosearch/Getty Images)

that large military forces were essential for their national existence. Never had the European states maintained such huge armies in peacetime as at the beginning of the twentieth century. One, two, or even three years of compulsory military service for all young men became the rule. In 1914 each of the Continental Great Powers had a huge standing army and millions of trained reserves among the civilian population. Few people wanted war; all but a few sensational writers preferred peace in Europe, but many took it for granted that war would come someday. Such expectations probably made some statesmen more willing to unleash their military forces. In any case, the popular assumptions about future wars as well as the large standing armies helped to produce the Great War that exploded in 1914; but the war also came from other causes, including the interlocking system of international alliances, Germany's desire for a greater role in world affairs (which challenged Britain's earlier ascendancy and raised nationalist anxieties in France), and the ongoing conflicts in the Balkans.

The inevitability of war?

Rival Alliances: Triple Alliance versus Triple Entente

Political diagnosticians, from Richelieu to Metternich, had long thought that an effective union of Germany would revolutionize the relationships of Europe's peoples. After 1870 their anticipations were more than confirmed. Once united (or almost united), the Germans entered upon their industrial revolution. Manufacturing, finance, shipping, and population grew phenomenally. By 1900, for example, Germany produced more steel than France and Britain combined, though in 1865 the French alone had produced more than the Germans.

A "place in the sun"

People in Germany felt that they needed and deserved a "place in the sun," by which they vaguely meant some kind of acknowledged supremacy like that of the British. Neither the British nor the French, the leaders of modern Europe since the seventeenth century, could share in such German aspirations. The French nursed the chronic grievance of Alsace and Lorraine, annexed to Germany in 1871. The British saw German salesmen appear in their foreign markets, selling goods often at lower prices and using what they viewed as ungentlemanly methods; they saw Germans turn up as colonial rivals in Africa, the Middle East, and the Far East; and they watched other European states gravitate into the Berlin orbit, looking to the mighty German Empire as a friend to advance their interests.

Bismarck after 1871 feared that another European war might tear his new German Empire to pieces. He therefore followed, until his retirement in 1890, a policy of diplomacy and peace. We have seen him as the "honest broker" at the Berlin Congress of 1878, helping to adjudicate the Eastern Question, and again offering the facilities of Berlin in 1885 to bring some international order to Europe's imperial interventions in Africa. To isolate France, divert it from Europe, and keep it embroiled with Britain, he looked with satisfaction on French colonial expansion. He took no chances, however; in 1879 he formed a military alliance with Austria-Hungary, to which Italy was added in 1882. Thus was formed the Triple Alliance, which lasted until the First World War. Its terms were, briefly, that if any member became involved in war with two or more powers, its allies should come to its aid by force of arms. To be on the safe side, Bismarck signed a "reinsurance" treaty with Russia also. Because Russia and Austria were rivals and enemies in the Balkans, Germany needed considerable diplomatic finesse to stay allied to both at the same time. After Bismarck's retirement his system proved too intricate, or too lacking in candor, for his successors to manage. The Russo-German agreement lapsed. The French, faced by the Triple Alliance,

The Triple Alliance

soon seized the opportunity to form their own alliance with Russia, the Franco-Russian Alliance signed in 1894. In its time this was regarded as politically almost impossible. The French Republic stood for the legacy of the French Revolution and for everything radical; the Russian Empire, for everything reactionary and autocratic. But ideology was thrown to the winds, French capital poured into Russia, and the tsar bared his head to the *Marseillaise.*

The Continent was thus divided by 1894 into two opposed camps, the German-Austrian-Italian against the Franco-Russian. For a time it seemed that this rigid division might soften. Germany, France, and Russia cooperated in the Far Eastern crisis of 1895 to stem the expanding power of Japan. All were anti-British at the time of Fashoda and the Boer War. The Kaiser, William II, outlined tempting pictures of a Continental league against the global hegemony of England and its empire.

Much depended on what the British would do. They had long prided themselves on a "splendid isolation," going their own way, disdaining the kind of dependency that alliance with others always | *"Splendid isolation"* brings. European hostility toward Britain during the Fashoda crisis and the Boer War came as a shock. British relations with France and Russia were going badly. Some in England, including Joseph Chamberlain, therefore thought that a better understanding with Germany should be sought as part of a broader strategy to reduce British isolation. Arguments for "racial" affinities, in this race-conscious age, made some people in Britain and Germany favor more cooperation. But politically it was hard to cooperate. The Kaiser's Kruger Telegram of 1896, expressing support for the South African Boers in their conflict with Britain, was a studied insult. Then in 1898 the Germans decided to build a navy.

A new kind of race now entered the picture, the naval competition between Germany and Great Britain. British sea power for two centu- | *Naval race* ries had been all too successful. The American Admiral Mahan, teaching at this time in the American Naval War College and taking his examples largely from British history, argued that sea power had always been the foundation of Britain's greatness and that in the long run sea power must always choke off and ruin a power operating on land. Nowhere were Mahan's books read with more interest than in Germany. The German naval program, mounting rapidly after 1898, became a source of concern to the British, and by 1912 the German navy was perceived as an aggressive menace to Britain's global interests. The Germans insisted that they must have a navy to protect their colonies, secure their foreign trade, and "for the general purposes of their greatness." The British held with equal resolution that England, as a densely populated industrial island, dependent upon imports even for food, must at all costs control the sea in both peace and war. They adhered stubbornly to their traditional policy of maintaining a navy as large as the next two combined. The naval race led both sides to enormous and increasing expenditures. In the British it produced a sense of profound insecurity, driving them gradually toward new collaborations with Russia and France.

Slowly and cautiously the British emerged from their diplomatic isolation. We have noted that in 1902 they formed a military alliance with Japan against their common enemy, Russia. The decisive break, however, came in 1904, from which may be dated the immediate series of crises issuing ten years later in the First World War.

In 1904 the British and French governments agreed to forget their conflict at Fashoda and the accumulated bad feeling of the preceding 25 years. The French recognized the British occupation of Egypt, and the British recognized the French expansion into Morocco. They also agreed to support each other against protests by third parties. There was no specific military alliance; neither side said what it would do in the event of war; it was only a close understanding, an *entente cordiale.* The French immediately tried to reconcile their new friend to their ally, Russia. After defeat by Japan the Russians proved amenable. The British, increasingly uncertain of German aims, proved likewise willing. In 1907 Britain and Russia, the inveterate adversaries, settled their differences in an Anglo-Russian Convention. In Persia, the British recognized a northern sphere of Russian influence, while the Russians recognized a British sphere in the south and east. By 1907 England, France,

Triple Entente

and Russia were acting together. The older Triple Alliance faced a newer Triple Entente, the latter somewhat the looser, because the British refused to make any formal military commitments.

The Crises in Morocco and the Balkans

The Germans, who already felt encircled by the alliance of France and Russia, watched with concern as England drifted into the Franco-Russian camp. The Entente Cordiale was barely concluded when the German government decided to test it by seeing how far the

Testing the Entente

British would go in support of France. The French, now enjoying British backing, were taking over more police powers, concessions, and loans in Morocco. In March 1905 Kaiser William II disembarked from a German warship at Tangier, where he made a startling speech in favor of Moroccan independence. To diplomats everywhere this carefully staged performance was a signal: Germany was attempting to break up the new understanding between France and England. The Germans demanded and obtained an international conference at the Spanish port city of Algeciras, but the conference, which met in 1906, supported the French claims in Morocco, only Austria voting with Germany.

The German government had thus created an incident and been rebuffed. The British, disturbed by German diplomatic tactics, stood by the French all the more firmly. French and British army and naval officers now began to discuss common plans. The German attempt to break the Entente simply made it more solid. In 1911 came a second Morocco crisis. A German gunboat, the *Panther,* arrived at Agadir "to protect German interests." It soon became apparent that the move was a holdup; the Germans offered to make no further trouble in Morocco if they could have the French Congo. This crisis also passed, the Germans obtaining some small accessions in Africa, but it increased British hostility to Germany.

Crises in the Balkans

Meanwhile a series of crises rocked the Balkans. The Ottoman Empire, now in an advanced state of dissolution, still held a band of territory from Constantinople westward to the Adriatic (see map, p. 712), which included Bulgarians, Serbs, Albanians, and Macedonians. In the center and west of the peninsula, north of the Turkish belt, was the small,

ANGLO-GERMAN INDUSTRIAL COMPETITION, 1898 AND 1913
This diagram shows the huge increase in world trade in the years before the First World War and also the fact that German exports grew in these years more rapidly than British exports. The exports of both countries together multiplied no less than threefold in these 15 years. The increase reflected a small rise in prices, but it was mainly due to a real increase in volume of business. In 1913, total German exports about equaled the British, but German exports to the United States and Russia greatly exceeded the British exports to these countries. Note how the Germans even gained exports in British India, where the liberalism of British trade policy freely admitted competitive goods. In merchant marine, though the Germans doubled their tonnage, the British continued to enjoy an overwhelming lead.

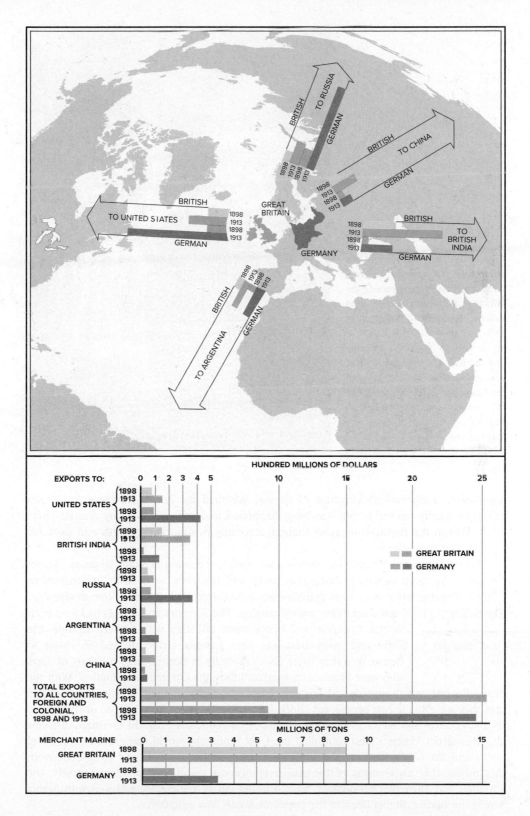

HUNDRED MILLIONS OF DOLLARS

EXPORTS TO:

UNITED STATES
- 1898
- 1913
- 1898
- 1913

BRITISH INDIA
- 1898
- 1913
- 1898
- 1913

RUSSIA
- 1898
- 1913
- 1898
- 1913

ARGENTINA
- 1898
- 1913
- 1898
- 1913

CHINA
- 1898
- 1913
- 1898
- 1913

TOTAL EXPORTS TO ALL COUNTRIES, FOREIGN AND COLONIAL, 1898 AND 1913
- 1898
- 1913
- 1898
- 1913

GREAT BRITAIN
GERMANY

MILLIONS OF TONS

MERCHANT MARINE

GREAT BRITAIN
- 1898
- 1913

GERMANY
- 1898
- 1913

Kaiser William II sought to strengthen Germany's international position by undermining the alliance between France and Britain. His visit to Morocco in 1905, as shown in this image of his arrival at Tangiers, exemplified the Kaiser's assertive style of personal diplomacy, but his call for Moroccan independence failed to weaken the French-British Entente.

(©Hulton Archive/Hulton Royals Collection/Getty Images)

landlocked, independent kingdom of Serbia, adjoined by Bosnia-Herzegovina, which belonged legally to Turkey but had been "occupied and administered" by Austria since 1878. Within the Austro-Hungarian Empire, adjoining Bosnia on the north and west, lay Croatia and Slovenia.

Serbs, Bosnians, Croats, and Slovenes all spoke basically the same language, Serbo-Croatian, the main difference being that Serbs and Bosnians wrote with the eastern or Cyrillic alphabet while the Croats and Slovenes wrote with the western or Roman alphabet. The difference reflected deep differences in religion. The Slovenes and Croats had long been

Ethnic and religious divisions

Roman Catholic, and hence more affiliated with western Europe; the Serbs and many Bosnians were Eastern Orthodox and so closer to Russia; and there were also, especially in Bosnia, large numbers of Slavs who were Muslims, converted during the Ottoman domination. With the Slavic Revival, which emphasized linguistic identities, many of these peoples came to feel that they were really one people, for which they took the name South Slavs, or Yugoslavs. By 1900 radical Slav nationalists within the empire had concluded that the German Austrians and Hungarian Magyars who controlled the Dual Monarchy would never grant them equal status and that all South Slavs should form an independent state of their own. Concretely, this meant that an element of the Austro-Hungarian empire's population, namely, the Croatian and Slovenian nationalists, wished to get out of the empire and join with Serbia across the border. Serbia became the center of South Slav agitation.

This brew was brought to a boil in 1908 by two events. First, the Young Turks, whose long agitation against Abdul Hamid has been noted, managed in that year to carry through a revolution. They obliged the sultan to restore the liberal parliamentary constitution of 1876. They showed, too, that they meant to stop the territorial dissolution of the Ottoman Empire by taking steps to have delegates from Bulgaria and Bosnia sit in the new Ottoman parliament. Second, Russia, its foreign policy in the Far East ruined by the Japanese war, turned actively to the Balkan and Turkish scene. Austria wanted full annexation of Bosnia, the better to discourage the pan-Yugoslav ideas that challenged Austria's influence in the former territories of the Ottoman Empire.

The Russian and Austrian foreign ministers, Alexander Isvolsky and Alois von Aehrenthal, came to a secret agreement in 1908. They would call an international conference, at which Russia would favor Austrian annexation of Bosnia and Austria would support Russia's long-sought opening of the Bosporus Straits to Russian warships. Austria, without waiting for a conference, proclaimed the annexation of Bosnia without more ado. This infuriated the Serbs, who had marked Bosnia for their own. Meanwhile, that same year, the Bulgarians and the Cretans broke finally with the Ottoman Empire, Bulgaria becoming fully independent, Crete uniting with Greece. Isvolsky was never able to realize the Russian plans for open access to the Bosporus Straits. His partners in the Triple Entente, Britain and France, refused to back him, and the projected international conference was never called. In Russia itself public opinion knew nothing of Isvolsky's secret deal. The known fact in Russia was that the Serbs, the little Slav brothers of Russia, had their toes rudely stepped on by the Austrian annexation of Bosnia.

The first Balkan crisis

This "first Balkan crisis" presently passed. The Russians, weakened by the Japanese war and by the domestic revolutionary turmoil of 1905, accepted the Austrian fait accompli. Austrian influence in the Balkans seemed to be growing. And South Slav nationalism was frustrated and inflamed.

In 1911 Italy declared war on Ottoman Turkey, from which it soon conquered Tripoli and the Dodecanese Islands near Turkey's Aegean coast. With the Ottomans thus embarrassed, Bulgaria, Serbia, and Greece joined together to launch their own war against Turkey, hoping to annex certain Balkan territories to which they believed they had a right. The Ottoman army was soon defeated again, but the Bulgarians claimed more of Macedonia than the Serbs would yield. The first Balkan war of 1912 was thus followed in 1913 by a second Balkan war over control of Albania. An agreement among the main European powers sought to resolve the conflict by creating an independent kingdom in Albania, which blocked Serbian access to the Adriatic Sea and aroused vehement new outcries in both Serbia and Russia. The Russians had again backed down, and Serbian expansionism was again frustrated and inflamed.

Two Balkan wars

The third Balkan crisis proved to be the fatal conflict that dragged all of Europe into the recurring violence in the borderlands of the Austrian and Ottoman Empires. The third crisis was fatal because two others had gone before it, leaving feelings of exasperation in Austria, desperation in Serbia, and humiliation in Russia.

The Sarajevo Crisis and the Outbreak of War

On June 28, 1914, a young Bosnian revolutionary, a member of the Serbian secret society called "Union or Death" and commonly known as the Black Hand, acting with the knowledge of certain Serbian officials, assassinated the heir to the Habsburg Empire, the Archduke

The assassination at Sarajevo

Francis Ferdinand, in the streets of Sarajevo, the Bosnian capital, which the Austrian Empire had annexed in 1908. The world was shocked at this terrorist outrage and at first sympathized with the protests of the Austrian government. Francis Ferdinand, who would soon have become emperor, was known to favor some kind of transformation of Austria-Hungary, in which a more equal place might be given to the Slavs; but the reformer who makes a system work is the most dangerous of all enemies to the implacable revolutionary, and it is perhaps for this reason that the archduke was killed by the Black Hand.

The Austrian government was determined to end the South Slav separatism that was gnawing its empire to pieces. It decided to crush the independence of Serbia, the nucleus of South Slav agitation, though not to annex it, because most Austrians thought too many Slavs were living within the empire already. The Austrian government consulted the German to see how far it might go with the support of its ally. The Germans, issuing their famous "blank check," encouraged the Austrians to be firm. The Austrians, thus reassured of strong German support, dispatched a drastic ultimatum to Serbia, demanding among other things that Austrian officials be permitted to collaborate in investigating and punishing the perpetrators of the assassination. The Serbs counted on Russian support, judging that Russia could not yield in a Balkan crisis, for the third time in six years, without losing its influence in the Balkans altogether. The Russians in turn counted on France; and France, terrified at the possibility of being someday caught alone in a war with Germany and determined to keep Russia as an ally at any cost, in effect gave a blank check to Russia.

The German "blank check"

The Serbs rejected the critical item in the Austrian ultimatum as an infringement on Serbian sovereignty, and Austria thereupon declared war upon Serbia. Russia prepared to defend Serbia and hence to fight Austria. Expecting that Austria would be joined by Germany, Russia rashly mobilized its army on both the German and Austrian frontiers. Because the power that first mobilized had all the advantages of a rapid offensive, the German government demanded an end to the Russian mobilization on its border and, receiving no answer, declared war on Russia on August 1, 1914. Convinced that France would in any case enter the war on the side of Russia, Germany also declared war on France on August 3. These German declarations of war would become the basis for later charges that Germany bore complete responsibility, or guilt, for the huge human and financial costs that all European nations would pay over the next four years.

The German decisions were posited on a reckless hope that Great Britain might not enter the war at all. England was bound by no formal military alliance. Even the French did not know for certain, as late as August 3, whether the British would join them in war. The British clung to scraps of their old proud isolation; they hesitated to make a final choice of sides; and as the foreign secretary Sir Edward Grey repeatedly explained, in England only parliament could declare war, so the foreign office could make no binding promise of war in advance. It has often been said that had the German government known as a positive fact that England would fight, the war might not have come. Hence the evasiveness of British policy is made a contributing cause of the war, and the guilt for what followed is expanded to include (at least to some extent) the government of every major European state. In reality, the probability that England would fight was so great that to underestimate it, as the Germans did, was an act of supreme self-deception. The British

English isolation

**Archduke Francis Ferdinand of Austria meets here with leaders of the Catholic Church during his visit
to Sarajevo on June 28, 1914. Shortly after this meeting, the Archduke (the tall man with a mous-
tache) and his wife were assassinated by a Bosnian terrorist who wanted Bosnia to separate from the
Austrian Empire and join with Serbia to form a larger Slavic state. The ensuing diplomatic crisis
quickly spread beyond Austria and Serbia, mobilized all of the nations in the European alliance system,
and led to the First World War of 1914–1918.**
(©Hulton Archive/Hulton Royals Collection/Getty Images)

government was deeply committed to France, especially through naval agreements, but
what swept the British public toward the French was the German invasion of Belgium.
The German plan to crush France quickly was such that it could succeed only by
crossing Belgium. When the Belgians protested, the Germans invaded anyway, violating
the treaty of 1839, which had guaranteed Belgian neutrality. England declared war on
Germany on August 4.

The mere narration of successive crises does not explain why the chief nations of
Europe within a few days became locked in combat over the murder of an imperial
personage in the Austrian Empire. Among more obvious general causes,
the alliance system and nationalist ideologies should be emphasized.
Europe was divided into two armed camps. Every incident tended to
become a test of strength between the two. A specific national incident,

*Causes of the First
World War*

such as German intervention in Morocco, or the assassination of Francis Ferdinand, could
not be settled on its own merits, merely by the parties concerned. However it was dealt
with, one of the two camps was deemed to have lost or gained and hence to have lost or
gained influence in other incidents, of perhaps greater importance, that would arise in

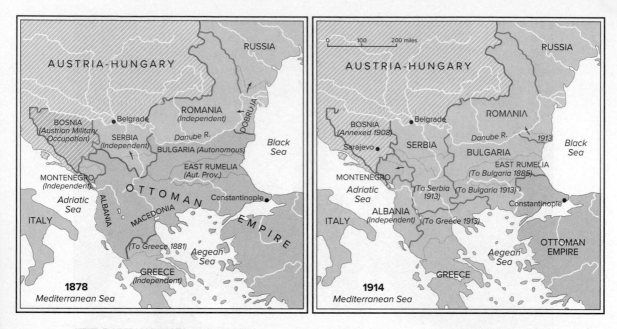

THE BALKANS, 1878 AND 1914
Austria and Russia had gradually pushed the Ottoman Empire out of Europe since 1699. The Congress of Berlin in 1878 attempted to stabilize the situation by recognizing Romania, Serbia, and Montenegro as independent monarchies, and northern Bulgaria as an autonomous principality within the Ottoman Empire. The ambitions and discontents of these new states, of Greece, and of non-Turkish people remaining within the Ottoman Empire culminated in the Balkan Wars of 1912–1913. Albania then became independent, and Serbia, Bulgaria, and Greece became contiguous. Austrian and Russian pressures meanwhile continued; in 1908 Austria annexed Bosnia, where the South Slav population, like the Serbs, was hostile to the Austrian annexation.

the future. The political leaders in each nation believed that they must stand by their allies whatever the specific issue; and every local conflict or confrontation became connected to wider anxieties about national security. This was because all lived in the fear of war, of some nameless future war in which allies would be necessary.

The Germans complained of being encircled by France and Russia. They dreaded the day when they might have to face a war on two fronts. Willing to accept even a Europeanwide war to break their threatened encirclement by the Entente powers, they were obliged to hold to their one ally, Austria-Hungary, which was in turn able to sell its support at its own price. The French dreaded a coming conflict with Germany, which in 40 years had far surpassed France in population and industrial strength; they were obliged to cling to their ally Russia, which therefore could oblige the French to yield to Russian wishes. As for Russia and Austria, they were both tottering empires. Especially after 1900, the tsarist regime suffered from endemic revolutionism and the Habsburg Empire from chronic nationalistic agitation. Authorities in both empires became desperate. Like the Serbs, they had little to lose and were therefore increasingly reckless in their foreign policies. It was Russia that drew France and hence England into war in 1914, and Austria that drew Germany. Seen in this light, the tragedy of

1914 is that the instability and nationalist conflicts in the deteriorating empires and least democratic parts of Europe, through the alliance system, dragged the more advanced parts automatically into ruin.

The German Empire, too, faced an internal crisis. The Social Democrats became the largest party in the Reichstag in 1912. Their sentiments for the most part were antimilitarist and antiwar. But the German imperial government recognized no responsibility to a majority in the chamber. Policy was determined by men of the old unreconstructed upper class, in which army and navy interests, now reinforced by new business interests, were strong; and many moderates and liberals also shared in the ambition to make Germany a world power, the equal of any. And while it is not true that Germany alone started the war, as its enemies in 1914 popularly believed, it must be granted that its policies had for some years been peremptory and obstinate. In a broad sense, the emergence of a consolidated industrial Germany after 1870, making its bid for world-power status through new competitions or conflicts with long-established states and empires, was a distant and basic cause of war.

The alliance system was only a symptom of deeper trouble. In a word, the world had an international economy but an anarchic system of competing, sovereign national states. Economically, each European people now required habitual contact with the world as a whole. Each national population was to that extent dependent and insecure. Industrial countries were especially vulnerable, relying as they did on the import of raw materials and food and on the expanding export of goods, services, or capital in return. There were, however, no global institutions to police or regulate the worldwide system, and each nation sought to take care of its own interests. This international competition for economic and political advantages generated much of the popular support for nationalist political ideologies and much of the drive for imperialism, in which each Great Power tried to stake out parts of the world system for itself. Both nationalism and the new imperialism intensified the quest for allies and for binding alliances. The alliances, in a world that was in the strict sense anarchic (and seemed likely to remain so), were a means by which each nation attempted to bolster its security; to assure that it would not be cut off, conquered, or subjected to another's will; and to obtain some hope of economic success in the competitive struggle for use of the world's goods.

82.   THE ARMED STALEMATE

The First World War lasted over four years, from 1914 to the end of 1918, the United States entering with effective result in the last year. Germany and its allies were called the Central Powers, while the Entente governments were termed the Allies. The war was appalling in its human costs; on the western front, more soldiers were used and killed in the First World War than in the Second.

At first a short war, as in 1870, was universally expected. The German General Staff had its plans ready for a two-front struggle against France and Russia. The disadvantage of fighting on two fronts was offset by the possession of good rail lines, which allowed the rapid shuttling of troops from one front to the other. *The Schlieffen Plan* The German war plan, known as the Schlieffen Plan, rested upon this fact. The idea was first to defeat France by the rapid wheeling motion of a tremendous army through Belgium and then to turn at more leisure against Russia, whose great size and less-developed railways would make its deployment much slower.

THE FIRST WORLD WAR
Land fighting in the First World War was mainly confined to the areas shown by the darker horizontal shading. The huge battles on the western front, which produced more casualties than all of the battles in the West during the Second World War, swayed back and forth over an area less than 100 miles wide.

The War on Land, 1914–1916

On August 3, 1914, the Germans launched 78 infantry divisions in a massive invasion toward the West. They were opposed by 72 French divisions, 5 British, and 6 Belgian. The Germans swept irresistibly forward. The Schlieffen Plan seemed to be moving like clockwork. Germany's civilian authorities made plans for the conquest and annexation of

Almost everyone in 1914 expected a short war and a quick resolution of the international crisis. These German soldiers at the Berlin railway station were preparing to board trains that would take them to the front. Accompanied by their wives or girlfriends and carrying flowers, they departed Berlin in early 1915 amid the patriotic fanfare that shaped public opinion during the first years of the war.
(©akg-images/Alamy Stock Photo)

large parts of Europe. Then a hitch occurred: the Russians were fulfilling the terms of their alliance; the 10 billion francs invested by the French in Russia now paid their most significant dividend. The Russians pushed two armies into Germany, penetrating into East Prussia. The German commander, Helmuth von Moltke, withdrew forces from the German right wing in France, on August 26, for service in the East. The Germans moved on, but their striking arm was weakened and their lines of communication were already overextended. General Joffre, the French commander, regrouping his forces with strong support from the relatively small British contingent and at exactly the right moment, ordered a counterattack.

The battle of the Marne

The ensuing battle of the Marne, fought from September 5 to 12, changed the whole character of the war. The German invasion was stopped, and the German army was forced to retreat. The plan for defeating France with a single blow had failed. Each side now tried to outflank and destroy the other until the battle lines extended to the sea. The Germans failed to win control of the Channel ports;

The German and Allied armies settled into trenches across the entire western front after 1914. Despite repeated, deadly attempts to achieve offensive breakthroughs, neither side could gain strategic advantages or significantly change the long-entrenched positions. These vulnerable French soldiers were stationed in a "departure trench," preparing for one of the many futile assaults during the protracted military stalemate.
(Library of Congress Prints and Photographs Division [LC-USZ62-93510])

French and British communications remained uninterrupted. For these reverses the great victories meanwhile won by the Germans on the eastern front, though of gigantic proportions (the battles of Tannenberg and the Masurian Lakes, at which 225,000 Russians were captured), were in the long run small consolation.

In the West the war of movement now settled into a war of position. The armies on the western front became almost immobile. The famous and once-important horse calvary units disappeared from the battlefield. Because aviation was barely beginning, and motor transport was still new (the armies had trucks, but no self-propelled guns, and no tanks until very late in the war), the basic soldier more than ever was the man on foot. The most deadly new weapon was the machine gun, which made it impossible for foot soldiers to advance across open fields without overwhelming artillery preparation. The result was a long military stalemate in which the indispensable infantry sought protection in a vast network of trenches.

War in the trenches

In 1915 the Germans and Austro-Hungarians put their main effort into an attempt to knock out Russia. They pressed far into the tsarist empire. The Russian losses were enormous—2 million killed, wounded, or captured in 1915 alone. But at the end of the year the Russian army was still fighting. Meanwhile the British and French, hoping to open up communications with Russia, launched a naval attack on Ottoman Turkey, which had joined the war as a German ally. Aiming at Constantinople by way of the Dardanelles, the British and French poured 450,000 men into the narrow peninsula of Gallipoli. Large contingents of the invading Allied army were drawn from colonized populations in Asia and Africa and from Australia and New Zealand, but the campaign soon stalled in another deadly stalemate. Almost 400,000 Ottoman and Allied soldiers were killed or wounded, including more than 140,000 in the British-French expeditionary forces. After almost a year the Allies abandoned the enterprise as a costly failure.

In 1916 both sides turned again to northern France in an attempt to break the deadlock. The Allies planned a great offensive along the river Somme, while the Germans prepared for a new assault near the town of Verdun. The Germans attacked Verdun in February. The French commander Joffre put in General Pétain to defend it but resisted committing his main reserves, holding them for the coming offensive on the Somme. Pétain and his troops, held to minimum numbers, thus had to take the full weight of the German army. The battle of Verdun lasted almost ten months, engaged about 2 million soldiers, and

The battle of Verdun

The miseries and dangers on the western front are conveyed in this photograph of soldiers in the battle of Passchendaele in 1917. Human life in such conditions became a raw struggle for survival; most soldiers reported that the grinding, daily experience on a battlefield seemed far removed from the nationalism or political concerns of civilians and government leaders.

(©Paul Popper/Popperfoto/Getty Images)

became a legend of determined French resistance ("they shall not pass"). The Germans finally abandoned the attack because they sustained almost as many casualties as the French—330,000 to 350,000.

While the inferno still raged at Verdun, the Allies opened their offensive on the Somme in July. They brought up vast amounts of artillery, and the newly raised British army was present in force. The idea was to break through the German line simply by stupendous pres-

The battle of the Somme

sure. On both sides, Allied and German, the art of generalship had sunk to an all-time low. Despite a weeklong artillery bombardment the British lost 60,000 men on the first day of the attack. In a week they had advanced only 1 mile along a 6-mile front. In a month they had advanced less than 3 miles. The battle of the Somme, lasting from July to October, cost the Germans about 500,000 men, the British 400,000, and the French 200,000. Nothing of any value had been gained. It was, indeed, at the Somme that the

The belligerent nations of Europe suffered more casualties in the First World War than in any previous European conflict. The fighting also destroyed millions of horses and large areas of the countryside as well as whole towns that became part of the battlefield. Examples of such destruction can be seen around these British soldiers who were advancing near the front in Flanders in 1917.
(©Ingram Publishing)

British first used the tank, an armored vehicle with caterpillar tracks that could crash through barbed wire, lunge over trenches, and smash into machine gun nests; but the tanks were introduced in such small numbers, and with such skepticism on the part of many commanders, that they had no effect on the battle.

The War at Sea

With land armies thus bogged down on all fronts both sides looked to the sea. The long preponderance of British sea power, and the more recent Anglo-German naval race, would now be tested. The British, with French aid, imposed a strict naval blockade on all German ports. International law at the time placed goods headed for a country at war into two classes. One class was called contraband; it included munitions and certain specified raw materials that might be used in the manufacture of military equipment. The other class, including foodstuffs and raw cotton, was defined as noncontraband. A country was supposed, by international law, to be able to import noncontraband goods even in wartime. These terms of wartime

Naval blockade

law had been set forth as recently as 1909 at an international conference in London. The purpose was to make it impossible for a sea power (that is, the British) to starve out an enemy in wartime or even to interfere with normal civilian production. The jealousy of Continental Europe for British sea power was an old story.

Such law, if observed, would make the blockade of Germany entirely ineffective, and the Allies did not observe it. To starve out the enemy and ruin the German economy was precisely their purpose. Economic warfare took its place alongside armed attack as a military weapon, as in the days of Napoleon. The Allies announced a new international law. The distinction between contraband and noncontraband was gradually abolished. The British navy (aided by the French) proceeded to stop all goods of whatever national origin or character destined for Germany or its allies.

The United States protested vehemently against these regulations and defended the trading rights of neutral nations. It reasserted the distinction between contraband and noncontraband, claimed the right to trade with other neutrals, and upheld the "freedom of the seas." These claims led to mutual bad feelings between the American and British governments in 1915 and 1916. But when the United States entered the war, it adopted the Allied position, and its navy joined in enforcing exactly the same regulations. International law was in fact changed. In the Second World War the very words "contraband" and "freedom of the seas" were never heard.

The Germans countered with an attempt to blockade England. A few isolated German cruisers were able for some time to destroy British shipping. But the Germans relied mainly on the submarine, against which the British naval power at first seemed helpless. The submarine was an unrefined weapon; a submarine commander could not always tell what kind of ship he was attacking, nor could he remove passengers, confiscate cargo, escort the vessel, or indeed do much except sink it. Citing British abuses of international law in justification, the German government in February 1915 declared the waters surrounding the British Isles to be a war zone, in which Allied vessels would be torpedoed and neutral vessels would be in grave danger.

Submarine warfare

Three months later the liner *Lusitania* was torpedoed off the Irish coast. About 1,200 persons were drowned, including about 120 American citizens. The *Lusitania* was a British ship; it carried munitions of war manufactured in the United States for Allied use; and the Germans had published ominous warnings in the New York papers that Americans should not take passage on it. Americans then believed that they should be able to sail safely, on peaceable errands, on the ship of a belligerent power in wartime. The loss of life shocked people in the United States. President Wilson informed the Germans that another such act would be considered "deliberately unfriendly." The Germans, to avoid trouble, refrained for two years from making full use of their submarines, and the Allied use of the sea during this time was only partly impeded.

The Lusitania

The dominance of Allied sea power was confirmed by the one great naval engagement of the war, the battle of Jutland. The German admirals became restless at seeing their newly built navy skulking behind minefields on the German shores, yet they could not presume to challenge the superior British Grand Fleet. They hoped, however, to decoy smaller formations of British ships, destroy them one by one, and perhaps eventually obtain enough of a naval balance to loosen the British blockade by which Germany was slowly being strangled. They were themselves, however, trapped into a major engagement in which the British Grand Fleet of 151 ships took them by surprise in the North Sea at the end of May in 1916. After a few hours of furious combat the Germans were able to withdraw into mined waters. They had lost less tonnage and fewer men than the British. They had proved themselves to be dangerously proficient in naval combat. But they had failed to undermine the British preponderance at sea.

Diplomatic Maneuvers, Secret Agreements, and Imperial Competitions

Italy joins the Allies

With no military solution in sight, both sides looked for new allies. The Ottoman Empire, fearing Russia, had joined Germany and Austria-Hungary as early as October 1914. The leading prospective ally was Italy, which, though formally a member of the Triple Alliance, had long ago drifted away from it. Both sides solicited the Italian government, which bargained imperturbably with both. The Italian public was divided, but extreme nationalists saw a chance to obtain their *irredenta,* the border regions in which Italians lived outside the national territory that had been incorporated at the time of national unification. The Italian government therefore cast its lot with the Allies in the secret treaty of London of 1915. It was agreed that if the Allies won the war, Italy would receive (from Austria) the Trentino, the south Tyrol, Istria and the city of Trieste, and some of the Dalmatian Islands. If Britain and France took over Germany's African colonies, Italy should receive additional territory in Libya and Somaliland. The treaty of London, in short, continued the most brazen prewar practices of territorial expansionism, but the Allies were desperate for additional military support. The Italian alliance was thus "bought" by the Allies, and Italy opened up a new front against Austria-Hungary in May 1915.

The Allies likewise made plans for a final partition of the Ottoman Empire, which still reached from Constantinople through the Middle East into Arabia and into Mesopotamia (modern Iraq). By another secret treaty they agreed that, upon an Allied victory, Mesopotamia was to go to Britain, Syria and southeastern Asia Minor to France, small portions to Italy, and Kurdistan and Armenia to Russia. The prewar attitudes and practices of European imperialism thus continued to guide the governments in every warring nation of Europe.

Each side also tampered with minorities and discontented groups living within the domains of the other. The Germans promised an independent Poland to embarrass Russia. They stirred up local nationalism in Ukraine. They raised up a pro–German Flemish movement in Belgium. They persuaded the Ottoman sultan, as caliph, to proclaim a holy war in North Africa, hoping that irate Muslims would drive the British from Egypt and the French from Algeria. This had no success. German agents worked in Ireland and one Irish nationalist, Sir Roger Casement, landed in Ireland from a German submarine, precipitating the Easter Rebellion of 1916, which was suppressed by the British.

The Zimmermann telegram

To Americans the most amazing German intervention appeared in the Zimmermann telegram. In 1916 an American military force had crossed the Mexican border in pursuit of a dissident revolutionary group that had raided a town in New Mexico. The Mexican government protested this American border crossing as relations between the United States and Germany were also deteriorating. In January 1917 the German state secretary for foreign affairs, Arthur Zimmermann, dispatched a telegram to the German minister at Mexico City, telling him to inform the Mexican president that if the United States went to war with Germany, the Germans would form an alliance with Mexico and if possible Japan, enabling Mexico to get back its "lost territories." These territories were in the region that the United States had conquered from Mexico in the 1840s–Texas, New Mexico, and Arizona (California was not mentioned). Zimmermann's telegram was

Colonel T. E. Lawrence emerged as the key British liaison to Arab forces fighting for independence from the Ottoman Empire during the First World War. He appears in this photograph at Versailles (wearing a British army uniform and Arab headdress) behind the left shoulder of Prince Faisal, who became the British-appointed King of Iraq in 1921.
(©Historical/Corbis Historical/Getty Images)

intercepted and decoded by the British, who sent it to Washington. Printed in the newspapers, it shocked public opinion in the United States.

The Allies were more successful in appealing to nationalist discontent, for the obvious reason that the most active national minorities were within the lands of their enemies. They were able to promise restoration of Alsace-Lorraine to France without difficulty. They promised independence to the Poles, though anticipating some difficulty as long as the Russian monarchy stood. It was easier for them to favor national independence for Czechs, Slovaks, and South Slavs, because an Allied victory would dissolve the Austro-Hungarian Empire.

But the Allied use of nationalist ambitions also extended from Europe into the Ottoman Empire and beyond. Within the Ottoman Empire the British aroused Arab hopes for independence. The British Colonel T. E. Lawrence led an insurrection against the Turks in the northwestern Arabian Peninsula—a region called the Hejaz that includes the Muslim holy city of Mecca. Encouraged by Lawrence and the British to pursue aspirations for an independent Arab state, the emir Hussein of Hejaz in 1916 took the title of King of the Arabs and established a kingdom that reached from the Red Sea to the Persian Gulf. Meanwhile, Zionists saw in the impending Ottoman collapse the opportunity to realize their dream for

Disruption in the Ottoman Empire

a Jewish state in Palestine. Because Palestine was peopled by Arabs (and had been for over 1,000 years) the Zionist program collided with British plans to sponsor Arab nationalism. Nevertheless, the British Foreign Secretary, Arthur Balfour, issued the famous Balfour Declaration in 1917, promising the British government's support for the idea of a "Jewish homeland" in Palestine (though with protection for the rights of non-Jewish peoples) and also setting the foundations for a clash between Jewish and Arab nationalisms, which has afflicted the Middle East down to the present.

For the Armenians these years were especially disastrous. They were a Christian people living in the eastern part of the Anatolian peninsula where it abuts on Russia. Like other peoples in the Ottoman Empire, including the Turks themselves, they had developed aspirations for a national state of their own, which conflicted with the plans of Turkish reformers to make the empire more Turkish. It was only 20 years since such clashes had produced the horrifying Armenian massacres of 1894. Now in 1915 the Turkish government, as the Russian army threatened its eastern frontier, ordered the deportation of Armenians from the war zone as potential sympathizers with Russia and the Western Allies. Supposedly they were to be resettled in Syria and Palestine. In fact, in the atmosphere of military crisis, political hatred, bureaucratic contempt, and wartime scarcities hundreds of thousands of Armenians perished in what most historians describe as a genocidal massacre. Virtually no Armenians remained within the territories that became the Turkish republic a few years later. The surviving Armenians became another of the world's scattered peoples with no state of their own except for a small Armenian republic, briefly independent after 1918, then part of the Soviet Union for 70 years, and finally independent again after 1991.

At the same time that they were seeking to disrupt and dismember the Ottoman Empire, the British and French were using the war as an opportunity to take control of the German colonies in Africa. The British foreign secretary, Sir Edward Grey, revealed to Colonel House, President Wilson's personal emissary, that the Allies did not intend that Germany should ever get its colonies back, though it also became clear that they did not intend to grant true independence to the people who lived there.

In China, too, the third important area of imperialist competition, the war accelerated the tendencies of preceding years. The Japanese saw their own opportunity in the self-slaughter of the Europeans. Japan had been allied to Britain since 1902, and in August 1914 the Japanese declared war on Germany. They soon overran the German concessions

Japan in China

in China and the German islands in the Pacific, the Marshalls and Carolines. In January 1915 Japan presented its Twenty-One Demands on China, a secret ultimatum for further concessions, most of which the Chinese were obliged to accept. Japan thereby proceeded to turn Manchuria and north China into an exclusive protectorate.

German expansionism

As for the Germans, their war aims were even more expansionist and more menacing to existing boundaries within Europe itself. Early in September 1914, when a quick victory seemed within their grasp, Bethmann-Hollweg, who remained chancellor until the summer of 1917, drew up a list of German war aims, which stayed unaltered until the end of hostilities. The plans called for an enlarged German Empire dominating all central Europe and annexations or satellites in both western and eastern Europe. In the east, Lithuania and other parts of the Baltic coast were to become German dependencies, large sections of Poland were to be directly annexed, and the remainder was to be joined with Austrian Galicia to form a German-dominated Polish state. In the west, Belgium was to become a German dependency to provide more direct access to the Atlantic, and French Lorraine with its rich iron ore was to be added to the already German parts of

Alsace-Lorraine. Colonial adjustments, including the acquisition of most of central Africa from coast to coast, were also projected. The political map of Europe and of colonial Africa would thus be transformed in Germany's favor.

All these developments, especially the Allied negotiations, whether accomplished facts or secret agreements, affecting Europe, the Middle East, Asia, or Africa, became very troublesome later at the peace conference. They continued some of the most unsettling tendencies of European politics before the war. It does not appear that the Allies, until driven by Woodrow Wilson, gave any thought to controlling postwar nationalism or what could be called international anarchy. As president of the United States, Wilson for a long time could see little to choose between the warring alliances, though his personal sympathies were with England and France. In 1916 he attempted to mediate, entering into confidential discussions with both sides; but both still hoped to win on their own terms, so negotiation was fruitless. Wilson judged that most Americans wished to remain uninvolved in European conflicts, and in November 1916 he was reelected to a second term, on the popular cry "he kept us out of war." Wilson urged a true international neutrality of thought and feeling, or a settlement, as he said, that should be a "peace without victory."

A "peace without victory"

The war had thus reached a deadly, global stalemate by the end of 1916; and it is hard to see how the First World War would have turned out had not two new sets of forces altered the military deadlock.

83. THE COLLAPSE OF RUSSIA AND THE INTERVENTION OF THE UNITED STATES

The Withdrawal of Russia: Revolution and the Treaty of Brest-Litovsk

The first great governmental victim of the First World War was the Russian Empire. As the Russo-Japanese War had led to the Revolution of 1905 in Russia, so the more ruinous conflict in Europe led to the far greater Revolution of 1917. The story of the Russian Revolution is told in the following chapter. It is enough to say here that war offered a prolonged test that the tsarist government could not meet. Bungling, dishonest, and secretive, incapable of supplying the materiel required for modern fighting, driving hordes of peasants into battle in some cases even without rifles, losing men by the millions yet offering no goal to inspire sacrifice, the tsarist regime lost the loyalty of all elements of its people.

In March 1917 the troops in St. Petersburg mutinied, while strikes and riots desolated the city. The Duma, or Russian parliament, used the occasion to press its demands for reform, which the tsarist government was unwilling and unable to address. On March 15 Nicholas II abdicated. A provisional government took over, made up of liberal noblemen and middle-class leaders, generally democrats and constitutionalists, with at first only one socialist. The provisional government held power from March to November 1917. Its members, who shared in the liberalism of western Europe, believed that a liberal and parliamentary regime could not succeed in Russia unless the German Empire were defeated. They took steps, therefore, to prosecute the war with a new vigor. In July 1917 a new offensive was opened, but the demoralized Russian armies again collapsed.

The provisional government

The mass of the Russian people would no longer support a war in which they were asked to suffer so much for so little. Nor did Russian peasants or workers feel any enthusiasm for the European-style intellectuals and professional men who headed the provisional government. Ordinary Russians, insofar as they held clear political views, were mostly drawn to one or another of numerous forms of socialism, Marxist and non-Marxist. The Russian Marxist Party, the Social Democrats, was divided between Menshevik and Bolshevik factions, the latter being more radical. The Bolshevik leaders had for some time lived as exiles in western Europe. Their principal spokesman, V. I. Lenin, with a few others, had spent the war years in Switzerland. In April 1917 the German government offered safe passage to Lenin through Germany to Russia. A railway car full of Bolsheviks, carefully "sealed" to prevent infection of Germany, was thus hauled by a German train to the frontier, whence it passed on to St. Petersburg, or Petrograd, as the city was renamed during the war. The aim of the Germans in this affair, as in the sending of Roger Casement to Ireland in a submarine, was of course to undermine the enemy's home front. It was to promote rebellion against the provisional government and thus at last to eliminate Russia from the war.

The Bolsheviks return from exile

The position of the Provisional Government became rapidly more untenable until by November 1917 the situation was so confused that Lenin and the Bolsheviks were able to seize power. The Bolsheviks stood for peace with Germany, partly to win popular favor in Russia and partly because they regarded the war as a struggle among capitalist, imperialist powers that should be left to exhaust and destroy each other for the benefit of socialism. On December 3, 1917, a peace conference opened between the Bolsheviks and the Germans at Brest-Litovsk. Meanwhile the peoples within the western border of the old Russia—Poles, Ukrainians, Bessarabians, Estonians, Latvians, Finns—with German backing, proclaimed their national independence. The Bolsheviks, because they would not or could not fight, were obliged to sign with Germany a treaty to which they vehemently objected, the treaty of Brest-Litovsk of March 3, 1918. By this treaty they acknowledged the "independence," or at least the loss to Russia, of Poland, Ukraine, Finland, and the Baltic provinces.

The treaty of Brest-Litovsk

For the Germans the treaty of Brest-Litovsk represented their maximum success during the First World War. Not only had they neutralized Russia, they also now dominated eastern Europe through political puppets placed at the head of the new independent states. A certain number of German troops remained in the East to preserve the new arrangements. But it was no longer a two-front war. Masses of the German army were shifted from east to west. The High Command, under the leadership of generals Hindenburg and Ludendorff since August 1916, prepared to launch a final assault in France to end the war in 1918.

The year 1918 was essentially a race to see whether American aid could reach Europe soon enough, in sufficient amount, to offset the added strength that Germany drew from the collapse of Russia. In March of that year the Germans, beginning with gas attacks and a bombardment by 6,000 artillery pieces, opened a formidable offensive before which the French and British both recoiled. On May 30, 1918, the Germans again stood at the Marne, 37 miles from Paris. There were still only two American divisions in action in France, though the United States had been at war for over a year. At this point in the story of the Great War there are therefore two open questions: how the United States entered the war and the length of time required for the buildup of its forces overseas.

American intervention

The United States and the War

We have seen how President Wilson clung persistently to neutrality. The American people were divided, in part because of their diverse historical connections with Europe. Many had been born in Europe or

America divided

were the children of immigrants. Those of Irish origin were anti-British; those of German origin were often sympathetic to Germany. On the other hand, since the time of the Spanish-American and Boer wars, a noticeable current of friendliness to the English had been running stronger than ever before in American history. The sale of war materiel to the Allies and the purchase of the bonds of Allied governments had given certain limited though influential circles a material interest in an Allied victory. American idealism was on the side of England and France, insofar as it was not isolationist. An Allied victory would affirm and advance the cause of democracy, freedom, and progress far more than a victory of the German Empire. On the other hand, England and France were suspected of somewhat self-interested, imperial motives, and they were allied with the Russian autocracy, the reactionary and brutal tsardom.

The fall of tsarism made a great impression. Democrats and progressives now came forward even in Russia. No one had heard of Lenin or could foresee the Bolshevik Revolution. It seemed in the spring of 1917 that Russia was struggling along the political path that England, France, and America had already taken. An ideological barrier had dropped away, and the demand for American intervention to safeguard democracy became more insistent.

The Germans gave up the attempt to keep the United States out. Constricted ever more tightly by the blockade, and failing to get a decision on land, the German government and High Command listened more readily to the submarine experts, who declared that if given a free hand they could force British surrender in six months. Civilian and diplomatic members of the government objected, fearing the consequences of war with the United States. They were overruled; it was a good example of the way in which, in Germany, the army and navy had taken the highest policy into their hands. Unrestricted submarine warfare was to be resumed on February 1, 1917. It was foreseen that the United States would declare war, but the German High Command believed that this would make no immediate difference. They *Unrestricted submarine warfare* estimated in 1917 (correctly) that there would be about a year between the time when the United States entered a European war and the time when it could take part with its own army. Meanwhile, the planners said, in six months they could force Britain to accept defeat.

On January 31, 1917, the Germans notified Wilson of the resumption of unrestricted submarine attacks. They announced that they would sink on sight all merchant vessels found in a zone around the British Isles or in the Mediterranean. Wilson broke off diplomatic relations and ordered the arming of American freighters. Meanwhile, the publication of the Zimmermann telegram convinced many Americans of German aggressiveness. German secret agents also had been at work in America, fomenting strikes and causing explosions in factories engaged in the manufacture of munitions for the Allies. In February and March several American ships were sunk. Americans regarded all these activities as an interference with their rights as neutrals. Wilson at last concluded that Germany was a menace. Having made his decision, he now saw a clear-cut issue between right and wrong. Wilson obtained a rousing *"To make the world safe for democracy"* declaration of war from Congress, on April 6, 1917, and the United States went to war against Germany "to make the world safe for democracy."

At first the German submarine campaign realized and even exceeded the predictions of its sponsors. In February 1917 the Germans sank 540,000 tons of shipping; in March, 578,000 tons; April, as the days grew longer, 874,000 tons. Something akin to terror seized the government in London. Britain was reduced to a six-week reserve of food. Gradually countermeasures were developed—mine barges, hydrophones, depth charges, airplane reconnaissance, and most of all the convoy. It was found that a hundred or more freighters together, though all had to steam at the pace of the slowest, could be protected by a sufficient concentration of warships to keep submarines away. The United States navy, which, unlike the army, was of considerable size and ready for combat, supplied enough additional force to the Allies to make convoying and other antisubmarine measures highly effective. By the end of 1917 the submarine was no more than a nuisance. For the Germans the great plan ultimately produced the anticipated penalty without the reward—its net result was only to add America to their enemies.

The French and British hold the line

On the western front in 1917, while the Americans desperately mobilized for the war they had entered, the French and British continued to hold the line. The French, finding in General Nivelle a commander who still believed in the breakthrough, launched an offensive so unsuccessful and so bloody that mutiny spread through the French army. Pétain replaced Nivelle and restored discipline to the exhausted and disillusioned soldiers, but he had no thought of further attack. "I am waiting for the Americans and the tanks," he said. The British then assumed the main burden. For 3 months late in 1917 they fought the dismal battle of Passchendaele. They advanced 5 miles, near Ypres, at a cost of 400,000 men. At the very end of 1917 the British surprised the Germans with a raid by 380 tanks, which penetrated deep into the German lines, but were obliged to withdraw, because no reserve of fresh infantry was at hand to exploit their success.

Meanwhile the Austro-Hungarians, strongly reinforced by German troops, overwhelmed the Italians in a decisive victory at the battle of Caporetto. The Central Powers streamed into northern Italy, but the Italians, with British and French reinforcements, were able to hold the line. The net effect of the campaigns of 1917 and of the repulse of the German submarine offensive was to reemphasize the stalemate in Europe, incline the weary Allies to await the Americans, and give the Americans what they most needed—time.

The Americans made good use of the time given them. Conscription, which was democratically called selective service, was adopted immediately after the declaration of

America mobilizes for war

war. The United States Army, whose professionals in 1916 numbered only 130,000, performed the mammoth feat of turning over 3.5 million civilians into soldiers. With the navy, the United States came to have over 4 million in its armed services (which may be compared with over 12 million in the Second World War). Aid flowed to the Allies in Europe. To the loans already made through private bankers were added some $10 billion lent by the American government itself. The Allies used the money mainly to buy food and munitions in the United States. American farms and factories, which had already prospered by selling to the Allies during the period of neutrality, now broke all records for production. Civilian industry was converted to war uses; radiator factories turned out guns, and piano factories manufactured airplane wings. Every possible means was employed to build up ocean shipping, without which neither American supplies nor American armies could reach the theater of war. Available shipping was increased from one million to ten million tons.

Civilian consumption was drastically reduced. Eight thousand tons of steel were saved in the manufacture of women's corsets and 75,000 tons of tin were spared in the making of children's toy wagons. Every week people observed meatless Tuesday, and sugar was rationed. Daylight-saving time, invented in Europe during the war, was introduced to save coal. By such means the United States made enormous stocks available for its European Allies as well as itself, though for some items, notably airplanes and artillery ammunition, the American armies, when they reached France, drew heavily on British and French manufactures. The deepening involvement in Europe's Great War therefore pushed the United States to develop a more active national government and to collaborate more closely than ever before with the western European states and peoples.

The Final Phase of the War

The Germans, as we have seen, victorious in the east, opened a great final offensive in the west in the spring of 1918, hoping to force a decision before American participation turned the balance forever. To oppose the new German assault, a unity of command was achieved for the first time when a French general, Ferdinand Foch, was made commander in chief of all Allied forces in France, with the national commanders subordinate to him, including Pershing for the Americans. In June the Germans first made contact with American troops in significant force, meeting the Second Division at Château-Thierry. The German position was so favorable that civilians in the German government thought it opportune to make a last effort at a compromise peace. The military, headed by Hindenburg and Ludendorff, successfully blocked any such attempts; they preferred one final gamble. The German armies reached their farthest advance on July 15 along the Marne.

There were now nine American divisions in the Allied line. Foch used them to spearhead his counterattack on July 18. The badly overstrained Germans began to falter. Over 250,000 American troops were now landing in France every month. The final Allied offensive that opened in September, with American troops in the Argonne occupying an eastern sector, proved more than the Germans could withstand. The German High Command notified its government that it could not win the war. The German foreign office made peace overtures to President Wilson. An armistice was arranged, and on November 11, 1918, firing ceased on the western front.

The armistice

Because Germany's allies had surrendered during the preceding weeks, the deadly, grinding battles were finally over, but the war continued to affect almost every aspect of European politics and society. The horror it brought to individual lives cannot be told by statistics, which dryly report that almost 10 million men had been killed and 20 million had been wounded. Each of the European Great Powers (except Italy) lost from 1 million to 2 million in killed alone. The United States, with some 330,000 casualties of all types (of whom 115,000 died) lost in the entire war fewer men than the main combatants had lost in single battles such as Verdun or Passchendaele; but American assistance was decisive in the defeat of Germany. It came late in the war, when the others had been struggling for almost 4 years, so that the mere beginnings of American military action were enough to turn the scale. On the date of the armistice there were 2 million American soldiers in France, and another million were on the way. But the American army had really been in combat only 4 months. During the whole year of 1918, out of every hundred artillery shells that were fired by the three Allied armies, the French fired 51, the British fired 43, and the Americans fired only 6.

Casualties of war

The war was thus less costly for the United States than for any of the other major military powers. About 50,000 Americans were killed in battle. Most other deaths were caused by disease, including the deadly influenza epidemic of 1918—which killed as many as 43,000 U.S. soldiers over several months. The horrible toll of military deaths in all countries during the World War was actually far surpassed in 1918-1919 by the worldwide influenza pandemic that caused at least 50 million deaths across the globe. A virulent new strain of virus (called the Spanish flu) was the source of the disease which became one of the most deadly pandemics in all of world history and deepened the profound sense of loss that affected people everywhere after the Great War.

These soldiers were in two of the American divisions that served in France during 1917–1918. Most American soldiers did not arrive in Europe until 1918, and they were segregated into white and black military units. The fresh troops from the United States enabled the Allied commanders to launch a decisive final offensive, forced the German commanders to recognize that Germany could not win the war, and contributed to America's expanding involvement in all aspects of modern European history.
(Left: ©Hulton Archive/Getty Images; Right: ©PhotoQuest/Archive Photos/Getty Images)

84. THE COLLAPSE OF THE AUSTRIAN AND GERMAN EMPIRES

The war proved as fatal to the German and Austro-Hungarian Empires as to the Russian. The subject nationalities in the Austro-Hungarian Empire, or the "national councils" representing them in the Western capitals, obtained recognition from the Allies, and in October 1918 declared their independence. The last Habsburg emperor, Charles I, abdicated on November 12, and on the next day Austria was proclaimed a republic, as was Hungary in the following week. Before any peace conference could convene, the new states of Czechoslovakia, Yugoslavia, an enlarged Romania, a republican Hungary, and a miniature republican Austria were in existence by their own action.

Nationalities gain independence

The German Empire stood solid until the closing weeks. Liberals, democrats, and socialists had lately begun to press for peace and democratization. Yet it was the High Command itself that precipitated the debacle. In the last years of the war dictatorial powers had become concentrated in the hands of General Ludendorff, and in September 1918 only he and his closest military associates realized that the German cause was hopeless. On September 29, at supreme headquarters at Spa in Belgium, Ludendorff informed the Kaiser that Germany must ask for peace. He urged that a new government be formed in Berlin reflecting the majority in the Reichstag, on democratic, parliamentary principles.

In calling for immediate peace negotiations, Ludendorff seems to have had two ideas in mind. First, he might win time to regroup his armies and prepare a new offensive. Or if collapse became unavoidable, then the army would not be blamed for the defeat because the civilian or democratic elements would be the groups in Germany that sued for peace.

The liberal Prince Max of Baden was recruited to head a cabinet in which even socialists were included. In October various reforms were enacted, the Bismarckian system was ended, and Germany became a liberal constitutional monarchy. These changes served the purpose of Ludendorff and other generals because the German military caste, at the moment of Germany's crisis, was more eager to save the army than to save the empire. The army must never admit surrender. Emperor, High Command, officers, and aristocrats were frantically unloading the humiliating tasks of surrender upon civilians.

President Wilson unwittingly played into their hands. Speaking now as the chief of the Allied coalition, the one to whom peace overtures were first made, he insisted that the German government must become more democratic. It may be recalled how Bismarck, after defeating France in 1871, demanded a general election in France before making peace. Wilson, unlike Bismarck, really believed in democracy; but in a practical way his position

Democracy in Germany

was the same. He wanted to be sure that he was dealing with the German people rather than with a discredited elite. He wanted the broader German nation to apply for and accept the Allied terms. In Germany, as realization of the military disaster spread, many people began to regard the Kaiser as an obstacle to peace. Or they believed that Germany would obtain better terms if it appeared before the Allies as a republic. Even the officer corps, to halt the fighting before the army disintegrated, began to talk of abdication. The socialists threatened to withdraw from the newly formed cabinet (that is, go into opposition and end the representative nature of the new government) unless William II abdicated. A general strike, led by minority socialists and syndicalists, began on November 9. "Abdication," Prince Max told the emperor, "is a dreadful thing, but a government without the socialists would be a worse danger for the country." William II abdicated on November 9, and slipped across the frontier into Holland, where despite cries to try him as a "war criminal" he lived quietly until his death in 1941. Germany was proclaimed a republic on the day he abdicated. Two days later the war stopped.

The fall of the empire in Germany, with the consequent adoption of the republic, did not arise from deep revolutionary action or change of basic sentiment in the German people. It was an episode of the war. The republic (soon called the Weimar Republic) arose because the victorious enemy demanded it, because the German people craved peace, because they wished to avoid forcible revolution, and because the old German

The Weimar Republic

military class, to save its face and its future strength, wished at least temporarily to be excused from its previous role in the German government. When the war ended, the German army was still in France, its discipline and organization still apparently unimpaired. No hostile shot had been fired on German soil. It was said later, by some, that the army had not been defeated, that it had been "stabbed in the back" by a dissolving civilian home front. This was untrue, but the myth became popular among many postwar German nationalists. It was actually the panic-stricken Ludendorff who first cried for "democracy." But the circumstances in which the German republic originated made its later history, and hence all later history, very troubled.

85. THE ECONOMIC, SOCIAL, AND CULTURAL IMPACT OF THE WAR

Effects on Capitalism: Government-Regulated Economies

European society was forced by the First World War into many basic changes that were to prove more lasting than the war itself. First of all, the war profoundly affected capitalism as previously known. Essential to the older capitalism (or economic liberalism, or free private enterprise) had been the idea that government should leave business alone, or at the most regulate a few general conditions under which businesses went about their affairs. Before 1914 governments had increasingly entered the economic field. They had put up tariffs, protected national industries, searched for markets or raw materials by imperialist expansion, or passed protective social legislation to benefit children and the wage-earning classes. During the war, however, all governments controlled their economies far more minutely. Indeed, the idea of the "planned economy" was first applied in the First World War as the warring states attempted to direct all the wealth and collective purpose of their societies to a single end.

The "planned economy"

Historians often describe this vast conflict as an example of the modern "total war." Such wars differ from "limited wars" or from earlier dynastic conflicts, which often had little direct effect on most people in a warring society. The term "total war," by contrast, suggests how the various European states mobilized every component of their armed forces, civilian populations, government institutions, economic resources, social organizations, and cultural systems against enemies that were deemed a mortal threat to the very existence of their nations. The war's enormous human and financial costs required constant propaganda campaigns to sustain civilian morale, recruit more soldiers, and counter a growing disillusionment with leaders who could never achieve a decisive victory. "Total war" thus directly affected every social group and almost every person in the belligerent countries.

Total war

Because in 1914 no one had expected a long war, no one had made plans for industrial mobilization. Everything had to be improvised. By 1916 each government had set up a system of boards, bureaus, councils, and commissions to coordinate its war effort. The aim was to see that all labor was effectively utilized and that all natural resources within the country, and all that could possibly be imported, were employed where they would do the most good. In the stress of war free competition was found to be wasteful; undirected private enterprise was found to be too uncertain and too slow. The profit motive came into disrepute. Those who exploited shortages to make big profits were stigmatized as profiteers. Production for civilian use, or for mere luxury purposes, was cut to a minimum. Businesses were not allowed to set up or close down factories as they chose. It was impossible to start a new business without government approval, because the flotation of stocks and bonds was controlled and raw materials were made available only as the government permitted. It was equally impossible to shut down a business engaged in war production. If a factory was inefficient or unprofitable, the government kept it going anyway, making up the losses, so that in some cases management came to expect government support. Here too the tests of competition and profitability were abandoned.

The "rationalization" of production

The new goal was coordination or "rationalization" of production in the interests of the country as a whole. Labor was discouraged from protesting against hours or wage scales, and the big unions generally agreed to refrain from strikes. For the upper and middle classes it became embarrassing to show their comforts too openly. It was patriotic to eat meagerly and to wear old clothes as a wartime strategy that enlisted rich and poor alike in a common cause.

Military conscription was the first step in the allocation of manpower. Draft boards told some men to report to the army, granting exemptions to others to work safely in war industries. Given the casualty rates at the front, state determination over individual life could hardly go farther. With the insatiable need for troops, drawing in men originally exempted or at first rejected as physically inadequate, great numbers of women poured into factories and

The allocation of manpower

offices, and in Britain even into newly organized women's branches of the armed forces. Women took over many jobs that most people had thought only men could do. Women did not remain in the labor force after the war in such large numbers because they often gave way to returning veterans; but the wartime experience was part of the social transition by which the labor force in all countries was enlarged, women's place in modern society was revolutionized, and the lives and outlook of millions of individual women were turned more actively toward public participation in national economies. The First World War thus contributed to the redefinition or reorganization of women's work—a social process that had begun in the early Industrial Revolution and that would be intensified during the Second World War and in the years that followed.

During the war governments did not directly force men or women to drop one job and take another. There was no systematic labor conscription except in Germany. But by influencing wage scales, granting draft exemptions, forcing some industries to expand and others to contract or standstill, and propagandizing the idea that work in an arms factory was patriotic, the state shifted vast numbers of workers to war production. Impressed or "slave" labor was not used in the First World War, nor were prisoners of war obliged to give labor service, though there were some abuses of these rules of international law by the Germans, who were possibly the least scrupulous and certainly the most hard-pressed.

Governments controlled all foreign trade. It was intolerable to let private citizens ship off the country's resources at their own whim. It was equally intolerable to let them use valuable foreign exchange by *Export controls* importing unneeded goods or to drive up prices of necessities by competing with one another. Foreign trade became a state monopoly, in which private firms operated under strict licenses and quotas. The greatest of the exporting countries was the United States, whose annual exports rose from $2 billion to $6 billion between 1914 and 1918. The endless demand for American farm and factory products naturally drove up prices, which, however, were fixed by law in 1917, for the most important items.

As for the European Allies, which even before the war had exported less than they imported and were now exporting as little as possible, they could make purchases in the United States only by enormous loans from the American government. British and French citizens, under pressure from their own governments, sold off their American stocks and bonds, which were bought up by Americans. The former owners received pounds sterling or francs from their own governments, which in return took and spent the dollars paid by the new American owners. In this way the United States ceased to be a debtor country (it had owed some $4 billion to Europeans in 1914), and became the world's leading creditor country. Taxes rose in all the belligerent countries, but Europe's long-term borrowing and debts increased even more than taxes. By 1919 Europeans were in debt to the United States by about $10 billion—an economic transformation that also affected transatlantic politics and cultural exchanges.

The Allies controlled the sea, but they never had enough shipping to meet rising demands, especially with German submarines taking a *Shipping and imports* steady though fluctuating toll. Each government set up a shipping board to expand shipbuilding at any cost and to assign available shipping space to whatever military or economic purposes the government considered most urgent in view of overall plans. Control and allocation eventually became international under the Interallied Shipping Council, of which the United States was a member after entering the war. In England and France, where all manufactures depended on imports, government control of shipping and hence of imports was itself enough to give control over the whole economy.

The need for workers during the First World War opened opportunities for women in jobs that were traditionally open only to men. These German women, who were working in a munitions factory in 1916, exemplified this trend in the workforce and also the general mobilization of an entire population to serve the demands of modern warfare.

(©Mary Evans/Robert Hunt Collection/ The Image Works)

Germany, denied access to the sea and also to Russia and western Europe, was obliged to adopt unprecedented measures of self-sufficiency. The Germans went with less food than other belligerents. Their government controls became more thorough

German "war socialism"

and more efficient, producing what they called "war socialism." In Walter Rathenau they found a man with the necessary ideas and organizing skills. He was a Jewish industrialist, son of the head of the German electrical trust. One of the first to foresee a long war, he launched a program for the mobilization of raw materials. Early in the war it seemed that Germany might be soon defeated by lack of nitrogen, necessary to make explosives. Rathenau sweepingly requisitioned every conceivable natural source, including the very manure from the farmers' barnyards, until German chemists succeeded in extracting nitrogen from the air. The German chemical industry developed many other substitute products, such as synthetic rubber. German production was organized into war companies, one for each line of industry, with private business firms working under close government supervision.

The other warring governments also replaced competition between individual firms and factories with coordination. Consortiums of industrialists in France allocated raw materials and government orders within each industry. The War Industries Board did the same in the United States. In Britain, similar methods became so efficient that by 1918, for example, the country produced every two weeks as many shells as in the whole first year of the war and turned out 70 times as much heavy artillery.

Inflation, Industrial Changes, Control of Ideas

No government, even by heavy taxes, could raise all the funds it needed except by printing paper money, selling huge bond issues, or obliging banks to grant it credit. The result, given heavy demand and acute shortages, was rapid inflation of prices. Prices and wages were regulated but were never again so low as before 1914. The hardest hit by this development were those whose income could not easily be augmented—people living on supposedly safe investments, those drawing annual salaries, professional people, government employees. These classes had been one of the most stabilizing social influences in Europe before the war. Everywhere the war threatened their status, prestige, and standard of living. The huge national debts meant higher taxes for years to come. The debt was most serious when it was owed to a foreign country. During the war the Continental Allies borrowed from Britain, and they and the British both borrowed from the United States. They thereby mortgaged their future. To pay the debt, they were bound for years to export more than they imported—or, roughly, to produce more than they consumed. It may be recalled that in 1914 every advanced European country habitually imported more than it exported. That fact, basic to the European standard of life, was now threatened with reversal.

Mortgaging the future

Moreover, with Europe torn by war for four years, the rest of the world accelerated its own industrialization. The productive capacity of the United States increased immensely. The Japanese began to sell in China, in India, and in South America, providing civilian goods that had previously come from Europe. Argentina and Brazil, unable to get locomotive parts or mining machinery from England, created their own industries to manufacture such items for themselves. In India the Tata family, controlling $250 million of native Indian capital, developed numerous manufacturing enterprises, one of which became the largest iron and steel works in the British Empire. With Germany entirely out of the world market, with Britain and France producing desperately for their armies, and with the world's shipping commandeered for war uses, the position of western Europe as the world's workshop was undermined. After the war Europe had new competitors. The economic foundations of the European-centered global trading system had slipped away. The age of Europe's economic and political supremacy was in its twilight.

Industry spreads

All the belligerent governments during the war attempted to control ideas as they did economic production. Freedom of thought, respected everywhere in Europe for half a century, was discarded. Propaganda and censorship became more effective than any government, however despotic, had ever been able to devise. No one was allowed to sow doubt by raising basic questions about the rationale for the war or the actions of government leaders.

It must be remembered that the facts of the prewar international crises, as related above, were then largely unknown. People were trapped in a nightmare whose causes they could not comprehend. Each side wildly charged the other with having started the war from pure malevolence. The long attrition, the fruitless fighting, the unchanging battle lines, and the appalling casualties were a severe ordeal to morale. Civilians had to be kept at a high

Propaganda and public opinion

Every nation in the First World War used propaganda posters to rally public support, recruit soldiers, and show the evil actions of the enemy. The picture on the left is an Austrian postcard with the typical image of a soldier defending the "Fatherland, Family, and Future." The child represents the nation's future. The poster on the right portrays the female symbol of the French Republic, Marianne, who is calling on the French to buy war bonds "for the flag and for victory." This money will support the soldiers who stand behind Marianne and defend the French nation.

(Left: ©akg-images/The Image Works; Right: ©Derek Bayes/Lebrecht/The Image Works)

emotional pitch during the demoralizing years in which they were deprived of their usual liberties, grieving the loss of family and friends, working harder, eating dull food, and seeing no military victory. Placards, posters, schoolbooks, public lectures, religious services, solemn editorials, patriotic speeches, and slanted news reports all conveyed the national message. The new mass press and the new motion pictures proved to be ideal media for the direction of popular thinking. Intellectuals and professors advanced complicated reasons, usually historical, for loathing and crushing the enemy. In Allied countries the Kaiser was portrayed as a demon, with glaring eyes and abnormally bristling mustaches, bent on the mad project of conquest of the world. In Germany people were taught to dread the day when Cossacks and Senegalese soldiers might rape German women and to hate England as the cruel enemy that starved little children with its blockade. Each side convinced itself that all right was on its side and all wrong, wickedness, and barbarity were on the other. An inflamed opinion helped to sustain men and women in such a fearsome struggle. But when it came time to make peace the rooted convictions, fixed ideas, profound aversions, hates, and fears became an obstacle to balanced political judgment.

Wilfred Owen, pictured here in his army uniform, was one of the English war poets who described the horrors of the First World War. He was killed in France, one week before the armistice in November 1918.

(©Fotosearch/Getty Images)

Cultural Pessimism

We have seen how many European intellectuals in the decades before 1914 began to question the theories of classical liberalism and to celebrate the social value of human struggle and violence. Such ideas, widely disseminated by popular writers and intellectuals, contributed to the nationalist enthusiasm that accompanied each nation's entry into the Great War. Indeed, some of the best-known younger writers, including Charles Péguy in France and Rupert Brooke in England, went off to die in the early battles, leaving literary testaments about the spiritual nobility of sacrifices for the nation. But as the war dragged on through more than four murderous years, much of the early literary patriotism turned into cynicism, pessimism, and despair. By 1918, famous war poets such as Siegfried Sassoon and Wilfred Owen were condemning the horrors of a senseless war and mocking the propaganda that flowed from every national government. Irony and bitterness became pervasive themes in the creative works of post–World War I European culture.

War poets

The war's most widespread cultural consequence thus emerged in new forms of cultural pessimism. The psychological studies of Sigmund Freud, for example, increasingly emphasized the raw power of human aggression—what Freud began to call the death instinct—which could never be completely tamed in even the most advanced modern societies. His famous postwar book, *Civilization and Its Discontents,* offered pessimistic descriptions of the endless struggle between humanity's deep irrational drives and civilized moral standards, a struggle in which the unconscious instincts of both individuals and

Historical Documents
Wilfred Owen, "Dulce et Decorum est" (1918)

Although all warring governments used nationalist beliefs and symbols to justify the Great War's huge financial and human costs, many soldiers in the trenches felt detached from the nationalism that sustained the home-front patriotism. Wilfred Owen (1893–1918) was one of the English soldiers whose poetry expressed a growing disillusionment with nationalist propaganda. He wrote this poem shortly before he was killed in France. The title and last lines drew ironically on the ancient Roman writer Horace, whose Latin poem had famously affirmed that it was both "sweet" and "honorable" to die in battle for your country.

Bent double, like old beggars under sacks,
Knock-kneed, coughing like hags, we cursed through sludge,
Till on the haunting flares we turned our backs,
And towards our distant rest began to trudge. . . .

Gas! GAS! Quick, boys!—An ecstasy of fumbling
Fitting the clumsy helmets just in time,
But someone still was yelling out and stumbling
And flound'ring like a man in fire or lime.—
Dim through the misty panes and thick green light,
As under a green sea, I saw him drowning.

In all my dreams before my helpless sight
He plunges at me, guttering, choking, drowning.

If in some smothering dreams, you too could pace
Behind the wagon that we flung him in,
And watch the white eyes writhing in his face,
His hanging face, like a devil's sick of sin,
If you could hear, at every jolt, the blood
Come gargling from the froth-corrupted lungs
Bitter as the cud
Of vile, incurable sores on innocent tongues,—
My friend, you would not tell with such high zest
To children ardent for some desperate glory,
The old Lie: *Dulce et decorum est*
Pro patria mori.

Wilfred Owen, *Poems*, with an Introduction by Siegfried Sassoon (London: Chatto & Windus, 1921), p. 15.

Freud and Spengler

social groups seemed constantly to overwhelm the precarious defenses of civilization. A different kind of pessimism appeared in the influential work of Oswald Spengler, the German philosopher-historian whose book *The Decline of the West* (1918) became a best-selling account of how Western civilization had fallen into crisis and decay. Drawing on cyclical theories of life and death, Spengler traced the history of Europe from its energetic youth (the Renaissance) to a creative middle passage (the eighteenth century) to a declining old age (the twentieth century). Spengler's historical theories, so alien to the nineteenth-century liberal confidence in Western progress and expansion, attracted attention far beyond Germany because they offered explanations for events that seemed otherwise to be simply chaotic and absurd.

Historical Interpretations and Debates
Cultural Responses to the First World War

Historians often describe the First World War as the decisive, transformative event in modern European history. In addition to the horrific loss of human lives, the war undermined Europe's pre-1914 supremacy in global political affairs, international trade, and colonial empires. At the same time, the war shattered much of the cultural confidence and optimism that had character- ized nineteenth-century European intellectual life. A younger generation of writers, artists, and skeptics emerged from the war with a sense of pessimism and alienation that altered European politics and social life as well as postwar philosophies and cultural movements. Compare the ways in which the historians Paul Fussell and Robert Wohl interpret the cultural responses to the "Great War" among those who returned from the battlefields and remembered their wartime experiences.

Paul Fussell, *The Great War and Modern Memory* (1975)

Every war is ironic because every war is worse than expected. Every war constitutes an irony . . . because its means are so melodramatically disproportionate to its presumed ends. In the Great War eight million people were destroyed because two persons, the Archduke Francis Ferdinand and his Consort, had been shot. . . .

The Great War was more ironic than any before or since. It was a hideous embar- rassment to the prevailing Meliorist myth which had dominated the public conscious- ness for a century. It reversed the Idea of Progress. . . .

No man in the prime of life knew [in 1914] what war was like. All imagined that it would be an affair of great marches and great battles, quickly decided.

Out of the world of summer, 1914, marched a unique generation. It believed in Progress and Art and in no way doubted the benignity even of technology. The word *machine* was not yet invariably coupled with the word *gun*. . . .

The innocent [British] army fully attained the knowledge of good and evil at the Somme on July 1, 1916 [when 60,000 were killed or wounded on the first day of battle]. That moment, one of the most interesting in the whole long history of human disillusion, can stand as the type of all the ironic actions of the war. . . .

Robert Wohl, *The Generation of 1914* (1979)

What intellectuals [of this generation] found most difficult to accept about the war was its mechanical and impersonal quality. Death and wounds were not ordinarily doled out in hand-to-hand combat, but in the whizzing and hissing and booming of shells fired by an unseen foe. Soldiers lay huddled like animals in craters and dugouts. . . .

What of value could intellectuals have found in the ugliness and the senseless slaughter of European trench warfare? . . .

The theme that comes back most fre- quently in the literature of the war is the discovery of comradeship. . . . Comradeship arose out of the sharing of a common danger and a common disillusion that was "beyond all hope." It was sharpened . . . by a sense of alienation from those [left] behind—those who had not been there, who had not seen the horrors, who had not experienced the fear of dying and the relief of survival. . . .

The front experience appears to have weakened some and strengthened others; to have driven some toward the Right and others toward the Left; to have given some the taste for war and violence and to have persuaded others to preserve the peace at any cost. . . . No unitary pattern of response emerges.

But one thing seems clear: The front taught an unforgettable lesson in generation- alism to those who came to know it. . . . Hence the dichotomy of young versus old was invested with a new and powerful emotional charge. . . .

(continued)

Paul Fussell . . . *(contd. . . .)*	**Robert Wohl . . .** *(contd. . . .)*
I am saying that there seems to be one dominating form of modern understanding; that it is essentially ironic; and that it originates largely in the application of mind and memory to the events of the Great War.	The younger men . . . were haunted by the memory of an experience that would overshadow everything that would happen to them during the rest of their lives.

Sources: Paul Fussell, *The Great War and Modern Memory* (Oxford: Oxford University Press, 1975), pp. 7–8, 21, 24, 29, 35; Robert Wohl, *The Generation of 1914* (Cambridge, MA: Harvard University Press, 1979), pp. 218–220, 222.

This sense of a crisis in Western culture spread also through new literary and artistic movements, most notably perhaps, in the nonsensical productions of Dadaism. The Dada movement, developing in Switzerland after 1915 and promoted by the poet Tristan Tzara, rejected the structures of traditional literature and generated nihilistic criticisms of European rationality, aesthetic ideals, and social conventions. After a brief moment of postwar popularity in Paris, Dadaism vanished from the scene, but its fascination with irrational impulses, "spontaneous" writing, and strange dreams passed into the more enduring ideas of Surrealism. Meanwhile, even the most sober-minded European authors believed that the war had exposed a sickness in the heart of European civilization. The great German writer Thomas Mann, for example, set his postwar novel *The Magic Mountain* within a Swiss sanatorium, where everyone is ill and where tubercular characters from all parts of Europe debate the flawed traditions of Western civilization. And the Irish poet W. B. Yeats, also seeing that something in Europe had gone terribly wrong, summarized the anxiety of a whole generation in his famous poem "The Second Coming" (1919):

Tzara, Mann, Yeats

> *Mere anarchy is loosed upon the World,*
> *The blood-dimmed tide is loosed, and everywhere*
> *The ceremony of innocence is drowned;*
> *The best lack all conviction, while the worst*
> *Are full of passionate intensity.*

86.   THE PEACE OF PARIS, 1919

The late ally, Russia, was in the hands of the Bolsheviks by 1919, completely ostracized and taking no part in international relations. The late German and Austro-Hungarian empires were already defunct, and more or less revolutionary regimes struggled to replace them. New republics already existed along the Baltic Coast, in Poland, and in the Danube basin but without effective governments or acknowledged frontiers. Central Europe was in a state approaching chaos, with Russian-style revolution threatening to break out in most countries. Western Europe needed vast reconstruction in all areas around the recent western front. The Allied blockade of Germany continued. In these circumstances the victors assembled in Paris, in the bleak winter of 1919, to reconstruct the world. During 1919 they signed five treaties, all named after Paris suburbs: St Germain with Austria, Trianon with Hungary, Neuilly with Bulgaria, Sèvres with Turkey (1920), and especially, with Germany the Treaty of Versailles.

Europeans looked with awe and expectation to one man—the president of the United States. Woodrow Wilson occupied a lone eminence and enjoyed a universal prestige. Victors, vanquished, and neutrals admitted that American intervention had decided the conflict. Everywhere people who had been long tried, confused, and bereaved were now stirred by Wilson's thrilling language in favor of a higher cause, of a great concert of right in which peace would be forever secure and the world itself would be at last free. Wilson reached Europe in January 1919, visiting several Allied capitals. He was wildly acclaimed, and almost mobbed, greeted as the man who would lead European civilization out of its wasteland.

Woodrow Wilson

The Fourteen Points and the Treaty of Versailles

Wilson's views were well known. He had stated them in January 1918 in his Fourteen Points—the principles upon which, after victory, peace was to be established. The Fourteen Points demanded an end to secret treaties and secret diplomacy; freedom of the seas "alike in peace and in war"; removal of barriers and inequalities in international trade; reduction of armaments by all powers; colonial readjustments; evacuation of occupied territories; self-determination of nationalities and a redrawing of European boundaries along national lines; and, last but not least, an international political organization to prevent future wars. On the whole, Wilson stood for the fruition of the democratic, liberal, progressive, and nationalistic movements that had evolved from the ideals of the Enlightenment, the French Revolution, and the revolutions of 1848. As Wilson saw it, and as many believed, the World War should end in a new type of treaty. There was thought to be something sinister about peace conferences of the past, for example, the Congress of Vienna of 1815. The old diplomacy was blamed for leading to war. Lenin in his own way and for his own purposes was saying this in Russia too. It was felt that treaties had too long been wrongly based on a politics of power or on unprincipled deals and bargains made without regard to the people concerned. Democracy having defeated the Central Powers, people hoped that a new settlement, made in a democratic age, might be reached by general agreement in an atmosphere of mutual confidence. There was a real sense that a new political era was dawning.

A new era

Wilson had had some difficulty, however, in persuading the Allied governments to accept his Fourteen Points. The French demanded a guarantee of German payment for the war damages in northern France. The British vetoed the freedom of the seas "in peace and war"; it was naval rivalry that had estranged them from Germany, and they had fought the war to preserve British command of the sea. But with these two reservations the Allies expressed their willingness to follow Wilson's lead. The Germans who asked for the armistice believed that peace would be made along the lines of the Fourteen Points with only the two modifications that were demanded by France and Britain. In addition, the socialists and democrats now trying to rule Germany thought that having overthrown the Kaiser and the war lords, they would be treated by the victors with moderation and that a new democratic Germany would reemerge to take its rightful place in the world.

Twenty-seven nations assembled at Paris in January 1919, but the full or plenary sessions were unimportant. Matters were decided by conferences among the Big Four—Wilson himself, Lloyd George for England, Clemenceau for France, Orlando for Italy. The conjunction of personalities was not a happy one. Wilson was stern and stubbornly righteous; Lloyd George, a savvy politician and longtime leader of Britain's Liberal Party; Clemenceau, an aged patriot, the "tiger of France," who had been politically

CHRONOLOGY OF NOTABLE EVENTS, 1879–1920

1879	Germany signs military alliance with Austria-Hungary
1894	France and Russia create the Franco-Russian alliance
1904	France and Britain establish close relations in the Entente Cordiale
1905	Germany challenges French-English relations by calling for Moroccan independence from France
1912–1913	Two Balkan wars contribute to Serbian and Russian hostility toward Austria
June 1914	Austrian Archduke Francis Ferdinand is assassinated by Bosnian terrorist in Sarajevo
August 1914	Germany declares war on Russia and France; England declares war on Germany
September 1914	Battle of the Marne stops German advance in France and leads to trench warfare on the Western front
1916	Battles of Verdun and the Somme confirm military stalemate in France
March 1917	Revolution in Russia overthrows Tsar Nicholas II; provisional government takes power and continues the war
April 1917	United States declares war on Germany
November 1917	Britain issues "Balfour Declaration," promising support for a Jewish homeland in Palestine; Bolshevik Revolution in Russia
March 1918	Treaty of Brest-Litovsk ends war between Russia and Germany
November 1918	Collapse of German and Austrian Empires
November 1918	Armistice ends the fighting on the Western Front
1919	Western Allies complete the Versailles treaty and recognize new nations in eastern Europe; Germany is charged with war guilt and reparations
1920	Treaty of Sèvres breaks up the Ottoman Empire and leads to French and British "mandates" in Middle East

active since the Franco-Prussian War of 1870; Orlando, a passing phenomenon of Italian politics. None of them was especially equipped for the task in hand. Clemenceau was a pronounced nationalist, Lloyd George had always been mainly concerned with domestic reforms, Orlando was by training a professor like Wilson, and Wilson, a former college president, was imbued with a sense of mission. Wilson arrived in Europe with a plan for future international relations, but he lacked concrete knowledge of peoples other than his own. However, all of the Big Four democratically represented the governments and peoples of their respective countries, and thus they could speak with an authority denied to professional diplomats of the old school.

A League of Nations

Wilson first fought a hard battle for a League of Nations, a permanent international body in which all nations, without sacrificing their sovereignty, would meet together to discuss and settle disputes, each promising not to resort to war. Few European statesmen had any confidence in such a League. But they yielded to Wilson, and the covenant of the League of Nations was written into the treaty with Germany. In return, Wilson had to make concessions to Lloyd George, Clemenceau, Orlando, and the Japanese, thereby compromising the idealism of the Fourteen Points. Probably compromise and bargaining would have been necessary anyway, for such general principles as national self-determination and colonial readjustment invariably led to differences of opinion in concrete cases. Wilson allowed himself to believe that if a League of Nations were established and operating, faults in the treaty could later be corrected at leisure by international discussion.

A special kind of disagreement arose over the covenant of the League. Wilson wished to include a clause endorsing religious freedom. The Japanese insisted that it be broadened to condemn racial discrimination as well. The Americans and British were opposed to the latter for fear that an international authority might interfere with the discriminatory racial laws within their nations and empires or with their race-based immigration practices. In the end both proposals were abandoned.

The great demand of the French at the peace conference was for security against Germany. The war in the West had been fought almost entirely on French soil, and the French wanted above all else to prevent another such war in the future. To trim Germany down more nearly to French size, they proposed that the part of Germany west of the Rhine be set up as an independent state under Allied auspices. Wilson and Lloyd George objected, sagely observing that the resulting German resentment would only lead to another war. The French yielded, but only on condition that they obtain their security in another way, namely, by a promise from both Britain and the United States to join them immediately if they were again attacked by the Germans. An Anglo-French-American guarantee treaty, with these provisions, was in fact signed at Paris. France obtained control over the Saar coal mines for 15 years;
during that time, a League commission would administer the Saar   *Alsace and Lorraine*
territory, and in 1935 a plebiscite would be held. Lorraine and Alsace
were returned to France. German fortifications and troops were banned from a wide belt in the Rhineland. Allied troops would occupy the Rhineland for 15 years to ensure German compliance with the treaty.

In eastern Europe the Allies wished to set up strong buffer states against Bolshevism in Russia. Sympathies with Poland ran high. Those parts of the former German Empire that were inhabited by Poles, or by mixed populations of Poles and Germans—Posen and West Prussia—were assigned to the new Polish state. This gave Poland a corridor to the sea, but this Polish corridor also cut off the bulk of Germany from East Prussia. Danzig, an old German town, became a free city, belonging to no country. Upper Silesia, a rich mining country, went to Poland after a disputed plebiscite. In Austria and among the Sudeten Germans of Bohemia, now that there was no longer a Habsburg Empire (whose prominence and power had blocked an all-German union in 1848 and also a few years later in the time of Bismarck), a feeling developed for annexation to the new German republic. But the feeling was unorganized, and in any case the Allies naturally refused to make Germany bigger than it had been in 1914. Austria was thus reduced to a small republic; and Vienna, a former imperial capital cut off from its empire—a head severed from its body and scarcely more capable of sustaining life. The Sudeten Germans became disgruntled citizens of the new state of Czechoslovakia.

Germany lost all its colonies. Wilson and the South African General Smuts, to preserve the principle of internationalism against   *Germany loses its*
any imputation of raw conquest, saw to it that the colonies were actually   *colonies*
awarded to the League of Nations. The League, under "mandates," then assigned them to various powers for administration. In this way France and Great Britain divided the

best of the African colonies; the Belgian Congo was slightly enlarged; and the Union of South Africa took over German Southwest Africa. In the colonial world, Italy got nothing. Japan received the mandate for the German Pacific islands north of the equator; Australia, for German New Guinea and the Solomon Islands; New Zealand, for German Samoa. The Japanese claimed rights over the German concessions in China. The Chinese at the Paris conference tried to get all special concessions and extraterritorial rights in China abolished. No one listened to such proposals. By a compromise, Japan received about half the former German rights. The Japanese were dissatisfied, and the Chinese walked out of the conference. Meanwhile, the young Vietnamese nationalist Ho Chi Minh, who was then living in Paris, wanted Wilson to recognize that France was violating the principles of national self-determination in Indochina, but such criticisms of European colonialism were ignored at Versailles. The western European powers continued to control their large Asian empires, and the new mandate system of the League of Nations expanded their imperial influence in Africa and the Middle East.

The Allies took over the German fleet, but the German crews, rather than surrender it, solemnly scuttled it at Scapa Flow. The German army was limited to 100,000. Because the Allies forbade conscription, or the annual training of successive groups of young civilians, the army became exclusively professional, the officer class retained political influence within the much-reduced but intensely self-conscious German military forces, and the means the Allies used to demilitarize Germany served if anything the contrary purpose. The treaty forbade Germany to have any heavy artillery, aviation, or submarines. Wilson saw his plan for universal disarmament applied to Germany alone.

The French, even before the armistice, had stipulated that Germany must pay for war damages. The other Allies made the same demand. Wilson, at the conference, was stupe-

War damages

fied at the size of the bills presented. The Belgians suggested, for their own share, a sum larger than the entire wealth of all Belgium according to officially published Belgian statistics. The French and British proposed to charge Germany with the entire expenses, including war pensions, they had incurred during the war. Wilson observed that "total" reparation, while not strictly unjust, was absolutely impossible, and even Clemenceau noted that "to ask for over a trillion francs would lead to nothing practical." The insistence on enormous reparations was in fact largely emotional. No one knew or considered how Germany would pay, though all dimly realized that such sums could only be made up by German exports, which would then compete with the Allies' own economic interests. The Germans, to avoid worse, even offered to repair physical damages in Belgium and France, but were brusquely refused on the ground that the Belgians and French would thereby lose jobs and business. No monetary total was set for reparations in the treaty; it was made clear that the sum would be very large, but it was left for a future commission to determine. The Allies, maddened by the war and themselves loaded with huge debts to the United States, had no desire to listen to economic reason and regarded the reparations as simply another means of righting a wrong and of putting off the dangers of a German revival. As a first payment on the reparations account the treaty required Germany to surrender most of its merchant marine, make coal deliveries, and give up all property owned by German private citizens abroad. This last proviso ended Germany's prewar career as an exporter of capital.

It was with the specific purpose of justifying the reparations that the famous "war guilt" clause was written into the treaty. By this clause Germany explicitly "accepted

The "war guilt" clause

the responsibility" for all loss and damage resulting from the war "imposed upon them (the Allies) by the aggression of Germany and her allies." The Germans themselves felt no such responsibility as they were now obliged formally to accept. They considered their honor as a people to be impugned. The war guilt clause gave a ready opening to agitators in Germany and made even moderate Germans regard the treaty as something to be overturned as a matter of self-respect.

The Treaty of Versailles was completed in three months. The absence of the Russians, the decision not to give the Germans a hearing, and the willingness of Wilson to make concessions in return for obtaining the League of Nations, made it possible to dispose of

The Treaty of Versailles

intricate matters with considerable facility. The Germans, when presented with the completed document in May 1919, refused to sign. The Allies threatened a renewal of hostilities. A government crisis ensued in Berlin. No German wished to damn himself, his party, or his principles, in German eyes, by putting his name to a document that all Germans regarded as outrageous. A combination drawn from the Social Democratic and Catholic parties finally consented to shoulder the hateful burden. Two abashed and virtually unknown representatives appeared at the Hall of Mirrors at Versailles and signed the treaty for Germany in the presence of a large concourse of Allied dignitaries.

These four men represented the leading Allied powers at the Versailles peace conference in 1918: (from left to right) Vittorio Emanuele Orlando of Italy, David Lloyd George of Great Britain, Georges Clemenceau of France, and Woodrow Wilson of the United States. Neither the Germans nor the Russians were represented at Versailles. The decisions of the peace conference, including a war guilt clause that blamed Germany for the recent war, produced deep resentments among the excluded peoples.

(©Bettmann/Getty Images)

The other treaties drafted by the Paris conference, in conjunction with the Versailles treaty, laid out a new map for eastern Europe and confirmed the recession of the Russian, Austrian, and Ottoman Turkish empires. Seven new independent states now existed: Finland, Estonia, Latvia, Lithuania, Poland, Czechoslovakia, and Yugoslavia. Romania was enlarged by adding areas formerly Hungarian and Russian; Greece was enlarged at the expense of Turkey. Austria and Hungary were now small states, and there was no connection between them. The belt of states from Finland to Romania was regarded as a *cordon sanitaire,* a quarantine zone, to prevent the infection of Europe by communism. The creation of Yugoslavia (or the Kingdom of the Serbs, Croats, and Slovenes, as it was called until 1929), although dominated by the Serbs and under the Serbian monarchy, seemed to fulfill the aims of the South Slav movement that had set off the fatal crisis of 1914. The fact, however, that Italy received Trieste and some of the Dalmatian Islands (in keeping with the secret treaty of 1915) left the more ambitious South Slavs discontented.

The treaty of Sèvres transformed the political order in the Middle East. The Ottoman Empire completely disappeared. Turkey emerged as a smaller republic confined to Asia Minor and the area around Constantinople, but most other people in the former empire fell under the control of France or Britain. Syria and Lebanon went to France as mandates of the League of Nations. Palestine and Iraq went to Great Britain on the same basis, though the British had to wage a military campaign to suppress strong nationalist resistance in Iraq before they could establish a cooperative government under the ruler they had chosen, King Faisal. The Kingdom of Hejaz in Arabia was recognized as an independent state; by 1924, however, it fell under the control of what was to become the kingdom of Saudi Arabia. In general, the breakup of the Ottoman Empire left a vast area of the Middle East unsettled. Indeed, the complex legacy of the Ottoman Empire as well as the British and French mandates continued to shape the enduring conflicts in this region down to the twenty-first century; and Europeans would remain deeply involved in Middle Eastern wars and revolutions long after their neocolonial mandates had given way to independent nation-states.

Significance of the Paris Peace Settlement

National self-determination

The most general principle of the Paris settlement was to recognize the right of national self-determination within Europe, though the right was not extended to Europe's colonies in Africa and Asia. Each European people or nation, as defined by language, was in principle set up with its own sovereign and independent national state. Czechoslovakia, a special case, had two national components, as its originally hyphenated name Czecho-Slovakia made clear. Nationalism triumphed as a culmination of the nineteenth-century belief that it went along naturally with liberalism and democracy. It must be added that the peacemakers at Paris had little choice in this matter, for the new states had already declared their independence. Because in eastern Europe the nationalities were in many places intermixed, and because the peacemakers did not contemplate the actual movement and exchange of populations to sort them out, each new state found alien minorities living within its borders or could claim that people of its own kind still lived in neighboring states under foreign rule. Hence minority problems and irredentism troubled eastern Europe, as they had before 1914. The Germans in the Sudetenland of Czechoslovakia, for example, soon described themselves as an oppressed minority; and this complaint–amplified by the irredentist demand of Germany to bring these outlying

Germans into the fatherland–would produce the Munich crisis preceding the Second World War. The Germans thus became militant advocates for their own "rights of national self-determination," which the peacemakers themselves, in 1919, had established as an essential principle of postwar European political boundaries.

The Treaty of Versailles was designed to put an end to the German menace. It was not a successful treaty. The wisdom of the treaty has been debated without end, but a few comments may safely be made. For practical purposes, with respect to Germany, the treaty was either too severe or too lenient. It was too severe to conciliate, but not severe enough to destroy German power. Possibly the victors should have dealt more moderately with the new German republic, which professed their own ideals, as the monarchical victors over Napoleon, in 1814, had dealt moderately with the France of the restored Bourbons, regarding it as a regime akin to their own. As it was, the Allies imposed upon the German Republic about the same terms that they might have imposed upon the German Empire. They innocently played the game of Ludendorff and the German reactionaries; it was the Social Democrats and liberals who bore the "shame" of Versailles. The Germans from the beginning showed no real intention to live up to the treaty. On the other hand, the treaty was not sufficiently disabling to destroy Germany's economic and political strength, which had in any case become a central fact of modern European history. Barring a complete (and now impossible) dismemberment of the unified German state, there was no way for the Allies permanently to reduce Germany's power and influence in European or world affairs. Even the severities that the Versailles treaty incorporated soon proved to be more than the Allies were willing to enforce.

The failure of Versailles

The treaty makers at Paris in 1919, working hastily and still in the heat of war, under pressure from press and propaganda in their own countries, drafted a set of terms that they themselves did not in the long run wish to impose. As the years passed, many people in Allied countries declared various provisions of the Versailles treaty to be unfair or unworkable. The loss of faith by the Allies in their own treaty only made easier the task of those German agitators who demanded its repudiation. The door was soon opened for Adolf Hitler.

The Allies began to express doubts about the treaty even before it was signed. Lloyd George, in the last weeks before the signing, vainly called for certain amendments. British opinion, in 1919, was shifting somewhat from fear of Germany to the fear of Bolshevism, and already the idea of using Germany as a bulwark against communism was expressed. The Italians disliked the whole settlement from the beginning; they observed that the spoils of Africa and the Middle East went only to France and Great Britain. The Chinese were also deeply dissatisfied with Japan's acquisition of Germany's former concessions within China. The Russians, when they reentered the international arena some years later, found a situation that they did not like and had played no part in making. They objected to being faced with a *cordon sanitaire* from Finland to Romania and soon remembered that most of this territory had once belonged to the Russian Empire.

Victors' uneasiness

The United States never ratified the Treaty of Versailles at all. A wave of isolationism and disgust with Europe spread over the country; and this feeling, together with some rational criticism of the terms and a good deal of party politics, caused the Senate to repudiate Wilson's work. The Senate likewise refused to make any promises of military intervention in a future war between Germany and France and hence also declined to ratify the Anglo-French-American guarantee treaty on which Wilson had persuaded Clemenceau to rely. The French considered themselves duped, deprived both of the Rhineland

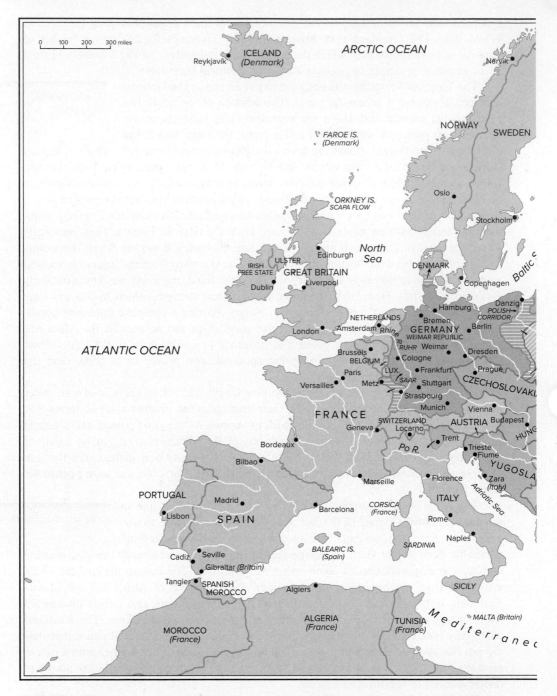

EUROPE, 1923

The map shows European boundaries between the two World Wars after the Peace of Versailles and certain other agreements. Germany returned Alsace-Lorraine to France and lost the region around Danzig (the "Polish corridor") to Poland. In place of the Austro-Hungarian Empire we find the "succession states"—Austria, Hungary, Czechoslovakia, Yugoslavia, and Romania. Poland regained its independence, and Finland and the three Baltic states—Estonia, Latvia, and Lithuania—emerged from the tsarist empire. Most of Ireland became a "free state" in the British Commonwealth of Nations, only Ulster remaining in the United Kingdom. These boundaries lasted until 1938, when Germany annexed Austria and the Sudeten part of Czechoslovakia.

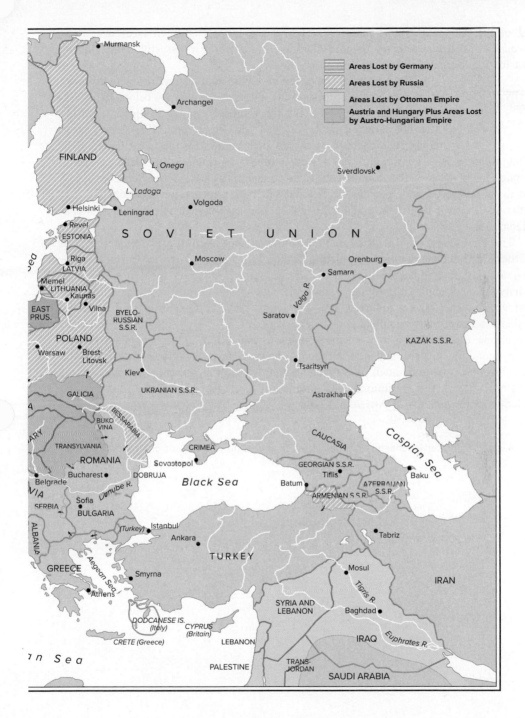

Areas Lost by Germany
Areas Lost by Russia
Areas Lost by Ottoman Empire
Austria and Hungary Plus Areas Lost by Austro-Hungarian Empire

Murmansk

Archangel

FINLAND

L. Onega

Sverdlovsk

L. Ladoga

Helsinki
Revel
ESTONIA

Leningrad

Volgoda

S O V I E T   U N I O N

Riga
LATVIA

Moscow

Orenburg

Memel
LITHUANIA
Kaunas

Samara

Vilna

Volga R.

KAZAK S.S.R.

BYELO-
RUSSIAN
S.S.R.

EAST
PRUS.

POLAND

Warsaw
Brest
Litovsk

Saratov

Kiev

Tsaritsyn

UKRANIAN S.S.R.

GALICIA

Astrakhan

BUKO
VINA

BESSARABIA

CAUCASIA

Caspian Sea

TRANSYLVANIA

CRIMEA

GEORGIAN S.S.R.

ROMANIA

Sevastopol

Tiflis

Baku

Belgrade
Bucharest

DOBRUJA

Black Sea

Batum

AZERBAIJAN
S.S.R.

VIA

Sofia

Danube R.

ARMENIAN S.S.R.

SERBIA

BULGARIA

ALBANIA

(Turkey)
Istanbul

Tabriz

Ankara

GREECE

TURKEY

Aegean Sea

Smyrna

Mosul

IRAN

Athens

Tigris R.

DODCANESE IS.
(Italy)

CYPRUS
(Britain)

SYRIA AND
LEBANON

Baghdad

CRETE (Greece)

LEBANON

IRAQ

Euphrates R.

n Sea

PALESTINE

TRANS-
JORDAN

SAUDI ARABIA

and of the Anglo-American guarantee. They raised more anguished cries over their insecurity and decided to try to hold Germany down while it was still weak, thereby contributing to many subsequent complications.

The League of Nations

The League of Nations was established at Geneva. Its mere existence marked a great step beyond the international anarchy before 1914. Wilson's vision did not die. But the United States never joined; Germany was not admitted until 1926, nor was Russia until 1934. The League could handle and dispatch only such business as the Great Powers were willing to allow. It was associated with a West European ascendancy that no longer corresponded to the facts of the world situation. Its covenant was part of the Versailles treaty, and many people on both sides in the late war saw it as a means for maintaining a new status quo in favor of Britain and France rather than as a system for true international adjudication.

The First World War dealt a last blow to the ancient institutions of monarchy and aristocratic feudalism. Thrones toppled in Turkey, in Russia, in Austria-Hungary, in the German Empire and in the individual German states; and with the kings went the courtly retainers and all the social preeminence and special advantage of the old landed aristocracies. The war was indeed a victory for democracy, though a bitter one. It carried further a transformative political and social process as old as the French and American revolutions. But for the basic problems of modern civilization, industrialism and nationalism, economic security and international stability, it gave no answer. And it left the major European nations much weaker than before to face the rising economic power of the United States, the revolutionary government of the Soviet Union, and the emerging anticolonial movements of Africa and Asia.

Suggested Further Readings can be found in the ebook, on Connect, or online at www.mhhe .com/kramer12e.

Chapter 18

THE RUSSIAN REVOLUTION AND THE EMERGENCE OF THE SOVIET UNION

The Russian Revolution became almost as important as the First World War in its influence on later twentieth-century events and global conflicts. Although the war of 1914–1918 was one of the decisive, short-term causes of the revolution, the far-reaching upheaval came also from numerous other social and political problems in Russian society—and the revolutionary ideas of the Bolshevik Party attracted followers far beyond Russia itself. The Russian Revolution of 1917 can thus be compared in its historical magnitude with the French Revolution of 1789. Both originated in deep-lying and distant causes, and both made their repercussions felt in many countries for many years. The present chapter will examine the revolutionary process in Russia over half a century. We begin with a brief overview of the old regime before 1900, pass through the two revolutions of 1905 and 1917, and survey the Union of Soviet Socialist Republics down to 1939, at which time a new order had been consolidated under Joseph Stalin, a form of "planned economy" had been realized, and the last of the original revolutionaries, or Old Bolsheviks, either had been silenced or put to death.

The comparison of the Russian Revolution to the French is enlightening in many ways. Both claimed to be movements of liberation—the one against "feudalism" and "despotism"; the other against "capitalism" and "imperialism." Neither was a strictly national movement dealing with merely domestic troubles; both claimed a universal historical significance and addressed their message to all the world. Both overthrew traditional monarchies, passed through phases of increasing radicalism, and attracted followers and critics in all countries. Both aroused a strong reaction on the part of those whose view of life was endangered. And both showed the same pattern of revolutionary politics: a relative unity of opinion so long as the problem was to overthrow the old regime, followed by disunity and conflict over the founding of the new, so that one set of revolutionaries eliminated others, until a small,

French and Russian revolutions

Chapter emblem: Families of soldiers marching in St. Petersburg in 1917 to demand more rations for Russian troops. (©Sovfoto/UIG via Getty Images)

organized, and determined minority (Jacobin democrats in 1793; Bolshevik communists in 1918) suppressed all opposition in order to defend or advance the revolutionary cause; and in short order (within a matter of months in France; years in Russia), many of the most intensely revolutionary leaders were themselves suppressed or liquidated.

The differences are equally deserving of notice. Relatively speaking, or compared by many criteria with other European societies, Russia in 1900 was among the least advanced countries and France in 1780 in many ways was in the lead. The main strength of the French Revolution lay in the middle classes, who soon managed to prevail over more extreme pressures from lower-class activists. In the Russian Revolution middle-class people were also active, especially at first, but they proved unable to cope with mass discontents and succumbed to a more radical party that appealed to workers and peasants. In France the Revolution just "happened," so to speak, in that ordinary people from many walks of life unexpectedly found themselves in a revolutionary situation, and even the Jacobin dictatorship was improvised by individuals who had spent their lives thinking of other things. In Russia professional revolutionaries worked for the revolution long in advance, and the dictatorship of the Bolsheviks realized the plans and preparations of 20 years.

In France the Revolution was followed by a reaction in which émigrés returned, dispossessed classes reappeared in politics, and even the Bourbons were restored. The French Revolution was followed by a century of uneasy compromise. The Russian Revolution effectively wiped out its opposition; few émigrés returned; no Romanovs regained their throne. The Russian Revolution was in this sense more immediately successful. But in the long run other significant differences reemerged. By the 1990s the ideas proclaimed in Russia in 1917 were in ruins, while those proclaimed in France in 1789 were widely accepted—representative constitutional government, equal civil rights under national sovereignty, and legal safeguards for persons and property.

Repercussions of the revolution in Russia

The repercussions of the Russian Revolution were felt widely around the world because of Russia's special position in global politics and economic affairs. Since the days of Peter the Great and before, it had always faced toward both Europe and Asia. It was European, yet it was also outside Europe and even opposed to it. If about 1900 it was the least developed of the major European countries, it was at the same time one of the most developed, industrialized, or modernized parts of the world outside the "inner zone" of European nations. Its revolution could win sympathy on the left in Europe because it reinforced the old European socialist objections to capitalism. It aroused the interests of peoples in other continents because it also denounced economic imperialism and the possession of colonies by Europeans, affirming that imperialism was merely the "highest stage" of capitalism and that both must be overthrown together. The Soviet Union, once established, came to occupy an intermediate position between Europe and the colonial world (or what later came to be called the Third World). In Europe and America it would long be feared or admired as the last word in social revolution. In the colonial, or formerly colonial, world it suggested new beginnings, a new way to become modern without being capitalistic or Western, a step in a worldwide rebellion against Europe's imperial ascendancy. The Russian Revolution thus not only produced communism and a fascist reaction in Europe but also added strength to the emerging anticolonial movements in Asia and elsewhere.

Although professional revolutionaries worked for revolution in Russia, they did not "cause" it. Lenin and the Bolsheviks did not bring about the Russian Revolution. They captured it after it had begun. They boarded the ship in midstream. The Russian Revolution, like all great revolutions, originated in many strands of previous history, in diverse local causes, and in the prolonged dissatisfaction of many kinds of people.

87.   BACKGROUNDS

Russia after 1881: Reaction and Progress

We have seen in earlier chapters how the tsarist autocracy ruled as a machine superimposed upon its subjects, how the upper class became increasingly connected with western European cultures while the masses sank further into serfdom, how a developing intelligentsia was divorced both from the work of government and the activities of the people, and how Alexander II freed the serfs in 1861 and created provincial and district councils or zemstvos.

In 1881 Alexander II was assassinated by members of the revolutionary group called the People's Will. His son, Alexander III (1881-1894), tried to stamp out revolutionism and to silence even peaceable criticism of the government. Revolutionaries and terrorists were driven into exile. Jews were subjected to pogroms, by far the worst of any (until then) in modern times. For the first time the empire adopted a program of systematic Russification. Poles, Ukrainians, Lithuanians, the peoples of the Caucasus, the scattered German communities, the *Russification in the old regime* Muslim groups in central Asia—all faced the prospect of forcible assimilation to Russian culture. The philosopher and chief official of this movement was Pobiedonostsev, procurator of the Holy Synod, or layman head of the Russian Orthodox Church, who wanted a disciplined clergy to protect the faithful from insidious European influences.

This is not, however, what happened. In the closing decades of the nineteenth century Russia became more than ever before a part of European civilization. Almost overnight it presented Europe with great works of literature and music that Europeans could appreciate. The nineteenth-century Russian novel became known throughout the Western world. All could read the novels of Tolstoy (1828-1910) without a feeling of strangeness; and if characters in the novels of Turgenev (1818-1883) and of Dostoevski (1821-1881) behaved more strangely, the authors themselves were obviously within the broad European cultural traditions and debates. The melodies of Tchaikovsky (1840-1893) and of Rimsky-Korsakov (1844-1908) became familiar throughout Europe and America; if they sometimes seemed hauntingly wild, distant, or sad, they still betrayed no more than the usual amount of national idiosyncrasy. Russians also contributed to the sciences, notably chemistry, physics, and higher mathematics; and Russia produced internationally acclaimed chess players.

Russia also, from the 1880s, began to pass through the Industrial Revolution and take its place as an integral part of the world economic system. European capital entered the country, financing railways, mines, and factories (as well as government and the army) until by 1914 Europeans had about the same *Industrialization before 1914* amount invested in Russia as in the United States, some $4 billion in each case. In 1897, under the reforming ministry of Count Witte, Russia adopted the gold standard, making its currency readily convertible with all others. In the quarter-century between 1888 and 1913 the Russian railway mileage more than doubled, the miles of telegraph wires multiplied fivefold, the number of post offices trebled, and the number of letters carried by the mails multiplied seven times.

Although still industrially undeveloped by European standards, Russia was industrializing rapidly. Exports rose in value from 400 million rubles in 1880 to 1.6 billion in 1913. Imports, though smaller, grew more rapidly, quintupling in the same period. They consisted of such items as tea and coffee and of the machines and industrial goods made in western Europe.

Industrialization, in Russia as in all countries, brought an increase both of the business and of the wage-earning classes. Though growing, they were still not numerous by comparison to similar social classes in the more industrialized nations. Factory workers, laboring for 11 or more hours a day for low wages under hard conditions, were in somewhat the same position as in England or France before 1850. Unions were illegal and strikes were prohibited. Russian workers were heavily concentrated in larger industries, however, and half of all industrial workers were employed in factories employing over 500 persons. It was easier for workers under such circumstances to be organized economically and at the proper time to be mobilized politically. As for the Russian business and capitalist class, it was relatively the weaker because of several features in the situation. Ownership of much of Russia's new industrial plant was in foreign hands. Much was owned by the tsarist government itself; Russia already had the largest state-operated economic system in the world. Moreover, the Russian government itself borrowed heavily from Europe; hence it was less dependent financially on its own people and more able to maintain an absolutist regime.

Nevertheless, the rising business and professional classes, reinforced by enterprising landowners, were strong enough to form a liberal segment of public opinion, which emerged in 1905 as the Constitutional Democratic Party (or "Cadets").

The "Cadets"

Many of those who were active in the provincial zemstvos also became Constitutional Democrats. They were liberals, progressives, or constitutionalists in the western European sense, thinking less about the troubles of factory workers and peasants than about the need for a nationally elected parliament to control the policies of state.

Russia remained predominantly agricultural. Its huge exports were mainly farm and forest products. The peasants formed four-fifths of the population. Free from their former lords since 1861, they lived in village communes called *mirs*. In most communes much of the land was divided and redivided among peasant households by agreement of the village community, nor could anyone leave without communal permission. Until 1906 the peasants continued to pay redemption money arising from the Emancipation of 1861, and they paid other onerous fees even after the redemption payments ended. They also paid high taxes, for the government defrayed the interest on its foreign loans from taxes raised at home. The constantly rising export of cereals (also used to pay off Russia's foreign debts) tended to keep food from the farmer's table; many peasants raised the best wheat for sale and ate black bread themselves. The farm population, in short (as in other countries in similar stages of their development), bore a considerable share of the costs of industrialization.

Under such pressures, and because of their crude methods of cultivation, the peasants were forever demanding more land. "Land hunger" was felt both by individual families and by the mirs. The Emancipation had turned over roughly half the land to peasant ownership, individual and collective; and in the following half-century the peasants added to their share by buying from nonpeasant owners. The *mirs* were by no means obsolescent. They were in fact flourishing; they acquired far more land by purchase than did individual buyers, and perhaps half or more of the peasants valued communal security above the uncertain pleasures of private property. The exceptions were the minority of more enterprising and wealthier peasants, later called the kulaks, whom the most impoverished peasants often disliked.

Peasant demands

The Emergence of Revolutionary Parties

After the Emancipation in 1861 many peasants continued to believe that they had some kind of rights in *all* the land of former estates on which they had formerly been serfs—not merely in the portion that had been allotted to peasant possession. They demanded (and obtained) credit from the government to buy from the big landowners or former masters. Their land hunger could not be appeased. They remained jealous of the landed aristocrat's very existence. In Russia, as elsewhere in Europe, the rural population was divided into two sharply distinct classes—on the one hand, the peasants of all types who worked the soil, and on the other, the gentry who resided upon it. The two never intermarried. They differed not merely economically but in speech, dress, and manners, and even in their physical appearances. But in the last three decades of the nineteenth century the Russian peasants were notably quiet, and older forms of peasant insurrectionism seemingly subsided.

The other traditional source of revolutionary disturbance lay among the intelligentsia. Russia's most radical intellectuals and writers (as distinguished from those who were simply liberal or progressive) held a violent contempt for the Russian Empire and yearned for a catastrophic overthrow of the tsardom. The revolutionary intelligentsia, because there was normally little that they could do, spent their time in vehement discussion and interminable refinement of doctrine. By 1890 the terrorism and nihilism of the 1870s were somewhat passé. The great question was where these willing officers of a revolutionary movement could find an army. Disputation turned upon such topics as whether the peasants or the new factory workers were the true revolutionary class, whether the peasants were potentially proletarian or incurably petty bourgeois, whether Russia was bound to experience the same historical process as the other countries of Europe, or whether it was different; and, specifically, whether Russia had to go through capitalism or might simply skip the capitalist stage in reaching the socialist society.

The intelligentsia

Most of the revolutionary intelligentsia were "populists." Some continued to approve of terrorism and assassination as morally necessary in an autocratic country. They generally had a mystical faith in the vast inchoate might of the Russian people, and because most Russians were peasants, the populists were interested in peasant problems and peasant welfare. They believed that a great native revolutionary tradition existed in Russia, of which the peasant rebellion of Pugachev, in 1773, was the chief example. The populists admired the mir, in which they saw the European socialist idea of a "commune" represented. They read and respected Marx and Engels; but they did not believe that an urban proletariat was the only true revolutionary class or that socialism had to evolve historically out of capitalism. They addressed themselves to the plight of the farmer and the evils of landlordism, favored strengthening the mir and equalizing the shares of all peasants in it; and, because they did not believe that socialism would have to emerge from the prior triumph of capitalism in Russia, they thought that revolution might come quite soon. This populist sentiment crystallized in the founding in 1901 of the Social Revolutionary Party.

Populism

Two populists, Plekhanov and Axelrod, fleeing to Switzerland in the 1870s, founded in exile the organization from which the Russian Social Democratic or Marxist Party was to grow. A few Marxists began to declare themselves (though not publicly) in Russia itself. The fact that the peasants in the 1890s were disappointingly quiescent while machine industry, factory labor, and strikes were developing rapidly turned many of the revolutionary intelligentsia, though still only a minority, from populism to Marxism. To Plekhanov and Axelrod were added, as young leaders, Vladimir Ilyich Lenin (1870-1924), Leon Trotsky (1879-1940), Joseph V. Stalin (1879-1953), and others.

Marxism

Of these it was Lenin who, after Marx, was to be claimed by communism as a theoretical father. Lenin was a short almost rotund man,

Lenin

Although new industries began to develop in Russia during the early twentieth century, most people continued to live and work in the countryside. This picture of peasants harvesting hay around 1900 shows that women performed much of the labor and that workers still used only simple hand tools on Russian farms.
(©Historical/Getty Images)

with a bounding quickness and intense, penetrating gaze. His hair receded in early youth, leaving a massive forehead, behind which a restless mind was inexhaustibly at work. Even in his 20s he was called the Old One. He was of upper-middle-class origin, son of an inspector of schools who rose in the civilian bureaucracy to a rank equivalent to major general. Lenin's boyhood was comfortable and even happy, until the age of 17, when his elder brother, a student at St. Petersburg, became somewhat incidentally involved in a plot to assassinate Alexander III, for which he was put to death by order of the tsar himself. Because of this blot on the family record it became impossible for Lenin to continue with his law studies. He soon joined the ranks of professional revolutionaries, having no other occupation and living precariously from meager party funds.

Arrested as a revolutionary, he spent three years of exile in Siberia. Here the tsarist government treated educated political prisoners with an indulgence not later shown by the Soviet regime. Lenin and most of the others lived in cottages of their own or boarded with local residents. No labor was required of them. They borrowed books from Europe; met and visited with one another; debated, played chess, went hunting, and wrote. After his release from Siberian exile, Lenin moved in 1900 to western Europe, where except for short secret trips to Russia he remained until 1917. His intellectual vigor, irresistible drive, and shrewdness as a tactician soon made him a force in the party. Genius has been called the faculty for everlasting concentration upon one thing. Lenin, said his one-time close associate Axelrod, "for twenty-four hours of the day is taken up with the revolution, has no thoughts but thoughts of revolution, and even in his sleep dreams of nothing but revolution." Such accounts of his intensely focused activism suggest why and how Lenin would come to lead the Bolshevik Party.

In 1898 the Marxists in Russia, spurred on by émigrés, founded the Social Democratic Labor party. They were not more revolutionary than the larger group of Social Revolutionaries. They simply had a different conception of the revolution. As good theoretical Marxists, they were more inclined to see the revolution as an international movement, part of the dialectical process of world history in which all countries were involved. They expected the world revolution to break out first in the industrial societies of western Europe. They particularly admired the German Social Democratic Party, the largest and most flourishing of all the parties that acknowledged the fatherhood of Marx.

The Social Democrats

If the Social Democrats were more oriented to Europe than the Social Revolutionaries, it was because so many of their spokesmen lived there in exile. They tended to think that Russia must develop capitalism, an industrialist proletariat, and the modern form of class struggle before there could be any revolution. Seeing in the urban proletariat the true revolutionary class, they looked upon the peasantry with suspicion, ridiculed the mir, and abhorred the Social Revolutionaries. Like Marx himself, the Russian Marxists disapproved of sporadic terrorism and assassination. For this reason, and because their revolutionary doctrines seemed somewhat academic, the Marxists were for a time actually favored by the tsarist police, who regarded them as less dangerous than the Social Revolutionaries.

Split in the Social Democrats: Bolsheviks and Mensheviks

The Russian Marxists held a second party congress in Brussels and London in 1903. The purpose of the congress was to unify all Russian Marxism, but in fact it split it forever. The two resulting factions called themselves Bolshevik, or majority, and Menshevik, or minority. Lenin was the main author of the split and hence the founder of Bolshevism. Although after 1903 it was usually the Mensheviks who had the majority, Lenin clung proudly and stubbornly to the term Bolshevism, with its favorable connotation of a majority in his support. For a number of years after 1903 the Social Democrats remained at least formally a single Marxist Party, but they were now irreconcilably divided into two wings. In 1912 the Bolshevik wing organized itself as a separate party.

Bolshevism, or Leninism, originally differed from Menshevism mainly on matters of organization and tactics. Lenin believed that the party should be a small revolutionary elite, a hard core of reliable and zealous workers. Those who favored a larger and more open party, with membership for mere sympathizers, became Mensheviks. Lenin insisted upon a strongly centralized party,

Leninism

without autonomy for national or other component groups. He demanded strong authority at the top, by which the central committee would determine the doctrine and control personnel at all levels of the organization. The Mensheviks favored a greater degree of influence by the membership as a whole. Lenin thought that the party would strengthen itself by purges, expelling all who developed deviations of opinion. The Mensheviks, by contrast, came to recommend cooperation with liberals, progressives, and bourgeois democrats. Lenin regarded such cooperation as purely tactical and temporary. The Mensheviks, in short, came to resemble the Marxists of western Europe, insofar as that was possible under Russian conditions. Lenin stood for a rigid, exclusionary reaffirmation of Marxian fundamentals—dialectical materialism and irreconcilable class struggle.

Lenin accepted and added little to Marx's main governing ideas: that capitalism exploited the workers; that history was shaped by economic forces and was moving toward socialism; that class struggle was the law of society; and that existing forms of religion, government, philosophy, and morals were weapons of the ruling class. He did, however, develop certain theories of imperialism and of the "uneven development of capitalism" that had been propounded in only general terms by Marx and Engels. According to this Leninist

Imperialism and development

elaboration of earlier Marxist theory, "imperialism" was exclusively a product of monopoly capitalism, that is, capitalism in its "highest" and "final" stage, which develops differently and at different times in each country. The unceasing drive for colonies and markets in a world already almost completely partitioned was leading inevitably to international imperialist wars for the redistribution of colonies, as well as to intensified national colonial struggles for independence; both would provide new revolutionary opportunities for the proletariat.

In other respects, Lenin roundly denounced all who attempted to add anything to the fundamental principles of Marx. Nothing infuriated him so much as revisionist efforts to tone down the class struggle or hints that Marxism might in the last analysis perhaps find

Lenin built the Russian Bolshevik Party into a disciplined revolutionary movement by insisting that a small, centralized elite should make all of the party's key strategic decisions. When the opportunity for revolutionary action finally arrived during the First World War, the Bolsheviks had an effective, centralized political organization, a well-defined Marxist conception of class conflict, and the strong-willed leadership of Lenin—who is shown here addressing a crowd in the spring of 1920.
(©UniversalImagesGroup/Getty Images)

room for some kind of religion. Lenin was a militant convert who viewed Marxism as a coherent system of historical truth. He found in it a theory of revolution that he accepted without reservation as scientific and on which he was more outspokenly dogmatic even than Marx himself. His powers of mind, which were great, were spent in demonstrating how the unfolding events of the twentieth century confirmed the analysis of the master.

Although Leninism contributed little to Marxism as a theory of history, it contributed a great deal to it as a political movement. Lenin was the supreme agitator, a field commander in the class war who could dash off a polemical pamphlet, dominate a party congress, or address throngs of workers | *Lenin as activist* |
with equal ease. Beside him, Marx and Engels seem almost to be reclusive sociologists. Marx and Engels had preferred to believe that the dictatorship of the proletariat, when it came, would represent the wishes of the great majority in a society in which most people had become proletarians. Lenin more frankly foresaw the possibility that the proletarian dictatorship might represent the conscious wishes of a small vanguard and might have to impose itself on great masses by an unshrinking use of force.

Above all, Lenin developed Marx's idea of the role of the party by drawing on his own experience as a revolutionary activist in an autocratic Russian society. The party was an organization in which intellectuals provided | *The party* |
leadership and understanding for workers, who could not see so clearly for themselves. For trade unionism, concerned only with the day-to-day demands of workers, Lenin had even less patience than Marx. "The unconscious growth of the labor movement," he wrote, "takes the form of trade unionism, and trade unionism signifies the mental enslavement of the workers to the bourgeoisie." The task of intellectuals in the party was to transform the trade unions and the workers into class-conscious revolutionaries. Armed with "objective" knowledge, the party leadership naturally could not listen to the subjective opinions of others—the passing ideas of laborers, peasants, mistaken party subordinates, or other parties pretending to know more than Marx himself. The idea that intellectuals supply the brains and workers the brawn was understandable as an outgrowth of modern Russian social history, which had created on the one hand a highly self-conscious intelligentsia and on the other a repressed working class and peasantry deprived of all opportunity for political experience of their own. The insistence on a leading and powerful role for the party elite became one of the most distinctive traits of Leninism and one of the ideas most foreign to the democratic movements in other parts of Europe.

Leninism accomplished the marriage of Russian revolutionary traditions with the western European doctrine of Marxism. It was an improbable marriage, whose momentous offspring was to be communism. But at the time, when Bolshevism first appeared in 1903, it had little or no effect. When revolution first broke out in Russia in 1905, it took the revolutionary émigrés almost entirely by surprise.

88. THE REVOLUTION OF 1905

Background and Revolutionary Events

The almost simultaneous founding at the turn of the century of the Constitutional Democratic, Social Revolutionary, and Social Democratic parties was clearly a sign of mounting discontent. All three parties were essentially propaganda agencies for liberal constitutionalism or for various socialist theories. They had more leaders than followers, and they consisted mainly of intellectuals who argued about different lines of thought.

Growing discontent
At the same time, however, there were also signs of growing popular unrest. Peasants were trespassing on lands of the gentry and even rising in local insurrections against landlords and tax collectors. Factory workers sporadically refused to work. But with these popular movements none of the new parties had formed any solid links, in part because there were still no elections in Russia above the provincial zemstvo level.

The government refused to make concessions of any kind. The tsar, Nicholas II, who had mounted the throne in 1894, was a man of narrow outlook. Tutored in his youth by the lay leader of the Russian Orthodox Church, he regarded all ideas questioning autocracy, Orthodoxy, and Great Russian nationalism as un-Russian. For the tsar, the tsarina, and their leading advisors, autocracy was the best and only form of government for Russia.

The chief minister, Plehve, and the circles at court hoped that a short successful war with Japan would create more attachment to the government. The war went so badly that its effect was the reverse. Critics of the regime (except for the handful of the most inter-

Response to military defeat
nationalist Marxists) were sufficiently patriotic to be ashamed at the ease with which Russia was defeated by an upstart, Asian power. As after the Crimean War, there was a general feeling that the government had exposed its incompetence to all the world. Liberals believed that its secret methods, its immunity to criticism or control, had made it sluggish, obstinate, and inefficient, unable either to win a war or to lead the economic modernization that was taking place in Russia. But there was little that the liberals could do.

The police had recently allowed a priest, Father Gapon, to try to organize the St. Petersburg factory workers, hoping thus to counter the propaganda of revolutionaries. Father Gapon took up the workers' grievances in all seriousness. They believed, as uneducated peasants only recently transplanted to the city, that if only they could reach the ear of the tsar, whom they called the Little Father, he would hear their complaints with shocked surprise and rectify the evils that afflicted Russia. They drew up a petition, asking for an eight-hour day, a minimum daily wage of 1 ruble (50 cents), a repudiation of bungling bureaucrats, and a democratically elected Constituent Assembly to introduce representative government into the empire. Unarmed, peaceable, respectful, singing "God save the Tsar," a crowd of 200,000—men, women, and children—gathered before the tsar's Winter Palace one Sunday in January 1905. But the tsar was not in the city, and his officials were fearful. Troops marched up and shot down the demonstrators in cold blood, killing several hundred.

Reactions to "Bloody Sunday"
"Bloody Sunday" in St. Petersburg snapped the moral bond upon which all stable government rests. The horrified workers saw that the tsar was not their friend. The autocracy stood revealed as the force behind the hated officials, the tax collectors, the landlords, and the owners of the industrial plants. A wave of political strikes broke out. Social Democrats (more Mensheviks than Bolsheviks) appeared from the underground or from exile to give revolutionary direction to these movements. Councils or "soviets" of workers were formed in Moscow and St. Petersburg. The peasants, too, in many parts of the country spontaneously began to erupt, overrunning the lands of the gentry, burning manor houses and doing violence to their owners. Social Revolutionaries saw opportunities for a radical political upheaval and tried to take over this movement. The liberal Constitutional Democrats—professors, engineers, business people, lawyers, and leaders in the provincial zemstvos founded 40 years before—tried also to seize leadership or at least use the crisis to force the government's hand. All agreed on one demand: that there should be more democratic representation in the government.

The angry response to "Bloody Sunday" in early 1905 erupted in a wave of strikes, demands for political reform, and militant demonstrations, including this protest march in St. Petersburg. Most of the protestors in this photograph were students, and they were marching behind red flags that had become a modern symbol for revolutionary political movements.
(©TASS/Getty Images)

The tsar yielded grudgingly and as little as possible. In March 1905 he promised to call to office men "enjoying the confidence of the nation." In August (after a ruinous defeat in the naval battle of Tsushima) he agreed to call a kind of Estates General, for which peasants, landowners, and city people should vote as separate classes. Still the revolution raged unchecked. The St. Petersburg Soviet, or workers' council, led mainly by Mensheviks (Lenin had not yet reached Russia), declared a great general strike in October. Railroads stopped, banks closed, newspapers ceased to appear, and even lawyers refused to go to their offices. The strike spread to other cities and to the peasants. With the government paralyzed, the tsar issued his October Manifesto. It promised a constitution, civil liberties, and a Duma to be elected by all classes alike, with powers to enact laws and control the administration.

The tsar and his advisers intended to divide the opposition by releasing the October Manifesto, and in this they succeeded. The Constitutional Democrats, with a Duma promised, began to hope that social problems could henceforth be dealt with by parliamentary methods. Liberals were now afraid of revolutionaries, industrialists feared the strength shown by labor in the general strike, and landowners demanded a restoration of order among the peasants. The more militant peasants and workers, however, were not yet satisfied: the former still wanted more land and less taxation; the latter, a shorter working day and a living wage. The several branches of revolutionary intellectuals hoped to carry the

The October Manifesto

popular agitation forward until the tsarist monarchy was abolished and a socialist republic was established with themselves at its head. They believed also (and correctly) that the October Manifesto was in any case a deception, which the tsar would refuse to implement as soon as revolutionary pressure was removed. The soviets continued to seethe, local strikes went on, and there were mutinies among soldiers at Kronstadt and sailors in the Black Sea fleet.

But the government was able to survive and maintain its power. With the middle-class liberals now inactive or demanding order, the authorities arrested the members of the St. Petersburg Soviet. Peace was hastily made with Japan, and reliable troops were recalled from the Far East. The revolutionary leaders fled back to Europe, or again went underground, or were caught and sent to prison or to Siberia; executions were carried out in the countryside. The Revolution of 1905 would prove to be only a dress rehearsal for the revolution to come in 1917.

The Results of 1905: The Duma

The chief apparent result of the Revolution of 1905 was to reorganize Russia's government, at least ostensibly, into a parliamentary system that resembled the governments in other European states. The promised Duma was convoked. For ten years, from 1906 to 1916, Russia had at least the superficial attributes of a semiconstitutional monarchy.

But Nicholas II soon showed that he did not intend to yield much. He drew the teeth of the new Duma before the assembly could even be born, by announcing in advance, in 1906, that it would have no power over foreign policy, the budget, or government personnel. His attitude toward constitutional monarchy continued until 1917 to be entirely negative; the one concession that tsarism would not allow was any real participation in government by the public. Within this "public" the two extreme fringes were equally impervious to liberal constitutionalism. On the Right, stubborn upholders of pure autocracy and the Orthodox Church organized the Black Hundreds, terrorizing the peasantry and urging them to boycott the Duma. On the Left, in 1906, the Social Revolutionaries and both the Bolshevik and Menshevik wings of the Social Democrats likewise refused to recognize the Duma, urged workers to boycott it, and refused to put up any candidates for election.

The first Duma The short-lived first Duma was elected in 1906 by a system of indirect and unequal voting, in which peasants and workers voted as separate classes, and with proportionately far less representation than was granted to the landlords. The socialist boycott and the system of indirect voting gave the liberal Constitutional Democrats (the Cadets) a sweeping majority. The Cadets, when the Duma met, demanded true universal male suffrage and the responsibility of ministers to a parliamentary majority. The tsar's response was to dismiss the Duma after two months.

Later Dumas A second Duma was elected in 1907. The government sought again to control the elections, but because Social Revolutionaries and Mensheviks now consented to take part, some 83 socialists were elected. The Second Duma came to an abrupt end, however, when the government denounced and arrested some 50 socialists as revolutionaries bent only on destruction. A third Duma, elected after an electoral change that gave increased representation to the landed propertied class and guaranteed a conservative majority, managed to hold several sessions between 1907 and 1912, as did a fourth Duma from 1912 to 1916. The deputies, by following the lead of the government and by avoiding the basic question of where supreme power lay, kept precariously alive a modicum of parliamentary institutions in the tsarist empire.

The Stolypin Reforms

Some officials believed that the way to checkmate the revolutionaries and strengthen the hold of the monarchy was for the government, while keeping all controls in its own hands, to attract the support of moderate people by a program of reforms. One of these reformers was Peter Stolypin, whom the tsar retained as his principal minister from 1906 to 1911. Stolypin's aim was to build up the propertied classes as friends of the state. He believed, perhaps rightly, that a state actively supported by widespread private property had little to fear from doctrinaire intellectuals, conspirators, and émigrés. He therefore broadened the powers of the provincial zemstvos, in which the larger landowners took part in administering local affairs. For the peasantry he put through legislation more sweeping than any since the Emancipation, allowing peasants to sell their shares in the communal land of the mirs and leave their villages. Peasants also gained the right to acquire private control over land and to buy property from the communes or the gentry.

The Stolypin policy was successful. Between 1907 and 1916, 6.2 million families out of 16 million who were eligible applied for legal separation from the mir. There was no mistaking the trend toward individual property and independent farming. But the results of the Stolypin program must not be exaggerated. *Success of the* The mir was far from broken. A vast majority of peasants were still *Stolypin program* involved in the old system of common rights and communal restrictions. The land shortage was still acute in the agricultural areas where yields were highest. Land hunger and poverty continued in the countryside. There were the new big farmers—the *kulaks*—to be resented and envied, but the largest landed proprietors were still the traditional gentry. About 30,000 landlords owned nearly 200 million acres of land.

Stolypin's program provoked widespread opposition. The tsar gave him only an unwilling support. Reactionary circles disliked his tampering ways and his European orientation. Social Revolutionaries cried out against dissolution of the communes. Even Marxists, who should in theory have applauded the advance of capitalism in Russia, feared that Stolypin's reforms might do away with agrarian discontent. Stolypin was shot dead while attending the theater in Kiev, in the presence of the tsar and tsarina, in 1911. The assassin, a member of the terrorist wing of the Social Revolutionaries, is thought also to have been a secret agent of the reactionary tsarist police. It may be added that Stolypin's predecessor, Plehve, and about a dozen other high officials within the past few years had similarly died at the hands of assassins.

But all in all, despite its violence and repression, the Russian Empire on the eve of the First World War was moving toward the kinds of political and social institutions that had developed earlier in the more industrialized societies of western Europe. Its industries were growing, its railways were expanding, and *Social and economic* its exports were almost half as great in value as those of the United *changes* States. It had a parliament, if not a parliamentary government. Private property and individualist capitalism were spreading to new social layers of the population. There was a guarded freedom of the press, illustrated, for example, by the legal and open establishment of the Bolshevik Party paper, *Pravda* (or *Truth*), in St. Petersburg in 1912. It is not possible to say how far this development might have gone, for it was menaced on both the Right and the Left by obstinate reactionaries upholding the absolute tsardom and by revolutionaries whom nothing but the end of tsardom and wholesale transformation of society could appease. But both extremes were discouraged. The desperation of extreme reactionaries in the government, the feeling that they might soon lose their position, perhaps made them the more willing to precipitate a European war by armed support of Serbian nationalists. As for the revolutionary parties, and especially the Bolsheviks, they were losing membership on the eve of the war; their leaders lived year after year in exile, dreaming of the great days of 1905 and sometimes pessimistically admitting, as Lenin did, that there might be no revolution in their time.

89.   THE REVOLUTION OF 1917

End of the Tsardom: The Revolution of March 1917

War again put the tsarist regime to a test that it could not meet. In the new kind of total war after 1914, willing cooperation between government and people was indispensable to success. This essential prerequisite the tsarist empire did not have. National minorities— Poles, Ukrainians, the peoples of the Caucasus, Jews, and others—were disaffected. As for the socialists, who in every other European parliament voted for funds to finance the war, the dozen otherwise disunited socialists in the Duma refused to do so and were promptly jailed. Ordinary workers and peasants marched off with the army, but without the sense of personal conviction felt in 1914 by common people in other European nations. More decisive was the attitude of the middle class. Because they patriotically wished Russia to win, the glaring mismanagement of the government was the more intolerable to them. The Russian disasters at the battles of Tannenberg and the Masurian Lakes, with which the war opened in 1914, were followed by the advance of the Central Powers into Russia in 1915, at the cost of 2 million Russian soldiers killed, wounded, or captured.

Middle-class support

At the war's outbreak middle-class people, as in all countries, offered their assistance to the government. The provincial zemstvos joined together to form a union of zemstvos and to mobilize agriculture for the war effort; and business groups at Petrograd (as St. Petersburg was renamed during the war) formed a commercial and industrial committee to get the factories into maximum production. The government distrusted these signs of public activity arising outside official circles. On the other hand, organized in this way, middle-class people became conscious of their own strength and more critical of the bureaucracy. Rumors spread that some officials in the war ministry itself were pro-German, reactionaries who feared the liberalism of Britain and France with which Russia was allied.

Life at court was increasingly bizarre. The tsarina Alexandra, German by origin, looked upon all Russians outside her own circle with contempt, incited her husband to play the proud and pitiless autocrat, and took advice from a self-appointed holy man, the mysterious Rasputin. She was convinced that Rasputin possessed supernatural powers, because he had apparently cured her young son of hemophilia. Rasputin, by his influence over her, had a voice in appointments to high office. All who wished an audience with the imperial pair had to go through him. Patriotic and enlightened persons of all classes vainly protested. In these circumstances, and given the military defeats, the members of the zemstvos and other such wartime bodies increasingly complained about fundamental conditions in the state as well as governmental incompetence. The government responded by holding them at arm's length. The tsarist regime, caught in a total war, was afraid of the help offered by its own people.

Deepening of political divisions

During the war, in September 1915, the Duma was suspended. The war thus revived all the basic political issues that had been latent since the Revolution of 1905. The union of zemstvos demanded restoration of the Duma, which reassembled in November 1916 and expressed loud indignation at the way affairs were conducted. In December Rasputin was assassinated by nobles at the court. The tsar began to consider repression and again adjourned the Duma. Members of the Duma and of the new extragovernmental bodies concluded that the

Tsar Nicholas II, the last of the Romanov rulers in Russia, sought to wage war against Germany without mobilizing the popular support of the Russian people. This photograph shows the tsar with his wife and children at the beginning of the war. Nicholas abdicated the throne in March 1917, and the Bolsheviks put the entire family to death in the following year.
(©Popperfoto/Getty Images)

The mystical monk Rasputin gained a much-resented influence over tsarina Alexandra and the affairs of the Russian government because he seemed to cure the illness of the royal family's young son. Rasputin's mysterious personality is evoked in this picture, which was taken shortly before his enemies at court murdered him in 1916.
(©DEA/G. DAGLI ORTI/Getty Images)

situation could be saved only by force. It is when moderate persons, normally concerned with their own business, come to such conclusions that revolution becomes a political possibility. The shift of moderates and liberals, their need of a coup d'état to save themselves from reactionaries, likewise raised the long-awaited prospects of the most militant professional revolutionaries.

Again it was the workers of Petrograd who precipitated the crisis. Food had become scarce, as in all the belligerent countries. But the tsarist administration was too clumsy and too demoralized by graft to institute the controls that had become usual elsewhere, such as maximum prices and ration cards. It was the poorest who felt the food shortage most keenly. On March 8, 1917, food riots broke out, which soon developed, doubtless with the help of revolutionary intellectuals, into political insurrection. Crowds shouted, "Down with the tsar!" Troops within the city refused to fire on the insurgents; mutiny and insubordination spread from unit to unit. Within a few days a Soviet of Workers' and Soldiers' Deputies, on the model of 1905, had been organized in Petrograd.

Middle-class leaders demanded the formation of a new ministry commanding the confidence of a majority of the Duma. The tsar retaliated by again disbanding the Duma. The Duma set up an executive committee to take charge until the situation clarified. There were now two new authorities in the city: one, the Duma committee, essentially moderate, constitutionalist, and relatively legal; the other, the Petrograd Soviet, representing revolu-

The Petrograd Soviet

tionary forces arising by spontaneous upsurge from below. The Petrograd Soviet (or workers' "council") was to play in 1917 a role like that of the Paris Commune of 1792, constantly pushing the supposedly higher and more nationwide authority to the left. The Soviet became the public auditorium and administrative center of the working-class upheaval. Because it was generally socialist in its outlook, all the factions of doctrinaire socialists—Social Revolutionaries, Mensheviks, Bolsheviks—tried to win it over and utilize it for their own ends.

The Duma committee, under pressure from the Petrograd Soviet, on March 14 set up a provisional government under Prince Lvov. The Duma liberals, as a concession to the Soviet, admitted one socialist to the new government, Alexander Kerensky, a moderate, legal-minded Social Revolutionary; and they furthermore consented to demand the abdication of Nicholas II. The tsar was then at the front. He tried to return to his palace near Petrograd, but the imperial train was stopped and turned back by troops. The army, fatefully, was taking the side of the revolution. The very generals in the field, unable to vouch for the loyalty of their men, advised abdication. Nicholas yielded; his brother, the grand duke, declined to succeed him; and on March 17, 1917, Russia became a republic.

The Bolshevik Revolution: November 1917

The provisional government, following the best precedents of European revolutions, called for elections by universal male suffrage to a Constituent Assembly, which was to meet late in the year and prepare a constitution for the new regime. It tried also to continue the war against Germany. In July an offensive was mounted, but the demoralized Russian armies were quickly routed. Pending final decision by the Constituent Assembly, the provisional government promised wholesale redistribution of land to the peasants but took no action. Meanwhile, the peasants, driven by the old land hunger, were already overrunning the rural districts, burning and looting. At the front the armies melted away; many high officers refused to serve the republic, and masses of peasant soldiers simply turned their backs and went home, unwilling to be absent while land was being handed out. The Petrograd Soviet, opposing the provisional government, called for speedy termination of the war. Fearing reactionary officers, it issued on March 14 its Order No. 1, entrusting command within the army to committees elected by both officers and soldiers. Discipline collapsed.

Revolution advancing

The revolution was thus already well advanced when Lenin and the other Bolsheviks arrived in Petrograd in the middle of April. They immediately took sides with the Petrograd Soviet against the provisional

Russia's costly military defeats and the food shortages that developed because of the long war contributed decisively to the revolutionary uprising that overthrew Tsar Nicholas II. Similar discontents soon undermined popular support for the provisional government, which tried to continue the war. These women in Petrograd were demanding increased food rations for Russian soldiers, but their demonstration in 1917 is an example of the wider political mobilization that swept across Russia during that revolutionary year.
(©Sovfoto/Getty Images)

government, and with similar soviets that had sprung up in other parts of the country. In July an armed uprising of soldiers and sailors, which the Bolshevik central committee disapproved of as premature, was put down. The Bolsheviks were blamed, and Lenin had to flee to Finland. But as a bid for popular support the provisional government named the socialist Alexander Kerensky as its head in place of Prince Lvov in an uneasy coalition of moderate socialists and liberals. Kerensky's middle position was next threatened from the Right. The newly appointed military commander, General Kornilov, dispatched a force of cavalry to restore order. Not only conservatives but liberals wished him success in the hope that he would suppress the soviets. Kornilov's movement was defeated, but with the aid of the Bolsheviks, who rallied with other socialists, and of revolutionary-minded soldiers in the city who offered armed resistance. Radicals denounced liberals as accomplices in Kornilov's attempt at counterrevolution, and both camps blamed Kerensky for having allowed the plot to be hatched under his government. Both liberals and moderate socialists abandoned Kerensky, and he had to form a government of uncertain political support. Meanwhile the food shortage worsened with transport disarranged and the farm population in turmoil, so that workers in the city listened more willingly to the most extreme speakers.

The Bolsheviks adapted their program to what the most active elements in a revolutionary people seemed to want. Lenin concentrated on four points: first, immediate peace with the Central Powers; second, redistribution of land to the peasants; third, transfer of factories, mines, and other industrial plants from the capitalists to committees of workers in each plant; and, fourth, recognition of the soviets as the supreme power instead of the provisional government. Lenin, though a rigid dogmatist on abstract questions, was a flexible and bold tactician, and his program in 1917 was dictated more by the immediate situation in Russia than by considerations of theoretical Marxism. What was needed was to win over soldiers, peasants, and workers by promising them "peace, land, and bread." With this program, and by infiltration and parliamentary stratagems, as well as by their accuracy as political prophets—predicting the Kornilov counterrevolution and "unmasking" the trend of middle-way liberals to support it—the Bolsheviks won a majority in the Petrograd Soviet and in soviets all over the country.

"All power to the Soviets!"

Lenin thereupon raised the cry, "All power to the Soviets!" to crush Kerensky and forestall the coming Constituent Assembly; and he decided that the hour had come for the seizure of power. The Bolsheviks themselves were divided, but Lenin was backed by Trotsky, Stalin, and a majority of the party Central Committee. Troops garrisoned in Petrograd voted to support the soviets, which the Bolsheviks now controlled. On the night of November 6–7, 1917, the Bolsheviks took over telephone exchanges, railway stations, and electric power plants in the city. A warship turned its guns on the Winter Palace, where Kerensky's government sat. The latter could find almost no one to defend it. The hastily assembled Congress of Soviets pronounced the provisional government defunct and named in its place a Council of People's Commissars, of which Lenin became the head. Trotsky was named commissar for foreign affairs; Stalin, commissar for nationalities. Kerensky fled, eventually arriving in the United States, where he died in 1970.

Resolutions on peace and property

At the Congress of Soviets Lenin introduced two resolutions. One called upon the belligerent governments to negotiate a "just democratic peace," without annexations and without indemnities; the second "abolished all landlord property" immediately and without compensation. Although determined to establish a proletarian dictatorship, the Bolsheviks knew the importance of the Russian peasants. The millions of acres belonging to the large estates that were now expropriated provided a base of peasant support for the new regime without which it could hardly have survived.

Thus was accomplished the Bolshevik or November Revolution.[1] But the long-awaited Constituent Assembly remained to be dealt with. It finally met in January 1918. Thirty-six million persons had voted for it. Of these, 9 million had voted for Bolshevik deputies, showing that the Bolshevik program, launched less than a year before by a small band of émigrés, had a widespread mass appeal. But almost 21 million had voted for Kerensky's party, the agrarian, populist, peasant-oriented Social Revolutionaries. However, said Lenin, "to hand over power to the Constituent Assembly would again be compromising with the malignant bourgeoisie." The Assembly was broken up on the second day of its sessions; armed sailors dispatched by the people's commissars simply surrounded it. The forcible dissolution of the Constituent Assembly was a frank repudiation of majority rule in favor of "class rule"—to be exercised for the proletariat by the Bolsheviks. The dictatorship of the proletariat was now established. Two months later, in March 1918, the Bolsheviks renamed themselves the Communist Party.

---

[1]Also known as the October Revolution, because according to the Julian calendar used in Russia until 1918, the events described took place in October.

Historical Documents

John Reed, *Ten Days That Shook the World* (1919)

Government leaders in western Europe and America condemned the Bolsheviks' Marxist ideology and supported the anti-Bolshevik forces that opposed Russia's revolutionary regime after 1917, but some outsiders endorsed the revolution's ideas and goals. One such foreign sympathizer was the American journalist John Reed (1887-1920), who was in Petrograd during the revolution and who immediately wrote a controversial book to explain why the Bolsheviks had taken power. Although he did not foresee the Soviet regime's brutal violence or far-reaching repression, he was one of the first writers to argue that the Russian Revolution would have global historical significance.

Instead of being a destructive force, it seems to me that the Bolsheviks were the only party in Russia with a constructive program and the power to impose it on the country. If they had not succeeded to the Government when they did, there is little doubt in my mind that the armies of Imperial Germany would have been in Petrograd and Moscow in December, and Russia would again be ridden by a Tsar. . . .

It is still fashionable, after a whole year of the Soviet Government, to speak of the Bolshevik insurrection as an "adventure." Adventure it was, and one of the most marvelous mankind ever embarked upon, sweeping into history at the head of the toiling masses, and staking everything on their vast and simple desires. Already the machinery had been set up by which the land of the great estates could be distributed among the peasants. . . .

No matter what one thinks of Bolshevism, it is undeniable that the Russian Revolution is one of the great events of human history, and the rise of the Bolsheviks a phenomenon of world-wide importance. Just as historians search the records for the minutest details of the story of the Paris Commune, so they will want to know what happened in Petrograd in November, 1917.

John Reed, *Ten Days That Shook the World* (New York: Boni and Liveright, 1919), pp. xi-xii.

The New Regime: The Civil War, 1918-1922

In these same months, the Communists, or Bolsheviks, signed the peace of Brest-Litovsk with Germany, surrendering to Germany control over the Baltic provinces, Poland, and Ukraine. The Russian conquests of two centuries were thus abandoned, but to Lenin it made no difference. He was convinced that the events that he had just mastered in Russia were the prelude to a general upheaval; that the war, still raging in Europe, would bring all of the belligerent nations to the inevitable proletarian or Marxist revolution. Imperial Germany would therefore give way to a new socialist state, and borders would change again. In any case, it was largely by promising peace that Lenin had won enough backing to overthrow Kerensky, who on this deep popular demand had delayed too long, waiting for Britain and France to release Russia from its treaty obligations as an ally. But real peace did not come, for the country sank immediately into civil war.

Not only old tsarist reactionaries, and not only bourgeois liberals, zemstvo members, and Constitutional Democrats, but all types of anti-Leninist socialists as well, Mensheviks and Social Revolutionaries, scattered in all directions to organize resistance against the regime of soviets and people's commissars; and they soon obtained aid from the Western Allies. Both sides competed for the support of the peasants.

As for the new regime, the oldest of its institutions was the Bolshevik Party, founded as a wing of the Social Democrats in 1903; the next oldest were the soviets, dating from 1905 and 1917; and then came the Council of People's Commissars set up on the day of the coup d'état. The first institution founded under the new order was a political police, an Extraordinary All-Russian Commission of Struggle Against Counterrevolution, Speculation, and Sabotage, commonly known from its Russian initials as the Cheka and in later years, without basic change of methods or purpose, under such successive names as the OGPU, the NKVD, the MVD, and the KGB. It was established on December 7, 1917. In January 1918 the Red Army was founded, with Leon Trotsky as war commissar and virtually its creator. In July a constitution was promulgated.

In social policy the Bolsheviks at first adopted no long-range plans, contenting themselves with a mixture of principle and expediency known as "war communism." They nationalized some of the largest industrial enterprises but left the bulk under the control of workers' committees. The pressing problem was to find food, which had ceased to move through any normal channels. The peasants, very much as in the French Revolution under similar conditions—worthless money, insecure property titles, unruly hired hands, armed marauding, and a doubtful future—were producing less food than usual, consuming it themselves, or hoarding it on their own farms. The response of the government and city workers also resembled the French response in 1793. The new government levied requisitions, required the peasants to make stated "deliveries," and invited labor unions to send armed detachments into the country to procure food by force. Class war broke out between the larger landowning farmers who feared that their very subsistence as well as their property would be taken away and city people, often supported by hungry agricultural laborers, who were driven to desperation by famine. Many peasants, especially the larger farmers, therefore rallied to anti-Bolshevik political leaders.

Centers of resistance developed on every side. In the Don Valley a small force assembled under Generals Kornilov and Denikin, with many army officers, gentry landowners, and expropriated business people taking part in it. The Social Revolutionaries gathered followers on the middle Volga. Their most significant military support came from a force of some 45,000 Czechs, who had deserted or been captured from the Austro-Hungarian armies and had then been organized as a Czech Legion to fight on the side of Russia and the Allies. After the November Revolution and the peace of Brest-Litovsk, these Czechs decided to leave Russia by way of the Trans-Siberian Railroad, return to Europe by sea, and resume fighting on the western front. When Bolshevik officials undertook to disarm them, they allied with the Social Revolutionaries on the Volga.

The Allied governments believed that Bolshevism was a temporary madness that with little effort could be stopped. They wished above all to bring Russia back into the war against Germany, an objective they sought to achieve by launching a military intervention in East Asia, through Vladivostok. The Japanese, who had declined military aid to their allies in any other theater, viewed this action favorably, seeing in the ruin of the Russian Empire a rare opportunity to develop their sphere of influence in East Asia. It was agreed that an interallied military force should land at Vladivostok, cross Siberia, join with the Czechs, break up Bolshevism, and fall upon the Germans in eastern Europe. For this ambitious scheme Britain and France could supply no soldiers, engaged as they were on the western front. The force turned out to be American and Japanese, but predominantly Japanese; Japan contributed 72,000 men and the United States only 8,000. They landed at Vladivostok in August 1918.

The civil war lasted until 1920, or even later in some places. It became a confused melee in which the Bolsheviks struggled against Russian opponents, independence-minded

Leon Trotsky commanded the Red Army that defeated the Bolsheviks' many enemies in the Civil War of 1918–1922. He is seen here in the early years of the revolution, when he emerged as a key political and military leader of the Bolshevik Party and an influential theorist of international communism.
(©Hulton Archive/Getty Images)

nationalities, and foreign intervention. But the anti-Bolshevik forces could never unite. The anti-Communist Russians represented every hue of the political spectrum from unregenerate tsarists to left-wing Social Revolutionaries. Many of the rightist anti-Bolsheviks openly antagonized the peasants by proceeding to restore expropriated landed estates in areas they occupied; many engaged in vindictive reprisals in a kind of "white terror." Leon Trotsky, on the other hand, shaped in the civil wars a disciplined, effective Red Army, recruiting it, organizing it, unifying it, and equipping it as best he could, assigning political commissars to watch it, and assuring that trustworthy officers occupied its high command. The Bolsheviks could denounce the foreign intervention and appeal to national patriotism, and they could win peasant support by the distribution of land.

Disunity among anti-Bolshevik forces

By 1922 the Bolsheviks, or Communists, had established themselves up to the frontiers of the former tsarist empire in every direction except on the European side. There the band of Baltic states—Finland, Estonia, Latvia, and Lithuania—remained independent. Poland, as a result of its own war against the Bolsheviks in 1920, retained a frontier farther east than the Allies themselves had intended. Russia thus lost thousands of square miles of territory and buffer areas that the tsars had brought into their empire over the centuries. These territories remained lost to the new Soviet state until the Second World War. But peace was won and the regime stood.

It was during these civil wars that the Red Terror broke out in Russia. Like the famous Terror in France in 1793, it was in part a response to civil and foreign war. The Bolshevik Terror, however, went far beyond the

The Red Terror

The Bolsheviks' consolidation of power depended on the carefully controlled Red Army. These men were drafted into the army of peasants and workers that defeated anti-Bolshevik forces throughout Russia in the early 1920s.

(©Slava Katamidze Collection/Getty Images)

violence of the earlier Jacobin Terror. Thousands were shot in Russia merely as hostages (a practice unknown to Europe for some time); and other thousands were killed without even the summary formalities of revolutionary tribunals. The Cheka was the most formidable political police that had yet appeared. The Bolshevik Terror was aimed at the physical extermination of all who opposed the new regime. A bourgeois class background alone would go far to confirm the guilt of any person charged with conspiring against the Soviet state.

But a working-class background for a man or a woman made little difference. In 1918 a young woman named Fanny Kaplan shot at Lenin and wounded him. She deposed that she had favored the Constituent Assembly, that her parents had emigrated to America in 1911, that she had six working-class brothers and sisters; and she admitted that she had intended to kill Lenin. She was of course executed, as were others in Petrograd. When the sailors at Kronstadt, who were among the first adherents of the Bolsheviks, rose in 1921, objecting to domination of the soviets by the party (threatening a kind of leftist renewal of the revolution, like the Hébertists who had opposed Robespierre), they were branded as petty bourgeois and shot down by the thousands. The Terror struck at the revolutionists themselves quite as much as it did the bourgeoisie; it was to continue to do so long after the revolution was secure.

The Terror succeeded in its purpose. Together with the victories of the Red Army, it established the new regime. Those "bourgeois" who survived took on the protective coloration of "toilers." No bourgeois

A new regime

person as such presumed to take part in the new politics of Russia. Mensheviks and other socialists fleeing to Europe told appalling stories of the human toll taken by Lenin. Horrified European socialists repudiated communism as an atrocious, Russian perversion of Marxism. But, at whatever cost, Lenin and his followers were now able to start building the socialist society as they understood it.

90. THE UNION OF SOVIET SOCIALIST REPUBLICS

Government: The Nationalities and Federalism

With the end of the civil wars and foreign intervention, and with the termination of the war with Poland, it became possible in 1922 to establish the Union of Soviet Socialist Republics. There were at first four such republics in the Union, but political reorganization and the occupation of new territories at the beginning of the Second World War increased the number to 15 (see map, pp. 776–777). Although many of these new republics were established in central Asia, most of the Soviet Union's population lived in three large Slavic regions: the Russian Soviet Federated Socialist Republic, the Ukrainian Soviet Socialist Republic, and the Byelorussian Soviet Socialist Republic. The new Union geographically replaced the old Russian Empire, but the name Russia was not officially used. The guiding conception was a blend of the national and the international: to recognize nationality by granting autonomy to national groups, while holding these groups together in a higher union and allowing new groups to enter regardless of historic frontiers. In 1922 the expectation of world revolution was still alive. The constitution, formally adopted in 1924, pronounced the founding of the U.S.S.R. to be "a decisive step by way of uniting the workers of all countries into one World Soviet Socialist Republic." It made the Union, in principle, fluid and expansible, declared that any member republic might secede and that newly formed soviet socialist republics might join (none ever did voluntarily). When the U.S.S.R. occupied contiguous territories (once part of the tsarist empire) after the outbreak of the Second World War, these territories were also transformed into Soviet Socialist republics—the three independent Baltic states, Estonia, Latvia, and Lithuania; Bessarabia, detached from Romania; and Karelia, taken from Finland in 1940 after the Russo-Finnish War.

The federal principle in the U.S.S.R. was designed to resolve the problem of nationalism and nationalist discontent, which had been one of the forces that fatally weakened the late Russian empire. National-

An answer to the problem of nationalism

ism, the demand that national groups should have their own political sovereignty, had not only broken up the Austro-Hungarian empire but "Balkanized" central and eastern Europe. This might have happened after 1917 in Russia except for the fact that the Red Army during the civil wars occupied large parts of the tsarist empire that had broken away and declared their independence. As it turned out, by 1922 the U.S.S.R. occupied a sixth of the world's land area.

A hundred languages were spoken in the Soviet Union, and 50 distinct nationalities were recognized within its borders. All recognized nationalities received a cultural autonomy, or the right to use their own language, have their own schools, wear their own dress, and follow their own folkways without interference.

A good example of early "socialist realism" in Soviet art, this Soviet political poster from 1918 celebrates "One Year of Proletarian Dictatorship" and portrays the early achievements of the revolution. A worker and a peasant stand on the symbols and chains of the old regime. The happy people in the background are celebrating their triumph and moving confidently toward a prosperous, industrialized future.

(©Print Collector/Getty Images)

The Soviet republics   Administratively the nationalities were put on various levels, with varying degrees of separate identity according to their size and importance. The most important were the soviet republics themselves, but in practice the Russian S.F.S.R., with over half the population and three-fourths of the territory of the Union, predominated over all the others. Moreover all political and economic rights were severely limited by the concentration of authority in the hands of the central government. There was little substance in the formal claim that each constituent republic was sovereign and had the right to conduct its own foreign affairs. During the Second World War there was evidence that separatism had not wholly died down, remaining especially alive in Ukraine, and several autonomous areas were officially dissolved for separatist activities or even for collusion with the German invaders.

Government: State and Party

Government in the Union, and in each component republic, followed a pattern worked out during the revolution and written into the constitutions of 1924 and 1936. In theory, a principle of parallelism was adopted. On the one hand was the state: on the other, paralleling the state but technically not part of it, was the party. But the close interlocking relationship between the two made the parallelism virtually meaningless because the party actually controlled all of the state institutions.

The distinctive state institutions were the councils or soviets, from which authority theoretically ascended through a hierarchy of local, provincial, and national Soviets. Under the constitution of 1924 only "toilers" had the right to vote for soviet members, but in the later constitution of 1936 a more direct democratic procedure was introduced. Voters henceforth directly elected members of the higher soviets, a secret ballot was adopted, no class was any longer denied the vote, and a bicameral parliament was created. On the state side, as set forth in the constitution of 1936, the government embodied many seemingly democratic features.

Elections

Yet alongside the state, at all levels and in all localities, was the party. Only one party was allowed, the Communist, though nonparty members might be elected to the Soviets or to other official positions. In the party, authority began at the top and proceeded downward. At its apex stood the Central Committee, whose membership varied from about 70 in the 1930s to more than double that in later years. Within the Central Committee a powerful Politburo, or political bureau, of about a dozen members dominated discussions of policy and personnel. An even more powerful general secretary, the office that Stalin virtually fashioned, dominated the entire structure and apparatus with authority over appointments, assignments, and decisions at all levels. Thus power and authority in the Communist Party flowed downward and outward, as in an army, or as in a highly centralized government agency or large private modern corporation, except that the party was not subject to any outside control. Discipline was also enforced by the fearsome machinery of the secret police, which was used against party members as well as those outside.

The Central Committee of the party

The number of party members, men and women, which could not have been more than 70,000 at the time of the revolution, rose to about 2 million by 1930, 3 million by 1940, and to 19 million in the late 1980s. A party of 2 million members, though small in contrast to the population of the U.S.S.R., still represented an enormous growth for the party itself; for each old member who had joined before 1917 there were thousands of new ones. To preserve party unity under the new conditions strict uniformity was enforced. The base of the party structure consisted of small nuclei or cells. In each factory, in each mine, in each office, in each class at the universities and technical schools, in each labor union, in each of the larger villages, a few people belonged to the party and imparted party views and party momentum to the whole social group.

Growth and nature of the party

The party in the U.S.S.R. by the 1930s functioned as a tightly knit, highly disciplined leadership group. Those who joined it were willing to work hard, devote themselves to party matters day and night, absorb and communicate the party policy (or "party line"), go where they were sent, attend meetings, speak up, perceive and explain the significance of passing events for the Soviet Union or the world revolution, and master intricate technical details of farming, manufacturing, or the care of machinery. The party was a specially trained elite whose members were present at all levels of government and in constant touch with each other.

The party's leadership role

If the party was a leadership group, the corollary was that more than 95 out of 100 persons were condemned to be followers, and while it is perhaps true (as apologists for the system maintained) that under any system true leadership is exercised by a tiny fraction of people, the difference between Communist and non-Communist in the U.S.S.R. became a clear matter of social status. As the years passed, many Communists in the U.S.S.R. were less the revolutionary firebrand type than the successful and well-rewarded man or woman in any social system. They represented the satisfied, not the dissatisfied. They enjoyed extensive material privileges, not only for themselves but also for their children. They became a new vested interest. Within the party, members had to be not so much leaders as followers. From time to time a good deal of difference of opinion and open discussion was tolerated within the party, but in the end the entire membership had to conform. The party favored a certain fertility of mind in looking for ways to get tasks accomplished, but it did not favor, and in fact repressed, originality, boldness, risk-taking, or freedom of thought or action. The dangers of stagnation in such a one-party system became apparent within the Soviet Union itself in later times.

The New Economic Policy, 1921–1927

By 1920 "war communism" had hopelessly antagonized the peasants, who were cultivating less than two-thirds as much land as in 1914. This fact, together with a severe drought and the breakdown of transportation, produced a great famine. Millions of people died. The ravages of eight years—of the First World War, the revolution, the civil wars, the Terror, the famine—had left the country in ruins, its productive facilities thrown back by decades as compared with 1914. Lenin concluded that socialization had advanced too fast. He openly advocated a compromise with capitalism, a strategic retreat. The New Economic Policy, or NEP, adopted in 1921, lasted until 1927. Most of the decade of the 1920s saw a relaxation of tempo (and of terror) for most people in the U.S.S.R.

Private enterprise under the NEP

Under the NEP, while the state controlled the "commanding heights" of the economy, maintaining state ownership of the basic productive industries, it allowed a great deal of private trading for private profit. The basic problem was to restore trade between town and country. The peasants would produce only for their own subsistence unless they could exchange a surplus for city-made wares such as clothing or tools. The city people had to be fed from the country if they were to turn out factory products or even continue to live in the city. Under the NEP, peasants were allowed to sell their farm products freely. Middlemen were allowed to buy and sell farm products and manufactured articles at will, selling to whom they pleased at market prices and at a profit to themselves. The NEP thus fostered a new commercial class in the cities and favored the big individualist farmer or kulak in the countryside. Indeed, rural changes initiated before 1914 were still at work; peasant families consolidated millions of acres as private property in 1922, 1923, and 1924. Correspondingly, other peasants became "proletarians," wage-earning hired hands. Under the NEP the worst damages of war and revolution were repaired. But there was no real progress, for in 1928 Russia was producing only about as much grain, raw cotton, cattle, coal, and oil as in 1913, and far less than it presumably would have produced (given the rate of growth before 1913) had there been no revolution.

Social and Cultural Changes after the Revolution

Most Bolsheviks wanted their revolution to accomplish much more than the reconstruction of the state and economy; they wanted to revolutionize the daily lives of the workers, peasants, and "toilers," whom they now expected to construct a new classless society. The new Soviet society was supposed to destroy traditional gender hierarchies as well as the hierarchies of class and wealth. Under the legal reforms of the revolutionary regime, women received equal voting rights, the right to divorce, and access to birth control and abortion—which was legalized in 1920. The new

Women's rights

theoretical rights, however, did not have much immediate effect on the social or economic lives of most women in the Soviet Union. Some of the new rights soon lost significance (for example, the right to vote) or disappeared (for example, abortion became illegal again in the 1930s and 1940s), and traditional social relations among the rural masses could not simply be transformed by revolutionary decrees. But it is also true that many girls and young women, like the boys and young men from the working classes, began to receive more education, especially after the turmoil of the Civil War subsided in the early 1920s.

The campaign to improve prerevolutionary literacy rates was only one example of the early Bolshevik aspirations for radical cultural changes. Writers and artists rallied to the revolutionary cause, seeing the social upheaval as part of a wider rejection of traditional ideas and artistic forms. The creative film director Sergei Eisenstein joined with avant-garde theatrical groups to create imaginative new techniques for editing films, portraying dramatic action, and representing political themes. Using his new techniques, Eisenstein produced a famous film about the Russian Revolution of 1905, *Battleship Potemkin* (1925), which was commissioned by the Soviet government and which is still regarded by many critics as one of | *Art, literature, and film*

the most innovative films in the history of cinema. Meanwhile, some radical artists sought to combine "futurist" art with the socialist revolution, and the young Russian poet Vladimir Mayakovsky moved on from a famous "Ode to Revolution" to innovative experiments with a new poetic language. In the end, though, Mayakovsky fell into despair and committed suicide as Soviet society entered the Stalinist era of rigid social control. By the late 1920s the period of experimental art was over, and the new cultural orthodoxy of "socialist realism" was celebrating the beauty of large factories and tractors rather than the abstract mysteries of the artistic avant-garde. Like all other spheres of Soviet life, art fell under the strict control of the Communist Party and government institutions.

Stalin and Trotsky

Lenin died in 1924 prematurely at the age of 54 after a series of paralyzing strokes that left him incapacitated in the last two years of his life. His embalmed remains were put permanently on view in the Kremlin; Petrograd was renamed Leningrad; a leader cult was built up around his name and image. The party presented him as a deified equal of Marx himself, and it became necessary for all Communists in the Soviet Union to claim unflinching fidelity to the Leninist tradition. Actually, in his own lifetime, the Old Bolsheviks had never regarded Lenin as infallible. They had often differed with him and with each other. As he lay dying, and after his death, his old companions and contemporaries, carrying on the feuding habits of the émigré days, fought with each other for control of the party in Lenin's name. They disputed over Lenin's intentions, but behind the scenes, the general secretary of the party, Joseph Stalin, whom Lenin had warned against, was drawing all the strings of party control into his own hands. More openly and vociferously, Leon Trotsky, who as war commissar in the critical years had been only less conspicuous than Lenin himself, raised the basic issues of the whole nature and future of the movement.

Trotsky, in 1925 and 1926, inveighed against the lassitude that had descended upon socialism.[2] He developed his doctrine of "permanent revolution," an incessant drive for

---

[2]For Communists, though not for socialists, the terms "communism" and "socialism" were almost interchangeable, because Russian Communists regarded their own system as true socialism and all other socialism as opportunistic, reactionary, or false. Communism was also defined, in the U.S.S.R., as a future state of society toward which socialism, that is, Soviet socialism, was the intermediate stage.

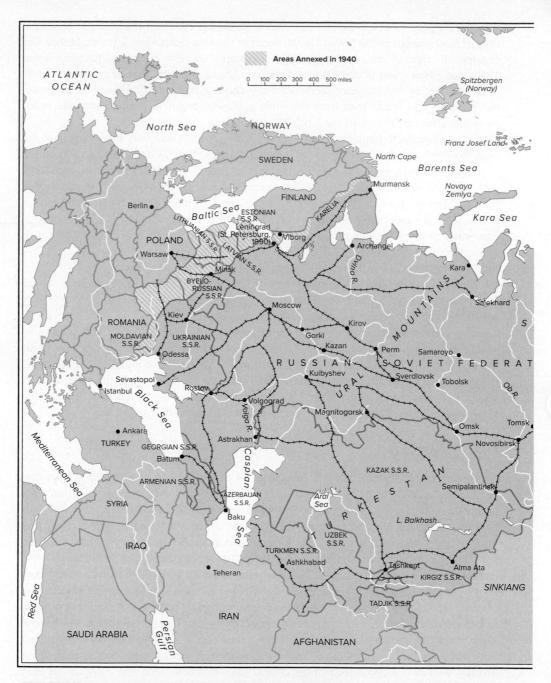

THE UNION OF SOVIET SOCIALIST REPUBLICS, 1922–1991

The U.S.S.R. was over 5,000 miles long and covered one-sixth of the land area of the globe. It was the only state that immediately adjoined so many important political areas—Europe in the west, the Middle East in the south, China along a long frontier, Japan across a narrow sea, and the United States on the coast near Alaska. The Union had 15 member republics (for a short time 16), of which the Russian was by far the largest. Most of it lay farther north than the Great Lakes of North America, but around Tashkent, in the latitude of New York and Chicago, cotton and citrus fruits were grown by irrigation. The diversion of rivers for this purpose led to environmental disasters such as the spread of deserts and the gradual drying up of the Aral Sea.

proletarian objectives on all fronts in all parts of the world. He championed world revolution, which many in the party were beginning to discard in favor of first building socialism in one country. He also called for more forceful development of industry and for the collectivization of agriculture, which had figured in Communist manifestos ever since 1848. Above all, he demanded immediate adoption of an overall plan, a central control and operation of the whole economic life of the country.

Permanent revolution

Trotsky failed to carry the party with him. He was charged with leftist deviationism, machinations against the Central Committee, and inciting public discussion of controversial issues outside the party. At a party congress in 1927, 95 percent of the delegates dutifully voted for Stalin and the Central Committee and fewer than 5 percent voted for Trotsky. Trotsky was first exiled to Siberia, then banished from the U.S.S.R.; he lived in Europe and then in Mexico, writing and propagandizing for the permanent revolution, condemning developments in the U.S.S.R. as a monstrous betrayal of Marxism-Leninism, and organizing an underground against Stalin as he had done in former days against the tsar. He was murdered in Mexico in 1940 by a Soviet agent. Not until the late 1980s was anyone in the U.S.S.R. permitted to talk or write about him and his contributions to the revolution.

91.   STALIN: THE FIVE-YEAR PLANS AND THE PURGES

Economic Planning

Hardly had Trotsky been expelled when Stalin and the party appropriated certain fragments of his program. In 1928 the party launched the First Five-Year Plan, aimed at rapid industrialization and the collectivization of agriculture. "Planning," or the central planning of a country's whole economic life by government officials, was to become the distinctive feature of Soviet economics and the one that for a time was to have the greatest influence on other parts of the world.

In retrospect, it seems strange that the Communists waited ten years before adopting a plan. The truth seems to be that the Bolsheviks had only vague ideas of what to do after their seizure of power. Marxism for the most part gave only general descriptions of a future classless society. The main constructive idea had been mapped out, most clearly by Engels. *Within* each private enterprise, Engels had observed, harmony and order reigned; it was only *between* private enterprises that capitalism was chaotic. In the individual factory, he noted, the various departments did not compete with each other; the output of all departments was planned and coordinated by management. The obvious next step, according to Engels and other socialists, was to treat *all* the economic life of a country as a single factory with many departments, a single enormous monopoly with many members under one unified, far-seeing management.

Engels's centralized economy

During the First World War the governments of belligerent countries had in fact adopted such centralized controls, not because they were socialist but because in time of war people were willing to subordinate their usual liberties to a single undisputed social purpose—victory. The "planned society" therefore made its first actual (though incomplete) appearance in the First World War. It was partly from socialist doctrine as exemplified by Engels, partly from experience of the war, and in even larger measure from the pressure to meet the continuing chronic problems of the country that Stalin and the party in Russia developed the idea of an economic plan.

Wartime conditions and economic planning

The U.S.S.R. decided to plan for five years into the future, beginning with the First Five-Year Plan in 1928. The aim of the plan was to strengthen and enrich the country, make it militarily and industrially self-sufficient, lay the groundwork for a true workers' society, and overcome the Russian reputation for backwardness. As Stalin said in a speech in 1929: "We are becoming a country of metal, a country of automobiles, a country of tractors. And when we have put the U.S.S.R. in a motor car and the *muzhik* in a tractor. . . . we shall see which countries may then be 'classified' as backward and which as advanced." The Plan was declared fulfilled in 1932, and a Second Five-Year Plan was launched, lasting until 1937. The Third, inaugurated in 1938, was interrupted by the war with Germany in 1941. New plans were introduced after 1945.

The First Five-Year Plan (like its successors) listed the economic goals to be achieved. It was administered by an agency called the Gosplan. Within the frame of general policy set by the party, the Gosplan determined how much of every article the country should produce, what wages all classes of workers should receive, and at what prices all goods should be exchanged. Because all decisions were made at the top, it was as much a command economy as a planned economy. The plan, in short, undertook to control, by conscious centralized state management, the flow of resources and workforce that was regulated in capitalist economies by shifts in demand and supply and through changes in prices, wage levels, profits, and interest rates. The system was exceedingly intricate. Countless reports, checkups, and exchanges of information were necessary. A huge class of bureaucrats came into existence to handle the paperwork. The plan achieved some of its goals, exceeded a few, and failed in some. The criteria for fulfillment were almost always quantitative, often to the complete neglect of quality control.

The First Five-Year Plan

The primary objective of the First Five-Year Plan was to build up the heavy industry, or capital wealth, of the U.S.S.R. The aim was to industrialize without the use of foreign loans.[3] Russia in 1928 was still chiefly an agricultural country. The world offered hardly any case of a country shifting from agriculture to industry without borrowing capital from abroad. Britain, the original home of the Industrial Revolution, was the best example, although even there in the eighteenth century a great deal of capital invested in England was owned by the Dutch. An agricultural country could industrialize from its own resources only by drawing upon agriculture itself. An agricultural revolution had been prerequisite to an industrial revolution in England. By enclosure of land, the squeezing out of small independent farmers, the introduction of scientific cultivation, and under the auspices of a growing class of wealthy landowners, England had both increased its production of food and released many of the rural population to find employment in industry. The First Five-Year Plan called for a similar agricultural revolution in Russia, without benefit to landlords and under the auspices of the state, but no one could foresee all of its social and economic consequences.

Building capital wealth

The Collectivization of Agriculture

The agricultural plan of 1929 set up collective farms, averaging a few thousand acres apiece, which were considered to be the property not of the state but of the peasants collectively who resided on them. (A few state-operated collective farms were also established, as models for the others.) Individual peasants were to pool their privately owned fields and livestock in these collectives. When those peasants who possessed fields or stock in considerable amount—the prosperous peasants or kulaks—resisted surrendering them to the new collectives, they were ruthlessly liquidated as a class. Zealous detachments of Communists from the cities used violence; poor peasants turned upon rich ones;

---

[3] The Bolsheviks had repudiated the entire debt of the tsarist empire. Their credit in capitalist countries was therefore not good, so that, in addition to fearing dependence upon foreign lenders, they were in any case for a long time unable to borrow large sums.

hundreds of thousands of kulaks and their families were killed and many more were transported to labor camps in remote parts of the Soviet Union. Collectivization was intended to convert the peasantry into a class of people who as individuals owned no capital and employed no labor and who would therefore fit better into a proletarian, socialist state. The year 1929, not 1917, was the memorable revolutionary year for most people in Russia.

The human costs of collectivization

Collectivization was accomplished at the cost of village class war in which many of the most capable farmers perished and at the cost also of a wholesale destruction of livestock. The big farmers slaughtered their horses, cattle, pigs, and poultry rather than give them up. Even middling and small farmers did the same, caring nothing about animals that were no longer their own. The ruinous loss of animals was the worst unforeseen food calamity of the First Five-Year Plan. The agricultural disorders led to a deadly famine in southeast Russia and Ukraine in 1932 that cost millions of lives. Despite the famine Stalin refused to cut back on cereal and other food exports because they were needed to pay for industrial imports under the Five-Year Plan.

Mechanization of agriculture

By introducing thousand-acre units in place of small ones, collectivization made it possible to apply capital to the soil. Formerly most peasants had been far too poor to buy a tractor and the fields had in any case been too small to use one; only a few kulaks had employed any such machinery. In the course of the First Five-Year Plan hundreds of Machine Tractor Stations were organized throughout the country. Each Station maintained a force of tractors, harvesting combines, and expert agronomists, which could be dispatched from one collective farm to another by local arrangement. Each collective was assigned a production quota. Members of the collective could sell in a free market any products they raised beyond this quota. Meanwhile the government knew the quantity of agricultural produce it could count on, either to feed the cities and other regions that did not produce their own food or for export in the world market to pay for imports of machinery from the West. By 1939 all but a negligible fraction of the peasantry was collectivized, but collectivization failed to increase agricultural output. The new collectives denied peasants the freedom to make their own economic decisions, destroyed their incentive to improve the land they worked, and prevented them from passing land on to their heirs. Agriculture therefore remained a troubled sector of the economy. Collectivization made possible, however, the success of industrialization by augmenting the supply of industrial workers. Because the villages needed less labor, 20 million people moved from country to city between the years 1926 and 1939 and became available for jobs in the new industries.

The Growth of Industry

While the agricultural base was being revolutionized, industrialization went rapidly forward. At first there was considerable dependence on the capitalist countries. Much machinery was imported. But the worldwide depression that set in about 1931, bringing a catastrophic fall of agricultural prices, made foreign-made machines more costly in terms of the cereals that were the chief Soviet export. The international situation also deteriorated. Both Japan and Germany in the 1930s showed overt hostility and began to pose a new military threat. The Second Five-Year Plan, launched in 1933, though in some ways less ambitious than the first, showed an even greater determination to cut down imports and achieve national self-sufficiency, especially in the heavy industry basic to war production.

The creation of collective farms during Stalin's First Five-Year Plan was one of the most radical and most resented economic actions of the new Communist regime. Millions of farm animals were destroyed by angry peasants and millions of people died in the subsequent period of repression and famine. But the creation of large-scale agriculture and tractor stations gradually made it possible for farmers to use new machinery in Russian fields. These people gathered to look at a new tractor that was delivered to their collective farm in the early 1930s.

(©TASS/Getty Images)

No ten years in the history of any industrializing country had ever shown such a rate of industrial growth as the decade of the first two plans in the Soviet Union. In Great Britain industrialization had been gradual; in Germany and the United States it had been more rapid, and

Rates of industrial growth

in each country there had been decades in which output of coal or iron doubled; but in the U.S.S.R., from 1928 to 1938, production of iron and steel expanded four times and that of coal expanded three and a half times. In 1938 the U.S.S.R. was the world's largest producer of farm tractors and railway locomotives. Four-fifths of all its industrial output came from plants built in the preceding ten years. In 1939 the U.S.S.R., as measured by purely quantitative standards, was surpassed in gross industrial output only by the United States and Germany.

These astounding developments were enough to change the relative economic strength of the world's peoples with respect to one another. It was significant that the five-year plans brought industrialization to central Asia and even to the most distant places in Siberia. In part

Changes brought by modernization

because of these developments in Asia, the Russia that went to war with Germany in 1941 proved to be a different antagonist from the Russia of 1914. Industrialization in the

Urals and in Asia enabled the U.S.S.R. (with Allied assistance) to survive the German occupation and destruction of the older industrial areas in the Don valley. The new "socialist fatherland" was able to absorb terrible losses and strike back, because a great deal of the increased industrial output helped to equip and modernize the Red Army.

At the same time, the degree of industrialization of the U.S.S.R. can easily be exaggerated. It was phenomenal because it started from so little. Qualitatively, by European criteria, standards of production were low, and many of the hastily constructed new plants suffered from rapid depreciation. In intensity of modernization, as shown by output of certain items in proportion to the whole population, the Soviet economy still lagged. Per capita comparisons with other industrial nations, in 1937, show that the U.S.S.R. produced less coal, electricity, cottons, woolens, leather shoes, or soap than did the United States, Britain, Germany, France, or Japan, and less iron and steel than any of them except Japan. Production of paper was a revealing benchmark because paper was used in so many different aspects of modern education, economic activity, communications, government affairs, and household life. Where the United States about 1937 produced 103 pounds of paper per person, Germany and Great Britain each produced 92, France produced 51, and Japan produced 17, the U.S.S.R. produced only 11.

Social Costs and Social Effects of the Plans

| Sacrifices and rewards |

Industrialization in Russia demanded huge and continuing sacrifices on the part of the people. It was not merely that kulaks lost their lives, or that millions of others, whose exact numbers have never been known, were condemned as enemies of the system and sent off to correctional labor camps. All were required to accept a program of austerity and self-denial, going without the better food, housing, and other consumer goods that might have been produced, in order that the capital wealth and heavy industry of the country might be built up. The plan required hard work and low wages. Morale was sustained by propaganda. One of the chief functions of party members was to explain why sacrifices were necessary. In the late 1930s life began to ease; food rationing was abolished in 1935, and a few more products of light industry, such as dishes and fountain pens, began to appear in Soviet retail stores. Living standards rose back to the level of 1927 with prospects brighter for raising them. But the need for war preparations, as international conflicts intensified, again drove back the vision of the Promised Land.

Socialism, as realized in the plans, did away with some of the evils of unrestrained free enterprise. There was no acknowledged unemployment or cycle of boom and depression. There was less misuse of women and children than in the early days of European industrialization. There was a minimum below which no one was supposed to fall. On the other hand, there was no economic equality. Marxism, indeed, had never seen complete equality of income as a principal objective. While there were no very rich people, as in other parts of Europe (where the income of the very rich often came from inherited property), the differences in income were nevertheless great. High government officials, managers, engineers, and favored artists and intellectuals received the highest rewards. People with large incomes could build precarious little fortunes for themselves and their children. They could not, however, under socialism, own any industrial capital, that is, buy shares of stock or other equities. There was, of course, no stock exchange.

| Competition |

Competition of a special kind developed. In 1935 a miner named Stakhanov greatly increased his daily output of coal by devising improvements in his methods of work. He also greatly increased his wages,

CHRONOLOGY OF NOTABLE EVENTS, 1894–1937

1894	Creation of Russian Marxist organization, the Social Democratic Party
1903	Social Democrats split into two factions, Bolsheviks and Mensheviks; Lenin leads Bolsheviks
January 1905	Economic hardship, "Bloody Sunday," and Russo-Japanese War spark Revolution of 1905 in St. Petersburg
October 1905	Tsar's October Manifesto establishes new parliamentary body, the Duma
1906–1911	Stolypin's reforms promote growth of prosperous farmers (kulaks)
1914	Russia enters war with Germany and suffers crushing military defeats
March 1917	Tsar Nicholas II abdicates; Russia becomes a republic under provisional government and continues war with Germany
April 1917	Germany provides safe passage for Bolshevik leaders to enter Russia
November 1917	The Bolshevik Revolution: Lenin and the Bolshevik-led Soviets overthrow the provisional government in Petrograd
January 1918	Bolsheviks dissolve Constituent Assembly and establish the Red Army
1918–1922	Bolsheviks consolidate power and suppress all opponents in Civil War and Red Terror
1919–1920	Creation of Third, or Communist, International (the Comintern)
1921–1927	New Economic Policy allows more independent commercial activity
1922	Establishment of the Union of Soviet Socialist Republics (U.S.S.R)
1925–1927	Stalin prevails over Trotsky to take control of the Bolshevik Central Committee
1928	Stalin launches the First Five-Year Plan for economic development
1929	Soviet regime begins the collectivization of agriculture; resistance from kulaks and others leads to widespread repression and famine
1936–1937	Public "purge trials" remove Old Bolsheviks from Communist Party; many are executed or imprisoned

because Soviet workers were paid at piece rates. His example proved contagious; workers all over the country began to break records of all kinds. The government publicized their achievements, called them Stakhanovites and "labor heroes," and pronounced the movement to be "a new and higher stage of socialist competition." In labor circles in the United States such straining to increase output was called a speed-up, and piecework wages had long been anathema to the organized labor of all countries. Nor was management free from competitive pressure. A factory manager who failed to show the net income (or "profit") upon which the plan counted, or who failed to meet his quota of output, might lose not only his job but also his social status—or even his life.

The government supervised everything with totalitarian methods, and conformity was the social and cultural ideal. There was no room for skepticism, independence of thought, or any criticism that weak-

The price of solidarity

ened the will to achieve. As in tsarist times, no one could leave the country without special permission, which was given far more rarely than before 1914. There was, of course, only

The rapid industrialization of the Soviet Union emphasized heavy machinery rather than consumer goods, but the Soviets also began to produce their own cars. This automobile factory in Nizhny Novgorod (a city the Soviets renamed as Gorky in honor of the Russian writer Maxim Gorky) represented the new industrial economy and also expressed the requisite political loyalty to Stalin.

(©Sovfoto/Getty Images)

one political party. There were no free labor unions, no free press, no freedom of association, and at best only an irritable tolerance for religion. Soviet Jews who adapted to the system found themselves in a more favorable position than ever before; some even attained positions of high importance. Many still faced lingering suspicion and distrust, however, and in religious matters they met harassment. Art, literature, and even science became vehicles of political propaganda; creative, experimental works—and the people who promoted them—disappeared from Soviet cultural life. As for the number of people sacrificed to Stalin's brutal Juggernaut—liquidated bourgeois, liquidated peasants, purged party members, disaffected persons sentenced to long terms in labor camps—a precise figure will never be known, but it certainly reached many millions over the years in which the various Soviet plans were implemented.

The Purge Trials of the 1930s

In 1936 socialism was judged to have proved so successful that a new constitution for the U.S.S.R. was proclaimed. It enumerated, as rights of Soviet citizens, not merely the usual civil liberties of modern democracies but the rights to steady employment, rest, leisure, economic security, and a comfortable old age. All forms of racism were condemned. It reorganized the Soviet republics and granted equal and direct universal suffrage.

The constitution of 1936 received favorable comment in western Europe, where it was hoped that the Russian Revolution, like former revolutions, had at last turned into quieter channels. It was nonetheless apparent that the Communist Party remained the sole governing group in the country, that Stalin was tightening his dictatorship, and that the party was racked by internal troubles.

Throughout the 1930s Stalin acted preemptorily to suppress all dissent. As early as 1933, the party underwent a drastic purge, in which *Stalinist repression* a third of its members were expelled. Even the faithful were appalled at Stalin's growing ruthlessness. Serge Kirov, an old friend and revolutionary companion of Stalin since 1909, head of the Leningrad party apparatus, and member of the Politburo since 1930, showed signs of leading the disaffected. In 1934 he was killed at his office by a gunman who was almost certainly an agent of Stalin's police. The assassination gave Stalin an excuse to strike out at his opponents, imagined or real, by a revival of terror, immediately executing over a hundred persons and launching extraordinary purges that continued during the next four years.

A series of sensational trials took place. In 1936, 16 Old Bolsheviks were brought to trial. Some had been expelled from the party in 1927 *Trials of the Old* *Bolsheviks* for supporting Trotsky and subsequently, after the proper recantations, had been readmitted. Now they were charged with the murder of Kirov, with plotting the murder of Stalin, and with having organized in 1932 under Trotsky's inspiration a secret group to disrupt and terrorize the Central Committee. To the amazement of the outside world, all the accused made full confession to the charges in open court. All blamed themselves as unworthy and erring reprobates. All were put to death. In 1937, after similar trials, 17 other Old Bolsheviks met the same fate or received long prison sentences; and in 1938 a group of "rightists" were executed after they were charged with wanting to restore bourgeois capitalism. The same confessions and self-accusations followed in almost every case, with no other verifiable evidence adduced. How these confessions were obtained in open court from hardened revolutionaries apparently in full possession of their faculties and bearing no sign of physical harm mystified the outside world. Only later did it become clear that psychological torture had broken the will of those accused and that threats against their families (or promises to spare them) had played the major part.

In addition to these public trials there were other arrests, private inquisitions, and executions that extended from the highest levels of the party, government, and military into intellectual and scientific circles and the lesser echelons of state institutions. In later years the KGB itself disclosed that in the years 1930–1953 (the year of Stalin's death) 3,778,334 persons had been tried and sentenced for "counterrevolutionary" activity and crimes against the state, most of them in the Great Terror of 1934–1938, and that 786,098 were executed; unknown others died in prison camps. The innocence of many of Stalin's victims was thus officially confirmed and their reputations posthumously restored.

By these purges Stalin rid himself of all possible rivals for his own position. He disposed of former Bolshevik colleagues who could *Reinforcing* remember the old days, who could quote Lenin as a friend, or belittle *the dictatorship* the reality of 1937 by recalling the dreams of 1917. After 1938 there were virtually no Old Bolsheviks left. A younger group, products of the new order, practical, constructive, impatient of "agitators," and acquiescing in Stalin's dictatorship, were operating what was now an established system.

ДА ЗДРАВСТВУЕТ СТАЛИНСКОЕ ПЛЕМЯ ГЕРОЕВ СТАХАНОВЦЕВ!

Soviet propaganda portrayed Stalin as a benevolent leader and worthy successor of Lenin. This typical poster by the artist Gustav Klutsis (1895–1938), which is entitled "Long Live Stalin's Generation of Stakhanov Heroes" (1936), links Stalin to a bust of Lenin, depicts the support of admiring Soviet citizens, and celebrates the "Stakhanovites" who worked overtime in Soviet factories and mines. Klutsis produced a wide range of imaginative artwork for the Soviet state, but like many longtime Bolshevik activists he was executed during one of Stalin's party purges.

(©Heritage Images/Getty Images)

92. THE INTERNATIONAL IMPACT OF COMMUNISM, 1919–1939

The Background: Socialism and the First World War

Marxism had always described the class struggle as an international movement and analyzed transnational economic systems more than the governments of specific national states. After Marx's death, however, as Marxist parties grew in numbers, and as the states of western Europe became more democratic, most people who called themselves Marxists accepted the national state, seeing in it a means by which the workers' lot could be gradually improved. This view was part of the movement of revisionism, or what more rigorous Marxists called "opportunism." In the First World War national loyalty proved its strength. The socialist parties in the Reichstag, the French Chamber, and other parliamentary bodies voted for war credits without hesitation. Socialist workers reported for mobilization like everyone else.

Small minorities of socialists in every country nevertheless broke with the nationalist majority and refused to accept the war. They met in international conferences with each other and with socialists from the neutral countries. Active among them had been Lenin and other Russian Social Democrats then in Switzerland. The minority or antiwar socialists met at the small Swiss town of Zimmerwald in 1915, where they drew up a "Zimmerwald program," calling for immediate peace without annexations or indemnities; and then the Zimmerwald group itself began to split. Most Zimmerwalders regarded peace, or the repudiation of the war, as their aim. But a "Zimmerwald Left" began to develop, inspired mainly by Lenin and the Russian émigrés. This faction made its aim not peace but revolution. It hoped that the war would go on until it caused social revolution in the belligerent countries.

Class solidarity vs. nationalism

Then in April 1917, as we have seen, with the German imperial government arranging their trip, Lenin and the other Bolsheviks went back to Russia and accomplished the November Revolution. Lenin, until his death in 1924, believed that the Russian Revolution was only a local phase of a world revolution—of *the* revolution of strict Marxian doctrine. Because he expected proletarian upheaval to follow soon in Germany, Poland, the Danube Valley, and the Baltic regions, he accepted the treaty of Brest-Litovsk. He took no pride in Russia; he was no patriot or "social-chauvinist," to use his own term. In the founding of the U.S.S.R. in 1922 he saw a nucleus around which other and greater soviet republics of any nationality might coalesce.

The First World War was in fact followed by attempted revolutions in Germany and eastern Europe. With the German and Austro-Hungarian empires wrecked, socialists and liberals of all descriptions strove to establish new regimes. Among socialists the old differences persisted, between those favoring gradual, nonviolent, and parliamentary methods and a more extreme group who saw in postwar disintegration a chance to realize the international proletarian revolution. The first group looked upon the Bolshevik Revolution with horror; the second looked upon it with admiration. The first group included not only trade union officials and practical socialist politicians but also major prewar Marxist writers such as Karl Kautsky and Eduard Bernstein. The mass of European socialists remained relatively moderate. Marxist in principle, they were in fact more than ever wedded to gradual, peaceable, and parliamentary methods. The second group, radical Leninists, continued to agitate for the forcible overthrow of European capitalism and European political institutions; and they began to join together in the Bolsheviks' new organization for promoting world revolution, the Third, or Communist, International, which was created in March 1919.

Attempted revolutions in Europe

The Founding of the Third International

The Second International, which since its foundation in 1889 had met every two or three years until 1914, held its first postwar meeting at Berne in 1919. It represented socialist parties and labor organizations of all countries. The Berne meeting was stormy, for a small minority vehemently demanded "revolution as in Russia, socialization of property as in Russia, application of Marxism as in Russia." Overruled at Berne, they went to Moscow and there founded a new International in conjunction with the Russian Communist Party, and with Lenin and the Russians dominating it completely. It was Lenin's hope, by founding a new International of his own, to discredit moderate socialism and to claim for the Communists the true line of succession from the First International of Karl Marx.

The Third
International

The first congress of the Third International in 1919 was somewhat haphazard, but at the second, in 1920, the extreme left parties of 37 countries were represented. The Russian Party was supposedly only one component. Actually, it supplied most of the personnel and most of the funds; the Bolshevik Zinoviev was its first president, remaining in this office until his disgrace as a Trotskyist in 1927. The Third, or Communist, International—the Comintern—was in part a spontaneous rallying of Marxists from all countries who viewed the Bolshevik Revolution as the true fruition of Marxism; but, even more, it was the creation and weapon of the Bolsheviks themselves, by which they wished to discredit and isolate the moderate socialists and bring about world revolution. Of all enemies the Communists hated the socialists most, reserving for them even stronger epithets than they bestowed upon capitalists and imperialists, because Communists and socialists were competing for the same objective, the leadership of the world's working class.

*Lenin's Twenty-One
Points*

The second congress of the International, in 1920, endorsed a program of Twenty-One Points, written by Lenin. These included the requirements that each national party must call itself Communist, repudiate "reformist" socialism, propagandize labor unions and get Communists into the important union offices, infiltrate the army, impose an iron discipline upon members, require submission to the orders of the international Executive, use both legal channels and secret underground methods, and expel promptly any member not hewing to the party line. Making no pretense of respect for parliamentary democracy, the Comintern was a weapon for revolution, organized by revolutionaries who knew how to seize power by revolutionary methods. In most countries, as in France, there were many socialists who could not accept the Twenty-One Points. Once unified socialist parties therefore broke up. Communists and socialists went their separate ways.

*Promoting world
revolution*

For several years the U.S.S.R., using the Comintern or more conventional diplomatic channels, promoted world revolution as best it could. Communists from many countries went to Russia for extended study of Marxist ideas or revolutionary tactics, and Comintern agents traveled widely around the world. In 1924, in England, publication of the "Zinoviev letter," in which the Comintern allegedly urged British workers to provoke revolution, led to a great electoral victory for the Conservative Party. The Bolshevik menace, real and imagined, produced everywhere a strong reaction. It was basic to the rise of fascism described in the chapters to follow.

In 1927, with the suppression of Trotskyism and world revolutionism in Russia, and with the concentration under Stalin on a program of building socialism in one country, the Comintern moderated its activities. In 1935, as fascist dictators became noisily bellicose and threatened the Soviet Union, the U.S.S.R. through the Comintern instructed all Communist parties to enter into coalitions with socialists and activist liberals in what were called "popular fronts" to combat fascism and reaction and support the national defense of their own countries. During the Second World War (in 1943), as a gesture of goodwill to Great Britain and the United States, the U.S.S.R. abolished the Comintern entirely. It reappeared for a few years from 1947 to 1956 under a new name, the Communist Information Bureau or Cominform, and was then disbanded.

The U.S.S.R.'s impact

It was not through the Comintern that the U.S.S.R. exerted its greatest global influence in the years after 1917. It exerted its influence by the massive fact of its very existence, which showed that a new type of modern economic system could emerge from a revolution. Before 1917 no one in Europe or Asia had thought that anything was to be learned from Russia. Twenty years

The Russian Revolution brought about a split between socialists who favored parliamentary politics and those who supported the revolutionary methods of the Bolsheviks. The latter group met in Russia to form the Third, or Communist, International. It adhered to the views of Lenin, who is speaking here to a meeting of the Third International in 1920.

(©Hulton Deutsch/Getty Images)

later even critics of the U.S.S.R. feared that it might represent the wave of the future. Its sheer power was soon demonstrated in the Second World War. Marxism was no longer merely a theory; there was an actual society, embracing a sixth of the globe, which called itself Marxist.

In every country those who were most critical of capitalist institutions compared them unfavorably to those of the Soviet Union. With the appearance of Communism and Communist parties, socialism and socialist ideas seemed in contrast to be middling and respectable. Everywhere in the 1930s the idea of planning began to find favor. Workers obtained more security against the fluctuations of capitalism. Colonial and formerly colonial peoples, especially in Asia, were particularly impressed by the achievement of the U.S.S.R., which had shown how a traditional society could modernize without falling under the influence of foreign capital or foreign guidance.

For a long time the Communist Party in the Soviet Union presented itself as the innovative leader of world revolution and tried to exert control over Communist parties in all other countries. This became increasingly difficult. Over the years the U.S.S.R. pursued diplomatic and military policies and engaged in acts of aggression and territorial expansion that resembled the actions of other ambitious global powers. By the late 1980s nobody was describing the U.S.S.R. as an innovative society, and many people both *Waning Soviet influence in later years* within the Soviet Union and in the former colonial world came to believe that it could not adapt to modern social realities. Its economic system was in a shambles; the component republics demanded autonomy or independence. The revelation from within the Soviet Union itself of the persecution and deaths of tens of millions of innocent victims, along with the restiveness of its own nationalities, undermined its claim to be a leader of oppressed peoples elsewhere. European Communist parties proclaimed their independence from Moscow. Meanwhile a new and influential form of communism emerged after 1949 in the People's Republic of China. Yet all Communist parties, including the Chinese, were derived from Marxism and from the Russian Revolution of 1917, once hailed as the first great victory over capitalism and imperialism. It was thus a revolution that profoundly influenced fervent supporters throughout much of the twentieth century. But the repressive political system, stifling cultural policies, brutal purges, and economic failures of the Soviet state also produced passionate opponents and a widespread hostility to Communism, even among many of its former advocates and supporters.

 Suggested Further Readings can be found in the ebook, on Connect, or online at www.mhhe .com/kramer12e.

Chapter 19

DEMOCRACY, ANTI-IMPERIALISM, AND THE ECONOMIC CRISIS AFTER THE FIRST WORLD WAR

We have discussed events that took place in Russia and the Soviet Union during the two decades after the First World War, but we have left the story of Europe and European empires at the signing of the peace treaties of 1919. We turn now to the wider historical changes in the period between the two world wars. These far-reaching, destructive wars reshaped modern European and global history, but there were also influential political and economic changes during the interwar decades. In these 20 years before 1939 Europeans passed through various (sometimes overlapping) cycles of optimistic confidence, disillusionment, hope, and fear. There were a few years of superficial prosperity, abruptly followed by unparalleled economic disaster.

For a time, in the 1920s, democracy and democratic reforms seemed to be advancing; then, in the difficult economic conditions of the 1930s, dictatorship began to spread in countries that had earlier tried to move toward greater democracy. Meanwhile, during these same decades, new political and social movements in Asia were challenging the European empires and colonial economic systems that had long given the European powers their dominant position in global affairs. The Great War, the Russian Revolution, and the changing world economy all affected European relations with the peoples and cultures of Asia, where anticolonial and nationalist campaigns attracted growing popular support. The apparent postwar triumphs of European democracy coincided with a growing opposition to European imperialism in the 1920s; and the devastating economic effects of the Great Depression affected politics, cultures, and international relations throughout the world in the 1930s.

93. THE ADVANCE OF DEMOCRACY AFTER 1919

The first years following the war were a time of social troubles. The victors and losers alike faced serious difficulties in the economic reconversion from war to peace. Veterans demobilized from the huge armies found themselves unemployed and psychologically

Chapter emblem: Mahatma Gandhi leading a group of nonviolent protestors in 1930 during the political campaign for India's national independence. (©Hulton Archive/Getty Images)

restless. Farms and factories geared to maximum production during the war faced a sudden disappearance of markets. They produced more than could now be sold, so that the war was followed by a sharp postwar economic depression, which, however, had run its course by 1922. Basically, the economic position even of the victors was seriously damaged, for the war had disjointed the pre-1914 commercial system, in which industrial western Europe had lived by exchange with eastern Europe and with overseas colonies and trading partners.

Gains of Democracy and Social Democracy

The war, President Wilson had said, was fought to make the world safe for democracy. Political democracy, to be sure, now made numerous advances. The new states that emerged from the war all adopted liberal democratic principles such as written constitutions and universal suffrage. Democracy also made advances in countries that had long sought to defend or expand democratic ideas and institutions. Great Britain, for example, dropped the last barriers to universal male suffrage in 1918. The most conspicuous innovation in many countries was the growing enfranchisement of women. We have seen how the women's suffrage movement in Great Britain achieved an important breakthrough in 1918, when women received a somewhat restricted right to vote; in 1928 the restrictions were dropped and the vote was granted on an equal basis with men. In 1920, through an amendment to the Constitution, female suffrage became general in the United States. Women voted also in Germany and in most of the new states of Europe. In the Soviet Union women received the vote on an equal basis with men after the revolution in 1917.

In most European countries the successors of the old prewar socialists gained in strength. With the left wings of the old socialists generally seceding, calling themselves Communists, and affiliating with each other and with Moscow in the Communist International, the European socialists or social democrats were preponderantly parties of peaceable or revisionist Marxism, entirely willing to pursue their political and social goals by legislative methods. Labor unions, with new self-confidence gained from their role in wartime economies, grew in membership, prestige, and importance.

Social legislation that before the war would have seemed radical was now enacted in many places. An eight-hour legal working day became common; and government-sponsored insurance programs against sickness, accident, and old age were either adopted or extended; an act of 1930, in France, insured almost 10 million workers. An air of progressive democracy pervaded Europe and the European world. The social service, or welfare, state, already beginning to emerge in most European countries in the late nineteenth century, was becoming more firmly established.

Social legislation enacted

Among the states that might have been expected to continue their prewar democratic gains in the postwar years, only Italy turned away from democracy. Italy had been a parliamentary state since 1861 and had introduced a democratic male suffrage in the elections of 1913. In 1919 the Italians held their second such elections. But Italian democracy soon abruptly ended. In 1922 an agitator named Benito Mussolini, leading a movement that he called Fascism (thereby adding a new word to the world's political vocabulary), ended Italian parliamentary government and founded his Fascist regime. Lenin in his way had already created the first single-party state; Mussolini became the first of the dictators in postwar Europe outside the Soviet Union. Fascist Italy in the 1920s was the chief exception in what seemed to be a rising tide of democracy.

Mussolini

The 19th Amendment to the U.S. Constitution, which gave American women the right to vote in all elections, was part of a more general expansion of women's political rights in the Atlantic world after the First World War. This poster was published by the American League of Women Voters shortly after the amendment was approved in 1920, but its message became relevant wherever women gained their long-delayed right to vote.
(©MPI/Getty Images)

The New States of Central and East-Central Europe

In central and east-central Europe—in Germany, in the territory of the former Austro-Hungarian Empire, and in the western fringe of former tsarist Russia—new states and new governments struggled to establish themselves. The new postwar states included, besides republican Germany, the four successor states to the Habsburg Empire—Austria, Hungary, Czechoslovakia, and Yugoslavia; and the five states that had broken away from the Russian Empire—Poland, Finland, Estonia, Latvia, and Lithuania (see map, pp. 746–747). The other small states in eastern Europe, Romania, Bulgaria, Greece, and Albania, had already been independent before 1914; their boundaries underwent some modification and their governments underwent considerable reorganization after the war. Turkey, the successor to the Ottoman Empire, was also a new republic.

Although many people in all countries had developed nationalist identities and aspirations, the new states in Europe (except possibly in Poland) did not emerge from a long-maturing revolutionary or republican sentiment. Only an infinitesimal number of Germans in

Weakness of republicanism

1914 would have voted for a republic. Even among the nationalities of Austria-Hungary in 1914 few persons would have chosen the complete breakup of the Habsburg Empire.

The republicans, moderate socialists, agrarians, or nationalists who now found themselves in power had to improvise governments for which there had been little preparation. They had to contend with reactionaries, monarchists, and members of the old aristocracy. They had also to deal with Communist revolutionaries, who, inspired by Lenin's success, hoped to bring about a dictatorship of the proletariat. A Communist revolt broke out in Germany in 1919 but was quickly suppressed; Soviet regimes were actually set up and soon crushed in Hungary and in the German state of Bavaria; and as late as 1923 there was a Communist uprising in the German state of Saxony.

Self-determination

The new central European states all embodied the principle of national self-determination, which held that each nationality should enjoy political sovereignty—one nation, one government. But people and cultures in this region had always been locally intermixed. Each of the new states therefore included minority nationalities; with the exception of a disruptive, forced exchange of populations between Greece and Turkey arranged in 1923, there was no thought of the actual physical removal of "alien" groups. Poland and Czechoslovakia each had many disaffected Germans. In Czechoslovakia the Slovaks resented Czech domination and in Yugoslavia, where the Serbs were in control, Croatian and other separatist movements actively opposed the Serb domination.

Nevertheless, despite economic and nationalist troubles, the new states and governments attempted at the outset to make themselves democratic. All the newly created states were republics except Yugoslavia, where the monarchy was under the older Serbian dynasty. Hungary started out in 1918 as a republic, but the attempt of the Communist leader Béla Kun to found a Hungarian Soviet Republic in 1919 brought back the counter-revolutionaries who restored the Habsburg monarchy in principle, though they were prevented by foreign pressure from restoring the king in person. Hungary emerged in 1920 as a monarchy with a perennially vacant throne, under an authoritarian regency exercised by Admiral Horthy. All smaller states of Europe, including Hungary, possessed at least the machinery of democracy until the 1930s; that is, they had constitutions, parliaments, elections, and a diversity of political parties. If civil liberty was sometimes violated, the right to civil liberty was not denied; and if elections were sometimes rigged, they were at least in principle supposed to be free.

Economic Problems of Eastern Europe; Land Reform

Eastern Europe for centuries had been an agrarian region of large landed estates. The wealthy, landowning aristocracy had been the chief support of the Austro-Hungarian Empire and an important pillar of the old order in the tsarist empire and in eastern Prussia. The mass of the rural population through all this region owned little or no property and had been free from serfdom only since the middle of the preceding century. The middle class of business and professional people was small except in Austria and Bohemia, the western portion of Czechoslovakia. In general, people in this whole region were conscious of lagging behind western Europe, not only in industry, factories, railroads, and great cities, but also in literacy, schooling, reading habits, health, death rates, length of life, and material standards of living.

Obstacles to modernization

The new states set out to modernize themselves, generally on the model of the western European nations. In addition to introducing democratic and constitutional ideas, they put up protective tariffs, behind which they tried to develop factories and industries of their own. But the new national boundaries created difficulties. Where Europe had

The peace settlements after the First World War transformed Vienna from its previous status as the capital city of a large empire into the capital of a small republic, but the city managed to sustain much of its earlier cultural vitality during the 1920s. This bustling outdoor cafe and dance suggest how the Viennese found ways to enjoy themselves in the diminished political context of the postwar Austrian state.

(©Popperfoto/Getty Images)

6,000 miles of frontiers in 1913, it had almost 10,000 after the war, and all the increase was in eastern Europe. Goods circulated much less easily. Protected industries in the old agricultural regions produced inefficiently and at high cost. Old and established industries in Austria, Czechoslovakia, and western Poland, cut off by the new frontiers and new tariffs from their former markets, fell upon hard times. The working class of Vienna lived in misery. Vienna, a city of 2 million persons, formerly the capital of an empire of 50 million, was now the capital of a republic of 6 million. In Czechoslovakia the German minority living in the Sudetenland complained that in hard times the German business-people and workers, because of government policies, always suffered more than their Czech counterparts. Economically, the carving up of eastern Europe into a dozen independent states was self-defeating.

The greatest of reforms undertaken by the new eastern European states was the reform of landownership. Although this reform could not solve basic economic problems in the area, it did have substantial

Land reform

effect on the pattern of land distribution. The work of the revolutions of 1848, which, in the Habsburg lands, had liberated the peasants from legal dependency but left them landless, was now carried a step further. The example of the Russian Revolution provided a powerful stimulus, for in Russia in 1917 peasants had driven off landlords, and Communists won a hearing among discontented and propertyless peasants from Finland to the Balkans. Not until 1929, it should be recalled, did the Soviet Union embark on the collectivization of agriculture; until then, communism appeared to favor the small individual farmer. But it may be said with equal truth that the model for agrarian reform lay in western Europe, especially in France, the historic land of the small peasant proprietor.

Land reform worked out differently in different countries, but large estates were generally broken into smaller farms throughout the Baltic states and in much of Czechoslovakia. This transformation reflected nationalist sentiment as well as a new social policy because most of the large landowners in all of these places were German. In Romania and Yugoslavia the breakup of large estates, though considerable, was less thorough. In Finland, Bulgaria, and Greece the issue hardly arose, because small landownership was already common. Land reform had least success in Poland and Hungary, where the landed magnates were exceptionally strong and well-rooted.

Peasant and small-holder parties

After the land reforms, political parties of small landholders became the chief democratic force within the various states on the western border of Russia. Often they inclined to socialism, especially because capitalism was associated in their minds with foreign investors and outsiders. On the other hand, the great landowners, the former aristocrats of the prewar empires, whether already expropriated or merely threatened with expropriation, were confirmed in a reactionary outlook. Although the land reforms provoked political fears among traditional social elites, the changes in land ownership did not destroy the social and economic hierarchies in eastern European societies. The new landowners' farms were small, frequently no more than ten acres. The peasant owners lacked capital, agricultural skill, and knowledge of the market. Farm productivity did not rise. In place of old differences between landlord and tenant there developed new differences between the more comfortable peasants and the proletarian hired hands. The continuance of relative poverty, the obstinacy of reactionary upper classes, the new economic tensions among the peasants themselves, the economic distortions produced by numerous tariff walls, and the lack of any sustained tradition of self-government all helped to frustrate the democratic experiments launched in the 1920s.

94.   THE GERMAN REPUBLIC AND THE SPIRIT OF LOCARNO

The keystone of Europe was Germany, which also had its revolution in 1918. But it was a revolution without revolutionaries, a negative revolution caused more by the disappearance of the old than by any decisive arrival of the new. The emperor and the High Command of the army, in the last weeks of the war, had bowed out of the picture, leaving it to others to face defeat and humiliation. For a time after November 1918, the political leaders in charge of affairs were mainly Social Democrats. The Social Democrats were Marxists, but their Marxism was the tamed, toned down, and revisionist Marxism that had prevailed for 20 years before the advent of Lenin. They were trade union officials and party managers. They could look back, in 1918, on decades spent in developing labor organizations and building up the Social Democratic Party, which in 1912 had become the largest single party in the Reichstag. Now, in 1918, they were a cautious and prudent group, more anxious to preserve what they had already achieved than to launch audacious new social experiments. Before 1917 the Social Democrats considered themselves well to the Left. But the Bolshevik Revolution in Russia and the emergence of a pro-Bolshevik or Communist element in Germany put the Social Democrats in the middle. The middle is an awkward spot, especially in disturbed times; the Communists regarded the Social Democrats as reactionaries, despicable traitors to the working-class movement, whereas the true reactionaries, recruited from old monarchists, army officers, Junker landowners, and big business groups, saw in social democracy, or professed to see in it, a dangerous flirtation with Bolshevism.

The middle group in Germany, the Social Democrats reinforced by the Catholic Center Party and others, was more afraid of the Left than of the Right. They were appalled in 1918 and 1919 by the stories brought out of Russia, not merely by bourgeois and aristocratic exiles but by refugee Social Democrats, Mensheviks, and anti-Leninist Bolsheviks, many of whom the socialists had long known and trusted in the Second International. In January 1919 the Sparta-cists,[1] led by Karl Liebknecht and Rosa Luxemburg, attempted to bring about a German proletarian revolution, like that in Russia. Lenin and the Russian Bolsheviks aided them. For a time, there seemed to be a possibility that the Spartacists might succeed in imposing a communist dictatorship of the proletariat in Germany. But the Social Democratic Provisional Government crushed the Spartacist uprising, turning for that purpose to demobilized army officers and volunteer vigilantes recruited from the disbanding army. The Spartacist leaders Liebknecht and Luxemburg were arrested and shot while in police custody. The events of "Spartacus Week" widened the chasm between Social Democrats and Communists.

The Spartacists

Shortly after the suppression of the Spartacists, elections were held for a National Constituent Assembly. No single party received a majority, but the Social Democrats were the leading party. A coalition of Social Democrats, Center Party, and liberal democrats dominated the Assembly. After several months of deliberations at the city of Weimar, in July 1919, a constitution was adopted establishing a democratic republic. The Weimar Republic (as the regime in Germany from 1919 to the advent of Hitler in 1933 is called) was soon threatened ominously from the Right. In 1920 a group of disaffected army officers staged a *Putsch,* or armed revolt, put the republican government to flight, and attempted to place a puppet of their own, one Dr. Kapp, at the head of the state. The Berlin workers, by turning off public utilities, stopped the Kapp *Putsch* and saved the republic. But the Weimar government never took sufficiently firm measures to put down private armed bands led by reactionary or outspokenly antidemocratic agitators. One of these was soon to be Adolf Hitler, who as early as 1923 staged an abortive revolt in Munich. Being democratic and liberal, the Weimar government would not deny the rights of free speech or of election to the Reichstag to even the most radical antidemocratic groups on the Left or the Right.

The Weimar Republic was in principle highly democratic. The constitution embodied all the devices then favored by the most advanced democrats, including universal suffrage, the vote for women, proportional representation, and procedures for referendums and petitions on public issues. But except for the legal eight-hour day and a few other such safeguards to the workers' welfare

The Weimar Republic

[1] So named from Spartacus, a Roman slave who led a slave revolt in south Italy in 72 B.C.E.

The Spartacists in Germany tried to provoke a Soviet-style, Communist revolution in early 1919, but their uprising was suppressed by the Social Democratic Provisional Government. These people are burning political pamphlets that they had seized from Spartacist newspaper offices.

(©Central Press/Hulton Archive/Getty Images)

the republic of which the Social Democrats were the main architects in its formative years was remote from anything socialist. No industries were nationalized. No property changed hands. No land laws or agrarian reforms were undertaken, as in the new states of eastern Europe; the East Elbian Junkers remained untouched in their landed estates. The very statues of Germany's earlier emperors, kings, princes, and grand dukes were left standing in the streets and squares. Officials, civil servants, police agents, professors, and schoolteachers of old imperial Germany remained at their respective duties. The army, though limited by the Versailles treaty to 100,000 men, remained the old army in miniature, with all its essential organization intact, and lacking only in numbers. In the officer corps the old professional and aristocratic influences remained strong.

Never had there been a revolution so mild, so reasonable, so tolerant. There was no terror, no fanaticism, no stirring faith, no expropriation, and no émigré migration. There had in truth been no revolution at all in the sense in which England, France, the United States, Russia, and other countries either recently or in the more distant past had experienced revolutions.

The German Democracy and Versailles

The supreme question for Europe and the world after 1920 was how Germany would adjust to the postwar conditions. How would the Germans accept the new internal regime of democracy? How would they accept the new German frontiers and other provisions of the Treaty of Versailles? The two questions were unfortunately interconnected. The Weimar Republic and the Treaty of Versailles were both products of the defeat of Germany in the war. There were many Germans who favored democracy, notably the numerous Social Democrats, and many more possibly could have been won over to it, given time and favorable conditions. But no one, not even the Social Democrats, accepted the Treaty of Versailles or the new German frontiers as either just or final. If democracy in Germany meant the perpetual acceptance of the treaty without amendment, or if it meant economic distress or hardship that could either reasonably or unreasonably be explained as consequences of the treaty, then democracy would lose such appeal as it had for the Germans.

The Versailles treaty as "Diktat"

The German republicans, as we have seen, protested against the Versailles treaty before signing, and signed only under pressure. The Allies continued the wartime naval blockade after the armistice, thus confirming, in German eyes, the argument that the Treaty of Versailles was a *Diktat,* a vengeful, dictated peace. The "war guilt" clause may have satisfied a deeply felt Anglo-American sense of morality, but it offended the strong belief in national honor that most Germans continued to affirm after 1919. Neither the reparations demanded of them nor the new frontiers were accepted by the Germans as settled. They regarded reparations as a perpetual mortgage on their future, and they generally expected some day to revise their eastern frontier, recover at least the Polish corridor, and merge with German-speaking Austria.

The French lived in fear of the day when Germany would recover. Their plans for their own security and for the collective security of Europe against a German revival had been disappointed. They had been unable to detach the Rhineland from Germany. The United States Senate had refused to ratify the treaty that Wilson signed at Paris, by which the United States was to support France against any future German invasion. Both Britain and the United States showed a tendency to isolation, to pull away from the Continent, to get back to "normalcy," to work mainly for a restored trade in which a prosperous Germany would be a large customer. The League of Nations, of which the United States was not a member and in which every member nation had a veto, offered little assurance of safety to the French. The French began to form alliances against a potentially resurgent Germany with Poland, Czechoslovakia, and other eastern European states. They insisted also on German payment of reparations. The amount of reparations, left unstated in the treaty, was fixed by a Reparations Commission in 1921 at 132 billion gold marks (the equivalent at the time of $35 billion), a sum that even non-German economists said was more than Germany could possibly pay.

French fear

The Weimar government in these circumstances looked to the Soviet Union, which had been no party to the Versailles treaty and claimed no reparations. The Soviet government meanwhile, concluding from the failure of proletarian revolution in Germany and Hungary that the time was not ripe for the sovietizing of Europe, prepared to enter into normal diplomatic relations with established governments. Germany and the Soviet Union, despite ideological repugnance, thus signed the treaty of Rapallo in 1922. In the following years the Soviet Union obtained needed manufactures from Germany, and German factories and workers were kept busy by orders from the Soviets. The German army dispatched officers and technicians to give instruction to the Red Army. Obliged by the Treaty of Versailles to restrict its activities, the German army was in fact able, through its work in Russia and through a number of subterfuges at home, to maintain a high standard of training and technical knowledge of new weapons and equipment.

Soviet-German relations

Reparations, the German Inflation of 1923, Recovery

The French, blocked in the attempt to collect reparations and assisted by the Belgians, in 1923 sent units of the French army to occupy the industrial sites of the Ruhr Valley. The Germans responded by general strikes and passive resistance. To sustain the workers the Weimar government paid them benefits by grinding new paper money off the printing presses. Germany, like other belligerent countries, had suffered from inflation during and after the war; neither the imperial nor the Weimar government had been willing to impose heavier taxes to offset it. But what now swept Germany was different from ordinary inflation. It was of catastrophic and utterly ruinous proportions. Paper money became literally worthless. By the end of 1923 it took over 4 trillion paper marks to equal a dollar.

A social revolution

This inflation brought far more of a social revolution than the fall of the Hohenzollern Empire had ever done. Debtors paid off debts in worthless money. Creditors received baskets full of meaningless paper. Salaries even when raised lagged behind the soaring cost of living. Annuities, pensions, proceeds of insurance policies, savings accounts in the banks, income from bonds and mortgages—every form of revenue that had been arranged for in the past, and which often represented the economy, foresight, and personal planning of many years—now turned to nothing. The middle class was pauperized and demoralized. Middle-class people were now materially in much the same position as workers and proletarians. Their whole view of life, however, made it impossible for them to identify themselves with the laboring class or to accept its socialist ideologies. They had lost faith in society itself, in the future, in the old burgher codes of self-reliance and rational planning of their own lives in an understandable world. A kind of moral void was created, with nothing for them to believe in, hope for, or respect.

The inflation, however, by wiping out all outstanding indebtedness within the country, made it possible, once the losses were written off and accepted, to start up economic production afresh. The United States was persuaded to play a reluctant role, in part because it was demanding the payment of huge war debts by the Allies. The Allies—Britain, France, Belgium—insisted that they could not pay these debts to the United States unless they collected reparations from Germany. In 1924 the Dawes Plan, named for the American Charles G. Dawes who negotiated the agreement, provided Germany with a new means to ensure the flow of reparations. By the Dawes Plan the French evacuated the Ruhr, the reparations payments were cut down, and arrangements were made for the German republic to borrow abroad. A good deal of American private capital was invested in Germany in the following years, both in German government bonds and in German industrial enterprises. Gradually, so at least it seemed, Germany was put on its feet. For four or five years the Weimar Republic even enjoyed a bustling prosperity, and there was new construction in roads, housing, factories, and ocean liners. But the prosperity rested in good measure on foreign loans, and the Great Depression that began in 1929 reopened all the old questions.

The Dawes Plan

The Spirit of Locarno

These years of economic prosperity were years also of relative international calm. Yet none of the fundamental international issues were addressed or resolved. The universal German hatred for the Treaty of Versailles elicited no concessions from the Allies. Conceivably, had the Allies been willing at this time to amend the treaty by international agreement, they might have taken the wind from the sails of nationalistic rabble-rousers in Germany and so spared themselves much later grief. It may be, however, that no possible concession would have sufficed. The great problem was to prevent a German overthrow of the treaty structure by violence, especially in eastern Europe where the Germans regarded the new frontiers as very much subject to revision. After the Ruhr incident in 1923 and adoption of the Dawes Plan in 1924, a group of moderate and peace-loving national leaders shaped the foreign policy of the principal countries—Gustav Stresemann in Germany, Édouard Herriot and Aristide Briand in France, and Ramsay MacDonald in England.

The charter of the League of Nations provided for international sanctions against potential aggressors. Like the system of congresses after the Peace of Vienna, the League was designed to assure compliance with the peace treaties or at the very least their

The catastrophic German inflation of 1923 destroyed the value of wages, savings, and investments. Consumers held millions of worthless marks and struggled to buy even the most essential goods. This woman used her paper money to light a fire in her kitchen stove.
(©Historical/Corbis Historical/Getty Images)

modification without resort to force. No one expected the League, by any authority of its own, to prevent war between Great Powers; but the League achieved various minor pacifications in the 1920s, and in any case its headquarters at Geneva offered a convenient meeting place in which statesmen could talk.

As a further assurance against war, in 1925, the European powers signed a number of treaties at Locarno, Switzerland. These marked the highest point in international goodwill reached between the two World Wars. Germany signed a treaty with France and Belgium guaranteeing their respective frontiers unconditionally. It signed arbitration treaties with Poland and Czechoslovakia —not guaranteeing these frontiers as they stood but undertaking to attempt changes in them only by international discussion, agreement, or arbitration. France signed treaties with Poland and Czechoslovakia promising military aid if they were attacked by Germany. France thus fortified its policy of balancing German power in the East by its own diplomatic alliances and by supporting the Little Entente, as the alliance of Czechoslovakia, Yugoslavia, and Romania was called. Great Britain "guaranteed"—that is, promised military aid in the event of violation—the frontiers of Belgium and France against Germany. It did not give an equivalent guarantee with respect to Czechoslovakia or Poland. It was on the borders of Czechoslovakia and Poland, 14 years later, that the Second World War began. Had Britain gone along with France in 1925 in guaranteeing these two countries, then abided by the guarantee, the Second World War might possibly have been prevented. On the other hand, no war ever depends on any single decision. It is the accumulation

The Locarno treaties

of many decisions that matters; and the expansionist ambitions of Hitler and the German Nazis would not have disappeared in 1939 if the British had simply "guaranteed" the protection of eastern national borders in the 1920s.

In 1925 people talked with relief of the "spirit of Locarno." In 1928 international harmony was again strengthened when the French foreign minister Briand and the United States Secretary of State Frank B. Kellogg arranged for the Pact of Paris. Ultimately signed by 65 nations, it condemned recourse to war for the solution of international controversies (though it provided no measures of enforcement).

In the mid-1920s the outlook for European international relations was therefore full of hope. At Locarno, Germany had of its own voli-

A hopeful outlook

tion accepted its borders both east and west, to the extent of abjuring violence and unilateral action even in the east. In 1926 Germany joined the League of Nations. Germany appeared to be developing a democratic republic. Democracy also seemed to work, as well as could be expected, in most of the new states of eastern Europe, and Communist Russia itself had halted its postwar revolutionary offensive. The world economy was again expanding, and the major European nations seemed to be more prosperous. World production was at or above the prewar level. World trade, by 1929, measured in hard money—gold—had almost doubled since 1913. The war and the postwar troubles were remembered as a nightmare from which Europe had finally escaped. It seemed that, after all, the world had been made safe for democracy.

But complacency was shattered by the great world Depression, by the growth of a malignant nationalism in Germany, due in part to the Depression, and by the assertion of a new militancy in Japan, which also gained influence during the Depression. But let us turn first to the postwar Asian nationalisms that rose up against European imperialism and challenged Europe's once-dominant position in the global economy.

95. ANTI-IMPERIALIST MOVEMENTS IN ASIA

Resentments in Asia

The peoples of Asia had never been satisfied with the position in which they found themselves after the great European expansion of the nineteenth century. Increasingly they condemned everything associated with "imperialism." In this respect there was little difference between countries actually governed by Europeans as parts of European empires in the nineteenth century, such as British India, the Netherlands Indies, and French Indochina, and countries that remained nominally independent under their own government, such as China, Persia, and the Ottoman Empire. In the former, as new national movements began to develop, there was objection to the monopoly of Europeans in the important offices of government. In the latter, there was objection to the special rights and privileges enjoyed by Europeans, the widespread impounding of customs revenues to pay foreign debts, the special privileges for foreigners in Turkey, the extraterritorial rights in China, and the spheres of influence in Persia that divided the country between British and Russians.

By imperialism, in either case, Asians meant a system whereby the

Imperialism in Asia

affairs of their own country were conducted, its resources exploited, and its people employed for the benefit of foreigners, Europeans, or white people. They meant the system of absentee capitalism, by which the plantations, docks, or factories on which they themselves labored, were the property of owners thousands of miles away whose main interest was a regular flow of profits. They meant the constant threat that an alien civilization would disintegrate and eat away their own ancient cultures. They meant the burden of having to speak a European language or the disagreeable prospect of having to fight in wars originated by Europeans. And they meant the airs of superiority assumed by white people, the race consciousness exhibited by all Europeans, the color line that was everywhere drawn, the attitudes varying between contempt and condescension, the relation of native "boy" and European "sahib." Imperialism to them signified the gentlemen's clubs in Kolkata to which no Indian was ever admitted, the hotels in Shanghai from which Chinese were carefully kept out, or the park benches in various cities on which no "native" could ever sit. In deeper psychology, as well as in economics and politics, the revolt of self-conscious Asians was a rebellion against an imperial system that reduced them to social inferiority and humiliation in their own societies.

The revolt against European imperialism was generally ambivalent or two-sided. It was a revolt against Western supremacy; but at the same time, in most cases those who revolted meant to learn from and imitate numerous components of European cultures. By using the methods and knowledge of European science, industry, governmental organization, and other sources of European power, they sought to preserve their own identity and achieve political and economic equality with the European nation-states. Anti-imperialist movements and intellectuals thus borrowed from European cultures even as they vehemently rejected European ideologies that assumed the superiority of European institutions or races.

The twentieth-century challenge to European imperialism in Asia had broken out with the Russo-Japanese War, when an Asian people in 1905 defeated a major European power for the first time. In 1906 revolution began in Persia, leading to the assembly of the first *majlis,* or parliament. In 1908 the Young Turks staged a successful revolution in Constantinople and summoned a parliamentary assembly to represent all regions then in the Ottoman Empire. In 1911 the revolutionists in China, led by Sun Yat-sen, overthrew the Manchu (or Qing) dynasty and proclaimed the Chinese Republic. In each case the rebels charged their old monarchs—shah, sultan, emperor—with subservience to European imperialists. In each case they summoned national assemblies on the prevailing democratic model of Europe, and they also proposed to use various European practices and technologies when such adaptations could help them resist or avoid domination by the imperial powers.

Anti-imperialist revolts

First World War and Russian Revolution

In the First World War almost all the Asian peoples were somehow involved. The Ottoman Empire, allied with Germany, immediately repudiated all the capitulations, or special legal rights of Europeans. In Persia, where Russian and British intervention in 1907 had blocked the developing movement for constitutional reform, there was a concerted attempt to maintain Persian neutrality in the war and to get rid of the foreign spheres of influence that Russia and Britain had imposed through agreements between themselves. Persian territory became a battleground of British, Russian, and Turkish forces; and a large number of Persians died from wartime violence, disruption, and disease. China, which joined the Allies, attempted at the peace conference to have the extraterritorial rights in China abolished. We have seen how this request of the Chinese Republic was refused, and how the Allies instead transferred many of the prewar German concessions to the Japanese. The colonized regions of Asia, the Dutch, French, and British possessions, were stimulated economically by the war. The Netherlands Indies, though remaining neutral, increased its output of foodstuffs, oil, and raw materials. India developed its steel industry and textile manufactures and contributed over a million soldiers to the British cause. All the colonized regions were stirred by Woodrow Wilson's call to make the world safe for democracy.

*Home government
concessions*

The European imperial governments made concessions, but they were always afraid they might go too far. They insisted that their subject peoples were not yet capable of self-government. Huge investments were at stake, and the whole world economy depended on the continuing flow of raw materials from tropical and subtropical countries. But they did compromise. In 1916 the Dutch created a legislative assembly to advise the governor general of the Indies; half its members were Indonesians. In 1917 the British agreed to a measure of self-government in India; an Indian legislative assembly was set up with 140 members, of whom 100 were elected, and in the provinces of British India the number of elected representatives and of local Indian officials was increased. The French in 1922 provided for a somewhat similar assembly in Indochina. Thus all three colonial powers at about the same time began to experiment with consultative bodies whose membership was partly elective and partly appointive, partly non-European and partly European.

*Bolshevik
anti-imperialism*

The Russian Revolution added a new stimulus to unrest in Asia. In Marxist-Leninist ideology imperialism was described as the "highest" or "final" phase of capitalist societies. Colonial peoples also tended to identify the two, not so much for Marxist-Leninist reasons as because modern capitalism was a foreign or imperialist phenomenon in colonial countries, where the ownership and the management of large enterprises were foreign. Nationalist movements in Asia thus easily shaded off into socialism and the denunciation of capitalist exploitation. The Bolsheviks were quick to see the advantages for themselves in this situation. As it became clear that the world revolution, as expected by Lenin, would not soon come to pass in Europe, the Russian Communists turned to Asia as the theater in which world capitalism might be attacked by a great flanking movement. In September 1920 a "congress of oppressed Eastern peoples" assembled at Baku, on the coast of the Caspian Sea. Zinoviev, head of the Communist International, called for war upon "the wild beasts of British capitalism." In the following years a few future radical leaders from Asian countries sojourned in Moscow. Meanwhile, Communists dispatched from Moscow stirred up the discontents which existed, quite without Russian instigation, all over Asia.

The postwar situation in Asia was thus extremely fluid. People who were not Communists hailed communism as a liberating force. Anti-European activists declared that their countries must use certain aspects of European science, technology, and social organization. Nationalism overshadowed all other "isms." In the Indian National Congress rich Indian capitalists worked together with socialist leaders in relative harmony so long as the common enemy was the British.

The Turkish and Persian Revolutions

The most immediately successful revolutionary movement took place in Turkey. The Young Turks at first, in 1908, had meant to prevent the further dissolution of the Ottoman Empire. This proved to be impossible. In the Balkan wars of 1912–1913 the Ottoman power was almost totally excluded from the Balkan Peninsula. In the First World War, in which the Turks were on the losing side, the Arabs with a great deal of British assistance broke away. After the war, in 1921, the Greeks invaded the Anatolian Peninsula.

They dreamed of a greater Greece embracing both sides of the Aegean. Western Europeans still regarded Turkey as "the sick man of Europe," the Ottoman state as doomed to extinction, and the Turkish people as barbarous or incompetent. The Allies had agreed in 1915 to partition the Ottoman Empire; and after the war the western European powers favored the Greek invasion. Italian and French forces occupied parts of Anatolia; and Italians, French, and British wanted to take Constantinople from Turkish rule, though its disposition remained uncertain. In these circumstances a powerful army officer named Mustapha Kemal rallied Turkish national resistance. Within two years, and with aid from the Soviet Union, the Turks drove out the Greeks and the European Allies. They affirmed their hold on the Anatolian Peninsula, and on both shores of the Straits, including Constantinople, which in 1930 was renamed Istanbul.

The Nationalists, under the energetic drive of Mustapha Kemal, now put through a sweeping revolution. They abolished the sultanate and the caliphate, because the sultan had compromised himself with foreigners and was also, as caliph or commander of the faithful, a religious leader for all Islam and hence a conservative link with the past. The Turkish Republic was promulgated in 1923.

The Turkish Republic

Whereas the Ottoman Empire had been a composite organization made up of diverse religious communities, among which the Muslims were the ruling group, the Turkish Republic was conceived as a national state in which the "people," that is, the Turkish people, were sovereign. Universal suffrage was introduced, along with a parliament, a ministry, and a president with strong powers. Non-Turks in Asia Minor now became "foreign" in a way they had not been before. We have seen that the Armenians were deported and massacred during the First World War. The other large non-Turkish and Christian people were the Greeks. After the war about 1.4 million Greeks either fled or were officially transported from Asia Minor to Greece and in exchange some 400,000 Turks residing in northern Greece were transported to Turkey. This forcible exchange of peoples became an early example of what would later be called "ethnic cleansing." The forced migration caused great hardship, it uprooted most of the Greek population that had lived in Asia Minor since antiquity, and it overwhelmed the impoverished Greek kingdom by obliging it suddenly to absorb a mass of destitute refugees, who were a quarter as numerous as the population of Greece itself. But the expulsion of the Greeks enabled the Turkish Republic to acquire a relatively homogeneous population (except for a Kurdish minority in eastern Turkey), and it ended minority disputes between Greece and Turkey until new problems arose after the Second World War.

For the first time in any Muslim country the spheres of government and religion were sharply distinguished. The Turkish Republic affirmed the total separation of religion and the state. It declared religion to be a private belief, and it tolerated all religions. Government was reorganized on secular and nonreligious principles stemming from the French Revolution. The law of the Qur'an was thrust aside. The new law was modeled on the Swiss Code, the most recently codified European legislation, itself derived from the Code Napoleon.

Mustapha Kemal urged women to put aside the veil, to come out of the harem, to vote, and to occupy public office. He made polygamy a crime. Men he required by law to discard the fez. He fought against the fez as Peter the Great had fought against the beard, and for the same reason, seeing in it the symbol of backward habits. The hat, "headgear of civilization," correspondingly became the symbol of progress. The people of Turkey shifted to European dress. The European alphabet became mandatory; literate Turks had to learn

Separation of religion and state

The governments of Greece and Turkey agreed in the early 1920s to force the migration of Muslims from Greece and of Christians from Turkey. This dual expulsion caused great hardship for hundreds of thousands of displaced people, including these beleaguered Muslim refugees who moved into Turkey during the fall of 1923.

(©Topical Press Agency/Hulton Archive/Getty Images)

to read again, and illiteracy was reduced. The European calendar and the metric system were adopted. Turks were required to assume hereditary family surnames, like Europeans; Kemal himself took the name Atatürk, or Great Turk. The capital was moved from Istanbul to Ankara. The republic put up a high tariff. In 1933 it adopted a five-year plan for economic development. The Turks, having shaken off foreign influence, were determined not to become again dependent on European capital or capitalism. The five-year plan provided for mines, railroads, and factories, mainly under government ownership. The Turks wanted a modern Turkey—by and for the Turks; and the Turkish government (like the late nineteenth-century Japanese government) set out to gain its full independence from the western European powers by imposing European-style reforms on its own people and institutions.

New regime in Persia

Persia experienced a different kind of political revolution, but there were comparable attempts to reduce the influence of foreign powers. When the British tried to establish a postwar colonial protectorate there in 1919, they were stymied by strong national resistance.

Meanwhile, the new Soviet regime withdrew from Persia and renounced all claims of the previous Russian government. In 1921 an army officer named Reza Khan overthrew the older ruling Qajar dynasty and in 1925 became shah (with British and Soviet support). Henceforth known as Reza Shah Pahlavi, he established a repressive regime that sought to modernize the country and to break away from various agreements with the British government. Earlier concessions, capitulations, and spheres of influence were abolished, and Reza Shah renegotiated the British oil contracts. There were also efforts to assert greater control over foreign corporations and to collect more taxes. Beginning in 1935, the government affirmed its national identity by changing the country's official international name to Iran, which had for some time been used within the nation itself.

The National Movement in India: Gandhi and Nehru

India at the close of the First World War was on the verge of revolution against British rule. Discontented Indians looked for leadership to Mohandas K. Gandhi, the Mahatma, or Holy One, who in the following decades, though hardly typical of modern Asia, attained a worldwide eminence as the champion of subjected peoples. Gandhi had been educated in England in the 1890s and had practiced law in South Africa, where he became aware of racial discrimination as a worldwide problem. In India, after 1919, he led a movement for self-government and economic and spiritual independence from Great Britain. He also sought greater tolerance within India itself, both between Hindus and Muslims, and between upper-caste Hindus and the depressed outcastes and untouchables. The weapons he favored were those of nonviolence, passive resistance, civil disobedience, and the boycott. He took to self-imposed fasts and hunger strikes to cope with his British jailers and later with the Indians themselves.

Gandhi and his most loyal followers, as the troubles mounted, refused to be elected to or take part in the partially representative institutions that the British had cautiously introduced. They also undermined the British economic position in India by refusing to buy or use goods imported from England. The latter touched the British in a sensitive spot. Before the World War half of all exports of British cotton cloth went to India, but by 1932 this proportion had fallen to a quarter. Gandhi turned against all industrialism, even the mechanized industry that was growing up in India itself. He put aside European clothing, took to using a spinning *Gandhi's campaign* wheel and living on goat's milk, urged Indian peasants to revive their old handicrafts, and appeared on solemn occasions clad in no more than a homespun loincloth. By the high level of his principles Gandhi made himself an inspiration to many groups that differed on more mundane matters. Even in Britain and other Western countries he came to be regarded as one of the great spiritual leaders of all time.

India was very much divided within, and the British resisted the growing Indian nationalist movement by arguing that the end of British rule would precipitate anarchy. There were Hindus and Muslims, *Divisions in society and politics* between whom clashes and terrorist outrages were chronic. (Gandhi was himself assassinated in 1948 by an anti-Muslim Hindu fanatic.) There were the hundreds of minor potentates of the native states. There were Indian capitalists and wealthy industrialists, like the Tata family, and growing masses of proletarians produced by Indian industrialization. There were the higher castes and the outcastes, and there were hundreds of millions of peasants living in rural poverty. In politics, there were those who demanded full independence, boycotted the British, and spent years in jail, as did Gandhi and his more practical-minded but devoted follower Jawaharlal Nehru; and there were the

The president of the new Turkish Republic, Mustapha Kemal Atatürk, sought to reduce the influence of Islam and to bring more European cultural practices into Turkish society. In this photograph from about 1925, he shows his support for such changes by wearing European-style clothes and by dancing at his daughter's wedding.

(©Hulton Archive/Getty Images)

moderates who believed that they might best advance the welfare of India by accepting government office, cooperating with the British, and working for dominion status within the British Empire. Marxism exerted a strong appeal, not indeed on the spiritual and pacific Gandhi, but on Nehru and even many of the less radical leaders. In the 1920s the Soviet Union stood in their eyes for the overthrow of imperialism; in the 1930s it pointed the way toward economic development by its adoption of five-year plans. For a people wishing to move from poverty to industrial strength and higher living standards without loss of time, and without dependence on foreign capital and capitalism, the Soviet Union with its economic planning seemed to offer a more appropriate model and more practical lessons than the rich democracies of western Europe, with their centuries of gradual progress behind them.

Continuing struggle for independence

The 20 years between world wars were for India a period of repeated disturbance, rioting and repression, sporadic violence despite the exhortations of Gandhi, conferences and round tables, reforms and promises of reform, with a shift in the 1930s toward more Indian participation in the governing institutions of the colonial system. Independence from Britain, however, was not won until after the Second World War; and in this transition to independence the Indian subcontinent was partitioned into two new nations, a predominantly Hindu India and a predominantly Muslim Pakistan.

National Movements in French Indochina and the Netherlands Indies

Resistance to European imperialism developed also in French-controlled Indochina and in the Netherlands Indies. We have seen how the Vietnamese nationalist Ho Chi Minh urged President Wilson to recognize the rights of colonized people in French Indochina

Historical Documents
Sarojini Naidu, "India's Future" (1929)

The nationalist movement in India mobilized wide opposition to British imperial rule after the First World War. Like most anti-imperialist activists throughout Asia, the Indian National Congress and other groups demanded national independence and condemned the destructive effects of European colonialism. Mohandas Gandhi became the most famous symbol of Indian nationalism, but the movement was also led by many women, including the poet and political activist Sarojini Naidu (1879-1949). Naidu served as president of the Indian National Congress in the mid-1920s and traveled around the world calling for Indian independence. This speech, which she presented in New York, summarized her political goals and linked India's struggle to America's earlier revolution against the British Empire.

[Some people say] it is necessary that India shall continue to be under benevolent tutelage for a century or two longer. . . .

Today we stand, we, the representatives of the great Indian nation, for the inalienable birthright of the people known as liberty, for that same liberty for which America fought. . . .

It is only the tragedy of historic circumstances that has brought us together as subjects and master, and we feel today in India, all of us, that the only vindication for a nation to live is that it is free . . . to formulate its own laws, establish its own policies, defend its own frontiers . . . [and] hold aloft that square yard of colored rag called the flag, which is the symbol of its national honor. . . .

But nothing, no repression, no ridicule, can stop our progress, no more than all the dams across the river stop the river from reaching its ultimate goal, the sea. Can anything stop the ultimate liberation which is the birthright of all people? . . .

I want only to say to you that I am the voice, the authentic and accredited voice of my nation. I speak in the name of my nation. I speak of a day when India shall stand free.

Sarojini Naidu, "India's Future" (New York: Foreign Policy Association Pamphlet #57, 1929), pp. 6, 8-10.

at the time of the Versailles peace conference, but his petition was ignored. The Bolshevik denunciation of European imperialism therefore attracted Ho's sympathetic attention. He moved from France to Moscow, where he became active in the Comintern and began to develop his ideas for an anticolonial revolution in Indochina. He spent most of the 1920s and 1930s in the Soviet Union or in China, however, so that his slowly emerging communist movement had little direct influence in Vietnam before the Second World War.

Meanwhile, a new nationalist party was established within Vietnam in 1927. Drawing on both socialism and the ideas of the Nationalist Party in China, anticolonial activists formed the Viet Nam Quoc Dan Dang (VNQDD). This group and others launched an anti-French campaign that included targeted assassinations of French officials and support for disaffected Vietnamese soldiers who served in the French colonial army. Some of these soldiers, encouraged by civilian nationalists, mutinied against their French commanders in 1930, but the revolt was quickly suppressed. In the aftermath of this brief rebellion, the French colonial government executed or imprisoned the main nationalist agitators. Other Vietnamese nationalists fled to China, and the anticolonial movement stalled until the Second World War, when Ho Chi Minh arrived to lead a new Viet Minh nationalist and communist movement against both the Japanese and (after 1945) the French.

In the Netherlands Indies, where the nationalist movement was less developed than in India, the interwar independence movement somewhat resembled the anticolonial activities in Indochina. The Bolshevik critique of imperialism drew some Indonesian nationalists to communism, and a serious rebellion, in which communists took part, broke out in 1926. But the Dutch quickly suppressed the revolt and cracked down on both the communist and the noncommunist elements of the nationalist movement. In the following year a new Indonesian National Party (PNI) was created by young Indonesians who wanted to build a unified, anticolonial movement. Although the Dutch soon arrested the party's leaders, including the future first president of Indonesia (Sukarno), the independence movement continued to gain support.

The peoples of the Indonesian archipelago were almost as diverse as those of India. Only the Dutch empire had brought them politically together. Opposition to the Dutch gave them a common program. In 1937 the legislative council petitioned for dominion status. But not until after the Second World War and the failure of a military effort to repress the nationalists did the Dutch, in 1949, concede independence.

The Chinese Revolution: The Three People's Principles

The Chinese Revolution had opened in 1911 with the overthrow of the Manchu (Qing) dynasty, which itself had belatedly begun to introduce modernizing reforms. A Chinese Republic was proclaimed, but the immediate result was the establishment in Peking (now Beijing) of a military dictatorship exercised by General Yüan Shih-kai, who had been a close adviser to the Manchus. In the south the veteran revolutionary Dr. Sun Yat-sen reorganized the Guomindang (National People's, or Nationalist Party), successor to the prerevolutionary network of underground societies of which he had been the chief architect.[2] Sun, elected the first president of the republic by a revolutionary provisional assembly, resigned within a few months in favor of General Yüan, who he mistakenly believed would unite the country under a parliamentary regime. Subsequently, in the confusion that followed Yüan's death in 1916, Sun was proclaimed president of a rival government in the south at Canton (now Guangzhou), which remained separate from the northern government and exercised a nominal power over the southern provinces. Not until 1928 could any government have any basis for claiming actual rule over China—and even then, there were important exceptions.

Sun Yat-sen and the Nationalists

It was Sun Yat-sen who best expressed the ideas of this phase of the Chinese Revolution. Born in 1867 and educated under American influence in the Hawaiian Islands, he received a medical degree in Hong Kong, traveled and lived around the world, studied European and American ideas, lectured to Chinese audiences in America, collected money for his conspiracies against the Manchus, and returned from Europe to take part in the revolution. Shortly before his death in 1925 Sun gathered the lectures that he had been expounding for years into a book, *The Three People's Principles*. The book sheds much light on the revolt of China and of all Asia against the supremacy of the Western imperial powers.

Democracy, nationalism, livelihood

The three people's principles, according to Sun Yat-sen, were democracy, nationalism, and livelihood. Livelihood meant social welfare and economic reform—a more equitable distribution of wealth and land, a gradual end to poverty and unjust economic exploitation. By nationalism

---

[2]The Pinyin system, adopted in 1979 by the People's Republic of China, is now widely used for the transliteration of Chinese into languages like English that use the Latin alphabet, replacing the older Wade-Giles spelling. For a few names like Sun Yat-sen or Chiang Kai-shek, however, the older spellings are often retained in English.

The nonviolent principles of Mohandas Gandhi profoundly shaped the Indian movement for national independence after the First World War. He is shown here in typically simple clothing as he led a nationalist "walk to the sea" to collect salt as part of a boycott of British goods and to promote his nonviolent campaign for Indian national independence. The woman in darker clothing on his left is Sarojini Naidu, who was a poet, a founding member of the Women's Indian Association, and President of the Indian National Congress in 1925–1926.

(©Hulton Archive/Getty Images)

Dr. Sun meant that the Chinese who had always lived mainly in the clan and family had now to learn the importance of the nation and the state. They were in fact a great nation, he taught, the world's most cultured, and they had once prevailed from the mouth of the Amur to the East Indies. But they had never been cohesive. The Chinese had been "a sheet of loose sand"; they must now "break down individual liberty and become pressed together into an unyielding body like the firm rock which is formed by the addition of cement to sand."

By democracy Sun Yat-sen meant the sovereignty of the people. Like Rousseau, he gave little attention to voting, elections, or parliamentary processes. He believed that while the people were sovereign, the able should govern. Adhering in this respect to traditional Confucian teachings, he believed that government should be conducted by experts, a principle he criticized the Western powers for neglecting. Dr. Sun felt a warm sympathy for Lenin. Yet he was by no means a doctrinaire Marxist. Marxism he thought inapplicable to China, arguing that the Chinese must take Marxism as they took all other European ideas, avoiding slavish imitation, using, adapting, amending, or rejecting as they saw fit. China had no native capitalism in any European sense. The "capitalists" in China, he said, were owners of land, especially in cities such as Shanghai, where the coming of Europeans had raised land values to dizzy heights. Hence if China could get rid of imperialism it would take a long step toward getting rid of capitalism also; it could begin to equalize landowning and confiscate unearned rents. Because China, he observed, had no true capitalists, the state itself must undertake capitalist and industrial development. The Chinese therefore needed a strong and economically active national state.

With Sun Yat-sen, in short, democracy easily shaded off into a theory of benevolent and constructive dictatorship. Marxism, communism, socialism, "livelihood," the planned society, welfare economics, and antiforeign and anti-imperialist sentiment were all mixed together in a complex combination of European and Chinese ideas and political aspirations. The new nationalism in China (as well as the new Chinese Communism that was beginning to develop at the same time) may therefore be seen as an example of the ways in which the emerging campaigns against European imperialism often drew on European ideologies and intellectual traditions, even as they denounced the actions of European governments or corporations and the racism of European cultures.

Antiforeign sentiments

The first aim of Sun Yat-sen and of the revolutionists in China was to shake off the "treaty system" that had bound China to European interests since 1842. In this respect the Paris peace conference had been as disappointing for the Chinese as it had been for other explicitly colonized peoples. The Chinese not only failed to obtain the abolition of foreign privileges and extraterritorial rights but also could not win back the former German concessions that the Japanese had taken over during the war. Widespread student and worker demonstrations directed against the Western powers took place at the time of the Paris peace conference on May 4, 1919. The May Fourth movement heightened antiforeign consciousness.

As the western European powers proved obdurate, Sun and the Guomindang turned to Russia. They declared the Russian and Chinese revolutions to be two aspects of the same worldwide movement of liberation. The Chinese Communist Party, organized in 1921, became allied with the Guomindang in 1923. The Soviet Union, following its strategy of outflanking world capitalism by penetrating Asia, sent military equipment, army instructors, and party organizers into China. It also surrendered the Russian concessions and extraterritorial rights that the tsars had acquired in China. The Chinese policy of friendliness to

Alliances with the Soviet Union

Russia began to produce the hoped-for effects; the British, to draw China from Russia, gave up a few of their lesser concessions at Hankow and other cities.

China: Nationalists and Communists

The Guomindang, its armies reorganized and strengthened, displayed a fresh vitality and after 1924 launched a military and political offensive against its political rivals. The new offensive was planned with assistance from some recently arrived Russian advisers, supported by the Chinese Communists, and headed by Chiang Kai-shek, who succeeded to the leadership of the Nationalist party upon Sun's death in 1925. Chiang's main objectives were to compel the independent war lords and the northern regime still holding office in Beijing to accept the authority of a single Nationalist government. By the end of 1928 Chiang's armies had swept northward, occupied Beijing, and transferred the seat of government to Nanjing. The outside powers, acknowledging the accomplishments of the Guomindang, extended diplomatic recognition to the Nanjing government and conceded its right to organize and run the country's tariff and customs affairs. They also partially surrendered their extraterritorial privileges and pledged to abolish them completely in the near future.

In 1927, while a measure of national unity was being forged in the country, an open break occurred between the Guomindang and its left wing. In the course of the northern military campaign, and particularly in the seizure of Nanjing, popular disturbances and excesses, including the killing of a number of foreigners, had taken place, allegedly fomented by the Communists. Chiang himself had never apparently considered the alliance with either the Communists or the Russians as anything more than one of convenience. He now took decisive action, purging Communists and Russian advisers from the party, executing many people who were affiliated with left-wing groups, and suppressing a Communist-led uprising in Guangzhou. A number of armed Communist groups fled to the safety of the mountain regions in the south and joined other guerrilla contingents. In that way the Chinese Red Army was formed; among its leaders was Mao Zedong, a former librarian, teacher, newspaper editor, and union organizer, who had been one of the founding members of the party.

Communists purged from the Guomindang

The Communists, operating in southeast China, fed on popular discontent and drew support from the peasantry by a systematic policy of expropriation and distribution of large landed estates as well as by intensive propaganda. Organizing a network of local soviets, in 1931 they proclaimed a Chinese Soviet Republic in the southeast. When the Nationalist armies succeeded in dislodging them, the Communists, under Mao's leadership, undertook in 1934–1935 an amazing 6,000-mile march over near-insuperable terrain to north-central Yenan, where they were closer to Soviet supply lines. About 90,000 began the Long March, of which only half survived. They entrenched themselves again, fought off the Nationalist armies, and built up a popular following among the rural masses. The Chinese Communists thus survived all attempts to destroy their army and their base of popular support; and after a long struggle against the Japanese invasion of China during the Second World War, the Communists eventually defeated the Guomindang. Taking power in all China by 1949, Mao and his allies finally drove both the Europeans and the Americans from their long-established positions in the Chinese cities and economy—thereby becoming also an international symbol for other anti-imperialist movements in late twentieth-century Asia. The Chinese Revolution was a prolonged, ruthless conflict, and it never established

Advance of Chinese Communism

Mao Zedong and Zhou Enlai led nearly 100,000 Communists on the famous "Long March" from southeast China to the northwest province of Yenan in 1934–1935. They were escaping the armies of the Nationalist Guomindang and seeking to establish new bases near their allies in the Soviet Union. This picture shows Mao and Zhou as they appeared at the time of the march, which crossed almost 6,000 miles of remote terrain. The Chinese Communist Party, after 1949, would become the most powerful opponent of European imperial interventions in Asia.

(©Keystone/Hulton Archive/ Getty Images)

a democratic political system. It also differed from the national movements that challenged the European colonial systems in India, Indochina, and the Netherlands Indies, but it became a widely influential force in the broader Asian rejection of European imperialism during the decades after the First World War.

96.   THE GREAT DEPRESSION: COLLAPSE OF THE WORLD ECONOMY

The European economy, like the economies in all other regions of the world, was deeply entangled in a global system of trade and production because many basic commodities prices were determined by the free play of supply and demand in a worldwide market. There was much regional division of labor; large areas lived by producing a few specialized articles for sale to the world as a whole. A great deal of production, both local and international, especially in the 1920s, was financed by credit, that is, by promises of repayment in the future. The system rested upon mutual confidence in the processes of mutual exchange—on the belief of lenders, creditors, and investors that they would get their money back and on the belief of borrowers that they could pay their debts. This vast interlocking system also depended on the ability of farms and factories to market their products at prices high enough to bring a net return, so that farmers and factory people might purchase the output of other factories and farms—all this round and round in countless circles of mutual interdependence and throughout the world as a whole.

CHRONOLOGY OF NOTABLE EVENTS, 1911–1935

1911	Revolution in China ends the Qing (Manchu) dynasty
January 1919	Spartacist attempt at proletarian revolution is suppressed in Berlin
July 1919	Weimar Republic is established in Germany
1919	Gandhi launches campaign in India for independence from Britain
1922	Germany and the Soviet Union agree to diplomatic relations in Treaty of Rapollo
1923	French occupation of the Ruhr Valley and ruinous German inflation
1923	Turkish Republic is established under the leadership of Kemal Atatürk, who launches modernizing reforms
1925	Treaties at Locarno recognize the postwar European national borders
1925	Reza Khan becomes shah of Iran and seeks to curb British and other foreign concessions
1925	Death of Sun Yat-sen is followed by conflicts between Nationalists and Communists in China and gradual decline of European influence
October 1929	Stock market crash in New York leads to the Great Depression
1932	Governments respond to economic crisis with national protectionism
1932–1939	Writers respond to social crisis with new "social realism"
1934–1935	Chinese communists make the 6,000-mile Long March and claim to lead the "anti-imperialist" movement in China

The Prosperity of the 1920s and Its Weaknesses

The five years after 1924 were a period of prosperity in that there was an expansion of international trade, building, and new industries. The automobile, for example, still in very limited use before 1914, became an article of mass production after the war. Its widespread use increased the demand for oil, steel, rubber, and electrical equipment, caused the building of tens of thousands of miles of roads, and created whole new occupations for truck drivers, garage mechanics, and gas station attendants. Similarly the new mass popularity of radios and movies had repercussions in all directions. The economic expansion was most phenomenal in the United States, but almost all European countries enjoyed it in greater or lesser degree. "Prosperity" became a magical term, and some thought that it would last indefinitely, that the secret of human plenty and of progress had been found, and that science and invention were at last realizing the hopes of ages.

But there were weaknesses in this prosperity, various imperfections in this or that gear or valve of the mechanism, flaws that, under stress, were to bring the whole intricate structure to a halt. The expansion was largely financed by credit, or borrowing. Laboring people received less *A prosperity financed by credit* than a proportionate share; wages lagged behind profits and dividends; mass purchasing power, even when inflated by installment buying (another form of credit), was inadequate to pay for the vast output that it was technically possible to produce. And throughout the world the whole decade of the 1920s was a time of chronic agricultural depression, so that farmers could neither pay their debts nor purchase manufactures to the degree required for the smooth functioning of the system.

Movies became one of the most popular entertainments in European cities during the early twentieth century. This crowd was waiting to enter London's Brixton Astoria Theater in December 1930. Similar movie theaters attracted large audiences throughout Europe, even amid the economic crisis of the Great Depression.

(©Fox Photos/Hulton Archive/Getty Images)

Worldwide agricultural depression

Military operations in the First World War had reduced wheat fields under cultivation in Europe by a fifth. The world price of wheat went up, and farmers in the United States, Canada, and elsewhere increased their acreage. Often, to acquire land at high prices, they assumed mortgages that in later years they were unable to repay. After the war Europe restored its wheat production, and eastern Europe reentered the world market. Agriculture everywhere was increasingly mechanized, farmers rapidly increased their output of wheat by using a tractor-drawn harvester-thresher combine, and scientific research helped to increase the yield per acre. The result of all these agricultural developments was a super-abundant global output of wheat. But the demand for wheat was what economists call "inelastic." By and large, within the area of Europe and the wider Western world, people already ate as much bread as they wanted and would buy no more; and the undernourished masses of Asia, who in pure theory could have consumed the excess, could not pay even low costs of production or transportation. The price of wheat fell to incredibly low levels, disrupting farm life in almost every country of the world. In 1930 a bushel of wheat, in terms of gold, sold for the lowest price in 400 years.

Wheat growers everywhere were faced with ruin. Growers of many other crops faced the same dismal prospect. Cotton and corn, coffee and cocoa all collapsed. Brazilian and African planters were caught by overproduction and falling prices. In Java, where the acreage in sugar had been extended and the unit yield from the sugar cane had also multiplied ten times under scientific cultivation over the past century, prices bottomed out of the world market.

The acute phase of the Great Depression, which began in 1929, was made worse by this chronic background of global agricultural distress, because there was no reserve of purchasing power on the farms. The farmer's plight became even worse when city people, struck by depression in industry, cut down their expenditures for food. Agricultural depression, rather than industrial depression, was at the root of widespread troubles in the inter-war years throughout eastern Europe and the colonial world.

The Crash of 1929 and the Spread of Economic Crisis

The Depression, in the strict sense, began as a stock market and financial crisis. Prices of stocks had been pushed upward by years of continuing expansion and high dividends. At the beginning of 1929 prices on the European stock exchanges began to weaken. But the real crisis, or global turning point, came with the crash on the New York Stock Exchange in October 1929. Here values had been driven to fantastic heights by excessive speculation. Not only professional speculators, but quite ordinary people bought stock with borrowed funds. Often trading on "margin," they "owned" five or ten times as much stock as the amount of their own money put into it; the rest they borrowed from brokers, and the brokers borrowed from banks, the purchased stock in each case serving as collateral. With money so easy to obtain, people pushed up American stock prices by bidding against each other and enjoyed huge fortunes on paper; but if prices fell, even a little, the hapless owners would be obliged to sell their stock to pay off the money they had borrowed. Hence the weakening of values on the New York Stock Exchange set off uncontrollable tidal waves of selling, which drove stock prices down irresistibly and disastrously. In a month stock values dropped by 40 percent, and in three years, from 1929 to 1932, the average value of 50 industrial stocks traded on the New York Stock Exchange dropped from 252 to 61. In these same three years 5,000 American banks closed their doors.

The crisis passed from finance to industry and from the United States into Europe and the rest of the world. The export of American capital came to an end. Americans not only ceased to invest in Europe but sold the foreign securities that they had. This pulled the foundations *Economic crisis becomes global* from under the postwar revival of Germany and hence indirectly of much of Europe. Americans, their incomes falling, ceased to buy foreign goods; people in Europe saw their American markets slip away, and prices tumbled. Everywhere business firms and private people could not collect what was owed them or even draw on money that they thought they had in the bank. They could not buy, and so the factories could not sell. Factories slowed down or closed entirely. Between 1929 and 1932, the latter year representing the depth of the Depression, world production is estimated to have declined by 38 percent, and the world's international trade fell by two-thirds. In the United States national income fell from $85 billion to $37 billion.

Unemployment, a chronic disease ever since the Great War, assumed the proportion of a plague. In 1932 there were 30 million *Unemployment* unemployed persons reported in the world; and this figure did not include the further millions who could find work only for a few hours in the week, or the masses in Asia or Africa for whom no statistics were reported. The worker's wages were gone, the farmer's income touched bottom; and the decline of mass purchasing power forced more idleness of machinery and more unemployment. People in the prime of life spent years out of work. Young people could not find jobs or establish themselves in an occupation. Skills and talents of older people grew rusty. Millions were reduced to living and supporting their families on the pittances of charity, doles, or relief. Great modern cities saw an outburst of sidewalk art, in which jobless able-bodied men drew pictures on the pavement with colored chalk, in the hope of attracting a few sixpence or dimes. People were crushed in spirit by a feeling of uselessness; months and years of fruitless job hunting left them demoralized, bored, embittered, and resentful. Never had there been such waste, not merely of machinery that now stood idle but also of the trained and disciplined labor force on which all modern societies were built. And people chronically out of work turned to new and disturbing political ideas.

Political and Economic Reactions to the Crisis

Optimists at the time, of whom President Herbert Hoover in the United States was one, declared that this Depression, though a severe one, was basically only another periodic low point in the business cycle, or alternation of expansion and contraction, which had ebbed and flowed in the Western world for over a century. Prosperity, they blithely said, was "just around the corner." Others came to believe that the crisis represented the breakdown of the whole system of capitalism and free private enterprise. These people in many cases looked for signs of the future in the planned economy then being introduced in the U.S.S.R. There was some truth in both views. After 1932, in part for purely cyclical reasons—because the Depression cut down indebtedness and reduced the costs of doing business—it again became possible to produce and sell. World steel production, for example, which had stood at 121 million tons in 1929, and then collapsed to 50 million in 1932, by 1936 again reached 122 million. To a considerable degree, to be sure, revival was due to rearmament, especially in Europe. On the other hand, the Great Depression did put an end to some aspects of the older free-market economic system. Even if such a stricken economy had internal powers of full recuperation, people would not stand for such terrifying insecurity in their personal lives. The horrors of mass unemployment were long remembered.

All governments took new steps to provide work and incomes for their people. All in one way or another strove to free themselves from dependency on the uncertainties of the world market. The interlocking world economy collapsed both from the Depression itself and from the measures adopted to cure it. One of the most marked economic consequences of the Depression was a strong movement toward economic nationalism—toward greater self-sufficiency within the sphere that each government could hope to control.

Economic nationalism   The international trading systems that had developed through easy money exchanges, the gold standard, and the free convertibility of currencies gradually broke down. Countries specializing in agricultural exports were among the first to be pinched. Agricultural prices were so low that even a large quantity of exports failed to produce enough foreign currency to pay for needed imports; hence the exporting country's currency fell in value. The currencies of Argentina, Uruguay, Chile, Australia, and New Zealand all depreciated in 1929 and 1930. Then came the turn of the industrial countries. England, also, as the Depression went on, could not

Rising unemployment in Depression-era Britain led to widespread protests such as this "Hunger March." Unemployed workers demanded more access to the government assistance that helped impoverished people buy food.
(©Keystone/Hulton Archive/Getty Images)

sell enough exports to pay for imports. It had to pay for imports in part by sending gold out of the country; thus the gold reserve supporting the pound sterling declined, and people who had pounds sterling began to convert their pounds into dollars or other currencies for which they thought the gold basis was more secure. This was known, in the poetic language of economics, as the "flight from the pound." In 1931 Great Britain went off the gold standard, which is to say that it devalued the pound. But after Britain devalued, some 20 odd other countries, to protect their own exports and their own industries, did the same. Hence somewhat the same relative position reappeared. Even the United States, which possessed most of the world's gold supply, renounced the gold standard and devalued the dollar in 1934. The purpose was mainly to help American farmers; with dollars cheaper in terms of foreign currencies, foreigners could afford to buy more American agricultural products. But it became harder for Europeans and other foreigners to sell to the United States.

Hence the Depression, adding its effects to those of the World War and postwar inflation, led to chaos in the international monetary exchanges. Governments manipulated

International monetary exchanges in chaos

their currencies to uphold their sagging exports. Or they imposed exchange controls, which required that foreigners from whom their own people purchased, and to whom they gave their own currency, should use this currency to buy from them in return. Trade, which had been multilateral, became increasingly bilateral. Sometimes, notably in the relations between Germany and eastern European countries in the 1930s, bilateralism degenerated into actual barter. The Germans would exchange a certain number of cameras with Yugoslavia in return for a certain number of pigs. In such cases the very conception of a market disappeared.

Currency control was one means of keeping one's own factories from idleness by holding or capturing export markets in time of depression. Another way of keeping one's own factories going was to shut out competitive imports by the old device of protective tariffs. The United States enacted the unprecedentedly high Hawley-Smoot tariff in 1930, which soon contributed to the further decline of international trade. Other countries, equally or more distressed, now could sell less to America and hence buy fewer American goods. Other countries likewise raised their own tariffs in the desperate hope of reserving national markets for their own people. Even Great Britain, citadel of free trade in the nineteenth century, turned to protectionism. It also revived and adopted Joseph Chamberlain's old idea of an imperial tariff union. In 1932, by the Ottawa agreements, Britain and the British dominions adopted a policy of lower tariffs against one another and higher tariffs against the rest of the world.

Quotas

Even tariffs were not always enough for economic nationalists. Quotas or quantitative restrictions were adopted in many nations. By this system a government said in effect not merely that goods brought into the country must pay a high tariff duty but that above a certain amount no goods could be brought in at all. Increasingly both importers and exporters worked under government licenses, in order that a country's entire foreign trade could be centrally planned and managed.

Thus the world economy disintegrated into fiercely competing national economic systems. In the oceanic wreckage of the Great Depression, each state tried to create an island of economic security for its own people. Some efforts were made to break down the rising barriers. An International Monetary and Economic Conference, meeting in London in 1933, attempted to open the clogged channels of world trade; it ended in failure, as did attempts to stabilize the exchange rates of various currencies. Soon thereafter, the wartime Allies defaulted on their postwar debt payments to the United States. Legislation in Congress then denied them the right to float bonds or obtain new loans in the American securities market. American actions thus reinforced economic nationalism. The era that had opened with Woodrow Wilson's dream of international economic cooperation was ending with an unprecedented intensification of economic rivalry and national self-centeredness; it was only one of the promises of the postwar world to be blasted by the Great Depression.

Cultural Reactions to the Crisis

The effects of the economic crisis spread to the cultural and intellectual life of the 1930s. Responding to the despair and social dislocation of the masses of unemployed, artists and writers turned to describing painful social realities and committed themselves to political activism.

Modernism

All this was in contrast to the 1920s. The postwar decade had been a period of great achievement in what is generally called "modernist" art and literature. Painters projected disjointed dreamlike scenes

The economic turmoil of the Great Depression caused social instabilities and disruptions throughout most of Europe and the world. These German women were receiving food from German soldiers at a soup kitchen in November 1931, but their experiences exemplified a wider social disorientation that reshaped personal lives and political cultures in all industrial countries during the global economic crisis.

(©Popperfoto/Getty Images)

evoking their personal memories or disorienting personal experiences, and writers emphasized their own personal vision and the innermost lives of the characters whom they depicted. These writers were responsible for remarkable explorations of memory, time, and the internal workings of the human mind. The Irish writer James Joyce published his famous novel *Ulysses* portraying the life and thoughts of its leading character during a single day in Dublin, contributing with it to a new literary fascination with interior monologues and "stream of consciousness" writing. The French novelist Marcel Proust also developed lengthy descriptions of personal and emotional experiences in his multivolume *Remembrance of Things Past,* and the English writer Virginia Woolf examined the complex passage of time through the characters she created in novels such as *To the Lighthouse.* A generation of American writers, including Gertrude Stein and Ernest Hemingway, had even settled in Paris after the First World War to pursue experimental forms of literature and art. The political and social world by no means disappeared from modernist literature, but these writers were more concerned with exploring the inner complexities of human psychology, partly in response to the horrors of the First World War.

Now, under the harsh economic conditions of the 1930s, it became common to reject the literary exploration of psychological anxieties as inadequate or even as self-indulgent. A new kind of "realist" literature and a literature of political engagement won support from intellectuals in all industrial societies, especially among those who believed that the Great Depression had grown out of fundamental flaws and injustices in the capitalist economy. Some writers, like the French novelist André Gide, as well as some poets, artists, and film-makers, temporarily embraced communism and praised the social experiments of the Soviet Union. Others simply decided that they should set aside the arcane language of the literary avant-garde and write about the social suffering among unemployed or impoverished workers. A new genre of proletarian literature came into being. Many of the American expatriates who had settled in Paris to pursue avant-garde art or literature returned to the United States in the early 1930s. As the American critic Malcolm Cowley noted in his *Exile's Return,* the new social problems called for new kinds of writing. Joyce's *Ulysses* was a classic modernist work of the 1920s, but the literary style of high Modernism gave way to a new kind of "social literature" and nonfiction in the 1930s. A younger generation of socially conscious authors, such as the English writer George Orwell, published Depression-era books that focused on poverty and the economic realities of daily life. Describing his own encounters with impoverished living conditions in *Down and Out in Paris and London* (1933) and *The Road to Wigan Pier* (1937), Orwell emphasized the "real world" social experiences of people who struggled simply to survive. His themes and those elaborated by others expressed the social and cultural anxiety that affected Europeans of all social classes in the wake of the unprecedented economic crisis. Meanwhile, the anxiety

Realism and extremism

that fostered a new literary and artistic realism also contributed in very different ways to the rise of an angry, polarizing political extremism, which was now attracting new support among disillusioned and displaced people in every part of Europe and the wider Atlantic world.

Suggested Further Readings can be found in the ebook, on Connect, or online at www.mhhe .com/kramer12e.

Chapter 20

DEMOCRACY AND DICTATORSHIP IN THE 1930S

In the 1920s many people believed, or hoped, that despite the horrors of the World War, Europe could begin moving again toward material and political progress. In the 1930s they began to fear that "progress" was a phantom and that Europe could relapse into barbarism and a new world war.

The Great Depression ushered in the nightmare of the 1930s. Everywhere the demand was for security. Each nation tried to live, insofar as possible, within itself. Each regulated, controlled, guided, planned, and tried to rescue its own economic system, attempting to escape from the influence or unpredictable behavior of other countries. Within each country the same search for security encouraged the advancement of the welfare state and social democracy.

Where democratic institutions were strong and resilient, governments took steps to protect individuals against the ravages of unemployment and destitution and to help guard against future catastrophes. This political response to the economic crisis shaped new democratic social reforms in northwestern Europe and in the United States, where President Franklin Roosevelt's "New Deal" legislation brought numerous European-style social welfare policies into American society. On the other hand, where democratic governments were not well established or taken for granted, which was the case in many countries after the First World War, dictatorship spread rapidly as authoritarian political leaders claimed they could respond more efficiently to the economic problems of the 1930s. Democracy was said to be suited only to wealthy or prosperous countries. Unemployed people generally cared far more for economic help or for promises of economic help than for any theory of how persons wielding public power should be selected. The cry was for a leader, someone who would act, make decisions, get results, inspire confidence, and restore national pride. The Great Depression opened the way for unscrupulous and ambitious political adventurers, for dictators like Adolf Hitler in Germany, whose solution to all political and international problems, it turned out, was war.

Chapter emblem: Benito Mussolini addressing a Fascist meeting in Italy in 1932. (©Keystone/Hulton Archive/ Getty Images)

97.   TRIALS AND ADJUSTMENTS OF DEMOCRACY IN BRITAIN AND FRANCE

British Politics: The 1920s and the Depression

Britain, like the United States, even in the troubles of the Depression, remained firmly attached to representative institutions and democratic principles. The Great Depression aggravated and intensified Britain's older economic difficulties. More dependent on overseas markets than any other people, the British until 1914 had managed to hold their lead, exporting industrial products and investment capital, selling insurance and other services, and importing foodstuffs. But in the years before 1914 the British had begun to lose markets because of the emergence of other economically aggressive industrial nations, the growth of tariff barriers, the development of indigenous textile and other industries in India and elsewhere in Asia, the competition of new textile products with British cottons and woolens, and the substitution of new sources of fuel for British coal. The losses were accelerated by the economic disruption of the First World War, the disappearance of many overseas investments, and the postwar disorganization and impoverishment of markets. The widespread rise in tariffs after the war and the customs barriers in the new small states of Europe also hurt British exports. After 1918 Britain lived in a world no longer dependent on, or eager for, its manufactures. Britain's historical primacy as the pioneer industrial country also became a handicap. Both labor and management had developed their ideas and methods under older conditions, and the more recently industrialized countries were using newer techniques and machinery.

The net result of all this was that in the interwar years, even in times of relative prosperity for the rest of the world, Britain was in Depression and suffered severely from unemployment. The unemployment insurance adopted in 1911 was called heavily into play. By 1921 over 2 million unemployed were receiving benefit payments, contemptuously called the "dole" by those who disliked it. Unemployment insurance, an expanded old-age pension system, medical aid, government-subsidized housing, and other social welfare measures helped to relieve economic distress and to prevent any drastic decline in the living standards of British workers. The welfare state was already well established in Britain before the Labour Party took office after the Second World War.

Unemployment insurance

The labor unions made a strenuous effort to retain wage gains and other concessions won in wartime. Industry, hard-pressed itself, resisted. This situation reached a climax in 1926 in the coal-mining industry, which was in a particularly bad plight; government subsidies had not helped and even conservative investigators had recommended some form of amalgamation and public management. A strike by the coal miners led to a "general strike" supported by the other British unions; about half of the 6 million organized workers in Britain left their jobs as a token of sympathy and solidarity. But the government declared a state of emergency and made use of military personnel and middle-class volunteers to take over essential services. The strike ended in failure, and even in a setback for the trade unions. They were put under stricter control by the Trades Disputes Act of 1927, which declared all general or sympathy strikes illegal and even forbade the unions from raising money for political purposes.

The Labour Party

After the election of 1922, the Labour Party displaced the Liberal Party as the second of the two great parties of the country and faced the Conservatives as the official opposition. The Labour Party, which

The British coal miners' strike in 1926 generated a massive "general strike" by sympathetic workers throughout Britain. These well-dressed engineers joined the strike and marched across London to show their solidarity with the miners, but the government soon responded to this broad-based labor action with legislation that made all such sympathy strikes illegal.
(©G. Adams/Hulton Archive/Getty Images)

had been no more than a loose federation of trade union and socialist organizations before the war, tightened its organizational structure, promoted labor legislation, and, bridging the gap between the trade unionists and the socialists, committed itself to a program of socialism. But it was a program of gradualist, democratic socialism operating through customary British parliamentary procedures and hence able to gain the goodwill of large sections of the middle classes.

Twice, in 1924 and in 1929, Labour governed the country as part of a coalition government in which Ramsay MacDonald served as prime minister. In 1924 Labour demonstrated its moderation. It did no more than extend unemployment relief and inaugurate housing and public works projects; indeed it acted firmly in the face of strikes that broke out. But it aroused opposition when it gave diplomatic recognition to the Soviet Union and pledged a loan to the Soviets for the purchase of British goods. Meanwhile newspapers published the so-called Red (or Zinoviev) letter purporting to be secret instructions from the head of the Communist International for British Labour groups to prepare for a Communist uprising in Britain. The document's authenticity has never been established, but the Conservatives successfully exploited it in an election that restored their earlier governing majority.

In the election of May 1929, however, Labour's representation almost doubled, and the Conservative representation dropped proportionately. MacDonald again became prime minister. The Wall Street crash and the worldwide Depression came during this second period of Labour Party government. The effects of the Depression were quickly felt. Unemployment, which had hovered about the 1 million mark in 1929, soon approached the 3 million figure. The government expended large sums to supplement the unemployment insurance payments, and the public debt began to grow. Alarmed by the mounting deficit, MacDonald made plans to introduce a severe retrenchment policy, even to the extent of reducing the dole payments. The Labour Party was outraged, and some of the Labour ministers in his cabinet refused to support him.

Critics such as the British economist John Maynard Keynes argued that the government's deficit spending was in fact essential for economic recovery. Keynes had begun to put forward this view of government expenditures even before the Great Depression struck, and he would soon bring his theories together in his most famous book, *The General Theory of Employment, Interest, and Money* (1936). In this book and other writings, Keynes argued that if private investment funds were idle, government funds must be employed to encourage or stimulate economic activity and to increase purchasing power until such time as private funds flowed again. Governments should therefore get money into circulation and "prime the pump" of industrial production. According to Keynes and others who criticized MacDonald's policies, the British government should set aside old orthodoxies about the dangers of deficit financing, because such policies were actually the most direct and rapid method for preventing a more general collapse of the capitalist system. Keynes's ideas attracted the interest of some policymakers in other countries (including the United States) and later gained wide international influence, but MacDonald rejected the new economic theories and continued to promote austerity measures. He was read out of the Labour Party, along with those ministers who had gone along with him. MacDonald thereupon formed an all-party coalition cabinet known as the National government, which in an election of 1931 won an overwhelming victory, but it was the Conservative members of the coalition who took a majority of the seats in Parliament.

Theories of Keynes

The formation of the National government

The National government coped with the Depression chiefly along retrenchment lines, under Ramsay MacDonald from 1931 to 1935, Stanley Baldwin to 1937, and Neville Chamberlain after 1937. In addition to retrenchment and budget balancing, the government encouraged industry to reorganize and rationalize production by providing low-interest loans. Mainly, the government concentrated on economic nationalist measures rather than on fundamental changes in the capitalist economic system. Despite some recovery from the depths of the Depression, none of the government's nationalist policies brought full recovery or full employment. Unemployment persisted until military conscription and a growing armament program absorbed the jobless through a kind of inadvertent "Keynesian" expansion of government expenditures.

Britain and the Commonwealth: Imperial Relations

To the older British Empire—India, the crown colonies, protectorates, and spheres of influence—the postwar settlement added a number of League of Nations mandates. British rule in its various forms extended after 1919 to almost 500 million people, a fourth of the earth's population and land surface. It was principally in Palestine, Egypt, India, and Ireland that the British faced complex political or social problems and growing opposition to their imperial control. In Palestine, where Britain exercised a League of Nations mandate following the breakup of the Ottoman Empire, a bitter conflict developed as Jewish emigrants moved into the territory after 1919 (at which time there had been a relatively small population of about 570,000 Muslims, 75,000 Christians, and 60,000 Jews). The emigration increased rapidly during the 1930s, when Jews were escaping from Nazism and the rising anti-Semitism in Europe. Arabs and Jews began to struggle with each other and with Britain for control of lands that both groups claimed on the basis of long ancestries and ancient religions, inflamed now by modern nationalisms. In Egypt, in 1922, Britain formally ended the protectorate it had established 40 years earlier. The British retained the right to station some troops on Egyptian territory, however, and many political questions, especially the status of Sudan, remained unresolved. In India the agitation for national independence, as we have seen, grew more intense. In all of these areas, from the Middle East to South Asia, the British were unable or unwilling to make major changes in their imperial system until after the Second World War. In Ireland, however, the independence movement finally managed to establish a separate Irish state.

The Irish question had disoriented English politics for 40 years. Home rule, authorized by Parliament in 1914, had been deferred for   *The Irish question* the duration of the war. During the hostilities the Irish nationalists even accepted German support and rose in rebellion against the British in 1916. The rebellion was suppressed, but after the war the Irish nationalists, led by the Sinn Fein Party, fought a small but savage war of independence against the British. In 1922 the British finally recognized the Irish Free State, granting it dominion status within the British Commonwealth. But the Protestants in Ulster, the northern counties of Ireland where Presbyterians of Scottish origin had lived for three centuries and where they comprised a majority of the population, insisted on remaining outside the new state. Despite the vehement dissatisfaction of Irish nationalists, Ulster continued to be part of what was now called the United Kingdom of Great Britain and Northern Ireland. In 1937 the Irish Free State affirmed its full sovereignty and took the name Eire. In 1949 it broke all ties with the British Commonwealth and renamed itself the Republic of Ireland. The Irish question, however, remained unsettled throughout the rest of the century and beyond because Catholic activists in both Northern Ireland and the new Irish Republic agitated for the Irish annexation of Ulster. The conflict pitted Irish moderates against Irish extremists, the latter perpetrating assassinations, bombings, and other disturbances to further their cause of uniting all Ireland within the Irish Republic. The Protestants in Ulster meanwhile remained obdurate about retaining their own religious and cultural identity and maintaining their political affiliation with Britain.

As for the dominions, the political status of these areas of European settlement overseas was now more clearly defined than ever before. The   *The dominions* white-controlled dominions—Canada, Australia, New Zealand, and the Union of South Africa—had long pursued their own independent policies, even levying tariffs against British goods. They had all joined loyally with Great Britain in the First World War, but all were stirred by a nationalism of their own and desired their independence to be regularized and promulgated to the world. An imperial conference in 1926 defined "dominion status," which was then corroborated by the Statute of Westminster of 1931. The dominions became legally equal with each other and with Great Britain. No act passed by the British Parliament would apply to a dominion except by the dominion's own consent. Despite independent policies in economic matters and even in foreign affairs, the bonds between the dominions and Britain remained firm; the support of the dominions in the Second World War was to be vital in Britain's survival. In the postwar world, with decolonization, the Commonwealth became a larger, more heterogeneous, and even more flexible institution.

France: The 1920s and the Coming of the Depression

When the Depression came to France, right-wing agitation of fascist type made more headway than in Britain or the United States. Earlier, in the 1920s, France was preoccupied with recovery from the physical destruction of the war, the instability of public finances, and the fear of a resurgent Germany. Immediately after 1919, and for most of the 1920s, the government was run by coalitions of parties of the conservative Right, that is, parties supported by business and financial interests, well disposed toward the army and church, and determined to maintain the traditional order in domestic affairs. In contrast to Britain, Germany, and the United States, for example, France continued to exclude women from the right to vote. For a brief time, from 1924 to 1926, the Radical Socialists were in control; this party of the moderate Left, whose leader was Edouard Herriot, served as spokesman for the lower classes, small business, and farmers; it advocated progressive social legislation but only so long as increased taxes were not necessary. Despite its name, a carryover from an earlier era, it was firmly committed to private enterprise and private property (and was often described as "neither radical nor socialist"). It was staunch in its defense of individual liberties, and it carried the memory of the Dreyfus Affair into a fervent anticlericalism. This enduring anticlerical fervor sometimes seemed to serve as a substitute for a more positive legislative program.

Although the Radical Socialists cooperated in parliamentary elections with the Socialists, the other major party of the Left, the two parties differed too profoundly on economic policies to preserve stable coalitions. In the 1920s the Socialists were still recovering from the secession of the more orthodox Marxists who had formed a French Communist Party. Both Left and Right in France shaded off into antidemocratic groups that were hostile

Hostility to the republic

to the parliamentary republic. These included the Communists on the Left, who sat in Parliament and took part in elections; and on the extreme Right, royalists of the *Action Française* and other antirepublican organizations, which also remembered the Dreyfus Affair (as a struggle against the dangers of French republicanism) and which operated principally outside the Chamber as militant and noisy pressure groups.

Poincaré's measures

The outstanding figure of the moderate conservative Right was Raymond Poincaré, who sent troops into the Ruhr in 1923 when the Germans failed to pay reparations, and who also "saved" the franc. The reparations question was extremely important for French finances. The country had undertaken a large-scale reconstruction program to repair the wartime devastation of northern and eastern France, and the French government had counted upon the defeated enemy to pay. When German reparations were not paid as anticipated, the public debt mounted, a balanced budget became impossible, and the franc declined precipitously. The huge war expenditures, heavy loss of foreign investments, notably in Russia, and an outmoded taxation program that invited widespread evasion added to French difficulties. After 1926, when the financial crisis reached a climax, a "national union" ministry under Poincaré inaugurated new taxes, tightened tax collection, cut down drastically on government expenditures to balance the budget, and eventually stabilized the franc—at about one-fifth its prewar value. The internal debt was thus in effect largely repudiated, to the despair of many bondholders, but the threat of a runaway inflation like that of Germany's Weimar Republic was avoided. From 1926 to 1929 France prospered. New factories, replacing those destroyed in the war, were modern and up to date. The index of industrial production rose; tourists flocked in. As in many other countries, however, workers did not share proportionately in the prosperity of the 1920s, and labor unions still had little influence on the French government's social policies.

The Great Depression came later to France and was less severe than in the United States or Germany. Trade declined. Unemployment increased; in 1935, close to 1 million

Britain repeatedly used its armed forces to suppress the movement for Irish independence during and after the First World War. The British army thus operated in Ireland's cities as a kind of special police force. These troops were holding back the crowd in a Dublin street while other soldiers conducted a raid on Irish nationalists in 1921—shortly before the Irish Free State was finally established.

(©Hulton Archive/Getty Images)

workers were unemployed, and half of those employed worked part-time. Industrial production, which in 1930 was 40 percent above the prewar level, sank by 1932 back to the production rates of 1913. Faced with such economic challenges, the government returned to an older pattern of unstable, short-lived ministries. Five ministries rapidly succeeded one another in 1933, and there were some 40 during the interwar years. The Depression-era cabinets followed a policy of national retrenchments, tried to reduce government expenditures, clung to the gold standard, and faced the threat of an aggressive new government in Germany, where Adolf Hitler had become chancellor in 1933.

Depression Ferment and the Popular Front

In the uneasy years of the Great Depression, the latent right-wing hostility to the French republic came to the surface. Fascist-type "leagues" appeared in open imitation of Italian and German fascist organizations, many obtaining funds from wealthy industrialists; the

Although the Great Depression was at first less severe in France than in other European countries, rising unemployment eventually contributed to a new political mobilization of French workers. The Popular Front government that came to power in 1936 thus enacted legislation to support collective bargaining and to establish a 40-hour week for people like these workers at a Parisian subway construction site.

(©Imagno/Hulton Archive/Getty Images)

older *Action Française* and right-wing veterans' associations like Colonel de le Rocque's *Croix de Feu* continued to be active. The same elements that had been antirepublican, antidemocratic, or monarchist since the French Revolution, and that in the nineteenth century had rallied behind Boulanger and denounced Dreyfus, now grew more strident in their attacks on the parliamentary republic.

In 1934 it seemed for a moment that the long-awaited opportunity for an antirepublican breakthrough had emerged. A political and financial scandal shook the country. A financial manipulator and adventurer with important political connections, Serge Alexandre Stavisky, induced the municipal authorities at Bayonne to launch a flotation of worthless bonds. When the scheme was exposed, Stavisky fled and apparently committed suicide; the sensationalist press and right-wing political agitators encouraged the rumor that he had been shot by the police to prevent the implication of high-ranking politicians. A clamor went up accusing the government of involvement in the financial

Scandals

scandal. Where such an affair in other countries might simply have forced the incumbents out of office, in France it supplied ammunition for those who demanded the end of the republic itself, which they now equated with corruption and venality.

The agitation reached a climax in street riots in February 1934. A crowd of angry antirepublican activists and right-wing extremists assembled in Paris at the Place de la Concorde, where they threatened the nearby Chamber of Deputies and battled violently with the police; several were killed and hundreds were injured. French liberals and democrats, organized labor, and socialists angrily denounced this threat to the republic from violent agitators who resembled the fascist groups that had seized power elsewhere in Europe. The Communists, though hostile to the fascist groups, were also unfriendly to the government and critical of the moderate Socialist Party. Guided by the Comintern, however, they sensed that a fascist triumph in France would endanger the Soviet Union.

The French Popular Front brought the leftist, antifascist political parties together in a governing coalition that held power for about a year in 1936–1937. Despite its brevity, the Popular Front government introduced numerous reforms that became permanent features of French social and economic life. This photograph shows Premier Léon Blum addressing socialist supporters of the Popular Front in November 1936.

(©Keystone-France/Gamma-Keystone/Getty Images)

Moving away from their sectarian revolutionary isolation, the Communists in France (and elsewhere) entered new political coalitions that widened their influence and appeal. An impressive labor-sponsored general strike mobilized French workers a week after the Parisian riot. Shortly thereafter, Radical Socialists, Socialists, and Communists joined together in a political movement that came to be known as the Popular Front. This movement provided a model for new kinds of left-wing solidarity that spread to other countries during the 1930s; and it pledged to defend the republic against fascism, to develop stronger policies against the Depression, and to introduce labor reforms. In the spring of 1936 the Popular Front won a decisive victory at the polls. The French Socialists, for the first time in their history, became the leading party in the Chamber of Deputies. The Socialist leader Léon Blum, long a spokesman for democratic and socialist reforms, became premier of a coalition cabinet of Socialists and Radical Socialists; the Communists, who had increased their representation in the Chamber from 10 to 72 seats, did not join the cabinet but pledged their support.

The emergence of the Popular Front

The Popular Front and After

Blum's Popular Front ministry, although it lasted little more than a year, put through a program of far-reaching legislation. This legislation was due, in part, to the Popular Front election program, but it also emerged from unforeseen events. The tremendous enthusiasm generated by the victory led to a spontaneous nationwide wave of "sit-down strikes," in which the striking workers refused to leave their factories or shops until Blum pledged a number of immediate reforms.

The Chamber of Deputies quickly passed laws providing for a 40-hour week, vacations with pay, and a collective bargaining law. The encouragement given to collective bargaining led to the nationwide signing of collective labor contracts for the first time in the country's history and to enormous growth in trade union membership, from about 1 million to 5 million over a year's time. Other legislation was important too. Steps were taken to nationalize the armaments and aviation industry; the fascist armed leagues were, at least in theory, dissolved; the Bank of France was reorganized and placed under government control to break the power of the nation's close-knit economic elite, the so-called "two hundred families." Machinery was established for the arbitration of labor disputes. Aid was given to farmers through price fixing and government purchases of wheat. All these measures aimed at both economic recovery and social reform.

Overdue measures for reform and recovery

Blum spoke openly of his program as a "French New Deal," thus suggesting that the actions of the Popular Front were similar to President Roosevelt's social reforms in the United States. But French conservatives, and the quasi-fascists to their Right, cried revolution; they uttered dark predictions that a French Lenin would follow Blum. They did not conceal their sullen resentment at what had come to pass: the fate of Catholic France in the hands of a leftist, a Socialist, and a Jew. Some believed that political interventions by a conservative warrior from outside the country, one who had demonstrated his anti-Bolshevism, would be preferable to the Popular Front. They envied the protection given to established interests by Mussolini, and there were those who, it was said, even muttered "better Hitler than Léon Blum."

The Popular Front reforms, long overdue though they were, came to France at a time when the sands of the postwar international treaties were rapidly running out. While France had a 40-hour week, German arms plants were operating at full capacity. In the shadow of Nazi remilitarization a rearmament program had to be undertaken at the very same time as reform; even moderates argued that the country could not afford both. Opposition from many quarters hindered success. French employers balked at cooperating in the new labor reforms and tried to pass on rising production costs to consumers. Disgruntled workers were unhappy about the price rises that canceled out their wage gains. Both employers and labor applied the 40-hour week in such a manner that plants were shut down for two days a week instead of operating in shifts, as the law had made possible. Nothing could check the flight of gold from the country. Industrial production hardly rose; even in 1938, when production showed substantial recovery in other countries, it was only 5 percent higher in France than at the depth of the Depression.

In July 1936 the Spanish Civil War had broken out. The Communists attacked the Blum government for refusing aid to the hard-pressed Spanish Popular Front government, which was fighting fascist forces across the Pyrenees; Blum, following the lead of Britain

The overthrow of Blum's government

and fearful also of opposition within an already divided France, resisted involvement. In 1937, after a year in office, the Blum government was overthrown by the Senate, which refused to grant it emergency financial powers. The Popular Front coalition rapidly disintegrated. By mid-1938 the Radical Socialists had abandoned their allies on the Left and formed a new conservative ministry under Edouard Daladier, whose attention was increasingly occupied by the international crisis. Little remained of the Popular Front, or indeed of the strength of labor,

**The French Popular Front ministry introduced
numerous social changes after coming to power
in 1936. One of the most popular reforms
required employers to offer paid vacations, so
this dancing couple was able to enjoy a new paid
holiday at a seaside café.**
(©Roger Viollet/Getty Images)

which declined rapidly and exhausted itself further by an unsuccessful general strike that
protested nullification of the 40-hour week. Although the conservative government did not
overturn all of the recent social reforms, French workers found that 1936 had gone the
way of other "great years" in French history; the comfortable classes had been thrown into
panic by the social turmoil; internal division and class hatreds had grown sharper. Yet the
French democracy, the Third Republic itself, had been successfully preserved and its
domestic enemies repulsed, at least for a time.

Western Europe and the Depression

Britain and France, and indeed all western Europe, Europe's inner zone, never fully recovered from the Great Depression before the Second World War. When economic expansion resumed after the war, the interwar years seemed like a deep trough in Europe's economic history. Western Europe barely maintained its old industrial equipment during the Depression and was unable to utilize even its existing machinery to capacity. Moreover, as the events of 1929 had clearly shown, Europe's economy was increasingly affected by industrial and financial systems in the United States, and the U.S.S.R. was becoming an industrial giant. Europeans in the 1930s could see that they were gradually losing control of their own economic destiny.

Other signs of decline

There were other signs of decline. The birth rate in western Europe in the 1930s fell to its lowest recorded levels as people postponed marriage or limited the size of their families because of economic and psychological stresses. Birth rates did not run significantly higher than death rates; the population was stagnating and growing older. There was a scarcity of middle-age men because of the casualties of the First World War. Politically neither British nor French democratic political leaders were able to cope with the economic dilemmas of the Depression era. The socialists also struggled to propose new responses to the continuing economic crisis. Finding little practical guidance for specific policies in Marxian economics, they were unable to renew or reinvigorate their own doctrines in any significant way.

98.   ITALIAN FASCISM

Though they shade into each other imperceptibly, it is possible to distinguish dictatorship from totalitarianism. Dictatorship, an old phenomenon in history, has commonly been regarded as a mere expedient, designed for emergencies and believed to be temporary; at most, it is a theory of government to justify the authoritarian exercise of state power. Totalitarianism as it arose after the First World War, was not merely a theory of government but a more comprehensive theory of life and of human nature. It claimed to be a permanent form of society and civilization, and insofar as it appealed to emergency for justification, it regarded life itself as an everlasting emergency. This new kind of totalitarianism, when it emerged in western Europe, came from the political Right and carried significant theoretical differences from Russian Communism—which it vehemently rejected. Yet the repressive methods, the cult of the leader, and the system of one-party rule characterized totalitarian regimes on both the Left and the Right. The first of the new right-wing totalitarian movements to seize power in Europe appeared somewhat unexpectedly in Italy in the form of fascism.

Mussolini and the Fascist Seizure of Power

The post-1919 belief that democracy was generally advancing was not deeply disturbed by the failure of Russia or Turkey or China to develop effective parliaments or liberal institutions. Most Europeans regarded these regions as lagging countries that were still mired in the throes of revolution; someday, when conditions quieted down, it could be supposed, they would move toward the kinds of democratic systems that had been established earlier in Europe. Italy thus became a jarring exception to the apparent victory of

democracy in European societies because the Italians had always been
an integral part of European history. Although Italy had accepted parliamentary liberalism and other democratic institutions since 1861,
Benito Mussolini seized control of the Italian government in 1921 and
proclaimed the new ruling ideology and political system of *Fascismo.*

*The birth of
Fascismo*

Mussolini, born in 1883, the son of a blacksmith, was a fiery and pugnacious character, who before the war had followed the career of professional revolutionary, left-wing
socialist, and radical journalist. He had read and digested Marxist writings but also
works such as Sorel's *Reflections on Violence* and the writings of Nietzsche. During the
war he turned intensely nationalist, clamored for Italian intervention on the side of the
Allies, and demanded the conquest from Austria of *Italia irredenta,* the "unredeemed"
Italian lands to the north and across the Adriatic. In the war he served as a corporal.
In March 1919 he organized, mainly from demobilized and restless ex-soldiers, his first
fighting band, or *fascio di combattimento. Fascio* meant a bunch or bundle, as of sticks;
it called to mind the Latin *fasces,* or bundle of rods, carried by the lictors in ancient
Rome as a symbol of state power—for Mussolini loved to conjure up ancient Roman
glories.

In 1919 Italian glories were dim. Italy had entered the war on the side of the Allies
quite frankly to gain new territorial and colonial spoils; the secret treaty of London in
1915 had promised the Italians certain Austrian lands and a share in German and Ottoman Turkish possessions. During the war Italian arms did not especially shine, and Italian
troops suffered a disastrous defeat in a battle against the Austrians at Caporetto in 1917.
Yet Italy lost over 600,000 lives in the war, and the Italian delegates came to the Versailles
peace conference confident that their sacrifices would be recognized and their territorial
aspirations would be satisfied. They were rapidly disappointed. Wilson refused to honor
the provisions of the London secret treaty and other demands of the Italians. Britain and
France displayed no eagerness to side with Italy. The Italians received some of the Austrian
territories promised to them, but to their resentment they were given no part of the former
German or Ottoman Turkish possessions as mandates.

After the war Italy, like other countries, suffered from the burden of wartime debt
and from acute postwar depression and unemployment. Social unrest spread. In the countryside land seizures took place, not in any significant proportions but
enough to spread concern among landowners; tenant farmers refused
to pay rents; peasants burned crops and destroyed livestock. In the

Social unrest

cities great strikes broke out in heavy industry and in transportation. Some of the strikes
turned into sit-down strikes, the workers refusing to leave the plants; demands were raised
even for worker control of the factories. Moderate socialist and labor leaders disavowed
all such extremism, but left-wing socialists who, as elsewhere, had turned Communist and
joined the Third International, fanned the existing discontents. Meanwhile, armed bands
of young men, most prominent of whom were the Blackshirts or Fascists, brawled with
Communists and ordinary workers in the streets. By the late summer of 1920 the strikes
and the agrarian unrest had subsided, although violence in the streets persisted.

During the months of turmoil the government refrained from any bold action, and
the already low respect for Italy's parliamentary system sank even lower. In 1919 the first
postwar election gave impressive victories to the Socialist Party and a new Catholic
Popular Party (the latter were also called Christian Socialists). In 1921, in the wake of
the postwar disturbances, new elections were held. Despite concerns about the recent
social turmoil, liberals and democrats, moderate socialists, and the Catholic Popular Party

Fascist groups joined a "March on Rome" that sought to displace Italy's liberal-democratic government in October 1922. Mussolini joined the March as the Blackshirts entered the capital, and he is seen here (in civilian clothes) leading his Fascist followers through the city—shortly before he became prime minister in a new coalition ministry.

(©Ullstein bild Dtl./Getty Images)

were all returned in large numbers. Mussolini's Fascist Movement won only 35 of the 500-odd seats. This less than impressive showing was the best the Fascists ever achieved in a free election, but the Fascist ranks were nonetheless swelling outside the regular channels of electoral politics—in the backwash, as it were, of the postwar unrest.

Mussolini and the Fascists at first went along with the radical tide; they did not disapprove the factory seizures; they inveighed against plutocracy and war profiteers and called for a high levy on capital and profits. But Mussolini was more interested in seizing power than in defending principles or the economic interests of the lower classes, and he soon came forward with

Mussolini: Upholding order and property

his Fascists as the upholders of national law and order, and hence property; he now pledged battle "against the forces dissolving victory and nation." Although the social agitation subsided, burning itself out on its own, and there had never been any real threat of a Soviet-style revolution in Italy, the propertied classes had gone through a great fright; they found comfort in the Fascist Movement and were willing to lend it financial support. Patriots and nationalists of all classes rallied to it, as well as the lower middle class, which was pinched by economic inflation and, as elsewhere, was unable to find protection or solace in labor unions or socialist movements. The black-shirted upholders of national order proceeded methodically to administer beatings (and doses of castor oil) to Communists and alleged Communists, to Socialists and Christian Socialists, and to ordinary persons who did not support them; nor did they refrain from arson and murder. Vigilante Fascist squadrons, the *squadristi*, broke up strikes, demolished labor union headquarters, and drove from office duly elected Socialist and Communist mayors and town officials. Mussolini nevertheless reinforced his claim as paladin of law, authority, and order by declaring his loyalty to king and church; a few years earlier he had been a rabid republican and anticlerical. Now he saw a new pathway toward a seizure of power.

Benito Mussolini liked to portray his Fascist regime in Italy as a restoration of the power and grandeur of ancient Rome. Speaking here at a Fascist rally in 1932 and surrounded by uniformed followers as well as symbols of the Roman Empire, Mussolini struck a characteristic stance to convey a public image of decisive, powerful leadership in the authoritarian Italian state.

(©Keystone/Hulton Archive/Getty Images)

In October 1922 the "March on Rome" took place. The Blackshirts mobilized for a threatened coup and began to converge from various directions on the capital; Mussolini remained at a safe distance in Milan. The liberal-democratic coalition cabinet had viewed the events of the past two years with disapproval but at the same time saw with satisfaction that the Blackshirts were serving a useful national purpose by suppressing troublemakers on the Left. Now they made belated but ineffectual gestures to save the situation by seeking a declaration of martial law, but the king refused to approve. The cabinet resigned and Mussolini was named premier. It was all quite legal, or almost so. Indeed Italy was still in form a constitutional and parliamentary monarchy. Mussolini headed only a coalition ministry and received from parliament no more than a year's grant of full emergency powers to restore order and introduce reforms.

The "March on Rome"

But Mussolini wanted to create a permanent authoritarian government, and it soon became clear that the Fascists were undermining democratic institutions as they consolidated state power in their own hands. Before the expiration of his emergency powers Mussolini forced through parliament a law providing that any party securing the largest number of votes in an election should automatically receive two-thirds of the seats in the legislature. The two-thirds law was not even necessary. In the 1924 elections, although seven opposition slates appeared, the Fascists, aided by control of the electoral machinery and the use of squadristi, received well over three-fifths of the total vote.

After the elections of 1924 the highly respected Socialist deputy Giacomo Matteotti publicly exposed hundreds of cases of armed Fascist violence, fraud, and chicanery. He was murdered by Fascists. There was widespread indignation in the country, and the press clamored for Mussolini's

Matteotti's murder

resignation. The left and centrist parties, in an act that proved to be a serious miscalculation, withdrew in protest from the Chamber, wanting to have nothing to do with such a government. Mussolini, not directly involved in the assassination, expressed a willingness to punish the perpetrators but eventually took full responsibility and moved to consolidate his dictatorship. Within a few years he reduced the Italian parliament to a nonentity, placed the press under censorship, abolished the labor unions, deprived labor of the right to strike, and abolished all political parties except the Fascist Party.

The Fascist State

Fascism in the 1920s was an innovation that the rest of the world was slow to understand. In his more flamboyant moments Mussolini strutted, stuck out his jaw, and glared ferociously; he jumped through flaming hoops to show his virility and had his chief subordinates do likewise; to the outside world this seemed an odd way of demonstrating fitness for public office. He denounced democracy as historically outmoded and declared that it accentuated class struggle, split people into countless minority parties, and led to selfishness, futility, evasion, and empty talk. In place of democracy he preached the need for vigorous action under a strong leader who had no need for parliamentary institutions or a free press; he himself took the title of Leader, or *Duce*. He denounced liberalism, free trade, laissez-faire, and capitalism, along with Marxism, materialism, socialism, and class consciousness, which he said were the evil offspring of liberal ideas and capitalist economies. In their place he preached national solidarity and state management of economic affairs under the same Leader's farseeing and audacious vision. And in fact Mussolini's authoritarian methods may have brought a limited kind of new efficiency to Italian society; as the saying went, he made the trains run on time. Popular protests, democratic rights, and independent labor unions were all suppressed, however, and Italians paid a high political price for whatever limited changes he imposed on the Italian economy.

The corporative state

Mussolini introduced, at least in theory, the syndical, or corporative state, which had been discussed in both left- and right-wing circles for many years. Left-wing syndicalism, especially before the First World War, looked to revolutionary labor unions to expropriate the owners of industry and then to assume the direction of political and economic life. A more conservative syndicalism had been endorsed and encouraged by the Catholic church, with which Mussolini made his peace when he signed with the papacy the Lateran accord in 1929 recognizing the independence and sovereignty of Vatican City. The more conservative type of syndicalism looked nostalgically toward a revival of the medieval guilds, or "corporations," in which master and journeymen, employer and employees, had labored side by side in a supposedly golden age of social peace.

The Fascist corporative system, however, did not resemble the older syndicalist theories because in practice the hand of the state was writ large, something that neither of the earlier corporative doctrines had anticipated. The system went through a number of complicated stages, but as it finally emerged in the 1930s, it provided for the division of all economic life into 22 major areas, for each of which a "corporation" was established. In each corporation representatives of Fascist-organized labor groups, employers, and the government determined working conditions, wages, prices, and industrial policies; and in a national council these representatives were supposed to devise plans for Italy's economic self-sufficiency. In each case the role of government was decisive and the whole structure was under the jurisdiction of a minister of corporations. As a final step, these corporative economic chambers were integrated into the government proper so that in 1938 the old

The Italian Fascist Party sought to bring all individuals and social groups under the control of an authoritarian national state. This woman at a Fascist rally in Rome exemplified a disciplined, nationalized gender identity that the Italian government regularly promoted during the 1930s.
(©Hulton Archive/Getty Images)

Chamber of Deputies was superseded by a Chamber of Fasces and Corporations representing the corporations and the Fascist party, all of its members selected by the government and not subject to popular ratification.

None of this was democratic, but the Fascists claimed that their corporative system was an improvement over democracy. A legislature in an advanced economic society, they said, should represent not political parties and geographical constituencies but economic occupations. Organization along such lines would do away with the anarchy and class conflict engendered by free capitalism, which only sapped the strength of the national state. In the end real authority rested with the government—the head of the government, the *Duce*, who settled most matters by decree. In point of fact, social unrest and class conflict were "ended," not by the corporative system as such, but by the prohibition of strikes and lockouts and the abolition of independent labor unions. The corporative system represented the most extreme form of state control over economic life within a framework of private enterprise and a capitalist economy, that is, one in which ownership continued to rest in private hands. It was the Fascist answer to Western-style democracy and to Soviet proletarian dictatorship. Fascism, said Mussolini, is the "dictatorship of the state over many classes cooperating."

State control of economic life

When the Depression struck, none of Italy's economic controls availed very much. Mussolini was eager to lay upon the world Depression the blame for Italy's continuing economic ills. He turned to a vigorous program of public works and to increasing economic self-sufficiency. Throughout the Fascist era, however, no fundamental reform changed the status of the farmers and peasants. The existing structure of society, which in Italy meant social extremes of wealth and poverty, remained unaltered. Fascism provided neither the economic security nor the material well-being for which it had demanded the sacrifice of individual freedom and democracy. It undeniably, however, substituted a widespread psychological exhilaration, a feeling that Italy was undergoing a heroic national revival; and after 1935 to support that feeling Mussolini turned increasingly to military and imperialist adventures.

Some people in other countries came to regard fascism as a possible alternative to democratic or parliamentary government, as an actual corrective to troubles whose reality no one could deny. All Communists hated it, and so did all socialists, labor leaders, moderate leftists, idealistic liberals, and many traditional conservatives. Wealthier or established people, because of fear of Bolshevism, made more allowances in its favor. In eastern European countries, often highly nationalistic, or influenced by disgruntled landowners, fascism had considerable appeal. In the Latin countries, in Spain, Portugal, and France,

The appeal of fascism

Mussolini's corporative state found champions and admirers. Sometimes, in Europe and elsewhere intellectuals spun sophisticated theories about the new order of discipline and authority, forgetting how Mussolini himself with unusual candor had written, "Fascism was not the nursling of a doctrine worked out beforehand with detailed elaboration; it was born of the need for action."

99. TOTALITARIANISM: GERMANY'S THIRD REICH

The Rise of Adolf Hitler

It was in Germany that Mussolini found his aptest pupil. Born in 1889 in a small Austrian town near the border with Bavaria, Adolf Hitler did little before the First World War. He was not an intellectual, like the prewar leftist journalist Mussolini. He was never a socialist, but he fell into a restless and racist type of radicalism. Son of an Austrian customs official, he lost his father at 14 and his mother a few years later. He dropped out of high school at 16 and at 19 came to the great metropolis of Vienna as an art student but was never accepted into the academy to which he sought admission. When the small inheritance left by his parents ran out and a government grant for orphan students ended, he drifted into various menial jobs, occasionally selling a few of his postcard and poster paintings but mainly eking out a marginal existence with hardly any friends, money, or livelihood.

Hitler's dislikes

The young Hitler did not like what he saw in Vienna: neither the trappings of the Habsburg court, nor the nobility of eastern Europe who rode by in their carriages, nor the mixed nationalities of the Danubian Empire, nor the Vienna worker's attachment to international Marxism, nor above all the Jews, who thanks to a century of liberal influences had become assimilated into the German culture and now occupied many distinguished positions in Viennese business, law, medicine, and journalism. He became exceedingly race conscious and racist, not unlike others in many countries at the time. The youthful Hitler took a special satisfaction in thinking of himself as a pure German of the good old German stock. He became violently anti-Semitic, and he also disliked aristocracy, capitalism, socialism, cosmopolitanism, internationalism, and "hybridization."

His aversion to Austria led him in 1913 to move to Munich, capital of the South German state of Bavaria. Once again he drifted without livelihood except by occasionally selling a few of his watercolors. When the war broke out, he volunteered for the German army. He served as a dispatch runner to the front line, and at one point was the victim of a gas attack that temporarily blinded him and injured his vocal cords. Although he rose in rank only to the rough equivalent of corporal, he received important military decorations. For Hitler, as for Mussolini and others, the war was a thrilling, noble, and liberating experience. Many individuals in modern societies became isolated or demoralized. They viewed peacetime life as a routinized, dull existence from which war was an exciting emancipation. Human atoms, floating in an impersonal and unfriendly world,

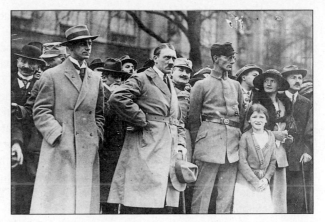

The small Nazi Party gained enough followers by 1923 for Adolf Hitler to believe that a popular revolt or *Putsch* might cause the collapse of Germany's Weimar Republic. Hitler appears here (holding a hat) with his supporters at the time of the "beer hall Putsch" in Munich, an almost farcical event for which he was sentenced to a brief term in prison.

(©Keystone/Hulton Archive/Getty Images)

they were stirred by the wartime nationalism into a sense of belonging to, believing in, and fighting for something greater than themselves, but that was yet their own. When peace returned, they felt a letdown.

When the war ended, Hitler remained for a time on active duty and was transferred to Munich. Bavaria in 1919 was a principal focus of the Communist expansion in central Europe; a Bavarian Soviet Republic even existed for about three weeks until crushed by the federal government in Berlin. The Communist threat made Bavaria a busy center for anticommunist, antisocialist, antirepublican, and antidemocratic agitation of all kinds, and the seat of a disgruntled illiberalism. It swarmed with secret societies and paramilitary organizations led by discontented army officers or others who remained alienated from civilian society and hostile to the new Weimar democracy. Hitler, working with the army's political instruction program, which had been created to combat socialist and democratic propaganda among the demobilized veterans and workers, joined at the army's behest a tiny party called the German Workers' Party and soon became its leader. Early in 1920 he proclaimed its 25-point program, the party now calling itself the National Socialist German Workers' *Nazi origins* Party. Thus were born the Nazis, so called from the German way of pronouncing the first two syllables of "National." Now demobilized, Hitler was fully launched on a career of radical politics.

We have earlier noted the beginnings of the Weimar Republic and the burdens it was compelled to bear from the start—the Versailles peace, reparations, the catastrophic inflation of 1923. Something has been said also of the failure of the republicans to inaugurate the kind of deeper social changes that might have democratized the political and social structure of German society and thereby strengthened republican forces. For five years after the war, violence remained sporadic in Germany. Communist agitation continued; but more dangerous, because they attracted more sympathy among the Germans, were the militant monarchist and antirepublican organizations, which maintained armed bands and staged uprisings like the unsuccessful Kapp Putsch of 1920. One such private "army" was the Brownshirts or Storm Troopers maintained by the Nazis. The armed bands fought their political opponents in the streets, and they also resorted to political assassinations. Thus Walter Rathenau was murdered in 1922; he had organized German production during the war, and in 1922 he was foreign minister, but he had democratic and internationalist inclinations—and was a Jew. Another victim was Matthias Erzberger, a leading moderate politician of the Catholic Center Party—he had helped "betray" the army by signing the armistice.

In 1923, when reparations payments were not forthcoming, the French army occupied the Ruhr region in western Germany. A clamor of national indignation swept over Germany. Hitler and the National Socialists, who since 1919 had obtained a considerable following, denounced the Weimar government for shameful submission to the French. They judged the moment opportune for seizing power; and at the end of 1923, in imitation of Mussolini's march on Rome the year before, the Brownshirts staged

The beer hall Putsch

the beer hall Putsch in Munich. Hitler jumped on the platform, fired a revolver at the ceiling, and shouted that the "national revolution has broken out." But the police suppressed the disturbance, and Hitler was sentenced to five years in prison. He was released in less than a year; the Weimar democracy dealt mildly with its enemies.

In prison Hitler wrote his book, *Mein Kampf (My Struggle),* a turbid stream of personal recollection, racism, nationalism, collectivism, the-

Mein Kampf

ories of history, Jew-baiting, and political comment. *Mein Kampf* sold widely. The book and the publicity that had accompanied the five-week trial converted Hitler into a political figure of national prominence. The former soldier was not alone in his ideas; no less a person than General Ludendorff, who had distinguished himself in the war, and after the war became one of the most grotesquely unbalanced of the old officer class, gave his warm support to Hitler and even took part in the beer hall Putsch.

Beginning in 1924, with the French out of the Ruhr, reparations adjusted, a new and stable currency adopted, and loans from foreign countries, mainly the United States, Germany began to enjoy an amazing economic revival. National Socialism lost its appeal; the party lost members, Hitler was regarded as a charlatan, and his followers as a lunatic fringe. All seemed quiet. Then came the Great Depression in 1929. Adolf Hitler, who might have faded out of history, was transformed by the circumstances attending the Depression in Germany into a figure of Napoleonic proportions.

No country suffered more than Germany from the worldwide economic collapse. Foreign loans abruptly ceased. Factories ground to a halt. There were 6 million unemployed. The middle class had not really recovered from the great inflation of 1923; struck again, after so brief a respite, they lost all faith in the economic system and in its future. The Communist vote steadily mounted; large numbers of the middling masses, who saw in communism their own death warrant, looked about desperately for someone to save them from Bolshevism. The Depression also stirred up the universal German loathing for

The crisis confronting Germany

the Treaty of Versailles. Many Germans, still mourning the huge loss of lives in the World War, explained the ruin of Germany by the postwar treatment it had received from the Allies—the constriction of its frontiers; the loss of its colonies, markets, shipping, and foreign investments; the colossal demand for reparations; the occupation of the Ruhr; the inflation; and much else.

Any people in such a trap would have been bewildered, resentful, and even receptive to demagogues. But many Germans responded to their crisis with ideas and actions that may have reflected or grown out of Germany's political experience and position in Europe over the previous three or four centuries. Democracy—the agreement to obtain and accept majority verdicts, to discuss and compromise, to adjust conflicting interests without wholly satisfying or wholly crushing either side—was hard enough to maintain in any country in a crisis. In Germany democracy was itself an innovation, which had yet to

Nazi Party members and paramilitary groups often marched around German cities in the decade before Hitler came to power. This parade through Nuremberg in 1929 was thus one of the recurring demonstrations of Nazism's racist nationalism during the last decades of the Weimar Republic.
(©Keystone-France/Gamma-Keystone/Getty Images)

prove its value, which could easily be called un-German, an artificial or imported doctrine, a foreign system foisted upon Germany by the victors in the late war.

Hitler inflamed all such feelings by his propaganda. He denounced the Treaty of Versailles as a national humiliation. He denounced the Weimar democracy for producing class struggle, division, weakness, and wordy futility. He called for "true" democracy in a vast and vital stirring of the people, or *Volk,* behind a Leader who was a man of action. He declared that Germans, pure Germans, must rely only on themselves. He inveighed against Marxists, Bolsheviks, Communists, and Socialists, throwing them all together in a deliberate beclouding of the issues; but he claimed to favor a unique kind of socialism for German workers, that is, the doctrine of the National Socialist German Workers' Party. He ranted against unearned incomes, war profits, the power of the great trusts and chain stores, land speculators, interest slavery, and unfair taxes. Above all, he denounced the Jews, who, like individuals in other social and religious groups, could be found in all political camps. They now came under attack from anti-Semitic extremists on all sides of the political spectrum. To the Left, Jewish capitalists were anathema. To the Right, Jewish revolutionaries were a horror. In anti-Semitism Hitler found a lowest common denominator upon which to appeal to all parties and classes. At the same time the Jews were a small minority (only 600,000 in all Germany), so that in an age of mass politics it was safe enough to attack them.

Hitler's propaganda

In the election of 1930 the Nazis won 107 seats in the Reichstag; in 1928 they had won only 12; their popular vote went up from 800,000 to 6.5 million. The Communist representation rose from 54 to 77. By July 1932 the Nazis more than doubled their popular vote, won 230 seats, and were now by far the largest single party though because of the multiplicity of parties they fell well short of a majority. In another election, in November 1932, the Nazis, though still well out in front, showed some loss of strength, losing 2 million votes, and dropping to 196 seats. The Communist vote had risen progressively to a peak of 100 in November 1932.

After the relative setback of November 1932 Hitler feared that his movement was passing. But certain conservative, nationalist, and antirepublican elements—old aristocrats, Junker landowners, army officers, Rhineland steel magnates, and other industrialists—had conceived the idea that Hitler could be useful to them. From such sources, which supported other reactionary causes as well, came a portion of Nazi funds. This influential group, mainly from the small Nationalist Party, was confident that it would be able to control Hitler and hence control the wave of national and mass discontent that he was leading.

Amid the continuing economic crisis in 1932, Franz von Papen became the leader of a Nationalist cabinet with the backing of the influential army leader General Kurt von Schleicher. In December 1932 Schleicher forced Papen's downfall and succeeded him.

Hitler named chancellor

When he too was compelled to resign a month later, both men, intriguing separately and against each other, prevailed upon President Hindenburg to name Hitler chancellor of a coalition cabinet. On January 30, 1933, by entirely legal means, Adolf Hitler became chancellor of the German Republic; other positions in the new cabinet were filled by the Nationalists, with whom the Nazis were to share power.

But to share power was not the Nazis' aim. Hitler called for another election. A week before election day in March the Reichstag building caught fire. The Nazis, without any real evidence, blamed it on a plot among the Communists. They frightened the population with a Red scare, suspended freedom of speech and press, and set loose the Brownshirts to bully the voters. Even so, in the election, the Nazis won only 44 percent of the vote; with their Nationalist allies, they had 52 percent. Hitler, trumpeting a national emergency, was voted dictatorial powers by a pliant Reichstag from which the Communist deputies by now had been excluded. The Nazi revolution began.

The Nazi State

Hitler called his new order the Third Reich. He declared that following the First Reich, or Holy Roman Empire, and the Second Reich, the empire founded by Bismarck that had ended with the war in 1918, the Third Reich would carry on the process of true German history, of which, he said, it was the organic outgrowth and natural culmination. The Third Reich, he prophesied, would last a thousand years.

Like Mussolini, Hitler took the title of Leader, or, in German, the *Führer*. He claimed to represent the absolute sovereignty of the German people. Jews were considered un-German. Democracy, parliamentarianism, and liberalism were condemned and together with communism were labeled as "Jewish." Women who were defined as "true Germans" were supposed to bear numerous children, but they could not play an active role in the Nazi

Anti-Semitism

government or in the leadership of the Nazi Party. Concentration camps were set up for opponents of the regime. The new "racial science" classified Jews as non-Aryans and included as Jewish anyone who

The Nazi-orchestrated attack on Jewish shops and businesses in November 1938 carried the official anti-Semitism of the Nazi state to a new level of violence in German cities. The shattered windows and signs at this Jewish store in Berlin convey the hostile meaning of *Kristallnacht*—the night of broken glass. Pedestrians continued to go about their daily lives, however, even as they passed by the evidence of escalating Nazi violence against Jews on their own city streets.

(©UniversalImagesGroup/Getty Images)

had one Jewish grandparent. Almost at once Jews were driven from public office, the civil service, teaching, and other professions. The Nuremberg laws of 1935 deprived Jews of all citizenship rights and forbade intermarriage or even sexual relations between Jews and non-Jews. On November 9, 1938, *Kristallnacht,* the "night of broken glass," the anti-Semitism of Nazi Germany turned to fierce violence. When a 17-year-old Polish-Jewish student, distraught by the mistreatment of his parents, shot and killed a German diplomatic official in the German Embassy in Paris, Nazi storm troopers in a savage orgy of vandalism, looting, and incendiarism smashed Jewish shops, businesses, and syna-gogues in German cities; beat up thousands of Jews; and rounded up 30,000 to be sent to concentration camps. Party and government leaders moved in to control the storm troopers and to use anti-Semitism for their own purposes. The government levied a 1 billion-mark fine on the Jewish community for provoking the assault and collected the insurance payments for the shattered glass and other property damage. Jews who in the wake of these events belatedly tried to flee the country discovered that neither they nor their families could readily find places of refuge; the doors in Europe and the United States were for the most part closed to them. The events of 1938 in Germany still resem-bled an older-style pogrom, but they also expressed a radical new racism and foreshadowed the state-organized systematic destruction, in the Holocaust, of 6 million European Jews and of others in the grisly death camps.

The new totalitarian order was thought of as absolutely solid, and monolithic, like one huge single slab of rock in which no particle had any separate structure. Germany ceased to be federal; all the old states such as Prussia and Bavaria were abolished. All political parties except the National Socialists were destroyed. The Nazi Party was itself violently purged on the night of June 30, 1934, when many of the old Brownshirt leaders, those who represented the more social revolutionary wing of the movement, were accused of plotting against Hitler and were summarily shot. A secret political police, the Gestapo (*Geheime Staatspolizei*), and a system of permanent concentration camps, in which thousands were detained without trial or sentence, suppressed all persons who were deemed to be "un-German" and all ideas at variance with the Nazi Party and the dictates of the Leader.

Law itself was defined as the will of the German people operating in the interests of the Nazi state (and with the Nazi regime as the sole interpreter of the German "will"). Churches, both Protestant and Catholic, continued to function but were "coordinated" with the new regime; their clergy were forbidden to criticize its activities, international

"Coordinating" German society

religious ties were discouraged, and efforts were made to keep children out of religious schools. The government encouraged anti-Christian pagan movements and worship of the old Teutonic gods, but nothing was sponsored so much as worship of Nazism and its *Führer*. A Nazi Youth Movement worked in schools and universities to indoctrinate the rising generation in the new concepts and to carry older nationalist ideas to new racist extremes. The total, all-encompassing repression thwarted the efforts of a few dedicated Germans to develop a broad resistance movement.

Labor unions also were "coordinated"; they were replaced by a National Labor Front. Strikes were forbidden. Under the "leadership principle" employers were set up as small-scale *Führers* in their factories and industries and given extensive control, subject to close government supervision. On the positive side (if such a term may be used for any aspect of this totalitarian system), an extensive public works program was launched, reforestation and swamp drainage projects were organized, housing and super-highways were built. A vast rearmament program absorbed the unemployed and within a short time unemployment disappeared. Even under Nazi statistics labor's share in the national income was reduced, but workers had jobs; and an organization called Strength Through Joy attended to the needs of people with small incomes, providing entertainment, vacations, and travel for many who could never otherwise afford them. The constant Nazi propaganda and the improving economy and social programs—for those not directly suppressed or excluded—steadily increased the popular support for Hitler's regime, even as personal and political freedoms rapidly disappeared.

The government assumed increasing controls over industry, while leaving ownership in private hands. In 1936 it adopted a Four-Year Plan of economic development. All countries after the Great Depression tended to economic nationalism, but Nazi Germany

Economic autarky and self-sufficiency

set up the goal of autarky and self-sufficiency—absolute independence from foreign trade. German chemists developed artificial rubber, plastics, synthetic textiles, and many other substitute products to enable the country to do without raw materials imported from overseas.

For Europe as a whole one of the basic economic problems, especially after the World War, was that while the Continent was economically a unit dependent on exchange between diverse regions, politically it was cut to pieces by tariff restrictions, currency differences, and hothouse industries artificially nurtured by nationalist ambition. Although the Nazis also favored nationalist economic policies, they claimed they could solve the

Historical Interpretations and Debates
Women in Fascist Italy and Nazi Germany

The fascist parties relegated women to a secondary position in all spheres of public and economic life, which partly explains why early historians of the twentieth-century right-wing totalitarian states in Italy and Germany gave relatively little attention to the experiences or roles of women. A more recent generation of historians, however, has described how fascism tried to control women and (with discomforting historical examples) how women also supported or contributed to the functioning of fascist societies—noting that many women were not simply passive victims. Compare the themes that the historians Victoria De Grazia and Claudia Koonz emphasize in their accounts of women's social positions within Fascist Italy and Nazi Germany.

Victoria De Grazia, *How Fascism Ruled Women: Italy, 1922-1945* (1992)

Fascism took as axiomatic that women and men were different by nature. The government politicized this difference to the advantage of males and made it the cornerstone of an especially repressive, comprehensive new system for defining female citizenship, for governing women's sexuality, wage labor, and social participation. Every aspect of being female was thus held up to the measure of the state's interest and interpreted in light of the dictatorship's strategies of state building. . . .

In fascist statecraft, the duty of women toward the nation lay first and foremost in making babies.

Women's procreative role now potentially defined every aspect of their social being. Thus, Italian women not only confronted their exclusion from politics . . . , but they also risked exclusion from the entire public sphere: their rights in the workplace, their contributions to culture, and their service as volunteers were all called into question by the official message that their preeminent duty was to bear the nation's children. . . .

Above all, fascist policy fought against an especially dangerous notion, that work was a universal right—for women as for men—and that for women, it should also open the door to social emancipation. . . . If [women] held jobs, it had to be out of family necessity or because no men would take them. Thus Mussolini's "civilization of labor" belittled women's professional abilities and vocational skills not only in the eyes of government, employers, and men but in the view of women themselves.

Claudia Koonz, *Mothers in the Fatherland: Women, the Family, and Nazi Politics* (1987; new edition, 2013)

What, then, did women do for the [Nazi] men who ignored them [in public life]? . . . They gave men Nazis the feeling of belonging not just to a party but to a total subculture that prefigured the ideals of the Nazi state for which they fought. . . . While Nazi men preached race hate and virulent nationalism that threatened to destroy the morality upon which civilization rested, women's participation in the movement created an ersatz gloss of idealism. The image did not, of course, deceive the victims, but it helped Nazis . . . to continue their work under the illusion that they remained decent. . . .

For women, belonging to the "master race" opened the option of collaboration in the very Nazi state that exploited them . . . [and] denied them access to political status. . . . Far from remaining untouched by Nazi evil, women operated at its very center.

Wives, when they remained in their "proper place," kept their family world apart from the masculine sphere of brutality, coercion, corruption, and power. As with so many other aspects of Nazi ideology, this vision of womanhood embodied a traditional ideal carried to extremes. . . .

In Hitler's Germany, women provided in a separate sphere of their own creation the image of humane values that lent the healthy gloss of motherhood to the "Aryan" world of the chosen. . . . [Wives] gave the individual men who confronted daily murder a safe place where they could be respected for who they were, not what they did.

Sources: Victoria De Grazia, *How Fascism Ruled Women: Italy, 1922-1945* (Berkeley: University of California Press, 1992), pp. 7, 41, 44, 168; Claudia Koonz, *Mothers in the Fatherland: Women, the Family, and Nazi Politics* (New York: Routledge, 2013), pp. 5-6, 419.

problem of trade barriers through a network of bilateral trade agreements assuring all neighboring peoples an outlet for their products. But it was a solution in which Germans were to be the most industrial and most advanced, the most powerful and wealthiest. Other Europeans were to be relegated to permanently inferior status. What could not be accomplished under trade agreements and economic penetration could be accomplished by conquest and war. Within a few years after 1933, although the regime had its share of bureaucratic confusion and personal rivalries, the Nazi revolution had turned Germany into a huge disciplined war machine, its internal foes liquidated or silenced, its mesmerized masses roaring their approval in giant demonstrations, ready to follow the *Führer* in storming new Valkyrian heights. "Today Germany," went an ominous phrase; "tomorrow the whole world."

Totalitarianism: Some Origins and Consequences

Totalitarianism was a many-sided thing. It had appeared first with the Bolshevik Revolution, for in the denial of individual liberty the Communist regime did not differ from the most extreme right-wing totalitarianism as manifested in Germany. Although Mussolini was the first to use the term "totalitarian," and advance it explicitly as an ideology, the Fascist regime that he established lacked the all-embracing control over people's lives to merit that term in its full political meaning. The Catholic Church came to terms with the regime, anti-Semitism did not appear until much later, the Italian upper legislative house or Senate continued to function, and the king retained many of his prerogatives. As to the differences between Soviet totalitarianism and Nazism, they were important, at least in principle. Theoretically, the proletarian dictatorship was temporary; it did not at first glorify the individual Leader; and it was not nationalistic, for it rested on a principle of worldwide class struggle in all nations alike. It adopted a democratic-sounding constitution and claimed (in theory) to respect individual rights. Its constitution officially condemned racism, and it did not deliberately and consciously cultivate an ethics of war and violence. But as time passed, Soviet totalitarianism or Communism became harder to distinguish from totalitarian regimes like Nazism. The Soviet dictatorship and one-party state seemed permanent; the hollowness of the constitution and the falsehood of claims to guarantee individual rights became more apparent; a cult developed around the person of Stalin; the political emphasis became more nationalistic, falling less on the workers of the world and more on the glories of the Soviet motherland; and it sent untold numbers to perish in the harsh labor camps of the Gulag.

The evolution of totalitarianism

Totalitarianism, as distinct from mere dictatorship, though it appeared rather suddenly in Europe after the First World War, was no historic freak. It was an outgrowth of a good deal of development in the past. The state was an institution that had continuously acquired new powers ever since the Middle Ages. The First World War continued and advanced the process. The twentieth-century totalitarian state, mammoth and monolithic, claiming absolute dominion over every department of life, carried this old development of state sovereignty to a new extreme. For centuries, for example, the state had clashed with the church. The twentieth-century dictators did the same. In addition, however, they were in most cases not merely anticlerical but explicitly anti-Christian, offering, or imposing, a "total" philosophy of life. They also rejected all democratic theories that called for a "division of power" or for intermediary institutions that could challenge the authoritarian actions of repressive national states.

The new fascist and Nazi philosophy drew heavily upon historic nationalism, which it distorted, exaggerated, and militarized. It rejected classical liberalism, which stressed the autonomy of rational individuals, and promoted instead an organic theory of society. It held that society was a kind of living organism within which the individual person was but a single cell. Individuals, in this theory, had no independent existence; they received life itself and all their ideas from the society, people, nation, or culture into which they were born and by which they were nurtured. In Marxism, the absolute subordination of individuals to their class came to much the same thing. Individuals were a microscopic cell, meaningless outside the social body. It made little sense, given such theories, to speak of the individual's "reason" or "freedom," to allow individuals to have their own opinions or to count up individual opinions to obtain a merely numerical majority. Valid ideas were those of the group as a whole, of the people or race or nation (or, in Marxism, the class) as a solid block. Even science was a product of specific societies; there was a "Nazi science," which was bound to differ in its conclusions from democratic bourgeois, Western European, or "Jewish" science; and for the Soviets there was a Soviet science, consistent with dialectical materialism and better equipped to see the truth than the decadent bourgeois, capitalistic, or fascist science of the non-Soviet world. All art, too—music, painting, poetry, fiction, architecture, sculpture—was good art insofar as it expressed the unifying cultural identity of the society or nationality in which it appeared.

Reliance on historic nationalism

The avowed philosophy of totalitarian regimes was subjective. Whether an idea was held to be true depended on whose idea it was. Ideas of truth or beauty or right were not supposed to correspond to any outer or objective reality or to the critical evaluations of rational thought; they had only to correspond to the inner nature, interests, or point of view of the people, nation, society, or class that entertained such ideas. The older Enlightenment concepts of universal reason, natural law, natural right, and the ultimate alikeness of all human beings disappeared.

The totalitarian regimes did not simply declare, as a dry finding of social science, that peoples' ideas were shaped by environment. They set about actively shaping ideas through the constant use of propaganda and by establishing propaganda offices as a principal branch of government. Propaganda was hardly new, but in the past, and still in the democratic countries, it had been a piecemeal affair, urging the public to accept this or that political party, or rally to this or that campaign. Now, like all else, it became "total." Propaganda was monopolized by the state, and it demanded faith in a whole view of life and in every detail of this coordinated whole national system. Formerly the control of books and newspapers had been mainly negative; under Napoleon or Metternich, for example, censors had forbidden statements on particular subjects, events, or persons. Now, in totalitarian countries, control of the press became frighteningly positive. The government manufactured thought and actively spread false information. It manipulated opinion. It rewrote history. Writers were required to adopt whole ideologies; books, newspapers, magazines, and the radio diffused an endless and overwhelming cloud of words. Loudspeakers blared in the streets; gigantic blown-up photographs of the Leader looked down in public places. The propaganda experts were sometimes fanatics, but often they were cynics like Dr. Joseph Goebbels in Germany, too intelligent to be duped by the rubbish and misinformation with which they duped their country.

Propaganda

The very idea of empirical truth evaporated. No norm of human utterance remained except political expediency—the wishes and self-interest of those in power. No one could learn anything except what the government wanted people to know. No one could escape

CHRONOLOGY OF NOTABLE EVENTS, 1922–1938

1922	Britain recognizes the Irish Free State with dominion status; first step toward full sovereignty as Republic of Ireland
October 1922	Mussolini takes power in Italy after the Fascist March on Rome
1923	Nazis fail to mobilize political support during an attempted Putsch in Munich
1924	First Labour government is elected in Britain under Ramsey MacDonald
January 1933	Hitler comes to power in Germany; Nazis soon take control of all state institutions and suppress opposition
March 1933	Franklin D. Roosevelt introduces the "New Deal" in the United States to mitigate economic effects of the Great Depression
1934	Right-wing and fascist groups in France challenge the Third Republic with riots during the Stavisky Affair
1935	Nazis adopt Nuremberg laws against Jews
1936	Left-wing Popular Front comes to power in France under Léon Blum and enacts notable social reforms
1938	The Nazi regime encourages violent attacks on Jews and Jewish property during Kristallnacht—the night of broken glass

the omnipresent official doctrine or the images of the great leader. People came to accept and even to believe the most extravagant statements when they were endlessly repeated, year after year. Bombarded by lies or systematic distortions of public events and barred from all independent sources of information, having no means by which any official allegation could be tested, the peoples in totalitarian countries became increasingly, in fact and not merely in sociological theory, incapable of the use of reason.

Racism

Racism, more characteristic of Nazi Germany than of totalitarianism in general, was a further exaggeration, or degradation, of older ideas of nationalism and national solidarity. It defined the nation in a tribal sense, as a biological entity, a group of persons possessing the same physical ancestry and the same or similar physical characteristics. Non-European peoples were condemned as "inferior" to white Europeans, but anti-Semitism became an especially venomous form of racism within Europe itself. While a latent hostility to Jews had always been present in the Christian world, modern anti-Semitism had little to do with Christianity. It arose in part from the fact that in the nineteenth century with the removal of religious barriers, the Jews entered into general society and many achieved prominent professional positions. Jews had therefore made notable social advances in Germany and other regions of central Europe, so that resentful individuals increasingly blamed their problems on Jewish competitors in business or the professions. But most of all, anti-Semitism was inflamed by propagandists who wished people to feel their supposed racial purity more keenly or to forget the deeper problems of society, including poverty, class divisions, and economic inequities.

Totalitarianism "resolves" class conflict

Totalitarianism emphasized national unity as a way of pretending that differences between rich and poor were of minor importance. Typically, a totalitarian regime came into power by stirring up class fears, then remained in power, and represented itself as indispensable

The Nazis promoted racist definitions of German nationhood and created racial propaganda to show the "ideal" German family. This image of the new "people's community" appeared on a Nazi poster in 1936 and conveyed the Nazis' view of gender identities as well as the regime's racial portrait of the German nation.

(©Universal History Archive/Universal Images Group/Getty Images)

by declaring that it had solved the problem of class conflict. Thus Mussolini, Hitler, and certain lesser dictators before seizing office pointed alarmingly to the dark menace of Bolshevism, and once in power, declared that all classes stood shoulder to shoulder in slablike solidarity behind the Leader.

Nor were events in Russia (or in China after the Second World War) altogether different. The Bolsheviks in 1917, armed with the ideas of Marx, aroused the workers against capitalists, landlords, the middle classes, and rich peasants; once in power and after extensive liquidations, they declared that the classless society had arrived, that no true social classes any longer existed, and that all citizens stood solidly behind a regime from which, they said, all good citizens benefited equally. Only the democracies admitted that they suffered from internal class problems, from maldistribution of wealth, or from social distinctions between favored and unfavored groups in society.

The dictatorships blamed their troubles on forces outside the country. They accused dissatisfied persons of conspiring with foreigners or refugees—with being the tools of Trotskyism, imperialism, or international Jewry. Or they talked of the struggle (as Mussolini did) between rich nations and poor nations, or between the "have" and the "have not" countries. In the distinction between have and have not countries there was, of course, more than a grain of truth; in more old-fashioned language some countries (such as the European democracies, as well as the United States and the British dominions of the 1930s) had progressed farther than others in their economic productivity and accumulation of

The Nazi regime used public spectacles to send a message of irresistible national power to both the German people and foreign observers. The annual Nazi rallies at Nuremberg became the most carefully organized expressions of allegiance to the Third Reich and the Nazi ideology. The salute to Hitler, as shown in this photograph of the *Führer* leading his officers between rows of soldiers and cheering onlookers at Nuremberg in 1937, suggests the fervent loyalty and emotion that such events were designed to evoke.

(©Past Pix/SSPL/The Image Works)

wealth. It is probable that any propaganda is more effective if partly true. But when the totalitarians blamed their troubles on other countries and transformed the conflict between have and have not into a struggle between nations, they gave the signal that war might be a solution for social ills that had not yet disappeared.

The glorification of violence

Violence, the acceptance and even glorification of violence, was indeed one of the characteristics that most clearly separated the totalitarian from the democratic systems. We have seen how a cult of violence, or belief that struggle was beneficial, had arisen before the First World War. The war itself habituated people to violence and direct action. Lenin and his followers showed how a small group could seize the helm of state under revolutionary or chaotic conditions. Mussolini in 1922 taught the same lesson, with further refinements; for the Italy in which he seized power was not at war, and it was merely the threat or possibility of revolution, not revolution itself, that provided him with his opportunity. In the 1920s, for the first time since the seventeenth century, some of the most civilized parts of Europe, in time of peace, saw private armies marching about the country, bands of uniformed and organized ruffians, Blackshirts or Brownshirts, who manhandled, abused, and even killed law-abiding citizens with impunity. Nor would anyone in the 1920s have believed that by the 1930s Europe would see the reintroduction of torture.

The very ethics of totalitarianism was violent and neopagan. It borrowed from and distorted Nietzsche and other prewar theoreticians, who, safe at their desks, had declared that people should live dangerously, avoid the flabby weakness of too much thought, and throw themselves with red-blooded vigor into a life of action. The new regimes all instituted youth movements. They appealed to a simplistic juvenile idealism in which young people believed that by joining some kind of squad, donning some kind of uniform, and getting into the fresh air they contributed to a great moral resurgence of their country. Young men were taught to value their bodies but not their minds, to be tough and hard, and to regard mass gymnastics as patriotic demonstrations. Young women were taught to breed large families without complaint, to be content in the kitchen, and to look with awe upon their virile mates.

The body cult flourished while the mind decayed. Especially in National Socialism the ideal was to turn the German people into a race of splendid blond Nordics. Contrariwise, euthanasia was adopted for the chronically ill and the insane and was proposed for the aged. Nazi ideologists produced pseudoscientific racist theories to explain and justify their actions. Later, in the Second World War, when the Nazis overran eastern Europe, they committed Jews and others to gas chambers, destroying over 6 million human beings by the most scientific methods. Human beings were viewed as some people had long and coldly viewed animals; one bred the kind of persons one wanted and killed the kind one did not.

The Spread of Dictatorship

The trend toward dictatorship, if not necessarily of the totalitarian variety, spread in Europe in the 1930s. By 1938 only 10 out of 27 European countries remained democratic, in the sense that different political parties honestly competed for office and that citizens within generous limits thought and acted as they pleased. They were Great Britain and France; Holland, Belgium, and Switzerland; Czechoslovakia and Finland; and the three Scandinavian countries Denmark, Norway, and Sweden.

The democratic aspirations of the nineteenth century as well as the post-1919 hopes for liberal democracies collapsed across most of southern, central, and eastern Europe. The weakness or absence of a parliamentary or democratic tradition, low education and literacy standards, the hostility of reactionary elements, the fear of Bolshevism, and the dissatisfaction of existing national minorities, all coupled with the economic strains resulting from the Great Depression, contributed to the collapse of representative institutions. Democracy was more fragile and vulnerable than Wilsonian optimists had imagined. Apart from the avowedly totalitarian or fascist regimes of Germany and Italy, the new dictatorships and authoritarian systems generally rested on a combination of personal and military power, but several reflected or absorbed some of the ideological features of a generic fascism. In Portugal, Salazar inaugurated a clerical-corporative dictatorship in 1932 that lasted for over four decades. In Austria, Dollfuss fused various right-wing political and military elements into a clerical-fascist "Christian" dictatorship that violently suppressed the Socialists and sought in vain to counter the German threat. In Spain General Franco established a right-wing authoritarian government after a bloody civil war (described in the next chapter).

The collapse of democratic governments

The authoritarian regimes were alike in repressing individual liberties, banning opposition parties, abolishing or nullifying parliamentary institutions, and blocking the development of independent judicial systems. Many borrowed features of fascism, establishing a corporative state, outlawing independent labor organizations, and forbidding strikes; many, like Hungary, Romania, and Poland, enacted anti-Semitic legislation. None of the right-wing regimes went as far as Hitler's Third Reich in the total coordination of all political, economic, intellectual, and biological activities in a revolutionary, mass-based dictatorship.

The acceptance and glorification of violence, it has been noted, was a cultural and political feature that clearly distinguished the totalitarian from the democratic systems. War in the Nazi and Fascist ethics was a noble thing, and the love of peace a sign of decadence. The Soviet regime by its own theory regarded war with non-Soviet powers as inevitable someday, but did not preach it as a positive moral good. The exaltation of war and struggle, the need for maintaining national solidarity, and the habit of blaming foreign countries for social troubles helped to make violence seem like a normal and appropriate means for strengthening the nation. These general ideological themes were intensified by the considerable armaments programs on which the dictatorships embarked and by the personal ambition and egotistical mania of individual dictators. All of this made the decade of the 1930s a time not only of domestic political reaction but of recurrent international crises that led finally, in 1939, to a second and even greater world war.

Suggested Further Readings can be found in the ebook, on Connect, or online at www.mhhe .com/kramer12e.

Chapter 21

THE SECOND WORLD WAR

Peace in the abstract, the peace that is the mere absence of war, does not exist in international relations. Peace is never found apart from certain conditions; it means peaceable acceptance of given conditions, or peaceable and orderly transformation of conditions by negotiation and agreement. The international conditions and borders in the 1930s were basically those laid down by the Paris peace conference of 1919. In the 1930s neither Germany, Italy, Japan, nor the U.S.S.R. was content with these conditions; they were "revisionist" or dissatisfied powers; and the first three were willing to undertake war itself to make changes in the outcome of the First World War. Great Britain, France, and the United States were satisfied powers, expecting no benefit from change in the conditions; but on the other hand they had lost faith in the conditions of the postwar settlement and were unwilling to risk war for the sake of upholding them. They had written a treaty in 1919 that a dozen years later they were unwilling to enforce. They stood idly by, as long as they could, while the dissatisfied powers tore to pieces the states recognized, the frontiers drawn, and the terms agreed to at the Peace of Paris. From the Japanese invasion of Manchuria in 1931 to the outbreak of European war in 1939, force was used by those who wished to upset the post-1919 international order, but never by those who wished to maintain it. A new world war was therefore launched by nations that had never accepted the outcome of the last one.

The war that raged across the world from 1939 to 1945 was the most destructive conflict in human history. It was also the most widely dispersed global war that has ever been fought. The Second World War affected nations on every continent; caused the deaths of almost 60 million people (at least two-thirds of whom were civilians); produced vast physical damage in cities, factories, and countrysides; generated new forms of genocidal mass murder as well as new military weapons of mass destruction; and contributed decisively to the new global influence of two superpower nations—the United States and the Soviet Union.

Chapter emblem: German troops entering a destroyed Polish village in September 1939. (©Historical/Corbis Historical/Getty Images)

Historians often disagree about the social or political consequences of warfare, but the Second World War was unquestionably one of the definitive, shaping events in modern world history. Both the haunting memories and complex legacy of the Second World War still influence modern cultures and people everywhere in the twenty-first century.

100.   THE WEAKNESS OF THE DEMOCRACIES: AGAIN TO WAR

The Pacifism and Disunity of the West

While dictators asserted their aggressive, authoritarian nationalisms in the 1930s, the Western democracies were swayed by a profound pacifism. Many people responded to the vast human and financial costs of the recent world war by insisting on peace regardless of consequences. They came to believe (especially in Britain and the United States) that the First World War had been a mistake, that little or nothing had been gained by it, that they had been deluded by wartime propaganda, and that wars were really started by armaments manufacturers. They believed also that Germany had not really caused the war of 1914, that the Treaty of Versailles was too hard on the Germans, that democracy was after all not suited to all nations, that it took two to make a quarrel, and that there need be no war if one side refused to be provoked—a whole system of pacific and tolerant ideas in which there was perhaps both truth and misunderstanding.

The pacifism in western Europe also had other roots, most evident in France. About 1.4 million Frenchmen had died in the First World War; half of all French males between the ages of 20 and 32 in 1914 had been killed. To the French it was inconceivable that such a human disaster should be repeated. French strategy was therefore defensive and sparing of manpower. If a new war came, the French expected to fight it mainly in the elaborate fortifications, called the Maginot Line, which they built on their eastern frontier facing Germany, from the Swiss to the Belgian border; to its north the Ardennes forest was to be a barrier to any invader. During the Depression, France was torn by internal class conflict and by fascist or quasi-fascist agitation. Many French on the Right, historically unsympathetic to the republic and seeing a threat of social revolution in movements such as the Popular Front, did not conceal their admiration for Mussolini or even for Hitler. Abandoning their traditional role as ardent nationalists, they would do nothing to oppose the dictators. On the other hand, many on the Left looked with sympathy upon the Soviet Union. France was ideologically too divided in the 1930s to possess a firm foreign policy, and all elements took false comfort from the supposed impregnability of the carefully constructed Maginot Line.

The pacifism in western Europe

A similar situation, in lesser degree, prevailed in Great Britain and the United States. The loss and bloodshed of the First World War were remembered with both mourning and anger. It was well known that another world war would be even more horrible; there was an unspeakable dread of the bombing of cities. Typical of the time was a resolution adopted by students at Oxford in 1933 that they would never take up arms for their country under any conditions. In the 1930s, when any international action seemed to favor either the U.S.S.R. on the one hand, or Hitler and Mussolini on the other, it was hard to establish any foreign policy on a firm basis of national unity. In Britain some members of the upper classes were overtly sympathetic to the fascist dictators or saw in them a bulwark against communism. The government itself tried to be noncommittal;

it believed that some means of satisfying or appeasing the more legitimate demands of the dictators might be found. Neville Chamberlain, the British prime minister after 1937, became the principal architect of the appeasement policy.

The United States government, despite President Roosevelt's repeated denunciation of the aggressors, followed in practice a policy of rigid isolation in both Europe and Asia. Neutrality legislation, enacted by a strong isolationist bloc in Congress in the years 1935 to 1937, forbade loans, export of munitions, and use of American shipping facilities to any belligerent once the president had recognized a state of war in a given area. From this American neutrality legislation the European aggressors of the 1930s derived great benefit, but the victims of aggression lost a key source of possible assistance.

As for the rulers of the U.S.S.R., they were revisionist and dissatisfied in that they did not accept the new frontiers of eastern Europe nor the territorial losses incurred by Russia in the First World War. They resented the *cordon sanitaire* created in 1919 against the spread of Bolshevism, the ring of small states on their borders from Finland to Romania, which were almost without exception vehemently anti-Soviet. They were thus obsessed by fear of foreign intrusions and military attacks. Their Marxist doctrine taught the inherent hostility of the entire capitalist world; the intervention of the European Allies in the revolution and civil wars confirmed their Marxist theory. Resentful and suspicious of the outside world, in the 1930s the Bolshevik leaders were alarmed primarily by Germany. Hitler, in *Mein Kampf* and elsewhere, had declared that he meant to obliterate Communism and subordinate large stretches of eastern Europe to Germany.

Russian resentment

The Soviets thus became interested in collective security, in international action against aggression. In 1934 they joined the League of Nations. They instructed Communist parties to work with socialists and liberals in popular fronts. They offered assistance in checking fascist aggressors, signing mutual assistance pacts with France and Czechoslovakia in 1935. But many Europeans fled from the Soviet embrace with a shudder. They distrusted Soviet motives, or they were convinced that the purges and trials of the 1930s had left the Soviets weak and undependable as allies, or they felt that the fascist dictators might be diverted eastward against the Soviets and so spare the western European democracies. Here again, though the Soviet Union was ostensibly willing, no effective coalition could be formed to oppose the growing threat of German aggression.

The March of Nazi and Fascist Aggression

Adolf Hitler perceived these weaknesses with uncanny genius. Determined to wreck the whole treaty system, which most Germans, to be sure, found humiliating, he employed tactics of gradual encroachment that played on the hopes and fears of the democratic peoples. He inspired in them alternating tremors of apprehension and sighs of relief. He would rage and rant, arouse the fear of war, take just a little, declare that it was all he wanted, let the former Allies naïvely hope that he was now satisfied and that peace was secure, then rage again, take a little more, and proceed through the same cycle.

Each year he precipitated some kind of emergency, and each time the French and British saw no alternative except to let him have his way. In 1933, soon after seizing power, he took Germany out of the League of Nations and out of the international Disarmament Conference then taking place. He successfully wooed Poland, long France's ally, and in 1934 the two countries signed a nonaggression treaty. That same year the Nazis of Austria attempted a Putsch, assassinated the Austrian chancellor, Dollfuss, and demanded the union of Austria with Germany. The Western

Hitler's triumphs

Hitler lived in Vienna as an unknown artist before the First World War, but he returned as the all-powerful German *Führer* after the union of Austria and Germany in March 1938. Proceeding through Vienna in this triumphant motorcade, he was hailed by Austrian Nazis and others who celebrated the long-anticipated *Anschluss* on the city's streets.

(©De Agostini Picture Library/De Agostini/Getty Images)

powers did nothing. It was Mussolini who acted. Not desiring to see Germany installed at the Brenner Pass, he mobilized large Italian forces on the frontier, discouraged Hitler from intervening openly in Austria, and so preserved the independence of Austria for four more years. In January 1935 a plebiscite was conducted in the Saar territory by the League of Nations as stipulated under the Versailles treaty. The Saar was a strategic area along the French border, and amidst intense Nazi agitation the voters overwhelmingly favored reunion with the Reich. Two months later, in March 1935, Hitler dramatically repudiated those clauses in the Versailles treaty intended to keep Germany disarmed; he now openly built up the German armed forces. France, England, and Italy protested such arbitrary and one-sided denunciation of an international treaty but did nothing about it. Indeed, Great Britain entered into a naval agreement with Germany, to the consternation of the French.

On March 7, 1936, using as his justification the new Franco-Soviet pact, Hitler repudiated the Locarno agreements (which had confirmed post–World War I national borders) and reoccupied the Rhineland; that is, he sent German troops into the German territory west of the Rhine, which by the Treaty of Versailles was supposed to be a demilitarized zone. The French government considered possible military action to force the German army to leave the Rhineland; and at this time Hitler might have been checked, for German military strength was still weak and the German army was prepared to withdraw, or at least consult, at signs of resistance. But the French government was divided, preoccupied with internal issues, and unwilling to act without Britain; and the British would not risk war to keep German troops from occupying German soil. The following year was quieter, but Nazi agitation flared up in Danzig, which the Treaty of Versailles had set up as a free city. In March 1938 German forces moved into Austria, and the union of Austria and Germany, the *Anschluss,* was at last consummated. In September 1938 came the turn of Czechoslovakia and the Munich crisis. To understand the context for the events in Munich, we must first pick up other threads in the story.

Mussolini, too, had his ambitions and required sensational foreign triumphs to magnetize the Italian people. Since 1919 the Italians had been dissatisfied with the peace arrangements. They had received none

of the territories of the former Ottoman Empire, and they were excluded from the former German colonies that had been liberally parceled out as mandates to Great Britain, France, and other countries. They had never forgotten the humiliating defeat of Italian forces by Ethiopia at Adowa in 1896, which had blocked Italy's imperial ambitions in northeast Africa. Ethiopia remained the only part of black Africa (with the exception of Liberia) that was still independent.

In 1935 Italy invaded Ethiopia. The League of Nations, of which Ethiopia was a member, pronounced the Italian action an unwarranted aggression and imposed sanctions on Italy, by which members of the League were to refrain from selling Italy either arms or raw materials—oil was excepted. The British even gathered large naval forces in the Mediterranean in a show of strength. In France, however, there was considerable sympathy for Mussolini among influential political factions, and in England there was the fear that if sanctions became too effective, by refusal of oil or by closure of the Suez Canal, Italy might be provoked into a general war. Mussolini was thus able to defeat Ethiopia in 1936 and to combine it with Italian Somaliland and Eritrea in an Italian East African empire. Haile Selassie, the Ethiopian emperor, made futile pleas for further action at Geneva. The League of Nations again failed, as in an earlier Japanese invasion of Manchuria in 1931, to provide machinery for disciplinary action against a wayward Great Power.

The Spanish Civil War, 1936–1939

The invasion of Ethiopia therefore gave the Italian aggressor exactly what he wanted, but the international system immediately faced another crisis in Spain. In 1931, after a decade of political disturbance, a rather mild revolution had driven out Alfonso XIII, of the Bourbon family, and brought about the establishment of a democratic Spanish Republic. Old hostilities within the country came to a head. The new republican government undertook a program of social and economic reform. To combat the long-entrenched power of the church, anticlerical legislation was enacted: church and state were separated, the Jesuit order was dissolved and its property confiscated, and the schools were removed from clerical control. An enduring movement for Catalan independence was somewhat mollified by the grant of considerable local autonomy. To placate the peasantry the government began to break up some of the larger landed estates and to redistribute the land. The government's program was never pushed vigorously enough to satisfy the more radical social and political groups, who manifested their dissatisfaction in strikes and uprisings, particularly in industrial Barcelona, the Catalan capital, and the mining areas of the Asturias, but it was radical enough to antagonize the great property owners and the church. After 1933 the government fell into the hands of rightist and conservative parties, who ruled through ineffective and unpopular ministries. An insurrection of the miners in the Asturias was put down with much brutality. Agitation for Catalan independence was repressed.

In February 1936 new elections were held. All groups of the Left—republicans, socialists, syndicalists, anarchists, communists—joined in a Popular Front against monarchists, clericals, army officers, other adherents of the old regime, and Falangists, or Spanish fascists. The Left won a victory at the polls, and pressed forward with a reform program. In July 1936, a group of military men led an insurrection against the republican government; General Francisco Franco emerged as leader. The parties of the Left united in

Right-wing forces launched a military insurrection against Spain's republican government in July 1936. In the civil war that followed, Germany and Italy sent aid to General Francisco Franco, but antifascist groups mobilized everywhere to fight for the Republic. These men and women distributed arms to antifascist fighters in Barcelona, where the Republic had strong support. General Franco and his fascist allies won the civil war, however, and Franco became the leader of another right-wing authoritarian regime.

(©Hulton Deutsch/Corbis Historical/Getty Images)

resistance and the whole country fell into civil war. It was the most devastating war in all Spanish history; over 600,000 people lost their lives, and it was accompanied by extreme cruelties on both sides. For nearly three years the republican or loyalist forces held their own before finally succumbing to the insurgents led by Franco, who in March 1939 established an authoritarian, fascist-type rule over the exhausted country.

Francisco Franco

Spain provided a rehearsal for the greater struggle soon to come. The republican government had needed and expected to purchase arms abroad to suppress the rebellion, but Britain and France feared that the war might expand into a general conflict. Although pro-republican groups and individuals in Europe and the United States wanted to send military assistance to the antifascist forces, the British and French governments forbade the shipment of all war materials to Spain; even the French Popular Front government put obstacles in the way of aid to the hard-pressed Spanish Popular Front. The United States extended its neutrality legislation to cover civil wars and placed an embargo on the export of arms to Spain. At British and French instigation 27 nations, including all the major European powers, agreed not to intervene or take sides. But the nonintervention policy proved a fiasco. Germany, Italy, and the Soviet Union intervened anyway. The two fascist powers supported Franco and denounced the republicans as the tools of

GUERNICA
by Pablo Picasso (Spanish, 1881–1973)

Picasso painted this famous picture shortly after the fascist bombing of the Spanish city of Guernica in 1937. Although it expressed Picasso's response to a specific event in the Spanish Civil War, its disjointed images of the death, suffering, and destruction in modern warfare quickly gave this work a haunting, universal meaning.

Bolshevism, while the U.S.S.R. supported the Republic, reinforced the growing strength of the Spanish Communists, and stigmatized the rebels under Franco as the agents of international fascism. Germans, Italians, and Russians sent military equipment to Spain, testing their tanks and planes in battle. The fascist bombings of Guernica, Madrid, and Barcelona horrified the democratic world. The Germans and Italians sent troops (the Italians over 50,000); the Soviets if only for geographical reasons did not send troops but sent technicians and political advisers. Thousands of volunteers of left-ist or liberal sympathy from the United States and Europe went to Spain to serve with the republican forces. Spain became the battlefield of contending ideologies. The Spanish Civil War split the world into fascist and antifascist camps.

Ideological split in Spain

As in the earlier case of Ethiopia, the war in Spain helped bring Germany and Italy together. Mussolini had at first, like others, feared the revival of a militant Germany. He had successfully opposed Hitler when the latter threatened to absorb Austria in 1934, but Mussolini's view of Germany changed in the following years. The Ethiopian war, Italian ambitions in Africa, and a clamorous Italian demand for ascendancy in the Mediterra-nean, the *mare nostrum* of the ancient Romans, estranged Italy from France and Britain. In 1936, soon after the outbreak of the Spanish Civil War, Mussolini and Hitler came to an understanding, which they called the Rome-Berlin Axis—the diplomatic axis around which they hoped the world might turn. That year Japan signed with Germany an Anti-Comintern Pact, soon ratified by Italy too; ostensibly an agreement to oppose communism, it was actually the foundation for a diplomatic alliance. Each, thus furnished with allies, was able to push its interna-tional aggression with more success. In 1937, Japan launched a brutal,

Alliance of Germany, Italy, and Japan

full-scale invasion of eastern China, where the Japanese quickly gained control of much of the country; and in 1938 Mussolini accepted what he had denied to Hitler in 1934—the German absorption of Austria.

The Munich Crisis: Climax of Appeasement

Czechs divided

By annexing Austria in March 1938 Hitler added about 6 million Germans to the Reich. Another 3 million Germans lived in Czechoslovakia (see maps, pp. 484, 746–747). All those who were adults in 1938 had been born under the Habsburg Empire. They had never, since 1918, been content with their new position as a minority in a Slavic state and had long complained about various forms of subtle discrimination. There were Polish, Ruthenian, and Hungarian minorities also, and because even the Slovaks had a strong sense of separate identity, there was in actuality no preponderant national majority of any kind. The fact that Czechoslovakia had one of the most enlightened minorities policies in Europe, enjoyed the highest living standard east of Germany, and was the only country in central Europe in 1938 that was still democratic only demonstrated the difficulty of maintaining a democratic, multiethnic state even under the most favorable of conditions.

Czechoslovakia had become the strategic keystone of Europe. It had a firm alliance with France, by which the French pledged to defend it against German attack, and an alliance with the Soviet Union, which, however, was contingent on the functioning of the French alliance. It had a well-trained army, important munitions industries, and strong fortifications against Germany, which, however, were located in precisely the Sudeten border area where the population was almost all German. When Hitler annexed Austria —because Vienna is further east than Prague—he enclosed Czechoslovakia in a vise. From the German point of view it could now be said that western Czechoslovakia, which was almost a third German anyway, formed a bulge protruding into the German Reich.

The Sudeten Germans of Czechoslovakia, whether Nazis or not, fell under the influence of agitators whose aim was less to relieve their grievances than to promote National Socialism. Hitler fomented their demands for union with Germany. In May 1938 rumors of an imminent German invasion caused the Czechs to mobilize; Russia, France, and England issued warnings to Germany. Hitler gave assurances but was nevertheless determined to smash the Czechs in the autumn. France and England were appalled by their narrow escape from war. The nervous French acquiesced in the leadership of Britain, which in the following months strove to avoid any firm stand that might precipitate war. The Czechs, under pressure from Britain and France, accepted British mediation on the Sudeten issue and in the summer of 1938 offered wide concessions to the Sudeten Germans amounting to regional autonomy, but this was not enough to satisfy Hitler, who loudly proclaimed that the plight of the Germans in Czechoslovakia was intolerable and must be corrected. The Soviets urged a firm stand, but the Western powers had little confidence in Soviet military strength and, given the Soviet geographical situation, their ability to render assistance to Czechoslovakia. Moreover, they feared that firmness might mean war. They could not be sure whether Hitler was bluffing. He might, if opposed, back down; but it seemed equally likely, or indeed more so, that he was entirely willing to fight.

As the crisis grew in September 1938, the British prime minister, Neville Chamberlain, who had never before traveled on an airplane, flew to Germany twice to discuss Hitler's terms for a possible solution to the Czech issues. The second time Hitler raised his demands so that even the British and French could not accept them. Mobilization began; war seemed

Britain and France accepted Hitler's demand for German control over the Sudetenland of Czechoslovakia at the Munich conference in September 1938. Although most people in Czechoslovakia deeply resented the western European appeasement of Hitler's aggressive demands, these Sudeten women welcomed the German troops who streamed into their region almost immediately after the Munich meetings adjourned.

(©Keystone-France/Gamma-Keystone/Getty Images)

imminent. Suddenly, in the midst of the unbearable tension, Hitler invited Chamberlain and Edouard Daladier, the French premier, to a four-power conference at Munich, to be attended by his ally, Mussolini. The Soviet Union and Czechoslovakia itself were excluded. At Munich Chamberlain and Daladier accepted Hitler's terms and then put enormous pressure on the Czech government to yield—to sign its own death warrant. France, urged on by England in an appeasement course that it was only too willing to follow, repudiated its treaty obligation to protect Czechoslovakia, ignored the Soviets who reaffirmed their willingness to aid the Czechs if the French acted, and abandoned its whole alliance system of a Little Entente (which had also linked Romania and Yugoslavia with the Czechs in a partnership to protect national boundaries in eastern Europe). The Munich agreement permitted Germany to annex the adjoining fringe of Bohemia in which the majority of the people were Germans. This fringe contained the mountainous approaches and the Czech fortifications, so that its loss left Czechoslovakia militarily defenseless. After promises to guarantee the integrity of what remained of Czechoslovakia, the conference disbanded. Chamberlain

Appeasement: the Munich agreement

and Daladier were welcomed home with cheers. Chamberlain reported that he had brought "peace in our time." Again the democracies sighed with relief, hoped that Hitler had made his last demand, and told themselves that, with wise concessions, there need be no war.

Western democratic weakness

The Munich crisis, with its death sentence to Czechoslovakia, revealed the weak position into which the western European democracies had fallen by 1938. There may have been little that the French and British could have done at Munich to save Czechoslovakia. Their countries lagged behind Germany in military preparedness. They had little confidence in and were suspicious of the Soviets; and they were impressed by the might of the German army and air force. Bolder leaders than Daladier and Chamberlain, knowing the state of their own armed forces, may well have declined to risk a quarrel. The French and British governments (and many of the people they represented) desperately wanted peace and would buy it at a high price, not daring to believe that they were dealing with a blackmailer whose price would always be raised.

The western Europeans suffered, too, from another moral uncertainty. By the Wilsonian principle of national self-determination, accepted by the victors after the First World War, Germany could argue that it had a right to all that it had hitherto demanded. Hitler, in sending German troops into the German Rhineland, annexing Austria, stirring up Danzig, and incorporating the Bohemian Germans, had only asserted the right of the German people to have a sovereign German state. Moreover, if Hitler could be diverted eastward, enmeshed in a war with Russia, then communism and fascism might destroy each other—so many in France and Britain might hope. Possibly it was one of Hitler's motives, in the Munich crisis, to isolate the Soviet Union from the major western European states. If so, he achieved this goal at the same time he was seizing the Sudetenland.

End of Appeasement

The final disillusionment came in March 1939. Hitler took control of Bohemia-Moravia, the really Czech part of Czechoslovakia, which he transformed into a German protectorate. Exploiting Slovak nationalism, he declared Slovakia "independent." Czechoslovakia, merely trimmed down at Munich, completely disappeared from the map. Having promised to take only a bite, Hitler swallowed the whole. He then seized Memel from Lithuania and raised demands for Danzig and the Polish Corridor. A horrible realization now spread in France and Britain. It was clear that Hitler's most solemn guarantees were worthless, that his designs were not limited to "German self-determination," but reached out to all eastern Europe and beyond, that he was essentially insatiable, that he could not be appeased. In April 1939 his partner in aggression, Mussolini, took over Albania.

The western European powers belatedly began to make preparations for a military stand. Britain, changing its previous appeasement policies at the eleventh hour, gave a guarantee to Poland and followed that with guarantees to Romania and Greece. That spring and summer the British tried to form an anti-German alliance with the U.S.S.R. But Poland and the Baltic states were unwilling to allow Soviet armies within their borders, even for the purpose of defending themselves against the Germans. The Anglo-French negotiators refused to put pressure on them. Because the Poles, in 1920, had conquered more eastern territory than the Allies had meant them to have, pushing their eastern border well into Byelorussia, almost to Minsk, the Anglo-French territorial scruples seemed to the Soviets unnecessarily delicate. They did not wish the Germans to launch an attack on them from a point as far east as Minsk. They may have thought also that what the French and British really wanted was for the Soviet Union to take the brunt of a Nazi attack. They considered it an affront that the British sent lesser officials as negotiators to Moscow when the prime minister himself had three times flown to Germany to deal with Hitler.

The climax came when the Soviets, having quietly undertaken negotiations earlier that spring, on August 23, 1939, openly signed a treaty of nonaggression and friendship with Nazi Germany. In a provision kept secret at the time, it was agreed that in any future territorial rearrangement the Soviet Union and Germany would divide Poland between them, that the Soviet Union would enjoy a preponderant influence in the Baltic states and receive recognition for its claim to Bessarabia, lost to Romania in 1918. In return the Soviets pledged to stay out of any war between Germany and Poland or between Germany and the western European democracies.

The Nazi-Soviet Pact

The Nazi-Soviet Pact stupefied the world. Communism and Nazism, supposed to be ideological opposites, had come together. A generation more versed in ideology than in power politics was dumbfounded. The pact was recognized as the signal for war. The Germans invaded Poland on September 1. On September 3 Great Britain and France declared war on Germany. The second European war in a generation thus began in Poland, but it soon spread very widely and became the Second World War.

101. THE YEARS OF AXIS TRIUMPH

Nazi Europe, 1939-1940: Poland and the Fall of France

The Second World War opened with a fast-moving German assault across the western borders of Poland. German forces totaling over 1 million men, spearheaded by armored divisions and supported by the concentrated air power of the *Luftwaffe,* rapidly overran western Poland and subdued the ill-equipped Polish armies. The outcome of the campaign, a spectacular example of *Blitzkrieg,* or lightning warfare, was clear within the first few days; organized resistance ended within a month. The Germans set about to integrate their Polish conquest into the Reich.

German Blitzkrieg

Simultaneously, the Soviet Union, acting under the secret clauses of the Nazi-Soviet Pact, moved into the eastern half of Poland two weeks after the German invasion; the territory occupied was roughly equivalent to what the new Soviet state had lost to Poland in 1920. The Soviets proceeded also to establish fortified bases in the Baltic states—Estonia, Latvia, and Lithuania. Finland resisted Soviet demands and refused to cede border territories sought by the Russians. The Soviets insisted; Leningrad, the second major city of the U.S.S.R., lay only 20 miles from the Finnish frontier. When negotiations foundered, the Soviets attacked in November 1939. Finnish resistance was valiant and at first effective, but the small country was no match for the U.S.S.R. Western European sympathies were with the Finns; the British and French sent equipment and supplies and even planned an expeditionary force. The Soviet Union was expelled from the League of Nations for the act of aggression—the only power ever to be expelled. By March 1940, however, the fighting was over. Finland had to yield somewhat more territory to the U.S.S.R. than originally demanded but retained its independence.

Meanwhile all was deceptively quiet in western Europe. The main armies did not even move. The French stayed behind their Maginot Line; the British had few troops on the continent; the Germans did not stir from behind their Siegfried Line, or West Wall, in the Rhineland. Hardly any air action took place. It was called the "phony war." The western European democracies rejected

The "phony war"

The German army launched the massive, far-reaching violence of the Second World War with its motorized assault on Poland. The new term *Blitzkrieg* was used to describe this kind of rapid military advance, which is represented here by the arrival of German troops in a bombed-out Polish village. Closely supported by air power and moving quickly on motorcycles, trucks, and armored vehicles, the Germans showed how the new tactics of offensive warfare could overwhelm the defensive strategies that had stopped advancing armies in the First World War.

(©Historical/Corbis Historical/Getty Images)

Hitler's peace overtures after the conquest of Poland but clung to their peacetime outlook. The hope still lingered that somehow a real clash might even yet be averted. During this same strange winter, a cold and bitter one, the Germans put their forces through special training, whose purpose became apparent in the spring.

On April 9, 1940, the Germans suddenly attacked and overran Norway, ostensibly because the British were laying mines in Norwegian waters in an endeavor to cut off German sources of Swedish iron ore. Denmark, too, was overrun, and an Allied expeditionary force with inadequate air strength had to withdraw. Then on May 10, the Germans delivered their main blow, striking at the Netherlands, Belgium, Luxembourg, and France itself. Nothing could stand against the German armored divisions and dive bombers. The Nazi use of massed tanks, though already demonstrated in Poland, took the French and British by surprise. Strategically, the Allies expected the main advance to be in central Belgium, as in 1914, and indeed as in the original German plan, which had been altered only a few months earlier. Hence the French and British sent into Belgium the best-equipped troops they had.

But the Germans delivered their main armored thrust, seven divisions, through Luxembourg and the Ardennes forest, long considered by the French General Staff impassable to tanks. In France, skirting the northwestern end of the Maginot Line, which had never been extended to the sea, the German armored divisions crossed the Meuse, drove deep into northern France against confused and ineffective resistance and, racing westward toward the Channel ports, cut off the Allied armies in Belgium. The Dutch, fearful of further air attack on their crowded cities, capitulated. The Belgian king sued for an armistice, and a large part of the French armies surrendered. The British fell back upon

Dunkirk and could hope only to salvage their broken forces before the trap closed completely. Fortunately for the retreating British army, Hitler had halted the advance of his overextended armored divisions. In the week ending June 4 an epic evacuation of over 330,000 British and French troops was successfully executed from the beaches of Dunkirk, under air cover, with the help of all kinds of British vessels, manned in part by civilian volunteers, even though the precious equipment of the shattered army was almost totally abandoned.

In June the mechanized German forces drove relentlessly southward. Despite attempts at fragmented resistance by French forces (about 100,000 French soldiers died in the Battle of France), Paris itself was occupied on June 13, and Verdun was occupied two days later; by June 22 France sued for peace and an armistice was signed. Hitler danced with glee.

France, obsessed by a defensive military psychology at the outset of the war, its armies unprepared for mechanized warfare, its government divided, its people split into hostile and suspicious factions, had fallen into the hands of an openly defeatist group of leaders. The collapse of France left the world aghast. Everyone   *Fall of France* knew that France had suffered great losses in the earlier world war and that it was no longer its former self, but it had still been considered a Great Power. Its collapse in one month seemed inconceivable. Some French, fleeing to England, established a Free French movement under General Charles de Gaulle; others soon began to form a resistance movement within France. The British made the bitter decision to destroy a part of the French fleet anchored in the Algerian harbor of Oran to prevent its falling into enemy hands.

France itself under the terms of the armistice was occupied in its northern two-thirds by the Germans. The Third Republic, its capital now at Vichy in the unoccupied southern third, was transformed by vote of a confused and stunned parliament into an authoritarian regime headed by the 84-year-old Marshal Pétain and the cynical and unscrupulous Pierre Laval. The republic was dead; the very slogan "Liberty, Equality, Fraternity" was banned from official use and replaced by a new right-wing ideology of "Work, Family, Fatherland." French fascist groups, long frustrated in their campaigns to destabilize or destroy the Third Republic, now saw their opportunity to undermine republican traditions in French politics and society. Pétain, Laval, and others, claiming that they were acting to shield France from further suffering, proceeded to collaborate with the Nazis and to integrate Vichy France into the "new order" in Europe (see map,   *Vichy France* p. 876). The Vichy government cooperated in sending hundreds of thousands of French workers as slave laborers to Germany and even took the initiative in identifying and deporting thousands of French Jews to places that would soon become Nazi death camps. The French people themselves had hard choices to make. Some chose to cooperate with the collaborators and the victorious Germans; others chose in a variety of ways to resist, some even joining the underground Resistance; most went about their daily lives, trying to survive amid the dangerous and oppressive conditions until the fortunes of war might change. Not for many years after the war did the French admit responsibility as a nation for the misdeeds and collaborations of the Vichy era.

Mussolini attacked France in June 1940, as soon as it was clear that Hitler had defeated the French armies. Shortly thereafter, he invaded Greece and moved against the British in Africa. The *Duce* tied his own destinies, for good or ill, to those of the *Führer*. Because the Germans were emphatically the senior partner in this combination, because they were on good terms with Franco in Spain, and because the U.S.S.R. was benevolently neutral, the aggressive Nazi war machine now dominated the European continent.

History seemed to repeat itself, in the distant and unreal way in which it ever repeats. The Germans controlled almost exactly the same geographical area that Napoleon had controlled in the early nineteenth century. Organizing a new "continental system," they made plans to govern, exploit, and coordinate the resources, industry, and labor of Europe. Not having planned for a long war, and only belatedly mobilizing their resources for a sustained military effort, they intensified the exploitation of their conquered subjects. They impressed millions, prisoners of war or civilians, as slave labor, to work under close control in the German war industries. They garrisoned Europe with their soldiers, creating

Festung Europa

what they called *Festung Europa,* the Fortress of Europe. In every country they found sympathizers, collaborators, or "quislings"—the prototype was Vidkun Quisling, who had organized a Norwegian Fascist Party in 1933 and was Norwegian premier from 1942 to 1945. When Hitler later was at war with the Soviet Union, some Europeans joined Hitler in the crusade against Bolshevism; 500,000 non-Germans fought in the divisions of the Waffen SS.

The Battle of Britain and American Aid

In 1940, as in 1807, only Great Britain remained at war with the conqueror of Europe. After Dunkirk the British awaited the worst, momentarily expecting invasion. Winston Churchill, who replaced Chamberlain as prime minister in May 1940 during the military debacle, rose to the summit of leadership in adversity. To Parliament and the British people he promised nothing but "blood, toil, tears, and sweat." He pledged implacable war against "a monstrous tyranny, never surpassed in the dark, lamentable catalogue of human crime." To the American democracy across the Atlantic he appealed, "Give us the tools, and we will finish the job." The United States began to respond.

American "neutrality"

Since 1939, and even before, the American government had been anything but neutral. Opinion was excitedly divided. One group, called isolationist, opposed involvement in the European war, believing that Europe was hopeless, or that the United States could not save it, or that the Germans would win anyway before America could act, or that Hitler, even if victorious in Europe, constituted no danger to the United States. Another group, the interventionists, urged immediate aid to the European Allies, believing that Hitler was a menace, that fascism must be destroyed, or that the Nazis, if they subjugated all Europe, would soon tamper with the Latin American republics. President Roosevelt was an interventionist, convinced that American security and vital interests were endangered by Nazi aggression; he tried to unite national opinion by declaring that the United States might openly assist the Allies without itself fighting, by using "measures short of war."

"The great arsenal of democracy"

The neutrality legislation of the mid-1930s was amended in November 1939, when the ban on the sale of arms was repealed. Roosevelt described Britain as "the spearhead of resistance to world conquest"; the United States was to be "the great arsenal of democracy." Both were fighting for a world, he said as the British continued their war against Nazi Germany in early 1941, in which the Four Freedoms were to be secure —freedom of speech, freedom of worship, freedom from want, and freedom from fear. In June 1940, immediately after Dunkirk, the United States had sent a small initial shipment of arms to Britain. A few months later the United States gave the British 50 overage destroyers in return for the right to maintain American bases in Newfoundland, the Bermudas, and the British Caribbean islands. In 1941 it adopted Lend-Lease, a policy of

The rapid, complete military collapse of France in 1940 stunned the French people and indeed the entire world. Parisians faced this humiliating sight of German troops marching through the great symbol of French nationalism, the Arc de Triomphe, as they began to cope with an oppressive German military occupation that would last more than four years.

(©Bettmann/Getty Images)

providing arms, raw materials, and food to powers at war with the Axis. At the same time, in 1940 and 1941, the United States introduced conscription, built up its army and air force, and projected a two-ocean navy. To protect its shipping it secured bases in Greenland and Iceland and convoyed Allied shipping as far as Iceland.

After the fall of France, the Germans stood poised for an invasion of Britain. But they had not calculated on such rapid and easy successes in Europe, they had no immediately practical plan for an invasion, and they needed to win control of the air before

Historical Documents

Franklin D. Roosevelt, "The Four Freedoms" (1941)

Following the Nazi conquest of France, President Franklin Roosevelt sought to strengthen America's connections with Britain. The United States sent military assistance as the British continued the war and fought against German air attacks on their cities. Roosevelt also began to explain why Americans had a stake in the European war, stressing that Nazism posed a dire threat to all democratic societies. The following excerpts from Roosevelt's famous "Four Freedoms" speech to the U.S. Congress in January 1941 show how he interpreted the war as a global struggle for freedom—and hence as a conflict in which America's democratic society was already under assault from the fascist expansion in Europe.

The Nation takes great satisfaction and much strength from the things which have been done to make its people conscious of their individual stake in the preservation of democratic life. . . .

For there is nothing mysterious about the foundations of a healthy and strong democracy. . . .

These are the simple, basic things that must never be lost sight of in the turmoil and unbelievable complexity of our modern world. . . .

[W]e look forward to a world founded upon four essential human freedoms.

The first is freedom of speech and expression—everywhere in the world.

The second is freedom of every person to worship God in his own way—everywhere in the world.

The third is freedom from want—which, translated into world terms, means economic understandings which will secure to every nation a healthy peacetime life for its inhabitants—everywhere in the world.

The fourth is freedom from fear—which, translated into world terms, means a worldwide reduction of armaments to such a point and in such a thorough fashion that no nation will be in a position to commit an act of physical aggression against any neighbor—anywhere in the world.

That is no vision of a distant millennium. It is a definite basis for a kind of world attainable in our own time and generation. That kind of world is the very antithesis of the so-called new order of tyranny which the dictators seek to create with the crash of a bomb.

"100 Milestone Documents," compiled by the National Archives and Records Administration, "President Franklin Roosevelt's Annual Message (Four Freedoms) to Congress (1941)," https://www.ourdocuments.gov/doc.php?flash=false&doc=70&page=transcript.

a sea invasion could take place. Moreover, there was always the hope, in Hitler's mind at least, that the British might sue for peace, or even become an ally of Germany. The air assault on Britain began that summer and reached its climax in the autumn of 1940. Never until then had any bombing been so severe. But the Germans were unable to win control over the air in the battle of Britain. Gradually the British Royal Air Force fought

Air war over Britain

off the bombers with more success; new radar devices helped detect the approach of enemy planes. Although Coventry was wiped out, the life and industry of other cities badly disrupted, and thousands of people killed, 20,000 in London alone, still the productive activity of the country carried on. Nor, contrary to the predictions of air power theorists, did the bombings break the morale of the civilian population.

In the winter of 1940–1941 the Germans began to shift their weight to the east. Hitler set aside the planned invasion of Britain, for which he seems never to have had much enthusiasm anyway. He had already decided, like Napoleon before him, that before committing his resources to an invasion of England he must first dispose of a disliked "ally" in Russia, a project much closer to his ideology and his illusions.

The Nazi Invasion of Russia: The Russian Front, 1941–1942

The Nazi-Soviet Pact of 1939, which had precipitated the war, like the alliance between Napoleon and Alexander I, was never a warm or harmonious understanding. Both parties probably entered it mainly to gain time. The Soviets gained space as well, pushing their borders westward. Stalin, incredibly, seems to have convinced himself that he could remain uninvolved in the war going on. But he and the Nazis soon fell into disputes over eastern Europe. The Soviets, with the Nazis preoccupied by the war, hoped to win complete control over the Baltic and to gain influence in the Balkans as well. They had already occupied eastern Poland and the three Baltic states and won territory from Finland. In June 1940, to the chagrin of the Germans, they aggressively sovietized and converted the three Baltic states into member republics of the U.S.S.R. The old German landowning class, the famous "Baltic barons," who had lived there for centuries, were uprooted. At the same time, the Soviets seized from Romania the Bessarabian province that they had lost in the First World War and incorporated it too as a Soviet republic. The Soviets were expanding toward the Balkans, an area of historic Russian interest, and they seemed bent on winning control over eastern Europe.

This the Germans viewed with dismay. The Nazis wished to reserve eastern Europe for themselves as a counterpart to industrial Germany. Hitler therefore moved to bring the Balkans under German control. By early 1941 he blackmailed or, by territorial concessions, cajoled Romania, Bulgaria, and Hungary into joining the Axis; they became Axis lesser partners and were occupied by German troops; Yugoslavia also was occupied despite resistance by *Hitler takes the Balkans* the army and population. Greece, too, was subjugated, the Germans coming to the rescue of Mussolini's hard-pressed troops. Hitler thus barred Soviet expansion in the Balkans and made the Balkan states part of the Nazi new order. The Balkan campaigns delayed his plans, but now, to crush the Soviets and to gain the wheat harvests of Ukraine and the oil wells of the Caucasus, the core of the Eurasian "heartland," Hitler launched a massive invasion of the U.S.S.R. on June 22, 1941. Stalin, refusing to heed several warnings he had received, was caught completely by surprise, and momentarily seemed incapable of mounting any kind of defense.

The German army threw 3 million men into Russia along a vast 2,000-mile front. The Russians gave way. One swift moving battle melted into another. By the autumn of 1941 the Germans had overrun Byelorussia and most of Ukraine, where the brutal military occupation led imme- *The Nazi invasion of Russia* diately to Nazi mass murders of Jews, Bolshevik government officials, and other civilians. In the north, Leningrad was in a state of siege; in the south, the Germans had entered the Crimean Peninsula and were besieging Sebastopol. And toward the center of the vast front, the Germans stood, exhausted, but apparently victorious, within 25 miles of Moscow. But the overconfident German forces had not calculated on the stubbornness of Soviet resistance once Stalin recovered from his initial shock, replaced some of his military commanders, and rallied the country to the defense of the Russian motherland. Nor were the Germans prepared to fight in an early and extraordinarily bitter Russian winter, which suddenly descended upon them. A counteroffensive, launched by the Red Army that winter, saved Moscow.

Hitler, disgusted and impatient with his subordinates, took over direct command of military operations; he shifted the main attack to the south and began a great offensive in the summer of 1942 directed toward the oil fields of the Caucasus. Sebastopol soon fell; the siege of Stalingrad began. After the failure to take Moscow, Hitler, aware now that the war would not be brief, took steps to mobilize the German economy on a fuller wartime basis. Germany had been ready for war in 1939 as no other major power had been, but lacked preparation in depth for a protracted conflict. In the early months of 1942 Hitler found in Albert Speer an organizing genius who, despite all kinds of obstacles from party leaders and government functionaries, coordinated labor and resources in the next two years and tripled armaments production. Nazi Germany and all of its hard-pressed enemies entered into the absolute mobilization of total war.

1942, the Year of Allied Dismay: Russia, North Africa, the Pacific

A year after the invasion of the Soviet Union, in the summer of 1942, the German line reached from beleaguered Leningrad in the north, past the western outskirts of Moscow, past Stalingrad on the Volga southward to the Caucasus Mountains; the Germans were within a hundred miles of the Caspian Sea. But the Russians had traded space for time. Though the industrial Don Basin and the food-producing regions of Ukraine were overrun, and the deliveries of Caucasus oil rendered hazardous and uncertain, the Russians continued to fight. Industries were shifted to the new Ural and Siberian cities; and neither the Soviet economy nor the Soviet government was yet struck in a vital spot. A "scorched earth" policy, in which the retreating Russians destroyed crops and livestock, and guerrilla units wrecked industrial and transportation facilities, guaranteed that Russian resources would not fall into the hands of the advancing German armies.

The desert campaigns

Simultaneously, late in 1942 the Axis also moved forward in North Africa. Here the desert campaigns started in September 1940 with an Italian eastward offensive from Libya, which succeeded in crossing over into Egypt. The stakes were high—control over the Suez Canal and the Mediterranean. At the height of the battle of Britain, Churchill made the decision to send troops and supplies, much needed at home, to North Africa. A British counteroffensive against vastly superior numbers swept the Italians out of Egypt and by early 1941 the British moved deep into Libya. Shortly thereafter the British overran Ethiopia and ended Mussolini's short-lived East African Empire. But in North Africa fortunes were fickle. A German elite force, the Afrika Korps under General Rommel, in the spring of 1941 attacked in Libya and drove the British back to the Egyptian frontier. A few months later, once more on the offensive, the British advanced into Libya. Again fortunes shifted. By mid-1942 Rommel had repulsed the British and penetrated Egypt. The British took up a stand at El Alamein, 70 miles from Alexandria, their backs to the Suez Canal. Here they held the Germans.

But it seemed in 1942 that the Axis armies, breaking through the Soviet Caucasus and across the isthmus of Suez in North Africa, might enclose the whole Mediterranean and Middle East in a gigantic vise, and even, moving farther east, make contact with their allies the Japanese, who were at this time penetrating into the Indian Ocean. For the Pacific situation in the latter half of 1941 had also exploded. It was Japan that finally drew the United States into war.

The Japanese, in 1941, had conducted a war against China for ten years. With the war raging in Europe and the European imperial powers unable to deploy military forces in their Asian colonies, Japanese expansionists saw a propitious moment to assert themselves throughout east Asia. In 1940 they cemented their alliance with Germany and Italy in a new three-power

Japan and the Pacific

The German army's advance across the Soviet Union displaced millions of people and opened the way for murder squads to execute large civilian populations whom the Nazis deemed to be "inferior" people. These desperate Russian refugees were fleeing from cities that the Germans occupied during the early months of the invasion in 1941.

(©SVF2/Universal Images Group/Getty Images)

pact; the following year they concluded a neutrality treaty with the Soviet Union. From the Vichy French government the Japanese obtained a number of military bases and other concessions in Indochina. The new Japanese prime minister, General Hideki Tojo, a staunch champion of the Axis, publicly proclaimed that the influence of Britain and the United States was to be totally eliminated from Asia, but he agreed to send representatives to Washington for negotiations on a recently imposed American trade embargo.

At the very time that the Japanese representatives in Washington were carrying on conversations with the Americans, on December 7, 1941, without warning, the Japanese launched a heavy air raid on the American naval base at Pearl Harbor in Hawaii and began to invade the Philippines. Simultaneously, they launched attacks on Guam, Midway, Hong Kong, and Malaya. The *Pearl Harbor* Americans were caught off guard at Pearl Harbor; close to 2,500 were killed, the fleet was crippled, and the temporary disablement of the American naval forces allowed the Japanese to roam at will in the western Pacific. The United States and Great Britain declared war on Japan on December 8. Three days later Germany and Italy declared war on the United States, as did the Axis puppet states; the war had become a global struggle.

The Japanese, working overland through Malaya, two months later captured Singapore, a British colonial city and naval base long famous for its supposed impregnability, the veritable Gibraltar of the East. In 1942 the Japanese conquered the Philippines, Malaya, and the Netherlands Indies. They invaded New Guinea and threatened Australia; they moved into the Aleutians. They streamed into the Indian Ocean, threatening the main centers of the British Empire in South Asia. They took control of Burma and seemed about to invade India. Everywhere they found ready collaborators among Asian enemies of European imperialism. They held up the idea of a Greater East Asia Co-Prosperity Sphere under Japanese leadership, in which the one clear element (apart from the dominance of Japan) was that the Europeans should be ejected.

Meanwhile, as noted, the Germans stood at the Caucasus and almost at the Nile. And in the Atlantic, German submarines were sinking Allied ships at a disastrous rate. The Mediterranean was unusable. For the Soviet-Western alliance, 1942 was the year of

The year of dismay

dismay. Despite Allied naval and air victories in the Pacific, the late summer and autumn of 1942 was the worst period of the war. Few realized, wrote the United States Chief of Staff General George C. Marshall some years later, how "close to complete domination of the world" were Germany and Japan and "how thin the thread of Allied survival had been stretched." That Germany and Japan had no plans to concert their strategy and operations was no small factor in the eventual Allied victory.

102.   THE WESTERN-SOVIET VICTORY

Plans and Preparations, 1942–1943

By January 1942 there were 26 nations, including the three Great Powers—Britain, the United States, and the U.S.S.R.—and representing every continent, aligned against the Axis, a combination to which President Roosevelt gave the name the United Nations. Each pledged to use all its resources to defeat the Axis and never to make a separate peace. The Grand Alliance against the Axis aggressors, which could not be created in the 1930s, had at last been consummated.

The two Atlantic democracies, the United States and Great Britain, pooled their resources under a Combined Chiefs of Staff. Never had any two sovereign states formed

A unified strategy

so close a coalition. In contrast with the First World War an overall strategy was in effect from an early date. It was decided that Germany was the main enemy, against which it was necessary to concentrate first. For the time being the Pacific war was relegated to the background. Australia became the chief base for operations against the Japanese. The American navy and air force soon brought Japanese southward expansion to a halt and frustrated Japanese efforts to cut off supply lines to Australia; and the Americans won naval and air victories in the spring of 1942 in the battle of the Coral Sea and at Midway, the only relief to the overall Allied gloom of that period. The Japanese threat to Britain's imperial position in South Asia began to recede. In the summer American forces landed at Guadalcanal in the Solomon Islands. A long ordeal of "island hopping" began, but the Americans and British built up their main forces for the war in Europe.

The first point of concentration for the British-American strategic war plan in Europe was an air bombardment of Germany. Meanwhile Stalin called for a true "second front," an immediate invasion by Allied ground forces that would relieve the pressure of the German divisions that were devastating the Soviet Union. Suspicious as ever of the Western capitalist governments and their military priorities, the Soviet government regarded the failure to establish a second front as new evidence of anti-Soviet feeling. But neither the United States nor Britain, in 1942, was ready to undertake land action by a direct assault on *Festung Europa*. In the Second World War, as in the First, more than two years elapsed between the outbreak of war in Europe and the major military intervention of the

The Second World War quickly became a "total war" for which men and women were widely mobilized in every warring nation. These women were receiving their pay as members of Britain's Auxiliary Territorial Service (ATS), a women's branch of the British army that supported diverse military operations both within Britain and in other countries.

(©Popperfoto/Getty Images)

United States. Although in the second war American military preparations began much sooner, the United States in 1942 was still involved in the cumbersome processes of mobilization, converting its industry to the production of war materials for itself and its Allies, imposing controls on its economy to prevent a runaway inflation, and giving military training to its profoundly civilian-minded people, of whom over 12 million men and women eventually served in the armed forces—over three times as many as in the First World War.

War preparations

The American home front was transformed like the societies of other warring nations into a war economy. The government introduced the kinds of wartime policies and economic controls that had already been enacted in Britain; and it worked closely with the nation's industrial companies to produce vast quantities of ships, warplanes, tanks, and every kind of military armament and equipment. Persons of all racial and ethnic groups found new jobs in the expanding industrial workforce. The total mobilization, however, led also to new forms of racial exclusion. Black Americans remained segregated in the armed forces; and more than 100,000 Japanese-Americans on the West Coast were forcibly evacuated to internment camps, where they remained until the end of the war. The national mobilization had

The home front

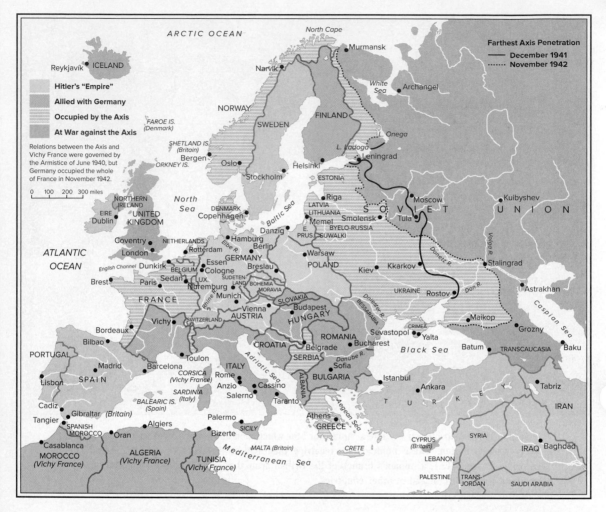

EUROPE 1942

The map shows Europe at the height of Axis military success during the Second World War. Austria, the Sudetenland, Bohemia-Moravia, Poland, and Alsace-Lorraine were all joined to Hitler's Reich. The Atlantic Coast from southern France to northern Norway was under German military occupation, as was much of Russia. Southern Europe from Vichy France to Romania was also occupied or allied with Germany.

different effects on the social and economic positions of women. Large numbers of American women, as in Britain, and more so than in the First World War, took wartime jobs in the military, in defense industries, and in other spheres of the national economy. In contrast, almost to the end, Nazi ideology placed obstacles in the way of utilizing women in German factories.

During the first year after the United States entered the war, German submarines controlled enough of the Atlantic shipping lanes to threaten the transport of American troops and war supplies. The American and British navies, however, gradually won the battle of the Atlantic; the submarine menace was reduced to tolerable proportions by the first part of 1943. The Americans and British decided to begin the assault upon Germany, from Great Britain as a base, with a massive and prolonged air bombardment. Because precision bombardment of factories and other military targets proved difficult either by

The destruction of cities and loss of life on the eastern front during the Second World War went far beyond the destruction and losses in all other theaters of the war. This photograph of refugees in Stalingrad at the time of the huge, extended battle for that city suggests the incredible desolation and losses that resulted from the fighting and the vast movement of armies across the Soviet Union and all of eastern Europe.

(©Sovfoto/Universal Images Group/Getty Images)

day or by night, the air assaults became area bombings; German cities were bombed mercilessly, and (as in the German air attacks on British cities) most of the casualties were civilians. In Hamburg in 1943 fires raged on and destroyed most of the city after several days of incessant bombing. Because not everything could be shipped across the Atlantic at the same time, and because the United States and Britain were engaged in war with Japan as well, land invasion had to be deferred until 1944. The embattled Russians questioned whether the Western Allies ever meant to face the German army at all.

The Turning of the Tide, 1942–1943: Stalingrad, North Africa, Sicily

Meanwhile, at the end of 1942 the tide had begun to turn. In November an Anglo-American force under the command of General Dwight D. Eisenhower gained control of the French-held territories in Algeria and Morocco after an amphibious operation of unprecedented proportions. In the competition that developed in the succeeding months for leadership of the French liberation committee, newly established in Algiers, General de Gaulle, though virtually ignored by President Roosevelt, pushed aside all rivals and moved forward with plans for France's revival.

After the North African landings, the Germans took over control of unoccupied France as well; they were frustrated, however, in the effort to seize the remainder of the French fleet when French crews scuttled their ships at Toulon. In North Africa the Allied forces fought their way eastward into Tunisia. Meanwhile British forces under General Montgomery, having held the Germans at El Alamein in June 1942, had already launched their third (and final) counteroffensive in October; they now pushed the Germans westward from Egypt until a large German force was crushed between the two Allied armies in Tunisia. By May 1943 Africa was cleared of Axis forces. Mussolini's dream of an African empire had been thwarted; the Mediterranean was open; the threat to Egypt and the Suez Canal ended.

Africa cleared of Axis forces

At the same time it became clear, in the winter of 1942–1943, that the Germans had suffered a catastrophic reversal in the Soviet Union in the titanic battle of Stalingrad. In August 1942 massive German forces, an army of well over a quarter million, began an all-out assault on Stalingrad, the vital key to all transport on the lower Volga River; by September they had penetrated the city itself.

Stalingrad

Stalin ordered his namesake city held at all costs; Russian soldiery and the civilian population mounted a desperate defense. Hitler, still gambling on a decisive, crushing victory, was as obstinate in ordering the city taken. After weeks of fighting, the Germans occupied most of the city when suddenly a great Red Army counterattack, led by General Zhukov, trapped the German army and took a terrible toll. Fewer than 100,000 German soldiers were still alive in Stalingrad when their commander finally surrendered in February 1943; and the aura of Germany's military invincibility was permanently shattered. The Soviets followed up their victory with a new counteroffensive, a great westward drive that regained for them what they had initially lost in the first year of the war. After Stalingrad, despite some setbacks, the Soviet Union was on the offensive for the remainder of the war. Stalingrad (or Volgograd as it was later renamed) became a turning point not only in the history of the war but in the history of central and eastern Europe as well.

American equipment meanwhile arrived in the Soviet Union in prodigious quantities. The terms of Lend-Lease were liberally extended to the Soviets; a stream of American vehicles, clothing, food, and supplies of all kinds made its way laboriously to the U.S.S.R. through the Arctic Ocean and through the Persian Gulf. Machinery and equipment were sent for the Soviet arms plants, which were themselves vastly increasing their output. Anglo-American bombing meanwhile was cutting into German airplane production at home. The Allied contribution to the Soviet war effort was indispensable, but Russian human losses were tremendous. Between 20 and 25 million people in the Soviet Union died from war-related causes. More than two-thirds of these casualties were civilians; many had been killed early in the war by Nazi murder squads whose assignment was to eliminate all so-called "undesirable" persons from territories occupied by the German army. But the number of battle deaths alone went far beyond Allied losses in other military theaters of the war. The Soviet Union lost more men in the battle of Stalingrad, for example, than the United States lost in combat during the entire war in all theaters combined.

With contemporary American successes against Japanese forces in the Solomon Islands at the end of 1942 and the slow throttling of German submarines in the Atlantic,

New advances for the Allies

there were new advances for the Allies on all fronts. In a spectacular campaign in July–August 1943, the British, Canadians, and Americans conquered the island of Sicily. Mussolini fell from power, and the 21-year-old Fascist regime came to an end. Mussolini set up an "Italian Social Republic" in the north, but it was no more than a German puppet government. Some months later, in April 1945, the *Duce*, as he attempted to flee the country, was seized and shot by anti-Fascist Italians. When the new Italian government under Marshal Badoglio, in August 1943, tried to make peace, the German army occupied Italy. The Allies, having crossed to the Italian mainland from Sicily, attacked from the south. In October the Badoglio government declared war on Germany, and Italy was recognized by the Allies as a "cobelligerent." But the Germans stubbornly blocked the advance of the Allies to Rome despite new Allied landings and beachheads. The Italian campaign turned into a long and disheartening stalemate because the Allies, concentrating troops in Britain for the approaching cross-Channel invasion, could never spare enough for the Italian front.

The vast German-Soviet war mobilized huge Russian armies, but the armies were also supported by guerrilla fighters throughout the countryside. These women were active in one of the partisan groups that resisted the German army far beyond the main battlefronts and brought civilians into armed action against the Nazi occupation of Soviet territory.

(©Library of Congress/Corbis Historical/Getty Images)

The Allied Offensive in Europe, 1944–1945

Festung Europa, especially along its western approaches, the coasts of Holland, Belgium, and France, bristled with every kind of fortification that German scientific and military ingenuity could devise. A seaborne attack upon these coasts clearly differed from the earlier amphibious attacks on Algeria, Sicily, or the Pacific islands in that the German defenders, in the part of Europe where the road and railway network was thickest, could immediately rush overwhelming reserves to the spot attacked—except insofar as feinting tactics kept the Germans uncertain, air power destroyed their transport, or the Russians held the bulk of their forces tied down on the eastern front. Precise and elaborate plans were developed for the Allied assault. Ten thousand aircraft were to provide aerial protection, scores of warships were to bombard the coast, 4,000 ships were to carry the invading troops and their supplies across the Channel, and artificial harbors were to be created where none existed.

The Allied invasion of western Europe began before dawn on June 6, 1944. The spot selected was the coast of Normandy directly across the Channel from England; false intelligence reports, planted by the Allies, led the Germans to expect the main thrust, when it occurred, to be at Calais. An unparalleled combination of forces—British, Canadian, and American, land, sea, and air, backed up by huge accumulations of supplies and troops assembled in Great Britain, and the whole under the unified command of General Eisenhower—assaulted the French coast, established a beachhead, and maintained a front. The Allies poured in their strength, over 130,000 men the first day, 1 million within a month. After heavy fighting around the town of Saint-Lô in early July, the Germans were thrown back more easily than had been expected. By August Paris was liberated. In France, Italy, and Belgium the men and women in the underground Resistance movements, which had grown up in secret during the years of German occupation, came into the open and drove out Germans and pro-German collaborators. In Germany itself no widespread or deeply rooted Resistance movement ever developed, but a small group of Germans, military and civilian, formed an underground. On July 20, 1944, after the failure of earlier efforts, the members of this group attempted to assassinate Hitler by exploding a bomb at his military

The invasion of Europe

The Allied landing in Normandy on June 6, 1944, launched a complex, costly military campaign that led within ten weeks to the liberation of Paris. The invading forces included these British troops who came ashore on the first day of a vast amphibious operation that extended across 50 miles of open beaches. Thousands of American, British, and Canadian soldiers died in the invasion, but the Allied armies overwhelmed the German defensive positions and began to advance into France.

(©Hulton Archive/Getty Images)

headquarters in East Prussia; Hitler was only injured and took a fearsome revenge on the conspirators.

In August, in another amphibious operation, the Allies landed on the French Mediterranean coast and swept up from southern France to join the Allied forces advancing against stiffening resistance. At one point, as the Allied forces moved beyond France, their offensive suffered a serious reversal. A sudden German attack under Hitler's direct personal orders in December 1944 was launched against thinly held American lines on the Belgian sector in the Ardennes, creating a vulnerable "bulge" in the advancing armies and causing heavy losses and confusion. But the Allies rallied, and Hitler used up his last armored reserves in the effort. Neither the Ardennes counteroffensive nor the new destructive weapons rained on Britain, jet-propelled flying bombs and rockets, opening up the missile age, availed the Germans. All this time the Americans and British kept up their massive air bombardments, destroying many of Germany's industrial cities and killing over 50,000 civilians in the fire-bombing of Dresden in February 1945. On the ground they smashed through the heavily fortified Siegfried Line. The last natural obstacle, the Rhine, was crossed when in March 1945 American forces by a stroke of luck discovered an undestroyed bridge at Remagen; they poured troops over it and established a bridgehead —the first troops to cross the Rhine in combat since the armies of Napoleon. The main crossing, under the British, subsequently took place farther to the north. Soon the Allies were accepting wholesale surrenders in the Ruhr Valley.

The eastern front

Meanwhile in 1944 the Russian armies swept the Germans from Ukraine, Byelorussia, the Baltic states, and eastern Poland. By August they reached the suburbs of Warsaw. The Polish underground rose against the Germans, but the Soviets, determined that Poland not be liberated by non-Communist Polish leadership, refused to permit aid to the rising, and it was crushed, with a heavy loss of Polish lives. Earlier, in 1943, the mass graves of thousands of Polish prisoners of war, mainly officers, had been found by the Germans in the Katyn Forest.

Despite continuing Soviet denials at the time, documents in the Russian archives later revealed that they had been shot by the Red Army on Stalin's orders in 1940, after the Soviet Union had joined with Germany in partitioning Poland. The Russians, their lines now overextended, and checked for several months by German strength in Poland, pushed southward into Romania and Bulgaria; both countries changed sides and declared war against Germany. Early in 1945 the Soviets, reopening their offensive, forced their way into East Prussia and Silesia and by February reached the Oder River, 40 miles from Berlin, where Zhukov paused to regroup his forces. In March and April Russian forces occupied Budapest and Vienna.

The final drive on Germany began. In April the Americans reached the Elbe, about 60 miles from Berlin, with hardly any obstacles before them; but here they halted, by decision of General Eisenhower. The Americans, whose supply lines were already overextended, wanted a clear line of demarcation from the Russians; they also believed it necessary to divert forces southward against a possible German last stand in the Alps. But mainly the decision was made as a gesture of goodwill toward the Russians, who were to be permitted to take Berlin as compensation for their heavy sacrifices in the common cause, and to preserve the Western-Soviet coalition until final victory. Similarly, the American troops that moved southward were held back from taking Prague, and the Soviets were permitted to take the Czech capital too. At the end of the war the Soviets were therefore in control of all the major capitals of central and eastern Europe—a military situation that would soon carry major political consequences.

The final drive on Germany

The Allies offered no terms to Hitler nor to any Germans. They demanded unconditional surrender, and the Germans fought on in the very streets of Berlin. On the last day of April Hitler perished by his own hand in the ruins of his capital after denouncing some of his closest party subordinates as traitors. Admiral Doenitz, designated by Hitler as his successor, went through the formalities of surrender on May 8, 1945. Because fighting had already ceased on the Italian front a few days earlier, the war in Europe was over.

The Holocaust

Meanwhile a generation reared to mistrust the fabricated atrocity tales of the First World War painfully and belatedly became aware of the real German horrors of the Second —hostages rounded up and shot in reprisal for resistance; whole villages like Lidice in Czechoslovakia or Oradour-sur-Glane in France razed to the ground and their inhabitants slain or deported; concentration camps like Dachau and Buchenwald, where the prisoners were given minimal rations and worked to death, and where Allied troops found only pitifully emaciated survivors; above all, the mass death camps with gas chambers and crematory ovens at Auschwitz (where at its peak 12,000 victims a day were gassed to death), Treblinka, Belzéc, Sobibor, and others, where peoples whom the Nazis deemed "inferior" could be systematically liquidated.

In the areas of Nazi domination in eastern Europe, the Nazis first used special firing squads and mobile gas units to kill "undesirables," but Hitler's murderous ambitions could not be achieved through such temporary or improvised methods of killing in the countryside. As the war went on, the more unstructured forms of mass murder were replaced by a systematically organized, European-wide system for gathering people at "collection" centers and transporting millions of men, women, and children in railroad cattle cars to the mass death camps where some were worked to death and others were put to death at once. By far the largest proportion killed were some 6 million Jews, but millions of other

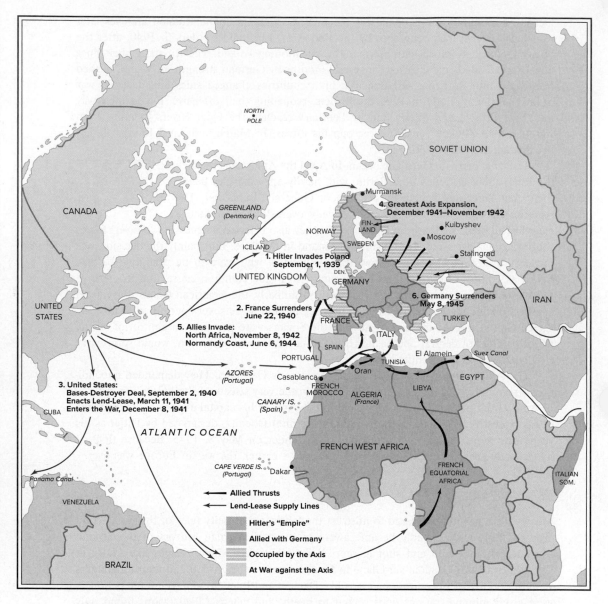

THE SECOND WORLD WAR

These two maps show the global character of the war and the central position of the United States with respect to the European and Pacific theaters. The numbered legends summarize the successive stages of the war in both the Eastern and Western Hemispheres. In 1942, with the Germans reaching as far east as Egypt and Stalingrad and the Japanese as far west as Burma, the great danger to the Soviet-Western alliance was that these two might join forces, dominate southern Asia, control the oil resources of the Persian Gulf, and stop the flow of Western supplies to the Soviet Union from this direction. The almost simultaneous Soviet-Western successes, late in 1942, at Stalingrad and El Alamein, and in the invasion of Morocco-Algeria and of Guadalcanal, proved to be the turning point of the war. In 1943 the German submarine campaign in the Atlantic was defeated, so that American troops and supplies could move more freely to Europe. The invasion of Normandy in June 1944, with continuing

Russian pressure from the east, brought about the German surrender in May 1945. Meanwhile, in the Pacific, American occupation of the islands and reoccupation of the Philippines prepared the way for the surrender of Japan, which followed the dropping of two atomic bombs in August 1945.

Poles, Russians, other Slavic peoples, Gypsies, and others were slain as well—either in the death camps or in various killing fields throughout Europe.

Many of the plans for systematic annihilation of the Jews, which would come to be known and remembered after the war as the Holocaust, were decided upon at a high-level Nazi meeting at Wannsee in January 1942. In the genocidal view of Nazi planners such as Heinrich Himmler, these policies would provide the wartime "Final Solution" to the so-called "Jewish problem" that Hitler had agitated with maniacal racist fury for so many years.

The "Final Solution"

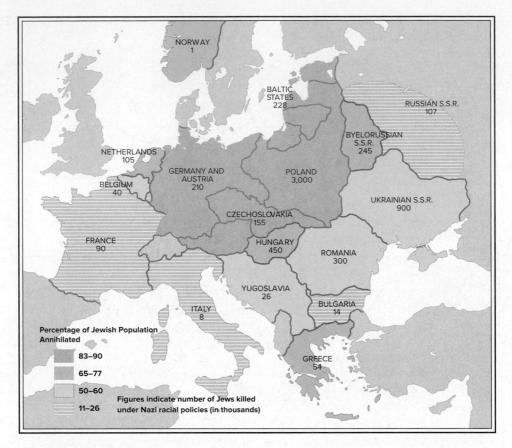

THE HOLOCAUST

This map shows the loss of life that resulted from what the Nazis called their "Final Solution"—that is, their systematic genocidal program of destroying the Jews and Judaism. Before the Second World War most European Jews lived in Poland and the adjoining parts of the Soviet Union. The Germans occupied all of these areas during the war, and most deaths occurred in these territories. The map shows both the number killed in each country and the percentage of its Jewish population that were victims of this deliberate genocide. The numbers add up to about 6 million men, women, and children, or an estimated two-thirds of the Jewish population of Europe as a whole. Although word of this annihilation policy reached the outside world through the Vatican and other sources, the Allied leaders at first disbelieved the reports, and then, giving priority to their military objectives, did nothing to stop the systematic slaughter.

Genocide, the planned, systematic effort to destroy a whole people, was the greatest of the Nazi sins against humanity. Although there have been mass murders in many other places and eras of human history, the genocidal attack on European Jews had a uniquely modern scale and scientific organization, which explains in part why it has produced such painful memories and questions for later generations. How could such murderous events occur in the heart of modern European civilization? The fact that the Holocaust was carried out by ordinary people and bureaucrats raises pointed questions about individual and collective responsibilities for deadly government policies,

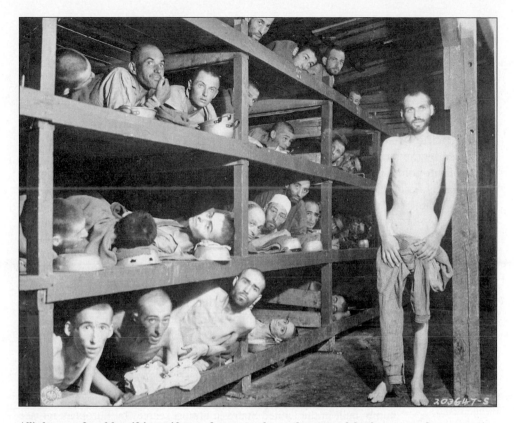

Allied troops found horrifying evidence of mass murder as they entered death camps and concentration camps that the Nazis had constructed throughout Germany and central Europe. These emaciated survivors were liberated from the camp at Buchenwald, where they had been forced to work as slave laborers and where more than 40,000 people had died. This group includes Elie Wiesel (seventh from left in second level, near the vertical beam), who would later write searing descriptions of the camps and of the Holocaust.

(National Archives and Records Administration (NWDNS-208-AA-206K(31)))

about the danger of misused, modern technologies, and about the destructive consequences of racist ideologies.

Survivors described extraordinary acts of courage and human will among the prisoners in Nazi death camps, but the Holocaust has become the modern world's most terrifying example and memory of systematic murder and human brutality. And although it was easy enough to blame the Holocaust on Hitler and the other rabid leaders of the Nazi regime, the most haunting aspect of these massive crimes may have come from the unquestioning participation of so many anonymous followers. One of the few survivors from the camp at Auschwitz, the Italian Jewish writer Primo Levi, summarized the problem that reappears constantly in later historical, ethical, and political reflections on the Holocaust and suggests why this event remains so memorable in modern world history. "We must remember," Levi wrote, "that these faithful followers, among them the diligent executors of inhuman orders, were not born torturers, were not (with a few exceptions) monsters:

Levi describes "Ordinary Men"

they were ordinary men. Monsters exist, but they are too few in number to be truly dangerous. More dangerous are the common men, the functionaries ready to believe and to act without asking questions."

The Last Phase of the War in the Pacific and the Atomic Bomb: 1944-1945

In the Pacific, American operations against Japan had dragged on for three years, hampered by the strategic decision of the Allies to concentrate against Germany first. Slowly, from points in the Solomon Islands, the easternmost fringe of the Indonesian archipelago, American forces worked their way in a northwesterly direction toward faraway Japan, fighting against stubborn entrenched Japanese resistance and at heavy cost. Finally, in a protracted and bloody battle lasting over 2½ months, in the spring of 1945 they won the island of Okinawa, only 300 miles from Japan itself. Okinawa was captured just as the Germans collapsed in Europe. From the new Allied bases on islands that the Americans had won in their long offensive campaign and from aircraft carriers at sea, a crushing air offensive was launched against Japan, shattering Japanese industry, destroying the remnants of the Japanese navy, and compelling the Japanese government to give serious thought to suing for peace. The Allied leaders did not believe, however, that Japanese defenses were ready to crumble or that the Japanese were ready to negotiate. The American army prepared to shift combat troops from the European theater to Asia. The stage was being set for a full-scale invasion of Japan itself.

The atomic bomb   Then, on August 6, 1945, an American aircraft dropped an atomic bomb—built in the United States in utmost secrecy by European refugee and American scientists—on the city of Hiroshima, with a population of 200,000 people. The city was destroyed in this single explosion, and about 100,000 lives were lost; thousands of others were injured or suffered the long-term effects of radiation. Two days later, the Soviet Union, which had pledged to enter the conflict in the East within three months after the surrender of Germany, declared war on Japan and invaded Manchuria. On August 9 a second American atomic bomb struck Nagasaki and killed approximately 60,000 more. The atomic bombs and the Soviet declaration of war drove the Japanese to make peace at once. On September 2, 1945, the formal surrender was signed. The emperor was permitted to remain as head of state, but Japan was placed under a United States army of occupation.

Meanwhile, the atomic bomb, like the death camps of the Holocaust, became another haunting memory and symbol of the new forms of violence and mass destruction that a staggeringly costly global war had bequeathed to humanity. It was probably true, as American leaders insisted at the time and in retrospect, that the atomic bomb was the least costly way (in terms of American and European lives) for the United States to bring the war in Japan to a rapid, victorious conclusion; but it is also true that the introduction of this hugely destructive weapon brought instant death to large civilian populations, created an unprecedented new threat to human survival, and set up an endless danger that has loomed over the modern world ever since. European history would thus evolve, after 1945, in an international context that always included the annihilating possibilities of atomic weaponry.

The human consequences of Nazi brutalities appear in this picture of a Nazi concentration camp near the German city of Ohrdruf in early May 1945. American soldiers were making their way through the camp, where the Nazis had subjected Poles, Czechs, German Jews, and German political prisoners to forced labor and then shot or flogged to death the internees who could no longer work.

(©Keystone-France/Gamma-Keystone/Getty Images)

The atomic bomb that was dropped on Hiroshima was the most destructive weapon in the long history of warfare. This photograph shows a view of the city after the single American bomb had reduced the buildings to rubble and killed 100,000 people. The bomb helped to end the Second World War in Japan, but it also altered Europe's influence in global affairs and created an enduring atomic threat to the future of human civilization.

(©Roger Viollet/Getty Images)

The Second World War of the twentieth century was over, the greatest conflict in human history. The same cold impersonal statistics that had recorded 10 million killed in the First World War reported 15 million military deaths and (unlike the First World War) more than twice as many civilian fatalities. Soviet military deaths were estimated at over 6 million, German at 3.5 million, Chinese at 2.2 million, Japanese at 1.3 million, Polish at 700,000. British and Commonwealth losses were over 400,000, American about 300,000, French about 200,000. Over 25 million suffered battle wounds. The military death figures would have been higher except that one of every two of those wounded was saved by new sulfa and penicillin drugs and blood plasma transfusions. None of these statistics could be more than approximate; and no one could estimate the complete toll of human lives lost from Allied and Axis bombings, Nazi mass slayings of Jews in the Holocaust and of other people in all the German-occupied nations, Nazi and Soviet deportation policies, and postwar famines and epidemics. Some estimates place the total at 60 million men, women, and children, but at such figures the human mind retreats and human sensitivities are dulled.

CHRONOLOGY OF NOTABLE EVENTS, 1935–1945

October 1935	Mussolini launches an Italian invasion and conquest of Ethiopia
March 1936	German troops enter Rhineland; France and Britain do not intervene
July 1936	Fascist groups under General Franco in Spain rise against the Spanish Republic; Franco takes power after three-year Civil War
March 1938	Hitler annexes Austria to Nazi Germany
September 1938	French and British leaders meet with Hitler in Munich and accept German takeover of Sudetenland in Czechoslovakia
August 1939	Nazi-Soviet Nonaggression Pact includes plan for division of Poland
September 1939	Nazi invasion of Poland begins the Second World War
May–June 1940	Nazis conquer the Netherlands, Belgium, and France
July 1940	French collaborators set up a pro-fascist regime in Vichy
September 1940	German air attacks on Britain are repelled in Battle of Britain
June 1941	Germany launches massive invasion of the Soviet Union
December 1941	Japanese attack on U.S. Pacific fleet at Pearl Harbor brings the United States into war with Japan and then Germany
January 1942	Nazi leaders launch plans to build death camps for genocidal killing of European Jews and others, leading to over 6 million deaths in the Holocaust
February 1943	Soviet forces defeat the Germans in decisive battle at Stalingrad
June 1944	Allied Armies open a "western front" in France after D-Day landings at Normandy
February 1945	Churchill, Roosevelt, and Stalin agree on postwar arrangements at meeting in Yalta
May 1945	Germany surrenders after Hitler commits suicide in Berlin
September 1945	Japan surrenders after the United States drops two atomic bombs and the Soviet Union declares war on Japan

---

103.   THE FOUNDATIONS OF THE PEACE

Whereas the First World War had been concluded by a peace conference a few months after the close of hostilities, the Second World War ended in no such clear-cut settlement. Nothing like the Treaty of Versailles of 1919 followed the defeat of Germany in 1945. The peace terms emerged episodically, at first during a series of conferences among the Allied nations during the war, and then in a series of de facto arrangements in the years after 1945.

The foundations for a peaceable postwar world were being laid, it was thought, at various meetings where the strategy of the war itself was gradually planned. As early as August 1941, before the United States had entered the war, Roosevelt and Churchill met at sea off the coast of Newfoundland and drew up the Atlantic Charter. Later, there were meetings in 1943 at Casablanca, at Cairo, and at Tehran (which was close enough to the Soviet Union for Stalin to participate); and in the final phase of the war, in February 1945, at Yalta (a Crimean resort city in the Soviet Union), and in July 1945 at Potsdam in the environs of shattered Berlin.

The Atlantic Charter, issued jointly by Roosevelt and Churchill at their first meeting, resembled in spirit the earlier Fourteen Points of Woodrow Wilson. It pledged that sovereign rights and self-government would be restored to all who had been forcibly deprived of them, that all nations would have equal access to world trade and world resources, that all peoples would work together to achieve improved living standards and economic security. The postwar peace, it promised, would assure people of all lands freedom from fear and want; and it would end force and aggression in international affairs. Here, and in the Four Freedoms enunciated by President Roosevelt before the United States had entered the war, the ideological basis of the peace was proclaimed. At the 1943 conferences, and through other consultations, the Allies endeavored to concert their military plans. At Casablanca in January 1943, they resolved to accept nothing less than the "unconditional

"Unconditional surrender"

surrender" of the Axis powers. This vague formula, adopted somewhat cavalierly at American initiative, and without much thought to possible political implications, was intended mainly to prevent a recurrence of anything like the ambiguity surrounding the armistice of 1918, when nationalist Germans complained that Germany had not been defeated on the battlefield but had been "stabbed in the back" by a dissolving home front.

At Tehran in December 1943, Roosevelt and Churchill met with Stalin for the first of two wartime meetings. They discussed the postwar occupation and demilitarization of Germany, laid plans for a postwar international organization, and debated strategy for winning the war. Throughout the war Roosevelt, unwilling to disturb the unity of the Western-Soviet coalition in the global struggle in which America was engaged, followed a policy of postponing controversial territorial and political decisions until victory was assured. Churchill was more apprehensive. Steeped in traditional balance-of-power politics, he sensed that without prior diplomatic bargaining and political arrangements, the victory over the Nazis would leave Russia dominant over central and eastern Europe. At Tehran he proposed operations in the Mediterranean and an invasion through the Balkans, both for political reasons and out of concern for the casualties that a cross-Channel invasion would involve. But Roosevelt persuaded him otherwise. It was agreed that a landing in France would take place in the spring of 1944; thus the major second front that Stalin had been promised would finally be opened. Stalin pledged that he would launch a simultaneous offensive on the eastern front.

The strategy that would win the war in the next 18 months was decided upon at Tehran, but that strategy, without prior political agreements, all but guaranteed the Soviet domination of postwar eastern Europe. Later, in October 1944, as the Russian armies advanced westward, Churchill visited Stalin and sketched out a demarcation of spheres of influence for the Western powers and the Soviets in the Balkan states (a Soviet preponderance in Romania and Bulgaria, a Western preponderance in Greece, and an even division of influence in Hungary and Yugoslavia). Soviet control over the Baltic states had virtually been conceded by the British earlier. Roosevelt, however, would not agree to any such arrangement, which he considered old-fashioned and a dangerous revival of the worst features of pre-1914 diplomacy.

The agreements at Yalta

The two conferences that arrived at the most important political decisions were the meetings at Yalta and at Potsdam in 1945. The Yalta meeting in February 1945 took place when the Allies were close to final victory—closer than anyone at the time could realize. The three Allied statesmen met at the old tsarist Crimean summer resort on the

Black Sea, toasted their common triumphs, and, as at Tehran, took the measure of each other. Roosevelt thought of himself as a mediator between Churchill and Stalin where European issues were involved. He took pains to avoid giving Stalin the impression that he and Churchill were in any sense united against him; in point of fact, Roosevelt was suspicious of Churchill's devotion to empire and the British colonial system, which he considered anachronistic for the postwar world. Despite differences, the Big Three reached agreements, at least formally, on Poland and eastern Europe, the future of Germany, the war in Asia, and the projected postwar international organization—the United Nations.

The discussion of Poland and eastern Europe raised the most serious difficulties. Stalin's armies, having driven the Nazi forces to within 40 miles of Berlin, were in control of Poland and of almost all eastern and central Europe. The Russians remembered these areas as anti- *Poland and eastern Europe* Soviet, and Poland particularly as the perpetrator of aggression against Soviet territory in 1920. Stalin had already taken steps to establish a "friendly" government in Poland, which meant a government subservient to the Soviets. Neither Roosevelt nor Churchill had fought the war against the Nazis to leave the Soviet Union the undisputed master of central and eastern Europe and in a position to impose a totalitarian political system on all this vast area. At Yalta, Roosevelt and Churchill extracted from Stalin a number of promises for the areas he controlled. In accordance with the Atlantic Charter, the liberated states were to be permitted provisional governments "broadly representative of all democratic elements in the population," that is, not consisting merely, as in the case of the provisional government of Poland already established, of authorities subservient to the Soviets. They pressed Stalin to pledge also the "earliest possible establishment through free elections of governments responsive to the will of the people." The pledge was a verbal concession that cost the Soviet leader little; he rejected the suggestion of international supervision over the elections. The Declaration on Liberated Europe, promising sovereign rights of democratic self-determination, provided a false sense of agreement; there would actually be no free postwar elections in Soviet-controlled eastern Europe.

A number of territorial changes were also accepted, pending final settlement at a post-war peace conference. The Russian-Polish boundary would be set roughly at the so-called Curzon line, the Polish frontier contemplated by the Allies in 1919 before the Poles conquered territory to their east. The Poles would be compensated, in the north and west, at the expense of Germany (see map, p. 922). On this and on other matters relating to Germany there was a large area of accord; the three were united in their hatred of German Nazism and militarism. Germany was to be disarmed and divided into four occupation zones under the administration of the Big Three powers and France—the latter at the insistence of Churchill. There was vague talk, at Yalta and earlier, of dismembering Germany, of undoing the work of Bismarck; but the difficulties of such an undertaking were understood and the proposal was eventually discarded. The Americans and British rejected as excessive the Soviet proposals for reparations, a sum of $20 billion to be paid in kind, half to the Soviets. It was agreed, however, that reparations would go to those countries that had borne the main burdens of the war and suffered the heaviest losses. The Soviet Union was to receive half of whatever total sum was set.

To the satisfaction of everyone, the participants agreed on plans for a postwar international organization, to be called the United Nations. Roosevelt believed it essential to win the Soviets over to the idea of an international organization. He was convinced that the Great Powers, cooperating within the framework of the United Nations and acting as international police, could preserve the future *The United Nations* peace and security of the world. No less than Stalin or Churchill,

The final meeting of Roosevelt, Churchill, and Stalin took place in the Crimean resort city of Yalta in February 1945. Roosevelt's position here between the other two leaders suggests his mediating position at the conference. The agreements reached at Yalta shaped the postwar organization of eastern Europe, laid the foundation for the United Nations, and eventually brought the Soviet Union into the war against Japan, but some critics in the Western democracies later complained that the Yalta accords made too many concessions to Stalin and opened the way for Soviet domination of central Europe.
(Library of Congress Prints and Photographs Division [LC-USZ62-7449])

he emphasized the importance of the Great Powers in the new organization, although he accepted a dignified role for the smaller nations as well. All agreed that each of the Great Powers, the permanent members of the new organization's Security Council, would have a veto power on important decisions. The Soviets pressed for 16 votes in the General Assembly of the new organization, arguing that their constitution gave sovereign rights to each of their then 16 constituent republics and also that the British dominions would each have a seat. In the interests of harmony, at Churchill's behest, they were given three.

Critical agreements were reached on new plans for eastern Asia. The Soviets had remained neutral in the Pacific war despite their historic interests in that part of Asia. Given the magnitude of the Soviet war effort on the European front, no one had pressed them to enter the Pacific war earlier. It was agreed to wait at least until the Germans were on the verge of defeat. At Yalta, Stalin agreed to enter the war against Japan, but Soviet "public opinion," he averred, would demand compensation. The U.S.S.R. would enter the war against Japan "two to three months" after Germany had surrendered. In return, the Soviets would receive territories and rights that tsarist Russia had lost to Japan 40 years before in the Russo-Japanese war of 1904–1905 (see map, p. 697), with the addition of the Kurile Islands, which had never been Russian before.

Roosevelt made controversial concessions at Yalta because he believed he needed Soviet support in the last phase of the war against Japan and because he wished to preserve the Western-Soviet coalition until final victory was guaranteed. He believed also that wartime cooperation would produce postwar harmony. Churchill, less sanguine about the future and about "diplomacy by friendship," preferred a franker definition of spheres of influence. Such ideas were ruled out as the thinking of a bygone era. Yet the spirit of the Atlantic Charter, so closely identified with the American president, the pledge of sovereign self-determination for all peoples, was already being contravened.

These people celebrated as news of the German surrender spread across Paris on May 8, 1945. Despite the vast destruction, the horrific loss of life, and the continuing struggle to rebuild shattered lives, the women and children in this Parisian street still found reasons to smile, to play music, and to look toward the future. The Second World War was a catastrophic event, but the Allied military victory revived possibilities for European democracy and cultural freedom that Nazism had almost destroyed. (©AFP/Getty Images)

At Potsdam, in July 1945, after the German collapse, the Big Three met again. A new American president, Harry S. Truman, represented the United States; President Roosevelt had died in April, on the eve of final victory. Churchill, in the midst of the conference, was replaced by a new British prime minister, Clement Attlee, after the Labour Party's victory at the polls. Stalin still represented the Soviet Union. By now, disagreements between the Western

The Potsdam Conference

Allies and the Soviets had deepened, not only over Soviet control in Poland, eastern Europe, and the Balkans, but over German reparations and other matters. Yet Truman and Attlee were still prepared to make concessions in the hope of establishing harmonious relations. Agreements were announced on the postwar treatment of Germany, which included German disarmament, demilitarization, "denazification," and the punishment of war criminals—who were soon prosecuted for war crimes in trials at Nuremberg. Each power could take reparations in kind from its occupation zone and the Russians would get substantial additional deliveries from the Western zones so that the original $10 billion Soviet demand was virtually met.

Pending the final peace treaty, German territory east of the Oder-Neisse rivers had been committed to Polish administration at the Yalta meeting, but the Polish-German boundary was now set at the western

Germany divided

Neisse, even further west than originally envisaged. Poland thus extended its territorial boundaries about a hundred miles westward as compensation for Russian westward expansion at Polish expense. German East Prussia was divided between the Soviet Union in the north and Poland in the south. Königsberg, founded by the Teutonic Knights and for centuries the coronation city of Prussian kings, became the Russian city of Kaliningrad. The ancient German cities of Stettin and Breslau became the Polish cities of Szczecin and Wroclaw. Danzig became Gdansk. The de facto administration of these areas hardened into permanent rule. The transfer of the German population in these eastern areas was supposed to be effected in an orderly and humane fashion, but millions of Germans were driven from their homes or fled westward within a few months. For them (and for the Sudeten Germans who were expelled from Czechoslovakia) this forced migration toward the west was a final, unsettling consequence of Hitler's aggressive, failed plan to expand German territories and power toward the east.

The Potsdam participants agreed that peace treaties would be signed as soon as possible with the former German satellite states; the task of preparing them was entrusted to a council of foreign ministers representing the United States, Britain, France, the Soviet Union, and China. In the months that followed, the widening chasm between the Soviets and their recent Western Allies manifested itself in stormy meetings in London, Paris, and New York, as well as in a peace conference held in Paris in 1946, at which were represented the 21 states that had contributed substantial military forces to the defeat of the Axis powers. In February 1947 treaties were finally signed with Italy, Romania, Hungary, Bulgaria, and Finland, all of which paid reparations and agreed to certain territorial adjustments. In 1951 a peace treaty was signed with Japan, but not by the Soviets, who signed their own treaty in 1956. The years went by, but no final treaty was signed with Germany, which for many years to come remained divided into western and eastern zones. The wartime Western-Soviet coalition had fallen apart, shattering the dreams or aspirations for a lasting peace among those who had fought the Second World War to a decisive triumph over one kind of aggression and totalitarianism, but who now found themselves confronted with a new age of crisis.

Suggested Further Readings can be found in the ebook, on Connect, or online at www.mhhe .com/kramer12e.

Chapter 22

THE COLD WAR AND RECONSTRUCTION AFTER THE SECOND WORLD WAR

Every age has its share of social conflicts, economic problems, political upheavals, wars, and cultural changes, but the first half of the twentieth century must surely be ranked as one of the most deadly and disorienting periods that people have ever known. During these decades, over the course of a single lifetime, the world passed through the Great War of 1914–1918, a global influenza pandemic (which killed at least 50 million people), the collapse of long-standing dynasties in Europe and the Middle East, the Russian Revolution, the worldwide Great Depression, the rise of aggressive fascist and Nazi dictatorships, the Second World War (stretching from Europe and North Africa to all of east and southeast Asia), the Holocaust in Nazi-occupied Europe, the first use of atomic bombs, the rise of Communist China, and the breakup of the Ottoman and European empires into new nations in the eastern Mediterranean and South Asia.

These events brought massive disruptions to individual lives, caused more millions of deaths than can ever be accurately counted, and produced far-reaching changes in global political and economic systems—including the rapid, international ascendancy of the United States and a steady decline in Europe's previous control over people or economies in much of the non-European world. In short, the upheavals of the early twentieth century profoundly transformed the course of modern world history. Yet people everywhere, like their ancestors after earlier upheavals, moved on from these cataclysms to rebuild their lives, their societies, their political institutions, and their economic activities. History did not end, of course, and the age-old resilience of human beings and their cultures appeared again in the decades that followed the Second World War.

The end of that titanic war marks a transition for historians as well as for the people who lived through it, because the era that historians often call "contemporary history" began in the decades after 1945. Although that postwar era is increasingly distant from

Chapter emblem: Hungarian protestors mock a toppled statue of Joseph Stalin in 1956. (©Hulton Archive/ Getty Images)

our own time and several later generations have reshaped modern societies, the historical consequences of many events and conflicts since the Second World War are still part of our contemporary world. Recent history arouses strong feelings. It created many of the world's still unresolved international problems, and it continues to influence the ideas and social positions of most people who are now alive. Contemporary history poses even more challenges for historians than the history of earlier eras because many sources are still unavailable, or because present-day conflicts distort the historical analysis of recent events, or because the lasting influence of ongoing social and economic changes cannot yet be known. These open-ended aspects of contemporary history will become apparent in the later chapters of this book as we examine the unsettled events and trends of the contemporary world, which continues to evolve more rapidly and in more ways than any historical narrative can describe with the long-range perspectives of historical analysis.

104.   THE COLD WAR: THE OPENING DECADE, 1945–1955

Certain issues that had confronted humankind for over a century became even more complex and more urgent in the second half of the twentieth century. Three can be singled out: science, the organization and environmental consequences of industrial society, and national sovereignty.

The atomic bomb

The atomic bomb dramatized the new problem of science. People in all parts of the world shuddered at the instantaneous destruction of Hiroshima. The postwar contest to produce more sophisticated nuclear weapons spurred the realization that a third world war would be unthinkable. Human beings now possessed the means to annihilate not only civilization but even human existence on the planet, a thought especially shocking to people who had long praised the social value of scientific progress.

Science and its partner, invention, had for a long time transformed both industry and war. It had conquered many of the dreaded plagues and diseases of the world. Everyone had long known that science could be applied either constructively or destructively, but the extreme violence of the two world wars suggested that the destructive uses were becoming more common. It was the magnitude of the new destructive possibilities that now made thoughtful people worry. Scientists themselves, after the Holocaust and the first atomic explosion, affirmed the need for a moral regeneration. They insisted that science itself was neutral, free from blame for the horrors of Auschwitz and Hiroshima and Nagasaki, that the trouble lay not with science but with the uses to which scientific knowledge was put.

Organizing industrial society

The problems of organizing industrial economies and adapting to the environmental effects of industrialization were also unresolved after 1945. There were in theory two opposite social-economic poles. At one, best represented by the Union of Soviet Socialist Republics (until its demise in 1991), all capital was owned by the state and supplied to managers and workers as needed, and all production and interchange were planned in advance by public authorities. In the Soviet form of communist socialism (as well as in the People's Republic of China after 1949), the government's role was all-encompassing. At the other pole, best exemplified by the United States, economic exchange took place through the mechanism of the market, and capital was owned by private persons who chose the channels of investment and determined the availability of jobs.

Neither the socialist nor the capitalist system was pure in practice, and even in capitalist countries mixed economies became the rule, with varying degrees of government intervention. Most western European countries developed such mixed economies after 1945 and also expanded their social welfare systems, in part to reduce the kinds of social instability that had contributed to the political extremism and dictatorships of the 1930s. Many Europeans looked for a "middle way" between the Soviet and American systems. They favored "democratic socialist" institutions that might avoid or mitigate the contrasting drawbacks of both the communist and capitalist systems. The chief drawbacks in the Soviet system appeared in the lack of political and economic freedom and in its stifling of individual initiative; in the American system, the drawbacks appeared in the periodic economic crises and in the threats to the economic security of individual workers. In the years after the Second World War, the Europeans and Americans expended much more effort trying to correct the lack of economic security than the Soviets did to correct the lack of freedom. By the later twentieth century, however, it was also becoming apparent that all advanced industrial systems—communist, democratic socialist, capitalist—polluted the natural environment and created environmental problems that threatened the future well-being of people across the whole planet.

Another postwar question hinged on the nationalism and political disunity of the modern world. It was indisputably one world in the sense that there existed a close-knit, interdependent economy, that political events and environmental changes affected the whole globe, and that world cultures and religions interacted as never before. But this interconnected world was far from homogeneous. All admired the steam turbine and stood in awe of nuclear fission, but beyond the material level schemes of values diverged. No people wished to be subordinated to another, or to an international body, or to lose its way of life in a uniform global civilization.

After the Second World War, as after the First, an international organization was set up to prevent war in the future. A conference of all anti-Axis powers, held at San Francisco in 1945, founded the United Nations (UN) and drew up its charter. The new organization was designed to maintain international peace and security and to encourage cooperative solutions to international problems. Although it was widely acknowledged that peace would depend primarily on the Great Powers, all states, regardless of size, would be represented. Two agencies were central. The General Assembly was a deliberative body in which all member states, however small, had an equal vote. The Security Council, whose primary responsibility was to preserve peace, consisted of the five Great Powers, who were to be permanent members, and ten rotating members chosen for two-year terms. Apart from the two superpowers, the United States and the U.S.S.R., it was not easy to define the Great Powers in 1945, but the permanent seats were assigned to the United States, the Soviet Union, Great Britain, France, and China.[1] Despite the decline of Europe's economic and political influence in other regions of the world, the traditional western European powers retained their prominent, prewar positions in the new international organization.

The United Nations

Each permanent member had a veto power. Thus the Security Council could act on important matters only if the Great Powers were unanimous. Although widely criticized, the veto was accepted as necessary. In major crises the agreement of the Great Powers

---

[1] Nationalist China (the Republic of China, or Taiwan) occupied the seat until 1971, when the People's Republic of China (Communist China) replaced it. In the early twenty-first century there were growing demands to expand the number of permanent seats on the Security Council by adding other large nations from Asia, Africa, and Latin America.

The UN was established to resolve international conflicts and to foster peaceful exchanges between nations. It also soon adopted a Universal Declaration of Human Rights, though (as can be seen here) there was virtually no gender or racial diversity among the early UN representatives themselves. This picture of an early UN meeting shows a representative of the Philippines, Pedro Lopez, calling for the establishment and protection of a free press in all nations of the world.

(©Hulton Deutsch/Corbis Historical/Getty Images)

would be needed to maintain world peace. The U.S.S.R. demanded the veto most frankly, but the United States would not have joined without this safeguard. In the following years, however, even small countries refused to abide by judgments of the UN. No nation, large or small, was yet willing to forgo its sovereign independence or subordinate itself to an international body with the authority to put down violence, but there was much hope, and even confidence, that the authority and prestige of the UN would grow with time.

Membership expands

The UN had 51 original members. To symbolize the strong American commitment (and the contrast with America's earlier refusal to join the League of Nations), its headquarters was located in New York. The charter provided for the admission of new members, including the former Axis countries and their satellites, and also wartime neutrals, so that it could be truly international. From 1947 to 1955 a few additional states were admitted; in 1955, 16 more; and in the next several decades, after decolonization and other changes, the organization expanded so that by the third decade of the twenty-first century it had over 190 members. In 1948, in good part because of the persuasive powers of the American delegate Eleanor Roosevelt, it adopted a sweeping Universal Declaration of Human Rights. The Declaration included rights to individual freedoms, education, participation in government, and diverse forms of social welfare, but it did not propose specific methods for implementation or enforcement.

The UN and its Security Council failed to fulfill the role projected for it in the early postwar era because of the tensions between the American-led Western nations and the Soviets. Although the UN remained one of the few arenas where the Americans and Soviets could meet and debate, it was powerless to prevent the two superpowers from drifting further and further apart. On the other hand it helped from the beginning to mediate regional disputes and to play a role in peacekeeping missions. Most Europeans supported the UN as part of a new international order that might reduce the kinds of national wars that had nearly destroyed their twentieth-century societies. But the UN also evolved away from the preoccupations of the older European powers as it expanded to include new nations in regions that later twentieth-century diplomats called the "Third World." Many of these newer members of the UN were former colonies of the European empires, and they became known as the Third World because they chose not to align themselves during the 1950s and 1960s with either the Western or the Soviet camp in international affairs. Such nations increasingly used the General Assembly of the UN as a forum in which to express their grievances against global economic and political systems, which they criticized for protecting the interests of the wealthier European and American nations.

The Cold War: Origins and Nature

The Second World War left only the United States and the Soviet Union still standing with major military strength. The United States also emerged physically unscathed from the war, its economy stronger than ever before. Although it demobilized much of its wartime military force, it alone possessed the atomic bomb. The Soviet Union had been economically devastated by the war, in which over 20 million of its population had perished, but it was still a formidable military power, with 4 million soldiers under arms and in control of eastern European populations and territories well beyond its pre-1939 boundaries. It became common to speak of the two countries as superpowers—continental land giants, possessing enormous resources and overshadowing all other states, including the long-dominant nations of western Europe.

In the kind of two-superpower system that emerged after the Second World War, each power can readily identify its only dangerous enemy. A diplomatic equilibrium is difficult to sustain in such situations because each views the other power's every action as possible aggression or provocation; and each, ignorant of the other's strength, exaggerates the power and danger of its enemy. After 1945 the United States and the U.S.S.R. fell into this unhappy relationship, which began to develop conflicts as soon as the two superpowers attempted to devise postwar settlements in Europe. The emerging diplomatic conflicts were compounded by a deep-seated ideological tension between capitalist democracy and Marxist-Leninist communism that dated back to the Bolshevik Revolution of 1917. The widening diplomatic, geopolitical, and ideological clash of interests came to be known as the Cold War, so called because the antagonisms and rivalries, intense though they were, always fell short of open or direct military hostilities between the two powers.

The Cold War

It was not possible for anyone to know what Stalin, who dictated the Soviet decisions, or his lieutenants in the Kremlin, really believed or intended at the end of the Second World War. Probably they considered a clash between the U.S.S.R. and the Western capitalist powers as inevitable at some point in the future. Probably they were disturbed by the ambitious goals of American capitalism, which sought markets in eastern Europe and elsewhere, and by the American monopoly of the atomic bomb. They themselves

The Allied military victory over Nazi Germany was followed by new distrust and conflict in Europe. The Soviet Union took control over Communist satellite states, creating what Winston Churchill called an "iron curtain" against free institutions and ideas. This picture shows Churchill giving a famous speech in March 1946 in Fulton, Missouri, where he first described the new iron curtain that had descended across eastern Europe.

(©PA Images/Getty Images)

undoubtedly saw an opportunity to consolidate their hold over European territories gained during the war (or regained, given that the new Soviet state had lost control of some of these territories at the end of the First World War), and to create an outer buffer zone for Soviet national security. Undoubtedly they also saw in the aftermath of the Second World War, as of the First, an opportunity to promote the international Communist cause in the shattered nations of central Europe and among the still-colonized peoples within the large European empires.

Whether the Soviets were acting to protect their national security, fulfill old Russian territorial ambitions in eastern Europe, or promote communism on a world scale, the political leaders of the United States and a great majority of the American people became convinced that the Soviets were bent on consolidating their grip on central and eastern Europe and then embarking on a worldwide Communist offensive. The American government therefore developed a global strategy of "containment," by which the United States and its allies would seek to contain this new Soviet offensive. Although the American government would take direct military steps mainly in reaction to Soviet expansion or threats of expansion, many people in the United States came to ascribe almost all of the complex social and political unrest on the globe to initiatives launched by the Kremlin;

Containment

and in contrast to its rapid military withdrawal from Europe in 1918–1919, the United States maintained a strong military and political presence in European affairs long after 1945.

In Europe, at the close of hostilities, Soviet armies occupied eastern Europe and Germany as far west as the Elbe River. American, British, and French armies held the remainder of Germany, most of Austria, and all of Italy. During the war, the armed forces liberating an area exercised political authority. In that way, the sweep of the Red Army gave the Soviets political control over millions of people in central and eastern Europe. On the other hand, the United States excluded the Soviets from any active role in its occupation of Italy and Japan. For the Soviet Union, occupation meant full control over a nation's political, economic, and social institutions and the right to shape the occupied country in its own image. The Western powers, on the other hand, had hoped that postwar eastern Europe would develop pluralist and democratic societies, which would have been open to Western trade and influence. During the war the Americans and British had conceded Soviet predominance in eastern Europe, which the Soviets had liberated from the Nazis, but they soon resented the transformation of Poland and other East European countries into Soviet-dominated Communist states.

For Stalin, however, this kind of transformation was the only way to guarantee "friendly regimes" on his borders. Beginning as early as the Potsdam conference in July 1945, Truman denounced the Soviets for violating their pledge to allow free elections in the eastern European states and for failing to cooperate in the joint occupation of Germany. American diplomats began to believe that Soviet control over eastern Europe was similar to the Nazi and Fascist aggression of the 1930s, to which Truman himself frequently compared it. Stalin may have been acting more as a Russian nationalist bent on protecting Russian national security than as a champion of worldwide Communist revolution, but his stubbornness and paranoia about capitalist encirclement, and his lack of concern for world public opinion, made it difficult for the Americans and western Europeans to deal with him in the Cold War or to distinguish between legitimate Soviet security needs and an expansionist, Communist missionary zeal.

Concerns about Soviet expansion

A series of Soviet actions fed the belief that Stalin's ambitions transcended eastern Europe. In Asia, as pledged at Yalta, the Soviets had declared war on Japan in August 1945 and moved into Manchuria, where they were well positioned to help the Chinese Communists. In Korea, once the Japanese were defeated, the Soviets by agreement occupied the northern part of the country but also took steps to consolidate their occupation zone into a Communist government. Iran was another trouble spot. The Americans, British, and Russians had jointly occupied Iran during the war to forestall a Nazi takeover, but the Soviets refused to evacuate their troops at the stipulated time and pressed for oil concessions (such as the British and Americans already enjoyed).

The Soviets also massed troops on the Turkish border, pressing for joint control over the Black Sea straits and for naval access to the Mediterranean through the Dardanelles—an old tsarist goal. The British, acting again in their earlier role as the "Western" guardians of the Mediterranean and Middle East, bolstered the Turkish defenses despite their own financial weakness. In Greece, in a civil war that raged from 1946 to 1949, Communist guerrillas battled the British-supported royalist, or nationalist, army. Stalin, perhaps recognizing his wartime agreement with Churchill that Greece would remain in a sphere of Western influence, lent little aid to the Communists, but Tito's new Communist regime in Yugoslavia helped the Communist guerrillas. The Communist pressures on Turkey, Greece, and Iran aroused British and American concerns about Soviet strategic designs on the eastern Mediterranean and on the oil reserves of the Middle East.

One casualty of the postwar tension was a plan for international supervision of nuclear weapons. The United States knew that it was only a matter of time before the Soviets (and other nations) could build the atomic bomb, because the scientific basis for it was known. The United States proposed in 1946 that atomic energy be controlled by an international authority and that its use be limited to peaceful purposes. Such an international body would have the right to send inspectors into any country to check violations and enforce sanctions that would not be subject to veto in the Security Council. The Soviets objected and would not give up their veto. The idea of foreigners freely examining their society was

Mutual mistrust

Historical Documents

Winston Churchill, "The Sinews of Peace" (1946)

The Allied military victories at the end of the Second World War raised cautious hopes for a more peaceful European future, but new conflicts soon arose between the Soviet Union, the United States, and Great Britain. Winston Churchill (1874–1965) warned about Joseph Stalin's postwar policies in eastern Europe during a visit to the United States, which included this famous speech at Westminster College in Fulton, Missouri, on March 5, 1946. Using the term "iron curtain" as a metaphor for the Soviet barriers to freedom, Churchill summarized the emerging European and American perspectives on global tensions that would soon come to be known as the Cold War.

A shadow has fallen upon the scenes so lately lighted by the Allied victory. . . .

From Stettin in the Baltic to Trieste in the Adriatic, an iron curtain has descended across the Continent. Behind that line lie all the capitals of the ancient states of Central and Eastern Europe. . . . [A]ll are subject in one form or another, not only to Soviet influence but to a very high and, in many cases, increasing measure of control from Moscow. . . . The Communist parties . . . are seeking everywhere to obtain totalitarian control. Police governments are prevailing in nearly every case. . . .

[T]his is certainly not the Liberated Europe we fought to build up. Nor is it one which contains the essentials of permanent peace.

The safety of the world requires a new unity in Europe, from which no nation should be permanently outcast. . . .

These are somber facts for anyone to have to recite on the morrow of a victory gained by so much splendid comradeship in arms and in the cause of freedom and democracy; but we should be most unwise not to face them squarely while time remains.

Winston Churchill, "The Sinews of Peace," delivered March 5, 1946 at Westminster College, Fulton, Missouri. National Churchill Museum.

repugnant to them. They questioned the good faith of the United States, which would not destroy its atomic bombs or halt further testing and production until the proposed international authority was established (many Americans also opposed international controls on their own nuclear arms). The British, in turn, fearful of an American relapse into isolationism, undertook to become a nuclear power on their own. The plan for international control foundered on mutual suspicion and mistrust. The Soviets proceeded with their own atomic research (and efficient espionage), which yielded results even sooner than expected. In 1949 the Soviets successfully tested an atomic bomb, and the nuclear arms race, universally dreaded, now began. The British also moved forward with the independent development of their own atomic bomb, which they first tested in 1952.

The political conflicts had meanwhile deepened in 1946 and 1947. The American policy of containment, as formulated by the State Department, postulated that the Russians would expand wherever a power vacuum existed. Advocates for the strategy of containment argued that the Western powers should show both patience and firmness, and in time Soviet society itself might change. In the meantime, however, the United States and its European allies needed to maintain their military strength and use economic and other counterpressures to resist the Soviets. Containment, the cornerstone of American policy, came to be interpreted in more rigorously military terms than some of its early proponents had intended. Even before the Soviets had fully completed the transformation of eastern Europe into Communist satellites, Churchill had eloquently described the "iron curtain" that had descended between eastern and western Europe. Shortly after Churchill's "Iron Curtain" speech, in 1946, the United States turned down a pending Soviet request for a reconstruction loan, Congress having decided that Lend-Lease should end with the war, and also cut off reparations deliveries to the Soviets from the American occupation zone of Germany.

In 1947 financially strained Great Britain, forced to cut back on its commitments in the Mediterranean, informed Washington that it could no longer aid the anti-Communist forces in Greece or support Turkey in its resistance to Soviet pressures. The United States quickly moved to fill the vacuum. Truman agreed to provide the necessary assistance in the Mediterranean and also formulated in March 1947 a broad national policy to contain communism everywhere—"to assist free peoples who are resisting attempted subjugation by armed minorities or by outside pressures." The Truman Doctrine committed the United States to unprecedented involvement in global military and economic affairs. The Marshall Plan, which would provide billions of dollars for reconstruction of the war-damaged European economies and infrastructure, was announced by the American secretary of state, George Marshall, in 1947. Although the plan was designed to hasten European economic recovery, it also served the political purpose of checking Communist expansion in western Europe.

The Truman Doctrine

The American national security state began to take shape. A National Security Council was created to advise the president on security matters, and a Central Intelligence Agency (CIA) was created to coordinate the gathering of intelligence. The CIA soon received authorization to conduct covert operations as well, so that American agents began operating widely in both western and eastern Europe.

The Soviets in their turn denounced the American capitalist and imperialist "warmongers." With the United States arming Greece and Turkey; American air bases established in the Middle East; American armed forces in occupation of Japan, Okinawa, and South Korea; and the Americans possessing the atomic bomb, the Soviets felt threatened and encircled. Soviet suspicions mounted after 1947, but they also drew on memories that went back to the foreign intervention in the Russian Revolution and civil war in 1917–1920, the Soviets' exclusion from the Munich Pact, and the delay in opening up a second front in the Second World War as well as the cessation of Lend-Lease at the end of the war and the rejection of a requested postwar loan.

Soviet suspicions

In 1947 the Soviets decided they needed to reassert closer control over all Communist parties in every part of the world. They therefore reestablished in new form the old Communist International, or Comintern, which had been abandoned in 1943 as a gesture of wartime cooperation, renaming it the Communist Information Bureau, or Cominform. The Soviets also replaced coalition governments in central and eastern Europe, in which the Communists had formerly shared power, with regimes dominated by Communist parties. In Czechoslovakia, for example, where President Benes's democratic coalition had been viewed as a possible bridge between eastern and western Europe, the Czech Communist Party, faced with defeat in a forthcoming election, seized power in February 1948. By this time, the postwar Soviet-American conflicts had created a mutual perception of permanent dangers, which each side sought to counter by its own assertive political or military actions. The increasingly bitter Cold War therefore spread into the local disputes and political confrontations that were constantly developing in Europe, Asia, and elsewhere around the globe.

The Soviet closure of the railways and roads into Berlin provoked one of the most dramatic events of the early Cold War: the Berlin Airlift. For almost a year (1948–1949) the Americans and their Western allies flew supplies into the isolated city on military aircraft such as the plane in this picture. Images of the airlift became part of the evolving Cold War struggle for international public opinion and an enduring symbol of the new links between West Berlin and the postwar Western Allies.

(©Bettmann/Getty Images)

Germany: The Berlin Blockade and the Airlift of 1948–1949

The key to the rebuilding of Europe, and the most critical area of Soviet-Western contention, was Germany, divided by Allied agreement into four zones and occupied by the United States, the Soviet Union, Britain, and France. The Allies had agreed to joint Allied policies for a defeated Germany, even though each of the four powers was to occupy its separate zone. Berlin also was divided into four separate Allied sectors, with joint

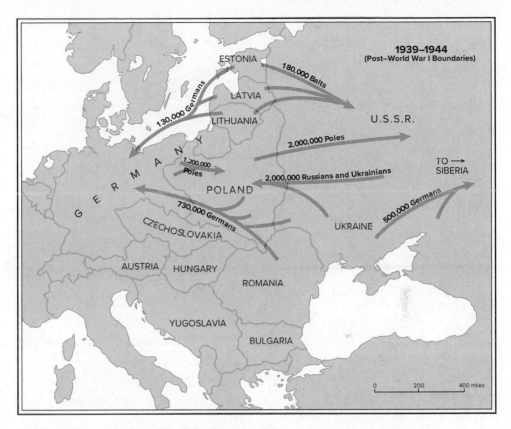

DEPORTATION AND RESETTLEMENT, 1939–1950

The age-old distribution of nationalities in central and eastern Europe was radically transformed between 1939 and 1950. About 6 million Jews died in the Holocaust, with over 300,000 survivors emigrating to Israel by 1950, and millions of Germans, Poles, and others were forcibly uprooted.

The first stage began with the Nazi-Soviet Pact of 1939, after which the Germans occupied western Poland, while the Russians annexed eastern Poland and the three Baltic republics. Western Poland received Poles expelled from Germany, while in eastern Poland about 2 million Poles were deported to Siberia, being replaced by about the same number of Russians and Ukrainians. Many Estonians, Latvians, and Lithuanians were moved to other parts of the Soviet Union. Thousands of Germans were "returned" to Germany from the Baltic republics and from places such as Romania, where they had long formed German enclaves. The "Volga Germans," Tatars, and others in south Russia were sent to Siberia.

administration for the city as a whole. All had agreed that Germany should pay reparations, both in capital equipment and current production, mainly to the Soviet Union, which had suffered most from German military destruction, and that limits should be placed on German productive capacity.

At the war's end the Americans, supported by the British, quickly came to favor the economic reconstruction of Germany to accelerate European recovery and to reduce European dependence on American financial aid. The Ruhr, in the western zone, was still Europe's industrial heartland. The Soviets, on the other hand, were determined to use German resources to repair the devastation in their own country. They removed large amounts of food and stripped entire plants of machinery in their zone. The Western Allies refused to permit

Two Germanys emerge

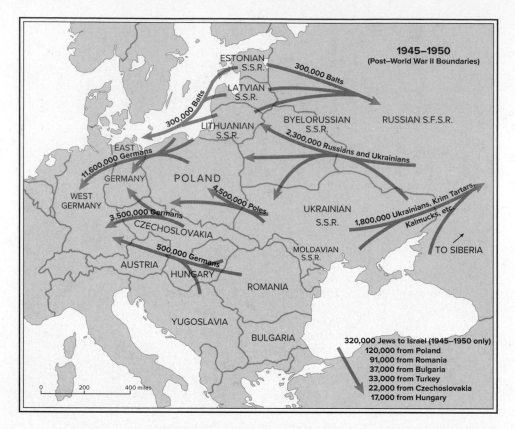

A second stage of displacements came with the Soviet victory and collapse of Hitler's Reich. The German-Polish frontier was now moved westward to the Oder River. Millions of Germans from east of the Oder, along with other millions from the Sudeten regions of Czechoslovakia, from Hungary, and from Romania, were thrown back into what remained of Germany, most fleeing to the western zones. Poles streamed into what had been Germany east of the Oder; others came into Poland from Ukraine. Russians moved into what had been eastern Poland and the Baltic states. Ukrainians and various non-Russian minorities were sent to Siberia. Some Balts escaped to western Europe; others were redistributed to various places in the Soviet Union.

Amid all of these movements of people, the most conspicuous, long-term changes, in addition to the virtual disappearance of east European Jews, were the expulsion of the Germans from eastern Europe and a westward movement of Poles and Russians.

(Westermanns Atlas zur Weltgeschichte)

the dismantling of factories in their zones and insisted that the Soviets take their share of current production only from their own zone. By May 1946 joint administration of Germany had all but broken down. Early in 1947 the United States and Britain united their two zones; the French, overcoming their initial reluctance to see a revived Germany, soon merged their zone as well. The Western powers encouraged the reconstruction of governments in the individual German states and the convening of a constituent assembly to set up a federal republic. The Soviets, in their zone, took steps to establish a Communist-dominated government. Two Germanys were emerging.

In June 1948 the Western powers, recognizing the need for drastic currency reform to cope with inflation and encourage West German economic revival, suddenly revoked the old worthless currency and at a 1-to-10 ratio issued a new German mark, the Deutsche mark. The Soviets, who had not been consulted, objected to this violation of the wartime agreement to treat Germany as a single economic unit. In retaliation

they blockaded all road and rail access to Berlin, which lay 100 miles deep within the Soviet zone. The blockade was a sharp challenge to the Western Allies. If they abandoned Berlin, they could also lose authority in other parts of Europe and open the way for Soviet expansion in Europe and perhaps elsewhere. Knowing that they could not resort to military measures against the much stronger Soviet ground forces, the Allies responded with a massive airlift. For close to a year, American and western European aircraft flew in thousands of tons of food and other supplies to the occupation forces and to the 3 million inhabitants of West Berlin. The Soviets harassed the planes but avoided direct confrontation and, finally, in May 1949 lifted the blockade.

Each side now proceeded with the formation of a German government. The Federal Republic of Germany, its capital in the small Rhineland city of Bonn, came into existence in September 1949; the German Democratic Republic, its capital in the eastern sector of Berlin, one month later. There were now two Germanys, and the postwar division of Europe hardened along a rigid new political boundary.

The Atlantic Alliance

In 1948 Britain, France, Belgium, the Netherlands, and Luxembourg formed a West European Union for collective self-defense, but it had only limited military resources. In 1949 the United States took the lead in creating a larger military alliance and collective security system. The United States, Canada, and ten European nations met in Washington and agreed to military arrangements for the joint defense of western Europe. The Atlantic Pact was a military alliance of unlimited duration and broad scope: "an armed attack against one or more" was to be considered "an attack against all." The United States formally committed itself to the security of western Europe and agreed to supply funds and equipment for European rearmament. It was the first such military alliance of its kind in American history and another example of the deepening American involvement in the multiple spheres of European political and economic life. Breaking with the isolationist views of past generations, American political leaders had come to believe that their own national security was inextricably linked to the security of western Europe.

The North Atlantic Treaty Organization (NATO) emerged with a network of military arrangements and a chain of command headed by

General Eisenhower. Because West Germany remained the most vulnerable target for Soviet expansion, large numbers of American troops (eventually over 300,000) were stationed there as the nucleus of the NATO armed forces. But with overwhelming Soviet superiority in ground forces, the NATO defense strategy was based primarily on American air power rather than on ground troops alone. The treaty solemnly affirmed American determination not to abandon the Continent. In later years the West Europeans became restive with American leadership, or, alternatively, feared an American decoupling from Europe, but NATO remained western Europe's shield against Soviet aggression. The Truman Doctrine, the Marshall Plan, and NATO were the three prongs of the American and western European response to a potential Soviet challenge.

Meanwhile the West European countries, with the aid of the Marshall Plan, were making an impressive economic recovery and cooperating with each other (the Marshall Plan is discussed in the next section of this chapter). The Soviets became increasingly wary about the revival and growing unity of western Europe. American financial and military assistance, NATO, the containment policy, all defensive in Western eyes, and indeed provoked by Soviet expansionism, were hostile acts from the Soviet perspective. The Soviet Union drew its six eastern European satellite or client states, variously styled people's republics or people's democracies, closer to it. It formalized economic ties by creating in 1949 a Council for Mutual Economic Aid and a few years later coordinated the existing network of military alliances in the Warsaw Pact of 1955.

By 1949, however, Stalin's postwar expansion seemed contained and Truman could claim success for his policies. The Soviets had dropped their demands on Turkey and departed from Iran. Insurrectionary strikes launched by Communist parties in western Europe had failed, as did a Communist bid for power in Italy. Marshal Tito in 1948 successfully defied the Cominform, and Yugoslavia went its separate Communist way. In Greece the American- and British-backed Greek royalists triumphed in 1949 against the Communist guerrillas. The Soviet blockade of Berlin had failed to drive the Americans and West Europeans from the city.

The rivalry over Europe thus led to a stalemate by about 1950. The Soviet threat to western Europe diminished. The continent remained divided into a western and eastern

Stalemate in Europe

Europe, Germany into two Germanys, Berlin into West and East Berlin. After the failure of the Soviet blockade of Berlin, there was no such overt conflict or military confrontation within Europe. Despite renewed threats to Berlin, each side recognized the strength and security concerns of the other. But any thoughts that the world might settle into peace, no matter how uneasy, were shattered in June 1950. The Western-Soviet struggle shifted to Asia.

America, Europe, and New Conflicts in Asia

In Asia new conflicts also developed during the early postwar years. The Chinese Communists triumphed over the Nationalists, and Mao Zedong proclaimed the People's Republic of China in 1949. In Japan the United States excluded the Soviet Union from its military occupation, which lasted from 1945 to 1952. The Americans sought to foster stable parliamentary institutions and revive the Japanese economy, but a new war in Korea disrupted the Asian revival and drew both American and European troops into difficult military campaigns.

The Western Allies and the Soviet Union had agreed during the Second World War that Korea, once an object of imperialist rivalry between tsarist Russia and Japan, but under Japanese control since 1910, would become free and independent after Japan's

Korea after 1945

defeat. In 1945 the United States, for reasons of military expediency, proposed that Soviet troops temporarily occupy the northern part of the country down to the 38th parallel; American troops would temporarily occupy the southern half. But postwar negotiations for a unified Korea foundered. The U.S.S.R. established a satellite government in its occupation zone and built up North Korean military strength. The United States developed its own client state in the south and lent economic and military assistance. Despite the original plans for a united Korean state, two Koreas had come into existence.

Following a series of border skirmishes between North and South Korea, the North Koreans launched a sudden, full-scale invasion of the south in June 1950. American and western European leaders saw the invasion as an open act of Communist military aggression, the first such clear-cut military aggression of the Cold War. The timing of the invasion seems to have surprised the Soviets, however, because they were then boycotting

The Korean War was a key test for the American and western European policy of containing communism, yet, like all modern wars, it disrupted the lives of millions of civilians, including those who knew little about the larger political issues at stake. This Korean girl and her baby brother were photographed near an American tank in the summer of 1951, but their expressions convey some of the timeless, local struggle to survive amid the violent international conflicts of governments and global powers.

(©Interim Archives/Archive Photos/Getty Images)

the Security Council of the UN to protest the exclusion of the People's Republic of China. They were thus unable to exercise their veto when the Council condemned the invasion and authorized military countermeasures; but the Soviets quietly furnished military aid to North Korea and denounced the Americans and western Europeans for intervening in Asian affairs. President Truman, who viewed the North Korean invasion as a new example of Soviet expansionism, used the authority of the Security Council resolution to send American combat troops to Korea and to approve air strikes on North Korean territory. General MacArthur, the wartime hero of the Pacific War who had successfully presided over the American military occupation of Japan, was named commander of the UN multinational forces. Although these forces consisted largely of Americans, a number of western European nations also sent troops and supported the Korean campaign.

UN authorizes military action

After early setbacks, the American-led UN army drove the North Koreans back above the 38th parallel, and then rapidly moved toward the Yalu River, the boundary between Korea and the People's Republic of China. Mao, incensed at the arrival of a multinational army on the Chinese border, took action to assert China's new international influence. In late October 1950 a large Chinese army suddenly appeared and drove the advancing UN forces back below the 38th parallel. It was now an entirely new war, to which China had committed major military resources. The European allies, at first gratified by the American show of determination in Asia, grew worried that the war would escalate into a global, possibly nuclear conflict. President Truman, also growing concerned about a wider war in which the United States would lack the full support of its European allies, replaced the belligerent General MacArthur with another commander and sought to negotiate a truce.

Chinese army enters Korea

In July 1951 a cease-fire agreement brought large-scale fighting to a halt, but armistice negotiations dragged on until 1953. An armistice was eventually signed, drawing the line of partition between North and South Korea roughly where the fighting had begun three years earlier, at the 38th parallel. Korea thus became officially divided, like Germany, into communist and anticommunist countries.

In addition to the costly loss of life on all sides, the Korean War also affected the global economy. The United States itself could not supply all of the military needs and expenditures of the war, so the conflict became a stimulus for the economic growth of western Europe and Japan. It also contributed to a growing Western desire for German rearmament. In American eyes, the costs of the war were justified because a flagrant act of aggression had been checked in Asia. Most western Europeans, even those who were concerned about the recklessness of General MacArthur, found reassuring implications for Europe in the firm American response to Communist military aggression.

Economic effects of Korean War

The Korean War also had direct political repercussions in Europe. Despite some concerns among the French and other Europeans who still feared a revival of German military strength, the American government pressed for West German rearmament. When a French proposal for a European Defense Community (with a "European army," in which the Germans were to serve as "European soldiers") failed to pass the French legislature in 1954, West Germany was authorized to create its own army under the overall command of NATO.

Political effects in Europe

Anxieties about a resurgent German militarism steadily receded in the context of the Cold War. The West German constitution guaranteed civilian control over the military. A strong antimilitarist movement emerged within Germany itself, and a new democratic political culture developed during the 1950s. In 1955 the Federal Republic of Germany became a full member of NATO.

The decades that followed the conflicts of the early Cold War in Europe and Asia brought new crises, including confrontations over Berlin, Cuba, Vietnam, and the Middle East, to name only the most important. Above all, a mounting nuclear arms race between the two superpowers and the stockpiling of the most formidable weaponry ever assembled continued to threaten Europe and the wider world. Amid the ongoing conflicts of the Cold War, however, Europeans steadily rebuilt their cities, industries, commercial infrastructures, and social systems. This era of remarkable economic recovery and political reconstruction brought Europeans back into the global economy and contributed to the growth of Europe's population, even as European governments confronted a new wave of anticolonial movements in their empires and the evolving challenges of eastern European communism.

105.   WESTERN EUROPE: ECONOMIC RECONSTRUCTION

The Second World War had left Europe in a worse state of disorder than the First. It had ruined one of the world's chief industrial areas and brought its economic system to collapse. Even when the worst local devastation was repaired, suffering and distress persisted. Europe could no longer pay for the imports that it needed. During the war the West Europeans, and especially the British, had used up their overseas investments and lost a good share of the shipping services they had once provided. Overseas countries had built up their own industries and needed those of Europe less, and the United States had taken over markets once in European hands.

At the same time, western Europe retained diverse and still-valuable economic resources. Its population exceeded that of either of the superpowers. Even in ruins, it still possessed one of the world's leading industrial plants and an educated workforce with the skills needed to rehabilitate and run it. The Europeans did not wish to be rescued by either of the superpowers. Most rejected communism as a modern form of enslavement. Yet they also feared excessive dependence on the United States. Memories of the stock-market crash of 1929, the economic collapse of Europe after the withdrawal of American capital, and the Great Depression bred skepticism about American capitalism.

The Marshall Plan and European Recovery

For the non-Communist world, the single most important economic reality in the early postwar years was the productivity of the American economic system. The American economy had expanded enormously during the war. At the war's end the United States accounted for two-thirds of the world's industrial production and held two-thirds of the world's gold. Its gross national product was two and a half times higher than in 1939; its exports were three times greater. Despite predictions about postwar economic collapse, its economy grew at unprecedented rates in the 1950s and 1960s.

U.S. economic strength

When the Lend-Lease export of equipment and supplies ended after the war, the United States sent billions of dollars worth of goods to western Europe to relieve distress and made loans to individual states, especially to Britain. But the Europeans themselves quickly set about to rebuild their economies. Within two years, by 1947, the economies of western Europe were approaching prewar levels of production. American aid was still desperately needed, however, to continue the purchase of food, fuel, raw materials, and industrial parts essential to full recovery. By the spring of 1947 that recovery appeared at risk. The poorest harvest in a century was feared. With Cold War tensions mounting, Communist parties in France and Italy moved away from earlier cooperation in postwar reconstruction and launched a wave of strikes. Even if the Soviet Union was not actively promoting social unrest or revolution in western Europe, the Americans were concerned about European stability. Between the two superpowers the Soviets had more to gain by chaos in western Europe and the United States had more to gain by its rebuilding.

American economic aid so far had been improvised and piecemeal. In June 1947 Secretary of State George C. Marshall used the occasion of his Harvard commencement address to invite the Europeans to cooperate in drawing up blueprints for a broad program of reconstruction, for which the United States would provide the financial support. The plan, as formulated, was "directed not against country or doctrine, but against hunger, poverty, desperation, and chaos." To reinforce its nonpolitical character, the United States extended the invitation to all European governments, including the Soviet Union and the East European states. The Soviet Union rejected the proposal and forbade the participation of its East European satellites, denouncing the plan as "a new venture in American imperialism."

The Marshall Plan

The West European countries, by contrast, responded eagerly. Under the Marshall Plan, or European Recovery Program, as enacted by Congress, American aid was coordinated with each country's needs and with joint European priorities to maximize the benefits. The Office for European Economic Cooperation (OEEC) in Paris worked closely with the Americans to identify projects, coordinate the planning, and allocate the funds.

The results of the Marshall Plan exceeded the boldest anticipations of its American sponsors. The West Europeans utilized their technical and managerial skills to improve transportation facilities, modernize their infrastructure, and expand their productive capacity. They reduced trade barriers among themselves and facilitated trade by setting up a payments union. Hard currency, now available for imports, reduced the financial pressures on the western European governments and thus curtailed the need for further austerity. The Marshall Plan accelerated the recovery already under way, enhanced the economic exchanges with the United States, and encouraged the economic cooperation of the European countries with each other.

Results of the Marshall Plan

While the United States thus used its economic resources to help revive its competitors, the Marshall Plan also served American interests by restoring a world market, of which the United States would be a principal beneficiary. By creating markets for American exports in Europe, it helped fuel the postwar economic boom in the United States. The Americans satisfied their humanitarian impulse, served their economic needs, and reduced the possible drift of Europeans toward the Communist camp. At the same time the Marshall Plan sharpened the division between the Soviet bloc and western Europe.

Economic Growth in Western Europe

For West Germany the currency reform of 1948, Marshall Plan aid, and the economic opportunities opened up by the Korean War ignited a stunning economic revival and expansion, the *Wirtschaftswunder,* or "economic miracle." By 1950 the Federal Republic of Germany was exceeding prewar Germany's production levels, and by 1958 it was the leading industrial country of western Europe. France, Italy, and other West European countries experienced an "economic miracle" also. For two and a half decades, from 1948

The silver '50s and golden '60s

to 1974 (when a global recession set in), the western European economies expanded at unprecedented and uninterrupted rates of growth. The West Europeans basked in prosperity and rising living standards. Europeans would later speak of the "silver '50s" and the "golden '60s"; the French would speak also of the "30 glorious years." Although Britain's economy, burdened by older industries and the loss of overseas markets, lagged behind the growth in other countries, it too grew faster than at any time in the interwar years.

The prosperity of western Europe in this era derived from a competitive, capitalist, free-market and private-enterprise economy, but it was accompanied almost everywhere

Economic planning and government intervention

by economic planning, systematic government intervention, and new social services to help people cope with the instability of competitive capitalism and the business cycle. No one anywhere wished to repeat the hard times and suffering of the Great Depression. Keynes's theories about the wider economic stimulus of government spending, first formulated in the 1930s but without many adherents at that time, took hold in the postwar era and dominated government policy in the 1950s and 1960s even when conservative governments were in control. Governments kept their economies under close surveillance and used their fiscal and monetary powers to promote investment, production, and employment and to control inflation. They took "countercyclical" measures; that is, at signs of decline in the business cycle they increased government spending. Full employment was accepted as a goal. Improved statistical techniques and economic forecasting, although far from precision instruments, made economic planning and "fine-tuning" feasible. Such planning, however, took the form of guidance and direction, not coercion, and differed markedly from the rigid, detailed, and doctrinaire centralized planning of the Soviet Union and the eastern European Communist states.

In Britain, France, and Italy (less so in West Germany, which had lived through state control under the Nazis), the postwar governments also nationalized a number of the key sectors of the economy to bring them under government control. But even in these mixed economies, the private capitalist sector represented the major share of economic activity. In all western Europe economic growth became virtually an obsession as governments, business leaders, and workers came to expect growth rates far exceeding those of the past.

When the sustained economic growth led to a labor shortage, West Germany and other countries invited foreign workers to join their labor force. Turks, Greeks, Yugoslavs, Spaniards, Portuguese, and Italians (mostly from southern Italy) were invited in as "guest workers." Four and a half million workers arrived in the Federal Republic of Germany

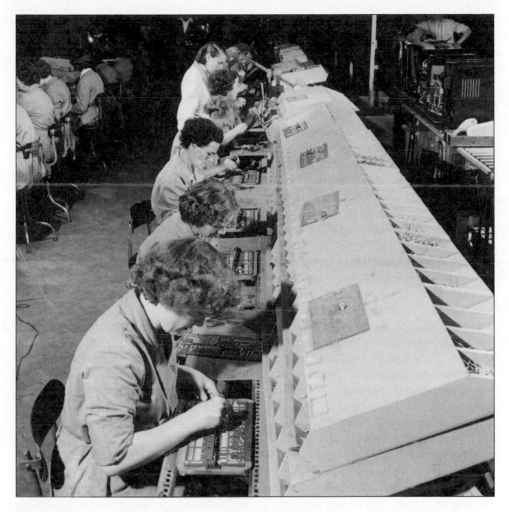

The European "economic miracle" of the 1950s and 1960s brought new jobs and wealth to workers throughout Europe. This picture of British workers in 1957 shows women assembling circuit panels for television sets, one of the important new consumer products in post-World War II economies and social life.

(©Arthur Tanner/Hulton Archive/Getty Images)

alone, over half of them Turks, who did not return home but often formed large enclaves in which people maintained many of their own cultural traditions and identities. After the postwar collapse of the European colonial empires, many immigrants from the former European colonies in Asia, Africa, and the Caribbean islands also arrived in western Europe. Beginning in the 1950s, a steady stream of immigrants flowed into Britain from India, Pakistan, the West Indies, and Africa. France drew large numbers from its former North African colonies, especially Algeria, and from its former colonies in western Africa. The Netherlands became home for many Indonesians. Later political refugees also arrived in Europe from Vietnam and other parts of Asia. The new Europeans often brought different cultures and religions into European cities. Most European societies became more multicultural, and there was more racial diversity everywhere. Mosques became a common sight in

A steady stream of immigrants

neighborhoods where previously there had been only churches or synagogues. The influx of guest workers and large immigrant populations later created new social conflicts and resentments, especially in less affluent times after the 1970s. The growing presence of diverse immigrant communities led to new social friction, often overtly racial or religious, testing the flexibility and tolerance of increasingly multiethnic and multicultural European societies.

A postwar baby boom and the arrival of at least 13 million immigrants and refugees increased the population of western Europe by 25 percent between 1945 and 1970. But by the 1960s the birth rate of the West Europeans began to level off and western Europe's population began to show signs of long-term decline—a demographic pattern that has also reappeared in other modern, wealthy societies around the world.

Growth of the welfare state

In these same postwar years the welfare state grew well beyond its pre-1914 origins and its earlier expansion in the interwar years. The postwar governments gave a high priority to social objectives, to what the French Resistance charter had called "a more just social order": the right to a suitable job, government compensation in the event of unemployment or disability, social security in old age, free or subsidized health care, and the redistribution of wealth and income through progressive taxation. The protection of the welfare state was intended to be universal, not confined, as in earlier times, to the poor and disadvantaged. Its social objectives could be achieved in the 1950s and 1960s because of a salutary interplay of government, management, and labor, which all shared in the consensus about investment and growth. Only later, from the late 1970s on, did a growing number of critics attract political support by arguing that all these entitlements had become excessive or an impediment to economic growth or a too-expensive benefit for immigrant populations.

106. WESTERN EUROPE: POLITICAL RECONSTRUCTION

Western Europe also confronted overwhelming challenges of political reconstruction at the end of the war. Britain was economically exhausted and in the process of liquidating its empire. France, recovering from the collapse of 1940, the occupation, and the wartime Vichy regime, became engaged in costly colonial wars in Indochina and Algeria. Italy had to renew its political life after two decades of fascism. Germany, after the Nazi defeat, was divided and under military occupation. Nevertheless political reconstruction went forward. Britain resumed its role as the world's oldest parliamentary democracy; France and Italy adopted new constitutions; out of the western zone of occupied Germany the Federal Republic of Germany emerged in 1949.

The smaller states of western Europe also reestablished their parliamentary democracies. Only Spain and Portugal remained under prewar dictatorships until those regimes also came to an end in the mid-1970s. The right to participate in political life continued to expand throughout western Europe. Women finally received the vote in France and Italy as the war drew to a close and in Switzerland in 1971. And in another suffrage reform that went almost unnoticed, the legal voting age in most countries was reduced to 18 during the 1970s.

The spirit of reform

The earliest postwar elections showed the strong political desire for social reforms, which also advanced because right-wing political groups, as in France, lost influence after their wartime collaborations with the Nazis. The Resistance movements had called during the war for a federal union of Europe to prevent future wars and had emphasized the need for economic and social rights as well as political freedom. Postwar governments were therefore asked to provide protection against the insecurities of old age, disability, ill health, and unemployment. Such ideals shaped the new political debates and popular social reforms in the first years after 1945, but western European politics also reverted to older democratic patterns of bargain and compromise.

The welfare state idea persisted, as did the evolving desire for a more integrated Europe, but (by comparison to the 1930s) politics became less rigidly ideological. Socialists, following the Scandinavian model, became Social Democratic reformists, accepting capitalism but insisting that they could manage capitalist economies more effectively than liberals, centrists, or conservatives. In France and Italy the large Communist parties, with strong attachments to the Soviet Union in the early postwar years, complicated or challenged the search for pragmatic solutions to social problems, yet the Communists also participated in parliaments and rejected revolutionary violence within their own societies. In the Federal Republic of Germany, Italy, and France, the Christian Democrats, drawing inspiration from Roman Catholic religious and ethical precepts, played a key role in shaping and governing the new regimes. They accepted the welfare state but backed away from the egalitarianism of the socialists and, over time, increasingly came to represent conservative and business interests.

All of the major national governments in postwar western Europe were able to establish stable economic and social systems that raised the standard of living, reduced the dangers of political extremism, and fostered transnational exchanges rather than nationalist violence. In striking contrast to the era after the First World War, the western European nations decisively and permanently rejected warfare as a means to settle disagreements or conflicts among themselves.

Great Britain: Labour and Conservative

In Great Britain, the first parliamentary elections in ten years, in July 1945, unseated Winston Churchill and the Conservative-led wartime coalition and voted in a Labour government. For the first time in its history the Labour Party had a majority of its own. Governing from 1945 to 1951, with Clement Attlee as prime minister, it set Britain on a new course of parliamentary socialism and the modern welfare state.

On the premise that the country's basic industries could not be left to the unplanned anarchy of capitalism and unregulated competition, the Labour government nationalized the Bank of England, the coal mines, electricity and gas, iron and steel, and other parts of the economy. Because four-fifths of industry remained in private hands, it was a mixed economy that emerged. At the same   *Labour government* time Labour greatly expanded and revamped the social insurance program inherited from the Liberal reforms of 1906-1914. During the war, in 1942, the British economist William Henry Beveridge had prepared a government report that proposed to guarantee "full employment in a free society" and social security for all "from the cradle to the grave." Drawing on the Beveridge Report, Labour now extended insurance coverage for unemployment, old age, and other contingencies; inaugurated a comprehensive national health service; and increased taxes on income and inheritances.

In the elections of 1951 Labour lost its majority in Parliament. The Conservatives returned to office and governed for the next 13 years under a succession of prime ministers. After 1964 the two parties alternated in office. The shifting electoral fortunes stemmed from disagreement within the country over the welfare state, dissatisfaction with the performance of the economy, concerns about the processes of decolonization in the British Empire, and frustration at Britain's diminished global status.

During their years in office, the Conservatives restored some nationalized industries to private control but did little else to dismantle the welfare state. Both parties recognized, however, that the social reforms of the welfare state would require a prosperous, expanding economy. But there were nagging economic problems. The liquidation of investments to pay for the Second World War, the loss of export markets, and a decline in income from shipping and other commercial services adversely affected the country's balance of payments and weakened the British pound. With American financial aid, an intensified export drive, an austerity program that reduced imports, and a curtailment of military and imperial commitments, the economy gradually improved, but the British failed at the time to rebuild their obsolescent capital equipment and infrastructure as effectively as their West European neighbors.

Britain's economic challenges

Such problems made British workers vulnerable to competition from more efficient foreign industries. When inflation set in during the late 1960s and intensified in the 1970s, the trade unions demanded wage increases to match rising prices. Strikes and prolonged work stoppages troubled the economy and divided British society. Until the late 1970s, when a new political era opened, the main disagreements focused on how or if Labour or the Conservatives could better manage British decline, not how economic and imperial decline itself could be overcome.

Troubles in Northern Ireland

Meanwhile troubles in Northern Ireland persisted. After the partition in 1922, as noted earlier, the six predominately Protestant counties of Northern Ireland had remained part of the United Kingdom. The Catholic minority, about one-third of the population, protested militantly that they were victims of political and economic discrimination and pressed for annexation to the Republic of Ireland, which the Protestants vehemently opposed. Open violence broke out in 1969, inflamed by the Irish Republican Army on the one hand and Protestant extremists on the other. In the sectarian violence that followed, over 3,000 persons lost their lives.

The French Republic: Fourth and Fifth

After the liberation of France, General Charles de Gaulle, the very incarnation of the French Resistance, became provisional president and elections were held for a Constituent Assembly that would create a new republican government. The parties of the Right were discredited by their role in the Vichy regime, but the Left emerged from the war with new strength and prestige. The Communists, the Socialists, and the Popular Republican Movement (*Mouvement Républicain Populaire,* or MRP), a Catholic progressive party akin to Christian Democrats elsewhere on the Continent, formed the provisional government. The Left pressed for a systematic purge of collaborators, despite the difficulties in determining levels of guilt. The purge had begun as soon as the Free French military forces reached French soil, taking the form of angry drumhead trials and executions. Gradually, the process was brought under more orderly judicial procedures. Even so, the trials of Marshal Pétain and Pierre Laval were impassioned showpieces. The debate over collaboration and trials of collaborators continued to divide the country in later decades, in part because some of the most egregious acts of violence against the French Jews and others had originated with the French Vichy government and not the Nazi occupiers. Such issues were critically examined in memoirs,

Purging collaborators

French leaders sought to revive the national economy and demographic vitality after the Nazi occupation and the collapse of international trade during the Second World War. Although France struggled to establish a stable political system, a postwar "baby boom" (encouraged by government benefits for families) led to a rapid population growth, an expansion of schools such as this Parisian kindergarten, and a steady increase in trade and industrial production.

(©Popperfoto/Getty Images)

controversial history books, and films, including, for example, the much-debated documentary *The Sorrow and the Pity* (1969) by the filmmaker Marcel Ophuls.

The Fourth Republic's machinery of government differed in only a few details from the prewar Third Republic. Once again the presidency was only ceremonial and the premier and cabinet were responsible to an all-powerful National Assembly. De Gaulle made no secret of his dislike for the new constitution, the ceremonial presidency, the return of party rivalries, and the dominant role of the legislature, all of which interfered with his vision of a strong France ready to resume a leadership role in world affairs. He resigned in protest in December 1946. The Communists, Socialists, and MRP continued their tripartite coalition under Socialist leadership until the Communists, in the heightened tensions of the Cold War, fomented a series of strikes and were expelled from the cabinet in May 1947.

Parliamentary division and ministerial instability grew more acute. Periodically de Gaulle returned to the political scene, heading a movement called the "Rally of the French People," which he described as "above parties." Except for the brief

"Rally of the French People"

reform ministry of Pierre Mendès-France in 1954–1955, governmental ineffectiveness in the midst of colonial wars as well as recurring domestic and foreign crises led to public cynicism and constant turnover in the governing ministries.

Yet despite its record of political instability—25 cabinets from 1946 to 1958—the Fourth Republic enacted significant legislation. The provisional government had quickly nationalized several key industries, and as in Britain a mixed economy gradually emerged. The existing social security legislation was expanded. An economic plan, drawn up by Jean Monnet, a farsighted economist and public official who later played a large role in the creation of the European Economic Community, enlarged and modernized the country's economic base, paving the way for industrial expansion. By 1952 production levels were 1½ times those of 1938, and industrial output was growing at an annual rate of over 5 percent. From 1946 to 1966 production tripled. (In the half-century from 1889 to 1940, it had no more than doubled.) The country also displayed a demographic vitality, at least for a time, that confounded pessimists who had long worried about France's low birth rate.

What finally brought down the Fourth Republic was the strain of trying to preserve the old French colonial empire. France alone, of all the major powers, was almost continuously engaged in colonial wars for 15 years after the Second World War. It faced

Colonial wars

economic problems that resembled the need for postwar reconstruction in Germany, Italy, and Japan, but the former Axis nations emerged from their defeats with no restless colonies to subdue. The new French constitution of 1946 recognized the emergence of new political aspirations in the French empire by giving the colonies representation in Paris but such reforms did not satisfy nationalists pressing for independence. From 1946 to 1954 the French forces unsuccessfully fought against independence movements in Indochina until they finally had to withdraw. Then, within a matter of months, the Arab movement for independence in Algeria rose up in another anticolonial war, which further drained France's material resources, political morale, and national confidence. The European settlers in Algeria and army leaders adamantly opposed French withdrawal and staged an insurrectionary coup in Algiers in May 1958. When civil war threatened, France turned to the one man whom many believed could save the situation—Charles de Gaulle, then living quietly in self-imposed retirement. The army leaders, the settlers in Algeria, and the parties of the Right were convinced, given de Gaulle's solicitude for the army and French national pride, that he would maintain French control of Algeria. De Gaulle accepted the summons. In June 1958 the National Assembly approved his appointment as premier, giving him emergency powers for six months, including the authority to prepare a new constitution.

The Fifth French Republic thus emerged from the crisis in Algeria and from the political program of Charles de Gaulle. In the autumn of 1958 the new constitution was overwhelmingly accepted in a popular referendum, and de Gaulle was shortly thereafter elected president. The presidency, as de Gaulle had long urged, became the fulcrum of power. The president was the final authority in foreign affairs and national defense. The president named the prime minister (as the premier was now called) and had the right to dissolve the National Assembly, call for new elections, submit important questions to popular referendums, and assume emergency powers, all of which de Gaulle did during his years in office. Political instability disappeared; in the first 11 years of the Fifth Republic there were only three cabinets.

De Gaulle settled the Algerian crisis in his own way. Sensitive to the revolution sweeping the colonial world, he came to recognize that France must accept a policy of independence for Algeria, which the people of both France and Algeria voted to approve in separate refer-

France under de Gaulle

endums in the spring and summer of 1962. Even earlier he granted independence to all of the French colonies in sub-Saharan Africa. With peace, governmental stability, and economic prosperity, the French reconciled themselves to the loss of their empire and looked for new strategies to have international influence under de Gaulle. France became the world's fifth largest industrial power in the 1960s, behind only the United States, the U.S.S.R., West Germany, and Japan. Seeking to maintain its status in global affairs, in 1960 France became the fourth nation to develop a nuclear bomb. De Gaulle even created an independent nuclear strike force, but the French also became western Europe's largest producers of nuclear energy for peacetime energy needs.

After the settlement of the Algerian crisis, de Gaulle built a kind of plebiscitary democracy by direct appeals to the electorate. Although civil liberties were preserved and free elections were maintained, much of France's usual democratic ferment seemed to disappear. Skilled technicians ran the affairs of state, and de Gaulle, an uncrowned republican monarch, presided as arbiter over the nation's destinies.

The nation grew restless, however, and there was increasing skepticism about de Gaulle's technocratic system of government and his extravagant posturing in world affairs. Suddenly, in May 1968, grievances in the overcrowded universities sparked a revolt that led to demonstrations by hundreds of thousands of students and then brought 10 million workers out on strike, paralyz-

May 1968

ing the economy and threatening the regime itself. Students demanded reforms in the education system, but many also supported the striking workers who agitated for new rights in their factories as well as better wages. De Gaulle survived the revolt but only after assuring himself of army support. Stressing the threat of communism and domestic chaos, he won an overwhelming majority for his party in new elections. Although there was wide support for institutional reforms in French society, the country as a whole rejected the outburst of radical political agitation, which resembled the revolts of students and a youthful "New Left" all over the globe in 1968. Educational reforms and other changes were gradually introduced, but the strikes and social disruptions of 1968 hurt the French economy. In 1969 de Gaulle chose to turn a referendum on various constitutional and regional reforms into a vote of confidence in himself. When his proposed reforms lost by a small margin, he resigned and retired to his country estate, where he died a year later, an august, heroic, austere, and always controversial figure whose exploits in war and peace assured him a lasting place in France's history.

The Federal Republic of Germany

To communicate to the German people and to the entire world the enormity of the Nazi crimes, the four wartime Allies convened an international trial in 1945–1946 at Nuremberg. Hitler, Himmler, and Goebbels were already dead, but 22 other Nazi leaders and the major Nazi organizations were indicted for crimes against peace, that is, plotting and waging a war of aggression; war crimes, which were defined as violations of the accepted laws and con-

The Nuremberg Trials

ventions of warfare; and crimes against humanity, that is, acts of mass murder and genocide. The evidence of evil deeds, massive and incontrovertible, was set down for posterity in many volumes of recorded testimony. Despite the high moral purpose of the trials and

Demonstrations and strikes swept across France in May 1968, evoking memories of nineteenth-century revolutionary battles in the barricaded streets of Paris, but President de Gaulle was more successful than earlier French kings in quelling crowds and protests. As this photograph suggests, however, clashes between the police and student demonstrators produced strong reactions throughout French society during the weeks before de Gaulle and his followers consolidated their power by winning new national elections.
(©JACQUES MARIE/AFP/Getty Images)

an honest effort to establish fair judicial procedures for the accused, some critics questioned their appropriateness, especially the decision to try the leaders of a defeated sovereign nation for planning and waging war and to indict an agency of government such as the General Staff of the military. Some also questioned the propriety of having the Soviet Union sit in judgment of the Nazis. These critics argued that the Soviets were themselves guilty of crimes because they had contributed to the outbreak of the war, shared in the partition of Poland, and incorporated the Baltic states into the Soviet Union. Others dismissed the trials as victors' justice. Yet the Nuremberg trials served in a singular way to reinforce international standards of civilized behavior and to describe the meaning of "crimes against humanity." The court condemned 12 of the defendants to execution. Seven received prison terms of varying length, including life sentences; three were acquitted.

Denazification

The four occupation authorities also carried out a "denazification" program, which produced mixed results. Because so many professional Germans had been members of Nazi organizations, it became difficult to exclude all of them from public life if the normal processes of economic and governmental institutions were to resume. Some individuals guilty of the more heinous Nazi crimes fled the country and were still being apprehended and tried many decades after the war's end by the Germans themselves or in French or Israeli courts. But the people who survived the Nazi camps and the families of Nazi victims only began to receive some financial restitution at the end of the twentieth century.

Divided Germany (and Berlin) meanwhile gained new international significance as a central arena of the Cold War. The German Democratic Republic became one of the most loyal client states of the Soviet Union. The Federal Republic of Germany became a prosperous parliamentary democracy, a full partner of the West, and also made efforts to atone for the horrors of the Nazi regime.

The West German government encouraged private industry and a capitalist, competitive economy; but it also shaped overall economic policies and provided broad social services, so that West Germany emerged with what became known as a "social market economy." The guaranteed benefits came to exceed those of other major industrial Western countries. The Federal Republic also pioneered in bringing labor and capital together. The labor unions accepted a role as social partners in the expanding economy, moderating wage demands to avoid inflation. A "codetermination" law gave workers seats on the boards of directors of larger firms.

A "social market economy"

After independent state governments had been set up in each state (or *Land*) in West Germany with the encouragement of the occupying powers, a constitutional convention representing the ten German states met in 1948–1949 in Bonn. The convention produced a Basic Law (or *Grundgesetz*) and officially established the Federal Republic of Germany. The Basic Law, by design not called a constitution, was to be temporary, valid only until at some future date the two parts of Germany could be reunited, but it remained the governing system even after German unification eventually took place in 1990. An extensive bill of rights was one of its most prominent features. Power was decentralized under a federal system.

The founders deliberately set out to avoid the weaknesses of the Weimar Republic. The president, elected indirectly and not by popular vote, was a ceremonial figure with limited political power; a president of stature could, however, as the years revealed, exercise substantial moral authority. The head of government, or real executive, was the chancellor, responsible, along with the cabinet, to the majority in the popularly elected lower house, the *Bundestag*. To avoid instability, a chancellor could be overthrown only when a new majority was ready with an immediate replacement. Proportional representation guaranteed that each party would be apportioned seats equivalent to its share of the popular vote, but to prevent splinter parties and political fragmentation, a party received seats in the legislature only if it won at least 5 percent of the national vote. The Christian Democratic Union and the Social Democrats emerged as the two chief parties and shared between them a large proportion of the popular vote.

The power of the chancellor

The Christian Democratic Union governed uninterruptedly for 20 years, from 1949 to 1969. In reaction to the Nazi barbarism, it sought to infuse politics with a moral idealism and ethical purpose. Although its name suggested a religious identity, it was not a confessional party. It appealed to Protestants and Catholics alike, who were almost equally represented in West Germany, and it received strong support from the business community and large segments of the middle classes. The dominating figure in the party and government in the early years was Konrad Adenauer, who had begun his political career in the Catholic Center Party during the pre-1914 imperial era. A patriarchal, strong-willed

Christian Democrats and Konrad Adenauer

GERMANY AND ITS BORDERS, 1919–1990

Upper panel: **The boundaries established after the Treaty of Versailles. Note the Free City of Danzig and the Polish Corridor.** *Middle panel:* **Germany's borders at the height of the Second World War in 1942. The Reich proper had then annexed (1) Luxembourg, (2) Alsace and Lorraine from France, (3) Carniola from Yugoslavia, (4) Austria, (5) the Sudeten regions and a Bohemian-Moravian protectorate from Czechoslovakia, (6) the Free City of Danzig, and (7) Poland.** *Lower panel:* **Germany after Hitler's defeat. East Prussia was divided between Poland and the U.S.S.R., and Poland reached westward almost to Berlin. A Communist East Germany (the German Democratic Republic) and a democratic West Germany (the Federal Republic of Germany) grew out of the zones occupied respectively by the Soviets and the West. After the fall of the Communist regime in East Germany, Germany was reunited in 1990.**

personality, his ambition was to regain for Germany a position of dignity and international respect while moving away from the extreme nationalism that had been such a destructive force in modern German and European history. He became chancellor in 1949 at the age of 73 (with only a slim majority) and governed for 14 years. Opponents criticized *der Alte* ("the old man") for creating a "chancellor's democracy"; but he provided the resolute leadership, stability, and continuity that made possible the remarkable economic expansion of the 1950s and the regaining of full West German sovereignty.

Adenauer successfully integrated the Federal Republic of Germany into the emerging political, economic, and military structures of western Europe, strengthening ties with

The new spirit of international cooperation in postwar Europe was expressed in the collaboration of French President Charles de Gaulle and German Chancellor Konrad Adenauer (standing next to de Gaulle here and waving to a crowd in Reims, France, in 1962). The two leaders met often to create a partnership that became the foundation for a new Europe. After fighting three major wars in the heart of Europe over a period of 75 years, Germany and France established a peaceful alliance that brought stability to the continent and eliminated the traditional problem of warfare between two former enemies.

(©ullstein bild/Getty Images)

France, cooperating in the movement for European economic integration, and winning the support and confidence of the United States and the other Western powers. Indeed, within a decade after the disastrous military defeat that had left a shattered and occupied country, West Germany was a major economic power, a coveted ally of the West and an equal member of NATO. The major opposition party, the Social Democrats, heirs to the Social Democratic Party founded in the 1870s, criticized Adenauer for his overly close identification with the United States and for ignoring the issue of national reunification. But the Social Democrats abandoned their traditional Marxist ideology at a party congress in 1959 and steadily broadened their appeal to the middle classes and younger voters.

In 1965 the Social Democrats, who had softened their neutralist stand in foreign affairs, joined the Christian Democrats and the Free Democrats (a small liberal centrist party) in a "grand coalition." Willy Brandt, the former Social Democratic mayor of West Berlin, became foreign minister and launched his "Eastern policy," or *Ostpolitik,* a policy that encouraged building bridges to the Soviet Union and eastern Europe, including East Germany. In 1969, with the support of the Free Democrats, he became chancellor

Willy Brandt's "grand coalition"

of a new coalition that ended the 20-year tenure of the Christian Democrats. Brandt negotiated treaties with the Soviet Union and Poland in 1971, formally accepting the German eastern border at the Oder and West Neisse River line that the Allies had established at the end of the Second World War. His government officially recognized the

German Democratic Republic and promoted close economic ties with it and other countries of eastern Europe. When a spy scandal in his own entourage cut short his chancellorship in 1974, his Social Democratic colleague Helmut Schmidt took over and continued his policies. Not until 1982 would the Christian Democrats return to office with Helmut Kohl as chancellor. Meanwhile, in the early 1980s, reunification with East Germany still seemed to be only a remote possibility.

The Italian Republic

During the struggle to oust the German armies from the Italian peninsula after the fall of Mussolini in 1943, the Italian political parties, repressed for over two decades under Fascism, sprang to life. In 1946 the country voted by a narrow margin to abolish the Savoy monarchy, never distinguished, and now tarnished by its cooperation with the Fascist regime. A constitution for the new Italian Republic established a ceremonial presidency, cabinet government, and legislative supremacy. Proportional representation guaranteed equitable representation for all political parties, large and small.

The Christian Democrats quickly became the dominant party. It appealed to all classes and sectors of Italian society, successfully blending support for democratic political principles, a moderately regulated free-enterprise economy, and the labor tenets of social Catholicism. In Alcide De Gasperi, who had survived the Fascist years as a librarian in the Vatican, the Chris-

Alcide De Gasperi's Christian Democrats

tian Democrats found an effective leader. For seven formative years from 1946 to 1953 he presided over a series of coalition governments, which made possible postwar economic reconstruction and expansion. In the Cold War he kept Italy firmly in the Western camp. As in France, the Communist Party's role in the resistance to Fascism helped to establish its position as a leading party in postwar politics. Communists at first held seats in the cabinet and cooperated in economic reconstruction, but when they fomented politically inspired strikes in 1947, De Gasperi dismissed them from his ministry. In 1948, during the early years of the Cold War, the United States intervened openly for the first time in its history to influence a European election, throwing its weight behind the Christian Democrats to thwart the Communists. The Christian Democrats for the first and only time won an absolute majority in the legislature.

After later electoral setbacks in 1953, however, De Gasperi resigned, and the Christian Democrats governed under a succession of short-lived coalition cabinets formed with small centrist parties. Over the years the Christian Democrats became faction-ridden and less interested in reform than in patronage. Abandoning their initial idealism, they catered to narrow, propertied interests, and many in the party profited from business connections. In the early 1960s the Socialists became part of the governing coalition, but this "opening to the Left" did not alter political rigidities, and the country grew impatient with the uninterrupted tenure of the Christian Democrats.

The Communists gained further strength in the 1960s. They weakened their ties with Moscow, renounced tenets of orthodox Marxist-Leninism, and tempered their assault on

Eurocommunism

religion. Leading architects of what came to be known as "Eurocommunism," they declared that each nation, without deferring to Moscow, must find its own way to a new society through parliamentary democracy and national consensus. The Italian Communist Party became the strongest Communist faction in the Western world, counting 1.8 million members at its peak in the mid-1970s and winning the support of 35 percent of the electorate. Communist mayors and municipal councils governed in many major cities, including Rome. But the Christian Democrats continued to reject the Communist bid for seats in the national government.

The unstable political scene did not interfere with Italy's postwar economic growth. The industrial triangle of Genoa, Milan, and Turin in northern Italy provided the nucleus for recovery and expansion. By 1949 industrial production reached 1939 levels, and by the early 1950s Italy's rate of industrial growth rivaled that of West Germany and France. Italy was transformed from a primarily agricultural country into one of the world's leading industrial nations. An economic revolution dramatically elevated living standards for most Italians. Only the underdeveloped south remained a troubled economic region, even in times of advancing prosperity. In general, however, Italy joined the other nations of western Europe in a remarkably rapid political and economic recovery from the catastrophic events of the Second World War.

A prosperous economy

107.   EUROPE AND THE GLOBAL ECONOMY

Even before the close of hostilities in 1945, the United States, with British support, developed a bold initiative to reshape the postwar world economy. Determined to avoid the economic nationalism, trade restrictions, and currency instability of the interwar years, the planners sought to restore the free flow of trade and the stable currencies of the pre-1914 era. In 1944 the United States convened an international conference of 44 nations at Bretton Woods, New Hampshire. The participants pledged to reduce trade barriers and work for stable currencies in the postwar world.

An effort to establish a formal world trade organization to oversee international commerce foundered, but an alternative strategy proved successful. The United States had earlier negotiated bilateral trade agreements with a number of countries to reduce tariffs on a reciprocal basis, with each agreement carrying a "most-favored nation" clause whereby concessions to one country were extended to all. These piecemeal arrangements led in 1948 to a broader arrangement, the General Agreement on Tariffs and Trade (GATT), embodying the same negotiating principle. Subscribed to initially by 23 nations, GATT became the foundation of a postwar global commercial system in which tariffs steadily declined and in which Europeans gradually regained part of the international economic influence they had lost during the Second World War.

GATT

The General Agreement laid down rules to prevent discrimination in international trade, set up procedures for handling complaints, and provided a framework for continuing negotiation through lengthy bargaining sessions, or "rounds," designed to lower tariffs and remove nontariff barriers. By the 1990s over 100 countries were participating. GATT was only a partial substitute for a formal international trade organization, but it contributed to the vast expansion of world trade beginning in the 1950s. Not until 1995 was a formal World Trade Organization (WTO) established, with enlarged powers to mediate agreements and settle trade disputes. The WTO in its turn faced new problems and recurring controversies as it tried to resolve the conflicting claims of different nations in the global economy.

The "world economy" in the early postwar years meant the world's non-Communist or free-market economies. The strategic centers were North America and western Europe, with the addition of Japan, which doubled its share of world trade between 1951 and 1960. Latin America, Asia, the Middle East, Australasia, and Africa were also integrated into the postwar world economy, so that the new commercial networks had truly global dimensions. The Soviet Union

Global participation

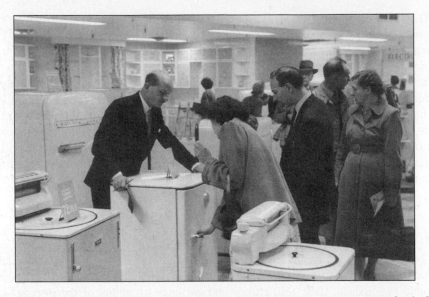

The postwar economic expansion enabled Europeans to purchase new consumer goods, including modern appliances such as refrigerators and washing machines. These shoppers were looking at the newest refrigerators in a London department store in the mid-1950s, when postwar consumers bought goods and services within a global commercial system of declining tariffs and fluctuating currency values.

(©John Murray/Picture Post/Getty Images)

played no part in any of the postwar trade negotiations and restricted its commerce principally to its East European bloc of satellites. In the late 1960s the Soviets and the East European countries opened up trade and economic relations with western Europe and the United States but not until the late 1980s did they seek integration into the global economy.

Currency Stability: Toward the "Gold-Dollar" Standard

If the first objective of the wartime Bretton Woods conference was to liberalize trade, the second was to stabilize the world's currencies. The chaos of the interwar years when nation after nation abandoned the gold standard and competed in currency devaluations to gain trade advantages haunted everyone. The Bretton Woods conference sought to restore the equivalent of the pre-1914 gold standard, which had provided for fixed exchange rates and the convertibility of all currencies into gold or into the equivalent at the time, British pounds sterling.

Currency stabilization, however, turned out to be more difficult than anticipated. The stable conversion of different currencies into gold or dollars at fixed exchange rates did not become possible until the end of 1958. For about a dozen years, until 1971, each major currency had a par value in gold and in dollars. For that same short time the American dollar, like the British pound before 1914, was accepted as the equivalent of gold itself. But the postwar economic situation changed rapidly as the American share of world commerce declined in the 1960s; the era of the "gold-dollar standard" proved short-lived, and a system of "floating currencies" and fluctuating exchange rates took its place.

Currency stabilization

Meanwhile two important agencies established after the war helped in international financial settlements. The International Monetary Fund (IMF) provided loans to governments to manage temporary balance of payments difficulties and to help reduce the need for currency devaluations. The International Bank for Reconstruction and Development (or World Bank) made long-term loans to the governments of poorer countries for economic development.

The IMF and the World Bank

Both agencies played a larger role in later years than in the immediate postwar era, and both became controversial when critics complained that their policies did not really benefit the world's poorer nations or people. Both were located in Washington, their major funding provided by the United States. The economic center of gravity for the North Atlantic world, like the political and the military, lay after 1945 on the American side of the ocean.

European Integration: From the Common Market to the European Community

As western Europe expanded economically, it also drew together in a more integrated economic system. The war, the wartime Resistance movements, the Marshall Plan, European cooperative recovery efforts, and the threat from the Soviet Union in the Cold War all contributed to the idea that western Europe's future lay in unity. A number of European leaders pressed for the creation of a "United States of Europe." In 1949 delegates representing the parliaments of ten countries met in Strasbourg to establish a Council of Europe with the hope that it might

Expansion and unity

become a legislative body for a federated Europe. Although the Council of Europe grew in membership over the years and continued to support the idea of federation, it never became an important political force. It confined itself to humanitarian, cultural, and social issues. In 1959 it set up a European Court of Human Rights to protect the rights of individuals in its member nations against arbitrary government actions. It banned corporal punishment in the schools and outlawed the death penalty for convicted criminals.

European integration itself, however, took a different path, beginning in the economic area. In 1948 Belgium, the Netherlands, and Luxembourg created a customs union, called Benelux, which provided the benefits of an expanded free trade area for the three small countries. At the same time the visionary but pragmatic French administrator Jean Monnet, who had helped reorganize the postwar French economy, recognized that the first steps toward greater European unity had to develop along modest economic lines and begin with specific objectives.

In 1952, under a plan designed by Monnet, six West European countries—France, the Federal Republic of Germany, Italy, and the three Benelux nations—placed their coal and steel industries under a form of supranational authority. They established the European Coal and Steel Community, its headquarters in Luxembourg. The six nations not only agreed to eliminate import duties and quotas on coal and steel but also placed production under a common High Authority with decision-making powers. A council of ministers represented the six governments, but the High Authority carried out major administrative functions.

The European Coal and Steel Community

Monnet was the first president of the European Coal and Steel Community, which paved the way for economic integration that would extend far beyond a single sector of the West European economy. In a momentous second step, the same six nations on March 25, 1957, signed the Treaty of Rome, creating a large free-trade area or customs union, the European Economic Community, or Common Market, its headquarters in Brussels, with

The Common Market
the goal of moving toward full economic and even political integration. The six nations pledged to eliminate tariff barriers, develop a common tariff with respect to the outside world, harmonize social and economic policies, and work toward the free movement of capital and labor. Under a separate treaty the member countries also agreed to coordinate their nonmilitary atomic research and technology in a European Atomic Community.

The six-nation Common Market, encompassing 175 million people in 1958, quickly became one of the thriving economic aggregates of the expanding world economy. By 1968, even earlier than anticipated, the last internal tariff was dropped and trade among the six nations grew at a rate double that of trade with outside countries. Its influence spread to the former European colonies, with which it worked out preferential trade arrangements. Through the Common Market, western Europe set about to recapture a key role in the new configuration of global affairs, which had been dominated since 1945 by the two superpowers. The Common Market also helped further absorb a revived democratic West Germany into western Europe and to nurture reconciliation between France and Germany, ending the internecine rivalries that had devastated the European continent in the first half of the twentieth century.

In 1967 the three "Communities" consolidated themselves into what now came to be called the European Community. Their high commissions became the European

*The European
Community*
Commission and their assemblies became the European Parliament, meeting in Strasbourg. The members of the European Parliament took seats by party affiliation and not by nation. In 1979, for the first time, they were not chosen by their respective governments but were elected by a European-wide electorate. The Parliament enjoyed only limited legislative authority, but it supervised the budget and the European Commission and kept alive the idea of unity. Final decision making still rested with the council of ministers representing each of the member nations, whose decisions on important matters had to be unanimous.

Great Britain initially refrained from joining the Common Market. Its economic ties to the Commonwealth, its dependence on low-priced food imports, and its unwillingness to accept any supranational authority kept both Labour and Conservative governments from seeking to join. But Britain's economy continued to lag behind the economic growth of the major western European nations, prompting the British government to advance the nation's economic interests by applying for membership in the Common Market in 1963. Britain's request was vetoed by President de Gaulle, however, because he regarded Britain and its admittedly "special relationship" with the United States as a threat to French leadership on the Continent. Not until after de Gaulle retired from the political scene in 1969 did Britain gain admission; but British ambivalence about closer integration with other European economies never entirely disappeared.

*Advance toward
political unity*
If the years 1958–1968 showed remarkable gains in economic integration, the advance toward political unity was slower. Although de Gaulle understood the contribution of the Common Market to the prosperity of western Europe and envisioned a strong western Europe as a counterpoise to the two "hegemonic superpowers," he opposed political or supranational authority for the Community. Europe had to be a Europe of sovereign states, a *Europe des patries.* The more dedicated Europeanists were disappointed. Yet the supranational economic and political machinery of the Community, the day-to-day cooperation of the European civil servants or bureaucrats (inevitably called "Eurocrats") in Brussels and Strasbourg, and the close consultation on common interests were favorable signs for

unity, even apart from the military and defense ties that brought the western Europeans together in NATO. French-German friendship, cemented by de Gaulle and Adenauer and reinforced by their successors, remained the linchpin of cooperation within the Community.

The Europeans showed no haste to surrender their national sovereignty and independence. National identities remained powerful and influential, but the European Community created a strong sense of common destiny, a shared faith in democratic institutions and market economies and a concern for human rights and social needs. It contributed immeasurably to the economic and political strength of western Europe and also helped Europeans regain a larger role in world affairs; and by the beginning of the twenty-first century the European Community was projecting its own transnational military force.

Western Europe accounted in the 1960s for one-fourth of all imports and one-fifth of all exports in the world economy; for a time its exports equaled those of the United States and Japan combined. *West European competition* One-third of the largest multinational corporations, that is, corporations that set up subsidiaries outside their own country for manufacturing or sales, were European. London, Frankfurt, and Paris were again important financial centers. In 1971 West European steel production surpassed that of the United States. European (and Japanese) automobiles cut sharply into American domestic and foreign markets. Self-sufficient in food, western Europe became the world's largest exporter of dairy products. The Federal Republic of Germany, in the 1960s, enjoyed a gross national product exceeded only by the economies of the United States and the U.S.S.R., even though it had only one-fourth the population of each; it accounted for one-third of the Common Market's gross national product. Western Europe and Japan were whittling away at the American economic lead in production and trade and ending the era of the dollar's unchallenged supremacy.

End of the Gold-Dollar Standard, 1971

The new trading patterns created monetary problems for the global financial system that had developed after the Second World War. Because America's exports no longer exceeded its imports, American trade shifted to an unfavorable balance of payments. The United States spent more abroad than it earned abroad. *Trade imbalances* Western Europe accumulated large dollar reserves (or "Eurodollars"), some $50 billion by 1971; oil-rich Arab states held "petrodollars." The number of dollars held abroad exceeded American gold reserves.

The shift in the American economic position undermined confidence in a dollar that many now viewed as overvalued. De Gaulle, resentful of American political and economic power, demanded an end to the gold-dollar standard and a return to gold itself. In 1965 France redeemed hundreds of millions of its dollar holdings for gold. Other central banks in Europe and Japan did not follow suit, but private investors speculated against the dollar. American gold and foreign currency reserves dropped precipitously.

In 1971 President Nixon unilaterally suspended gold convertibility and thus devalued the dollar against European and other currencies. A second devaluation came in 1973. The global monetary system projected at Bretton Woods ended. Despite many proposals, there was no formal revision of the postwar methods for currency exchanges. Instead, on a day-to-day basis and with considerable success, the world's major currencies were allowed to "float," that is, to fluctuate *Floating currencies*

The global economy of the 1970s and the "floating" of national currencies gave a new importance to the world's leading financial markets and stock exchanges. Governments in Europe and around the world found that the value of their money and the stability of their economies were constantly affected by the speculations of influential investors. The traders in this photograph were active at the London stock exchange, where financial speculators helped Britain regain much of its earlier prominence in international markets.

(©George W. Hales/Hulton Archive/Getty Images)

daily against each other and against the dollar in world markets. Gold itself fluctuated freely and official gold prices were abolished. Although the American dollar remained the world's principal reserve currency, the West German mark and the Japanese yen took their place beside the dollar as key international currencies.

The breakdown of the postwar monetary arrangements did not seriously affect the world economy. Currencies did not collapse because they were no longer exchangeable for gold. For currency stability the financial markets and global trading companies learned to rely mainly on international consultation and rapid exchange of information, but governments found their currencies and economic policies vulnerable to speculators and fast-moving exchanges in a global financial system that crossed all national boundaries.

108. COMMUNIST SOCIETIES IN THE U.S.S.R. AND EASTERN EUROPE

Stalinism in the Postwar Years

In March 1953 Russia's twentieth-century Peter the Great died. Like his eighteenth-century tsarist predecessor, Stalin had a massive impact during his almost 30 years in power. He was responsible for industrialization in the 1930s, the rallying of the country in the Great Patriotic War, the expansion of the nation's borders, the consolidation of Communist regimes in eastern Europe, and the emergence of the Soviet Union as a nuclear power. But the human costs of the Stalinist transformation of the country were staggering. Millions had fallen victim in the 1930s to his forced collectivization of the countryside and the ensuing famine, and additional millions had died as a result of his purges. Western and Soviet scholars alike have estimated the total figure of Stalin's victims at least as high as 20 million, quite apart from the millions of lives lost in the Second World War. Because the earlier civil war and war communism under Lenin had also taken millions of lives, the Communist regime from its emergence in 1917 to its demise in 1991 must be counted among the costliest experiments in social engineering in all history.

The Stalinist terror had continued during the war. Entire ethnic groups like the Crimean Tatars and the Volga Germans, suspected of collaboration with the Nazis, were forcibly moved east to Siberia. Mass | **Stalinist terror**
deportations took place from Estonia, Latvia, and Lithuania, the three Baltic republics that had been formally annexed in 1940. At the war's end, returning Soviet soldiers who had been prisoners of war and civilian deportees forced to work for the Nazis in Europe were sent off to labor camps because their exposure to other European societies made them suspect. The unbridled authority of the secret political police (the NKVD, later the KGB) continued to increase, and the network of forced labor camps grew in size. Stalin's personal suspicions, growing sharper with the passage of the years, filled even his closest associates with dismay. In later years, in a freer atmosphere both before and after the dissolution of the U.S.S.R., Russians debated whether Stalin's dictatorship represented a logical outgrowth of the Bolshevik Revolution itself or was his own personal distortion.

Controls over intellectual life in the postwar years took on a vehemently nationalistic and xenophobic tone; deviations from Stalin's "line" in economics, music, genetics, history, and linguistics were forbidden. An officially inspired anti-Semitism, thinly disguised as anti-Zionism, accused Jewish intellectuals of being "rootless cosmopolitans." The political police meanwhile fabricated conspiracies to justify the terror. In the fictitious "doctors' plot," officially announced in early 1953, a score of Jewish doctors were arrested for plotting to poison Stalin and other Kremlin leaders; one month after Stalin died, his successors withdrew the charges and freed the imprisoned physicians.

Khrushchev: The Abortive Effort at Reform

After Stalin's death the party leaders resolved to exercise collective control, determined that no single leader should again dominate party and government. In the struggle for power, however, authority gradually shifted to Nikita S. Khrushchev. Outwardly jovial and ebullient, Khrushchev was a tough party stalwart who had enforced Stalin's purges in Ukraine and had long been a member of the Central Committee and Politburo, but he was shrewd enough to recognize the need for change.

CHRONOLOGY OF NOTABLE EVENTS, 1945–1962

1945	The UN is established at a conference in San Francisco
1947	Secretary of State George C. Marshall announces U.S. plan to aid the rebuilding of Europe
1948–1949	American airlift of supplies sustains West Berlin during Soviet blockade
1949	The Soviet Union successfully tests an atomic bomb
1949	United States and western Europe create NATO
1949	Mao Zedong and the Communist Party proclaim the People's Republic of China
1950–1953	Korean War demonstrates new American policy to "contain" communism
1953	Death of Stalin opens new era in Soviet and East European history
1956	Unsuccessful revolts against Soviet control in Poland and Hungary
1957	Six western European nations establish a new Common Market for trade
1958	France establishes the Fifth Republic with Charles de Gaulle as president
1962	French war in Algeria ends with recognition of Algerian independence

In part to win allies against those in the party who were opposed to change, Khrushchev encouraged a greater measure of cultural and intellectual freedom—a "thaw." He put restraints on the still formidable powers of the political police. He surprised many with an attack on Stalin's record. In a speech to the twentieth party congress in 1956, he officially revealed or corroborated the "crimes of the Stalin era," making partial but nonetheless startling disclosures of the Stalinist terror. Stalin had been personally responsible for the purges and executions of the 1930s, and millions of victims had been innocent of the charges against them; his most intimate colleagues had lived in fear for their lives. Khrushchev also revealed Stalin's initial loss of nerve and ineptitude at the time of the German invasion in June 1941.

Khrushchev's "thaw"

Although Khrushchev criticized Stalin, the thaw in Soviet society was never systematic or thorough. In 1958 Boris Pasternak was forbidden to accept the Nobel Prize in literature because his novel, *Dr. Zhivago,* by stressing individual freedom, implicitly condemned the oppressiveness of Soviet society. But in 1962 Alexander Solzhenitsyn was permitted to publish his *One Day in the Life of Ivan Denisovich,* a depiction of human suffering in the forced labor camps. Khrushchev continued the de-Stalinization campaign. Cities named in Stalin's honor were renamed: Stalingrad, the most famous, became Volgograd. Stalin's body was removed from the mausoleum on Red Square, where it had lain next to Lenin's, and buried outside the Kremlin Wall.

Decentralization

For the economy Khrushchev pressed decentralization, attempting to loosen tight central economic controls by creating regional economic councils and offering factory managers greater autonomy and incentives for efficiency and profitability. Meanwhile the country successfully tested the hydrogen bomb; launched its first space satellite, Sputnik, in 1958; and built its first intercontinental ballistic missiles. The Soviet economy was second only to that of the United States in gross national product, though it lagged far behind in the production and consumption of

The Cold War did not end after the death of Joseph Stalin, but the new Soviet leader Nikita Khrushchev spoke of "peaceful coexistence" with Western nations and even traveled to the United States. Wearing his Soviet medals, Khrushchev appears in a congenial mood during a White House meeting in 1959 with the American President Dwight Eisenhower and Vice President Richard Nixon.
(©Sovfoto/Getty Images)

modern consumer goods. Within a decade, Khrushchev boasted in the early 1960s, the Soviet economy would surpass the American. The stress on heavy industry and on military expenditures meant continuing privation for the ordinary citizen, and the emphasis on quantity to the neglect of quality concealed deep flaws in the system as a whole.

Khrushchev's most ambitious effort lay in agriculture, the weakest sector of the economy ever since Stalin's forced collectivization. His agricultural reforms did little to alter the bureaucratized system of collective and state farms, however, or to inspire the collective farmers to increase their output. For the party itself he unsuccessfully sought fixed terms of office for important party posts. Few of his reforms were acceptable to the government and party bureaucrats, who saw their privileged positions threatened and who mustered opposition to his "hare-brained" schemes.

Khrushchev pursued a truculent foreign policy. Proclaiming that war was not inevitable with the United States and other capitalist countries, he spoke of "peaceful coexistence," and relations for a time improved. But the Cold War conflicts by no means disappeared. In 1960 he scuttled a summit meeting with Allied leaders and in 1962, following new tensions in Berlin, Khrushchev overreached himself in a confrontation with the United States during the Cuban missile crisis (to be described in a subsequent chapter). His boastfulness and recklessness, his retreat in Cuba, the failure of his agricultural and other economic policies, and his attempt to reform the party itself led to his downfall. In 1964 the party leadership ousted him from

Khrushchev's fall

office. He lived quietly in Moscow until his death in 1971. In the post-Stalin era, a reformer did not necessarily have to fear for his life, but there were clear limits to the reforms the party and bureaucracy would tolerate. Leonid I. Brezhnev, who had helped engineer Khrushchev's downfall, soon emerged as the new Soviet leader.

Eastern Europe: The Decades of Dictatorship

Although nothing like the Russian Revolution of 1917 erupted in Europe after the Second World War, communism made dramatic advances in central and eastern Europe through the Red Army's military presence and the support given to local Communist leaders. Eleven European states and 100 million Europeans fell under Communist-style governments. The areas considered in 1919 by the Allied peacemakers to be a protective buffer against Bolshevism were now under Communist domination.

The three Baltic states, Estonia, Latvia, and Lithuania, came under Soviet control under the terms of the Nazi-Soviet pact, and in 1940 they were incorporated into the U.S.S.R. as Soviet socialist republics. Later, in the sweep of military operations during the last months of the war, Poland, Hungary, Romania, Bulgaria, and Czechoslovakia fell into the orbit of Soviet influence. East Germany, initially part of the joint Allied occupation of Germany, was shaped into a sixth Soviet satellite as the German Democratic Republic. Yugoslavia and Albania, liberated by their own partisan leaders rather than by the Red Army, were governed by Communist regimes but with looser ties to the Soviet Union and soon broke with the Soviets. Despite its defeat in the Soviet-Finnish War in 1940, Finland escaped Communist domination. Accepting its wartime territorial losses, it maintained its independence by a cautious neutrality in foreign policy and a discreetly correct relationship with the Soviets. Austria, after a decade of joint occupation by the four Allied powers, gained independence as a neutral state in 1955.

Soviet satellites

Consolidation of Communist Control

The Soviets consolidated control in eastern Europe in stages. Soviet military occupation made it possible for local Communist leaders, many returning from exile in Moscow, to dominate Left coalition governments. In the early coalition governments everywhere, the Communists shared power but held the key ministries of interior, propaganda, and justice, and controlled the police, the army, and the courts. Individuals alleged to have been "fascist" or to have collaborated with the Nazis were barred from public life and from voting; the loose definition of "fascist" and "reactionary" barred many who were only anti-Communist. In the first elections, in Poland and elsewhere, purges and disfranchisement made a mockery of Stalin's pledge at Yalta to hold "free and unfettered elections" in eastern Europe. Protests by the United States and Great Britain only hardened the Soviet position.

Agrarian reform and nationalization

The new regimes confiscated and redistributed large estates and put uncultivated land to use, so that 3 million peasant families acquired about 6 million acres of land; the agrarian reforms were the final blow to the landed aristocracy that had once ruled in eastern Europe. They also nationalized the economy. As they struggled with postwar reconstruction, the new regimes had lent a sympathetic ear to the American invitation in 1947 to accept Marshall Plan aid. But Stalin blocked their participation in the Marshall Plan, fearing that the East European countries would drift into the Western economic orbit.

After the summer of 1947, wherever non-Communists were still strong, the Communists ousted their political rivals and banned or reduced to impotence all other political parties. In Czechoslovakia the coalition government lasted longer than elsewhere but fell victim to a Communist coup in February 1948.

With the Communists in control, the leaders of the opposition political parties were forced into flight, imprisoned, or in other ways silenced. The new regimes, notably in Poland and Hungary, clashed also with the Roman Catholic Church; high-ranking prelates were brought to public trial and imprisoned, and church property was confiscated. The Communist leaders themselves soon became Stalin's victims. From 1949 to 1953, reflecting the repression in the Soviet Union in Stalin's last years, purges, arrests, trials, confessions, and executions occurred in the highest ranks of each party. Leaders were accused of nationalist deviations and of conspiring with Tito, the independent-minded Communist leader of Yugoslavia.

The new "people's democracies" took steps to collectivize agriculture in countries where peasants had long struggled to gain more control over the lands on which they worked. Collectivization was often resisted, however, and agriculture in the people's republics, as in the Soviet Union, remained the weakest part of the economy. Farmers diligently cultivated their individual plots *Collectivization* of land but worked reluctantly on the large collectives. All of the East European societies also entered a new phase of industrialization. But the emphasis on heavy industry rather than consumer goods and the pressures to complement the economy of the Soviet Union severely limited the improvement of East European living standards—an enduring economic problem that ultimately weakened the internal political power of every eastern European Communist regime.

The Soviets formalized their economic relationship with eastern Europe through the Council for Mutual Economic Assistance, but the *Economic and* Council (established in 1949) never worked as cooperation among *political cooperation* equals. The Soviets provided low-cost raw materials and oil and provided a large market for East European goods, regardless of their quality, but much of the economic cooperation principally benefited the Soviet Union. Militarily, the Warsaw Pact, signed in 1955, brought the six East European countries together into a mutual defense alliance, and Soviet troops remained stationed in eastern Europe in large numbers.

Yugoslavia, freed from the Nazis largely by its own partisan armies, made a remarkable show of resistance to the Soviets. The Yugoslav Communist leader, Marshal Tito, kept a tight grip on the multinational state but loosened centralized controls over the economy and abandoned collectivization of agriculture. He pursued an independent foreign policy, openly defied Moscow, and took his stand with the neutralist nonaligned nations of Asia and Africa. The first major Communist figure to declare his independence from Moscow, Tito established a model of national autonomy for other Communist leaders and parties to follow.

Ferment and Repression in East Germany, Poland, and Hungary, 1953–1956

The changes in the Soviet Union after Stalin's death directly affected the Soviet satellites. The East Europeans chafed at the collectivization of agriculture, forced industrialization, austere living standards, subservience to the Soviets, and harsh rule by Stalinist-type leaders. An initial outburst, riots in East Berlin in June 1953, was quickly suppressed. New ferment rose to the surface, however, after Khrushchev denounced the brutal

The demand for political reforms spread across Hungary during the fall of 1956. Emboldened by changes in Communist Poland and by the policies of the Hungarian reformer Imre Nagy, the people of Budapest protested the Soviet Union's repressive control of their economy, fought with the Communist state's security forces, and tore down this statue of Joseph Stalin. The Soviets responded with a decisive military intervention. Nagy was secretly tried and executed, and the new Soviet-supported Hungarian regime crushed all anti-Communist dissent.

(©Hulton Archive/Getty Images)

character of the Stalin dictatorship and, in an attempt to win back Yugoslavia, made the official concession that "different roads to socialism" were possible. This concession and his de-Stalinization speech in 1956 opened a Pandora's box; undermining Stalin's infallibility undermined Soviet infallibility as well.

<table>
<tr><td>

Revolt in Poland and Hungary

</td><td>

In 1956 open revolt broke out in Poland and Hungary. In Poland, where national sentiment and church attachments ran deep, pressures for internal freedom and for independence from Moscow led to riots and demonstrations. The Communist leader Wladyslaw Gomulka

</td></tr>
</table>

relaxed political and economic controls, halted collectivization, improved relations with the church, and took steps to loosen the bonds to Moscow. The country welcomed an alternative to direct Soviet control. Khrushchev threatened military action but backed down. For a few years, Gomulka curbed police terror and created a freer atmosphere, but the reform era was short-lived, and Gomulka's regime controlled Poland with growing repression throughout the 1960s.

In Hungary, in 1956, events took a tragic turn. When news of Gomulka's success in Poland reached Budapest, demonstrations broke out; young rioters even toppled a statue of Stalin. The reform-minded Communist leader Imre Nagy, who had earlier been driven from the premiership, returned to power. His reform program and release of political prisoners ignited pressures not only for democratization and parliamentary government but also for the severance of ties to Moscow. Alarmed, the Soviets forced the party leadership to remove Nagy from power and to replace him with the more subservient János Kádár, who accepted Soviet intervention. Khrushchev dispatched troops, tanks, and artillery to suppress the "counterrevolution" and reestablish Communist rule. Severe reprisals followed. Nagy himself was imprisoned, then tried and hanged, and his body was thrown into a mass grave. In the wake of the repression, 200,000 Hungarians fled into exile, mainly to the United States, a larger number than at any time since the crushing of the European revolutions of 1848–1849. The Soviet tanks in Budapest weakened any remaining illusions about the liberalism of Stalin's successors, provoked international condemnation, and drove many Communists in western Europe and elsewhere to renounce their affiliations with Communist parties.

By the late 1950s the Soviet Union and the United States had therefore established opposing "spheres of influence" in eastern and western Europe, but these arrangements became relatively stable during the Cold War because neither superpower was able or willing to challenge the ascendancy of the other power within its own European sphere. Although the Americans and their western European allies harshly condemned the Soviet repression in Hungary, for example, they did not take steps to intervene with military force. The Cold War thus never evolved into a new international war on the European continent, despite the bitter confrontations, mutual suspicions, and ongoing arms race.

In this same era, however, both the Europeans and the Americans became involved in wars outside of Europe, especially when the expanding anticolonial movements were viewed as part of a global communist challenge to either the European imperial systems or the interests of the United States. Most of Europe's far-flung Asian and African colonies faced new anticolonial and nationalist agitation after the Second World War—agitation that developed into prolonged guerrilla wars in places such as Vietnam and Algeria. These campaigns against European empires often became entangled in the wider conflicts of the Cold War; and the new nations that emerged from the struggles for decolonization also became new sites for the interplay of global political forces and for the destabilizing social transitions of the turbulent world economy.

 Suggested Further Readings can be found in the ebook, on Connect, or online at www.mhhe .com/kramer12e.

Chapter 23

DECOLONIZATION AND THE BREAKUP OF THE EUROPEAN EMPIRES

Among all of the global, political, and cultural changes in the three decades after 1945, nothing was more revolutionary, more dramatic, or perhaps more unexpected in Europe than the rapid and almost complete demise of the European overseas colonial empires. Although all of the European nations that held colonial empires were weakened or even defeated during the various phases of the Second World War, Britain, France, the Netherlands, Belgium, and Portugal still governed large parts of the world's population in 1945. Within 30 years, however, these colonial empires all disintegrated. Hundreds of millions of people around the world became citizens of new states whose governments, economies, and cultures became independent after long periods of European colonial control; and European interactions with the peoples of their former empires entered a new era of postcolonial exchanges in which Europe's global ascendancy came to an end.

The Second World War reinforced nationalist agitation for independence and freedom. It was difficult to wage war in the name of self-determination and democracy, often with the colonized countries as supportive participants and allies, without recognizing the contradictions of colonialism. Colonized peoples were claiming the very rights that the anti-fascist Allies had advocated during the recent world war. The Japanese conquests in Asia had also undermined the image of European invincibility. After the war the Europeans, economically exhausted, learned that they could rule their empires only at prohibitive military cost and only by ignoring their own condemnations of the racist regime in Nazi Germany and their own professed ideals of democratic self-government.

Contradictions of empire

In some instances the colonial powers, bowing to agitation for independence, liquidated their colonial holdings without armed struggle, as in the British withdrawal from the Indian subcontinent in 1947. Elsewhere the European powers withdrew only after protracted bloody wars, as in the case of the Dutch in Indonesia, the French in Indochina

Chapter emblem: Independence parade in Kuala Lumpur in 1957. (©Keystone/Hulton Archive/Getty Images)

*Revolutionary wars
in Asia and Africa*
and Algeria, the British in Malaysia, and the Portuguese in Angola and
Mozambique. The United States also participated in the transformation
of colonialism. It granted independence to the Philippines, changed
Puerto Rico's status into a new kind of "commonwealth" territory, and
admitted Alaska and Hawaii as new states of the federal union, but it also waged a long,
unsuccessful war in the 1960s against a communist-nationalist movement in Vietnam that
had earlier driven out the French. The last prominent vestiges of the European empires
in Asia disappeared when Britain surrendered Hong Kong to China in 1997 and Portugal
transferred Macao to China in 1999.

The Europeans also withdrew from Africa and from the various post-1919 "mandates"
that they had received from the League of Nations after the breakup of the Ottoman Empire
in the Middle East. By the mid-twentieth century, nationalist movements had emerged throughout this region, challenging the weakened European powers and demanding the establishment
of new African and Arab states as well as the creation of an independent Israel. European
governments lacked the political will and the resources to maintain imperial rule in their
African colonies and Middle Eastern mandates, but the transitions in this region—as in parts
of Asia—were often delayed by widespread violence and local wars.

The French resisted the nationalist upsurge in Algeria, the British suppressed anticolonial militants in Kenya, and the Portuguese fought to keep their colonies in Angola and

*Africa and the
Middle East*
Mozambique, but the independence movements would ultimately manage to free every African country from European control. Meanwhile,
the Arab countries that emerged from the European mandates and
colonial systems in North Africa and the Middle East entered into a
prolonged conflict with the new Jewish state of Israel, which was established in 1948 after
the British withdrew from the mandate they had exercised over Palestine. The creation of
Israel represented the triumphant fulfillment of a Zionist movement that had grown
steadily in Europe since the late nineteenth century and gained new support after the
genocidal Nazi Holocaust, but it also brought about the displacement of a large Palestinian
Arab population and a series of regional wars that would repeatedly involve the governments and peoples of Europe. The legacy of Europe's entanglement in the Middle East
and the former Ottoman Empire would therefore remain an important component of
European international affairs long after the earlier mandates and colonies had dissolved
into independent states and national economies.

The breakup of the European empires in the second half of the twentieth century led
to the largest liberation of colonized peoples and transfer of political power in all of
human history. This era could, in fact, be called "The Age of the Asian and African
Revolutions." Extending and revising the ideas of the earlier "Age of the Atlantic Revolutions," the twentieth-century upheavals destroyed previously existing colonial systems,
overthrew "old regime" governments, and claimed everywhere to represent the national

New nations
sovereignty of oppressed peoples. The processes of decolonization
eventually contributed to the emergence of over 100 new nations—a
political upheaval that must count among the most far-reaching consequences of the two world wars, and especially of the second. Like the earlier postcolonial
states in the Americas, many of the new nations were still-fragile political entities rather
than coherent national communities with shared cultures, languages and traditions. By
the late twentieth century, however, they were internationally recognized as independent
sovereign states and as members of the United Nations.

Although the new nations broke free from European political control, Europe's colonial legacy was still influential in many of the postcolonial states, partly because older

The British departure from India in 1947 may have been the most momentous transition from European colonialism to national independence in all of Asia. The presentation of the new Indian flag at this Home Guard ceremony in Mumbai was one of countless symbolic affirmations that a new era had begun. New problems soon emerged, but Britain was relinquishing its long-held imperial power to intervene in other societies and to control the governments of other peoples.

(©Keystone/Hulton Archive/Getty Images)

colonial borders were mostly retained as new national boundaries and partly because European colonial languages were often used as cultural tools for building national unity in multilingual societies. More generally, however, many people in the former colonies maintained long-established connections with European institutions and schools, migrated to join family members in Europe, or continued to sell goods and commodities to European consumers. The end of colonialism, in short, opened a new phase of European exchanges with the non-European world, but it by no means ended the many economic and cultural interactions that had deeply influenced European societies during every era of modern global history. This chapter focuses on the diverse history of the most significant anticolonial movements and transitions to independent statehood between the late 1940s and 1970s, by which time the European control of colonized territories and peoples had almost completely disappeared.

109. THE EMERGENCE OF INDEPENDENT NATIONS IN SOUTH ASIA AND SOUTHEAST ASIA

The End of British Rule in India and Pakistan

The end of British rule in India, the largest and most populous of all colonial areas ruled by Europeans, was epoch-making. Unfortunately, it fueled an explosion of ethnic and religious conflicts on the Indian subcontinent. The Indian National Congress, founded in 1885, had developed strength in the interwar years under the leadership of Gandhi and Nehru. The Congress Party leaders demanded independence but also wished to avoid social revolution in the complex multiethnic country. Along with the British-trained Indian civil service, they considered themselves well prepared to govern an independent state. But the Muslim League, founded in 1906, claimed to speak, under Muhammad Ali Jinnah's leadership, for millions of Muslims unwilling to live in an India dominated by the Hindus and the Congress Party. The Muslims insisted on their own national state, rooted in Islam. The Congress leaders, in contrast, pressed for a unified, secular India, with religion separated from politics and with freedom of worship for all religions. British colonial administrators sought to maintain political peace by negotiating with both the Muslim League and the Congress Party, but there was clearly no way for the British to satisfy both factions.

During the Second World War India supported the British, but at the same time the Congress Party and the Muslim League stepped up a "quit India" campaign. To retain Indian support for the war effort and to counter Japanese anti-Western propaganda, the British pledged independence. At the war's end, the British under Labour Party leadership were poised to honor their pledge, but the Congress Party and the Muslim League continued to have irreconcilable differences as plans were developed for an independent Indian state. To end the impasse the British decided on partition. In 1947 Britain granted independence to two nations: to India, predominantly Hindu, with a population of 350 million at the time, which became the Republic of India; and to Pakistan, mainly Muslim, with a population of 75 million, which became the Islamic Republic of Pakistan. Large Muslim populations were concentrated in two widely separated regions of Britain's former Indian Empire, and Pakistan was established as a state with two disconnected parts, West and East Pakistan, separated by a thousand miles of Indian territory. About 60 million Muslims were also left in India, which helped keep India the multireligious secular state that Gandhi and Nehru desired. Ceylon (later renamed Sri Lanka) and Burma (later called Myanmar) in South Asia also received independence from Britain at this time.

Partition of India

The partition, overly hasty and ill-conceived, led immediately to violence and a vast social upheaval. Independence in August 1947 brought with it terrible communal riots between the Hindu and Muslim communities costing at least a million lives in a matter of weeks; some 17 million Hindus and Muslims were caught up in mass expulsions and turbulent migrations. In the worst of the tragedies, in the northern province of Punjab, Hindu and Sikh religious zealots ambushed and slaughtered trainloads of Muslim refugees fleeing west to Pakistan, and Muslim fanatics did the same to Hindus and Sikhs migrating east to India. Gandhi, while praying for civil peace, was himself assassinated in 1948 by a Hindu extremist protesting his program for religious toleration. Only after the uglier features of the communal warfare subsided could the tasks of governing begin.

Jawaharlal Nehru, the British-educated leader of the Congress Party and a close associate of Gandhi, became the leader of the new Indian government, serving as prime minister from 1947 until his death in 1964. Nehru set the country on the path of British-style parliamentary democracy and even a kind of Fabian socialism. With no effective opposition, Nehru's program was more paternalistic than democratic. In economic matters Nehru, a moderate socialist who had studied law and economic theory in Britain, understood the need for private capitalist enterprise; but he believed that economic planning, government controls, and the nationalization of key industries were also necessary. Under his leadership a modern industrial India with a mixed economy began to take shape and in many ways grew impressively in the years that followed.

Nehru's paternalism

Meanwhile, the British-designed partition of South Asian territories and populations did not solve the problems of Hindu-Muslim relations. India and Pakistan fell into a recurring pattern of conflict, centered in part on the former princely state of Kashmir (officially, Jammu and Kashmir) in the Himalayas. Although three-fourths of the population were Muslim, the Hindu maharajah opted to take Kashmir into India. Open fighting over the issue of Kashmir broke out between India and Pakistan in 1948, and tense relations and intermittent conflicts continued over the following decades. War again broke out over Kashmir in 1965–1966, ending in an uneasy truce. In 1971 India went to war with Pakistan, but this time to support Bangladesh in its bloody war of secession from Pakistan. Although the British could not be blamed for all of the enduring conflicts between India and Pakistan, the continuing tensions between these two nations showed how the borders and politics of the postcolonial states were still affected by British colonial policies for many decades after the imperial system was dissolved.

Pakistan's independence leader Muhammad Ali Jinnah was, like Nehru, a British-educated lawyer. He was by no means an Islamic extremist and might have made a significant difference in the country's history, but he died shortly after independence, and his successor was assassinated. Despite the machinery of British-style parliamentary democracy, the Islamic Republic of Pakistan soon succumbed to military rule and over the years oscillated between periods of military rule, restoration of constitutional government, which generally meant civilian misrule, and the return of military dictatorship. By the end of the century military dictators had run the country for half of its years of independence.

The awkward postcolonial arrangement for uniting the widely separated Muslim populations of South Asia in a single nation collapsed in violence. In East Pakistan, which had been carved out of the old Indian state of Bengal during the hasty British partition in 1947, most of the population lived in congested, impoverished conditions that fueled political and social resentments against the West Pakistani leaders who dominated the government of Pakistan. These resentments exploded into a war of secession in 1971, when East Pakistan proclaimed its independence and with the help of Indian military forces established the new state of Bangladesh (or "Bengali nation"). The postcolonial, two-state political settlement was thus permanently altered, and yet Britain's earlier colonial influence on South Asian politics, cultures, and economic life never completely disappeared. There was also a continuing migration of South Asians into the cities of modern Britain, so that by the early twenty-first century more than 3 million people of Indian, Pakistani, or Bangladeshi origin were living around London or in the English midlands. This growing South Asian population played an increasingly prominent role in Britain's commerce and culture, bringing new global trade as well as diverse religions, foods, music, and transnational communities into British society.

Bengali secession and war

The British Withdrawal from Burma (Myanmar), Malaysia, and Singapore

Burma, India's neighbor to the east, embarked on a unique path of isolation and repression after it gained independence in 1948. Britain had annexed the country to its Indian Empire in 1885; and gradually, over the next half century, the British built a railway network, developed the country's mining and forest resources, and encouraged rice cultivation. Burma became for a time the world's largest exporter of rice. In the interwar years the British encouraged limited self-government but also imprisoned nationalist leaders such as Aung San, who pressed for immediate independence. After the Japanese invasion of Burma in the Second World War the nationalist leaders took up arms against the Japanese but also took advantage of the Japanese conquest to advance Burma's independence from Britain.

Burmese independence

After the war the British recognized Burma's independence, but Aung San, who was to become prime minister, was assassinated and his associate, U Nu, a devout Buddhist

**The British partition of its South Asian colonial empire into mostly Muslim Pakistan and preponder-
antly Hindu India led to chaotic mass migrations and expulsions as people fled across the new borders
in all directions. These trains in Amritsar, India, were swamped with Indian refugees who were trying
to move to other Indian cities after fleeing from West Pakistan in October 1947.**
(©Bettmann/Getty Images)

and somewhat doctrinaire socialist, became the first prime minister. In contrast with the
pattern in many former British colonies, almost all connections with European commerce
and culture were severed. There was little money, however, so it was difficult to import
machinery and to train workers; "the Burmese path to socialism," as it was styled, became
impossible. In addition to economic chaos, there was recurring unrest among the ethnic
minorities who made up about one-third of Burma's population. Many of these minorities
were incensed by Nu's plan to make Buddhism the official state religion, and the government's suppression of minorities such as the mostly Muslim Rohingya people would
continue long after independence and into the twenty-first century.

   Despite the official political framework of a multiparty parliamentary democracy, the
military exercised a parallel power with the civilian authorities. As ethnic insurgencies
became more threatening to the governing elite, the army head General Ne Win staged
a military takeover in 1962. He would retain power for the next 26 years in a one-party

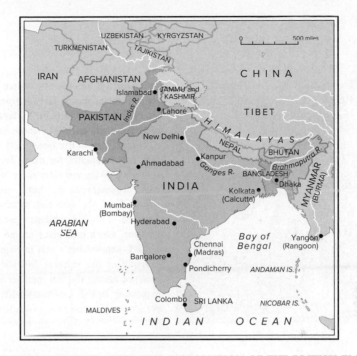

THE INDIAN SUBCONTINENT AFTER THE DISSOLUTION OF THE BRITISH EMPIRE, 2000
The map shows nations that emerged from the dissolution of the British Empire in South Asia. East Pakistan was part of Pakistan until its war of secession in 1971 led to the establishment of an independent Bangladesh; Pakistan and Bangladesh are predominantly Muslim. India is predominantly Hindu, but large Muslim and Sikh minorities live there. The political ascendancy of a Hindu nationalist party in the 1990s altered India's pluralistic political culture and also changed the names of cities that were known during and after the British colonial era as Bombay, Calcutta, and Madras (Mumbai, Kolkata, and Chennai). Political movements have changed other colonial-era names in the region, including the name of the country now called Myanmar, which was known as Burma throughout the era of British control and early independence. The island called Ceylon in the time of the British Empire is now Sri Lanka. The dispute between India and Pakistan over the status of Jammu and Kashmir has remained unresolved. Conflicts in this disputed territory, intensified by the development of nuclear weapons in India and Pakistan, as well as international wars in Afghanistan and continuing internal conflicts in Sri Lanka and Myanmar, made South Asia one of the world's politically volatile regions in the early twenty-first century.

state still dedicated to pursuing the "Burmese path to socialism," but in effect a military regime that carried the country into deeper isolation. Seeking to affirm its complete break from the earlier colonial era, the government later changed the nation's name to Myanmar. Movements for democratic reform were stifled; and few countries of the former British Empire moved away from Britain as quickly or decisively as Burma.

Meanwhile, a different movement toward nationhood developed in Malaysia. In the Malayan Peninsula British plans for independence after the Second World War were delayed because of tensions between the country's Muslim Malay majority and its sizable Chinese and Indian minorities. These large minority populations had lived in Malaysia since the nineteenth century when the British had imported workers from China and India to work in the tin and rubber mines. The Chinese had come to play a dominant role in the economy. At the same time a militant Communist movement had emerged, and the British for several years fought a

Malaysian independence

This image of an elegantly attired British High Commissioner waving farewell from his airplane as British rule ended in Malaya became an often-repeated, post-1945 scene in all parts of Asia and Africa. Europeans left colonies that they had dominated for many decades or even centuries, giving way everywhere to new national political movements that both rejected and borrowed from the imperial systems that they replaced. This independence parade in Kuala Lumpur, which took place on the day after the High Commissioner's exit in September 1957, exemplifies the cultural hybridity that often emerged among the new member nations of the expanding British Commonwealth.

(©Central Press/Hulton Archive/Getty Images; ©Keystone/Hulton Archive/Getty Images)

Communist insurgency. In 1957, with the rebellion mostly subdued, Britain granted independence. Five years later Malaya joined with Singapore and other former British dependencies to create the Federation of Malaysia.

Singapore withdrew in 1965 to become a small island-nation with a flourishing modern economy and high living standards but governed by a semi-authoritarian, paternalistic regime under Lee Kuan Yew. Singapore thus resembled other East Asian countries that made rapid economic advances without establishing full-fledged democracies. British culture remained influential in Singapore, however, and English became the official language—a cultural strategy that unified diverse ethnic groups and effectively linked Singapore to the global economy. There was no absolute repression, but no genuine democracy either. Singapore nevertheless differed from Burma and other inward-looking countries by embracing international economic institutions and maintaining strong connections with British culture.

Singapore

The transitions out of the British Empire thus took different forms, but the British surrendered almost all of their vast Asian Empire within about a decade after the end of the Second World War. However, most of the former British colonies in Asia (as well as in Africa, the Caribbean, and the Pacific) agreed to retain a voluntary association with Britain and each other in a new Commonwealth of Nations. Both Malaysia and Singapore, for example, became members of this Commonwealth, which grew into an association of over 50 independent nations. The Commonwealth did not force its members to act in concert on international issues, but it helped to promote useful interchange between the diverse peoples who had once lived within Britain's far-flung empire.

The Dutch Withdrawal from Indonesia

Another major European empire in Southeast Asia, the Dutch East Indies, also faced new opposition and came to an end. Agitation for independence, as in India, went back to pre-1914 days, but the Indonesian Nationalist Party, founded in 1927, and a growing Communist Party made little political progress in the interwar years. The Japanese could thus appeal to anti-Western sentiment during the Second World War, and they found Indonesian nationalist leaders who were willing to collaborate in their military occupation of the East Indies. At the same time, a broad nationalist movement emerged to oppose and resist the occupation. Once the Japanese were ousted at the war's end in August 1945, before the Dutch could return, the Indonesian Nationalist leader Sukarno (Indonesians often use only their family name in public life) proclaimed the country's independence. The Dutch soon tried to reassert their colonial control, however, and they stubbornly fought the nationalist movement during a bloody four-year struggle before finally ceding independence in 1949.

Sukarno began with a parliamentary constitutional program, but in 1959 he dissolved the Constituent Assembly and governed in the following years under a populist dictatorship that he called "guided democracy"; and he sought to play a prominent, independent role in Cold War diplomacy.

Sukarno's "guided democracy"

Sukarno became one of the chief spokesmen for the postcolonial and developing nations of Asia and Africa. He hosted the meeting in Bandung in 1955 at which leaders of 29 of the new nations celebrated their new sovereignty, condemned Western imperialist and capitalist exploitation, and pledged neutralism and nonalignment in the Cold War. For a time Sukarno managed to work with and control Indonesia's large Communist Party, but in 1965 leftist army officers attempted a coup. A relatively unknown army leader,

Indonesian President Sukarno emerged from the independence movement against the Dutch Empire to become a leader of the world's new and developing nations during the era of decolonization. He is shown here in 1955, addressing the international meeting at Bandung, where representatives of nonaligned nations affirmed their independence, pledged to remain neutral in the Cold War, and condemned the legacies of Western imperialism.

(©Lisa Larsen/The LIFE Picture Collection/Getty Images)

General Suharto, suppressed what was alleged to be a Communist rebellion, but he also ousted Sukarno. Suharto ruled Indonesia for the next 32 years, continuing the economic and cultural transitions from Dutch colonialism that had begun under Sukarno. The Suharto regime, which began with the brutal repression of the Communists, maintained power through a centralized, authoritarian political system. Yet Suharto (like a number of other undemocratic leaders in postcolonial nations) was steadfastly supported by Western governments during the Cold War as a bulwark against the Asian influence of Communist China and as an alternative to the kind of postcolonial movement that had emerged from the French Empire in Indochina.

The Independence Movement in Indochina

The French colonial empire also fell apart in the decades after the Second World War. France tried to repress the nationalist movements that arose in both Asia and Africa, but its military campaigns could not stop the anticolonial surge that quickly spread across the whole French Empire. France offered new autonomy to the colonized people of Indochina at the end of the Second World War, proposing that they occupy a more autonomous position within a French federation. Leaders in Cambodia and Laos accepted this plan, but Vietnam demanded full independence. When France rejected this demand, the Vietnamese launched a well-organized armed resistance in 1946, and French armies fought against the Communist-led Vietnamese forces for more than seven years.

The Communist leader Ho Chi Minh, who headed the independence movement in Vietnam, had spent years in London and in Paris (where, as noted earlier, he had first called for the "self-determination" of Indochina during the Versailles peace conference and witnessed the founding of the French Communist Party in 1920). He later lived in Moscow and in China. He returned to Vietnam in 1941, organized a Vietnamese independence movement (the Viet Minh), and mobilized guerrilla armies to fight the Japanese. At the war's end he proclaimed Vietnam's independence, and when France rejected the Vietnamese declaration of independence, Ho turned his armies against the French. Because the Communists led the anticolonial movement, the French could claim that they

The French defeat at Dien Bien Phu in 1954 effectively ended the era of European colonialism in Indochina. Vietnamese soldiers led these captured French troops toward a prison camp in the last days of a war that showed the limits of European power and overturned the social-political hierarchies of France's collapsing Asian Empire.

(©AFP/Getty Images)

were fighting to stem the tide of world communism, not to preserve nineteenth-century colonial privileges. Yet communism here, as often in Asia, gained local support because it mobilized nationalism, anticolonialism, anti-Westernism, and genuine popular discontent.

Communism and imperialism

Under President Eisenhower the United States, anticolonial but ready to champion anti-Communist causes in the Cold War, aided the French financially but refrained from open military intervention. The war drained French morale and resources. In the spring of 1954 at the very time that an international conference was meeting in Geneva to arrange a settlement in Indochina, the French army suffered a severe defeat at the battle of Dien Bien Phu. The conference, with French acquiescence, recognized the independence of Vietnam, as well as of Cambodia and Laos.

Vietnam was provisionally partitioned at the 17th parallel into a northern and southern sector until elections could be held for the entire country, but the elections never took place. Neither the Hanoi-based Communist regime in the north nor the Western-backed anticommunist regime in the south viewed the 1954 Geneva plan as an acceptable political settlement, and a civil war soon began. The United States, taking up the struggle that France had abandoned, became deeply involved in the war by the early 1960s. The American government saw the war in Vietnam as part of a global Communist challenge that had to be contained, so that a conflict that began in the anticolonial upheavals of the late 1940s became one of the most protracted and costly conflicts of the Cold War era. Meanwhile, France's entire colonial empire in Indochina—like the British and Dutch empires in the same region—had given way to new national states. Such transitions redefined Europe's interactions with Asian peoples and societies, but the irreversible collapse of empires also transformed national identities within those European countries (such as France) that had long viewed their colonial systems as tangible and symbolic expressions of their national power and influence in global affairs.

110.   THE AFRICAN REVOLUTION

Africa is a large continent, considerably larger than North and Central America combined. Its estimated population grew from 220 million in 1950 to more than 1 billion in the early twenty-first century, so that it has had one of the fastest-growing populations in

North and sub-Saharan Africa

the modern world. A distinction may be made between North Africa and sub-Saharan Africa. North Africa, stretching from Mauritania and Morocco to Egypt, mostly Muslim and Arab, belongs as much to the Mediterranean world (and even more to the Islamic Middle East) in ethnic composition, culture, geography, and history. The history of northern Africa has always included commercial, cultural, and population exchanges with southern Europe. In sub-Saharan Africa the population is predominantly black, and in addition to large Islamic communities, there are many people who adhere to African animist faiths or to Christianity. An ethnographic and linguistic map of Africa would reveal hundreds of different ethnic groups and some 800 African languages, of which about 50 are spoken by a half million people or more. A large number of Africans since the colonial era also speak English or French, and there are also numerous descendants of European and South Asian settlers and immigrants, most notably in South Africa. Europe's involvement with sub-Saharan Africa, which first developed with the early modern trade in gold, ivory, and enslaved people, was most pervasive during the era of modern European imperialism, but European influences and exchanges remained significant in many of the region's postcolonial societies.

In 1945 the map of Africa was scarcely different from what it had been in 1914. All of Africa was European-governed with the exceptions of Egypt, Liberia, and Ethiopia (the latter had regained its independence from Italy during the Second World War). By the early 1960s, however, there were 35 independent states, and most of Africa was either

Independence movements

independent or close to achieving independence from dissolving European empires. By the early twenty-first century there were 53 independent African states, making up more than a fourth of the membership of the UN. Of the 53 states, all but five were in sub-Saharan Africa.

The cultures in these new states generally differed from European nationalist descriptions of national cultural coherence (which was actually rare in European countries too). Africa's territorial boundaries, as we have seen, were drawn hastily during the era of European imperial expansion in the late nineteenth century, and the new states usually accepted these earlier political boundaries. Most of the new states therefore contained highly diverse ethnic and linguistic groups who lacked the national affinities that are associated with the concept of a modern, imagined "nation-state." At the same time, people who shared cultural or ethnic similarities were frequently distributed over two or more countries. The age of European imperialism also left the African states economically underdeveloped, dependent on world markets, and with little political experience within constitutional systems or large self-governing institutions; the very rapidity of the transition to independence added to their difficulties. Ethnic or civil wars and regional conflicts marked much of Africa's first half-century of independence. The following survey of anticolonial movements and the emergence of postcolonial African states can only sketch the broad outlines of decolonization, which sometimes led to protracted wars with European colonial powers and always led to complex political, economic, and cultural transitions.

French North Africa and the War in Algeria

During the Second World War the Allied leaders had made various commitments to self-determination. With Italy defeated (and Ethiopia liberated), the wartime Allies in 1951 granted independence also to the former Italian colony of Libya, and the British took steps to end what was left of their privileged position in Egypt. These events galvanized French North Africa, where Arab nationalist leaders, often French-educated, had pressed for independence since the 1920s. In Morocco, Tunisia, and Algeria—the Maghreb, as these Arab states of northwest Africa are called—the nationalists mounted a vigorous campaign. Morocco and Tunisia were not outright colonies but French protectorates under their traditional rulers, the Moroccan sultan and the Tunisian bey. The French in 1956 granted independence to both countries. The Moroccan sultan became king as a constitutional monarch, but as the years went by, the monarchy increasingly enlarged its powers. Tunisia became a republic and was governed for its first 30 years by Habib Bourguiba, who introduced many democratic reforms (including rights of divorce for women) but insisted on being named president for life. In both countries the push for political, economic, and cultural liberalization continued long after independence, often against counterpressures from Muslim traditionalists.

Algeria's story was very different. In the early nineteenth century the French had invaded and occupied Algeria, which was part of the weakening Ottoman Empire. After several brutal military campaigns Algeria became a fully controlled French colony. Later in the nineteenth century French and other Europeans settled there in substantial numbers, creating large immigrant communities that came to dominate the political and economic life of the country and its Arab population. The French meanwhile provided a few limited measures for Algerian self-rule and representation along with a promise that further concessions could be made when the country became fully assimilated to French and European ways. Some additional political concessions were granted in the interwar years, but after 1945 Algerian nationalists pressed for full independence. Although Algeria was represented in the French legislature in Paris, the suffrage in Algeria was heavily weighted in favor of the European settlers to the distinct disadvantage of the Arab majority. Of the 9 million or so inhabitants, about 1 million were Europeans. Many of the *colons*, or European settlers, mostly

French colons in Algeria

French, belonged to families that had lived in Algeria over several generations. Because the Europeans controlled the economy and owned most of the land and industry, they feared for their political and economic privileges if Algeria were cut loose from France and governed by an Arab Muslim majority that had long lived under discriminatory laws and

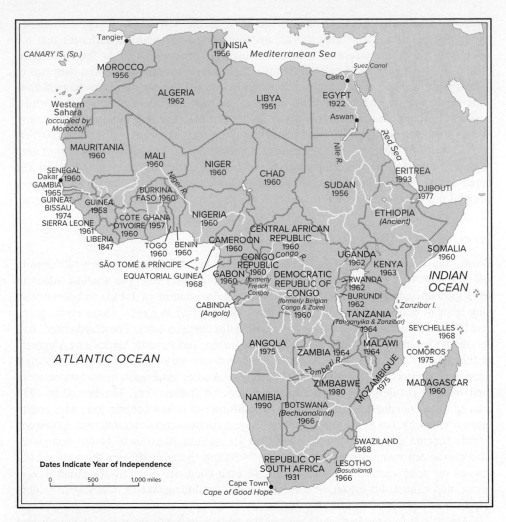

AFRICA AT THE END OF THE TWENTIETH CENTURY
This map shows the emergence of independent African states (with dates of independent nationhood) and may be compared with earlier maps for precolonial Africa (p. 681) and for Africa in 1914 at the height of European imperialism (p. 684). The first of the new sub-Saharan, postcolonial states was Ghana, which gained independence from Britain in 1957 and took its name from a medieval African kingdom that had been located further north. The last transitions to independent nationhood (after long struggles) extended from Zimbabwe (1980) and Namibia (1990) in southern Africa to Eritrea (1993) in northeastern Africa. By the end of the twentieth century all of the European colonial empires had disappeared and the white-controlled apartheid regime in South Africa had given way to a nonracial, democratic political system.

unequal social opportunities. The French military suppressed initial postwar uprisings, but the nationalist movement grew, and in the autumn of 1954 the National Liberation Front (FLN) launched a fierce guerrilla war against the French.

The French-Algerian War

The French-Algerian war lasted 7½ years, involving at its peak 500,000 French troops and provoking sharp political divisions within France itself. There were numerous demonstrations and protests, some of which led to violence in French cities. At one such demonstration in Paris, in 1961, the police attacked a large crowd, killing dozens of protestors in what later came to be called the Paris "massacre." Meanwhile, the Algerian armed forces received aid and support from Egypt and other Arab states. Torture and cruelty became common on both sides. In the spring of 1958, during a French cabinet crisis in which the Europeans in Algeria feared that a negotiated settlement might be arranged, an insurrection by army leaders and diehard European settlers in Algiers brought political changes in Paris and General Charles de Gaulle's return to power. To the dismay of the army leaders, however, de Gaulle unexpectedly arranged a cease-fire and soon spoke of autonomy and self-determination for the Algerians. In 1962, in a referendum, he won the backing of the French electorate for full independence. Army leaders thereupon rebelled, and some of his closest former associates helped form a secret army of terrorists who bombed and killed, and even attempted his assassination. Nevertheless, de Gaulle pressed on with negotiations for Algerian independence, and in 1962 French rule ended. The long and brutal war had cost the lives of 10,000 French and 100,000 Algerian combatants as well as many thousands of Algerian civilians.

After independence there was a mass exodus of Europeans from Algeria. Some of the immigrants (who were known as *Pieds-Noirs* in France) remained bitter critics of de Gaulle's Algerian policies, but most people in France and Algeria were grateful that de Gaulle had negotiated an end to the ordeal and withdrawn the French army. The French accepted the loss of Algeria and other parts of their empire in West Africa, recognizing that a large overseas colonial system was no longer in France's economic interests or essential for the nation's influence in Europe and the wider world. With a prospering economy in the later 1960s, the French turned their attention to other matters. Although deeply hostile to European colonialism, the new Algerian government accepted French technical assistance for the development of the country's extensive oil and natural gas resources. The FLN, for its part, retained power and governed under a military-dominated one-party regime for the next 30 years, gradually producing political and economic resentments that would lead to future internal conflicts. The long period of French control had ended, however, and Algeria could move on to a new era of political and cultural independence. More generally, after 1962 the Algerian revolutionary movement became a widely studied example of anticolonial campaigns, in part because the French-educated writer Franz Fanon wrote about the war's cultural and psychological meaning for colonized persons in his influential book *The Wretched of the Earth* (1961)—a work that continued to attract international attention during the postcolonial era. Fanon was originally from the French island of Martinique, but he participated in the Algerian Revolution and drew on his training as a psychiatrist to describe the corrosive effects of violence in colonial societies and anticolonial warfare.

Algerian independence

End of British Rule in West Africa: Ghana and Nigeria

In North Africa nationalist agitation for independence, already under way in the interwar years, might have been expected, but south of the Sahara the anticolonial movement was less advanced before the Second World War. Here black African populations still lived in colonial empires that Europeans had carved out either in the colonial age that opened in the fifteenth century or in the "scramble for Africa" in the brief decade and a half of European imperialist competition after 1885.

Yet independence movements, barely in existence before 1945, rapidly developed after the end of the Second World War. The British first resisted the mounting nationalist pressures, imprisoning or exiling

From colonies to independent republics

The Algerian war for independence from France was one of the most bitter, protracted struggles for decolonization, in part because a large French population had lived in Algeria for several generations and had representatives in the French legislature. France sent about 500,000 soldiers to maintain control of Algeria, including these troops in the city of Oran. Despite this large deployment, the French army could not defeat the Algerian FLN or regain control of the Algerian countryside. Algeria became an independent nation in 1962.

(©Keystone/Getty Images)

nationalist leaders, but then, recognizing the strength of the liberation movements and the pressures of their own postwar economic problems, they decided in the 1950s to change their imperial policies. Britain thereafter moved quickly to grant autonomy to its colonies, which soon became dominions and then independent republics.

The Gold Coast (soon renamed Ghana) was the first British colony to win independence, and its history both before and after independence exemplified political and economic patterns that would reappear in many of Britain's African colonies. The British initially tried to repress a militant civil disobedience movement led by the nationalist leader Kwame Nkrumah, whom they imprisoned. But in 1951 they freed Nkrumah and conceded self-government. Nkrumah's party overwhelmingly won the elections that followed, and he became prime minister. In 1957 the colony won full independence with dominion status, and in 1960 Nkrumah transformed it into a republic with himself as president. The country shed the name of Gold Coast, which was too closely identified with the centuries of imperialist exploitation and the slave trade. It called itself Ghana, recalling an African kingdom somewhat to the north

Nkrumah's Ghana

Ghana was the first African nation to gain independence from Great Britain during the 1950s. The president of the new nation, Kwame Nkrumah, appears in this picture, waving to supporters at a national celebration in 1957. Nkrumah led the struggle for independence and became a key figure in the Pan-African movement, but his autocratic methods of governing and his extravagances provoked a military coup that ousted him from power in 1966.
(©Bettmann/Getty Images)

that had flourished from the sixth to the eleventh centuries. Nkrumah quickly gathered extensive power into his own hands, banned opposition parties, governed autocratically, and declared himself president for life. The early postcolonial history of Ghana thus showed an antidemocratic political evolution that would reappear often in Africa (and in Asia): Charismatic nationalist leaders who led the struggles for independence repeatedly turned into authoritarian dictators once independence was won, and the party of the independence movement often became the basis for one-party governments.

Nkrumah adopted an anti-Western stance, championed a nonalignment policy in the Cold War, and sought a leading role in a pan-African movement, hosting in 1958 the first All-African People's Congress in Ghana's capital, Accra. Nkrumah's arbitrary rule, unbridled extravagances, and cult of personality provoked growing opposition, however, and military leaders ousted him in 1966. There then followed a series of military coups until a more democratic system of multiparty elections developed in the 1990s. Every phase of Ghana's postindependence history—especially the gradual evolution from authoritarian rule toward more democratic government in the early twenty-first century—resembled general trends that could be seen in much of postcolonial Africa.

Similar political patterns developed in Nigeria, which was the largest British-governed colonial territory and population in Africa (its population would exceed 150 million by the early twenty-first century). British-educated Nigerians, who had pressed for political representation in the 1920s, stepped up pressure against the British colonial system after the Second World War. Britain granted independence in 1960, and in 1963 Nigeria became a republic with a constitution, political parties, and guarantees of civil rights. The postcolonial political system soon broke down, however, because of regional and ethnic tensions, a series of military coups, and a secessionist movement that led to a devastating civil war in the late 1960s. Despite this internal violence, the recurring coups, and the conflicts between religious and ethnic groups, Nigeria—like Ghana—moved eventually toward a more stable democratic system in the late 1990s, supported in part by a booming oil industry. The Nigerian social elites also retained various links with British society, and postcolonial Nigeria was one of the largest member states in the British Commonwealth of Nations.

Nigeria

End of British Rule in East Africa: Kenya and Uganda

In East Africa, especially in Kenya, the independence movements after 1945 encountered obstacles, but the struggles to establish new nations moved through the usual political stages to achieve sovereign statehood. In the 1920s and 1930s young nationalist leaders, many of whom, like Jomo Kenyatta, had studied in Britain, agitated for land reform and African representation in government. After the Second World War a movement for independence led by Kenyatta and his party gathered momentum. European settlers, who had arrived during the early twentieth century and developed large coffee and tea plantations, stubbornly resisted pressures for independence. The Kenyan militants responded with violence and acts of terrorism, to which the European settlers retaliated with their own mounting cycles of violence. The British declared a state of emergency and imprisoned or removed from the troubled area many of the nationalist leaders. Eventually, however, the British faced up to the inevitable movement toward decolonization. They ended the state of emergency, released Kenyatta, and in 1963 granted Kenya independence. Over 55,000 Europeans left the country. Kenya became a republic in 1964 with Kenyatta as its first president. Until his death 14 years later he completely dominated political life, following the all-too-familiar pattern of the independence leader's turning dictator after independence. Like other new African leaders he championed pan-Africanism and neutralism in the Cold War.

Kenyatta and Kenyan independence

Uganda, which Winston Churchill once described as the "pearl of Africa" because of its natural beauty, won independence in 1962. It, too, encompassed many ethnic groups, who had been brought together in a British protectorate during the 1890s. Some permanent European settlers established large plantations, but the African farmers mostly cultivated small plots of cotton, tea, and coffee. Meanwhile, following the kind of migration that the British often facilitated between various parts of their global empire, South Asians settled in Uganda to play a leading role as merchants. In 1921 Britain established a legislative council, but the first African members were admitted only in 1945, and not until several years later did they receive a substantial number of seats. Pressure for independence

Uganda

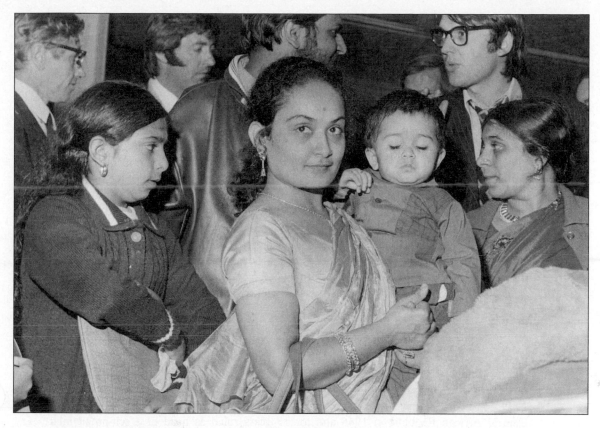

Uganda's postcolonial dictator Idi Amin expelled thousands of Asians who had played a key role in the country's colonial economy. The refugees pictured here left Uganda in 1972 and were among the first to arrive in London, where they joined a multicultural population that brought new cultural perspectives and practices into late twentieth-century British society.
(©George W. Hales/Hulton Archive/Getty Images)

continued to develop until the British officially withdrew in the early 1960s. A new constitution, approved in 1963, transformed the Ugandan state into a republic, which fell almost immediately into the hands of dictatorial leaders, including (after 1971) the notorious Idi Amin. Centralizing all power under his own control, Amin brutalized the country for eight years with repressive policies that shocked both the recently departed British and all of Africa. As many as 300,000 Ugandans may have lost their lives in executions and massacres. Professionals and intellectuals fled the country; and in 1972 Amin expelled some 60,000 Asians, mostly the Indian community, which had been a strong presence in the country's commerce. These exiles scattered in all directions, forming a new South Asian immigration into Britain and joining the far-flung Indian diaspora of the 1970s.

Amin was finally overthrown in 1979 with the help of outside forces from Tanzania, but the history of his Ugandan regime had shown how the transitions to postcolonial independence could carry former British colonies into authoritarian quagmires, some of which lasted for

Problems of decolonization

decades. The British people and government had reached a general consensus, by the 1960s, that their vast empire must be dissolved. Yet the messy conflicts of decolonization in both western and eastern Africa showed (as in Asia) that the British imperial system had never fully established the public institutions, economic opportunities, mass education, and political values that would be needed to sustain stable democratic states in the postcolonial era.

The French Sub-Saharan Empire

The French, largely as a consequence of the bloody war in Algeria, dissolved the remainder of their vast colonial empire in sub-Saharan Africa peacefully. After the Second World War they had hoped that a French-educated and assimilated African elite would maintain ties to France in a loosely organized French Union. They gave the African colonies representation in the French National Assembly and promised self-governing institutions, but control remained centralized in Paris, and by the mid-1950s the African colonies, inspired by nationalist movements elsewhere, pressed for independence. De Gaulle recognized the inexorable pressure for independence and offered the sub-Saharan colonies their freedom of choice. By 1960 all 15 colonies had chosen independence, though these new nations—like the former British colonies—were often slow to develop democratic political institutions.

French aid and cooperation

Many of the African countries that emerged from the French Empire retained close ties with France for economic aid and cultural cooperation. France remained a strong presence among the African francophone nations (and indeed the strongest presence of all the European countries on the African continent), training the armies of the new states, lending financial assistance, and taking a leading role in economic development.[1] On numerous occasions after 1960 the French intervened in Africa with military force. In 1979, for example, they helped overthrow a brutal dictator who had seized power in the Central African Republic in 1966 and for 13 years ruled as head of a self-proclaimed Central African Empire; and they later sent troops to intervene in other conflicts in places such as Chad and Ivory Coast.

France thus continued to see itself as a key international power in African affairs. The French organized the African Financial Community, which helped stabilize African currencies in the postcolonial era, and became the largest donor of aid to the continent. While some African leaders criticized such actions as neocolonialism, others viewed the French presence more as a partnership than an intrusion. As elsewhere in Africa, the early aspirations for democratic government in the former French colonies were often crushed by civilian or military dictatorships, even if the degree of repression varied. Here too the independence party frequently became the sole legally recognized political party. Presidents concentrated power in their own hands, often holding office for 20 years or more. Meanwhile, the economic and political problems in France's former colonies contributed to a continuing migration of people from West Africa to France, where the immigrants became increasingly prominent in the social and cultural life of French cities.

---

[1]The francophone, or French-speaking, sub-Saharan African states emerging from the French colonial empire in 1960 were Benin (until 1975 called Dahomey), Cameroon, Central African Republic, Chad, Republic of Congo (Brazzaville), Gabon, Guinea, Ivory Coast, Madagascar (or Malagasy Republic), Mali, Mauritania, Niger, Senegal, Togo, and Burkina Faso (until 1984 called Upper Volta). Comoros became independent in 1975; Djibouti in 1977. Morocco, Algeria, and Tunisia, in North Africa, are also part of francophone Africa as former French protectorates. The former Belgian colonial territories must also be included: the Democratic Republic of Congo (once the Belgian Congo, and from 1971 to 1997 called Zaire), and Burundi and Rwanda (once Belgian trusteeships).

Independence Movements in the Belgian Congo and Portugal's African Colonies

European decolonization also took place in the African territories of Belgium and Portugal. Both of these smaller European countries had sustained a certain international status by holding large colonies in Africa, and influential groups in each nation had long-standing interests in the colonial economies. The demise of the Belgian and Portuguese colonies thus became a final sign of the disintegrating European imperialism in Africa.

The Belgian Congo was a byword for European imperialist exploitation and cruelty in the late nineteenth century. Some of the most abusive features were remedied before 1914, but political control remained concentrated in Brussels and little was done to prepare the large colony (it was 80 times the size of Belgium) for self-government. Agitation for independence intensified when the neighboring French Congo, its capital at Brazzaville, won independence in 1960 and became the Republic of Congo.

Faced with pressure for independence, the Belgian government, which had first proposed a transition period of 30 years, decided against gradualism and in 1960 announced its intention to withdraw in six months' time. Chaos followed. The key nationalist leaders were at odds with one another, ethnic and regional antagonisms ran deep, and no one was prepared to carry out governmental responsibilities. The army mutinied, and the soldiers turned against the European officers who had remained to command the new nation's military forces. Belgian paratroopers hastily flew back, and a UN international military force was sent to restore order. The troubled situation became even more volatile in 1961 because the main leftist leader, Patrice Lumumba, was assassinated (with evidence of American connivance) and because of a threatening Soviet-Western confrontation within the context of wider Cold War conflicts in Europe. The Soviets charged the Europeans and their American supporters with deliberately creating the chaos so that the Europeans might return.

Eventually, in 1965, Colonel Joseph Désiré Mobutu established a dictatorship that would last for the next 32 years. He at once nationalized the large mining enterprises and set out to break the country's historical connections to Belgian colonialism. To symbolize the new era, | *Cold War entanglement*

all geographical and personal names were Africanized. He himself took the name Mobutu Sese Seko. The country became Zaire, as did the famous river. The capital city of Leopoldville and the second largest city, Stanleyville, both carrying names reminiscent of European imperialism, became Kinshasa and Kisangani; Lake Albert became Lake Mobutu. (After the Mobutu era, the lake was renamed again as Albert and Zaire became known again as the Democratic Republic of the Congo.) Although he sought to efface the former European presence in his country, Western governments continued to support Mobutu in future years because of his anticommunism and his willing- | *Mobutu and Zaire* ness to provide a base for operations against leftist movements and governments in neighboring countries such as Angola. Once again the postcolonial transition out of a European empire became entangled in the global conflicts of the Cold War; and this broader international context also affected the anticolonial war in Angola.

Among all the European colonial powers in Africa, Portugal, itself under authoritarian dictatorship until 1974, clung longest to its colonies, symbols of grandeur from the days of Vasco da Gama's late fifteenth-century explorations and the early age of European expansion. To retain Angola, on the southwestern | *Portuguese withdrawal from Angola* African coast, and Mozambique, on the southeastern, both of which at

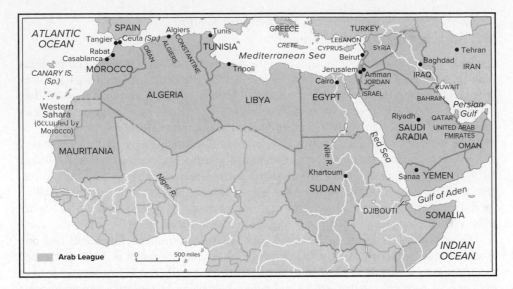

THE MODERN ARAB WORLD
The Arabic language zone is one of the most extensive in the world, reaching from the Atlantic Ocean to the Persian Gulf. In 1945 the Arab states formed a league, which was to provide an Arab counterweight to Europe's twentieth-century influence in the region and which eventually came to have 22 members. The Arab League proved to be rather loose and its members often disagreed, but after 1948 all Arab nations expressed varying levels of suspicion and hostility toward the Israeli state in the midst of an otherwise predominantly Arab world.

one time had been flourishing centers of the slave trade and had been under Portuguese rule for over 400 years, the Portuguese dictatorship stubbornly suppressed anticolonial revolts that broke out in 1961. As the fighting dragged on, disaffected officers and soldiers in the army, radicalized by the prolonged colonial war, turned against the Portuguese regime and overthrew the authoritarian government in 1974. The following year Portugal granted independence to Angola, Mozambique, and its smaller African colonies.

A new postindependence war soon began in Angola as Soviet-supported Marxist forces fought American-supported, anti-Marxist groups for control of the country, but the only remaining European empire in Africa had finally collapsed. Hundreds of thousands of Portuguese migrated to Portugal or to cities in South Africa, where the last white-controlled government in sub-Saharan Africa would hold on to power until the early 1990s.

The African Revolution against European colonialism now came to an end, at least as a political/military upheaval; and like earlier anticolonial revolutions in the Americas and in Asia, it ushered in a new era of independence and national sovereignty. European cultures and trading systems were still influential in much of postcolonial Africa (as in the earlier postcolonial societies of the Atlantic world), but the new nations did not quickly construct democratic governments, protect human rights, resolve regional conflicts, or bring about significant changes in the economic conditions of the most impoverished social classes. There were new civil wars and social conflicts that could be compared to the political and cultural struggles that had also developed in other places after European colonial powers withdrew or, indeed, that had long afflicted societies within Europe itself. Yet the African revolutions, for all their problems and disappointments, represented another major phase in Europe's changing relations with the wider world—relations that were now finally moving beyond the long, complex history of European empires.

111.   EUROPE AND THE MODERN MIDDLE EAST

The Islamic and the Arab World

In the Islamic societies of the modern Middle East the era of European colonial domination also came to an end, and a powerful renewed sense of Muslim identity emerged. Most people in Islamic societies wanted

Islamic identity

to share in the economic and material advances that had enriched modern Europe, but many Muslims also wanted to develop or reform their societies without assimilating European or American cultural patterns. Religious and cultural traditions thus provided alternatives to Europeanizing reforms and influenced the political institutions in the diverse, new independent nations. In many cases strong tensions developed as Islamic traditionalists resisted secular changes. Turkey made a concerted effort to protect the secular society decreed by its founder, Kemal Atatürk; but elsewhere, in Saudi Arabia, Iran, Afghanistan, Sudan, and other countries, strong Islamic movements tried to establish governments that defended religious values or even created virtual theocracies, thereby affecting the interactions between Islamic societies and Europe.

The Arab states that emerged from the collapse of the Ottoman Empire at the end of the First World War became League of Nations mandates under British or French administration, with the expectation

The Arab states

of one day receiving independence. Egypt became nominally independent in 1922 and Iraq in 1932, although the British retained treaty rights in each until after 1945. The other Arab states became independent during or after the Second World War, when the British and French ended their mandates. In 1945 Egypt, Iraq, Lebanon, Saudi Arabia, Syria, and Jordan formed the influential League of Arab States, or Arab League. Libya, after gaining independence in 1951, also became a member. In the decades that followed, newly independent Arab states as well as the Palestinian National Authority joined so that it grew to have 22 members by the early twenty-first century.

Although Europeans sometimes imagined a united Arab or Islamic culture, the Arab world and diverse Islamic societies were far less unified

Arab rivalries

or coherent than generalizing theories suggested. Divisive rivalries persisted between Sunni and Shiite Muslims and between secular and religious political movements. The pan-Arabism advocated by Egypt's Colonel Nasser in the 1950s failed to rally lasting support. A United Arab Republic joining Egypt and Syria in 1958 was short-lived. After the Second World War, however, the Arab states found common cause in their opposition to the state of Israel, which itself had emerged as a new sovereign state from a British mandate in the Middle East in 1948. The Arab states viewed Israel as a Western-backed intrusion into their land, and the result was a series of continuing tensions and conflicts that frequently brought wider international forces into play and also affected people in Europe.

The Emergence of Israel

Zionism, evolving in the late nineteenth century as a response to European anti-Semitism, became a movement to establish (or reestablish) a Jewish homeland in Palestine, then part of the Ottoman Empire. A small number of Jewish pioneers from Russia and eastern Europe had made their way to Palestine before 1914. During the First World War, while Britain was at war with the Ottoman Empire, the British Foreign Secretary Arthur Balfour issued the "Balfour Declaration" of 1917, which stated his government's support for "a Jewish homeland in Palestine." In other ways, however, Britain's wartime policies supported

CHRONOLOGY OF NOTABLE EVENTS, 1946–1979

1946	Communist-led independence movement launches war against French control of Vietnam
1947	Britain ends its imperial rule in South Asia, partitioning most of the region into the two new nations of India and Pakistan
1948	Burma gains independence from Britain
1948	Republic of Israel is established in former British mandate of Palestine; Arab states go to war against Israel
1949	Indonesia wins independence from the Netherlands
1954	France withdraws from Indochina; two governments emerge in North and South Vietnam
1954–1962	Algerian nationalists wage war for independence from France
1955	Leaders of 29 "new nations" meet in Bandung, Indonesia, to affirm "nonalignment" in the Cold War and condemn Western imperialism
1956	Britain, France, and Israel attack Egypt after it nationalizes Suez Canal
1957	Ghana is the first British colony in Africa to win independence
1960	France's 15 sub-Saharan colonies complete their voting for independence
1960	Congo gains independence from Belgium, but falls into violent conflict
1963	Federation of Malaysia is established, temporarily uniting Malaya and Singapore after independence from Britain
1963	Kenya wins independence from Britain
1965	Singapore breaks away from Malaysia to become an independent nation
1965	General Suharto overthrows Sukarno; begins 32-year rule in Indonesia
1971	India intervenes militarily to help Bangladesh gain independence from Pakistan
1973	Yom Kipper War: Egypt and Syria fight new war with Israel; conflict leads to Arab oil embargo as a geopolitical weapon, creating an oil crisis in Europe
1975	Angola and Mozambique gain independence from Portugal, completing the breakup of European empires in Africa
1979	Ayatollah Khomeini returns from exile to lead Islamic Revolution in Iran

emerging Arab nationalisms. After the demise of the Ottoman Empire, the British received a League of Nations mandate for Palestine, where a growing number of Jewish settlers arrived throughout the 1920s and 1930s.

The question of Palestine

The whole question of Palestine poignantly and urgently reemerged at the end of the Second World War when the homeless survivors of the Nazi Holocaust, which had all but wiped out central and eastern Europe's Jews, sought out Palestine as a place of refuge. But in deference to Arab protests the British limited immigration from Europe and turned away whole shiploads of refugees. Jewish leaders contested the British restrictions on refugee migrations and pressed their campaign for an independent Jewish state at the UN and among sympathetic American political groups. Meanwhile, some Zionist militants launched more forceful actions within Palestine, resorting at times even to terrorist attacks against British forces and the British mandate government. In 1947 the UN in a vote supported by both the United States and

The creation of the State of Israel in 1948 marked the triumphant culmination of a long-developing campaign in Europe and Palestine to establish an independent Jewish state. The first prime minister of Israel, David Ben-Gurion, who was originally from Poland, joined the Zionist migration to Palestine in the early twentieth century. He is pictured here, signing the proclamation that established the new Israeli state, opened an important new era in Jewish history, and led to a long conflict with the surrounding Arab nations.

(©Universal History Archive/Universal Images Group/Getty Images)

the Soviet Union recommended partition of Palestine into two parts: a Jewish sector and an Arab sector, with the area around Jerusalem under international control.

The Arabs, who had boycotted the UN committee hearings, rejected the partition, complaining that they were being asked to make sacrifices for Europe's persecution of the Jews. Both sides prepared for conflict. On May 14, 1948, when the Zionist leaders proclaimed the Republic of Israel, Israel's five Arab neighbors—Syria, Lebanon, Jordan, Egypt, and Iraq—refused recognition and invaded the new state. The Israelis (as the citizens of the new republic called themselves) not only defended themselves but also counterattacked. In the course of the fighting at least 600,000 Palestinian Arabs fled, or were forced by the Israelis to flee, to Jordan, Lebanon, Syria, and other Arab where they lived in overcrowded refugee camps or joined a growing global Palestinian diaspora. The Israelis withstood the Arab assault and even increased their originally allotted lands before an armistice ended the hostilities in 1949; and Israel emerged from the British mandate and the war as a viable, independent nation.

The New State of Israel

The Israelis saw themselves as creating a Jewish homeland after the Holocaust, so that persecuted Jews in Europe and other parts of the world would never again be without a refuge. Under a Law of Return Jewish immigrants from anywhere in the Jewish diaspora were automatically entitled to citizenship. After independence Israel over the years built a modern, European-style, urban, industrial society with a democratically elected parliament, the Knesset, and a lively political culture. For many years the moderately socialist Labor Party governed. The country provided a large role for labor unions and agricultural cooperatives (famous as *kibbutzim*), extensive health and educational services, and support for scientific and

A Jewish homeland

The creation of Israel and the subsequent Arab-Israeli war of 1948–1949 drove some 600,000 Palestinian Arabs into neighboring countries and refugee camps. These Palestinians were living in 1956 at a camp on the West Bank of the Jordan River—an area that came under Israeli control after the Six-Day War in 1967 and remained a source of international conflict as the Palestinians later sought to establish an independent state in this territory.

(©John Chillingworth/Picture Post/Getty Images)

| Economic growth |

technological research. Implementing European conceptions of a mixed economic system, the Israelis at first developed an economy that was about half government-controlled until a later shift to privatization. Economic development took off swiftly, and industry expanded. Living standards compared favorably to those of western Europe.

Over 2 million immigrants arrived in the decades after 1948. Some Jews continued to migrate from Europe, but many also arrived from the Arab states in North Africa or from Arab and non-Arab Muslim states in Asia, forced to abandon established communities where their families had lived for centuries but where Jews were now persecuted. From 1989 to 1992 about 400,000 Soviet Jews, finally permitted by the Soviet government to migrate, moved to Israel from Russia and other areas of the dissolving Soviet Union. The population of 870,000 in 1948 rose to more than 8 million by the second decade of the twenty-first century.

European Involvement with Later Arab-Israeli Wars

Arab-Israeli wars continued to affect Europe and global diplomacy after the emergence of new Arab states and the creation of Israel. Britain and France, in an early example of European involvement, joined Israel in a brief war against Egypt in 1956. The war erupted as a European response to Egypt's nationalization of the Suez Canal and Egyptian attempts to block Israeli shipping. The American president, Dwight Eisenhower, opposed

British and French troops entered the Sinai Peninsula in 1956 as part of a joint military operation with
Israel to stop Egyptian nationalization of the Suez Canal and to weaken Egyptian President Nasser.
The American government strongly opposed the Suez campaign and took diplomatic steps to bring about
the withdrawal of European forces. These British soldiers were part of the expeditionary force that took
over the road leading to Port Said and thus blocked Egyptian forces from the Suez Canal.
(©Popperfoto/Getty Images)

the British-French intervention, however, fearing the implications for Cold War conflicts
in other regions, the possible effects on NATO, and the threat of a wider war. In a rare
break with its key European allies, the American government demanded that the attack
on Egypt should stop and worked with others to pass a UN resolution
calling for a cease-fire. The assault was therefore suspended and the   *The Suez Crisis*
British-French forces soon withdrew from Egyptian territory.

  After the crisis passed, the United States reaffirmed its support for Israel, but the
Suez Crisis pushed some European states in different directions. France had been a
staunch Israeli ally before and during the Suez crisis. The French had also regularly supplied weapons for the Israeli military, but its policies evolved after Charles de Gaulle
became president in the late 1950s. De Gaulle sought to expand French influence and to
restore a regional balance of power by developing closer relations with postcolonial Arab
nations, especially in the aftermath of France's withdrawal from Algeria. The Soviet

Union, another original backer of the Jewish state, also changed its strategic goals in the later 1950s and sent arms to Arab nations. The American government, seeking to prevent the expansion of Soviet influence, pledged to support countries in the region that would oppose communism. For the Europeans and Americans alike, the Middle East became another contested site in the Cold War struggle for global advantages.

Israel's later wars with Arab countries in 1967 and 1973 also had wider international effects. In the brief Six-Day War against Egypt, Syria, and Jordan, Israel gained control over the Sinai Peninsula and Gaza Strip (formerly held by Egypt) and the West Bank of the Jordan River (formerly held by Jordan). Palestinians in the newly occupied territories developed a stronger nationalist identity, opposed the development of new Jewish settlements on these lands, and demanded an independent state for themselves. The conflict spread into Europe as radical Palestinian groups began to launch terrorist attacks against Israelis, including a deadly attack on Israel's athletes at the Olympic Games in Munich in 1972. Another Arab-Israeli war broke out in the following year, when Egyptian and Syrian forces attacked Israeli forces on the Jewish holy day Yom Kippur. The Israelis recovered swiftly from the attack, but the League of Arab States responded to Israeli

Arab Oil Embargo

military advances by introducing an embargo on oil shipments to Western nations. Although the embargo was aimed specifically at the United States and at a few European countries such as the Netherlands, and although it was lifted early in 1974, the price of oil quadrupled. This rapid price rise disrupted the European economy and deeply affected global commerce. The war's economic impact therefore lingered for years after the Americans mediated an end to the fighting. Israel withdrew from the east bank of the Suez Canal, but continued to occupy most of the Sinai Peninsula until the early 1980s and the Gaza Strip until 2005.

Other conflicts continued to generate violence and terrorism across the Middle East long after the Yom Kippur War, the oil embargo, and Israel's withdrawal from the Sinai Peninsula. Each new crisis, however, seemed to confirm that Europe's influence in the region had declined, that the Israeli-Palestinian conflict defied all outside attempts to mediate a solution, that Europe would remain vulnerable to fluctuating oil prices, and that refugees from Middle Eastern wars would continue to flee toward Europe. The breakup of the Ottoman Empire after the First World War thus presented people in the Middle East and in Europe with various political challenges and intractable problems that constantly affected later generations, even in the twenty-first century. European societies remained deeply entangled with Middle Eastern history—which continued to affect everything from oil prices and immigration patterns to the threat of terrorist attacks and the rise of new Islamic religious movements in European cities.

The Revolution in Iran

Where change occurred rapidly in the Middle East, it was clear that traditionalists often resented the European and American influence that accompanied modern economic and cultural changes. They opposed secularism and the disruption of older religious and cultural institutions as a Western subversion. Yet most people in other parts of the world were not prepared for the fierce anti-Westernism of the Islamic revolution that erupted in 1979, not in an Arab state, but in Iran, where the principal language was Persian (or Farsi). Iran was a Shiite state, whereas nine-tenths of the Islamic world adhered to the Sunni branch of Islam, but the Shiite revolutionary leaders in Iran helped to foment a new religious revivalism everywhere in the Muslim world.

Foreign domination

Over the centuries of modern history Persia (or Iran, as it was known after 1935) had often faced the disruptions of foreign domination. At the opening of the twentieth century, as we have seen, Britain and Russia, coveting its newly discovered oil resources, divided it into spheres of European influence. After the First World War the British had tried to retain control, but in 1921 an army officer, Reza Khan, seized power, assumed the title of shah, or hereditary ruler, in 1925, and embarked on a program of modernization. During the Second World War, however, in 1941, when some of his machinations brought him threateningly close to the Axis, the British and Russians occupied the country and forced him to abdicate in favor of his son, Muhammad Reza. The young shah identified with western Europe and the United States.

After the war American influence became dominant. When Prime Minister Mossa-degh and a leftist parliament moved to nationalize and control the oil industry in the early 1950s, the shah, with clandestine support from the American CIA, ousted him and blocked the attempt. With oil wealth and extensive American military and economic aid, the shah embarked upon an ambitious development program. The pace and breadth of secularization and economic reforms pleased urban business and professional interests but alienated others, especially in the countryside. Moreover, the shah presided over an increasingly authoritarian regime, crushing opposition and dissent with his secret police. The United States, pleased with the policies of its anti-Soviet ally in a strategic part of the world, ignored the swelling internal restlessness. In 1978 religious-inspired protests and strikes and riots broke out as the opposition coalesced around Islamic clerics. A tidal wave of demonstrations forced the shah to flee the country in January 1979.

In February the aged leader of Iran's Shiite community, Ayatollah Ruhollah Khomeini (ayatollah is the highest rank in the Shiite religious hierarchy), returned to Iran from Paris. The ayatollah had lived in France during the last phase of a 15-year exile (he spent most of these years in Iraq), but he had closely followed the Iranian protests and denounced the shah's pro-Western, anticlerical, and irreligious regime. Ayatollah Khomeini quickly assumed leadership of the revolution and proclaimed an "Islamic republic." Supreme control rested with the ayatollah and his council of religious guardians, appointed to guarantee the new regime's strict commitment to Islam and to ensure control of the revolution through a network of mosques.

Ayatollah Khomeini's "Islamic republic"

The revolutionary authorities forcefully rejected the European and American influences in Iranian society and set out to restore traditional Islamic ways of life. Women were ordered to wear the chador, the traditional long black dress covering them from head to toe. The necktie was outlawed for men, who were also encouraged to grow beards. The authorities banned Western music, classical and popular, from radio and television and enforced the Islamic prohibition on alcohol. Islamic law, to be interpreted by the clerics, took precedence over secular law. Thousands were executed for religious, moral, or political offenses. The ayatollah's theocracy pushed aside moderate leaders, even those who had welcomed the overthrow of the shah. The first president was forced to flee into exile in France; the foreign minister was executed.

Militants, many of them university students, aroused by the ayatollah's fervid denunciations of the United States as "the great Satan," took decisive action on their own. Reacting to the admission of the ailing shah to the United States in the autumn of 1979, revolutionary activists and students seized the American embassy in Tehran and held 50 American hostages for almost 15 months, demanding the return of the shah and his wealth to Iran. The American hostages were finally released in early 1981 (the shah died in 1980), but the new Iranian Islamic Republic continued to repress its internal critics. Meanwhile, the Iranian revolutionaries sought to eradicate secular and Western influences that would never completely disappear from Iranian politics, culture, and economic life.

"The great Satan"

Although the Iranian Revolution mobilized new political movements of radical Muslims in other countries, condemned American policies in the Middle East, and altered the

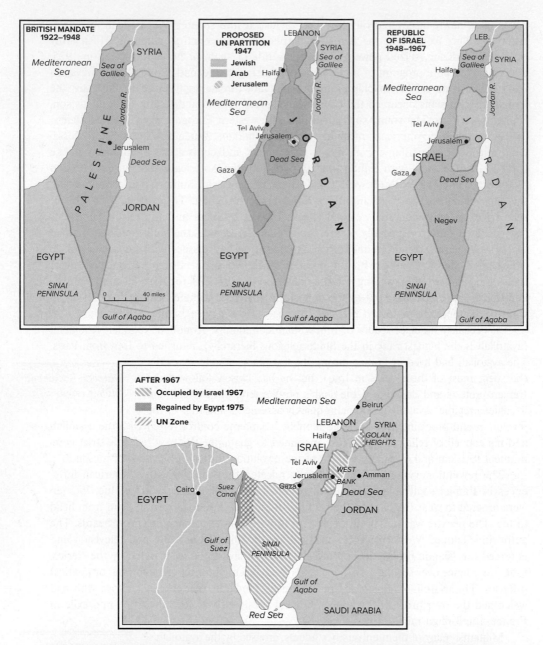

ISRAEL AND ADJOINING REGIONS AFTER THE ERA OF THE BRITISH MANDATE

"Palestine" is the term by which Europeans long designated a small region of predominantly Arab population on the east coast of the Mediterranean. The area belonged to the Ottoman Empire until the end of the First World War. In 1922 the League of Nations made the territory a Mandate of Great Britain, which soon responded to Arab dissatisfactions by placing restrictions on the migration of European Jews, who had been moving into Palestine since the rise of Zionism in the late nineteenth century. After the deaths of millions of Jews in the Holocaust during the Second World War, the Zionist aspiration for an independent Jewish state won new international support, especially in Europe and North America. In 1947 the UN proposed a partition of Palestinian lands to create a new Jewish state and a division of the city of Jerusalem into separate zones. The Arabs rejected this plan, but in the Arab-Israeli war of 1948 the Israelis won control of wider boundaries than those first proposed.

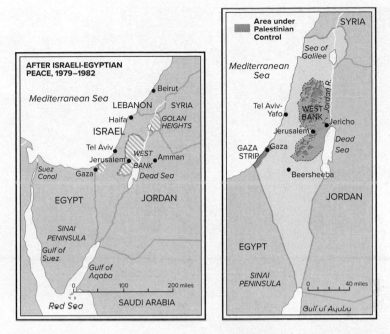

The Arab states still refused to recognize Israel. In the Six-Day War of 1967 the Israelis occupied additional territory, as shown in the fourth panel, labeled after 1967. In 1973, in the Yom Kippur War, Egypt and Syria attacked to regain their lost lands, but Israel defeated them and continued to occupy the Sinai Peninsula and other territories, although Egypt eventually won control of the east bank of the Suez Canal. Under a peace treaty that Israel and Egypt negotiated in 1979, Israel returned the Sinai to Egypt, but retained the small area known as the Gaza Strip. In 1993 Israel agreed to begin withdrawing from some areas of the occupied territories and allow the first steps toward self-government for the Palestinians. A new Palestinian Authority emerged to govern the autonomous Palestinian communities, but a long series of later conflicts and negotiations had still not led to a final peace settlement or an independent Palestinian state in the early twenty-first century. In 2005, however, Israel removed all Jewish settlements and its military forces from the Gaza Strip.

balance of power between the major Islamic states, it may be best understood in relation to modern European history as a final great upheaval in the vast movement toward decolonization that swept across the world between the late 1940s and the late 1970s. Whatever else might be said about the specific ideas and aspirations of the Islamic Revolution, it clearly represented another popular campaign for the expulsion of Western political and economic interests from a society that was long dominated by the outside power of Britain and then the United States. A religious movement that may have attracted much less support in a different context or time therefore generated strong nationalist passions among the huge crowds, political activists, and intellectual elites who saw Islamic clerics as an expression of Iranian national sovereignty and as the leaders of a mass movement for true national independence.

The anticolonial and anti-imperialist movements that developed in South and Southeast Asia during the late 1940s and spread across all of Africa and the Middle East in the 1950s and 1960s ultimately came to a final explosion in the Iranian Revolution of 1978–1979. To be sure, the Iranian anger was directed more at the United States than at Europe. Yet the Iranian critique of modern secular cultures and social practices was also part of a broader rejection of the whole European ascendancy that had held sway over

The revolution in Iran brought on a wave of militant, anti-Western demonstrations. These Iranian women, wearing the chador to assert their strong Islamic values, showed their determined support for Islamic religious traditions and the new political order as well as their opposition to European-style clothing by wielding powerful, modern weapons.

(©Keystone/Hulton Archive/Getty Images)

most of Asia and Africa since the later nineteenth century and that was now ending in the global processes of decolonization. The Islamic themes of the Iranian Revolution and of other radical religious movements in the Arab world differed enormously from the ideas of the secular Communists who led the anticolonial movements in places such as Vietnam, and yet similar challenges to European power and culture could be found wherever anticolonial or anti-Western movements emerged between the 1940s and 1970s. The "Age of the Asian and African Revolutions" changed Europe's position in global history, much like the previous "Age of the Atlantic Revolutions" had transformed Europe's position in the Americas. European culture, science, commerce, and political theories remained powerful forces in the modern world, but Europe's relations with non-European peoples and societies, after decolonization, would never again return to the hierarchical global systems of earlier historical eras.

Suggested Further Readings can be found in the ebook, on Connect, or online at www.mhhe .com/kramer12e.

Chapter 24

COEXISTENCE, CONFRONTATION, AND THE NEW EUROPEAN ECONOMY

We must turn from the breakup of empires to other political and economic changes that affected the internal development of European societies as well as Europe's position in global affairs during the late twentieth century. By the end of the 1950s western Europe and Japan had drawn on American aid and their own technical expertise to rebuild their war-damaged cities and factories. Responding to the new challenges of a bipolar world and the global ambitions of two competing superpowers, western Europe joined together economically in the evolving European Community (EC) and buried many of its old antagonisms. Regions of the world that formerly were part of European colonial empires were everywhere asserting their new social and cultural autonomy. The global economy grew increasingly interdependent and the social effects of economic expansion and contraction reverberated worldwide. Older distinctions between "industrialized" Europe and "nonindustrialized" societies became blurred, and even the Soviet bloc in eastern Europe expanded its trade and financial exchanges with non-Communist countries.

Yet the Cold War continued to manifest itself in an escalating nuclear arms race and in the worldwide confrontation of the two superpowers, each of which attempted to prevent the other from gaining strategic or military ascendancy. The stockpiling of nuclear arms and the development of sophisticated long-range delivery systems led to the accumulation of unparalleled destructive power. The nuclear missiles supposedly were built for deterrence and not for use, and a new kind of balance of power emerged that preserved the peace. The people of Europe (like others around the world) nonetheless lived under the threat of a possible nuclear catastrophe, and neither economic nor intellectual life could fully escape from the global shadow of the Cold War.

As time passed, the phenomenon of bipolarity, or the predominance of the two superpowers, the United States and the Soviet Union, gave way to new global configurations; and Europe gradually became a more independent force within the context of superpower

Chapter emblem: Citizens of Prague celebrate the destruction of a tank in 1968, after the Soviet invasion of Czechoslovakia. (©Reg Lancaster/Hulton Archive/Getty Images)

conflicts. Many Europeans, for example, became strong advocates for human rights, or they protested the escalating arms race that led to the placement of nuclear weapons in the densely populated countries of both eastern and western Europe. But while the charged atmosphere of the Cold War lasted, despite periods of détente, Europeans were forced to live with repeated international crises that were often beyond their control.

112.   CONFRONTATION AND DÉTENTE, 1955–1975

The Soviet leaders who succeeded Stalin after 1953 seemed at times more conciliatory and willing to acknowledge the need for arms control and cooperation in the nuclear age, and there were even recognizable periods of détente, or formal relaxation of tensions. But

Periods of détente

dangerous confrontations recurred, the nuclear arms buildup assumed unprecedented forms and dimensions, and relations seesawed over the next several decades between conciliation and crisis.

By 1955 the Cold War had stabilized, especially in Europe. The North Atlantic Treaty Organization (NATO), strengthened by the West German armed forces, faced the Warsaw Pact nations of the Soviet bloc. The iron curtain still divided Europe, but the threat of direct military confrontation receded. The Western powers and the Soviet Union were even able to agree in 1955 on a treaty with Austria, ending the joint Allied occupation and leaving Austria independent and neutral.

We have seen how Khrushchev had emerged as the dominant Soviet leader after the death of Stalin. Sharp-tongued, volatile, boastful, he announced that the Soviets would

Pressures for coexistence

abandon their revolutionary principles only "when shrimp learn to whistle" and pledged that the Soviets would "bury" Western capitalism. Nonetheless he rejected the inevitability of war and emphasized the "possibility and necessity of peaceful coexistence." President Eisenhower, in office from 1953 to 1961, continued the policy of containment and the American military buildup, but both superpowers recognized the need for coexistence in the nuclear age.

In 1955 President Eisenhower, along with the leaders of Britain and France, met at Geneva with the new Soviet leaders in a friendlier atmosphere than any since the Second World War. Although they reached no new agreements, the American president could speak of "a new spirit of conciliation and cooperation." But tensions mounted over Berlin. The Soviets, who were incensed that East Germans were fleeing in large numbers to West Berlin and then to the Federal Republic of Germany, demanded that the Western powers end their occupation of West Berlin, but Eisenhower forcefully rejected the ultimatum, and the crisis passed. In 1959, when Khrushchev visited President Eisenhower at his weekend retreat in Camp David, they spoke of peaceful coexistence and even of mutual disarmament.

At a second summit conference in Paris, the superpowers continued to recognize their common interests in preserving stability and peace. But by then Khrushchev, under criticism at home and from Mao in China for being too conciliatory toward the West,

Cooperation fades

produced irrefutable evidence of American reconnaissance flights over Soviet territory and broke up the conference. By the summer of 1960 the "spirit of Geneva" and the "spirit of Camp David" had faded. When Khrushchev spoke before the United Nations, he boasted of Soviet arms production and denounced the United States.

The United States, unwavering in its resolve to maintain the defense of western Europe, accepted Soviet hegemony east of the iron curtain. The Americans and their western European allies protested but did not intervene when the Soviets put down anti-government riots in East Berlin, or when the Soviets exerted pressure on Poland to curb its reform movement, or when the Soviets, even more dramatically, sent troops and tanks to crush the Hungarian revolt in 1956 and the Czech attempt to democratize their government in 1968. The United States offered little more than moral encouragement to dissident groups in all of these eastern European states.

At the same time one part of the world after another was brought into the American strategic defense system. American foreign policy in the Cold War remained based on the premise that unrest on every continent was Soviet-inspired—a premise that led the United States to build military bases throughout the world. It was also an overarching geopolitical theory that sometimes prevented Americans from understanding the complex local causes of conflicts within Europe or within postcolonial societies in Asia and Africa. The nuclear arms race continued. In October 1957 the Soviets, to the world's astonishment, demonstrated their prowess in the new era of rocket technology when they successfully launched *Sputnik,* the first artificial satellite to orbit in outer space. A few months later the United States launched its own space satellite, *Explorer I.* The space age had opened, and the military implications of space rocketry quickly became apparent.

American Cold War policy

A new kind of arms race emerged, using the technology of intercontinental ballistic missiles and the idea of "mutual deterrence." Given the destructive capability of the new weaponry, it became impossible to promote a strategy of "massive retaliation." Now that American cities were vulnerable to nuclear destruction, anxiety spread in western Europe that the United States might not so readily defend it. The French president, Charles de Gaulle, voiced such misgivings in the 1960s as he built up a French nuclear force and called for a more independent role for the West Europeans. Rejecting the rigid bipolar patterns of the Cold War and viewing postwar international relations as a traditional struggle between great powers rather than as a conflict of ideologies, de Gaulle urged Europeans to recognize their own spheres of national interest and to promote Europe's reunification—"from the Atlantic to the Urals." He declined to follow the American lead in foreign policy in Europe or elsewhere. Although he kept France in the Atlantic alliance, he withdrew France from the integrated NATO military command in 1966 and pressured NATO into moving its headquarters from French soil. His aspirations for a leadership role on the international scene troubled many Europeans, but he nevertheless articulated European uneasiness with American hegemony over western Europe's policies in world affairs.

A new kind of arms race

The Cold War in the 1960s

The gravest Soviet-American confrontations came during the early 1960s. President John F. Kennedy heightened the rhetoric of the Cold War in these years, proclaiming that the United States "had to pay any price, bear any burden, meet any hardship, support any friend or oppose any foe in order to assure the success and survival of liberty." Kennedy took steps to close what he called a "missile gap" with the Soviets; and shortly after becoming president he supported Cuban exiles who launched an unsuccessful assault on Cuba—where the revolutionary leader Fidel Castro was developing close relations with the Soviet Union. The new tensions spilled over into Europe later in 1961. At a meeting with

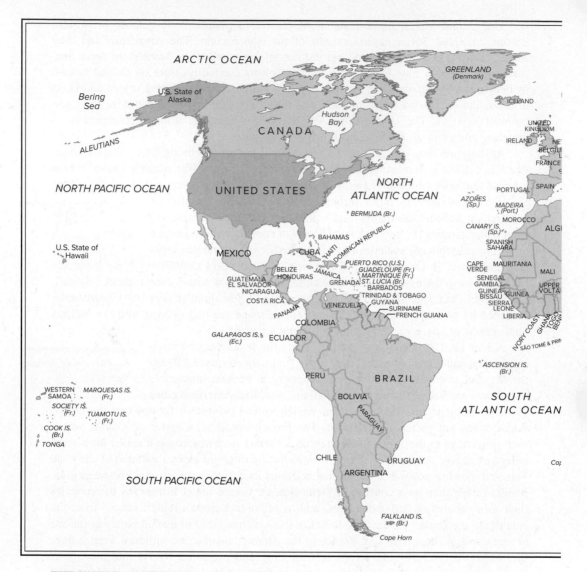

THE WORLD ABOUT 1970

This political map of the world about 1970 shows a number of important changes that reduced Europe's global influence after the end of the Second World War: the breakup of the European colonial empires in Asia and Africa, the emergence of some 50 independent republics in Africa and of several new states in Asia, the emergence of the People's Republic of China, and the peripheral expansion of the Soviet Union.

Kennedy in Vienna that year, Khrushchev delivered a new Soviet ultimatum for the western European powers and the United States to leave Berlin. Kennedy, smarting over the recent defeat in Cuba, reaffirmed the Western resolve to remain in Berlin. The European members of the Atlantic alliance backed him, and the immediate crisis passed. But in the summer of 1961 the Soviets, exasperated at the continuing exodus from East Berlin (over 3 million East Germans had already fled), constructed the Berlin Wall, a 28-mile rampart of concrete and barbed wire, with armed sentry stations. The Wall stood as a grim physical reminder of the Cold War

The Berlin Wall

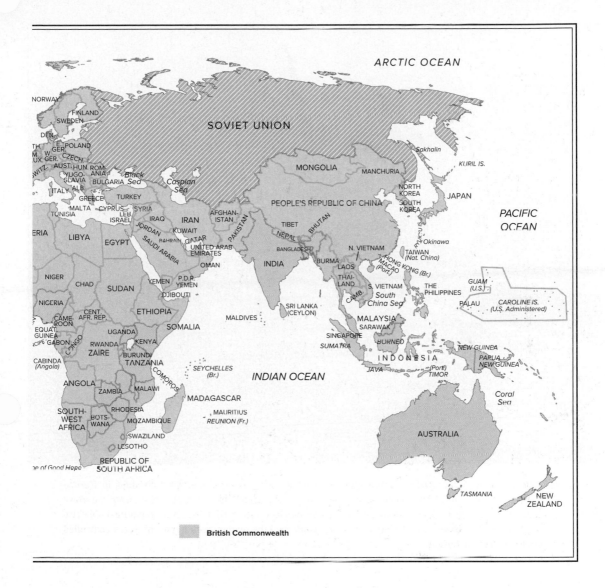

British Commonwealth

and of the enduring postwar division of Germany; hundreds of East Germans who attempted to cross the barrier met their deaths. Meanwhile, both the Soviets and the Americans resumed their testing of nuclear weapons.

The most dangerous Western-Soviet confrontation occurred not in Berlin but in Cuba, where in the fall of 1962 Khrushchev dispatched Soviet soldiers and technicians to construct missile sites that would have brought the American mainland within target range. For the United States this Soviet intrusion on America's own doorstep was a completely unacceptable military threat.

During 13 tense days in October President Kennedy and his advisers resolved not to take any hasty military action but to stand firm against the Soviet military presence in Cuba, fully aware that the showdown could lead to nuclear war. Kennedy imposed a blockade (or quarantine) of the island, forbidding further deliveries of arms and supplies. The launching of any nuclear

Cuban missile crisis

The Berlin Wall became both a concrete and symbolic expression of the bitter divisions in Europe during the Cold War. This photograph shows how workers built the Wall in 1961 under the close supervision of armed guards. Although the Wall accomplished the Soviets' short-term political objective by stopping the exodus of East Germans, it also confirmed the repressive character of Soviet-controlled states in eastern Europe.

(©Popperfoto/Getty Images)

An eyeball-to-eyeball confrontation

missile from Cuba, he made clear, would lead to a "full retaliatory response upon the Soviet Union." Although Khrushchev blustered that the blockade was illegal, he backed down. He recalled Soviet ships that were en route to Cuba and also accepted Kennedy's demand that the missiles be withdrawn from the Cuban bases. In one note Khrushchev agreed to remove the missile sites in return for an American pledge not to invade Cuba. In a second note, more aggressive in tone, he demanded the removal of American missile sites in Turkey. Kennedy replied only to the first message, but privately let it be known that the United States would eventually remove its missiles from Turkey (though nuclear bombs remained). By late October the most ominous crisis of the Cold War, an "eyeball-to-eyeball" confrontation, as the American Secretary of State Dean Rusk described it, was over.

Khrushchev had lost face; he was weakened still further by economic problems within the Soviet Union, and he was ousted from power in 1964. Tensions once again eased, but the Cuban crisis had a direct effect on the arms race. Both the Soviet Union and the United States moved to expand their nuclear arsenals, and the Soviets under Khrushchev's successors were determined to achieve nuclear parity.

The Americans drew their own lessons from the Cuban missile crisis. Reaffirming a global policy of resisting Communist forces wherever they appeared, the United States soon became deeply involved in the continuing conflict in Vietnam. Like other countries in this era, Vietnam had been divided into Communist and non-Communist sectors after the French left in 1954, but American policymakers feared that the French withdrawal from Indochina would open the way for Communist expansion across Southeast Asia. American presidents therefore intervened with   *The Vietnam War* increasingly large military forces to fill the vacuum that was created in this region by the collapse of France's colonial system. During the decade after the construction of the Berlin Wall and the Cuban missile crisis, the United States sent an American army of well over 500,000 troops to support the anti-Communist regime in South Vietnam, launched wide-ranging attacks on Communist guerrilla forces, and conducted massive air bombardments of territories and supply lines that were controlled by Ho Chi Minh's North Vietnamese government. The death of Ho himself in 1969 had little effect on the war, which continued into the 1970s. The anti-Communist regime was unable to establish a stable government or expel the Communists from the countryside, however, and the United States—facing domestic unrest and broad-based criticism in Europe—ultimately withdrew its forces. The war ended in 1975 when the Communists took complete control of South Vietnam and united the country under one government.

The American war in Vietnam significantly affected European views of the United States. America's allies in western Europe were generally critical of the deepening American military involvement, which coincided with Europe's own political and military withdrawal from empires in Asia and Africa. Europeans became skeptical of the strategic value as well as the morality of the American war.   *Critiques of* President de Gaulle, a moralizer when it suited his vision of the French   *Vietnam War* role in world affairs, saw the American intervention in Vietnam as the doomed follow-up to France's own colonial failures in Indochina; and he claimed that it was "detestable" for "a great nation to ravage a small one." The United States, which had been hailed as a great liberating force in Europe in the 1940s, was now condemned by antiwar protestors in the cities and universities of Germany, France, Britain, and other European countries. The critique of American policies in Vietnam, however, did not push Europeans toward a new sympathy for the Soviet Union. In fact, by the late 1960s a new generation of Soviet leaders had shown most people in western Europe why they had good reasons to sustain their political, economic, and cultural alliances with the United States—even in the worst years of the Vietnam War.

Brezhnev and the Prague Spring in Eastern Europe

Leonid I. Brezhnev, who emerged as the dominant Soviet leader after Khrushchev's fall from power in 1964, was intent on building the country's military and naval strength to compete with the United States. Yet he avoided direct confrontation and saw political and economic advantages in a relaxation of tensions and arms negotiations. A widening rift with Communist China made détente with the Western powers even more important. But the two superpowers continued to vie with each other for influence in the Middle East,

The American war in Vietnam provoked frequent protests across Europe, including this antiwar demonstration in London in the spring of 1968. Despite the widespread opposition to American policies in Vietnam, however, western European nations maintained their strong political and military alliance with the United States during every decade of the long Cold War.

(©Evening Standard/Hulton Archive/Getty Images)

Africa, and other strategic areas of the world; and the Soviets consolidated their hold on eastern Europe.

Despite the failure of the Hungarian uprising in 1956, the longing for freedom and independence in eastern Europe could not be suppressed. A new movement for liberalizing reforms emerged in Czechoslovakia during the spring of 1968 as the Communist leader Alexander Dubček allowed more open political debates that threatened one-party rule in the Czech state. Brezhnev and the Soviet party leadership ruthlessly crushed this "Prague spring" movement by dispatching 250,000 troops to suppress the incipient revolution and remove Dubček and his reformist allies from power. The "Brezhnev Doctrine" that year proclaimed the Soviet right to intervene in the name of "proletarian internationalism" in any Communist country to protect "socialism" against "internal or external forces" and prevent the "restoration of a capitalist regime." It was in its own way a kind of mirror image of the Truman Doctrine. Czechoslovakia returned to a tight dictatorship ruled by

The Brezhnev Doctrine

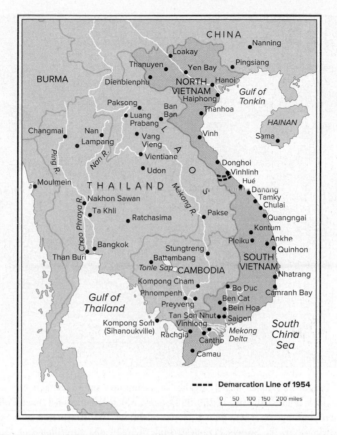

VIETNAM AND ITS NEIGHBORS AFTER THE ERA OF FRENCH COLONIALISM, SHOWING BOUNDARIES IN 1970

The French built up their colonial empire in Indochina during the 60 years before the Second World War, controlling the old Asian territories of Cambodia, Laos, and Vietnam. Shaken by Japanese occupation of the region during the Second World War, the French were unable to defeat a postwar Vietnamese movement for independence that drew strength also from Communist affiliations. When the French withdrew in 1954, the Geneva Accords provided for partition of Vietnam until national elections could take place and unity could be restored, but the elections never took place. Because the north was now Communist, the United States provided economic and military support for an anti-Communist regime in South Vietnam. This involvement grew in the 1960s as the conflict between North and South Vietnam developed into a large-scale war. The United States intervened with over 500,000 troops and heavy air bombardments, but the American forces (like the French before them) could not defeat the Vietnamese Communists—who were supplied with arms by the Soviet Union. American troops were gradually withdrawn in the early 1970s, and North Vietnam eventually won the war. Hostilities ended in 1975 with Communist regimes in control of a unified Vietnam and of Laos and Cambodia.

party bosses with close ties to Moscow. The United States did no more than protest the armed intervention in Czechoslovakia, demonstrating once again that it would not openly challenge Soviet control over eastern Europe in what was tacitly accepted as a sphere of Soviet influence. But the invasion of Czechoslovakia, like the suppression of the 1956 Hungarian uprising, alienated many Communists in other parts of the world and undermined the Soviet influence on the western European Communist parties, which strongly denounced the military intervention.

The citizens of Prague responded angrily to the Soviet military forces in their city in August 1968, but they could do little against an army of 250,000 troops, which also included token Polish, Hungarian, and East German contingents. These young people celebrated the destruction of a Soviet tank; elsewhere in the city, however, the Soviets were destroying the reformist government of Alexander Dubček and suppressing the movement that had attempted to create a more democratic political system in Czechoslovakia.

(©Reg Lancaster/Hulton Archive/Getty Images)

Brezhnev and Nixon

Although President Nixon, who took office in 1969, continued and even intensified the war in Vietnam, he introduced greater flexibility into the American policy of containment

Nixon and détente

and pursued a policy of systematic détente in the Cold War. Like his national security advisor, Henry Kissinger (and somewhat like President de Gaulle in France), Nixon believed in the balance of power diplomacy of an earlier age, and he assumed that each country's long-range national self-interest and geopolitical concerns should count more than ideology.

Under the Nixon-Kissinger policy the United States linked Western technology, trade, and investment to Soviet cooperation in international affairs. The economic inducements were important because the Soviet Union's economic difficulties were aggravated by its growing arms burden. The Soviets badly needed Western technology, investment credits, and even Western grain. In the new atmosphere American and West European private bankers made large loans to the East European nations, which benefited even more than the Soviets from détente. The two Germanys moved closer together in economic relations, recognized each other diplomatically, and were admitted to the United Nations in 1973 as two separate sovereign states.

The Nixon-Kissinger policies in Europe were developed out of a reassessment of these evolving global realities. Unlike the bipolar situation after 1945, when there were only two superpowers, there were now other centers of power in both Europe and Asia, including the

People's Republic of China. In 1971 the United States withdrew its objections to the entry of the People's Republic of China into the United Nations as a replacement for Taiwan. The American opening to China increased pressure on the Soviets to pursue détente. The Soviet arms buildup under Brezhnev signified that the Soviets were approaching nuclear parity, and both the United States and the Soviet Union became more willing to negotiate arms reduction. In 1972 Nixon and the Soviet leaders reaffirmed the goal of peaceful coexistence and signed the SALT I treaty. Each nation agreed to reduce its antimissile defense system to make it possible to work toward equality in offensive weapons. After the Watergate scandal forced Nixon to resign from the pres-

idency in 1974, détente continued under his successor, President Gerald Ford.

Détente offered an opportunity to settle or phase out some unresolved European issues of the Second World War. In 1975, in what resembled a peace conference for Europe, three decades after the Second World War had ended, 35 nations—the 16 members of NATO, the 7 Warsaw Pact states, and 12 European countries not formally members of either alliance—met at Helsinki over a period of two years in a Conference on Security and Cooperation in Europe.

They pledged to work for peace, economic and cultural cooperation, and the protection of human rights. The Helsinki Accords, although not a formal treaty, confirmed that postwar Europe had regained the political and economic vitality that was shattered in the chaos and destruction of 1939–1945. The accords ratified the European territorial boundaries established after the Second World War and set up "Helsinki watch committees" for the surveillance of human rights in nations that signed the agreements. The U.S.S.R. considered the commitment to human rights a small price to pay in exchange for the economic and territorial benefits of détente. It still expected to keep strict limits on dissent within its own country and in its East European satellites, but it failed to see how much the Helsinki Accords would encourage dissenters to defy repression. The Helsinki agreements helped to create a new political environment in which dissident movements gained support in eastern Europe and gradually mobilized opposition groups that would bring about the collapse of every Communist regime in the Soviet bloc by the end of the 1980s. The Helsinki conference was thus the high point of Cold War détente. It showed the growing importance of human rights as a key issue in European political life, and it became the starting point for wider historical changes, though in the short run, in 1979, Soviet-Western relations took another downward turn. But we must first turn to the changing world economy, to which the Soviet Union and the countries of eastern Europe were now more closely tied than ever before.

113. COLLAPSE AND RECOVERY OF THE EUROPEAN AND GLOBAL ECONOMY: THE 1970S AND 1980S

Interdependence is a form of dependency, and the expansion of the global economy after the Second World War made each country more vulnerable to events in distant places. In 1974, after two and a half decades of spectacular growth, the European economic boom came to an abrupt end. Signs of economic slowdown and inflationary pressures were already visible in the late 1960s, and recession might have occurred in any event, but it was the oil embargo growing out of the Arab-Israeli war in the autumn of 1973 that precipitated the crisis.

Oil had replaced coal as a major source of energy in industrial economies. Readily available at low prices, it came primarily from the vast reserves of the Middle East and was transported easily and economically into Europe by tankers through the Persian Gulf and Suez Canal. The major international oil companies, mostly American, for a long time controlled prices and production, and purchasers paid for the oil in dollars. The Western economies had come to depend on cheap oil. Oil-exporting countries in the Middle East and Latin America formed the Organization of Petroleum Exporting Countries (or OPEC) in 1960 to curb the monopoly concessions enjoyed by foreign companies and to assume a larger share of authority over production and prices.

OPEC

Several African nations also joined OPEC in later decades, but the Arab states of the Middle East were the most assertive leaders. The oil issue turned intensely political during the Arab-Israeli war of October 1973 when the Arab oil-producing states embargoed the shipment of oil to states accused of supporting Israel. The OPEC cartel cut back production and quadrupled oil prices. Apprehension spread in western Europe, Japan, and the United States, which needed foreign oil to supplement its domestic resources. Never had an essential commodity risen in price so rapidly; the entire global industrial complex seemed vulnerable. The oil shortage and the price escalation, coming on the heels of the international monetary difficulties and devaluations of the dollar in 1971–1973, sharply increased the balance of payment deficits for all oil-importing countries, undermined currencies, accelerated an inflationary spiral already underway, and seriously interrupted the spectacular growth of the West European economies.

Dependence on oil

The immediate panic caused by the oil embargo passed, but prices remained at a much higher level. Later in the decade, in 1979, a second oil crisis occurred when Iran, in the midst of its revolution, halted oil exports and the OPEC cartel again doubled prices. Eventually, however, the oil cartel proved less cohesive and influential than Europeans had originally feared. Additional energy resources became available within Europe itself, easing some of the dependence on Middle Eastern oil imports. After the discovery of oil in the North Sea, Britain and Norway became exporters of oil. The Netherlands and other countries turned to natural gas; France, to nuclear energy. Many European countries also initiated energy conservation measures, but frequent fluctuations in oil prices continued to affect Europe's economy and political relations with the oil-producing Arab states.

The Recession: Stagnation and Inflation

The recession that began in 1974 was severe, although it never approximated the crisis of the Great Depression. What set it apart from previous economic declines was the accompanying inflation, which raced on in major industrial countries at double-digit annual figures.

In some European countries the annual rate of inflation rose to over 20 percent; it reached 27 percent in Britain in 1975. In the United States prices doubled over the course of the decade, thus reshaping trade on both sides of the Atlantic. For a time economic growth ground to a standstill in western Europe. By the late 1970s the recession was worldwide. Bankruptcies shook several countries; production declined; economic growth slowed or even halted. Over 10 percent of the West European labor force were unemployed.

Effects of recession

New economic problems in the mid-1970s led to the restructuring of older European industries, rising unemployment, and high inflation. Facing the loss of jobs and the stagnation of wages, labor unions responded with strikes and other protests such as this "litter assault" on the Champs Élysées by striking Parisian newspaper workers. These kinds of actions brought public attention to the workers' grievances, though this particular protest clearly ignored the environmental concerns that were also developing in this era.

(©Hulton Archive/Getty Images)

The economic troubles were somewhat cushioned for the unemployed in industrial countries. Labor unions were still active, although declining in membership and influence, and welfare benefits were more advanced than they had been in the 1930s. Workers in all the western European countries could count on severance pay, trade union benefits, and government unemployment compensation far beyond the welfare payments and dole of earlier generations. These benefits reduced human suffering and also limited the decline in consumer purchasing power. The recession, how-   *Structural*
ever, aggravated the problem of "structural unemployment." Because of   *unemployment*
automation, high technology, and the dwindling importance of older, less-efficient sectors of the economy (such as coal mining, shipbuilding, and other so-called smokestack industries), many workers would never return to their old jobs or use their old skills again; and labor unrest spread into many of the European industries in which earlier generations of workers had built up strong unions.

The combination of stagnation and inflation (dubbed "stagflation"   *Stagflation*
by journalists) created unprecedented problems for governments. Keynesian theory, which had gained a wide following in Europe after 1945, called for government spending and deficit financing in slow times to buoy demand and keep employment stable. With inflation rampant, such measures became questionable. The dilemma centered on whether curbing inflation or reducing unemployment should claim the highest priority. Efforts to fight inflation by tight money and high interest rates would discourage investment, aggravate the business slowdown, and swell the ranks of the unemployed. Government spending to prime the pump or reducing interest rates to facilitate private borrowing could feed inflation.

With the American economy troubled, the western European industrial countries looked to the Federal Republic of Germany and its powerful economy to take the lead in expanding investment and production. Germany, however, mindful of the hyperinflation of the 1920s, set its highest priority on controlling inflation; it kept interest rates high and rejected expansionist policies. Other countries followed the same track. By the early 1980s inflation was brought under control in the United States and in western Europe, but European unemployment continued at levels well above the unemployment rates in the early postwar decades. The high unemployment put new pressures on government budgets, which had risen steadily in all the "welfare state" societies of the industrial world.

From 1950 to the mid-1970s the percentage of gross national product spent on social measures in the industrial countries more than doubled, creating a pattern of rising taxes and government expenditures that came to be criticized as an obstacle to economic growth.

Faith in Keynes shaken

The established tenets of Keynesian economics were now challenged by resurgent conservative and neoliberal political parties. The British Conservative Party leader Margaret Thatcher, who became prime minister in 1979, gained international prominence by leading a campaign against the welfare state that had developed in Britain since the Second World War. She attacked the welfare state as costly, wasteful, paternalistic, and bureaucratic and blamed it for eroding individual initiative and responsibility. Nationalized industries and some public services also faced mounting criticism from Thatcher and other European conservatives.

Although conservative governments in Britain and elsewhere continued to make significant expenditures for national defense, they sought to curb government spending on social measures. Meanwhile to stimulate production they offered numerous incentives to private enterprise, including tax reductions, deregulation, and restraints on unions that interfered with technological innovation. "Supply side" economics, as these ideas were labeled by conservative economists in the United States, emphasized increased production rather than the hitherto prevailing notion of increased consumer demand as most important for economic growth. The results were then expected to "trickle down" for everyone's benefit, with a safety net in place for the truly disadvantaged.

Supply side economics

The gradual return of prosperity in the 1980s reinforced faith in the free-market economy, despite uneasiness about the continuing volatility of global business cycles. Conservative or neoliberal economic theories and policies appeared to be confirmed by a worldwide movement toward market economies and away from centralized planning, which in its rigidly Marxist form had manifestly failed in the Soviet Union and eastern Europe. Defenders of the European welfare state systems, however, continued to stress the importance of supplementing market economies with direct action by governments to manage business cycles, help unemployed workers, and provide essential health care. The welfare, or interventionist, state still served important social needs and seemed destined to survive, even if in modified form. A new generation of liberal, labor, and socialist leaders came to preach the virtues of a "new middle way" that leaned heavily on market economies as the key to economic growth but without surrendering the prerogatives of government in confronting the social and economic problems of modern societies.

Economic and Political Change in Western Europe

Britain was especially hard hit by the recession of the 1970s. Of all the industrial nations, it suffered the highest rate of inflation. Unemployment climbed, and the pound dropped to a new low in global financial markets. The trade unions refused to accept the sacrifices that even their own Labour Party believed necessary to revive the economy, and disruptive strikes in coal and transportation exasperated much of the country. Radical factions in the Labour Party pressed for increased nationalization of industry and for nonalignment

Conservatives sought to reduce or dismantle various social programs of the modern welfare state after they came to power in the 1980s. British Prime Minister Margaret Thatcher was the best-known European advocate for the reduction of government participation in domestic economic life, though she favored higher government expenditures for military forces. She is shown here in 1985 with President Ronald Reagan, her close American political ally who was attending a meeting with Thatcher and other government leaders in Germany.

(©Pool APESTEGUY/IIIRES/Gamma-Rapho/Getty Images)

in the Cold War. Alienated by the economic confusion and changing social conditions in British society, which they blamed on Labour governments that had been in power since 1974, the voters in 1979 turned to the Conservatives, who now resolved to address Britain's economic problems by changing the welfare state.

Margaret Thatcher, the first woman prime minister in any major Western country, decisively cut government expenditures, reduced imports, and resisted trade union wage demands. The focus of government policies shifted to investment, productivity, and economic growth. Inflation was curbed, but unemployment rose. The Thatcher government in its early years seemed headed for political trouble, but in 1982 Thatcher stirred Britain's patriotic and imperial memories by dispatching a small armada 8,000 miles to the coast of South America, thwarting the attempted takeover of the Falkland (or Malvina) Islands by Argentina. The Conservatives won a sweeping parliamentary majority the following year.

Margaret Thatcher

For a time in the 1980s the Thatcher policies successfully implemented the main Conservative goals. The government curtailed the power of the unions, returned over one-third of the nationalized industries to private enterprise, and made credit more readily available for business and for home buyers. Britain could soon point to the highest economic growth rate of all the European countries. Unemployment, however, remained high; fiscal retrenchment hurt education, especially the universities; and pockets of deep depression persisted, especially in the north of England and in Scotland and Wales, where traditional industries such as coal mining and shipbuilding faced difficulties competing in the new global economy. The south and southeast enjoyed a bustling prosperity, particularly in the high-technology industries around London and Cambridge. Meanwhile London reinforced its position as a world financial center, and the United Kingdom became once again a leading creditor nation. Decades of economic decline and demoralization seemed to have been reversed. The opposition was disunited and in disarray. In the elections of 1987, Labour's popular vote dropped to its lowest point in decades, and union membership steadily declined.

But when economic growth slowed and the initial stimulus of privatization and deregulation wore off, Thatcher introduced new tax and fiscal measures that led to her fall in 1990. Her successor as prime minister, John Major, had to cope with a new recession that set in after 1990, a weakened pound, and persistent unemployment. Labour, meanwhile, under new leadership that abandoned older ideas of class struggle and attracted a broad range of middle-class support, continued to challenge the Conservatives, arguing that the Thatcher era had favored the rich and fostered a less equitable society. Finally,

New Labour

under the moderate "New Labour" leadership of Tony Blair, the Labour Party won the parliamentary elections in 1997 and regained control of the government for the first time since 1979. Blair and the increasingly moderate Labour Party would remain in power through the opening decade of the twenty-first century, winning a third consecutive electoral victory in 2005 and seeking to promote a "middle way" between earlier welfare state policies and the free-market policies of the Thatcher era.

In France, politics in the 1980s veered toward the Left. An austerity program adopted in the 1970s by the conservative parties to combat inflation was unpopular, and the government's aloofness, elitism, and seeming unconcern with social issues under de Gaulle's successors helped the Socialist-led opposition gain electoral strength. In 1981 François Mitterrand became the first Socialist president in the French Fifth Republic, thus achieving a long-sought goal he had set for himself and the Socialist party. Mitterrand had a varied and complex career, some aspects of which were unknown until the last years of his life, including his association with right-wing causes in the early 1930s and his wartime service to the Vichy government before joining the Resistance Movement. He was known as a moderate Socialist, whose socialism owed more to liberal idealism than to Marxism. A consummate politician, he revitalized the Socialist Party and reached out to many who chafed at the social insensitivities of the Gaullists and Conservatives. "Changer la vie"

*Mitterrand and
"Changer la vie"*

—change life for everyone—was his campaign slogan. Mitterrand's new cabinet moved quickly to introduce social reforms when subsequent legislative elections gave the Socialist party an absolute majority in the National Assembly.

The workweek was reduced from 40 to 39 hours and a fifth week of annual paid vacation was added. Expanding on the nationalizations of 1945, Mitterrand nationalized the remaining large banks as well as several leading industrial corporations. One of the European leaders still faithful to Keynesian precepts in the 1980s, Mitterrand rejected the kind of deregulation and free-market philosophy that Thatcher was then advocating in Britain. He expected government spending and labor reforms to raise purchasing power, stimulate the economy, and thus absorb the costs of the expanded welfare state. But increased labor costs reduced French competitiveness abroad, and private investment also dried up. The immediate consequences were slow economic growth, trade deficits, inflation, unemployment, and a weakening franc. Within two years Mitterrand abruptly changed course. He halted further nationalization and other reforms, insisted on retrenchment and austerity to cope with inflation, and placed a strong emphasis on modernization. Cutting off subsidies to decaying industries, he shifted government support to high technology. The new policies encouraged economic growth but contributed little to reducing unemployment. Many of his Socialist followers became disenchanted, and French political culture began to suffer from a deepening public frustration with the nation's governing elite.

Renewed economic problems cost the Socialist Party popular support. It lost its parliamentary majority in 1986 and Mitterrand was forced to govern with a Conservative prime minister. The term "cohabitation" entered the political language to signify a popularly elected president of one party governing with a prime minister who represented the opposing parliamentary majority. It was a precedent that de Gaulle never foresaw. But as an established practice that was repeated over the years to come, it became a legacy of Mitterrand that demonstrated the resiliency of the Fifth Republic, even as it seemed also to impede decisive government action. In the Gaullist tradition, however, the president continued to determine defense and foreign policy.

"Cohabitation"

When in 1988 Mitterrand was reelected president, the Socialists regained a small plurality in the National Assembly. But unemployment and political scandals involving Socialist ministers led to a socialist rout in 1993 and the return of a large conservative majority. Cohabitation resumed under the conservative Gaullist Prime Minister Jacques Chirac, who was then elected to the presidency in the elections of 1995 and 2002, and the seesaw pattern of French politics continued in his administration. Although the French economy strengthened impressively in the 1990s, unemployment remained a persistent problem, especially for young people. A growing political movement on the Far Right, the National Front, attracted disaffected voters who blamed French economic problems on the nation's growing immigrant as well as the long-entrenched "political class" in French society. The leader of the National Front, Jean-Marie Le Pen, became a prominent figure in French politics and even reached the final round of voting in the presidential election of 2002.

Meanwhile, in response to the ongoing problems of unemployment, a Socialist prime minister in yet another cohabitation government, Lionel Jospin, had secured passage of a new labor law that reduced the workweek in France from 39 to 35 hours to create new jobs. The measure met with strong opposition from most employers, but it exemplified ongoing attempts to deal with structural problems in the economy that contributed to an enduring disillusionment and anger on both the left and right wings of French political culture. During these same years, there were also new attempts to enhance the influence of women in French public life. Women played a much larger role in French government and public institutions than ever before, occupying key ministries and high-level posts in business and professional life. A new law, implemented in stages after 2000, provided that women were to be candidates in elections for representative bodies in equal numbers with men. A few women writers and scholars were even admitted to the French Academy, a male bastion since 1635.

Socialists and Social Democrats holding office in western Europe during the new era of neoliberal economic theories increasingly championed modernization, market economies, and economic growth as the path to the good society; and their policies often won broad support, even as conservatives pushed for changes in the economic policies of the welfare states. Moderation and pragmatism overshadowed older Marxist ideologies. Helmut Schmidt, the Social Democratic chancellor in West Germany from 1974 to 1982, was one leading exemplar of the new pattern. In Italy, Bettino Craxi and a Socialist coalition in 1983 ended the long tenure of the Christian Democrats, who had formed 40 consecutive cabinets since 1945. The Italian Socialists governed for an unprecedented four years but were barely distinguishable in policies and practices from the long-entrenched Christian Democratic establishment. In Spain the popular Socialist Party leader, Felipe Gonzalez, in 1982 headed the first Left government since the Spanish Civil War of the 1930s and governed on into the mid-1990s. Europe's democratic socialist parties, in short, had moved from their once-marginal positions in European states to the center of governing coalitions.

West European Socialists

French workers, like workers in all the major industrial countries of Europe, were increasingly drawn from the diverse immigrant communities that grew rapidly during the later decades of the twentieth century. These workers, who were protesting the policies of a French automobile company in 1983, represented the evolving multiculturalism of the modern French workforce.
(©Daniel SIMON/Gamma-Rapho/Getty Images)

In West Germany Helmut Schmidt's Social Democratic government sought to control inflation through policies of retrenchment and fiscal conservatism, but the industrial slowdown of the late 1970s brought unemployment to a country that for years had known only labor scarcity. Even after recovery, unemployment persisted for several years at about 8 percent. The doors once open to guest workers began to close; bonuses were offered to those who would return home; activist reactionary groups (as in Britain, France, and Austria) alarmingly exploited anti-immigrant and antiforeign sentiment in new political groups that would later gain more influence in the twenty-first century. Amid these evolving economic and social conditions, the Christian Democrats returned to office with Helmut Kohl as chancellor. Kohl would remain chancellor for 16 years, leading the German Federal Republic through a period in which the economy resumed its earlier growth and accounted for about a third of the combined output of the EC. But heavy labor costs, resulting from high wages and generous social benefits, reduced German competitiveness in world markets until the

"One nation and two states"

late 1990s—when the Germans brought more flexibility into their labor practices and wage system. Meanwhile the prospects in the 1980s for reunification of the two Germanys still seemed remote—Germany would apparently remain "one nation and two states," in Willy Brandt's phrase.

The Enlarged European Community: Problems and Opportunities

After de Gaulle left the political scene in 1969, the way opened for enlarging the six-nation EC. In 1973 Britain, Denmark, and Ireland were admitted; the six became nine. In the next decade, with the admission of Greece in 1981 and Spain and Portugal in 1986, the

Although skeptics questioned and resisted the growing integration of the European Union (EU), most political leaders continued to promote a more unified European economy and culture during the late twentieth century. German Chancellor Helmut Kohl, for example, visited Strasbourg, France in 1986 to give a speech on European unity and to honor Robert Schuman—a leading French architect of the post-1945 transnational cooperation. Schuman's portrait and an EU pennant were placed behind Kohl to affirm the themes of his speech.

(©STAFF/AFP/Getty Images)

9 became 12. In 1995, with the admission of Austria, Finland, and Sweden, the numbers grew to 15. The largest expansion made possible by momentous changes in eastern Europe after 1989 and by the collapse of Soviet communism, would take place at the beginning of the twenty-first century, in 2004, when 10 more nations from eastern and southern Europe (from Estonia to Malta) joined what had come to be known as the European Union (EU) in 1993.[1] Other states joined the EU during the next decade, so that by the second decade of the twenty-first century there were 28 members—until Britain voted to leave the EU in 2016 and moved haltingly thereafter toward a messy "divorce."

Expansion of the European Union brought new difficulties, aggravated by the economic slowdown of the 1970s and then by the wage differentials between richer and poorer countries. A food importer, **Growing pains** Britain objected to the "common agricultural policy" agreed upon in 1968, whereby countries such as France and Italy received large subsidies for their farmers, whose products were withheld from the open market and stored at great expense to keep prices artificially high. The admission of the less industrially advanced southern Mediterranean states in the 1980s (and of eastern nations in the early twenty-first century) introduced serious regional differences in wages and government budgets. Despite the original promise and accomplishments of the Community as a whole, the free trading area remained far from complete. Countries still placed quotas on agricultural imports; France kept out Italian wines. Burdensome administrative regulations at some borders persisted amid the general development of a transnational economy.

---

[1] By 2013 the EU member states were Austria, Belgium, Bulgaria, Croatia, Cyprus, Czech Republic, Denmark, Estonia, Finland, France, Germany, Greece, Hungary, Ireland, Italy, Latvia, Lithuania, Luxembourg, Malta, the Netherlands, Poland, Portugal, Romania, Slovakia, Slovenia, Spain, Sweden, and the United Kingdom (which, by its "Brexit" vote in 2016, chose to leave the EU).

Except for a limited circle of Europeanists, the enthusiasm for closer political integration seemed to decline. With enlargement and greater diversity, the Community became even more intergovernmental and less supranational. Britain was always reluctant to support additional supranational authority for the Community. In periods of economic slowdown and monetary instability the national governments themselves had to cope with the problems. In 1973 the government leaders began meeting as a council on a regular basis, the presidency rotating among the member states. The first elections to the European Parliament in 1979 were more symbolic than substantial, and the Parliament's role as a legislature failed to grow significantly. While the more ambitious dream of a United States of Europe went unrealized, the Community, for all its problems, became a key, transnational institution in Europe's increasingly integrated economy and culture.

Toward a "Single Europe": The European Union

After the 1970s Europe entered a new phase of industrialism, a "third industrial revolution," marked by the introduction of automation, computers, and other forms of advanced technology. Progress would no longer be measured in coal and steel or in ships and textiles but in nuclear reactors, microelectronics, telecommunications, computers, robotics, and space technology. In the "postindustrial" age data processing, information storage and retrieval, and more sophisticated communications capabilities were the keys to competitive success. In 1977 the first personal computer was produced for what would soon become

The postindustrial age

a mass market, with rapid improvements to follow in speed and capacity. More workers were employed in the service sector than in the older basic industries, and the service economy was growing faster than either agriculture or industry. It was widely noted that the global economy was eroding the economic and political autonomy of the nation-state. Using new technologies, the multinational corporations of the industrial world invested capital and developed new operations across all national boundaries and on every continent; and this new global production system weakened Europe's competitive position in many of its traditional industries.

As new forms of technology emerged in the late twentieth century, Europeans found themselves for a time outdistanced by the Americans and the Japanese. American multinational corporations controlled most of the high-technology industries in Europe—before the Japanese arrived to compete. Trade competition from Japan and the rapidly developing industrial countries of the Pacific Rim posed new economic challenges for all national governments and for most of Europe's major commercial institutions. The post-1974 recession made it difficult for the Europeans to promote research and technological development, and they lagged behind other parts of the world in recovering economically after the mid-1970s.

The EC therefore launched new initiatives to reinvigorate itself in the 1980s. Although internal tariffs had disappeared, nontariff obstacles still impeded the flow of trade, and

The Single European Act

there were different national standards of production and quality. In 1987, by the "Single European Act" the 12 member-nations agreed to establish common production standards, remove impediments to the flow of capital, seek uniform tax rates, recognize each other's professional and commercial licensing, and honor a common charter of labor rights. They would create an integrated "single Europe," a "Europe without borders." A unified European

CHRONOLOGY OF NOTABLE EVENTS, 1957–1995

1957	Soviet Union launches first satellite into outer space
1961	Soviet Union constructs the Berlin Wall to stop exodus from East Germany
1962	United States compels the withdrawal of Soviet missiles from Cuba
1968	Protests spread across Europe in response to the American war in Vietnam
1968	Soviet troops enter Czechoslovakia to crush reform movement in Prague
1974	High oil prices and inflation contribute to European and global economic recession
1979	Margaret Thatcher becomes prime minister in Britain; introduces Conservative reforms
1979	Soviet Union invades Afghanistan to protect a left-wing regime
1981	François Mitterrand becomes president of France; introduces Socialist reforms
1982	Helmut Kohl becomes chancellor of West Germany
1983	Protests in western Europe against deployment of new intermediate-range nuclear weapons on European bases
1987	Ronald Reagan and Mikhail Gorbachev reach a U.S.-Soviet agreement to withdraw intermediate-range nuclear weapons from Europe
1992	Treaty of Maastricht establishes the European Union (EU)
1995	EU expands to include 15 nations, creating a foundation for further expansion in the early twenty-first century

currency and central banking system were projected for the end of the 1990s, and even common defense and foreign policies were envisaged for the future. These arrangements were confirmed in a Treaty of European Union signed at Maastricht in the Netherlands at the close of 1991, and ratified after protracted debate by the parliaments or electorates of the member states by the end of 1992. Opponents in every affiliated country raised objections to the loss of national control over various economic or public policies, but the treaty was adopted. The EC became the EU. The way was open to closer European integration.

The EU represented a domestic market of 345 million people (one-third larger than that of the United States) and by the early 1990s it was the largest trading bloc in the global economy, accounting for 40 percent of all international trade. With the new steps toward European integration and the later expansion of EU member-ship, European leaders hoped to enlarge investment, develop high tech-nology, stimulate productivity, end the lagging rate of economic growth, and reduce an unemployment rate that was still distressingly high.

Dangers of protectionism

In the world as a whole, a possible turn toward protectionism was always a lurking international danger for Europe's continental and global commercial system. Advocates of tariffs on imported goods could be found in most industrial nations, so the possible creation of new competitive barriers could still threaten the free trade that had contributed so much to post-1945 prosperity. Meanwhile, there were growing concerns about the effects of "globalization" on the industrial and agricultural economies within Europe itself.

The Treaty on European Union, which was signed by twelve nations in the Dutch city of Maastricht in 1992, became the key statement of EU policies on government budgets, national debts, the new European currency, and other economic and legal issues. This voter was among those who encountered the arguments for and against EU policies in France, where a contentious referendum on ratification of the Maastricht agreements led to a narrow approval in September 1992.

(©FRANCOIS XAVIER MARIT/AFP/Getty Images)

114.   THE COLD WAR REKINDLED AND DEFUSED

The complex flow of international events and Cold War conflicts continued to influence European politics and cultures throughout the era of growing economic integration. The election of Jimmy Carter to the presidency of the United States in 1976 led to a new American foreign policy that linked détente more closely to progress on human rights in the Soviet

Human rights

Union and eastern Europe. The theme of human rights had also become a major issue for many Europeans in the years after the Helsinki agreements of 1975. The Americans proposed, for example, that economic aid would be forthcoming only if the Soviets permitted freedom to dissenters, the right of emigration for Soviet Jews and others, and an end to the coercion of Poland. Both the Americans and the Soviets meanwhile reinforced their military and nuclear strength, even as they negotiated a new strategic arms treaty. But before the new treaty could be ratified by the U.S.

Soviet invasion of Afghanistan

Senate, the Soviet Union moved troops into the neighboring state of Afghanistan to bolster a weak pro-Soviet leftist regime. It was the first Soviet military intervention of that kind outside eastern Europe, and it was widely denounced on both sides of the Atlantic.

Carter condemned the Soviet invasion, withdrew the arms treaty from the Senate, embargoed sales of grain and high technology to the Soviets, took measures to increase the military budget, and set up procedures at home for a renewal of the draft. The invasion of Afghanistan, Carter informed the U.S.S.R., was the most serious threat to world peace since 1945. The European allies, however, generally viewed the Soviet intervention as a less threatening event. Some Europeans argued that the Afghanistan episode was a regional matter, that the Soviet Union was acting to prevent instability on its borders, and that détente should continue. Unwilling to disturb commercial relations with the Soviets and eastern Europe, they refused to support the economic embargo, which, among other consequences, would have interfered with the completion of a Soviet natural gas pipeline to western Europe. As it developed, Afghanistan turned out to be the U.S.S.R.'s Vietnam. Some 100,000 Soviet troops fought for more than 8½ years before withdrawing ignominiously in 1989. Like the Americans in Vietnam, the Soviets were unable to use their overwhelming military power to defeat the Muslim guerrillas who, armed with American weapons and supported by Pakistan, fought stubbornly from their Afghan mountain strongholds.

In the midst of these expanding international tensions (which included the Iranian Revolution and hostage crisis), the new Republican president, Ronald Reagan, came to office in the United States and affirmed his commitment to a hard line in the Cold War. The Soviet Union, Reagan asserted in 1983, represented "the focus of evil in the modern world." It was "an evil empire" with "dark purposes." Despite the strain on its economy, the Soviet Union during the 1970s had built up its military strength, modernized its conventional fighting forces, created a powerful navy, and achieved nuclear parity. Reagan substantially increased defense appropriations, sponsored the largest peacetime military spending in American history, and took a confrontational stand against communism everywhere. He stepped up arms shipments to the Muslim guerrillas in Afghanistan and sent aid to Pakistan, which was backing the Afghan rebels. Reagan also favored strong anti-Communist actions in Europe. He reinforced the embargo on the sale of high technology to the Soviets and to eastern Europe, but the embargo on grain sales was dropped because of opposition from American farmers. Yet Reagan would also move gradually toward his own policies of détente and negotiation with the Soviet Union during the later years of his presidency.

> *Reagan and the "evil empire"*

Nuclear Arms Control

No nuclear weapons were used in any conflict in the years after 1945, yet over every crisis hung the ultimate threat of a nuclear clash. We have seen how the earliest negotiations on nuclear disarmament, at a time when the United States alone possessed the atomic bomb, were broken off in 1947; how in 1949 the Soviets successfully tested their first atomic bomb, ending the American monopoly; and how the United States in 1952 and the Soviet Union shortly thereafter developed the hydrogen or thermonuclear bomb, which by its chain reaction had vastly more destructive capacity than the mere 20,000 tons of TNT of the Hiroshima bomb. By the 1960s both superpowers were building intercontinental ballistic missiles capable of delivering their nuclear warheads accurately and swiftly to targets in each other's homeland.

> *The ultimate threat*

The arms experts insisted that nuclear arms were increasingly built for deterrence rather than for use in an intercontinental war. The international balance of power came to be described as a "balance of terror," and military strategists referred to "mutually assured destruction" (the acronym for which, ironically, was MAD). Deterrence became the accepted formula. Although

> *MAD: Mutually assured destruction*

Historical Interpretations and Debates
The Nature and Legacy of the Cold War

Europeans emerged from the devastating human and material losses of the Second World War in a weakened position between the ascendant American and Soviet superpowers. The competing ambitions of the United States and the Soviet Union often played out after 1945 on the European continent as both sides developed spheres of influence and also used their European bases in the NATO and Warsaw Pact countries as a front line in their global military strategies. After several decades of conflict and confrontation, however, the Soviet system in eastern Europe collapsed, creating a sense of triumph in the Western countries and opening new opportunities for the increasingly unified European economy. Compare the views of Eric Hobsbawm and John Lamberton Harper as they explain how the Cold War affected Europeans and why the Western powers ultimately prevailed.

Eric Hobsbawm, *The Age of Extremes: A History of the World, 1914–1991* (1994)

The peculiarity of the Cold War was that, speaking objectively, no imminent danger of world war existed. More than this: in spite of the apocalyptic rhetoric on both sides, . . . the governments of both the superpowers accepted the global distribution of force at the end of the Second World War. . . .

Once the USSR acquired nuclear weapons . . . both superpowers plainly abandoned war as an instrument of policy against one another, since it was the equivalent of a suicide pact. . . .

All Western European governments . . . were without exception wholeheartedly anti-communist, and determined to protect themselves against possible Soviet military attack. . . . . Yet [fear of] the "communist world conspiracy" was not a serious part of the domestic politics of any of those who had some claim to being political democracies. . . .

However, the effect of the Cold War on the international politics of Europe was more striking than on the Continent's domestic politics. It created the "European Community" with all its problems; an entirely unprecedented form of political organization, namely a permanent . . . arrangement to integrate the economies, and to some extent the legal systems, of a number of independent nation-states. . . .

John Lamberton Harper, *The Cold War* (2011).

The Cold War was a competition between social-economic systems that regarded each other as natural enemies. Each side's ideology, or secular religion, conditioned its choice of friends and determined its basic objectives: safeguarding and advancing capitalism and democracy, on one hand; protecting and expanding Communism, on the other. Each side espoused a directional and messianic view of history, believing its cause would prevail. . . .

In its central theater [in Europe], the conflict was a total mismatch. Thanks to the way World War II ended, most of the rich, industrially advanced regions of Europe fell into the Western sphere. The EEC's founding members were the main beneficiaries of the US-Soviet confrontation as well as important protagonists of the eventual Western victory. Thanks partly to U.S. aid and protection, they recovered quickly, developed generous welfare systems, and pursued a successful strategy of integration. . . .

In the 1980s Western Europe restructured industry and embarked on a new round of integration. Central and Eastern Europe's per capita GDP was 51 percent (on average) of Western Europe's in 1950; 47 percent in 1973; a mere 40 percent in 1989. By then, countless Eastern Europeans, including once-loyal Communists, were ready to reinvent themselves as capitalists. . . .

Eric Hobsbawm . . . *(contd . . . .)*

The "Community" was, like so many other things in post-1945 Europe, created both by and against the USA. It illustrates both the power and ambiguity of that country and its limits; but it also illustrates the strength of the fears that held the anti-Soviet alliance together. . . .

[E]ven though the USA was unable to impose its politico-economic plans on the Europeans in detail, it was strong enough to dominate their international behavior. The policy of the alliance against the USSR was the USA's, and so were its military plans.

John Lamberton Harper . . . *(contd . . . .)*

[T]he West won the contest partly because the playing field was always tilted in its favor, and the United States shared the laurels . . . with Europe. . . . A degree of Western triumphalism was understandable in 1989–90. But a clear look back on the Cold War battlegrounds, along with a sense of relief that the world survived forty-five years of confrontation, evokes feelings of humility and regret.

Sources: Eric Hobsbawm, *The Age of Extremes: A History of the World, 1914-1991* (New York: Pantheon, 1994), pp. 226, 229, 236-237, 239-241; John Lamberton Harper, *The Cold War* (Oxford: Oxford University Press, 2011), pp. 244-246, 250.

Britain and France had developed their own nuclear weapons by the early 1960s, and the People's Republic of China also became a nuclear power in that era, the arms race developed mainly in the competition of the American and Soviet superpowers. Europeans lived between the two great nuclear forces, but they could only be worried spectators as the superpowers on each side amassed huge stockpiles of arms, capable of destroying each other and Europe many times over, in what was described as "overkill." When the Soviets developed antiballistic defense missiles, which undermined deterrence, the United States responded by building its own defense system and more powerful offensive weapons—such as the MIRV (a "multiple independently targeted reentry vehicle"). The MIRV was a delivery system carrying up to 10 nuclear warheads, each guided to separate targets and each many times more powerful than the Hiroshima bomb. Meanwhile, shorter-range missiles with nuclear warheads were also deployed in Europe for use as possible strategic support in the event of a European land war. The   *Overkill* Americans placed the intermediate-range Pershing missiles in Germany, for example, and the Soviets placed comparable nuclear weapons along the borders that divided the eastern and western European nations. For the first time in its long history, the very survival of Europe rested in the military hands of others.

By the 1980s each superpower possessed about 25,000 nuclear weapons, of which roughly 12,000 on each side were strategic, that is, long-range, or intercontinental; but many were also designed for shorter-range use in places such as the European borderlands. Together the arsenals of the two major nuclear powers exceeded 500,000 megatons (millions of tons) of explosive power, dwarfing the total explosive power used in all the previous wars of human history. This was the context in which the American and Soviet leaders began to rethink their strategic interests and to initiate new negotiations that would also alter the "balance of terror" within Europe.

Early in the Reagan administration, in 1981, Soviet and American officials resumed low-level talks on strategic arms limitations, but in an atmosphere of Cold War mistrust, suspicion, and continuing arms buildup. Especially disturbing for the western European and American governments was the deployment in eastern Europe of new Soviet intermediate-range nuclear missiles capable of reaching a radius of 600 to 1,500 miles. As the Soviets developed   *New missiles and European protests*

The nuclear arms race evolved during the early 1980s as both the Soviets and Americans deployed new intermediate-range missiles within Europe. The new strategic weapons provoked deep concern among Europeans who feared that they could be caught in a devastating nuclear exchange between the opposing superpowers. The German protestors at this demonstration therefore represented a broader antimissile movement that spread across western Europe, but the new missiles were nevertheless installed. Later Soviet-U.S. negotiations, however, led to the removal of these weapons and the easing of Cold War tensions.

(©Sahm Doherty/The LIFE Images Collection/Getty Images)

this new force in the late 1970s and early 1980s, the United States joined with its European allies to reinforce existing defenses in western Europe with a new generation of intermediate Pershing and cruise missiles. These missiles were to serve as a new deterrent against Soviet military action, but they were also deployed as a forceful encouragement for the Soviets to remove or reduce their own missiles from eastern Europe. The construction of the new American missile sites set off mass antimissile protests in much of western Europe and provoked a new European wave of post-Vietnam criticisms of American military policies. The West European governments, however, remained firm in their support of the new missiles, and the new weapons were installed at strategic military bases.

High-level arms negotiations between the Soviet and Western governments all but ceased during the first years of the Reagan presidency, in part because Soviet leaders such as Leonid Brezhnev were ailing and in part because Western leaders such as Reagan and Thatcher were not eager to negotiate with Communist regimes. Beginning in 1985, however, the emergence of the new Soviet leader Mikhail Gorbachev offered an opening for new negotiations on nuclear weaponry. Unlike his predecessors, Gorbachev seemed to view détente

New arms negotiations

as a means to help the weak Soviet economy and as an essential diplomatic process for avoiding catastrophe in the nuclear age. For his part, Reagan was confident that American military strength would give the Americans and western Europeans a stronger position from which to negotiate; and Reagan would ultimately hold four summit meetings with Gorbachev in the later 1980s.

At their third meeting, in December 1987, the American and Soviet leaders made a remarkable breakthrough by consenting to remove the intermediate-range missiles that each country had installed in Europe. Gorbachev also agreed to reduce the number of short-range nuclear missiles; in fact, the Soviets were   *Removal of missiles* willing to destroy over four times as many missiles as the United States. Even more unprecedented, the Soviets agreed to allow the United States to verify the destruction of the weapons through on-site inspections. Negotiations for the further reduction of long-range nuclear weapons would continue after Reagan left office and would lead finally to another strategic arms treaty in 1991, pledging each of the superpowers to reduce its arsenal by about a third of its missiles.

All of these remarkable changes in the nuclear arms race altered the political and strategic context for the people of western and eastern Europe as well as for the Americans and the Soviets. The international conflicts of the Cold War came to an end. Equally important for Europeans, a new wave of political dis-   *End of Cold War* sent gathered force in eastern Europe, leading to the collapse of the   *conflicts* Communist regimes, the free movement of people across formerly rigid national boundaries, and the unexpected demise of the Soviet Union itself. New problems emerged, of course, including ethnic and national violence in southeastern Europe; but the protracted European transition out of the Second World War finally came to a close. The Cold War threat of Communist expansion in Europe disappeared, providing new possibilities for a more unified Europe that would link the continent's western and eastern nations in new forms of commerce, cultural exchange, and political cooperation. The challenges of "globalization" remained an ongoing problem for European economies, but the diminution of the nuclear arms race—which had seemed almost impossible to many Europeans in the early 1980s—was soon followed by an equally unexpected upheaval across all of eastern Europe in 1989.

Suggested Further Readings can be found in the ebook, on Connect, or online at www.mhhe .com/kramer12e.

25

THE INTERNATIONAL REVOLT AGAINST SOVIET COMMUNISM

Most Europeans and other people around the world were astonished in the mid-1980s to see some of the basic structures of Soviet communism begin to come apart. The transitions in the Soviet Union also opened the way for other extraordinary events, in 1989, in central and eastern Europe, where the existing Communist regimes collapsed one by one and were replaced with virtually no violence. In an even more epochal event, in 1991, the Communist regime of the Soviet Union itself came to an end after holding absolute power since the Russian Revolution of 1917; and the U.S.S.R. disintegrated into Russia and its other component republics.

In a strict sense, if revolutions are defined as violent political and social upheavals, there was no actual revolution in 1989–1991. Indeed, it was a source of wonder and satisfaction that such sweeping change could occur without armed struggle or a wider European war. The older regimes disappeared less by explosion than by implosion—a breakup from within. The "revolution" of 1989 could remain peaceful because (in contrast to the French Revolution of 1789) it faced no strong internal resistance or threat of foreign intervention. Yet the upheavals were revolutionary in that they demolished repressive governments and brought abrupt, radical change. They reasserted political ideals that were revolutionary when proclaimed in America in 1776, in France in 1789, throughout Europe in 1848, and in many of the anticolonial movements after 1919 or 1945—ideals that were now called human rights and the principles of a democratic civil society. These ideals had been incorporated into the American Declaration of Independence and the French Declaration of the Rights of Man, and they had become the guiding ideals for democracies in most of the modern world. Democracy meant representative and constitutional government and freely contested elections; and freedom and independence meant guarantees against repression by one's own government or dictatorial foreign rule. Such ideas were now invoked again to support the new political revolutions of 1989, though the actual practice of democracy in post-Communist societies (as in even the oldest democratic societies) often fell short of the professed ideals, and some post-Communist states gradually drifted toward new anti-democratic practices.

Chapter emblem: Germans destroying the Berlin Wall in November 1989. (©Patrick PIEL/Getty images)

The Revolution of 1989 gave the people of central and eastern Europe a long-deferred opportunity to decide their own destiny. With the collapse of the U.S.S.R. one of the two superpowers that had dominated international affairs and a European sphere of influence since 1945 abruptly disappeared. The Cold War, as the world had known it, came to an end, though Russia remained a large, important power and other strategic conflicts soon emerged. A new global and European political era opened, leading to new challenges and frustrations, but also raising expectations and possibilities for a more peaceful international order.

115.   THE CRISIS IN THE SOVIET UNION

Neither the transformation of central and eastern Europe nor of the Soviet Union could have taken place as they did without the changes in the U.S.S.R. that began in 1985. A new reformist Soviet leader, Mikhail S. Gorbachev, unexpectedly rose to supreme power from within the constraining Soviet system of centralized control and one-party government. The country was in dire straits, however, and the party leadership itself was desperately looking for some way to revitalize the state's political and economic policies. As a young man Gorbachev studied at the university in Moscow and at the agricultural institute in Stavropol, his home city in southwestern Russia. After working as an agricultural researcher, he received a full-time party assignment in the region and came to the attention of Yuri V. Andropov (soon to be the party general secretary) and other party leaders in Moscow. His appointment to the party secretariat in Moscow in 1978, with special responsibility for agriculture, afforded him a privileged view of the country's deep economic troubles. By 1980 he was a member of the Politburo, and by 1984 he was being groomed by Andropov for top party leadership. After struggling with the weakening leadership of an incapacitated Brezhnev, who clung to power during a long period of declining health, and then seeing his two successors, Andropov and Konstantin U. Chernenko, die in office after only brief terms, the Politburo in March 1985 decided that it was time for a forceful, younger leader. At 54, Gorbachev was by far its youngest member. Andrei Gromyko, for many years foreign minister of the U.S.S.R., ultimately endorsed Gorbachev and is said to have reassured those with doubts: "He has a nice smile but he has iron teeth."

Gorbachev at once demonstrated a dynamism and vigor that had been absent from recent Soviet leadership. His first task was to convince the party and country that fundamental economic restructuring was needed to break a pervasive pattern of economic

Perestroika

stagnation. He called this restructuring *perestroika,* by which he meant a drastic modification of the centrally planned command economy inherited from Stalin and carried forward with only minor changes since. However well the older system may have served the industrialization of the country, the test of the Second World War, and the projects of postwar reconstruction, it was ill-suited for the rapidly evolving technologies and production systems of the global industrial era. Industry and agriculture urgently needed freedom from restraints to release creative energies, provide incentives for productivity, introduce new technologies, raise quality levels, and satisfy consumer needs. Gorbachev's proposed remedies included decentralization, self-management for industry and agriculture, an end to the rigidity imposed by the party and government bureaucracy, and incentives for productivity. He moved cautiously, believing that exhortation and a sense of urgency would bring results, but his proposed reforms quickly evoked opposition from entrenched Soviet bureaucrats.

For his economic restructuring to succeed, Gorbachev needed broad popular support from others both within and outside the Communist Party, which he hoped to gain through political change. Thus he also called for *glasnost,* or "openness," which he closely linked to economic reform. By *glasnost* he meant the right to voice the need for change, the freedom to criticize the existing system, and the willingness to reexamine past mistakes and wrongdoings. Even if this new openness originally had a more limited objective, *glasnost* soon took on a dynamic of its own. It led to an unprecedented liberalization of Soviet society, a freer press, and an end to the decades of totalitarian control over political, cultural, and intellectual life. The ferment that had been choked off after Khrushchev's brief "thaw" in the 1950s now reappeared and quickly expanded. Newspapers, theater, the arts, and political discourse opened up as at no time before. Books and plays written in the 1960s or earlier but never permitted publication or performance made their appearance, including Pasternak's *Dr. Zhivago* and eventually even Solzhenitsyn's *Gulag Archipelago,* the novel that gave the outside world a concise and widely used name for Stalin's network of forced labor camps. Gorbachev permitted the physicist Andrei Sakharov, a leading dissenter and committed opponent of the regime, to return to Moscow from exile and take an active part in political life. Soviet Jews, who had earlier been refused permission to leave the country, were now allowed to emigrate in larger numbers. The atmosphere changed visibly. People became freer and less fearful. The legal codes were revised to encompass a measure of civil liberties, allow freedom of expression, and reduce police abuses. The KGB itself came under public and legislative scrutiny. Gorbachev even spoke of freedom of conscience and tolerance for religion, negotiating a rapprochement with the Orthodox Church.

Glasnost

In 1987, on the very occasion of the 70th anniversary of the Bolshevik Revolution, Gorbachev spoke publicly of "Stalin's enormous and unforgivable crimes." A monument to Stalin's victims was planned, while the press openly discussed their total number, clearly in the tens of millions. New history textbooks were prepared, as well as a revised history of the party. Gorbachev told the country that there should be "no forgotten names or blanks in history or literature."

Although Gorbachev did not challenge the role of the Communist Party as the directing agent of Soviet society, he was clearly introducing changes that would curb its monopoly on power. Reform could not simply be imposed from above. The people, he said, needed more than a "good tsar," and new government institutions would thus be required. Constitutional reforms in 1988 created a new national legislature, and multicandidate elections were to replace the traditional one-party slate of nominees. Gorbachev began with a technocratic vision of a more efficient economy, but he and his supporters were moving the country toward a sweeping transformation of Soviet life and society.

Gorbachev's constitutional reforms

In the freer atmosphere the government released long-suppressed information about poor grain harvests, inefficient state enterprises, and nuclear accidents that had occurred before the worst nuclear disaster at the Chernobyl power plant in 1986. At party meetings and at the new Congress of People's Deputies the public heard for the first time outspoken critiques of Soviet society: descriptions of poverty, corruption, crime, alcoholism, and drugs; of serious shortcomings in medicine, health, and housing; of environmental decay. Tens of millions, perhaps one-fifth the population, lived in poverty.

Gorbachev soon recognized that the country's economic problems were more intractable than he had thought, but he persisted with his gradualist reform program. Private enterprise and state industries were one day to be integrated into a market-based economy, linked to the outside world. Foreign capital for trade and investment and joint

Limited economic reforms

ventures with foreign firms were to be welcomed. Soviet managers were encouraged to travel abroad to learn advanced (sometimes elementary) business and accounting practices. But many of these reforms remained paper decrees only; party officials and government bureaucrats helped checkmate others. The older economic system remained virtually unchanged. Gorbachev shrank from moving more rapidly to a market-oriented competitive economy. His concerns about painful short-term dislocations and political unrest reinforced his commitment to reform rather than abandon the older Communist system in its entirety.

The party's grip loosened

But the constitutional and political changes that Gorbachev had initiated significantly loosened the monopoly grip of the party. In March 1989 openly contested, multicandidate elections were held, the first since 1917, though well over half the seats were reserved for the party and various state-sponsored associations. Voters elected a Congress of People's Deputies, which in turn chose a smaller standing legislative body to meet more frequently. Both were empowered to initiate legislation and freely debate issues. In 1990, under another constitutional reform, the Congress of People's Deputies created a presidency with broad executive powers modeled on the American and French examples. The Congress elected Gorbachev president.

Gorbachev brought about stunning political changes, unprecedented in the years since the revolution. Western political leaders in the era of the Great Depression had sought to save capitalism by reforming it. Gorbachev was likewise bent on saving the Communist system by reform. Yet the country remained divided and disoriented. It was torn between

Criticisms of Gorbachev

the old guard, who resisted the Gorbachev changes, and a growing group of democratic reformers in the central legislature and in the newly elected parliaments of the restless component republics who believed that Gorbachev had not gone far enough in either political or economic matters. Praise for his policies gave way to criticism for the still-dismal economic record and the continuing weakness of agricultural production. Critics condemned his indecisive, sometimes contradictory, steps in shaping a market economy and his reluctance to revamp the collectivized agrarian system. He also seemed determined to repress ethnic unrest and to reject the demands of the constituent republics for greater freedom from central control. The military, the industrial bureaucrats, and the party were still in command.

The loosening of totalitarian controls unleashed nationalist movements and long-suppressed ethnic tensions. Every one of the 15 federated constituent republics of the Soviet Union began to raise demands for independence. Secessionist pressures developed most quickly and went furthest in the three Baltic republics. People in Latvia, Lithuania, and Estonia remembered their 20 years of independence between the two world wars; how they had fallen victim to the Nazi-Soviet pact of 1939; and how one-third of their population had been killed, deported, or driven into exile in the war and postwar years. In the freer atmosphere of *glasnost,* the constituent republics, which had come to consider themselves trapped within the Soviet Empire, were able to denounce Soviet control. For his part Gorbachev was willing to create a federation council to advise on matters relating to the republics, but he would not risk the wrath of the old guard by going beyond that.

Gorbachev and the West

As the new era evolved, Communist ideology and the view of world affairs that had helped to create and prolong the Cold War were also transformed. Gorbachev repudiated ideological struggle. In an interdependent globe besieged by nuclear, ecological, and economic

Mikhail Gorbachev advocated economic and cultural reforms that came to be known in general terms as the call for *glasnost,* **or "openness," and** *perestroika,* **or "structural reforms." Gorbachev expected the reforms to benefit agriculture as well as the industrial sector of the Soviet economy, and he campaigned for his program among both farmers and workers. He is shown here (smiling, on the right) during a meeting with workers on a collective farm near Moscow in 1987. Such contacts with people in the countryside affirmed the spirit of** *glasnost,* **but the reforms on state-owned farms did not go far enough to bring about a rise in agricultural production.**
(©SVF2/Universal Images Group/Getty Images)

dangers, the highest concern must be "universal human interests" and the "universal human idea." Because Marx and Lenin had argued that "universal" ideals were usually a smoke screen for class rule and oppression, the turnabout was startling.

Gorbachev changed the image of the Soviet Union as a military threat and promoter of world revolution. He became a familiar and popular figure in Western capitals as a negotiator, diplomat, and often Western-style politician. He followed his conciliatory words with deeds. He removed troops and weapons *Encouraging détente* from eastern Europe, negotiated nuclear arms reduction agreements with the United States, ended the Russian war in Afghanistan, and helped to resolve Cold War regional conflicts. He spoke up for human rights, paid tribute to the standards embodied in the Helsinki Accords, and called for a "common European home" for western and eastern Europe. We have seen how Gorbachev extended the earlier policies of détente, believing that the reduction of nuclear arms was essential for the relief of intolerable military burdens on the Soviet economy. Gorbachev's support for détente thus went hand in hand with his plans for domestic economic reform. From their low point in the early 1980s, relations between the Soviet Union and the United States, as noted earlier, abruptly changed after 1985. A series of meetings between Gorbachev and President Ronald Reagan led to major new agreements on the reduction of nuclear weapons.

In summit meetings in Washington and Moscow, the Soviet and American leaders had closer contact with each other's people than ever before. Gorbachev mingled with throngs in crowded Washington streets. Reagan, in the shadow of Lenin's tomb in Moscow, spoke openly about the Soviet repression of dissidents, the refusal to permit Jews to emigrate, religious persecution, and the ongoing war in Afghanistan. Gorbachev eventually committed his country to the withdrawal of Soviet troops from the unwinnable war against Muslim insurgents in Afghanistan—a "bleeding wound" he called it. Meanwhile Gorbachev encouraged the reforms and vast changes that spread across eastern Europe in the late 1980s. By 1990 Gorbachev and Reagan's successor, President George H. W. Bush, could jointly hail the end of the Cold War. In 1991 they signed a strategic arms treaty pledging each nation to scale down by about a third its arsenal of long-range nuclear missiles.

116. THE COLLAPSE OF COMMUNISM IN CENTRAL AND EASTERN EUROPE

While Gorbachev began to introduce reforms in the mid-1980s, central and eastern Europe remained under Stalinist-type party bosses, some in office for over 30 years, impervious to pressure for reform. But cracks and fissures were apparent even before Gorbachev launched his new policies in the Soviet Union. The years of détente had already opened up the East European states to Western loans and investments and to closer contacts with the West. Dissidents called for a recognition of the human rights guaranteed by the Helsinki Accords in 1975, to which the Soviet Union and the East European bloc had subscribed. They wrote about ending party-state dictatorships and restoring a "civil society" in which people could live their lives free from the dictates of the state.

Economic stagnation

As in the Soviet Union itself, East Europeans discussed the shortcomings of their centrally planned economies, which had stagnated since the 1970s. Initiative and productivity were stifled, and large subsidies propped up inefficient state-run monopolies unchallenged by competition. The older plants and industrial infrastructure were decaying; the environment was deteriorating. A scarcity of investment capital prevented the growth of new industries. Even if state-run planned economies were to continue, many argued for new market competition, incentives for entrepreneurs and workers, and encouragement of joint ventures with the outside capitalist world.

Poland: The Solidarity Movement

In the 1970s and 1980s demands for economic reform and political liberalization surfaced almost everywhere, but nowhere so forcefully as in Poland. Gomulka, who governed Poland for 14 years after 1956, disappointed the reformers. He used troops to put down strikes, persecuted church leaders, and permitted an anti-Semitic campaign against the small number of Jews still living in Poland. In 1970, after riots over food prices, the party replaced him with the reform-minded Edmund Gierek, who embarked on an ambitious economic development program, financed by heavy borrowing from western Europe. The initial results were promising and the economy began to improve, but to meet its rising debt obligations, the country expanded exports at the expense of production for domestic Polish consumers. Economic conditions again deteriorated, sparking a new wave of social unrest.

In 1980 the rise in food prices led to widespread strikes, which began in the Lenin shipyards in Gdansk and spread rapidly to other cities. A somewhat freer political atmosphere made it possible for workers to create an aggressive independent trade union federation, Solidarity, the first of its kind in any Communist country. The new workers' movement found a militant leader and national symbol of protest in Lech Walesa. Before long Solidarity claimed a national membership of 10 million industrial and agricultural workers. With backing from leaders of the Polish Catholic Church, its leaders called for free elections and a role for Solidarity in government. The Soviet government, still led in this era by Leonid Brezhnev, once again saw a socialist regime threatened. They put heavy pressure on the Polish government and party to curb Solidarity, oust Gierek, and install the more dependable General Wojciech Jaruzelski as party head and premier. When strikes and demonstrations continued to mobilize wide popular support, raising the threat of Soviet military intervention, Jaruzelski, in 1981, imposed martial law, banned Solidarity, and arrested its leaders.

Lech Walesa

But once the power of Solidarity was curbed and the Soviet threat of intervention passed, Jaruzelski himself took a different tack. To placate labor he lifted martial law and initiated a reform program of his own. International pressure also contributed to liberalization. John Paul II, the first Polish pope to head the Roman Catholic Church, inspired huge demonstrations for freedom during visits to Poland after his elevation to the papacy in 1978; and Lech Walesa was honored with a Nobel Peace Prize in 1983. Polish dissidents thus became international symbols of the growing European campaign for human rights.

Jaruzelski's efforts at economic reform failed to improve the economy or mollify widespread resentments. Meanwhile, in the late 1980s, Gorbachev's liberalizing reforms in the Soviet Union encouraged further reforms in Poland and suggested that the Soviets would not intervene to check liberalization in eastern Europe. The recognition that the "Brezhnev Doctrine" was no longer operative encouraged a movement for reform even within the Polish Communist Party itself.

In June of 1989 Jaruzelski and the party leadership permitted parliamentary elections, in which Solidarity and other groups were free to put forward candidates, although the Communist Party was guaranteed a fixed number of seats. The first open elections in Poland in over 40 years gave Solidarity a landslide victory in all contested seats. A Solidarity-led coalition cabinet was formed in which the Communists were a minority. The party took steps to transform itself into a Western-type socialist party, but many of its members drifted away. The party-state dictatorship ended without bloodshed. The authoritarian walls in eastern Europe were breached, thus allowing political and economic reforms to flow into Polish society.

Reforms within the party

The new government moved at once to restructure the economy along free-market lines. Sharp differences emerged between Lech Walesa, elected president in 1990, and his one-time political allies; and former Communists soon returned to the political scene, but Poland was finally and henceforth in charge of its own national political destiny. Like most other former Communist nations, Poland's government alternated between left-leaning and right-leaning factions in the new era of national autonomy. The Poles adopted a democratic Constitution in 1997, joined the NATO alliance in 1999, and entered the European Union in 2004. In the first decade of the twenty-first century, however, a new nationalist, conservative movement called the Law and Justice Party came to power under the leadership of two brothers (Lech and Jarosław Kaczyński) and continued to control the government after Andrzej Duda was elected as president in 2015. Although Duda and his political allies won wide support in Polish elections, critics within Poland and other members of the European Union condemned the president's growing control of the judiciary, the government's attempt to deny any Polish involvement in the Holocaust, the harassment

Law and Justice Party

of opposition groups, and a general embrace of populist or anti-immigrant nationalism. The long transition out of the postwar Communist era in Poland thus continued into the following century and included a resurgence of nationalist political ideas that explicitly challenged the transnational, democratic goals of the European Union.

Hungary: Reform into Revolution

In Hungary the attempt at reform in 1956, initiated by the Communist Party leadership itself, had been brusquely interrupted when the Soviets intervened with troops and tanks to suppress the "counterrevolution." For the next 32 years, hard-liner János Kádár ran the country. But even under Kádár the party, without relinquishing its monopoly on political control, moved away from an inflexible centrally planned economy, encouraged a degree of private enterprise, and turned to Western countries for capital investment. For a time the economy expanded and standards of living rose, but the limited reforms accomplished no fundamental change. After 1985, as Gorbachev's reforms were implemented in the Soviet Union, a new drive for political and social change began to develop also within Hungary.

In 1988 the party sought to show its support for change and also to maintain power by easing Kádár out of office. The new Hungarian leadership allowed opposition parties and multiparty elections and began to dismantle the older party-state apparatus. It even

Party initiatives

dissolved the Communist Party, reconstituting it along socialist and social–democratic lines, and a wide range of independent political groups came forward. Reform was therefore initiated by the party itself, and it had turned into a revolution without bloodshed. The new leaders reclaimed the memory of the suppressed 1956 uprising as a progressive movement and formally condemned those who had invited Soviet intervention. By sweeping aside the humiliation of 1956, the country reasserted its national independence, restored self-government and civic freedom, and opened the way to a market-oriented economy and a pluralist democracy.

The developments in Hungary soon precipitated even more dramatic events. The new Hungary, looking westward, symbolically demolished a portion of the barbed-wire barrier on its Austrian border. A few months later, in September 1989, when large numbers of East Germans vacationing in Hungary sought to emigrate to the West, Hungary opened its border with Austria and allowed the Germans to exit. For the first time since 1961 East Germans found a safe way to leave their country, and this exodus helped to bring about a dramatic political transformation in all of Germany.

In the decades after 1989, Hungary resembled Poland and other post-Communist states that sought to create free-market economies and democratic governments. Political parties of the left, right, and center held power at different times in various coalitions, and Hungary (also like Poland) joined NATO in 1999 and the European Union in 2004. But a nationalist, conservative movement called the Hungarian Civic Alliance (FIDESZ was the Hungarian acronym) came to power in the twenty-first century, and under Prime Minister Victor Orbán the Hungarian government moved after 2010 toward a more authoritarian nationalism that gradually broke away from the more multilateral themes of the EU. Orbán won large majorities in Hungarian elections, but his opponents inside and outside the country condemned his centralizing control of political power, the decline of the free press, the hostility for the Central European University (which eventually moved out of Hungary), and the virulent, anti-Semitic attacks on critics such as the Hungarian-American philanthropist George Soros. History never exactly repeats itself, but many Europeans became deeply concerned that Orbán and other twenty-first-century political leaders were reasserting nationalist ideologies and policies that had shattered European democracies in the twentieth century. The collapse of Communism was viewed in the expanding European Union of the 1990s as a new opportunity for building democracies and transnational collaborations, but the demise of Communism also offered new opportunities for nationalist movements that mobilized deep fears of foreigners or immigrants and challenged the essential tenets or institutions of liberal democratic societies.

The German Democratic Republic: Revolution and Reunification

Gorbachev's positive attitude toward reform also hastened the pace of change in the other hard-line dictatorships of eastern Europe—the German Democratic Republic, Czechoslovakia, Bulgaria, and Romania. A surge of new political upheavals during the fall of 1989 overthrew the Communist regimes in all of these countries at almost the same time.

In the German Democratic Republic Erich Honecker, in power since 1961, stubbornly held the line against reform. Although East Germany boasted the strongest economy and highest per capita income in eastern Europe, its citizens enjoyed far fewer amenities than the prosperous West Germans, and the Berlin Wall still blocked the free movement of people across the border. Although Honecker had agreed to the closer economic and political relations with West Germany that Willy Brandt had initiated with his *Ostpolitik* in 1969, he refused to relax controls at home. But the East Germans were watching the Gorbachev changes in the Soviet Union and the rush of events in Poland and Hungary; and when the opening of Hungarian borders offered a new passageway into western Germany, thousands of people seized the opportunity to migrate in the autumn of 1989. The trickle soon became a flood, as East Germans fled the repression and drabness of the German Democratic Republic to find better economic opportunities in the Federal Republic of Germany, where as Germans they were entitled by law to receive citizenship and assistance in finding homes and jobs. By the end of 1989, more than 350,000 among East Germany's population of 17 million had left, and many more emigrated in the early months of 1990.

Flight from Honecker's rule

Demonstrations against the Communist government meanwhile mounted throughout East Germany, but Gorbachev clearly signaled that Honecker could not expect the Soviet troops stationed in East Germany to save the regime; and he even warned against the use of force to prevent reform. In Leipzig, over 100,000 demonstrators, assembling in churches, marched in solemn procession with lighted candles, calling for the resignation of party and government leaders and for an end to the police state. The party forced Honecker to resign.

The new leadership promised elections and confirmed the right of free and unrestricted travel. On November 9, 1989, when the government opened up the hated symbol of confinement itself, the Berlin Wall, excited Berliners on both sides of the barrier tore it down. The exodus to West Germany continued. Many East Germans were infuriated by public disclosure of the corruption and luxurious living that Honecker and the party elite had enjoyed while ordinary people suffered over the years. The entire party structure now came crashing down. The Politburo and Central Committee resigned. Honecker and other leaders were arrested on charges of corruption and embezzlement, and younger reformers assumed control. Delegates from a wide variety of opposition groups, exultant over their "gentle" revolution, met with reform-minded representatives of the former Communist Party to oversee the transition to a new constitutional regime, which many still envisaged as a socialist society that could now truly embody its democratic name.

Corruption within the party

The independent Polish trade union movement, Solidarity, gained the support of millions of workers in the early 1980s. Solidarity organized strikes and demonstrations, demanding better wages for workers and major reforms in the Communist political system. These demonstrators gathered to support Solidarity at a rally outside the court buildings in Warsaw in November 1980. The Solidarity movement was suppressed after martial law was imposed the following year, but the Polish Communist Party could never destroy the movement's popular appeal. Solidarity eventually won control of Poland's first new government in free elections that took place at the end of the decade.

(©Keystone/Hulton Archive/Getty Images)

Once the German Democratic Republic was no longer Communist, however, pressure for reunification with West Germany began to build. Helmut Kohl, the Christian Democratic chancellor in West Germany, took the initiative to reunite the two Germanys. For many of the wartime Allies the prospect of a reunified Germany of close to 80 million people, possessing one of the world's most powerful economies, stirred grim ghosts of the past. The "German question" resurfaced. The entire postwar European settlement stood at issue. Because no final peace treaty had ever been signed, reunification required the approval of the

The "German question" revived

The destruction of the Berlin Wall in November 1989 provided dramatic physical and symbolic evidence of the collapse of Communist regimes in eastern Europe. Young people, like the men swinging their hammers here, shattered the Wall in a great celebration that released long-suppressed political anger and marked the culmination of a nonviolent revolution in East Germany. Within a year, the two postwar German states were united in a new, enlarged Federal Republic of Germany, which faced the social and economic challenges of bringing two different societies into an integrated national political system. (©Patrick PIEL/Getty images)

four major Allied powers of the Second World War. There was hesitation, especially in France and Britain, but it was difficult, as the Americans argued, to deny the German people the right of self-determination 45 years after the end of the war. Moreover, the Federal Republic of Germany had demonstrated its commitment to democracy. There was confidence that a reunified Germany could integrate East Germany and remain part of democratic western Europe and the European Community. Despite the unspeakable crimes of the Nazi era, it seemed unreasonable to insist upon unalterable traits of national character or to punish future generations for atrocities of the past.

Reunification therefore moved forward swiftly. The four Allied powers, including the U.S.S.R., gave their approval and relinquished their occupation rights. Germany confirmed the earlier cession of territories in the east to the U.S.S.R. and Poland and pledged the inviolability of the German-Polish border. The two German states merged their economies and the West German mark became the common currency. On October 3, 1990, the two states formally united to become an enlarged Federal Republic of Germany, its capital to be reestablished within a few years in Berlin. In the first nationwide elections, Chancellor Kohl and his Christian Democrats, who played a key role in the reunification, won a sweeping victory. Although the nation's postelection exhilaration was soon tempered by the gigantic problems of absorbing the thoroughly decayed East German economy, a key component of post-1945 European politics and conflicts—the division of Germany—permanently disappeared. Equally important, Germany had been reunited through democratic processes rather than through violence or the actions of an authoritarian government. The united German state would face complex challenges as the former

The "Velvet Revolution" in Czechoslovakia exemplified the nonviolent overthrow of late twentieth-century communist regimes in central Europe. Czech dissidents, including the playwright Vaclav Havel, had led anti-Soviet campaigns for human rights since the 1960s, so the upheaval in November 1989 reaffirmed political aspirations that had flourished during the "Prague spring" of 1968. These two historical moments were linked in this photograph as the younger Havel took the hand of his predecessor Alexander Dubček and made his way with the dissident singer Marta Kubisova toward a vast Prague rally against Czechoslovakia's discredited Communist government.
(©LUBOMIR KOTEK/AFP/Getty Images)

Communist regions were integrated into the country's democratic political culture, and right-wing nationalist groups would reappear in Germany as in other central European countries. The reunited Germany, however, remained a key pillar of the European Union and the strongest economic force in Europe's transnational commercial system.

Czechoslovakia: "'89 Is '68 Upside Down"

In Czechoslovakia the ruling hard-liners who took power after Soviet military forces had ruthlessly crushed the "Prague spring" in 1968 disapproved of Gorbachev's reforms in the Soviet Union and stifled dissent at home. But the dissidents quietly grew in numbers and influence. Charter '77, an organization of intellectuals formed after the Helsinki Accords of 1975, became a rallying point for the struggle against the dictatorship. The Czech public observed the steady disintegration of Communist power in Poland, Hungary, and East Germany. Demonstrations also broke out in Prague in the autumn of 1989, and the government responded with the usual arrest of the dissident leaders. But thousands of demonstrators went into the streets to call for the release of the imprisoned dissidents and for the government's resignation. Reformers came together in a loose coalition and found inspiring leadership in the ideas and activism of the dissident writer Vaclav Havel, an outspoken opponent of the regime who had repeatedly suffered persecution and imprisonment for his views.

The demonstrations grew in intensity. When 350,000 demonstrators gathered in Prague on November 24 to demand an end to the party-state dictatorship and when a general strike threatened to bring the whole country to a standstill, the government and party leaders all at once resigned. Alexander Dubček, the hero of 1968, dramatically appeared on a balcony alongside a new reform-minded Communist prime minister, who appointed opposition leaders to his cabinet, pledged a free press and free elections, dissolved the secret police, and abolished the compulsory teaching of Marxism-Leninism in the universities. The party's 41-year monopoly on power was finally broken. Havel became provisional president and led a new cabinet in which the Communists were a minority. Gorbachev took steps to withdraw the 75,000 Soviet troops that had been stationed in the country since 1968. In the excitement someone exultantly observed: "'89 is '68 upside down." The people had wrested control without bloodshed in a "velvet revolution" that destroyed an "iron curtain" regime.

A "velvet revolution"

Of all the nations in the disintegrating Soviet bloc, Czechoslovakia had the strongest democratic traditions. Despite long-standing ethnic tensions, it had developed a genuine parliamentary democracy in the interwar years, and it was the last of the eastern European states to fall under Communist dictatorship after the Second World War. It moved rapidly after 1990 toward a market-oriented economy and a pluralist democracy—the kind of civil society that had been sought by dissidents such as Havel, who was now elected president of the new republic. But an unexpected political sequel followed within three years. The country came apart when Slovak political leaders pressed for an independent Slovakia, which some had wanted since 1918. A negotiated settlement arranged for the peaceful division of the country in January 1993 into two independent and sovereign nations—the Czech Republic and Slovakia. Both nations later joined NATO and the European Union; and both built democratic institutions that continued to develop amid the political transitions in central Europe during the first decades of the twenty-first century.

Bulgaria's Palace Revolution, Bloodshed in Romania

Even Bulgaria, considered the most docile of the Soviet client states, succumbed to the new revolutionary contagion. Mass demonstrations in Sofia demanded an end to the Communist dictatorship, and pressure from within the party forced the resignation of the party chief who had run the country for 35 years. The revolution in Bulgaria was essentially a palace coup within the party, but it, too, arose in response to deep national resentments. In a country that had known little freedom even in the pre-Communist years, the question was whether the reform-minded former Communists who, like many others elsewhere, renamed themselves Socialists, could work together with the new opposition to create a true democracy.

Only in Romania did events take a violent turn in 1989. It seemed at first as though the revolution would not even reach Bucharest. Since 1965, the dictator Nicolae Ceausescu had firmly controlled party and government, ruling with the help of his wife and family and building a cult of personality around himself. His Stalin-like ambition was to transform a largely agrarian society into a modern industrial society regardless of the human cost. For his modernization program he borrowed heavily from Western institutions, but to remain independent of the outside world he insisted that the country regularly pay the burdensome interest on its debt. All dissent was kept under tight surveillance and control. What was distinctive about Ceausescu was his independent position in foreign and military affairs. Unlike the other members of the Warsaw Pact, he had supported Israel in the Arab-Israeli wars and had refused to join the invasion of Czechoslovakia in 1968.

The Ceausescu regime

Throughout the revolutionary autumn of 1989 Ceausescu ignored the upheavals in central and eastern Europe. But in December protest riots broke out in Timisoara, a key provincial capital. The military refused to fire on the demonstrators, but the dictator's private security forces took over, killing hundreds. Word of the brutality spread, sparking new protests. When the security forces attempted to suppress demonstrators in Bucharest, angry crowds forced the dictator to flee the capital.

For days a battle raged between Ceausescu's security forces and regular army units supporting the revolutionists until the security forces were routed. Ceausescu and his wife were apprehended in the provinces and executed by a firing squad. A National Salvation Front, consisting of former officials of the Ceausescu regime and emergent opposition leaders, took control. Although former Communists dominated the new regime and the strength of the democratic forces remained limited, the party's authority ended and the most repressive dictatorship of the Eastern bloc came to an ignominious end.

The Revolutions of 1989 in Central and Eastern Europe

Except in Romania, the eastern European revolutions of 1989 were carried out everywhere by placards and candles, not by rifles. Solidarity's early struggle in Poland and Gorbachev's liberalization in the Soviet Union made it possible for revolutionary changes in central and eastern Europe to take place as they did. With a suddenness that took even the closest observers by surprise, smoldering discontents flared up all at once in a revolutionary firestorm that transformed the region more decisively than the famous revolutions of 1848. The long-sought goals of national independence and political democracy, which many people in eastern Europe had been trying to reach since the nineteenth century, would mostly become a political reality during the decade after 1989, though concerns about new authoritarian threats to democracy would develop in the early twenty-first century—especially in Poland and Hungary. In the immediate aftermath of the firestorm that "burned down" every government in eastern Europe, however, the collapse of the Communist regimes greatly advanced the long-developing European campaign for human rights and seemed all the more remarkable because almost no human lives were lost in the conflagration. Gorbachev, committed to curtailing economic and military obligations for the sake of the Soviet economy, accepted the end of the Communist regimes that Stalin had imposed after the Second World War.

The groundwork for change had been prepared by the growing economic ties and contacts with western Europe during the years of détente, the Helsinki Accords, the stubborn challenge of Solidarity, and the courage of the dissidents. But

it was Gorbachev's clear signal that the Soviets would not intervene outside their own borders that made the stupendous chain of revolutionary events possible, toppling one regime after another. The revolutionists, armed only with a moral cause, would have found it difficult to prevail if any of their own governments had chosen to use the full power of the army and police. During this same year, in June 1989, the Communist government of China violently repressed pro-democracy demonstrations at Tiananmen Square in Beijing, and such repression might have been repeated in eastern Europe. But the ruling elites, without Soviet support to bolster them, yielded; they simply lacked the will to govern under a system that had lost legitimacy and credibility, even among those who controlled it.

117. THE COLLAPSE OF THE SOVIET UNION

Before the stunning developments in eastern Europe could be fully absorbed, an even more epochal event occurred. An all but bloodless revolution brought the collapse of communism in 1991 in the very epicenter of world communism, undoing the Russian Revolution of 1917 and ending three-quarters of a century of Communist Party rule. The Union of Soviet Socialist Republics, heir to the one-time tsarist empire, dissolved into its component republics. Russia reemerged as a single state without its Soviet-controlled national appendages.

How did this collapse of a seemingly impregnable regime with a heavy apparatus of military and police security occur? We have already seen how Gorbachev in the years after 1985 opened up Soviet society to revitalize the system but avoided the more decisive measures that might have ended the hegemony of the Communist Party. Gorbachev vacillated between the reformers and the hard-line conservatives. A superb political tactician—few leaders could have brought the party and the system as far as he had within five years—he nonetheless gave the impression that he did not know how thorough a transformation he would ultimately permit. The old guard became further embittered as they witnessed the loss of Soviet control over eastern Europe. Meanwhile the economy worsened, and by 1990 production was in steep decline. Gorbachev tried plan after plan, but the economic structure remained virtually unchanged. In addition, not only the Baltic republics, as might have been expected, but the Russian republic itself and all the other component republics of the U.S.S.R. were pressing for sovereignty—self-government and control over their political and economic fortunes.

The "Creeping Coup d'État"

In the autumn of 1990 Gorbachev decided for strategic political reasons to replace reform-minded ministers and other key officials with old-guard appointees unsympathetic to his reform program. He summarily abandoned an important "500-Day" economic plan that would have freed prices and moved more swiftly to a market economy. The plan would also have curtailed the military budget and given broad economic powers to the republics. It now appeared that military force would be deployed against the secessionist Baltic republics, which earlier, in the spring of 1990, had proclaimed their independence. In January 1991 Soviet troops, apparently taking matters into their own hands without Gorbachev's prior approval, used military force against demonstrators in Lithuania, with a loss of lives; and there was anxiety about where the military might move next.

The democratic reformers grew alarmed by the turn of events. Some spoke of "six wasted years of reform communism" and of a "creeping coup d'état." They had concluded that the country's economic problems could not be resolved short of demolishing the entire central planning structure, and also that each republic must be allowed to work out its own destiny. To the reformers Gorbachev seemed a barrier to further change, and he in turn grew increasingly hostile to them, convinced that he alone knew the proper pace of reform.

Uneasiness of reformers

The democratic reformers turned to a political figure who on the surface seemed an unlikely choice as their leader. Boris N. Yeltsin was blunt and outspoken, not by any definition an intellectual. His personal style made a striking contrast to the suave, smooth, and urbane Gorbachev, but Yeltsin knew the Communist Party well, and all its secrets. He had been party boss in Moscow and a member of the Politburo. When in 1987 he openly attacked the privileges, perquisites, and downright incompetence of Communist

Party officials, he had been dismissed from his posts, vilified in the press, and sent off into the political wilderness. Humiliated by Gorbachev and the party, he found allies among the democratic reformers, who saw in him a populist figure around whom they could rally public support. They helped polish some of his rough edges, undertook his political reeducation, and converted him into an opposition leader of stature.

Yeltsin becomes opposition leader

Elected to the Soviet legislature in March 1989, he soon played a key role in the opposition. With the encouragement of his political allies, however, he turned to a new, and seemingly unpromising, power base, the Russian legislature, that is, the legislature of the Russian constituent republic. Yeltsin was elected to this formerly insignificant legislative body in 1990. Becoming chair of the legislature almost immediately, he used his position to step up his attacks on Gorbachev, the party, and the central government. When Gorbachev conceded to demands that the constituent republics should choose their presidents in direct popular elections, Yeltsin won election in June 1991 as president of the Russian republic in an overwhelming victory over his Communist opponents—the first president in Russian history to be elected by popular vote. It was a distinction that Gorbachev, elected president of the U.S.S.R. solely by the Soviet Congress, could not claim. (It was at the time of Yeltsin's election that Russia's second largest city voted to change its name from Leningrad back to St. Petersburg, as it had been called before 1914.) From his new position of strength Yeltsin demanded immediate independence for the three Baltic states and self-government for Russia and the other Soviet constituent republics.

Gorbachev, intent on keeping the country and the union intact, began negotiations with the presidents of the increasingly independent republics. He agreed to surrender considerably more autonomy to the 15 republics, including substantial control over the economic and financial resources that Moscow had always tightly guarded. The three Baltic republics, insisting on full independence, refused to participate in the negotiations, as did Georgia, now embroiled in its own internal turmoil. But in August 1991 the Russian republic and eight other constituent republics agreed to sign Gorbachev's "union treaty," which created a framework for the republics to share power within a new political federation.

The Failed August Coup

For the old-guard hard-liners in the party, the military, and the secret police the treaty was the final straw—the end of the union as originally created by Lenin in 1922 after the Bolshevik Revolution of 1917 and the ensuing civil wars. Despite lip service to the sovereignty of the republics and the federal structure set forth in the Soviet constitution, the Soviet Union was from the beginning, and increasingly under Stalin, a Russian-dominated centralized nation, virtually the successor to the empire of the tsars. To abandon the union was more than many of the old guard could tolerate. The day before the treaty was to be signed, a small coterie of eight hard-liners acted to seize power. They included high-ranking party and government functionaries, among them, the head of the KGB and the commander of the Soviet land forces. All key figures were Gorbachev appointees. Several of the plotters, including the chief of Gorbachev's personal cabinet, arrived at Gorbachev's summer home in the Crimea, possibly hoping to win him to their side. After he refused to cooperate or yield to pressure, they proclaimed a Committee of State Emergency to replace him.

The *Putschists* expected the coup to be a simple operation. Resistance in the country, they were convinced, could be overcome by a simple show of military strength. But they

The failed coup

miscalculated, underestimating the new political forces alive in the country. Gorbachev disavowed the plotters. In Moscow Yeltsin gained additional stature when he rallied the Russian legislature in defense of

Gorbachev, warned that anyone supporting the coup would be subject to grave criminal charges, and appealed for popular support against any military show of force. But the assault never came. At least one KGB unit disobeyed orders to attack; other tank units advanced only half-heartedly. There was some sporadic street fighting, and three civilian deaths, but the coup gained little support and collapsed within four days.

Gorbachev, his ordeal over, returned to Moscow. He had demonstrated with courage that he was not the prisoner of the old guard and now went further. Because of the Communist Party's complicity in the attempted coup, he resigned as general secretary. Yet he still failed to comprehend how far matters had gone. He believed it sufficient only to replace the traitors and "return to the business of reform." Once again he defended "socialism" as "the choice made in 1917" and stressed the need to preserve the unity of the U.S.S.R. so that the country would not fall apart.

Yeltsin acted immediately and decisively on an entirely different agenda. As president of the Russian republic, he issued a series of decrees, describing the Communist Party as "not a political party but an unlawful apparatus that took over the Soviet state" and denouncing it as "one of the principal villains" in the attempted coup. *Yeltsin dissolves* Suspending its activities throughout the Russian republic, he transferred to *the regime* the state the party's vast property, along with its files and archives. The Soviet Congress of People's Deputies meeting in Moscow soon validated the decrees for the entire country before voting itself out of existence. In many ways what happened in the aftermath of the failed coup was the culmination of the Gorbachev six-year reform era. But the dissolution of the party-state regime, at Yeltsin's hands, was the revolution.

All that remained of the earlier framework was a federation council consisting of the presidents of the constituent republics, over which Gorbachev continued to preside. It immediately recognized the independence of the three Baltic republics. For the country as a whole Gorbachev still hoped to salvage his older idea, a "union of sovereign states," which, while granting self-government to the republics, would retain a central authority. But the republics pressed for full independence; hostility toward central authority had intensified after the bungled coup. The very party leaders, as in the Ukrainian S.S.R., who themselves once suppressed separatist movements, had by now taken over the leadership of nationalist independence movements.

The Ukrainian S.S.R. proclaimed itself independent as Ukraine (never again to be called *the* Ukraine) immediately after the August coup. In December, Yeltsin announced that Russia would not remain in the union without Ukraine. Thereupon the three Slavic states—Russia, Ukraine, and Belarus (the new name for Byelorussia), the states that had originally created the Union of Soviet Socialist Republics in December 1922—dissolved it. Gorbachev resigned as president. Yeltsin at once occupied his office in the Kremlin.

The other republics of the Soviet Union also agreed to its dissolution. A loose organization called the Commonwealth of Independent *The U.S.S.R. dissolves* States (CIS) consisting of Russia and ten other republics came into existence.[1] The Baltic states had already gone their separate ways. The Union of Soviet

---

[1]The 11 republics affiliating themselves with the Commonwealth of Independent States (CIS), created in December 1991 as successor to the U.S.S.R., in order of population (with their capitals in parentheses) were as follows: Russian Federation (Moscow), Ukraine (Kiev), Uzbekistan (Tashkent), Kazakhstan (Alma-Ata), Belarus (Minsk), Azerbaijan (Baku), Tajikistan (Dushanbe), Moldova (Chisinau), Kyrgyzstan (Bishkek), Turkmenistan (Ashkhabad), and Armenia (Yerevan). Georgia (Tbilisi) joined in 1993, but withdrew in 2009. Turkestan and Ukraine were affiliated states rather than official members. Ukraine stopped participating in the CIS after changing its government in 2014, and the Ukrainians officially broke their affiliation in 2018. Former Communist leaders retained control of most of the new governments until the early twenty-first century, when revolutionary, democratizing changes took place in several of the republics.

Boris Yeltsin's firm resistance to an attempted coup against the government of Mikhail Gorbachev by old-guard Communists in August 1991 confirmed Yeltsin's stature as the most popular political figure at the time. He is shown here waving to the huge crowd that gathered outside the Parliament building to show its support for the political reforms that were transforming the Soviet Union. Yeltsin was the first popularly elected president of Russia when it was still part of the U.S.S.R., a position he continued to occupy after the formal dissolution of the Soviet Union in December 1991.
(©Wojtek Laski/Hulton Archive/Getty Images)

Socialist Republics, for close to seven decades the world's largest multinational state, stretching over one-sixth the earth's surface and 11 time zones, with close to 300 million people, one of the world's two superpowers for over 40 years after the Second World War, simply disappeared as a geographic entity. Russia, still the world's largest nation in area and itself a mixture of many peoples, succeeded to the Soviet Union's permanent seat on the UN Security Council.

Gorbachev returned to private life, declaring "the main task" of his life to have been accomplished. He has to be counted as one of the great reformers in history. The "Gorbachev factor," as it has been called, made an immeasurable difference. His political flaw was that he failed to build a new

Gorbachev's legacy

system to replace the communism that he had undermined. He unleashed powerful winds of change that ultimately he could not direct or control. He drastically altered a totalitarian system yet refused to recognize that the demolition of the entire structure was necessary. Eventually he became a danger to the old order and an impediment to the new. Yeltsin, who took undisguised satisfaction in the fall of his once all-powerful rival, said of him: "We, like the world, respect him for what he did, especially in the first years of *perestroika* beginning with 1985 and 1986." After that, he said, the "errors" began. Russia, predicted George Kennan, one of America's preeminent diplomat-historians and Russian specialists, would eventually regard Gorbachev as the "person who led it out of bondage" even if "he was unable to reach the Promised Land." But it was not yet time to render final historical judgments, and the continuing transitions in post-Communist Russia did not lead easily or directly to a fully democratic political system.

118.   AFTER COMMUNISM

Marxist-Leninist ideology as the undergirding for one-party dictatorship still persisted at the opening of the twenty-first century in the People's Republic of China, the world's most populous country, and in the smaller states of North Korea, Vietnam, and Cuba. Albania, the last of the Communist regimes in Europe, and the most impoverished, threw off Communist rule in 1991. Yugoslavia's disintegration after the end of communism, as we shall see, unfolded separately. In western Europe, most notably in France, Italy, Spain, and Portugal, once strong Communist parties reexamined their beliefs, at times abandoned the party name, and adapted to changed circumstances. Marxism, born in the mid-nineteenth century in response to the instability and inequities of industrial capitalism, would survive as a scholarly, analytical tool; but Communism held little or no popular appeal as a political philosophy and program of political action. Democratic Socialist parties remained active and won elections in numerous democratic societies, but revolutionary "Proletarian internationalism" lost much of its appeal because the term had often been used simply to support repressive Soviet hegemony in eastern Europe or to promote Soviet interests in various international conflicts.

The late-twentieth-century overthrow of Communism in the Soviet Union and eastern Europe seemed to herald the international triumph of the political liberalism that had emerged in the late eighteenth century and *Triumph of liberalism* shaped the political cultures and institutions of the modern, western European democracies. Like earlier advocates of political democracy (but with adjustments to their own cultural contexts), the eastern European reformers sought free elections, political and civil rights, individual liberties, and respect for human dignity. The peoples of their various nations had too long been the pawns of totalitarian party-state regimes that self-righteously demanded sacrifice and subservience in the name of an ultimate utopia. The reformers objected to the centrally planned bureaucratic command economies, which had deprived almost everyone of decent living standards. They envied the immeasurably more prosperous economies of the United States, western Europe, and elsewhere, even if these other nations also had their share of inequalities, economic insecurity, and social and ethnic conflicts. The official claim that all citizens in "socialist" societies enjoyed equal rights and privileges had only concealed the realities of political repression, economic stagnation, and social immobility. For many, the public revelation of the Communist Party elite's special privileges and luxuries proved the final shock.

The revolutionary changes in 1989–1991 made possible, but did not guarantee, democratic and pluralist societies in which the citizens themselves through responsible government could shape their political and economic future. The transition to democracy and free economies was complex, and it continued in the twenty-first century. If democratic governments failed to take root, new authoritarian political parties and repressive governments could reemerge. The revolutionary changes soon released many ugly currents, ominous for the future—anti-Semitism, xenophobia, chauvinistic nationalism, irredentism—all easily mobilized when discontented people sought scapegoats for their frustrations. We have seen that some of these authoritarian and nationalist currents gained wide influence in countries such as Poland and Hungary during the early twenty-first century, but these nations were by no means the only countries in which liberal democracies faced new threats.

Difficult economic and political transitions

Russia, the other former Soviet republics, and the countries of eastern Europe thus entered a difficult period of protracted transitions. In principle, they were transforming their political systems into representative democracies and their centrally planned economies into competitive market economies. But bureaucrats and managers of the old order often remained in control under new labels, giving rise, in turn, to demands for more complete removal of the Communist-era legacies. Despite infusions of international aid, the new regimes struggled to cope with the disorienting challenges of a free market, capitalist economy, new technologies, and a global financial system.

The market economy could take many forms. The state had always played a large role in central and eastern Europe. It was unlikely that the new regimes would turn to a pure laissez-faire model of private enterprise, which did not actually exist in even the most capitalist Western economies. Governments would remain actively engaged, seeking to ensure a protective network of social services. The ideals and policies of democratic socialism still had more appeal in western and eastern Europe than in the United States or in some of the other industrial societies around the world.

The Soviet experience had tarnished, even poisoned, the image of authoritarian socialism (or Communism); but the egalitarian message of many socialist policies retained an attraction when the policies were clearly linked to respect for democracy and individual rights by the various European Socialist and Social Democratic parties. Meanwhile all countries with capitalist market economies and democratic political systems, in western Europe and elsewhere, were challenged to create societies that could overcome economic instability, individual insecurity, unemployment, and gross social and economic injustices. Democracies and market economies offered a means toward desired ends, not final goals in themselves. It was now generally assumed, however, that prosperity and productivity could do far more to overcome social inequities than the would-be utopias of repressive Communist regimes.

Russia after 1991

At the close of 1991 the Russian flag replaced the Soviet hammer and sickle over the Kremlin. As of January 1, 1992, the Union of Soviet Socialist Republics ceased to exist. The 15 former Soviet republics were now independent states. Officially, the Russia that emerged from the Soviet Union was the Russian Federation, with 21 "federated republics" of its own and with numerous additional ethnic-based territorial units. With almost twice the land area of the United States and a population of almost 150 million, Russia, even if in desperate economic straits, was still a significant world power.

The most pressing international concern was the nuclear weaponry of the former U.S.S.R. Yeltsin had worked out an agreement with the other former Soviet republics whereby Russia alone was to retain nuclear weapons. Although four-fifths of the nuclear

weapons were located on Russian soil, nuclear arms were positioned in
Ukraine, Kazakhstan, and Belarus. The United States mediated an

Nuclear arms

agreement under which the three republics consented to dismantle their
weapons in return for generous financial reimbursement. Russia for its part soon began
the initial stage of dismantling its vast arsenal of strategic weapons in accordance with
the arms reduction treaty that had been signed with the United States in 1991.

The new Russia, like the Soviet Union in its final stages, faced
separatist threats. Several of its "federated republics" adopted their own

Separatist pressures

constitutions, flags, and anthems and before long enjoyed considerable
de facto independence from Moscow. Only in the southern Chechen Republic did the
secessionist threat become reality, and before long Russia was involved in a brutal, draining war to prevent secession by Chechnya. Meanwhile 25 million Russians who had long
made their home in other parts of the former Soviet Union came to be regarded in those
places as foreigners and in some instances were treated with hostility.

In domestic affairs Yeltsin faced severe economic problems. He and his succession
of prime ministers met with little success in making the transition to a market economy.
In the first four years of Yeltsin's presidency production declined, the ruble fell in value,
standards of living sank, and new forms of corruption spread throughout the country.
Economic life at times seemed more trying for the average citizen than before the collapse
of communism.

After temporizing at first, Yeltsin turned to a Western-oriented economist as his key
adviser and economics minister in the belief that a swift transition to a market economy
would be the least painful course toward economic development. From late 1991, a flood
of decrees deregulated prices, ended or cut subsidies to state-owned industries, and moved
forward with privatization. But most Russians suffered a serious decline in living standards
by the spring of 1992 while privatization enriched others who bought into former state
industries at bargain prices. An industrial and financial oligarchy of "robber barons"
developed a system of crony capitalism; and a shadow economy run by mafia-type gang-
sters appeared on the borderlines of the legal system.

In the spring of 1993 a frustrated Yeltsin appealed to the country to support a new
constitution that would provide for "a strong presidential republic." That September Yeltsin
dissolved the legislature and called for new elections as well as for a referendum on his
proposed constitution. For two weeks the lawmakers, denouncing the
dissolution as "a coup d'état," refused to leave the parliament building.

*Yeltsin's new
constitution*

Demonstrators, incited by the legislative leaders, threatened insurrection.
Yeltsin felt bound to act. On October 4 tanks fired on the building and
set it ablaze. The legislators were evacuated and the leaders were arrested. Over 100 persons
died in the confrontation and many more were injured. In fact, both sides shared in the
blame for the conflict, but the violence showed that Russia was still going through its
revolution.

The new constitution, approved in December 1993, gave broad political authority to
the president, including the right to dissolve the legislature. A popularly elected lower
house, the State Duma, the old name deliberately chosen because of its
pre-Soviet roots, replaced the former Congress of People's Deputies. In

Yeltsin's problems

a stinging rebuke to Yeltsin, the new Duma in one of its first acts voted
amnesty to the legislative leaders arrested in October—and to the hard-line old-guard plotters against Gorbachev in the failed coup of August 1991. Lacking the necessary political
support, Yeltsin's ministers abandoned many of the economic reforms and restored
government controls on wages, prices, and profits.

RUSSIAN FEDERATION IN 2000
The map shows the territories of the Russian Federation, the largest and most important of the republics to emerge from the breakup of the former Soviet Union (U.S.S.R.) in 1991. The hatched lines indicate the lands of the other former Soviet republics, which are clustered to the south and west of the Russian Federation. The Federation itself consisted of some 21 "federated units," including Chechnya, where the Russians waged a military campaign to suppress a Chechen independence movement. The vast lands of the Russian Federation made it territorially the largest nation in the world. Much of this land was sparsely populated, however, and Russia's twenty-first century population has been gradually declining. The Federation's 143 million people ranked ninth on the list of the world's most populous nations in 2015.

Meanwhile, Yeltsin's political troubles continued in the Chechen Republic. Chechnya, in the oil-rich Caucasus, its population mostly Islamic, had a long tradition of rebellion and stubborn resistance to Russian domination. In 1991, as the Soviet Union was collapsing, the Chechens had demanded independence, or at least equal partnership with Russia. Militant guerrilla forces now proclaimed independence, but Russia was intent on retaining control of its southern borderlands and the links to central Asia as well as strategic oil resources and pipelines.

For three years Yeltsin supported covert efforts to overthrow the rebel regime, but, toward the end of 1994, at the urging of his entourage who expected to make political capital out of a quick victory, Yeltsin suddenly gave orders to invade Chechnya. In a grievous failure of military intelligence the invasion led to disastrous results. For close to two years the Russian army sank into a frustrating guerrilla war for which its poorly trained conscript army was

Chechnya invaded

The Russian campaign to suppress a secessionist movement in the Republic of Chechnya during the 1990s included two brutal wars against Chechen guerilla forces. The Russian army eventually regained control of Chechen towns and the capital city of Grozny, but only after bombardments had killed thousands of civilians and forced people such as this grieving woman to flee from their bombed-out homes. (©Konstantin Zavrazhin/Hulton Archive/Getty Images)

ill-prepared and ill-equipped. When the army failed to take the capital city of Grozny, the military resorted to air bombing and rockets, killing thousands of civilians. In April 1996 Yeltsin, admitting that the military action in Chechnya was "the greatest mistake" of his first four years as president, withdrew the army. Although numerous Chechen towns had been destroyed and some 20,000 to 40,000 of Russia's Chechen citizens had been killed, the Chechen independence struggle was not yet over.

In the presidential elections of June 1996 Yeltsin's political agility enabled him to win reelection, but only after he was forced into a run-off with the Communist Party's candidate. The economic stagnation and draining budgetary deficits continued well into Yeltsin's second term, bringing further political instability. Yeltsin made frequent, short-lived cabinet appointments and changed his prime minister five times in 18 months. Finally, in August 1999, he appointed as his prime minister Vladimir V. Putin, a former intelligence operative who had been stationed in East Germany and then served as head of the domestic security agency, the reorganized KGB. It soon became apparent that Yeltsin was choosing his successor to run in the presidential elections in 2000.

Putin chosen as successor

New trouble had meanwhile developed in Chechnya. In the fall of 1999 mysterious explosions in Moscow and nearby cities took the lives of some 300 civilians. Prime Minister Putin at once blamed the explosions on Chechen terrorists and the government proceeded to take drastic military measures. Intent on avoiding the costly Russian mistakes of the earlier war, the army launched large-scale air and artillery attacks on the Chechen cities and countryside. Russian military forces again suffered significant losses, but the results for the Chechen population were far more deadly. At least 35,000 Chechen fighters and civilians were killed, and over 200,000 refugees were forced to flee their homes. The Chechen capital was destroyed. The United States and its European allies condemned the Russian response, but the Russian army reestablished control over Chechnya, and the government's aggressive action was popular in Russia. Putin's decisiveness greatly enhanced his political stature.

On the last day of December 1999 Yeltsin dramatically announced his resignation and, in accordance with the constitution, appointed Putin acting president. The date of the presidential elections was advanced by three months. In the elections that followed in the spring of 2000 Putin readily won election.

Yeltsin left a mixed record. He was the first democratically elected president of the Russian republic while it was still part of the U.S.S.R., and he supported the independence movements of the other Soviet republics. He rallied the population to reject the hard-liners'

An ambiguous legacy

coup against Gorbachev and became a chief architect of the Soviet Union's dissolution, but he was not able to stimulate a post-Communist expansion of the Russian economy. Although his two terms as president often disappointed his western European sympathizers and the democratic reformers within Russia as well, he left the country with a constitutional system intact, and the way was still open for democracy to take root.

Yeltsin's historical legacy would depend in part on the policies and democratic commitments of his successor. Putin's proclaimed dedication to a "strong state" aroused concerns, however, and his governing methods seemed to become more authoritarian over the course of his first term and after he won reelection to the presidency in 2004. Responding in part to the continuing problem of Chechen terrorism (which included shocking terrorist attacks on a large Moscow theater and a public school in a small town), Putin promoted the centralization of state power and suppressed his opponents in the government, in the media, and in elite business circles. He went on to serve as an exceptionally influential prime minister during the presidential term of his own chosen successor, Dmitry Medvedev, who was elected in 2008 (when Putin was constitutionally barred from a third consecutive presidential term). In 2012 Putin was again elected to the presidency. The Russian Constitution had meanwhile been amended to extend the presidential term to six years, and after the election of 2012 Medvedev moved to the position of prime minister. By the time Putin returned to the president's office for a third term, a growing anti-Putin "democracy movement" was organizing large demonstrations and gaining support among disaffected Russians who viewed him as a throwback to an earlier kind of Russian ruler who would never voluntarily relinquish power.

Concerns about Putin's strong-willed consolidation of power continued to grow after he was reelected to a fourth presidential term in 2018. Facing only token opposition from other candidates, Putin won another landslide electoral victory and reappointed Medvedev as his prime minister. Although he suppressed his political opponents, cracked down on public demonstrations, restricted freedom of the press, and favored government power over the protection of individual human rights, Putin remained remarkably popular within

Putin's forceful policies

Russia. This popularity depended, in part, on Putin's appeal to Russian nationalism, which he promoted in actions such as Russia's seizure of the Crimean peninsula from Ukraine in 2014. Asserting his views of national interests with carefully targeted force (as in earlier interventions in Chechnya), Putin managed to annex Crimea, assist pro-Russian separatists in eastern Ukraine, mobilize public support within Russia, and withstand the foreign economic sanctions that his Crimean invasion provoked.

Vladimir Putin consolidated his dominant position in post-Communist Russia after a series of increasingly lopsided victories in presidential elections. He is shown here at one of his public rallies in 2012, surrounded by Russian flags and a large crowd of loyal supporters. Putin used his expanding power to maintain tight control over government policies and to suppress critics within Russian society; and his interventionist foreign policies strongly asserted Russian interests throughout the world.

(©Sasha Mordovets/Getty Images News/Getty Images)

Putin sought constantly to expand Russia's international power, influence, and independence. He opposed the American-British invasion of Iraq in 2003, improved relations with China, supported the Syrian regime of Bashar Assad in a brutal civil war that began in 2011, and intervened in American and European elections with cyberattacks or Internet misinformation campaigns that intelligence agents directed against candidates deemed hostile to Russian interests. Russia became a leading global exporter of petroleum, natural gas, and coal, which strengthened the Russian economy and helped Putin pursue his wide-ranging efforts to restore Russia's status as a great power. His international goals were entangled with his autocratic political methods, however, and his hostility for democratic institutions expanded the antidemocratic threats that twenty-first-century liberal democracies faced in Europe and in other places around the world.

Three decades after the collapse of the Soviet Union, the old Leninist-Stalinist communism was gone, but Russia's global aspirations had not disappeared and the Russian government had developed new autocratic tendencies that raised new foreign concerns. No one expected Russia to return to a command economy and the rigidities of central planning or to put together the pieces of the old Russian Empire of the tsars or the Soviets. Putin's critics nevertheless had good reasons to complain about growing threats

CHRONOLOGY OF NOTABLE EVENTS, 1980–2018

1980–1981	"Solidarity" labor movement leads campaign for reform in Poland
1985	Mikhail Gorbachev assumes leadership of the Soviet Union
1986	Nuclear accident at Chernobyl releases dangerous radioactivity in Ukraine
1989	Soviet Union withdraws its military forces from Afghanistan
1989	Berlin Wall is dismantled; Communist regime collapses in East Germany
1989	Communist regimes are dissolved in Poland, Czechoslovakia, Bulgaria, Hungary, and Romania
1990	German reunification creates an enlarged Federal Republic of Germany
1991	Boris Yeltsin is elected president of Russia and leads resistance to attempted coup by antireform faction of Communist Party
1991–1996	Yugoslavia breaks apart; Serbian and Croatian forces pursue "ethnic cleansings" in Bosnia and Croatia
1992	The Union of Soviet Socialist Republics is officially dissolved
1994–1996	Russia wages military campaign against secessionist movement in Chechnya
1999	NATO forces launch air attacks on Serbia to stop Serbian assaults on Muslims in the province of Kosovo
2000	Vladimir Putin succeeds Yeltsin as president of the Russian Federation
2000–2001	Slobodan Milosevic is forced out of power in Serbia and sent to stand trial at the war crimes tribunal in The Hague
2008	Kosovo proclaims its independent status as the "Republic of Kosovo"
2010	Victor Orbán is elected prime minister of Hungary; begins nationalist campaign to reshape the country's political culture and relations with the European Union
2015	Andrzej Duda is elected president of Poland; promotes the nationalist goals of the Law and Justice Party in reforming the judiciary and challenging EU policies
2018	Vladimir Putin is elected to a fourth term as president of Russia; consolidates personal political power and asserts Russian power abroad

to democratic political institutions, even though Russia had not gone back to Stalin's dictatorial system of the 1930s or tried to reestablish political control over the former Soviet republics. Some of these republics had even joined the NATO military alliance. The Putin-era nation (as compared with its Soviet-era predecessor) had much more commerce and cultural contact with other European nations, all of which might provide longer-term openings for future changes in Russia's political culture too.

The Resurgence of Nationalism: The Breakup of Yugoslavia

Of all the explosive issues that confronted Europe after the downfall of communism in 1989, ethnic nationalism proved especially intractable. Nationalist passions resurfaced after a long period of political suppression during the decades of Communist rule.

Czechoslovakia, as we have seen, divided peacefully in 1993 in response to Slovak pressures. But in Yugoslavia, the large multiethnic, multinational federation that had been created at Versailles in 1919, politically ambitious leaders stirred up old national and even religious tensions that tore the state apart and confronted Europe and the international community with violence, armed combat, atrocities, floods of refugees, and civilian suffering not seen within Europe since the Second World War.

What happened in Yugoslavia was rooted in historical animosities that were awakened and exploited for selfish political purposes by nationalist political leaders after communism collapsed in eastern Europe. To go back in time, *Political leaders and* the Balkan Peninsula had been conquered by the expanding Ottoman *historical animosities* Turks in the fourteenth century. Serbia, once a powerful medieval kingdom attached to the Eastern Orthodox Church, fell under Ottoman rule in 1389 and remained under Ottoman rule for close to 500 years. In 1878 it broke away from the weakening Ottoman Empire and regained its status as an independent kingdom. Its neighbors Croatia and Slovenia had also been ruled by the Ottomans, but Croatia and Slovenia rejoined the Austrian Habsburg Empire in the late seventeenth century and reaffirmed their ties with Roman Catholicism and central Europe. Bosnia (more precisely Bosnia and Herzegovina) long had a mixed population of Serbs, Croats, and Muslims; many Bosnians of Slavic ancestry in the long years of Turkish rule had adopted Islam. Bosnia also broke free from Ottoman rule in 1878 but was taken over by the Habsburg Empire.

When both the Austrian and Ottoman empires collapsed at the end of the First World War, Serbia together with other South Slav nationalists in 1918 proclaimed a "Kingdom of the Serbs, Croats, and Slovenes." At the Paris Peace Conference in 1919 it was permitted also to annex Bosnia, Montenegro (also ethnically Serb), and other formerly Ottoman territories. For many years these diverse nationalities held together in a somewhat uneasy alliance under a kind of royal dictatorship. In 1929 King Alexander changed the multinational country's name to Yugoslavia (or South Slav state). Croat separatism remained alive and a Croat nationalist assassinated King Alexander in 1934. Yet many people spoke of themselves as Yugoslavs and regarded Belgrade as their capital, and the outside world accepted an increasingly unified Yugoslav national identity.

During the Second World War, after the Nazis invaded Yugoslavia in 1941, the internal tensions in the Serb-dominated country reemerged. Croatia proclaimed its independence and for a time was governed as a separate Nazi puppet state. A Croat fascist organization, the Ustachi, collaborated with the Nazis in rounding up and brutally mistreating Serbs, Jews, and others. For the country as a whole the Yugoslav military resistance to Hitler eventually evolved into a civil war between the royalist (mostly Serb) army and guerrilla forces (mainly non-Serb) led by the prewar Communist leader Marshal Tito. By his greater effectiveness against the Nazis, Tito won the support of Churchill and Roosevelt and then triumphed in the civil war.

After its wartime ordeal, with some 2 million of its people dead, Yugoslavia emerged in the postwar years under a Communist regime headed by Tito, who soon broke with Moscow. In 1946 he set up a federal republic with six *Marshal Tito* component "republics" (Serbia, Croatia, Slovenia, Bosnia, Montenegro, and Macedonia), along with two "autonomous provinces," one of which was Kosovo. Although himself a Croat, he suppressed all separatist movements with an iron hand, but allowed each of the republics a degree of autonomy. In Bosnia he recognized the Bosnian Muslims as a distinct "national group" and gave them equal status with the Serbs and Croats. So long as Tito lived, Yugoslavia retained its national unity and identity. His death in 1980, however, was soon followed by the reemergence of the latent separatist

NATIONALITIES IN CENTRAL AND EASTERN EUROPE AT THE END OF THE TWENTIETH CENTURY
The map shows national boundaries and the location of various peoples after the collapse of the Communist governments and the conflicts in the Balkans during the 1990s. East Germany was reunited with the rest of Germany.
Czechoslovakia was broken into the Czech Republic and Slovakia. The state of Yugoslavia lost control over Slovenia,
Croatia, Bosnia, and Macedonia, all of which became independent nations. Yugoslavia itself dissolved into the separate
states of Serbia and Montenegro in 2006. A large Serbian population remains in Bosnian territory, along with Croats
and a large number of Slavic-speaking Muslims. The population in Macedonia includes many Albanians. The region
of Kosovo has a preponderantly Albanian Muslim population; it remained under the control of NATO military forces
for almost a decade after NATO intervened to stop Serbian suppression of a Kosovar separatist movement in 1999.
Kosovo proclaimed itself to be an independent republic in 2008, but this change was not recognized by Serbia. There
are many Hungarians in the countries that surround Hungary, and about 1 million Turks live in Bulgaria. Moldova
has been an independent nation since 1991 (it was part of the Soviet Union from 1940 to 1991), but much of its
population speaks Romanian. Although the region's diverse ethnic groups often lived together peacefully for long
periods of their history, the modern nationalist emphasis on cultural differences and identities, at times inflamed by
political leaders, produced strong ethnic hostilities and recurring cycles of violence.

After the breakup of Yugoslavia in 1991, Serbs and Croats sought to create their own national enclaves in Bosnia by driving Bosnian Muslims from territories where they had lived for centuries. This violent process of "ethnic cleansing" led to Serbian massacres of Muslims in cities such as Srebenica and Sarajevo, where this woman and her son mourned the loss of her husband and his father at a Muslim cemetery.

(©Patrick Robert - Corbis/Sygma/Getty Images)

movements. Tito's successors tried various solutions, including a rotating federal presidency, but separatist agitation continued. When communism collapsed all over eastern Europe, the regime in Yugoslavia collapsed as well. Yugoslavia's reform Communists (now calling themselves Socialists) relaxed the party's authoritarian grip on the country, faced up to its nationalities problem, and held open elections on the country's future. Only Serbia and Montenegro (the two Serb states were always closely allied) voted to maintain the federal republic. Croatia, Slovenia, Macedonia, and Bosnia all voted for parties committed to independence.

Former Communist leaders, like Slobodan Milosevic in Serbia and Franjo Tudjman in Croatia, seeing power slip away, placed themselves at the head of nationalist crusades. Milosevic, the Serbian president, rallied Serbs in Bosnia, Croatia, and Slovenia to fight to remain under Serb control whenever secession from the federal republic might take place. His fiery speeches and tactics backfired. Alarmed by Serb militancy, both Croatia and Slovenia quickly held a referendum and in 1991 proclaimed their national independence. They received immediate recognition from the international community, which was persuaded that prompt recognition would forestall Serb military action.

In Bosnia, the situation was even more complicated. The Serbs and Croats together comprised over half the population, but the Muslims, as the largest single national group, dominated the government; over the opposition of the Serb and Croat representatives, the Muslim nationalist leaders declared Bosnia's independence. The secession of Croatia, Slovenia, and Bosnia and their immediate international recognition infuriated Milosevic, who now governed the former Yugoslavia as a rump state consisting of only Serbia and Montenegro.

Open warfare broke out in the various seceding states in mid-1991. Local Serb paramilitary forces, reinforced by army units from Belgrade, proceeded to carve out enclaves in the secessionist states, where Serbs lived in significant numbers, and to drive out non-Serbs. In the fighting in Croatia and Slovenia Serb forces continued to seize territory until a temporary cease-fire was arranged.

Tudjman meanwhile goaded the Croat nationalists into action, mainly against the Serbs. The worst violence occurred when both Serbs and Croats attempted to create enclaves for themselves in Bosnia. For years the mixed population there, despite ethnic and religious differences, had lived peacefully side by side and had even intermarried. In the war that ensued, the Serb military forces brutalized the Muslim population. The barbaric deeds, labeled "ethnic cleansing," included large-scale expulsions, wholesale civilian slaughter, pillage, and rape. A prolonged siege of Sarajevo took place. At Srebenica, in eastern Bosnia, Serb militia executed some 8,000 Muslim men and buried them in mass graves. Europeans could scarcely believe such events were occurring on their own continent in the closing decade of the twentieth century.

In 1994, to end the siege of Sarajevo, the United Nations (UN), the United States, and NATO mediated a cease-fire and threatened air strikes if it were violated. For Bosnia a partial diplomatic settlement was negotiated. Croats and Muslims agreed to create a Croat-Muslim federation in what remained of Bosnian territory after the Serb conquests. The Serbs now occupied two-thirds of Bosnia and one-third of Croatia, with no intention of surrendering their gains. By 1994, 200,000 people were dead or missing, mostly in the fighting in Bosnia since 1991; there were about 4.4 million displaced persons. And still the fighting went on. In 1995 the Croatian army repulsed the Serb military and recovered most of the territory it had lost to the Serbs four years earlier. The Croats undertook their own ethnic cleansing program, expelling over 200,000 Serbs. In Bosnia the Serb offensive failed as well. Finally, in 1996, Serbia agreed to terms mediated by the United States at a meeting in Dayton, Ohio, accepting the new boundaries of Croatia and Bosnia and agreeing that UN peacekeepers would supervise the settlement in Bosnia.

An additional source of trouble soon developed, this time within Serbia itself in its province of Kosovo, where a growing separatist movement alarmed the Serbs. Ethnic Albanians, Muslim in religion, had long lived in Kosovo; through immigration from Albania and with large families, they had grown in such numbers that they now made up 90 percent of the population of 2 million. The Kosovars, as they were known, considered themselves related in religion, language, and culture to fellow Albanians in Albania. The Serbs were especially concerned because they themselves viewed Kosovo as a kind of holy land, where their ancestors had fought and lost the famous battle of Kosovo in 1389 to the Ottoman Turks.

The separatist movement grew at first under moderate leadership, but the Kosovars soon turned to their small but militant liberation army. In 1998 Milosevic launched a military offensive aimed at wiping out the Kosovar forces. Serb military and police units blasted villages

Kosovar separatism repressed

and towns to root out the rebels, killing civilian men, women, and children as well. International efforts to mediate failed. In 1998 the United States and NATO, acting not only because of the egregious human rights violations but because of the threat to the stability of the wider Balkan region, warned Milosevic that it would not allow the Serbs to do in Kosovo what they done in Bosnia a few years earlier. Milosevic nonetheless continued the wholesale Serb offensive, with mandates for ethnic cleansing that seemed intended to destroy the Kosovars or drive them into exile. By that time over 800,000 Kosovars had been forced to flee; at least 10,000 were dead.

In March 1999 NATO, for the first time in its 50-year history, undertook a military offensive, launching large-scale air attacks against Serbia. The bombing, led by the United States, continued for 78 days with severe damage in Belgrade and elsewhere before Milosevic yielded.

The NATO air offensive

It was an attack upon a sovereign European state not charged with external aggression, and it was controversial because it seemed to violate a fundamental principle of national sovereignty. But the egregious abuses by Serbia and the violations of human rights against its own citizens were viewed as illegal, murderous actions that required and justified what was described as "humanitarian intervention." New international law was being made. The United States and its European allies were compensating for the failure of the international community to act against the mass killings in Bosnia (and in the African state of Rwanda) a few years earlier; and the Europeans had decided that they could no longer tolerate such brutal abuses of human rights within a European nation. In the end Milosevic had to yield, but a Russian-backed UN Security Council resolution confirmed Yugoslav sovereignty over Kosovo even if Milosevic had to accept 50,000 armed NATO troops as peacekeepers there.

Kosovars returned to their homes under international protection. NATO forces and UN administrators moved into Kosovo, but they faced the difficult task of offering relief and reconstruction and of providing security for both Kosovars and Serbs. The indictment of Milosevic as a war criminal by the international court at The Hague and his international isolation added to his unpopularity, but he did not give up power until he unexpectedly lost an election in the fall of 2000 and was forced to resign after massive demonstrations demanded the recognition of his

Milosevic ousted

opponent, Vojislav Kostunica, a respected law professor who had kept aloof from the regime. Under international pressure, Milosevic was handed over in 2001 to the war crimes tribunal at The Hague, where he died in detention, in 2006, before the completion of his long trial for war crimes. Meanwhile, the Serbian political situation remained unsettled as die-hard nationalists continued to oppose those who favored closer economic and political relations with western Europe. Despite this opposition, the campaign for new relations with Europe gained support, and Serbia applied for membership in the European Union (EU). In 2012 the EU officially recognized Serbia as a candidate for future membership. There were still tensions, however, and negotiations continued, in part because of the situation in Kosovo. The Kosovars remained under UN administration until they proclaimed an independent "Republic of Kosovo" in 2008. Although Serbia, Russia, and other nations strongly objected to the creation of an independent Kosovar state, most members of the EU and NATO recognized the new republic and established diplomatic relations. Meanwhile, Montenegro also separated from Serbia to become an independent

The post-Communist, nationalist surge, which spread violently across southeastern Europe, gained strong support among separatists in Serbian-controlled Kosovo. Most Kosovars were ethnic Albanians who strongly supported the proclamation of a new Republic of Kosovo in 2008. Although Serbia denounced and rejected an independent Kosovar state, the European Union and the United States accepted the new republic, which these people celebrated with nationalist pride in the streets of the capital, Pristina.
(©DANIEL MIHAILESCU/AFP/Getty Images)

country; and two other former Yugoslavian states, Slovenia and Croatia, became members of the European Union and of NATO. The post-Communist transformation of the Balkans thus brought the whole region into closer connection with western European commerce, cultures, and politics.

Central and Eastern Europe after 1989

But we must return to central and eastern Europe, where developments took place more peacefully than in the former Yugoslavia. Most eastern European nations moved toward democracy, the rule of law, and a free economy. Former Communists often reconstructed their parties under various names and gradually learned to live and work with the newer democratic parties. Virtually every country in the former Soviet bloc for a time had either a head of state or head of government who had once been a Communist political leader. Many of the post-Communist societies experienced a repetition of the greed and rapaciousness of early Western capitalism. As in Russia, the former ruling and managerial elites profited personally from the newly privatized state industries, accumulating economic power and wealth. But most people had to cope with continuing economic challenges, which contributed to the rise of the nationalist political parties that gained influence in many post-Communist political cultures.

Some observers judged the revolution of 1989 harshly, arguing that despite its significance in overthrowing a failed system and casting off foreign domination, the new regimes were bent mainly on emulating the material successes of western European consumer societies. The goal of a democratic, civil society to supplement the organized state seemed to fade. Party politics and party maneuvering became the rule. Governmental problems thus added political anger to the economic frustrations; and EU membership did not solve either the political or economic issues that fueled resurgent nationalisms.

The 1989 revolution assessed

There were also complaints about the lingering influence of pre-1989 regimes, even though each state tried to reckon with the repressive institutions of the recent past. The former German Democratic Republic conducted trials and purges and opened the files of the East German secret security police, the Stasi, dramatically revealing wide networks of informers; and investigations of the Stasi continued after the completion of German reunification. The Czechs tried to ban men and women accused of serving as informers or collaborators from participation in political life for stipulated time periods, but that led to abuses and was abandoned. The Poles at first sought to draw a "thick line," as they described it, between past and present, but then they too conducted purges and opened police files. Some said the Europeans might have benefited from "truth commissions," as in Latin America or South Africa, before which past offenders against human rights could come forward to admit their misdeeds without necessarily expecting forgiveness.

Confronting the past

Poland, Hungary, and the Czech Republic took the lead in the transition to democratic freedoms, market economies, the rule of law, and pluralist societies, closely followed by the three Baltic states, Estonia, Latvia, and Lithuania. They all sought admission to the EU, which eventually took place in 2004. The most prosperous eastern European countries were those that adopted the most drastic economic measures, even though the initial social consequences at the time were painful. Poland was the best example of a country that benefited from such "shock therapy" and from the mid-1990s enjoyed a vigorous expanding economy. Despite persistent problems, the overall economic balance sheets showed progress throughout central and eastern Europe. The revolutionary upheavals of 1989 and their aftermath would long be remembered as the final events in the Cold War of the second half of the twentieth century.

More generally, the revolutions of 1989 helped to stimulate new cultural contacts, economic exchanges, and migrations of people between eastern and western Europe. The political and social differences that had often separated these regions of the continent began to break down as the EU later expanded to include eastern Europe and as people in every country increasingly identified themselves as "Europeans." New social and economic conflicts emerged, but the long, violent history of warfare and military confrontations between the major European nations seemed to have come to an end. At the beginning of the twentieth century, in 1914, a crisis in the Balkans had swept the European powers into the catastrophic First World War. At the end of the twentieth century, by contrast, another crisis in the Balkans led to a European-American collaboration that kept the conflict within the region, ended the violence, and ultimately brought most Balkan countries into new affiliations with the wider EU.

The new eastern European affiliations with the EU, however, would spark a new kind of crisis after 2010 as millions of refugees fled into Europe to escape violence, warfare, and economic problems in the Middle East and northern Africa. The EU had created open borders among the member nations and established processes for asylum seekers to settle in Europe; but the unprecedented wave of twenty-first-century immigration provoked nationalist anger in every European country, gave anti-immigrant and nationalist political parties new popular support, and generated widespread hostility for the EU and its system of open borders within Europe. The anger about Middle Eastern immigrants added to the already existing political and economic unhappiness that had pushed many European voters away from the policies and institutions of the transnational European Union. Despite these ongoing social and political challenges, the post-Communist transitions in eastern Europe and even the violence in the Balkans had not caused a new European wide conflagration. Nobody could predict the future, of course, yet the end of warfare between the major European nations had to be seen as one of greatest changes and signs of progress in modern world history.

Suggested Further Readings can be found in the ebook, on Connect, or online at www.mhhe .com/kramer12e.

Chapter 26

EUROPE AND THE CHANGING MODERN WORLD

The demise of Soviet-style Communist regimes in Europe after 1989–1991 suggested to some observers that the history of the modern world would henceforth evolve in only one direction. All modern societies, according to such theorists, were in fact already moving on their own erratic paths toward a universal system of liberal democracies and free market economies. But it soon became evident that this imagined "end of history" was by no means the only direction in which history could evolve. New movements arose to challenge the global capitalist economy, the ascendancy of Western political theories, the institutions of liberal democracies, the secularism of modern cultures, and the powerful influence of the United States—which had emerged from the Cold War as the world's sole superpower.

There were new and continuing conflicts among competing religious or ethnic groups and among nations that competed for power and commercial advantages in the global economy. Warfare itself changed when militant, extremist groups increasingly dramatized their grievances or waged violent political campaigns through the indiscriminate tactics of terrorist bombings. Facing such opponents, the most powerful national governments found that traditional methods of international warfare—invasions, the surrender of enemy governments, military occupations—could no longer achieve the decisive political and military closure that modern nation-states expected to reach at the end of their wars.

No sooner had the Cold War receded into historical memory than global struggles over natural resources, economic interests, political power, and cultural values began to shape new international conflicts and wars. In the early twenty-first century, various European nations joined with the United States to become deeply involved in new conflicts in central Asia and the Middle East. Responding to the attacks and continuing

Chapter emblem: View of the planet Earth, photographed from Apollo 17 in December 1972. (©NASA/Getty Images)

threats of radical terrorists, the North Atlantic Treaty Organization (NATO) allies participated in extended "peacekeeping" and military campaigns against Islamic groups in Afghanistan; and (in a separate war) the British sent their army into Iraq as part of an American-led invasion of that country in 2003. The much-anticipated post–Cold War "peace dividend" disappeared almost immediately in a new cycle of military interventions outside of Europe, shadowy intelligence operations, and deadly terrorist attacks.

Amid these cycles of international violence and conflict, however, the deeper historical patterns of human migration, global economic exchange, technological innovation, transnational cultural interaction, and changing social mores continued to develop in Europe and in every other region of the world during the postcolonial era. Computer technologies and communications systems now moved information around the globe with instantaneous speed; a global "culture industry" spread the same music, films, foods, and fashions throughout Europe and the wider world; evolving conceptions of knowledge and scientific research reshaped intellectual debates as well as artistic creativity; and new opportunities for the education, professional careers, and social and political rights of women continued to expand in Europe and in most modern nations everywhere. The pace of change seemed to be increasing in all spheres of modern life, placing Europeans in a "global village" that was both united and divided by the processes of contemporary globalization.

All of these twenty-first-century events, the transnational violence and the transnational exchanges alike, evolved on a planet whose changing climate was transforming global environmental conditions. People in Europe and throughout the world faced unprecedented dangers from rising air temperatures and ocean waters, intense storms, and other climatic transitions that affected human health, agricultural production, economic planning, and the migration of peoples from increasingly dangerous environments. Despite all of their cultural or political differences and conflicts, everyone on the planet would eventually have to respond to shared climatic problems that human actions were creating and that future human actions would have to address.

119.   WESTERN EUROPE AFTER THE COLD WAR

*Economic Changes, Political Transitions, and Immigration
in a New International Context*

It was generally expected that the nations of central and eastern Europe would suffer political and social problems in the post-Communist transition to democracies and market economies. What was unanticipated was the burden of political and economic troubles that western Europe found itself confronting after 1990. Buoyant and self-confident because of continuing prosperity during the 1950s and 1960s, the people of western Europe were first jolted by the recession of the 1970s that combined economic stagnation with inflation. By the mid-1980s the economies of the European democracies had recovered, although with lower growth rates than in the past and with discomfiting levels of unemployment.

Costs of German reunification

In Germany the economic situation after 1989 was complicated by the reunification with East Germany. The steep costs of absorbing East Germany's decayed economy and the decision to convert the East German mark on an equal basis with the West German created a threat of inflation. To combat it the German Bundesbank kept interest rates high. But tight money choked off credit and investment when downturns occurred in the early 1990s, delaying economic recovery for itself and its European neighbors and leading to currency devaluations and instability. The German economy remained sluggish long after political unification was completed.

Despite gradual improvement in the overall western European economy, many workers remained unemployed, and unemployment rates rose to postwar highs in the early 1990s. For the members of the European Union (EU) the unemployment figures approached 19 million, or more than 12 percent of the workforce. Long-term unemployment became a structural problem, and many workers would never again find jobs for which they could still use their old skills. Young people were especially hurt by shrinking job prospects as Europe's older industrial economy evolved toward a new kind of service economy, which would become even more pervasive in the early twenty-first century.

The Europeans slowly came to realize what had only been suspected in the earlier recession: The problem of unemployment was not temporary, but was deep-seated, structural, and connected to the movement of industrial production toward parts of the world where workers *Persistent unemployment* earned lower wages. High labor costs that included generous welfare-state benefits for unemployment, disability, retirement, and extended paid vacations undercut western Europe's ability to compete globally. An aging population raised health care costs as well as the expense of state pension systems. Many European corporations, like their American counterparts, began to restructure, sharply reducing employment rolls and introducing new technologies that required fewer workers. European multinational corporations moved many of their manufacturing operations to Asian or Latin American nations in which the costs for labor and social benefits were significantly lower. For the first time since 1945 the West European nations, echoing the British example under the Thatcher government, took steps to roll back the welfare state as it had evolved by consensus after the Second World War.

Western Europe: Political Crises and Discontents

There was widespread dissatisfaction with the governing political parties of the center and Center-Left, which were judged to have held office too long and seemed incapable of providing innovative new plans for the future. The rising dissatisfaction with European political cultures could perhaps be seen most clearly in Italy, where anger against the governing elite became symptomatic of the wider European response to political cronyism.

For years the Christian Democrats had dominated the political scene, forming successive coalition governments, with the Right in the 1950s *Italy's Christian Democrats* and with the Socialists and other parties in the 1960s. By the 1970s in the midst of economic setbacks their popular support shrank rapidly. In the 1980s the Socialists replaced them, heading a cabinet for a record four years. Meanwhile the country's second strongest party, the Italian Communist Party, which had earlier demonstrated its independence from Moscow, won numerous mayoralties and control of municipal councils (though it was excluded from the national government). In 1989, with the collapse of communism and end of the Cold War, the party renamed itself the Democratic Party of the Left and began a new quest for participation in the national government.

Over the years the Christian Democrats had kept a tight grip on power and patronage and maintained close ties both to state-owned enterprises and private business. In good part because the Christian Democrats projected themselves as Italy's defenders against communism they were shielded from scrutiny or criticism. But in the early 1990s the

The populations of all European nations have become increasingly diverse as immigrants and mobile workers stream across national borders in search of better jobs, education, cultural freedom, and basic human rights. These children at a primary school in contemporary London represent the diverse racial, ethnic, and cultural backgrounds of the people who live in the multicultural nations of modern Europe. Immigration is constantly changing the workforce, schools, food, music, and neighborhoods of European cities; it also at times provokes anti-immigrant political movements and affects the political culture of every nation.

(©Gideon Mendel/Corbis Historical/Getty Images)

Italian public learned of bribes, kickbacks, and payoffs for government contracts up to the highest political levels. There had been illegal payments to the political parties and even widespread collusion with organized crime. Former prime ministers, cabinet ministers, and parliamentary deputies of all political parties as well as top business executives were implicated. So tainted was the Christian Democratic Party that it returned to an earlier name for itself, the Popular Party.

All the Italian governments of the 1990s inherited public deficits, economic slowdown, unemployment, social tensions, and continuing inquiries into corruption. Neither the new political parties nor the

New parties

governing elites could provide stability or serve as public models. Recognizing and also manipulating the wide discontent with Italian politicians, the conservative media magnate Silvio Berlusconi headed a coalition that won national elections in 2001; its Center-Right majority promised stability but also aroused misgivings about the ambitious prime minister and his assertive *Forza Italia* Party (the name itself derived from the championship soccer team that he owned). Berlusconi nevertheless remained in office longer than most of his predecessors. Fending off charges of corruption and criticism of his support for the U.S.-led invasion of Iraq, he overcame losses in a number of elections and managed to retain power in the face of mounting domestic opposition. Berlusconi was widely criticized for his flamboyant personal lifestyle, for his self-interested uses of government power, and for his tendency to fuse his private financial interests with his political career, but he remained prime minister until 2011. Although Berlusconi was only one of the many European political leaders whose self-absorbed lives and corruption seemed to undermine their ability to serve general public interests, his career exemplified the kinds of leadership problems that discredited political elites in numerous European countries as people struggled with new economic challenges or with enduring unemployment. Berlusconi himself was not really a major historical figure, but he represented and contributed to a historical pattern that reappeared in much of Europe during the early twenty-first century.

Berlusconi's break with traditional political coalitions and practices also became the starting point for later developments in Italian politics, which showed the weakness of conventional parties and the appeal of new populist movements. Many Italians disliked the European Union's economic guidelines (which restricted deficit spending) and immigration policies (which urged member nations to accept numerous refugees). In this evolving social context, Italy's postwar political parties lost influence. Berlusconi had created his own political organizations and shown how the political establishment could be challenged, but a new coalition of the right wing "Northern League" and the left-leaning "Five-Star Movement" carried the challenge even further in 2017-18. Despite their disagreements on some issues, these two movements shared a common critique of the EU, a vehement rejection of traditional

Italian Populist Parties

political parties, and a strong demand to stop the constant flow of refugees and immigrants who were coming into Italy from North Africa and the Middle East. Winning the election of 2018 with majorities in different regions of the country, the Northern League and Five-Star Movement formed a coalition government that immediately demanded changes in EU policies on government spending and immigration. The Italian upheavals—from the Berlusconi era to the economic and anti-immigrant populism of the 2018 elections—thus showed how European political culture was changing as public concerns shifted from the late twentieth-century Cold War toward twenty-first-century anxieties about transnational economic systems and the massive migrations of displaced persons.

Europe's Immigrants and Refugees

We have already seen how the influx of millions of immigrants and refugees since the 1960s was altering the nature of European societies. In the 12 years from 1980 to 1992, 15 million new immigrants arrived to make their home in western Europe; and the patterns of immigration continued over the following decades. By the end of the first decade in the twenty-first century, roughly 8 percent of the population in countries such as Germany, France, Britain, Spain, and the Netherlands consisted of immigrants who were born outside of Europe, and millions of other people in European nations were the children of recent immigrants.

The European Union's official statistics in early 2017 showed that almost 37 million people then living in the 28 EU countries had been born outside an EU nation, and about 22 million still held citizenship in a non-EU country. There were also large migrations of

Immigration to EU Countries

EU citizens who moved to other EU countries within Europe, so that roughly 20 million EU country citizens were living in places outside the EU nation in which they were born. These foreign populations became significant demographic groups within all the major European countries. In Germany, for example, there were 9.2 million non-national residents by 2017, and the United Kingdom (6.1 million), Italy (5 million), France (4.6 million), and Spain (4.4 million) all had large immigrant populations from both non-EU countries and other EU nations. These growing, multicultural populations provided valuable workers for the various national economies, but they also evoked hostile social and political responses from anti-immigrant groups that gained influence within every national society.

The EU launched a controversial new program in 2009 to provide "EU blue cards" for skilled workers who came to Europe from other parts of the world, thereby recognizing the growing economic role of highly educated persons who looked for professional opportunities in Europe (even as some European professionals were also leaving for the Americas or Asia). Skilled workers also formed part of the large migration within the EU as people from eastern European countries such as Poland moved to Britain or other western European countries in search of higher wages.

Middle Eastern wars and political repression pushed many immigrants toward Europe, where they sought personal safety or political asylum; but many also moved in search of economic opportunities that they could not find in their own impoverished countries. Many immigrant workers regularly sent part of their earnings back to families in the places from which they had immigrated. They worked in both the private and the public sectors of the European economy, often taking lower-paid, less desirable jobs that Europeans did not want. When the Cold War ended, some eastern Europeans joined family members who had earlier gone into exile to escape the repression of Communist regimes; and many refugees streamed into western Europe from the former Yugoslavia during the era of intense ethnic violence in the 1990s.

Shifts in Europe's ethnic composition

The steady flow of immigrants visibly changed the ethnic composition of Europe, especially during the decades after 1990. In Germany Turkish workers settled in with their families as permanent residents; many reared their children as Muslims. In France in a population of 57 million in the mid-1990s, at least 4 million were foreign-born—mainly Arabs from North Africa and immigrants from other former French African colonies but also Vietnamese from Southeast Asia. In Britain, with a population of 56 million, at least 2.5 million had emigrated from various parts of Asia, Africa, and the Caribbean. Nations that had long sent emigrants to all parts of the world now found themselves absorbing large new populations from abroad.

The xenophobic hostility that had manifested itself earlier in western Europe again flared up. In Germany there were physical assaults on Turks, firebombings, and other acts of violence. Neo-Nazis in Germany, "skinheads" in Britain (who dated from the 1950s), neo-Fascists in Italy, and followers in France of Jean-Marie Le Pen's National Front agitated the immigrant issue and even resorted to racist violence. Governments adopted laws to reduce or eliminate further immigration. Germany in 1993 repealed a constitutional provision that had offered asylum to "all persecuted on political grounds," but it became virtually impossible to distinguish between political and economic refugees. France moved toward "near-zero" immigration and abandoned a tradition going back to the Revolution of granting citizenship to any child born on French soil. Unemployment and troubled economies made the social tensions potentially explosive and fed prejudices of all kinds, including anti-Semitism.

In the 1990s the European Union had adopted the "Schengen Convention," which extended earlier travel agreements and allowed the free movement of persons across the borders of the EU's member states. People could travel freely between most EU countries without showing passports, and EU citizens could work or attend universities in other EU nations without visa applications and other cumbersome restrictions. Europeans in every social group—commercial entrepreneurs, skilled workers, students, professional experts, performing artists, and others—moved constantly around the continent and enjoyed the convenience of open borders; and non-EU citizens (once admitted to a Schengen-area nation) could also move freely between most EU nations. The open borders policy became increasingly controversial, however, after 2004, when numerous eastern European countries joined the EU; and it was criticized even more widely after 2011, when refugees from the Middle East and North Africa began streaming into eastern and southern Europe. Millions of migrants fled through Turkey or across the Mediterranean in dangerous, overcrowded boats, seeking safety from the horrendous Syrian civil war and other regional conflicts.

Schengen Area and Immigrants

The flood of immigrants from mainly Muslim countries sparked a new anti-immigrant backlash. Political leaders and nationalist political parties condemned the free movement of refugees who (if they could enter a Schengen-area country) might move across national borders as they sought asylum in various EU nations. When terrorists launched new attacks in some European cities, the fear of immigrants intensified (even though most refugees were desperately fleeing for their own safety). Anti-immigrant politicians won electoral victories in numerous countries, including Austria, Hungary, and Poland—where, as we have seen, more authoritarian political leaders were consolidating their control of state power. Defying the EU's plans for refugees to settle in various EU nations, for example, the Polish government and leaders of the Law and Justice Party expressed the views of most citizens in their predominantly Catholic nation by resisting all efforts to resettle Muslim refugees who had recently come into countries such as Greece or Italy. But Poland was by no means the only country that resisted refugee resettlement plans. Stranded refugees lived throughout Europe in camps or isolated settlements from which they were unable to leave; and the EU faced an ongoing immigrant-refugee crisis that threatened the stability of the European Union itself as well as the internal political stability of most European nations.

Resistance to Refugees

Western Europe seemed to settle into a new cultural era of persistent gloom and political frustration in the early twenty-first century. The end of the Cold War had not automatically ushered in peace, prosperity, and harmony. Unemployment and industrial dislocation marred the economic scene. In the euphoria following the collapse of communism, few had anticipated the resurgence of the explosive nationalism and religious conflict that brought bloodshed to the Balkans and new violence to the nearby Middle East. Western Europe, for all its announced commitment to democratic institutions and for all its military strength, feared the entanglements of military intervention so much that until the American-led air offensive in Kosovo it refrained from decisive action. On the political scene conservative and centrist political leaders offered few new initiatives, and the Left seemed in disarray. On the other hand, many still believed, or hoped, that western Europe

Post-Cold War gloom

Wars in Syria, Iraq, and other Middle Eastern countries drove millions of people from their homes. Although many of these displaced persons moved to nearby nations in the region, others fled by sea on overcrowded boats that brought them into southern Europe. These refugees were disembarking at a Greek port in 2015, but their quest for asylum within the EU would be a long, complicated process, in part because there was strong opposition to new immigrants in most European nations. (©Milos Bicanski/Getty Images News/Getty Images)

would reach out to central and eastern Europe, continue to work toward a united Europe, and play a central role in the world's economy and international affairs. But even the most optimistic Europeans increasingly recognized that the pursuit of such goals would require bold new economic or political initiatives, new responses to populist nationalisms, and new solutions for the misery that arose from massive immigration.

120. NATION-STATES AND ECONOMIES IN THE AGE OF GLOBALIZATION

Economic Recovery and a "Third Way" in Politics

In the 1990s the American President Bill Clinton helped to set the tone for a new type of democratic politics in the Atlantic world. Clinton promoted a pro-business program that favored economic growth and productivity but combined it with social issues such as health care and education and concern for the disadvantaged and minorities. Clinton

Clinton and Blair

found a kindred political spirit in the buoyant British Labour Party leader Tony Blair, who also adopted many conservative pro-business policies and became the Labour leader in 1994. Calling for a "New Labour" framework, Blair reduced the traditional influence of trade unions and persuaded his party to abandon what still remained of its earlier socialist and welfare-state platform.

The best prescription for prosperity, as Blair described it, was to encourage economic growth and industry but without neglecting social needs, which he argued that Thatcher and the Conservative Party had done in their uncritical support for free-market capitalism. After four Conservative electoral victories since 1979 and 18 years of Conservative leadership, the country gave the Labour Party in 1997 its largest margin of victory since 1945. Blair thus launched his new policies as a "third way," seeking to move Britain forward on a middle path between unbridled capitalism and the most intrusive policies of state-directed socialism.

As in the United States, the economy turned upward in Britain. Blair's political strength and popularity also enabled him to institute a number of constitutional changes. The United Kingdom had long had a highly centralized government, with all power emanating from the Westminster Parliament in London. The Labour Party with its large majority in the House of Commons took unprecedented steps toward a devolution of power to a new parliament in Scotland, where the reform was intended to defuse a strong separatist movement, and to a new legislative assembly in Wales. Each gained broad jurisdiction over its internal affairs. Voters in Scotland for the first time since the Act of Union of 1707 went to the polls to elect their own parliament, and in Wales voters elected an assembly for the first time ever. Critics saw the devolution of authority as the "undoing of Britain" and an erosion of parliamentary sovereignty. Meanwhile, some Scottish nationalists pressed for more autonomy and even, in some cases, for complete independence from Britain. Others recognized the need for more Scottish autonomy, though they also wanted Scotland to remain within the United Kingdom. No one wished to repeat the mistakes of Britain's long resistance to home rule for Ireland, which had led to continuing violence, partition, and prolonged strife.

In Northern Ireland matters seemed to be taking a more peaceful turn. The Protestant and Catholic parties finally reached an agreement in 1998, moving to end a violent conflict that over the past 30 years had cost the lives of over 3,000 people. The new arrangements authorized a legislative council of representatives from Britain, Northern Ireland, and the Republic of Ireland, and a sharing of power in a joint cabinet. Northern Ireland thus gained a new opportunity for self-government, but the introduction of the new self-governing institutions was delayed when the Irish Republican Army (IRA) and other paramilitary groups resisted calls for complete disarmament. By 2005, however, the IRA had in fact given up its weapons. The recurring violence between Catholics and Protestants thus gave way to a more peaceful era in politics and social life. Northern Ireland remained within the United Kingdom, but subsequent political agreements somewhat revised the "Northern Ireland Assembly" and the system for power sharing between Protestant and Catholic leaders. Although political tensions did not disappear and later debates about Brexit created new conflicts, problems were now managed through the new institutional structures. The people of Belfast and other Northern Irish cities accepted the political settlement, and in 2007 the British army ended its long deployment in the region.

The settlement in Northern Ireland

Tony Blair's popular support declined after he brought the country into a joint British-U.S. invasion of Iraq in 2003. Many in Britain opposed the war, and approval for Blair's leadership fell rapidly as the country tired both of the war and of Blair's apparent deference to American foreign policy during the era of George W. Bush's presidency. In 2007 Blair resigned his position as leader of the Labour Party, giving way to Gordon Brown, who had served as Blair's chief economic minister and whose own term as Labour leader and prime minister was dominated by the pervasive financial problems of a major recession. British voters, who became increasingly disenchanted with Labour policies and

Women played an increasingly important role in twenty-first-century European elections and national governments. Although she held different political views, German Chancellor Angela Merkel welcomed France's Socialist presidential candidate Ségolène Royal (on the left) to Berlin in the spring of 2007. Royal lost the election, but women were everywhere asserting their rights to the highest levels of national political leadership.

(©Andreas Rentz/Getty Images News/Getty Images)

Cameron and the Conservative coalition

with the bland personality of Gordon Brown, turned toward the Conservative Party in new elections in 2010. The Conservatives were unable to win a clear majority in the new Parliament, however, without the support of the moderate Liberal Democrats—a third party, which joined an unusual coalition government that would be led by a new Conservative prime minister, David Cameron. The Conservatives introduced new austerity measures to balance the British budget and to encourage more private investment in new economic enterprises.

The economic recovery nevertheless lagged, and Cameron's domestic policies sparked strong opposition from government workers, educators, and others who feared that the budget cuts and other reforms would hamper an economic recovery. The British stead-

British economic policies

fastly kept their own currency and maintained their separation from other aspects of European economic life, but they resembled the people of other European countries in their growing disillusionment with the nation's political elites. Like many Europeans in the early twenty-first century, the British often expressed concern about their government's inability to solve intractable economic and social problems that threatened to diminish the infrastructure and welfare of their modern national life.

Britain's nationalism remained an influential cultural and political force. The British celebrated both the diamond jubilee of Queen Elizabeth's reign and the London Summer Olympics in 2012; and they affirmed their nationalism even more forcefully in 2016 when

Brexit

they voted in a referendum to exit from the European Union. Prime Minister Cameron had promised a vote on a possible "Brexit" to placate anti-Europe factions of the Conservative Party, but he was surprised by the outcome and immediately resigned from office. The next Conservative leader, Theresa May, struggled to implement a Brexit agreement, which was supposed to go into effect in 2019. Although the people of London and Scotland had voted to remain in the EU, the Brexit faction won by a small margin—perhaps because of traditional British suspicion of Europe or because of rising concerns about immigration or because of anger about EU bureaucrats and economic policies. In any case, Britain became the first nation that ever voted to leave the European Union. There were concerns that other countries might also want to leave, and the postwar European project would be permanently weakened. Meanwhile, Britain struggled to develop new national policies that would alter its economy as well as its future political culture.

The governments of Germany and France also alternated between the politics of the Left or Left-Center and the politics of resurgent conservative parties. In Germany the Social Democratic Chancellor, Gerhard Schröder, replaced Helmut Kohl in 1998. Schröder was a new kind of Social Democrat who wanted to curb the generous provisions of the postwar welfare state, which had driven up labor costs *Schröder* and made it difficult to hire new workers. He too spoke of his program as a "middle way," and—despite the problem of chronic unemployment—the Social Democrats held on to power into the early twenty-first century. Subsequent elections in 2005, however, failed to produce a clear majority for either of the major German parties, and a coalition government emerged after extended negotiations. Angela Merkel, the leader of the Christian Democrats, became Germany's first woman chancellor as well as the first chancellor to reach that office from the former East Germany. Half of the cabinet ministries went to Social Democrats, however, creating an unusual Left—Right collaboration.

Merkel and her Christian Democratic Party went on to win the German elections in 2009, which gave her party an absolute majority and enabled her to lead the country without the constraints of a coalition government. Much of her new term in office was devoted to the problems of the European recession *Merkel* and to the crisis of the "euro debt." Merkel and her German political allies favored a strong euro zone economy, but they worried about inflation and pushed for austerity measures when EU countries such as Greece and Spain fell deeply into debt. Drawing economic strength from reforms that they had made in both the labor wage system and government spending, the Germans gained a new dominance in European affairs on the basis of their economy. The old German militarism had disappeared, but the new Germany still played a decisive role in European affairs and contributed disproportionately to the EU's broader influence in the world economy.

Merkel and her Christian Democratic Party lost support, however, as she advocated a more welcoming policy for refugees from the Middle East. A rising right-wing movement called "Alternative for Germany" (AfD) condemned Merkel's immigration policies and (as in other countries) launched critiques of the EU and the "non-democratic" imposition of EU guidelines in German society. By 2017 the AfD was expanding its influence in state governments and becoming a leading opposition party in the national Bundestag. Nationalism thus seemed to be gaining a new kind of political support within Germany, though the country remained firmly embedded in the European Union—even after Merkel announced that she would not seek another term as chancellor in 2021.

In France the conservative Gaullist Jacques Chirac was elected president in 1995, but the Socialists soon won a majority in the legis- *Chirac and Jospin* lature; under the now established practice of "cohabitation" the president appointed Daniel Jospin prime minister. Jospin, though resolutely committed to a large role for government on social issues, believed in moderation and pragmatism, favored a market economy, and moved forward with the privatization of state-owned industries. The constitution meanwhile was amended to curtail the powerful role of the Gaullist-inspired French presidency by reducing the term of office from seven to five years. Many socialists became disenchanted with Jospin and refused to vote for him in the 2002 presidential election, thus opening an opportunity for the extremist right-wing candidate Jean–Marie Le Pen to face Chirac in the second round of voting. Leftist and other voters, to their consternation, had to rally to Chirac, who easily won reelection, but the disillusionment with France's traditional political parties continued to grow.

Chirac's government became mired in various scandals and political conflicts that undermined his effectiveness during his second term as president, but his conservative party found a new leader for the elections in 2007. Nicholas Sarkozy mobilized popular nationalist sentiments and distrust of the Socialist candidate, Ségolène Royal, to win a narrow victory. Royal's candidacy marked another milestone in French politics, because she was the first woman to be nominated for the presidency by a major French political party. She lost the election, but Sarkozy soon alienated much of the French electorate as he introduced new austerity measures, attempted to reduce the influence of French labor unions, and also came to be viewed as more concerned with the interests of wealthy supporters than with the needs of workers or the lower classes. These issues, when combined with ongoing economic problems and questions about Sarkozy's own mercurial

Sarkozy and Hollande

personality, led finally to the election of another Socialist president in 2012. François Hollande entered office with plans to stimulate the French economy through new government initiatives, but he was like other modern European Socialist leaders in that he advocated a mixed economy that was by no means truly "socialist" in its organization or distribution of wealth. The "middle way" had become a familiar formula for Left-leaning political leaders, but Hollande's policies soon lost support on all sides. Indeed, the Socialist Party essentially collapsed by 2017. A young, former cabinet minister in Hollande's government, Emmanuel Macron, won election to the presidency as the leader of a new movement ("En Marche") that claimed to be neither Left nor Right nor beholden to any previously existing political party. Significantly, Macron's opponent was Marine Le Pen, leader of the far-right National Front (renamed in 2018 as "National Rally"), which had now eclipsed traditional conservative parties to become the main right-wing faction in France. Populist Nationalism had thus become a major force in French elections, but Macron won a decisive majority and his supporters also won control of the National Assembly.

In contrast to the Brexit campaign in Britain, Macron staunchly defended the EU and criticized Europe's surging populist nationalisms. He also became a leader of global

Macron's Policies

attempts to combat climate change. Yet his economic policies soon evoked strong opposition, and his reforms were widely condemned on both the Left and the Right. Macron seemed to embody and also to provoke a deep hostility for French political parties and governing elites. Lacking a traditional political base, Macron's own popularity rapidly declined. France thus struggled like other nations to reconstruct its political culture and public policies as older political affiliations or identities continued to break down.

Government leaders who were looking for a middle way between conservatism and welfare-state socialism thus found themselves under attack from new populist and nationalist movements throughout Europe. Pragmatic, moderate leaders embraced various neoliberal policies that altered the welfare-state ideologies which had generally prevailed after the Second World War. But the social effects of deindustrialization, the economic impact of global production systems, the cultural anxiety about massive immigration, the political frustration with corruption or stagnation in long-ruling parties, and the growing disenchantment with EU bureaucracies all weakened support for traditional governing elites and shaped the rise of new nationalist political movements throughout Europe.

The European Union: Economic Cooperation, the Euro, and the Debt Crisis

By the early twenty-first century European integration had made remarkable progress since six West-European nations had created the Common Market in the 1950s. The European Economic Community, established in 1957, became the European Community in 1965, and it in turn became the European Union (EU) under the Treaty of Maastricht signed in 1991. Having grown to 28 member nations by 2013 (before Brexit), the EU was an economic superpower. The total annual gross domestic product (GDP) rose to more than 18 trillion dollars in 2018, which was almost equal to the annual GDP of the United States and considerably larger than China's GDP (12 trillion dollars).

As agreed under the Maastricht treaty, the EU embarked in the 1990s on one of its most ambitious enterprises, the voluntary adoption of a common currency. Twelve EU nations began to use the new "euro" in 2002 for financial transactions and the cash payments of daily life, replacing such historic national currencies as the franc, the mark, and the lira. The number of euro *A common currency* zone countries gradually increased, reaching 19 by 2018 and creating new problems for the stability of the currency when several national governments fell into financial crises as they struggled to pay their accumulating national debts.[1] The euro's value fluctuated in global financial markets, but it quickly became a major international currency and competed strongly against the American dollar. Several EU members chose not to adopt the euro, and many of the new states that joined the EU after 2002 remained outside the euro currency zone, pending further internal economic reforms. In another unprecedented step a European Central Bank was established in Frankfurt with the authority to set monetary policy for the member countries. The effects of this monetary policy on each country's social and economic policies became a controversial issue in European politics as the various national economies came under a more centralized system of monetary management and as a "sovereign debt crisis" developed in 2009–2010.

The debt crisis emerged as several euro zone countries, including Greece, Ireland, and Portugal, accumulated debts that far exceeded the levels they could manage. Having borrowed extensively during the expansive early years of the "euro era," these countries now faced escalating interest costs, difficulties in procuring new loans, and a possible default on their payments. The problems of the euro zone, on the most basic political and economic levels, resulted from the fact that all member nations used the same monetary system but continued to follow their own fiscal policies for expenditures, borrowing, and taxation. In short, the monetary union of different national states had never expanded into the kind of fiscal union that would normally shape the government budget within a single national economy. When countries such as *Greek debts* Greece seemed to be heading toward default on their loans, the whole European economy was threatened because the major European and American banks had loaned large amounts of money to governments that could no longer repay their debts or the accumulating interest; the banks themselves could therefore collapse because of their own financial exposure. In earlier eras, a country such as Greece might have worked its way out of such a crisis by devaluing its currency in ways that allowed for more flexibility in making repayments or in stimulating foreign trade, but the unified Euro currency precluded strategies of devaluation or inflationary adjustments. The euro debt crisis thus

---

[1]The 19 euro zone countries in 2018 were Austria, Belgium, Cyprus, Estonia, Finland, France, Germany, Greece, Ireland, Italy, Latvia, Lithuania, Luxembourg, Malta, the Netherlands, Portugal, Slovakia, Slovenia, and Spain.

spread from Greece and Portugal into the broader European financial system, even though Greece itself, for example, accounted for less than 2 percent of the total euro zone economy.

The European Central Bank and other agencies of the EU began providing emergency loans, or "bailouts," worth hundreds of billions of euros to avert the defaults that might have caused a collapse of the major European banks and a possible breakdown of the entire euro system. European political and financial leaders were determined to avoid such a breakdown, but the emergency loans were provided with the condition that the countries receiving such assistance must introduce rigorous austerity measures to bring down the deficits in their current and future government budgets. Such measures inevitably meant reductions in salaries, pension benefits, and other support for public sector workers; and the falling government expenditures, in turn, reduced demand in the private spheres of national economic life. Unemployment rose to very high levels, and the weakening economies undermined the secure standard of living that most Europeans had come to expect. Protests spread across Greece, Spain, and other countries where workers were faced with major cutbacks in salaries and benefits; and some Europeans proposed that Greece should be expelled from the euro zone. Meanwhile, many people in the most affected countries blamed Germany and Chancellor Angela Merkel for the austerity measures that accompanied each bailout, but the Germans were understandably hesitant to provide a large share of the emergency funds unless the governments and populations in the most indebted nations also agreed to reduce their expenditures.

Austerity measures

The leaders of the European Central Bank, the EU, and private banking groups all looked for new strategies to defuse the debt crisis, restore financial stability, avoid a deeper recession, and create a more reliable euro zone system for fiscal management. Representatives of the various euro zone governments—spurred on by the Germans and the French—thus negotiated a plan to create a European Stability Mechanism (ESM), which was a new organization that would raise money in the financial markets of member nations (and also raise funds by selling ESM bonds) and then provide loans for indebted governments or for government-funded bailouts of major banks that fell under extreme financial stress. In return for receiving such loans, however, a national government had to show that it was adopting fiscal reforms to ensure that its annual budget deficit remained below a fixed percentage of the national GDP—that is, the deficit in any year's budget was not to exceed 3 percent of the national GDP.

European Stability Mechanism

This new "mechanism" went into operation in 2013. It helped to restore some of the financial stability that was needed to ensure the long-term viability of the euro currency. The ESM was expected to collect more than 500 billion euros for future bailouts or "firewalls" to protect vulnerable governments, but the capital fund actually lagged well below this ambitious goal. It was nevertheless apparent that Europe's political and economic elites—and much of the population in their various nations—remained strongly committed to the euro as an essential economic foundation for the integrated European economy and as a symbolic affirmation of the "European project" that had been developing since the end of the Second World War. Although the debt crisis became the greatest economic threat that had yet arisen to the campaign for greater European integration, it seemed that Europe's collective historical memories would help to ensure the survival of the euro zone. To be sure, opinion polls showed that support for the EU fell significantly as people faced new austerities or considered the unattractive plan for diverting national financial resources into the collective funds of the European Stability

Mechanism. Neither austerity nor bailouts were popular political policies, and the EU restrictions on deficit spending provoked opposition and challenges in most member nations. Yet those many Europeans who remembered the devastating history of the twentieth-century world wars were not inclined to aban- don their visions of a united, peaceful Europe because of their concerns about a sovereign debt crisis. It was definitely a crisis, but the human suffering that accompanied this crisis could scarcely be compared to the earlier European tragedies of the "Western Front" or the Great Depression or the death camp at Auschwitz or the "ethnic cleansing" in Bosnia.

Commitment to EU

The European project, in short, seemed likely to survive the early twenty-first-century economic crisis, because the demise of a carefully constructed EU and common currency was a highly unattractive alternative. The nationalist anger about EU economic policies, however, increasingly fused with the rising nationalist anger about EU immigration policies, so that the European Union's long-term survival seemed more precarious than anyone could have imagined in the optimistic, post–Cold War era of the Maastricht Treaty (1991).

The European Union: Politics and Transnational Collaborations

Amid the political, economic, and social challenges of the debt crisis and immigration crisis, the EU remained firmly attached to liberal political and economic models. Although Britain voted to withdraw from the EU, several countries in the Balkans continued to negotiate for possible admission. An applicant nation had to demonstrate its commitment to "liberty, democracy, respect for human rights and fundamental freedoms, and the rule of law," which meant, among other stipulations, that would-be members had to have abolished capital punishment. A functioning free market economy was also required.

Meanwhile, the EU was "deepening" in additional ways. The Maastricht treaty had called for the continued development of common foreign and defense policies. In June 1999 the EU foreign ministers resolved to develop a capacity for collective military action of their own. The EU began to move toward creating an armed force supplementary to but not supplanting NATO. The Atlantic alliance would remain firm, but a new "European Defense Agency" came into full operation after 2005. The new military cooperation sig- naled Europe's intention to end its long-term dependence on the United States and to reject the status of "an American protectorate." These developments both pleased and disturbed American policy makers who wanted Europe to play an independent role, espe- cially in European matters, but did not wish to see resources drained off from NATO.

The EU political and bureaucratic structures did not change as rapidly as the evolving economic or defense policies. The European Commission, with an extensive civil service bureaucracy in Brussels, served as its executive and administrative branch and had the right to initiate proposals for legislation. The European Parliament, elected by a European-wide electorate, supervised the budget and debated Commission proposals. This representative body never aroused much enthusiasm, and voter turnout in the member nations at election time remained low. Although the heads of government held regularly scheduled meetings, the foreign ministers of the member-nations meeting as a council also convened frequently to discuss and vote on matters of common interest. The meetings of this council provided an opportunity for the EU to take positions on international issues that extended well beyond Europe itself. It had not been anticipated that the ministers would evolve into the chief policy-making body, but in some ways it tied the EU to democratic support in a way that the European Commission had failed to do.

Common foreign and defense policies

Historical Documents

Emmanuel Macron, "The Illusions of Nationalism" (2018)

The European Union (EU) provided a late-twentieth-century framework for the transnational economic and cultural collaboration of Europe's diverse national cultures. By the second decade of the twenty-first century, however, resurgent populist nationalisms were denouncing numerous EU actions and the EU bureaucracy. Britain voted to leave the EU, and the hostility to EU policies threatened traditional political parties and governmental stability in other countries. In this changing political context, the French President Emmanuel Macron (1977-) spoke at the European Parliament in Strasbourg, strongly reaffirming (in these excerpts) the importance of the European Union and condemning populist nationalisms that drifted away from democratic principles.

[We meet in] a context where a sort of European civil war is reappearing, where our differences, sometimes our national egoisms, appear more important than what unites us. . . .

Our discussion also takes place at a time of great transformations brought about by digital technology, climate change, and its consequences. . . .

I firmly believe that European democracy is our best chance in this world at this difficult time. Abandoning our model, and I would go as far as to say our identity, would be the worst mistake. . . .

I do not wish to let this fatal illusion take hold once again, which has, lest we forget, . . . pushed our continent towards the abyss. The illusion of strong power, nationalism, and the abandonment of freedoms. . . . Faced with the authoritarianism which

surrounds us on all sides, the answer must not be authoritarian democracy but the authority of democracy. . . .

This [European] union for peace and solidarity offers the world a unique space of stability and security. . . .

I belong to a generation which has never experienced war and I belong to a generation which is allowing itself the luxury of forgetting what its forebears lived through. . . .

I don't want to belong to a generation of sleepwalkers, I don't want to be part of a generation which has forgotten its own past. . . .

I want to belong to a generation which will defend European sovereignty because we fought for it, because it means something and because it is this sovereignty which will enable future generations to choose their own futures.

L'actualité présidentielle en continu [News from the French Presidency], Speech of the President of the Republic at the European Parliament, April 17, 2018, https://www.elysee.fr/emmanuel-macron/2018/04/20/european-parliament.

Cooperation or supranationalism?

The early impetus for supranationalism in the Union faded, but what remained was the close cooperation of the ministers representing the member-states, discussing and making decisions on the basis of a half-century of common values and experience and a large body of jurisprudence and legal principles under the jurisdiction of the Union's Court of Justice. Each nation saw its stability, prosperity, and security enhanced by membership in the Union and recognized that the loss of sovereignty had been less than feared.

Opposition to EU Constitution

But there was strong opposition to a proposed EU constitution that would have created the framework for a more coherent, integrated political union. Although a majority of EU countries supported the proposed constitution, voters in France and the Netherlands rejected the proposal in 2005, thus stopping the plan for a shared constitution and throwing open the whole question of how the EU might proceed with further political integration. Many

Europe's transnational integration contributed to a collective "European project" in many spheres, including sports. The Euro Cup soccer tournament has taken place every four years since 1960, creating an intense, continent-wide interest and new national rivalries in which young men collided on athletic fields rather than battlefields. This photograph of the French national team in a 2016 Euro Cup stadium suggests the intensity of modern European sports as well as the diversity of the athletes in contemporary European societies.

(©Clive Rose/Getty Images Sport/Getty Images)

Europeans favored the proposed constitution, particularly for its broad guarantees of social and economic rights and entitlements, but many others expressed concern about perceived threats to European living standards and social values or to specific national interests—especially after the major expansion of the EU membership in 2004.

The EU was therefore not likely to develop in the foreseeable future as its more visionary advocates had once anticipated, and the electoral success of nationalist, populist parties in the various member nations posed a developing threat to Europe's entire transnational project. New conflicts created new wedges between the European Union and various national governments. Indeed, the EU itself launched an "infringement procedure" against Poland in 2018, charging that the Polish government's judicial reforms violated the EU's core principles of democracy and rule of law; and the EU initiated "disciplinary action" against the Italian government for violating budgetary debt guidelines. Such actions exemplified the rising tensions between the EU and its many national critics; and each conflict showed the challenges that European integration would continue to face. The broader historical transition toward European peace, however, remained the EU's enduring achievement because (as noted earlier) the continent had entered an unprecedented historical era in which war between the leading European powers seemed unimaginable.

Recognizing the significance of this historical transition, the Nobel Prize committee in Norway awarded the 2012 Nobel Peace Prize to the EU for its multiple contributions to "the advancement of peace and reconciliation, democracy and human rights in Europe." The EU faced multiple threats to its vitality and even its survival in the wake of the debt and immigration crises, but the continuing collaboration within the EU, as the Nobel Prize committee suggested, still affirmed the wide support for democracy, peace, and human rights throughout Europe.

French–German cooperation, which had been the original driving force behind the success of European integration, remained crucial. No one could predict, however, the future evolution of an enlarged EU that could conceivably still unravel or that could become a potential rival to the global political and economic power of the United States. In Europe the older strategic threat from the Soviet Union was gone, but many Europeans now saw a threat to the European way of life in American-led "globalization," which Europeans criticized as a worship of mass consumerism and a materialistic abandonment of social and cultural values. To Europeans, even among admirers of American accomplishments, the EU provided an essential balance to American economic power and to the unpredictable directions of American diplomacy (which broke away from Europe and numerous EU policies after Donald Trump became President of the United States in 2017).

Uneasiness over American-led globalization

The "New Economy": The 1990s and Beyond

The global economy that reemerged after the Second World War seemed to enter a new phase in the 1990s. Globalization was the key word. It meant the more rapid and efficient movement of capital and technology worldwide across all geographical and political boundaries. The United States played a key role in the evolving global economy, but large multinational corporations in Europe and Asia also developed new operations in all regions of the world.

An information economy

The new economy was an information economy. At its base was the computer revolution and the Internet, a word scarcely known before the early 1990s. By the early twenty-first century the Internet was in everyone's vocabulary, and the new technology was used by billions of people throughout the world. It provided instant access to all kinds of information and became available through mobile telephones and computers in even the most remote towns, homes, and offices. It also helped to produce a new wave of social and economic transformations, bringing new communications and commercial systems that developed and spread more quickly than any previous industrial changes. Trade expanded. The flow of private investment capital from the industrial nations to the developing countries quickened. Living standards in many parts of the world rose, all tied to the growing trade and investment that linked Europe to the global economy; but the new technologies also widened the economic gap between wealthy and poorer nations.

The processes of globalization often threatened salaries and employment in Europe, however, as industrial production shifted to lower wage countries in Asia, Africa, and Latin America. To enhance competitive power in the global marketplace large corporations in the United States, Europe, and Asia turned to low-wage labor in poorer countries and bought other companies to become even larger, within and across national lines. Multinational corporations grew in numbers and size everywhere, and there seemed to be little concern over foreign companies' taking over domestic corporations. London regained much of its financial prestige and strength as the financial center for European mergers and amalgamations, which accelerated as never before.

Multinational corporations

Despite warnings from some quarters against "irrational exuberance," stock values and other speculative investments in real estate kept climbing in the late 1990s and early

The EU fostered international political cooperation as well as economic collaborations. This picture shows national representatives at a meeting of the European Parliament in 2018. They were listening to French President Emmanuel Macron in their flag-draped Strasbourg Chamber as he criticized anti-EU nationalisms and affirmed the value of the EU's transnational goals and institutions.
(©SOPA Images/LightRocket/Getty Images)

years of the twenty-first century. Although some believed that the new era of economic expansion would continue in both America and Europe, others recalled past speculative fever and manias in history: tulips in the seventeenth century; colonization schemes in the eighteenth; canals, railroads, gold, and silver in the nineteenth. Persons with broad historical perspectives were thus not surprised when both the housing "bubble" and stock values collapsed in America and much of Europe after 2007, setting off a major recession.

The computer revolution was meanwhile creating a new economy in many ways. Computer technologies helped the economy to grow through greater productivity and helped fuel the rising prices in global stock markets. Computer wizards as well as brokers, financial executives, and entrepreneurs of all kinds often became extremely wealthy at the same time that the older industrial infrastructure was declining in many European and American cities.

The Internet and the global communication system of the World Wide Web changed politics, culture, and social relations as well as commerce and economic production. New social media (promoted by global companies such as Facebook and Twitter) and new Internet search engines such as Google became enormous enterprises, eclipsing the capital investment in older industries and reshaping both public cultures and private lives on every continent. European political life took on the characteristics of a direct democracy as activists rallied supporters and spread information (or misinformation) via the instant communication of social media—which carried early Internet networks into vast new spheres of nongovernmental messaging and action.

The Internet had begun from modest beginnings in the late 1960s in the United States as a government-sponsored project to enhance communications. Computer scientists around the world enlarged its scope and made it easier for individuals and companies to utilize in their daily work. The World Wide Web was first developed in 1980 at a nuclear physics research center near Geneva when the young English physicist Tim Berners-Lee developed a program to process information through electronic associations and linkages. For a time it remained neglected, but by 1990 he and others had revived and perfected it. By means of the Internet, the World Wide Web became a mass medium for billions of people around the world, and its users continued to multiply. It revolutionized communications, especially as it overlapped with the new social media. People sent electronic mail and text messages (by telephones) to each other, negotiated financial transactions, made purchases, read the daily news, pursued online education, and used the Web for every form of entertainment. Many compared the significance of the new computer technology to the invention of the printing press in the fifteenth century. So rapidly was the new technology developing in speed, efficiency, and versatility that new, more powerful computer models became available almost immediately after earlier ones had first come into use.

English became the dominant language of the Internet, but the use of computers and Internet communications also developed rapidly in Europe. Some Europeans expressed concern that the Internet represented not only an immense step toward globalization but also toward Americanization. However, global competition continued. A Finnish company held an early lead in the cellular phone market, computer specialists developed innovative software programs in India, and companies in Taiwan manufactured many of the most advanced computer chips.

The worldwide faith in the market and market forces presented other challenges for those who wanted to reduce the growing gap in the wealth of different countries around the world. Faith in a kind of oversimplified laissez-faire market economy spread in Europe and in other industrialized countries. Europeans often referred to the new economic creed as "neo-liberalism," thereby evoking the classical era of nineteenth-century political economy. There was a kind of "market fundamentalism," not unlike a religious faith. Globalization and the world's market economy, its advocates claimed, made intervention by governments much less necessary than the advocates of Keynesian theories or European-style welfare states had assumed. The neo-liberal argument, however, was also opposed by critics everywhere. In France, for example, where unemployment was high and where labor unions had wide influence, protesting workers argued that it was immoral for corporations to earn large profits while at the same time laying off workers or closing factories.

The founding of the WTO

Meanwhile the growth in world commerce led to the creation in 1994 of a more formal World Trade Organization (WTO) to replace the General Agreement on Tariffs and Trade (GATT) in effect since 1948. GATT had been immensely successful in lowering tariffs and enlarging world trade through informal bargaining procedures and agreements. By 1986 it had grown to include 92 nations. In 1995 the United States succeeded in creating a permanent, more formal organization. The WTO was based in Geneva, Switzerland, and authorized to draw up and oversee agreements, enforce trade rules, and settle disputes. It grew to 162 members by 2016, but its large ministerial meetings often met with opposition and demonstrations in the streets. All European nations as well as the EU as a whole belonged to the WTO and often appealed to the organization to mediate trade disputes with countries throughout the world. The negotiated free trade agreements, in the view of protestors and other critics, paid little attention to environmental and labor

The computer revolution transformed modern culture, education, entertainment, and social life as well as politics, governments, and commercial systems. These people were working on their computers and telephones at a Parisian cafe, using twenty-first century technologies that enabled them to look for digital information or to communicate instantly with people around the world from a sidewalk table.
(©Christian Science Monitor/Getty Images)

conditions, or even to the widespread exploitation of child labor in the poorer, industrializing countries outside Europe and North America. The poorer nations, for their part, saw themselves at risk of losing out on cheaper labor costs, one of their chief competitive advantages in relation to Europe; and they pointedly underscored the large share of ecological damage for which the industrial nations were responsible. Subsidies to agriculture in Europe and other wealthier regions placed the less industrial nations, dependent on either the export or import of food, at a disadvantage. Critics of the new international trade system therefore rejected arguments for free trade as a means of enhancing living standards for all. The violence of the popular protests at WTO meetings in Europe and elsewhere sometimes expressed an angry anarchism rather than specific economic goals, but the protests also aroused new sensitivities to social issues worldwide.

Globalization, already visible in earlier periods of the world's history, and especially so in the nineteenth and twentieth centuries, seemed to be the defining social and economic theme for Europeans in the twenty-first century. National boundaries, though not disappearing, were increasingly transcended by cross-boundary transactions and global exchanges in the world of communications, industry, culture, travel, food, popular entertainment, even apparel. Some Europeans still viewed globalization as a form of "Americanization," but by the early twenty-first century the global system was by no means simply an American export. The giant multinational corporations, no longer exclusively European or American but home-based in nations all over the world, depended as never before on the

Critics of globalization

movement of capital, goods, trained personnel, technology, and ideas that flowed across traditional national boundaries. A new global culture that was never just "European" or "American" or "Asian" or "African" circulated everywhere and drew on a vast multicultural exchange among people and social institutions on every continent.

121.   INTELLECTUAL AND SOCIAL TRANSITIONS IN MODERN CULTURES

Intellectual and cultural life does not usually evolve through the dramatic public events or conflicts that reshape politics and economic relations. Yet the transitions in modern intellectual life and social mores have transformed modern history during all the years of international conflict and revolutionary change that we have discussed. People define themselves and their cultures in activities that go far beyond politics and economics. They constantly develop new forms of knowledge, philosophy, religious belief, creative art, and social life, all of which both influence and respond to the transformations of the modern world. Although much of twentieth-century culture had its origins in the years 1871 to 1914, science, philosophy, the arts, and religion crossed new frontiers or took new directions over the course of the twentieth century and set the stage for new trends in the early twenty-first century. Even to single out a few of these developments will suggest the wide-ranging changes of the contemporary era.

The Advance of Science and Technology

Science and technology expanded rapidly in the half-century before the First World War, but scientific knowledge changed even more quickly in the twentieth century. Scientific discoveries advanced more rapidly in this era than in all previous human history. For one thing, more scientists were at work. At the opening of the twentieth century, about 15,000 scientists were exploring scientific problems; in the latter half of the century, over a half-million scientists were engaged in research around the world, more than in all previous centuries combined. Over 85 percent of all scientists who have ever lived have been at work over the last century.

Medicine and public health

The average person in Europe and other industrialized societies experienced the triumphs of science most dramatically in medicine and public health. Nothing in previous medical discovery could equal the contributions of sulfa drugs, antibiotics, cortisone, and other substances used to combat formerly crippling or deadly diseases, including pneumonia and tuberculosis; hormones, adrenaline, and insulin were also available to promote health or relieve suffering. Vaccines combated a number of dread diseases, including, after 1955, poliomyelitis; by 1975 smallpox (a dreaded disease in early modern Europe) had been all but eradicated worldwide. Remarkable accomplishments in surgery included the transplanting of vital organs. Apart from the advances in medical science, Europeans benefited from modern technology in almost every aspect of their daily lives. For entertainment, radio and the motion picture became available everywhere. Television appeared after the Second World War, and twenty-first century computers and mobile phones brought music, films, and other arts within a click of every nimble finger. Washing machines, freezers, frozen foods, and microwave ovens lightened household duties. After 1947 airplanes could fly faster than the speed of sound; giant aircraft could traverse huge distances in a few hours; tourist travel to distant parts of the earth became commonplace. A world of electronics, robotics, rocketry, and space technology opened. Many people came to believe that technological solutions could be found for every problem.

It was therefore a shattering experience when the fatal disease AIDS (Acquired Immuno-Deficiency Syndrome) appeared in the early 1980s and by the 1990s was assuming global epidemic proportions. Deaths from the disease mounted, and it was estimated that as many as 2.3 million Europeans were living with the HIV infection in 2010. The disease spread especially in Russia, Ukraine, and some other countries of eastern Europe, but the new illness affected people in every European society. While medical scientists worked in the early twenty-first century to devise a preventive vaccine or to prolong the lives of its victims, educational efforts to stop its spread focused on sexual practices, intravenous drug use, and the protection of blood supplies. Uncertainty and anguish increased as people struggled with a physiological threat that was sometimes compared to the Black Death of the fourteenth century or the deadly worldwide flu pandemic of 1918.

Nuclear Physics

In pure, or theoretical, science the transformation of physics in the twentieth century could be compared only to the scientific revolution of the sixteenth and seventeenth centuries. Early in the twentieth century scientists had discovered the natural radioactivity of certain elements, German physicists such as Max Planck and Albert Einstein had developed quantum physics and relativity theory, and Einstein had propounded his now famous formula for the conversion of mass into energy ($e = mc^2$). After 1919 a series of discoveries led to a deeper understanding of the atom. The cyclotron, developed by British scientists in 1932 at Cambridge University, made it possible to penetrate or "bombard" the nucleus of the atom at high speed. The nucleus, scientists learned, consisted not only of protons but of other particles like neutrons as well. In 1938 the German chemist Otto Hahn discovered that when he bombarded the atomic nucleus of the heavy radioactive element uranium with neutrons, it became unstable and split into two, which meant that energy trapped within the atom could be released.

The implications of this breakthrough in theoretical science were clear. If the atoms in a large amount of uranium were split in a chain reaction, enormous amounts of energy would be released. In the troubled atmosphere of 1939 the possibility arose of its use for military purposes. When the war came, scientists in the United States, including Einstein and others who had fled from Nazi anti-Semitism and oppression in Europe, prevailed upon the American government to explore its military use before the Germans succeeded in doing so. In 1942 American and British scientists and European refugee scientists such as the Italian Enrico Fermi brought about the first sustained nuclear chain reaction. This in turn led to the secret preparation of the atomic bomb at Los Alamos, New Mexico and to its use by the United States against Japan at Hiroshima and Nagasaki in August 1945.

The first atomic bomb

After the war even more staggering technical developments followed. The hydrogen or thermonuclear bomb was built independently by the Americans and by the Soviets in 1952–1953; it involved nuclear fusion, or the joining together of hydrogen and other elements at great heat, using the atomic or fission bomb as a detonator with a stupendous chain reaction. The first use of nuclear energy was therefore for military purposes, but it held constructive peacetime potential; a tiny grain of uranium (or plutonium, another radioactive element) could produce power equal to almost three tons of coal. By the 1990s over 15 percent of the world's electricity was generated by nuclear power plants; in France, over 65 percent. At the same time, the dangers of radioactivity became more apparent and alarming. Accidents in nuclear power plants, including the 1986 accident at Chernobyl in Ukraine, threatened the surrounding population and environs with the release of radioactive gases; nor could nuclear meltdowns be ruled out. Popular opposition to the building of nuclear power plants grew in many European countries, as did concern over their proper design and the disposition of nuclear waste. This opposition became most influential in Germany, where the government announced plans, in 2011, to phase out all nuclear power plants; but France also began to reduce its reliance on nuclear power after 2018. Meanwhile, Europeans turned increasingly to the renewable power of wind turbines and solar panels to replace nuclear power, coal, and other fossil fuels. By 2015, about 30 percent of the power consumed in the EU came from renewable sources and 28 percent from nuclear energy.

New sources of power

In later years of the twentieth century and continuing into the twenty-first century scientists used linear accelerators like the cyclotron and even more powerful colliders and supercolliders as atom smashers to explore the nature of the atom and the behavior of its subatomic particles. Theoretical physicists continued to advance complex new concepts such as string theory and thus persisted in their search for an overarching theory that would explain the interrelationship of gravity, electromagnetism, and nuclear force, all of which could be found in the subatomic world and in the cosmos as a whole.

Social Implications of Science and Technology

As in the case of nuclear physics, science in the contemporary age was closely allied with technology and the organized effort to exploit new scientific findings. Governments and industries subsidized most scientific research. Laboratory equipment was expensive, and complex investigation required large-scale collaborative efforts; the solitary scientific investigator virtually disappeared. The subsidization of research for national purposes raised fears that scientific discoveries might serve political goals rather than meet pressing social or human needs.

Science had always affected the way people thought about themselves and their universe. The Copernican revolution had removed the earth from its central position in the scheme of things; Darwinian evolution had demonstrated that *Homo sapiens* was biologically a species that had evolved and survived. The philosophical implications of contemporary physics were only vaguely understood, yet they reinforced theories of relativism in all spheres. Ironically, at the very time that the average person was awed by the capabilities of science, scientists themselves recognized that they did not possess a magic key to the nature of things. Generally they claimed no more than the ability to determine, or guess at, relationships, which in the world of the atom (as in the cosmos itself) remained mysterious and uncertain.

Questioning scientific advances

Some thoughtful persons questioned scientific and technological advance and asked whether modern technology had grown beyond human control. Ecologists pointed to the wastage and despoliation of natural resources and the threat to the environment, thus helping to shape the political agendas of "Green" parties in various European nations. The life-preserving features of modern medicine also affected the environment in that much-desired improvements in public health could contribute to overpopulation and to perhaps unmanageable pressure upon the limited resources within Europe and around the globe. The techniques developed to save or prolong human life also raised ethical and legal issues, including new definitions of life and death, and the rights in such matters of patients, families, hospitals, and physicians. Questions arose over new forms of artificial conception, and later over stem-cell research using human embryos, and over prenatal DNA testing. Those who condemned modern technology sometimes extolled the virtues of a prescientific and preindustrial age; others called for sharper awareness of how scientific advances often posed new dangers or new ethical dilemmas, even when the new science seemed to enhance human health or life expectancy. In an age of destructive weaponry and threats to the environment, the advance of science and technology was no longer unequivocally equated with the idea of progress.

Meanwhile, in the quest to understand nature the old divisions between the sciences broke down and new sciences appeared. Biochemistry, cell and molecular biology, biophysics, astrophysics, geophysics, and other subdisciplines arose; and all made intensive use of mathematics. In biology genetics made striking advances. While physicists discovered new atomic particles, biochemists isolated the organic substance found in the genes of all living cells, the chemical carriers of all hereditary characteristics. When scientists deciphered the genetic "code" and synthesized the basic substance of heredity (DNA), it became possible by splicing genes to alter the characteristics of plant and animal species and to clone or reproduce in the laboratory an animal such as a frog or a sheep with desired hereditary characteristics. The implications for the possibility of even human cloning at some future date were staggering. Biotechnologists were also revolutionizing food production by genetically engineering new varieties of crops, which provoked strong objections from European critics who saw such modifications as a threat to safe food and human health. European scientists meanwhile became deeply involved after 2000 in the international research on the human genome—the more than 3 billion chemical units of DNA that control the human body and also contribute to genetic-based illnesses.

The other life sciences and social sciences also grew steadily as fields for modern European research. Psychological exploration of human behavior, as well as the treatment of mental and emotional disorders through psychiatry and psychoanalysis, expanded rapidly. Freud, who had first developed his theories of psychoanalysis before 1914, became more widely known in the 1920s. His emphasis on the human sex drive and sexual repression was later much modified. Many students of human behavior argued that his contributions were not universally or scientifically valid but reflected the values of pre-1914, middle-class, male-dominated Viennese society. A variety of schools emerged with different interpretations and techniques, and drugs were developed to treat psychological depression and other mental illnesses. But the search, initiated by Freud, for the unconscious sources of individual and collective human   *Impact of Freud* conduct remained a hallmark of contemporary thought and culture.

Anthropologists and other social scientists increasingly stressed the relativism of all culture. They denied notions of cultural superiority or hierarchies of cultural values, or even that there were objective criteria of historical progress. If Western societies, they noted, made notable progress in science and technology, other cultures accomplished more in self-discipline, individual integrity, and human happiness. The adjective "primitive," as opposed to "civilized," tended to disappear, and a new cultural humanism recognized and esteemed values that had evolved outside the European tradition. The French anthropologist Claude Lévi-Strauss exemplified this tendency in a series of influential books that developed the ideas of "structuralism" during the 1950s and 1960s. Arguing that deep cultural structures and rituals in all societies serve common symbolic purposes and help sustain social practices such as family life or respect for ancestors, Lévi-Strauss emphasized the underlying similarities in human cultures—even when the specific content of rituals varies widely in different places and times. Such theories spread from anthropology into the humanities and challenged earlier hierarchical beliefs about Europe's superiority to non-European cultures.

Space Exploration

Among the most dramatic developments in science and technology in the second half of the twentieth century was space exploration. In the 1950s the Soviets and the Americans competed with each other as part of the Cold War; each made important advances in rocket research. Both the United States and the U.S.S.R. mastered multistage rocket launching. The Soviets opened the space age when in 1957 they launched *Sputnik,* the world's first artificial satellite; in 1961 they sent the first human, Yuri A. Gagarin, in orbital flight around the earth. The Americans sent their own astronauts into space in 1961 and 1962. In the 1960s both countries launched unmanned automated spaceships to probe and explore the moon and then the planets of the solar system and their satellites. Early in the 1960s President Kennedy responded to the Soviet advances in space exploration by pledging that Americans would land on the moon before the end of the decade. In 1969 three American astronauts, as planned in Project Apollo, made the quarter-million-mile journey to the moon, and millions of viewers around the globe watched on television as Neil Armstrong took his first steps on the moon's surface.

The Soviets conducted their own impressive space probes to the moon, to Mars, and to Halley's Comet, whose behavior had been predicted in the seventeenth century and

U.S.-Soviet competition

European space missions provided another opportunity for international cooperation in the late twentieth century. These cosmonauts were preparing for a rocket launch that would take them to an orbiting space station in 2001. Their mission was an example of transnational space programs, because the crew included a French woman and two Russian men, and they were launched on their flight from a site in Kazakhstan.

(©MIKHAIL GRACHYEV/AFP/ Getty Images)

Existential philosophy attracted many adherents in Europe and North America during the decades after the Second World War, partly because it emphasized human freedom and affirmed the significance of individual actions in an impersonal, modern world that seemed to lack inherent meanings. The influential existential author Jean-Paul Sartre sits here in one of his characteristic philosophical and social places—alone at a Parisian cafe.

(©Dominique BERRETTY/Gamma-Rapho/Getty Images)

which once again returned close enough for observation in 1986. The Soviets also built a permanent space station and set records in testing human endurance in weightless space. As time went on, Cold War rivalries played less of a role in space exploration, but military objectives were never completely absent. The United States and U.S.S.R., and other countries in later decades, launched spy satellites for reconnaissance and information gathering.

International cooperation

In the 1980s space enterprise showed promise of international cooperation and was no longer confined to the military superpowers. France, Japan, China, and other countries became spacefaring nations, planning and launching satellites and space probes of their own. The European Space Agency carried out its own operations, launching communication satellites and also sending astronauts to work with the Russians on orbiting space stations. After the Cold War the Americans and the Russians began to cooperate in space, most notably in the development and joint use of a Russian-built space station. On the other hand, the need for human space expeditions came under serious scrutiny. Many objected to the enormous expense of space exploration when acute social needs at home remained unfulfilled. But its champions in Europe and elsewhere defended space exploration as part of the continuing human effort to cross new frontiers, expand horizons, and explore the unknown. The twentieth century may ultimately be remembered, apart from the destructiveness of its terrible wars, as the century in which humans first set foot on the moon, and with robot spaceships devised and guided by human intelligence, began to explore the universe.

Philosophy: Existentialism in the Postwar Years

In the early years after the Second World War, a new group of philosophers in Europe developed a loosely organized body of ideas called "existentialism." The existentialists formed no one school of thought and held no coherent body of principles. There were religious and atheist existentialists. Yet all held some beliefs and attitudes in common. All reflected a troubled civilization, a world disturbed by war and oppression, a civilization of material progress and moral uncertainty in which the individual could be crushed by the very triumphs of science and technology, and in which human life itself seemed to have lost inherent meaning or to have become absurd.

Existentialist thought owed a debt to Pascal, Nietzsche, and others who had underscored the tragic element in human existence and the limitations on the power of human reason. More directly it owed a debt to Søren Kierkegaard, the nineteenth-century Danish religious philosopher. But it was French writers, and especially Jean-Paul Sartre, who after the Second World War developed existentialist thought in literature and philosophy in an accessible form that for a time gave it a wide popular following. In a hostile world that lacked higher purpose or universal truths, the existentialists contended, human beings had to make choices and commitments on their own. They were "condemned to be free" and were alone responsible for the choices and actions that defined their very existence; for most existentialists, the nature of a human being's existence was defined by what he or she did rather than by some deeper spiritual essence. Authentic existentialists therefore had to move beyond philosophical contemplation and take action in the world, even though they were aware that human action might fail to change the world. Albert Camus, influenced by the existentialists, drew upon the myth of Sisyphus, who was condemned continuously to roll his stone uphill, though it always rolled back down again. The very humanity of Sisyphus grew out of courage and perseverance at a hopeless and absurd task. Existentialism emphasized the anguish of human existence, the frailty of human reason, the fragility of human institutions, and the need to reassert and redefine human freedom. Although its popular following waned and Sartre himself was dislodged from his earlier lofty eminence, existentialism never completely disappeared from contemporary philosophy or religion.

Jean-Paul Sartre

Philosophy: Logic and Language; Literary Criticism; History

Professional philosophy in the twentieth century seemed to contribute less to an understanding of contemporary problems than in the past. Always concerned with the origins and nature of knowledge, it had also shared an interest in metaphysics and ethics. In the early twentieth century it became highly analytical, focusing especially on the limits and criteria of knowledge. In the formal study of logic, mathematical symbols replaced the use of traditional language. On the eve of the First World War the English philosophers Bertrand Russell and Alfred North Whitehead had explored logic and mathematics in their monumental *Principia Mathematica*. In the 1920s an influential group of philosophers and mathematicians in Vienna, among them Ludwig Wittgenstein, sought to introduce the methodology and precision of mathematics into the study of philosophy as a whole, in what they called logical positivism. They rejected the ambiguities of language used in traditional speculation on morals and values, turning away from the nondemonstrable—that is, "God, death, what is higher," in Wittgenstein's phrase. The Vienna group disintegrated in the 1930s and Wittgenstein himself moved to England, but logical positivism remained influential. Most professional philosophers continued to emphasize scientific rigor and linguistic analysis. A smaller but growing number, responsive to contemporary ethical concerns, devoted themselves to questions about moral choices and the most ethical human responses to social dilemmas.

New studies in philosophy, linguistic analysis, and semiotics (that is, the study of signs and symbols in communication) drew attention to the complex relation between language and reality. Philosophers also challenged many of the dualisms taken for granted in traditional European thought. In literary studies "deconstruction" or "poststructuralist" theory emerged after the 1960s to offer new methods of analysis and criticism. Its proponents sought to analyze, or "deconstruct," a body of writing or "text" (which could be a painting or other kind of cultural object as well as a traditional narrative) to examine its implicit cultural assumptions and its indebtedness to its cultural traditions. No single valid meaning was to be attached to any individual work. According to its advocates, deconstruction made it possible to reveal the philosophical, class, racial, ethnocentric, or sexual assumptions hidden in the language of a work. It also contested older hierarchical standards of literary quality, blurred distinctions between elite and popular culture, made less of a dichotomy between fact and fiction (and other dualisms), and broadened the existing canon of writings studied in literature, history, law, religion, and other disciplines.

Deconstruction

The work of the critic was said to be as much a creative enterprise as literary or artistic creation itself. Propounded originally in the late 1960s in broad philosophical terms by the French philosopher Jacques Derrida, and developed further by other writers and scholars of various disciplines and nationalities, deconstruction also attracted a wide following in the United States. Its opponents viewed it as abandoning traditional literary history and rejecting rational, critical standards that had shaped modern thought since the Enlightenment.

The writing of history also underwent a profound change. A group of French historical scholars (called the *Annales* school, from a journal with which they were associated) gained wide influence after the Second World War. They focused on long-term elements in historical change such as population, economy, climate, and natural resources; relegated politics to a lesser role; and avoided the traditional narrative of public events. They studied also the lives of ordinary people in the past and tried to reconstruct the collective outlook of social classes. The newer social history in France, England, Italy, and Germany also paid special attention to the inarticulate and illiterate and to all those with strong oral traditions, such as the enslaved people whom Europeans had transported to the Americas, the English working classes, the common people in Renaissance cities, or the bourgeois families in German principalities. The goal of such historical work was to reconstruct the cultures and everyday lives of people who left few written sources. There was also an important expansion in the historical study of women from antiquity to the present, leading to cultural and social reassessments of entire historical eras and a new interest in how ideas or assumptions about gender shaped political systems and workplaces as well as the relationships within European families. A variety of social themes received new historical attention as historians redefined their more traditional studies of politics and society: marriage, divorce, the family, childhood, sexuality, even insanity and death through the ages. The French historian and social theorist Michel Foucault, for example, helped to stimulate new historical studies of psychology, education, and hospitals by stressing that the knowledge of "experts" always became linked to the exercise of social power. For their part, many traditional historians who had not been wholly insensitive to these concerns widened their narratives to include such social and cultural themes, or to expand their analysis of how hierarchical uses of power shape the social relations of daily life.

New interests among historians

The Creative Arts

The revolution against older traditions in the creative arts assumed new dimensions. Ever since the Renaissance, visual artists had followed certain norms of representation and space perspective. But much of twentieth-century art prided itself on being nonobjective; it rejected the idea of imitating or reconstructing nature, or mirroring it with realism or photographic fidelity. The artistic revolution inaugurated in France before 1914 accelerated in the interwar years and after 1945. It seemed to mirror the political turbulence of the times and the disillusionment with rationalism and optimism. It reflected the influence of Freudian and other schools of psychology and the emphasis on the unconscious and irrational, as well as the relativity of the new physics and its uncertainties about the nature of matter, space, and time.

Artists continued the pre-1914 experimentation in color, form, and use of materials, but went well beyond earlier innovations as they responded to later wars, suffering, and social disorientation. The innovative work of artists such as Picasso—whose cubist paintings had systematically distorted and deformed material objects or human figures—was followed by increasingly abstract artistic experiments during the later twentieth century, as may be seen by comparing Picasso's *Les Demoiselles d'Avignon* (see p. 647) with Willem de Kooning's *Woman VI* (see. p. 1063). Some artists expressed themselves through geometric form; others left reality behind and tried to represent their own unconscious fears or desires. The results were fascinating but frequently baffling, so that the abstract works of artists such as de Kooning offered questions rather than answers for those who wanted art to provide stable cultural meanings. Other art provided haunting reminders of World War II and the Holocaust, as in the work of Felix Nussbaum—a German-Jewish surrealist painter who died in the death camp at Auschwitz (see p. 1064). After the Second World War many European artists worked in the United States, but new experimental painting and sculpture continued to develop in Europe's major cities and in creative artistic communities that were scattered across the continent.

Seeing the world in new ways

Contemporary art resulted in original and striking expressions of form and color, but the conscious subjectivism widened still further the gap between artist and public. The artist, painter, and sculptor (and the poet, musician, playwright, and novelist, who were also rejecting the older conventions) were conveying their own visions of the world, not an objective reality that could easily be understood by others. Perhaps the greatest innovation was that the public, baffled as it was by much of contemporary art, came to accept the avant-garde as normal, even if on occasion it rebelled against it. Democratic societies accepted the need for artistic experimentation and innovation, which had been frowned upon or banned as degenerate and socially dangerous in totalitarian societies like Nazi Germany and the Soviet Union. Representational art, of course, never completely disappeared anywhere, and many artists reaffirmed it, contributing to a growing pluralism in contemporary artistic styles.

Subjectivism and the unconscious in literature

The focus on subjectivism and the unconscious was reflected in literature too. The reconstruction of lost time and the unfolding of the individual's innermost experience through a stream of consciousness and flood of memories, which had appeared first in the work of Marcel Proust and James Joyce shortly after the First World War, remained important for a new generation of novelists and playwrights after 1945. Not only writers but also cinematographers experimented with probing the unconscious in evocative but mystifying ways. All of this cultural experimentation contrasted with the popular entertainment provided through the mass media, especially movies and daily diets of television "soap operas" and "sit-coms."

WOMAN VI
by Willem de Kooning (Dutch, lived in the United States, 1904–1997)
This work is an example of the post-1945 trend toward increasingly abstract art. Painted in 1953 by the Dutch artist Willem de Kooning, who had moved to the United States and was working in New York, this abstract portrayal of a "woman" suggests how later-twentieth-century artists often abandoned the traditional representation of people and objects. Color and shapes replaced recognizable human features in the work of de Kooning and numerous other artists of his generation.
(©akg-images/The Image Works; ©2019 The Willem de Kooning Foundation/Artists Rights Society (ARS), New York)

Sometime in the early 1970s the phenomenon of postmodernism emerged in architecture, literature, and other art forms. In all areas the postmodernists borrowed from the past and mixed the old and new, and the popular and elite, to suit their tastes. Unlike modernists from the late nineteenth century on, the postmodernists did not reject the commercialization and materialism of

> *Postmodernism*

SELF-PORTRAIT IN HIDING
by Felix Nussbaum (German, 1904–1944)
The terrifying, disorienting experience of personal danger and exile is conveyed in this self-portrait, which Nussbaum painted while hiding from the Nazis in Belgium. Nussbaum belonged to a patriotic German-Jewish family (his father was a veteran of World War I), but he was forced to flee from Hitler's Germany in the 1930s. He continued to paint as he lived secretly in an attic during the early Nazi occupation of Brussels, but he was found there in 1944 and sent to the death camp at Auschwitz, where he and his wife were killed. His parents and siblings also died in the Holocaust. Many of Nussbaum's paintings survived, however, giving later generations powerful visual images of the horrendous pain and human costs of genocidal violence.
(©Heritage Images/Hulton Fine Art Collection/Getty Images)

contemporary culture but embraced it and incorporated it in new ways, often with humor. The American architect Robert Venturi and his collaborators wrote a book called *Learning from Las Vegas* (1972). American cities, in fact, represented a kind of postmodern landscape for many European theorists, such as the French writer Jean Baudrillard, for whom the millions of speeding cars on Los Angeles freeways or the flickering advertisements on American television screens expressed the anomie of fragmented, postmodern societies. Composers introduced street noises (and silences) into their music. Repetition, as in the

Nonrepresentational art became as common in sculpture as it was in twentieth-century painting. This work by the influential English sculptor Henry Moore (1898–1986), *Two Large Forms*, was placed in a London park. It shows how the modern representation of classical artistic themes radically altered Western sculptural traditions that went back to the Renaissance and even to antiquity.
(©Joe Schilling/The LIFE Images Collection/Getty Images)

commercial world of packaging, marketing, and television advertising, was adopted as an artistic technique. The American artist Andy Warhol attracted attention in Europe by painting serial pictures of Coca-Cola bottles and of the film star Marilyn Monroe—notable icons of popular culture on both sides of the Atlantic. In fiction the postmoderns mingled actual events and fantasy. A play by Harold Pinter, winner of the Nobel Prize for literature in 2005, Samuel Beckett, or Eugène Ionesco challenged traditional theatrical conventions. Indeed, a Pinter play such as *The Homecoming* or a Beckett play such as *Waiting for Godot* could be as baffling as the other postmodernist arts; and the dialogues and staging of contemporary plays created a postmodern theatrical culture that disoriented audiences long accustomed to the classic works of Shakespeare, Molière, Ibsen, or Shaw. The postmoderns rejected traditional ideas of structure, seeing no need in literature or art for a beginning, a middle, and an end. Postmodernism was both a phase of the modernist rebellion against traditionalism and a fragmented sequel in which new theorists extended modernism's critique of Enlightenment traditions. Where modernism typically sought to convey an artist's unique personal vision, postmodernists insisted that writers inevitably expressed the language and values of their culture rather than a distinctive individual consciousness. Because the writer's life and personal experience were now deemed less important for the study of literature, it even became possible to speak metaphorically of the "death of the author."

Religion in Modern Europe

Like other ideas and practices in modern European culture, religion was changing and evolving in new directions. With the continuing inroads of secularism, the challenges of science, and the post-1945 advances of communism in eastern Europe, organized religion encountered many obstacles. Attendance and membership in Christian churches declined almost everywhere in Europe, but the churches in eastern Europe survived the Communist regimes and often retained their vitality as an alternative to the dominant state institutions. Statistics on religious affiliation are never exact, but some figures on the religions with the largest number of adherents in the early twenty-first century were clear. Islam, with roughly 1.8 billion adherents worldwide, was the fastest-growing faith in many European countries, but Christianity remained the largest religion throughout Europe and in the world as a whole (2.3 billion). The historic divisions within Christianity—Roman Catholic, Protestant, Eastern Orthodox—still followed the broad geographical patterns that had emerged after the sixteenth-century Protestant Reformation. Older conflicts between Christian groups, however, gradually gave way to more collaboration and cooperation, perhaps because the declining number of European Christians and growing secularism in European societies encouraged Christians to emphasize their shared beliefs more than their theological differences.

The ecumenical movement

The ecumenical movement in Christianity, that is, the organized effort to unite the many branches of Protestantism, and eventually all Christianity, which began in the nineteenth century, made headway throughout the half-century after the Second World War. A World Council of Churches was founded in 1948. In historic breakthroughs toward the end of the century Lutheran churches announced a reconciliation and alliance with the Episcopalian churches, and Lutherans and Calvinists resolved theological differences over Luther's definition of salvation, "justification by faith." When in the 1960s the Roman Catholic Church abandoned its insistence on a privileged position within Christianity, it too encouraged ecumenicism. All Christian churches also moved toward a closer dialogue with non-Christian world faiths as well.

Religious tensions

As in the late nineteenth century, tensions between modernism (in its religious sense) and fundamentalism continued. Many of the twentieth-century Protestant churches reconciled their traditional teachings with science and Biblical scholarship, minimized the supernatural and dogmatic aspects of their faith, and sought to adapt the teachings of the gospel to the social needs of the contemporary world. But the two world wars and other social and cultural upheavals dealt a blow to theological modernism and to the inherent optimism of the social gospel. Evangelical or fundamentalist beliefs were reasserted in some Protestant churches, and an intellectual reaction also set in among Protestant theologians who emphasized revealed religion and elements of faith. The Swiss theologian Karl Barth in his writings from 1919 to the 1960s endeavored to lead Protestantism back to the root principles of the Reformation. There was much interest in Kierkegaard who, like Luther, had resolved his own deep anguish by a personal commitment to religious experience. During the Second World War, the German Lutheran theologian and activist Dietrich Bonhoeffer helped to sustain the small, anti-Nazi religious resistance, a courageous expression of Christian faith for which he was imprisoned and executed. After 1945, as a result of the work of Barth, Paul Tillich, and others, a powerful movement in Protestantism reasserted its dependence on revealed religion and denied that human reason could ever properly judge divine revelation. Some church writers, unable to explain the wrenching experience of the Second World War and the Holocaust, spoke of "post-Auschwitz theology" and of "God's removal from history." Evangelical Protestantism, with its literal adherence to the gospel, spellbinding preachers, and revivalist emotional appeal flourished much more widely in the United States than in Europe. Most European Protestants accepted the rigorous scholarship of religious historians and the intellectual validity of modern scientific knowledge, but this cultural reconciliation with modern science may have reduced religious passions or commitments among the members of Europe's main Protestant churches.

The Roman Catholic Church was passing through one of its great historic phases beginning in the second half of the century. Although the church no longer actively suppressed all forms of modernism, the Vatican in the early postwar years reaffirmed dogmatic training in the seminaries. In 1950 Pius XII (1939–1958), who headed the church during the Second World War (and was condemned by many critics for insufficiently opposing the terrible Nazi atrocities against the Jews), proclaimed the Assumption, the literal, or bodily ascent of the Virgin Mary into heaven, the only new Roman Catholic dogma to be promulgated in the entire twentieth century.

Pius XII was succeeded in 1959 by John XXIII. Although elected at the age of 77, and reigning for only four years until his death in 1963, John proved to be one of the most innovative popes of modern times, working to bring the church and its teachings into greater harmony with the contemporary world. His powerful encyclicals gave a global emphasis to the older social teachings of the church and called upon the wealthier nations to share their resources with the less favored. The first encyclical ever addressed to Catholics and non-Catholics alike, *Pacem in Terris* (1963), appealed for peace and human rights. A champion of ecumenicism, he opened dialogues with other faiths. In 1962, against the advice of his own theologians, he convened the Second Vatican Council, the first such council since 1870, and as it turned out, the most important since the sixteenth-century Council of Trent. Vatican II, as it came to be called, reshaped contemporary Catholicism.

John did not live to see the Council's labors completed, but was the principal inspiration for its reforms. His successor Paul VI (1963–1978) shared John's social concerns and encouraged ecumenicism, but *Vatican II* was more conservative in other ways. The Council completed its work in 1965. Accepting the principle of religious pluralism, it abandoned the older insistence on a Catholic monopoly on religious truth. It affirmed the principle of collegiality, which had gone into eclipse in the modern centuries, the view that the pope must share his authority with the prelates of the church, thus strengthening the authority of the national churches on substantive matters. It revised the liturgy and various church practices. The Mass, henceforth, would be conducted in vernacular tongues instead of in Latin, which had been the rule for centuries. The Council relaxed restrictions on dress for priests and nuns. In one historic declaration, the Council explicitly absolved the Jewish people from the charge of deicide that had fed and inflamed anti-Semitism over the ages. John XXIII's goal—the revitalization and updating of church teachings and practices—was amply fulfilled by the Council. There were limits to the changes, to be sure. The Council reaffirmed celibacy for the clergy and refused to sanction the ordination of women as priests. Paul VI, meanwhile, upheld papal supremacy and took a firm conservative stance on moral issues, especially against all artificial means of birth control.

After Paul VI's death in 1978 (and when a successor, John Paul I, died after only 34 days in office), John Paul II, the archbishop of Cracow, became the new head of the church, the first Polish pope ever elected, and the first non-Italian pontiff in over 450 years. Robust, earthy, energetic, versatile in languages, *John Paul II* and with a keen sense of pageantry and papal majesty, he brought an added dynamism to the church. He reaffirmed papal support for the Christian ecumenical movement, but he also reached out to non-Christians as well, traveling widely in Asia, Africa, and Latin America. During the Cold War years he entered into diplomatic

Pope John Paul II combined a defense of the traditional values and institutions of Roman Catholic Christianity with the frequent use of modern travel and communications. He is shown here during a trip to Poland in 1979. This much-acclaimed papal visit to his native country was an early example of John Paul's determination to speak out on public issues, promote social justice, and assert the importance of religious life in Communist countries.

(©Francois Lochon/The LIFE Images Collection/Getty Images)

negotiations with the Soviet Union and the Communist countries of eastern Europe to improve the status of the church, thereby contributing to the revolutionary transformation of his own country and eastern Europe in the 1980s.

In his indefatigable global travels John Paul presided over Mass for millions of Roman Catholics, and he offered apologies for past wrongs going back to the Crusades and including the abuses of the Inquisition, whose archives he opened to historians. He apologized for the Inquisition's condemnation of scientists like Galileo. In formal statements and documents he offered specific apologies to the Jews for abuses they had suffered over the centuries and especially for the ordeal of the Holocaust, and in a historic visit to Jerusalem he prayed at the Western Wall.

Although John Paul held progressive views on social and economic issues, in matters of church doctrine and governance he favored orthodoxy and papal supremacy. He appointed conservative archbishops, bishops, and cardinals, silenced dissenting theologians, and curbed the growing assertiveness of national churches. He would not countenance marriage for the clergy, the ordination of women as priests (an innovation accepted by the Church of England in 1994), rights of divorce (or of remarriage for the divorced), or homosexuality.

Objections to Vatican centralism

John Paul's stance on many issues engendered protest against the "new Roman centralism," the failure to modernize the church more thoroughly, and the unwillingness to respect the spirit of shared authority promised by the Council. His defenders argued that in upholding tradition he was restoring a balance upset by overly rapid changes in the church introduced by Vatican II. Although weakened by declining health in his later years, John Paul remained active in setting church policies and in defending his theological principles until the last days of his life in 2005. The church cardinals quickly chose a 78-year-old German theologian who had been a close aide of John Paul to serve as the next pope. Entering office as a well-known spokesman for his predecessor's policies, the new pope, Benedict XVI, reconfirmed the church's opposition to the ordination of women priests and strongly opposed the developing European campaigns for same-sex marriages. He thus sought generally to uphold Catholic traditions rather than to push the church toward major theological or institutional reforms, but he also broke with tradition when he became the first pope to resign from the papacy since the early fifteenth century. He was succeeded, in 2013, by Pope Francis, who had been a cardinal in Argentina, and who provoked new controversies by favoring more liberal policies on social issues. Pope Francis strongly favored more assistance for impoverished people and urged the peaceful resolution of ongoing conflicts, but he was also criticized for not acting more aggressively to punish priests or high church officials accused of sexual abuse. New investigations of cases in which the church had long failed to remove or prosecute clergy charged with sexual misconduct, especially the abuse of young parishioners, became a major concern for the Catholic Church during the early twenty-first century.

Judaism was haunted in the years after 1945 by the traumatic experience of the Holocaust. In the early twenty-first century there were about 14.5 million Jews in the world, but the Jewish population in **Judaism**
Europe had fallen to about 1.4 million by 2010 (from roughly 9.5 million in 1939). Whereas European Jews had accounted for about 57 percent of the global Jewish population before the Second World War and the Holocaust, there were now far more Jews living in other nations, including about 6.3 million in Israel and 5.7 million in the United States. Anti-Semitism and attacks on Jewish institutions became more widespread, and fears about the resurgence of anti-Semitic groups contributed to a gradual increase in Jewish migration out of some European countries after 2010. The earlier trend to secularism persisted, but more striking was the vitality of all its branches, Orthodox, Conservative, and Reform. Jews everywhere, including many who were not Zionists, lent moral and financial support to the state of Israel, although many were troubled by Israeli diplomatic intransigence or by the influence of right-wing political parties and ultraorthodox religious groups that refused to accept a secular state. But there were also concerns in Europe and elsewhere that anti-Zionism could serve as a thin screen for anti-Semitism. In the former Soviet Union and in some parts of eastern Europe, Jews had met harassment and persecution and, when permitted, emigrated in large numbers. The collapse of communism also reignited some older currents of anti-Semitism in eastern Europe.

Other world religions, including Islam, Hinduism, and Buddhism, attracted new adherents in Europe and also made efforts to adjust millennia-old doctrines to the secular tendencies of the contemporary age. Religious criticisms of modern secular societies, however, attracted significant support within Europe's growing immigrant communities—especially among certain Muslim groups in the multicultural European cities. Although Muslims became active in many commercial and social **Islam**
spheres of modern European life, the rise of militant reform movements (often called "fundamentalist" by outsiders) in the Islamic societies of North Africa and the Middle East also influenced some Muslims in Europe. All such movements condemned modern secularism and turned to what they took to be a literal reading of the Qur'an for their own guidance and for the imposition of rules of conduct on other

Radical Muslim groups

Muslims. A few of the most radical Muslims organized terrorist attacks within Europe, thereby trying (in their view) to express solidarity with international terrorist organizations such as al-Qaeda. Muslim terrorists set off deadly bombs on four Spanish trains in 2004, killing almost 200 commuters in Madrid. The following year, in July 2005, other terrorists exploded bombs in the London subway and bus system, killing more than 50 people. Even more deadly attacks came later in France, where Muslim extremists in Paris attacked newspaper offices and a concert hall in 2015, causing over 140 deaths; and a terrorist assault in Nice killed almost 90 people who were celebrating Bastille Day in 2016.

Such extremism evoked strong reactions against Muslims within the various European countries. There were new concerns about young Muslims who became radicalized after growing up in Europe as well as new fears about radicals who might be coming into EU countries among the refugees from the Middle East. The French government declared a state of emergency, which allowed special investigations and prolonged detentions of persons suspected of terrorist connections. The new antiterrorist measures gained wide political support, though they sometimes also affected the great majority of Muslims who practiced their faith peacefully and constructively in the mosques and Islamic community centers that were expanding across Europe. Some far-right groups agitated against all immigration from Muslim societies, and even mainstream political parties sometimes pushed for new actions to regulate Muslim religious practices. These regulatory interventions in specific aspects of Muslim culture usually developed as the legislative expression of broader assumptions about the "otherness" of Muslim communities rather than as a reaction to specific events, so the debates about new laws also sparked wider debates about religious and cultural diversity in European societies. In France, for example, legislators asserted their support for French "secularism," in 2004, by enacting a ban on the wearing of Islamic head scarves by Muslim girls in the French public schools; and in 2011

New laws affecting Muslims

it became illegal for women in France to wear a face-covering veil or burqa in public places. Meanwhile, voters in Switzerland, also in 2011, approved a ban on the construction of new minarets at the mosques in Swiss cities. Critics of this ban and of the ban on head scarves in French schools charged that such laws violated religious freedoms, but supporters of the new laws generally believed that regulations were needed because Muslim "fundamentalism" was hostile to European cultural traditions or conceptions of human rights.

Fundamentalism could also be found in evangelical Christian sects and in extremist Orthodox Jewish quarters as well as among the radical Muslim groups. Although they rarely became violent, fundamentalist movements easily bred intolerance and separatism, and they ran counter to the secularism and blending of cultures in modern European nations. The separation of political and religious authority had become so widely accepted throughout contemporary Europe that it often became difficult for secular persons and moderate religious believers to understand the strength and appeal of the religious ferment in other societies around the world.

Activism: The Youth Culture and Rebellion of the 1960s

In the second half of the twentieth century young people acquired a collective cultural and generational identity that young people seemed not to have possessed in earlier historical periods. It was now possible to speak of a youth market, a youth culture, youth movements. In part the phenomenon was demographic in origin, the result of the extraordinary number of births in the decade and a half after the Second World War—the

The growing Muslim population in European countries became more visible and well established in the early twenty-first century. Muslims entered widely into the workforce, developed new social institutions, and built new mosques. The Great Mosque in Paris, pictured here as people gathered for prayers, became one of the many centers for Muslim life in France.
(©Godong/BSIP/The Image Works)

"baby boom." A large cohort grew up in a rapidly changing world, and they developed a generational identity through a new popular culture that appeared in music, fashion, films, and advertising. Youth culture became a key component of modern European and global culture.

In the 1960s a new youth political activism made a startling appearance, marked by a widespread student rebellion. Young people born after 1945 attended institutions of higher learning in larger numbers than ever before. It was a generation that grew up in an era of global change and scientific breakthroughs, to which their elders were not dependable guides. They took for granted the scientific, technological, and economic accomplishments of their world and concentrated on its deficiencies—the flagrant contradictions of wealth and poverty within and among nations, racial injustice, discrimination, colonialism, the impersonal quality of mechanized society and bureaucratized institutions (including colleges and universities), the violence that destroyed human beings in continuing wars, the pollution of natural environments, and the ominous threat of nuclear destruction. The rebelliousness extended beyond the traditional generation gap; it was directed at all established society and reiterated romantic or utopian themes that had influenced social criticism since the beginnings of modern history.

Youth activism

The revolt burst forth in the late 1960s in widely separate parts of the world, extending from North America and Asia to the main cities and universities in western Europe. At the peak of the movement, in

1968

A global youth culture emerged in the 1960s and 1970s, creating distinctive styles of dress and an international market for new forms of popular music. Rock musicians such as this English band, the Rolling Stones, toured the world and wrote songs that helped to shape a generational identity spanning nations and cultures. The lead singer Mick Jagger is seen here with other members of the band at a show in London in 1968.

(©Mark and Colleen Hayward/Redferns/Getty Images)

1967–1968, students demonstrated and rioted on campuses and battled police all over the world; American, Canadian, Mexican, West German, French, Italian, and Spanish universities were heavily involved.

France was one center of the storm. Demonstrations there reached near-revolutionary dimensions in the spring of 1968 and, as we have seen, the protests threatened to overthrow the de Gaulle government when 10 million workers also went out on strike, partly in sympathy with students and partly for their own grievances. But the government eventually restored order, and many of the initial grievances in the overcrowded, impersonal universities were almost forgotten in the wider, but quickly passing, French upheaval. Other large demonstrations and student strikes disrupted universities in West Germany, Italy, and Great Britain, often pitting the younger generation of the "New Left" against the more culturally conservative leaders of well-established leftist political parties. The American war in Vietnam was one of the issues that mobilized student protestors, but the demonstrations also focused on specific local concerns—ranging from inadequate urban housing or social services to the traditional curriculum in European universities.

The rebelling students often defined their collective identities through rock music, unconventional styles of dress, and a language of their own. Some activists also made icons out of controversial revolutionary leaders who symbolized opposition to the established Western political order: Fidel Castro and his martyred lieutenant Che Guevara, Ho Chi Minh, Mao Zedong, militant American black leaders like Malcolm X, the heralds of the colonial revolution such as Frantz Fanon (the West Indian author of *The Wretched of the Earth*), and others. They read the neo-Marxist German philosopher Herbert Marcuse, who warned that the very tolerance of bourgeois society was a trap to prevent true protest against injustice; they learned from him that the industrial working class, co-opted by the existing system, was no longer a revolutionary force. The "New Left" also dismissed older revolutionaries in the Soviet Union as stodgy bureaucrats and affirmed that future revolutionary leadership should come from Maoist China or other places in Asia, Africa, and Latin America. They attacked materialism, affluence, and conformity, and the power structure of contemporary society. Many believed in militant confrontations that recalled an older anarchism and nihilism. They wanted to transform or destroy various social, political, and cultural traditions, assuming that their generation could overcome the social hierarchies and injustices in modern democratic societies.

Emergence of the New Left

The rebellion in its mass political phase faded by the early 1970s. Only a small number of extremists carried on a kind of urban guerrilla war through underground terrorist organizations—the Bader–Meinhof gang in Germany, the Red Brigades in Italy. Mostly, the rebels of 1968 moved on to places in established society. While many people condemned the disruptive attacks on traditional institutions and orderly processes, others were shaken out of their complacency about social or racial inequities. Efforts were made to reform university administration and to provide better teaching facilities. The youth movement, even after its political radicalism subsided, had a continuing cultural effect on all European age groups in loosening older standards of language, dress, and sexual mores.

The Women's Liberation Movement

The feminist, or women's liberation, movement was another, but more enduring, manifestation of twentieth-century and contemporary social ferment. From the time of the French Revolution, as noted earlier, a few advanced thinkers in France and England had argued that women should have equal legal and political rights, and a women's political movement had also developed in the United States by the mid-nineteenth century. Elizabeth Cady Stanton and a small group of associates in 1848, inspired in part by revolutionary developments in Europe that year, had proclaimed a declaration of independence for women, demanding the right to vote, equal compensation for work, legal equality in property and other matters, and expanded educational opportunities. In Britain, later in the century, the suffragettes raised similar demands in their militant campaign for the vote. Women won the right to vote before the First World War in a few of the smaller European countries such as Finland and Norway; after 1918, in many more nations, including Britain, Germany, and the United States; and eventually after 1945, in all other European countries. But other social objectives went unrealized.

A new twentieth-century phase of the women's movement began in the United States in the mid-1960s, partly as a parallel to the African American civil rights movement, but it also spread across much of Europe over the following decades. The women's liberation movement, inspired by such books as Simone de Beauvoir's *The Second Sex,* published in France in 1949, and Betty Friedan's *The Feminine Mystique,* which appeared in the United States in 1963, contended that women had always been and continued to be oppressed by a male-dominated society and that women were systematically denied access to positions of authority, leadership, property, and power.

Although the more blatant forms of legal discrimination in voting and property rights had been removed, twentieth-century feminists demanded an end to all barriers to equal participation in every public, economic, and social institution. Betty Friedan's influential

The French writer Simone de Beauvoir, shown here in 1947, wrote about the social position of women in her widely read book *The Second Sex* (1949). Beauvoir analyzed the constraints and myths that affected women in what she described as patriarchal societies and called for the independence or liberation of women in contemporary social and political life. Her work became an influential statement of themes and ideas that helped shape a new international women's movement in the 1960s and 1970s.
(©Hulton Archive/Getty Images)

Inspirations and demands

book, which was translated into multiple European languages, described the frustrations of women who were blocked from professional careers; and it strongly encouraged women to move beyond traditional work within the home and family and to utilize their education, skills, and abilities in the outside world as well. Large and constantly increasing numbers of women pursued advanced professional training and entered the job market during the 1970s, shaping permanent transformations in gender roles, higher education, and workplace cultures. These transitions continued to evolve in the twenty-first century as women made their way into new kinds of jobs and professional positions and as they pushed for often-resisted adjustments in family responsibilities or in the social policies of their employers. Parental leave and child care facilities, for example, became common forms of support for Europeans who worked in both public and private institutions—though many EU countries still lagged in providing adequate child care options.

Some women, more so than in the past (when only a few reigning women sovereigns were able to exercise political power), came to hold positions of the highest authority in their countries in the years after 1945. Among them were prominent women leaders in former European colonies such as Indira Gandhi in India and Benazir Bhutto in Pakistan. Women also rose to the highest government positions in numerous European countries. Margaret Thatcher in Britain and Angela Merkel in Germany became especially influential, but there was also a growing list of women presidents, prime ministers, and cabinet ministers in France, Italy, Spain, Portugal, Norway, Iceland, Ireland, Poland, Finland, and almost every other nation in Europe. Women were thus entering widely into modern political life, but it was also true, as feminists and others continued to stress, that men still dominated legislative assemblies and government ministries in most European countries in the early twenty-first century.

Meanwhile the development of advanced contraceptive technology, especially the birth control pill in the early 1960s, and the legalization of abortion procedures in most of Europe,

Ideas about marriage and family life changed rapidly in contemporary Europe, leading almost everywhere to more autonomy for women, more acceptance of same-sex partnerships, and new marriage laws. These Spaniards celebrated in 2005 as the Spanish Parliament passed legislation giving same-sex couples the equal legal right to marry and adopt children.
(©AFP/Getty Images)

provided a new biological freedom and autonomy for women. Changing social mores tolerated more sexual freedom and fostered more equality between women and men within marriages and other relationships. The campaigns for women's rights also led in many places to new calls for recognition of same-sex relationships. Both women and men began to live more openly in same-sex partnerships, and several European countries—including the Netherlands, Spain, Portugal, Belgium, France, England, Germany, and Denmark—gave full legal status to same-sex marriages in the first decades of the twenty-first century. Other countries recognized "civil unions" and **New marriage laws** new legal or economic rights for same-sex partners, thereby providing new security and social stability for women and men who did not live within traditional marriages. Although the advocates and opponents of same-sex marriages continued their debates in European courts, legislatures, and newspapers, there was clearly a general movement toward equal rights for gay women and men in European political, social, and cultural life.

In the twenty-first century women were filling a larger share of places in higher education and in professional schools than ever before. As more women became part of the labor force at all levels, a new wave of feminist activism demanded not only equal compensation for equal work, still far from realized, but also better pay for jobs that were poorly compensated because they had been traditionally filled by women. Although there were disagreements within and outside the women's liberation movement on the methods and tempo of change, wide agreement existed on the need to utilize fully all human resources in the economy and in all the institutions of public and private life. If that could be accomplished, the changing social, economic, and political position of women would count among the most significant changes in contemporary European history.

122. EUROPE AND INTERNATIONAL CONFLICTS IN THE EARLY TWENTY-FIRST CENTURY

The end of the Cold War and the demise of the U.S.S.R. in 1991 transformed the foundations on which international relations had rested since 1945. The end of the American and European campaign to contain communism raised new questions about how the United States would use its post–Cold War power with consideration for its allies and other nations; and these questions became even more complex after the American President Donald Trump (elected in 2016) challenged long-standing assumptions about the need for close collaborations within NATO and the transatlantic alliance system. A new configuration of world affairs began to emerge, but peace and security remained the world's most pressing problems in this era of global economic exchanges. Two new challenges appeared: the eruption of conflicts more frequently within nations than between nations and the danger of terrorism, which spread into almost every region of the world.

It became clear that the end of the Cold War had not brought peace to the world, but the older patterns of warfare between nation-states seemed to be breaking down by the early twenty-first century. The new wars tended to be conflicts between religious or ethnic groups within a national territory or between guerrilla forces and high-tech national armies that sought to suppress them. These new wars could last for years, in part because they were no longer waged by opposing national governments that were able to negotiate a truce or a peace settlement. European governments, like all others, struggled to redefine their new role in such international conflicts.

Some analysts of international affairs maintained that the new world order might best be understood in the context of rivalries and conflicts between religion-based civilizations, not between nation-states. The Russian offensive against Chechnya, for example, had anti-Islamic overtones, as did the Serb and Croat attacks on Muslims in Bosnia and the

Religious divisions could shape conflicts

Serb war against the Albanian Muslims in Kosovo. The conflicts between Israel and its Arab neighbors in the Middle East had distinctive religious overtones. The wars launched by the United States and its European allies against governments and radical Muslim groups in Afghanistan and Iraq during the early twenty-first century also took on religious meaning because some saw these conflicts as a battle between different religious and cultural traditions and values.

But nonreligious factors remained preponderant in international affairs after the Cold War, and even within each religion there was marked diversity. The world's religions were far from homogeneous, and all had been touched to some degree by secularism and globalization. There were enduring conflicts between branches of the major religions—Catholics and Protestants in Northern Ireland, for example, and Shiites and Sunnis in many Muslim countries of the Middle East.

Recognizing global diversity

It was nevertheless important to call attention to the global diversity of traditions, cultures, and religions if only to shed earlier illusions among people in Europe and North America that they were destined to spread their ideas and values across the world unchallenged. Western civilization, with its Judeo-Christian heritage, had always been enriched by interaction with other civilizations. Although European and other Western cultures still had far-reaching global influence in the twenty-first century, people in Western countries had to recognize and respect diverse cultural identities in every part of the world and to understand the deep influence of different cultural traditions in diplomatic affairs, economic exchanges, and political conflicts.

The United Nations

The much-used term "international community" was indispensable but defied precise definition. The closest approximation to it was the United Nations (UN). The UN counted over 190 members by the early twenty-first century, but the Security Council was its dominant institution. The original roster of five permanent members of the Council, the victors in the Second World War, had been modified only in 1971 when the People's Republic of China replaced Nationalist China and in 1991 when Russia succeeded to the seat of the dissolved U.S.S.R. The political and economic changes in the world spurred proposals for giving other large powers permanent seats (other nations rotated among the ten non-permanent seats), so that they might exercise international responsibilities commensurate with their economic and military resources. Even the veto power of the five permanent powers came into question.

UN membership expands

Debate went on in the UN, the EU, and elsewhere over the interpretation of human rights. The Universal Declaration of Human Rights, adopted by the UN in 1948, had described political and civil rights, emphasizing protection from arbitrary arrest, imprisonment, and torture, but it also noted social and economic rights for individuals living within each country. The UN's member nations continually disagreed, however, as they debated the meaning of these basic rights and as they responded to specific events and conflicts.

Defining human rights

Diverging interpretations of human rights thus divided nations within both the UN and the EU—which had become a strong advocate for the modern legal defense of human rights. People in different nations at times contended that the political and civil rights generally described as universal were really a specific aspect of Western political or cultural traditions and should thus be modified to fit the culture, history, and religions of other societies. Equality for women or the rights of children, in this interpretation, could have different meanings in countries whose cultural traditions differed from those of Europe. But many across the globe maintained that human rights, no matter how difficult to define, of European origin or not, represented a common core of values that should protect every individual human being against enslavement, violation, or discrimination. Respect for cultural pluralism or local traditions should not cover or excuse any form of human indignity. European values, in short, were now seen as part of a universal campaign, even in societies far outside Europe.

Although the UN was often criticized for its inability to prevent wars or act decisively on global social problems, its broad goals remained as formulated in 1945: to control and reduce the scourge of war, advance human rights, promote equality, protect the independence of nations, encourage social progress, raise living standards, and work for peace and security. But the world's nations, large and small, were not willing to subordinate their national interests or sovereignty to any international organization. Without armed power of its own, the United Nations could not prevent civil wars within its member nations or prevent powerful sovereign nations from using their own military forces whenever they decided to go to war.

CHRONOLOGY OF NOTABLE EVENTS, 1949–2016

1949	Simone de Beauvoir's publication of *The Second Sex* helps to launch a new international campaign for women's rights
1968	Youth movements in many nations press for political and social change
1969	American astronauts land on the surface of the moon
1978	John Paul II becomes Pope—the first Pole ever elected to the papacy
1991	Treaty of Maastricht establishes the new European Union (EU)
1994	World Trade Organization (WTO) is established to mediate international trade
1997	Labour Party wins elections in Great Britain; Tony Blair becomes prime minister
1998	Political agreement in Northern Ireland offers plan to end violence between Protestants and Catholics
1998	Social Democrats win elections in Germany; Gerhard Schröder becomes chancellor
2001	Al-Qaeda terrorist attacks on New York and Washington; United States and its allies overthrow Taliban regime in Kabul; NATO forces are authorized to enter Afghanistan
2002	The euro becomes the common currency of 12 European nations
2003	American and British forces invade Iraq and overthrow the regime of Saddam Hussein, but begin prolonged war against "insurgents"
2004	EU membership grows to 25 nations
2005	Angela Merkel of the Christian Democratic Party becomes the first woman chancellor of Germany and an influential leader of the EU
2009	Sovereign debt crisis threatens the financial stability of the EU
2011	British and American troops withdraw from Iraq
2015	Mass migration of refugees from the Middle East sparks anti-immigrant backlash in EU nations
2016	The British vote to leave the EU, launching a prolonged "Brexit" process

U.S. leadership in international affairs

The United States, as the sole superpower after 1991, exercised a leading role in international affairs during the post–Cold War era, though often in concert with its European allies and other major powers. At times, however, it took initiatives that made it difficult to distinguish between American unilateralism and international action. The Security Council in 1990 condemned Iraq's invasion and occupation of Kuwait, but it was the United States that assembled a formidable multinational military force that could take decisive action. This well-equipped international army, which included over a half-million American troops along with deployments of more than 70,000 troops from Britain and France (and smaller contingents from numerous other countries), launched a massive assault in early 1991 that forced the Iraqi withdrawal from Kuwait.

Although it was never easy to mobilize broad international coalitions, Europeans joined with the United States in a number of global military interventions. As we have noted earlier, the massive American-led air offensive by NATO against the former Yugoslavia in 1999 set a precedent for multinational "humanitarian intervention" within

The debate about human rights continued in Europe and around the world as people argued about how to balance "universal" rights with respect for specific "cultural" rights or traditions. In 1998, on the fiftieth anniversary of the UN's Universal Declaration of Human Rights, the United Nations Educational, Scientific and Cultural Organization (UNESCO) convened a meeting in Valencia, Spain, to discuss the meaning of human rights. The assembled delegates endorsed a new "Declaration of Human Duties and Responsibilities," which reaffirmed the original declaration while also adding new emphasis on the need for individual security, free expression of ideas, and protection of minorities. This picture shows the Nigerian writer and political activist Wole Soyinka as he read the new declaration at the UNESCO meeting in Valencia.
(©DOMINIQUE FAGET/AFP/Getty Images)

a sovereign state, although no ground troops were used. The UN did not join the war, but played a major role in postwar peacekeeping in Kosovo. An international military force that included participants from several European countries also intervened to protect the people of East Timor after they voted in a UN-sponsored referendum for independence from Indonesia and then faced virtual butchery by Indonesian paramilitary forces. It nevertheless remained a formidable challenge for Europeans and other members of the UN to decide on the legitimate use of international force against sovereign nations to protect threatened or abused populations.

Multinational humanitarian intervention

NATO, Russia, and the New International Cooperation

The new American President, elected in late 2000, George W. Bush, son of the former President Bush, reassessed the concept of humanitarian intervention, but soon initiated other military actions when he decided that American interests were at risk. Meanwhile the Europeans took steps to strengthen the independent military and defense role for the EU. The French, following the precedent of de Gaulle in the Cold War years, called for recognition of a "multipolar world," in which the EU would be a more equal partner, and they objected, if only in rhetoric, to the hegemony of the "American hyperpower."

The role of Russia in the new world order was critical but not yet precisely defined. That it was still a major power and not ready to abandon aspirations to an important role in world affairs was evident in its pro-Serb stance in the Balkans. How to deal with an assertive Russia still armed with thousands of nuclear

Russia's role undefined

weapons was a major challenge. NATO, meanwhile, at American initiative, admitted Hungary, Poland, and the Czech Republic as full members in 1999; and seven other countries of formerly Soviet-controlled central and eastern Europe joined in 2004. The Central and East European nations not only wished to be full partners in Europe but also saw their membership in NATO as the best guarantee of their future security. The admission of several states on the very borders of Russia, however, was regarded by many Russians as a provocation. On the other hand, Russia's president became a member of what was now the Group of 8, the heads of government of the major industrial democracies; and there were regular consultations with NATO through a council established in 2002 to facilitate cooperation on various international issues.

Nuclear disarmament loomed as another key issue in the post–Cold War international order. The collapse of the U.S.S.R. promised to end the "balance of terror" that had resulted from the nuclear buildup of the two superpowers. Despite some initial obstacles, the United States and Russia agreed on the voluntary reduction of nuclear arms. The number of nuclear warheads in the world, of which the largest number were held by the United States and the U.S.S.R., had been reduced between the mid-1980s and 2000. Nonetheless the head of the UN's nuclear monitoring agency reported at the close of 2005 that there were still 27,000 nuclear warheads in various parts of the world, which, he said, could mean "the destruction of entire nations in a matter of minutes."

By the end of the twentieth century 187 nations had signed the 1968 Nuclear Non-Proliferation Treaty. At one of the periodic meetings held to review the status of the treaty, in May 2000, the five major nuclear powers—the United States, Russia, Britain, France, and China—in the first such declaration ever made pledged themselves "unequivocally" to the eventual elimination of all nuclear weapons. There was satisfaction and reassurance also that since August 1945 no nuclear bomb had been exploded in warfare. That additional nations such as North Korea and Iran might be developing nuclear arms nevertheless gave cause for continuing concern. A major setback to the progress of nuclear arms control was the refusal of the United States Senate in late 1999 to ratify the Comprehensive Nuclear Test Ban Treaty because the United States insisted that the nation's security and the security of other states required periodic testing of the American nuclear

Nuclear Weapons

arsenal. Almost all other countries ratified this treaty, which would have prohibited all nuclear weapons testing. Negotiations for nuclear arms reductions continued in the early twenty-first century, however, and a later American President, Barack Obama, eventually signed a new START treaty with Russian president Medvedev. The new treaty, which was narrowly approved by the United States Senate in 2010, carried provisions for verifiable and significantly reduced new limits on the numbers of Russian and American missiles and nuclear warheads, thus marking another milestone in the long transition away from the earlier Cold War nuclear arms race. President Obama, who was reelected to a second term in 2012, made the reduction and elimination of nuclear weapons a key foreign policy objective of his administration. Speaking in Prague during a European tour in 2009, Obama had declared his aspiration to reduce and even eliminate nuclear weapons in all parts of the world. "We must stand together," Obama emphasized to his large audience in a Czech public square, "to live free from fear in the twenty-first century"—a distant, perhaps elusive, goal that, he said, could ultimately be achieved through "the peace and security of a world without nuclear weapons." Obama's presidential successor, Donald Trump, rejected this disarmament goal, however, and announced that the United States would withdraw from the nuclear arms control treaty that Ronald Reagan and Mikhail Gorbachev had signed in 1987. A new, twenty-first-century arms race could thus develop, threatening Europeans and others with future nuclear dangers.

The United States remained deeply involved in European affairs after the Cold War. European-American trade, travel, and cultural exchanges were influential on both sides of the Atlantic, and the NATO military alliance continued to shape national defense policies. This picture shows President Barack Obama during one of the many post-1945 American presidential visits to Europe. Obama was speaking in 2009 to a large crowd in Prague, where he called for the international reduction of nuclear arms and also proposed a long-term, future campaign for the global elimination of such weapons of mass destruction.

(©JOE KLAMAR/AFP/Getty Images)

Terrorism and Wars in Afghanistan and Iraq after September 11, 2001

We have seen how the United States and the western European countries became steadily more involved in the Middle East during the latter part of the twentieth century—in the Persian Gulf War that drove Iraq out of Kuwait in 1991 and in other episodes; but involvements of Americans and Europeans entered a new phase of extended military conflict in the new century, when on September 11, 2001, radical Islamic terrorists carried out a surprise attack against the United States. Dispatched to America by the extremist Islamic organization known as al-Qaeda, committed terrorists from the Middle East set out on a carefully prepared suicide mission. The terrorists hijacked four large American commercial airliners, each loaded with passengers, and crashed two of the planes into the towers of the World Trade Center in New York; the third plane crashed into the Pentagon in northern Virginia; the fourth crashed to the ground in rural Pennsylvania without reaching its intended target.

September 11, 2001

There had never been a terrorist attack of this kind or on this scale in the whole deadly history of terrorism throughout the world. Almost 3,000 people died in the attacks, which stunned Europeans almost as deeply as the Americans. An article in the French newspaper *Le Monde,* for example, proclaimed on September 12, "Today we are all Americans," expressing a solidarity that most Europeans reaffirmed in the following months. Many saw the terrorist attack in September 2001 as a turning point in modern American history, in part because it destroyed the assumption that wide oceans protected the United States from the kinds of direct assaults that had long threatened the nations and peoples of Europe.

European support for United States

President George W. Bush received authorization from the American Congress to use all necessary resources to mount a counterattack against the terrorist al-Qaeda organization and its supporters. The al-Qaeda leader, Osama bin Laden, had lived for many years outside his native Saudi Arabia. He found welcome support from the radical Islamic Taliban regime in Afghanistan, yet he controlled no government or armies or industrial infrastructure that might be attacked in conventional military operations. The al-Qaeda organization had emerged in the aftermath of the 1991 American-European Gulf War against Iraq, when bin Laden had vehemently condemned the permanent stationing of American forces near Islamic holy sites in Saudi Arabia and when he had also begun to organize terrorist operations.

NATO role in Afghanistan

The United States immediately received strong support from its European allies in NATO, whose members had always pledged to defend other member nations if they were attacked from abroad. American forces therefore launched an air assault on Afghanistan with NATO assistance, and by working also with Afghan forces opposed to the Taliban, the United States quickly brought about the overthrow of the Taliban regime in Kabul. A large number of al-Qaeda militants were captured or killed, but bin Laden escaped and remained at large until he was eventually killed, in 2011, by American special forces in Pakistan. A new Afghan government was established in Kabul, and a large NATO force moved into Afghanistan to conduct peacekeeping operations, support the development of Afghan police forces, and fight Taliban guerillas, who soon launched an insurgent campaign against the foreign troops as well as the new government.

The Afghan war would continue for more than a decade, and even then it was difficult to see a clear resolution emerging. The NATO deployment in Afghanistan, which was officially called the International Security Assistance Force (ISAF), was authorized by the UN in late 2001 and composed of troops from almost every NATO country. The largest contingent came from the United States, but over the following years there were always significant forces from Britain, Germany, France, Italy, Poland, Spain, and other European nations as well as Canada and Australia. All participating forces suffered significant casualties, and there were thousands of Afghan deaths during every phase of the war.

European troop deployments

Many in Europe complained that NATO, which had been created to defend against Soviet threats in post-1945 Europe, was now being used inappropriately to maintain a far-distant peacekeeping force and to wage a counterinsurgency war against Muslim fighters in Afghanistan. Even after a decade, however, there were still thousands of European troops stationed in Afghanistan and working closely with the Americans—whose 70,000 soldiers formed roughly 70 percent of the total ISAF/NATO deployment. The NATO countries and the United States officially concluded the ISAF military operations at the end of 2014, but they continued their Afghan involvement by supporting a "Resolute Support Mission" (RSM). The RSM trained and advised Afghan forces, and it required a steady rotation of NATO personnel. In 2018 there were still 16,000 troops from NATO countries in Afghanistan, participating in the longest military conflict in the history of the transatlantic alliance.

Meanwhile, the NATO alliance faced other challenges as the American and British governments launched a campaign to remove "weapons of mass destruction" from Iraq and to overthrow the regime of the brutal Iraqi dictator Saddam Hussein. President Bush and British prime minister Tony Blair successfully pushed for UN resolutions demanding that teams of UN-appointed inspectors be allowed to enter Iraq to search for weapons.

U.S.-British view of Iraq

When the inspectors could not find chemical stockpiles or other weapons of mass destruction, the American and British governments insisted that the Iraqis were concealing evidence and that the UN should sanction military action to enforce compliance with UN resolutions. Britain

The deployment of NATO forces in Afghanistan marked a new era in the long-established European-American military alliance. The Afghan War was the first conflict in which NATO troops were sent to wage war in a country far outside Europe, but this mission was organized and sustained as the central Asian component of a broad European-American campaign against terrorist groups. These German soldiers were part of a NATO detachment that was guarding sites such as this Afghan gasoline station in 2009, eight years after the war had begun.
(©MICHAEL KAPPELER/AFP/Getty Images)

was the only permanent member of the Security Council to support the United States, but President Bush and Prime Minister Blair resolved to go to war without a UN resolution and (in contrast to Afghanistan) without the endorsement of the NATO alliance. The governments and populations in France and Germany, where support and sympathy for the United States had been strong and widespread after the terrorist attacks in 2001, became outspoken in their opposition to the American-British campaign in Iraq—which they saw as unconnected to the war on terrorism and as a destabilizing intervention in a sovereign nation that had not attacked members of NATO. Some European countries, notably Spain and Italy, contributed small contingents to the "allied" forces, but strong public opposition led them to withdraw their troops well before the main American and British armies had completed their military campaigns.

The American-British invasion began in March 2003 and rapidly destroyed Saddam Hussein's regime in Baghdad. Hussein himself was captured by American troops and executed by a later Iraqi government. It appeared that the military intervention had achieved a complete success, but no weapons of mass destruction were ever discovered, thus calling into question the main rationale for the invasion. Meanwhile, a violent insurgency erupted as Iraq's multiple

Iraq War

religious and ethnic groups sought to protect their diverse, often conflicting interests by opposing the military occupation of their country. American and British forces found themselves mired in a protracted war as they struggled to establish a new government, restore the production of oil and electricity, and also contain the escalating conflict between Sunni and Shiite groups that struggled for ascendancy within the fragmented Iraqi society. Tens of thousands of Iraqis died in the violence, and casualties steadily mounted in the American and British armies.

As the number of deaths rose on all sides, support for the war declined in the United States, in Britain, and in most of Europe, where public opinion had never really favored the American-British invasion. The war provoked even more international criticism when it was revealed that American soldiers had humiliated and tortured Iraqi prisoners. Such revelations further undermined support for the war, especially in Britain—where, as we have seen, approval of Tony Blair plummeted in public opinion polls. Indeed, Blair himself resigned from office in 2007, having sacrificed much of his former popularity to his close alliance with President Bush and to the Iraqi war.

The extreme internecine violence, suicide bombings, and roadside attacks on American-British forces slowly subsided. A somewhat more stable Iraqi government con-

U.S.-British withdrawal from Iraq

solidated its political control, but sectarian conflicts continued to divide the population. A new, radical Islamic group, known as ISIS, later gained control over large territories in northern Iraq, from where militant fighters intervened in Syria's brutal Civil War and also supported terrorist attacks in Europe. Meanwhile, new leaders in the United States and Britain, Barack Obama and David Cameron, set timetables for the withdrawal of American and British military forces, and by the end of 2011 both countries had moved their armies out of Iraq.

The Iraq War by no means ended the involvement of the United States and European countries in the Middle East, but there was a growing reluctance to commit ground forces in later conflicts. When rebels rose up against Libyan dictator Muammar al-Qaddafi in 2011, for example, countries such as Britain and France joined the United States in an

Intervention in Libya

air campaign against Qaddafi's forces; but the NATO countries would not send ground troops to support the insurrection that ultimately overthrew the Qaddafi regime. Similarly, a violent uprising by opponents of the Syrian regime of President Bashar al-Assad attracted sympathy, weapons, and political support from the European and American governments, but the NATO alliance refused to intervene with more direct military assistance for the Syrian rebels. Most Europeans also favored opposition groups in other Arab countries, where political movements during the "Arab Spring" overturned authoritarian governments in 2011 and continued to push for democratic reforms in the following years. Yet even the most sympathetic European governments did not send military support as the new movements challenged "old regime" authorities and institutions; and we have seen how the later refugee migrations from Middle Eastern conflicts evoked strong opposition in most EU countries.

European governments were thus engaged in numerous international conflicts during the early twenty-first century, though European populations were generally more skeptical of warfare than in any previous era of their modern history. New wars were fought outside

European views of war

Europe by relatively small professional armies, but these conflicts never resembled the "total wars" that European powers had once fought between themselves. Although Europe's role in future international conflicts could not be known, it seemed likely that most Europeans would

This photograph of British soldiers on patrol in a southern Iraqi city in 2004 suggests the challenges that European and American troops faced as they tried to discern the social, political, and religious complexities of an unfamiliar Middle Eastern society during the second Iraq War. As military outsiders in this cultural context, heavily armed British troops often provoked suspicion or resistance, even when they sought to promote humanitarian goals.

(©Marco Di Lauro/Getty Images News/Getty Images)

support only limited "humanitarian interventions" or specific campaigns for human rights. The legacy of imperialism and the memory of the costly world wars, however, had shaped a broad-based European resistance to most contemporary wars and military interventions, including the American-British invasion of Iraq and the lingering NATO involvement in Afghanistan.

123. SOCIAL AND ENVIRONMENTAL CHALLENGES IN THE TWENTY-FIRST CENTURY

The Population Explosion

Of all the social developments in the late twentieth century one of the most spectacular was the growth of the world's population. From about 1950, as a result of medical discoveries, improved health and sanitation measures, declining infant mortality, and more efficient food production and distribution, death rates declined dramatically while birth rates rose. In India, for example, the death rate in 2000 was half the 1950 figure and its population rose from 350 million in 1950 to over to 1 billion at the beginning of the twenty-first century. Globally, the number of human beings grew so rapidly that demographers spoke of a population explosion. In 1950, when the contemporary takeoff began, world population totaled 2.5 billion; at the end of the century it exceeded 6 billion. Never before had human beings lived through a doubling of the world's population in their own lifetime; nor had they ever faced the kinds of environmental changes that accompanied this huge population increase.

It took the world millions of years for its human population to reach the quarter-billion mark some 2,000 years ago. Not until about 1650 did the population double to a half-billion. It then doubled in less than two centuries to reach its first billion about 1830. By about 1930, in only one century, it again doubled to reach 2 billion. By 1960, in a little over 30 years, it grew to 3 billion; 14 years later, in 1974, to 4 billion; 13 years later, by 1988, to 5 billion; in 1999 after only 11 years, it passed the 6 billion mark; and by 2018 demographers reported that the world's population had reached 7.7 billion. The time required to add a billion people to the world's population, and for the population to double in size, had grown shorter than ever before in history. The annual growth rate for much of this time, close to 2 percent, meant the addition of roughly 80 million people each year.

Growth in the late twentieth century

Although predictions were never certain, demographers began to find indications of a slowdown in the rate of growth. Sometime between 1965 and 1970 the global annual growth rate seems to have peaked at about 2 percent, and then the rate began to decline, unevenly and irregularly, to less than 1.5 percent. Nonetheless, because of the huge population base demographers still pushed well into the future the time and estimated figure at which stabilization might be achieved. Even with a continuing decline in the growth rate, the world population figure was projected for 2050 at a range between 9 to 11.5 billion. A debate continued over the "carrying capacity" of the earth, the maximum number of humans that the earth's resources could sustain.

The population growth rate after about 1965 gradually declined because of declining birth rates, a pattern that first appeared in the most industrialized countries and then spread to other parts of the world as well. The population increase in the second half of the twentieth century took place largely in Asia, Africa, and Latin America, where three-fourths of the world's population lived and where birth rates were highest. By contrast, in North America and especially in Europe birth rates were already lower. Industrialization, urban life, education, and social pressures for smaller families had begun to reduce birth rates ever since the late nineteenth century. In the industrially developed countries of western Europe growth rates were now below the population replacement rate of 2.1 children. Italy and Spain had the lowest rates with an average of 1.2 children per woman of child-bearing age, and Italy's population was expected to decline steadily over the next 25 years (unless the Italians began to accept a much larger immigrant population). In the United States the population was still growing, in good part because of immigration and immigrant families. Europe and North America in general, however, had a shrinking share of the world's population as the number of people in Asia, Africa, and Latin America continued to grow. Several of the world's major religions still discouraged or forbade artificial birth control measures, numerous societies restricted educational and vocational opportunities for women, and social customs in many regions of the world, especially the poorest, encouraged large families for the sustenance and support of the elderly. The impact of the global population explosion in the second half of the twentieth century would therefore be felt in Europe and the whole world far into the future.

Changing birth rates

The Environment

In addition to the environmental challenges that emerged from the sheer growth of the world's population, other dangers grew with the worldwide expansion of industry, automobile and truck transportation, coal-burning power plants, and deforestation. From 1950 to 2000 world industrial production grew more than fivefold, burning vast amounts of oil, coal, wood, and natural gas and steadily increasing the atmospheric carbon dioxide, methane, and other "greenhouse gases" that trap heat in the atmosphere. Although the full implications remained a subject of political controversy, almost all scientists and environmentalists were certain that the increasing modern emission of these gases was causing temperatures to rise. The decade of the 1990s was *Climate change* the warmest in 600 years, and the global warming trend continued in the new century. The five warmest years ever recorded in human history all came after 2010. The effects of greenhouse gas emissions over the course of the twenty-first century were projected (on the basis of current trends) to bring about increases of at least 3 to 5 degrees Fahrenheit (1.7 to 2.8 degrees Celsius) in the earth's mean surface temperatures. Some projections suggested that temperature increases could possibly go as high as 10 degrees Fahrenheit (5.6 degrees Celsius)—a change that would produce highly dangerous ecological effects.

Although nobody could predict the precise consequences of global warming, the changing climate was expected to alter agricultural production, water supplies, and coastlines. There was already clear evidence that polar ice caps were melting, glaciers were receding, sea levels were rising, and weather patterns were becoming more turbulent. European societies would face major economic challenges as these changes continued to develop. Wheat-producing areas in France, for example, would have lower yields as the French climate became warmer and drier; and some of the soils that support the vineyards for Europe's diverse wines would no longer be hospitable for the delicate grapes that have been cultivated for centuries in Spain or Italy or *Economic effects of* France. The European Environmental Agency, a component of the EU, *climate change* collected extensive information on the continent's climate and developed recommendations to cope with the various environmental threats. Greenhouse gases and rising temperatures posed a greater long-term threat to the European economy than government debts or changes in global trade and industry. Recognizing these dangers, European governments tried to reduce the emission of greenhouse gases, expand public transportation, protect forests, and sustain the productivity of traditional farmlands.

Europeans also made new efforts to reduce the pollution of their air and water. Industrial pollution caused the acid rain that laid waste to many forests, lakes, and rivers in the industrial nations. Severe environmental damage in the former Soviet Union, the former Communist nations in eastern Europe, and the People's Republic of China confirmed that pollution was not confined to any single economic system; Central planners had pressed development with little regard for the ecological consequences. Many other nations in both the wealthier and poorer regions of the world had long paid little attention to their environment. Under the pressure of expanding population and rapid urbanization, they permitted the slashing and burning of forests for ranching, timber exports, urban expansion, and resettlement.

By the 1970s a newly sensitized international community began to speak of sustainable growth rates, growth that could be maintained *Sustainable economic* without the destruction of humanity's natural habitat. Alternative forms *growth*

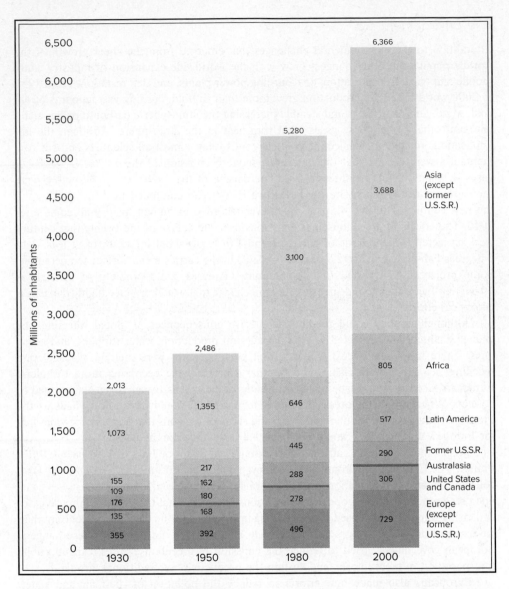

THE GLOBAL POPULATION EXPLOSION

The world's population has more than tripled in size since 1930, but the growth has been most rapid over the last five decades, especially in Latin America, Africa, and Asia. Before the twentieth century, world population had never before doubled in any half-century, so the recent increase can truly be called an "explosion." The world's population passed the 6 billion mark in 1999 and reached 7.7 billion in 2018. Although wealthy societies have lower growth rates than most poor nations, the wealthy societies consume the largest portion of the world's resources. Future population growth is expected to occur mainly in the less industrialized regions of the globe, but demands on the earth's limited resources will continue to grow in both the wealthy and poor nations. The question is whether the growth of population and the growing demand for resources can be slowed in ways that will protect the earth's increasingly overstrained environment.

(United Nations Demographic Yearbook)

The United Nations sponsored numerous meetings on the growing challenges of global climate change and rising temperatures. The 2015 Climate Change Conference in Paris produced new plans for the reduction of greenhouse gas emissions (with the goal of keeping future temperature increases below 2 degrees Celsius), but critics argued that the Paris agreements were still inadequate for the twenty-first century's widening climate problems. These protestors were among the thousands who converged on Paris, urging governments to counter global environmental dangers with strong actions that would also protect the world's poorest nations.

(©FRANCOIS GUILLOT/AFP/Getty Images)

of energy, some as old as the sun and the wind, others new, like nuclear energy (with proper safeguards, to be sure) were proposed. Emissions from industrial factories and from vehicles came under stricter controls. A number of industrial nations, including all the countries of Europe, agreed to stop production of chlorofluorocarbons, which were widely used in air-conditioning and in aerosol propellants and which damaged the earth's ozone by releasing dangerous amounts of chlorine into the upper atmosphere. Other UN-sponsored meetings and treaties followed. In 1992, at the first "Earth Summit" meeting in Rio de Janeiro, representatives of 178 countries pledged to protect plant and animal species and to take steps in a "climate treaty" to halt global warming. In 1997 representatives from 150 countries met at Kyoto, where they agreed to reduce the emission of so-called greenhouse gases by 50 percent. Another climate plan emerged in 2015 when 195 nations signed the Paris Climate Agreement. This new agreement, which sought to keep the rise in global temperatures below 2 degrees Celsius over the remaining decades of the twenty-first century, called for steady reductions of greenhouse gas emissions in every signatory nation and provided financial support for poor nations that faced the greatest economic challenges. The reduction guidelines were voluntary, however, and there was no assurance that the Paris Agreement's goals could be met—though yet another UN Climate Conference in Poland, in 2018, produced more plans for actually reducing the key emissions.

As awareness of ecological dangers grew, grass-roots environmental organizations multiplied, and in several countries emerged as "Green" political parties. Despite the numerous pledges and measures to counter the threat of environmental deterioration, there was opposition to strict environmental regulations in some poor countries and in industrialized countries, including China, India, Australia, and the United States. The American government, for example, withdrew from the Kyoto agreement in 2001; and in 2017 President Trump announced that the United States would also withdraw from the Paris Agreement, further threatening global attempts to control dangerous carbon fuel emissions.

Population growth and the threat to the environment added to Europe's concerns at the beginning of the twenty-first century and the new millennium. Many of the most pressing concerns, however, were not new: the social implications of contemporary science and technology, the sovereignty of nations, peace among nations, and the quest within nations for freedom, dignity, and economic well-being. All were aspects of one overriding problem. How could human beings in each generation, regardless of sex, color, creed, religion, nationality, or ethnic background—beings said by some to be made in the image of God, by others to have a natural right to life, liberty and happiness, by still others to have the freedom to create meaning in a meaningless universe—live out their lives in peace, fulfill their destiny, protect the environment, and pass on their heritage to future generations?

The constant changes and upheavals in contemporary human history might be compared to cataclysms in the natural world. A cataclysm is not a time of downfall only. Mountains crumble, but others are thrust up. Lands vanish, but others rise from the sea. So it is with the political and social cataclysm of our times. Old landmarks are worn down. Empires and older ideologies pass away; new nations and ideas arise in their place. The ascendancy of Europe and the European nations closes; they learn to negotiate with others, not to rule them. There is a greater fluidity in social relationships. Women and marginalized social groups struggle for equal places in society. But social justice and peace remain elusive goals. The gap between rich and poor among nations, and within nations, takes new forms, but never disappears and often grows. Old and new diseases, natural catastrophes, and armed conflicts exact their toll. Resurgent nationalisms feed on intolerance and hatred. Never has war been so potentially destructive; the menace of a nuclear war that would blight much of civilization wanes but does not disappear. Uncontrolled economic development threatens the environment, and population growth presses on natural resources. International cooperation and intervention are needed to protect human rights, end or prevent wars, and sustain the earth's billions.

Change across time

But people everywhere recognize these concerns and seek new solutions. To close this long history on a note of complacent optimism would be naive and inappropriate, but it would also be wrong to close on a pessimistic note of doom. The history of Europe and the wider modern world shows the astonishing range of human imagination and ingenuity, and there are good historical reasons to believe that people will continue to confront human conflicts and environmental dangers with the determination, creativity, and new ideas that lead slowly and eventually toward social progress.

Suggested Further Readings can be found in the ebook, on Connect, or online at www.mhhe.com/kramer12e.

APPENDIX, INDEX, SUGGESTIONS FOR FURTHER READING

Log on to Connect or visit www.mhhe.com/kramer12e for access to Suggestions for Further Reading

RULERS AND REGIMES
In Principal European Countries since 1500

HOLY ROMAN EMPIRE

Habsburg Line
Maximilian I, 1493–1519
Charles V, 1519–1556
Ferdinand I, 1556–1564
Maximilian II, 1564–1576
Rudolph II, 1576–1612
Matthias, 1612–1619
Ferdinand II, 1619–1637
Ferdinand III, 1637–1657
Leopold I, 1658–1705
Joseph I, 1705–1711
Charles VI, 1711–1740

Charles VI was succeeded by a daughter, Maria Theresa, who as a woman could not be elected Holy Roman Emperor. French influence in 1742 secured the election of

Bavarian Line
Charles VII, 1742–1745

On Charles VII's death, the Habsburg control of the emperorship was resumed.

Lorraine Line
Francis I, 1745–1765 (husband of Maria Theresa)

Habsburg-Lorraine Line
Joseph II, 1765–1790 (son of Francis I and Maria Theresa)
Leopold II, 1790–1792
Francis II, 1792–1806

The Holy Roman Empire became extinct in 1806.

AUSTRIAN DOMINIONS

The rulers of Austria from 1438 to 1740, and at least titular kings of Hungary from 1526 to 1740, were the same as the Holy Roman Emperors. After 1740:

Habsburg Line (through female heir)
Maria Theresa, 1740–1780
Joseph II, 1780–1790
Leopold II, 1790–1792
Francis II, 1792–1835

In 1804 Francis II took the title of Emperor, as Francis I of the Austrian Empire. Austria was declared an "empire" because Napoleon proclaimed France an empire in that year, and because the demise of the Holy Roman Empire could be foreseen.

Ferdinand I, 1835–1848
Francis Joseph, 1848–1916
Charles I, 1916–1918

The Austrian Empire became extinct in 1918.

BRITISH ISLES

Tudor Line
Kings of England and Ireland
Henry VII, 1485–1509
Henry VIII, 1509–1547
Edward VI, 1547–1553
Mary I, 1553–1558
Elizabeth I, 1558–1603

In 1603 James VI of Scotland, a great-great-grandson of Henry VII, succeeded to the English throne.

Stuart Line
Kings of England and Ireland, and of Scotland

James I, 1603-1625
Charles I, 1625-1649

Republican Interregnum
The Commonwealth, 1649-1653
The Protectorate
Oliver Cromwell, 1653-1658, Lord Protector
Richard Cromwell, 1658-1660

Restored Stuart Line
Charles II, 1660-1685
James II, 1685-1688

In 1688 James II was forced out of the country, but Parliament kept the crown in a female branch of the Stuart family, calling in Mary, the daughter of James II, and her husband William III of the Netherlands. Mary died in 1694.

William III and Mary II, 1689-1702/1694
Anne, 1702-1714

In 1707, through the Union of England and Scotland, the royal title became King (or Queen) of Great Britain and Ireland. The Stuart family having no direct Protestant heirs, the throne passed in 1714 to the German George I, Elector of Hanover, a great-grandson of James I.

Hanoverian Line
Kings of Great Britain and Ireland

George I, 1714-1727
George II, 1727-1760
George III, 1760-1820
George IV, 1820-1830
William IV, 1830-1837

William IV having no heirs, the British throne passed in 1837 to Victoria, a granddaughter of George III. Though the British family has continued in direct descent from George I, it has dropped the Hanoverian designation and is now known as the House of Windsor. From 1877 to 1947, the British rulers bore the additional title of Emperor (or Empress) of India.

Victoria, 1837-1901
Edward VII, 1901-1910

George V, 1910-1936
Edward VIII, 1936
George VI, 1936-1952
Elizabeth II, 1952-

FRANCE

Valois Line
Louis XI, 1461-1483
Charles VIII, 1483-1498
Louis XII, 1498-1515
Francis I, 1515-1547
Henry II, 1547-1559
Francis II, 1559-1560
Charles IX, 1560-1574
Henry III, 1574-1589

In 1589 the Valois line became extinct, and the throne passed to Henry of Bourbon, a remote descendant of French kings of the 14th century.

Bourbon Line
Henry IV, 1589-1610
Louis XIII, 1610-1643
Louis XIV, 1643-1715
Louis XV, 1715-1774
Louis XVI, 1774-1792

The Republic
Convention, 1792-1795
Directory, 1795-1799
Consulate, 1799-1804

The Empire
Napoleon I, 1804-1814, Emperor of the French and King of Italy

Restored Bourbon Line
Louis XVIII, 1814-1824

(Royalists counted a Louis XVII, 1793-1795 and dated the reign of Louis XVIII from 1795.)

Charles X, 1824-1830

The Revolution of 1830 gave the throne to the Duke of Orleans, descendant of Louis XIII.

Orleans Line
Louis-Philippe, 1830-1848

Second Republic
1848-1852

Second Empire

Napoleon III, 1852-1870, Emperor of the French

Third Republic

1870-1940

Vichy Regime

1940-1944

Provisional Government

1944-1946

Fourth Republic

1946-1958

Fifth Republic

1958-

PRUSSIA (AND GERMANY)

A continuous Hohenzollern line ruled until 1918.

Electors of Brandenburg and Dukes of Prussia

George William, 1619-1640

Frederick William, 1640-1688, the "Great Elector"

Frederick III, 1688-1713

In 1701 Frederick III was permitted by the Holy Roman Emperor to entitle himself King in Prussia, as Frederick I.

Kings of Prussia

Frederick I, 1701-1713

Frederick William I, 1713-1740

Frederick II, the "Great," 1740-1786

Frederick William II, 1786-1797

Frederick William III, 1797-1840

Frederick William IV, 1840-1861

William I, 1861-1888

In 1871 William I took the title of German Emperor.

German Emperors

William I, 1871-1888

Frederick III, 1888

William II, 1888-1918

The German Empire became extinct in 1918. It was succeeded by the

Weimar Republic

1919-1933

(The Weimar Republic is an unofficial title for what was still called the Deutsches Reich, a phrase not easy to translate accurately.)

The Third Reich

1933-1945

(The Third Reich is an unofficial title for the Deutsches Reich under Adolf Hitler.)

Allied Military Government in 1945 was followed by

German Federal Republic (West Germany)

1949-1990

German Democratic Republic (East Germany)

1949-1990

The two Germanys were united in 1990.

German Federal Republic

1990-

SARDINIA (AND ITALY)

In 1720 Victor Amadeus II, Duke of Savoy, took the title of King of Sardinia, having acquired the island of that name. The kingdom was often called Piedmont because of the king's older mainland domain.

Kings of Sardinia

Victor Amadeus II, 1720-1730

Charles Emmanuel III, 1730-1773

Victor Amadeus III, 1773-1796

Charles Emmanuel IV, 1796-1802

Victor Emmanuel I, 1802-1821

Charles Felix, 1821-1831

Charles Albert, 1831-1849

Victor Emmanuel II, 1849-1878

In 1861 Victor Emmanuel II took the title of King of Italy.

Kings of Italy

Victor Emmanuel II, 1861-1878

Humbert I, 1878-1900

Victor Emmanuel III, 1900-1946

(Benito Mussolini's Fascist regime governed Italy, 1922-1943.)

Humbert II, 1946

In 1946 the Kingdom of Italy became extinct and was succeeded by the

Italian Republic

1946-

SPAIN

Ferdinand and Isabella, 1479–1504/1516

Isabella died in 1504, but Ferdinand lived until 1516, whereupon the Spanish thrones were inherited by their grandson Charles, who became Charles V of the Holy Roman Empire, but was known in Spain as Charles I.

Habsburg Line
Charles I, 1516–1556
Philip II, 1556–1598
Philip III, 1598–1621
Philip IV, 1621–1665
Charles II, 1665–1700

With Charles II the Spanish Habsburg line became extinct, and the throne passed to the French Bourbon grandson of Louis XIV of France and great-grandson of Philip IV of Spain.

Bourbon Line
Philip V, 1700–1746
Ferdinand VI, 1746–1759
Charles III, 1759–1788
Charles IV, 1788–1808

Bonaparte Line
Joseph, 1808–1813 (brother of Napoleon)

Restored Bourbon Line
Ferdinand VII, 1813–1833
Isabella II, 1833–1868

In 1868 Isabella abdicated; after a regency, and a brief reign by Amadeus I (Savoy), 1871–1873, there was a short-lived First Republic, 1873–1874, succeeded by

Alfonso XII, 1874–1885
Alfonso XIII, 1885–1931

In 1931 a republican revolution unseated Alfonso XIII.

Second Spanish Republic
1931–1936

Spanish Civil War
1936–1939

Regime of General Francisco Franco
1939–1975

Upon the death of Franco the Bourbon family was restored.

Juan Carlos I, 1975–2014
Felipe VI, 2014–

RUSSIA (AND U.S.S.R.)

Grand Dukes of Moscow
Ivan III, the "Great," 1462–1505
Basil III, 1505–1533
Ivan IV, the "Terrible," 1533–1584

In 1547 Ivan IV took the title of Tsar of Russia.

Tsars of Russia
Ivan IV, the "Terrible," 1547–1584
Theodore I, 1584–1598
Boris Godunov, 1598–1605

Time of Troubles
1604–1613

Romanov Line
Michael, 1613–1645
Alexis, 1645–1676
Theodore II, 1676–1682
Ivan V and Peter I, 1682–1689
Peter I, the "Great," 1689–1725
Catherine I, 1725–1727
Peter II, 1727–1730
Anna, 1730–1740
Ivan VI, 1740–1741
Elizabeth, 1741–1762
Peter III, 1762
Catherine II, the "Great," 1762–1796
Paul, 1796–1801
Alexander I, 1801–1825
Nicholas I, 1825–1855
Alexander II, 1855–1881
Alexander III, 1881–1894
Nicholas II, 1894–1917

In 1917 the tsardom became extinct.

Provisional Government
1917

Communist Revolution
1917

Union of Soviet Socialist Republics
1922–1991

In 1991 the Communist regime ended, and the U.S.S.R. dissolved into its component republics (Russia, Ukraine, Belarus, etc.), loosely associated with each other in a Commonwealth of Independent States.

Russian Federation
1991–

Dates given after names of rulers and popes are the years of reigns or pontificates; those given for all others are the years of birth and death.

Pronunciation is indicated where it is not obvious. With foreign words the purpose is not to show their exact pronunciation in their own language but to suggest how they may be acceptably pronounced in English. Fully Anglicized pronunciations are indicated by the abbreviation *Angl*. Pronunciation is shown by respelling, not by symbols, except that the following symbols are used for vowel sounds not found in English:

ø   indicates the sound of ö as in Göttingen. To form this sound, purse the lips as if to say *o,* and then say *ay* as in *ate*.

U   indicates the sound of the French *u,* or of German *ü*. To form this sound, purse the lips as if to say *oo,* and then say *ee* as in *eat*.

aN,   oN, uN, iN indicate the sounds of the French nasal vowels. Once learned, these are easily pronounced, roughly as follows: For aN, begin to pronounce the English word *on,* but avoid saying the consonant *n* and "nasalize" the *ah* sound instead. For oN do the same with the English *own;* for uN, with the English prefix *un-;* for iN, with the English word *an*.

The sound of *s* as in the word *treasure* is indicated by *zh*. This sound is common in English, though never found at the beginning or end of a word. *igh* always indicates the so-called long *i* as in *high*. The vowel sound of *hoot* is indicated by *oo*, that of *hood* by *ŏo*.

Compared with English, the European languages are highly regular in their spelling, in that the same letters or combinations of letters are generally pronounced in the same way.

Index

G

H

L

S